SIXTH EDITION

Applying Educational Research

How to Read, Do, and Use Research to Solve Problems of Practice

M. D. Gall
Professor Emeritus, University of Oregon

Joyce P. Gall
Independent Researcher

Walter R. Borg
Late of Utah State University

PEARSON

Boston   New York   San Francisco
Mexico City   Montreal   Toronto   London   Madrid   Munich   Paris
Hong Kong   Singapore   Tokyo   Cape Town   Sydney

Editor-in-Chief: Paul A. Smith
Series Editorial Assistant: Matthew Buchholz
Vice President, Marketing and Sales Strategies: Emily Williams Knight
Vice President, Director of Marketing: Quinn Perkson
Marketing Manager: Erica DeLuca
Production Editor: Paula Carroll
Editorial Production Service: Omegatype Typography, Inc.
Composition Buyer: Linda Cox
Manufacturing Buyer: Megan Cochran
Electronic Composition: Omegatype Typography, Inc.
Interior Design: Omegatype Typography, Inc.
Cover Designer: Linda Knowles

For related titles and support materials, visit our online catalog at www.pearsonhighered.com

Between the time website information is gathered and then published, it is not unusual for some sites to have closed. Also, the transcription of URLs can result in typographical errors. The publisher would appreciate notification where these errors occur so that they may be corrected in subsequent editions.

Library of Congress Cataloging-in-Publication Data

Gall, Meredith D.
  Applying educational research : how to read, do, and use research
to solve problems of practice / M. D. Gall, Joyce P. Gall,
Walter R. Borg.—6th ed.
        p. cm.
  Includes bibliographical references and index.
  ISBN-13: 978-0-205-59670-6 (pbk.)
  ISBN-10: 0-205-59670-3 (pbk.)
  1. Education—Research—Handbooks, manuals, etc.   I. Gall, Joyce P.
II. Borg, Walter R.   III. Title.
  LB1028.B59   2010
  370.7'2—dc22

                                        2009023024

Printed in the United States of America

10 9 8 7   EBM   14 13

Allyn & Bacon
is an imprint of

www.pearsonhighered.com

ISBN-10: 0-205-59670-3
ISBN-13: 978-0-205-59670-6

Meredith "Mark" Gall, professor emeritus, has a bachelor's degree and master's degree in education from Harvard University and a Ph.D. in psychology from the University of California at Berkeley. He was an R & D specialist at the Far West Laboratory for Educational Research and Development and then a professor of education at the University of Oregon, where he served in various capacities, including head of teacher education and director of graduate studies in curriculum and instruction. His specializations include research methodology, teacher development, teaching strategies, and the psychology of studying. He has served on the editorial boards of several journals, including the *Journal of Experimental Education, Journal of Educational Research,* and *Elementary School Journal.* Among his other book publications are *Educational Research: An Introduction* and *Clinical Supervision and Teacher Development.*

Joyce P. "Joy" Gall has a bachelor's degree in journalism from the University of Illinois at Urbana-Champaign and a Ph.D. in psychology from the University of California at Berkeley. She has worked as a trainer-developer at the Far West Laboratory for Educational Research and Development, the American Institutes for Research, ROLM Corporation, and the University of Oregon. Her specializations include educational leadership, the psychology of studying, and training and development in education and industry. Her other books include *Educational Research: An Introduction, Making the Grade, Help Your Son or Daughter Study for Success,* and *Tools for Learning: A Guide to Teaching Study Skills.*

Brief Contents

Contents

2   Doing Your Own Research: From Proposal to Final Report   25

PART two   APPLYING THE RESEARCH LITERATURE TO PROBLEMS OF PRACTICE

3   Conducting and Writing Your Own Literature Review   49

---

4   Using Search Engines in a Literature Review   74

---

5   Making Use of Available Literature Reviews   91

PART *three*

USING QUANTITATIVE METHODOLOGY TO STUDY PROBLEMS OF PRACTICE

6   Analyzing and Evaluating Reports of Quantitative Research Studies   122

9   Tests of Statistical Significance   189

13   Experimental Research   292

PART
four

USING QUALITATIVE METHODOLOGY
TO STUDY PROBLEMS OF PRACTICE

14   Case Studies in Qualitative Research   336

15   Narrative Research   372

PART
five

COMBINING QUANTITATIVE AND QUALITATIVE METHODOLOGIES TO STUDY PROBLEMS OF PRACTICE

18   Mixed-Methods Research   460

PART
six

USING OTHER RESEARCH METHODOLOGIES TO STUDY PROBLEMS OF PRACTICE

19   Action Research   487

20   Evaluation Research   511

Reprinted Articles

The following articles are reprinted exactly as they appeared in the original source, except that the format of the original articles (e.g., column layout) has been standardized for presentation in this text.

Preface

Goals of This Book

Educators do their best for students, but their efforts are often hampered by difficult problems. In this book, we call them "problems of practice" to denote our emphasis on resource needs, knowledge gaps, conflicts, and other challenges that arise in educators' professional work. The primary goal of *Applying Educational Research* is to help educators learn the many ways in research can enable them to think methodically about problems of practice and work toward their solutions.

To achieve this goal, the book focuses on helping educators develop three skills. The first skill is the ability to search the educational literature for research articles and other publications relevant to specific problems of practice. The second skill is the ability to comprehend technical research reports and draw appropriate conclusions from their findings. The third skill is the ability to do one's own research.

In addition to developing these skills, *Applying Educational Research* encourages educators to look beyond their daily routines and ask questions about why problems of practice occur and how to solve them. By asking such questions, educators should come to realize that the research community is one of their profession's best resources for answering them and paving the way for new, more effective practices.

New to This Edition

This book is a major revision of the fifth edition of *Applying Educational Research*. This new edition places much more emphasis on problems of practice that preservice and professional educators face in their workplace and on how they can use the findings of their own or others' research to solve them. Also, it presents developments in research methodology that have occurred since the fifth edition.

- This edition contains five new chapters. Chapter 2 describes in detail the complete process of doing a research study, from preparing an initial proposal to writing a final report of the completed study. Chapter 8 explains how to determine the practical significance of statistical results. Chapter 9 provides a more extensive explanation of tests of statistical significance than was provided in the fifth edition. Chapter 15 describes the approach and purpose of narrative research. Chapter 18 describes the methods and benefits of mixed-methods research.
- The book presents more than 100 examples of current problems of practice, most of them new to this edition. We selected problems that confront educators at all levels of schooling, from kindergarten through graduate school, and educators who serve in a variety of roles, including teachers, administrators, counselors, school psychologists, higher education personnel, staff development specialists, and teacher educators. Some of these problems involve the need to better serve students who are struggling with discrimination, health risks, substance abuse, bullying, underachievement, learning disabilities, or autism; some involve school dropouts or students whose talents are not adequately addressed by current educational systems. Other problems of practice involve the current quality of instruction in school subjects such as reading, mathematics, social

studies, science, and industrial arts. Still other problems involve the challenges created by recent policy initiatives such as the No Child Left Behind Act, alternative teacher certification programs, charter schools, national curriculum standards, online courses, the accountability movement, and stakeholders' calls for educational innovation.

- Nearly 80 research studies conducted in the United States or other countries, most published since 2005 and new to this edition, are described. Most of the studies are directly relevant to problems of practice that concern educators and other stakeholders who wish to improve education for all students.

- Several chapters from the previous edition have been reorganized. Two chapters in the fifth edition on ethnographic research and critical theory research have been reorganized into one chapter on ethnography and critical research (Chapter 16). The fifth edition's chapter on descriptive and causal-comparative research has been expanded into two chapters, one on descriptive research (Chapter 10) and the other on causal-comparative research, now called group comparison research (Chapter 11). The previous edition had one chapter on statistical analysis of research data. One of the topics of that chapter, descriptive statistics, has been expanded into a chapter of its own (Chapter 7), and two other topics, statistical significance and practical significance, now are organized as separate chapters (Chapters 8 and 9).

- The previous edition of this book included 13 full-text research articles selected from the education literature. This new edition includes 18 full-text research articles, all but two of which are new to this edition. Thirteen of these articles were published in 2007 or later, and all address significant problems of practice that confront educators today.

- Several chapter features in the sixth edition are new or have been updated. For most chapters, there is a new feature titled *An Example of How [chapter topic] Can Help in Solving Problems of Practice.* This feature, located near the end of the chapter, first presents a problem of practice that was recently reported in a newspaper or other news source. Then an example is given of how a research study, based on the concepts and procedures described in the chapter, could be designed to address that problem of practice. This feature shows readers how real-life problems of practice can be productively addressed by the research methods covered in the book.

- Another new chapter feature is a section on evaluation criteria near the end of each of the chapters about a particular research methodology (Chapters 10–20). Readers can apply these criteria to evaluate the quality of research studies that interest them or that they plan to include in a literature review. All these design-specific criteria are then organized and repeated in an appendix new to this edition (Appendix 4).

- A feature in previous editions, *Resources for Further Study,* is retained in this edition. Located near the end of each chapter, it has been updated to include articles, books, and other publications that have appeared since the previous edition. These resources enable the reader to explore further the topics covered in the chapter.

Organization of the Book

Parts I through VI

Part I begins with a chapter that provides an overview of the nature of educational research and its relevance to solving problems of practice in education. Chapter 2 helps educators develop an understanding of all the steps involved in designing and completing a research study. They can use these steps as a guide for conducting their own research studies. It is supplemented by an appendix (Appendix 1), which contains a form for outlining a research proposal.

Part II is about how to review the literature reporting educational research studies, syntheses of research evidence, theories, practices, and opinions. Chapter 3 presents a systematic process for locating and writing a report about the literature on any educational topic of interest. Chapter 4 describes how to use search engines to access the education literature, and Chapter 5 explains how to access literature reviews that have been prepared by authorities on particular problems and topics.

Part III is about quantitative methods used in educational research. It starts with Chapter 6, which provides an overview about how to read and evaluate reports of studies that primarily use quantitative methods. Next, three chapters explain various types of statistical analysis: descriptive statistics (Chapter 7), the relevance of statistical results for educational practice (Chapter 8), and tests of statistical significance (Chapter 9). The remaining chapters in Part III concern particular quantitative methodologies used by educational researchers: descriptive research (Chapter 10), group comparison research (Chapter 11), correlational research (Chapter 12), and experimental research (Chapter 13).

Part IV includes four chapters on research methodologies that are entirely or mostly qualitative in nature. The first of these chapters (Chapter 14) presents methods that are used in case study research but that also can be applied to the other qualitative research approaches explained in this part of the book: narrative research (Chapter 15), ethnography and critical research (Chapter 16), and historical research (Chapter 17).

Part V consists of a single chapter (Chapter 18), which is about mixed-methods research. This type of research methodology is discussed separately because it incorporates both quantitative methods, which is the subject of Part III, and qualitative methods, which is the subject of Part IV.

Part VI includes chapters on action research (Chapter 19) and evaluation research (Chapter 20). Both of these approaches to research can employ either quantitative or qualitative methods, or both, and they are especially relevant to the improvement of educational practice.

Chapter Organization

Each chapter begins with a list of the important ideas and key terms in the chapter. Next comes the main body of the chapter. The end section includes a self-check test (with answers provided at the end of the book), chapter references, and resources for further study.

The end section of most chapters also includes an introduction to a full-text article that explains how it addresses a particular problem of practice. Next comes the article, which is reprinted in full. Chapters 5, 13, and 14 each include two reprinted articles that illustrate different sets of concepts and procedures covered in the chapter.

In addition, the end section of most chapters includes a feature *An Example of How [chapter topic] Can Help in Solving Problems of Practice.* We described this feature on the previous page.

Suggested Study Strategy

Examine the Book's Organization.   Before you start reading the book, explore its layout: table of contents, list of reprinted articles, organization of each chapter, and end matter (self-check test answers, appendixes, glossary, and name and subject indexes).

Start Each Chapter by Reading the Lists of Important Ideas and Key Terms. Each chapter begins with a list of important ideas in the approximate order in which they are discussed in the chapter. Next follows a list of key terms that refer to important concepts and techniques covered in the chapter. Studying these lists will give you a good idea of what you already know about the topics covered in the chapter and what will be new to you.

Read the Body of the Chapter.   As you read the chapter, try to locate the information relating to each important idea and key term. Also, look for the examples of research studies that illustrate them. In addition to reading these examples, reflect on how the concepts and techniques represented in the lists of important ideas and key terms might relate to an educational context that is familiar to you. Wherever a key term is defined in a sentence in the text, the term appears in boldface. In a few instances, a key term is defined in a table. All key terms also appear in the glossary.

Read the Full-Text Article or Articles.   As you read each reprinted article, consider how it employs the concepts and techniques described in the chapter. Also, consider how the findings of the study contribute to your understanding of problems of practice that you encounter in your work. If you come across an unfamiliar technical term while reading a full-text article, you most likely will find it defined in the glossary. Also, you can look for it in the subject index and then read the section of the book that explains it.

Check Your Mastery   After reading the chapter, return to the list of important ideas and see whether you can elaborate on them in your own words. Similarly, check whether you can provide your own definition for each term in the list of key terms. If you find any topic that you have not mastered, engage in further study of the chapter or other resources, such as those on the Internet. Also, consider entering a key term or terms in a search engine like Google, which often yields informative websites. Then take the self-check test in the chapter, which includes multiple-choice items related to the chapter's important ideas and key terms. If you wish to expand your understanding of particular topics, you can read the resources for further study listed at the end of the chapter.

Prepare for Tests.   You can prepare for the instructor's tests by rereading the relevant lists of important ideas and key terms, any chapter material that you highlighted, and your class notes. Another useful strategy is to have a review session with one or more of your classmates. You can take turns with them in playing the role of the instructor, making up questions about the chapter content, and asking classmates to answer them.

Complete Homework Assignments.   If your instructor gives you assignments that involve preparing a research proposal or conducting a study, you can refer to Chapter 2 and the guide in Appendix 1 to help you. If you are given assignments involving the preparation of a literature review, you can refer to the chapters in Part II for guidance.

If you are given assignments that require you to evaluate a full-text research article in the book or a research report in another source, you can refer to Appendix 2 (general criteria for evaluating quantitative research studies), Appendix 3 (general criteria for evaluating qualitative research studies), and Appendix 4 (evaluation criteria that are specific to a particular research design). Also, you can read about these evaluation criteria in the chapter where they are introduced and explained.

If you are asked to identify a problem of practice and explain how research might shed light on it, you should find it helpful to refer to the section titled *An Example of How [chapter topic] Can Help in Solving Problems of Practice* at the end of most chapters.

Instructor's Manual

The Instructor's Manual has been thoroughly revised for the sixth edition of *Applying Educational Research*. It includes suggestions for designing an introductory research course for undergraduate or graduate students in education and related fields, teaching activities related to each chapter's content, and a test-item bank with both multiple-choice and short-answer items covering the content of each chapter.

Acknowledgments

We thank our many colleagues who have shared with us their knowledge, insights, and experiences relating to educational research. In particular, we express deep appreciation to the following reviewers of portions of the manuscript: Dale I. Foreman, Shenandoah University; Deborah J. Hendricks, West Virginia University; Jean Krows, Emporia State University; and Marylin Lisowski, Eastern Illinois University. Thank you for spending time carefully reading chapter drafts and giving us feedback to help us refine this new edition of *Applying Educational Research*.

M. D. (Mark) Gall
Joyce P. (Joy) Gall

chapter 1

Using Research Evidence to Improve Educational Practice

IMPORTANT *Ideas*

1. Educational research is having an increasing impact on educational policy and practice.
2. Evidence-based practice is becoming more prevalent in medicine, psychology, education, and other professions.
3. Teachers' traditional motivations and workplace conditions have not been conducive to evidence-based practice.
4. Evidence-based practice in education has four key elements: (1) focus on problems of practice, (2) reliance on research evidence, (3) clinical expertise, and (4) respect for stakeholders' values.
5. An important impetus for improving education is heightened awareness of pressing problems of practice and a commitment to solve them.
6. Educators need to understand research methodology so they can evaluate the quality of others' research or conduct their own research.
7. Educators need to view research evidence from multiple ethical perspectives.
8. Educators can collaborate productively with researchers by participating in research or program evaluation or by joining with researchers in influencing policy agendas for educational change.
9. Research differs from other forms of inquiry in its emphasis on (1) making direct observations of phenomena; (2) taking steps to eliminate personal bias in data collection, analysis, and interpretation; and (3) carefully determining the generalizability of findings to individuals and situations other than those that were studied.
10. Research produces four types of knowledge: (1) descriptions, (2) predictions, (3) evidence about the effects of experimental interventions, and (4) explanations.
11. The purpose of basic research is to understand fundamental processes and structures that underlie observed behavior, whereas the purpose of applied research is to develop and validate interventions that can be used directly to improve practice.
12. Postmodernists believe that no one method of inquiry is inherently better than any other, whereas social scientists believe that their methods of inquiry have a special legitimacy and claim to authority, based on use of (1) explicitly defined concepts or procedures available for inspection by anyone; (2) replication studies to test the soundness of findings from a single study; (3) knowledge claims that can be tested, and possibly refuted, by empirical data; and (4) explicit procedures to minimize researcher errors and biases.

13. Quantitative and qualitative research differ in various ways, but chiefly in epistemology. Quantitative researchers assume an objective social reality that exists independently of observers and participants, whereas qualitative researchers assume that social reality is continuously constructed by observers and participants.

14. Mixed-methods research studies make use of both quantitative and qualitative research methods. ■

Key TERMS

action research	educational research	progressive discourse
APA Presidential Task Force on Evidence-Based Practice	epistemology	qualitative research
	evaluation research	quantitative research
applied research	evidence-based practice	reflexivity
basic research	interpretivism	refutation
clinical expertise	No Child Left Behind Act	replication
Cochrane Collaboration	positivism	theory
construct	postmodernism	triangulation
descriptive research	prediction research	What Works Clearinghouse

Each of the principal authors of this book (Mark Gall and Joy Gall) has had a career in education spanning more than 40 years. From our current vantage point, we stand in awe of the many educational practitioners (called *educators* in this book) who do such a remarkable job of teaching increasingly diverse students while maintaining schools and other learning institutions in the face of ever-present budgetary challenges and shifting policy initiatives.

In addition, we are impressed by the expansion of educational research over the past 40 years. An ever-growing worldwide network of educational researchers have developed sophisticated methods for studying the complexities of the educational enterprise, producing a substantial body of research knowledge and highly efficient electronic methods for accessing it.

Unfortunately, something is missing from this picture of progress. We have not yet witnessed a meaningful bridge between educational research and educational practice. Researchers and educators live mostly in separate worlds. They come together only occasionally in university courses, workshops, conferences, and journals that both groups read.

There are signs, though, that the two worlds—the world of educational practice and the world of educational research—are coming closer. The signs, mostly seen at the level of national legislation and policy making, point to a sea change in education. The findings of educational research are becoming increasingly influential in shaping national legislation about education, which in turn is creating changes in educational practice.

If you are an educator, these changes mean that you will need to study research so that you can enter into a dialogue with researchers and the policy makers who make decisions based on research findings. Otherwise, you and your colleagues might find yourselves in the uncomfortable position of trying to implement programs and policies that you did not have a voice in shaping.

In short, we claim that educational research is becoming too important for anyone interested in schools and students to ignore. In the next sections, we make our case for the validity of this claim. We invite you to reflect on the soundness of the claim and, if you think it has merit, how you plan to respond in your role as an educator.

Evidence-Based Professional Practice

The movement called **evidence-based practice** represents a striking change in the relationship between educational research and practice. This relatively new approach to professional decision making relies on rigorous research findings rather than custom, personal experience, or intuition. For example, suppose a teacher recommends that a student needs one-on-one tutoring to come up to grade level in writing skills. Suppose the parents ask whether tutoring is likely to help their child. A teacher who is well versed in evidence-based practice would be able to refer to research findings demonstrating the effectiveness of tutoring and justify the applicability of this research to their child's needs.

Evidence-based practice is changing the foundations of various professions. We will consider two of these professions—medicine and clinical psychology—before discussing evidence-based practice in education. Our purpose is to help you see that evidence-based practice is a large-scale professional movement, not just a passing fad.

Evidence-Based Practice in Medicine

Suppose you have a heart problem and seek treatment for it. How do you decide which is the best treatment? You might try to contact other patients with the same problem. Perhaps they will offer testimonials about some medicine or individual who helped them. Another option is to seek a professional opinion, probably by making an appointment to see a doctor with expertise, such as a board-certified doctor in cardiology.

Testimonials, case examples, and expert opinion can be worthwhile. On the other hand, they might lead you astray if they are based on untested beliefs, inaccurate observations, or reliance on outmoded research. Evidence-based practice in medicine represents an effort to avoid such pitfalls. It does so by basing treatment decisions on the best possible research evidence about a patient's condition.

Evidence-based medical practice has two significant features. The first involves the need to identify good research evidence. The fact that a research study has been published does not necessarily guarantee that its findings are sound. Professionals need to sift through research findings to determine which ones hold up well under critical scrutiny. Although researchers might be in the best position to do this screening, medical practitioners also need to understand research methodology to validate for themselves what others consider good research evidence for a particular treatment option. Researchers use systematic procedures to synthesize evidence collected across research studies on a particular medical intervention, such as meta-analysis, which we describe in Chapter 5. Several organizations coordinate and publish these research syntheses. Among the most prominent is the **Cochrane Collaboration,** whose website (www .cochrane.org) publishes reviews of research on interventions for various medical problems. For example, when we visited the site, we found featured reviews on antioxidant supplements to enhance health and nonsteroidal antiinflammatory drugs for low back pain, as well as on strategies for preventing the transmission of meticillin-resistant staphylococcus.

The second feature of evidence-based medical practice is the use of clinical expertise in applying research evidence. A treatment option that is generally effective might be harmful for a particular patient. For this reason, the Cochrane Collaboration states: "Evidence-based medicine is the conscientious, explicit and judicious use of current best evidence in making decisions about the care of individual patients" (Cochrane Collaboration, n.d.). **Clinical expertise** is the ability to make informed ethical judgments about whether a particular professional intervention is both evidence based and appropriate for the needs of an individual client.

Evidence-based medicine follows the principle that research evidence by itself does not lead to good medical practice. Neither does clinical expertise. Both are necessary in order to create a sound bridge between medical research and medical practice.

Evidence-Based Practice in Psychology

Psychological practice, whose practitioners receive training to help clients with various emotional, cognitive, and medical problems, has grown enormously over the past half-century. In 2005, the American Psychological Association commissioned the **APA Presidential Task Force on Evidence-Based Practice** (2006). The work of this task force should be of interest to educators, because educational practice has been influenced greatly by psychology, especially in the areas of achievement testing, instructional design, and behavior management.

The APA Task Force defined evidence-based practice in psychology as "the integration of the best available research with clinical expertise in the context of patient characteristics, culture, and preferences" (2006, p. 273). This definition is similar to the Cochrane Collaboration's definition of evidence-based medicine, but with an even greater emphasis on the importance of the client's individual characteristics in determining an effective intervention.

The Task Force concluded that a variety of research methods can generate evidence to guide psychological practice, among which are methods that are also commonly used in educational research and covered in different chapters of this book:

- Clinical observation, including individual case studies (Chapter 14)
- Single-case experimental designs (Chapter 13)
- Ethnographic research (Chapter 16)
- Experiments on treatment efficacy (Chapter 15)
- Meta-analysis to synthesize research results from multiple studies (Chapter 5)

Keep in mind, then, that learning about the methods of educational research described in this book has multiple benefits. Your learning will apply to education but also generalize to research as it is conducted in other professions, including psychology and medicine, as well as business, science, and technology.

The Task Force (2006) analyzed eight components of clinical expertise in psychology. Struck by their applicability to clinical expertise in teaching, we list them in Figure 1.1. As you study the list, we invite you to draw parallels to the teaching process and to reflect on how it is possible to interweave clinical expertise and research evidence.

Evidence-Based Practice in Education

Robert Slavin (2002) provides us with a concise statement about the history of educational practice and its current status:

> At the dawn of the 21st century, education is finally being dragged, kicking and screaming, into the 20th century. The scientific revolution that utterly transformed medicine, agriculture, transportation, technology, and other fields early in the 20th century almost completely bypassed the field of education. If Rip Van Winkle had been a physician, a farmer, or an engineer, he would be unemployable if he awoke today. If he had been a good elementary school teacher in the 19th century, he would probably be a good elementary school teacher today. It is not that we have not learned anything since Rip Van Winkle's time. It is that applications of the findings of educational research remain haphazard, and that evidence is respected only occasionally, and only if it happens to correspond to current educational or political fashions. (p. 16)

We believe that Slavin's assessment is accurate. This leads us to ask, Why has education been so resistant to research?

Traditional Educational Practice

Most educators start their careers by preparing to be teachers. Their motivations often involve a love of children, personal gratification in seeing students learn and develop, a passion for par-

FIGURE *1.1*   Components of Clinical Expertise in Evidence-Based
Psychological Practice

1. *Diagnostic judgment and treatment planning.* "The clinically expert psychologist
   is able to formulate clear and theoretically coherent case conceptualizations,
   assess patient pathology as well as clinically relevant strengths, understand
   complex patient presentations, and make accurate diagnostic judgments."
2. *Treatment implementation and monitoring.* "Clinical expertise entails the skillful
   and flexible delivery of treatment. Skill and flexibility require knowledge of and
   proficiency in delivering psychological interventions and the ability to adapt the
   treatment to the particular case."
3. *Interpersonal expertise.* "Central to clinical expertise is interpersonal skill, which is
   manifested in forming a therapeutic relationship, encoding and decoding verbal and
   nonverbal responses, creating realistic but positive expectations, and responding
   empathically to the patient's explicit and implicit experiences and concerns."
4. *Self-reflection and self-development.* "Clinical expertise requires the ability to
   reflect on one's own experience, knowledge, hypotheses, inferences, emotional
   reactions, and behaviors and to use that reflection to modify one's practices
   accordingly."
5. *Evaluation and application of research evidence.* "Clinical expertise in psychology
   includes scientific expertise. . . . An understanding of scientific method allows
   psychologists to consider evidence from a range of research designs, evaluate
   the internal and external validity of individual studies, evaluate the magnitude of
   effects across studies, and apply relevant research to individual cases."
6. *Sensitivity to individual differences.* "Clinical expertise requires an awareness of
   the individual, social, and cultural context of the patient, including but not limited
   to age and development, ethnicity, culture, race, gender, sexual orientation,
   religious commitments, and socioeconomic status."
7. *Willingness to draw on other resources.* "When research evidence indicates
   the value of adjunctive services or when patients are not making progress as
   expected, the psychologist may seek consultation or make a referral."
8. *Planning phase prior to treatment.* "Clinical expertise requires a planful
   approach to the treatment of psychological problems. . . . Psychologists rely
   on well-articulated case formulations, knowledge of relevant research, and the
   organization provided by theoretical conceptualizations and clinical experience to
   craft interventions designed to attain desired outcomes."

Source: Adapted from APA Presidential Task Force on Evidence-Based Practice (2006). Evidence-
based practice in psychology. *American Psychologist 61*(4), 271–285.

ticular subject areas (e.g., science, social studies, literature), and a desire to instill this passion
in others. Another motivating factor is that the teaching profession allows for independence and
creative freedom; teachers typically have responsibility for their own classroom with minimal
supervision by others. The desire to apply research to practice, if present, does not have nearly
the same priority as these other motivations for entering the teaching profession.

   Another attraction of teaching is that the professional preparation program is not as demanding as that for other professions, such as medicine and psychology. In fact, in regions
with teacher shortages, college graduates are typically able to begin teaching immediately if
they agree to professional preparation, either concurrently or over several summers. There
is relatively little opportunity for research training within the typical teacher preparation
curriculum.

   After becoming licensed and employed by a school system, teachers typically find
that the work of a classroom teacher is very time-consuming and often stressful. They also

experience professional isolation, because they and their colleagues spend most of their time meeting their students' needs. There is little free time to discuss issues and ideas, or how to apply research evidence to problems of practice.

Many teachers are able to develop increasing expertise as their careers progress, but they have little opportunity to share it with others. They eventually retire and take their hard-won expertise with them. There is no system for recording that expertise, testing its validity through systematic research, and then making it available to novice teachers.

During their careers, some teachers earn additional licenses and degrees. With these credentials, they can assume positions as instructional specialists, school administrators, or education professors. Their basic outlook on education, however, continues to be shaped by their experiences as classroom teachers, not by their knowledge of research evidence.

Other roadblocks exist to building bridges between research and existing educational practice. Even if researchers have strong evidence to support a new instructional method, they lack authority to institute them. Also, researchers who ask educators to join in seeking legislation to fund educational research find that educators generally would rather seek funding to serve pressing needs in their own practice.

The Movement toward Evidence-Based Education

As we have noted, the American Psychological Association (APA) has created an official definition of evidence-based practice in psychology. We have modified this description to define evidence-based practice in education as the art of solving problems of practice through the integration of the best available research combined with educators' clinical expertise and values. Clinical expertise involves the types of skills listed in Figure 1.1. Values, as we explain later in this chapter, govern the ethics of both research and practice.

The federal government has moved strongly in the direction of evidence-based education. The **No Child Left Behind Act** of 2001 (NCLB) requires all states to specify standards of achievement in basic skills that all students in certain grades are expected to meet. Furthermore, educators are required to use scientifically based research evidence in choosing programs and procedures to help students achieve those standards. NCLB administrators and many researchers believe that randomized experiments (see Chapter 13) produce the best possible research evidence for improving educational practice.

NCLB has been heavily criticized (e.g., Darling-Hammond, 2007) for various reasons, such as imposing requirements on schools without providing adequate funding, focusing only on basic skills, forcing teachers to "teach to the test," and threatening public education by allowing parents with children in "failing" schools to transfer them to nonpublic schools.

We do not know whether NCLB will survive in the political arena. However, we believe that there will be a continued press to base educational practice on the best possible research evidence. Because medicine, psychology, and other professions appear to have made a long-term commitment to evidence-based practice, it will be difficult for education to stand alone against this movement.

Another sign of the movement toward evidence-based education is the establishment of the Institute of Education Sciences (IES) by the U.S. Department of Education in 2002. The mission of this institute is "to provide rigorous evidence on which to ground education practice and policy" (U.S. Department of Education, n.d.). IES currently includes four centers, all of which support scientifically based research to improve student learning outcomes.

IES also administers the **What Works Clearinghouse** (WWC), whose mission is "to promote informed education decision making through a set of easily accessible databases and user-friendly reports that provide education consumers with high-quality reviews of the effectiveness of replicable interventions (programs, products, practices, and policies) that intend to improve student outcomes" (Institute of Education Sciences, n.d.). WWC's syntheses of research on educational interventions are similar to those of the Cochrane Collaboration, described earlier in the section on evidence-based medicine. We describe WWC in more detail in Chapter 5.

Problems of Practice in Education

The greatest impetus for improving professional practice is the acknowledgement of problems. The medical profession is a good example of this principle. Disease and injuries, and the human suffering that accompanies them, are problems that cry out for solutions. For this reason, basic and applied medical research is heavily funded by governmental agencies and the private sector all over the world. New treatments that ameliorate a medical problem, even to a modest degree, gradually find their way into medical practice.

Serious problems abound in education, and the news media continually bring them to the public's attention. Consider this statement by Dana Hawkins-Simons (2008) in *U.S. News & World Report:*

> Each week seems to bring more evidence of how the United States is losing step with the rest of the developed world when it comes to educating children. Seventy percent of eighth graders are not proficient in reading, over a million high schoolers drop out each year, and nearly one third of college freshmen must take remedial math or English courses. (p. 29)

If evidence-based programs and procedures are available to lessen the severity of these problems, the education profession has a moral imperative to examine them closely and to consider adopting them.

You can develop your own sensitivity to the problems that educators need to solve by reading various news sources, including daily newspapers. Some newspapers, such as the *New York Times,* are available in an online version, with free subscriptions. They often publish articles about school incidents, academic achievement data, poll results, and policy debates that highlight problems of educational practice. In fact, most of the problems of practice that we present as features near the end of each chapter in this book (including this chapter) are drawn directly from news sources.

ASCD SmartBrief is a particularly informative news source about problems—and successes—that are likely to be of interest to educators. Each item in the newsletter summarizes a recent newspaper article, journal article, or institutional report that has educational relevance. Published by the Association for Supervision and Curriculum Development, one of the largest professional organizations for educators in the United States, it is available online at no cost (www.smartbrief.com/ascd).

We reviewed newsletter items from 2008 to identify which educational problems were the frequent subject of news reports. A sample of the problems revealed by our search is shown in Figure 1.2.

Individual teachers and school districts might try to solve problems like these on their own. However, their magnitude is so great that more systematic, well-funded efforts are likely necessary, such as innovative programs and procedures whose effectiveness is tested by researchers. On the other hand, some problems require **basic research,** which seeks to go beyond the surface manifestations of a problem and study it at a more fundamental level to identify underlying processes and structures. Eventually, basic research should yield insights that have practical applications.

In summary, evidence-based practice in education that addresses compelling problems of teaching and learning appears to be our best long-term approach to improving education. For this approach to work, every educator and policy maker will need to understand how research evidence is generated and the factors that differentiate high-quality research from weak research. The purpose of this book is to help you acquire this understanding, either for the purpose of doing your own research or for judging whether research done by others is sound and applicable to your own professional practice.

The Ethics of Educational Research and Practice

Education is a thoroughly human enterprise. This is true both of educational research and educational practice. As humans, our values can, and should, influence our judgments and behavior. For example, researchers might identify an effective set of procedures for

FIGURE *1.2*   Significant Problems of Practice in Education

Teacher expertise.

Data indicate that students with science degrees can earn thousands of dollars more annually by opting to go into fields other than teaching, writes Gerald F. Wheeler, the executive director of the National Science Teachers Association. Perhaps that's why nearly half of high school biology students and roughly two-thirds of chemistry and physics students are taught by teachers without majors or certification in the relevant field, he writes.

(*Education Week,* May 13, 2008)

Educating the talented and gifted.

Dalton Sargent's poor grades despite his high IQ are emblematic of the nation's failure to address the needs of the 3 million U.S. children identified as gifted and more who are never labeled, advocates say.

(*Los Angeles Times,* May 12, 2008)

Mathematics education.

California's requirement that each high school graduate pass algebra was meant to better prepare students for college, but instead community colleges are finding more students lacking in both algebra and basic math skills. "It's the million-dollar question," said Mary Martin, who chairs the math department at a community college where nearly 52% of students require remedial math courses, up from 43% in 2003. "We are asking more of our high school students, so why isn't it transferring over to college?"

(*The Sacramento Bee,* May 12, 2008)

Fostering student creativity.

Many employers value workers with creative skills, yet new research suggests most high schools provide the problem-solving or artistic endeavors believed to foster creativity only on an elective basis. "The findings . . . present an opportunity for school systems and business leaders to further engage in a dialogue about how best to foster creativity among students, not only to produce a competitive workforce, but also to help all students succeed in life," said Paul D. Houston, executive director of the American Association of School Administrators.

(*eSchool News,* May 2, 2008)

Student boredom.

Teens capable of producing YouTube videos, publishing anime or podcasting are likely to be underwhelmed by school, researchers say. "Kids associate one word with school: 'boring,'" Deborah Stipek, a Stanford professor and dean of education, said, adding, "The question becomes what is the role of school in this larger environment."

(*CNET,* April 24, 2008)

Student bullying.

Students who self-report regular bullying behavior are more likely than their classmates to experience difficulty in relating to their friends or parents, are apt to associate with other bullies, display aggressive tendencies and lack strong moral values, according to a study of 871 students, conducted by researchers at York University and Queens University.

(*ScienceDaily,* March 26, 2008)

Source: News items in *ASCD SmartBrief,* a publication of the Association for Supervision and Curriculum Development.

---

reducing the incidence of student misbehavior in school. However, the procedures might have harmful effects on students' self-esteem, motivation, or respect for teachers. Other solutions that are effective for students and without bad side effects might be so expensive that they diminish the budget for other educational priorities.

Evidence-based practice, then, must not endorse blind use of research evidence, no matter how sound it is. For example, in medicine, doctors might have effective procedures for prolonging the life of a patient, but at the cost of great suffering and exorbitant expense. All stakeholders, therefore, including the patient and the patient's loved ones, need to weigh treatment effectiveness and values in reaching a decision. Some professionals, called medical ethicists, specialize in identifying and weighing the values that are an inextricable part of medical research and practice. Similarly in education, all stakeholders concerned about students' well-being need to examine research evidence from the perspective of their own personal values as well as the shared values of society.

Keep in mind, too, that the relationship between research and practice is a two-way street. Educators need to make value judgments about research evidence as it becomes available. However, they also need to realize that their willingness to support research and seek out research findings is itself a value judgment. Educators who prefer to rely only on their own beliefs and experiences, without considering research evidence, might be denying students access to more effective programs and procedures than they are providing. In other words, the dismissal of evidence-based practice is a value-laden decision that should not be made lightly.

Collaborating with Researchers

In order for educational research to play a role in improving practice, educators need to participate in an ongoing dialogue with professional researchers. Maintaining a dialogue is no easy matter, though. One challenge is that researchers and educators tend to have very different views about knowledge and research. According to Lilian Katz and Dianne Rothenberg (1996), researchers' main interest in knowledge is scientific. When confronted with a problem, they seek to explore and discover the nature of the problem, no matter how long that might take. In contrast, educators' main interest in knowledge is clinical. When confronted with a problem, they seek information that will allow them to solve it, usually under the pressure of a time limit. Katz and Rothenberg also note that effective practice "depends to some extent on the certainty with which the practitioner approaches his or her task. And by definition, the researcher's task is to prize doubt and uncertainty and be open to being wrong" (p. 8).

Nonetheless, researchers and educators have a shared desire to improve educational practice. Therefore, they should take steps to understand each other's needs and to communicate clearly with each other. For example, researchers can develop research agendas that are responsive to educators' needs. Also, they can write reports of their findings in nontechnical language and spell out their implications for practice. In turn, educators need to make an effort to understand the language and methods used by researchers. In addition to improving lines of communication, educators and researchers can strengthen the application of research to practice through collaboration, as described in the following sections.

Being a Research Participant

Researchers often ask educators to participate in their studies. The effort required might be minimal (e.g., filling out a questionnaire) or more extensive (e.g., volunteering your class to be part of the experimental group or control group in an experiment). By volunteering to participate, you might find that you are eligible to receive special training, consultation, or free use of innovative curriculum materials. You also will have the opportunity to learn how research is actually done.

Participating in Program Evaluations

Educational institutions occasionally receive grants from private or government funding sources to implement experimental programs. These grants typically require the grantee to carry out an evaluation of the program. If your institution employs evaluation specialists, you can work alongside them to design an appropriate evaluation study. For this collaboration to happen, however, you need to be knowledgeable about evaluation research. If no evaluation specialists are available to help you in securing a grant and satisfying its criteria for evaluation, you will need to know even more about evaluation research to deal effectively with the grant's requirements.

Chapter 20 explains how to conduct an evaluation study and also how to decide whether you can apply the findings of an existing evaluation study to your own situation. Because evaluation research typically involves one or more of the research approaches described in Parts III and IV of this book, study of those chapters will be helpful to you too.

Influencing Policy Agendas for Education

Various policy-making bodies, ranging from national and state legislatures to the central offices of local school districts, are constantly proposing changes in educational practice that directly affect educators' work. We have described one such change, the No Child Left Behind Act, earlier in the chapter.

Some policy-driven changes are sound, but others make little sense to the educators who must implement them. For example, many states have implemented or are considering mandatory achievement testing of all students in order to make educators accountable for student learning outcomes. Many teachers are concerned about the validity of these tests and whether they respect the huge individual differences in students' learning needs and family situations. However, without knowledge about research on achievement testing and student characteristics, teachers and other educators are handicapped in their ability to influence statewide testing programs.

Ill-considered policies perhaps could be avoided if educators and researchers would collaborate to make their views and knowledge known to policy makers. For this to happen, though, researchers and educators must be familiar with each other's knowledge, goals, and perspectives.

The Purpose of Educational Research

Up to this point in the chapter, we have discussed the relationship between educational research and practice, showing how evidence-based education can bridge them. We need now to explore the nature of educational research and how it differs from other forms of inquiry.

We start with a definition. **Educational research** is the systematic collection and analysis of empirical data in order to develop valid, generalizable knowledge that involves (1) descriptions of educational phenomena, (2) predictions about future events or performance, (3) evidence about the effects of experimental interventions, and (4) explanations of observed phenomena in terms of the basic processes that underlie them.

This definition will become clearer to you as you study the chapters of this book. For now, we wish to highlight the fact that research seeks to produce *valid* knowledge, meaning that it uses special methods to control for personal biases and confounding factors that might compromise the soundness of its findings. Also, research seeks to produce *generalizable* knowledge, meaning that it uses special methods to produce knowledge applicable to other situations besides the one that was investigated. Finally, research relies on *empirical data,* meaning that it uses special methods to make replicable observations of the phenomena being studied.

Other forms of inquiry, such as personal observations and intuitive thinking, can also result in useful knowledge. However, they do not employ the special methods of educational research.

Our previous definition of educational research asserts that it produces four types of knowledge: (1) descriptions, (2) predictions, (3) evidence about the effects of experimental interventions, and (4) explanations. In the next sections of this chapter, we discuss how research produces each of these types of knowledge.

Descriptive Research

The purpose of **descriptive research** is to make careful, highly detailed observations of educational phenomena. For example, Marilyn Adams's monumental synthesis of research on learning to read includes findings about how an individual's eyes move while reading text (Adams, 1990). Contrary to popular belief, researchers have found that good readers process every word in the text rather than engage in selective scanning, a finding with important implications for teaching children to read.

Descriptive research is particularly good for discovering problems of practice. For example, Mary McCaslin and her colleagues (2006) observed 145 teachers' classrooms (grades 3–5) during 447 visits for 2,736 10-minute intervals. Among their many research findings they discovered:

the cognitive demands of most observed instructional opportunities were judged as only basic facts and skills content (37%) or a mixture of basic facts and skills, elaborations, and related thinking (37%). In comparison, 3% of the instructional opportunities were judged to involve students only in tasks that involved higher-order thinking/reasoning. (p. 324)

McCaslin and colleagues note that these observations of normative practice are discrepant from "best practice" recommendations of groups such as the National Association for the Education of Young Children and the National Council of Teachers of Mathematics. These groups recommend "considerably more opportunities for 'constructive' learners to think, reason, and construct personally meaningful learning than we observed" (McCaslin et al., 2006, p. 327).

This discrepancy between normative and best practice in elementary schools is a serious problem whose solution would greatly improve education. If individuals claim that the problem might exist elsewhere but not in their particular school system, we might reasonably ask them to present empirical data to back their claim.

You will study methods of descriptive research in Chapters 7 and 10 involving the collection of numerical data. Other types of descriptive research rely primarily on verbal data, such as interviews, historical records, or ethnographic data. This research approach—often called qualitative research—is explained in the chapters of Part IV of this book.

Prediction Research

Prediction research seeks to determine whether data collected at one point in time can predict behavior or events that occur at a later point in time. This type of research can be helpful in solving problems of practice. For example, we know that a substantial percentage of students drop out of high school or have poor academic achievement. If we could identify these students at a younger age, we might be able to provide them with instruction and other interventions to prevent these problems. Prediction research can provide knowledge to guide this identification process.

Another example involves college administrators, who often face the problem of having more applicants than they can accept. Prediction research can be helpful in identifying characteristics of students who will do well academically and in other aspects of college life. Future applicants then can be assessed on these characteristics in order to select those most likely to be successful in a particular college.

Prediction studies typically involve the use of group comparison or correlational methods, which are explained in Chapters 11 and 12.

Experimental Research

Some research studies try to determine the effects of a particular intervention in a natural or laboratory setting. Studies of this type use what is commonly called the experimental method. For example, many researchers have conducted experiments to determine whether introducing cooperative learning into a classroom improves students' learning. Any observed improvement in student learning can be considered an *effect* of the intervention or an indicator of the intervention's *effectiveness.*

The findings of experimental research are particularly important to educators. Virtually everything they do is an intervention of some sort. For example, teachers intervene in students' lives in order to facilitate their learning or to help them with their personal problems. Administrators intervene by engaging in leadership behavior that facilitates the work of other individuals in the organization or that solves workplace problems. Experiments can determine which types of interventions are most likely to be successful.

Methods of experimentation involving quantitative data are explained in Chapter 13. Some researchers study the effects of an intervention by in-depth exploration of its use in one or a few situations. This type of research involves the use of case study methodology, which we explain in Chapter 14.

Educators, either on their own or in groups, can do small-scale experiments to improve local practice. They can test locally developed programs, or they can determine whether evidence-based programs developed elsewhere are effective in their particular school system. This approach, called **action research,** is explained in Chapter 19.

Educators, working together or with a professional researcher, can do studies to determine not only the effects of an intervention, but also the value or worth of the intervention. For example, they might wish to determine whether the intervention is cost-effective, better than other possible interventions, or valued by the community. This type of investigation, called **evaluation research,** is explained in Chapter 20.

Explanatory Research

The purpose of some research studies is to explain individual or group behavior. Explanatory research, as we use the term here, involves statements about cause-and-effect relationships. For example, a common explanation of the finding that students in some schools do better than average on state or national tests is that they come from families with a high socioeconomic status. In other words, socioeconomic status (the cause) is invoked as an explanation of students' academic achievement (the effect).

All the research methods previously mentioned, with the exception of purely descriptive methods, can be used to investigate cause-and-effect relationships. The researchers hypothesize that one or more factors are causes and one or more factors are effects. They then collect data to determine whether variations in the presumed cause (e.g., schools with high teacher morale versus schools with low teacher morale) are associated with variations in the presumed effect (e.g., high student attendance rate versus low student attendance rate).

Some researchers study cause-and-effect relationships to satisfy their curiosity about particular phenomena or problems. Other researchers investigate cause-and-effect relationships to develop and test theories. Indeed, some researchers believe that the ultimate goal of educational research is to develop theories that explain various aspects of education. A **theory** is an explanation of particular phenomena in terms of a set of underlying constructs and principles that relate these constructs to each other. **Constructs** are structures or processes that are presumed to underlie observed phenomena.

Theories about brain structures and processes are currently of great interest to professionals in various disciplines, including education. If researchers can determine how the brain works to facilitate or hamper students' learning and motivation, this understanding might well lead to new solutions to problems of practice. The journal article reprinted at the end of this chapter presents brain theories that help us understand why some students have difficulty learning to read. It also includes suggestions about how to enhance all students' motivation to enjoy reading. The author of the article is a neurologist who became a classroom teacher.

Basic and Applied Research

Researchers do not use a single approach to inquiry. Some of their investigations can be characterized as basic research, whereas others can be characterized as applied research. The purpose of basic research, as previously noted, is to understand fundamental processes and structures that underlie observed behavior.

For example, we can observe teachers and students in a classroom as they engage in their activities. We might note that the teacher distributed a worksheet to the students and gave directions for completing it and that students took a writing instrument and made marks on their worksheet. These behavioral observations might be useful information, but they do not tell us what the teacher and students were thinking or what neural–chemical processes were activated in students' brains as they learned new skills and concepts by completing the worksheet. The study of processes that underlie observed behavior is the province of **basic research.**

In contrast to basic research, the purpose of **applied research** is to develop and test interventions that can be used directly to improve practice. In education, the development and testing of a new method to help students engage in mathematical problem solving would be an example of applied research. The published research articles that are included in Chapters 13 (Experimental Research), 19 (Action Research), and 20 (Evaluation Research) are examples of applied research.

Some educators believe that applied research is more valuable as a guide to their work than basic research and that it should therefore have funding priority over basic research. A study of medical research by Julius Comroe and Robert Dripps (1976) raises doubts about this view. Comroe and Dripps studied the advances in research knowledge that were necessary for innovations in the treatment of cardiovascular and pulmonary disease (e.g., cardiac surgery and chemotherapy). Surprisingly, many more basic research studies were instrumental in the development of these innovations than were applied research studies. Basic research leads to theoretical understanding of underlying processes and structures, and this understanding is the best foundation for constructing interventions that are likely to be effective.

Characteristics of Research as an Approach to Inquiry

Some philosophers and social critics question the relevance of research to understanding human behavior and society. Their critique of social science has led to a movement called **postmodernism.** Postmodernists (e.g., Graham, Doherty, & Malek, 1992) acknowledge that science has contributed to an understanding and control of the physical world, but they argue that no one method of inquiry can claim to be true, or better than any other method, in developing knowledge about the human condition. For example, postmodernists would argue that the methods of social science inquiry are not superior to personal reflection or other forms of investigation such as aesthetic and religious studies.

The postmodern critique of scientific inquiry has caused social science researchers (including educational researchers) to rethink their claims to authority in the pursuit of knowledge. They have identified several characteristics of research that establish its claim to authority and that differentiate it from other forms of inquiry. We describe these characteristics in the following sections.

Use of Concepts and Procedures That Are Shared, Precise, and Accessible

Social science researchers have developed specialized concepts (e.g., test reliability), procedures (e.g., purposeful sampling), and carefully defined terminology. Their terminology, concepts, and procedures are explicit and accessible. Everyone is free to learn and use them. Indeed, most journals that publish research reports use a "blind" review procedure, meaning that reviewers do not have access to the authors' names or other identifying information.

Of course, there are power struggles in the arenas of funding and publicity for research findings, but it is highly unlikely that important theories or findings can be suppressed over the long term, because researchers generally are committed to **progressive discourse** (Bereiter, 1994). Anyone at any time can offer a criticism about a particular research study or research methodology, and if it proves to have merit, that criticism is listened to and accommodated.

Many educators perform their work at a high level of excellence and have developed many insights from their personal inquiries. However, they lack carefully refined concepts and forums for making their ideas widely accessible. Hence, their knowledge cannot be publicly debated, and it generally disappears when they retire. By contrast, new researchers are able to learn from experienced researchers, and the results are available in research journals for all to study.

Replicability of Findings

For researchers to have their findings published, they must be willing to make public the procedures by which those findings were obtained. Because the procedures are public, other researchers can conduct similar studies to compare results. Called **replication** studies because they involve repetition of the original study under similar conditions but with a new sample of participants, such studies can provide additional confidence in the original findings, or refutation of them.

Individuals who engage in nonscientific inquiry might discover potentially important interventions and insights. However, their inquiries are of limited value because they do not make their procedures sufficiently explicit for others to replicate. Thus, we have no way to know whether an individual's claimed findings and insights are unique to that individual or can inform the work of other individuals.

Refutability of Knowledge Claims

Karl Popper (1968) proposed a standard for testing knowledge claims that has won general acceptance among social science researchers. Popper argued that science advances through the process of **refutation,** which involves submitting knowledge claims (theories, predictions, hunches) to empirical tests that allow them to be challenged and disproved. If the data are inconsistent with the knowledge claim, we can say that it is refuted. The knowledge claim must then be abandoned or modified to accommodate the negative findings. If the data are consistent with the knowledge claim, we can conclude that it is supported, but not that it is correct. We can say only that the knowledge claim has not been refuted by any of the tests that have been made thus far.

Refutation tests knowledge claims more rigorously than we usually test everyday knowledge claims. For example, suppose a school administrator visits a teacher's classroom one day and discovers that (1) the teacher has attended a recent workshop on classroom management, and (2) the teacher's class is unusually quiet and orderly. The administrator might conclude that the workshop is effective and therefore mandate participation from all teachers. In effect, the administrator made an observation first and then formulated a broad knowledge claim. In contrast, researchers who follow Popper's logic make a knowledge claim first, perhaps based on a similar observation, and then test it by making further observations before reaching any conclusions.

Control for Researcher Errors and Biases

Researchers acknowledge the likelihood that their own errors and biases will affect their data collection. Therefore, they design research studies to minimize the influence of such factors. For example, in making observations, researchers often seek to reduce error by using multiple observers and training them beforehand in the system for collecting data on observational variables. In addition, they typically use statistical procedures to estimate the observers' level of agreement. While the observations of different observers rarely agree perfectly, a certain level of agreement must be achieved before the observational data are accepted as valid.

An approach often used in case study research is to validate findings by triangulation of data sources. **Triangulation** refers to researchers' attempts to corroborate data obtained by one method (e.g., observation of individuals) by using other methods (e.g., interviews of individuals or examination of documents).

Other research procedures described throughout this book are also intended to minimize various researcher errors and biases in data collection and analysis. We invite you to compare the rigor of these methods with the everyday methods that individuals use to arrive at and justify knowledge claims.

Quantitative and Qualitative Research

Educational research is not a unified enterprise. The approaches to research described in Part III, called **quantitative research,** involve the study of samples and populations and rely heavily on numerical data and statistical analysis. In contrast, the research traditions described in Part IV, called **qualitative research,** rely on the study of individual cases and make little use of numbers or statistics, preferring instead verbal data and subjective analysis.

Why does educational research include such diverse approaches? To answer this question, we need to consider the different **epistemologies**—that is, views about the nature of knowledge—that guide educational researchers.

Some researchers assume that features of the human environment have an objective reality, meaning that they exist independently of the individuals who created them or are observing them. These researchers subscribe to a positivist epistemology. **Positivism** involves the belief that there is a real world "out there" available for study through scientific means similar to those developed in the physical sciences.

Most quantitative research is carried out by researchers who subscribe to the positivist epistemology. They define their topics of interest in terms of observable behavior (e.g., "feeling good about one's teacher" might become "students report positive attitudes"). They attempt to define that behavior in terms of the specific operations used to measure it (e.g., "students with positive attitudes gave average ratings of 3 or higher on 5-point scales"). They also are concerned about generalizing what they discover about a research sample to the larger population from which that sample was presumably drawn.

Other researchers take the epistemological position known as interpretivism (Erickson, 1986), believing that aspects of the human environment are constructed by the individuals who participate in that environment. **Interpretivism** involves the belief that social reality has no existence apart from the meanings that individuals construct for it. For example, a teacher might form the construction that the students in his first-period class are "13 boys and 16 girls," or "29 unique individuals each with their own needs," or "easier to teach than students I've had other years," depending on when the teacher is thinking about them. If the principal steps into the teacher's classroom, her construction of the students in the class might vary depending on how they are behaving at the moment, how the principal is feeling, or many other factors.

Most qualitative research is carried out by individuals who subscribe to interpretivist epistemology. These researchers believe that scientific inquiry must focus on the study of the different social realities that different individuals in a social situation construct as they participate in it. Because of the complexity of these constructions, qualitative researchers usually study single individuals or situations, each of which is called a *case*. They determine the applicability of case findings to other situations mainly by comparing cases or suggesting that educators do this comparison with their own situation.

Qualitative researchers also acknowledge their own role in constructing the social realities that they describe in their research reports and thus often include their own experiences in their reports. This focus on the researcher as a constructor of social reality is called **reflexivity.**

While some scholars refer to positivism and interpretivism to distinguish these two approaches to research, quantitative research and qualitative research are more commonly used and we will use these terms in this book. The words *quantitative* and *qualitative* highlight the differences in the kinds of data that typically are collected by researchers and how these data are analyzed and interpreted. Table 1.1 provides a further elaboration of the distinguishing characteristics of quantitative and qualitative research.

Given that both quantitative and qualitative methods are used to study education, several questions arise. Is one approach better than the other? Do they complement each other in some way? Do they produce conflicting findings? We address these questions in Chapter

TABLE **1.1**   Differences between Quantitative and Qualitative Research

Quantitative Researchers	Qualitative Researchers
Assume an objective social reality.	Assume that social reality is constructed by the participants in it.
Assume that social reality is relatively constant across time and settings.	Assume that social reality is continuously constructed in local situations.
View causal relationships among social phenomena from a mechanistic perspective.	Assign human intentions a major role in explaining causal relationships among social phenomena.
Take an objective, detached stance toward research participants and their setting.	Become personally involved with research participants, to the point of sharing perspectives and assuming a caring attitude.
Study populations or samples that represent populations.	Study cases.
Study behavior and other observable phenomena.	Study the meanings that individuals create and other internal phenomena.
Study human behavior in natural or contrived settings.	Study human actions in natural settings.
Analyze social reality into variables.	Make holistic observations of the total context within which social action occurs.
Use preconceived concepts and theories to determine what data will be collected.	Discover concepts and theories after data have been collected.
Generate numerical data to represent the social environment.	Generate verbal and pictorial data to represent the social environment.
Use statistical methods to analyze data.	Use analytic induction to analyze data.
Use statistical inference procedures to generalize findings from a sample to a defined population.	Generalize case findings by determining their applicability to other situations.
Prepare impersonal, objective reports of research findings.	Prepare interpretive reports that reflect researchers' constructions of the data and an awareness that readers will form their own constructions from what is reported.

Source: Table 1.2 on p. 32 in Gall, M. D., Gall, J. P., & Borg, W. R. (2007). *Educational research: An introduction* (8th ed.). Boston: Allyn & Bacon. Copyright by Pearson Education. Reprinted by permission of the publisher.

18. For now, we will observe that many researchers believe that the methods of qualitative research and quantitative research are complementary and that researchers who use a combination in mixed-methods research studies are in the best position to give a full picture of educational practices and problems.

A Personal Note: The Research "Spark"

We are well aware that some people do not have an interest in formal research methodology, which is what this book is primarily about. They might take great interest in new discoveries, such as breakthroughs in medicine or alternatives sources of energy or how the brain affects our ability to learn, but not in the research processes that led to those discoveries.

We believe that interest in research methodology is set off by some "spark" that differs among people. Since we (Mark and Joy Gall) know our own "sparks" best, we will recount them briefly here.

Mark Gall

I began my doctoral studies with the intention of becoming a clinical psychologist in private or group practice. Gradually, I began to wonder whether psychotherapy was actually as effective as claimed. That was the "spark" that led to my interest in research; I wanted to know what researchers had learned about the effectiveness of different psychotherapeutic approaches (e.g., Freudian, Jungian, Adlerian) and how I could do my own research to determine their effectiveness.

Later in my career, after I became a teacher educator, I became interested in teacher enthusiasm, which some research studies had found to be positively associated with student learning. Several of my doctoral students wondered whether it was possible to train teachers to become more enthusiastic during classroom instruction. That question was the "spark" for a series of doctoral studies that I chaired. To do these studies, both the students and I needed to learn how to use particular research methods. In particular, we needed to study methods for conducting experiments (see Chapter 13), because each study involved training some teachers to use indicators of enthusiasm (the experimental group) but not others (the control group) and then observing the effects of this intervention on their students' learning and behavior.

Joy Gall

I began my doctoral studies with an interest in social psychology, and the ways in which groups such as families, work organizations, or schools shape individuals' thinking, emotions, and behavior. While doing my doctoral studies, I was hired by two psychology professors who had a funded grant to develop curriculum materials for young students based on the latest principles of scientific discovery. I developed materials that were designed to bring science alive for young learners. The work of developing curriculum or training materials based on the findings of research is known as research and development. My understanding of how research and practice could be connected began with this work.

During my career, I have continued to apply my psychological research and writing skills by developing research-based curriculum and training materials for educational administrators, teachers, and students. I also have addressed the learning needs of various community groups, including parents of students. My "spark" involves the desire to discover ways to help individuals understand and improve their social environment through individual and joint learning endeavors.

You

You might already have experienced your own "spark." Perhaps that spark is a desire to find answers to a question or problem that you can't stop thinking about. Perhaps it is a desire to test a personal theory about a better way to teach. If you have a research "spark" for this or another reason, you have the requisite motivation to study this book.

If your primary "spark" is a desire to get into schools and help students learn, we encourage you to be on the lookout for *what works* and also for *problems* that trouble you and your colleagues. You might find answers in the workplace, but we encourage you to look also at the research literature on education. You might find answers there, or at least new ways of thinking about what works, and what doesn't, in education.

We encourage you to keep an open mind about the value of research. If you do, the chapters of this book will reveal new ideas and develop new skills that will enhance your expertise as a professional educator.

An example of
HOW RESEARCH CAN HELP IN SOLVING PROBLEMS OF PRACTICE

Note to the reader. You will find features similar to this section in most of the other chapters of this book. We present a problem of practice that has reached public attention through newspapers or other media. Then we suggest how the research methodology described in the particular chapter can be used to design studies that address the problem.

These vignettes are designed to develop your understanding of the relationship between educational problems and educational research. Most important, we hope you will see that conventional wisdom and individual effort are insufficient to solve these problems. Empirical knowledge generated by well-designed research studies is also necessary. This type of knowledge enables us to test the validity of our claims about how to solve these problems. Moreover, research knowledge facilitates discoveries that can lead to innovative, effective solutions that we might not think of on our own.

An editorial about the status of educational research in the United States appeared in November 2008 in *The Boston Globe*. The following excerpts are from the newspaper editorial:

> Grover Whitehurst, who heads the research arm of the U.S. Department of Education says that the quality of education research today is the rough equivalent of medical research in the 1920s.
>
> [Whitehurst recommended] operating a national education department that spends just $575 million—1 percent of its budget—on research.
>
> Editorial (2008, November 1). Healing America's schools. *Boston Globe*. Retrieved from www.boston.com/bostonglobe

Medical research has led to huge advancements in practice. Could research do the same for educational practice? Some educators believe that research can accomplish this goal. Other educators, however, believe that federal monies, including the $575 million recommended by Grover Whitehurst, would best be used for direct service to students. A research study might help educators and their professional organizations decide what the priority should be.

A simple survey study should be sufficient to learn educators' views. For example, a sample of educators could be asked to read the *Boston Globe*'s editorial and then respond to a question—for example, "Based on what you just read and what you know about research, do you think that the U.S. Department of Education should allocate 1 percent of its budget for research?"

In designing this study, we would need to pay particular attention to the sampling procedure. The population should be defined as all educators in the United States. A large random sample should be drawn from that population, so that we have confidence that the survey results represent the views of educators in general, not just educators from one region or educators who volunteer to complete the survey.

Self-Check Test

1. Evidence-based practice requires that educators
   a. collect evidence on their own instructional effectiveness.
   b. make use of relevant research findings in solving problems of practice.
   c. disregard stakeholders' values in decision making unless they are consistent with research evidence.
   d. use instructional programs and procedures that do not rely on educators' clinical expertise.

2. The Institute of Education Sciences and the What Works Clearinghouse exemplify education's movement in the direction of
   a. basic research.
   b. qualitative research.
   c. postmodernism.
   d. evidence-based practice.
3. Assuming that policy agendas for education become more evidence based, educators will most likely
   a. seek to develop greater understanding of research concepts and procedures.
   b. use their professional organizations to resist such agendas.
   c. argue that education's problems are unique and cannot be solved by research.
   d. claim that evidence does not lead to improvement in professional practice.
4. Educational research emphasizes
   a. collection of empirical data.
   b. control for personal biases in collecting, analyzing, and interpreting empirical data.
   c. study design such that findings can be generalized to other individuals and situations.
   d. All of the above.
5. The role of theory in educational research is primarily to
   a. develop precise descriptions of educational phenomena.
   b. evaluate the effectiveness of specific instructional interventions.
   c. explain phenomena in terms of constructs and principles.
   d. provide a language that facilitates collaboration between researchers and educators.
6. Postmodernists argue that
   a. contemporary research methods have overcome serious deficiencies of research methods used in the first part of the twentieth century.
   b. educational research is not superior to other forms of inquiry about problems of practice.
   c. basic research is ultimately more important than applied research in solving problems of practice.
   d. any knowledge claim can be refuted.
7. Triangulation is a method by which researchers
   a. look for explanations about why a finding from one research study fails to replicate in a subsequent study.
   b. obtain data from different sources in order to check for errors and biases in their findings.
   c. determine whether a problem of educational practice can be studied by collecting empirical data.
   d. collaborate with educators and policy makers in the design of an empirical study.
8. Positivist researchers
   a. subscribe to the belief that there is an objective reality that exists independently of the observer.
   b. believe that aspects of the human environment are constructed by the participants in the environment.
   c. emphasize description as the goal of scientific inquiry.
   d. disregard the possible effects of their own biases on research findings.
9. Qualitative researchers typically
   a. focus on making subjective judgments about the quality of educational programs and procedures.
   b. include quantitative measures to represent the qualities of each case they study.
   c. argue that the methods of social science inquiry are not superior to other forms of investigation.
   d. emphasize the study of individual cases of a phenomenon.
10. Mixed-methods research
    a. is designed to produce descriptive and predictive findings within a single study.
    b. was developed to speed up the transfer of research findings into educational practice.
    c. uses a combination of quantitative and qualitative research methods.
    d. uses theories from multiple disciplines to study problems of practice.

Chapter References

Adams, M. J. (1990). *Beginning to read: Thinking and learning about print.* Cambridge, MA: MIT Press.

APA Presidential Task Force on Evidence-Based Practice. (2006). Evidence-based practice in psychology. *American Psychologist, 61*(4), 271–285.

Bereiter, C. (1994). Implications of postmodernism for science, or, science as progressive discourse. *Educational Psychologist, 29,* 3–12.

Cochrane Collaboration. (n.d.). *Evidence-based medicine and health care.* Retrieved from www.cochrane.org/docs/ebm.htm

Comroe, J. H., Jr., & Dripps, R. D. (1976). Scientific basis for the support of biomedical science. *Science, 192,* 105–111.

Darling-Hammond, L. (2007, May 21). Evaluating "No Child Left Behind." *The Nation.* Retrieved from www.thenation.com/doc/20070521/darling-hammond

Erickson, F. (1986). Qualitative methods in research on teaching. In M. C. Wittrock (Ed.), *Handbook of research on teaching* (3rd ed., pp. 119–161). New York: Macmillan.

Graham, E., Doherty, J., & Malek, M. (1992). Introduction: The context and language of postmodernism. In J. Doherty, E. Graham, & M. Malek (Eds.), *Postmodernism and the social sciences* (pp. 1–23). Basingstoke, UK: Macmillan.

Hawkins-Simons, D. (2008, May 19). Not a primary concern. *U.S. News & World Report,* 29–31.

Institute of Education Sciences. (n.d.). *What Works Clearinghouse.* Retrieved from http://ies.ed.gov/ncee/wwc/overview

Katz, L. G., & Rothenberg, D. (1996). Issues in dissemination: An ERIC perspective. *ERIC Review, 5,* 2–9.

McCaslin, M., Good, T. L., Nichols, S., Zhang, J., Wiley, C. R., Bozack, A. R., Burross, H. L., & Cuizon-Garcia, R. (2006). Comprehensive school reform: An observational study of teaching in grades 3 through 5. *Elementary School Journal, 106*(4), 313–331.

Popper, K. (1968). *Conjectures and refutations.* New York: Harper.

Slavin, R. E. (2002). Evidence-based education policies: Transforming educational practice and research. *Educational Researcher, 31*(7), 15–21.

U.S. Department of Education. (n.d.). *About the Institute of Education Sciences.* Retrieved from www.ed.gov/about/offices/list/ies/index.html

Resources for Further Study

Moss, P. A. (Ed.). (2007). *Evidence and decision making* (106th Yearbook of the National Society for the Study of Education, Part I). Malden, MA: Blackwell.

The chapter authors examine the process by which educators use information to improve schools. They consider the use of both quantitative and qualitative research evidence, standardized test scores, and survey and interview data, and also examine various materials, including samples of students' works. This book identifies the difficulties, but also the promise, of evidence-based practice in education.

Phillips, D. C., & Burbules, N. C. (2000). *Postpositivism and educational research.* New York: Rowman & Littlefield.

Most of us understand something about how scientists, including educational researchers, work. However, few of us are aware of the fundamental assumptions that underlie scientific inquiry and also the ongoing controversies about these assumptions. If you wish to deepen your understanding of science, this book will enlighten you.

Taber, K. S. (2007). *Classroom-based research and evidence-based practice: A guide for teachers.* Los Angeles: Sage.

This book is written for teachers who are interested in incorporating evidence-based practice into their instructional repertoires. The author describes skills needed to critically evaluate research reports and to carry out one's own school-based research.

Sample Educational Research Study

The Gully in the "Brain Glitch" Theory

Willis, J. (2007). The gully in the "brain glitch" theory. *Educational Leadership, 64*(5), 68–73.

The author of the following journal article notes that 20 to 35 percent of students have significant reading difficulties. In addition to being a major problem for these students, as most school learning involves reading, reading difficulties are also likely to handicap these students in their career choices and career advancement.

In reading this article, will see how current research and theory is pointing to promising new approaches to solving this problem of educational practice. The author of the article is both a board-certified neurologist and middle school teacher.

The article is reprinted in its entirety, just as it appeared when originally published.

The Gully in the "Brain Glitch" Theory

Judy Willis
*Santa Barbara Middle School,
Santa Barbara, CA*

Learning to read is not a natural part of human development. Unlike speech, reading does not follow from observation and imitation of other people (Jacobs, Schall, & Scheibel, 1993) and has no specific regions of the human brain dedicated to it. Reading requires multiple areas of the brain to operate together through intricate networks of neurons; thus, many different brain dysfunctions can interfere with the complex process of learning to access, comprehend, and use information from text. Knowing how interdependent these areas of the brain are, we should hardly be surprised that an estimated 20 to 35 percent of students experience significant reading difficulties (Schneider & Chein, 2003). In fact, it is wonderful that anyone learns to read at all.

Unfortunately, misinterpretations of recent neurological research have ignored the complexity of the cognitive processes involved in learning to read. Some education policymakers have used the conclusions of this research to claim that neuroscience proves the necessity of intensive phonics instruction for students who struggle with reading. This oversimplified interpretation of the cognitive research harms students and schools.

AN OVERSIMPLIFIED PICTURE OF THE BRAIN

During more than 20 years of practicing neurology and conducting electron microscope research analyses of the neurophysiology of the cerebral cortex, I have been fascinated by the connections among many parts of the brain that neuroimaging revealed. Since leaving my medical neurology practice to become a classroom teacher, I have felt compelled to respond to research analyses that oversimplify and misinterpret the results of neuroimaging scans.

Unfortunately, federal policymakers are currently using flawed research analyses to advance a narrow approach to reading instruction. When President George W. Bush promoted the Reading First program and introduced Head Start legislation that heavily favored phonics reading instruction, he assured the nation that "scientific" brain research had produced definitive data proving the merits of this approach. To support such claims, phonics advocates often cite research conducted by Shaywitz and colleagues (1998, 2002, 2003)—research that falls far short of the medical scientific model. I have read this research, and I believe that its conclusions are based on flawed studies and misinterpretations of the findings.

Shaywitz and colleagues used functional magnetic resonance imaging (fMRI) to measure differences in the brain activity of normal and dyslexic readers as they performed such tasks as reading a list of rhyming nonsense words. Because the dyslexic readers' brains showed a disruption at the rear area of the brain, where visual and sound identifications are made during reading, the researchers concluded that a "glitch" in the brain circuitry holds the key to reading difficulties.

The major flaw in the brain glitch research was its assumption that subjects were actually *reading* during the fMRI scans. The reading tasks evaluated were not authentic reading. Rather, they were phonics-based sound-and-symbol tasks.

The researchers' interpretations of the fMRI scans considered only one portion of the brain's complex—and still not completely defined—reading network, focusing on a brain region known to be more active during phonics processing. Predictably, this brain region became more metabolically active when the test subjects performed phonics processing activities. Also predictably, when students receive intensive phonics instruction, this region of the brain shows more activity, and the students' performance on tests designed to measure phonics skills improves. But we cannot generalize from these findings that *all* reading improves when the so-called phonics center becomes more active.

Such a conclusion would be like taking a patient who has suffered permanent right-arm paralysis that has spared, but weakened the right pinky finger and treating the patient by performing intensive physical therapy on that one finger. If the patient moves that finger during an fMRI scan, the brain region with neurons dedicated to movement of the right pinky finger (there is such a place in the left frontal lobe) will show, an increase in metabolic activity, use more glucose and oxygen, and light up the colors of the fMRI scan. If the patient receives physical therapy exercising that finger, a subsequent fMRI scan could show that the brain has responded by building more cellular connections around the neurons in that dedicated section. Yet, no improvement would necessarily occur in the movement of any other part of the patient's arm; the therapy would not affect the damaged neurons that control the whole arm.

In the same way, it is faulty science to conclude that reading ability has improved just because phonics-intense instruction has produced changes in phonics-functioning brain regions and improved performance on phonics-weighted post-tests. Nevertheless, researchers have used the brain glitch theory to lump diverse reading differences and learning styles under a single label of phonics impairment. And policymakers have used that label to promote one-size-fits-all, phonics-heavy reading instruction (Coles, 2004). A generation of students is paying the price.

LIMITATIONS OF NEUROIMAGING

Functional magnetic resonance imaging and other neuroimaging technologies—which show increased blood flow and blood oxygenation in parts of the brain that are activated during various cognitive tasks—are exciting tools for studying what happens in the human brain as people learn. But it's important that we use caution in drawing conclusions from the results of brain scans. The brain glitch researchers' conclusions reached far beyond the current limitations of neuroimaging.

As an example of one such limitation, the observation that a brain area is metabolically active *during* a reading task does not prove that it is active explicitly *in* the reading task. To increase scan analysis precision somewhat, we can use subtraction analysis (Friston, Zarahn, Joseph, Henson, & Dale, 1999). This technique takes baseline scans when the subject performs a task identical to the task being studied in all but one cognitive variable and then subtracts the baseline scan's areas of metabolic activity from the overall metabolic activity shown during the experimental scans. This presumably leaves only the single cognitive operation as the remaining part of the brain that is different from the baseline scans. The brain glitch analyses did not use this technique and thus did not account for the complex patterns of brain activity that are involved in the reading process.

Another problem with current neuroimaging technology is speed. Both fMRI and positron emission tomography (PET) neuroimaging scans show changes in metabolism over seconds, but many parts of the reading process take place during the 20 to 200 milliseconds before the *eyes* move from one word to the next. To "see" cognitive events occurring that rapidly, such as individual word identification or naming, some research has used time-precise neuroelectric monitoring systems that measure the activation of small clusters of cells (Kail, Hall, & Caskey, 1999). The brain glitch scanning studies did not use such technology and thus relied on the gross metabolic activations of fMRI scans to represent the complex brain activity that occurs as children read.

THE COMPLEX BRAIN

Although the brain glitch theory treats learning to read as an isolated, independent cognitive process, reading is actually a complex process connecting multiple learning and association centers in the brain. Neuroimaging shows that specific sensory inputs (sound, visual images, and so on) are received in the brain lobes specialized to accept them. Any new information en route to its designated lobe passes through a type of alerting system in the limbic system (parts of the temporal lobe, hippocampus, and amygdala). Here, the sensory information is linked to previously learned memory, connecting new data with the prior information and thus forming long-lasting relational memory. After the initial response to the new input, feedback goes back to the medial temporal lobe where the relational memory is sent along neural circuits to long-term memory storage areas. This process both reinforces and expands brain neurodendritic circuits that connect the multiple brain lobes.

Just because fMRI scans during sound-and-symbol phonics activities show activation in one brain center, that does not prove that other brain areas are not equally or more metabolically active during other types of reading tasks or for children with different learning styles. Regardless of which center shows initial activation or even sustained activation, all brain operations are complex and involve communication among multiple lobes. At the minimum, reading stimulates the limbic system, occipital cortex, associational subcortical frontal lobe centers, and medial temporal lobe. Reading instruction that stimulates multiple brain areas is likely to be more successful for different styles of learners and more efficient in facilitating the multicentric, dynamic process of reading.

COMBINING SCIENCE WITH THE ART OF TEACHING

The implications of neuroimaging for education and learning research are still largely suggestive. Researchers have not yet established a solid link between how the brain learns and how it metabolizes oxygen or glucose. It is premature to claim that any instructional strategies are firmly validated by a solid combination of cognitive studies, neuroimaging, and classroom research. For now, educators must be guided by a combination of the art of teaching and the science of how the brain responds metabolically and electrically to stimuli. Here are some promising areas of research and practice.

The Amygdala—Where Heart Meets Mind

The education literature has included theories about the effects of emotion on language acquisition for decades. Dulay and Burt (1977) and Kraslen (1982) proposed that strong positive emotion reinforces learning, whereas excessive levels of stress and anxiety interfere with learning. Educators know from subsequent cognitive psychology studies and firsthand classroom experience that high stress, boredom, confusion, low motivation, and anxiety can hinder students' learning (Christianson, 1992).

Research using neuroimaging and neuroelectrical brain wave monitoring supports the connection between emotion and learning, enabling us to see what happens in the brain during stress (Introini-Collison, Miyazaki, & McGaugh, 1991). The amygdala, part of the limbic system in the temporal lobe, senses threat and becomes overactive, delaying or blocking electrical activity conduction through the higher cognitive centers of the brain. When the amygdala is in the overactive metabolic state associated with stress, the rest of the brain's cortex does not show the usual fMRI or PET scan activation that represents the processing of data (Chugani, 1998; Pawlak, Magarinos, Melchor, McEwen, & Strickland, 2003). New information coming through the sensory intake areas of the brain cannot pass as efficiently through the amygdala's affective filter to gain access to the brain's cognitive processing and memory storage areas such as the left prefrontal cortex.

Additional evidence of the amygdala's role as an affective filter comes from real-time neuroelectric studies, which demonstrate that the somatosensory cortex areas are the most active areas of the brain during the moments when new information is received. These are regions found in each brain lobe that receive input from each individual sense—hearing, touch, taste, vision, and smell (Andreasen et al., 1999). Mapping studies show that bursts of brain activity from the somatosensory cortex are followed milliseconds later by bursts of electrical activity in the hippocampus, the amygdala, and then the other parts of the limbic system (Sowell, Peterson, & Thompson, 2003). This is one of the most exciting areas of brain-based learning research because it shows which strategies stimulate and impede communication among the parts of the brain when an individual processes and stores information (Shadmehr & Holcomb, 1997).

This brain research supports educators' firsthand experience, which tells us that superior learning takes place when learning activities are enjoyable and relevant to students' lives, interests, and experiences (Puca & Schmalt, 1999). Teachers recognize the state of anxiety that occurs when students feel alienated from their reading experiences or anxious about their lack of understanding. I witnessed this response when, as a student teacher, I worked in a school district that had implemented time-and-page synchronization of its phonics-heavy reading program (Open Court). All teachers were required to cover material at a mandated pace, so that students at each grade level were on the same page of the program each day. Second graders were brought to tears or outbursts of frustration when they were confused, their requests for help went unheeded as teachers struggled to keep to the timetable. Students were told, "Don't worry if you don't understand or finish now, you'll be taught this same material in a lesson some time in the future."

Neurochemical, neuroimaging, and neuroelectric research support a learning model in which reading experiences are enjoyable and relevant. The brain research evidence reinforces the need for classrooms to become places where students' imaginations and spirits are embraced when reading time begins.

The Chemistry of Motivation

Research on neurochemistry also supports the benefits of intrinsically rewarding, positive experiences associated with the learning process. Chemical imbalances in the brain enable information to travel across nerve synapses—the gaps between neurons. (Information travels along the nerve cells' branching and communicating sprouts—axons and dendrites—as electrical impulses and is temporarily converted from an electrical impulse into a chemical one to travel across the synapses.) Neurotransmitters, such as dopamine, are brain proteins that are released by the electrical impulse on one side of the synapse and then float across the synaptic gap carrying the information with them to stimulate the next nerve ending in the pathway.

Neurochemical neuroimaging analyses show that dopamine release increases in response to pleasurable and positive experiences (Brembs, Lorenzetti, Reyes, Baxter, & Byrne, 2002). Early studies suggested that when an individual engages in certain activities (for example, playing, laughing, exercising, being read to, and recognizing personal achievements), the amount of dopamine released by the brain increases. Later studies discovered that neuron circuits going from the limbic system into the frontal lobe and other parts of the cerebrum, rich in dopamine receptors, respond to this dopamine release (Wunderlich, Bell, & Ford, 2005). Follow-up research has also shown increased release of dopamine even when subjects *anticipated* pleasurable states (Nader et al., 2002).

Because dopamine is the neurotransmitter associated with attention, memory, learning, and executive function, it follows that when the brain releases dopamine in expectation of pleasurable experience, this dopamine will be available to increase the processing of new information.

Unfortunately, most phonics-based reading curriculums do not place a priority on providing enjoyable reading materials that induce pleasurable states in the brain, pacing lessons at comfortable speeds, giving students opportunities for self-satisfaction, and acknowledging authentic achievement. The decodable reading books in phonics-heavy reading systems are often overly simplistic, and their language sounds unnatural because of the limitations of phonetically decodable vocabulary. Such books lack personal relevance or interest to many young readers. They do not stimulate a student's intrinsic interest in reading.

Brain Stimulation in Action

Researchers at the University of Maryland (Guthrie, Wigfield, Barbosa, & Perencevich, 2004) mixed reading strategy instruction and motivation support in a paradigm called Concept-Oriented Reading Instruction (CORI). The program helped students establish content goals for reading, allowed students to choose texts, used interesting texts, and encouraged social collaboration during reading. It also employed the cognitive strategies of generating related questions, activating background knowledge, summarizing text, searching for information, organizing information graphically, learning the structure of stories, and monitoring comprehension.

Concept-Oriented Reading Instruction was implemented in whole classrooms of elementary students. Using a variety of standardized tests to measure understanding, reading strategies, and motivation, the researchers found that classrooms that used the combined CORI formula scored significantly higher on standardized tests of reacting comprehension and on measures of reading motivation than did classrooms that used strategy instruction alone. The researchers concluded that teaching reading strategies is effective for improving reading, but not nearly as effective as coupling those strategies with motivational strategies. Considering the research on the amygdala, limbic system, and dopamine, it is not surprising that the motivation support paradigm of this program was so successful.

WHERE ARE WE NOW?

The stated goal of much education legislature is for all students to learn to read. The goal of most educators extends beyond that—for students not only to learn the mechanics of reading, but also to develop a love of reading. We can begin to achieve these goals when we teach students to read in nonthreatening, engaging, and effective ways.

Cognitive psychology, affective filter data, and neuroimaging, neuroelectric, and neurochemical evidence do not support an approach that puts phonics first at the expense of intrinsic appeal and significance to the young reader. They do support a phonics-embedded approach that uses literature as a medium through which motivated, engaged students can enjoyably learn reading skills and strategies.

Although valid neurological research offers exciting possibilities and must continue, we should not be fooled by policymakers or program developers who use the term *brain-based learning* in ways that many medical and teaching professionals consider irresponsible. Until there is a direct connection between double-blind, variable-controlled analysis and confirmed results, interpretations of data to "prove" that certain instructional strategies are superior fall into the realm of speculation. As educators, we can only evaluate the research, read objective evaluations by neutral third-party reviewers, and create or use strategies that are compatible with what we know about the brain. Teaching reading is still far from being pure science, and educators need to call on their training and experience as well as consider the findings of neurological research to shape their instruction.

References

Andreasen, N. C., O'Leary, D. S., Paradiso, S., Cizadlo, T., Arndt, S., & Watkins, G. L. (1999). The cerebellum plays a role in conscious episodic memory retrieval. *Human Brain Mapping, 8*(4), 226–234. Iowa City, IA: Wiley-Liss.

Brembs, B., Lorenzetti, F., Reyes, F., Baxter, D., Byrne, J. (2002). Operant reward learning in aplysia: Neuronal correlates and mechanisms, *Science, 31,* 1706–1709.

Christianson, S. A. (1992). Emotional stress and memory: A critical review. *Psychological Bulletin, 112*(2), 284–309.

Chugani, H. (1991). Biological basis of emotions: Brain systems and brain development. *Pediatrics, 102,* 1225–1229.

Coles, G. (2004). Danger in the classroom: "Brain glitch" research and learning to read. *Phi Delta Kappan, 85*(5), 344–351.

Dulay, H., & Burt, M. (1977). Remarks on creativity in language acquisition. In M. Burt, H. Dulay, & M. Finocchiaro (Eds.), *Viewpoints on English as a Second Language* (pp. 74–83). New York: Regents.

Friston, K. J., Zarahn, E., Joseph, O., Henson. R. N. A., & Dale, A. (1999). Stochastic designs in event-related fMRI. *Neuro-Image, 10*(5), 609–619.

Guthrie, J., Wigfield, A., Barbosa. P., & Perencevich, K. C. (2004). Increasing reading comprehension and engagement through concept-oriented reading instruction. *Journal of Educational Psychology, 96*(3), 403–423.

Introini-Collison, I., Miyazaki, N., & McGaugh, J. (1991). Involvement of the amygdala in the memory-enhancing effects of denbuteral. *Psychopharmocology, 104*(4), 541–544.

Jacobs, B., Schall, M., & Scheibel, A. B. (1993). A quantitative dendritic analysis of Wernicke's area in humans: Gender, hemispheric, and environmental factors. *Journal of Comparative Neurology, 327*(1), 91–111.

Kail, R., Hall, L., & Caskey, B. (1909). Processing speed, exposure to print, and naming speed. *Applied Psycholinguistics, 20,* 303–314.

Krashen, S. (1982). Theory versus practice in language training. In R. W. Blair (Ed.), *Innovative Approaches to Language Teaching* (p. 25). Rowley, MA: Newbury House.

Nader, M. A., Daunais, J. B., Moore, T., Nader, S. H., Moore, R. J., Smith, H. R., et al. (2002). Effects of cocaine self-administration on striatal dopamine systems in rhesus monkeys: Initial and chronic exposure. *Neuropsychopharmacology, 27*(1), 35–46.

Pawlak, R., Magarinos, A. M., Melchor, J., McEwen, B., & Strickland, S. (2003). Tissue plasminogen activator in the amygdala is critical for stress-induced anxiety-like behavior. *Nature Neuroscience, 55*(2), 100–174.

Puca, M., & Schmalt, H. (1999). Task enjoyment: A mediator between achievement motives and performance. *Motivation and Emotion, 23*(1), 15–29.

Schneider, W., & Chein, J. M. (2003). Controlled and automatic processing: Behavior, theory, and biological mechanisms. *Cognitive Science, 27,* 525–559.

Shadmehr, R., & Holcomb, H. (1997). Neural correlates of motor memory consolidation, *Science, 277*(5327), 821.

Shaywitz, S. E. (2003). *Overcoming dyslexia: A new and complete science-based program for reading problems at any level.* New York: Knopf.

Shaywitz, S. E., Shaywitz, B. A., Pugh, K. R., Fulbright, R. K., Constable, R. T., Menci, W. E., et al. (1998). Functional disruption in the organization of the brain for reading in dyslexia. *Proceedings of the National Academy of Sciences, 95,* 2636–2641.

Shaywitz, B. A., Shaywitz, S. E., Pugh, K. R., Menci, W. E., Fulbright, R. K., Skudlarskie, P., et al. (2002). Disruption of posterior brain systems of reading in children with developmental dyslexia. *Biological Psychiatry, 52,* 101–110.

Sowell, E. R., Peterson, B. S., & Thompson, P. M. (2003). Mapping cortical change across the human life span. *Nature Neuroscience, 6,* 309–315.

Wunderlich, K., Bell, A., & Ford, L. (2005). Improving learning through understanding of brain science research. *Learning Abstracts, 8*(1) 41–43.

chapter 2

Doing Your Own Research: From Proposal to Final Report

IMPORTANT *Ideas*

1. Preparing a proposal for your research study increases the probability that all the subsequent steps of the research process will be successful.

2. A good way to start identifying a research problem to study is by reading literature reviews and articles in your areas of interest.

3. Replication of previous research findings is important for the advancement of research knowledge.

4. You are more likely to write a successful research proposal if you follow a standard proposal guide from your university or other authoritative source.

5. Test your understanding of your proposed research study by attempting to state its purpose in one or two sentences.

6. After stating the purpose of your study in general terms, you should make it more specific by formulating research questions or hypotheses and by identifying the variables (in quantitative research) or case features (in qualitative research) that you plan to study.

7. A systematic literature review will help you prepare a sound research proposal and solve problems of practice.

8. In preparing a research proposal, you need to decide on the research design that is most appropriate for answering your research questions or testing your hypotheses.

9. It usually is impossible to study everyone in the population that interests you, so you need to select a sample from that population and specify your sampling procedure in the research proposal.

10. Careful identification of variables or case features will make it easier to identify all the measures or cases needed for your proposed study.

11. Specify your data analysis procedures in the research proposal to ensure that your eventual data can be analyzed appropriately.

12. You probably will need to submit your research proposal to an institutional review board, which will determine whether it adequately protects the research participants from certain risks.

13. In planning your research proposal, you need to think about the steps you will take to gain the cooperation of the research participants.

14. You should create a timeline for all the steps of your proposed study to ensure that there are no conflicts with your own time limitations or those of your research participants.

15. A pilot study of your measures and procedures, preferably completed as part of the proposal preparation process, helps to ensure that you will not encounter unexpected difficulties when you actually conduct the study.

16. Unexpected problems often arise while a study is being conducted, and you will need to find ways to solve them without compromising the integrity of the study.

17. To help in preparing the report of your completed research study, first read exemplary reports that are similar in format (e.g., dissertation, journal article) to the one that you are writing. ■

Key TERMS

construct	institutional review board	replication
database	*Publication Manual of the*	search engine
descriptor	*American Psychological*	theory
hypothesis	*Association*	variable

If you are enrolled in a university degree program, you might be required to complete a research project. It might consist of library research, meaning a literature review on a topic that you select. A step-by-step process for doing a literature review is presented in Chapter 3, with several of the steps explained in more detail in Chapters 4 and 5.

Another possible degree requirement is to conduct your own research study, which is the subject of this chapter. In describing how to do a research study, we refer to concepts and procedures that we explain in depth in other chapters. We recommend that you read this chapter first, though, because it provides a framework for understanding those chapters.

Doing a research study involves three major steps:

1. Preparing a proposal that describes the study to be done and its significance
2. Collecting and analyzing data
3. Writing a report of the completed study

The first step, preparing the proposal, is the most crucial because it provides the foundation for the two other steps of the research process. Others can review the proposal for flaws and offer suggestions while there is still opportunity to benefit from them. Obviously, the reviewers can provide better feedback if the proposal is well detailed.

Still another benefit of a well-prepared proposal is that it will serve as the basis for the final report and thereby speed up the process of writing it. For example, if your proposal contains a good literature review and descriptions of tests or other measures, you can incorporate them directly into the final report.

If you publish your completed study as a master's thesis or doctoral dissertation or present it at a professional conference, you will be required to submit the proposal, perhaps in modified form, to an institutional review board. It will determine whether you have included adequate procedures for protecting the rights of your research participants. If the board rejects your proposal, you will need to revise it. Revision will delay the start of data collection, which can be a serious problem for studies that are dependent on the schedule of schools or other organizations.

Identifying a Research Problem

The critical first step in doing a study is identifying a suitable problem to investigate. How you frame the problem determines everything that follows and often is the difference between a study that genuinely advances knowledge about education and one that does not. Therefore, we advise you to take your time with this step.

Novice researchers often attempt to identify a problem solely by reflecting on their experience as educators, or by simply thinking about education in general. Reflection is fine, but it needs to be supplemented by reading the research literature in an area of interest to you. You can start by reading a published literature review in your area of interest (see Chapters 4 and 5 for guidance on locating a suitable review) or by reading research articles in a relevant journal. Before long, you should come across a research study, or set of related studies, that attract your interest. It is highly likely that you will be able to identify a research problem by building on this study or set of related studies.

Some educators think that this approach does not lead to an "original" study or that they are somehow "cheating" by building on the ideas of others. In fact, the goal of research in the physical and social sciences is to construct a cumulative body of knowledge and theory, not to create a series of original findings that are unrelated to each other.

It is legitimate and useful to pursue this goal by doing **replication** research, which is an investigation that uses the methods of a previous study to determine whether the same findings are repeated. The replication study does not need to copy the previous study's methods exactly, though. For example, it might include a sample drawn from a different population to determine whether the original study's findings are generalizable beyond the sample that the researchers used.

If you have any doubts about the value of replication, we suggest that you study the work of Albert Einstein, who is considered one of the most creative scientists who ever lived. In a recent biography of his life, Walter Isaacson (2007) showed how Einstein drew on the writings of physicists, philosophers of science, and inventors to frame the problems that led to his theories of general and special relativity. Because Einstein was a theoretical physicist, it was left to others to study these theories and design empirical studies to test their soundness.

In other words, Einstein was not a lone, creative mind. His contributions to knowledge built on the research and speculations of other scientists and in turn provided a basis for investigations by still other scientists.

Even a simple replication of a previous study can make an important contribution to knowledge about education. Anthony Kelly and Robert Yin (2007) make the point this way:

> A limitation of both qualitative and quantitative studies in education is that they are difficult to replicate, which has led to many one-time-only study reports in both genres. However, the findings from any single study cannot be the basis on which a practitioner or policymaker draws a conclusion about a phenomenon or takes action. The most responsible use of research articles follows an accumulation of knowledge across multiple research studies. (p. 133)

The phrase "accumulation of knowledge" in this statement expresses well the idea that one research study builds on another. In doing a research study, you should consider yourself a member of a community of fellow researchers, not a lone explorer.

We recommend that you read some research articles in refereed journals. In the vast majority of them, you will find statements that indicate how the researchers grounded their study in the existing literature on the problem being studied. Also, you will find statements about possible directions that future research might take in light of the research results that they reported.

To illustrate the process of identifying a research problem, we start with a newspaper article that was cited in the *ASCD Smartbrief,* an online newsletter published by the Association for Supervision and Curriculum Development (see Chapter 1). The article, which appeared in the *Christian Science Monitor* (April 17, 2008), has the provocative title, "Good Teachers Teach to the Test." The author, Walt Gardner, starts the article with this comment: "I have a confession to make. For the entire 28 years that I taught high school English, I taught to the test. And I'm proud to finally admit it." Gardner goes on to note that, for him, teaching to the test means teaching the body of skills and knowledge represented by the test, not teaching the exact test items.

Gardner proceeds to make this claim: "If we're being honest, teaching to the test is done by almost all other effective teachers." We think that this claim frames a good problem for a research study. The problem to be investigated is whether the claim is true. We might put the claim to an empirical test by determining whether effective teachers spend more of their instructional time "teaching to the test" (as defined by Gardner) than do ineffective teachers.

Of course, we could not investigate this problem without defining what we mean by "effective" and "ineffective" teachers. Most likely, we would define teacher effectiveness, as many other people do, as the teacher's ability to promote student learning. By this definition, students would learn more from a highly effective teacher than from a less effective teacher.

Teacher effectiveness could be defined differently. That is the researcher's choice. However, the researcher has the responsibility to provide an explicit definition and defend it. You might recall from Chapter 1 that the use of explicitly defined concepts and procedures is one of the hallmarks of scientific research.

At this point, our research problem is firmly grounded in practice. It was stated by a highly experienced teacher. Also, we know from reading newspapers and professional journals that many educators are critical of "teaching to the test," especially the high-stakes tests mandated by the federal No Child Left Behind Act. A common criticism is that preparing students for these tests takes too much time away from instruction. Another criticism is that the tests focus on certain learning outcomes, to the detriment of other important learning outcomes.

Our next step is to start reading the research literature. We want to know how researchers have conceptualized the problem and what they have learned about it. Exploring the literature, we find that researchers typically conceptualize the problem as a "curriculum alignment" issue. They have investigated the extent to which state tests are aligned with state curriculum standards and the extent to which teachers align their classroom instruction with their own tests as well as with state tests and curriculum standards.

The claim underlying much of this research is that aligning instruction with one's own tests, as well as with other tests required by government agencies, is part of good teaching. Similarly, Walt Gardner (2008), the teacher whose article we cited above, claims that it is a good idea to "teach to the test," which can be rephrased as a claim that teachers should "align" their instruction with the test. Of course, this is just a claim until it is tested by research involving empirical data. The data either will support or reject the claim.

Outlining a Research Proposal

The process of identifying an idea for a research study and developing it into a proposal is challenging, even for an experienced researcher. A research proposal includes many elements, each of which requires careful thought. For this reason, you will benefit from a guide that specifies each element of the proposal and the order in which it appears, as shown in Figure 2.1. The guide will help you organize your thinking and ensure that you have not overlooked any part of the process of getting the proposal approved, collecting and analyzing data, and writing the final report.

The guide shown in Figure 2.1 organizes a research proposal into nine sections. Your university or other institution might require a different format for research proposals. It is unlikely, though, that their format differs markedly from the one shown in Figure 2.1. Also,

This form consists of a list of items in the form of questions and directions. By completing each item, you can create an outline of a research proposal. The outline then can be elaborated into a formal research proposal.

1. Purpose of Study
   A. The purpose of this study is to . . . (State the purpose succinctly in one or two sentences)
   B. What previous research is your study most directly based on? (Select three to five publications that are absolutely central)
   C. How does your study build on previous research?
   D. How will your study contribute to educational research and practice?

2. Research Questions, Hypotheses, Variables, and Case Delineation
   A. List your research questions or hypotheses.
   B. If you propose to test hypotheses, describe briefly the theory from which the hypotheses were derived.
   C. If your study is quantitative in nature, list the variables that you will study. For each variable, indicate whether it is an independent variable, a dependent variable, or neither.
   D. If the study is qualitative in nature, describe the case features on which data collection and analysis will focus.

3. Literature Search
   A. List the search engines and indexes that you will use to identify relevant publications.
   B. List the keywords and descriptors that you will use with search engines and indexes.
   C. Identify published literature reviews (if available) relating to your study.

4. Research Design
   A. Describe the research design that you selected for your study: descriptive, causal–comparative, correlational, experimental, case study or specific qualitative research tradition, evaluative, or action research.
   B. If your study is quantitative in nature, what are the threats to the internal validity of your research design? (Internal validity means the extent to which extraneous variables are controlled, so that observed effects can be attributed solely to the independent variable.) What will you do to minimize or avoid these threats?
   C. If your study is quantitative in nature, what are the limitations to the generalizability (i.e., external valid-ity) of the findings that will result from your research design? What will you do to maximize the generaliz-ability of your findings?
   D. If your study is qualitative in nature, what criteria do you consider to be relevant to judging the credibility and trustworthiness of the results that will be yielded by your research design?

5. Sampling
   A. If your study is quantitative in nature, describe the characteristics of the population that you will study.
   B. If your study is qualitative in nature, describe the phenomenon you wish to study and the cases that comprise instances of the phenomenon.
   C. Identify your sampling procedure and sampling unit.
   D. Indicate the size of your sample, and explain why that sample size is sufficient.
   E. Indicate whether the sample will be formed into subgroups, and if so, describe the characteristics of the subgroups.
   F. If your study will involve the use of volunteers, explain whether their characteristics will affect the generalizability of the research findings.

6. Methods of Data Collection
   A. For each of the variables that you plan to study (see 2.C), indicate whether you will measure it by a test, questionnaire, interview, observational procedure, or content analysis. Indicate whether the measure is already available or whether you will need to develop it.
   B. For each measure stated above, indicate which types of validity and reliability are relevant and how you will check them.
   C. If your study is qualitative in nature, indicate whether your data collection will focus on etic or emic perspectives, or both; how you will collect data on each case feature that you have chosen for study (see 2.D); and the nature of your involvement in the data-collection process.

7. Data-Analysis Procedures
   A. What descriptive statistics and inferential statistics, if any, will you use to analyze each of your research questions or hypotheses?
   B. If your study is qualitative in nature, indicate whether you will use an interpretational, structural, or reflective method of analysis.

8. Ethics and Human Relations
   A. What risks, if any, does your study pose for research participants? What steps will you take to minimize these threats?
   B. Will the study need to be approved by an institutional review board? If yes, describe the approval process.
   C. How will you gain entry into your proposed research setting, and how will you gain the cooperation of your research participants?

9. Timeline
   A. Create a timeline listing in order all the major steps of your study. Also indicate the approximate amount of time that each step will take.

most journals require or recommend that authors organize their research manuscripts into the sections stated in the ***Publication Manual of the American Psychological Association*** (2001, pp. 15–27):

- Introduction—the research problem and its importance; literature review; definition of the variables; hypotheses
- Method—research participants; materials; procedures used in the research design
- Results—statistical or other analysis of the data; tables and figures
- Discussion—confirmation or disconfirmation of hypotheses; interpretation of the results; contribution of the study to theory and real-life phenomena

Comparing the APA guidelines and the proposal guide in Figure 2.1 shows that they are quite similar. For this reason, following the proposal guide will facilitate not only the process of conducting your study, but the preparation of a final report (e.g., a thesis or dissertation) and a manuscript submitted to a journal for publication.

The next sections of the chapter explain each section of the proposal guide and illustrate it by using the research problem about curriculum alignment that we introduced above.

You will note that the guide shown in Figure 2.1 specifies various ways in which a proposal for a quantitative research study differs from a proposal for a qualitative research study. We explain these differences in this chapter, and they are further elaborated in other chapters of the book.

Because we will continue to refer to Figure 2.1 throughout the book, we have helped you locate it easily by repeating it as Appendix 1.

Purpose of Study

A good self-check on whether you understand your proposed study is to attempt to state your research purpose in one or two sentences. Using our "teaching to the test" example, we might state our purpose in these words:

> The main purpose of my study is to determine the extent to which teachers design their classroom instruction and assessments so that they are aligned with state standards and assessments. A related purpose is to determine whether students perform better on their teachers' assessments and on state assessments if teachers improve their curriculum alignment.

This statement is brief but sufficiently detailed to give direction to the design of the study. Note that we used the term *assessment* because it connotes a broader range of possible tests (e.g., projects, essays, class presentations) than the term *test*, which has more limited connotations (typically multiple-choice or brief-response items).

Before you can state your research purpose in such a concise form, you will need to review relevant educational literature, including articles and books written for practitioners and reports of research studies. You are likely to find many publications on important topics, but typically just a few that strongly influence the design of your study. You should discuss these publications in some depth to give the reader a sense of what is known about the topic and what you propose to study in order to advance knowledge about it.

We found a substantial number of research articles, opinion articles, and books about curriculum alignment in the literature. One research article and one book appeared to be particularly useful:

> Parke, C. S., & Lane, S. (2008). Examining alignment between state performance assessment and mathematics classroom activities. *Journal of Educational Research, 101*(3), 132–146.
>
> Squires, D. A. (2008). *Curriculum alignment: Research-based strategies for increasing student achievement.* Thousand Oaks, CA: Corwin.

The studies included in these sources are relevant to our study's purpose and therefore would facilitate the preparation of our own literature review.

Parke and Lane (2008) note how school systems currently are attempting to revise their curricula and assessments so that they can increase the percentage of their students who do well on these assessments. It is unlikely that mandates for state standards and assessments will disappear in the foreseeable future, so if we do a good study, it can help to improve educational practice while also increasing research knowledge about curriculum alignment.

Research Questions and Hypotheses

A purpose statement provides a general description of what you hope to learn by doing your research study. This statement should then be elaborated to make it more specific. Typically, specificity is achieved by preparing a set of research questions. The following research questions reflect the purpose statement in the previous section:

1. To what extent are teachers' instructional activities in science aligned with state assessments in science that are administered to fourth-grade and sixth-grade students?
2. To what extent are teachers' classroom assessments in science aligned with state assessments that are administered to fourth-grade and sixth-grade students?
3. Do fourth-grade and sixth-grade students whose teachers align their instruction to a greater extent with state assessments perform better on the state assessments than students whose teachers align their instruction to a lesser extent?
4. Do fourth-grade and sixth-grade students whose teachers align their classroom assessments to a greater extent with state assessments perform better on the state assessments than students whose teachers align their classroom assessments to a lesser extent?

As we proceed to other sections of the research proposal, these questions will help us select appropriate procedures for data collection and data analysis. As we select each procedure, we will need to ask ourselves how appropriate it is for answering our research questions.

The four questions stated above were written with the intent of doing a quantitative research study. Research questions for a qualitative research proposal typically will be written in a different style, because qualitative researchers do not dictate the specific direction of data collection and analysis in advance. They need to remain open to what they observe and what their research participants tell them; these observations and comments often open up new lines of inquiry within the study.

Now let us consider a possible qualitative research proposal. Suppose we find that a state is conducting professional development workshops to help teachers understand instruction–assessment alignment and incorporate it into their lesson planning. Further suppose that the purpose of our qualitative study is to learn about the benefits and drawbacks that teachers see in their state's alignment program (i.e., state standards and state assessments aligned to them) and the problems that they see in trying to alter their classroom teaching to accommodate the alignment program.

The following are examples of research questions that might follow from this purpose statement if we chose to make an intensive qualitative case study of professional development workshops in one school district:

1. What benefits and drawbacks about the state's alignment program and proposals for classroom implementation do teachers mention during the workshops?
2. What other benefits and drawbacks do they mention in a confidential setting where state-level officials and workshop leaders are not present?
3. How do teachers who welcome the state's alignment program differ from teachers who question its value and resist implementing it in their classrooms?

Note that these research questions do not restrict the kinds of data collection and analysis procedures that can be used.

Depending on the qualitative study's purpose, other research questions can be framed. For example, we might focus on just one school and pose research questions about how various stakeholders (e.g., teachers, administrators, specialists, students, parents) respond to the state's alignment program over a designated period of time.

In qualitative research we typically avoid seeking to predict our findings (or even specify all our data-collection methods) in advance, but instead allow them to emerge. Therefore, we are unlikely to state research hypotheses in our proposal.

Returning to quantitative research study proposals, we might choose to state research hypotheses that will guide our study instead of framing research questions. In simple terms, a **hypothesis** in a research study is a prediction about expected findings. For example, we posed the following research question: "Do fourth-grade and sixth-grade students whose teachers align their classroom assessments to a greater extent with state assessments perform better on the state assessments than students whose teachers align their classroom assessments to a lesser extent?"

This question instead can be stated as a hypothesis: "Fourth-grade and sixth-grade students whose teachers use classroom assessments that are well aligned with state assessments will achieve higher scores on the state assessments than students whose teachers use poorly aligned classroom assessments."

Before you consider stating research hypotheses, you should be aware that hypotheses are a particular form of prediction, derived from theories. As stated in Chapter 1, a **theory** specifies a set of **constructs** and how they relate to each other. We also stated that constructs are structures and processes that are believed to underlie observed events and behavior. For example, intelligence is a construct, because many people believe that it is a real but unobservable structure that enables some students to learn better than others.

Hypotheses are more commonly used in basic research than in applied research, because the main goal of basic research is to deepen our collective understanding of phenomena through the development of good theories. The soundness of a theory is determined by doing empirical tests of hypotheses derived from it.

Quantitative Variables and Case Delineation

Once you have stated your research purpose and research questions or hypotheses (items 1.A, 1.B, 1.C, 1.D, 2.A, and 2.B in Figure 2.1), the next step is to specify the variables (in quantitative research) or aspects of cases (in qualitative research) that you will study. If specification of variables or case aspects is too difficult, it probably means that you need to read and think about the research literature in more depth.

If you are planning a quantitative study, you will need to identify each variable that you intend to measure. We explain the importance and meaning of variables in Chapter 7. For now, you can think of **variables** as anything you wish to study that has some degree of variability. For example, if students vary in the scores they receive on a test, we can say that student test performance is a variable. If all students take the same test, the test itself has not varied. In this case, a researcher would say that the test is a "constant," not a variable.

Three main variables are expressed in the four research questions stated previously for the proposed quantitative study:

1. The degree of alignment of teachers' instructional activities with the state assessment in science (Instructional alignment can vary among teachers)
2. The degree of alignment of teachers' classroom assessments with the state assessment in science (Assessment alignment can vary among teachers)
3. Student performance on the state assessment in science (Test performance can vary among students)

Each of these variables will be studied at two grade levels (fourth grade and sixth grade). Therefore, we have a total of six variables.

Qualitative researchers usually do not think in terms of variables. Instead, they select a case, or several cases, for intensive study. Then they think about which features of the case to study. We cannot study everything about a case. Instead, we must focus our study by identifying a limited number of features of the case about which we will collect data. This process is explained in Chapter 14.

We stated three research questions for a proposed qualitative research study. Although a state curriculum alignment program involves many stakeholders, we limited our case study to the perspectives of teachers. We also delineated which features of their perspectives to study, choosing to examine their perceptions toward two aspects of the program (benefits and drawbacks) and whether their general attitude is welcoming or resistant. Also, we chose to collect data about their perspectives in two contexts: public workshops and confidential meetings.

The third research question implies an interest in personal characteristics and how they affect teachers' perceptions and attitudes. Therefore, we will need to decide which aspects of the teachers' personal characteristics to study. For example, we might study their personality patterns, upbringing, level of schooling, academic achievement, views about students, and political attitudes. As we start collecting data, we might find ourselves generating additional research questions, each of which will require us to consider the possibility of new cases, and new features of those cases, to study.

Literature Search

We stated earlier in the chapter that a good research study is built on a strong understanding of the existing literature on the problem that you wish to investigate. Chapters 3, 4, and 5 will help you conduct a literature review in order to identify a suitable research problem and to find what has been learned about it, as reported in books, journal articles, institutional reports, conference reports, and other media.

We explain in these chapters that professional associations, governmental agencies, and commercial publishers have created bibliographic citations for these publications and organized them into electronic **databases.** You can explore these databases by the use of **search engines** and keywords. Most likely, you are already familiar with electronic databases, search engines, and keywords, even if you have not studied research methodology. For example, you probably use Google, Yahoo!, or something similar to search for information.

We used a general search engine for educators, ERIC (Education Resources Information Center), to look for studies relating to our research problem. We entered two **descriptor** phrases, "teaching to the test" and "curriculum alignment," in the ERIC search engine, which generated hundreds of relevant citations and brief summaries (abstracts) that helped us develop an understanding of what is already known about our research problem.

Your ability to search the education literature will enhance your professional expertise, whether you are preparing a proposal for a research study or looking for ideas to solve a problem of practice.

Research Design

The fourth set of items in the proposal guide shown in Figure 2.1 involves the design of your research study. Over time, researchers have developed standard approaches (called *designs*) for answering their questions or testing their hypotheses. In fact, much of this book is concerned with explaining and illustrating the most commonly used, or otherwise noteworthy, research designs.

To illustrate how research designs can differ, consider the problem of investigating teachers' reactions to a state-mandated curriculum alignment program. We might use a case study design to study in depth a few teachers at one school. We could interview them extensively to learn what they think about the alignment program.

Alternatively, we could use an experimental design in which we compare two groups of teachers: One group participates in a workshop that attempts to help them develop positive attitudes toward instruction–assessment alignment; a control group of teachers does not participate in the program. We measure the attitudes of both groups of teachers by a quantitative scale before and after the workshop interval.

The case study design is not better or worse than the experimental design. Both are well-established research designs, each of which has advantages depending on the researchers' preferences, needs, and constraints. Also, each is susceptible to different flaws. You need to be aware of these flaws and take steps to avoid them. That is why we explain not only the features of each research design in this book, but also their potential weaknesses and how to minimize them.

Sampling

It is nearly impossible to study every instance of the phenomenon that interests you. For example, if you are interested in investigating teachers' reactions to state-mandated tests administered in their classroom, you cannot study the entire population of teachers. It simply would be too expensive and time consuming. However, there are ways to select a sample that is representative of the population that concerns you. By using an appropriate sampling procedure, you can generalize your findings from the sample to that population if you have done a quantitative research study. If you have done a qualitative research study involving one or several cases, you can consider the applicability of your findings to other cases.

The section on sampling in the proposal guide shown in Figure 2.1 specifies various factors that you will need to consider in selecting a sample for your study. Sampling procedures in quantitative and qualitative research are described in Chapters 6 and 14, respectively.

Methods of Data Collection

Whatever your research design may be, you will be collecting empirical data. In fact, the collection of empirical data to answer questions or test hypotheses is the very essence of research. Empirical data are direct observations of the phenomena that we are studying. By contrast, beliefs, ideas, and theories are claims about what we would find if we collected empirical data. The major advances that we have seen in medicine, engineering, and other professions over the past century have come about, in large part, because researchers have collected empirical data to make discoveries or to test beliefs, ideas, and theories.

Section 6 of the proposal guide shown in Figure 2.1 will help you identify the measures you will use to collect empirical data and how to ensure that these measures will hold up to critical scrutiny by others.

Careful and complete listing of your variables or case features (Section 2 of the proposal guide) will help you greatly in selecting methods of empirical data collection. If your list is complete, you will not find later on, to your dismay, that you failed to measure an important variable or case feature during the data-collection phase of your study.

Chapters 6 and 14 present a range of data-collection procedures used in quantitative and qualitative research, respectively. Other chapters describe measurement procedures that have been developed specifically for use with particular research designs.

Data-Analysis Procedures

Raw data do not speak for themselves. They need to be analyzed and interpreted. Therefore, your research proposal should include a section on how you plan to analyze your data. The items in Section 7 of the proposal guide in Figure 2.1 provide an overview of the types of information that need to be included.

This planning will help you determine whether your research design will result in data that can be analyzed by statistical or qualitative procedures and are relevant to your research questions and hypotheses. You certainly want to avoid a situation in which you have completed your data collection, only to find that you have insufficient or inappropriate data for addressing one of your research questions or hypotheses.

The analysis of quantitative data involves the use of statistical techniques, which are described in Chapters 7, 8, and 9. Some qualitative data are also amenable to statistical analysis, but more likely you will use the analytical techniques described in Chapter 14. Other chapters present methods of data analysis that are specifically intended for a particular research design.

Ethics and Human Relations

As we have explained, the federal government requires that most research studies involving the study of humans must be evaluated by an institutional review board (IRB) before data collection can begin. The purpose of an **institutional review board** is to ensure that research participants are protected from harm or risk of harm.

The IRB will ask you to include a section in your research proposal, or complete a special form, in which you describe how you will protect research participants. For example, data about the research participants might expose them to risk if the data became public. You can avoid this risk by taking steps to ensure the participants' anonymity. Some research studies have unavoidable risks, but the IRB might tolerate them if the risks are minor and if the potential benefits of the study outweigh the risks.

Each IRB has its own procedures for reviewing research proposals. If you are doing a research study as a university degree requirement, it is likely that the university has an IRB and that the IRB has published its procedures. Because these procedures vary, we do not describe this aspect of proposal preparation in detail in Section 8 of the proposal guide in Figure 2.1.

You will note that Section 8 also refers to human relations. You cannot take it for granted that your intended research participants will allow you to collect data from them directly or from their students or clients. Whether your participants are individuals in a professional role (e.g., school staff) or community representatives (e.g., residents of a household), they typically will want assurance that you are conducting a research study that has the seal of approval from an institution they respect. They also will want assurance that you are trustworthy and will treat participants and the data they provide with respect.

These assurances can come from the IRB, which typically has a standard form that indicates its approval of your research study. Assurances also can come from representatives of an institution that the research participants respect, possibly in the form of a letter on official letterhead, indicating that they have studied your proposal and approve of it. Ideally, the letter would also state what benefits are expected and who would benefit from the findings of your study.

Timeline

As you see, a research study involves many steps. The process might seem overwhelming, but you should be able to complete a successful research project if you are systematic in your approach.

To be systematic, it is helpful to analyze all the steps in your proposed study and estimate a completion date for each step. This process is particularly important if you plan to collect data in schools. For example, if you plan to collect data from teachers, you most likely will need to do it when school is in session. If you plan to collect data from students, you probably will need to do it on days when they are not involved in such activities as taking tests or going on field trips.

Other Steps in the Research Process

We believe that the intellectual exercise of preparing a thorough research proposal is at the heart of the research process. A detailed proposal greatly increases the likelihood of a successful study, and it also facilitates other steps in the research process, which we describe next.

Pilot Study

A pilot study of key measures and procedures helps to ensure the success of any research study. For example, if you plan to develop a questionnaire, test, or other data-collection instrument, it is helpful to try it out with a few research participants prior to formal data collection. You might discover that some of your questions and directions are unclear or require skills that data collectors or research participants do not possess. You can ask these individuals for guidance in revising the items and directions as needed.

The ideal situation is to conduct a pilot study of key measures and procedures before or during preparation of the research proposal. Reviewers of the proposal, including an IRB, will look at the proposal more favorably if you can state that your measures and procedures have been piloted and revised as needed.

If necessary, it might be possible to do a pilot study after the proposal has been reviewed and approved. However, you will probably need to submit to the IRB or review board any substantial changes made as a result of the pilot study.

Data Collection

The vast majority of research studies in education involve collecting data from humans, and there is always the possibility that your best-laid plans will go astray. For example, suppose your study involves administration of a test to a class of students. It might well be that some students will be absent for various reasons. Make-up sessions are an option if they do not interfere with your research timeline.

Many other problems can occur during the data-collection phase of a research study. You will need to exercise judgment and ingenuity in dealing with them. More experienced researchers can help you devise the best solution for a particular situation. Most problems can be managed if you have designed the proposal well, pilot-tested key measures and procedures, and built good relations with all stakeholders involved with the study.

Writing a Research Report

Writing a research proposal that includes the items shown in Figure 2.1 will greatly facilitate the last step—writing your final report. The proposal is an outline, or framework, for the finished report, and most parts of a proposal are included in final reports, such as theses, dissertations, journal articles, and conference papers. If your university or other institution has a required format for writing a research report, you simply need to follow that format.

We find it particularly helpful to locate good examples of research reports and adopt their organization and style. If you are writing a course paper, master's thesis, or doctoral dissertation, you can ask your advisors to recommend completed papers, theses, or dissertations that they consider exemplary.

Another approach is to read articles in refereed journals that publish research studies similar to yours. After reading five or so articles, you will begin to develop a sense of the writing style and format that are appropriate for formal research reports.

Many universities require that their students in education and related disciplines follow the style specifications of the *Publication Manual of the American Psychological Association* (2001). We referred to this manual's specifications for the format of research reports earlier in the chapter. In addition, the manual contains a great many other specifications, which have to do with such matters as language bias, statistical symbols, tables and figures, and bibliographic citations.

The APA manual is approximately 400 pages long and can seem intimidating. We do not recommend that you study it page by page. Instead, review the table of contents to get a sense of the topics that it covers. Then refer to it as you have questions about the preparation of your research report, such as how to construct a table or prepare a list of references that you have cited.

A Final Note about Using a Proposal Guide

This concludes our explanation of how to conduct a research study. As you read the remaining chapters of the book, each step of the process should become clearer to you.

If you are planning to do a research study, we recommend that you review the proposal guide in Figure 2.1, or another suitable guide, as you read each chapter. After reading a chapter, determine how its content pertains to a particular section, or sections, of the guide. Then complete the sections if they are relevant to your proposed study. Over time, you will see your study gradually taking shape.

We recommend that you occasionally show your evolving proposal to your research advisor for feedback and assurance that you are on the right track. It is relatively easy to revise an outline for a proposal, or trash it and start over again. It is much more difficult and emotionally draining to write a complete, polished proposal only to learn that it must undergo extensive revision or be scrapped.

An example of
OUTLINING RESEARCH PROPOSALS

We have created two proposal outlines to illustrate the process of using the proposal guide shown in Figure 2.1. The proposals are for a research study about curriculum alignment. They are similar in certain respects to the example already presented in this chapter.

The first proposal outline is presented in Appendix 2.1. It is for a quantitative research study. If you are planning to do a quantitative study using one of the research designs presented in Part III, this example will be helpful.

The second proposal outline is presented in Appendix 2.2. It is for a qualitative research study. If you are planning to do a qualitative study using one of the research designs presented in Part IV, this example will be helpful.

APPENDIX *2.1* Outline of a Proposal for a Descriptive Research Study

1. Purpose of Study

A. Purpose Statement
The purpose of this study is to learn how educators go about aligning curriculum content with instruction and test content under conditions involving a federal or state mandate to improve students' learning.

B. Relevant Previous Research
Among the studies we have identified in our literature review, the following three studies, all involving quantitative research designs, are particularly relevant to our research purpose. We provide the bibliographic citation and the abstract for each study as it appears in the ERIC database.

Blank, R. K., Smithson, J., Porter, A., Nunnaley, D., & Osthoff, E. (2006). Improving instruction through schoolwide professional development: Effects of the data-on-enacted-curriculum model. *ERS Spectrum, 24*(3), 9–23. (ERIC Reference Number EJ795681)

Abstract. The instructional improvement model Data on Enacted Curriculum was tested with an experimental design using randomized place-based trials. The improvement model is based on using data on instructional practices and achievement to guide professional development and decisions to refocus on instruction. The model was tested in 50 U.S. middle schools in five large urban districts, with half of the schools in each district randomly assigned to receive the 2-year treatment. Each school formed an improvement leadership team of five to seven members, including teachers, subject specialists, and at least one administrator. Teams received professional development on data analysis and instructional leadership and then the teams provided training and technical assistance to all math and science teachers in their school. The central premise of the treatment model is to provide teachers with data on their instructional practices and student achievement, to teach them how to use that data to identify weaknesses and gaps in instruction compared with state standards, and to focus school-level professional development on needed curriculum content and classroom practices. After a 2-year period of implementing the improvement model, the analysis of change in instruction showed significant effects of the model. The longitudinal analysis of instruction before and after treatment showed math teachers in treatment schools had significant improvement in alignment of instruction with standards compared with teachers in control schools, and the math teachers on the leader teams showed significantly greater gains than all other teachers.

Parke, C. S., & Lane, S. (2008). Examining alignment between state performance assessment and mathematics classroom activities. *Journal of Educational Research, 101*(3), 132–147. (ERIC Reference Number EJ787815)

Abstract. The authors describe research on the extent to which mathematics classroom activities in Maryland were aligned with Maryland learning outcomes and the Maryland School Performance Assessment Program (MSPAP; Maryland State Department of Education, 1995, 2000). The study was part of a larger research project (S. Lane, C. S. Parke, & C. A. Stone, 1999) that focused on the overall impact of MSPAP on schools, teachers, and students. The authors collected 3,948 instruction, assessment, and test-preparation activities from a statewide stratified random sample of 250 teachers in the tested grades (3, 5, and 8) and nontested grades (2, 4, and 7). The authors describe the methods used to collect, code, and analyze teachers' classroom activities concerning 7 components: (a) mathematics process outcomes; (b) mathematics content outcomes; (c) student response types; (d) interpretation of charts, tables, and graphs; (e) use of manipulatives and calculators; (f) integration with other subject areas; and (g) overall similarity to MSPAP. They also highlight results for overall degree of alignment as well as differences in alignment across grade levels and type of activity (instruction vs. assessment). Most classroom activities aligned with aspects of state assessment and standards. Only minimal differences occurred across grades. However, degree of alignment was higher for instruction than assessment activities. This research approach can be useful to other educators and researchers interested in studying alignment among standards, assessment, and instruction.

Roach, A. T., Niebling, B. C., & Kurz, A. (2008). Evaluating the alignment among curriculum, instruction, and assessments: Implications and applications for research and practice. *Psychology in the Schools, 45*(2), 158–167. (ERIC Reference Number EJ783243)

Abstract. Alignment has been defined as the extent to which curricular expectations and assessments are in agreement and work together to provide guidance for educators' efforts to facilitate students' progress toward desired academic outcomes. The Council of Chief State School Officers has identified three preferred models as frameworks for evaluating alignment: Webb's alignment model, the Surveys of Enacted Curriculum model, and the Achieve model. Each model consists of a series of indices that summarize or describe the general match or coherence between state standards, large-scale assessments, and, in some cases, classroom instruction. This article provides an overview of these frameworks for evaluating alignment and their applications in educational practice and the research literature. After providing an introduction to the use of alignment to evaluate large-scale accountability systems, the article presents potential extensions of alignment for use with vulnerable populations (e.g., students with disabilities, preschoolers), individual students, and classroom teachers. These proposed applications can provide information for facilitating efforts to improve teachers' classroom instruction and students' educational achievement.

C. Building on Previous Research

Previous research has found promising evidence that alignment of curriculum with instruction and test content improves students' academic achievement (e.g., Blank, Smithson, Porter, Nunnaley, & Osthoff, 2006, cited above). Also, some research studies have examined the existing degree of alignment among curriculum, instruction, and tests in schools (e.g., Parke & Lane, 2008, cited above). However, we could find no studies that examined the process used by schools to improve these alignments.

Our proposed study extends previous research by examining the alignment process.

D. Contribution to Educational Research and Practice

Research on other school improvement initiatives demonstrates that the reform process often is beset with problems and that educators' success in solving these problems affects how well the initiative is institutionalized and how much it benefits students. By examining the process of curriculum alignment at selected school sites, we hope to identify factors that facilitate or hinder the process.

Identification of these factors might help other schools plan their alignment process in ways that increase their likelihood of success in improving students' academic achievement.

The proposed study, once completed and reported, might stimulate other researchers to conduct additional studies on this particular approach to school improvement to identify how best to plan and conduct it.

2. Research Questions, Hypotheses, Variables, and Case Delineation

A. Research Questions

We have three research questions:

1. What percentage of schools in the state have engaged in curriculum alignment?
2. For schools that have engaged in curriculum alignment, what is their frequency of use of various alignment procedures?
3. What problems do these groups encounter as they engage in planning and conducting the alignment process?
4. What are the solutions that these groups attempt as they cope with problems in planning and conducting the alignment process?

B. Hypotheses

Not relevant to this study.

C. Variables

The questionnaire described in section 6.A below includes items asking about a school's involvement in a curriculum-instruction-test alignment process during the previous 2 years and about problems and solutions during the process. For now, we'll assume that the items include three problems (A, B, C) and their corresponding solutions (A, B, C).

In this scenario, there are a total of 13 variables:

1. The level of the school's involvement in an alignment process (a 7-point scale).
2. Occurrence of problem A (a yes-no scale)
3. Occurrence of problem B (a yes-no scale)
4. Occurrence of problem C (a yes-no scale)
5. Occurrence of solution A (a yes-no scale)

6. Occurrence of solution B (a yes-no scale)
7. Occurrence of solution C (a yes-no scale)
8. If problem A occurred, its level of severity (a 7-point scale)
9. If problem B occurred, its level of severity (a 7-point scale)
10. If problem C occurred, its level of severity (a 7-point scale)
11. If solution A was tried, its level of usefulness (a 7-point scale)
12. If solution B was tried, its level of usefulness (a 7-point scale)
13. If solution C was tried, its level of usefulness (a 7-point scale)

D. Case Delineation
Not relevant to this study.

3. Literature Search

A. Search Engines and Indexes
The ERIC search engine will be sufficient for our research purposes.

B. Keyworks and Descriptors
Our preliminary use of ERIC suggests that the keywords "alignment" and "curriculum alignment" by themselves or combined with the descriptors "achievement gains" and "academic achievement" will identify studies relevant to our research purpose.

C. Published Literature Review
The following literature review appears pertinent to our research studies. It is an article in a journal's theme issue about how educators have developed and studied methodological procedures involved in curriculum alignment over the past decade.

Beck, M. D. (2007). Commentary: Review and other views—"Alignment" as a psychometric issue. *Applied Measurement in Education, 20*(1), 127–135.

4. Research Design

A. Type of Design
The research questions call for a descriptive research design using quantitative methodology. The first question requires us to determine the *percentage* of schools having a certain characteristic, namely, involvement in curriculum alignment. The other three questions require us to determine the *frequency of use* of various alignment procedures, the *frequency* of various problems that occur during the alignment process, and the *frequency* of various solutions to these problems.

B. Threats to Internal Validity
Not relevant to this study.

C. Threats to Generalizability
The study will include a random sample of schools drawn from one state. The results should generalize at least to other schools in this state and possibly to other states having similar characteristics.

D. Criteria for Judging Credibility and Trustworthiness of Results
Not relevant to this study.

5. Sampling

A. Population Characteristics
All school systems in the United States are experiencing the need to improve student learning because of the No Child Left Behind Act. Our resources do not enable us to study all 50 states and U.S. territories. Therefore, we will focus on the state in which we reside. In the future, we or other researchers can replicate our study in other states.

B. Cases and Phenomena
Not relevant to this study.

C. Sampling Procedure

We will obtain a list of all schools in our selected state from the state department of education. We then will draw three random samples of schools from this list. Specifically, we will draw a random sample of elementary schools, a random sample of middle schools, and a random sample of high schools. There will be an equal number of schools in each of these samples.

Our sampling unit is schools. The sampling procedure is stratified random sampling, because we are drawing random samples from three different types of schools.

D. Sample Size

We do not have sufficient resources to study every school in the state. However, we wish to be able to make reasonably accurate generalizations from our sample to the population (i.e., all schools in the state). We will consult with a statistician to determine a sample size that will yield an acceptable margin of error for our statistics.

E. Sampling Subgroups

As we stated in section 5.C above, the sample will include three subgroups: elementary schools, middle schools, and high schools.

F. Use of Volunteers

We hope to obtain the participation of all schools included in our random sample. If a school does not wish to participate, we will randomly draw another school of the same type (elementary, middle, high) from the list of all schools in the state.

We will keep track of the number of schools in the original sample that decline participation in the sample. We realize that each declining school creates a risk for the generalizability of our findings to the target population (i.e., all schools in the selected state).

6. Methods of Data Collection

A. Measures

We will use a questionnaire as our data-collection instrument. It will be mailed to the principal of each school, unless the principal has been in this position at the school for less than 2 years. If that is the situation, we will not include the school in the sample, but will randomly draw another school from the list of all schools in the state.

The questionnaire will include a scale on which the principal will rate his school's involvement in a curriculum-instruction-test alignment process. The lowest point on the school indicates no involvement in this type of process. The highest point indicates a major change in the school's curriculum and instructional/testing practices as a result of an alignment process.

The questionnaire also will include a list of problems (e.g., school staff members who question the need for an alignment process) and solutions (e.g., recruiting an external consultant) that are commonly found in the literature on school improvement. The questionnaire will ask the principal to rate each problem on a scale from 0 (it did not occur) to 7 (it was a major stumbling block for the process). It also will ask the principal to indicate whether the solution was used, and if it was used, to rate its effectiveness on a scale from 0 (it was not useful) to 7 (it was a substantial aid in moving the alignment process forward).

The questionnaire also will include space for the principal to indicate problems and solutions not on the list, and also to make comments about the alignment process.

B. Validity and Reliability

We will ask a small sample of principals not involved in the study to evaluate the questionnaire items for clarity and relevance to the alignment process. We will make changes to the questionnaire based on their feedback.

We will select a small group of principals in the research sample for a reliability check. We will ask each of these principals to nominate another educator in the school (e.g., a teacher or assistant principal) who is knowledgeable about the school's activities over the past year.

We will ask each of these nominated individuals to complete the same questionnaire. If the questionnaire is reliable, we should find a high level of agreement between the principal's responses and the other individual's responses.

C. Emic and Etic Perspective
Not relevant to this study.

7. Data-Analysis Procedures

A. Statistical Analysis
We will compute the percentage of schools that reported one of the three problems or three solutions listed in the questionnaire. Also, we will report the mean and standard deviation for each of the seven rating scales. We will do these analyses separately for each of the three subgroups: elementary, middle, and high schools.

We will do an analysis of variance for each of the rating scale scores to determine whether there is a significant difference in the ratings of the elementary, middle, and high schools. Also, we will do a chi-square analysis to determine whether the percentage of each of the problems and solutions differs significantly at each of these levels of schooling.

We will do a content analysis of the principal's comments about problems and solutions not included in our list. We will identify each problem and solution that was mentioned, and then count the frequency with which each one was mentioned by each subgroup of principals (elementary, middle, and high school).

B. Qualitative Analysis
Not relevant to this study.

8. Ethics and Human Relations

A. Ethical Risks
Principals might feel that they are at risk if their ratings of the alignment process were revealed to school staff and other administrators. Therefore, we will assure them that their identities will be concealed in the data analyses and final report.

We will report demographic data about the schools included in the sample, but in a manner that makes it impossible to link demographic data about a particular school with the ratings of that school's principal.

B. Approval by an Institutional Review Board
The study will need to be reviewed by an institutional review board, especially because it poses risks for some participants. We will identify the appropriate board and follow its designated procedures.

C. Gaining Entry and Cooperation
We think that the proposed study will be of great interest to state departments of education that are concerned about improving student achievement because of federal and state legislative mandates. We would like to get a letter from the selected state department of education that endorses our study and encourages principals to complete the questionnaire. We propose to include the letter with the questionnaire.

9. Timeline
We would like to mail the questionnaire several months after the school year begins. Although principals are always busy, they are likely to be less busy at this time than at the start of the school year.

By mailing the questionnaire early rather than late in the school year, we will have sufficient time for several follow-up mailings in order to increase the response rate to the questionnaire.

APPENDIX 2.2   Outline of a Proposal for a Case Study

---

1. Purpose

A. Purpose Statement
The purpose of this study is to learn how educators go about aligning curriculum content with instruction and test content under conditions involving a federal or state mandate to improve students' learning.

B. Relevant Previous Research
Among the studies identified in our literature review, three studies are particularly relevant to our research purpose.

Foley, E. M., Klinge, A., & Reisner, E. R. (2007). *Evaluation of New Century High Schools: Profile of an initiative to create and sustain small, successful high schools. Final report.* Policy Studies Associates, Inc. (ERIC Document Reproduction Service No. ED498781)

> *Abstract.* "The most important school-level influence on student performance, as measured by credit accrual, was 'the quality of instructional systems,' including measures of the perceived alignment of instruction with Regent standards. . . . Case studies in the 2005–06 school year and earlier evaluation findings illuminated the influence on student outcomes of conditions that were fairly uniform across NCHS schools. Influential factors included: (1) Small enrollments; (2) Close student-teacher relationships and adult mentoring of youth; (3) Extension of student learning outside the regular school setting and school day; and (4) Use of data to track student performance."

Larson, W., & Howley, A. (2006). *Leadership of mathematics reform: The role of high school principals in rural schools.* Appalachian Collaborative Center for Learning, Assessment, and Instruction in Mathematics. (ERIC Document Reproduction Service No. ED498435)

> *Abstract.* "This monograph presents the results of qualitative interviews of seven selected principals [in remote Appalachian schools]. . . . The principals' responses revealed six categories . . . [The second category is] Strategies: Two strategies were used by most schools: curriculum alignment and individualization."

Campbell, T. (2007). *The science laboratory experiences of Utah's high school students.* (ERIC Document Reproduction Service No. ED497728)

> *Abstract.* "This research investigated the extent to which science laboratory experiences encountered by Utah high school students aligned with reform efforts outlined in national standards documents. Through both quantitative and qualitative methods the findings revealed that while there were instances of alignment found between science laboratory experiences and national standards documents when considering scientific content emphasis, this same alignment was not found when considering whether the experiences emphasized scientific processes."

C. Building on Previous Research
Previous research has found promising evidence that aligning of curriculum with instruction and test content improves students' academic achievement. However, we could find no studies that examined the actual alignment process. Our proposed study extends previous research by looking at this process in depth.

D. Contribution to Educational Research and Practice
Research on other school improvement initiatives demonstrates that the reform process often is beset with problems and that educators' success in solving

these problems affects how well the initiative is institutionalized and how much it benefits students. By examining the process of curriculum alignment at selected school sites, we hope to identify factors that facilitate or hinder the process.

Identification of these factors might help other schools plan their alignment process in ways that increase their likelihood of success in improving students' academic achievement.

The proposed study, once completed and reported, might stimulate other researchers to conduct additional studies on this particular approach to school improvement to identify how best to plan and conduct it.

2. **Research Questions, Hypotheses, Variables, and Case Delineation**

   A. **Research Questions**

   We have three research questions:

   1. What procedures do administrators, teachers, and specialists use in planning and conducting a process to align curriculum content with instruction and test content?
   2. What problems do these groups encounter as they engage in planning and conducting the alignment process?
   3. What are the solutions that these groups attempt as they cope with problems in planning and conducting the alignment process?

   B. **Hypotheses**

   Not relevant to this study.

   C. **Variables**

   Not relevant to this study.

   D. **Case Delineation**

   We plan to focus on (1) the problems that occur during the process and how those problems get resolved, and (2) alignment procedures and products for which there is consensual agreement and those for which consensual agreement could not be reached.

3. **Literature Search**

   A. **Search Engines and Indexes**

   The ERIC search engine will be sufficient for our research purposes.

   B. **Keywords and Descriptors**

   Our preliminary use of ERIC suggests that the keywords "alignment" and "curriculum alignment," by themselves or combined with the descriptors "achievement gains" and "academic achievement," will identify studies relevant to our research purpose.

   C. **Published Literature Review**

   We have not yet identified a literature review on curriculum-instruction-test alignment.

4. **Research Design**

   A. **Type of Design**

   The research design is a case study. This choice is based on our desire to produce a thick description of the process of curriculum alignment. We wish to understand in depth the experiences of a few school sites, from the perspective of those directly involved in the process, rather than to grasp at a surface level the experiences of many school sites.

   B. **Threats to Internal Validity**

   Not relevant to this study.

   C. **Threats to Generalizability**

   Our plan to use a volunteer sample might limit the applicability of our findings to other schools undergoing an alignment process. We will provide an intensive description of the school's characteristics to help readers of our final report decide whether our findings apply to their situation.

D. Criteria for Judging Credibility and Trustworthiness of Results

We will create a chain of evidence by making a record of all data collected in the study, the individuals involved in the data collection, and the dates of data collection. Constructs and themes identified in the data analysis will be related to specific examples of data sources from which they were inferred.

We will write detailed vignettes of critical incidents in the curriculum alignment process, so that the process becomes clear and real for readers of the study. We will have several educational practitioners involved in the process read and evaluate the report in terms of its soundness and usefulness to them. Their feedback will be used to revise the report.

The primary methods of data collection will be interviews, direct observations of critical events, and inspection of documents generated as part of the curriculum alignment process. The collected data will be analyzed to determine whether they provide corroborative evidence for constructs and themes that we identify in the curriculum alignment process.

The soundness of data coding will be checked by having several researchers code samples of the data to determine whether they derive similar constructs and themes from the data.

The soundness of the interview data, observational data, and documents selected for analysis will be checked by having selected participants in the study check them for accuracy, bias, and completeness.

To ensure thoroughness of data collection, we will continually check with participants that we have identified all the individuals involved in the curriculum alignment process and that we have identified all relevant events leading up to initiation of the process and the process itself. The check will include a list of the individuals and events we have identified, showing the list to a sample of participants, and asking them whether any person or event is missing from the list.

5. Sampling

A. Population Characteristics

Not relevant to this study.

B. Cases and Phenomena

The phenomenon of interest to us is the process of curriculum alignment as enacted at the school level, although we realize that administrators at the district and state level also might influence it. Therefore, our case will comprise a school involved in this process.

C. Sampling Procedure

Because of the intensive data collection required by this study, we will select just one school (the case). The sampling strategy will be to select a typical case, which for us means a school that has a recent history of neither being a district leader in school change nor a reluctant participant.

We believe that this sampling strategy will enable us to identify typical (rather than atypical) problems, solutions, and products that result from a curriculum alignment process. To an extent, sampling also will involve a convenience strategy in that the school will be selected from a district that is near the researchers' work site. The proximity will permit the researchers to make frequent trips to the school to collect data and make validity checks.

D. Sample Size

We will select just one school for the case study. However, the sample will include anyone in the school, community, school district, or other agency who has an involvement in the alignment process within this school.

E. Sampling Subgroups

Participants in the study will be selected to represent all the stakeholders in the curriculum alignment process. The known stakeholders include district-level specialists, the principal, teachers on the alignment team, and teachers not on the team but affected by the alignment outcomes.

If additional stakeholders are identified as the study progresses, they will be invited to participate in the study. If the number of individuals in a stakeholder group is large, a purposeful sample of these individuals will be selected.

F. Use of Volunteers

We will need to identify a school that has a mandate to engage in a curriculum-instruction-test alignment process but has not yet started it. We will attempt to identify several schools that are near our work site and inquire about their willingness to volunteer as study participants.

The volunteer nature of the sample might limit its applicability to other schools undergoing an alignment process. We will provide an intensive description of the school's characteristics to help readers of our final report decide whether our findings apply to their situation.

6. Methods of Data Collection

A. Measures

The case study is exploratory, so we will use measures that capture a wide range of data.

We will observe and take notes on significant events in the process. These notes will provide the basis for interviewing event participants about their perceptions of specific incidents that occurred during an event.

If an upcoming event seems particularly significant, efforts will be made to videotape it. We will watch the video with the event participants to obtain their perceptions as the event unfolds.

Furthermore, we will interview stakeholders who were not directly involved in the event but who will be affected by it. We also will collect significant documents prepared by stakeholders during the alignment process.

B. Validity and Reliability

One researcher will be the primary observer and interviewer. However, another researcher occasionally will observe the same event as a check on inter-observer reliability. Also, another interviewer will interview research participants who have the same perspective (e.g., two teachers at the same grade level) to determine whether both interviewers ask designated questions and collect similar kinds of data.

C. Emic and Etic Perspective

The procedures for data collection will focus on an emic perspective, that is, the perspective of the stakeholders as they experience the curriculum alignment process.

The researchers who collect data will not participate in the alignment process. They will maintain a supportive perspective but will act primarily as observers. If asked their opinion or advice, they will defer from offering it.

7. Data-Analysis Procedures

A. Statistical Analysis

We do not anticipate that we will collect quantitative data.

We likely will report school-level results for standardized tests mandated by the school district or state. Those results would have been statistically analyzed by the agency.

B. Qualitative Analysis

An interpretational approach to data analysis will be used. The interview and observational data will be entered into computer files and analyzed using the software program Ethnograph to analyze qualitative data. We will focus on identifying constructs, themes, and patterns relating to problems and problem-resolution processes and also on alignment procedures and products.

8. Ethics and Human Relations

   A. Ethical Risks

   Some participants in the alignment process might feel that they will incur the displeasure of colleagues and administrators if they criticize the alignment process during the research interviews.

   Another risk is that the presence of a researcher during meetings associated with the alignment process might influence what participants say and do.

   We will try to minimize these risks by assuring participants that the identity of all participants will be concealed in the final report. Also, we will assure participants that any comment they make to us will not be passed on to anyone, except to researchers directly involved in the study.

   B. Approval by an Institutional Review Board

   The study will need to be reviewed by an institutional review board, especially because it poses risks for the participants. We will identify the appropriate board and follow its designated procedures.

   C. Gaining Entry and Cooperation

   We will meet initially with the school board, local school administrators, and representatives of the local teachers association. If they appreciate the benefits of the study and of the safeguards we describe to minimize risks to participants, their endorsement should help us gain the cooperation of teachers and others who are directly involved in the study.

   Also, we will tell the participants that they can express concerns about data collection or other research matters at any time. We will inform them that we will make appropriate adjustments to the research design to the extent that they do not compromise the integrity and overall purpose of the study.

9. Timeline

   We are particularly interested in the initial stages of a curriculum alignment process. The process generally occurs in the summer with workshops and meetings of planning groups. Therefore, we will need to have obtained all necessary permissions and specified our data-collection procedures prior to the summer.

   Depending on our resources, we might need to limit data collection to the summer months. If resources permit, we will continue data collection into the start of the new school year until the winter break.

Self-Check Test

1. A study that seeks to replicate findings of previous research
   a. adds nothing of value to the research literature.
   b. is a worthwhile contribution to the research literature.
   c. should only be conducted by the researchers who reported the original findings.
   d. is important for theory building but not for an applied discipline like education.

2. Reviews of the research literature in your areas of interest
   a. should only be read after you have formulated your research questions.
   b. should usually be read after you have formulated your research design.
   c. are most useful when you are attempting to interpret the results of your data analyses.
   d. are particularly useful for generating ideas for your own research project.

3. Hypotheses are
   a. predictions about what you expect to find when you analyze your research data.
   b. statements of the constructs that will best describe your research data.
   c. primarily useful when conducting a replication study.
   d. most useful in applied research.

4. Which of the following is the best example of a variable?
   a. All students in the research sample will read the same chapter in a history textbook.
   b. A researcher will study one teacher's written comments on students' essays over an entire school year.
   c. A researcher will measure individual differences in students' academic self-esteem.
   d. A researcher states a hypothesis about the relationship between class size and students' off-task behavior.

5. If a researcher is interested in how teachers view students with autism, case delineation would be particularly useful for
    a. determining which features of a teacher's views will be the focus for interviews and classroom observation.
    b. determining how many teachers to include in the study.
    c. eliminating teachers who have difficulty in reflecting on their instruction.
    d. All of the above.

6. Search engines, databases, and descriptors are most useful for
    a. conducting complex data analyses.
    b. conducting a literature review.
    c. deciding whether quantitative or qualitative research is most relevant to answer your research questions.
    d. deciding which sampling procedure will yield the most appropriate sample size.

7. Procedures for data analysis
    a. should be specified in a research proposal only for a quantitative study.
    b. should be specified in a research proposal only for a qualitative study.
    c. are the only part of the research process that cannot be specified in a research proposal.
    d. can be specified in a research proposal, even if no data of any sort have been collected.

8. The main function of an IRB (institutional review board) is to determine whether the research proposal
    a. conforms in all respects to the *Publication Manual of the American Psychological Association.*
    b. follows all the specifications of the proposal guide published by the researcher's university or other source.
    c. includes procedures that will avoid or minimize harm to the research participants.
    d. specifies procedures to maximize fidelity of implementation by the research participants.

9. Pilot studies and timeline specifications
    a. are best completed as part of the process of writing a research proposal.
    b. are not necessary for a research study that is intended as a replication of previous research findings.
    c. are always required by an IRB (institutional review board).
    d. are only useful for a study that will use quantitative research methodology.

10. If a study has fidelity of implementation, this means that
    a. it has been reviewed and approved by an IRB (institutional review board).
    b. the research participants have followed the study's procedures in the manner prescribed by the researcher.
    c. each research participant has signed a statement indicating that they will follow the researcher's prescribed procedures.
    d. each variable or case feature specified in the research proposal has been measured.

Chapter References

American Psychological Association. (2001). *Publication manual of the American Psychological Association* (5th ed.). (2001). Washington, DC: Author. See also www.apastyle.org

Gardner, W. (2008). Good teachers teach to the test. *Christian Science Monitor.* Retrieved from www.csmonitor.com

Isaacson, W. (2007). *Einstein: His life and universe.* New York: Simon & Schuster.

Kelly, A. E., & Yin, R. K. (2007). Strengthening structured abstracts for education research: The need for claim-based structured abstracts. *Educational Researcher, 36*(3), 133–138.

Resources for Further Study

Henson, K. T. (2003). Writing for professional publication: Some myths and some truths. *Phi Delta Kappan, 84*(10), 788–791.

> The author provides advice about how to prepare a publishable manuscript and select an appropriate journal to which to submit it. The article includes an extensive list of education journals, with information about such matters as rejection rates and how to communicate with journal editors.

Kilbourn, B. (2006). The qualitative doctoral dissertation proposal. *Teachers College Record, 108*(4), 529–576.

> This article will give you ideas for writing a proposal for a qualitative research study, whether for a dissertation, thesis, course requirement, or other purpose. The author provides suggestions for preparing various sections of a proposal, such as specifying a research problem, conducting a literature review, providing a theoretical perspective, and selecting methods of data collection. The author includes examples drawn from actual qualitative research proposals.

Krathwohl, D. R., & Smith, N. L. (2005). *How to prepare a dissertation proposal: Suggestions for students in education and the social and behavioral sciences.* Syracuse, NY: Syracuse University Press.

> This book is a revision of a classic text on preparing a dissertation proposal. Although intended for doctoral students, anyone who is preparing a research proposal of any type can benefit from it.

chapter 3

Conducting and Writing Your Own Literature Review

IMPORTANT *Ideas*

1. The quality of a research journal partly depends on whether it is peer reviewed and on the reputation of its editorial board.

2. A formal review of the literature can help you (1) develop expert knowledge about an educational topic or problem of practice, (2) select or develop methods for your own research study, and (3) identify a research problem that you can study with some assurance that it is considered significant by other researchers.

3. Framing specific research questions or hypotheses relating to your research problem helps you focus your literature search and thereby reduce the risk of information overload.

4. Search engines, bibliographic indexes, and experts in your area of interest can help you greatly improve the efficiency and effectiveness of your literature search.

5. It is helpful first to read secondary source publications in order to acquire a broad understanding of existing research knowledge about a topic or problem of practice and then to read selected primary source publications to acquire a deeper, more nuanced understanding of this knowledge.

6. One of the most convenient ways to obtain a copy of a publication is to download it as a pdf file (Chapter 4) on your computer.

7. As you identify publications for your literature review, you should develop categories for classifying them; the categories will help you decide which publications to read first and how to synthesize their findings.

8. A report of a literature review typically has four sections: (1) introduction, (2) presentation of findings, (3) discussion, and (4) list of references.

9. In writing a report of a literature review, you should make the findings section as objective as possible, but in the discussion section you can provide your own interpretation of the findings and make your own recommendations for future research and practice.

10. If you are writing a literature review for a university or other institution, you will need to learn what bibliographic style it requires for the reference list. ■

Key TERMS

In this and next two chapters, we describe a process for reviewing literature on educational topics and problems of practice. Also, we describe two types of literature reviews, formal and informal.

Our starting point is an explanation of what we mean by the term *literature.* Virtually any written document can be considered literature. In the context of educational research, though, literature has the connotation of being authoritative. We might view a journal article, newspaper article, or book as authoritative because the authors generally are considered by others to be experts on the subject about which they are writing.

Research articles generally are considered to be more authoritative if they are published in a **peer-reviewed journal,** a type of journal in which the peers are authorities who review the research manuscript and decide whether it merits publication. The reviewers might reject the manuscript outright or accept it after it has been revised in accordance with the reviewers' criticisms and suggestions. Journals are considered to be more or less authoritative depending on the reputation of the journal editor and the editorial board. These individuals and their institutional affiliations typically are listed at the front of each issue.

You can use the procedures described in this chapter to search for any kind of publication. However, our emphasis is on publications that are authoritative in the sense that we just described.

Informal Literature Reviews

Literature searches can vary in purpose and depth. For example, suppose you hear a news report about cyberbullying in schools, and it arouses your curiosity. You might ask yourself questions such as:

1. Exactly what is cyberbullying?
2. What are some instances of cyberbullying in schools?
3. Is it a problem in our local school district?

A quick way to satisfy your curiosity is to "google" the term *cyberbullying,* which, being curious ourselves, we did using the search engine Google on January 18, 2009. Google listed 286,000 websites. We went to one website, http://en.wikipedia.org/wiki/Cyber-bullying, which contained an encyclopedia entry about this topic.

This entry was sufficient to satisfy our immediate curiosity about the first two questions. To answer the third question, we most likely would need to talk to educators in our school district. However, we should also consider the possibility that, if cyberbullying is a problem in our district, the local newspaper might have run an article about it. To find out, we would need to search the newspaper literature. In fact, we did that, again using Google. We entered "Cyberbullying Eugene Register-Guard" (the *Register-Guard* is the name of our local newspaper). Google produced a list of 170 websites, some of which were directly relevant to our third question.

Formal Literature Reviews

An informal literature search, such as the one just described, is a quick and useful way to learn about many problems of practice. However, our primary focus in this and next two chapters is on literature reviews that are scholarly. These formal literature reviews are done for one of two main purposes.

One purpose is to review the literature in order to develop a personal understanding about what is known about a particular educational topic or problem of practice. You might do this type of literature review for self-education or to complete a course or degree requirement, as for the literature review presented at the end of this chapter. We describe procedures that will enable you to do a high-quality literature review of this type.

The other main purpose for conducting a formal review of the literature is to initiate planning for your own research study. If you think about it, the reason for doing any research study is to add to what is already known about a particular problem or topic. If you have no idea of what is already known about that problem or topic, you will be unable to determine whether you have contributed anything to research knowledge. Certainly, we want to avoid the embarrassment of claiming an original discovery in our research study, only to discover that the same findings have already been reported in the literature.

A formal literature review, then, will tell you what is already known about the research problem that you intend to investigate. Equally important, the literature review will inform you about the research designs, sampling methods, and measures that other researchers have used. It might well be that you can adopt or adapt some of them for your study, thereby saving you the enormous amount of time often required to develop one's own procedures and materials from scratch. Moreover, researchers often discuss pitfalls and limitations of their investigations, which can provide an entry point for further research. You can address such problems in your study and thereby make a significant contribution to research methodology for investigating the problem.

Last but not least, a formal literature review can help you identify a research topic worthy of study. In the discussion section of their reports, researchers often identify problems in need of further investigation. If you are just learning how to do research, reading the discussion section of recent research reports can get you off to a good start. You can learn from more experienced researchers about the problems that, if investigated, will advance research knowledge. If you investigate one of these problems, you have some assurance that your research journey will lead you to discoveries that contribute to the improvement of educational practice.

A Systematic Procedure for Doing Formal Literature Reviews

It will be easier to conduct a good literature review if you use a systematic procedure. The systematic procedure that we will describe consists of a series of steps, which are summarized in Figure 3.1 (p. 52). Each step is described in this chapter, and occasional references are made to Chapters 4 and 5, where certain aspects of the steps are described in more depth.

Step 1: Framing Questions to Guide the Literature Search

It is easy to get lost in the information explosion that has been occurring over the past 50 years or so. Even a simple Google search, such as the one relating to cyberbullying, yields information spread over thousands of websites. To avoid information overload, you will need to focus your literature search. One way to do this is to reflect on your information needs and then frame them as a set of questions, as in the following examples:

- An elementary school teacher is concerned about students fighting during and after school. She has heard that anger management and conflict resolution programs have been developed for schools and wants to learn about them. She formulates the following questions to guide her literature search: "What anger management and conflict resolution programs, if any, have been developed for use at the elementary school

FIGURE *3.1*   A Systematic Process for Conducting a Formal Review
of the Research Literature

---

1. Frame your information needs as a set of questions or hypotheses that will guide your literature search.

2. Contact experts who can answer your research questions directly or guide you to relevant publications.

3. Select bibliographic indexes and search engines that will help you identify publications that are relevant to your research questions.

4. Read secondary sources (i.e., published literature reviews) to obtain an overview of relevant publications and a foundation on which to develop your own literature review.

5. Read and evaluate primary sources that are relevant to your research questions.

6. Classify the publications that you have identified as relevant to your literature review into meaningful categories.

7. Prepare a report of the findings of your literature review.

---

level? What are the characteristics of these programs? Is there any evidence that they are effective?"

- A committee of school superintendents has met with officials from the state department of education to learn more about plans for statewide mandatory testing of student achievement at selected grade levels. The superintendents expressed several concerns about the testing program. State officials work with the superintendents to frame questions for which the state department agrees to seek answers. "What have other states with mandatory testing programs done to ensure that the tests accurately reflect the school curriculum? What have other states done to ensure that the tests are administered and scored fairly? What percentage of students fail to earn each state's criterion score on the tests? What remediation programs, if any, have these states developed to help students who fail to achieve the criterion score? How effective are these remediation programs?"

- An educator from an Asian country is enrolled in a master's degree program at a U.S. university and wants to learn teaching methods that she can use in a private school she operates in her home country. In particular, she is interested in the latest methods for teaching English as a second language (ESL), which is the subject of her final master's degree project. She frames the following questions for this project: "What methods are currently used to teach ESL in U.S. schools? What is the theoretical basis, if any, for these methods? How effective are these methods? Are particular teaching resources needed in order to use these methods effectively?"

Framing questions to guide a literature search can be modified for different circumstances. For example, as you start reading publications identified through an initial literature search, you might generate new questions for which you would like answers. These questions can be added to those that you framed initially, and you can then reorient your literature search accordingly.

Another possible goal is to find research evidence to support or refute a knowledge claim of interest to you. For example, you might be convinced that students would perform much better in college if they could take their course examinations without the pressure of time limits. In this case, the purpose of your literature search is to find evidence to support a belief rather than to answer a question.

Step 2: Consulting with Experts

Educators occasionally call on experts when they have a pressing need for information and advice. More than likely, they will pay a fee to the experts for their time. However, many experts are willing to help you as a professional courtesy without charge if your information need involves a research study and if the need is clearly defined. They often are willing, even eager, to tell you their ideas and can point you to the most important publications relating to your information needs. With their expert knowledge as an initial framework, you can carry out a literature search with greater confidence and efficiency.

Educators in your local community might know an expert in your area of interest or can refer you to someone who is likely to know of such an expert. For example, the principal of a high school in Portland, Oregon, recently was planning to switch to block scheduling. (In block scheduling, fewer classes are offered, but they meet for longer time periods than in conventional scheduling of classes.) He wanted information about how best to implement block scheduling so that teachers would "buy into it" and so that students' learning would be enhanced.

He mentioned his information need to a member of his teaching staff, who in turn called us. We are not experts in the practice of block scheduling, but we know a colleague who is. We referred the principal to our colleague, and he was able to obtain an orientation to block scheduling from her. Thus, he had a strong initial background of information prior to conducting his own search of the literature on this practice.

A good way to contact experts outside your geographic area is to send them an email message. You can use various search engines (e.g., Yahoo!) to help you find the types of people, or specific individuals, with whom you wish to communicate. If you know the individual's institutional affiliation, you often can get their contact information by going to the institution's website and searching for the individual there.

Educators have formed many computer networks through which members engage in discussions or post information or queries of various types, such as announcements of upcoming conferences and requests for members' opinions and experiences. Called *bulletin boards* or *discussion forums,* these Internet sites are often managed by the computer software program **Listserv.** Some Listserv bulletin boards are moderated and others are unmoderated, depending on whether someone monitors the contributed messages and decides which ones will be posted.

Step 3: Using Bibliographic Indexes and Search Engines

The education literature consists of hundreds of thousands of publications—books, journal articles, technical reports, papers presented at professional conferences, curriculum guides, and so forth. Even if you limit your literature search to publications that have appeared in the past five or ten years, the number of retrieved publications can be overwhelming. For this reason, professional organizations and publishers have created bibliographic indexes and search engines to help you navigate the literature and retrieve citations only for the publications most relevant to your topic or research problem.

A bibliographic index is a list of publications on a particular topic or topics, usually in alphabetical order by author or title. The index typically appears in book form or, increasingly, on a website. A **search engine** is software that looks for publications or other information in a database, based on user-defined criteria. Chapter 4 describes various bibliographic indexes and search engines that you can use to retrieve citations for relevant publications. These indexes and search engines differ in their database of publications and in the procedures that you follow in order to retrieve relevant publications from the database.

Bibliographic indexes and search engines also differ in the amount of information about each publication in their database. The particular entry for each publication is sometimes referred to as a **bibliographic citation.** Most citations include the authors' names, title of the publication, publisher, and publication date. If the publication is a journal article, the page numbers of the article will also be included. Some bibliographic citations also include an abstract, which is a brief summary (typically, 100 words or less) of the information contained in the publication.

Bibliographic indexes and search engines generally include both secondary source and primary source publications. The distinction between secondary and primary sources is important, as discussed in the following sections.

Step 4: Reading Secondary Sources

Once you have identified the questions that you want to answer through a literature review, we recommend that you read several secondary sources in order to form a general picture of the research that has been done on your topic. A **secondary source** is a publication in which the author reviews research studies, theories, and educational practices and programs that others have generated about a particular problem or topic.

Some of the secondary sources described in Chapter 4 contain literature reviews on a wide variety of educational topics. The *Encyclopedia of Educational Research* is an example of this type of secondary source. Other secondary sources are more specialized. They focus on a single topic or set of closely related topics. The *Handbook of Research on Multicultural Education* is an example of this type of secondary source.

In Chapters 4 and 5, our discussion of secondary sources emphasizes published reviews of the research literature. However, we describe other types of secondary sources as well, such as published reviews of educational programs, curriculum guides and materials, tests, and measures.

Step 5: Reading Primary Sources

In contrast to secondary sources, a **primary source** is a publication written by the individual or individuals who actually conducted the work presented in that publication. Examples of primary sources include a journal article that reports a research study conducted by the author of the article, a curriculum guide prepared by the developers of the curriculum, a diary of reflections and experiences in the form that its author prepared it, or a report describing the author's opinions about a particular educational phenomenon or practice.

In short, a secondary source is a publication that is written by author A about the writings of authors X, Y, and Z, whereas a primary source is the actual writings of authors X, Y, and Z.

It sometimes is necessary to read primary sources directly rather than to rely on the summary of the primary source contained in a secondary source. For example, if you conduct a research study and report it in a master's thesis or doctoral dissertation in education, the report must include a review of relevant literature. This literature review consists of a detailed analysis of selected primary sources and their relationships to the problem that you investigated.

Other situations also require you to read primary sources. Suppose you read a secondary source that reviews research evidence about a program that you want your school or organization to consider adopting. This research evidence might play a critical role in convincing others to adopt the program. Therefore, you most likely will want to read the actual primary sources that produced this evidence, rather than relying on a secondary source review of it.

Similarly, you most likely will want to read program materials and documents written by the program's developers (i.e., primary sources) rather than relying on others' description of them in secondary sources. The reason is that a secondary source almost inevitably gives a briefer treatment of the research or development process than a primary source does. Also authors of secondary sources typically are less familiar with details of the program and so might skip or even misreport some of them.

Searching for a primary source in a library or ordering it through interlibrary loan can be time-consuming. Imagine, then, the frustration if you finally get hold of it and discover that it is irrelevant to your information needs. To avoid this problem, we recommend a careful study of the abstracts that often are included in the bibliographic citations. These abstracts usually contain sufficient information for you to decide whether particular publications are relevant to your information needs.

If you plan to read a set of research studies, it usually is a good idea to start with the most recent. Most recent studies use earlier research as a foundation and thus are likely to help you understand what already has been learned about the problem under investigation. It then will be easier to read the older studies.

Most reports of research studies in education follow the format of the *Publication Manual of the American Psychological Association* (American Psychological Association, 2001), as we noted in Chapter 2. The format is as follows:

1. Title, author, and author's affiliation
2. Abstract
3. Introduction: the research problem, research questions or hypotheses, and literature review
4. Method: the sample, tests and other measures, and data-collection procedures
5. Results: statistical procedures and findings, qualitative analyses and descriptions
6. Discussion: answers to the research questions, support or refutation of research hypotheses, contribution of the study to the research literature, practical applications of the findings, suggestions for future research on the topic
7. References: publications cited in the report
8. Appendix: more detailed descriptions of measures, materials, and procedures than is appropriate to include in the body of the report

Research articles might use slightly different or additional headings, but generally the variations are not substantial. Therefore, once you learn the APA publication format for journal articles, you will be able to read a research article more efficiently and find specific information within it more quickly.

Obtaining Copies of Primary and Secondary Sources.   You might find that a primary or secondary source you need is available only at the library, or can only be checked out from the library for a short period of time. You can take notes on the source, and these notes possibly will be sufficient for your literature review and other uses. However, if the publication is important to your study, you should consider photocopying it. Copying costs money, but is probably less expensive than repeated trips to the library to study the publication for details on which you did not take notes the first time.

Another option is to scan the publication if you have a scanner, computer, and scanning software. However, scanning can be difficult or impossible if the publication is bound, such that the pages cannot be placed flat on the scanning surface.

The best option, if available, is to use a search engine linked to a publication reprint service. We describe this capability in Chapter 4. Briefly, it involves using a search engine to identify relevant publications and then following a link to a source where you can obtain an electronic copy at no or minimal cost.

Step 6: Classifying Publications into Meaningful Categories

As you begin reading the publications identified in your literature search, you should also start the process of developing categories for grouping them. For example, suppose you are reviewing the literature to help your school system plan a staff development program for its administrators. As you read the literature, you might observe that some publications concern school administrators specifically, whereas others concern administrators in business and industry or administrators generally.

This observation suggests grouping the publications into three categories: (1) school administrators, (2) administrators in business and industry, and (3) general. You also might find that different publications concern different purposes of staff development, leading you to formulate the following subcategories under each of the three main categories: (a) staff development to help administrators improve staff morale, (b) staff development to help administrators lower their stress and maintain a healthy lifestyle, (c) staff development to help administrators achieve organizational efficiencies, and (d) staff development for other purposes.

Developing a set of categories can help you set priorities for reading the publications that you identified as relevant to your topic or problem. The categories also can help you organize your findings into meaningful clusters, which in turn can help you write a report of your literature review.

Categories are easier to use if you develop a code for each one. The codes can be written on your note card for, or photocopy of, each publication. Another option is to enter the codes as descriptor labels in a bibliographic software program such as Endnote or Procite (described in Chapter 4).

Step 7: Preparing a Report of a Literature Review

The literature review in a typical journal article is generally brief, even though a great deal of work might have gone into its preparation. Reading some articles in research journals will give you a sense of how literature reviews are written and how they fit into the overall organization of the article. Typically, key studies and trends in findings are reported in the introductory section. These topics usually are revisited in the discussion section, which considers how the study's findings contribute to what is already in the literature.

Parts and Presentation of a Literature Review

Some university programs make the completion of a formal literature review a degree requirement. Also, a literature review by itself might constitute a thesis or dissertation, especially if it involves an exhaustive search for research evidence relating to a problem and if it uses a formal analytic process, such as meta-analysis (described further in Chapter 5). The typical sections of these types of literature reviews are introduction, findings, discussion, and references.

Introductory Section

The introductory section of the report should state the research questions or hypotheses that motivated your literature review and the reasons why you chose to investigate them (step 1 in Figure 3.1). The introduction also should include a description of your literature search procedures, indicating the bibliographic indexes and search engines that you consulted (step 3 in Figure 3.1), the years that were covered, the descriptors and keywords (explained in Chapter 4) that were used, and any special problems that you encountered. If you read particular secondary sources that provided a historical background or conceptual framework for your literature review, they can be highlighted in the introduction.

Section on Findings

You can organize the findings of your literature review by the questions or hypotheses that guided your literature search (step 1 in Figure 3.1) or by the categories that you created to organize the publications identified in your search (step 6 in Figure 3.1).

You will need to decide on the order in which to present your questions, hypotheses, or categories. Then for each question or category, you can decide on the order in which to present relevant research studies, theories, programs, methods, and opinions. By grouping closely related publications, you can emphasize areas of agreement and disagreement that will be of interest to readers. A particular publication might be pertinent to several questions or categories and thus might be cited several times in your report.

Recommendations for writing the findings section of your report are presented in Figure 3.2. Also, this chapter includes a literature review by a graduate student in education,

FIGURE *3.2*   Recommendations for Writing a Report
of a Literature Review

1. Use straightforward language that clearly expresses whether you are reporting someone's research findings, theories, or opinions. For example, an author might have described a new program and its advantages but not reported any empirical evidence. In this case you might write, "Jiminez (1991) claims that . . ." If the author conducted a research study, you might write, "Jiminez (1991) found that . . ." If the author developed a theory or referred to another's theory, you might write, respectively, "Jiminez (1991) theorized that . . ." or "Jiminez (1991) referred to Piaget's theory of . . ."

2. Use frequent headings and subheadings to help the reader follow your sequence of topics more easily.

3. Describe the strengths and weaknesses of the methods used in important studies, so that readers have sufficient information to weigh the results and draw their own conclusions.

4. Discuss major studies in detail, but devote relatively little space to minor studies. For example, you might first discuss the most noteworthy study in depth and then briefly cite others on the same topic: "Several other studies have reported similar results (Anderson, 1989; Flinders, 1991; Lamon, 1985; Moursund, 1990; Wolcott, 1990)."

5. Use varied words and phrases, such as: "Martinez found that . . . ," "Smith studied . . . ," "In Wychevsky's experiment the control group performed better on . . . ," "The investigation carried out by Singh and Yang showed that . . ."

6. Use a direct quotation only when it conveys an idea especially well or when it states a viewpoint that is particularly worth noting.

and Chapter 4 includes a reprint of two published literature reviews. Studying how each of these reviews is organized will give you additional ideas for organizing the findings of your literature review. Also, you can find examples of high-quality literature reviews in the journal *Review of Educational Research.*

Discussion Section

When you write the findings section of the literature review, it is important to be objective and therefore fairly literal in presenting research findings, theories, program characteristics, and other types of information. In the discussion section, however, you are free to provide your own interpretation and assessment of this information.

As an example, suppose that your literature review is aimed at determining the effectiveness of programs to help teenage mothers complete their high school education. Also suppose that you will present a brief report of your literature review to state legislators, who are considering a bill to provide funds for such programs.

In writing the findings section of your report, you will need to state objectively what researchers have discovered about these programs and what experts think about them. In the discussion section of your report, however, you need to reach your own conclusions based on what you learned in reviewing the literature. For example, you might conclude: "The research evidence shows consistently positive effects of high school completion programs for teenage mothers. However, some studies have found that programs that isolate teenage mothers from mainstream students or that separate them from their children have lower retention rates."

A good procedure for writing the discussion section is to start by listing the main findings of your review. You can compile this list by asking yourself, "What did I learn from this review?" and then attempting to answer this question without looking at your report of the findings. By relying on memory, you are more likely to focus on the major findings rather than on a variety of specific details. If necessary, you then can check the findings against your discussion to be sure you did not miss any important findings.

Now list the findings in order of importance, reflecting on each one. You might ask yourself questions such as these: "To what extent do I agree with the overall thrust of the research evidence, theories, descriptions, and expert opinions that I examined? Are alternative interpretations possible? How can I explain the contradictions in the literature, if any? What is the significance of a particular finding for the problem of practice I need to solve or the question I want to answer?"

The discussion also should contain your recommendations regarding the problem or questions that initiated your literature review. The recommendations should be stated clearly and, if possible, without qualification. If you are tentative or indirect, readers of your report will not know where you stand. They want to know your opinions and recommendations, because you were the one who did a review of the literature. Therefore, you are an expert compared to policy makers or colleagues who do not know the literature.

For example, in the example of programs for teenage mothers, you might make a recommendation such as the following: "I recommend targeted funding for programs that create a school within a school for teenage mothers and also an on-site daycare center for their children. These recommendations are based on research findings demonstrating that teenage mothers are likely to have better self-esteem if they go to classes with mainstream students and are less likely to drop out of school if they can check on their child occasionally during the school day."

References

All the publications that you cite in your report should be included in the reference list at the end of the report. Conversely, the list should not contain any publications that were not cited in the report. If you wish to provide noncited publications for some reason, you should present them in a separate list, with a heading such as "Supplemental References" and an explanatory note about why they are being cited.

Different bibliographic indexes and search engines use different citation styles, and the bibliographies in the secondary and primary sources you read also might have different styles. It is important that you convert all the citations to the same style, namely, the style required by your institution or the journal or conference to which you might submit the literature review.

If no particular style is required, we recommend that you use the citation style of the American Psychological Association (APA), because it is the most widely used style in educational and psychological journals. For example, the chapter references and list of resources for further study at the end of each chapter in this book are written in APA style. To learn APA style, obtain a copy of the fifth edition of the *Publication Manual of the American Psychological Association* (American Psychological Association, 2001). Various guides and other aids to write bibliographic citations in APA style can be found at the website http://apastyle.apa.org.

Preparing a Visual Presentation of a Literature Review

Perhaps you plan to present the findings of your literature review to an audience that does not understand the technical aspects of research studies. In such cases, it is helpful to present your findings in an interesting nontechnical format that your audience will understand.

Figure 3.3 shows an example of a **chart essay,** a format using charts to focus the audience's attention on aspects of the literature review in which they are likely to be in-

FIGURE 3.3   Visual Presentation of Selected Findings from a Literature
Review on Cooperative Learning

---

*Research Question 1: How effective is cooperative learning relative to traditional
instruction in fostering academic achievement?*

In 60 studies, there were 68 comparisons of cooperative learning classes and
traditional classes on an achievement measure. Achievement was:

significantly higher in the traditional classes in:	not significantly different in the cooperative learning and traditional classes in:	significantly higher in the cooperative learning classes in:
4%	34%	62%
of the comparisons.	of the comparisons.	of the comparisons.

*Research Question 2: How important is it that group goals and individual
accountability both be present for cooperative learning to be effective?*

Percentage of studies showing significantly positive achievement effects for
cooperative learning when group goals and individual accountability are:

Present	Absent
80%	36%

Trends

Cooperative learning is more effective than traditional instruction in promoting
student achievement.

Cooperative learning is most effective when it includes both group goals and
individual accountability.

Source: Based on data from Slavin, R. (1992). Cooperative learning. In M. C. Alkin (Ed.), *Encyclopedia
of educational research* (6th ed., vol. 1, pp. 235–238). New York: Macmillan.

terested. The chart essay format was originally designed to summarize the findings of a
single research study (Haensly, Lupkowski, & McNamara, 1987; Jones & Mitchell, 1990).
Here we have adapted it to illustrate the value of a visual format for presenting the findings
of a literature review in a nontechnical form. The chart essay in Figure 3.3 is a graphic
presentation of two findings from a review of research on cooperative learning (Slavin,
1992).

You can see that the chart poses one research question, immediately followed by the
empirical research findings that pertain to it. The second research question is presented in
similar fashion. The chart concludes with two trend statements, which are generalizations
that can be inferred from the empirical findings. These statements are called *trends* because
the evidence pertaining to each question was not always consistent. However, there was
sufficient consistency to identify a trend that can serve as a guide to improving educational
practice.

The chart essay in Figure 3.3 is shown as a single chart. However, if you were to show
the chart essay to an audience as a PowerPoint presentation, a set of overhead transparen-
cies, or handouts, you might want to use three charts—one for each of the research questions shown in Figure 3.3 and a third for the trend statements.

Self-Check Test

1. One of the most common problems that educators encounter in conducting a literature search is
   a. a lack of sufficient information relevant to their research problem.
   b. an overabundance of information relevant to their research problem.
   c. a shortage of primary sources in the education literature.
   d. a shortage of secondary sources in the education literature.

2. Consulting an expert prior to conducting a literature review is particularly helpful for
   a. developing a theory relating to the topic of your review.
   b. identifying critical primary and secondary sources to include in the review.
   c. establishing the credibility of your review.
   d. determining an appropriate bibliographic citation style.

3. Search engines
   a. are equivalent to bibliographic indexes in literature coverage and citation style.
   b. share a universal standard for bibliographic citation style.
   c. vary in the amount of information that they provide about each publication in their database.
   d. provide less information about each publication in their database than does the typical bibliographic index.

4. A report of a research study written by the individuals who conducted the study is
   a. a primary source.
   b. a secondary source.
   c. both a primary and a secondary source.
   d. exempt from using a peer review process.

5. Most published reports of educational research follow the style specifications established by
   a. Google.
   b. the American Educational Research Association.
   c. the American Psychological Association.
   d. the most widely used bibliographic indexes and search engines.

6. Articles in research journals
   a. are available only by obtaining a hard copy of the journal in which they appear.
   b. are typically included in their entirety in bibliographic indexes.
   c. cannot be subjected to computer-based scanning devices.
   d. sometimes can be electronically downloaded directly from a search engine.

7. The most useful system for classifying publications obtained through a review of the literature is likely to be one that sorts publications by
   a. year of publication.
   b. topics relevant to the research questions or hypotheses.
   c. magnitude of the statistical results.
   d. the search engines and bibliographic indexes by which they were identified.

8. The report of a literature review
   a. should include a description of your literature search procedures.
   b. should cite mainly primary sources.
   c. should emphasize findings that agree across studies rather than findings that disagree across studies.
   d. All of the above.

9. Recommendations for further research or applications to practice are most commonly found in
   a. the introductory section of a literature review.
   b. the findings section of a literature review.
   c. the discussion section of a literature review.
   d. a separate section of a literature review, following a list of supplemental references.

10. The primary advantage of a chart essay over a written report of a literature review is that a chart essay
    a. identifies the particular studies on which the findings of the literature review are based.
    b. focuses on the statistics that were used to test the significance of the research findings.
    c. highlights the categories that were used to cluster the publications included in the review.
    d. is easier to understand by individuals without sophisticated knowledge about research methodology.

Chapter References

American Psychological Association. (2001). *Publication manual of the American Psychological Association* (5th ed.). Washington, DC: Author. See also www.apastyle.org

Haensly, P. A., Lupkowski, A. E., & McNamara, J. F. (1987). The chart essay: A strategy for communicating research findings to policy makers and practitioners. *Educational Evaluation and Policy Analysis, 9,* 63–75.

Jones, B. K., & Mitchell, N. (1990). Communicating evaluation findings: The use of a chart essay. *Educational Evaluation and Policy Analysis, 12*(4), 449–462.

Slavin, R. (1992). Cooperative learning. In M. C. Alkin (Ed.), *Encyclopedia of educational research* (6th ed., vol. 1, pp. 235–238). New York: Macmillan.

Resources for Further Study

Cooper, H. M. (1998). *Synthesizing research: A guide for literature reviews* (3rd ed.). Thousand Oaks, CA: Sage.

> You will find this book helpful if you plan to do a literature review as your primary requirement for completion of a master's or doctoral degree and if the studies you review are primarily quantitative in design.

Dunkin, M. J. (1996). Types of errors in synthesizing research in education. *Review of Educational Research, 66,* 87–97.

> The author identifies nine types of errors that sometimes occur in literature reviews. For example, reviewers might exclude relevant literature, report details of a study incorrectly, or draw unwarranted conclusions from the literature reviewed.

Maxwell, J. A. (2006). Literature reviews of, and for, educational research: A commentary on Boote and Beile's "Scholars before Researchers." *Educational Researcher, 35*(9), 28–31.

> This article and an earlier article by Boote and Beile in the same journal list common flaws in published literature reviews. The authors present their views on the purpose of a literature review in a research study.

Sandelowski, M., & Barroso, J. (2007). *Handbook for synthesizing qualitative research.* New York: Springer.

> This book will be useful if your literature review focuses primarily on qualitative research. The author presents procedures for planning the review, searching for qualitative research reports, evaluating the quality of the reports, synthesizing their findings, and writing the literature review report.

Sample Literature Review

Shifting the Paradigm from "At Risk" to "At Promise": A Review of the Construct of Resilience and Its Educational Applications

Kappa, S. L. (2002). Shifting the paradigm from "at risk" to "at promise": A review of the construct of resilience and its educational applications. Unpublished master's paper. Eugene: University of Oregon.

The following section of the chapter presents a literature review prepared by a student as part of the requirements for a master's degree in educational leadership. The paper is reprinted in full, just as it appeared when submitted to the university awarding the degree. Where appropriate, we have added footnotes to help you understand the information contained in the paper. The article is preceded by comments prepared by the author, Sandra Price (formerly Sandra Kappa), for the fifth edition of this book.

RESEARCHER'S *Comments*

Prepared by Sandra Price

I did this review of the literature on resilience to fulfill the University of Oregon's requirement of a capstone research project for a master's degree combined with initial administrator licensure. I began the review two months prior to the tragic events of September 11, 2001, and completed it about a year later. The resilience I observed in the United States in the face of growing insecurity and profound change in our collective way of life makes this time frame significant to my project.

I began by brainstorming about educational research topics I found interesting, followed by an initial meeting with my project guide, Joy Gall. Joy was quick to pinpoint the area (at risk students) about which I was most passionate. Joy shared my concern that so much emphasis was being placed on early interventions as the only viable course for changing the direction of an "at risk" student's life. This prompted me to look at the issue of "at risk" students in a wider sense that, in turn, helped me draw broader conclusions from the literature review that can be applied to students of any age.

As an aspiring school administrator, I recognize the importance of facilitating teacher growth and development. I want to foster student growth by nurturing teachers' professional development and ensuing continuous school improvement and reform (Henderson & Milstein, 2003). I felt that having a deeper understanding of how to help "at risk" students would provide me with a means to assist teachers in their endeavors in this challenging area of educational life. As I immersed myself in the literature, I came to realize that not only could I create a learning environment in the classroom that would help students build resilience, but I could, as an educational leader, help build teacher resilience, too.

The initial questions to which I wanted answers from the literature developed from my own childhood experiences with abuse, poverty, and neglect. As a child I succeeded brilliantly in school, and I have had a rich and happy personal life in spite of the adversity and hardships I faced in my childhood. Unfortunately, my younger brother, who was raised with the same hardships, has not "bounced back." I remember discovering the term "invulnerable" to describe children who flourish in spite of adversity. Are there such children, and had I been one, or was my resilience explainable in some other way?

I started with a very scattered set of questions about the impact I was potentially having on my students and the transformation that I hoped to bring about but did not see much evidence of, despite my best efforts. I felt that my personal experiences put me in a better position to understand others who had experienced adversity and connect with them. I postulated that this connection would help me to magically help them transform as I had transformed. Surely, I thought, caring deeply about the children should make a difference and should be a successful means to make such transformations happen.

My initial search keyword was "at risk," and I found a wealth of literature relating to that liberally used term. I wondered how I would ever wade through the mountain of books and journal articles and make some meaningful synthesis of it. In particular, I wondered whether I would find research-based methods for "fixing" the "at risk" students I care about so deeply.

I thought I would have plenty of time during the course of the year to go back and reread material for the purpose of highlighting ideas for possible citation in the report of the literature review. The truth is, an effective method of coding the "big ideas" early on would have saved me much time. On the other hand, because I cast my net very wide in my literature search, I was able to draw from other disciplines, such as rehabilitative studies. As a result, I stumbled upon the concept of salutogenesis, the idea that people who are sick or injured will naturally try to adapt or return to the initial state of health. Applying this concept to kids who are "at risk" led me to the discovery of the website of the National Resilience Resource Center (2003), where I first saw the term "at promise." I was already seeking to shift my thinking away from the idea that there was some hopeless group of children who, because of risk factors, were doomed to lifelong failure. I began to believe that even if there was no "magic bullet," there might be an innate push towards adaptation that could be fostered by focusing on children's strengths. The term "at promise" helped to crystallize this shift in my thinking.

Based on what I know now, I would have started this literature review by first trying to find and talk with experts in the field of at risk and resilience research, noting the authors and seminal works they mentioned. I would then start my review with that background information. Then I'd go back to talk to the experts again. I believe that this approach would have helped me find more meaning in the literature and draw stronger conclusions from it. The prospect of actually writing the literature review was daunting in spite of my usual enjoyment of the writing process. I didn't feel I was enough of an expert in spite of the countless hours and numerous articles and books I had read. There were so many sources and related subjects that I could have kept reading for another year easily.

I found, though, that a deeper understanding of the literature began to develop as I started to write. The paper went through many drafts, and the collaborative style of my project guide, Joy, was invaluable because her questions helped me to clarify, expand, and relate the synthesis of the findings to my own experiences in a powerful way. Indeed, Joy fostered my own resilience as a researcher by asking questions that prompted a deeper view of the literature and, as important, demanded a personal connection between my experiences as a teacher and application of the research findings to those experiences. This dialogue profoundly affected my confidence as a writer, researcher, and educator, particularly at a time in my life when I could easily have been overwhelmed with all of the work I was simultaneously responsible for besides this project: mother, teacher, graduate student and aspiring educational administrator.

I found it helpful to evaluate and synthesize the literature around the question, "What can I do as an administrator to make my school one that fosters resilience?" Howard and Johnson's study, cited in my paper, was particularly relevant to this question. They found a "pervasive theme concerning the need for help with school work" (p. 328) when students were asked what schools could provide them to help overcome their hardships. Some of the suggestions students made for how the school could help them were to provide additional learning assistance programs, special tutors, individual attention, and patient help from teachers when tasks proved too difficult for the students. Ironically, the teachers who were surveyed had barely mentioned formal learning at all, focusing instead on the importance of social skills training and making children feel comfortable and secure within the school. These findings illustrate how research can help teachers question and improve their taken-for-granted practices.

Indeed, I've learned that research related to the improvement of one's professional practice never ends. Each research study leads to new questions and new understandings. As a researcher and educator, one must have a willingness to ask fresh questions, consider new directions, and shift paradigms in the face of research-based evidence.

As I researched and wrote this paper, my incredulity regarding the events of 9/11 gave way to a realization of the tremendous vulnerability we all share as Americans and as human beings on this planet. I concluded my paper with the idea that applying the paradigm shift of considering our society "at promise" rather than "at risk" may be a more constructive response to the troubling world climate. It stands to reason that applying the precepts of caring, authentic helpfulness, responsiveness to individual needs, and a shift in our thinking from a deficit model to one of possibility and promise will help our country continue to be resilient in the face of great challenges.

References

Henderson, N., & Milstein, M. (2003). *Resiliency in schools: Making it happen for students and educators.* Thousand Oaks, CA: Corwin.

National Resilience Resource Center. Retrieved January 17, 2003, from www.cce.umn.edu/nrrc/research .shtml

Shifting the Paradigm from "At Risk" to "At Promise": A Review of the Construct of Resilience and Its Educational Applications

Sandra Kappa
Unpublished Master's Paper
University of Oregon,
Eugene, Oregon

ABSTRACT ■ Teachers and administrators who seek to make a difference in the lives of students "at risk" of failure in schools can assist students by promoting protective factors within the school to foster students' resilience. This resilience building can affect school climate, student achievement and, potentially, successful adaptation in adult life. Research on independent variables associated with the study of resilience theory shows promising results, but more research and standardized definitions of terms and methodologies are needed to move education from the theoretical to the practical with valid interventions.

INTRODUCTION

This literature review began with the research question "How can I know if what I do is having a positive effect on kids in my classroom who are clearly 'at risk' of failure?"

I wanted to focus on "problem" kids—those whose behavior is never quite transformed but is merely managed. I postulated that such "at risk" students must be victims

Kappa, S. L. (2002). Shifting the paradigm from "at risk" to "at promise": A review of the construct of resilience and its educational applications. Unpublished master's paper. Eugene, OR: University of Oregon. Reprinted by permission of Pearson Prentice Hall.

of some sort of deficit, whether social, economic, emotional, behavioral or intellectual, which caused them not to fit within the normal boundaries of school achievement and participation. As a teacher I was frustrated to feel that the students I had the most trouble managing hadn't really changed over the course of a school year. I knew I had done my best to move them forward, but I had a gnawing sense that I had failed to do my job—transform their behavior. I wondered if anything I had done might at some point in their future emerge as having had a transformational positive impact, and if I could do anything differently that might be more effective with my future students.

I have served mainly in rural school districts since I began teaching ten years ago, teaching almost all levels from grades 1 to 6 during my career. Currently, I teach third grade and have taught at this level for the past four years. Given the population I am currently serving, the question of risk and its relationship to student performance and future prospects for success is compelling, The Peridot Elementary and Middle School where I teach (a pseudonym) is a small, rural school of about 300 students in a formerly prosperous logging town. Fifty-eight percent of the students qualify for free or reduced lunch. This indicator of poverty significantly exceeds the state average of 36 percent. Indeed, many of the children of the community are fed their only meals by the school. The population of ethnic minority students is quite low (approximately three percent), and only one English as a Second Language student is currently being served. The turnover rate for students is high, with many families moving and then returning to the area in an almost cyclical fashion. Rural schools tend to have, comparatively, more "at risk" conditions such as poverty and student attrition, along with a lack of resources (Helge, 1992). The idea of tapping into resilience-building protective factors to help "at risk" students succeed potentially fits the needs of this population.

Reflecting on the more challenging students I've had in my class over the years, I realized that the classroom management techniques I used were generally the same, and involved, in order of increasing severity, verbal reprimand, parent contact, or other punitive measures such as "time out" or office referrals. For continued transgressions, the student would receive a loss of privileges such as recess time. On the positive side, I also relied on reward systems such as giving extra time on the computer for work completed or additional recess time for consistently good behavior. In more severe individual cases, I would develop an individualized tracking system of specific goals that, when met, would result in some sort of treat or other reward. Often I have used preferential seating combined with close physical monitoring to help students stay on-task. My "bag of tricks" also included some proactive, whole group, small group and individual social skills training from the program *Tribes* (Gibbs, 2001).

Academically, I survey and carefully observe students in an effort to choose material that directly interests them for their use in reading, writing, science and art activities. I also use diagnostic, formative and summative assessments in varied ways to better individualize instruction by addressing individual needs.[a] I feel that it is very important to identify the academic or social strengths of students and

to plan curriculum and classroom management to put such strengths to use.

As I reflected on my own experiences with "at risk" students, I began to assess my classroom management methods for protective characteristics. What I was aiming for was something beyond mere management of problematic behavior. I wanted to address the underlying risk factors to actually help these children transform into more productive, settled, purposeful and happy students.

As I reflected, three students came to mind who defined for me the three areas of concern I have encountered in the classroom: behavioral, academic, and, social. It is important to note that while the source of the risk factor can generally be categorized in this way, the actual presentation of the problem is primarily behavioral for all three categories. I've categorized them so that I can address the core problematic mechanism that I felt served as their greatest barriers to success in the classroom. It is interesting to note that for two of these students standardized academic measures revealed high scores, but for all three students regular classroom academic achievement showed significant deficits.

John (not his real name), a third-grade male, had been identified as emotionally disturbed. He was under the care of a psychiatrist, and his recommended placement was a self-contained behavior management classroom. The self-contained classroom in the area was full. Therefore John was placed in my classroom, with no additional interventions provided except for the after-school counseling program he attended with his mother and older brother, who himself was in the self-contained behavior management classroom mentioned earlier. Although John was on medication for the control of his temper, it seemed to have little or no effect on his behavior. Through my talks with John's mother, it came to light that John had witnessed her being physically and verbally abused by the father. She had separated from the father and kept custody of the two boys. The family lived in a poverty situation in this small, rural area. Although John performed well on standardized tests, his behavior was so disruptive that he spent a great deal of time out of the classroom and, consequently, achieved very little success academically. He was very much in danger of failing. Examples of his acting out included threatening other students, shouting obscenities for no apparent reason, fighting, throwing chairs and other destructive behavior, and frequent, attention-seeking verbal outbursts.

I was afraid of John. I remember talking to anyone I could find about strategies I might put in place before school began so as to get off on the right track with him. Right off the bat, I made the decision to control my tone of voice and to give as much positive feedback as I could. Even the smallest actions on his part that were positive or appropriate, I rewarded with praise. I set up a reward sys-

---

a. In formative assessment, the teacher uses students' performance on homework, tests, and other tasks as feedback to make decisions about next instructional steps (e.g., remediation or introduction of new curriculum content). In summative assessment, the teacher judges students' level of mastery at the end of instruction for the purpose of assigning course grades or other summary indicator of learning.

tem in which I would place colorful, die-cut paper shapes of computer disks in a large, transparent plastic jar on John's desk whenever he did anything remotely positive or in the absence of negative behavior. When the jar was full, John could go to the computer in the classroom and play a game of his choice for 15 minutes. We would then start the process again.

I also invited John's mother to help in the classroom. She and I had several very open and honest discussions about John. At first John was very rude to his mother in class, but we made the decision to ignore the rude behavior. She spent much of her time with other students, and John was able to see them treating her with respect. His behavior improved somewhat, but his rude manner toward his mother was never fully extinguished. After the winter break when I returned to school, I was told that John and his family had moved to another town several miles away. John's mother had often complimented me on my handling of her son and although his problematic behavior continued, it had, indeed, improved to some degree. That was six or seven years ago, and I often wonder if anything I did made any difference in John's life later on.

Steven, also a third-grade male student but in a different year and school than John, had many behavioral issues in the classroom. At first I thought his severe behavioral outbursts and agitation were due to the poor circumstances of his life outside school. It wasn't until the spring of that school year that I came to realize that most of his difficulties, including his behavior problems, were more likely due to academic deficits. It puzzled me that I was unable to get Steven, a verbally capable child, to produce much written work of any quality or substance. Unlike John, he was rarely violent but could be impulsively aggressive with other students when provoked in some manner. Steven had numerous risk factors in his life. His mother gave birth to him when she was only 14 years old. He, like many of the children in the area, lived in poverty. His mother suffered ongoing problems with drug and alcohol abuse. Steven was often shuttled back and forth between his mother and his grandmother's home. I knew that he might not have been capable of achieving as high a scholastic standard as I set for him, but I was fairly relentless in my manner regarding the high expectations I had for him. I was fairly tough on him: redirecting his attention several times an hour to the work at hand; sending work back to be redone; and keeping him in at recess to finish work others had long since finished. I did all this in a warm and caring manner, although at times I would feel very frustrated with Steven. However, I truly felt that firm structure, high expectations and consistent follow-through would make a difference in helping him become a successful student. I welcomed his mother in the classroom and spent a lot of time helping her to understand how she could best help Steven at home.

In the spring, after reviewing the final reading scores, I finally decided to refer Steven to the special education teacher for testing to see if he had some discernible learning difficulty that was the root of his trouble in school. Testing revealed that Steven's IQ was in the high 70's. Because there was no discrepancy between his low performance and his low test scores, Steven was not eligible for special education services. Previously I hadn't considered Steven

to be a slow learner. He had seemed capable and bright to me, and I had honestly thought that he could do the work but chose not to. I often wonder if my relentlessly high expectations for him would have been lower but more realistic if I'd referred him for testing sooner. I wonder, too, though, if he is better off today because of my having had those high expectations of him.

Jenna was also a third-grade student of mine. She could sometimes produce outstanding work, but usually she would simply sit and appear to be paying attention while not actually engaged in work. She was not disruptive to the other students and when called upon directly she would usually respond in some way, however minimal, but generally she did not participate in classroom activities. Jenna, too, lived in poverty. Her mother fought constantly with Jenna's father, who lived in another state, for custody of Jenna and her two younger sisters, with each parent accusing the other of child abuse and substance abuse. Jenna had been referred to the school's student services team almost every year of her school life. Testing showed that scholastically she was capable of a very high level of achievement. The state program involving services to children and families had been contacted numerous times regarding allegations of abuse and neglect but no action had yet been taken.

The passive-aggressive nature of Jenna's refusal to do work in the absence of any verbal refusals or other negative active behaviors was frustrating and puzzling, especially considering the few times she did choose to display her more than adequate skills. I tried using timers and rewards to get at least a minimal amount of work from her in order to keep her from failing.

Jenna's mother and stepfather were frequent visitors to the school but were inconsistent in their efforts to follow through on steps we agreed upon to help Jenna complete unfinished work that was sent home. The stepfather would often arrive unexpectedly to check up on Jenna, while clearly under the influence of alcohol. The mother, during meetings, would often forget details of previous meetings, especially regarding suggestions she had made to help Jenna and her own agreements for taking responsibility at home for encouraging Jenna to finish work sent home. It was difficult to maintain a consistent set of supports for Jenna under these conditions.

As with the other students I've described, my efforts with Jenna were largely focused on management rather than effecting any kind of transformation of her behavior. Jenna is now in sixth grade and continues to struggle with work completion and on-task issues. There is a strong social risk component evident in her interactions with others. She would often mope around at recess time and rarely interacted with other students. At the end of the year, I wondered if any of my attempts at "dangling the carrot on the stick" in front of her in order to get her to complete the bare requirements of the grade had made any lasting difference. Even more, I wondered what other things I could or should have been doing to help Jenna.

All three of these students—John, Steven, and Jenna—represent many others with whom I have worked over the years. These students have caused me to question my efficacy as a teacher. I want to make a difference to children.

That's why I am a teacher. That's why I want to be an administrator. These three students are symbolic of the types of challenges a caring teacher who wants to make a difference faces. The question remains in my mind: What can I do to help them more effectively to succeed?

WHY THE CONSTRUCT OF RESILIENCE?

In my review of the literature I found many research articles devoted to identifying vulnerabilities and testing corresponding remedial interventions for students "at risk." As I pondered the huge body of information about all the different things that can go wrong in a child's world and the desire on my part to be a teacher who can make a difference for every child in my care, I felt overwhelmed. I found it difficult to focus on a single risk factor, yet that seemed necessary if I was to have any reasonable chance of completing this master's paper.

It was the sense of feeling overwhelmed that caused me to choose the framework of a literature synthesis for my master's project. I knew I had some very important burning questions, but the questions themselves were quite unfocused and uninformed. I needed much more information, and a clearer focus for my research. I could have chosen to work on developing a model for applying resilience theory in the school or classroom. I felt my time would be better served to first learn all I could about the construct and its components through a thorough literature review. However, my review provides numerous suggestions for the promotion of resilience in the classroom and in the school. Indeed, my attitude toward teaching has been fundamentally affected by this literature review, such that my awareness of the protective mechanism school can afford students in need will surely have a positive effect on my current and future classroom teaching and schoolwide leadership endeavors. I feel so strongly about my findings that I fervently hope to continue working in this area.

In my literature review I was struck by the optimism of a few articles that referred to something called "resilience." I decided to pursue my research on this theoretical construct. Its holistic and optimistic nature appealed to me on a philosophical level. I was gratified to find a substantial and growing body of research, mostly theoretical but with some very important practical successes (Luthar, Cicchetti & Becker, 2000a&b; Miller, Brehm & Whitehouse, 1998).

Some studies of resilience show the positive effects of teacher rapport on student achievement (Bowen & Bowen, 1998). In one study, abused students who were provided with a "supportive and nurturing network of services" in the school had a significantly lower likelihood of engaging in risky behaviors (Brown & Block, 2001). In another study, an early intervention program, with aspects similar to a mentoring program for young students (grades 1 to 4) identified as being "at risk" for social adjustment, resulted in significant and positive changes in social variables associated with adaptive behavior (Nafpaktitis & Perlmutter, 1998). An action research study designed to assess a resilience-building program for sixth graders showed promise for reducing violence and promoting resilience in youth who are "at risk" from environmental factors (Meyer & Farrell, 1998).

I found that the construct of resilience incorporates a multidisciplinary approach to a cluster of psychological, educational and emotional concerns. This approach can be likened to medical research on physical health concerns that seeks to promote health and prevent disease rather than simply prescribe treatments when ill health arrives (Howard & Johnson, 2000; Luther, et al., 2000a&b). This multidisciplinary approach promotes "out of the box" strategies to restructure the school environment, such that the school can act as a catalyst and an agent of resource management to meet the varying needs of students who would not otherwise be ready or able to participate in the fundamental activity of academic learning for which schools were built (Maeroff, 1998).

New research questions emerged as I followed this new path: What is resilience? What are protective factors? How can protective factors or processes be used in the classroom? Are the programs or models that operationalize protective factors supported by action research findings?

WHAT IS RESILIENCE?

Resilience is "the power or ability to return to the original form or position after being bent, compressed, or stretched" (*Random House Dictionary*, 1968, p. 1123). Resilience is further defined as, "the ability to recover readily from illness, depression, adversity or the like." Buffering or protective factors are commonly evident in resilient children, that is, students who seem to rise above the social, economic and environmental deficits in their lives and avoid the potential harmful effects of such adversity (Rak & Patterson, 1996). Studies suggest that by helping students develop or tap into such protective factors, schools enable students to help themselves achieve and succeed in school and in life.

Resilience has been shown to be a cluster or combination of protective factors that operate together during times when risk factors (such as illness, depression, and adversity) are present and offer the student the best chance to build a capacity for recovery. "Resiliency is more appropriately understood as a continuum" (Bradley, et al., 1994) and ". . . adaptive functioning is subject to change over time . . ." thus indicating the need for a process or set of processes that create a mechanism within which risks can be ameliorated depending on individual needs."Just as risks seem to accumulate to the detriment of children's health and development, protective mechanisms seem to accumulate to their benefit" (Bradley, et al., 1994).

Resilience is not one single moment in time in which a person "bounces back" and is forever free from the negative effects of risk (Bradley, et al., 1994). Because the continuum of risk and resilience is fluid and ever-changing, because labeling students for the purpose of direct interventions that focus on deficiencies about which they may have little control poses dangers, and because of children's natural and innate advancement toward health, it would seem that a focus on promoting resilience and providing the means for children to build their resilience capabilities is an important and worthwhile goal for schools to adopt.

Resilience is related to the medical concept of saluto-genesis: the origin of health. Salutogenesis refers to the time and place before which maladjustment begins to oc-cur, as well as the consistent and innate push to grow in a healthy way in spite of trauma, disease or adverse condi-tions (Levenstein, 1994; Lustig, et al., 2000; Rak & Patter-son, 1996; Strumpfer & Mlonzi, 2001). Resilience research involves efforts to glean understanding from this process and then search for practical applications through the pro-motion of such factors and processes to help children build their capacity for achieving good outcomes in the face of adversity (Luthar, et al., 2000a&b).

DEFINITIONS OF "AT RISK" AND ADVERSITY

The term "at risk" is reminiscent of medical terminology re-garding the potential for poor health outcomes as a result of behaviors or conditions present in the patients' lives. It is a broad, loosely defined term that has a variety of negative predictive outcomes, including being "at risk" of dropping out of school several years down the road, being "at risk" for perpetrating violence in the classroom as a result of abuse suffered, and the prediction of a life lived in poverty and hopelessness as a result of social capital deficits.

Similarly, adversity, as defined by Irwin Sandler, is that which, ". . . threatens the satisfaction of basic human needs and the acquisitions of competencies to carry out valued social roles" (Sandler, 2001). Further, ". . . an ad-verse condition [is] a relation between children and their environments that threatens the satisfaction of basic hu-man needs and goals and impedes the accomplishment of age appropriate developmental tasks" (Sandler, 2001, p. 20).

Adverse conditions include internal risk factors like learning disabilities and physical handicaps. External risk factors can include family violence, parental substance abuse, parental criminality, divorce, large family size, single parenthood, child abuse and neglect, poor child rearing skills and poverty (Howard & Dryden, 1999). Risk factors associated with institutions like schools include bullying by peers, unsympathetic teachers, inappropriate boundaries and rules, or doing little to invite or encour-age parental/school communication (Howard & Dryden, 1999).

MOVING FROM REACTIVE TO PROACTIVE

The traditional "at risk" intervention model, wherein the school seeks to respond or react to deviant behavior, can actually increase student risk by placing students in a lose/lose situation (Osterman, 2000). If the student is acting out on the basis of some non-school related difficulty and the school's response is to further penalize or stigmatize the student, the school is then further harming the student

and, consequently, contributing to the risk (Osterman, 2000).

For instance, one day Steven came to school wearing pink fingernail polish and eye shadow. I'm not sure exactly what the motive was, but I got the distinct impression that his mother and he had been playing "dress-up" together and he decided to wear the makeup to school. This could have been a disruptive event if I had chosen a course of action that would have escalated it, such as sending him to the office on a behavior referral. Needless to say, his behavior was inappropriate and unexpected, but to draw undue attention to it and/or to invite peer scorn would have done Steven a great disservice. I venture a guess that in a classroom not so forgiving this could have resulted in a traumatic event for Steven; school could have put him at further risk if he'd been teased or disproportionately punished.

Although there was some twittering from a few students in the class, all I had to do was remind the students of the rules we'd agreed upon, which included "no put-downs," and Steven's unusual appearance was dismissed quietly and without incident. The next day he came to school without makeup, and he did not repeat that behavior. What could have put him at greater risk, instead, became an experience of acceptance and kindness. This example is somewhat simplistic in nature, but it does illustrate the importance of having an environment set up such that strengths have been built up and children feel safe that even if they are different in some way, they will still be ac-cepted members of the group.

To move to a more proactive strategy that would seek to help students succeed given the likelihood of problem-atic responses to certain behaviors (such as a boy wearing makeup to class), one must set up the environment so that the likelihood of these responses is decreased (Krovetz, 1999). For instance, if the culture of the school is such that teasing or making fun or put-downs are not permitted, if Steven shows up with nail polish on, we already have the means in place to diffuse the situation, keep the disruption to a minimum, and thus protect Steven's self-esteem and sense of belonging (Osterman, 2000).

SHIFTING THE PARADIGM FROM "AT RISK" TO "AT PROMISE"

The nature of the pathogenic term "at risk," especially when combined with the deleterious effects of labeling students, can operate as a self-fulfilling prophecy. How-ard & Dryden state, ". . . students labeled by schools as vulnerable or "at risk" are often those whose appearance, language, culture, values, home communities, and fam-ily structures often do not match those of the dominant culture . . ." (Howard & Dryden, 1999). From this subjec-tive ideological perspective, the effect of assigning a self-fulfilling label ("He's the troublemaker" or "He's certainly going to wind up on the front page of the crime section someday") can further alienate students identified as "dif-ferent" and can work against the more inclusive provisions of promoting the protective mechanism (Osterman, 2000). Potentially, we all could be assigned the label of "at risk," given the nature of our stress-laden culture and current world events today. "Life inevitably entails threats, after all, no matter how comfortable one's circumstances" (Finley, 1994). In some ways, if the wrong combination of challenges and deficits in resources combined to prohibit or preclude success in any given instance, any student could potentially be "at risk" for failure in a given developmental task.

Identifying and labeling students as "at risk" focuses on intervening to change children and/or families in order to better fit into the school structure, rather than changing the school structure to accommodate the needs of the students (Howard & Dryden, 1999). Adopting a more proactive approach, in which the school assumes students have a diversity of needs, identifies students' strengths, and builds on those strengths by creating an environment of emotional safety, can better serve as a protection to those students who are facing adversity outside the school environment (Krovetz, 1999).

Werner and Smith, in their seminal longitudinal study of over 600 people in Kauai, Hawaii, over a 40-year period, found that most children have an innate push to develop positively even in the face of adversity, and that their caring relationships, competent behavior and positive self-concept can flourish even in the face of extraordinary life difficulties (Werner & Smith, 1982, 1992). Children who live in the shadow of major external challenges (like abuse, neglect, poverty), who have faced some overwhelming trauma (like the death of a parent or sibling) or who struggle with personal disadvantage (like physical or learning disabilities), frequently surmount such difficulties and succeed beyond the predicted inferior outcome one might expect would result from such bleak circumstances (Werner & Smith, 1982, 1992).

One compelling story is told in an article written by one of the "at risk" children originally identified in the Werner & Smith study (Kitashima, 1997). Mervlyn Kitashima, now grown, wrote about the things that made a difference to her that she believes are responsible for her having grown up into a successfully adapted adult. Of her childhood, she writes:

> We were "those children." You know what "those children" are?—the ones where you as parents say to your own, "I don't want you playing with 'those children.' I don't want you going to 'those people's house.'" We were the "those children" that nobody wanted around.

Mervlyn lists a number of factors that she feels made a difference in her life. One struck me as particularly poignant. From time to time her grandmother would look after her when her parents, both alcoholics, were incapacitated. Mervlyn writes, "My Grandma Kahuanaele never treated me like one of 'those children.'" When Mervlyn stayed at her Grandma's house during her mother's institutionalization, she suffered from nightmares. Mervlyn's Grandma, who had had a leg amputated in childhood, would crawl on her hands and knees down the hall to make sure that

Mervlyn was okay in the night; she wouldn't even spare the time to put her wooden leg back on. Mervlyn writes of " . . . an example, a memory, of caring and support unsurpassed by anything else for me." This simple yet courageous act demonstrated the level of love and devotion this caregiver had for the child, and the child, long since grown, remembers. This child, born into poverty, surrounded by disadvantage, went on to become a successful adult and contributing member of society.

Even better news is that, of Mervlyn's seven siblings, six are doing well in their lives. Only one sister succumbed to drug abuse and a life on the streets. Mervlyn writes, "Six out of seven, not bad." This mirrors Werner and Smith's findings: Most "at risk" children overcame their adversity-filled childhoods to become successful adults (Werner & Smith, 1982, 1992). Considering children who are facing adversity to be "at promise" rather than "at risk" will help to prevent such children from fulfilling a negative self-concept imposed on them by others. It is amazing to realize how many people do succeed in life despite the challenges, trauma and mistreatment they might have experienced as children, but it gives much hope to those of us who seek to make a difference for them.

KEY PROTECTIVE FACTORS

Studies of children who demonstrate resilience have found some common factors that are present either internally, as part of their personality or way of dealing with the world, and externally, from family, school and community influences that buffer the child (Anthony & Cohler, 1987; Seligman, 1995; Werner & Smith, 1982, 1992). Such protective factors seem to work together in a process whereby adverse conditions are ameliorated (Benard, 1997; Werner & Smith, 1982, 1992). This is not a prescriptive, step-by-step process (Bradley, et al., 1994; Christiansen, 1997; Doll & Lyon, 1998). Not all protective factors are present at all times in the resilient child (Bradley, et al., 1994). Development of resilience is fluid, complicated, and more an evolving process than a single experience. That is, the risk and protective factors interact in such a way that the outcome ends up being positive in spite of the risk factor or factors present, and the outcome is not a particular occurrence but, instead, a continual adjustment and growth mechanism operating in the face of challenges or traumas as they arise (Bradley, et al., 1994; Looper & Grizenko, 1999).

Protective factors or mechanisms ameliorate the effects of disadvantage or adversity (Dugan & Coles, 1989; Garmezy, 1991; Henderson, Benard & Sharp-Light, 2000; Krovetz, 1999). Protective factors work together to support the strengths the child possesses (Dugan & Coles, 1989; Garmezy, 1991; Krovetz, 1999). They come to the fore when risk factors might otherwise overcome. Focus on protective factors contrasts with a risk-management model for "at risk" students (Bowen & Bowen, 1998). The use of an approach that focuses on children's strengths rather than deficiencies, is flexible to address individual differences rather than seeking to fit the child to a preconceived mold, and changes school structures to serve individual needs can result in more positive outcomes (Bowen & Bowen, 1998; Howard & Dryden, 1999; Miller, 1997).

INTERNAL PROTECTIVE FACTORS

Internal protective factors include temperament, cognitive skills, and a special kind of persistence and positive responsiveness (Dugan & Coles, 1989).[b] Children who have an internal locus of control are less vulnerable to the outside influences of risk factors (Dugan & Coles, 1989). Children who have a sense of "power rather than powerlessness" seem to bounce back more readily than those who do not (Garmezy, 1991). Being active rather than passive, being persistent in a flexible manner such that the same mistakes are not made again and again, and garnering support from adults are all examples of internal attributes that act as protective factors in the face of adversity (Bowen & Bowen, 1998; Garmezy, 1991). Children who possess such internal protective factors tend to show social competence that invites positive relationships with others. Despite the difficulties in their lives, they tend to have an effective problem-solving approach to such situations and a sense of independence, purpose and future (Werner & Smith, 1982, 1992).

EXTERNAL PROTECTIVE FACTORS

External protective factors include the presence of a parental surrogate figure such as a neighbor, teacher or other authority figure in the absence of responsive parents (Krovetz, 1999; Werner & Smith, 1982, 1992). A supportive family culture in which there are appropriate boundaries and rules also promotes resilience in children who are otherwise "at risk" (Garmezy, 1991).

INSTITUTIONAL PROTECTIVE FACTORS

Institutional structures can also serve as protective factors if the student finds warmth, cohesion and a sense of belonging to a larger community (Barton-Arwood, Jolivette & Massey, 2000; Bowen & Bowen, 1998; Guetzloe, 1997; Osterman, 2000). It is important for children's resilience that they have at least one caring and nurturing relationship with an adult in the community or school (Werner & Smith, 1982, 1992). Indeed, "Schools serve as a critical support system for children seeking to escape the disabling consequences of poor environments" (Garmezy, 1991). Schools can offer children "at risk" stimulation, emotional support, structure, and physical safety, all of which are important protective factors in overcoming adversity (Bradley, et al., 1994). Schools can offer plentiful opportunities for students "at risk" to participate meaningfully in activities and within groups (Benard, 1997; Werner & Smith, 1982, 1992). School is an excellent place to promote "required helpfulness" in

which "at risk" students find meaning and purpose to their lives as they authentically participate in helping others (Benard, 1997; Werner & Smith, 1982, 1992).

Students who feel that teachers care about them and show an interest in them tend to have higher grades and to be more invested in their education (Bowen & Bowen, 1998). It is vitally important for teachers to become aware of how significant an impact we can have on "at risk" students' success. Having high expectations that are effectively and clearly communicated to the student is an important protective factor that teachers can provide (Benard, 1997). Research shows, unfortunately, that many "at risk" students already receive less teacher support than low risk students (Bowen & Bowen, 1998). It is imperative that teachers understand the importance of "conveying warmth, concern, respect and a desire to have students in attendance" and to specifically target "at risk" students to provide additional support and understanding (Bowen & Bowen, 1998).

SCHOOL AS A PROTECTIVE MECHANISM

In a qualitative study by Sue Howard and Bruce Johnson (Howard & Johnson, 2000), the students and teachers interviewed from several disadvantaged areas in South Australia expressed similar views on the role of family and the community pertaining to resilience but expressed different views on the role of the school. Teachers felt that they helped most by providing social and emotional support for children via both formal and informal contact. Surprisingly, only some of the children agreed with the importance of this aspect of support on the part of the school. When they did speak about teacher social support as important, it was generally in the context of intervening in bullying situations. Both teachers and students agreed on the importance of the school's role in promoting a good link of communication between home and school as a means of improving a child's circumstances. Interestingly, students were most concerned with and felt the most important aspect of school support needed was in the area of the school's ability to supply additional assistance with learning difficulties and challenges.

Howard and Johnson's study reflects an interesting and unexpected viewpoint for teachers to consider when questioning the efficacy of their teaching philosophy. Their study highlights the importance of student perceptions of their own academic successes in the promotion of resilience in these students. As mentioned previously, one protective factor that has been identified is that of high academic expectations being communicated to the student. This, along with the students' indications of the importance of extra help for succeeding academically, and the danger of "at risk" students having lower expectations and less teacher-initiated contact, points to one very powerful component of resilience: individual teachers individualizing instruction to maximize academic success in a meaningful, relevant and achievable but realistically high way (Howard & Dryden, 1999).

---

b. Individuals with an internal locus of control habitually believe their successes and failures are due to their own efforts or abilities rather than to luck or chance.

Concern has been expressed about systemic efforts in schools to promote resilience as faddish and consequently short-lived (Doll & Lyon, 1998). Nevertheless, the strong success for students when such protective factors have been operationalized into programs promoting resilience in the classroom provide compelling reasons for educators to shift their paradigm and promote an atmosphere in schools that, to borrow from the medical field again, will ". . . help, or at least to do no harm" (Hippocrates in *Epidemics*, Bk. I, Sect. XI; tr. by W. H. S. Jones). While caution is needed in implementing programs designed to promote resilience, the developing body of research does support the concept of institutionalizing those protective factors that are preventive or promotional for building individual resilience (Henderson, et al., 2000; Krovetz, 1999).

For example, in my school, Jenna, who awaits identification for special education and/or some type of home intervention by the state program involving services to children and families, likes to draw and will do so when given the opportunity. Building on her strength, I can modify the classroom assignments such that her drawing can be incorporated. This particular institutionalizing effect for building resilience involves individualizing instruction to build on student strengths rather than singling the student out and penalizing her with some ineffectual punitive action. I think it is important to note here that I am not suggesting that Jenna's difficulties be ignored. Instead I mean that Jenna will be more likely to succeed in the future if the school first recognizes her strengths and builds upon them.

Promoting resilience should be a priority of schools (Krovetz, 1999). Teachers need to change their thinking such that they take pride in ". . . the most worthy of societal enterprises—the enhancement of competence in their children and their tailoring, in part, of a protective shield to help children withstand the multiple vicissitudes that they can expect of a stressful world" (Garmezy, 1991). This competence refers to the child's ability to successfully adapt and respond to adversity and difficulty (Finley, 1994). Teachers need to realize that their ". . . appropriate role is to think of oneself as a protective figure whose task is to do everything possible to enhance students' competence" (Garmezy, 1991). We as educators may rarely be able to transform students' lives or behavior, but we can always teach skills, provide a caring, supportive atmosphere, and communicate high, realistic standards, thus enabling students to build such competence and ultimately experience success as we tap into the innate salutogenic pursuit of health evident in all living things.

HOW CAN PROTECTIVE FACTORS BE OPERATIONALIZED SCHOOLWIDE?

Resilience theory, when applied schoolwide, effects change in the school climate (Krovetz, 1999). A list of suggestions for promoting resilience building in schools emerged from the Werner and Smith study (Werner & Smith, 1982, 1992) and is echoed in several other articles (Benard, 1997; Henderson, et al., 1999; Krovetz, 1999; Osterman, 2000):

- Provide authentic and meaningful opportunities for children to be helpful
- Provide optimistic leadership
- Address individual and intensive academic or social interventions for those in need
- Assess strengths and protective factors along with deficits and risks
- Maintain caring connections with children who leave the school
- Refer to children in positive terminology
- Create an authentic atmosphere of an extended family at school
- Provide plentiful opportunities for meaningful participation
- Communicate high expectations and the belief that such expectations can be met by the child

The literature suggests that we can do more for "at risk" students by taking a preventive, proactive approach to bolstering students' strengths rather than waiting for failure to occur and then applying, or attempting to apply, remedies that are beyond the scope of the usual school boundaries (Henderson, et al., 2000; Krovetz, 1999). School is a good place to operationalize protective factors. Individual teachers using effective teaching techniques can provide the best environment for protective mechanisms to operate (Garmezy, 1991; Howard & Dryden, 1999). Building a "mentoring structure" or "protective community" within the school will effectively enhance student success at school and in life (Guetzloe, 1997; Henderson, et al., 2000; Miller, 1997; Osterman, 2000; Terry, 1999; Young & Wright, 2001). A significant connection between the quality of the teacher-student affective relationship and subsequent student academic performance has been demonstrated (Bowen & Bowen, 1998). This suggests that even an effort by individual teachers to communicate positive affect and demonstrate willingness to support students who are struggling can improve student achievement and is thus clearly a protective factor that can be easily operationalized in the school to the benefit of many.

A school climate that promotes pro-social bonding promotes resilience in students (Henderson, et al., 2000). Examples of such bonding include encouraging supportive and caring relationships with others in the school community. Mentoring programs can be viewed as one aspect of the protective mechanism schools can provide for students. A school environment that sets clear and consistent boundaries is another protective mechanism (Henderson, et al., 2000). Current research on Effective Behavioral Support (EBS) programs shows that such programs succeed by focusing on the positive while actually providing articulated behavior training to students (Lewis, Sugai & Colvin, 1998).[c]

---

c. Effective Behavioral Support is a research-based program that aims to improve student behavior and motivation. It involves a schoolwide effort to recognize and reinforce students' positive behaviors while extinguishing negative behaviors by reducing the attention given to them.

This study suggests that, "Critical to the success of any school-wide system is the reduction of risk factors among children during their life spans." Clearly, EBS systems can be school-wide resilience-building instruments. Cooperative learning programs, such as the *Tribes* program, can provide a means for social skills training that is also an operationalized resilience-building approach (Gibbs, 2001).

SUGGESTIONS FOR FURTHER RESEARCH

One potential problem, perhaps mostly political in nature, is the question of whether resilience depends more on experience (nurture) or the innate qualities (nature) of the child. That is, is the ability of children to "right themselves" over time more a function of their internal qualities or is their recovery largely due to environmental factors? Critics of school resilience-building programs may argue that students who succeed must do so by ". . . pulling themselves up by their own bootstraps" (Gelman, 1991). It would be interesting to see if there is indeed any difference in the relationship between populations of "at risk" children and their successful or unsuccessful adaptation when viewed by the number or quality of resilience-building experiences.

Von Eye and Schuster (2000) developed several sample research designs that can be used to analyze the construct of resilience from different perspectives. They make several suggestions for the development of more "controlled causal analysis of resilience." They also give voice to the dilemma that, as compelling and hopeful as resilience theory and its potential for therapeutic interventions, "the conceptual, empirical, and methodological bases are far from clear." As in many other murky areas of educational research, it may be, as von Eye and Schuster suggest, that quasi-experimental research designs that seek to control confounding effects may be the most appropriate methodology.[d]

Several researchers focused on the need for further definition and clarity of terms in resilience research (Jew, Green & Kroger, 1999; Luther, et al., 2000a&b; von Eye & Schuster, 2000). Continued work in this area, particularly in identifying controllable independent variables and developing meaningful and quantifiable assessment tools, will help to bring greater focus and reliability to this area of study. Currently, interaction effects are "at the heart of resilience research" (Luthar, et al., 2000a).[e] With more universal and standardized terminology and methodology in place, the identification of causal and main effect relationships, and, potentially, respondent intervention strategies, will have more validity (von Eye & Schuster, 2000).

CONCLUSION

School was my "safe place." I am a person who bounced back or, more accurately, continues to bounce back from the adversity I faced in my childhood. I am successful today because of teachers and other adults who cared about me, mentored me, respected me and believed in me.

Emmy Warner, a pioneer in the field of resilience research, wrote:

> Forget about getting results overnight (or within an hour!) Take a longer view! Just like the research on resiliency program building and evaluation take time and perseverance, but also an attitude of hopefulness. (Henderson, et al., 2000)

Through my life journey I've come to realize that my effect on students is not about big transformational successes skillfully manipulated by me, the idealistic and influential teacher. It is more about the little successes of the students themselves as they push forward with their strengths to grow in spite of adverse conditions. Focusing on the strengths and victories, no matter how small, can eventually lead to transformation (Benard, 1998). As a teacher or educational administrator, I can provide an environment in which such successes are more likely to happen. I can be, as Bonnie Benard (1998) puts it, a "turnaround teacher."

A key protective belief is that there are some things over which we have no control: ". . . the ultimate mystery of life . . . [we must] recognize that there are forces at work in all of our lives that are beyond human understanding" (Ridley, 1996). No matter how gifted we are as educators, we can only do so much to help students who are in need. On the other hand, if we're not there to "stand in the gap" and if we don't at least do what we can, who else will?

I know from my own life experience how important school can be in providing a protective atmosphere for student growth. My school experience was not perfect and, indeed, there were times that school itself operated in a detrimental way in my life. Certainly, bullying, unresponsive teachers, and systemic barriers and obstacles can make school difficult for students already facing adversity in their personal lives. Still, even with its flaws, without the protective mechanism of school I am unsure what course my life would have followed but fairly certain it would not be the positive road I am now on.

Unfortunately, the pathogenic concepts of risk and deficit are more prevalent among educators and policymakers than the more salutogenic concepts of resilience and protective factors and mechanisms (Finley, 1994). What I discovered in conducting this literature review is that true transformation of troubled children's lives is not so much within my sphere of influence as is the transformation within myself as an educator to better understand and promote

---

d. Quasi-experimental research is a quantitative research method involving an experimental group that receives the treatment and a control group that does not receive the treatment. Unlike a true experiment, participants in a quasi-experiment are not randomly assigned to the treatment or control conditions.

e. An interaction effect is said to have occurred if an experimental intervention is found to be more effective than a control condition, but only for a certain type of individual. In other words, the intervention "interacts" with individual characteristics to produce certain outcomes. For example, a particular intervention might make boys more resilient, but have no effect on girls' resilience.

those protective processes that can and do help children build capacity for transforming themselves.

Karen Osterman (2000) writes, ". . . many of the changes necessary to satisfy students' needs for 'belongingness' involve drastic changes in the cultural values, norms, policies, and practices that dominate schooling . . ." According to Nan Henderson (1996), effective education and resilience-building strategies are strongly related. She writes, ". . . effective school restructuring produces a resiliency-building school and resiliency building in schools is actually the foundation of effective education."

I urge busy teachers not to think that schoolwide reform to enhance resilience building is just "one more thing" they have to try to accomplish. In the course of addressing the steps to create a resilient learning community, effective teaching practices are symbiotic if not synonymous (Krovetz, 1999). Mary Finley (1994) writes:

> . . . educators need to understand more clearly what goes right even in risky circumstances, and why . . . [it's important to] regard students not as a problem to be "fixed," but as personalities to be protected—and in which to nurture internal resilience to the prevalent threats.

It is important, then, as educators, to change our thinking regarding students who are "at risk" if we truly want to make a difference in their lives—to view them as capable participants who aren't substandard or doomed to failure.

My reflection process has helped me find the commonalities between my own personal teaching philosophy and the articulated theory of resilience, and identify the protective mechanisms that my classroom management strategies mirrored. Some of the good things I did for the three children I mentioned as examples in the introduction include: showing a genuine concern and warmth for the students; inviting parents in and trying to work with them as equal partners in their child's education; setting the environment up for success; being proactive in my approach to potential problems and planning how to deal with them when they arise; and focusing on the positives while minimizing focus on the negatives.

The most obvious failure on my part was not coming to the realization that Steven really had some significant learning problems that needed to be identified and addressed outside the regular classroom setting. My assumption that his behavior was due entirely to his poor life circumstances rather than any learning disabilities or deficits, especially if I had merely passed him on to the next grade without referring him for identification in order to get him the assistance he needed, would have put him at greater risk for failure later. Indeed, in many ways, I was thinking of him as "one of those kids." One of the best things I did with these three students, and that I strive to do with all my students, is to tap into their strengths, communicate high expectations, and, most importantly, build a caring and authentic relationship with them.

Like other living things, schools as organizational entities have the same salutogenic tendency: a push towards organizational health and well-being. With all the stresses and responsibilities placed on public schools, resilience theory and its application to school climate is the key to effective school reform, especially at a time when society is more "at promise" than ever before.

References

Anthony, E., & Cohler, B. (1987). *The invulnerable child.* New York: The Guilford Press.

Barton-Arwood, S., Jolivette, K., & Massey, G. (2000). Mentoring with elementary-age students. *Intervention in School and Clinic, 36*(1), 36–40.

Benard, B. (1997). Turning it around for all youth: From risk to resilience. ERIC/CUE Digest, Number 126.

Benard, B. (1998). How to be a turnaround teacher/mentor. *Mentoring for Resiliency.* San Diego: Resiliency in Action.

Bowen, N., & Bowen, G. (1998). The effects of home microsystem risk factors and school microsystem protective factors on student academic performance and affective investment in schooling. *Social Work in Education, 20*(4), 219–232.

Bradley, R., Whiteside, L., Mundfrom, D., Casey, P., Kelleher, K., & Pope, S. (1994). Contribution of early intervention and early caregiving experiences to resilience in low-birthweight, premature children living in poverty. *Journal of Clinical Child Psychology, 23,* 425–434.

Brown, K., & Block, A. (2001). Evaluation of Project Chrysalis: A school-based intervention to reduce negative consequences of abuse. *Journal of Early Adolescence, 21*(3) 325–353.

Christiansen, J. (1997). Helping teachers meet the needs of students "at risk" for school failure. *Elementary School Guidance & Counseling, 31*(3), 204–211.

Doll, B., & Lyon, M. (1998). Risk and resilience: Implications for the delivery of educational and mental health services in schools. *School Psychology Review, 27*(30), 348–365.

Dugan, T., & Coles, R. (1989). *The child in our times: Studies in the development of resiliency.* New York: Bruner/Mazel.

Finley, M. (1994). Cultivating resilience: An overview for rural educators and parents. ERIC Digest: ED372904.

Garmezy, N. (1991). Resiliency and vulnerability to adverse developmental outcomes associated with poverty. *American Behavioral Scientist, 34*(40), 416–430.

Gelman, D. (1991). The miracle of resiliency. *Newsweek, 117*(22), 44–48.

Gibbs, J. (2001). *Tribes: A new way of learning and being together.* Windsor, CA: CenterSource Systems.

Guetzloe, E. (1997). The power of positive relationships: Mentoring programs in the school and community. *Preventing School Failure, 41*(3), 100–106.

Helge, D. (1992). Solving special education reform, problems in rural areas. *Preventing School Failure, 36*(4), 11–16.

Henderson, N. (1996). Integrating resiliency building and educational reform: Why doing one accomplishes the other. *Resiliency in Action: A Journal of Application and Research,* Spr. 1996, 35–36.

Henderson, N., Benard, B., & Sharp-Light, N. (1999). *Resiliency in action: Practical ideas for overcoming risks and building strengths in youth, families and communities.* San Diego: Resiliency in Action.

Henderson, N., Benard, B., & Sharp-Light, N. (2000). *Schoolwide approaches for fostering resiliency.* San Diego: Resiliency in Action.

Howard, S., & Dryden, J. (1999). Childhood resilience: Review and critique of literature. *Oxford Review of Education, 25*(3), 307–324.

Howard, S., & Johnson, B. (2000). What makes the difference? Children and teachers talk about resilient outcomes for children "at risk." *Educational Studies, 26*(30), 321–340.

Jew, C. L., Green, K. E., & Kroger, J. (1999). Development and validation of a measure of resiliency. *Measurement and Evaluation in Counseling and Development, 32,* 75–89.

Kitashima, M. (1997). Lessons from my life: No more "children at risk" . . . all children are "at promise." *Mentoring for resiliency.* San Diego: Resiliency in Action.

Krovetz, M. (1999). *Fostering resiliency: Expecting all students to use their minds and hearts well.* Thousand Oaks, CA: Corwin.

Levenstein, S. (1994). Wellness, health, Antonovsky. *The Journal of Mind–Body Health, 10*(3), 26–30.

Lewis, T., Sugai, G., & Colvin, G. (1998). Reducing problem behavior through a school-wide system of effective behavioral support: Investigation of school-wide social skills training program and contextual interventions. *School Psychology Review, 27*(3), 446–459.

Looper, K., & Grizenko, N. (1999). Risk and protective factors scale: Reliability and validity in preadolescents. *Canadian Journal of Psychiatry, 44*(2), 138–145.

Lustig, D., Rosenthal, D., Strauser, D., & Haynes, K. (2000). The relationship between sense of coherence and adjustments in persons with disabilities. *Rehabilitation Counseling Bulletin, 43*(30), 134–142.

Luthar, S., Cicchetti, D., & Becker, B. (2000a). Research on resilience: Response to commentaries. *Child Development, 71*(3) 573–575.

Luthar, S., Cicchetti, D., & Becker, B. (2000b). The construct of resilience: A critical evaluation and guidelines for future work. *Child Development, 71*(3), 543–562.

Maeroff, G. (1998). *Altered destinies: Making life better for schoolchildren in need.* New York: St. Martin's.

Meyer, A., & Farrell, A. (1998). Social skills training to promote resilience in urban sixth-grade students: One product of an action research strategy to prevent youth violence in high-risk environments. *Education & Treatment of Children, 21*(4), 461–480.

Miller, G., Brehm, K., & Whitehouse, S. (1998). Reconceptualizing school-based prevention for antisocial behavior within a resiliency framework. *School Psychology Review, 27*(3), 364–379.

Nafpaktitis, M., & Perlmutter, B. (1998). School-based early mental health intervention with at-risk students. *School Psychology Review, 27*(3), 420–432.

Osterman, K. (2000). Students' need for belonging in the school community. *Review of Educational Research, 70*(3), 323–367.

Rak, C., & Patterson, L. (1996). Promoting resilience in at-risk children. *Journal of Counseling & Development, 74*(4), 368–374.

Random House. (1968). *The Random House dictionary of the English language.* New York: Author.

Ridley, K. (1996). Protective beliefs are a key to professionals' and students' resiliency. *Resiliency in Action: A Journal of Application and Research,* Spr. 1996, 31–32.

Sandler, I. (2001). Quality and ecology of adversity as common mechanisms of risk and resilience. *American Journal of Community Psychology, 29*(1), 19–61.

Seligman, M. (1995). *The optimistic child.* New York: Houghton Mifflin.

Strumpfer, D., & Mlonzi, E. (2001). Antonovsky's sense of coherence scale and job attitudes: Three studies. *South African Journal of Psychology, 31*(2), 30–38.

Terry, J. (1999). A community/school mentoring program for elementary students. *Professional School Counseling, 2*(3), 237–241.

von Eye, A., & Schuster, C. (2000). The odds of resilience. *Child Development, 71*(3), 563–566.

Werner, E., & Smith, R. (1982). *Vulnerable, but invincible: A longitudinal study of resilient children and youth.* New York: McGraw-Hill.

Werner, E., & Smith, R. (1992). *Overcoming the odds: High risk children from birth to adulthood.* Ithaca, NY: Cornell University.

Young, C., & Wright, J. (2001). Mentoring: The components for success. *Journal of Instructional Psychology, 28*(3), 202–208.

chapter 4

Using Search Engines in a Literature Review

IMPORTANT *Ideas*

1. A search engine typically has thousands of bibliographic citations in its database and features that make it easy for you to identify the citations most relevant to your research problem or problem of practice.

2. Several search engines are comprehensive, free of charge, and useful to educators: Google (for websites), ERIC (for all kinds of educational publications), and the Library of Congress Online Catalog (for books).

3. Many search engines are designed to help educators locate particular types of publications: bibliographies, book reviews, books, dissertations and theses, journal articles, and magazine and newspaper articles.

4. ERIC's search engine has a variety of options to help you focus your literature search: keyword entry, truncation, connectors, a thesaurus of descriptors, and a selection of publication types and educational levels.

5. Maintaining a log of your search engine use will help you avoid repeating a search needlessly and enable you to include an accurate description of your search process when writing a literature review report.

6. You can save relevant bibliographic citations by using features that the search engine provides or by using a citation manager.

7. Search engines like ERIC provide information about how to obtain copies of the actual publications that you have identified as relevant to your needs.

8. Free online journals about education are increasingly available. ■

Key TERMS

AND connector	fugitive literature	search engine
bibliographic citation	keyword	truncation
citation manager	NOT connector	wildcard
citation pearl growing	OR connector	
ERIC (Education Resources Information Center)	pdf file	

The Purpose of Search Engines

In Chapter 2, we introduced search engines and bibliographic databases as important aids in conducting a literature review. In this chapter, we explain in detail how to use these resources.

The education literature is large. One of the main guides to this literature, called **ERIC (Education Resources Information Center),** included 1.2 million bibliographic citations in its database as of early 2009. If you wish to conduct an efficient, effective search of these citations, you will need to learn a systematic search strategy.

A good starting point is to consider what is meant by the term *publication.* Books and journal articles clearly are publications, but how about newspaper articles, government reports, curriculum guides, test manuals, tables of statistical data about education, conference papers, and websites? In this chapter, we consider all of them to be publications that you might wish to identify for your literature review. The term *publications* conveys one of their important features, namely, that they are publicly available to various extents.

A published book from a large publisher that is available from a bookstore or website such as Amazon.com is clearly "publicly available." Other publications, such as an out-of-print book that was published decades ago and in small quantities is still likely to be publicly available, but more difficult to locate. Even a paper that was presented at a conference that did not publish its proceedings is potentially publicly available, if you can locate the authors and they are willing to send you a copy. Publications like these sometimes are called **fugitive literature,** because, while not widely disseminated or easily obtained, they still exist and are part of the professional literature

In this chapter, we explain how to search for publications of many different types and degrees of availability. More precisely, we explain how to search for bibliographic citations to those publications. A **bibliographic citation** consists of information about a particular publication, such as its author, title, and year of publication. If you wish to examine the actual publication, the bibliographic citation might provide information about how to locate it.

Bibliographic Indexes and Search Engines

Until computers became widely available, **bibliographic indexes** (sometimes called *guides* or *indexes*) to the professional literature were available in the form of library card catalogs, books, or periodicals. These sometimes are called *hard-copy indexes,* because they have a physical entity.

Most hard-copy indexes have disappeared, and the information in them has been transformed into electronic databases and search engines. As we explained in Chapter 3, a **search engine** is computer software that helps a user explore relevant publications or other information in a database. The user can define what is relevant by selecting various search options included in the search engine.

The following sections of this chapter describe procedures for selecting and using a search engine. If you learn these procedures, you will be able to compile a list of publications that will provide the foundation for a good literature review.

Selecting a Useful Search Engine

ERIC might well be the only search engine you need to identify publications for your literature review. We make this statement, because its website home page (www.eric.ed.gov) describes ERIC as "the world's largest digital library of education literature." It is a free service funded by the U.S. government that can be easily accessed by your Web browser (e.g., Internet Explorer, Safari, Firefox).

If you are not familiar with the ERIC search engine, we recommend that you take a few minutes to access its website and do a basic search by entering any term of interest to you (e.g., "educational leadership," "classroom management"). Doing so will help you understand the rest of this chapter, which focuses primarily on ERIC.

Before ERIC created its search engine, it indexed educational publications in hard-copy format. The indexes were updated periodically during the year and then cumulated into an annual volume. The indexes were of two types. Journal articles were indexed in *Current Index to Journals in Education* (*CIJE*), and all other reports were indexed in *Resources in Education* (*RIE*). You might still find these indexes on the shelves of some university libraries and school offices. However, all the citations in these indexes, extending back to ERIC's inception in 1966, are now electronically filed in the search engine, which is much easier to use than the hard-copy indexes.

Some search engines require a subscription or fee. However, university libraries typically have a website that includes free access to a set of commercial search engines for their students, faculty, staff, and others. These search engines might be maintained by a commercial service, which organizes the search engines in a particular way. Therefore, you might find some differences between a commercial search engine that you access directly through the company's website and the same search engine that you access through a university library or other service. Generally, the differences are minor.

In this chapter, we describe search engines in each of the following categories: (1) comprehensive; (2) bibliographies; (3) books; (4) dissertations and theses; (5) journal articles, papers, and reports; and (6) magazines and newspapers. The lists are not exhaustive, but we have attempted to include the most important ones.

Most of the citations in these lists generally are not for the search engines but rather for their website home pages. You will need to determine whether your university or other institution has access to the actual search engine. Additional search engines are described in two other chapters of this book: search engines for tests and measures in Chapter 6 and search engines for historical publications in Chapter 17.

With experience, you will identify the search engines that are most relevant to your professional needs. For us personally, we rely most often on four search engines: Google (to identify relevant websites), ERIC (to identify a wide range of relevant publications, including journal articles), PsycInfo (to identify publications in journals and other sources not included in ERIC's database), and the Library of Congress Online Catalog (to identify relevant books). With the exception of PsycInfo, these are free search engines, accessible via the Internet.

Comprehensive Search Engines for Websites

Google, Yahoo!, AltaVista, HotBot, MetaCrawler, and AOL Search are among the comprehensive search engines whose databases include a great many of the world's websites.

You can use these search engines to identify websites that include databases of education literature by entering "literature search" and your topic as the keywords.

A **keyword** is a word or phrase that you enter in the appropriate search engine window to identify all entries (e.g., books, journals, websites) in its database containing that word or phrase. If you type quote marks around a particular phrase (e.g., "literature search"), you will retrieve only entries that contain those two words together, in that order.

We used a combination of two keyword phrases—"educational technology" "literature search"—to see which websites Google would retrieve from its database. It retrieved 1,050 websites, including the following:

- The Center for Comprehensive School Reform and Improvement (www.centerfor csri.org). We entered "technology" in its search window and obtained a list of 36 publications.
- Pennsylvania State University Program on Instructional Systems (www.libraries.psu .edu/ebsl/insy.htm). The home page contains links to many items of relevance to educational technology, such as professional associations, books, indexes and abstracts, journals, and instructional resources.

Websites such as these two provide a good initial overview of publications and other resources in the field of educational technology.

Search Engine for Bibliographies

Researchers sometimes compile bibliographies on specialized topics in education. They can provide a good starting point for your own literature review. The following search engine will help you identify bibliographies that are relevant to your research problem or problem of practice.

- Bibliographic Index Plus (www.hwwilson.com/databases/biblio.htm). This search engine includes citations for more than 450,000 bibliographies in its database. Of these, more than 136,000 are available in a full-text version.

Search Engines for Book Reviews

Some of the publications that you identify in your literature review are likely to be books. A review of a particular book can help you decide whether it is sufficiently relevant to take on the task of obtaining a copy. The following search engines are designed to help you determine whether reviews of your book are available.

- Books in Print with Book Reviews (www.bowker.com/catalog/index.htm#online). This index is currently available as a CD, including more than 500,000 full-text reviews of books.
- Book Review Index (http://library.dialog.com/bluesheets/html/bl0137.html). This search engine includes more than four million reviews of approximately two million books.
- Education Review (http://edrev.asu.edu). This search engine contains reviews of books relating to educational research and practice. It is a free service.
- PsycCritiques (www.apa.org/psyccritiques). This search engine includes reviews of books, films, videos, and software about psychology. Many of the reviews are about education-related publications.

Search Engines for Books

Books about education generally do not report original research, except for those that present extensive case studies (see Chapter 14). However, many education books are about research methodology and problems of practice in education. Also, there are numerous handbooks and encyclopedias that include contributed chapters synthesizing what is known about particular topics. The following search engines can help you identify these books.

- Books in Print (www.booksinprint.com/bip) This search engine includes bibliographic data about more than four million books, audios, and videos. If you go to the home page of its publisher (www.bowker.com), you will find information about more specialized search engines and hard-copy indexes, such as *El-Hi Textbooks and Serials in Print* and *Children's Books in Print.*
- Library of Congress Online Catalog (http://catalog.loc.gov). This search engine contains a comprehensive database of books, recordings, maps, and manuscripts. It is a free service of the U.S. government.

Search Engine for Dissertations and Theses

Reports of research studies conducted as a requirement for the doctorate are called *dissertations*. At the master's degree level, these reports usually are called *theses*. Some students rewrite their dissertation or thesis for journal publication, but many do not. If you want to do a comprehensive review of the literature, you should at least consider searching for relevant dissertations. An exhaustive review would include theses as well. The following search engine or its hard-copy indexes can be used for this purpose.

- Proquest Dissertations & Theses (www.proquest.com). The database for this search engine includes bibliographic citations for more than two million dissertations and theses around the world. The vast majority of these citations also include a full-text version of the dissertation or thesis. The following are hard-copy indexes of various subsets of the Proquest database: *Dissertation Abstracts International, Masters Abstracts International,* and *American Doctoral Dissertations.*

Search Engines for Journal Articles, Papers, and Reports

Certain search engines are designed to help you identify relevant journal articles, conference proceedings, agency reports, position papers on educational policy, descriptions of best practices, and statistical summaries, as in the following search engines with large, general databases.

- Education Index Retrospective: 1929–1983 (www.wilson.com). This search engine encompasses older education literature not included by ERIC, which extends back only to 1966. Related search engines produced by the same publisher are Education Full Text, Education Abstracts, and Education Index. Of these three, Education Full Text provides the most complete bibliographic information.
- ERIC (www.eric.ed.gov). This undoubtedly is the most frequently used search engine by educational researchers and educators. We discuss it extensively in later sections of this chapter.
- Google Scholar (http://scholar.google.com). The database for this search engine includes publications from many disciplines. Therefore, you might find relevant publications in it that are not included in education-specific search engines.
- National Center for Education Statistics (http://nces.ed.gov). This website includes a search engine and many publications and statistical tables pertaining to the demographics and performance outcomes of public and private K–12 schools, school districts, and postsecondary education. We recommend that you explore its resources by clicking the link Most Viewed NCES Sites. Among them are Nation's Report Card, Digest of Education Statistics, and Data Tools.
- PsycInfo (www.apa.org/psycinfo). This search engine is maintained by the American Psychological Association. Its database includes more than 2.4 million publications in more than 2,000 journals and other sources extending back to the 1800s. Its compre-

hensiveness might help you identify relevant publications not included in education-specific search engines.

- Web of Science (http://scientific.thomson.com). This search engine has a special feature. Suppose you identify a journal article that is critical to your research problem or problem of practice. You want to know whether other publications have referenced this article, because if they did, these publications also are likely to be relevant for your purposes. By using Web of Science, you can identify the journal article of interest and then search for other publications that have cited it.

Other search engines and a few hard-copy indexes are listed in Figure 4.1. The list is not exhaustive because education includes so many specialties, and new databases continue to be developed.

FIGURE 4.1   Search Engines and Bibliographic Indexes for Specific Topics in Education

- Catalog of U.S. Government Publications (http://catalog.gpo.gov/F). A free search engine for a database of U.S. government publications.
- Chicano Database (www.oclc.org). A search engine that includes approximately 60,000 publications about Chicanos, Puerto Ricans, Cuban Americans, and Central American immigrants.
- CSA Sociological Abstracts (www.csa.com). A search engine for publications relating to various aspects of sociology, including culture and social structure, evaluation research, management and complex organizations, sociology of education, and substance abuse and prevention.
- Education Policy Alliance (http://epicpolicy.org). A free search engine for locating policy research on many problems of practice in education. The research reports come from thirty-three leading university centers in twenty-three states.
- Educational Administration Abstracts (www.sagepub.com). A hard-copy index of publications about various aspects of educational administration.
- GPO Access (www.gpoaccess.gov/about/index.html). A free search engine for a wide range of information products produced by the U.S. government.
- International Index to Black Periodicals (http://iibp.chadwyck.com). A search engine for publications about African American studies that appear in more than 150 international periodicals.
- JSTOR (www.jstor.org). A search engine for an archive of important scholarly journals in various disciplines as they were originally designed, printed, and illustrated.
- PubMed (www.ncbi.nim.nih.gov/PubMed). A free search engine maintained by the U.S. National Library of Medicine. It includes over 17 million citations from the MEDLINE database and other life science journals.
- Sage Family Studies Abstracts (www.sagepub.com). A hard-copy index of publications about various aspects of family studies, such as family services, reproduction issues, courtship, and marriage.
- SportDiscus (www.sirc.ca/products/sportdiscus.cfm). A search engine for a database of publications relating to sport, health, fitness, and sports medicine.
- Women's Studies International (www.nisc.com/factsheets/qwri.asp). A search engine for a database of publications relating to a wide range of topics in women's studies, such as feminist studies, psychology and body image, women and the media, reproductive rights, racial/ethnic studies, and girl studies.

Search Engines for Magazine and Newspaper Articles

Articles in magazines and newspapers are good sources for identifying problems of practice and how educators, the community, and public officials are addressing them. The following search engines can help identify relevant articles.

- MagPortal (www.magportal.com). This search engine enables you to find online magazine articles on a wide range of topics, including education.
- Newspaper Source (www.epnet.com). The database for this search engine includes full-text coverage for 245 newspapers, newswires, and other sources, dating from the 1990s to the present.
- SearchEngineWatch (http://searchenginewatch.com). This website includes search engines for identifying news items.
- Ulrich's Periodicals Directory. (www.ulrichsweb.com). This is a comprehensive international search engine for journals, magazines, and newspapers. Ulrich's also publishes a hard-copy version of the directory.

Using a Search Engine to Focus a Literature Review

You probably have had the experience of entering a word or phrase (e.g., "No Child Left Behind Act") in a search engine like Google. Almost immediately, you get a list containing thousands, or even millions, of websites. Google helps you by listing what it thinks are the most relevant websites first. In this case, relevance is decided by a sophisticated algorithm developed by Google.

Some of the search engines described above or listed in Figure 4.1 are different in that they provide options to help you establish criteria of relevance *prior* to the search. To illustrate, we will describe the options available for the ERIC search engine.

We chose ERIC for three reasons. First, it is the search engine most widely used by educational researchers and practitioners. Second, the use of ERIC is free. Third, the search options are similar to those available for other well-developed search engines, such as PsycInfo.

As you read the next sections, we recommend that you go to ERIC's website (www .eric.ed.gov) so that you can see the search options on an actual computer screen as we describe them here.

Search Options in the ERIC Search Engine

Figure 4.2 shows the first screen (i.e., the home page) you see when you access the ERIC website. This screen includes two windows, Search Term(s): and Search In:, that you can use to do what is called a *basic search* of the ERIC database of publications. If you click on the Advanced Search link, you will see a new screen, part of which is shown in Figure 4.3. We will use the screen shown in Figure 4.3 to explain search options for ERIC. Once you understand these options, you will find it easier to do a basic search, if that serves your purpose best.

To explain the search options, we show in Figure 4.4 an example of the bibliographic citation that ERIC provides about each publication in its database. The bibliographic citation constitutes what ERIC refers to as a *record*.

We obtained this record by using the keyword phrase "questioning techniques" in an advanced search.

Pull-Down Menu for Keywords.   If you look at Figure 4.3, you will see the phrase "Search for: Keywords (all fields)." Immediately to the right of this phrase are two tiny

FIGURE *4.2*   ERIC Home Page

ERIC Education Resources Information Center

Home | ERIC Search | Thesaurus | My ERIC

>>> *The world's largest digital library of education literature*

Search ERIC

Search Term(s): [   ]

Search In: [Keywords (all fields) ▲▼]

[🔍 Search]   ⊙ Advanced Search   ⊘ Search Help

ERIC provides free access to more than 1.2 million bibliographic records of journal articles and other education-related materials and, if available, includes links to full text. ERIC is sponsored by the U.S. Department of Education, Institute of Education Sciences (IES).

 **ERIC Microfiche Digitization**

Microfiche to Megabytes
Help ERIC expand online access to nearly 340,000 documents indexed 1966–1992, now available only on microfiche. Click here to learn about our digitization project.

About the ERIC Collection

• What's in ERIC - Bibliographic records of education literature plus a growing collection of full text

• Journals Indexed in ERIC - Alphabetical list covering 1966 to the present

Contribute to the ERIC Collection

• Online Submission - Find out how individuals can contribute papers, reports, and other materials to ERIC.

• Publisher Information - Discover the benefits of indexing journals, books, and other education-related materials in ERIC. Learn how your titles can be included.

arrows, one pointing up and the other pointing down. These arrows indicate a pull-down menu, which you will see if you click on the phrase. The choices in the pull-down menu are Keywords, Title, Author, Descriptors (from Thesaurus), ERIC #, Source, Identifiers, ISBN, ISSN, Institution, and Sponsoring Agency. As indicated by the following description of the pull-down choices, each one enables you to focus your search for relevant publications in a different way.

Keywords.   A keyword is any word or phrase that you want ERIC to look for in its database. You can enter any keyword or key phrase in the window to the right of this item, as shown in Figure 4.3 (p. 82). ERIC's search engine will go through its entire database to find any record that contains this word or phrase in the text of any of its fields. (The term *field* refers to the information under each boldfaced heading in the record.) For example, we retrieved the record shown in Figure 4.4 (p. 82) by entering the phrase "questioning techniques" in the Keywords window. The phrase will be highlighted wherever it appears in the record.

FIGURE *4.3*   ERIC Advanced Search Screen

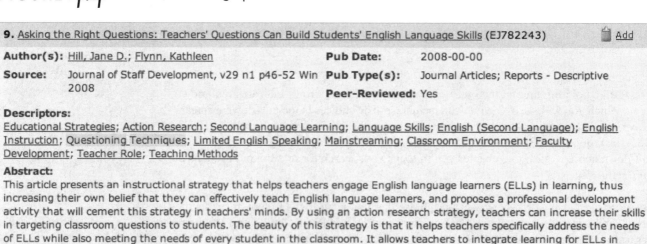

FIGURE *4.4*   An ERIC Bibliographic Citation

9. Asking the Right Questions: Teachers' Questions Can Build Students' English Language Skills (EJ782243)   🗑 Add

Author(s): Hill, Jane D.; Flynn, Kathleen	**Pub Date:**	2008-00-00
Source: Journal of Staff Development, v29 n1 p46-52 Win 2008	**Pub Type(s):**	Journal Articles; Reports - Descriptive
	Peer-Reviewed: Yes	

Descriptors:
Educational Strategies; Action Research; Second Language Learning; Language Skills; English (Second Language); English Instruction; Questioning Techniques; Limited English Speaking; Mainstreaming; Classroom Environment; Faculty Development; Teacher Role; Teaching Methods

Abstract:
This article presents an instructional strategy that helps teachers engage English language learners (ELLs) in learning, thus increasing their own belief that they can effectively teach English language learners, and proposes a professional development activity that will cement this strategy in teachers' minds. By using an action research strategy, teachers can increase their skills in targeting classroom questions to students. The beauty of this strategy is that it helps teachers specifically address the needs of ELLs while also meeting the needs of every student in the classroom. It allows teachers to integrate learning for ELLs in mainstream classrooms and to help these students achieve academic success at the same levels as their native English-speaking peers. Finally, it shows teachers one direction for creating a supportive environment for English language learners. (Contains 1 table.) ▲ Hide Full Abstract

Full-Text Availability Options:
Not available from ERIC | Find in a Library | Publisher's Web Site

If you put quotation marks around a phrase, as we did for "questioning techniques," the search engine will identify only those records that contain those two terms adjacent to each other. Each word in the phrase will be highlighted wherever it appears in the record, but there will be at least one instance in which the two words appear adjacent to each other in the order specified in the keyword window. In the record shown in Figure 4.4, that instance occurs under the field labeled Descriptors.

Suppose your keyword can have different endings. For example, consider teachers' questioning practices. Should we enter "teacher question," "teacher questions," "teacher questioning," or all three phrases? In fact, we only need to enter the stem of each word followed by an asterisk (*), which is called a **wildcard.** The use of just the word stem along with the wildcard sign (*) is called **truncation.**

When we entered "teacher questions" in the keyword window, the search engine retrieved 20,167 records. (This is the number of records for a search conducted in February 2008; the ERIC database keeps increasing, so you are likely to obtain a larger number of records for the same search and other searches described below.) When we entered "teacher question*" it retrieved 44,516 records. Clearly, use of the wildcard feature resulted in a more comprehensive set of potentially useful records.

Title.   If you are searching for a particular publication and know its title, you can select the Title option in the pull-down menu. You can enter all or part of the title.

Author.   Perhaps you wish to identify all publications by a particular author. Using the Author option, you will find these publications if you enter the author's last name (e.g., Brophy) or first and last name (e.g., Baxter, Juliet), or first and last name and middle initial (e.g., Teixeira-Dias, Jose J.).

Descriptors (from Thesaurus).   The use of a keyword will identify all records in the ERIC database containing that word in any field. However, you might fail to identify some relevant records because they do not include the particular keyword you have chosen. For this reason, the ERIC staff have developed a comprehensive list of descriptors, compiled into a thesaurus, that they use to classify each publication.

To access the thesaurus, we click on the Thesaurus link at the top of the basic/advanced search screens. A new screen appears, and we find that we can search the thesaurus alphabetically or by category to find relevant descriptors. Using the category option, we find what seems to be a relevant category for teachers' questioning practices, Educational Process; Classroom Perspectives. Clicking on that link, we find several relevant descriptors, such as Questioning Techniques, Classroom Communication, Discussion (Teaching Technique), and Discussion Groups. Using one or more of these descriptors, we are likely to retrieve more relevant records and obtain a better picture of the literature than if we just relied on a selection like "teacher question*" as the keyword phrase.

ERIC #.   This is a unique number that the ERIC staff assigns to the record for each publication in the database. The prefix for each ERIC # is either EJ, which indicates that the publication is a journal article, or ED, which indicates that it is some other kind of publication.

Other Options in the Keyword Pull-Down Menu.   You can click on the Search Help button of the Advanced Search screen to learn the meaning of the other search options of the keyword pull-down menu: Source, Identifier, ISBN, ISSN, Institution, Sponsoring Agency.

Pull-Down Menu for Connectors.   Look at Figure 4.3 and you will see three keyword pull-down menus. Next to two of them are two other pull-down menus labeled *AND*. The AND pull-down menu is an important aid for focusing your research. It includes three options: AND, OR, and NOT (not shown in Figure 4.3). These options sometimes are called *connectors* or *Boolean operators,* because they derive from a branch of mathematics known as Boolean logic. In the case of ERIC, a connector examines the relationship between two or more sets of publication records in the database.

To illustrate, we will continue to use the example of teachers' questioning practices. We retrieved 44,516 records when we entered "teacher question*" in the window for the first keyword pull-down menu. Suppose we wished to focus only on publications relating to teachers' questioning practices in mathematics education. The ERIC thesaurus indicates that "mathematics instruction" is a descriptor. A search for items categorized by that descriptor yields 19,081 records.

Now if we enter "teacher question*" as a keyword in the first window and "mathematics instruction" as a descriptor in the second window, using AND as the connector, we retrieve a set of 1,389 records. An **AND connector** identifies all publications in a database that have both keywords or both descriptors.

Examining these records, we find that some are not relevant, as they have to do with teacher questionnaires, which happen to include "teacher question*" in their labels. Therefore, we decide to redo the search, entering the thesaurus descriptor "questioning techniques" in the first window and the thesaurus descriptor "mathematics instruction" in the second window, connecting them by AND. (Note that each of these thesaurus descriptors needs to be enclosed by quotation marks.) This search yields 108 records, all of which appear highly related to our interest in the role of teachers' questioning practices in mathematics instruction.

Suppose we are interested in publications about either teachers' questioning practices or discussion practices. We can search for these publications by using the OR connector. We enter "questioning techniques" in the first window and "discussion (teaching technique)" in the second window, selecting OR as the connector. The ERIC search engine retrieves 7,270 records. Use of the OR connector almost invariably will retrieve more records than an AND connector, because an AND connector requires that a publication record include both keywords. However, an **OR connector** only requires that a publication include one of the two keywords in the publication record.

The **NOT connector** in the pull-down menu is used when you wish to exclude a set of published records having a characteristic that is not relevant to your literature review. For example, suppose we are interested in teachers' questioning techniques during classroom instruction. Our search of the ERIC database using the thesaurus descriptor "questioning techniques" yields 4,259 records. As we examine the records, we find that some of them concern questions on tests, not questions asked during classroom interaction between teacher and students.

To exclude the records involving test questions, we redo the search by entering "questioning techniques" in one window, entering "test*" as a keyword in another window, and selecting NOT as the connector to the left of the second window. This search yields a set of 3,482 records that are more relevant to our interests.

If you examine Figure 4.3, you will see a label "Add Another Row." By clicking on this label, you can add other keywords (or another option in the pull-down menu) and other connectors.

Other Advanced Search Options in ERIC

In the preceding section, we described some of the most important ways in which the advanced search option in ERIC allows you to define and focus your literature search. If you examine Figure 4.3, you will see additional search options, such as Publication Type(s) and Education Level(s). These options generally will not help you define the range of topics (as expressed by keywords or descriptors) that your literature review will encompass, but they can help you limit your search to a manageable, but relevant, set of publication records.

Full-Text Availability.   ERIC makes available at no cost the full text of some of the publications that are recorded in its database. Full-text availability is shown in the lower left corner of Figure 4.4. If the full text is available, you can view it as a pdf document on your computer screen and save it as a **pdf file,** a "portable document file" that can be opened by free software called Adobe Acrobat, in case you wish to view it again later or print a copy.

Publication Date.   The vast majority of the documents in the ERIC database were published between 1966 and the present. You might find a small number of documents published prior to 1966, depending on your topic. If you wish to search for older literature, we advise you to use the search engine Education Index Retrospective: 1929–1983. If your research problem has a psychological aspect, you can try using PsycInfo, which includes publications dating back to the 1800s in its database.

In general, we recommend that you start your literature search in ERIC by going back two years at a time for ten years, and then perhaps five years at a time for older publications. By starting with the two most recent years, you usually can get a manageable number of records to review. Reading the abstracts for these records (a sample abstract is shown in Figure 4.4) will give you a sense of recent knowledge and practice on your topic of interest. Then you can select a few of the most relevant records and read the complete journal article or other type of publication. These publications are likely to include a review of the literature, which will give you a sense of the knowledge that has accumulated over time and its significance from the perspective of the author.

You can continue going through this process two years at a time, using the Publication Date field. By the time you have gone back ten years, you should have a good sense of how knowledge about your topic of interest has developed and what the current state of knowledge is. You also will have a sense of who the leading experts are, based on the number and quality of their own publications and other publications whose authors have cited them.

Publication Types and Education Levels.   Figure 4.3 shows that you can limit your ERIC search to certain types of publications and education levels. The default option, as you can see, is Any Publication Type and Any Education Level. These options are appropriate if you wish to do a comprehensive literature review. However, if you have a limited focus, you can use other options to exclude nonrelevant publication records and thereby save time.

Figure 4.3 shows only a limited number of options in the pull-down menus for *Publication Type(s)* and *Education Level(s).* The full set of pull-down options for each field is shown in Figure 4.5.

Citation Pearl Growing.   Suppose that the journal article cited in Figure 4.4 is directly relevant to your literature review. In this case, you likely would want to find other publications similar to it. A process to help you do this, called **citation pearl growing,** uses a relevant article (the "pearl") to search for other relevant publications. One way to grow the pearl would be to examine the reference list for the article cited in Figure 4.4. At least some of these articles should be relevant to your topic.

Another way to grow the pearl is to examine the bibliographic citation for the article. The ERIC citation shown in Figure 4.4 includes thirteen descriptors. You can select the most relevant descriptors and then conduct ERIC searches using each of these descriptors as the "Search for:" term in the advanced search window (see Figure 4.3). Because your "pearl" article (the article cited in Figure 4.4) was classified by the descriptor selected, it might well be that other relevant articles in the ERIC database were classified by the same descriptor.

Still another way to grow the pearl is to use the search engine Web of Science, described earlier in the chapter, which will look for other publications that have included the article cited in Figure 4.4 in their reference list. If another publication cited our "pearl" article in its reference list, the authors of that publication considered the article to be relevant to their research problem or problem of practice. Thus, the publication is likely to be relevant to our interest in questioning techniques.

Part of the rationale for citation pearl growing is that researchers and educators who are strongly interested in a particular problem of practice are likely to begin communicating

FIGURE *4.5*   Pull-Down Menu Options for the Publication Type and Education Level Fields in ERIC's Advanced Search Window

Publication Types
1. Journal articles
2. Book/product reviews
3. Books
4. Collected works—general
5. Collected works—proceedings
6. Collected works—serials
7. Computer programs
8. Creative works
9. Dissertations/theses
10. Dissertations/theses—doctoral dissertations
11. Dissertations/theses—masters theses
12. Dissertations/theses—practicum papers
13. ERIC Digests
14. ERIC publications
15. Guides—classroom—learner
16. Guides—classroom—teacher
17. Guides—general
18. Guides—nonclassroom
19. Historical materials
20. Information analyses
21. Legal/legislative/regulatory materials
22. Machine-readable data files
23. Multilingual/bilingual materials
24. Non-print media
25. Numerical/quantitative data
26. Opinion papers
27. Reference materials—bibliographies
28. Reference materials—directories/catalogs
29. Reference materials—general
30. Reference materials—geographic
31. Reference materials—vocabularies/classifications

32. Reports—descriptive
33. Reports—evaluative
34. Reports—general
35. Reports—research
36. Speeches/meeting papers
37. Tests/questionnaires
38. Translations

Education Levels
1. Adult basic education
2. Adult education
3. Early childhood education
4. Elementary education
5. Elementary secondary education
6. Grade 1
7. Grade 2
8. Grade 3
9. Grade 4
10. Grade 5
11. Grade 6
12. Grade 7
13. Grade 8
14. Grade 9
15. Grade 10
16. Grade 11
17. Grade 12
18. High school equivalency programs
19. High schools
20. Higher education
21. Intermediate grades
22. Junior high schools
23. Kindergarten
24. Middle schools
25. Postsecondary education
26. Preschool education
27. Primary education
28. Secondary education
29. Two year colleges

with each other and reading each other's publications. Consequently, they will start citing each other's publications in their own writings. If you can find one relevant publication within this emerging community, you can use pearl growing as a strategy to find other relevant publications within the community.

Keeping Track of Your Search

In reality, the search for relevant publications for a literature review is a trial-and-error process. Within the ERIC search engine, you might try different keywords, thesaurus descriptors, connectors, and publication year intervals until you find the ones that retrieve relevant publications. Also, you might wind up using several different search engines, each in a different way.

The number of searches can increase rapidly. Typically, it is impossible to remember all these searches, especially after several days have passed. As a consequence, you might repeat searches needlessly, wasting valuable time. Therefore, we recommend that you keep a log of your searches, noting such details as (1) the date that you conducted the search; (2) keywords, descriptors, and connectors that defined the search; (3) additional limits on the search, such as publication type, education level, and publication date interval; and (4) the number of publication records yielded by the search. It takes just a minute or two to enter this information for each search, but doing so can save hours later.

A good report of a literature review will include information about the search procedure, so that readers can evaluate its soundness. If you have kept a detailed log of your searches, it will be easy to report this information.

Saving, Downloading, and Printing ERIC Records

Once you have specified all your search specifications (e.g., descriptors and connectors), you can click on the Search link (see bottom left corner of Figure 4.3), and the search engine will retrieve all the records that conform to these specifications. Your computer screen displays the retrieved set of records, each with the same format as the one shown in Figure 4.4. Near the top of the screen, you will see an option that allows you to sort the records in different ways (e.g., newest records first) and to determine the number of records to be displayed on your computer screen.

Suppose you want to save or print the displayed records. The ERIC search engine manages this process by a feature called My Clipboard. If you examine the upper right corner of Figure 4.4, you will see a tiny icon of a clipboard and the word Add. Clicking on Add changes this word to Added, meaning that the record has been added to your Clipboard. (By clicking Added, you can deselect the record from the Clipboard.) You can add up to 50 records to the Clipboard.

The top of the screen showing the retrieved records has a Clipboard icon and, to its right, a brief statement of the number of items you have saved to the Clipboard. Clicking on this statement will take you to a new screen, an example of which is shown in Figure 4.6. The information in this figure reflects the fact that we did an ERIC search for the descriptor

FIGURE 4.6   An ERIC Clipboard

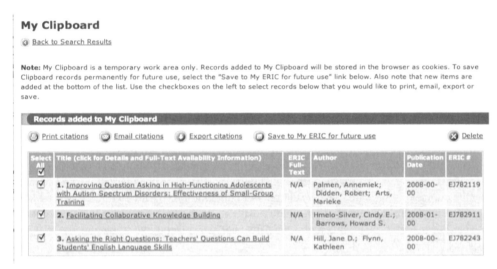

"questioning techniques," limiting the search to publications in 2008. We "added" (i.e., selected) three of the retrieved records to the clipboard.

The Clipboard gives you four options, which are shown in Figure 4.6 on a separate row:

1. *Print citations.* Clicking on this option takes you to a new screen that gives you the choice of printing (1) a brief citation, (2) a brief citation and abstract, or (3) a detailed citation and abstract.

2. *Email citations.* Clicking on this option takes you to a new screen. You enter an email address and a few other bits of information, and the records will be sent to your email box. The records can be emailed as brief citations, brief citations and abstracts, or detailed citations and abstracts.

3. *Export citations.* Clicking on this option takes you to a new screen that has two options. One option allows you to download the records to a "citation manager," such as Endnote or ProCite. (We describe citation managers in the next section.) The other option is "Text file," which enables you to directly download the publication record (brief citation, brief citation and abstract, or detailed citation and abstract) as an electronic file on your computer. Because the file is saved on your computer, you can look at it whenever you wish without opening the ERIC website.

4. *Save to My ERIC for future use.* Clicking on this option for the first time takes you to a window where you provide information to establish a free account. Once you have established your account, you can save your selected records for a particular search (up to a limit of 50 records) to the My ERIC website. Within this website you can save multiple searches, each in a separate folder, up to a limit of 10 folders. By logging into My ERIC, you can view your search results and the full record for each selected publication; you can also print this information. One advantage of My ERIC is that you can access your search results on a different computer than the one used to do the search.

An important feature of the Clipboard is that it allows you to select which record(s) to print, email, export, or save to My ERIC. For example, if you wish to print just one of the records yielded by your search, you can select just that one record. If you wish to print all the records, you can click the Select All link on the screen.

Citation Managers

A **citation manager** is software that enables you to record bibliographic citations so that they can be stored and retrieved easily and systematically. For example, the results of a literature search using ERIC or another search engine can be stored in a citation manager. You can classify each citation with your own list of descriptors and later retrieve all citations that have the specified descriptor. You also can integrate a citation manager with your word processing software, so that as you write a paper, its reference section is automatically prepared as you refer to particular citations within the body of the paper.

Two of the more commonly used citation managers in education are Endnote and ProCite. You can go to their websites (www.endnote.com and www.procite.com) to learn their specific capabilities. A comprehensive list of citation managers is available in the online encyclopedia Wikipedia. Go to its home page (http://en.wikipedia.org) and enter "comparison of reference management software" in the search window.

It might not be worthwhile to purchase a citation manager if you plan to use it only for a single project, such as a master's thesis. However, a citation manager can serve you well over the course of your career as a researcher or educator. From time to time, you are likely to come across publications that you find relevant to your work. You can jot a citation on a note card or piece of paper, but such items are easily misplaced over time.

A citation manager, by contrast, is software that is stored on your computer; and your "library" of citations is stored within the software. Your citations, then, are as close at hand as your computer is. You can add new citations whenever you wish, and they are easily retrieved whenever you need them. In short, a citation manager is a versatile professional tool that can serve you beyond the needs of a specific research project or paper assignment for a university course.

Obtaining a Publication after a Literature Search

A search engine provides a bibliographic citation for each relevant publication, not the publication itself. Our purpose in this section is to describe how to secure a copy of the actual publication, once you have determined that it is relevant to your literature review.

Keep in mind that obtaining the publication might be time-consuming, so reading the abstract can help you avoid the effort of obtaining publications that are not of sufficient relevance to include in the literature review. In some instances, it might be appropriate to mention publications in your literature review referring only to information provided in the abstract.

Figure 4.4 shows a bibliographic record retrieved by an ERIC search. The bottom of the record contains three aids for finding the publication to which the record refers:

1. *Availability from ERIC.* Although Figure 4.4 shows the first field as "Not available from ERIC," some of the publications referenced in the ERIC database are available directly from ERIC. In such cases, the first clickable button will state "ERIC Full Text." Clicking on the button brings up screens that present the publication as a pdf file.
2. *Find in a Library.* Clicking on this button will take you to screens with a list of libraries that have the publication. A nice feature of the list is that the libraries are ordered by their nearness to the location you indicate. For example, we entered our zip code in a window, and the list showed the libraries in order of their proximity to our zip code.
3. *Publisher's Website.* Clicking on this button will take you to the website, if there is one, for the publisher of the document cited in the ERIC record. The website might give you additional information about the publication, including information about how to secure a copy of it.

Another way to obtain copies of publications is directly from a university library, if you have an affiliation with it. A library with good electronic resources will have a Web-based catalog of its books and other holdings, so that from a computer you can find whether the library might have a copy of the book or of the journal containing the article that you want. The university library will also have a set of search engines that you can use without charge and subscriptions to services that allow you to download journal articles and other publications without charge. Before you begin a literature review, then, you should contact your library to determine the extent of its holdings and electronic resources for literature searching.

It is likely that, in coming years, an increasing number of professional journals will move toward online publication of their articles and charge no fee for viewing them on your computer screen, saving them as electronic files, or printing them. You can obtain a list of current electronic journals in education by going to the Web (http://aera-cr.asu.edu/ejournals). The list is limited to scholarly, peer-reviewed journals whose articles can be viewed in full-text format without cost.

Self-Check Test

1. Search engines for literature reviews typically
   a. include a collection of bibliographic citations and a procedure for converting them to the style format of the *APA Publication Manual.*
   b. include a collection of bibliographic citations and procedures for searching through them.
   c. can be purchased in hard-copy format.
   d. create a bibliographic citation for a publication one to two years after it has appeared in print.

2. If you use ERIC as a search engine, you
   a. will need to pay a small fee for every ten bibliographic citations that you wish to download.
   b. can only search for documents that have been published since the year 2000.
   c. can use features of its bibliographic citations for citation pearl growing.
   d. cannot link to any full-text publications cited in its database.

3. Search engines can be used to identify bibliographic citations for
   a. dissertations.
   b. book reviews.
   c. newspaper articles.
   d. All of the above.

4. In search engines, a wildcard enables you to
   a. search the database for all keywords that have a common stem, such as "instruction," "instructor," and "instructional."
   b. search the database for all keywords that consist of phrases, such as "instructional design" and "multiple intelligences."
   c. search for two keywords linked by all three types of connectors (AND, OR, NOT).
   d. use the same keyword with two databases simultaneously.

5. ERIC descriptors
   a. are listed in the ERIC Thesaurus.
   b. are available for searching journal articles but not conference proceedings or institutional reports.
   c. must be specified by the publication's authors prior to submission to ERIC.
   d. were created to avoid the necessity of using wildcards.

6. You are most likely to limit the number of bibliographic citations that you retrieve from a search of ERIC if you use
   a. a wildcard.
   b. an AND connector.
   c. an OR connector.
   d. descriptors.

7. Citation pearl growing is good technique to use if you
   a. do not have access to search engines.
   b. wish to contact the authors of publications cited in the ERIC search engine.
   c. need to increase the number of citations to be included in the reference list for your literature review report.
   d. wish to identify publications that share similar characteristics with a publication that you find particularly relevant to your research problem.

8. Keeping a continuous log of your use of search engines
   a. is necessary because it must be included in any research report that you write.
   b. is necessary because many search engines disappear from the Internet each year.
   c. will be a helpful resource when it comes time to write the report of your completed literature review.
   d. only needs to include the keywords and connectors that you used.

9. Citation managers
   a. provide a way to store bibliographic citations from search engines.
   b. enable you to classify bibliographic citations with your own descriptors.
   c. can be used to integrate bibliographic citations with word processing software.
   d. All of the above.

10. Online journals in education and other professions currently
    a. are very few in number.
    b. have increased in number over time.
    c. can only be accessed by using the ERIC search engine.
    d. are not peer reviewed and are thus of lower quality than hard-copy journals.

Resources for Further Study

Reed, J. G., & Baxter, P. M. (1994). Using reference databases. In H. Cooper & L. V. Hedges (Eds.), *The handbook of research synthesis* (pp. 57–70). New York: Russell Sage Foundation.

This book chapter provides detailed information about how to use search engines to identify publications that are relevant to your research problem or problem of practice. The second edition of this book is scheduled for 2009.

Schlosser, R. W., Wendt, O., Bhavnani, S., & Nail-Chiwetalu, B. (2006). Use of information-seeking strategies for developing systematic reviews and engaging in evidence-based practice: The application of traditional and comprehensive pearl-growing—A review. *International Journal of Language and Communication Disorders, 41*(5), 567–582.

The authors explain search engines and various kinds of pearl growing that can be used to search for relevant publications. They illustrate pearl growing with examples from research and practice involving individuals with speech and language disabilities.

chapter 5

Making Use of Available Literature Reviews

IMPORTANT
Ideas

1. Available literature reviews are time-saving and valuable resources, especially if experts on the topic of the review have prepared them.

2. Reading some of the primary sources cited in a published literature review can enhance your understanding of the literature and help you check for reviewer bias and errors.

3. Systematic literature reviews generally are written for the needs and interests of the research community; in contrast, professional literature reviews are written for educators and are focused on problems of practice.

4. Meta-analysis provides a way to determine the magnitude of an observed cause-and-effect relationship in a research study or across a set of research studies.

5. Methodologists disagree about the kinds of research studies that should be included in a meta-analysis.

6. Systematic reviews of qualitative research studies should identify the key constructs and causal relationships that emerge from the review, as well as the various types of publications that were included in the review.

7. Professional literature reviews generally are less formal than systematic literature reviews and more focused on the implications of published research findings for the improvement of educational practice.

8. Search engines such as ERIC, the Library of Congress Online Catalog, and Books in Print can help you identify literature reviews that other researchers and educators have done.

9. Useful literature reviews on various educational topics can be found in encyclopedias, handbooks, yearbooks, and journals.

10. In reading literature reviews, you should take note of the reviewer's search procedures, the time period and range of publications covered by the review, the amount of information provided about each publication, reviewer bias, and how the reviewer handled inconsistent findings across studies. ■

Key TERMS

construct	exploratory case study method	primary source
effect size	literature review	secondary source
ERIC	meta-analysis	

Advantages of Available Literature Reviews

To learn what is known about an educational topic, you can conduct your own literature review or rely on literature reviews done by others. Our purpose in this chapter is to help you locate and use literature reviews done by others.

Published literature reviews sometimes are called **secondary sources,** publications in which authors review the work of others—their research studies, theories, curriculum materials, experiences, and opinions.

As we explained in Chapter 3, secondary sources can be distinguished from **primary sources,** which are publications by authors who are describing their own work and ideas.

Reading primary sources obviously has some advantages over relying on secondary sources. For example, you will develop a deeper understanding of a particular research study, because you will have read the full report, as stated in the researcher's own words. You will learn the author's perspective directly without a reviewer's interpretation of what the author wrote.

Reading a long list of primary sources, however, has a major drawback—namely, the large amount of time and effort that is required, a requirement that exceeds the resources of most educators. Nonetheless, many policy makers and community members believe that educators working in school systems should inform their decision making with research evidence. You will also need to cite primary sources if you are doing a research study for a degree or credential program.

Reading a published literature review enables you to accomplish either goal with much less effort than is involved in doing a comprehensive search of primary sources and studying them. Even a published literature review that was written some years ago can save you a lot of time, because you will only need to search for recent sources to update the information contained in the review.

A published literature review has a special advantage if its authors are experts on the topic being reviewed. You reap the benefits of their expertise in finding, organizing, and interpreting research, theory, and opinion relevant to your problem of practice. It is difficult for most educators to develop the same level of skill as a reviewer who is familiar with the range of methodologies, measures, and statistical techniques that have been used to investigate a particular educational problem.

Still another advantage of reading a literature review published in a well-regarded journal or book is that it is authoritative. Therefore, policy makers are likely to view it as more credible than a literature review done by individuals whose time for such work is likely to be very limited. Furthermore, if you can cite well-documented literature reviews as the basis for your own opinions, policy makers and colleagues are likely to give your opinions more weight.

Despite these advantages, you cannot rely entirely on a published literature review to form your opinions. You still need to exercise independent judgment about the literature cited and use your own judgment to determine whether the reviewer's conclusions are justified by the body of research evidence included in the review. For example, reviewer bias can occur, as when reviewers omit important information from a primary source or interpret it in a way that reflects their own values. Therefore, it is wise to track down selected studies cited in the **literature review** and read them yourself. Reading primary sources selectively will give you more detailed information than is contained in a secondary source and will deepen your understanding of the research process.

In the next sections of this chapter, we distinguish between two types of published literature reviews—systematic syntheses of the literature and professional reviews of the literature—and explain their features.

Systematic Syntheses of Research Findings

We use the term *systematic literature review* to characterize literature syntheses that involve the use of standard procedures developed by the research community for the purpose of insuring that a comprehensive search of the literature has been conducted and evaluating the soundness of research evidence revealed by the search. The main audience for systematic literature reviews is the research community or educators who have sufficient expertise to understand the technical aspects of a research review.

The Cochrane Collaboration and the What Works Clearinghouse, both of which we describe in Chapter 1, exemplify the production of systematic literature reviews on particular topics. They make explicit their procedures for doing a literature review, and they continually refine these procedures.

The purpose of systematic literature reviews is to rigorously examine diverse research findings about a particular problem and create a coherent picture of the state of research knowledge about that problem. In addition, this type of literature review typically includes recommendations for future research on the topic and implications of the current state of research knowledge for the improvement of professional practice.

Meta-Analytic Syntheses of Quantitative Research

Some systematic literature reviews focus on findings from quantitative research studies that have investigated the same problem, but with different types of participants, measures, and statistical techniques. This type of literature review is becoming increasingly prevalent with the movement toward evidence-based practice in education (described at length in Chapter 1).

In recent years, meta-analysis has become the most widely used method for systematically combining results from different quantitative research studies. **Meta-analysis** involves translating the statistical results from each of a set of research studies on the same problem into a statistic called an effect size.

Effect Sizes in Meta-Analysis.   We explain the statistical basis of effect sizes in depth in Chapter 8. Here we provide a simple introduction to this concept.

Suppose the literature reviewer has found individual research studies that are experiments to test the effectiveness of a particular educational program. In this case, the **effect size** is a number that indicates the degree to which participants in the experimental group show superior performance compared to a comparison group, called the control group, that receives either no treatment or an alternative program.

The effect size typically is computed by a simple formula. The numerator is the difference between the mean score of the experimental group and the mean score of the control group on a criterion measure (for example, an achievement test). The denominator typically is the average of the two groups' standard deviations (a measure of score variability) on the criterion measure.

For example, imagine a study of the effect of small cash rewards on the achievement of students in an inner-city high school. For one school year, experimental students receive cash rewards for passing weekly quizzes, and control students receive no rewards. At the end of the year both the experimental and control group students take the same standardized achievement test, which is the criterion measure. For the experimental group, the mean score is 46.2 and the standard deviation is 4.0. For the control group, the mean score is 41.2 and the standard deviation is 3.6.

The numerator for the effect size is 46.2 minus 41.2, which equals 5.0. The denominator is the average of the two standard deviations: $(4.0 + 3.6) \div 2 = 3.8$. Dividing the numerator (5.0) by the denominator (3.8) equals 1.32, which is the effect size.

The practical significance of an effect size of 1.32 usually is determined by making percentile comparisons. In our example, an effect size of 1.32 means that a student who scores at the 50th percentile in the experimental group has a score that is equivalent to a score at the 91st percentile in the control group.

This type of percentile comparison is explained in mathematical terms in Chapter 8. We can explain it more simply here by asking you to suppose that you typically score in the 50th percentile among your fellow students on achievement tests. Suppose that the incentive of cash rewards motivates you to study harder and learn more. An effect size of 1.32 predicts that you are likely to score at or around the 91st percentile among your fellow students on achievement tests. That is quite a jump in achievement for you.

Students who typically score somewhat lower or higher than the 50th percentile also are likely to make substantial percentile gains from the cash reward relative to students not receiving the incentive. The specific gain will depend on their beginning percentile and the distribution of scores on achievement tests among their fellow students.

In our experience, educational researchers believe that an effect size of 0.33 or larger has practical significance. An effect size of 0.33 indicates that a student in the experimental group whose score is at the 50th percentile would be at the 63rd percentile of the other group's score distribution.

The advantage of the effect size over other methods of comparing performance is that it transforms the results from various studies into a comparable unit of measure. It does not matter that one study used the XYZ Mathematics Test, on which scores can vary from 0 to 70, and that another study used the ABC History Test, on which scores can vary from 0 to 100. An effect size can be calculated for the results of both studies, and these effect sizes can be directly compared. An effect size of 1.00 is twice as large as an effect size of 0.50, regardless of the measures and scoring systems that were used.

Not all studies in the research literature report the means and standard deviations for calculating an effect size in the manner described above. However, procedures exist for estimating an effect size from virtually any statistical data reported in a research study.

The means of the effect sizes from different studies can be combined to determine the average effect that the experimental program or method produces relative to a comparison intervention across the studies. For example, suppose that you find seven research studies on the effects of class size. In each study, a sample of large classes was compared with a sample of small classes. Also in each study, data on all students' performance on an achievement test were collected at the end of the school year.

Each of the seven studies would yield one effect size. Each effect size has the same meaning no matter how large or small the sample size or the type of achievement test or other measure. Therefore, you can synthesize the results across the seven studies by calculating the mean of the seven effect sizes across the seven studies. The mean effect size is likely to give you a more valid estimate of the effects of class size than the effect size derived from a single research study.

Meta-analysis has become a popular method for synthesizing research findings in medicine, psychology, education, and other fields. We illustrate its use at the end of this chapter with a meta-analysis of research on differentiating instruction based on students' learning styles.

Limitations of Meta-Analysis.   Meta-analysis is a powerful method of synthesizing quantitative studies for a literature review, but you must examine each meta-analysis that you read for potential limitations. In particular, you need to consider reviewer basis in selecting studies to include in a meta-analysis or a failure to locate all relevant studies in the literature.

For example, Haller, Child, and Walberg (1988) conducted a meta-analysis of research on the effects of metacognitive instruction on reading comprehension. (Metacognitive instruction involves teaching students how to regulate their own thinking and learning processes.) Haller and her colleagues state that they examined 150 references, but limited their analysis to 20 studies. These 20 studies met certain criteria: the use of metacognitive intervention, employment of a control group for comparison, and provision of statistical information necessary to compute effect sizes.

Gene Glass (1976), one of the primary developers of meta-analysis, would have advised Haller and her colleagues to include as many of the 150 original studies as possible in their analysis, even though some were methodologically more sound than others. Glass argues that either weaker studies will show the same results as stronger studies and thus should be included, or that a truer picture will emerge if weak studies are also analyzed.

In contrast, Robert Slavin (1986) argues against including every possible study in a meta-analysis. Slavin examined eight meta-analyses conducted by six independent teams of reviewers and compared their procedures and conclusions against the studies they analyzed. Slavin reported that he found errors in all eight meta-analyses that were serious enough to invalidate or call into question one or more of the major conclusions of each study.

Therefore, Slavin recommends that a meta-analysis should include only research studies providing "best evidence," that is, studies that meet criteria such as methodological adequacy and relevance to the issue at hand. He also makes a strong case for calculating not only an overall mean effect size, but also separate effect sizes for subsets of studies, for example, those that used the same measure of the dependent variable or those that studied a specific ethnic group.

Whether you agree with Glass or Slavin, we advise you not to accept an effect size in a meta-analysis at face value. At the least, you should examine several of the research studies that contributed statistical data for the calculation of the effect size. By taking this extra step, you can check how the literature reviewer synthesized these studies and judge the extent to which the studies actually investigated the particular educational practice or issue of interest to you.

Syntheses of Qualitative Research Studies

In the preceding section we considered procedures for reviewing research studies that involve quantitative methodology. As we explained in Chapter 1, qualitative research represents another approach to scientific inquiry. It involves the study of specific cases in an effort to understand the unique character and context of each case.

Ogawa and Malen (1991) suggested a method, called the exploratory case study method, for synthesizing qualitative research studies. Reviewers who use the **exploratory case study method** provide a synthesis of case studies on the same topic by identifying concepts and principles that are present across cases, while also acknowledging the unique characteristics of each case. Although the primary focus is qualitative studies, Ogawa and Malen's method allows reviewers to include other kinds of writings (e.g., newspaper editorials or articles in journals for practicing educators) in their synthesis of the literature on a particular educational topic.

A literature review by Bos, Krajcik, and Patrick (1995) illustrates several of the procedures that Ogawa and Malen recommend for reviewing qualitative research. Their review appeared in a special issue of the *Journal of Computers in Mathematics and Science Teaching,* devoted to the topic of telecommunications. It was intended to clarify the potential role of computer-mediated communications (CMC) in improving teaching practice in mathematics and science. The report described research on a selected number of projects (13) about which sufficient research was available. The literature review focused primarily on case studies of the projects, but some quantitative survey data were collected and analyzed as well.

One procedure Ogawa and Malen (1991) advocate is to clarify the focus of the review and define key constructs used in the review. A **construct** is a concept inferred from commonalities among observed phenomena that can be used to explain those phenomena.

Consistent with this recommendation, Bos and his colleagues identified a specific focus for their literature review: "This review will focus on computer networking projects that have been designed to support teacher practice" (1995, p. 188). They define computer-mediated communications as "e-mail networks, bulletin boards, listservers, and ftp libraries for teachers" (p. 188).

Ogawa and Malen (1991) recommend that reviewers classify the types of publications they identified in their search of the literature—for example, qualitative case studies, quantitative research experiments, and position statements. Bos and his colleagues do not classify the publications that they included in their review, perhaps because all of them were similar in being descriptions of specific CMC projects.

Ogawa and Malen also recommend that reviewers analyze the case studies by developing narrative summaries and coding schemes that take into account all the pertinent information in the documents. The literature review on CMC includes a table containing three columns: (1) the name of each CMC network, (2) the network's uses and purposes, and (3) research findings relating to the network.

According to Ogawa and Malen (1991), the goals of a review of qualitative research are to increase understanding of the phenomena being studied and to guide further research. These goals are achieved by searching the documents included in the review for relevant constructs and cause-and-effect relationships. A quantitative research review also has the goal of guiding further research, but its other goal is quite different, namely, to make generalizations based on statistical findings.

Bos and his colleagues identified several key constructs that helped them understand the potential benefits and limitations of CMC networks for teachers, among them reflective practice, support for innovation, professional isolation, and communities of learning. In addition, the authors developed several cause-and-effect propositions from their analysis of findings reported in the documents that they reviewed. For example, they proposed that CMC (the presumed causal agent) helps to create "a uniquely egalitarian online 'classroom' for mutual reflection and idea-sharing" (1995, p. 190), which is the presumed effect.

Ogawa and Malen (1991) caution reviewers of qualitative research to be aware of possible bias in their literature review procedures. For example, various statements in the literature review on CMC networks make evident that the authors strongly believe that these networks have great potential as a support for teachers. Therefore, Bos and his colleagues needed to be careful not to overlook any negative effects reported by the researchers whose studies were included in the research synthesis. To their credit, their published literature review included highlighted sections called "issues" to draw the reader's attention to several such limitations. They also suggested future directions for CMC development and research.

Professional Literature Reviews

Professional literature reviews synthesize research findings, but in a less formal manner than systematic literature reviews, because their primary audience is not researchers, but rather educators, policy makers, and other stakeholders whose research expertise is limited. The typical goals of professional literature reviews are to focus on a particular problem of practice, synthesize research and other literature about it, and, most important, draw implications for the improvement of educational practice.

Professional literature reviews generally use nontechnical language to describe research findings. They also tend to be brief and selective in their citations of primary sources. For example, the *Encyclopedia of Educational Research* consists primarily of professional reviews. Each review is about four pages and lists ten to fifteen references.

The reviewers who are invited to write articles for a publication like the *Encyclopedia of Educational Research* typically are recognized as experts on particular topics. For example, Slavin's research and development in the area of cooperative learning are well known both among educators and researchers. In the article, Slavin summarizes his own work and that of other researchers and educators.

Authors of professional literature reviews generally examine published research studies, syntheses of research, and theoretical writings to determine their implications for improving professional practice. Slavin, for example, cites a number of research studies that found positive effects of cooperative learning methods on various student outcomes. He also notes the conditions that are necessary to produce these effects in actual classrooms.

Unless a professional review is recent, it might not provide a sound basis for making decisions about improving educational practice. Over time, new advances in research and the changing conditions of educational practice might invalidate the reviewer's conclusions. Even so, a professional literature review can be useful as a reflection of the state of knowledge and practice that prevailed at the time it was prepared. You can supplement it by conducting your own literature search for publications that appeared subsequent to the review.

Professional reviews generally lack the rigor of meta-analyses, so you need to consider carefully whether the reviewer's conclusions and recommendations are warranted. Also, individuals with limited experience in conducting or interpreting research sometimes write a professional review. Therefore, you are advised to read for yourself some of the primary and secondary sources cited in a professional review before basing important educational decisions on the reviewer's conclusions.

Locating Published Reviews of the Education Literature

Fortunately, the increasing number of publications about education in recent decades has been accompanied by an increase in the number of literature reviews that synthesize the research findings and ideas in them. Therefore, a published literature review about a topic of interest to you probably is available. The question is how to find it. In the following sections, we describe various resources designed for this purpose.

Search Engines

We recommend search engines as the first resource to use when attempting to locate published literature reviews in your area of interest. We describe these resources in Chapter 4 and list many of them in Figure 4.1. Also in Chapter 4, we describe the **ERIC** search engine at length, because of its extensive coverage of many types of educational publications.

One way to use ERIC and similar search engines to identify literature reviews on a topic of interest is simply to enter "literature review" as a descriptor or keyword and your topic as another descriptor or keyword. Suppose that we are interested in literature reviews about writing instruction. Going to the ERIC website (www.eric.ed.gov), we use the advanced search feature and enter "writing instruction" as one descriptor (found in the ERIC thesaurus) and "literature review" (also found in the ERIC thesaurus) as another descriptor. The results of this search yielded 139 literature reviews on various aspects of writing instruction extending back many years. The following recent citations illustrate what we found:

Andrews, R., Torgerson, C., Beverton, S., Freeman, A., Locke, T., Low, G., Robinson, A., & Zhu, D. (2006). The effect of grammar teaching on writing development. *British Educational Research Journal, 32*(1), 39–55.

McMaster, K., & Espin, C. (2007). Technical features of curriculum-based measurement in writing: A literature review. *Journal of Special Education, 41*(2), 68–84.

Panofsky, C., Pacheco, M., Smith, S., Santos, J., Fogelman, C., Harrington, M., & Kenney, E. (2005). *Approaches to writing instruction for adolescent English language learners: A discussion of recent research and practice literature in relation to nationwide standards on writing.* Providence, RI: Education Alliance at Brown University. (ERIC Document Reproduction Service No. ED491600)

Stein, M., Dixon, R., & Barnard, S. (2001). What research tells us about writing instruction for students in the middle grades. *Journal of Direct Instruction, 1*(2), 107–116.

Another search option is to use "meta-analysis" as a descriptor, especially if you are searching for a review of quantitative research studies that relies on this approach. We repeated our search for literature reviews on writing instruction using "writing instruction" as one descriptor and "meta analysis" as another descriptor (the ERIC Thesaurus spells it as two words with no hyphen). The search yielded no results. This is an interesting finding in itself; it suggests that one might make a contribution by conducting a meta-analysis on some aspect of writing instruction that has been the subject of extensive research.

We determined how many meta-analyses are contained in the ERIC database from 1966 through June 2008. With "meta analysis" as the sole descriptor, ERIC located 2,027 publications in its database. The following are a few illustrations:

Merrell, K. W., Gueldner, B. A., Ross, S. W., & Isava, D. M. (2008). How effective are school bullying intervention programs? A meta-analysis of intervention research. *School Psychology Quarterly, 23*(1), 26–42.

Patall, E. A., Cooper, H., & Robinson, J. C. (2008). The effects of choice on intrinsic motivation and related outcomes: A meta-analysis of research findings. *Psychological Bulletin, 134*(2), 270–300.

Wang, S., Jiao, H., Young, M. J., Brooks, T., & Olson, J. (2008). Comparability of computer-based and paper-and-pencil testing in K–12 reading assessments: A meta-analysis of testing mode effects. *Educational and Psychological Measurement, 68*(1), 77–108.

Some of the major sources of literature reviews described in the next sections, such as encyclopedias and handbooks, can become dated or superceded by new editions. Therefore, we recommend using a search engine to check for the most recent editions of these sources as well as new sources. Good search engines for locating this purpose are the Library of Congress Online Catalog (http://catalog.loc.gov) and Books in Print (www.booksinprint.com/bip).

Encyclopedias

Many reviews of educational literature are published in encyclopedias. These books are characterized by the fact that they contain articles (also called *entries*) on a wide range of topics, but the articles typically are short, ranging from a few paragraphs to a few pages in length. However, they are useful in providing an overview on what is known about each topic.

A good way to search for encyclopedias about education is to use a search engine for books. The Library of Congress search engine (http://catalog.loc.gov) is good, because it is comprehensive and free. Using its advanced search feature, we looked for encyclopedias by using "encyclopedia" as a keyword, AND as a connector, and "education" as another keyword. Instead of "education," you could use your particular topic (e.g., "history education") as the keyword. We limited our search to encyclopedias published from 2000 to mid-2008. Figure 5.1 contains a list of general encyclopedias resulting from this search.

In additional to general encyclopedias, you can find a substantial number of encyclopedias that focus on limited areas of the educational enterprise. Our search of the Library of Congress search engine yielded the list of encyclopedias shown in Table 5.1. They are organized by topic. Keep in mind that there might be other specialized encyclopedias that do not appear in Table 5.1. We only relied on one search engine, albeit a comprehensive one, and we used a general keyword ("education") rather than keywords for specific educational topics.

FIGURE *5.1*   Encyclopedias Containing Literature Reviews of
a Comprehensive Range of Educational Topics

Alkin, M. C. (Ed.). (2001). *Encyclopedia of educational research* (6th ed.). New York:
Macmillan.

Guthrie, J. W. (Ed.). (2003). *Encyclopedia of education* (2nd ed.). New York:
Macmillan.

Husén, T., & Postlethwaite, T. N. (Eds.). (1994). *International encyclopedia of
education* (2nd ed.). New York: Elsevier. Entries in this encyclopedia relating to
certain subjects (e.g., educational technology, economics of education, teaching
and teacher education) subsequently were cumulated and published as separate
volumes.

McCulloch, D., & Crook, D. (Eds.). (2008). *Routledge international encyclopedia of
education*. New York: Routledge.

Salkind, N. J. (Ed.). (2008). *Encyclopedia of educational psychology*. Thousand Oaks,
CA: Sage.

Unger, H. G. (Ed.) (2008). *Encyclopedia of American education* (3rd ed.). New York:
Facts On File.

Handbooks

Handbooks are good sources of literature reviews. Whereas encyclopedias typically include
short entries on a large number of topics, handbooks cover a smaller number of topics, each
in a separate chapter. A handbook has one or more general editors who oversee the design
of the chapters and the authorities who write them. Table 5.2 (pp. 102–103) illustrates the
range of educational domains for which handbooks are available. With a few exceptions,
they have been published in or after the year 2000.

An effective way to search for a handbook on your topic of interest is to use the Library
of Congress Online Catalog as your search engine. Using the advanced search feature,
you can enter "handbook" as a keyword, AND as a connector, and your topic of interest
as another keyword. We recommend that you enter your topic in its least restrictive form
(e.g., "writing" instead of "writing instruction") to increase your likelihood of identifying
a relevant handbook.

Yearbooks, Journals, and Periodic Reports

Several yearbooks and journals primarily publish reviews of the education literature, usually with a focus on topics of current interest to educators. In addition, several organizations
publish periodic reports that involve literature reviews.

NSSE Yearbooks.   The NSSE Yearbooks are sponsored by the National Society for the
Study of Education. NSSE yearbooks published from 1977 to 2004 are listed at www.press
.uchicago.edu/Complete/Series/NSSE.html. More recent NSSE yearbooks are available as
journals in print or online format through Blackwell Publishing (www.blackwellpublish
ing.com).

Each yearbook covers recent research, theory, and commentary related to a major educational theme. In recent years, the themes have included

- Evidence and decision making (2007)
- Voices for democracy: Struggles and celebrations of transformational leaders (2006)
- With more deliberate speed: Achieving equity and excellence in education (2006)
- Media literacy: Transforming curriculum and teaching (2006)
- Uses and misuses of data for educational accountability and improvement (2005)

TABLE *5.1*   Encyclopedias Containing Literature Reviews on a Particular Domain of Education

Domain	Encyclopedia
Adult education	English, L. M. (Ed.). (2005). *International encyclopedia of adult education.* New York: Palgrave Macmillan.
Bilingual education	Cummins, J., & Hornberger, N. H. (Eds.). (2008). *Bilingual education* (2nd ed.). New York: Springer.
Early childhood education and human development	Farenga, S. J., & Ness, D. (Eds.). (2005). *Encyclopedia of education and human development.* Armonk, NY: M. E. Sharpe. New, R. S., & Cochran, M. (Eds.). (2007). *Early childhood education: An international encyclopedia.* Westport, CT: Praeger.
Foreign language education	van Deusen-Scholl, N., & Hornberger, N. H. (Eds.). (2008). *Second and foreign language education* (2nd ed.). New York: Springer.
Foundations of education	Kazdin, A. E. (Ed.). *Encyclopedia of psychology.* Washington, DC: American Psychological Association. Levinson, D. L., Cookson, P. W., Jr., & Sadovnik, A. R. (Eds.). (2002). *Education and sociology: An encyclopedia.* New York: RoutledgeFalmer.
Gender and education	Bank, B. J., Delamont, S., & Marshall, C. (Eds.). (2007). *Gender and education: An encyclopedia.* Westport, CT: Praeger. Martínez, A. M., & Renn, K. A. (Eds.). (2002). *Women in higher education: An encyclopedia.* Santa Barbara, CA: ABC-CLIO. Sears, J. T. (Ed.). (2005). *Youth, education, and sexualities: An international encyclopedia.* Westport, CT: Greenwood.
Higher education	English, L. M. (Ed.). (2005). *International encyclopedia of higher education.* New York: Macmillan. Forest, J. J. F., & Kinser, K. (Eds.). (2002). *Higher education in the United States: An encyclopedia.* Santa Barbara, CA: ABC-CLIO.

Each of these themes reflects problems of practice that are currently of great interest to educators.

Publications of the American Educational Research Association.   The *Review of Research in Education* is a yearbook published by the American Educational Research Association (AERA). Each volume contains chapters written by leading educational researchers who provide critical surveys of research on important problems and trends in education. For example, Volume 32, published in 2008, focuses on the theme of what counts as knowledge in educational settings. It includes 10 chapters on such topics as the sociology of the curriculum, art education, history education, foreign language education, mathematics education, and teachers' professional learning.

Review of Educational Research, also published by AERA, is a journal that consists entirely of reviews of research literature on educational topics. It is published quarterly, and each issue typically contains four to seven reviews. Another AERA publication is *Research Points*, a quarterly series of reports that connect research to educational policy. Recent reports include the following:

- Time to learn (Winter 2007)
- Science education that makes sense (Summer 2007)
- Do the math: Cognitive demand makes a difference (Fall 2006)
- Foreign language instruction: Implementing the best teaching methods (Spring 2006)

Domain	Encyclopedia
International education	Marlow-Ferguson, R. (Ed.). (2002). *World education encyclopedia : A survey of educational systems worldwide* (2nd ed). Detroit, MI: Gale Group/Thomson Learning.
Law in education	Russo, C. J. (Ed.). (2008). *Encyclopedia of education law.* Thousand Oaks, CA: Sage.
Literacy	Springer Publishing Company has published various encyclopedias about literacy since 2000 on a number of topics, including the following: • *Discourse and education* • *Language testing and assessment* • *Ecology of language* • *Literacy* • *Language policy and political issues in education* • *Research methods in language and education* • *Language socialization*
Mathematics education	Grinstein, L. S., & Lipsey, S. I. (Eds). (2001). *Encyclopedia of mathematics education.* New York: RoutledgeFalmer.
Middle schools	Anfara, V. A., Jr., Andrews, G., & Mertens, S. B. (Eds.). (2005). *The encyclopedia of middle grades.* Greenwich, CT: IAP-Information Age.
Multicultural education	Mitchell, B. M., & Salsbury, R. E. (Eds.). (1999). *Encyclopedia of multicultural education.* Farmington Hills, MI: Macmillan.
Peace education	Bajaj, M. (Ed.). (2008). *Encyclopedia of peace education.* Charlotte, NC: Information Age.
Special education	Reynolds, C. R., & Fletcher-Janzen, E. (Eds.). (2007). *Encyclopedia of special education* (3rd ed.). New York: Wiley.
Technology in education	Kovalchick, A., & Dawson, K. (Eds.). (2004). *Education and technology: An encyclopedia.* Santa Barbara, CA: ABC-CLIO.

• Early childhood education: Investing in quality makes sense (Fall 2005)
• Teaching teachers: Professional development to improve student achievement (Summer 2005)

The reports are free and available online (www.aera.net/publications/?id=314).

What Works Clearinghouse.   The Institute of Education Sciences, a branch of the U.S. Department of Education, sponsors the What Works Clearinghouse (WWC). WWC (http://ies.ed.gov/ncee/wcw) publishes periodic reports that review the scientific evidence for various educational programs and practices. The purpose of these reports is to help educators and policy makers choose those programs and practices that are most likely to improve student outcomes.

WWC currently focuses on reviewing research about interventions in the areas of beginning reading, character education, dropout prevention, early childhood education, elementary school math, English language learners, and middle school math curricula. If you click on What's New on WWC's home page, you will find an archive of its reports. Most of them present a synthesis of research on a particular intervention, or set of related interventions. The following are interventions that have been the subject of recent reports:

• Intervention: Job Corps (April 2008). A federally funded education and job-training program for economically disadvantaged youth.

TABLE 5.2   Handbooks Containing Literature Reviews on a Particular Domain of Education

Domain	Handbooks
Administration	Young, M., Crow, G., Ogawa, R., & Murphy, J. (Eds.). (2008). *Handbook of research on leadership education.* New York: Routledge.
Catholic education	Hunt, T. C., Joseph, E. A., & Nuzzi, R. J. (Eds.). (2001). *Handbook of research on Catholic education.* Westport, CT: Greenwood Press.
Classroom management	Damon, W., & Lerner, R. M. (Eds.). (2006). *Handbook of child psychology* (6th ed., Vols. 1–4). New York: Wiley. Evertson, C. M., & Weinstein, C. S. (Eds.). (2006). *Handbook of classroom management: Research, practice, and contemporary issues.* New York: Lawrence Erlbaum.
Early childhood education	Spodek, B., & Saracho, O. N. (Eds.). (2006). *Handbook of research on the education of young children* (2nd ed.). New York: Lawrence Erlbaum.
Educational psychology	Alexander, P., & Winne, P. (Eds.). (2006). *Handbook of educational psychology.* New York: Lawrence Erlbaum.
Experiential learning	Silberman, M. L. (Ed.). (2007). *The handbook of experiential learning.* San Francisco: Jossey-Bass.
Higher education	Smart, J. C. (Ed.). (2008). *Higher education: Handbook of theory and research.* New York: Springer.
Literacy	Flood, J., Heath, S. B., & Lapp, D. (Eds.). (2007). *Handbook of research on teaching literacy through the communicative and visual arts* (Vols. 1–2). New York: Lawrence Erlbaum. Neuman, S. B., & Dickinson, D. K. (Eds.). (2001–2006). *Handbook of early literacy research* (Vols. 1–2). New York: Guilford Press.
Mathematics education	English, L. D., Bussi, M. B., et al. (Eds.). (2008). *Handbook of international research in mathematics education* (2nd ed.). New York: Routledge.
Middle schools	Anfara, V. A., Jr. (Ed.). (2001). *Handbook of research in middle level education.* Greenwich, CT: Information Age Publishers.
Multicultural education	Banks, J. A., & Banks, C. A. M. (Eds.). (2004). *Handbook of research on multicultural education* (2nd ed.). San Francisco: Jossey-Bass.

- Intervention: Success for All (August 2007). A school reform model that includes a reading, writing, and oral language development program for students in pre-kindergarten through grade 8.
- Intervention: Peer-assisted learning strategies (July 2007). A program to improve the academic performance of children with diverse academic needs.

WWC publishes other kinds of reports as well, each intended to synthesize research evidence that can be used to improve educational practice.

Criteria for Evaluating Published Literature Reviews

The following criteria can help you judge the merits of published literature reviews in your area of interest.

Domain	Handbooks
Policy making	Cooper, B., Cibulka, J., & Fusarelli, L. (Eds.). (2008). *Handbook of education politics and policy.* New York: Lawrence Erlbaum.
Reading	Kamil, M. L., Moje, E., Mosenthal, P., Pearson, D., & Afflerbach, P. (Eds.). (1996–2008). *Handbook of reading research* (Vols. 1–4). New York: Lawrence Erlbaum.
School administration	Christenson, S. L., & Reschly, A. L. (Eds.). (2009). *Handbook of school-family partnerships.* New York: Routledge. Kowalksi, T., & Lasley, T. (Eds.). (2009). *Handbook of data-based decision making in education.* New York: Routledge. Randazzo, M. R. (Ed.). (2006). *Handbook of school violence and school safety: From research to practice.* New York: Lawrence Erlbaum.
Science education	Abell, S. K., & Lederman, N. G. (Eds.). (2007). *Handbook of research on science education.* New York: Lawrence Erlbaum.
Second language education	Hinkel, E. (Ed.). (2005). *Handbook of research in second language teaching and learning.* New York: Lawrence Erlbaum.
Social justice	Ayers, W. C., Quinn, T., & Stovall, D. O. (Eds.). (2008). *Handbook of social justice in education.* New York: Lawrence Erlbaum.
Social studies education	Levstik, L. S., & Tyson, C. A. (Eds.). (2008). *Handbook of research in social studies education.* New York: Lawrence Erlbaum.
Sport psychology	Tenenbaum, G., & Eklund, R. C. (Eds.). (2007). *Handbook of sport psychology* (3rd ed.). New York: Wiley.
Teacher education	Cochran-Smith, M., Feiman-Nemser, S., McIntyre, D. J., & Demers, K. E. (Eds.). (2008). *Handbook of research on teacher education: Enduring questions in changing contexts* (3rd ed.). New York: Routledge.
Teaching	Richardson, V. (Ed.). (2001). *Handbook of research on teaching* (4th ed.). Washington, DC: American Educational Research Association.
Technology in education	Carliner, S., & Shank, P. (Eds.). (2008). *The e-learning handbook: Past promises, present challenges.* San Francisco: Jossey-Bass.

1. *Reviewer's credentials.* The reviewer's reputation and experience with the topic are factors to consider when reading a literature review. One way to make this determination is to examine the reference list at the end of the source to see whether the reviewer has done research on the topic, and if so, where and when it was published. You can also check for information in the article itself about the author's affiliation, title, and experience related to the topic.

2. *Search procedures.* In older published reviews, it was not customary for reviewers to specify their search procedures. Thus, readers could not determine whether the research cited in the review resulted from a comprehensive or cursory search. Now it is customary for reviewers to identify the search engines and bibliographic indexes examined, the descriptors used, and the years covered. This is more likely to be the case in a systematic literature review than in a professional literature review.

3. *Breadth of the search.* Research reviews vary widely in their breadth, from an exhaustive search for all primary sources on a topic to a highly selective search. The advantage of a comprehensive search is that you have some assurance that no significant research evidence

or theoretical framework has been overlooked. A narrower search might be just as useful for your purposes, but in this case, knowing how the reviewer selected the publications included in the review is even more important. The following dimensions reflect the breadth of the reviewer's search of the literature.

    a. Period of time covered by the search. The publication dates of the most recent and oldest sources provide an indication of this time period. Keep in mind, though, that the time period might span beyond these dates if the reviewer's search did not yield older or more recent publications that were relevant to the topic.

    b. Types of publications reviewed. For example, the literature review might include only published journal articles, or it also might include dissertations and so-called fugitive literature, such as technical reports produced by a research team for its funding agency.

    c. Geographical scope of the search. Some reviewers examine only studies carried out in the United States, whereas others also include studies conducted in other countries.

    d. Range of grade levels and types of students, teachers, educational institutions, or other entities that were included in the literature review.

    e. Range of theoretical and ideological perspectives on the topic. For example, did the reviewer consider both studies based on behavioral theory and studies based on cognitive theory? Were different ideological perspectives considered, such as critical theory (see Chapter 16) and the accountability movement?

    f. Use of criteria to exclude any of the reports that were initially examined. For example, the reviewer might exclude research studies that involved atypical students or experiments that did not employ random assignment procedures. (Random assignment is explained in Chapter 13.)

    4. *Amount of information provided about the studies included in the literature review.* Reviewers have the challenging task of summarizing findings of a large number of studies briefly so as to be readable, yet in sufficient detail that the basis for the reviewer's conclusions and interpretations is reasonably clear. Simply including a citation or two in parentheses after making a sweeping generalization does not accomplish this goal. A better approach is for the reviewer to describe briefly the relevant information from a research study that demonstrates how it supports the generalization.

    5. *Exercise of critical judgment.* Research reviews range from those that reflect uncritical acceptance of research findings to those in which the reviewer finds flaws in every research study and asserts that no conclusions can be drawn from them. Neither extreme is likely to be justified for topics that have been extensively researched. Another aspect of critical judgment is whether the reviewer tended to lump studies together or discriminated among studies that appeared to deal with the same question but that were substantially different in design or purpose. The latter approach generally reflects better critical judgment.

    6. *Resolution of inconsistent findings.* Nearly every research review will reveal that the results obtained in some studies do not agree with those found in other studies. You should examine carefully how the reviewer dealt with these inconsistencies.

An example of
HOW LITERATURE REVIEWS CAN HELP IN SOLVING PROBLEMS OF PRACTICE

We occasionally read articles about the idea of giving students tangible rewards for good grades. The idea is controversial, with stakeholders providing arguments for and against the practice. Washington, D.C., is experimenting with this practice, and a retired teacher, Kathy Megyeri, wrote an article in the *Washington Post* about it. Based on her thirty-four years as an English teacher, she claimed that "little trinkets, treats and rewards" worked very well for her. She wondered whether cash payments would be any more effective than her small rewards. Megyeri observed positive effects of these small rewards on her students:

> My giving of those small prizes enhanced the cooperative atmosphere of learning, sharing and doing well in class, especially for students who did not usually succeed in school or are from impoverished homes.

Immediately after this comment, she states:

> Thus, I was shocked when my school's assistant principal called me in to complain that I "bribed" my students and complained that there was a plethora of research and literature that condemned this practice.

> Megyeri, K. A. (2008, November 6). Like Wall Street bonuses for doing well. *Washington Post*. Retrieved November 23, 2008, from www.washingtonpost.com

Is there, in fact, a substantial body of research evidence demonstrating the ineffectiveness or harm of small rewards?

One way to respond to this question—and to the complaint of Megyeri's assistant principal—is to look for literature reviews that summarize the research evidence. Literature reviews are particularly helpful if you do not have time to review individual studies directly.

We did a quick search of the literature using ERIC as our search engine. We used "literature reviews" and "rewards" in one search and "literature reviews" and "extrinsic motivation" in another search. We found a few literature reviews, with each summarizing a small body of studies. In general, the research evidence is inconclusive, and does not allow one to strongly endorse or condemn the use of small rewards, including cash. However, Megyeri's observations are compelling, and they lead us to recommend either formal experiments (see Chapter 13) or action research (see Chapter 19) to study this problem of practice. These studies should be designed to test the effectiveness of rewards like those used by this teacher.

Self-Check Test

1. Literature reviews are
   a. considered to be primary sources.
   b. of value only if the reviewers have done research studies similar to those in the review.
   c. of value only if they have been published within the past five years.
   d. of possible value even if they were published 10 or more years ago.
2. Meta-analysis
   a. is the standard procedure for synthesizing the findings of quantitative research studies.
   b. is the standard procedure for synthesizing the findings of qualitative research studies.
   c. avoids the need to compute an effect size for each research study included in a literature review.
   d. is used in systematic literature reviews to exclude studies with findings that are not statistically significant.
3. Effect sizes
   a. are calculated to determine whether the sample in a research study represents the population.
   b. cannot be used to make judgments about the practical significance of a research finding.
   c. provide information about the practical significance of a research finding.
   d. cannot be used to compare the findings of studies that investigated the same topic but used different measures.
4. There is general consensus among researchers that an effect size has practical significance if it has a value
   a. of 0.10 or larger.   c. of 0.33 or larger.
   b. of 0.20 or larger.   d. between –0.10 and 0.
5. Experts in meta-analysis
   a. disagree about whether a research study's methodological quality should be considered in determining whether to include it in a meta-analysis.

b. agree that a study of a specific program's effectiveness should be included in a meta-analysis even if the researchers were the program developers.

c. agree that only studies published in peer-reviewed journals should be included in a meta-analysis.

d. All of the above.

6. Reviewers who use the exploratory case study method

a. limit their focus to the unique characteristics of each case in a set of qualitative research studies.

b. seek to identify concepts and principles that are present across cases in a set of qualitative research studies.

c. calculate effect sizes with a different formula than that used in reviews of quantitative research studies.

d. may include various types of publications in their review except online sources.

7. Reviewers who use the exploratory case study method

a. rarely make generalizations or claims beyond those made by the researchers who conducted the studies included in the review.

b. use only constructs previously stated by the researchers who conducted the studies included in the review.

c. include only qualitative research studies in which data on multiple cases were collected.

d. attempt to increase educators' understanding of the phenomena that were studied in the publications included in the review.

8. Professional literature reviews

a. are more likely to present a meta-analysis of research findings than systematic literature reviews.

b. are more likely to present effect sizes than systematic literature reviews.

c. are less likely to present a meta-analysis of research findings than systematic literature reviews.

d. are less likely to draw implications for problems of practice than systematic literature reviews.

9. The ERIC search engine

a. cannot be used to identify literature reviews contained in fugitive literature sources.

b. can be used to identify both published literature reviews and meta-analyses.

c. can be used to identify educational encyclopedias, but not meta-analyses.

d. can be used to identify systematic literature reviews, but not professional literature reviews.

10. In writing their report of a literature review, the reviewers

a. should provide a detailed description of their search procedures.

b. do not need to provide a detailed description of their search procedures, because these procedures have been standardized by the American Psychological Association.

c. should explain the manner in which they located a copy of each publication that is included in the review.

d. should limit their search to U.S. publications if they hope to have their literature review published in a U.S. research journal.

Chapter References

Bos, N. D., Krajcik, J. S., & Patrick, H. (1995). Telecommunications for teachers: Supporting reflection and collaboration among teaching professionals. *Journal of Computers in Mathematics and Science Teaching, 14,* 187–202.

Glass, G. V (1976). Primary, secondary, and meta-analysis of research. *Educational Researcher, 5*(10), 3–8.

Haller, E. P., Child, D. A., & Walberg, H. J. (1988). Can comprehension be taught? A quantitative synthesis of "metacognitive" studies. *Educational Researcher, 17*(9), 5–8.

Ogawa, R. T., & Malen, B. (1991). Towards rigor in reviews of multivocal literatures: Applying the exploratory case study method. *Review of Educational Research, 61,* 265–286.

Slavin, R. E. (1986). Best-evidence synthesis: An alternative to meta-analytic and traditional reviews. *Educational Researcher, 15*(9), 5–11.

Resources for Further Study

Lather, P. (1999). To be of use: The work of reviewing. *Review of Educational Research, 69,* 2–7.

This article will help you understand how published literature reviews reflect to some extent the biases, values, and agendas of the reviewer. The author demonstrates that you need to use critical judgment when reading them.

Lipsey, M. W., & Wilson, D. B. (2000). *Practical meta-analysis.* Thousand Oaks, CA: Sage.

The authors explain how to decide which research reports to include in a meta-analysis, how to code information about each study's characteristics, and how to use computer software to analyze the resulting data.

Sandelowski, M., & Barroso, J. (2006). *Handbook for synthesizing qualitative research.* New York: Springer.

Although written for health disciplines, this handbook also will be helpful to educators interested in synthesizing qualitative research related to educational topics. The authors describe all aspects of the literature review process, from identifying relevant studies to synthesizing them, drawing valid conclusions, and writing a report of the review.

Sample Professional Review

The Case For and Against Homework

Marzano, R. J., & Pickering, D. J. (2007). The case for and against homework. *Educational Leadership, 64*(6), 74–79.

Arguments for and against homework appear in the media. Does homework take time away from students' pursuit of other important activities? Does homework help students reach a higher level of academic achievement, which could have long-term benefits?

These arguments are likely to confuse parents, students, educators, and others. The following journal article addresses the arguments by presenting a professional literature review about the effectiveness of homework. The authors refer to the results of research meta-analyses, but in a relatively nontechnical manner. They also make recommendations for professional practice.

The article is reprinted in its entirety, just as it appeared when originally published.

The Case For and Against Homework

Robert J. Marzano and
Debra J. Pickering

Robert J. Marzano *is a Senior Scholar at Mid-Continent Research for Education and Learning in Aurora, Colorado; an Associate Professor at Cardinal Stritch University in Milwaukee, Wisconsin; and President of Marzano & Associates consulting firm in Centennial, Colorado; robertjmarzano@aol.com.* **Debra J. Pickering** *is a private consultant and Director of Staff Development in Littleton Public Schools, Littleton, Colorado; djplearn@hotmail.com.*

Homework has been a perennial topic of debate in education, and attitudes toward it have been cyclical (Gill & Schlossman, 2000). Throughout the first few decades of the 20th century, educators commonly believed that homework helped create disciplined minds. By 1940, growing concern that homework interfered with other home activities sparked a reaction against it. This trend was reversed in the late 1950s when the Soviets' launch of *Sputnik* led to concern that U.S. education lacked rigor; schools viewed more rigorous homework as a partial solution to the problem. By 1980, the trend had reversed again, with some learning theorists claiming that homework could be detrimental to students' mental health. Since then, impassioned arguments for and against homework have continued to proliferate.

We now stand at an interesting intersection in the evolution of the homework debate. Arguments against homework are becoming louder and more popular, as evidenced by several recent books as well as an editorial in *Time* magazine (Wallis, 2006) that presented these arguments as truth without much discussion of alternative perspectives. At the same time, a number of studies have provided growing evidence of the usefulness of homework when employed effectively.

THE CASE FOR HOMEWORK

Homework is typically defined as any tasks "assigned to students by school teachers that are meant to be carried out during nonschool hours" (Cooper, 1989a, p. 7). A number of synthesis studies have been conducted on homework, spanning a broad range of methodologies and levels of specificity (see fig. 1). Some are quite general and mix the results from experimental studies with correlational studies.

FIGURE 1   Synthesis Studies on Homework

Synthesis Study	Focus	Number of Effect Sizes	Average	Percentile Gains
Graue, Weinstein, & Walberg, 1983[1]	General effects of homework	29	.49	19
Bloom, 1984	General effects of homework	—	.30	12
Paschal, Weinstein, & Walberg, 1984[2]	Homework versus no homework	47	.28	11
Cooper, 1989a	Homework versus no homework	20	.21	8
Hattie, 1992; Fraser, Walberg, Welch, & Hattie, 1987	General effects of homework	110	.43	17
Walberg, 1999	With teacher comments	2	.88	31
	Graded	5	.78	28
Cooper, Robinson, & Patall, 2006	Homework versus no homework	6	.60	23

Note: This figure describes the eight major research syntheses on the effects of homework published from 1983 to 2006 that provide the basis for the analysis in this article. The Cooper (1989a) study included more than 100 empirical research reports, and the Cooper, Robinson, and Patall (2006) study included about 50 empirical research reports. Figure 1 reports only those results from experimental/control comparisons for these two studies.

[1]Reported in Fraser, Walberg, Welch, & Hattie, 1987.

[2]Reported in Kavale, 1988.

Two meta-analyses by Cooper and colleagues (Cooper, 1989a; Cooper, Robinson, & Patall, 2006) are the most comprehensive and rigorous. The 1989 meta-analysis reviewed research dating as far back as the 1930s; the 2006 study reviewed research from 1987 to 2003. Commenting on studies that attempted to examine the causal relationship between homework and student achievement by comparing experimental (homework) and control (no homework) groups, Cooper, Robinson, and Patall (2006) noted,

> With only rare exceptions, the relationship between the amount of homework students do and their achievement outcomes was found to be positive and statistically significant. Therefore, we think it would not be imprudent, based on the evidence in hand, to conclude that doing homework causes improved academic achievement. (p. 48)

THE CASE AGAINST HOMEWORK

Although the research support for homework is compelling, the case against homework is popular. *The End of Homework: How Homework Disrupts Families, Overburdens Children, and Limits Learning* by Kralovec and Buell (2000), considered by many to be the first high-profile attack on homework, asserted that homework contributes to a corporate-style, competitive U.S. culture that overvalues work to the detriment of personal and familial well-being. The authors focused particularly on the harm to economically disadvantaged students, who are unintentionally penalized because their environments often make it almost impossible to complete assignments at home. The authors

called for people to unite against homework and to lobby for an extended school day instead.

A similar call for action came from Bennett and Kalish (2006) in *The Case Against Homework: How Homework Is Hurting Our Children and What We Can Do About It.* These authors criticized both the quantity and quality of homework. They provided evidence that too much homework harms students' health and family time, and they asserted that teachers are not well trained in how to assign homework. The authors suggested that individuals and parent groups should insist that teachers reduce the amount of homework, design more valuable assignments, and avoid homework altogether over breaks and holidays.

In a third book, *The Homework Myth: Why Our Kids Get Too Much of a Bad Thing* (2006a), Kohn took direct aim at the research on homework. In this book and in a recent article in *Phi Delta Kappan* (2006b), he became quite personal in his condemnation of researchers. For example, referring to Harris Cooper, the lead author of the two leading meta-analyses on homework, Kohn noted,

> A careful reading of Cooper's own studies . . . reveals further examples of his determination to massage the numbers until they yield something—anything—on which to construct a defense of homework for younger children. (2006a, p. 84)

He also attacked a section on homework in our book *Classroom Instruction That Works* (Marzano, Pickering, & Pollock, 2001).

Kohn concluded that research fails to demonstrate homework's effectiveness as an instructional tool and recommended changing the "default state" from an expectation that homework will be assigned to an expectation that homework will not be assigned. According to Kohn, teachers should only assign homework when they can justify that the assignments are "beneficial" (2006a, p. 166)—ideally involving students in activities appropriate for the home, such as performing an experiment in the kitchen, cooking, doing crossword puzzles with the family, watching good TV shows, or reading. Finally, Kohn urged teachers to involve students in deciding what homework, and how much, they should do.

Some of Kohn's recommendations have merit. For example, it makes good sense to only assign homework that is beneficial to student learning instead of assigning homework as a matter of policy. Many of those who conduct research on homework explicitly or implicitly recommend this practice. However, his misunderstanding or misrepresentation of the research sends the inaccurate message that research does not support homework. As Figure 1 indicates, homework has decades of research supporting its effective use. Kohn's allegations that researchers are trying to mislead practitioners and the general public are unfounded and detract from a useful debate on effective practice.[1]

THE DANGERS OF IGNORING THE RESEARCH

Certainly, inappropriate homework may produce little or no benefit—it may even decrease student achievement. All three of the books criticizing homework provide compelling anecdotes to this effect. Schools should strengthen their policies to ensure that teachers use homework properly.

If a district or school discards homework altogether, however, it will be throwing away a powerful instructional tool. Cooper and colleagues' (2006) comparison of homework with no homework indicates that the average student in a class in which appropriate homework was assigned would score 23 percentile points higher on tests of the knowledge addressed in that class than the average student in a class in which homework was not assigned.

Perhaps the most important advantage of homework is that it can enhance achievement by extending learning beyond the school day. This characteristic is important because U.S. students spend much less time studying academic content than students in other countries do. A 1994 report examined the amount of time U.S. students spend studying core academic subjects compared with students in other countries that typically outperform the United States academically, such as Japan, Germany, and France. The study found that "students abroad are required to work on demanding subject matter at least twice as long" as are U.S. students (National Education Commission on Time and Learning, 1994, p. 25).

To drop the use of homework, then, a school or district would be obliged to identify a practice that produces a similar effect within the confines of the school day without taking away or diminishing the benefits of other academic activities—no easy accomplishment. A better approach is to ensure that teachers use homework effectively. To enact effective homework policies, however, schools and districts must address the following issues.

GRADE LEVEL

Although teachers across the K–12 spectrum commonly assign homework, research has produced no clear-cut consensus on the benefits of homework at the early elementary grade levels. In his early meta-analysis, Cooper (1989a) reported the following effect sizes (p. 71):

- Grades 4–6: ES = .15 (Percentile gain = 6)
- Grades 7–9: ES = .31 (Percentile gain = 12)
- Grades 10–12: ES = .64 (Percentile gain = 24)

The pattern clearly indicates that homework has smaller effects at lower grade levels. Even so, Cooper (1989b) still recommended homework for elementary students because

> homework for young children should help them develop good study habits, foster positive attitudes toward school, and communicate to students the idea that learning takes work at home as well as at school. (p. 90)

The Cooper, Robinson, and Patall (2006) meta-analysis found the same pattern of stronger relationships at the secondary level but also identified a number of studies at grades 2, 3, and 4 demonstrating positive effects for homework. In *The Battle over Homework* (2007), Cooper noted that homework should have different purposes at different grade levels:

- For students in the *earliest grades*, it should foster positive attitudes, habits, and character traits; permit appropriate parent involvement; and reinforce learning of simple skills introduced in class.
- For students in *upper elementary grades*, it should play a more direct role in fostering improved school achievement.
- In *6th grade and beyond*, it should play an important role in improving standardized test scores and grades.

TIME SPENT ON HOMEWORK

One of the more contentious issues in the homework debate is the amount of time students should spend on homework. The Cooper synthesis (1989a) reported that for junior high school students, the benefits increased as time increased, up to 1 to 2 hours of homework a night, and then decreased. The Cooper, Robinson, and Patall (2006) study reported similar findings: 7 to 12 hours of homework per week produced the largest effect size for 12th grade students. The researchers suggested that for 12th graders the optimum amount of homework might lie between 1.5 and 2.5 hours per night, but they cautioned that no

---

[1]For a more detailed response to Kohn's views on homework, see Marzano & Pickering (2007) and Marzano & Pickering (in press).

hard-and-fast rules are warranted. Still, researchers have offered various recommendations. For example, Good and Brophy (2003) cautioned that teachers must take care not to assign too much homework. They suggested that

> homework must be realistic in length and difficulty given the students' abilities to work independently. Thus, 5 to 10 minutes per subject might be appropriate for 4th graders, whereas 30 to 60 minutes might be appropriate for college-bound high school students. (p. 394)

Cooper, Robinson, and Patall (2006) also issued a strong warning about too much homework:

> Even for these oldest students, too much homework may diminish its effectiveness or even become counterproductive. (p. 53)

Cooper (2007) suggested that research findings support the common "10-minute rule" (p. 92), which states that all daily homework assignments combined should take about as long to complete as 10 minutes multiplied by the student's grade level. He added that when required reading is included as a type of homework, the 10-minute rule might be increased to 15 minutes.

Focusing on the amount of time students spend on homework, however, may miss the point. A significant proportion of the research on homework indicates that the positive effects of homework relate to the amount of homework that the student completes rather than the amount of time spent on homework or the amount of homework actually assigned. Thus, simply assigning homework may not produce the desired effect—in fact, ill-structured homework might even have a negative effect on student achievement. Teachers must carefully plan and assign homework in a way that maximizes the potential for student success (see Research-Based Homework Guidelines).

PARENT INVOLVEMENT

Another question regarding homework is the extent to which schools should involve parents. Some studies have reported minimal positive effects or even negative effects for parental involvement. In addition, many parents report that they feel unprepared to help their children with homework and that their efforts to help frequently cause stress (see Balli, 1998; Corno, 1996; Hoover-Dempsey, Bassler, & Burow, 1995; Perkins & Milgram, 1996).

Epstein and colleagues conducted a series of studies to identify the conditions under which parental involvement enhances homework (Epstein, 2001; Epstein & Becker, 1982; Van Voorhis, 2003). They recommended interactive homework in which

- Parents receive clear guidelines spelling out their role.
- Teachers do not expect parents to act as experts regarding content or to attempt to teach the content.
- Parents ask questions that help students clarify and summarize what they have learned.

Good and Brophy (2003) provided the following recommendations regarding parent involvement:

Especially useful for parent-child relations purposes are assignments calling for students to show or explain their written work or other products completed at school to their parents and get their reactions (Epstein, 2001; Epstein, Simon, & Salinas, 1997) or to interview their parents to develop information about parental experiences or opinions relating to topics studied in social studies (Alleman & Brophy, 1998). Such assignments cause students and their parents or other family members to become engaged in conversations that relate to the academic curriculum and thus extend the students' learning. Furthermore, because these are likely to be genuine conversations rather than more formally structured teaching/learning tasks, both parents and children are likely to experience them as enjoyable rather than threatening. (p. 395)

GOING BEYOND THE RESEARCH

Although research has established the overall viability of homework as a tool to enhance student achievement, for the most part the research does not provide recommendations that are specific enough to help busy practitioners. This is the nature of research—it errs on the side of assuming that something does not work until substantial evidence establishes that it does. The research community takes a long time to formulate firm conclusions on the basis of research. Homework is a perfect example: Figure 1 includes synthesis studies that go back as far as 60 years, yet all that research translates to a handful of recommendations articulated at a very general level.

In addition, research in a specific area, such as homework, sometimes contradicts research in related areas. For example, Cooper (2007) recommended on the basis of 60-plus years of homework research that teachers should not comment on or grade every homework assignment. But practitioners might draw a different conclusion from the research on providing feedback to students, which has found that providing "feedback coupled with remediation" (Hattie, 1992) or feedback on "testlike events" in the form of explanations to students (Bangert-Drowns, Kulik, Kulik, & Morgan, 1991) positively affects achievement.

Riehl (2006) pointed out the similarity between education research and medical research. She commented,

> When reported in the popular media, medical research often appears as a blunt instrument, able to obliterate skeptics or opponents by the force of its evidence and arguments. . . . Yet repeated visits to the medical journals themselves can leave a much different impression. The serious medical journals convey the sense that medical research is an ongoing conversation and quest, punctuated occasionally by important findings that can and should alter practice, but more often characterized by continuing investigations. These investigations, taken cumulatively, can inform the work of practitioners who are building their own local knowledge bases on medical care. (pp. 27–28)

If relying solely on research is problematic, what are busy practitioners to do? The answer is certainly not to wait until research "proves" that a practice is effective. Instead, educators should combine research-based generalizations, research from related areas, and their own professional judgment based on firsthand experience to develop specific practices and make adjustments as necessary. Like medical practitioners, education practitioners must develop their own "local knowledge base" on homework and all other aspects of teaching. Educators can develop the most effective practices by observing changes in the achievement of the students with whom they work every day.

Research-Based Homework Guidelines

Research provides strong evidence that, when used appropriately, homework benefits student achievement. To make sure that homework is appropriate, teachers should follow these guidelines:

- Assign purposeful homework. Legitimate purposes for homework include introducing new content, practicing a skill or process that students can do independently but not fluently, elaborating on information that has been addressed in class to deepen students' knowledge, and providing opportunities for students to explore topics of their own interest.
- Design homework to maximize the chances that students will complete it. For example, ensure that homework is at the appropriate level of difficulty. Students should be able to complete homework assignments independently with relatively high success rates, but they should still find the assignments challenging enough to be interesting.
- Involve parents in appropriate ways (for example, as a sounding board to help students summarize what they learned from the homework) without requiring parents to act as teachers or to police students' homework completion.
- Carefully monitor the amount of homework assigned so that it is appropriate to students' age levels and does not take too much time away from other home activities.

References

Balli, S. J. (1998). When mom and dad help: Student reflections on parent involvement with homework. *Journal of Research and Development in Education, 31*(3), 142–148.

Bangert-Drowns, R. L., Kulik, C. C., Kulik, J. A., & Morgan, M. (1991). The instructional effects of feedback in test-like events. *Review of Educational Research, 61*(2), 213–238.

Bennett, S., & Kalish, N. (2006). *The case against homework: How homework is hurting our children and what we can do about it.* New York: Crown.

Bloom, B. S. (1984). The search for methods of group instruction as effective as one-to-one tutoring. *Educational Leadership, 41*(8), 4–18.

Cooper, H. (1989a). *Homework.* White Plains, NY: Longman.

Cooper, H. (1989b). Synthesis of research on homework. *Educational Leadership, 47*(3), 85–91.

Cooper, H. (2007). *The battle over homework* (3rd ed.). Thousand Oaks, CA: Corwin Press.

Cooper, H., Robinson, J. C., & Patall, E. A. (2006). Does homework improve academic achievement? A synthesis of research, 1987–2003. *Review of Educational Research, 76*(1), 1–62.

Corno, L. (1996). Homework is a complicated thing. *Educational Researcher, 25*(8), 27–30.

Epstein, J. (2001). *School, family, and community partnerships: Preparing educators and improving schools.* Boulder, CO: Westview.

Epstein, J. L., & Becker, H. J. (1982). Teachers' reported practices of parent involvement: Problems and possibilities. *Elementary School Journal, 83,* 103–113.

Fraser, B. J., Walberg, H. J., Welch, W. W., & Hattie, J. A. (1987). Synthesis of educational productivity research [Special issue]. *International Journal of Educational Research, 11*(2), 145–252.

Gill, B. P., & Schlossman, S. L. (2000). The lost cause of homework reform. *American Journal of Education, 109,* 27–62.

Good, T. L., & Brophy, J. E. (2003). *Looking in classrooms* (9th ed.). Boston: Allyn & Bacon.

Graue, M. E., Weinstein, T., & Walberg, H. J. (1983). School-based home instruction and learning: A quantitative synthesis. *Journal of Educational Research, 76,* 351–360.

Hattie, J. A. (1992). Measuring the effects of schooling. *Australian Journal of Education, 36*(1), 5–13.

Hoover-Dempsey, K. V., Bassler, O. C., & Burow, R. (1995). Parents' reported involvement in students' homework: Strategies and practices. *The Elementary School Journal, 95*(5), 435–450.

Kavale, K. A. (1988). Using meta-analyses to answer the question: What are the important influences on school learning? *School Psychology Review, 17*(4), 644–650.

Kohn, A. (2006a). *The homework myth: Why our kids get too much of a bad thing.* Cambridge, MA: Da Capo Press.

Kohn, A. (2006b). Abusing research: The study of homework and other examples. *Phi Delta Kappan, 88*(1), 9–22.

Kralovec, E., & Buell, J. (2000). *The end of homework: How homework disrupts families, overburdens children, and limits learning.* Boston: Beacon.

Marzano, R. J., & Pickering, D. J. (2007). *Response to Kohn's allegations.* Centennial, CO: Marzano & Associates. Available: http://marzanoandassociates.com/documents/KohnResponse.pdf

Marzano, R. J., & Pickering, D. J. (in press). *Errors and allegations about research on homework.* Phi Delta Kappan.

Marzano, R. J., Pickering, D. J., & Pollock, J. E. (2001). *Classroom instruction that works: Research-based strategies for increasing student achievement.* Alexandria, VA: ASCD.

National Education Commission on Time and Learning (1994). *Prisoners of time.* Washington, DC: U.S. Department of Education.

Paschal, R. A., Weinstein, T., & Walberg, H. J. (1984). The effects of homework on learning: A quantitative synthesis. *Journal of Educational Research, 78,* 97–104.

Perkins, P. G., & Milgram, R. B. (1996). Parental involvement in homework: A double-edge sword. *International Journal of Adolescence and Youth, 6*(3), 195–203.

Riehl, C. (2006). Feeling better: A comparison of medical research and education research. *Educational Researcher, 35*(5), 24–29.

Van Voorhis, F. (2003). Interactive homework in middle school: Effects on family involvement and science achievement. *Journal of Educational Research, 96,* 323–338.

Walberg, H. J. (1999). Productive teaching. In H. C. Waxman & H. J. Walberg (Eds.), *New directions for teaching practice research* (pp. 75–104). Berkeley, CA: McCutchen.

Wallis, C. (2006). Viewpoint: The myth about homework. *Time, 168*(10), 57.

Sample Meta-Analysis

A Meta-Analysis of the Effectiveness of Computer-Assisted Instruction in Science Education

Bayraktar, S. (2001–2002). A meta-analysis of the effectiveness of computer-assisted instruction in science education. *Journal of Research on Technology in Education, 34,* 173–188.

This article provides a good illustration of how the statistical methods of meta-analysis can be used to synthesize the findings of a large number of research studies on an important problem of practice in education.

This meta-analysis included research studies published between 1970 and 1999. Undoubtedly, research on computer-assisted instruction has advanced since then. However, this meta-analysis is useful, because it represents the cumulated state of research knowledge up to 1999. If you review subsequent studies, you will be able to determine whether their findings corroborate or fail to support this meta-analysis and also whether researchers have moved into new areas—such as other applications of technology to science education—since 1999.

This meta-analysis serves still another purpose. You can enter it into a search engine called Web of Science (see Chapter 4). This search engine will identify subsequent publications that have cited it. The authors of these publications most likely will state how their study was influenced by the meta-analysis and how their findings relate to it.

The article is reprinted in its entirety, just as it appeared when originally published. With the permission of the author and the publisher, we have corrected various errors that appeared in the published article.

A Meta-Analysis of the Effectiveness of Computer-Assisted Instruction in Science Education

Sule Bayraktar
Yuzuncu Yil University, Turkey

ABSTRACT ■ This meta-analysis investigated how effective computer-assisted instruction (CAI) is in raising student achievement in secondary and college science education when compared to traditional instruction. An overall effect size of 0.273 was calculated from 42 studies yielding 108 effect sizes, suggesting that a typical student moved from the 50th percentile to the 62nd percentile in science when CAI was used. The results of the study also indicated that some study characteristics such as student-to-computer ratio, CAI mode, and duration of treatment were significantly related to the effectiveness of CAI. (Keywords: academic achievement, computer-assisted instruction, instructional effectiveness, meta-analysis, science education.)

Computer use in classrooms as an aid to teaching and learning processes has become increasingly popular during the last two decades. According to National Assessment of Educational Progress (NAEP, 1996) statistics, in 1996 more than 80% of the K–12 students in the United States reported using computers for learning purposes in

Bayraktar, Sule (2001–2002). A meta-analysis of the effectiveness of computer-assisted instruction in science education. *Journal of Research on Technology in Education, 34,* 173–188. Reprinted with permission from the *Journal of Research on Technology in Education, 34*(2), Copyright © 2001, ISTE (International Society for Technology in Education), 1.800.336.5191 (U.S. & Canada) or 1.541.302.3777 (Int'l), iste@iste.org, www.iste.org. All rights reserved.

school or at home, though this proportion was just above 50 percent in 1984.[a] The number of computers used in education is consistently increasing. Research on the effectiveness of computer-assisted instruction (CAI), however, does not provide consistent results.

Educational research often produces contradictions. Even frequent replications might produce diversified results. Thus, research review has been a common practice to resolve this kind of conflict. A research review provides an overall conclusion by bringing separately published studies together and investigating if some study characteristics were related to outcomes of the studies (Kulik, Bangert, & Williams, 1983).

A quantitative research review method introduced by Glass (1976) is called meta-analysis. Meta-analysis typically follows the same steps as primary research. A meta-analyst first defines the purpose of the review and develops the research question(s) of interest. Second, the meta-analyst locates research studies conducted on the topic that meet the specified criteria. Typically, meta-analyses are comprehensive reviews of a full population of relevant research studies. Third, the meta-analyst collects data from studies in two ways: (1) study features are coded according to the objectives of the review and (2) study outcomes are transformed to a common metric so that they can be compared. A typical metric in education is effect size (d), the standardized difference between the treatment and control group means. Effect sizes provided from each study are then combined to obtain an overall effect size (grand mean effect size). Finally, statistical procedures are used to investigate relationships among study characteristics and findings.

Although several meta-analyses (e.g., Flinn & Gravat, 1995; Kulik & Kulik, 1991; Liao, 1992; Niemiec & Walberg, 1985) focused on the effectiveness of computers in general, only two studies (Christmann & Badget, 1999; Wise, 1988) focused exclusively on science education. Wise included 26 studies reflecting the situation of computer-based instruction prior to 1988. However, in that study, nearly half of the effect size measures came from studies investigating the effects of computer applications other than computer-assisted instruction.[b] Moreover, in the 12 years since that study, there have been enormous advances in computer technologies. Many other studies have been done and need to be taken into consideration in the research synthesis. In a more recent meta-analysis, Christmann and Badget compiled a total of only 11 studies consisting of CAI in the areas of chemistry, biology, physics, and general science. Thus, a comprehensive meta-analysis on the effectiveness of computer-assisted instruction in the science subject areas, covering a three-decade period, is needed to evaluate the status of this instructional method and to see overall trends clearly.

The purpose of the present meta-analysis is to determine the overall effectiveness of CAI on student achievement in secondary and college science education in the United States between 1970 and 1999 when compared to traditional instruction, by using meta-analysis as a research tool. In addition, the study also examines the effects of variables such as school level, CAI mode, and student-to-computer ratio on the effectiveness of CAI.

METHOD

The procedures used to conduct this meta-analysis will be described in detail in the following sections. First, criteria for studies included in the meta-analysis will be presented. Then, procedures for locating studies and coding study characteristics will be described. Finally, statistical techniques for investigating the relationships between study characteristics and effect sizes will be provided.

Inclusion Criteria

This study synthesized the research that investigated the effectiveness of CAI in the areas of physics, chemistry, biology, general science, and physical sciences at secondary and college levels. Studies included in this analysis were chosen from the experimental and quasi-experimental studies comparing the achievement of students who were taught science with a form of CAI and students who were taught science with traditional instruction.[c] The studies included in the synthesis were limited to those conducted in the United States. Designs including no comparison group were not used in the analysis. Studies that did not report effect sizes or adequate statistics for transformation into effect sizes were not included. Necessary statistics for these transformations are means, standard deviations, and number of subjects, or a variety of parametric statistics such as t and F test results where effect sizes were not reported.[d]

Locating the Studies

Studies included in the analysis were located by several approaches. A search was first conducted using electronic databases, including Educational Resources Information Center (ERIC), Social Science Citation Index (SSCI), PsycINFO, Education Abstracts, and Digital Dissertation Index PROQUEST.[e]

I also manually undertook a journal search for articles that may not have been included in the computer search databases. This search was conducted in the journals in

---

a. The NAEP is a congressionally mandated project of the U.S. Department of Education. It is a large-scale, continuing assessment of what a representative sample of students in the United States know and can do in various subject areas.

b. An effect size is a statistic based on a formula involving both the mean scores and standard deviations of the scores of two groups. It allows a precise calculation of how different the score distributions of the two groups are, and is adjusted so that it can be compared directly to effect sizes involving other samples or based on other measures.

c. A quasi-experiment is a type of experiment in which research participants are not randomly assigned to the experimental and control groups. Quasi-experiments are often contrasted with "true" experiments, which do involve random assignment of research participants to the experimental and control groups.

d. The mean is the average of a set of scores. The standard deviation is a measure of how much a set of scores deviates from the mean score. Parametric statistics make certain assumptions about the distribution and form of scores on the measured variable. A t test is a test of statistical significance that is used to determine whether the null hypothesis that two sample means come from identical populations can be rejected. An F test is similar to a t test, but is used when the null hypothesis involves more than two sample means.

e. These electronic databases are indexes to the education literature.

which most of the studies on the effectiveness of CAI have been published: *Journal of Research in Science Teaching, Journal of Computers in Mathematics and Science Teaching, Computers in the Schools, Journal of Research on Computing in Education* (now *Journal of Research on Technology in Education*), *Science Education, The American Biology Teacher, School Science and Mathematics,* and *Journal of Chemical Education.*

Coding Process

A coding sheet was prepared for translating critical study information into coded form. By using these sheets, variables and effect size information were coded for each study by two coders and me. Both coders were Ph.D. students who had taken a graduate course on meta-analysis before this study.

Assessing the Reliability

To determine reliability, a random sample of 5 of 42 studies were duplicated and distributed among the coders. Each coder was given a copy of the articles, coding forms, and instructions for coding. To assess the inter-coder reliability, *agreement rate* (AR), also called the *percent agreement index*, was used.[f] The formula for AR, as represented by Orwin (1994), is:

$$AR = \frac{\text{Number of observations agreed}}{\text{Total number of observations}}$$

An agreement rate of 0.85 or greater was predetermined to be considered sufficient. An agreement rate of 0.88 was obtained for my study.

Variables

The following variables were coded for each study:

- Course content: general science, biology, physics, chemistry
- CAI type: drill and practice, tutorial, simulation
- Instructor effect: studies were classified as either having the same teachers instructing both the experimental and comparison group or having different teachers instructing both groups.
- Duration of treatment: less or equal to four weeks, greater than four weeks
- School level: college, secondary
- Student-to-computer ratio
- Software: commercial, teacher or researcher designed
- Instructional role of computers: substitute, supplement
- Publication year: 1970–1999
- Publication source: journal article, ERIC document, dissertation, master's thesis

Statistical Analysis

The Unit of Analysis.   The unit of analysis for the present research was the effect size (*d*). Effect size was calculated by using the formula derived by Hunter and Schmidt (1990) for posttest comparisons of control and treatment groups. The formula is:

$$d = \frac{Xe - Xc}{SDp}$$

Xe is the experimental group mean, *Xc* is the control group mean, and *SDp* is the pooled standard deviation of the two groups.[g]

The formula for corresponding pooled standard deviation is:

$$SDp^2 = \frac{(Ne - 1)Se^2 + (Nc - 1)Sc^2}{(Ne + Nc - 2)}$$

Ne is the number of subjects in the experimental group, *Nc* is the number of subjects in the control group, *Se²* is the experimental group variance, and *Sc²* is the control group variance.[h]

In many cases, the primary researchers did not report the standard deviations or means of the separate groups; instead, they used *t, F,* or *r* values. For such cases, these values were converted to *d* statistics by using the following conversion formulas provided by Rosenthal (1991):[i]

For *t* test $\quad d = \dfrac{2t}{\sqrt{df}}$

For *F* test $\quad d = \dfrac{2\sqrt{F}}{\sqrt{df}\,(\text{error})}$

For *r* test $\quad d = \dfrac{2r}{\sqrt{1 - r^2}}$

Calculation of Mean Effect Sizes and Hypothesis Testing. MetaWin (Rosenberg, Adams, & Gurevitch, 1997), a statistical package designed to perform meta-analysis, was used to analyze the data. The variables and classes as well as the effect size information were recorded for each study. This particular software provides mean effect sizes with confidence intervals for each class of variable as well as the between-class homogeneity, Q_{Bet}, which allows one to compare classes.[j] Finally, MetaWin calculates

---

f. Inter-coder reliability is the degree to which two or more individuals are consistent in their coding of a document or other communication.

g. The pooled standard deviation is the average of the standard deviation of the mean for the treatment group (also called the experimental group) and the standard deviation of the mean for the control group. If the size of the treatment-group sample differs from the size of the control-group sample, the computation of the pooled standard deviations typically takes this difference into account.

h. The variance is a measure of the extent to which the scores in a distribution deviate from the mean score. It is equal to the square of the standard deviation.

i. A *d* statistic is a measure of effect size. Various statisticians have developed different formulas for calculating *d*. The larger the *d* value, the greater the difference between the two groups on the statistic (e.g., the mean) being compared.

j. A confidence interval is a set of values, derived by computing statistics for a sample, that is likely to contain the actual population value. For example, the mean for a sample on a particular measure might be 5.1, but the actual mean for the population from which the sample was drawn might be different. The confidence interval indicates a range of scores within which the population mean is likely to fall. The Q test is a test of statistical significance that is used to determine whether the null hypothesis that two sample effect sizes come from identical populations can be rejected.

the grand mean effect size, which is the mean effect size for all the effect sizes for all studies included in the meta-analysis.

The hypothesis that there are no effect size differences between classes of a variable was tested by utilizing the test of homogeneity between classes effect sizes (Q_{Bet}). Rejecting the Q_{Bet} implies that the effect sizes from the classes may not measure the same population parameter. In other words, there is a statistically signifi-

cant difference in the mean effect sizes for each class of a variable.

RESULTS

The first purpose of this study was to determine the overall effectiveness of CAI in science instruction. The literature search yielded 42 studies meeting the inclusion criteria, including 5 ERIC documents, 20 journal articles, 2 master's theses, and 15 dissertations (Table 1). Some studies

TABLE 1 The Primary Studies Included in the Meta-Analysis with Effect Sizes

Study	Subject Area	n of ES	ES Range
Akpan & Andre, 1999	Life sciences	1	1.295
Ayoubi, 1985	Chemistry	6	⁻0.487–0.077
Bennett, 1985	Biology	2	0.253–0.719
Bobbert, 1982	Chemistry	4	⁻0.087–0.893
Castleberry, Montague, & Lagowski, 1970	Chemistry	1	1.89
Cavin & Lagowski, 1978	Chemistry	4	0.152–1.124
Chien, 1997	Physics	1	⁻0.685
Choi & Gennaro, 1987	General	1	0.005
Cracolice, 1994	Chemistry	4	⁻0.272–0.345
Duffy & Barowy, 1995	Biology	1	⁻0.288
Eisenkraft, 1986	Physics	12	0.136–1.246
Faryniarz & Lockwood, 1992	Biology	1	0.672
Ferguson & Chapman, 1993	Biology	4	0.439–0.815
Fox, 1986	Earth science	1	⁻0.557
Hauben & Lehman, 1988	Chemistry	4	⁻0.245–0.683
Hoge, 1995	Biology	5	⁻0.49–0.215
Hounshell & Hill, 1989	Biology	1	0.406
Jackman, Mollenberg, & Brabson, 1987	Chemistry	2	0.279–0.375
Jensen, Wilcox, Hatch, & Somdahl, 1996	Biology	1	0.523
Jones, 1972	Chemistry	1	⁻0.171
Kelly, 1997–1998	Earth science	1	⁻0.276
Kromhout, 1972	Physics	1	0.702
Lasater, 1971	Chemistry	2	0.284–0.472
Leece, 1982	Biology	1	0.877
Lehman, 1988	Biology	10	⁻0.384–0.679
Milkent & Roth, 1989	Physical science	5	⁻0.453–⁻0.201
Miller, 1986	Biology	1	⁻0.220
Morrel, 1992	Biology	1	⁻0.566
Nicholls, Merkel, & Cordts, 1996	Biology	5	⁻0.016–0.439
Nishino, 1993	General science	1	0.457
Podell, Kaminsky, & Cusimano, 1993	Physical science	1	0.522
Rivers & Vockell, 1987	Biology	8	0.395
Shaltz, 1982	Biology	1	0
Shaw, 1984	General science	1	0.709
Stringfield, 1986	Biology	1	0.335
Summerlin & Gardner, 1973	Chemistry	1	⁻0.436
Tauro, 1980	Chemistry	4	⁻0.314–0.573
Tylinski, 1994	Biology	1	⁻0.472
Wainwright, 1985	Chemistry	2	⁻0.335–⁻0.148
Williamson & Abraham, 1995	Chemistry	1	0.54
Wyman, 1988–1989	Physics	1	⁻0.453
Ybarrando, 1984	Biology	1	0.051

performed multiple comparisons—that is, multiple experiments within the same study—thus producing multiple effect sizes. Thus, 108 effect sizes from 42 studies were included in the meta-analysis.

Only one of the 42 studies showed no difference between CAI and the traditional instruction group ($ES = 0$) in terms of science achievement outcome. The range of the ES's was from –0.685 to 1.89.

Grand mean effect size for all 42 studies with 108 ES's was 0.273, considered to be a small difference. This effect size can be interpreted as: an average student exposed to CAI exceeds the academic achievement of 62 percent of the students in the traditional classroom. Ninety-five percent confidence limits were from 0.240 to 0.305.[k]

Seventy of the 108 effect sizes included in this analysis were positive, favoring the CAI group, and 38 were negative, indicating that traditional instruction was found more effective than the CAI. Twenty-eight of the 108 effect sizes were equal to or greater than 0.5, which indicates moderate to large effects of CAI in science education. Forty-two of the effect sizes were positive and small in magnitude. A summary of the analysis results is presented in Table 2.

DISCUSSION OF FINDINGS

This study synthesized the results of 108 effect sizes included in 42 studies. The mean of the 108 effect sizes was determined to be 0.273 standard deviation, indicating that computer-assisted instruction has a small positive effect on student achievement in science education when compared to traditional instruction. An effect is considered to be small when $ES = 0.2$ standard deviation, medium when $ES = 0.5$ standard deviation, and large when $ES = 0.8$ standard deviation (Cohen, 1977). However small, the positive effect indicates that incorporating computers in science instruction can be beneficial.

An effect size of 0.273 standard deviation indicates that an average student exposed to CAI exceeded the performance of 62 percent of the students who were taught using traditional instructional methods. This finding can also be interpreted as: the typical student moved from the 50th percentile to the 62nd percentile in science when CAI was used.

This finding is consistent with the Christmann and Badget (1999) study. The authors found an effect size of 0.266 standard deviation when they synthesized the results of 11 studies comparing the effectiveness of CAI and traditional instruction in science. Although the number of studies included in this analysis was four times larger than their sample size, this study showed very similar results, a fact that points to an overall trend. Similar results have been reported in earlier studies. Flinn and Gravat (1995), for example, reported an effect size of 0.26 standard deviation for CAI in science plus medicine. Niemiec and Walberg (1987) reported the effect size for science from two studies as 0.28 standard deviation. Smaller effects ($ES = 0.13$)

for science were reported by Bangert-Drowns, Kulik, and Kulik (1985).

The results of this analysis also indicated that all variables except educational level were related to effect size. The strongest relationships were found for the following variables: length of treatment, student-to-computer ratio, and publication year. Effect sizes did not vary by publication status and educational level. The relationships between effect size and each variable will be discussed in the following sections.

The present meta-analysis detected significant differences in effectiveness for different CAI implementations. The results indicated that the most effective mode of CAI was simulation in science subject areas, followed by tutorial. A striking result of the analysis was that drill-and-practice CAI had a negative effect. This study supported the results of two previous meta-analyses (Liao, 1992, 1998) reporting that drill and practice is not as effective as simulation or tutorial. However, this finding was completely opposite that of earlier findings. Niemiec and Walberg (1985), for example, reported that CAI was most effective in drill and practice ($ES = 0.47$) and least effective in problem solving ($ES = 0.12$), with a moderate effect for tutorials ($ES = 0.34$). Similarly, Bangert-Drowns (1985) found that CAI is more effective in drill-and-practice form, followed by tutorial. However, it should be noted that these studies did not limit their primary studies to science and that these results were for all subjects in general.

This finding suggests that drill and practice might not be a good choice for science, although it might be beneficial in other subject areas. The higher effect sizes associated with studies using simulation might be partly because simulations create a more active learning environment, thus increasing student involvement and enhancing achievement. Drill and practice, on the other hand, is generally associated with rote learning. Science requires students, however, to be involved in higher-level cognitive processes such as questioning, hypothesizing, problem solving, analyzing, and synthesizing.

The majority of studies located for this meta-analysis were in the subject areas of biology and chemistry. The effects reported for these two subjects, however, were barely noticeable. Little research investigating the effectiveness of CAI in physics was available in the literature. However, the largest mean effect was found for physics ($ES = 0.555$), suggesting that CAI is most effective in physics. This result, however, should be viewed with caution, because the number of studies included was limited and the majority of them were conducted before 1990. Clearly, more research needs to be conducted to evaluate with confidence the effectiveness of CAI in physics teaching.

The majority of past meta-analyses reporting effect sizes for science did not distinguish between the subject areas. This analysis was consistent with the results of the only meta-analysis reporting the difference in effect sizes for different science subject areas, conducted by Christmann and Badget (1999). By synthesizing the results of 11 studies, the researchers concluded that CAI is most effective in general science ($ES = 0.707$), followed by physics ($ES = 0.280$), chemistry ($ES = 0.085$), and biology ($ES = 0.042$).

---

k. Confidence limits define the lower and upper limits of a confidence interval. Confidence limits at the 95 percent level of statistical significance define a range of scores that are very likely to contain the actual population score on the measure that was administered.

TABLE 2   Summary of Analysis Results

Variables and Classes	Between-Classes Effect (Q_{BET})	Number of Effect Sizes (N)	Mean Effect Size (d+)
Subject matter	178.16****		
Biology		45	0.167
Chemistry		36	0.108
Physics		16	0.555
General science		3	0.335
Physical science		5	0.025
Earth science		2	−0.507
Mode of CAI	115.60****		
Drill and practice		22	−0.107
Simulations		43	0.391
Tutorials		26	0.369
Combination		16	0.122
School level	0.003		
Secondary		53	0.273
College		55	0.272
Instructor effect	10.434****		
Same instructor		33	0.218
Different		37	0.328
Unspecified		36	0.226
Length of treatment	40.18**		
0–4 weeks		34	0.378
More than 4 weeks		72	0.219
Unspecified		36	0.273
Student-to-computer ratio	46.647***		
1		40	0.368
2		9	0.168
3 or more		23	0.096
Unspecified		36	0.273
Software author	7.01*		
Researcher/teacher		60	0.318
Commercial		41	0.229
Unspecified		7	0.251
Role of computer	5.32*		
Supplementary		81	0.288
Substitute		27	0.175
Publication date	93.13****		
1970–1979		10	0.615
1980–1989		69	0.212
1990–1999		29	0.159
Publication type	14.27**		
ERIC documents		16	0.337
Journal articles		44	0.293
Dissertations		42	0.229
Theses		6	0.013

*$p < .05$. **$p < .01$. ***$p < .001$. ****$p < .0001$.[1]

1. A p value (i.e., a probability value) represents the likelihood that a statistical result was obtained by chance. The lower the p value (e.g., .0001 is lower than .05), the less likely it is that the result was obtained by chance.

This study concluded that experimenter/teacher-developed software was relatively more effective than commercial software. Similar results were reported by several meta-analysts (Kulik et al., 1983; Niemiec & Walberg, 1985; Ryan, 1991). The explanation for this particular finding might be that an experimenter or teacher is more conscious of the specific objectives and desired outcomes of a course.

The results of this study suggested that the effects are smaller ($ES = 0.218$) when the same teacher taught both CAI and traditional classes and larger ($ES = 0.328$) when different instructors taught experimental and control classes. This result is consistent with the majority of research in the CAI literature. For example, Flinn and Gravat (1995) reported that, if the same teacher taught both groups, the effect size was 0.23 standard deviation; if different teachers taught, the effect size was 0.30 standard deviation. The instructor effect on CAI effectiveness was more impressive in a more recent study. Liao (1998) reported that the effect size was 0.782 for different and 0.068 for the same teachers. This finding is very crucial because it brings up the question of whether the instructional medium or the teachers' instructional effectiveness makes the difference in student achievement. As Kulik and Kulik (1991) suggested, assigning more effective teachers to the CAI group might account for higher effects found in different teacher experiments. However, this analysis showed that even when the same instructor was assigned to the control and treatment groups, student achievement was higher in the CAI groups, which shows a clear effect of CAI on student achievement.

This study detected a significant relationship between CAI effectiveness and the instructional role of computers. Effect sizes were higher ($ES = 0.288$) when computers were used as a supplement to the regular instruction and lower when the computer entirely replaced the regular instruction ($ES = 0.178$). This finding was consistent with the previous meta-analyses (Kulik et al., 1983; Liao, 1998), suggesting that using the computer as a supplement to regular instruction should be the preferred choice instead of using it as a replacement.

The results of the present study suggested a strong relationship between CAI effectiveness and student-to-computer ratio. The effect size difference between individual ($ES = 0.368$) and group ($ES = 0.096$) implementations was remarkable, suggesting that an individualized version of CAI would be preferable in educational settings. However, this finding is tentative, because some studies of the 36 relevant effect sizes did not specify the student-to-computer ratio. This variable has not been investigated extensively in the previous meta-analyses. One of the few studies reporting effect size differences with respect to the student-to-computer ratio was conducted by Liao (1998). That study, however, reported no significant relationship between effect size and the student-to-computer ratio.

This meta-analysis indicated that there were no significant effect size differences at different school levels. This result supports the meta-analysis conducted by Flinn and Gravat (1995), reporting an effect size of 0.26 standard deviation for elementary grades, an effect size of 0.20 standard deviation for secondary grades, and an effect size of 0.20 standard deviation for college. However, this finding is not consistent with the majority of meta-analyses (Bangert-Drowns, 1985; Burns & Bozeman, 1981; Liao, 1998; Roblyer, 1989), which report significant effect size differences for different school levels.

The results of this study indicated that the length of the treatment was strongly related to the effectiveness of CAI for teaching science. CAI was especially effective when the duration of treatment was limited to four weeks or less. The average effect of CAI in such studies was 0.378 standard deviation. In studies where treatment continued longer than four weeks, the effects were less clear ($ES = 0.219$). A similar relationship between length of treatment and study outcome has been reported in previous meta-analyses. Kulik et al. (1983), for example, reported an effect size of 0.56 for 4 weeks or less, 0.30 for 5–8 weeks, and 0.20 for more than 8 weeks. The higher effect sizes associated with shorter studies could be explained by the *Hawthorne effect*. A Hawthorne, or novelty, effect occurs when students are stimulated to greater efforts simply because of the novelty of a treatment. On the other hand, if the treatment extends over a long time period, it loses its attractiveness over time and the effects become less clear.

This study concluded that the results found in ERIC documents were more positive ($ES = 0.337$) than results found in journal articles ($ES = 0.293$) and dissertations ($ES = 0.229$). This variable was studied to investigate whether there is a publication bias in the research literature on the effectiveness of CAI. Publication bias is an alleged tendency of the editors or reviewers rejecting studies showing no significant results. This study did not show signs of any such bias, because the results found in ERIC documents were the most positive. The reason the results found in dissertations were remarkably smaller than journal or ERIC documents, however, remained unclear.

Year of publication was one of the most significant variables in this meta-analysis. A strong relationship between the effect size and the year of publication was determined. Results revealed that CAI was most effective ($ES = 0.615$) in science education between 1970 and 1979 and least effective ($ES = 0.159$) between 1990 and 1999. This finding is particularly surprising and contradictory to the earlier prediction that the effects of CAI on student achievement would be greater over the years, because software would be of better quality due to advances in computer technology. The result could be partly because computer use in schools was so new in the 1970s that a Hawthorne effect occurred.

CONCLUSION

The present meta-analysis detected a small positive effect for CAI use in science and determined that some characteristics of the study were related to the effectiveness of CAI. The small effect size seems to suggest that using CAI in the science classroom may not be highly effective at this point. However, investigation of effectiveness by variables revealed that CAI is more effective under particular conditions. CAI could be more beneficial in student learning in science when these conditions are fulfilled. The present analysis, for example, revealed that computers are more effective when used in simulation or tutorial modes. Consequently, tutorial and simulation CAI programs could be used in science classrooms to enhance student learning. This meta-analysis also revealed that CAI is more effective when computers are used individually. Supplying classrooms with a sufficient number of computers, thus allowing students to work individually rather than in groups, would be beneficial and is recommended for a higher level of effectiveness. According to the results of this study, CAI is more effective when used as a supplement to traditional instruction rather than as a substitute. Therefore, instead of devoting the entire class time to the use of computers, use of such technology in conjunction with other teaching strategies could be more beneficial for student learning in science subject areas. This analysis also revealed that experimenter- or teacher-developed programs were more effective than commercial software programs. This finding seems to indicate that teacher- or experimenter-developed software is more focused on the specific educational objectives of the lesson and the curriculum goals. Devoting more attention to these factors when designing software is recommended for a higher level of effectiveness.

Recommendations for Future Research

Although this analysis indicated that CAI was most effective in teaching physics, this finding is tentative. Because most studies investigating the achievement effects of CAI were done before 1990, this finding does not reflect recent trends. Therefore, more research on the effects of CAI in physics education is needed to reach a confident conclusion.

This research could not make use of some research studies because of the lack of necessary statistics, which are important elements of a meta-analysis. Educational researchers are advised to report all necessary statistics, such as number of subjects in treatment and control groups, standard deviations, and means, as well as significance levels.

Contributor

Sule Bayraktar *received her Ph.D. in curriculum and instruction with an emphasis on science education from Ohio University. She is currently affiliated with Yuzuncu Yil University in Turkey. Her research interests include (1) effects of computer technologies and constructivist teaching methods on student achievement in science and (2) gender differences in science education. (Address: Sule Bayraktar, Yuzuncu Yil Universitesi, Egitim Fakultesi, Zeve Kampusu, VAN/TURKEY; sulebayraktar@yahoo.com.)*

References

References marked with an asterisk (*) indicate studies included in the meta-analysis.

*Akpan, J. P., & Andre, T. (1999). The effects of a prior dissection simulation on middle students' dissection performance and understanding of the anatomy and morphology of the frog. *Journal of Science Education and Technology, 8*(2), 107–121.

*Ayoubi, Z. R. (1985). The effect of microcomputer assisted instruction on achievement in high school chemistry. (Doctoral dissertation, The University of Michigan, 1985). *Dissertation Abstracts International, 46,* A3310.

Bangert-Drowns, R. L. (1985, March–April). *Meta-analysis of findings on computer-based education with precollege students.* Paper presented at the annual meeting of the American Educational Research Association, Chicago. (ERIC No. ED 263 905)

Bangert-Drowns, R., Kulik, J. A., & Kulik, C. (1985). Effectiveness of computer-based instruction in secondary schools. *Journal of Computer Based Instruction, 12*(3), 59–68.

Bennett, R. F. (1985). The effects of computer-assisted instruction and reinforcement schedules on physics achievement and attitudes toward physics of high school students. (Doctoral dissertation, Boston University, 1985). *Dissertation Abstracts International, 46,* A3670.

*Bobbert, L. C. (1982). The effects of using interactive computer simulated laboratory experiments in college chemistry courses. (Doctoral dissertation, University of Cincinnati, 1982). *Dissertation Abstracts International, 43,* A2300.

Burns, P., & Bozeman, W. (1981). Computer-assisted instruction and mathematics achievement: Is there a relationship? *Educational Technology, 10*(2), 32–39.

*Castleberry, S. J., Montague, E. J., & Lagowski, J. J. (1970). Computer-based teaching techniques in general chemistry. *Journal of Research in Science Teaching, 7,* 197–208.

*Cavin, C. S., & Lagowski, J. J. (1978). Effects of computer simulated or laboratory experiments and student aptitude on achievement and time in a college general chemistry laboratory course. *Journal of Research in Science Teaching, 15*(6), 455–463.

*Chien, C. C. (1997). The effectiveness of interactive computer simulations on college engineering student conceptual understanding and problem solving ability related to circular motion. (Doctoral dissertation, Ohio University, 1997). *Dissertation Abstracts International, 58,* A2589.

*Choi, B., & Gennaro, E. (1987). The effectiveness of using computer simulated experiments on junior high students' understanding of the volume displacement concept. *Journal of Research in Science Teaching, 24*(6), 539–552.

Christmann, E. P., & Badget, J. L. (1999). A comparative analysis of the effects of computer-assisted instruction on student achievement in differing science and demographic areas. *Journal of Computers in Mathematics and Science Teaching, 18*(2), 135–143.

Cohen, J. (1977). *Statistical power analysis for the behavioral sciences* (rev. ed.). New York: Academic Press.

*Cracolice, M. S. (1994). An investigation of computer-assisted instruction and semi-programmed instruction as a replacement for traditional recitation/discussion in general chemistry and their relationships to student cognitive characteristics. (Doctoral dissertation, University of Oklahoma, 1994). *Dissertation Abstracts International, 55,* A2335.

*Duffy, M., & Barowy, W. (1995, April). *Effects of constructivist and computer-facilitated strategies on achievements in heterogeneous secondary biology.* Paper presented at the annual meeting of the National Association for Research in Science Teaching, San Francisco. (ERIC No. ED 406 207)

*Eisenkraft, A. J. (1986). The effects of computer simulated experiments and traditional laboratory experiments on subsequent transfer tasks in a high school physics course. (Doctoral dissertation, New York University, 1986). *Dissertation Abstracts International, 47,* A3723.

*Faryniarz, J. V., & Lockwood, L. G. (1992). Effectiveness of microcomputer simulations in stimulating environmental problem solving by community college students. *Journal of Research in Science Teaching, 29*(5), 453–470.

*Ferguson, N. H., & Chapman, S. R. (1993). Computer-assisted instruction for introductory genetics. *Journal of Natural Resources Life Sciences Education, 22*(2), 145–152.

Flinn, C. M., & Gravatt, B. (1995). The efficacy of computer assisted instruction (CAI): A meta-analysis. *Journal of Educational Computing Research, 12*(3), 219–242.

*Fox, J. A. (1986). A comparison of lecture based instruction and computer based individualized instruction. (Doctoral dissertation, University of Northern Colorado, 1986). *Dissertation Abstracts International, 47,* A2132.

Glass, G. V. (1976). Primary, secondary, and meta-analysis of research. *Educational Researcher, 5*(11), 3–8.

*Hauben, M. H., & Lehman, J. D. (1988). Computer assisted instruction for problem solving by dimensional analysis. *Journal of Computers in Mathematics and Science Teaching, 7*(3), 50–54.

*Hoge, P. S. (1995). The effect of computer-assisted instruction on the achievement levels of secondary biology students. Unpublished master's thesis, Central Missouri State University, Warrensburg.

*Hounshell, P. B., & Hill, S. R. (1989). The computer and achievement and attitudes in high school biology. *Journal of Research in Science Teaching, 26*(6), 543–549.

Hunter, J. E., & Schmidt, F. L. (1990). *Methods of meta-analysis: Correcting error and bias in research findings.* Newbury Park, CA: Sage Publications.

*Jackman, L. E., Mollenberg, W. P., & Brabson, D. G. (1987). Evaluation of three instructional methods for teaching general chemistry. *Journal of Chemical Education, 64*(9), 794–796.

*Jensen, M. S., Wilcox, K. J., Hatch, J. T., Somdahl, C. (1996). A computer assisted instruction unit on diffusion and osmosis with a conceptual change design. *Journal of Computers in Mathematics and Science Teaching, 15*(1/2), 49–64.

*Jones, J. E. (1972). Computer-simulated experiments in high school physics and chemistry. (Doctoral dissertation, Iowa State University, 1972). *Dissertation Abstracts International, 33,* A4200.

*Kelly, P. R. (1997–1998). Transfer of learning from a computer simulation as compared to a laboratory activity. *Journal of Educational Technology Systems, 26*(4), 345–351.

Kinzie, M. B., & Sullivan, H. J. (1989). Continuing motivation, learner control, and CAI. *Education Technology Research and Development, 37*(2), 5–14.

*Kromhout, O. M. (1972). *Effect of computer tutorial review lessons on exam performance in introductory college physics. Tech memo number 64.* Tallahassee: Florida State University. (ERIC No. ED 072 654)

Kulik, C., Kulik, J., & Bangert-Drowns, R. (1984, April). *Effects of computer-based education on elementary school pupils.* Paper presented at the annual meeting of the American Educational Research Association, New Orleans, LA. (ERIC No. ED 244 616)

Kulik, C. C., & Kulik, J. A. (1991). Effectiveness of computer-based instruction: An updated analysis. *Computers in Human Behavior, 7*(1–2), 75–94.

Kulik, J., Bangert, R., & Williams, G. (1983). Effects of computer-based teaching on secondary school students. *Journal of Educational Psychology, 75*(1), 19–26.

*Lasater, M. E. (1971). The development and evaluation of a computer assisted instructional program involving applications of selected chemical principles. (Doctoral dissertation, University of Texas, 1971). *Dissertation Abstracts International, 32*(10A), 5535.

*Leece, C. G. (1982). *The development and evaluation of the microcomputer modules entitled photophosphorylation.* Houghton: Michigan Technological University. (ERIC No. ED 223 469)

*Lehman, J. D. (1988, April). *Integrating computers in the biology education of elementary teaching majors.* Paper presented at the annual meeting of the National Association for Research in Science Teaching, Lake of the Ozarks, MO. (ERIC No. ED 291 579)

Liao, Y. C. (1992). Effects of computer-assisted instruction on cognitive outcomes: A meta-analysis. *Journal of Research on Computing in Education, 24*(3), 367–381.

Liao, Y. C. (1998). Effects of hypermedia versus traditional instruction on students' achievement. *Journal of Research on Computing in Education, 30*(4), 341–359.

*Milkent, M., & Roth, W. M. (1989). Enhancing student achievement through computer generated homework. *Journal of Research in Science Teaching, 26*(7), 567–573.

*Miller, D. G. (1986). The integration of computer simulation into the community college general biology laboratory. (Doctoral dissertation, Florida Atlantic University, 1986). *Dissertation Abstracts International, 47,* A2106.

*Morrel, P. D. (1992). The effects of computer assisted instruction on student achievement in high school biology. *School Science and Mathematics, 92*(4), 177–181.

National Assessment of Educational Progress. (1996). *Trends in academic progress, 1996.* Washington, DC: U.S. Department of Education, National Center for Education Statistics.

*Nicholls, C., Merkel, S., & Cordts, M. (1996). The effect of computer animation on students' understanding of microbiology. *Journal of Research on Computing in Education, 28*(3), 359–371.

Niemiec, R. P., & Walberg, H. J. (1985). Computers and achievement in the elementary schools. *Journal of Educational Computing Research, 1*(4), 435–440.

*Nishino, A. K. (1993). An exploratory investigation to determine the effects of a multimedia computer-based science learning environment and gender differences, on achievement, and attitudes and interests of students in an eighth-grade science classroom. (Doctoral dissertation, University of Southern California, 1993). *Dissertation Abstracts International, 54,* A4414.

Orwin, R. G. (1994). Evaluating coding decisions. In H. Cooper & L. V. Hedges (Eds.), *Handbook of research synthesis* (pp. 139–162). New York: Sage Publications.

*Podell, D. M., Kaminsky, S., & Cusimano, V. (1993). The effects of micro-computer laboratory approach to physical science instruction on student motivation. *Computers in the Schools, 9*(2/3), 65–73.

*Rivers, R. H., & Vockell, E. (1987). Computer simulations to stimulate scientific problem solving. *Journal of Research in Science Teaching, 24*(5), 403–415.

Roblyer, M. D. (1989). *The impact of microcomputer-based instruction on teaching and learning: A review of recent research.* Syracuse, NY: ERIC Clearinghouse on Information Resources. (ERIC No. ED 315 063)

Rosenberg, M. S., Adams, D. C., & Gurevitch, J. (1997). MetaWin: Statistical software for meta-analysis with resampling tests [Computer software]. Sunderland, MA: Sinauer Associates.

Rosenthal, R. (1991). *Meta analytic procedures for social research* (rev. ed.). Thousand Oaks, CA: Sage Publications.

Ryan, A. W. (1991). Meta-analysis of achievement effects of microcomputer applications in elementary schools. *Educational Administration Quarterly, 27*(2), 161–184.

*Shaltz, M. B. (1982). *Development and evolution of SUMIT microcomputer module entitled "Predator Functional Response."* Report submitted in partial fulfillment of the requirements for the degree of Master of Science in Biological Sciences, Michigan Technological University, Houghton. (ERIC No. ED 229 249)

*Shaw, E. L., Jr. (1984). Effects of the use of microcomputer simulations on concept identification achievement and attitudes toward computers and science instruction of middle school students of various levels of logical reasoning ability. (Doctoral dissertation, University of Georgia, 1984). *Dissertation Abstract International, 45,* A2827.

*Stringfield, J. K., Jr. (1986). The effects of reasoning ability and computer based instructional materials on the achievement and attitudes of high school students in a genetics unit in general biology. (Doctoral dissertation, University of North Carolina at Chapel Hill, 1986). *Dissertation Abstracts International, 48,* A1165.

*Summerlin, L., & Gardner, M. (1973). A study of tutorial type computer assisted instruction in high school chemistry. *Journal of Research in Science Teaching, 10*(1), 75–82.

*Tauro, J. P. (1980). A study of academically superior students' response to particular computer assisted programs in chemistry. (Doctoral dissertation, Syracuse University, 1980). *Dissertation Abstracts International, 42,* A643.

*Tylinski, D. J. (1994). The effect of a computer simulation on junior high students' understanding of the physiological systems of an earthworm (dissection). (Doctoral dissertation, Indiana University of Pennsylvania, 1994). *Dissertation Abstracts International, 55,* A923.

*Wainwright, C. L. (1985, April). *The effectiveness of a computer assisted instruction package in supplementing teaching of selected concepts in high school chemistry: Writing formulas and balancing chemical equations.* Paper presented at the annual meeting of the National Association for Research in Science Teaching, French Lick Springs, IN. (ERIC No. ED 257 656)

*Williamson, V. M., & Abraham, M. R. (1995). The effects of computer animation on the particulate mental models of college chemistry students. *Journal of Research in Science Teaching, 32*(5), 521–534.

Wise, K. C. (1988). The effects of using computing technologies in science instruction: A synthesis of classroom research. In J. D. Ellis (Ed.), *1988 AETS Yearbook* (pp. 105–118). Colorado Springs, CO: Office of Educational Research and Improvement, U.S. Department of Education.

*Wyman, N. R. (1988–1989). A computer-aided unit to teach reduction of experimental data to a functional relationship. *Computers in Mathematics and Science Teaching, 8*(2), 41–46.

*Ybarrando, B. A. (1984). *A study of the effectiveness of computer assisted instruction in the high school biology classroom.* (ERIC No. ED 265 015)

chapter 6

Analyzing and Evaluating Reports of Quantitative Research Studies

1. Most reports of quantitative studies in education follow the style specified in the *Publication Manual of the American Psychological Association.*

2. In reading research reports, you should identify the constructs that are mentioned, because these constructs determined which phenomena the researchers selected for study, how they measured those phenomena, and how they interpreted their data.

3. Constructs can be thought of as variables, meaning that research participants can differ quantitatively with respect to them. A construct is considered to be a constant if the participants do not vary with respect to it.

4. You should look for explicit research hypotheses, questions, or objectives in the introductory section of a research report, because you will judge the quality of the study by how well the hypotheses were tested, the research questions were answered, or the research objectives were achieved.

5. Space limitations in research journals do not allow for extensive literature reviews, but the authors should at least discuss the previous studies most relevant to their own study.

6. The authors of a research report should state whether they studied the entire population of interest or a sample from either the target population or the accessible population.

7. The authors of a research report should state whether they used stratified random sampling or proportional random sampling to ensure that subgroups in the population of interest were adequately represented in their sample.

8. Educational researchers typically study volunteer samples, because the legal requirements of informed consent allow individuals to refuse to participate in a study if they wish.

9. To determine whether findings for the research sample that was studied are generalizable to the target population, the accessible population, or your local setting, you need to compare your participants to these larger groups on important variables (e.g., socioeconomic status, age, gender, ethnicity). Therefore, the research report should contain information about these variables.

10. The authors of a research report should specify each variable and whether it was measured by a test, scale, questionnaire, interview, direct observation, content analysis, or other approach.

11. In evaluating a questionnaire described in a research report, you should check whether it was pretested, whether it included leading or psychologically threatening questions, and whether the research respondents could reasonably be expected to have the information that it requested.

12. In evaluating a research interview described in a research report, you should check whether it was pretested, whether the interviewers were trained properly, whether it included leading or psychologically threatening questions, and how the interview data were recorded for subsequent analysis.

13. In evaluating a direct observation procedure described in a research report, you should check whether the observed variables were high-inference or low-inference, whether the observers were adequately trained, whether a standard observation form was used, whether the observation period was of sufficient duration, and how conspicuous the observers were to the research participants.

14. In evaluating a content analysis described in a research study, you should check whether the content categories were well defined and worthy of study, whether the procedure for selecting a sample of documents was sound, and whether the observers who content analyzed each document created reliable data.

15. A test described in a research report is valid to the extent that interpretations of scores earned by the test-takers are supported by various types of evidence: content-related evidence, predictive evidence, convergent evidence, concurrent evidence, response-process evidence, and consequential evidence.

16. A test described in a research report is reliable to the extent that it is free of measurement error. Test reliability can be determined by calculating the consistency of its items, its stability across time, the consistency with which it can be administered and scored, and its standard error of measurement.

17. A test that is developed by the methods of item response theory consists of items that are ordered on a difficulty scale, such that an individual with a given amount of the ability measured by the test will be able to answer most of the items below a certain point on the scale and few or no items above that point.

18. Search engines and bibliographic indexes are available to help you locate or evaluate available tests and other measures described in a research report.

19. The methods section of a research report should explain details of the research design in sufficient detail that a reader can judge whether it achieves commonly accepted standards for that kind of design.

20. The results section of a research report is an objective presentation of the statistical findings, without interpretation. The discussion section provides an opportunity for the researchers' own interpretation of the results, evaluation of the study's methodology, and discussion of the significance of the study's findings for future research, theory development, and improvement of professional practice. ■

Key TERMS

abstract	inter-rater reliability	response-process evidence of test validity
accessible population	interview	
closed-ended item	item consistency	sampling error
concurrent evidence of test validity	item response theory	scale
consequential evidence of test validity	low-inference variable	simple random sampling
	measurement error	standard error of measurement
constant	open-ended item	*Standards for Educational and Psychological Testing*
construct	parameter	
content analysis	performance measure	stratified random sampling
content-related evidence of test validity	population validity	target population
	predictive evidence of test validity	test
convergent evidence of test validity	proportional random sampling	test–retest reliability
	Publication Manual of the American Psychological Association	test stability
Cronbach's alpha		test validity
direct observation		true score
face validity	questionnaire	variable
high-inference variable	reliability	volunteer sample
hypothesis	reliability coefficient	

Organization of a Quantitative Research Report

Chapter 1 describes quantitative research and qualitative research as two different approaches to scientific inquiry in education. Among the primary characteristics of quantitative research are an epistemological belief in an objective reality, the analysis of reality into measurable variables, the creation of generalizable knowledge through the study of samples that accurately represent a defined population, and reliance on statistical methods to analyze data.

You will read several quantitative research reports—reprinted articles from research journals—in this part of the book (Part III). In this chapter, we describe how to read such reports analytically and critically.

Most reports of quantitative research studies are organized similarly, because researchers typically follow the style guidelines in the ***Publication Manual of the American Psychological Association*** (2001). The guidelines specify the sections of a quantitative research report and their order of presentation, as follows:

> Abstract
> Introduction
> Methods
>   Sampling Procedures
>   Measures (or Materials)
>   Research Design and Procedures
> Results
> Discussion

Each of these sections is explained in this chapter.

Of course, it is not sufficient to be able to read a research report with good comprehension. You also need to be able to evaluate the soundness of the study that it reports. Therefore, as we explain the parts of a research study that are reported in each section of the report, we also explain how to judge whether each part is sound or flawed.

To make these judgments, it is helpful to ask yourself questions as you read each section of the report. A set of questions for this purpose is presented in list form in Appendix 2. Another list of questions, intended for specific research designs, is presented in Appendix 4.

Abstract and Introduction

A research report begins with an **abstract,** which is a brief summary (typically about 100 words) of the content of the report. Reading the abstract first will give you an idea of the purpose of the study, its methods of inquiry, and the major findings. With this overview in mind, you will find it easier to comprehend the many details included in the full report.

The following is an abstract for a research study (Ridley, Hurwitz, Hackett, & Miller, 2005) that was published in the *Journal of Teacher Education:*

> To date, the professional development school (PDS) preservice teacher preparation literature base is long on attitudinal analysis and short on comparative analysis of outcome variables. This article reports on a 2-year study comparing the lesson planning, teaching effectiveness, postlesson reflectivity, and content retention of professional teaching knowledge for teachers prepared at a PDS or campus-based program. The teaching outcome variables were a rubric scored by experienced raters blind to participants' teacher preparation program. Although the scores of PDS-prepared student teachers consistently trended higher than the campus-prepared cohort, no statistically significant differences were found. However, during the 1st year of teaching, PDS-prepared teachers scored significantly higher than campus-prepared teachers on teaching effectiveness. Potential explanations for the findings are provided. (p. 46)

This abstract concisely states the purpose of the study and its key findings. In the next sections of this chapter, we continue discussing this study to illustrate other features of a research report.

The introductory section of a quantitative research report comes immediately after the abstract. It describes the purpose of the study, relevant constructs and variables, and the specific hypotheses, questions, and objectives that guided the study. In addition, the introductory section includes a review of previous research findings and other information that is relevant to the study. We explain these features of a research report in the following sections.

Constructs and Variables

The introductory section of a research report should identify and describe each of the concepts that was studied. Examples of concepts studied by educational researchers are learning style, aptitude, academic achievement, intrinsic motivation, school leadership, and curriculum standards. Researchers typically refer to these concepts as constructs or variables.

A **construct** is a structure or process that is inferred from observed behavior. For example, psychologists have observed that some individuals tend to speak about themselves in consistent ways, such as "I'm very good at sports," "I am ambitious," or "I don't like to draw attention to myself." The consistency of these self-perceptions over time and situations has led social psychologists to infer that individuals have a psychological structure that they call *self-concept.* Self-concept, then, is a construct inferred from observed behavior; it cannot be observed directly. Other related constructs have been inferred as well, such as self-esteem, self-determination, and self-efficacy.

Some constructs are tied to a particular theory. For example, logical operations and sensorimotor intelligence are key constructs in Piaget's theory of human development. Metacognition, short-term memory, and long-term memory are key constructs in certain cognitive theories. Oppression and voice are key constructs in critical research (see Chapter 16).

Constructs are extremely important in all types of educational research. They determine how researchers view reality, the phenomena they study, their procedures for measuring these phenomena, and their interpretations of their empirical findings. If you do not accept a researcher's definition of a construct, you might very well reject the entire study as irrelevant to the improvement of educational theory and practice.

In the study of teacher education that we introduced in the preceding section (Ridley et al., 2005), two of the key constructs are (1) programs of teacher education based on professional development schools (PDS) and (2) campus-based teacher education programs. The value of the study to you and others depends on how the researchers defined these two constructs. The key features of each construct are shown in Table 6.1, just as they appear in the journal article. If you have a different conception of how PDS teacher education programs operate, or should operate, the researchers' study probably will have limited value for you.

Other key constructs in this study involve the outcomes of teacher education programs: (1) professional teaching knowledge, (2) the quality of teachers' lesson plans, (3) teaching

TABLE *6.1*   Comparison of Professional Development School (PDS) and Campus-Based Preparation Programs

PDS Teacher Education Program	Campus Teacher Education Program
Same teacher education coursework delivered in 1 calendar year (three semesters, including summer)	Same teacher education coursework delivered in 2 calendar years (four semesters, no summers)
Preservice teachers (PSTs) completely immersed on site every semester of their teacher preparation (i.e., all coursework and clinical preparation is site based)	PSTs' coursework is completed on campus with the exception of their method courses semester where they participate on site
PSTs are supervised and receive clinical feedback over the entire program	PSTs are supervised and receive clinical feedback during student teaching
PSTs are involved in extensive, ongoing classroom teaching (in teams and individually) throughout the program, including the teaching of summer school	PSTs individually teach from 3 days to 2 weeks per semester during their site-based semester
Most or all teachers at the school are involved and committed to the program	A select, usually small number of site teachers are involved and committed to the program
Cohort size is 18 to 20, and PSTs form very close bonds with one another as well as school and university faculty members (strong support system)	Cohort size is 35 to 36, and PSTs may or may not bond with one another
Inquiry through action research is a fundamental component of the teacher preparation program and school improvement efforts	Inquiry through action research is not necessarily an important component of the program
University faculty member housed at the PDS sites (Monday through Thursday) and actively contributes to the achievement of all four PDS goals	University faculty are campus based and not necessarily active in school improvement effort (unless paid as consultants)
Site teachers have an active role in program design and delivery	Site teachers are not necessarily active contributors to program direction

Source: Table 1 on p. 50 of Ridley, D. S., Hurwitz, S., Hackett, M. R. D., & Miller, K. K. (2005). Comparing PDS and campus-based preservice teacher preparation: Is PDS-based preparation really better? *Journal of Teacher Education, 56*(1), 46–56. Copyright © 2005 by Sage Publications. Reprinted by permission of Sage Publications.

performance in classrooms, and (4) the quality of teachers' postlesson reflections. Once again, you need to determine whether you agree with the researchers' definitions of these constructs. Also, you need to decide whether these actually are worthwhile outcomes of teacher education programs and whether other outcomes of value to you were not considered in this study.

Variables and Constants

Quantitative researchers generally use the term *variable* rather than *construct* when conceptualizing their studies and writing their reports. A **variable** is the quantitative expression of a construct. For example, we can think of the construct of self-concept as ranging from highly negative to neutral to highly positive. In thinking this way, we are viewing self-concept as a variable.

Variables usually are measured in terms of scores on a measure, such as an achievement test or attitude scale. Variables also can take the form of categories, for example, tall versus short, public versus private schools, or authoritarian versus democratic versus laissez-faire styles of leadership.

If a construct is part of the design of a research study but does not vary, it is called a **constant.** For example, suppose a researcher conducts an experiment to compare the effectiveness of teaching method A and teaching method B for community college students. The educational level of the students (that is, community college) is a constant because no other educational level is included in the research design. Suppose, however, that the experiment compares the effectiveness of the two teaching methods to see which is most effective for community college students and which is most effective for high school students. In this experiment, educational level is a variable because it takes on two values: community college and high school.

In reviewing a research report, you should examine carefully how each construct is defined, how it is treated as a variable, and how that variable is measured. If the definitions are unclear or nonexistent, the significance of the research results is cast into doubt. More doubts arise if the definitions of the constructs are inconsistent with the methods used to measure them.

In the teacher education study, the variable "teacher education program" includes two categories: PDS program and campus-based program. Additional categories could be imagined, for example, a teacher education program that has some features of the PDS model shown in Table 6.1 but not others.

Each of the outcome constructs are variables that can be measured by interval scales (explained in Chapter 7). Scores on the test of professional teaching knowledge can range from 0 to 38. The other outcome measures are rating scales that can range from 0 to 18 (quality of lesson plan), 0 to 22 (teaching performance), and 0 to 9 (postlesson reflection). Different researchers might consider other options. For example, a researcher might view the construct "quality of lesson plan" as a variable having three possible values: excellent, adequate, and not acceptable.

Research Hypotheses, Questions, and Objectives

A **hypothesis** in a research study is a reasoned speculation, or prediction, about how two or more variables are related to each other. For example, researchers might hypothesize that children's order of birth in their family relative to their siblings is related to their level of leadership in school activities, or that method A is more effective than method B for promoting the academic achievement of students involved in distance education. After formulating a hypothesis, researchers collect data to test it and then examine the data to decide whether or not to reject it.

Hypotheses usually are formulated on the basis of theory and previous research findings. For example, the study of PDS and campus-based teacher education programs was designed to test two explicit hypotheses:

Hypothesis 1. During student teaching, PDS-based students will be superior to campus-based students in lesson planning, teaching effectiveness, and postlesson reflections and will be equal in content retention of professional teaching knowledge. (p. 48)

Hypothesis 2. During their 1st year of teaching, PDS graduates will be superior to campus-based graduates in lesson planning, teaching effectiveness, and postlesson reflection. (p. 48)

The researchers' rationale for these hypotheses was based on their analysis of program features. They thought that a PDS program had several advantages over a campus-based program. A PDS provides more clinical experiences, and its preservice teachers receive clinical supervision from both school-based and university-based educators throughout the entire program.

You will note that, in Hypothesis 1, the researchers did not predict a difference in professional teaching knowledge between the two groups. They explained that they had no basis for predicting whether PDS-based students would attend more to the "theoretical content" (as compared with "practical classroom experiences") presented in their program than would campus-based students. Theoretical content presumably would be emphasized in the test of professional teaching knowledge.

If theory or previous research do not provide an adequate basis for formulating specific hypotheses, researchers instead will formulate questions or objectives to guide their investigation. For example, suppose a research team wondered about the effect of higher cognitive questions on students' learning in social studies classes but had no basis for formulating a hypothesis about what that effect might be. In this situation, they could pose a question such as "What is the effect of higher cognitive questions on students' learning in social studies classes?" Alternatively, they could state an objective: "The objective of this study is to determine whether higher cognitive questions improve students' learning in social studies classes."

The choice of research questions or objectives is generally a matter of personal preference. In our experience, research questions are more commonly stated than research objectives in journal articles.

The formulation of hypotheses, questions, or objectives is one of the first steps researchers take in planning a quantitative research study. They provide a foundation that guides the rest of the planning process, data collection, and data analysis. Therefore, you should look for hypotheses, questions, or objectives in the introductory section of the report. If none are present, you have reason to be concerned about the quality of the study and the validity of its findings. You also should be concerned if you find that hypotheses, questions, or objectives are stated, but the research design and statistical analyses do not address them directly.

Literature Review

If you are doing a comprehensive review of the research literature on a particular problem, you will soon notice that a few key studies are cited in many of the research reports. If these key studies are not reviewed in a particular research report, it might indicate that the researchers were careless in reviewing the literature. If important studies that disagree with the researchers' findings are omitted, bias might be involved.

Most research journals allow researchers limited space for reviewing previous research, so you should not expect detailed reviews. However, the five to ten most relevant previous studies should be discussed, if only briefly. Significant syntheses of the literature also merit discussion in a research report. Research reports not appearing in journals, such as doctoral dissertations, usually provide much more detailed reviews because they are not subject to space limitations.

The report of the PDS study included 27 references. The majority of them involved articles reporting on the purported benefits of PDS teacher preparation and previous empirical studies on its effectiveness.

The Researchers' Qualifications

Because quantitative researchers strive to be objective, they generally reveal little or nothing about themselves in their reports. Each author's institutional affiliation typically is listed beneath the author's name at the start of the report, and there might be a note indicating the author's job title. The literature review might refer to reports of other studies or scholarly work that the authors have written.

Knowledge about the researchers might provide some indication of whether researcher bias affected their study. For example, some research studies involve experimental tests of the effectiveness of an educational program or method. If we know that the researchers have a stake in the program or method (which is often the case), we should be on the alert for any indications that the design of the experiment was slanted to support its effectiveness.

Whenever researchers have reason for wanting their research to support a particular viewpoint, the likelihood of bias is greatly increased. Occasionally, the bias becomes so great that the researchers slant their findings or even structure their research design to produce a predetermined result. A famous case of researcher bias involved the study of twins by Sir Cyril Burt. It appears that Burt was so intent on proving that intelligence is inherited that he misanalyzed, or even fabricated, research data to support his hypothesis (Evans, 1976).

Method Section: Sampling Procedures

In conducting a study, researchers ideally would investigate all the individuals to whom they wish to generalize their findings. These individuals constitute a **target population,** meaning that they make up the entire group of individuals (or organizations, events, objects, etc.) having the characteristics that interest the researchers. Because of the great expense involved in studying most populations of interest, researchers are limited to studying a sample of individuals who represent that population.

For example, suppose the researchers wish to study the effect of a new reading program on the reading comprehension of visually impaired children in U.S. elementary schools but lack the resources to try out the new reading program with the entire population of such children. Therefore, they must first define an accessible population and then select a sample from this population. The **accessible population** is the entire group of individuals (or other entities) that can feasibly be included in the research sample. For example, the researchers might define the accessible population as all the students within a certain region of the state in which they work.

The researchers now have solved the problem of making the study feasible to conduct, but they have created a different problem in the process, namely, whether they can generalize their findings from a limited sample drawn from the accessible population to the entire population of visually impaired children in U.S. elementary schools. As we explain below, researchers can use various sampling procedures to increase the likelihood that their findings have valid generalizability.

Samples rarely will have exactly the same characteristics as the populations from which they are drawn. For example, suppose that you randomly select three male students from each class in a large high school and measure their height. Because each member of the population has an equal and independent chance of being included in the sample, your sampling procedure is random. Nonetheless, it is unlikely that the mean height of this sample will turn out to be identical to the mean height of all male students in the school (defined to be the target population in this example).

The difference between the mean height of this random sample and the population's mean height is a random sampling error. In technical terms, a **sampling error** is the difference between a statistic (e.g., a mean score) for a sample and the same statistic for the population. The technical term for a statistic that is based on measurement of the entire population is **parameter.**

Sampling errors are likely to occur even when the sample is randomly drawn from the population. The size of the errors tends to become smaller as we select a larger random sample. For this reason, we can be more confident in generalizing results from studies with a large random sample than studies with a small random sample. We describe the effects of sampling error in more detail in Chapter 10.

Despite the advantages of a random sample, researchers often must study nonrandom samples. Unfortunately, sampling errors in nonrandom samples cannot be estimated by mathematical procedures. Therefore, generalizations about populations based on nonrandom samples need to be viewed as tentative. If the research findings have theoretical or practical significance, researchers likely will do replication studies with other samples (random or nonrandom) to determine whether the original findings are generalizable to a defined population.

Types of Sampling

Researchers have developed various techniques for drawing random samples from a defined population. Two of the most common techniques are simple random sampling and stratified random sampling, which will be described in the next sections. Additional sampling techniques, intended specifically for longitudinal research, are described in Chapter 10.

Simple Random Sampling.   In **simple random sampling,** all the individuals in the defined population have an equal and independent chance of being selected as a member of the sample. By *independent,* we mean that the selection of one individual does not affect in any way the chances of selection of any other individual.

A simple random sample can be selected by various means. For example, the researchers might assign a number to each individual in the population and use a computer-based random number generator or a hard-copy table of random numbers to select the needed number of individuals.

Simple random sampling is most feasible in survey research. For example, if researchers wish to know the opinion of psychologists on some educational issue, they might be able to obtain a directory of a national organization for psychologists, such as the American Psychological Association. They then can draw a simple random sample of psychologists from the directory list and request the sample group to complete a mailed questionnaire or phone interview.

Not everyone in the sample is likely to agree to participate. In this case, the resulting sample of participants is no longer a random sample. If the response rate to the questionnaire or phone interview falls below 70 percent, you should be concerned about the randomness of the sample.

Stratified Random Sampling.   **Stratified random sampling** is a procedure for ensuring that individuals in the population who have certain characteristics are represented in the sample. For example, suppose that researchers are interested in whether boys and girls from four different home environments (single parent, mother; single parent, father; both parents together; guardians) have different attitudes toward mathematics.

If the researchers draw a simple random sample from a school district's list of students, there is a chance that they will get few or no students in one of these eight classifications: (1) boys with single parent, mother; (2) girls with single parent, mother; (3) boys with single parent, father; (4) girls with single parent, father; (5) boys with both parents together; (6) girls with both parents together; (7) boys with one or more guardians; and (8) girls with one or more guardians.

To ensure that all eight groups are represented in the sample, the researchers can use stratified random sampling. They would consider each of these groups (called *strata* or *levels* in sampling terminology) as a separate population. They then would draw a random sample of a given size from each group, thereby ensuring that each population is represented adequately in the sample.

Another option is to draw random samples of different sizes (but each size being an adequate number) so that the proportion of students in each group in the sample is the same as their proportion in the population. This procedure is called **proportional random sampling.**

Volunteer Samples

Educational research usually requires face-to-face interaction with individuals, as when the researcher needs to administer tests under standardized conditions or try out a new instructional method. It is expensive, though, to define a population that covers an extensive geographical area, randomly select a sample from that population, and then travel to the individuals in the sample in order to collect the necessary data. Therefore, researchers typically work with nonrandom samples.

Sampling is further complicated by the fact that researchers have the legal and ethical requirement to obtain informed consent from individuals or their guardians before involving them in a research project. An individual can refuse to participate for any reason. As a result, nearly all educational research is conducted with **volunteer samples,** that is, samples based on individuals' expression of willingness to participate in a research study rather than on systematic sampling strategies. Samples of this type sometimes are called *convenience samples*.

In the PDS study, the sample of preservice teachers was drawn from individuals enrolled in either a PDS teacher preparation program or a campus-based teacher preparation program, both of which were situated in the same university. The researchers note: "Entrance into the PDS program was voluntary" (Ridley et al., 2005, p. 48). Therefore, it seems reasonable to conclude that the total sample was a volunteer sample rather than a sample randomly drawn from a defined population. The name of the university is not stated, but it is likely the same one where three of the four authors work (Arizona State University).

Population Validity

The main difficulty with volunteer samples is that they might have different characteristics than the population that they are intended to represent. If the differences are large, the sample is said to have low population validity. The term **population validity** refers to the degree to which the sample of individuals in the study is representative of the population from which it was selected.

Population validity is established in part by demonstrating that the selected sample is similar to the accessible population, which is the immediate population from which the researchers drew their sample. The researchers also must demonstrate that the accessible population is similar to the target population, which is the population to which the researchers wish to generalize or apply their research findings.

For example, if researchers are interested in investigating career planning among high school seniors, the target population could be defined as all seniors in U.S. public and private high schools. This target population most likely would be too large from which to draw a sample. The researchers might then limit themselves to their local community—let's say, Denver, Colorado. In this case, Denver high school seniors would be the accessible population from which the sample would be drawn.

To establish population validity, the researchers need to demonstrate similarity on variables that are relevant to their research problem among (1) the sample, (2) the accessible population (Denver high school seniors), and (3) the target population (all U.S. high school seniors). For example, it seems reasonable to expect that career planning would vary by students' gender, socioeconomic status, and ethnicity. Therefore, the researchers should determine the extent to which their sample, the accessible population, and the target population are similar on these variables. Evidence of similarity helps to establish the population validity of their sample.

In making a critical evaluation of a research report, you should pay close attention to the target population, accessible population, and the sample. It also is important to determine the degree to which students, teachers, or other groups in the research sample are similar to the groups in the local setting to which you wish to apply the research findings. As the similarity between the research sample and the local group decreases, the research results are less likely to apply.

Comparison of the research sample with your local group sometimes proves to be a difficult task, for several reasons. First, researchers often include very little information in their reports about the sample and the accessible population from which it was drawn. Second, local educational organizations often can provide only limited information about the characteristics of the local group that is of interest to you. Third, it might be difficult to decide which differences between the research sample and the local group would actually affect the applicability of the research findings.

Given these problems, the best test of population validity might be to try out the educational practices suggested by the research findings and collect data to see how well they generalize to your local groups. This approach involves action research, which we describe in Chapter 19.

Method Section: Measures

Research data are only as sound as the measures used to obtain them. Therefore, the research report should include information about each measure that was used: the construct being measured, the scoring procedures for the measure, and evidence of the measure's validity and reliability. You might be able to find additional information you want about a measure by using one of the search engines or bibliographic indexes described later in the chapter.

Another good way to learn about a measure used in a research study is to examine a copy of it. Some school systems and universities maintain collections of commonly used tests and the manuals that accompany them. Otherwise you might be able to order a copy from the publisher. If the measure was developed specifically for the research study, you can write the researchers to request a copy. They should be willing to send you a copy if you state a reasonable purpose for your request and if you provide assurances that you will maintain the confidentiality of the measure.

Types of Measures

Four types of measures are commonly used in quantitative research studies: (1) paper-and-pencil tests and scales, (2) questionnaires, (3) interviews, and (4) direct observation. Each type is described in the following sections.

Tests, Scales, and Performance Measures.   **Tests** measure an individual's knowledge, skills, or depth of understanding within a curriculum domain. They typically yield a total score, based on the number of items answered correctly.

Scales measure an individual's attitudes, personality characteristics, emotional states, interests, values, and related factors. They typically yield a total score, which is the sum of the individual's responses to item scales. For example, a Likert-type scale item typically has five response options (such as 5 points for "strongly agree" to 1 point for "strongly disagree").

Many tests and scales are designed to fit on standard-size (8½" × 11") sheets of paper. Individuals can write their responses directly on the test sheets or on an answer sheet with a pen or pencil. For this reason, these measures traditionally have been called *paper-and-pencil measures.* Now that computers are commonly available, test and scale items often are displayed on computer screens, and research participants can enter their responses using the computer keypad.

Performance measures involve the evaluation of individuals as they carry out a complex real-life task. A driving test is an example of a performance measure, because the test requires that you drive a car while being evaluated by a state examiner.

Performance measures typically must be individually administered. Paper-and-pencil measures, or their computer counterpart, are used much more frequently in educational research than performance measures because they generally are less costly to administer and require less time. Also, because of the huge number and variety of paper-and-pencil measures, researchers usually can find at least one available measure for virtually any variable.

Paper-and-pencil tests and scales have certain limitations. First, most of them require that the person being tested be able to read and write. Thus, individuals who lack these skills will be unable to show what they know or think about the constructs measured by such tests and scales. Another limitation is that they rely on self-report. This is not a serious problem when measuring academic achievement, but in attitude measurement, for example, individuals might wish to hide their true attitude in order to produce a socially acceptable response. The third limitation is that many tests and scales are group administered. Thus, it is difficult for the researcher to determine the physical and mental state of the persons being assessed. If they happen to be ill, tired, or emotionally upset, they are likely to perform atypically on the measure.

One of the outcome measures in the PDS study was a 38-item multiple-choice test of professional teaching knowledge. Another was a written lesson plan prepared by each teacher in the sample. It seems reasonable to characterize it as a performance measure, because lesson planning is a real-life task required of teachers and because the teachers undoubtedly knew that their performance on this task would be rated for quality.

Questionnaires.   A paper-and-pencil test or scale usually measures one or two variables, such as knowledge of vocabulary or attitude toward school. In contrast, a **questionnaire** is a set of questions in paper-and-pencil or computer format that typically measures many variables. For example, a questionnaire might ask respondents about the type of computer they have, the software programs they use, the frequency of use of each program, their previous training in computers, and their intentions to expand their use of computers in the future. The response to each question constitutes a separate variable in the research study.

In evaluating a research questionnaire, ask yourself the following questions:

1. *Was the questionnaire pretested?* A research participant might interpret a questionnaire item differently than intended by the researcher. Therefore, the researcher should pilot, that is, try out, the questionnaire and analyze the responses of a small sample of individuals before starting the main study. Results of this pilot study should be used to refine the questionnaire. If a pilot study has been done, you can have more confidence that the findings reported in the main study are valid.

2. *Does the questionnaire include leading questions?* A copy of the questionnaire sometimes is included in the research report. Check it for leading questions, which are questions framed in such a way that individuals are given hints about the kind of response that is expected. Results obtained from leading questions are likely to be biased, so they should be interpreted with caution.

3. *Does the questionnaire include psychologically threatening questions?* The researcher should avoid questionnaire items that might be psychologically threatening to the respondents. For example, a questionnaire sent to school principals concerning the morale of their teachers would be threatening to some principals, because low morale suggests that they are failing in part of their job. If they feel threatened, the principals might not complete and return the questionnaire. If they do return it, little confidence can be placed in the accuracy of their responses because of their ego involvement in the situation.

4. *Do the individuals who received the questionnaire have the requested information?* Researchers inadvertently might send a questionnaire to a sample that does not have the

desired information. If this happens, the sample will provide inaccurate information or simply not complete the questionnaire.

In the PDS study, one of the outcome measures was postlesson reflection. The measure consisted of a questionnaire containing two open-ended items. One asked teachers to compare their lesson plan to the learning outcomes they actually achieved in the lesson. The other asked teachers to discuss how the lesson might be improved.

These were **open-ended items,** because teachers were required to write responses in their own words. Some questionnaires contain **closed-ended items,** which require individuals to make a forced choice among options. For example, some questionnaires include closed-ended items in the form of attitude scales. The individual might be asked to circle the number on the scale that best characterizes their level of agreement or disagreement with the item. For example, the statement "I believe that social justice should be a primary goal of schooling" might have the following choices: 5 = strongly agree, 4 = agree, 3 = neutral, 2 = disagree, 1 = strongly disagree. More information about the construction of questionnaires is provided in Chapter 10.

Interviews.   Unlike paper-and-pencil tests, scales, and questionnaires, **interviews** involve the collection of verbal—and sometimes nonverbal—data through direct interaction between the researcher and the individuals being studied.

The main advantage of interviews is their adaptability. The researcher usually creates a schedule of questions for the interview but allows the interviewers to ask additional questions in order to obtain the fullest possible response from the individual or to follow up on an unexpected response. Another advantage of interviews is that they can elicit data of greater depth than is possible with other measurement techniques. For example, most questionnaires tend to be shallow; that is, they fail to probe deeply enough to produce a full picture of the respondents' opinions and feelings.

The major disadvantage of interviews is that the direct interaction between researcher and interviewee makes it easy for subjectivity and bias to occur. The research participant may be eager to please the interviewer or may on the other hand feel a vague antagonism toward the interviewer. These interviewee feelings or the tendency of interviewers to seek out answers that support their preconceived notions are a few of the types of interview bias that can occur.

The following questions will help you evaluate research studies that use interviews to collect data.

1. *How well were the interviewers trained?* The level of training required for interviewers is directly related to the type of information being collected. Less training is required for structured interviews, because the interviewer asks specific questions from an interview schedule and does not deviate from them. More training is required for semistructured and unstructured interviews, because the interviewer does not employ a detailed interview guide. Instead, the interviewer has a general plan and decides on the spot what questions and comments to use in order to lead the interviewee toward the interviewer's objectives. Information on the training that interviewers received should be included in the research report.

2. *How was information recorded?* Audiotaping is the most accurate method of recording interview information. If interviewers take notes instead of audiotaping the interview, they might overlook important information or take biased notes.

3. *Were the interview procedures pilot tested before the study began?* Because interviewing tends to be highly subjective, the researcher must employ various safeguards to obtain objective data. A careful pilot study is necessary to develop these safeguards before data for the main study are collected. The pilot study should be described in the research report.

4. *Were leading or psychologically threatening questions asked?* As with questionnaires, leading and psychologically threatening questions can invalidate interview data.

If an interview was a primary measure in a research study, the report should include at least the main questions that were asked. You should study these questions for signs of bias. More information about the construction of interviews is provided in Chapter 10.

Direct Observation.   **Direct observation** involves an observer collecting data while an individual is engaged in some form of behavior or while an event is unfolding. The observer generally uses a standard observation form that defines each variable and provides directions for recording each observed occurrence of it.

Direct observation yields more accurate data about particular variables than questionnaires or interviews, because questionnaires and interviews rely on self-report, which is more susceptible to distortion and error than direct, impartial observation. However, a disadvantage of direct observation is that it tends to be very time-consuming. Also, the observer might change the situation being observed, albeit unintentionally.

In evaluating the use of observational procedures in a research study, you should consider the following questions.

1. *Were high-inference or low-inference variables observed?* Observational variables differ in the amount of inference required by the observer. A **high-inference variable** requires the observer to examine a behavior and then think carefully about whether it is the result of an underlying cognitive or emotional process. A **low-inference variable** only requires the observer to examine a behavior and then decide whether it is an instance of a behavioral construct. The validity of the observer's data will be more of an issue if the observational variables are high-inference than if they are low-inference.

For example, an observer will need to engage in a greater degree of inference to decide how much enthusiasm a teacher is exhibiting during a lesson than to decide how many verbal praise statements the teacher made. Enthusiasm is a cognitive and emotional construct that underlies and motivates behavior. A verbal praise statement is a construct that can be defined in terms of the language that a person uses. It does not require inferences about the individual's underlying cognitions and emotions.

2. *Were observers trained to identify the variables to be observed?* The researcher should describe the extent of training given to the observers.

3. *How long was the observation period?* The observation period should be of sufficient duration to obtain a representative sample of the behaviors being studied. Otherwise the observation data could yield atypical results. The necessary period of observation will depend on such factors as the nature of the behaviors being observed, the circumstances under which the behavior occurs, and its frequency of occurrence.

4. *How conspicuous were the observers?* For ethical reasons, observers in most research studies need to be visible to the research participants. Consequently, the observers are likely to have some impact on the participants. This problem can be overcome to a certain extent if the observers do not record any observational data initially. In classrooms, for example, students become accustomed to observers after a while and engage in their customary behavior. You should examine the research report to determine whether the researchers were sensitive to the possibility of observer effects and took steps to minimize them.

In the PDS study, each teacher was not observed directly while teaching a lesson. Instead, the researchers followed the common practice of videotaping the lesson, which is a form of direct observation, but with the advantage that the videotape can be viewed repeatedly for rating purposes. Raters observed each videotaped lesson and rated it on the following categories: "motivational set, instruction, classroom management, interest/engagement, feedback, assessment, and closure" (Ridley et al., 2005, p. 51).

Content Analysis.   Researchers sometimes focus their observations on documents produced or used by research participants. The investigation of data derived from documents is called **content analysis.** For example, researchers might study how males and females are portrayed in textbooks or the issues that are mentioned in the minutes of school board meetings.

Content analysis involves the development of categories and a frequency account of the occurrence of each category in the document. For example, a researcher might form the following categories for the analysis of elementary school mathematics textbooks: number calculation problems, word problems involving real-life situations that children might encounter, and word problems involving real-life situations that children are not likely to encounter. The researcher might collect data about the frequency and percentage of each type of problem in different textbook series.

In evaluating the soundness of a content analysis, you should look for evidence that (1) the categories are clearly defined and worthy of study, (2) the procedure for selecting a sample of documents is sound, and (3) different observers are able to use the categories reliably.

Validity of Measures

The definitive guide for determining the quality of tests and other measures is ***Standards for Educational and Psychological Testing*** (American Educational Research Association et al., 1999). We refer to this book hereafter as the *Standards*. According to the *Standards*, a good test is one that yields reliable test scores from which we can make interpretations that have strong validity.

The key concepts in this view of test quality are validity and reliability. We discuss validity in this section of the chapter and reliability in the next.

Test validity refers to the "degree to which evidence and theory support the interpretation of test scores entailed by proposed uses of tests" (*Standards*, p. 9). For example, if we administer a science achievement test to a group of students, each student earns a score on the test. We would interpret this score as a representation of how much each student has learned about science relative to other students. It is helpful to think about this interpretation as a claim that we make about the scores on this test.

Note that, according to the *Standards*, a test is neither valid nor invalid. Furthermore, the scores earned by individuals who take the test are neither valid nor invalid. Rather, it is our interpretations of the test scores—or, in other words, the claims that we make about the test scores—that are valid or invalid. Test developers and test users need to provide empirical evidence that their interpretations and claims are valid. We might find that one claim about the test scores is valid, but that another claim about the same test scores is invalid.

Five types of evidence and theory can be used to demonstrate the validity of the interpretations we might make from individuals' scores on a test or other measure:

1. Evidence from test content
2. Evidence from internal structure
3. Evidence from relationship to other variables
4. Evidence from response processes
5. Evidence from consequences of testing

Some types of evidence might be more important than others for judging the validity of a test used in a research study. To make this judgment, you need to be familiar with all five types. Also, you should be aware that authors of older research reports used different terms to refer to these types of evidence. The terms used in the 1999 edition of the *Standards* are intended to convey the fact that there are not different types of test validity. Rather, there are only different types of evidence to support test validity, which is a unitary construct.

Evidence from Test Content.   **Content-related evidence of test validity** involves a demonstration that the content of the test's items matches the content that it is designed to measure. For example, researchers might claim that the XYZ Test is a valid measure of how much students have learned about algebra in high school. To support their claim, they might argue that the test has **face validity,** which involves the degree to which the test *appears* to measure what it claims to measure. For example, we might examine the items of the XYZ Test and conclude that the test is valid because the items correspond to our view of what high school students typically are taught in an algebra course.

The evidence for test validity would be much stronger if we went beyond appearance (i.e., the "face" of the test) by systematically comparing the test content with course content. This comparison is time-consuming, because we need to analyze in minute detail the textbooks, lesson plans, handouts, classroom assignments, and teacher-made tests, as well as each item on the XYZ Test.

Content-related evidence of test validity is particularly important in research on how different teaching methods affect students' learning. The test of learning should measure as precisely as possible the curriculum content that was taught in the methods under investigation.

In the PDS study, the validity of the outcome measures was not discussed explicitly. However, the researchers' description of the scoring rubrics for the written lesson plans, videotape recordings of teaching performance, and responses to questionnaire items relating to postlesson reflection mentioned features of teaching that most educators would consider to be valid, in that they are generally accepted indicators of good teaching practices.

Evidence from Internal Structure. Nearly all tests and other measures have multiple items. These items and their relationship to each other constitute the internal structure of the test. An examination of a test's internal structure can provide evidence about its validity.

Suppose that researchers claim that a particular test, which has 10 items, measures a teacher's desire to engage in continuous professional development. If this claim is true, each of the 10 items should measure this variable. This means that if a teacher responded to an item in a certain way, we would predict a similar response to all the other items; conversely, a teacher who responded to the item in a different way should respond to the other items the same way. This prediction can be tested by the use of correlational statistics (see Chapters 7 and 11).

Evidence from Relationship to Other Variables. The *Standards* describes several types of validity evidence that have a common feature. The evidence is based on the degree of relationship between individuals' scores on the test and their scores on another measure. We consider several of these types of validity evidence in this section.

Predictive evidence of test validity involves a demonstration that individuals' scores on the test predict their future performance on another test or measure. For example, suppose that the developers of a test claim that it measures skill in reading comprehension among students in the upper grades. If the test in fact measures reading comprehension, it is reasonable to predict that eighth-grade students who earn higher scores on it will also earn higher grades in their high school courses, because good reading comprehension is necessary for success in these courses. The researchers can collect empirical data to test this hypothesis. If the results support the hypothesis, they can serve as evidence of the test's validity.

Another option is **convergent evidence of test validity,** which involves a demonstration that individuals' scores on the test are related to their scores on another test or measure of the same variable. For example, the developers can examine the relationship between an individual's scores on the test and scores on another test that purportedly also measures reading comprehension. If students who earn higher scores on the developer's test also earn higher scores on another test measuring the same variable, this can serve as evidence of both tests' validity. The evidence is even stronger if the other test has a well-established body of evidence supporting its validity.

Some tests are rather long, so developers might want to create a shorter version. Evidence supporting the validity of the longer test might be strong, but this does not mean that the shorter version also has validity. To demonstrate the validity of the shorter version, the developers need to do studies in which a sample of individuals take both versions. If individuals who earn higher scores on the long version also earn higher scores on the shorter version, this serves as evidence of the shorter test's validity. This type of evidence, based on administration of two versions of the same test within a brief time interval, is called **concurrent evidence of test validity** in the *Standards*.

Evidence from Response Processes.   Taking a test requires the test-taker to engage in particular cognitive and evaluative processes. Some of the processes engaged might be consistent with the variable that the test is designed to measure, but other processes that are also engaged during test-taking might not be. **Response-process evidence of test validity** involves a demonstration that the processes used by individuals in taking the test are consistent with the particular variable that the test presumably measures.

For example, a test of critical thinking might be designed to engage students' higher-order reasoning processes to solve certain types of mathematical problems. Suppose some students obtain high scores on the test because they had received extensive instruction on these problem types and thus were able to solve them by applying specific algorithms rather than by engaging in higher-order reasoning processes. In this case, the validity of the claim that the test scores reflect higher-order reasoning would be compromised.

Evidence from Consequences of Testing.   Individuals' scores on a test can have consequences for them. **Consequential evidence of test validity** is the extent to which the values implicit in the variables measured by a test and in the intended uses of the test are consistent with the values of test-takers, those who will use the test results to make decisions, and other stakeholders.

For example, students' low scores on a standardized achievement test might have the consequence of the students' being denied admission to the college of their choice. Children's scores on a test battery might have the consequence of labeling them as having a learning disability, with the further consequence that they might be assigned to special education teachers. These consequences need to be examined carefully to determine whether they are appropriate. Evidence resulting from this examination can and should be used in making judgments about a test's validity.

These examples illustrate the direct consequences for individuals that can result from interpretations of their test scores by others. At a more general level, policies about testing also have consequences. For example, some policy makers argue that preservice teachers should take and pass competency tests in order to obtain a teaching license, claiming that this requirement will result in a more effective teacher workforce (Mitchell, Robinson, Plake, & Knowles, 2001). More evidence relating to this claimed consequence of teacher competency testing needs to be collected. This evidence can be used to judge the validity of the competency tests for their intended use by policy makers.

The researchers who conducted the PDS study did not explicitly discuss the consequential validity of their outcome measures. Nonetheless, consequential validity is a legitimate concern related to these measures. For example, suppose that policy makers, teacher educators, and others conclude that graduates of PDS programs are better teachers than graduates of traditional campus-based programs, because they perform better on these outcome measures. Their conclusions might be used to put pressure on teacher educators to change their current programs to PDS programs. The process of change might be stressful and time-consuming, and university-based teacher educators might have to learn new skills and deal with budgetary problems.

In short, the measures used in the PDS study have potentially serious consequences. Both the researchers who conducted the study and readers of the study need to consider these consequences as part of their examination of the measures' validity.

Reliability of Measures

A test or other measure is considered to have **reliability** to the extent that it is free of measurement error. In classical test theory, **measurement error** is construed as the difference between the scores that individuals actually obtain on a test and their true scores.

A **true score** is the score that an individual would receive if it were possible to obtain a perfect measure of performance. For example, if two testers score an individual's test and obtain different total scores, measurement error has occurred. Because there is only one true score that an individual can earn on the test, the assumption is that at least one of the scorers has miscalculated.

Less obviously, suppose a student takes the same achievement test on two different days and obtains two different scores. These different results also constitute measurement error. They are not errors in the usual sense of the word, that is, mistakes resulting from the student's lack of skill. Instead, they reflect shortcomings in the test's ability to measure the student's performance in a stable manner. Because an individual can only have one true score on a test, the assumption is that at least one of the test administrations on the two days must have measurement error.

A variety of factors can create measurement error. Possible factors are differences in the skill of those who administer the measure, changes in measurement conditions from one day to the next, temporary fluctuations in how individuals respond to the measurement situation, and features of the measure's items that affect different individuals differently. It is virtually impossible to eliminate all these sources of error from a test or other measure.

If a test or other measure has very low reliability, it will produce large errors of measurement. These errors will obscure the effects of methods and programs or the magnitude of a relationship between variables. This problem can be understood by considering the case of a completely unreliable test. After the test is administered, the resulting scores will consist entirely of measurement error, meaning that they are essentially random numbers. Random numbers obviously cannot reveal the true effects of educational programs or the true relationships between variables. For this reason you need to check how reliable a measure is before you reach conclusions about research findings based on its use.

The degree of reliability of an educational measure is usually expressed by a **reliability coefficient.** A reliability coefficient is a type of correlation coefficient, which we explain in Chapters 7 and 12. For now it is sufficient for you to know that reliability coefficients range from .00, which indicates no reliability, to 1.00, which indicates perfect reliability. In other words, a reliability coefficient of .00 means that the test scores are meaningless because they consist entirely of measurement error; in contrast, a reliability coefficient of 1.00 means that the measure has absolutely no measurement error. As a rule of thumb, a measure is considered reliable for most research and practical purposes if its reliability coefficient is .80 or higher.

Procedures have been developed to estimate the magnitude of the different types of measurement errors in a test. We describe four of these procedures in the next sections. In doing so, we use the term *test* to refer generally to various forms of measurement, such as achievement tests, attitude scales, observational scales, and frequency counts of content analysis categories.

Item Consistency.   One type of measurement error is caused by inconsistencies in the items that make up the test. For example, if a test of visual creativity contains some items that measure one variable and other items that measure a somewhat different variable, the total score will be an inaccurate indicator of visual creativity. Therefore, test developers strive for **item consistency,** that is, a test in which all the items measure the same construct. In other words, they want the items to be consistent. If the items are perfectly consistent, individuals who score one way on an item should score the same way on all the remaining items. **Cronbach's alpha** is a reliability coefficient that is commonly used to quantify the extent to which an individual's scores across different items on a test are consistent with each another.

Stability of Measurement.   As stated above, measurement error often occurs when individuals take the same test on several different occasions. These variations can occur for several reasons. For example, an individual might be fatigued on one testing occasion and rested on the next. Or an individual might have reviewed a relevant item of information just before one testing occasion, but not just before the next.

If a test is free of this type of measurement error, individuals should earn the same score on each testing occasion. To determine the extent to which this is the case, researchers administer the test to a sample of individuals and then after a delay they administer the same test again to the same sample. Scores obtained from the two administrations are then correlated to determine their reliability, or in other words, their consistency across time. This type of reliability is called **test–retest reliability** or **test stability.**

Consistency of Administration and Scoring.   Individuals who administer or score tests can create measurement errors because of absentmindedness or some other reason, such as not knowing the correct procedures. Measures with highly objective scores, such as multiple-choice tests, tend to be free of this type of measurement error. However, even test-scoring machines have been known to make scoring mistakes because of mechanical defects. Measures with less objective scores, such as individually administered intelligence tests, personality tests, or high-inference observational scales, are more subject to administration and scoring errors.

The presence of test administration errors can be determined by having several individuals administer the same test to the same sample. Similarly, the presence of scoring errors can be determined by having several individuals or machines score the same set of tests. A reliability coefficient is calculated for the sets of scores to determine how well they agree. The degree of reliability among the individuals who administer or score measures is sometimes called **inter-rater reliability.** This type of reliability was an important consideration in the PDS study.

The multiple-choice test of professional teaching knowledge could be scored with virtually no likelihood of error, but the other outcome measures required rater or observer judgment. Therefore, the researchers had two individuals rate each lesson plan, videotape of teaching performance, and postlesson reflection. Moreover, these individuals were kept blind as to whether the teacher was in the PDS or campus-based program. This blind scoring feature is desirable because it eliminates, or at least greatly reduces, rater bias in judging each teacher's effectiveness.

In their journal article the researchers stated, "Initial interrater reliability for the lesson plan, video, and postlesson reflection averaged .82 for the student teacher and 1st-year teacher data" (Ridley et al., 2005, p. 51). A reliability coefficient of this magnitude generally is considered acceptable.

Standard Error of Measurement.   Another approach to expressing the magnitude of a test's reliability is to calculate the standard error of measurement. This reliability statistic is based on the assumption that each individual's score on a test has two components: the individual's true score and the measurement error.

Suppose that the test measures knowledge of vocabulary. The individual's true score would be a perfect measure of the amount of this ability that the individual actually possesses. The difference between the individual's obtained score on the test and the individual's true score is the measurement error. Although we cannot know the individual's true score (except on a perfectly reliable test), the **standard error of measurement** is an estimate of the probable range within which the individual's true score falls.

The calculation procedures and rationale for the standard error of measurement are fairly sophisticated. For present purposes, it is sufficient to know that the calculation of a standard error of measurement enables the researcher to make a statement like "The chances are about 95 in 100 that this sample's true score on the test lies between 12.75 and 16.63." It is advantageous for researchers to use a highly reliable test, because it reduces the range of values likely to contain the true score.

Evaluating Researchers' Determination of Reliability.   We have described four procedures for estimating a test's reliability: calculation of item consistency, stability of measurement, consistency of test administration and scoring, and the standard error of measurement. It is unlikely that researchers will determine all these types of reliability for each measure used in a study. Depending on the measure involved and the research situation, one of these types of reliability is usually of most concern.

Item Response Theory

It is very difficult to develop a test that is reliable for all individuals. For example, consider the measurement of mathematical problem-solving ability. This ability varies across a long continuum, from none at all, to the ability to solve the types of mathematical problems taught in school, and ultimately to the ability to solve complex problems in theoretical mathematics.

A test that contained primarily items in the mid-range of this ability would be unsuitable for estimating the true score of individuals having the most rudimentary problem-solving skills in mathematics or the true score of individuals with highly sophisticated problem-solving skills. Also, even for individuals in the mid-range of this ability, the test might have satisfactory reliability for individuals at some points in this mid-range but not for individuals at other points.

These problems can be overcome to a large extent by developing tests based on item response theory (IRT). **Item response theory** is based on the assumption that individuals with different amounts of an ability will perform differently on the items measuring that ability. For example, suppose we have a large sample of items that represents the entire continuum of mathematical problem-solving ability and a large sample of individuals who also represent the entire continuum of this ability. Most of the individuals will be able to answer the simplest items. As the items become more difficult, fewer individuals—the ones with more problem-solving ability—will be able to answer them.

By using individuals' item responses and IRT statistical procedures, test developers can order the items by difficulty level so that they can determine the level at which a particular individual "tests out." By this we mean that the test items are placed in order such that a particular individual is able to answer most of the items below that difficulty level and few or no items above that difficulty level. Once we find the difficulty level at which the individual tests out, we can administer more items at that difficulty level in order to improve the reliability of measurement.

Test development using IRT procedures is complex and expensive. Also, test administration typically requires a computer that presents items one at a time and that adjusts item difficulty based on the individual's responses to preceding items. However, because of the superior reliability of tests based on IRT, this approach is being used increasingly to develop high-stakes tests, such as those used to assess students' academic achievement or potential for success in university studies and different occupations. Scores from such test administrations are likely to be used increasingly in educational research studies.

Limitations to Tests of Validity and Reliability

Researchers sometimes determine the validity and reliability of their measures by using evidence from other studies. If these studies involve a different population from the one used in the researcher's study, the validity and reliability evidence might not be applicable. In other words, a measure might be valid and reliable for one population but not for another. Therefore, you need to check the source of the validity and reliability evidence that is presented in a research report.

Another problem sometimes found in research reports is that the researchers develop their own measure but do not adequately check its validity and reliability. A common reason for not making these checks is that they are time-consuming and expensive.

Rather than developing new measures, many researchers choose well-developed existing measures. If you are planning to do your own quantitative research study, you should consider whether you can frame your research problem in such a way that you can rely on existing measures of your variables rather than having to develop new ones.

Sources of Information about Established Measures

Thousands of measures have been developed for use in educational research and related disciplines. They measure a wide range of individual characteristics, including academic

FIGURE *6.1*   Sources of Information about Established Measures for Use in Education

Behavioral Assessment

Herson, M., & Bellack, A. S. (2002). *Dictionary of behavioral assessment techniques.* Clinton Corners, NY: Percheron.

Comprehensive Handbooks of Psychological Assessment

Hersen, M. (Ed.). (2004). *Comprehensive handbook of psychological assessment* (Vols. 1–4). Hoboken, NJ: Wiley. Each volume covers tests for a particular purpose: intellectual and neuropsychological assessment, personality assessment, behavioral assessment, and industrial and organizational assessment.

Exceptional Students

Taylor, R. L. (2009). *Assessment of exceptional students: Educational and psychological procedures* (8th ed.). Upper Saddle River, NJ: Pearson/Merrill.

Family Processes

Touliatos, J., Perlmutter, B. F., Straus, M. A., & Holden, G. W. (Eds.). (2001). *Handbook of family measurement techniques* (Vols. 1–3). Thousand Oaks, CA: Sage.

Mental Measurements Yearbooks

Geisinger, R. A., Spies, R. A., Carlson, J. F., & Plake, B. S. (Eds.). (2007). *Mental measurements yearbook* (17th ed.). Lincoln, NE: Buros Institute of Mental Measurements.

Continually updated to include new tests, revised tests, and frequently referenced tests. The online version of these yearbooks is Test Reviews Online (see below). Another relevant resource is *Tests in Print,* which is a hard-copy index, updated periodically, to all the Yearbooks.

Social Processes

Kempf-Leonard, K. (Ed.). (2004). *Encyclopedia of social measurement* (Vols. 1–3). Washington, DC: American Psychological Association.

Test Link

Website (www.ets.org/testcoll/index.html) maintained by the Educational Testing Service containing a database of information about more than 25,000 tests. A small number of these tests can be obtained at its website. In the search window on the home page, enter the phrase "Tests on Demand" or "Tests in Microfiche."

Test Reviews Online

Test Reviews Online (http://buros.unl.edu/buros/jsp/search .jsp) is a Web-based version of the *Mental Measurements Yearbook,* providing information on nearly 4,000 tests and critical reviews for many of them. The test information is free, but the critical reviews are fee based.

---

achievement, academic aptitude, learning styles, personality traits, self-concept, attitudes, and vocational interests.

As stated above, before developing your own measure for research or practice, you should consider searching for one that has already been developed and is suitable for your purposes. Various search engines and bibliographic indexes are available to help you conduct a search for suitable measures. The characteristics of search engines and bibliographic indexes are explained in Chapter 4.

Some of the more commonly used search engines and bibliographic indexes are listed in Figure 6.1. Of these, the *Mental Measurements Yearbook* probably is the best known and most used resource for obtaining information about measures used in education and other disciplines. These same resources also can help you evaluate measures encountered in research reports or school systems. These resources typically describe each measure and summarize what is known about its validity and reliability. Widely used measures, particularly aptitude and achievement tests, generally include manuals that provide some or all of this information. In addition, you can inspect the measure itself and make judgments about its soundness and applicability to your needs.

Developing a Measure

Developing a measure is a complex process involving many steps. This is particularly true for achievement tests, attitude scales, and personality scales. The development steps include the following:

- Define the construct that is to be measured and show how it relates to similar but different constructs. Justify the importance of the construct.

- Define the population for whom the construct and the measure is appropriate.
- Review related measures that have already been developed. Explain why your new measure is needed.
- Develop a prototype of the measure. Write an adequate number of items, with attention to the relationship of each item to the construct and to the other items in the measure. Write the items so that they will be comprehensible for the intended audience.
- Conduct a field test of the measure. Collect adequate data for an analysis of each item.
- Revise the measure based on the field results. Continue the cycle of field testing and revision until the measure has achieved accepted standards for validity, reliability, and usability by those who will administer it to individuals and samples in the target population.

This list of steps illustrates that developing a measure requires expertise and time. In fact, some researchers conduct studies whose only purpose is to determine the validity and reliability of measures that they or others have developed. The following citations represent examples of this kind of study:

Hager, K. D., & Slocum, T. A. (2008). Utah's alternate assessment: Evidence regarding six aspects of validity. *Education and Training in Developmental Disabilities, 43*(2), 144–161.

Smith, D. W., Lee, J. T., Colwell, B., & Stevens-Manser, S. (2008). Confirming the structure of the "Why Do You Smoke?" questionnaire: A community resource for adolescent tobacco cessation. *Journal of Drug Education, 38*(1), 85–95.

Thompson, T., Sharp, J., & Alexander, J. (2008). Assessing the psychometric properties of a scenario-based measure of achievement guilt and shame. *Educational Psychology, 28*(4), 373–395.

If you are planning to conduct your own research study, you should consider searching for well-developed measures for your variables. Otherwise, you will need to acquire expertise in measurement and extend the timeline for your study to include measure development.

Method Section: Research Design and Procedures

Research reports should describe the research design that was used to obtain the data needed to test the hypotheses, answer the questions, or achieve the objectives of the research study. Chapters 10 through 13 explain how quantitative studies vary in their research design.

As a simple illustration, consider this research question: Do students in small classes learn more than students in large classes? One research design for answering this question would be to find existing classes that are large or small, all of which have students at the same grade level learning the same curriculum subject. We can compare the two groups of classes on an achievement test administered after a certain period of instructional time has elapsed.

Another research design would be to start with a sample of teachers and randomly assign them to teach either a large or small class. This is a classic experimental design, because it involves manipulating a situation rather than studying a situation that is already in place. As in the research design described in the preceding paragraph, we can compare the two groups of classes on an achievement test after a certain period of instructional time has elapsed.

This illustration demonstrates that the same research question can be answered by two different research designs. The designs have advantages and disadvantages relative to each other—a matter that is discussed in subsequent chapters.

The descriptions of procedures in research reports vary in length. Because descriptive research designs (see Chapter 10) generally are simple, the researchers might consider it sufficient to mention how and when the measures were administered. If descriptive data were collected periodically, as in longitudinal research, the time intervals should be specified.

Other research designs, especially experimental designs (see Chapter 13), require more detailed explanations. For example, the report should indicate the timeline of the experiment so that readers know when the various measures and treatments were administered. Also, each of the experimental treatments (for example, a new teaching method) should be described so that other researchers could implement them as intended if they wish to replicate the study.

You will need a basic understanding of various research designs in order to evaluate the adequacy of the research design used in a particular quantitative research study. Chapters 10 through 13 are intended to help you develop this understanding. In addition to explaining each design, we present a report of an actual research study that used it.

Results Section

The results section of a quantitative research report presents the results of statistical analyses of the data from the measures that were administered to the sample. Interpretation of the results is left to the final section of the report, namely, the discussion section.

In the PDS study, the essential results came from comparisons of PDS-based and campus-based teachers on the outcome measures. These comparisons are shown in Table 6.2 in the form of descriptive statistics. The text of the journal article also reports tests of statistical significance. We explain commonly used statistical techniques and conditions for their appropriate use in Chapters 7, 8, and 9. Then in Chapters 10 through 13, we explain how these statistical techniques are commonly used in conjunction with particular quantitative research designs. If you are planning to do a quantitative research study, you might find that reading these chapters is sufficient for your professional needs. However, depending on your degree or credential program of studies, you might be required to take courses on the research statistics and measurement statistics used in test development. Such courses will enhance your capacity to do your own research or interpret research findings in the literature.

The mean scores shown in Table 6.2 are fairly straightforward and demonstrate that PDS teachers were superior to teachers prepared in campus-based programs on all outcome measures, except for the postlesson reflection measure administered to first-year teachers.

Discussion Section

The final substantive section of a quantitative research report is the discussion (sometimes called *conclusions*). Following the discussion section is a list of bibliographic citations for the publications mentioned in the body of the report. Next, there might be one or more appendices, such as a supplemental statistical analysis or copy of a measure that was used in the study.

The discussion section gives researchers the opportunity to express their own interpretations of the results, evaluate shortcomings in the design and execution of the study, draw conclusions about the practical and theoretical significance of the results, and make recommendations for further research.

In evaluating the discussion section, you must decide whether you agree with the researchers' judgments about how the results should be interpreted and their implications for theory and professional practice. The most critical factor in this evaluation is whether you think the researchers' judgments are supported by their empirical findings and the findings of previous research studies that they cited. Your ability to make this evaluation will

TABLE 6.2 Comparison of Mean Scores on Variables for Each Phase

| | Phase I: Student Teaching | | Phase II: First Year of Teaching | |
	Professional Development School	Campus	Professional Development School	Campus
Content retention				
Mean	26.10	26.68	Not measured	Not measured
Standard deviation	3.54	3.75		
N	10	12		
Lesson plan				
Mean	12	10.21	11.61	9.56
Standard deviation	3.3	4.26	3.7	3.59
N	10	14	14	12
Teaching effectiveness				
Mean	15.2	14.0	16.82	13.5
Standard deviation	2.35	3.96	2.90	4.58
N	10	14	14	12
Professional reflection				
Mean	3.78	3.57	4.29	5.04
Standard deviation	2.17	1.34	1.76	2.26
N	9	14	14	12

Source: Adapted from Table 2 on p. 52 of Ridley, D. S., Hurwitz, S., Hackett, M. R. D., & Miller, K. K. (2005). Comparing PDS and campus-based preservice teacher preparation: Is PDS-based preparation really better? *Journal of Teacher Education, 56*(1), 46–56. Copyright © 2005 by Sage Publications. Reprinted by permission of Sage Publications.

improve as you develop an understanding of research methodology and knowledge of the research literature to which a particular study contributes.

In the PDS study, the researchers reflected on their statistical results and the findings of previous related research and concluded, "The results . . . are beginning to suggest that teachers prepared at PDS-based preservice teacher education programs are indeed more instructionally effective than teachers prepared at a traditional campus-based program" (Ridley et al., 2005, p. 54).

As an educator, you might be called on to make a judgment about whether these "suggestive" findings are sufficiently compelling to warrant changing an existing campus-based teacher education program into a PDS-based program. If you decide to make this change, a lot of hard work will go to waste if there really is no difference in the effectiveness of the two types of programs. Conversely, if you decide not to make the change, you and your colleagues might continue preparing new teachers whose effectiveness is compromised by the fact that their program of studies did not include professional development schools.

Another conclusion you might reach is that further research is needed in order to be sure that PDS-based programs are superior to campus-based programs. If so, you will need to determine the shortcomings of existing research (including the study discussed in this chapter) and design a study, or group of studies, that would lead to conclusive results.

This situation illustrates the high stakes involved in conducting and interpreting research. If you wish to make a contribution to the improvement of education, you will need to learn all you can about research methodology. Otherwise, you and your colleagues might institute changes in practice that have no actual evidence to support them, or conversely, fail to make changes that would lead to genuine, demonstrable improvement of practice.

An example of
HOW QUANTITATIVE RESEARCH CAN HELP IN SOLVING PROBLEMS OF PRACTICE

The following problem of practice in education involves the science and math skills of American students relative to students from other nations.

> As the U.S. grows less competitive in terms of its scientific and technological prowess, competitive math bowls, robotics competitions and science fairs aim to draw in top student talent. "I think we have a generation where math and science became uncool," says Dr. Jim Hamos, program director of the National Science Foundation's Math and Science Partnership Program. "People are wondering what's the galvanizing moment [for math and science education], and competitiveness may be that galvanizer. It's one way to make science and math cool . . . as opposed to abstract and minimalist."
>
> *ASCD SmartBrief* news item, May 19, 2008, summarizing an article in the *Christian Science Monitor*, May 16, 2008

Are organized competitions the "galvanizer" to help the United States achieve excellence in science and math? We can't know for sure until we do research on this question. Here's one kind of research that might provide answers.

Quantitative researchers can do a longitudinal study to find out whether students who participate in these competitive activities go on to pursue science and math majors in college and subsequent careers in these fields to a greater extent than equally talented students who do not have this opportunity. If the research results favor the types of competitive activities featured in the article, they might cause policy makers to fund these activities and thereby increase the "scientific and technological prowess" of the United States.

Self-Check Test

1. Reports of quantitative research studies typically
   a. are written in a more personal style than are reports of qualitative research studies.
   b. follow the style guidelines of the American Psychological Association.
   c. do not include an abstract.
   d. begin with a description of the research design that was employed.

2. Many research studies in education are designed to test the effectiveness of different instructional methods. In this kind of research, the instructional method being studied constitutes a
   a. constant.
   b. scale.
   c. variable.
   d. research hypothesis.

3. In simple random sampling, researchers
   a. select a sample of individuals who are easily accessible in the target population.
   b. identify sample populations and randomly select one of them to be studied.
   c. ensure that each individual in the population has an equal chance of being in the sample.
   d. All of the above.

4. To evaluate population validity, researchers must analyze
   a. the selected sample, the accessible population, and the target population.
   b. the selected sample and the target population.
   c. the accessible population and the target population.
   d. the membership list used to define the target population.

5. A research questionnaire ideally should
   a. include several leading questions to put the respondent at ease.
   b. measure only one variable.
   c. be used instead of an interview to collect psychologically threatening information.
   d. undergo pretesting before being used with the actual research sample.

6. In a study that involves direct observation of classroom instruction, the best example of a low-inference observational variable would be
   a. teacher enthusiasm.
   b. amount of time allocated for seatwork.
   c. students' on-task behavior during seatwork.
   d. the cognitive level of students' responses to teacher questions.

7. If researchers want to develop a test whose items are ordered on a scale of difficulty, they will find it useful to
   a. do a content analysis to identify the constructs being measured.
   b. follow the procedures specified by item response theory.
   c. focus on collecting concurrent evidence of test validity.
   d. focus on collecting consequential evidence of test validity.

8. If a measure has high reliability, it means that it
   a. is relatively free of measurement error.
   b. can be understood and completed by most students.
   c. will yield valid results for most users.
   d. has a low Cronbach's alpha value.

9. All of the following typically appear in the discussion section of a quantitative research report, except
   a. summary of the statistical results.
   b. interpretation of the statistical results.
   c. speculations about the practical significance of the results.
   d. recommendations for further research.

Chapter References

American Educational Research Association, American Psychological Association, and National Council on Measurement in Education. (1999). *Standards for educational and psychological testing.* Washington, DC: American Educational Research Association.

American Psychological Association. (2001). *Publication manual of the American Psychological Association* (5th ed.). Washington, DC: Author. See also: www.apastyle.org

Evans, P. (1976). The Burt affair: Sleuthing in science. *APA Monitor, 12,* 1, 4.

Mitchell, K. J., Robinson, D. Z., Plake, B. S., and Knowles, K. T. (Eds.). (2001) *Testing teacher candidates: The role of licensure tests in improving teacher quality.* Washington, DC: National Academy Press.

Ridley, D. S., Hurwitz, S., Hackett, M. R. D., & Miller, K. K. (2005). Comparing PDS and campus-based preservice teacher preparation: Is PDS-based preparation really better? *Journal of Teacher Education, 56*(1), 46–56.

Resources for Further Study

Downing, S. M., & Haladyna, T. M. (Eds.). (2006). *Handbook of test development.* Mahwah, NJ: Lawrence Erlbaum.

The 32 chapters of this book cover all aspects of test development and use, including an extensive treatment of the kinds of evidence that can be used to establish a test's validity.

Fowler, F. J. (2008). *Survey research methods* (4th ed.). Thousand Oaks, CA: Sage.

This book provides a basic guide for designing and conducting research surveys involving questionnaires and interviews.

Among the topics covered are methods for constructing survey questions, methods for obtaining high response rates, and the use of computers, the Internet, landline phones, and cell phones to collect and analyze data.

Gall, M. D., Gall, J. P., & Borg, W. R. (2007). *Educational research* (8th ed.). Boston: Allyn & Bacon.

This book is intended for individuals who want to develop a deeper understanding of each of the topics covered in this chapter, usually as a basis for conducting one's own research.

Green, J. L., Camilli, G., & Elmore, P. B. (Eds.). (2006). *Handbook of complementary methods in education research*. Mahwah, NJ: Lawrence Erlbaum.

> The chapters in this book are written by experts in research methodology. Some of them cover topics that we discuss in Chapter 6, including direct observation, interviewing, measurement, item response theory, and survey research.

Krippendorff, K., & Bock, M. A. (Eds.). (2008). *The content analysis reader*. Thousand Oaks, CA: Sage.

> This book explains how to do a quantitative content analysis and provides examples of research studies that have employed this methodology.

Waxman, H. C., Tharp, R. G., & Hilberg, R. S. (Eds.). (2004). *Observational research in U.S. classrooms: New approaches for understanding cultural and linguistic diversity*. Cambridge, UK: Cambridge University.

> The chapters in this book describe various observational measures and how they can be used both in research and in the improvement of educational practice.

chapter 7

Using Descriptive Statistics to Study Problems of Practice

IMPORTANT *Ideas*

1. Quantitative data play an important role in improving educational practice.

2. A measure of a construct is not synonymous with the construct. It is possible to have different measures of the same construct, with each measure having particular strengths and weaknesses.

3. A construct can be represented as a variable, which represents how individuals differ with respect to the construct.

4. Nominal scales, ordinal scales, interval scales, and ratio scales differ from one another in terms of whether their values have orderable magnitude, equal distance between any two sets of adjacent values, and a true zero point.

5. A sample statistic or population parameter only becomes meaningful when we examine the construct, variable, measurement scale, and group of scores from which it was derived.

6. The mean, median, and mode are different ways of representing the point around which a distribution of scores is centered.

7. The standard deviation provides useful information about whether a distribution of scores varies widely or narrowly around its mean.

8. If a set of scores is normally distributed, standard deviation units enable us to estimate the percentage of the sample that has earned scores within a particular interval of scores.

9. Researchers can determine the strength of the relationship between one distribution of scores and another distribution by doing a correlational analysis or by making group comparisons.

10. Researchers increasingly favor the use of correlational analysis, because it provides a more mathematically precise representation of the strength of the relationship between two or more score distributions. ■

Key TERMS

bell-shaped curve	median	scale
categorical scale	mode	scattergram
central tendency	multivariate descriptive statistics	scatter plot
construct	nominal scale	skewness
correlation coefficient	normal curve	standard deviation
dependent variable	normal probability distribution	statistic
descriptive statistics	ordinal scale	sum of squares
Excel	outlier	value
independent variable	parameter	variable
interval scale	range	variance
mean	rank	
mean absolute deviation	ratio scale	

Individuals generally enter the education profession primarily because they are interested in helping others—children, adolescents, young adults, life-long learners. They do not go into education because they want to work primarily with numerical data. Yet as we shall show in this chapter, numerical data and statistics have much to do with real people, and they are essential to identifying and solving problems of practice in education.

Some educators are concerned that numbers, such as IQ and GPA (grade-point average), stereotype students in ways that negatively affect their self-concept as learners or block their access to certain educational opportunities. They also are concerned about the type of school "report cards" now required by the No Child Left Behind Act that hold educators accountable for student learning (Yell & Drasgow, 2008). They claim these number-based report cards ignore certain factors that affect student learning but are beyond educators' control.

What case can be made for the benefits of numbers and statistics in education? To answer this question, consider an example from medicine, described in an article that appeared in the *New York Times* (Abelson, 2007). It concerns the efforts of Cincinnati Children's Hospital to become a national center of excellence in pediatric medicine. The article states, "Cincinnati Children's is among the relatively few medical centers that meticulously collect a wide range of data, to let the hospital see whether patients are getting good, effective care—and to look for ways to improve." As an example, the hospital was able to reduce the number of surgical infections from 95 in 2005 to 42 in 2006; this is nearly a 50 percent improvement. This achievement required the hospital staff to collect quantitative data, identify it as representing a problem of practice, and use the data as a marker for determining whether improvement efforts were working.

The article cites other areas of improvement in the treatment of serious children's diseases. For example, through careful monitoring of quantitative data, hospital staff have helped children with cystic fibrosis improve their lung function, ward off infection through flu shots, and avoid being seriously underweight through good nutrition.

Can quantitative data be of similar help to educators? Consider, for example, an article in the *Oregonian* (Hammond, 2007). The newspaper reported 15,517 homeless children and youth in Oregon, a total 18 percent higher than the previous year and 37 percent higher than two years before. Furthermore, 2,500 of the 15,517 homeless children and youth lacked not only a home but also a parent or guardian. Clearly, this situation posed a problem of practice for educators and the community. Had this problem not been quantified, it might have gone unnoticed or underappreciated in terms of its severity.

Other serious problems of practice, such as the achievement gap between white students and ethnic-minority students, similarly might not have come to our attention if the achievement gap had not been quantified. The quantification is illustrated in Figure 7.1, which shows score comparisons on the the mathematics test of the National Assessment of Educational Progress for white and black students over a 30-year period (Perie, Moran, & Lutkus, 2005). Looking at these statistics, educators, policy makers, and others are compelled to see this achievement gap as a significant problem of practice that needs to be solved.

If you are persuaded by the argument that quantitative data can play an important role in education and other professions, your next step is to learn the characteristics of such data, how they are used in research, and how they are subjected to statistical analysis. That is the purpose of this chapter. Our focus is on quantitative data and statistical analysis in research studies, but much of the discussion applies as well to quantitative data and statistical analysis in educational practice.

Constructs, Variables, and Measurement Scales

Most of us experience tests, attitude scales, and other measures only in their final form. We read the title of the measure, perhaps some of its items, and a summary of a sample's

FIGURE 7.1   Gaps in Mathematics Test Scores between White and Black Students from 1973 to 2004

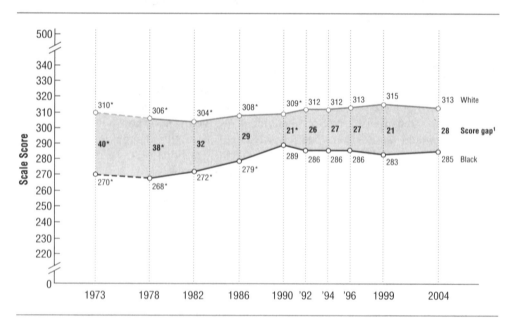

*Significantly different from 2004.

[1]White average scale score minus black average scale score.

Note: Dashed lines represent extrapolated data. Score gaps are calculated based on differences between unrounded average scale scores.

Source: Adapted from Figure 3.6 on p. 42 of Perie, M., Moran, R., & Lutkus, A. (2005). *The nation's report card. NAEP 2004 trends in academic progress: Three decades of student performance in reading, 1971–2004 and mathematics, 1973–2004.* Washington, DC: NCES. (ERIC Document Reproduction Service No. ED3460802)

scores on it. There is much more to the story, though. Measurement has a logic of its own. To understand measurement, then, we need to study its logic. We start by examining what it is we measure.

Constructs

By definition, quantitative data take the form of numbers. What do these numbers represent? One way to answer this question is to consider classroom tests. They typically measure how well students have mastered the facts, concepts, and skills covered in the curriculum. Suppose a test includes 30 items, with each item worth one point. Students' scores presumably measure how well they have mastered a curriculum unit or topic. A student with a score of 25 is considered to have learned more content than a student with a score of 18.

Researchers take a rigorous approach to this common educational practice. The starting point is to think of the test as measuring a particular construct or set of constructs. A **construct** in this context is a particular characteristic of individuals that is being measured. The construct might be mastery of a particular curriculum topic (as in the example above), but it also can be such things as an attitude, aptitude, personality trait (e.g., extraversion), or organizational characteristic (e.g., type of school).

It is important to realize that tests and other instruments measure particular constructs, but they are not identical to the constructs. For example, a teacher might assign students to write an essay (the measurement device) to demonstrate their understanding of freedom (the construct). However, the teacher could use other measures, such as a conventional multiple-choice test or oral presentation, to measure this construct. In other words, constructs are not directly measurable, but instead manifest themselves in forms of behavior—such as students' performance on tests and essays—that are measurable.

A measure might have a label indicating the construct it was designed to assess, but this is no guarantee that the measure is valid. For example, intelligence tests were developed more than a century ago, but there is still controversy over whether they actually measure intelligence (White, 2005).

Variables

If all individuals were the same, quantitative analysis would be simple. For example, if we were interested in the construct "attitude toward school," we could develop a measure of the construct and administer it to one individual. We then would know how well all other individuals would rate their attitude toward school. In reality, though, individuals vary, often greatly, on nearly any construct we can imagine. Quantitative research and statistical analysis are largely about the study of these variations.

When our interest is in how individuals vary with respect to a construct, it is useful to think of the construct as a variable. For example, if we think of attitude toward school as a variable, this means we are concerned about how individuals differ in their attitude toward school. A **variable** can be defined as the quantitative expression of a construct, with each difference in the quantity representing a difference in the amount of the construct. Each discernible difference in the quantity of a variable is called a **value** of the variable.

Given this definition of a variable, we would need to consider how many values can be distinguished in a variable of interest to us. For example, the variable of length can have virtually an infinite range of values, because objects can vary in length from, let's say, an electron to the size of the universe, and all points in between.

In thinking about attitude toward school as a variable, though, the number of values that constitute this variable is more difficult to conceptualize. We might distinguish two values—positive attitude toward school and negative attitude toward school. Or we might distinguish four values—very positive attitude, positive attitude, negative attitude, very negative attitude. Even more values of this attitude can be distinguished, but there is most likely an upper level. Individuals probably can distinguish where their attitude toward school falls on a continuum of 6 values (e.g., 6 points on a rating scale), but it is unlikely that they can do so on a continuum of 20 values.

The values of a variable can be expressed as numbers on a scale. For example, some school report cards use a 100-point scale, with 100 being perfect academic performance and some other point (perhaps 60) representing failing performance. In other situations, the values of a variable are represented by a symbol rather than a number. For example, some report cards use letters of the alphabet to represent academic performance (e.g., A+, A, A−, B+, B, and so forth). These are symbols, but they can be converted to numbers if one wishes.

Types of Measurement Scales

We stated above that a variable can have different values, each of which is expressed by a different number. These numbers are organized into scales for the purpose of measuring a construct. A **scale** is a set of numbers that represents the range of values of a variable. For example, currency in the United States is measured by a scale that represents money as a set of numbers that increase in value by one-penny intervals. (In some uses of currency, the values, called *mills,* are even smaller.)

In the following sections, we describe four types of scales used in educational research. Each type yields data that are amenable to different kinds of statistical analysis.

Nominal Scales.   A **nominal scale** is a set of numbers that represent a variable whose values are categories that have the properties of being mutually exclusive and not orderable. Marital status is a good example of a nominal scale. An individual can be married or not married, but not both. Also, a married individual is neither more nor less than a nonmarried individual. We can assign numbers to married and nonmarried individuals, such as a 1 to represent married individuals and 2 to represent nonmarried individuals. This numbering is arbitrary but useful for entering information about a research sample into a database for statistical analysis.

Nominal scales sometimes are called **categorical scales** because each number on the scale represents a different category. In a research study involving a variable that is measured on a nominal scale, researchers typically will report a frequency count of the number of individuals or objects that are members of each category. For example, researchers might be asked to determine the number of teachers in each of the 50 states and commonwealths. Each state and commonwealth is a separate category.

Ordinal Scales.   An **ordinal scale** is a set of numbers that represent a variable whose different values can be placed in order of magnitude, but the difference between any two sets of adjacent values might differ. The values often are called **ranks** (or rankings). We commonly see ordinal scales in sports. For example, in a golf tournament, the person with the best score occupies first place, the next best scorer occupies second place, and so forth. Each "place" represents a different rank.

One of the most widely cited ordinal scales is found in national rankings of colleges and universities, such as those reported in *U.S. News & World Report.* For example, law schools might be rated by various groups on different scales; then these scales are summated in some manner to yield a total score. If there are, let's say, 50 law schools in the survey, the top-scoring law school is ranked first, and the lowest-ranking law school is ranked 50th.

An important limitation of ordinal scales is that they yield numerical data in the form of ranks, but the ranks do not necessarily represent equal differences from one rank to the next. For example, suppose the top-ranked student in a class has a GPA of 3.98. The second-ranked student might have a GPA of 3.97 or 3.85 or 3.62. In other words, the second-place ranking only indicates that the student has the next-lower GPA than the student with the first-place ranking, but it does not indicate how much lower the GPA is.

Despite this limitation, the rankings produced by ordinal scales often are meaningful and important to various constituencies. For example, scholarships might be awarded to the top five students in a class, irrespective of how much or how little they differ on the criteria used to determine the rankings. In selecting candidates for a job, the search committee might select the top three candidates, as determined by their scores on rating scales, for an interview no matter how much their scale scores differ among each other and no matter how close the fourth-ranked candidate's scores on the scales are to the third-ranked candidate's scores.

Interval and Ratio Scales.   An **interval scale** is a set of numbers that represent a variable whose different values can be placed in order of magnitude, with an equal interval between any two adjacent values. An easy way to understand this type of scale is to think of an ordinary ruler. The distance between the 1-inch point and the 2-inch point is equal to the distance between the 5-inch point and the 6-inch point; the distance between the 17.4-inch point and the 17.8-inch point is equal to the distance between the 11.4-inch point and the 11.8-inch point, and so forth.

Interval scales are commonly found in measurement instruments used in the physical sciences and related professions. It is questionable whether any of the measures used in education, such as achievement and attitude scales, represent an interval scale. For example, the amount of learning needed to go from a score of 5 to a score of 10 on a 50-item achievement test is probably less than the amount of learning needed to go from a score of 45 to 50. For this reason, some researchers justifiably view educational tests and other measures as ordinal scales, which do not assume equal intervals between any two adjacent scores. However, for purposes of statistical analysis, these tests and measures usually are treated as if they were interval scales.

The reason is that the statistical procedures described in the next sections assume an interval scale of measurement. This assumption usually is not a problem, so long as one is cautious in drawing conclusions about such matters as achievement gains. For example, one student might show more gain than another student on an achievement test when it is readministered after remedial instruction, but the amount of gain might mean something different for the two students if their initial scores on the achievement test were different.

A **ratio scale** has the same characteristics as an interval scale—the values of the variable can be ordered, and the interval between any two adjacent values is equal—plus it has a true zero point. For example, currencies are ratio scales: a person can be in the position of having zero dollars, euros, shekels, or other currency.

Ratio scales are commonly found in the physical sciences and related professions, but not in education and related fields. As we indicated, a ratio scale has all the properties of an interval scale, and these properties are difficult to achieve in education. However, some educational constructs have a true zero point. For example, many individuals have absolutely zero knowledge about a particular language, country, or academic discipline.

Statistical Analysis of Data

A **statistic** is a number that describes some characteristic of quantitative data collected from a sample. The data take the form of a group's scores on a scale, or scales, and the scales represent measures of variables such as academic achievement and attitudes.

The calculation of a statistic, then, is one step in a chain of events. First, the researchers define a construct that is of interest to them. Second, they think about how individuals differ with respect to the construct, and that leads them to think of the construct as a variable. The third step is to develop a measure of the variable that will yield scores on a suitable scale (nominal, ordinal, interval, ratio). Next, they administer the measure to a sample, and each member of the sample receives a score on the measure. At this point, researchers can begin the process of statistical analysis to determine certain features of the collection of scores.

We see, then, a statistical analysis is not a stand-alone procedure. Its quality depends on the soundness of the steps leading up to it.

Statistics and Parameters

The focus of statistics is on a sample's distribution of scores on a measure, not on individual scores. To interpret a statistic, then, we need to understand the nature of samples. Chapter 6 provided a discussion of samples and sampling procedures in quantitative research. For the purposes of this chapter, it is sufficient to understand that a sample is a group of individuals who share a common characteristic. For example, the students in Mr. Smith's math class would be a sample; their common characteristic is that they are enrolled in that class. All the students in all the classes taught by Mr. Smith also would be a sample; their common characteristic is that they are taught by Mr. Smith.

A **parameter** is similar to a statistic, except that the numbers describe some characteristic of a population's scores on a scale or scales. Determining whether a group of individuals constitutes a sample or a population is a matter of perspective. If we are interested only in Mr. Smith's students, they would constitute the population. However, if Mr. Smith is a math teacher, and we are interested in learning how math teachers generally work with students, he and his students would be considered a sample that represents, in some manner, all math teachers.

The distinction between statistics (based on samples) and parameters (based on populations) affects the process of statistical analysis in various ways. It especially affects inferential statistics, which is discussed in Chapter 9.

Descriptive Statistics

Descriptive statistics are numerical summaries of a sample's distribution of scores on a scale, or scales. Suppose we ask a teacher how her class of 30 students did on a homework assignment. The teacher might say that the students did quite well, OK, or poorly. That is a descriptive summary. Descriptive statistics, used properly, would provide a fuller and more quantitatively precise description of the meaning conveyed by phrases like "quite well," "OK," or "poorly."

To illustrate descriptive statistics, we will consider teacher salaries in U.S. schools. We chose this variable because we consider it a problem of practice if teachers are not adequately compensated for their contributions to society in teaching students. Salaries that are too low might have an adverse effect on teachers' morale, and they might be a deterrent to attracting talented individuals to enter the teaching profession.

In this example, we view the underlying construct as financial compensation for full-time teaching. This construct can be refined further. We need to consider whether financial compensation will be defined just as regular salary, or whether it also will include extra-duty pay and employer contributions to pension plans and health insurance.

The salary statistics for teachers shown in Table 7.1 are a bit ambiguous on this point. The salary statistics for several states (e.g., Georgia and Oklahoma) include these salary supplements, but it is not clear whether other states pay for these supplements or whether they were reported. Nonetheless, the statistics shown in the table likely provide a fairly valid description of teacher salaries for the particular year (2004–2005) in which data were collected.

Table 7.1 shows that teacher salaries vary, so we can view the construct of salary as a variable that will have many values. We can measure the variable of salary as U.S. currency, which is a ratio scale because the interval between any two equal ranges—for example, $30,000 to $32,000 and $47,000 to $49,000—is identical and because there is an absolute zero (theoretically, a teacher could work for free and earn zero dollars).

The actual measurement of the variable can be done in several ways, such as asking each teacher to state his or her salary or examining salary reports generated by a school's business office. The measurement procedure used to generate salary statistics in Table 7.1 was a survey sent to state departments of education by a national teachers union (the American Federation of Teachers). It would be interesting to know the details of the survey procedure, but they are not provided on the website (www.aft.org/salary/2005).

TABLE 7.1   Descriptive Statistics for Teacher Salaries in Each State for 2004–2005

State	Teachers' Average Salary (2004–2005)	Deviations from the Mean ($44,916)	Squares for the Deviations from the Mean	Mean Household Income (2004)
Alabama	$38,186	6,730	45,292,900	$36,709
Alaska	$52,467	7,551	57,017,601	$57,027
Arizona	$39,095	5,821	33,884,041	$41,995
Arkansas	$41,489	3,427	11,744,329	$32,983
California	$57,604	12,688	160,985,344	$51,185
Colorado	$43,965	951	904,401	$48,198
Connecticut	$57,760	12,844	164,968,336	$60,528
Delaware	$52,924	8,008	64,128,064	$50,315
Florida	$43,095	1,821	3,316,041	$41,236
Georgia	$46,437	1,521	2,313,441	$43,037
Hawaii	$47,833	2,917	8,508,889	$53,554
Idaho	$40,864	4,052	16,418,704	$39,934
Illinois	$56,494	11,578	134,050,084	$48,953
Indiana	$46,591	1,675	2,805,625	$42,195
Iowa	$39,284	5,632	31,719,424	$41,350
Kansas	$39,351	5,565	30,969,225	$41,638
Kentucky	$41,075	3,841	14,753,281	$35,269
Louisiana	$39,022	5,894	34,739,236	$35,110
Maine	$40,935	3,981	15,848,361	$42,163
Maryland	$52,330	7,414	54,967,396	$57,424
Massachusetts	$54,688	9,772	95,491,984	$55,658
Michigan	$53,959	9,043	81,775,849	$44,905
Minnesota	$47,411	2,495	6,225,025	$50,860
Mississippi	$38,212	6,704	44,943,616	$31,642
Missouri	$39,064	5,852	34,245,904	$41,473
Montana	$38,485	6,431	41,357,761	$35,239
Nebraska	$39,441	5,475	29,975,625	$41,657
Nevada	$43,212	1,704	2,903,616	$44,646
New Hampshire	$43,941	975	950,625	$55,580

Measures of Central Tendency

Some descriptive statistics are intended to identify the **central tendency** of a sample's scores on a measure, which can be defined as a point in the distribution of scores around which a distribution of scores is centered. The most common measure of central tendency is the mean, but the median and mode are also reported in certain situations.

Mean.   The **mean** is a measure of central tendency that is calculated by summing the individual scores of the sample and then dividing the total sum by the number of individuals

State	Teachers' Average Salary (2004–2005)	Deviations from the Mean ($44,916)	Squares for the Deviations from the Mean	Mean Household Income (2004)
New Jersey	$56,635	11,719	137,334,961	$61,359
New Mexico	$39,391	5,525	30,525,625	$36,043
New York	$55,665	10,749	115,541,001	$47,349
North Carolina	$43,343	1,573	2,474,329	$39,428
North Dakota	$36,449	8,467	71,690,089	$39,447
Ohio	$49,438	4,522	20,448,484	$42,240
Oklahoma	$37,879	7,037	49,519,369	$35,357
Oregon	$48,320	3,404	11,587,216	$41,794
Pennsylvania	$53,281	8,365	69,973,225	$42,941
Rhode Island	$56,432	11,516	132,618,256	$48,722
South Carolina	$42,189	2,727	7,436,529	$39,837
South Dakota	$34,039	10,877	118,309,129	$38,472
Tennessee	$42,076	2,840	8,065,600	$38,794
Texas	$41,009	3,907	15,264,649	$41,759
Utah	$37,006	7,910	62,568,100	$47,074
Vermont	$44,346	570	324,900	$46,543
Virginia	$45,377	461	212,521	$51,689
Washington	$45,722	806	649,636	$47,659
West Virginia	$38,404	6,512	42,406,144	$31,504
Wisconsin	$43,099	1,817	3,301,489	$45,315
Wyoming	$40,487	4,429	19,616,041	$44,275

Mean Salary	$44,916
Mean Absolute Deviation	$5,562
Sum of Squares	2,147,072,021
Variance	43,817,795
Standard Deviation	6,553
Mean Household Income	$44,201
Correlation between teacher salaries and household income	$r = .73$

Source: The teacher salary statistics come from www.aft.org/salary, retrieved January 14, 2008.

in the sample. For example, if the ratings for four people on a scale are 1, 2, 4, 4, the mean is 2.75 (1 + 2 + 4 + 4 = 11; 11 ÷ 4 = 2.75). The statistics reported in Table 7.1 are labeled as *averages*, a term which almost always refers to means.

You will note that the descriptive statistic for the teachers in each state is their average salary, namely, the sum of all the teachers' salaries in that state divided by the number of teachers. In addition, the table reports the average of the averages ($44,916).

Actually, the mean salary across the 50 states, as reported by the American Federation of Teachers (AFT), is $47,602. This is because their analysis took into account the number of teachers in each state. For example, California had 299,660 teachers in 2004–05, and their average salary was very high ($57,760), whereas South Dakota had 8,988 teachers, and their average salary was low ($34,039).

Our calculation of the mean salary yields a lower number ($44,916). This is because we did not have access to data about the teacher population in each state. The AFT's mean salary is more accurate, but our data are sufficiently accurate for the purpose of illustrating descriptive statistics.

Median.   The **median** is the middle score in the distribution of scores. If there were 51 states, the median would be the average teacher salary for the state that ranked 26th in the distribution of states; half of the states would have a higher average salary, and half would have a lower average salary.

In reality, though, there are 50 states, so we cannot determine an exact middle score. In this situation, the usual procedure for determining the median is to use the two scores in the middle of the distribution and calculate the average of those two scores. In Table 7.1, Nevada ranks 25th (average salary is $43,212) and Wisconsin ranks 26th ($43,099). Therefore, the median salary is $43,166. This statistic indicates that almost half the states have a salary higher than $43,166, and almost half have a salary lower than that.

The mean is much more commonly reported than the median in educational research. The main reason for preferring the mean is that it has desirable mathematical properties for calculating other statistics, such as the standard deviation (explained below).

In some situations, though, the median is a useful measure of central tendency. For example, real estate professionals often report the median price of houses in a particular city. The reason is that the median price provides useful information to house hunters. If their financial status enables them to buy a house in the $200,000 range, then knowing that the median price of houses in their city is $190,000 tells them that they will be able to find a lot of affordable houses.

Mode.   The **mode** is the most frequently occurring score in the distribution of a sample's scores on a particular measure. It is seldom used as a measure of central tendency in educational research. Generally, the reason is that there is so much variation in scores on most measures that no one score stands out as representative of the central tendency of a score distribution. For example, all the state teacher salaries in Table 7.1 differ. In other words, they all occur with the same frequency, and so there is no modal salary. If there were multiple instances of a particular salary, this salary would constitute the mode, but we would not know where in the salary distribution it was located. Therefore, we would not know whether this modal salary was representative of all the state salaries.

It is possible to imagine situations where the mode would be a useful measure of central tendency. For example, suppose that educators are working with architects to design a new high school. They do a survey of class sizes in existing high schools in their region and find that classes of 26 students are most prevalent. This finding informs educators and architects that they should design an ample number of classrooms to accommodate classes with that number of students. They could examine the next most frequently occurring class size and make corresponding design decisions. This statistical approach is likely to be more informative than calculating the mean class size or median class size for all classrooms in the sample.

Outliers.   Some samples include **outliers,** that is, individuals who have an extremely high or low score on a measure. The presence of a few outliers in a sample can distort a measure of central tendency and lead to misinterpretations.

To illustrate this principle, suppose that California, Connecticut, and New Jersey had an unusually large number of highly experienced teachers and that these teachers were at the top end of the salary scale. Let's say their average salary is $10,000 higher than that shown in Table 7.1. California's would be $67,604, Connecticut's would be $67,760, and New Jersey's would be $66,635. They are outliers because their average salary is $10,000 higher than the next highest state, Illinois.

Now let's compute the mean salary for the 50 states with these three outliers included in the sample. The mean salary is $45,516, which is $600 higher than the actual mean salary ($44,916). The presence of these three outliers might lead to an interpretation that teachers nationwide are better compensated than is actually the case.

Educators might be justifiably concerned if a national or state mandate requires them to test all students in each class for accountability purposes. One teacher might have one or two students who score unusually low on the test for reasons beyond the teacher's control. Another teacher might not have such students, and the class's mean score would be higher for that reason alone.

This example does not imply some students should be excluded from testing simply because they are potential outliers. Rather, it makes a case for not relying on the mean as the sole measure of central tendency. The entire score distribution should be examined for outliers and other anomalies in order to develop a valid picture of how a class, school, district, or other grouping of students performed on the test.

Nominal Scale Data.   We explained in a previous section of this chapter that the values of a nominal scale—called *categories*—are not orderable. Therefore, it is not meaningful to use a measure of central tendency to determine a representative score for the score distribution of nominal scale data. Instead, researchers will calculate the number of individuals in a sample who fit into each category of the nominal scale. For example, marital status is a nominal scale. Categories typically used as values of the scale are never married, married, divorced, and widowed. The categories are not orderable, meaning that none of the categories is "more" or "less" than the other categories.

Suppose a sample includes 200 individuals, and the marital status of each individual is known. This information could be summarized as frequencies or percentages. Suppose the results are 70 never-married individuals, 100 married, 20 divorced, and 10 widowed. These frequency counts provide a meaningful summary of the data. Another meaningful summary would be a conversion of the frequency counts to percentages: 35 percent never married, 50 percent married, 10 percent divorced, and 5 percent widowed.

Measures of Variability

A measure of central tendency provides a score, typically the mean or median, that is representative of a sample's distribution of scores on a measure. This often is useful information in its own right. However, the variability of the scores is of most interest in identifying and studying problems of practice. To understand why this is true, let's examine Table 7.1. It shows that the mean state salary for teachers is $44,916. Suppose that all the states clustered tightly around this mean. For example, suppose that no state's teachers' salary was more than $1,000 above or below this mean. This low variability probably would attract no attention. However, the actual variability is substantial. The highest state salary, $57,760 (Connecticut) is almost $25,000 greater than the lowest state salary, $34,039 (South Dakota).

That's a lot of money, and it raises concerns. Does the salary variability mean that some states value their teachers much more than other states? Does it mean that higher-salary states attract better teachers than other states, and therefore the children in higher-salary states receive a better education? If true, is this fair? Should students' learning and potential be limited by the state in which they happen to reside?

Perhaps there is a more benign explanation. It might be that the variability in state teacher salaries simply reflects the different cost of living in each state. Perhaps the cost of living is much greater in Connecticut than in South Dakota. If so, the differences in state teachers' salaries might simply reflect this economic reality, and have no effect on teacher quality or morale or on students' opportunity to learn.

We see, then, that variability is an important aspect of a sample's scores on a measure. In following sections, we present several descriptive statistics that are designed to represent this variability. Each of them assumes that the scores have the key property of an interval or ratio scale, namely an equal interval between any two adjacent scores on the scale. Thus, these measures of variability are not appropriate for categorical or rank data.

Range.   The **range** is the largest score in the sample's score distribution minus the smallest score. In Table 7.1, the largest salary ($57,760) minus the smallest salary ($34,039) equals $23,721. The range, then, is $23,721. This is a useful indicator of the amount of variability in a score distribution.

A disadvantage of the range is that it can be distorted by an outlier at either end of the score distribution. If the highest salary ($57,760) was $10,000 greater or the lowest salary ($34,039) was $10,000 lower, the range would increase dramatically to $33,721. This large value for the range ignores the fact that the variability among the other 49 states did not change at all. The measure of variability described below—the standard deviation—is much less susceptible to this type of distortion.

Mean Absolute Deviation.   The **mean absolute deviation** is the mean of all the amounts by which each score deviates from the actual mean of the scores, ignoring whether the deviation from the mean is positive (i.e., a score greater than the mean) or negative (i.e., a score lower than the mean).

As an illustration of mean absolute deviations, Table 7.1 includes a column labeled "Deviations from Mean ($44,916)." The number in each row is the state's average salary minus the mean salary for all states, which is $44,916. For example, teachers' average salary in Alabama is $38,186, which "deviates" from the mean salary for all states by $6,730. The mean absolute deviation, which is labeled on a separate row near the bottom of Table 7.1, is $5,562.

The mean absolute deviation provides a simple, clear measure of how much variability there is in a set of scores. In the case of teacher salaries, the mean deviation of $5,562 indicates a fair amount of variability across states. The typical state is either approximately $5,000 higher or lower than the mean of all states ($44,916).

Sum of Squares.   The standard deviation is a more stable and mathematically useful measure of the variability of scores around the mean than the mean absolute deviation. To explain the meaning of a standard deviation, we must first introduce two other measures of variability: the sum of squares and variance.

Looking at Table 7.1, we see that Alabama's deviation from the mean is $6,730. The next column to the right (labeled "Squares for the Deviations from the Mean") shows the square of that deviation, which is 45,292,900. The same column also shows the square of the deviation for the other 49 states. The sum of all the squared deviations for a set of scores for a sample is called the **sum of squares.** This statistic, as shown in Table 7.1, is 2,147,072,021.

The sum of squares is one of the most important statistics used in statistical analysis. In simple terms, the sum of squares represents the total amount of variability in a set of scores. The purpose of many statistical analyses—for example, correlation, the t test, analysis of variance, multiple regression—is to determine whether other variables measured in a research study "explain" the variability that is expressed by the sum of squares.

Variance.   The variance is another measure of the variability of scores around the mean. It sometimes is calculated as part of a statistical analysis. The **variance** is simply the sum of squares divided by the sample size minus one ($n - 1$). In other words, it is the average of the squared deviations from the mean. If the data to be analyzed represent an entire population, the equation stated above is modified slightly: The sum of squares is divided by the population size (in this case, the 50 states); it is not necessary to subtract 1 from 50.

For our purposes here, we will assume that the American Federation of Teachers obtained salary data on a sample of teachers, albeit a very large sample. If you examine Table 7.1, you will see the variance on a separate line of the table (variance =

43,817,795). That number is the sum of squares (2,147,072,021) divided by the sample size minus 1 (50 − 1 = 49).

Standard Deviation.   The **standard deviation** is the square root of the variance of a sample's scores on a measure. In Table 7.1, the standard deviation of state teacher salaries is stated to be 6,620, which is the square root of the variance. You will note that the mean absolute deviation shown in Table 7.1 (5,562) is not much different in magnitude from the standard deviation (6,553), but the standard deviation is used because it has several desirable statistical properties. The standard deviation is the most commonly used measure of variability of a sample's scores in educational research. The term *standard deviation* is commonly abbreviated as SD in research reports. We follow this convention in the following sections of the chapter.

Normal Curve.   The standard deviation is a particularly useful statistic if the individual scores on the measure form a normal probability distribution, which is shown in Figure 7.2. To understand this figure, suppose that a large number of individuals are measured on a particular variable. The height of the curve at any point along the vertical line (i.e., the *y* axis) indicates the total number of individuals who obtained the score represented by that point. You will note that the mean of the sample's scores is indicated on the horizontal line (i.e., the *x* axis). If the sample's scores are normally distributed, more individuals will obtain the mean score than any other score in the distribution of scores.

Examining Figure 7.2 will help you understand that a **normal probability distribution** is a set of scores that are clustered around each side of the mean in a symmetrical pattern known as the **normal curve** or **bell-shaped curve.**

Note, too, that actual scores for a measure are not shown in Figure 7.2. Instead, the scores are represented immediately below the curve as standard deviation units (−3, −2, −1, etc.). To understand what these units mean, let's assume that we have a set of scores on a measure for a particular sample. The mean of these scores is 34.15, and the SD is 7.32. If an individual scored 1 standard deviation unit above the mean, it indicates that he or she obtained a score of 41, that is, 34.15 + 7.32 = 41.47, rounded to the whole number of 41.

FIGURE 7.2   Characteristics of a Distribution of Scores That Form a Normal Curve

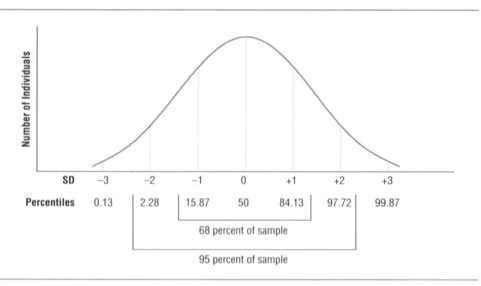

Note: The *x* axis in this figure represents standard deviation units. The *y* axis represents the number of individuals in a sample or population whose score on a measure has a particular SD/unit value on the *x* axis.

This score corresponds to the +1 in Figure 7.2. Individuals who score 1 standard deviation unit below the mean score would obtain a score of 27, that is, 34.15 − 7.32 = 26.83. This score corresponds to the −1 in Figure 7.2.

Now consider the case of an individual who scores 2 standard deviations above the mean, that is, 7.32 × 2 = 14.64. That individual's score would be 49, that is, 34.15 + 14.64 = 48.79. This score corresponds to the +2 in Figure 7.2.

The standard deviation units immediately beneath the normal curve shown in Figure 7.2 include a zero (0). The zero is the mean of the raw scores of the sample or population. If you think about it, there is no deviation of a mean score from itself. Therefore, it has a value of zero when expressed in standard deviation units.

The advantage of the standard deviation units shown in Figure 7.2 is that the raw scores for any measure can be represented by them, assuming that the scores are normally distributed. It does not matter whether one measure has 100 possible points and another has 20 possible points, or whether one measure employs an interval scale and another measure employs a ratio scale. The standard deviation units for each measure have the same meaning with respect to the normal curve.

The normal curve is helpful in interpreting the results of research studies. If you know the mean and standard deviation for the scores on a measure, you can use these two bits of information to determine the amount of variability in the scores (assuming the scores are normally distributed). Referring to Figure 7.2, you will see that scores 1 standard deviation below the mean are at approximately the 16th percentile, and scores 1 standard deviation above the mean are at approximately the 84th percentile. Thus, approximately 68 percent of the sample (84 − 16) will earn scores between +1 and −1 standard deviation. By a similar procedure, we can determine that approximately 96 percent of the sample (97.72 − 2.28) will earn scores between +2 and −2 standard deviations.

Suppose that, for a particular sample, the mean of their scores on a measure that has 50 possible points is 25 and the standard deviation is 2. Assuming the scores form a normal curve, we can conclude that most of the sample (approximately 96 percent) earned scores between 21 (−2 SD units) and 29 (+2 SD units). In other words, the scores are clustered tightly around the mean score, and so the mean is a good representation of the performance of the entire sample.

Suppose that, for another sample, the mean is again 25 but the standard deviation is 10. The variation in scores is quite large. If we consider only those individuals who scored within the range of +1 and −1 standard deviation units (approximately 68 percent of the sample), their scores are expected to vary from 15 (25 − 10) to 35 (25 + 10) if the distribution of scores follows the normal curve. In interpreting the research results, we need to keep in mind that the individuals in this research example are more different than alike with respect to the variable that was measured.

Standard deviation units also provide useful information about individual members of a sample. The row of percentiles in Figure 7.2 indicate each member's approximate percentile in the sample, based on his or her score. For example, an individual whose score places her two standard deviations above the mean would be at approximately the 98th percentile (97.72) relative to the rest of the sample. Statistics books contain tables that show percentiles for each standard deviation unit, usually to two decimal places (e.g., −1.37 SD units).

The mean and standard deviation are mathematically elegant, because these two statistics together provide a succinct summary of a sample's scores on a measure. Even if the sample includes one thousand individuals, we can learn a lot about how they performed on a measure just by calculating the mean and standard deviation of their scores on the measure.

Skewness.   Many of the variables measured by researchers and educators yield score distributions that follow a normal curve. However, some do not. In fact, this is the case with the teacher salary data in Table 7.1. The approximate shape of the distribution is illustrated in Figure 7.3.

If teacher average salaries across states were normally distributed, we would expect an approximately equal number of states above and below the overall mean, which is $44,916.

FIGURE *7.3*   Skewness in Distribution of Average Teacher Salaries across the United States

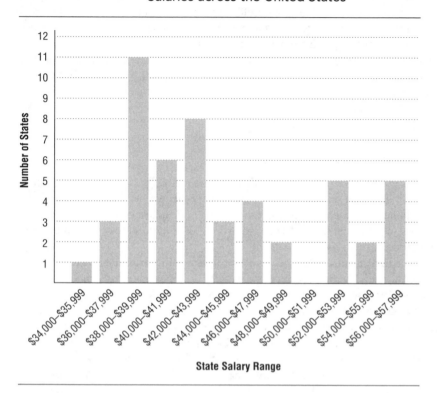

However, as shown in Figure 7.3, there are 29 states above the range of salaries ($44,000 – $45,999) that contains this mean and 18 states below it.

If the distribution of average state teacher salaries followed a normal curve, the salary range that contains the mean ($44,916) would have the largest number of states in it. This is clearly not the case, as we see in Figure 7.3. Only three states are in the salary range that contains the mean.

The kind of score distribution shown in Figure 7.3 exhibits a substantial degree of **skewness,** which is the tendency for a majority of scores to be bunched on one side of the mean and for the other scores to tail off on the other side of the mean. Skewness is neither good nor bad but is simply a feature of some score distributions. In fact, it is a research finding in its own right. One might wonder why so many states have salaries in the $34,000 to $40,000 range, while a smaller number have average salaries of $50,000 or more.

Multivariate Descriptive Statistics

The preceding sections of this chapter explained the use of descriptive statistics to reveal several features of a sample's scores on a single measure. We now move to descriptive statistics that reveal the relationship between score distributions on two or more measures. Statistics that describe this type of relationship between score distributions are called **multivariate descriptive statistics.**

To illustrate what it means for two score distributions to be related to each other, we will consider the question of why there is so much variability among states in average teacher salary. We speculated earlier in the chapter that perhaps some states value education more and compensate teachers accordingly. This would be a matter of concern, as educators undoubtedly expect all communities in all states to place high value on their work. Perhaps, though, variations in state teacher salaries are a reflection of variations in state economies.

Let's suppose that household income is an indicator of a state's economy: The more wealth a state's economy generates, the more money its residents should earn. Acting on this supposition, we found the median household income for each state in 2004, which is the same period of time for the state teacher salaries shown in Table 7.1. The source of these data is a U.S. government website (see footnote for Table 7.1).

The mean household income for each state is shown in a separate column in Table 7.1. The mean household income across all 50 states is $44,201, as shown near the bottom of the table. If you examine the column labeled "Mean Household Income (2004)," there is considerable variability around this mean. The range extends from a low of $31,504 (West Virginia) to a high of $61,359 (New Jersey).

Correlational Analysis

We wish to answer the following question: Is there a relationship between a state's teacher compensation and its overall economic status? To answer it, we need to view these two constructs as variables and then measure them on scales. Teacher compensation can be measured by salary, which is an interval scale, and states' economic status can be measured by household income, also an interval scale.

The next step is to determine whether variations in teacher salaries are related to variations in household income. More precisely, we wish to do a correlational analysis, which involves determining whether the distribution of scores (i.e., salaries) on one measure is related to the distribution of scores on the other measure.

A simple way to make this determination is to create a **scattergram** (also called a **scatter plot**), which is a chart having (1) two axes *(x and y)* representing the two scales and (2) a set of points, each of which represents a sample member's score on the two scales.

Figure 7.4 is an example of a scattergram. The horizontal *(x)* axis is a scale representing a range of teacher salaries, and the vertical *(y)* axis is a scale representing a range of household incomes. Each point in the scattergram is data for an individual state. Looking down from the point, we see the state's average teacher salary, and looking to the left of each point, we see the state's average household income.

FIGURE 7.4   Scattergram of the Relationship between Teacher Salaries and Household Income

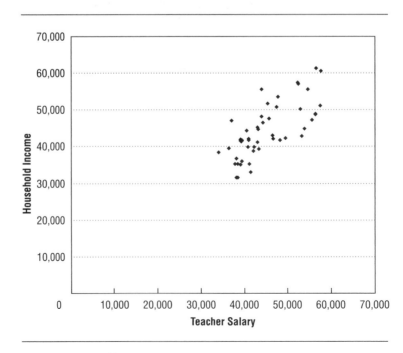

Visual inspection of the scattergram reveals a clear relationship between state teacher salaries and household incomes. States with higher household incomes are likely to have higher teacher salaries. The degree of this relationship can be mathematically described by a statistic called a **correlation coefficient,** which is explained in Chapter 12.

A closer inspection of Figure 7.4 indicates that there is more to the story than the finding that the strength of a state's economy is associated with teacher salaries. There are exceptions to this finding. Some states have similar household incomes but different state salaries. For example, looking back to Table 7.1, we find that Iowa and Oregon have similar household incomes ($41,350 and $41,794, respectively), but their average teacher salaries are quite different ($39,284 and $48,320, respectively). Another example is Illinois and Colorado: their average household incomes are similar ($48,953 and $48,198, respectively), but their average teacher salaries are quite different ($56,494 and $43,965, respectively).

Clearly, other variables besides the strength of a state's economy are associated with variations in state teacher salaries. Perhaps some states have stronger teacher unions or teachers with more experience or credentials, all of which might increase teacher salaries beyond the effect of the state's economy. Correlational techniques, described in Chapter 12, can tease out the relationship between these other variables and teacher salaries.

The study of teacher salaries becomes more complex—and interesting—when we investigate not only which factors determine variations in teacher salaries but how these variations in turn possibly affect student learning. Our research question is, Do teachers who are paid higher salaries produce more student learning?

This question can be answered by measuring each variable and using correlational analysis to examine whether scores on one measure are related to scores on the other measure. In this case, teacher salaries are the **independent variable** (i.e., the hypothesized cause) and student learning is the **dependent variable** (i.e., the hypothesized effect). In the previous example, the strength of the state economy, as measured by average household income, was the independent variable (the hypothesized cause) and teacher salary was the dependent variable (the hypothesized effect).

Group Comparisons

Correlational analysis is one way to describe the relationship between distributions of scores on two (and sometimes more) measures. Another approach is to consider scores on one of the measures as categorical, form groups based on those categories, and then compare these groups with respect to their scores on the other measure.

To illustrate this approach, we grouped states into two categories: high household income and low household income, depending on whether the state's household income is above or below the median. Table 7.2 shows the two types of states (high and low household incomes) and the average teacher salary in each state.

We then computed the average teacher salary across the 25 states of each type. As shown at the bottom of Table 7.2, we found that the mean teacher salary in high-household-income states is $49,541, and the mean teacher salary in low-household-income states is $40,292. These descriptive statistics make it easy to see that the salaries of teachers depend heavily on whether they reside in a high-household-income state or a low-household-income state.

A correlational analysis, as shown in Figure 7.4, would yield the same finding. Does it have any advantage over the group comparison shown in Table 7.2? A simple answer to this question is that correlational analysis provides a mathematically more precise description of the relationship between two or more score distributions than that provided by a group comparison. Also, correlational analysis makes it easier to look for relationships among multiple variables. For these two reasons, many educational researchers prefer correlational analysis to group comparisons.

Of course, readers of the research report will need to understand correlational statistics in order to interpret the results of this type of analysis. That is why reports written for a general audience often present statistics based on group comparisons. Most people find these statistics easier to understand.

TABLE 7.2   Comparison of Teacher Salaries in High-Income and Low-Income States

Average Teacher Salary in States with High Household Incomes		Average Teacher Salary in States with Low Household Incomes	
Alaska	$52,467	Alabama	$38,186
California	$57,604	Arizona	$39,095
Colorado	$43,965	Arkansas	$41,489
Connecticut	$57,760	Florida	$43,095
Delaware	$52,924	Idaho	$40,864
Georgia	$46,437	Indiana	$46,591
Hawaii	$47,833	Iowa	$39,284
Illinois	$56,494	Kansas	$39,351
Maryland	$52,330	Kentucky	$41,075
Massachusetts	$54,688	Louisiana	$39,022
Michigan	$53,959	Maine	$40,935
Minnesota	$47,411	Mississippi	$38,212
Nevada	$43,212	Missouri	$39,064
New Hampshire	$43,941	Montana	$38,485
New Jersey	$56,635	Nebraska	$39,441
New York	$55,665	New Mexico	$39,391
Ohio	$49,438	North Carolina	$43,343
Pennsylvania	$53,281	North Dakota	$36,449
Rhode Island	$56,432	Oklahoma	$37,879
Utah	$37,006	Oregon	$48,320
Vermont	$44,346	South Carolina	$42,189
Virginia	$45,377	South Dakota	$34,039
Washington	$45,722	Tennessee	$42,076
Wisconsin	$43,099	Texas	$41,009
Wyoming	$40,487	West Virginia	$38,404
	$M = \$49,541$		$M = \$40,292$
	$SD = 5,997$		$SD = 2,991$

Chapter 11 presents research designs based on group comparisons. Chapter 12 presents research designs based on correlational analysis. The designs use very different statistics to analyze data, but they are similar in their purpose, which is to investigate relationships between variables.

Calculating Descriptive Statistics

The calculations needed to generate a descriptive statistic for a set of scores can be done by hand, especially if the data set is small. Some handheld calculators can do these analyses. All you need to do is enter the data and then press the appropriate function key.

We find that the software program **Excel** works quite well for calculating descriptive statistics. If you have Office for Windows or Mac installed on your computer, you most likely have Excel included as part of Office. You can enter your data on an Excel spreadsheet and then use the Data Analysis feature in the Tools pull-down menu. We were able to generate the tables in this chapter, including the descriptive statistics shown in them, using only Excel. The Chart function under the Insert menu can create score distribution graphs, scattergrams, and other pictorial displays.

More complicated statistical analyses require software that is run on a personal computer or workstation. An example is the Statistical Package for the Social Sciences (SPSS). (Information about SPSS is available at www.spss.com.) SPSS enables you to do any of the statistical analyses described in this book. Because of its widespread use, you should be able to find someone in the research community who can help you learn how to use SPSS if needed. Another option is the Statistical Analysis System (SAS) (available at www.sas .com). SAS is more difficult to use than SPSS but has more capabilities.

Errors can easily occur while conducting a statistical analysis. Therefore, you should run checks on your data entry and software operations. One helpful check is to do a few statistical analyses by hand and compare the results with those generated by your statistical software.

An *example of* HOW DESCRIPTIVE STATISTICS CAN HELP IN SOLVING PROBLEMS OF PRACTICE

Many educators believe that emphasizing the learning of facts rather than the developing of thinking skills is a significant problem in education. The following is a description of a new resource for social studies teachers that might address this problem.

> Social studies teachers now have a new resource [the 21st Century Skills and Social Studies Map] to help them . . . : a free online document that maps various social studies projects, tasks, and outcomes to corresponding skills—such as problem solving and critical thinking—that are becoming increasingly important for 21st-century success.
>
> "For us, that is the promise of these maps—that it makes these skills understandable and achievable by practitioners . . ." [statement by Valerie Greenhill, vice president of the Partnership for 21st Century Skills]
>
> > Devaney, L. (2008, July 18). New resource helps teach 21st-century skills. *eSchoolNews*. Retrieved from www.eschoolnews.com

How do we help students acquire expertise in problem solving and critical thinking? Is the 21st Century Skills and Social Studies Map a solution? We need research to answer these questions. Research that produces descriptive statistics might help.

Researchers could collect descriptive data by installing software from the 21st Century Skills/Map website. The software would maintain a count of the visitors to the site, how much time they spent there, and whether they downloaded the social studies map (assuming it is downloadable).

The researchers could calculate the mean and standard deviation for the time measure to determine the average length of time spent by the population of visitors to the website and the amount of variability in time spent. They also could sum the visits to the site and calculate the percentage of visitors who downloaded the map.

Researchers also could ask the website visitors to complete a brief survey questionnaire. It would ask the visitors to provide demographic information and complete an attitude scale measuring the usefulness of the social studies map for their needs. The researchers could analyze the resulting data by computing descriptive statistics: the percentage of visitors having each demographic characteristic and the mean and standard deviation of the distribution of scores on the attitude scale.

If the descriptive statistics demonstrate positive results for the 21st Century Skills/ Map, this evidence can be used to advocate for resources from funding agencies to expand on and support this curriculum approach.

Self-Check Test

1. Quantitative data
   a. are useful only in basic educational research.
   b. are useful in identifying problems of practice.
   c. are not useful in identifying problems of practice.
   d. have been found to be useful in educational research but not in medical research.

2. An educational construct
   a. can only be measured by one instrument.
   b. cannot be represented as a variable.
   c. is a constant that does not vary across members of a sample.
   d. can be conceptualized as a variable on which members of a sample can differ.

3. An ordinal scale consists of
   a. categories that are not orderable.
   b. values that can be placed in order of magnitude but without an equal magnitude between any two adjacent values.
   c. values that can be placed in order of magnitude, with an equal magnitude between any two adjacent values.
   d. values that can placed in order of magnitude, with an equal magnitude between any two adjacent values and a true zero point.

4. An interval scale consists of
   a. categories that are not orderable.
   b. values that can be placed in order of magnitude but without an equal magnitude between any two adjacent values.
   c. values that can be placed in order of magnitude, with an equal magnitude between any two adjacent values.
   d. values that can placed in order of magnitude, with an equal magnitude between any two adjacent values and a true zero point.

5. A statistic is different from a parameter because it
   a. represents a sample, whereas a parameter represents a population.
   b. represents a population, whereas a parameter represents a sample.
   c. is derived from a random sample, whereas a parameter is derived from a nonrandom sample.
   d. is derived from a nonrandom sample, whereas a parameter is derived from a random sample.

6. As a measure of central tendency,
   a. the mode is more stable across samples drawn randomly from a population than is the median.
   b. the mean is more stable across samples drawn randomly from a population than is the median.
   c. the mode is more likely than the median to detect outliers in the sample.
   d. the mode is most favored by researchers for use in their studies because generally there is only a small range of individual differences in scores on most educational measures.

7. The sum of squares is
   a. the mean of all the amounts by which each score deviates from the actual mean of the scores.
   b. the square root of the variance.
   c. the total of all of a sample's scores on a measure, after each score has been squared.
   d. the total of all the squared deviations of each score from the sample mean.

8. If a distribution of scores is normally distributed, scores that are between +1 and −1 standard deviation unit would include
   a. 68 percent of the members of the sample.
   b. 98 percent of the members of the sample.
   c. fewer than 10 percent of the members of the sample.
   d. the top 10 percent of the members of the sample.

9. If the distribution of scores for a sample is skewed, we can infer that
   a. the sample was not randomly drawn from a population.
   b. a ratio scale was used to measure the variable.
   c. the majority of the scores are clustered to one side of the mean.
   d. the scores include no outliers.

10. A scatter plot is used primarily to determine whether
    a. the standard deviations of two distributions of scores are similar.
    b. the means of two distributions of scores are similar.
    c. there is skewness in one or both of two distributions of scores.
    d. there is a relationship between two distributions of scores.

Chapter References

Abelson, R. (2007, September 15). Managing outcomes helps a children's hospital climb in renown. *New York Times.* Retrieved from www.nytimes.com

Hammond, B. (2007). More kids have a school but not a home. *The Oregonian.* Retrieved from www.oregonlive.com

Perie, M., Moran, R., & Lutkus, A. (2005). *The nation's report card. NAEP 2004 trends in academic progress: Three decades of student performance in reading, 1971–2004 and mathematics, 1973–2004.* Washington, DC: National Center for Education Statistics. (ERIC Document Reproduction Service No. ED346082)

White, J. (2005). Puritan intelligence: The ideological background to IQ. *Oxford Review of Education, 31*(3), 423–442.

Yell, M. L., & Drasgow, E. (2008). *No child left behind: A guide for professionals* (2nd ed.). New York: Pearson.

Resources for Further Study

Leech, N. L., Barrett, K. C., & Morgan, G. A. (2007). *SPSS for intermediate statistics: Use and interpretation* (3rd ed.). Mahwah, NJ: Lawrence Erlbaum.

Morgan, G. A., Leech, N. L., Gloeckner, G. W., & Barrett, K. C. (2004). *SPSS for introductory statistics: Use and interpretation* (2nd ed.). Mahwah, NJ: Lawrence Erlbaum.

These two books describe the capabilities and procedures for SPSS, which is one of the most commonly used statistical software packages. Even if you turn your data over to an SPSS expert, these books will help understand SPSS so that you can consult with the expert about the statistical analyses you want done.

Smith, L. D., Best, L. A., Stubbs, D. A., Archibald, A. B., & Roberson-Nay, R. (2002). Constructing knowledge: The role of graphs and tables in hard and soft psychology. *American Psychologist, 57*(10), 749–761.

The authors discuss the various descriptive statistics presented in this chapter. They demonstrate the importance of these statistics not only in the social sciences but also in the physical sciences. The article illustrates how even simple statistical analyses can reveal important insights about the phenomena being studied.

Vogt, W. P. (2005). *Dictionary of statistics and methodology: A nontechnical guide for the social sciences* (3rd ed.). Thousand Oaks, CA: Sage.

This dictionary provides definitions of approximately 2,000 terms. Its comprehensive nature means that you are likely to find a definition of any statistical or methodological term that you encounter in reading research reports.

chapter 8

The Practical Significance of Statistical Results

IMPORTANT *Ideas*

1. A statistical result has practical significance if the result has important consequences for individuals for whom the result is relevant.

2. Statistical results can have practical significance when compared against personal standards, organizational standards, or curriculum standards.

3. A distribution of scores sometimes is converted into rank scores in order to determine prizes or awards, which often have practical significance for the winners.

4. Tables of norms based on grade equivalents, age equivalents, or percentile ranks have practical significance, because they inform educators whether an individual student or group of students is performing well or poorly relative to a norming group that the educators consider to be important.

5. Raw scores on a test or other measure can be converted into z-scores. These z-scores are helpful for interpreting how an individual compares with other individuals on a measure, how an individual's performance varies across different measures, or how one group compares with other groups on a measure.

6. The most common type of standard score is z, but some test developers convert raw scores on their measures to other types of standard scores.

7. An effect size is a useful statistic, because it provides a quantitative index of how much two groups differ on a measure or the strength of the relationship between two variables.

8. Gain scores and percentage increases or decreases are useful because they provide a quantitative index of how much an individual or group has changed over time as a result of instruction, maturation, or other factors.

9. In response to federal demands for school accountability, educators increasingly are using growth models as evidence of year-to-year improvement in student academic achievement.

10. The practical significance of statistical results can be quantified to an extent, but educators also must use their own expertise and judgment to determine whether statistical results indicate problems of practice or can help provide solutions to problems. ■

Key TERMS

age equivalent	normal curve	raw score
ceiling effect	normal curve area	standard score
effect size	norming group	statistic
gain score	norm-referenced test	status model
grade equivalent	percentile rank	table of norms
growth model	practical significance	z-score
National Assessment of Educational Progress (NAEP)	*Publication Manual of the American Psychological Association*	
No Child Left Behind Act (NCLB)	ranking	

The Practical Significance of Statistical Results

In the previous chapter, we explained **statistics** that describe a distribution of scores on a measure. These statistics include the mean, median, mode, and standard deviation. We also explained statistics that describe relationships between two or more distributions of scores, such as a correlation coefficient or comparison of groups.

These statistics have little meaning for professional practice by themselves. We need judgment and expertise to interpret the meaning of statistical results and their value, if any, for professional practice. In our view, a statistical result has **practical significance** if it has, or might have, important consequences for the individuals for whom the result is relevant.

Determining the practical significance of a statistical result often involves transforming raw scores on a test or other measure into some other metric, such as grade equivalents or rankings. The **raw score** is the numerical value that the individual obtains on a test or other measure. For example, on a multiple-choice test, each item usually is scored 1 (correct) or 0 (incorrect), and all the item scores are summed to yield a total score on the test. This is the individual's raw score. As you read this chapter, you will learn various ways in which raw scores can be transformed to make them more useful to educators and other groups.

Comparisons with Personal and Organizational Standards

In Chapter 7, our primary example for illustrating descriptive statistics involved state teacher salaries. The average teacher salary in each of the 50 states is shown in Table 7.1. Suppose you are an individual living in the state of Arizona, and you find that the average teacher salary there is $39,095. If you reside in Arizona and are thinking about teaching as a career, you might look at that salary and conclude: (1) This salary will support the lifestyle you desire, (2) this salary will not support your desired lifestyle, or (3) you want to learn more about the variability around this average salary to determine whether some teaching specialties have a higher-than-average salary that will support your desired lifestyle.

In each case, you are judging the statistical result (i.e., the state's average teacher salary) against a standard, namely, the salary needed to support your preferred lifestyle.

Thus, the statistical result has practical significance for making decisions about your choice of career. The statistical result also would have practical significance for anyone else for whom salary is a factor in making a decision about career choice.

Policy makers in various organizations (e.g., school boards, state legislatures, teachers unions) also might find that this statistical result has practical consequences for them. For example, suppose that school administrators in their state are experiencing difficulty in recruiting and retaining teachers, and they find that one of the main reasons is that their teacher salaries are insufficient. The teacher salary and household income statistics shown in Table 7.1, combined with other statistical data, can help them decide what level of salary increase might be necessary to improve teacher recruitment and retention. The enhanced salary becomes the standard against which existing salaries are compared, and also the standard that policy makers will need to justify in order to win taxpayers' support.

Comparisons with Ideal Standards

It might be difficult to find consensus on a standard for teacher salaries, but there is near universal agreement on standards that represent ideal conditions for educational practice. For example, it is difficult to imagine anyone who would disagree with the following standards: Schools should strive for a school dropout rate of 0 percent; school violence and vandalism should be nonexistent; all students should be physically fit; there should be a 100 percent rate of high school completion.

Descriptive statistics on actual rates of a phenomenon have practical significance when judged against the standard of the ideal rate. For example, if we find a school system with a dropout rate of 30 percent, we know that the system has a serious problem that needs to be solved. Statistical results from research studies have practical significance if they identify variables that affect dropout rates or experimental interventions that change the dropout rate in the desired direction.

Comparisons with Curriculum Standards

In recent years, educators have seen the development of new curriculum standards for various school subjects. National commissions formed by federal agencies and education organizations, as well as state departments of education, have been involved in this work. Their standards, often accompanied by the development of tests keyed to the standards, can be used to judge the practical significance of statistical results.

The **National Assessment of Educational Progress (NAEP)** is a major ongoing activity of the National Center for Education Statistics. The NAEP governing board and staff have been at the forefront of this focus on creating curriculum standards and tests to measure them.

Consider, for example, their identification of a curriculum standard for reading achievement for eighth-grade students. The standard identifies three levels of reading proficiency, as shown in Figure 8.1. NAEP developed a test keyed to the standard and cut-off scores for each level of reading performance, as shown in the figure.

Table 8.1 (on p. 174) shows statistical results for a national sample of eighth-grade students who took the reading test in 2007. The table includes the percentage of students at each level of reading proficiency for the total sample and also for five racial/ethnic groups.

The first data column shows the average score of each group on the reading test. What do these scores mean, and what is their practical significance? Elsewhere in the website containing these data, we find that the test is a scale whose scores range from 0 to 500 and that the test items assess three reading skills: reading for information, reading for literary experience, and reading to perform a task. This information gives us only a limited understanding of what the scores mean and what their significance is.

FIGURE *8.1*   NAEP's Curriculum Standard and Achievement Test
for Eighth-Grade Reading

At grade 8, equal proportions of assessment questions were devoted to reading for
literary experience and reading for information. The remaining assessment questions
were devoted to reading to perform a task, which was allotted one-half as much time
as either literary or information reading. The 2007 eighth-grade reading assessment
included a total of 13 reading passages and 140 questions.

The following descriptions are abbreviated versions of the full achievement-
level descriptions for grade 8 reading.* The cut score depicting the lowest score
representative of that level is noted in parentheses.

Basic (243): Eighth-grade students performing at the Basic level should
demonstrate a literal understanding of what they read and be able to make some
interpretations. When reading text appropriate to eighth grade, they should be able
to identify specific aspects of the text that reflect the overall meaning, extend the
ideas in the text by making simple inferences, recognize and relate interpretations
and connections among ideas in the text to personal experience, and draw
conclusions based on the text.

Proficient (281): Eighth-grade students performing at the Proficient level should
be able to show an overall understanding of the text, including inferential as well as
literal information. When reading text appropriate to eighth grade, they should be
able to extend the ideas in the text by making clear inferences from it, by drawing
conclusions, and by making connections to their own experiences—including other
reading experiences. Proficient eighth-graders should be able to identify some of the
devices authors use in composing text.

Advanced (323): Eighth-grade students performing at the Advanced level should
be able to describe the more abstract themes and ideas of the overall text. When
reading text appropriate to eighth grade, they should be able to analyze both
meaning and form and support their analyses explicitly with examples from the
text, and they should be able to extend text information by relating it to their
experiences and to world events. At this level, student responses should be
thorough, thoughtful, and extensive.

*The full descriptions can be found at www.nagb.org/frameworks/reading_07.pdf.

Source: p. 38 of http://nces.ed.gov/nationsreportcard/pdf/main2007/2007496_3.pdf

The other data columns are much more informative. The statistics are the percentage of
students who are reading at each level of reading proficiency. For example, we find in Table
8.1 that 83 percent of white students meet at least the basic standard of reading proficiency.
Looking at Figure 8.1, we can read descriptions of the reading standard represented by each
level to determine the reading skills that all these students have. We also can look at Figure
8.1 to determine the reading skills that the 38 percent of students who score at or above the
proficient standard have.

The statistics for ethnic-minority students are also easy to interpret. We find, for example, that a substantial percentage of students in each group lack basic proficiency in
reading skills, as defined in Figure 8.1.

The fact that the statistics (in this case, percentages) are tied to defined curriculum
standards makes it possible for educators to frame problems of practice and to set goals
for addressing them. In other words, the statistics have practical significance. Looking at
the statistics in Table 8.1, educators might decide that the achievement gap between white
students and other racial/ethnic groups in basic reading proficiency is the most serious problem and that resource allocation to reduce this gap should have greatest priority. Another

TABLE *8.1*   Performance on an NAEP Reading Test Taken by a National Sample of Eighth-Grade Students

Group	Average Scale Score	Percentage of Students Below Basic Level	Percentage of Students at or above Basic Level	Percentage of Students at or above Proficient Level	Percentage of Students at Advanced Level
White Students	270	17	83	38	3
Black Students	244	46	54	12	<1
Hispanic Students	246	43	57	14	1
Asian/Pacific Island Students	269	21	79	40	5
Alaska Native Students	248	42	58	19	2

Note: NAEP is an abbreviation for National Assessment of Educational Progress.

Source: http://nces.ed.gov/nationsreportcard/pdf/main2007/2007496_4.pdf

priority might be to increase the percentage of students, irrespective of their racial/ethnic status, who can meet the standard of proficiency, as defined in Figure 8.1.

Tests and other measures that are keyed to curriculum standards are not commonly used in educational research. However, as standards and standards-based measures become part of the mainstream of educational practice, they are likely to become a central focus of educational research methodology. As this happens, educators are likely to attend more closely to statistical results involving curriculum-based achievement tests because of their practical significance.

Comparisons Based on Rankings

A **ranking** expresses the position of an individual on a measure relative to the positions held by other individuals. Educators use rankings for various purposes. For example, a school might rank the students at a particular grade level with respect to academic achievement, or athletes might be ranked with respect to performance in a sports contest (e.g., first place, second place, and third place). These ranks can have important consequences for students' self-esteem and eligibility for future opportunities to learn and perform. Because of their significance, rankings sometimes are collected and analyzed by educational researchers.

Rankings typically have unequal intervals. For example, in one classroom there might be very little difference in academic achievement between the first-ranked and second-ranked student. In another classroom, however, these two rankings might reflect substantial differences in academic achievement. This limitation of rankings should be kept in mind when interpreting statistical results based on this type of score.

Comparisons Involving Tables of Norms

You probably are familiar with the height and weight chart available in doctors' offices. The chart shows the average height and weight for children at many age levels starting in infancy (e.g., 6 years old, 6 years 1 month old, 6 years 2 months old). It is constructed by gathering a large sample of children at different age levels who are representative of the general population. Using children at each age level, the researchers compute their mean height and weight.

When parents bring their child to a doctor's office, someone measures the child's height and weight. The doctor then uses these data to determine whether the child is above or below the mean height or weight of other children the same age. This comparison can have diagnostic value, especially if it is found that the child deviates markedly from the mean.

In this example, the large sample used to represent the general population's scores on a test or other measure is called the **norming group.** The chart of mean heights and weights for different age groups is typically called a **table of norms.** Comparing the score (or value, such as height or weight) of a particular individual or group of individuals with those of the norming group can have practical significance.

For example, if the table of norms involves scores on a particular test, we can determine whether our research sample's test scores are typical or atypical. Suppose the sample's test scores are much lower than the norming group's scores. This statistical result might prompt educators to take local action to remediate this problem. Also, educators can use these norm-referenced statistical results as a basis for securing additional federal and state funding to assist students identified as very low achieving or as gifted and talented.

Commercial tests intended for wide use often have tables of norms, so that local users can compare their students' scores with those of students in the general population who are at the same age or grade level. Tests that include tables of norms that are of practical use to educators for comparing their students' scores with a norming group often are called **norm-referenced tests.**

Norms can be of various types. The above example involving a medical setting included norms relating to height and weight. The following sections describe several types of norms commonly used in educational research and practice.

Grade Equivalents

Grade equivalents are a type of norm in which a student's score on a test is interpreted in terms of the grade level of other students who, on average, earn that score. For example, consider the Iowa Test of Basic Skills (ITBS), a widely used battery of tests of students' achievement in four school subjects—language arts, math, social studies, and science. The website for the ITBS explains grade equivalents:

> The GE [grade equivalent] is a decimal number that describes performance in terms of grade level and months. For example, if a sixth-grade student obtains a GE of 8.4 on the Vocabulary test, his score is like the one a typical student finishing the fourth month of eighth grade would likely get on the Vocabulary test. (www.education.uiowa.edu/itp/itbs/itbs_interp_score.htm)

The table of norms is created by administering a test each month of the school year to nationally representative samples of students at each grade level. The mean of the scores of each group (e.g., all students in the fourth month of the eighth grade) is computed, and this mean is considered the norm.

These norms have practical significance, because they tell educators whether a particular student or group of students is at, below, or above grade level. Of course, one would need to know what it means to have, let's say, the vocabulary of a typical eighth-grader in order to understand the actual meaning of a grade equivalent.

Age Equivalents

Age equivalents are similar to grade equivalents, except that a student's score on a test is interpreted as the average age of students in the norming sample who earned that score. The "average age" is the mean of the ages of the students who earned the score. The table of norms, then, would include a list of possible scores on the test, and next to each score would be the average age of students who earned that score.

If we know a student's age, we can say whether she is performing at the same level as her peer group (i.e., students of the same age) or like older or younger students. This is useful information if educators and researchers have an understanding of what students at different age levels know about the content that the test measures.

Percentile Ranks

Percentile ranks specify the percentage of students in a sample or population whose scores on a test are below a particular score. For example, if a research sample's mean on a test translates into a percentile of 72 in a table of norms, we can say that the sample's mean is at the 72nd percentile of students in the norming group. In other words, 72 percent of students in the norming group earned the same or lower score as the average score (i.e., the mean) of the research sample.

Calculation of percentile ranks is particularly appropriate if the test is designed for a particular age group or grade level. Students in the norming group would be approximately the same age and all would be in the same grade, so tables of age norms or grade norms would not make sense. However, calculation of percentile ranks makes it possible to determine the cumulative percentage of students who earned each possible score on the test, starting with the lowest score.

By consulting a table of norms based on these cumulative percentages, we can determine what percentage of students in the norming group earned the same score as a particular student or group of students. Knowledge about how well a research sample performed relative to a peer group might have practical significance in terms of whether their level of performance presents a problem of practice that needs to be addressed. For example, if the research sample has a low percentile rank, educators who serve students similar to the research sample might decide that special interventions should be put into place to help these students.

A table of norms based on percentile ranks is shown in Table 8.2. This table is for the SAT Subject Tests, which are used nationally and internationally for college admissions. The tests are developed by the Educational Testing Service (www.ets.org) and administered by the College Board (www.collegeboard.com).

The norming group for the percentile ranks was a large sample (numbers shown at the bottom of Table 8.2) of college-bound seniors in 2006. To illustrate use of the table, suppose that a student earned a score of 600 on the two biology tests. That would place the student in the 48th percentile of the norming group on the ecological biology test and the 34th percentile of the norming group on the molecular biology test.

In a preceding section, we described the use of rankings to determine the practical significance of a group's scores on a measure. Percentile ranks are similar, except that they are based on a norming group. If we have a sample's scores on a measure, we can rank each individual by comparing their scores. If a table of percentile ranks is available, we also can determine each individual's rank with respect to a norming group.

Comparisons Involving Standard Scores

In the preceding sections, we described how tables of norms can be used to understand the practical significance of raw scores on a test or other measure. In the next sections, we describe an approach to interpreting raw scores in terms of the score distribution itself. This approach involves the conversion of raw scores into standard scores. A **standard score** is a score that involves a transformation of an individual's raw score on a test or other measure by using the standard deviation of the score distribution. One advantage of standard scores is that they enable direct comparison of a student's performance across a range of measures.

TABLE 8.2   SAT Subject Test Percentile Ranks for Science

Score	Ecological Biology	Molecular Biology	Chemistry	Physics	Score	Ecological Biology	Molecular Biology	Chemistry	Physics
800	99	98	95	92	480	13	9	11	8
790	99	97	94	90	470	13	7	9	7
780	98	93	91	88	460	11	7	8	6
770	97	93	89	93	450	10	6	7	5
760	96	90	86	82	440	8	3	5	4
750	94	88	83	80	430	7	4	4	3
740	93	84	80	77	420	6	4	3	2
730	91	81	77	74	410	5	3	2	1
720	89	77	74	71	400	4	3	1	1
710	86	73	71	67	390	3	2	1	1–
700	83	69	67	64	380	3	2	1–	1–
690	81	66	64	60	370	2	1	1–	1–
680	77	62	61	57	360	2	1	1–	1–
670	74	58	58	54	350	1	1	1–	1–
660	70	55	54	51	340	1	1	1–	–
650	67	51	52	47	330	1	1–	1–	–
640	63	47	48	44	320	1–	1–	–	–
630	60	43	43	40	310	1–	1–	–	–
620	56	40	43	38	300	1–	1–	–	–
610	53	37	40	34	290	1–	1–	–	–
600	48	34	37	32	280	1–	1–	–	–
590	43	30	34	29	270	–	1–	–	–
580	42	28	32	26	260	–	1–	–	–
570	39	25	29	24	250	–	–	–	–
560	35	23	27	22	240	–	–	–	–
550	32	20	25	19	230	–	–	–	–
540	32	20	25	19	220	–	–	–	–
530	26	16	20	15	210	–	–	–	–
520	24	14	18	14	200	–	–	–	–
510	21	11	16	12	Number	32,546	38,171	54,652	32,895
500	19	11	15	11	Mean	591	630	629	643
490	16	10	13	9	SD	104	105	110	107

Note: These total group percentile ranks for SAT Subject Test scores appear on the SAT Subject Test score reports for the 2006–07 test administrations.

Percentile ranks are based on scores from the 2006 College-Bound Seniors cohort.

Source: www.collegeboard.com/prod_downloads/highered/ra/sat/SubjTestPercentileRanks.pdf

The Most Common Standard Score: The z-Score

To explain standard scores, we need to refer to the concept of a **normal curve,** which we explained in Chapter 7. We displayed a normal curve distribution of scores in Figure 7.2. For the sake of convenience, we show the same normal curve again in Figure 8.2.

If the scores for a sample of individuals approximate a normal curve, the mean and standard deviation of the raw scores can be used to transform them into standard scores. The process is fairly simple. We simply subtract the sample mean from the individual's raw score and divide that result by the standard deviation of the sample.

For example, suppose that a sample's mean score is 20 and the standard deviation is 5. If an individual in the sample earned a raw score of 20, we would subtract that score from 20, which is zero. Dividing zero by the standard deviation (5) equals zero. Therefore, the individual's standard score is zero. Looking at Figure 8.2, we see that a standard score of 0 puts the individual at 0 on the normal curve, which is the mean (20) and also the 50th percentile of the score distribution. Stated another way, a standard score of 0 is zero standard deviation units (the *x* axis in Figure 8.2) away from the mean.

Taking another example, suppose the individual's raw score is 25. Subtraction of the mean (20) from the raw score equals 5. Dividing 5 by the standard deviation (5) equals a standard score of 1.0. Looking at Figure 8.2, we see that a raw score of 25, which equals a standard score of 1.0, places the individual at the 84th percentile of the score distribution. Stated another way, a standard score of 1 is one standard deviation unit (the *x* axis in Figure 8.2) away from the mean.

Some standard scores have a negative value. Suppose the individual's raw score is 15. Subtraction of the mean (20) from 15 equals –5. Dividing –5 by the standard deviation (5) equals a standard score of –1.0. Looking at Figure 8.2, we see that a raw score of 15, which equals a standard score of –1.0, places the individual at approximately the 16th percentile of the score distribution.

In the preceding paragraphs, we referred to three standard scores: 0, 1.0, and –1.0. Another name for these standard scores is *z*-scores. A **z-score** is the expression of a raw score in terms of another type of score, namely, a standard score that is based on the stan-

FIGURE *8.2*   Characteristics of a Distribution of Scores That Form a Normal Curve

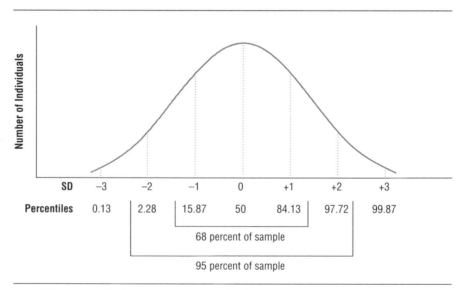

Note: The *x* axis in this figure represents standard deviation units. The *y* axis represents the number of individuals in a sample or population whose score or a measure is a particular SD unit value on the *x* axis.

dard deviation of the score distribution. In a subsequent section of this chapter, we describe several other types of standard scores.

As we explained, we can use z-scores to indicate an individual's percentile rank within the sample or population. For example, looking at Figure 8.2, we see that an individual whose raw score translates into a z-score of +2 is at approximately the 98th percentile of the score distribution. The 98th percentile means that 98 percent of the sample or population have earned z-scores that are at or below a z-score of +2.

Another way of stating this information is to think of the normal curve as containing a certain area. Segments within this total area consist of all the area between one of the curved lines and the vertical line that can be drawn at any point on the x axis. If the normal curve can be divided into areas, what does the 98th percentile mean? It means that 98 percent of the area of the normal curve lies below the z-score of +2. Conversely, we can interpret the 98th percentile to mean that 2 percent of the area of the normal curve lies above the z-score of +2.

As another example, consider a z-score of −1. If we examine the normal curve in Figure 8.2, we can interpret this z-score to mean that approximately 16 percent (or precisely, 15.87 percent) of the area of the normal curve falls below a z-score of −1, and approximately 84 percent of the area is above −1.

The Presentation of z-Scores in Table Form

The use of a typical normal curve to determine the percentile equivalent for a particular z-score is imprecise, because it only includes a small number of benchmark z-scores (−3, −2, −1, 0, +1, +2, +3). Therefore, statisticians have constructed tables that include a much larger number of units on an interval scale, usually to three or four decimal places. Table 8.3 presents a small number of z-scores to illustrate what these tables look like.

You will note that the table has a column that shows z-scores and a column that shows their corresponding normal curve area. The **normal curve area** is the amount of area in the normal curve between the mean, which has a z-score of 0, and the z-score of interest to us.

In Table 8.3, a z-score of 0 has a normal curve area of 0, meaning that there is no area between it and the mean. A z-score of 0.05 has a normal curve area of 0.0199 from the mean. If we round 0.0199 to 0.02, we can conclude that any individual with a z-score of 0.05 will be at the 52nd percentile of the score distribution (50 + 2 = 52).

Table 8.3 also can be used for negative z-scores. For example, an individual with a z-score of −0.10 will be at the 46th percentile of the score distribution (50 − 3.98 = approximately 46).

Table 8.3 shows a very small number of z-scores. A full table, found in most statistics textbooks, will show z-scores to two decimal places from 0.00 to 3.00. There is no need

TABLE 8.3   z-Scores and Normal Curve Areas

Normal Curve		Normal Curve		Normal Curve	
z-Score	Area	z-Score	Area	z-Score	Area
0.00	0.0000	0.05	0.0199	0.10	0.0398
0.01	0.0040	0.06	0.0239	1.00	0.3413
0.02	0.0080	0.07	0.0279		
0.03	0.0120	0.08	0.0319	2.00	0.4772
0.04	0.0160	0.09	0.0359	3.00	0.4987
				4.00	0.5000

to show *z*-scores beyond 3.00, because any individual with that *z*-score or higher is well beyond the 99th percentile (if the sign is positive) or well below the 1st percentile (if the sign is negative).

The Practical Significance of *z*-Scores

An individual's raw score on a test or other measure generally is not of much use to educators. A low score might indicate low achievement or a negative attitude, but perhaps that is typical of others in the same group that took the test or other measure. If we convert the raw score to a *z*-score, however, we now have information about where that individual stands relative to this group. The *z*-score tells us whether this individual is typical of others (a low *z*-score) or whether this individual is relatively or very atypical of others (high positive or negative *z*-scores).

The use of *z*-scores has another important application. Suppose that students have taken achievement tests in several subjects, such as chemistry, physics, and mathematics. Further suppose that each test has a different number of items. Raw scores, then, will have different meanings from one test to another. However, *z*-scores will have the same meaning across tests. For example, suppose that a student has a high *z*-score in mathematics and physics but a low *z*-score in chemistry. Educators might use this information to recommend that the student proceed to take more advanced coursework in mathematics and physics but do remedial study of chemistry before attempting advanced coursework in that subject.

Still another use of *z*-scores can be found when making group comparisons on a test or other measure. Suppose two groups, such as males and females, take the same test. We then calculate the mean score for each group and find that that they are different. Should we interpret the difference as trivial or sufficiently large to warrant further inquiry?

One way to answer this question is to first plot the score distribution for, let's say, females, so that it looks something like the normal curve shown in Figure 8.2. Next, we determine the average score (i.e., the mean) of the male group. Now we can ask the question: If a female had earned that score, where would that place her in the distribution of scores for the female group? To answer this question, we can convert the raw score to a *z*-score, calculated using the mean and standard deviation of the females' scores.

If we find that the *z*-score is +1, this would mean that the average male is at the 84th percentile of the females' score distribution. If we find that the *z*-score is −1, this would mean that the average male is at the 16th percentile of the females' score distribution. Depending on the actual percentile, educators might decide whether there is a gender gap and whether it is sufficiently large, in percentile terms, to constitute a problem of practice that needs to be addressed.

In fact, this use of *z*-scores to compare groups is of great importance in educational research. The calculations that we describe are the basis for calculating effect sizes, which we explain later in the chapter.

Types of Standard Scores

We explained in the preceding section that *z*-scores are a distribution of raw scores that have been converted into standard scores having a mean of 0 and a standard deviation of 1. Some test developers use a different type of standard score to represent the raw scores yielded by their measure. For example, raw scores on intelligence tests such as the Stanford-Binet Intelligence Scale and the Wechsler Adult Intelligence Scale are expressed as standard scores having a mean of 100 and a standard deviation of 16. An individual's standard score on these tests is commonly referred to as their IQ, which stands for intelligence quotient. An adult with an IQ of 100 is at the 50th percentile of the norming sample used to represent the population of U.S. adults. A person with an IQ of 116 would be approximately at the 84th percentile of the norming sample.

The College Board at the Educational Testing Service (ETS) has developed some of the most widely used tests in education—the SAT Reasoning and Subject Tests used for college admission; the Test of English as a Foreign Language (TOEFL) used to determine

English language proficiency (often administered to international students seeking admission to U.S. universities); the Graduate Records Examination (GRE) used for admission to graduate programs; and the Praxis tests administered to teacher education candidates.

Raw scores on these tests are converted to standard scores that can range between 200 and 800. The mean and standard deviation of the standard scores for each test can vary, so you need to obtain information for the test that is of interest to you. For example, you can access a website containing standard score distributions, means, and standard deviations for each SAT Subject Test for the 2006–2007 test administration (www.collegeboard.com/prod_downloads/highered/ra/sat/SubjTestPercentileRanks.pdf).

Effect Sizes

Imagine a research study that is designed to investigate the effect of small cash rewards on the achievement of high school students. For one school year, experimental students receive cash rewards for passing weekly quizzes, and control students receive no rewards. At the end of the year, both the experimental and control group students take the XYZ Mathematics Test, which is the criterion measure. The mean score for the experimental group is 46.2, and its standard deviation is 4.0. The mean score for the control group is 41.2, and its standard deviation is 3.8.

This hypothetical experiment demonstrates that cash rewards have a positive effect on student learning, because the experimental group scored 5 points higher than the control group on the math test. This result raises two questions. Just how large is a 5-point difference? Does it have practical significance?

Researchers increasingly answer these questions by calculating a statistic known as an effect size. An **effect size** is a mathematical expression that quantifies the magnitude of the difference between two groups or, more generally, the magnitude of the relationship between two variables. The calculation for determining the difference between two groups subtracts the mean score of Group 1 from the mean score of Group 2 and then divides this difference by the standard deviation (SD) of the control group. (In some experiments, the SD of the combined score distribution for the experimental and control groups is used instead.)

To illustrate this calculation procedure, consider the preceding experiment.

1. Subtract the control group mean (41.2) from the experimental group mean (46.2). The result is 5.0.
2. Divide 5.0 by 3.8, which is the control group's SD. The result is 1.32. This number (1.32) is the effect size.

Now we face the task of interpreting the significance of this effect size (1.32). It is very close in meaning to *z*-scores, which we explained earlier. The standard score for an individual in a sample involves subtracting his score from the sample mean and dividing that result by the sample's SD. We follow the same procedure in computing an effect size, except that we subtract one group's mean from the other group's mean, and we divide the result by the control group's SD.

Referring to Table 8.3, we see that an effect size of 1.32 is approximately at the 91st percentile (50 + 40.66 = 90.66). To interpret this result, consider experimental group students who earned the mean math test score ($M = 46.2$) at the end of the school year. These students would be in the 50th percentile of the experimental group score distribution but in the 91st percentile of the control group's score distribution. This is because students in the control group who have a score of 46.2 on the math test are at the 91st percentile relative to other students in their control group.

Of course, it is not only experimental group students with an average math test score (46.2) who made greater gains relative to the control group students. The entire score distribution of the experimental group moved up relative to the score distribution of the control group. In other words, most students who received cash rewards, no matter what their achievement test score was, performed better than if they had been in the control group.

Educators who are concerned about improving the mathematics achievement of high school students should take an effect size this large seriously. Of course, they also need to reflect on ethical concerns about giving cash rewards for learning. Statistical results have practical significance, but they cannot be the sole determinant of decision making in education.

In our experience, educational researchers consider an effect size of 0.33 or larger to have practical significance. An effect size of 0.33 indicates that a student in the group with a higher mean score whose score is at the 50th percentile would be at the 63rd percentile of the other group's score distribution.

Suppose that two research studies investigated the same variables but used different statistical analyses. For example, in Chapter 7 we showed how the relationship between a state's average teacher salary and its average household income can be analyzed using group comparisons or correlation. One researcher might investigate this relationship by making group comparisons, and another researcher might investigate this relationship by correlational analysis.

An advantage of effect size statistics is that the results of these two studies, each involving a different statistical approach, can be converted to a common metric, namely, an effect size. Readers of the two research reports can determine whether the observed relationship between teacher salaries and household income is similar in the two studies simply by comparing the two effect sizes.

Meta-analysis of research results across studies, which we explained in Chapter 5, relies on the effect size metric. Researchers can synthesize the findings of many studies by converting the results of diverse statistical analyses into effect sizes. It does not matter whether different studies measured the same variables using different measures. All the findings can be converted to the effect size metric.

Furthermore, suppose that the studies examined the effect of the same independent variable on different outcome variables. No matter what the outcome variable is or how it was measured, the statistical results can be converted to a single metric, namely, effect size. The individual doing a meta-analysis need only convert each finding of each study to an effect size, group effect sizes according to the outcome variable that was measured, and then determine whether the independent variable (e.g., an experimental intervention) had a different effect on different outcome variables.

Effect sizes commonly appear in reports of quantitative research, especially in recent years. In part, this is because the ***Publication Manual of the American Psychological Association*** (American Psychological Association, 2001) strongly recommends them: "For the reader to fully understand the importance of your findings, it is almost always necessary to include some index of effect size or strength of relationship in your Results section" (p. 25). Most educational journals follow APA publication guidelines, and therefore journal editors are likely to require authors to adhere to this recommendation.

The APA quote states that an index of either "effect size" or "strength of relationship" can be reported. Strength of relationship is a feature of correlation coefficients, which we explain in detail in Chapter 12. Properly interpreted, a correlation coefficient can be used to interpret the practical significance of a statistical result. Some researchers report both a correlation coefficient and its effect size equivalent.

Gain Scores

Educators' fundamental mission is to promote the learning and personal development of their students. Researchers think of learning and development as a series of changes that occur in students across time. They can detect these changes by administering the same measure to individuals at two or more points in time. The amount of change can be quantified by computing a **gain score,** which is simply the difference in an individual's score on the measure from one time to the next. Gain scores often are positive, but they also can be negative, as when a student forgets information learned earlier.

Researchers sometimes include gain scores in their reports, but you should view them with caution. For example, they are subject to the **ceiling effect,** which occurs when a student's academic achievement exceeds the highest achievement measured by the test. To understand this effect, suppose that a student scores 95 out of 100 possible points on initial testing. The student can improve by a maximum of only 5 points on this test when it is readministered. This 5-point range might be inadequate to measure all the new information or skills that the student has learned during the intervening time interval. In other words, the ceiling (100 possible points) is too low.

Another limitation of gain scores is that most tests are not true interval scales, meaning that they do not have equal intervals. For example, suppose a test has 50 items, with each item answered correctly earning a score of 1. Further suppose that the items vary in difficulty. Now consider the case of two students who earn the same gain score of 5, but one goes from a raw score of 10 to a raw score of 15, whereas the other goes from a raw score of 40 to a raw score of 45. It probably is more difficult for the second student to make a gain score of 5 than it is for the first student, because she will need to correctly answer test items that are greater in difficulty. If this is true, the same gain score does not have the same meaning for both students.

Still another problem is that most tests contain different types of items. For example, suppose that two students earn the same gain score on a subtraction test, but they do it by making gains on different types of subtraction items. Once again, the gain score is the same, but it does not have the same meaning for the two students.

Percentage Gains and Losses

Gains and losses occasionally are expressed in terms of percentages. For example, we might read that there has been a 50 percent increase in the number of students in a school who report being the victim of cyberbullying from one school year to the next. This statistic suggests a problem of practice that should be addressed, but exactly how big a problem is it?

The calculation procedure involves (1) subtracting the frequency of cyberbullying in Year 1 from the frequency in Year 2, (2) dividing that result by the frequency in Year 1, and (3) expressing that result in percentage form. Suppose the frequency of cyberbullying in Year 1 is 100, and the frequency in Year 2 is 150. Subtracting 100 from 150 equals 50. Dividing 50 by 100 equals $\frac{1}{2}$, and expressing $\frac{1}{2}$ in decimal form is 0.50. In percentage form, 0.50 equals 50 percent.

If only percentage increases or decreases are reported, faulty interpretations can result. In the example just reported, a 50 percent increase in cyberbullying appears ominous, because it represents 50 more students who report being cyberbullied. However, suppose the number of students who report being the victim of cyberbullying in Year 1 is 4, and the number in Year 2 is 6. The percentage increase is 50 percent ($[6 - 4] \div 4 = \frac{2}{4}$, which equals 0.50, or 50 percent).

In both examples, the percentage increase is 50 percent. However, in the second example, the increase is only 2 students, which might indicate a much less serious problem of practice for educators than an increase of 50 students, which was the case in the first example.

This illustration indicates the need to know not only the percentage of increase or decrease, but also the actual frequencies that are involved. Because of this need, some researchers and educators report ratios instead. For example, we found these statistics in a Wikipedia article about autism (http://en.wikipedia.org/wiki/Epidemiology_of_autism; retrieved May 15, 2009).

> Attention has been focused on whether the prevalence of autism is increasing with time. Earlier prevalence estimates were lower, centering at about 0.5 per 1,000 for autism during the 1960s and 1970s and about 1 per 1,000 in the 1980s, as opposed to today's 1–2 per 1,000.

In this example, the authors present the incidence of autism as a ratio. We can see that there has been an increase in the autism rate, but the prevalence at the present time (1 or 2 per 1,000) is still very low. From a human perspective, of course, even if one more child is diagnosed with autism from one year to the next, that is a great personal problem for the child, her parents, and the community.

Status Models and Growth Models for School Accountability

Policy makers are increasingly interested in collecting and analyzing gain scores for the purpose of holding schools accountable for student learning (Goldschmidt et al., 2005). To understand the reasons for this trend, we need to examine the accountability standards of the federal government's **No Child Left Behind Act (NCLB),** which we have discussed in Chapter 1 and elsewhere.

Among other things, NCLB requires that all students achieve proficiency in mathematics and reading by the 2013–2014 school year. To determine whether schools are making adequate gains toward this goal, educators must demonstrate that the percentage of students who achieve proficiency in mathematics and reading increases each year.

For example, if 60 percent of fifth-graders in a particular school achieved proficiency in reading in the 2008–2009 school year, then the children who are in fifth grade the next school year (2009–2010) must exceed that percentage (60%) by a particular amount. If the annual target is 10 percent improvement, educators will be expected to have 66 percent of the 2008–2009 fifth-graders achieving proficiency in reading.

This approach to school accountability sometimes is referred to as a status model. In a **status model,** students at a particular grade level are tested each year, and the achievement test scores of students at that grade level in year X are compared with the scores of students at the same grade level in year Y. Let's assume that it's the fifth grade and the year is 2009. The expectation is that the scores (or percentage of students achieving proficiency) will be higher for the fifth-graders enrolled in 2010 than the fifth-graders who were enrolled in year 2009.

There are several problems with this way of measuring gain. One is that the fifth-graders in year 2009 might be substantially different from fifth-graders in year 2010. If so, we are measuring gain using two different types of students, and therefore the amount of gain or loss might be impossible to interpret. Another problem is that the statistical results do not provide any information about the amount of gain that fifth-graders in 2009 made during year 2010 when they were sixth-graders.

A particularly serious problem with the status model occurs if students are assessed with respect to standards of performance, such as Below Basic, Basic, Proficient, and Advanced. (These standards are used by the National Assessment of Educational Progress, which we discussed earlier in the chapter.) Under NCLB, educators must bring all students up to the Proficient level within a certain number of years.

Suppose that 40 percent of students in a school are Below Basic and 40 percent are Proficient in year 2009. Suppose further that educators work intensively to improve students' learning the following school year, with these results: Only 10 percent of the students score at the Below Basic level; 30 percent score at the Basic level; and 40 percent score at the Proficient level. Student learning in this school has improved tremendously, but the statistical results show no gain in the percentage of students who score at the Proficient level. In both years, it is 40 percent.

Because of these and other problems with the status model for measuring gain, researchers and assessment experts have proposed using growth models. **Growth models** use tests to measure the same students' learning over time. For example, researchers and educators might administer a test to fourth-graders at the end of the school year, administer it again to the same students when they have completed fifth grade, and still again when these same students have completed sixth grade. Statistical analyses would focus on how much gain these students made on the test as they progressed across different grade levels.

One of the main advantages of growth models is that they provide relatively clear statistics describing whether a group of students is learning as they progress through school and whether each new cohort of students enrolled at the school learns more than previous cohorts. Among the disadvantages of growth models are that they require a lot of student testing and data analysis, as well as the development of tests that measure a span of curriculum content sufficiently wide to include several grade levels.

Practical Significance as an Interpretive Process

Statistical results do not speak for themselves. Means, standard deviations, ranges, correlation coefficients, and score distributions are not a direct guide to practice or to the development of theories that might affect practice. Educators and researchers must always use their expertise and apply judgment to determine whether a specific statistical result has practical significance.

In particular, they need to consider the variables to which the statistical results pertain. In discussing different approaches to determining practical significance, we primarily used examples that refer to academic achievement, as measured by scores on academic achievement tests. Most educators are interested as well in other academic outcomes, such as helping students develop creativity, improving students' self-esteem, eliminating school violence and bullying, or helping students develop habits that maintain physical health. A small effect size for one of these outcome variables might be more valued, and therefore have more practical significance, than a larger effect size for an outcome variable that is less valued.

An example of

HOW DETERMINING THE PRACTICAL SIGNIFICANCE OF STATISTICAL RESULTS CAN HELP IN SOLVING PROBLEMS OF PRACTICE

Educators often find that some students have personal problems that interfere with their learning. Some of these problems involve physical illness. Educators need to understand such illnesses, how they affect students, and what remedies are available.

One such illness is asthma. A recent literature review of research about asthma, reported in the medical journal *BMC Medical Practice*, was made available to the general public by various news services, including Reuters. The Reuters news item indicated that the researchers who did the literature review found that exercise can improve aerobic fitness and psychological well-being in asthmatic children. However, the researchers also found that children and young people with asthma

> tend to be less active than their peers without the disease [and] many young people with asthma didn't think they were able to fully participate in sports and physical activities.
>
> Retrieved from www.reuters.com/article/healthNews/idUSGOR18144620080731

The article states that asthmatic children and young people are "less active" than their peers. However, the article does not specify what "less active" means in quantitative terms. Thus, we do not know how serious a problem this is.

We can gain insight into the seriousness of the problem by obtaining a copy of the research team's literature review. Hopefully, the review contains effect sizes that can be analyzed to determine the percentile of the average asthmatic child's exercise level relative to the distribution of exercise levels for nonasthmatic children. If the average asthmatic child is at the 40th percentile, this suggests a less serious problem than if the average asthmatic child is at the 20th percentile.

The phrase "many young people with asthma" poses a similar problem. What does "many" mean? It would be helpful to compute percentages, so that we know exactly what percentage of young people with asthma have negative beliefs about their ability to participate in physical activities.

By precise quantification of "less active" and "many young people," we can develop a better understanding of the practical significance of the problem. If the effect sizes and percentages indicate a serious problem, this could spur policy makers and educators to institute programs that better meet the needs of asthmatic children. These programs might pay dividends by improving the health of such children and by possibly decreasing their absence from school because of illness.

Self-Check Test

1. Curriculum standards are
   a. not available for any school subject at the national level.
   b. useful for formulating research hypotheses.
   c. useful for judging the practical significance of statistical results.
   d. useful for developing tests but minimally useful for developing curriculum.

2. A norming group represents
   a. the entire population for whom a test was developed.
   b. a random sample of the population for whom a test was developed.
   c. the portion of the sample who fall between the 25th and 75th percentile in a table of norms.
   d. the sample or population used to create a table of norms for a test.

3. A grade equivalent for a test indicates
   a. the grade level of the average student who earned a particular raw score on a test.
   b. the grade level for which a test is most appropriate.
   c. the effect size for the difference in the mean scores of students at two different grade levels.
   d. the accuracy with which a particular test predicts the grades of a sample of students randomly selected from a population of students.

4. A standard score represents an individual's raw score in relation to
   a. the standard deviation of the score distribution.
   b. grade equivalents or age equivalents.
   c. percentile ranks based on a table of norms.
   d. All of the above.

5. If a group of individuals takes the same test, those with a z-score of +1.0 are
   a. one standard deviation below the group mean.
   b. one standard deviation above the group mean.
   c. at the 18th percentile of the score distribution.
   d. at the 99th percentile of the score distribution.

6. The z-score
   a. is not a type of standard score.
   b. is equivalent to an effect size.
   c. can be used to compare an individual's scores on different tests that vary in number of items.
   d. can be used to compare an individual's scores on different tests only if the number of items is constant across the tests.

7. The results of intelligence tests and SAT Subject Tests are commonly reported in terms of
   a. raw scores.
   b. standard scores.
   c. effect sizes.
   d. rank scores.

8. An effect size
   a. compares the standard deviation of Group A and Group B.
   b. compares the mean scores of Group A and Group B using a table of norms.
   c. compares the score distributions of Group A and Group B to the score distribution for a norming group.
   d. compares the mean score of Group A to the score distribution of Group B or the score distributions of the two groups.

9. The interpretation of gain scores can be difficult because
   a. there is the possibility of a ceiling effect.
   b. most tests tend to have unequal intervals between the points on the scale.
   c. most tests contain different types of items.
   d. All of the above.

10. The status model for school accountability is illustrated by
    a. selecting a group of students in fifth grade and tracking their learning for several years.
    b. selecting students who are in fifth grade in 2008 and comparing their learning with that of students who enter the fifth grade in 2009 at the same school.
    c. selecting fifth-grade classes of students across a sample of schools in 2008 and comparing them using a table of norms based on grade equivalents.
    d. selecting a sample of students at different grade levels in 2008 and comparing their test performance by calculating effect sizes.

Chapter References

American Psychological Association. (2001). *Publication manual of the American Psychological Association* (5th ed.). Washington, DC: Author.

Goldschmidt, P., Roschewski, P., Choi, K., Auty, W., Hebbler, S., Blank, R., & Williams, A. (2005). *Policymakers' guide to growth models for school accountability: How do accountability models differ?* Washington, DC: Council of Chief State School Officers. Retrieved from www.ccsso.org/publications/index.ctm

Resources for Further Study

In addition to the following resources, we suggest that you examine the resources for further study listed at the end of Chapter 7.

Bracey, G. (2006). *Reading educational research: How to avoid getting statistically snookered.* Portsmouth, NH: Heinemann.

> The author provides a list of 32 guidelines for avoiding being misled by statistical results presented in reports of educational research. The author presents many examples to illustrate how statistical results can be manipulated to support the biases and political agendas of researchers and funding agencies.

Coe, R. (2000). *What is an "effect size"? A guide for users.* Retrieved from www.cemcentre.org/File/CEM%20Extra/EBE/ESguide.pdf

> This guide, available free on the Web, provides a good introduction to the meaning and uses of effect sizes. The author provides examples of effect sizes found in research studies of various educational methods.

Sample Educational Research Study

Can Growth Ever Be beside the Point?

Popham, W. J. (2005). Can growth ever be beside the point? *Educational Leadership, 63*(3), 83–84.

The following article describes current statistical methods that are being recommended for determining whether schools are making year-to-year improvements in student achievement. Even though the author does not offer a solution to avoiding the flaws in such statistical methods, he performs a service to the education profession by identifying them.

The article demonstrates why educators and policy makers need to understand the practical significance of statistical results. Without this understanding, they might adopt a method that produces statistical results that hamper, rather than improve, educational practice.

The article is reprinted in its entirety, just as it appeared when originally published.

Can Growth Ever Be beside the Point?

W. James Popham
UCLA Graduate School of Education and Information Studies

A school is supposed to nurture children's intellectual growth—that is, to promote students' increasing command of significant bodies of knowledge and key cognitive skills. Consequently, if a school *does* promote greater intellectual growth in its students each year, you would think that any annual evaluation of the school's effectiveness would reflect that growth.

Although the architects of No Child Left Behind (NCLB) clearly wanted U.S. schools to foster gobs of student growth, this law's evaluative requirements currently don't function that way. Each state's success or failure under NCLB hinges on the particular cut score that a state's officials have selected, often arbitrarily, to determine whether a student's performance on a state accountability test classifies that student as proficient. On the basis of that cut score, a state identifies its students as either "not proficient" or "proficient or above." For simplicity's sake, I'll call this cut score the *proficiency point*. A state's proficiency point on each of its standardized tests becomes the most significant factor—by far—in determining how many schools will stumble during that state's annual NCLB sweepstakes.

If a designated percentage of a school's students don't earn proficiency on the state-mandated tests, that school is classified as having failed to make adequate yearly progress (AYP). Yet as odd as it may sound, such AYP failure can occur despite the fact that the school has promoted substantial overall growth in its students' achievement levels.

I can illustrate the absurdity of this situation with a fictitious school I'll call Pretend Prep. Let's locate Pretend Prep in a state that uses four levels of NCLB-determined proficiency—below basic, basic, proficient, and advanced. Two years ago, 50 percent of Pretend Prep's students earned such low scores on their state's standardized NCLB tests that they were classified as below basic. The other 50 percent of this imaginary school's students, because of their higher test scores, were classified as proficient.

However, because of an intense, yearlong instructional effort on the part of Pretend Prep teachers, last year all the below-basic students scored well enough on the tests to move up one level to the basic category. Moreover, all the school's proficient students improved their scores so that they, too, jumped up one category to the advanced classification. This represents astonishing academic growth on the part of the school's students. However, because NCLB success is *only* determined by the percentage of students who score at or above the state's proficiency point, Pretend Prep has shown no AYP-related progress. Despite the blatant evidence of remarkable growth in student achievement, 50 percent of the students remained below the proficiency point, and 50 percent remained above.

Although my example is both fictitious and extreme, it illustrates an important point: In real-world school evaluations, students will often improve on state-mandated tests, sometimes dramatically, but the improved scores will not influence a school's AYP status because those students' scores don't cross the proficiency point.

The major drawback of a school evaluation system that doesn't take growth into account is that it encourages teachers to focus excessive instructional attention on students who are at the cusp of proficiency—just above or below a test's proficiency point. Because students who are well above or well below that proficiency point won't affect a school's evaluation, teachers may be tempted to neglect those two categories of students.

Although I am urging the adoption of a growth-based approach to NCLB school evaluation, I am not advocating the adoption of "value-added" evaluative models,

such as those first used in Tennessee but now adopted by a number of other states. These value-added models are explicitly designed to monitor individual students' grade-to-grade achievement growth. By following individual students' growth across grade levels, value-added models can circumvent NCLB's "cross-sectional" analyses whereby test scores of this year's crop of 4th graders, for example, are compared with the test scores of last year's crop of 4th graders. Because of the sometimes considerable disparities in the abilities of different grade-level groups, any evaluative approach that doesn't depend on cross-sectional analyses has great appeal.

For Tennessee's version of the value-added method to work properly, however, student test scores must be statistically converted to a special kind of analytic scale so that student achievement gains in particular content areas represent the same amount of growth at different grade levels. Thus, an analytic scale must be generated so that a 6th grader's 10 percent improvement in mastering 6th grade math content, for example, will be equivalent to a 5th grader's 10 percent improvement in mastering 5th grade math content. Without such analytic scales, most value-added approaches just won't work.

These kinds of analytic scales are difficult to create, however. That's because substantial curricular variation exists between grades, even in the same content area. Moreover, children have an annoying habit of developing cognitively and emotionally in different ways at different times. Accordingly, the only statistically defensible analytic scales for value-added models are excessively general ones, such as scales measuring a student's "quantitative competence" or "language arts mastery."

But these overly general analytic scales supply teachers with no diagnostically useful information about *which* skills or bodies of knowledge a student has or hasn't mastered. Consequently, any useful diagnostic information instantly evaporates with the installation of value-added approaches. Regrettably, value-added methods sacrifice effective instructional diagnoses on the altar of statistical precision. We need to find better ways of measuring students' growth for our AYP analyses.

Fortunately, the U.S. Department of Education has appointed a number of study groups to advise Secretary of Education Margaret Spellings about how best to incorporate growth models into NCLB's accountability requirements. I'm hopeful that these advisory groups can come up with reasonable ways to incorporate growth into NCLB's school evaluations and that Secretary Spellings will heed their advice. Although advocates of a value-added strategy sure know how to belt out an alluring siren song, I suggest we all steer clear of that approach.

W. James Popham is Emeritus Professor in the UCLA Graduate School of Education and Information Studies; wpopham@ucla.edu.

chapter 9

Tests of Statistical Significance

IMPORTANT *Ideas*

1. Tests of statistical significance are used to make inferences about a population's scores on a measure when all that is available are the scores of a sample that is drawn, randomly if possible, from that population.

2. Confidence intervals around a sample statistic (e.g., the mean) enable us to estimate a range of values that are likely to include the actual population parameter for that statistic.

3. The null hypothesis is a prediction about population parameters, and a test of statistical significance is done to determine the likelihood that the prediction is correct.

4. A test of statistical significance is more likely to reject the null hypothesis when the sample is large or when there is a substantial real difference in the parameters of the populations that the samples represent.

5. Every test of statistical significance is susceptible to a Type I error and a Type II error. Generally, Type I errors are more acceptable than Type II errors.

6. There are many tests of statistical significance, each intended for a different type of null hypothesis or directional hypothesis. The *t* test, analysis of variance, and analysis of covariance are among the more commonly used tests of statistical significance.

7. Parametric tests of statistical significance make assumptions about a sample's score distribution and the scale properties of measures, whereas nonparametric tests do not make these assumptions.

8. Tests of statistical significance continue to be widely used in educational research, but they are problematic. These tests assume that the samples are randomly drawn from a defined population, but that is seldom true of actual educational research studies.

9. Education is a "people profession," and therefore it is easy to dismiss the seemingly "cold" numbers that statistics provide. However, statistics have an essential role to play in improving education. ■

Key TERMS

analysis of covariance	nonparametric test of statistical significance	Scheffé's test
analysis of variance		statistical significance
chi-square test	null hypothesis	test of statistical significance
confidence interval	one-tailed test of statistical significance	*t* test for independent means
confidence limit		*t* test for related means
directional hypothesis	parametric test of statistical significance	Tukey's test
F value		two-tailed test of statistical significance
inferential statistics	population	
interaction effect	*p* value	Type I error
margin of error	random sample	Type II error

The Logic of Statistical Significance and Confidence Intervals

Many quantitative research reports include tests of statistical significance and mathematical expressions such as "$p < .05$." For this reason, you need to develop an understanding of what these tests and expressions mean. Our explanation of tests of statistical significance focuses on their underlying logic and meaning rather than computational procedures. Hopefully, our nontechnical explanations and illustrations will help you understand statistics textbooks that present computational procedures for these tests and the mathematical reasoning that underlies them.

The concepts of practical significance and statistical significance are similar terms, but they have different purposes. Indicators of practical significance (e.g., gain scores and effect sizes) help us determine how important a statistical result is for educational practice. Practical significance is the subject of Chapter 8.

In contrast, tests of statistical significance help us to make inferences about a population's scores on a measure when we only have the scores of a sample that presumably is representative of the population. Because the focus is on making inferences from a sample to a population, tests of statistical significance often are called *inferential statistics*. The process by which these inferences are made is explained in the following sections.

Population Data and Sample Data

To illustrate population data, we will use a data set created by the Center for International Development (CID) at Harvard University. Researchers at this center determined the average number of years of schooling for citizens of 136 countries for the year 2000. For our purposes, we will consider these countries the population of interest. A **population** is the complete set of individuals, groups, events, or other entity that is of interest in a research study.

As a side note, other sources, such as the website About.com (http://geography.about .com/od/countryinformation/a/capitals.htm), state that the world actually contains 194 countries. We assume that CID included a smaller number of countries as their population because of difficulty in accessing relevant, current data from all countries.

The CID researchers determined the average number of years of schooling completed by each country's citizens, age 25 and older. Years of schooling is an important variable for educators and policy makers, because it has an important influence on individuals' lives and a nation's economic, political, and social well-being. A country with a poorly educated citizenry represents a problem of practice that should be addressed both by that country and by the world community.

Table 9.1 shows the mean number of years of schooling for each of the 136 countries that constitute the population studied by CID researchers. You will note considerable variation in years of schooling, ranging from a low of 0.76 years (Mali) to a high of 12.25 years (United States). As shown near the bottom of the table, the mean (*M*) number of years of schooling for all 136 countries is 6.14, and the standard deviation is 2.89.

TABLE *9.1*   Average Years of Schooling for the World's Countries (*N* = 136)

Afghanistan	1.14	Egypt	5.05
Algeria	4.72	El Salvador	4.50
Antigua & Barbados	4.80	Estonia	9.17
Argentina	8.49	Ethiopia	1.15
Australia	10.57	Fiji	7.96
Austria	8.80	Finland	10.14
Bahrain	6.09	France	8.37
Bangladesh	2.45	Gambia	1.86
Barbados	9.11	Germany, United	9.75
Belgium	8.73	Ghana	4.01
Benin	2.10	Greece	8.51
Bolivia	5.54	Guatemala	3.12
Botswana	5.35	Guyana	6.05
Brazil	4.56	Haiti	2.67
Brunei	5.81	Honduras	4.08
Bulgaria	9.74	Hong Kong	9.47
Burundi	1.23	Hungary	8.81
Cameroon	3.17	Iceland	8.75
Canada	11.43	India	4.77
Central African Republic	2.11	Indonesia	4.71
Chile	7.89	Iran	4.66
China	5.74	Iraq	4.34
Colombia	5.01	Ireland	9.02
Congo	4.68	Israel	9.23
Costa Rica	6.01	Italy	7.00
Croatia	6.49	Jamaica	5.22
Cuba	7.78	Japan	9.72
Cyprus	8.77	Jordan	7.37
Czechoslovakia	9.46	Kazakhstan	9.03
Denmark	10.09	Kenya	3.99
Dominica	4.54	Korea	10.46
Dominican Republic	5.17	Kuwait	7.05
Ecuador	6.52	Latvia	9.54

(continued)

TABLE *9.1*   *(continued)*

Lesotho	4.47	Sierra Leone	1.99
Liberia	2.26	Singapore	8.12
Libya	2.87	Slovakia	9.19
Lithuania	9.30	Slovenia	7.35
Malawi	2.58	Solomon Islands	2.53
Malaysia	7.88	South Africa	7.87
Mali	0.76	Spain	7.25
Malta	7.57	Sri Lanka	6.09
Mauritania	1.94	St. Kitts & Nevis	7.65
Mauritius	5.55	St. Lucia	4.22
Mexico	6.73	St. Vincent & The Grenadines	4.99
Moldova	9.07	Sudan	1.91
Mozambique	1.19	Swaziland	5.73
Myanmar (Burma)	2.44	Sweden	11.36
Nepal	1.94	Switzerland	10.39
Netherlands	9.24	Syria	5.74
New Zealand	11.52	Taiwan	8.53
Nicaragua	4.42	Tajikistan	9.62
Niger	0.82	Thailand	6.10
Norway	11.86	Togo	2.83
Pakistan	2.45	Trinidad & Tobago	7.62
Panama	7.90	Tunisia	4.20
Papua New Guinea	2.39	Turkey	4.80
Paraguay	5.74	Uganda	2.95
Peru	7.33	United Arab Emirates	2.88
Philippines	7.62	United Kingdom	9.35
Poland	9.90	United States	12.25
Portugal	4.91	Uruguay	7.25
Puerto Rico	9.14	Venezuela	5.61
Reunion	2.28	Vietnam	3.81
Romania	9.51	Western Samoa	6.65
Russia/U.S.S.R.	10.49	Yugoslavia	7.48
Rwanda	2.03	Zaire	3.18
Senegal	2.23	Zambia	5.43
Seychelles	5.79	Zimbabwe	4.88
		M = 6.14 (SD = 2.89)	

Source: Data in table is from Barro, R. J., & Lee, J. (2000). *International Data on Educational Attainment: Updates and Implications.* Center for International Development, Harvard University (www.cid.harvard.edu/ciddata/ciddata.html). Years of schooling are projections for 2000 based on data estimates for 1995.

As we explained in Chapter 7, the mean and standard deviation in this case are called *parameters,* because they refer to characteristics of the entire population of countries studied by the researchers. If we compute the mean and standard deviation for a sample of countries in this population, they are called *statistics.*

Drawing Random Samples from a Population

Suppose no one had collected data on years of schooling for the world's nations. Further suppose that we wished to have this information, but our funding for collecting it is limited. Faced with this situation, we would be well advised to study a random sample of the countries. A **random sample** is a group in which each member of the group was chosen entirely by chance from the population. The size of the random sample would be as large as our budget allowed.

This approach raises an important question: How well will the sample statistics match the actual population parameters? We can answer this question by playing with the actual population parameters shown in Table 9.1. We will draw random samples from this population and determine how well the sample statistics estimate the population of all 136 countries.

Our first step was to randomly select a sample of five countries, determine their years of schooling using the data shown in Table 9.1, and compute the mean and SD for these data. The results are shown in the first data row of Table 9.2 under the heading, "Five Random Samples ($N = 5$ for Each Sample)." The sample mean is 7.36, which overestimates the population mean (6.14) by 1.22 years, as shown in the column "Deviation from Population Mean (6.14)."

Our next step was to draw four more samples of five countries each to see what would happen. (We used a table of random numbers to select our samples.) None of the sample means matched the actual population mean. By chance, all five means were higher than the population mean; their average deviation from the population mean was 1.04, as shown on the line labeled "Mean Deviation."

The SD for each of the five random samples is also shown in the same section of Table 9.2. None of them matched the population SD (2.89). On average, they deviated from the population SD by 0.77 schooling years.

What happens if we double the size of the random sample ($N = 10$)? The second section of Table 9.2 shows the mean and SD for five samples, each including 10 countries that we drew randomly from the population of 136 countries. If you look at Table 9.2, you will see that none of the sample means and SDs matched the population mean and SD, but their deviations from these parameters were, on average, smaller when $N = 10$ than when $N = 5$. The average deviation from the population mean was 0.59.

Even still, one of the random samples yielded a mean of 7.51 years of schooling, which is a substantial deviation from the population mean. Thus, drawing a larger sample does not guarantee a better estimate of population parameters; it only increases the likelihood of obtaining a better estimate.

What happens if we increase the size of the random sample to 20 countries? The bottom section of Table 9.2 shows what happened when we did this five times. You can see that four of the five sample means were good estimates of the population mean; one of them (7.32) deviated substantially from the population mean, but less so than the worst estimate for the random samples with $N = 5$ (7.98) or with $N = 10$ (7.51). Also, the mean deviation for the sample SDs (0.28) was smaller than the corresponding number for random samples where $N = 5$ and $N = 10$.

These data analyses demonstrate that increases in sample size increase the likelihood of obtaining good estimates of the population parameters. Another conclusion is that even a random sample of 20 countries, which is only a fraction of the total number of countries ($N = 136$), is likely to yield a good estimate of population parameters. Thus, random sampling is a good option when funds are insufficient to study an entire population.

TABLE *9.2*   Years of Schooling Based on Random Samples of Different Sizes from the Defined Populations of 136 Countries

Sample Mean	Deviation from Population Mean (6.14)	Confidence Interval	Sample SD	Deviation from Population SD (2.89)
Five Random Samples (N = 5 for Each Sample)				
7.36	1.22	4.67–10.05	2.16	0.73
7.98	1.84	3.68–12.28	3.46	0.57
6.63	0.49	4.50–9.76	1.72	1.17
7.10	0.96	2.40–11.80	3.79	0.90
6.81	0.67	3.82–9.80	2.40	0.49
Mean Deviation	1.04			0.77
Five Random Samples (N = 10 for Each Sample)				
5.56	–0.58	3.03–8.09	3.54	0.65
6.08	–0.06	3.74–8.42	3.27	0.38
7.51	1.37	5.26–9.76	3.15	0.26
6.47	0.33	4.61–8.33	2.61	0.28
5.53	–0.61	3.32–7.74	3.10	0.21
Mean Deviation	0.59			0.36
Five Random Samples (N = 20 for Each Sample)				
6.38	0.24	4.86–7.90	3.25	0.36
7.32	1.18	5.89–8.75	3.05	0.16
5.88	–0.26	4.73–7.03	2.46	0.43
6.30	0.16	5.04–7.56	2.70	0.19
6.49	0.35	5.20–7.78	2.75	0.24
Mean Deviation	0.44			0.28

Survey studies of the U.S. population rely on these principles when trying to determine demographic characteristics (e.g., family size per household) or opinions about education and other matters. It is too expensive to collect data from every individual in the population, but a random sample can yield very good estimates of the population parameters. We discuss just how large a sample is necessary in the next sections of this chapter.

Confidence Intervals

In the preceding section, we had available to us both the population parameters (i.e., the population mean and standard deviation) and the sample statistics (i.e., the sample mean and standard deviation). Suppose we only had available the sample statistics for, let's say, one of the random samples of 20 countries. Can we use these statistical results to say anything about the population parameters? If not, we can only draw conclusions about these 20 countries, even though our real interest is the total population, that is, all 136 countries.

Fortunately, statisticians have developed mathematical equations that allow us to use our sample to determine a range of means that *probably* includes the actual population mean. The equations make use of the sample mean and SD, and they construct an interval around the sample mean that is likely to include the population mean.

For a mean of 7.36 and an SD of 1.22 (the first random sample of $N = 5$ in Table 9.2), the confidence interval is 4.67 and 10.05. In simple terms, the confidence interval tells us that there is a high likelihood that the actual population mean lies somewhere between 4.67 and 10.05. More exactly, the confidence interval tells us that if we took 100 random samples with $N = 5$ from a population, 95 of those samples would have a confidence interval that includes the actual population mean. Thus, it is very likely that our sample is one of the 95 samples whose confidence interval includes the population mean.

A **confidence interval** can be defined as a range of values, derived from known characteristics of a random sample (mean, SD, and sample size), that is likely to include a population parameter. In Table 9.2, you will see columns of confidence intervals that estimate the population mean. It is also possible to compute a confidence interval for the population standard deviation or other parameter (e.g., the correlation coefficient for two variables in a population).

If you look at Table 9.2, you will see that each of the confidence intervals includes the actual population mean. This is not surprising, because we computed confidence intervals that would include the actual population mean in 95 of every 100 random samples of a given size. If we continue to draw random samples, sooner or later we would come across one whose confidence interval did not include the population mean.

If researchers wish to be more certain that their sample includes the population interval, they will compute confidence intervals that contain the population parameter of interest for 99 of every 100 hundred samples randomly drawn from the population. However, the confidence interval will be larger.

The precision of our estimates is also a function of sample size. If you examine the confidence intervals in Table 9.2, you will find that they narrow as sample size increases. When $N = 5$, the average confidence interval is 6.82; when $N = 10$, it is 4.48; and when $N = 20$, it is 2.66.

Another way to understand the concept of confidence intervals is to consider a random sample whose mean score on a variable is 7.36 (the first mean shown in Table 9.2). Even if we do not know the population mean for this variable, it is easy to realize that the population mean is highly unlikely to be, let's say, 50. A population with a mean of 50 might have some scores of 7 or lower, but it is extremely improbable that we would draw a random sample that would consist of such low scores.

It is similarly improbable that a population whose mean is 30 would include sufficient low scores that we could draw a random sample and obtain a sample mean of 7.36. However, it is reasonable to imagine that a population whose mean score is 4.67 or 10.05 (the confidence intervals for 7.36 in Table 9.2) might yield a sample whose mean is 7.36.

Statisticians use the term **confidence limit** to label the upper or lower value of a confidence interval. For example, the confidence limits for our sample mean of 7.36 are 4.67 and 10.05. A population whose mean is above or below the confidence limits is highly unlikely to generate the mean that we obtained for our sample.

You are likely to find confidence intervals in reports or recent educational research studies. The *APA Publication Manual* (American Psychological Association, 2001), which is the standard style reference for educational researchers, states:

> The use of confidence intervals [in research papers] is . . . strongly recommended. As a rule, it is best to use a single confidence interval size (e.g., a 95% or 99% confidence interval) throughout the course of the paper. (p. 22)

Confidence intervals serve as a reminder that a sample mean or other statistic (e.g., a correlation coefficient or standard deviation) is only an estimate of the corresponding population parameter.

Margin of Error.   You probably have come across the term *margin of error* in popular media, such as newspapers. This term is often used in connection with political polls. For example, *The Boston Globe,* among many other newspapers, reported that, in a poll of likely Republican voters in New Hampshire leading up to the 2008 presidential election, Mitt Romney had the support of 28 percent of these voters and John McCain had the support of 25 percent. *The Boston Globe* also reported that the poll "has a margin of error . . . of plus or minus 4.9 percent" (Helman, 2007).

A **margin of error** has exactly the same meaning as a confidence interval. It is a range of values, derived from known characteristics of a random sample (mean, SD, and sample size), that is likely to include a population parameter. The margin of error is typically set at 95 percent. In the case of the New Hampshire poll, this margin of error means that there is a strong likelihood that Romney's level of support was between 25.55 percent (28 − half of 4.9) and 30.45 (28 + half of 4.9). The margin of error also tells us that McCain's level of support was between 22.55 (25 − half of 4.9) and 27.45 (25 + half of 4.9).

This information leads us to the conclusion that, in the actual population of likely Republican voters in New Hampshire (not the sample that was polled), there is a small probability that Romney's actual level of support might have been as low as 25.55 (or even lower) and McCain's level of support might have been as high as 27.45 (or even higher). Thus, it might be that McCain actually might have had more support than Romney, even though the poll found the opposite to be the case. The safest conclusion, based on the survey results and margin of error, is that Romney's and McCain's levels of support were approximately the same.

More certainty about the voters' preferences could be obtained if the pollsters surveyed every likely voter or increased their sample size to lower the margin of error. However, as the sample size increases, so does the cost of the poll. In general, a margin of error that yields a 95 percent confidence level is considered cost-effective. The poll is affordable, and the level of certainty is acceptable for those who want the survey information.

The preceding example comes from the world of politics, but polls are commonly done in education as well. For example, school districts regularly survey members of the community on issues such as the need for new school bonds and whether schools are adequately serving students with various characteristics. The cost of these surveys usually comes out of the district budget, so administrators need to select a sample size that is affordable yet likely to yield results that accurately reflect the total community.

Inferential Statistics

As we have explained, confidence intervals are useful because they enable us to estimate a population parameter, based on the sample mean. Another relationship between samples and populations is of great interest to researchers. It is the subject of the following sections of this chapter.

We start by considering the statistics shown in Table 9.2. Each of the sample means for the variable "years of schooling" was computed by drawing a random sample of a given size from a known population of 136 countries. Looking at the five random samples where $N = 20$, we see that the means fluctuate: 6.38, 7.32, 5.88, 6.30, and 6.49. These fluctuations are to be expected whenever we draw random samples from a population.

Although the means fluctuate and none of them is exactly the same as the population mean, we know one thing for certain: All five samples were drawn from the same population. Suppose, however, that we knew the sample means, but had no knowledge about the population mean. For example, suppose one researcher had studied 20 countries below the equator and found a mean of 6.38 years of schooling, and another researcher had studied 20 countries above the equator and found a mean of 7.32 years of schooling. (These are the first two means in Table 9.2 for samples where $N = 20$.)

It is possible to make one of two inferences from these sample means. One inference is that the mean number of years of schooling for the two samples are chance fluctuations from two populations (countries above and below the equator) that have identical means and score distributions. This is an entirely reasonable inference because, as we showed in Table 9.2, fluctuations in means occur for samples drawn from exactly the same population.

The other inference is that the two sample means differ because they were drawn from two different populations having different means. It is possible, for example, that the population of all countries below the equator has a lower average number of years of schooling, causing the obtained mean (6.38) to be lower than that for countries above the equator (7.32).

Which is the correct inference? Does the difference in the two sample means reflect chance fluctuations from identical populations? Or does it reflect a real difference between the two populations that the two samples were selected to represent?

An entire branch of statistics has been developed to answer these and similar questions that arise when researchers have collected data only on samples. This branch of statistics, sometimes called **inferential statistics,** involves statistical procedures for making *inferences* about characteristics of populations based on data collected from samples that were selected to represent those populations.

The Null Hypothesis

Inferential statistics follow a particular logic. In the case of two sample means, they test the validity of one of two possible inferences, namely, the inference that the samples come from identical populations. This possible inference is called the null hypothesis. In the case of comparisons involving two samples, we can define the **null hypothesis** as a prediction that there is no difference between the populations that the two samples are designed to represent; stated another way, it is a prediction that the two samples come from the same population.

A statistical procedure, called a test of statistical significance, is used to determine how likely it is that the null hypothesis is true. If the statistical test finds that the null hypothesis is unlikely to be true, we then make the opposite inference: We infer that the two samples come from different populations having different means. We do not know exactly what those means are or how different they are, but we can estimate them by computing confidence intervals.

The Meaning of p Values and Statistical Significance

A **p value,** in which p stands for probability, refers to the percentage of occasions that a chance difference between mean scores of a certain magnitude will occur when the population means are identical. The lower the p value, the less often a chance difference of a given magnitude will occur; therefore, the more likely it is that the null hypothesis is false.

For example, a p value of .001 indicates that it is much more likely that the null hypothesis is false than would a p value of .01. A p value of .001 indicates that a mean score difference between two groups as large as the mean score difference that was found in the research study would occur only once in 1,000 drawings of two random samples from identical populations. A p value of .01 indicates that a mean score difference as large as the obtained mean score difference would occur only once in 100 drawings.

In educational research, a p value of .05 generally is considered sufficient to reject the null hypothesis. This high a p value makes it fairly easy to reject the null hypothesis, because the observed difference between mean scores does not need to be large.

It is possible to reject the null hypothesis when it is true. In other words, we might conclude that the difference between the mean scores of two random samples occurred because they came from two populations with different mean scores when, in fact, they came from identical populations. This false rejection of the null hypothesis is more likely to occur when $p = .05$ than when $p = .01$. For this reason, you should be cautious about generalizing results from a sample to a population if the p value is .05 or higher (e.g., .10). You have less need for caution, though, if other research studies in the literature report findings similar to those that you obtain.

Some researchers will report p as less than .05 ($< .05$) rather than equal to .05 ($= .05$). Usually the p value is not exactly .05 but rather some value less than that. The symbol $<$ (meaning "less than") is a shorthand way of expressing this information.

If a p value reaches the desired level to reject the null hypothesis, researchers state that the difference between the two sample means is statistically significant. Otherwise, the result is not statistically significant. We can define **statistical significance** as a designation that an observed difference between two sample means is large enough to reject the null hypothesis.

The procedure used to determine whether an observed difference is statistically significant is called a **test of statistical significance.** A better label might be "test of the null hypothesis," because that is the purpose of the procedure—to determine whether the null hypothesis should be accepted or rejected.

Type I and Type II Errors

Keep in mind that tests of statistical significance are not perfect. They are educated guesses, based on mathematical logic, for estimating population means (or other parameters) from sample statistics. Therefore, erroneous inferences are possible. One kind of error, called a **Type I error,** involves rejection of the null hypothesis when it is actually true. Another kind of error, called a **Type II error,** involves acceptance of the null hypothesis when it is actually false.

Researchers can lower the risk of making a Type I error, but it is at the expense of increasing the risk of a Type II error. In medical research, the better risk usually is a Type I error. For example, suppose the researchers are testing a new drug with an experimental group of patients (they get the new drug) and a control group of patients (they get the conventional drug). If they reject the null hypothesis that the two drugs are equally effective and conclude that the new drug is more effective, the typical result will be more testing of the new drug. These additional tests should reveal whether the new drug truly is more effective or whether the initial test resulted in a chance difference between the two groups.

Consider now the case of a Type II error, that is, an acceptance of the null hypothesis when it is actually false. Suppose the conditions of the initial testing of the new drug are the same, but the observed difference between the experimental and control groups on the outcome variable is insufficiently large to reject the null hypothesis. This inference might lead the researchers to conclude that the new drug is a blind alley, and they and other researchers abandon it. This is indeed an unfortunate error, because an effective drug would be abandoned even though it is effective and would likely have been found effective with further testing.

Similarly, in educational research it is better to make the error of concluding that an ineffective new practice is effective than the error of concluding that an effective new practice is ineffective. Further research should eventually correct the error. Researchers do not want to waste valuable resources going down blind alleys, but neither do they want to prematurely abandon promising new practices. Therefore, the trade-offs between Type I and Type II errors in tests of statistical significance need to be carefully considered.

Directional Hypotheses

As we have stated, a null hypothesis predicts that there is *no* difference between the parameters of the populations that the samples represent. Most research studies test null hypotheses. However, in some studies, researchers predict that there actually is a difference between the populations that the samples represent. Furthermore, they predict the direction of the difference.

A prediction of this type is called a directional hypothesis. A **directional hypothesis** involves the assumption that a difference exists between the parameters of the populations represented by the samples, and that the difference is in a specific direction, that is, that one population will have a higher mean score than the other.

For example, researchers might predict that Population A, which is represented by sample A in their study, will have a higher mean score on the Iowa Test of Basic Skills than Population B, which is represented by sample B in their study. In order to specify a directional hypothesis rather than a null hypothesis, the researcher needs to justify it on the basis of theory or the findings of previous research studies.

The advantage of a directional hypothesis is that the test of statistical significance makes it easier to obtain findings that lead to acceptance of the directional hypothesis. Stated another way, the test of statistical significance makes it more difficult to reject the directional hypothesis. This is a desirable situation, because researchers typically do studies in order to find a difference (e.g., the innovative teaching method is better than the conventional teaching method) rather than to find no difference.

When possibilities of a difference in either direction are tested, the test is called a **two-tailed test of statistical significance.** When only a possibility of a difference in one direction is tested, the test is called a **one-tailed test of statistical significance.**

Tests of Statistical Significance

The following chapters present different quantitative research designs. These designs require different types of null hypotheses, each of which is accepted or rejected by a different test of statistical significance. We explain the more commonly used tests of statistical significance below. Table 9.3 lists these tests, the statistical value that each test yields, and the null hypothesis tested by each test of statistical significance.

TABLE **9.3**   Commonly Used Tests of Statistical Significance and Null Hypotheses

Test of Statistical Significance	Value	Description of Null Hypothesis Tested
t test for independent means	t	The observed difference between the mean scores of two samples are chance fluctuations between populations having identical mean scores.
t test for related means	t	The observed difference between the mean scores of two samples that are related to each other in some way are chance fluctuations between populations having identical mean scores.
analysis of variance (ANOVA)	F	The observed difference between the mean scores of three or more samples are chance fluctuations between populations having identical means. Follow-up tests can be done to determine whether the mean scores of any two of the samples are chance fluctuations between populations having identical mean scores. ANOVA also can be used to determine whether the interaction between a level of one factor and a level of another factor is a chance fluctuation between populations having identical mean scores on the specified level of one factor and the specified level of the other factor.
analysis of covariance (ANCOVA)	F	Used to test the same null hypotheses as ANOVA except that the different sample means are more-or-less equated on a pretest measure on which they might differ.
chi-square test	χ^2	The observed difference between the frequency counts on a nominal scale for two samples are chance fluctuations between populations having identical frequency counts on the nominal scale.
t test for correlation coefficients	t	The observed correlation coefficient for a sample is a random fluctuation for a population having a correlation coefficient of 0.00. Another null hypothesis that can be tested by t is that the difference between the correlation coefficients for two samples is a random fluctuation between populations having identical correlation coefficients.

Comparison of Two Sample Means

Many research studies involve the selection of two samples, each one being a group that represents a different population. For example, we might want to know whether U.S. males and females differ in their average years of schooling. Our resources might only allow us to collect data on 100 males and 100 females, who will represent the total populations of U.S. males and females, respectively.

The *t* **test for independent means** is used to determine whether to accept or reject the null hypothesis that two populations, each represented by a sample (in this case, males and females) have identical means on a variable (in this case, years of schooling). The *t* test is given that label, because it yields a value called *t*. The mathematical basis of *t* is beyond the scope of this book, but it can be found in statistics textbooks. For present purposes, though, you need to know that *t* can be converted to a *p* value. It is the *p* value that is used to decide whether to accept or reject the null hypothesis.

In some research studies, the scores of the two samples representing the two populations of interest are related to each other. For example, suppose that we administer a scale that measures interest in politics to a sample of high school seniors before and after they view a video about the importance of voting in a democracy. Prior to the video, the sample represents the population of all high school seniors who have not seen the film. After viewing the video, the sample represents the population of all high school seniors who have seen the video. Because the same group of individuals is in both samples, the *t* **test for related means** (also called the "*t* test for correlated means" or the "*t* test for dependent means") is used.

Comparison of More Than Two Sample Means

Some research studies involve more than two samples, each representing a different population. For example, suppose that we want to compare the grade point average (GPA) for four different types of college students: (1) students living in a college dormitory, (2) students living in a fraternity or sorority, (3) students living with other students off-campus, and (4) students living alone off-campus. Our null hypothesis is that the mean GPA for the four populations represented by these four groups is identical. The appropriate test of statistical significance would be **analysis of variance.** Analysis of variance is generally used to test differences when more than two means are being compared.

Analysis of variance yields an *F* **value.** You can consult a statistical table, found in most statistics textbooks, that converts *F* to a *p* value. If only two sample means are being compared, the *F* value and the *t* value (resulting from use of the *t* test) will be identical.

If the analysis of variance leads to the rejection of the null hypothesis, this result does not necessarily imply that all four populations represented by the four samples have different GPA means. It is possible that two of the populations have different GPA means (e.g., the groups designated "1" and "3" differ from each other). The null hypothesis for each pair of samples representing different populations can be tested with a special form of the *t* test, usually **Tukey's test** or **Scheffé's test.**

Comparisons of Sample Means in Complex Data Sets

Analysis of variance is a versatile statistical procedure because it can test several null hypotheses for a complex data set. To illustrate its versatility, we constructed data for a hypothetical experiment comparing two types of text. Two groups of students were formed prior to the experiment: students with high reading ability and students with low reading ability.

Students within each of these two groups were randomly assigned to experimental and control conditions. Students in the experimental condition read a text passage with inserted questions inviting them to relate the information being presented to something they already knew. Students in the control treatment read the same text passage but with no inserted questions. A multiple-choice test covering the content of the text passage was administered a day before students read the passage (the pretest) and a day after (the posttest).

Table 9.4 shows descriptive statistics for each subgroup (e.g., high-reading-ability students in the experimental group) on the posttest. Also shown are descriptive statistics for combinations of subgroups, for example, the mean score (*M*) and standard deviation for all experimental group students, whether they have high or low reading ability.

Many comparisons are possible for the mean scores shown in Table 9.4—for example, all experimental group students versus all control group students; high-ability students versus low-ability students in the experimental group; high-ability students in the experimental group versus high-ability students in the control group. One could do *t* tests for all these comparisons. However, not only is this procedure tedious, but as the number of comparisons increases, so does the likelihood of false conclusions. (It can be shown mathematically that, as the frequency of inferential statistics calculated for a set of data increases, so does the likelihood of falsely rejecting the null hypothesis.)

Analysis of variance is a more elegant and accurate method of making all the comparisons at once to determine which ones are likely to be chance differences. Table 9.5 shows a summary of the *F* values generated by the analysis of variance of the data presented in Table 9.4 and whether each *F* value is statistically significant ($p = .05$ or less). The first line of results shows the *F* value (49.88) for the comparison of all experimental group students ($M = 16.30$) and all control group students ($M = 8.55$) on the posttest, ignoring whether the students have high or low reading ability. This *F* value is statistically significant

TABLE 9.4 Posttest Scores for Students Classified by Reading Ability and Experimental Group or Control Group Assignment in Hypothetical Experiment on Inserted Questions in Text

Experimental Group		Control Group	
High Reading Ability	Low Reading Ability	High Reading Ability	Low Reading Ability
23	18	19	3
14	17	12	7
16	9	16	1
18	10	14	6
16	17	7	4
17	19	8	7
19	8	13	6
20	20	10	5
17	15	19	3
17	16	9	2
M = 17.70	*M* = 14.90	*M* = 12.70	*M* = 4.40
SD = 2.50	SD = 4.33	SD = 4.32	SD = 2.12

Subgroup Statistics			
Subgroup	*N*	*M*	SD
Experimental Group	20	16.30	3.73
Control Group	20	8.55	5.39
High-Reading-Ability Group	20	15.20	4.29
Low-Reading-Ability Group	20	9.65	6.33

TABLE 9.5   Summary of Analysis of Variance for Posttest Scores in Hypothetical Experiment on Inserted Questions in Text

Source	F	p
Treatment (T)	49.88	<.001
Reading Ability (R)	25.58	<.001
T × R Reaction	6.28	<.051

($p < .001$), meaning that the difference is generalizable to the populations represented by the samples.

The second line shows the F value (25.58) for the comparison of all high-reading-ability students ($M = 15.20$) and all low-reading-ability students ($M = 9.65$) on the posttest. This F value, too, is statistically significant ($p < .001$).

Interaction Effects

The next line of Table 9.5 shows an F value of 6.28 ($p < .05$) for the interaction effect. In educational practice, an **interaction effect** involves a finding that an intervention has a different effect on some members of the experimental group than on others. In statistics, an interaction effect is said to have occurred when the difference between two groups on variable B varies according to the value of variable A.

To understand what an interaction effect means, consider the research results shown in Table 9.4. For students with low reading ability (one level of variable B), the difference in the posttest mean scores of the experimental and control groups (variable A) is substantial ($14.90 - 4.40 = 10.50$ points). For students with high reading ability (the other level of treatment variable B), the difference in the posttest mean scores of the experimental and control students (variable A) is much smaller ($17.70 - 12.70 = 5.00$ points).

Thus, we find that the experimental text passage helped poor readers much more than it helped good readers. The significant F value for this interaction effect suggests that it is a real difference between the populations represented by the samples in the experiment.

Analysis of Covariance

We have not yet addressed the pretest results for our hypothetical experiment. The pretest was administered in order to determine how much students knew about the text passage content prior to the experiment. The pretest mean scores for each group are shown in Table 9.6. These results complicate our interpretation of the posttest results, because they show that the experimental group had higher scores on the pretest than did the control group. The experimental group's superior knowledge of the text passage content beforehand, rather than the inserted questions in the text passage, might be responsible for its higher score on the posttest.

We could eliminate superior pretest knowledge as an explanation for the results by doing another experiment in which the students selected for the experimental and control groups were equivalent on the pretest. This solution, however, is time-consuming and expensive. Another solution is to use gain scores, which are computed by subtracting the pretest score from the posttest score for each student in the experiment. However, gain scores have several limitations, so they are seldom used to analyze experimental data.

The best solution to the problem is to make the groups equivalent on the pretest by applying a statistical technique known as **analysis of covariance** (ANCOVA). ANCOVA adjusts each research participant's posttest score, either up or down, to take into account his

TABLE 9.6   Pretest Means for Students in Hypothetical
Experiment on Inserted Questions in Text

	Experimental Group M	Control Group M
High-Ability Readers	10.10	7.70
Low-Ability Readers	4.30	2.90

pretest score. Analysis of covariance yields F values similar in meaning to those described for analysis of variance.

The procedure used in analysis of covariance is somewhat similar to the handicapping procedure used in sports such as golf. Poor golf players can compete with good golf players by being assigned a handicap based on their past performance. Each golf player's score in a tournament is determined by how much better or worse she does than her handicap (that is, her previous performance).

Comparisons between Sample Frequencies

The tests of statistical significance described in the preceding sections involve comparisons of samples with respect to the mean of their scores on a particular measure. However, some measures yield frequency counts, because they constitute nominal scales. (We explained nominal scales in Chapter 7.) The **chi-square test** is the appropriate test for deciding whether to accept or reject null hypotheses that involve frequency data on nominal scales.

To illustrate the use of the chi-square test, suppose that we want to determine whether urban school districts are more likely to employ female school superintendents than are rural school districts. A random sample of 100 urban school districts and 100 rural school districts is drawn from a population of school districts. The gender of each district's superintendent is determined.

The two variables involved in this study are gender (male versus female) and type of school district (urban versus rural). Both variables are categorical because they cannot be ordered on a continuum. For example, a rural district is neither "more" nor "less" than an urban district.

Table 9.7 shows hypothetical data relating to our research question. The descriptive statistics are in the form of frequencies, each frequency being the number of superintendents in each gender category for a particular type of district. Table 9.7 shows that the distributions of male and female superintendents vary across districts. We need to determine whether these differences occurred by chance or are characteristic of the populations represented by the random samples.

TABLE 9.7   Distribution of Male and Female
Superintendents in Urban and Rural
School Districts

	Urban	Rural
Males	65	82
Females	35	18

The chi-square test is used to make this determination. It yields an inferential statistic known as *chi,* which is squared and represented by the symbol χ^2. Statisticians have created tables that convert χ^2 to *p* values. The χ^2 value for the distributions shown in Table 9.7 is 7.42. This value is associated with a *p* value that is less than .01. Therefore, we reject the null hypothesis that these results occurred by chance. Instead, we conclude that there are real differences in the proportion of male and female superintendents in the populations of districts represented by the two random samples.

Comparisons between Correlation Coefficients

The use of correlation coefficients in educational research is described at length in Chapter 12. We mention them here only to note that tests of statistical significance are available to accept or reject null hypotheses involving correlation coefficients. The most common null hypothesis is that the obtained correlation coefficient for a sample is a chance fluctuation from a correlation coefficient of zero ($r = .00$) for the population represented by the sample. A zero correlation coefficient means that there is no relationship between the two sets of scores. Therefore, an individual's score on one measure has no value in predicting his or her score on the other measure.

Even if the correlation coefficient for the population is zero, random samples drawn from that population might produce correlation coefficients that differ from zero. Some of these coefficients might be small; others might be large. Some of the coefficients might be positive, indicating that high scores on one measure are associated with high scores on the other measure. Other coefficients might be negative, indicating that high scores on one measure are associated with low scores on the other measure.

A test of statistical significance can be done to help us decide whether to accept the null hypothesis, namely, that the correlation coefficient for our sample is a chance deviation from the population coefficient, which is assumed to be zero. If the test yields a statistically significant result, we reject the null hypothesis and conclude that the correlation coefficient for the population represented by the sample is not zero. The test does not tell us what the correlation coefficient for the population is, but constructing confidence intervals (described earlier in the chapter) around the sample correlation coefficient can give us a range of correlation coefficients that are likely to include the population correlation coefficient.

Parametric versus Nonparametric Tests of Statistical Significance

The preceding sections explain commonly used tests of statistical significance for making decisions about whether to accept or reject null hypotheses and directional hypotheses. Other tests of statistical significance are used when the null or directional hypotheses involve multiple variables. If you understand the reasoning behind the simple tests of statistical significance, it should not be difficult to understand the basic features of more complex tests of statistical significance.

All the tests of statistical significance described above, with the exception of the chi-square test, are **parametric tests of statistical significance,** meaning that they make several assumptions about the measures being used and the populations that are represented by the research samples. These assumptions are that (1) there are equal intervals between the scores on the measures, (2) the scores are normally distributed about the mean score, and (3) the scores of the different comparison groups have equal variances.

Suppose the assumptions underlying parametric tests, especially the assumption of equal intervals, cannot be satisfied. In this case, researchers might use a parametric test anyway, if the assumptions are not violated seriously. Otherwise, they will use a **nonparametric test of statistical significance,** which makes no assumptions about the measures being used and the populations that are represented by the research samples. The chi-square test is the most commonly used nonparametric test, because many variables are in the form of categories, which do not form an interval scale.

Cautions in Interpreting Tests of Statistical Significance

It is easy to be misled by certain phrases in research reports such as, "The difference between the experimental and control group was statistically significant." The word *significant* might suggest that the research result is important. In fact, as we explained above, statistical significance only means that the null hypothesis or directional hypothesis can be rejected. Even then, a statistically significant result is subject to a Type I or Type II error.

Probably the most serious problem with tests of statistical significance is that education researchers seldom have the opportunity to work with random samples drawn from a defined population. This is unfortunate, because random sampling is essential to the mathematical logic of tests of statistical significance, and for that matter, to the logic of confidence intervals.

Instead of working with random samples, educational researchers typically work with volunteer samples, that is, a sample that happens to be accessible to them. (We explained volunteer samples in Chapter 6.) Volunteer samples might have characteristics that are representative of the population that interests the researchers, but they also might have distinctive characteristics.

For these and other reasons, research methodologists (e.g., Harlow, Mulaik, & Steiger, 1997) have expressed concerns about the appropriateness of tests of statistical significance in research about education and related professions. Our recommendation is that you view a statistically significant result as a tentative finding. Similarly, if the statistically significant result involves a positive difference favoring an innovative program or technique, we recommend that you look at the result as a promising finding that is reason for cautious optimism.

The critical next step is attempting to replicate the finding. Indeed, carefully designed replications are the most powerful way to determine whether a research finding has narrow generalizability or whether it applies to the entire population of interest. Different researchers should attempt to replicate the original study elsewhere with different samples (including volunteer samples) and with different measures of the same variables, if possible.

Over time, the results of different studies can be accumulated and analyzed to determine the features of the population to which the research result applies and the populations to which the research result does not apply. This accumulation and analysis is done most effectively by meta-analysis, which we explained in Chapter 5.

Jacob Cohen (1990), a statistician, succinctly explains both the limitations of tests of statistical significance and the superiority of replication research:

> The prevailing yes-no decision at the magic .05 level from a single research study is a far cry from the use of informed judgment. Science simply doesn't work that way. A successful piece of research doesn't conclusively settle an issue, it just makes some theoretical proposition to some degree more likely. Only successful future replication in the same and different settings (as might be found through meta-analysis) provides an approach to settling the issue. (p. 1311)

Cohen's recommendation echoes our own statements about replication as a research strategy in Chapter 1 and in other parts of this book.

If you are just learning how to do research, you can help to advance the field of research knowledge about education by replicating and extending previous research. This is a surer path to developing research expertise and making a research contribution than striking off in a new direction to study a problem about which little is known and for which measures and data-analysis procedures are either unavailable or uncertain.

Calculating Statistics

As we stated in Chapter 7, Excel, which is standard software on most computers, is an effective tool for calculating many statistics. You only need to enter the raw scores, double-check them for accuracy, and then use the appropriate Excel function. The Data Analysis function under the Tools menu can calculate descriptive statistics and some of the tests of statistical significance described in this chapter.

More complicated statistical analyses require software that is run on a personal computer or workstation. We described two of these software programs (SPSS and SAS) in Chapter 7.

In our experience, large data sets involving many variables and samples or populations require the services of expert statisticians and data managers. For example, if large groups of students have taken a standardized test, they typically record their response to each item on a sheet that can be optically scanned. The scanning process is complex, as is the process of transferring the scanning results into a data set that can be analyzed by statistical software. Each step in the process requires expert skill and judgment.

If your skills lie more in professional practice, you probably will find it best to consult statisticians and data managers who are trained to work with large data sets and to conduct tests of statistical significance. It would be a mistake, though, to simply turn over the data to these experts. It is best to work alongside them, so that both you and they understand the process. By doing so, you can answer questions raised by your colleagues and other stakeholders rather than having to plead ignorance and refer them to the experts. Also, you can help the experts identify possible errors that can creep in at each stage of data entry and analysis. (Just think of the errors that can creep into your checkbook entries and calculations.) Just as important, you can ensure that the data analyses actually answer your questions, not the questions that the experts might guess you want answered.

Using Statistics to Improve Professional Practice

Individuals enter the education profession because they wish to work with people, not numbers. Education is first and foremost a "people profession." The quality of the interpersonal relations teachers develop with students, parents, and their colleagues is critical to helping students learn. In contrast, statistical analysis deals with numbers and relies on mathematical logic, which can seem remote and arcane for those of us who do not have a strong background in mathematics.

Nonetheless, statistical analysis is an essential tool for improving educational practice. The history of educational research shows that it is possible to develop valid quantitative measures of learning, motivation, attitudes, interests, teaching behavior, and other constructs that are central to educational practice. These measures can be used to collect data that give us a reasonably objective picture of what actually occurs in schools. We can examine this objective picture to see how well it corresponds to ideal practice. Discrepancies between the actual and the ideal can and should be the stimulus for improving practice so that all students have the best opportunity to learn.

Moreover, quantitative data collection and statistical analysis can be used to identify whether promising innovations actually do improve learning, teacher morale, community support of schools, and other important outcomes. Statistical evidence of these improvements can provide the necessary leverage to obtain funding to disseminate and implement these innovations.

For these reasons and others, it is important for professional educators to learn the statistical concepts and procedures presented in this chapter. Statistical analysis is not an end in itself (except possibly for theoretical statisticians), but it is an important means to an end, namely, the improvement of educational practice.

An example of

HOW TESTS OF STATISTICAL SIGNIFICANCE CAN HELP IN SOLVING PROBLEMS OF PRACTICE

While Colorado as a state struggles to lift the scores of students who fail standardized tests, some schools have raised scores by testing regularly or involving parents. But the principals of such schools say no solution fits every school.

> *ASCD SmartBrief* news item, July 31, 2008, summarizing an article in *Teacher Magazine*, July 29, 2008.

It is good news when we learn that some schools have found a way to improve students' performance on achievement tests. We wonder, though, about the principals' claim that "no solution fits every school." Is the claim true? Experimental research can help provide an answer.

It is critical that the experiment involve a random sample of schools that represents a defined population, because a random sample provides a sound basis for generalizing the results beyond the sample to the population that it represents. The random sample would be divided into two groups: an experimental group of schools that receives training and support for testing regularly and parent involvement and a control group of schools that continues to use their regular practices.

A test of statistical significance can be done on the students' achievement test scores to determine the likelihood that any observed differences between the two groups are due to chance (the null hypothesis) or to real differences in the populations represented by the two samples.

Suppose the test of statistical significance leads to the rejection of the null hypothesis, and we find that the difference on the achievement test favors the experimental schools. These results might not allow us to conclude that the intervention will work in every school. However, the results do allow us to reach tentative conclusions about the percentage of schools in the population that will benefit from the intervention and by how much. These conclusions provide a better basis for deciding whether to promote the widespread adoption of the intervention than the simple assertion that "no solution fits every school."

Self-Check Test

1. The purpose of inferential statistics is to determine whether
   a. a set of scores forms a normal distribution.
   b. the sample size is sufficiently large to detect real differences between the experimental and control group.
   c. an observed statistical result for a sample randomly drawn from a population is a chance finding.
   d. the results of one study constitute a nonchance replication of the results of another study.

2. As the size of a research sample increases, the confidence interval
   a. around the mean score of a measure administered to the sample is likely to increase.
   b. around the mean score of a measure administered to the sample is likely to decrease.
   c. is less likely to include the population parameter.
   d. becomes more similar to the standard deviation of the population.

3. Researchers use the *p* value in a test of statistical significance to
   a. decide whether it is best to state a null hypothesis or a directional hypothesis.
   b. determine whether a Type I or Type II error has occurred.
   c. decide whether to accept or reject the null hypothesis.
   d. determine whether the sample size was sufficiently large.

4. The likelihood that the null hypothesis is false is greatest when the *p* value is
   a. .001.
   b. .01.
   c. .10.
   d. 1.00.

5. A Type I error means that the researcher has
   a. rejected the null hypothesis when it is actually true.
   b. accepted the null hypothesis when it is actually false.
   c. used the wrong test of statistical significance.
   d. used a volunteer sample rather than a random sample.

6. Suppose that researchers have administered a measure of open-mindedness to a sample of students at the start (pretest) and end (posttest) of their college careers. They would be well advised to determine the statistical significance of the difference between the pretest and posttest means on this measure by doing
   a. an analysis of covariance.
   b. an analysis of variance.
   c. the *t* test for related means.
   d. the *t* test for correlated means.

7. If the pretest scores of two groups in an experiment differ, researchers usually can compensate for this problem by
   a. using analysis of covariance.

   b. computing confidence intervals around the pretest mean scores.
   c. converting the pretest and posttest scores to gain scores.
   d. using a nonparametric test of statistical significance.

8. Researchers would conclude that an interaction effect occurred in an analysis of variance if they found that
   a. boys and girls had different pretest means on a measure of mathematics achievement.
   b. discovery learning was more effective for high-achieving students than low-achieving students.
   c. a statistically significant effect was found in the original experiment but not in the replication experiment.
   d. All of the above.

9. Nonparametric tests of statistical significance
   a. assume that the scores to be analyzed form an interval scale.
   b. do not assume that the scores to be analyzed form an interval scale.
   c. must be used even if the scores constitute a minor violation of the assumptions underlying analysis of variance.
   d. can be used only with continuous scores.

10. The most serious problem with tests of statistical significance is
    a. the prevalence of Type I errors.
    b. the prevalence of Type II errors.
    c. that educational researchers usually can only collect data that form a nominal scale.
    d. that educational researchers usually must work with volunteer samples rather than random samples.

Chapter References

American Psychological Association. (2001). *Publication manual of the American Psychological Association* (5th ed.). Washington, DC: Author.

Cohen, J. (1990). Things I have learned (so far). *American Psychologist, 45,* 1304–1312.

Harlow, L. L., Mulaik, S. A., & Steiger, J. H. (Eds.). (1997). *What if there were no significance tests?* Mahwah, NJ: Lawrence Erlbaum.

Helman, S. (2007, December 23). McCain closing gap with Romney. *The Boston Globe.* Retrieved from www.boston.com

Resources for Further Study

Fidler, F., & Cumming, G. (2007). Lessons learned from statistical reform efforts in other disciplines. *Psychology in the Schools, 44*(5), 441–449.

   The authors claim that tests of statistical significance have limited value, especially for the improvement of professional practice. They argue that effect sizes and confidence intervals provide stronger evidence for judging the practical significance of statistical results.

Thompson, B. (2006). *Foundations of behavioral statistics.* New York: Guilford.

   Many books about statistics are available. This one provides in-depth coverage of statistical significance and related topics.

chapter 10

Descriptive Research

IMPORTANT
Ideas

1. Descriptive research provides knowledge about the status quo, which is often the first step in improving educational practice.

2. Descriptive research studies identify characteristics of a group at one point in time or changes in such characteristics across time, but they do not explore cause-and-effect relationships involving these characteristics.

3. The Gallup Poll, the National Assessment of Educational Progress, and other organizations regularly collect descriptive data about various aspects of education.

4. Panel studies, trend studies, and cross-sectional studies use different sampling procedures to study human development or changes in a group or organization over a period of years.

5. Tests, questionnaires, observation schedules, interview guides, and other measurement methods can be used to collect data in a descriptive research study.

6. Researchers commonly analyze descriptive data to determine the central tendency and variability of score descriptions.

7. The findings of descriptive research studies can reveal the prevalence of problems, opinions, academic achievement, and other phenomena across an entire defined population. ■

Key TERMS

cohort study	margin of error	Phi Delta Kappa/Gallup Polls
confidence interval	mean	standard deviation
cross-sectional study	National Assessment of Educa-	survey research
descriptive research	tional Progress (NAEP)	trend study
longitudinal research	panel study	

The Relevance of Descriptive Research to Educational Practice

Educators and researchers are curious about what is happening in schools. Are teachers using research-based methods of instruction? How safe are schools? Are ethnic-minority students respected and supported? What problems do teachers face in their work? How does the public feel about school vouchers and charter schools?

Answering these questions about the status quo of education requires descriptive research. The knowledge gained by this type of research is often the first step in launching efforts to improve education. For example, knowledge about problems and successful practices in one school district can help educators in other school districts. Conversely, knowledge about problems and successful practices across many school districts can help educators in a particular school district.

The value of large-scale descriptive research is illustrated in the medical profession by a problem involving artificial joints (Meier, 2008). A surgeon discovered that several of his patients suffered greatly after being implanted with a metal hip socket, called the Durom cup, manufactured by Zimmer Holdings. He alerted colleagues in a professional association, and found that some of them, too, had found problems with this hip socket. Sales of the device were suspended until the problem was solved.

Meier notes that the patients' suffering might have been averted:

If those patients lived in other countries where artificial joints were tracked by national databases—including Australia, Britain, Norway and Sweden—many might have been spared that risk. And Zimmer might have suspended sales of the cup months ago.

But the United States lacks such a national database, called a joint registry, that tracks how patients with artificial hips and knees fare. The risk in the United States that a patient will need a replacement procedure because of a flawed product or technique can be double the risk of countries with databases, according to Dr. Henrik Malchau of Massachusetts General Hospital.

Educators often find that the most useful thing about conferences and workshops is the opportunity to share their local problems and practices with other educators. This sharing is undoubtedly useful, but educators also need to consider the value of national-level descriptive data about problems and practices. In this chapter, we consider how descriptive research can produce this type of knowledge, either for the nation as a whole or for particular defined populations within it.

The results of descriptive research about education are published in scholarly journals but also in popular media. Let's consider some examples.

Descriptive Research in Newspapers

In an article titled "Failing Schools See a Solution in Longer Day," the *New York Times* described a major problem in today's schools and a possible solution:

> States and school districts nationwide are moving to lengthen the day at struggling schools, spurred by grim test results suggesting that more than 10,000 schools are likely to be declared failing under federal law next year. . . .
>
> But the movement, which has expanded the day in some schools by as little as 30 minutes or as much as two hours, has many critics: among administrators, who worry about the cost; among teachers, whose unions say they work hard enough as it is, and have sought more pay and renegotiation of contracts; and among parents, who say their children spend enough time in school already. (Schemo, 2007)

Stories and statistics such as these are regularly reported in newspapers and other mass media. Success stories are reported, but problems and failings seem more prevalent. As an educator, you will want to take note of these reports, as they shape public opinion about schools generally and, fairly or not, about your own school and your own performance.

The Gallup Polls

You probably are familiar with the Gallup Polls, as their findings are widely disseminated by the mass media and various publications. The general purpose of Gallup Polls is to serve as a barometer of public opinion about various matters of interest to society.

One of the Gallup polls should be of particular interest to educators. It is the annual **Phi Delta Kappa/Gallup Poll** of the Public's Attitude toward the Public Schools. At their website (www.pdkintl.org/kappan/kpollpdf.htm), you can find the results of the most current annual poll and all other annual polls back to the first, conducted in 1969.

We refer here to PDK/Gallup Poll 38, conducted in 2006. The report includes 44 tables, which contain statistics describing the public's opinions about such matters as school governance, testing, the achievement gap, curriculum, teachers, and the No Child Left Behind Act. One of the tables is shown in Table 10.1, both because it is representative of most of the

TABLE *10.1*   Phi Delta Kappa/Gallup Poll: Question about Problems of Practice

What do you think are the biggest problems the public schools of your community must deal with?

	National Totals			No Children In School			Public School Parents		
	'06 %	'05 %	'04 %	'06 %	'05 %	'04 %	'06 %	'05 %	'04 %
Lack of financial support/funding/money	24	20	21	25	19	22	21	21	20
Overcrowded schools	13	11	10	12	9	9	16	15	13
Lack of discipline, more control	11	10	10	12	12	10	7	8	8
Use of drugs/dope	8	9	7	8	9	7	7	8	7
Pupils' lack of interests	6	*	3	6	*	4	6	*	2
Parents' lack of support	5	12	4	5	2	5	6	3	3
Fighting/violence/gangs	5	8	6	6	7	6	4	10	6

*Less than one-half of 1%

Source: Table 10 on p. 45 of Rose, L.C., & Gallup, A. M. The 38th annual Phi Delta Kappa/Gallup Poll of the public's attitudes toward the public schools. *Phi Delta Kappan, 88*(1), 41–56.

tables and because it highlights problems of practice in education. The problems identified through this type of descriptive research could shape future priorities for school improvement, research funding, and governmental intervention.

The PDK/Gallup polls are a form of survey research. We define **survey research** as the systematic collection of data about participants' beliefs, attitudes, interests, and behavior using standardized measures such as questionnaires, interviews, and tests. The measures are standardized in that each participant receives the same measure, administered in the same manner. The data typically are summarized in the form of descriptive statistics. (Descriptive statistics are explained in this chapter and in Chapter 7.)

The value of survey research, or any kind of descriptive research, depends on the sample from which data are collected. If the PDK/Gallup poll only reflected the views of educators, or of parents with school-age children, or people who were approached by data collectors in public settings, the usefulness and meaning of the results would be much different than if they represented the entire U.S. population.

In fact, the researchers who conducted Gallup Poll 38 wanted to represent the entire U.S. population, and so they used a systematic approach to achieve this goal. Among their procedures were the following:

- They used random-digit telephone dialing, so that households with unlisted telephone numbers were as likely to be included in the sample as households with listed telephone numbers.
- They used stratified sampling (see Chapter 6), so that all regions of the United States and communities of different sizes were represented equally.
- An interview was sought with the household member who had the most recent birthday, thus giving all members of the household an equal chance of being selected into the sample.
- Three calls were made to each selected household, and the time and day of callbacks were varied to ensure that household members who worked outside the home during the day had a fair chance of being selected.

These procedures illustrate what it means to take a scientific approach to surveying. It is far different than, for example, talking to one's circle of friends and neighbors about education and drawing conclusions from these conversations about what Americans think about the status of education.

National Assessment of Educational Progress

The **National Assessment of Educational Progress (NAEP)** is a congressionally mandated project of the National Center for Education Statistics (www.ed.gov/programs/naep). NAEP has been assessing U.S. students' performance since 1969 to determine how well students are learning school subjects such as reading, mathematics, science, writing, history, and geography.

Figure 10.1 illustrates the type of descriptive findings that NAEP produces. The bar graph shows the reading proficiency of a national sample of 17-year-old students. (Similar bar graphs for 9-year-olds and 13-year-olds can be found at http://nces.ed.gov/nations reportcard/ltt/results2004/nat-reading-perf.asp.) The bar graphs illustrate the percentage of students who achieved a particular proficiency level in a given year.

We will explain the bar graph by referring to the descriptive results for the year 2004. Using the legend in the top left of the bar graph, we see that 80 percent of the student sample scored at the 250+ level of reading proficiency, 38 percent of the student sample scored at the 300+ level of reading proficiency, and 6 percent of the student sample scored at the 350+ level of reading proficiency.

Of course, these statistical descriptions have little meaning unless we know what the different reading levels indicate. (Chapter 8 presented similar information about NAEP reading levels.) The following NAEP statements (National Center for Education Statistics, n.d.) provide the gist of their meaning:

- At Level 250, students can search for, locate, and organize information in relatively lengthy passages in literature, science, and social studies. They also can make inferences about main ideas in the passages and the author's purpose.
- At Level 300, students can understand complicated literary and informational passages about topics they study at school.
- At Level 350, students can understand ideas in specialized and complex texts, such as scientific materials, literary essays, and historical documents. Also, they can understand the links between ideas, even when those links are not explicitly stated.

With this information in mind, let's examine Figure 10.1 more closely. We see that 80 percent of 17-year-olds who were assessed in 2004 have reading skills that are at least at the 250+ level. That is good news. The bad news is that 20 percent of students have not achieved this basic level of reading proficiency. This finding, resulting from a descriptive research study, identifies a problem of practice that deserves serious consideration by educators, policy makers, and others.

Another finding is that 38 percent of 17-year-olds are at Level 300 or higher. Perhaps you will view this finding, as we do, disappointing. These are juniors or seniors in high school, and we would like to think that after 11 or 12 years of formal schooling, most students, not just 38 percent of them, would be sophisticated readers. Finally, we see in Figure 10.1 that only 6 percent of 17-year-olds are at Level 350 or above, meaning that they are prepared for the reading demands likely to be placed on them in college.

Now consider all the years included in Figure 10.1. The statistical results indicate no improvement in reading skills from 1971 to 2004. The percentage of students at each level is virtually unchanged. Other professions can report large improvements in their practice over the same time span. For example, medicine has improved the cure rate for certain diseases; public safety has seen drops in particular crimes; technological advances have resulted in better and more efficient engineering projects. As more educators become familiar with descriptive research and support it, we expect that they, too, will be able to make, and point to, demonstrable gains in their profession.

FIGURE **10.1**   The Reading Proficiency of 17-Year-Old Students from 1971 to 2004

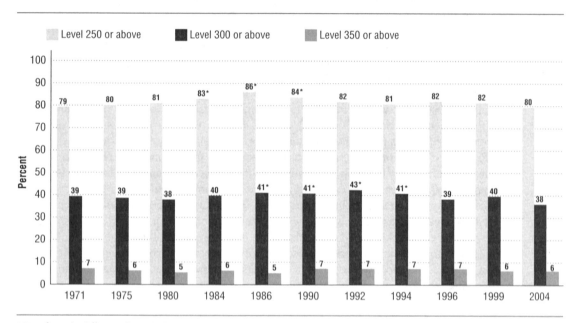

*Significantly different from 2004.

Source: U.S. Department of Education, Institute of Education Sciences, National Center for Education Statistics, National Assessment of Educational Progress (NAEP), selected years, 1971–2004 Long-Term Trend Reading Assessments. Retrieved from http://nces.ed.gov/nationsreportcard/ltt/results2004/not-reading-perf.asp

An Example of Descriptive Research: The Quality of Teaching in Low-Income Schools

Many descriptive studies are published in academic and practitioner journals. We will discuss one of them to illustrate the types of problems of practice that they can bring to light.

Mary McCaslin and her colleagues (2006) used a structured observation instrument to create a picture of how elementary teachers in low-income schools provide literacy and mathematics instruction to third-, fourth-, and fifth-grade students. The schools were selected because they were receiving supplemental funds from the Comprehensive School Reform Demonstration Act that would enable them "to adopt research-based, comprehensive whole-school improvement plans to enhance student achievement" (p. 314).

The researchers collected observational data on a total of 145 teachers for 2,736 10-minute intervals over the course of 447 classroom visits. Their data analyses led them to conclude that, by and large, the teachers were not engaged in "best practice" based on research about effective literacy and mathematics instruction. The challenge for educators then is how to provide "best-practice" instruction to children who are particularly in need of it.

An interesting feature of this descriptive research study is that it corrects misperceptions that some individuals might have about the classroom behavior of low-income children. Table 10.2 provides a summary of trained observers' data about the children's activity patterns during class.

Several of the results are particularly noteworthy. During 86 percent of the observed 10-minute intervals, at least 75 percent of the children were on task. Furthermore, students' on-task behavior was productive during 85 percent of the intervals.

McCaslin and her colleagues concluded from these results: "Contrary to the stereotypes of disruptive and disinterested students who attend high-poverty schools, the students in our study contributed to an orderly, safe, and predictable classroom" (p. 326). This finding reminds us that, although we emphasize the use of descriptive research to discover and document problems of practice, it also can be used to identify and report successes in educational practice.

Features of a Descriptive Research Report

What do the descriptive research studies we have discussed have in common? First, they seek to provide a quantitative representation of behavior, opinions, or other educational phenomena. Second, they focus on representative samples or entire populations, so that the researchers can draw conclusions about what is generally true rather than what is true of one individual, one group, or one institution. Third, the researchers specify the particular characteristics (technically, the variables) they wish to study in advance of data collection.

Given these three features, we can define **descriptive research** as the collection and analysis of quantitative data in order to develop a precise representation of a sample's behavior or personal characteristics with respect to predetermined variables. Other quantitative research designs (group comparison research, correlational research, and experiments) also describe behavior and personal characteristics, but their primary purpose is to identify cause-and-effect relationships involving behavior and personal characteristics. This differs from qualitative research, where you will find descriptions of individuals, groups, cultures, historical periods, and other phenomena. Unlike quantitative descriptive research, case studies are a voyage of discovery where the focus and methods of data collection can change as the researcher's questions and interests change over the course of the study. Table 10.3 (on p. 216) presents typical features of descriptive research studies that are reported in education journals, technical papers, or other formats. We discuss each of these features in the following sections.

Introduction

The introduction of a descriptive research report defines the problem and the particular aspects of the problem that will be investigated. Each aspect is a separate variable. For

TABLE *10.2*   Summary of Observations of Elementary Students'
Behavior in Low-Income Schools

Variable	Time-Sampled Intervals	
	Number	Percent
Student on task:		
1 = not evident/can't tell	12	.42
2 = 25% or fewer	34	1.2
3 = 25%–75%	351	12.36
4 = 75% or more	2,438	85.88
Level of productivity:		
1 = not evident/can't tell	132	4.65
2 = not productive	292	10.29
3 = productive	2,400	54.54
Student questions:		
1 = none	1,825	64.58
2 = task management	488	17.27
3 = task management and corrections	152	5.38
4 = correctness	268	9.48
5 = thinking included	93	3.29
Disruptions (coming/going):		
1 = none	2,504	88.2
2 = a few	304	10.71
3 = many	31	1.09
Disruptions (from main office):		
1 = none	2,670	94.21
2 = yes	164	5.78

Source: Table 3 on p. 321 of McCaslin, M., Good, T. L., Nichols, S., Zhang, J., Wiley, C. R. H., Bozack, A. R., Burros, H. L., & Cuizon-Garcia, R. (2006). Comprehensive school reform: An observational study of teaching in grades 3 through 5. *Elementary School Journal, 106*(4), 313–331.

example, there were two variables in our description of the NAEP study earlier in the chapter. One variable was the year in which a reading assessment occurred. Because 11 separate years were included, this variable had 11 values. The other variable was reading proficiency, which had three values (150+, 200+, and 300+). The researchers should state why they chose the particular variables to be studied. They also should provide a literature review that describes, among other things, what is already known about these variables.

Literature reviews and the measurement of variables (discussed below) are time-consuming, so it is better to study a few variables in depth than many variables superficially. To understand this point, think of educators you know who have become experts on a certain subject, such as multicultural education or classroom management. They could not have become experts without thoroughly studying past and current literature on their subject area, practicing the skills that the subject area involves, and observing various field settings in which the skills are relevant. Similarly, researchers tend to focus their investigations on a few central variables related to a problem of practice or theoretical framework so that they become recognized experts in them.

TABLE *10.3*   Typical Features of a Descriptive Research Report

Section	Content
Introduction	Hypotheses, questions, or objectives are stated. A review of relevant literature is presented. A common purpose is to study a problem of practice to determine its prevalence and severity.
Research design	The researchers select a sample that has the characteristic or problem of interest to them. The sample typically is studied at one point in time or at several predetermined points in time. The variables that are to be studied are specified in advance of data collection.
Sampling procedure	The researchers ideally select a sample that is representative of the population to which they wish to generalize their findings.
Measures	Virtually any kind of measure can be selected for data collection. Questionnaires, tests, and structured interviews are commonly used.
Data analysis	Descriptive statistics are computed and commonly presented in tables or graphs.
Discussion	The main findings are summarized. Flaws and limitations of the study are noted. Implications of the findings for further research and professional practice are discussed.

Research Design

The researchers should explain why they chose to use a descriptive research design to investigate the problems, questions, or objectives of interest to them. Typically, a descriptive research design is chosen because the educational phenomena that will be studied can be quantified and measured with a degree of objectivity.

Sampling Procedure

The soundness and utility of a descriptive research study is greatly affected by the procedure used to select a sample. Guidelines for good sampling were presented in Chapter 6.

If you are doing a descriptive research study, your primary concern will be to select a sample that is representative of the population of interest to you. If you are reading a descriptive research report, your primary concern will be to determine whether the sample selected by the researchers represents the individuals or groups of interest to you.

Sampling in Longitudinal Research.   **Longitudinal research** involves the collection of data about changes in a population's characteristics over a specified period of time. Sample selection in this type of research is more complex than a descriptive study that examines a problem or phenomenon at one point in time.

Suppose we wish to study a sample of talented middle school students to determine whether and how they develop their talents over a period of 5 years. This is called a **panel study,** which is a research study that surveys the same sample at each data-collection point. In contrast, a **cohort study** follows the same group over time, but not necessarily the same members of the group at each data-collection point. For example, we might identify a population of 1,000 talented students and draw a random sample from this population for each of the 5 years in which we collect data.

Another strategy for studying longitudinal changes is to conduct a trend study. **Trend studies** are research studies that describe change by selecting a different sample at each data-collection point from a population that does not remain constant. For example, suppose the researchers define a population of 1,000 talented students in Year 1 and randomly select a sample of 100 of them to study. In Year 2, they find that have lost contact with 75 students in the population, and so they must select 100 students from a slightly different population.

One of the most common sampling strategies in longitudinal research is to select samples that represent different stages of development and study all the samples at the same point in time. Longitudinal studies of this type are called **cross-sectional studies.** For example, Marilyn Nippold and her colleagues (2005) wished to study how syntactic complexity develops as children mature into adulthood.

Syntactic complexity involves such language factors as sentence length and frequency of subordinate clauses attached to the main clause of a sentence. Research knowledge about syntactic complexity can help educators in various ways, such as providing them with the ability to determine whether a child's use of language is developing in a typical manner or is better or worse than the norm.

Nippold and her colleagues (2005) studied syntactic complexity at six different age levels: 8, 11, 13, 17, 25, and 44. If she and her colleagues had started with a sample of 8-year-olds, they would have needed to follow them for 36 years until they reached the age of 44. Of course, this approach is not feasible, except in the case of large-scale, heavily funded longitudinal research. Lewis Terman's studies of gifted individuals who were followed from childhood into adulthood (e.g., Terman & Oden, 1959) are an example of that type of research.

Nippold and her colleagues solved the problem of sample selection by using cross-sectional sampling. They selected samples of individuals who represented each of the six age groups. This selection process probably required just a few weeks of the researchers' time, not the 36 years that would be required for a panel sample.

The downside of cross-sectional sampling is that the different age levels might represent different populations. For example, 44-year-olds might have had less opportunity to develop their language skills (e.g., less or no exposure to TV, computers, and other media) than the current generation of 8-year-olds. In reading the report, we found that these researchers did not consider the possibility of population differences as a threat to their goal of describing how syntactic complexity develops as individuals in our society mature.

Measures

The variables studied in descriptive research can be measured by any of the approaches described in Chapter 6: tests, scales, questionnaires, interviews, and direct observations. For example, the PDK/Gallup Polls, which we described previously, collect opinions by the use of attitude scales administered by telephone. The National Assessment of Educational Progress, which we have also described, relies heavily on standardized tests of academic achievement for its research data. The soundness of any descriptive research study is dependent on the quality of its measures. Validity and reliability, which were explained in Chapter 6, are the primary indicators of the quality of any measure.

Construction of Questionnaires and Interviews

Many novice researchers conduct surveys using questionnaires or interviews, because these measures appear simple to construct and administer. In fact, it might be relatively easy to develop questionnaire and interview items, but the collection of evidence to demonstrate the measure's validity and reliability requires expertise and resources. Without this evidence, educators will not be able to determine the soundness of research findings obtained by using the measure. We recommend that, whenever possible, you select a well-developed questionnaire or interview for use in your research study. By doing so, you will save the time required to develop your own measure.

If you find it necessary to develop your own questionnaire or interview, we explain several of the steps in the following sections. At the end of the chapter, Resources for Further Study lists books that provide a more detailed description of the development process. Our example is a questionnaire, the Stages of Concern Questionnaire (SoC). It has been widely used in educational research and practice since the 1970s. The measure, evidence for its validity and reliability, and administration procedures are freely available by finding the citation (Hall, George, & Rutherford, 1977) in ERIC and then using ERIC's full-text feature. (We explained the ERIC search engine in Chapter 4.)

Identification of Constructs.   You will need to identify the constructs that you wish to measure in your questionnaire or interview. (Constructs were explained in Chapter 6.) For example, the Stages of Concern Questionnaire (SoC) was designed to measure seven hypothesized stages of concerns that educators go through when considering whether to adopt an educational innovation in their local setting. Gene Hall and his colleagues did a literature review and found that concern is an important construct in educational practice. For example, researchers have found that teachers have many concerns about their instruction and that these concerns change in type and severity as their careers progress.

Hall and his colleagues (1977) (hereafter "the SoC developers") wondered whether educators had other concerns, namely, concerns about an innovation (e.g., a new organizational structure, program, textbook series, or teaching method) being considered for adoption in their schools. They defined the construct of concern as "the composite representation of the feelings, preoccupation, thought, and consideration given to a particular issue or task" (p. 5).

The SoC developers refined the construct of concern about an innovation into seven stages, each of which is a separate construct:

1. *Adoption.* Little concern about or involvement with the innovation.
2. *Informational.* General awareness of the innovation and interest in learning more about it.
3. *Personal.* Uncertainty about the demands of the innovation, one's adequacy to meet those demands, and what one's role will be if the innovation is adopted.
4. *Management.* Concerns about the efficiency, organizing, managing, scheduling, and time demands of the innovation.
5. *Consequence.* Concerns about the impact of the innovation on students within one's sphere of influence.
6. *Collaboration.* Concerns about coordinating and cooperating with others in using the innovation.
7. *Refocusing.* Exploration of more universal benefits from the innovation and concerns about whether a more powerful alternative to the innovation is possible.

A major hypothesis relating to these seven constructs is that each stage of concern must be resolved or lowered in intensity before the next stage can become the focus of the educator's attention.

It is common to include demographic questions in questionnaires and interviews. Demographic questions are queries about characteristics of the sample or population that readers of the research report would consider important or interesting. The following demographic questions were included in the questionnaire that also contained the SoC:

- What percent of your job is: teaching __%   administration __%   other (specify) __%
- Do you work: full time __   part time __
- Female __   Male __
- Total years teaching: __
- Number of years at present school: __ (Hall, George, & Rutherford, 1977, p. 69)

Each of these demographic characteristics is itself a construct that requires careful analysis. If you ask research participants to reveal information about personal characteristics, such as age, you should be able to justify the request. Researchers generally do not consider it ethical to ask participants to provide information unless it is relevant to the objectives of the research study.

In the case of the SoC, its developers asked these and other demographic questions to determine whether individuals' personal characteristics had an influence on their expressed concerns about an educational innovation. They report their findings as follows:

> It has been of interest to us, in our research to date, that there have been no outstanding relationships between standard demographic variables and concerns data. Rather, as our research unfolds, there is increasing support for the hypothesis that "interventions" and "conditions" associated with the implementation effort are more critical variables than age, sex, teaching experience, etc. (Hall, George, & Rutherford, 1977, p. 62)

We see then that the incorporation of demographic variables in the questionnaire yielded a useful finding. The research results suggest that educators who attempt to introduce an intervention into a school system should focus more on creating conditions that facilitate its adoption than on the personal characteristics of those who are part of the adoption and implementation process.

Writing Questionnaire and Interview Items.

Research methodologists have developed many guidelines for the writing of questionnaire and interview items. Items that are poorly written can create a negative impression on research participants. As a consequence, they might complete the items haphazardly or not respond at all. The following guidelines for writing questionnaire items are also applicable to writing interview items:

- Begin with a few interesting and nonthreatening items.
- Put threatening or difficult items near the end of the questionnaire.
- Include examples of how to respond to items that might be confusing or difficult to understand.
- Avoid terms like *several, most,* and *usually,* which have no precise meaning.
- Avoid negatively stated items, because they are likely to be misread by respondents.
- Avoid "double-barreled" items that require the participant to respond to two separate ideas with a single answer. For example, "Do you favor abstinence education and drug education?" is double-barreled, because it asks about two different types of education but only allows a single answer.
- Avoid biased questions, such as, "What do you see as the benefits of requiring all students to learn algebra in the eighth grade?" This question assumes that the respondent sees benefits when, in fact, they may not.

With the advent of Internet surveys, additional guidelines have been developed to accommodate the capabilities and limitations of this electronic medium. These guidelines are described in several of the publications in *Resources for Further Study* at the end of the chapter.

The SoC developers prepared an initial set of 544 items that they thought would measure the seven stages of concern in adopting an innovation. They submitted these items to various groups for their appraisal and also performed statistical analyses on them. They gradually whittled the 544 items to a 35-item questionnaire. Their item development process was unusually extensive, but even a more modest development process requires considerable effort.

Each of the 35 items ask the respondent to circle a number on an eight-point scale. A respondent circles one of the low numbers (0, 1, 2) if the concern is "not true of me now." The respondent circles one of the middle numbers (3, 4, 5) if the concern is "somewhat true of me now" and one of the high numbers (6, 7) if the concern is "very true of me now."

The following are seven of the items in the 35-item questionnaire. Each item represents a different level of concern, shown in parentheses.

1. I don't even know what the innovation is. (Awareness)
2. I would like to know what resources are available if we decide to adopt this innovation. (Informational)
3. I would like to know who will make the decisions in the new system. (Personal)
4. I am concerned about my inability to manage everything the innovation requires. (Management)
5. I am concerned about how the innovation affects students. (Consequence)
6. I would like to coordinate my effort with others to maximize the innovation's effects. (Collaboration)
7. I would like to modify our use of the innovation based on the experience of our students. (Refocusing) (Hall, George, & Rutherford, 1977, pp. 65–66)

Note that each item is simply worded and directly relevant to the construct it was designed to measure. This simplicity and relevance are among the reasons that the SoC questionnaire has been widely used by researchers and educators.

At the time that it was developed, the SoC questionnaire was administered as a paper-and-pencil measure. Now that the Internet has become universally available, questionnaires like this are increasingly administered online. There are three main types of Internet-based research surveys:

1. Researchers can send an email message to prospective survey respondents, with the survey embedded as a part of the message. Respondents can then reply to the message with their answers to the survey items.
2. Researchers can send an email message with a file attachment containing the survey. Respondents can then open the attachment, answer the questions, and return them as an attachment to an email message addressed to the researchers.
3. Researchers can send an email message with a direct link to an Internet website containing the survey, which has been designed using a Web-based software program. As the respondent responds to each item, the answer is transmitted directly back to the researchers via the Internet. Depending on the software program, it might be able to analyze the data and record which respondents in the sample have completed the survey.

The decision about which of these options to use depends on the respondents and the characteristics of the survey, such as its length. The third option (Web-based surveys) probably is now the most widely used in educational research studies. The reason is that the populations of interest to educational researchers generally have access both to the Internet and email and also the ability to follow the directions presented in Web-based software programs.

Evidence of Validity and Reliability.   Validity and reliability are often associated with achievement tests, because many of them are high-stakes measures. However, validity and reliability should be of equal concern when considering the soundness of questionnaires and interviews. For example, consider a questionnaire item that asks respondents to report age or occupation. How do we know that their responses are valid? A respondent might choose to report the correct information but might also provide inaccurate information for various reasons. Therefore, researchers should consider a validity check to corroborate the self-report information with other data, if possible. This type of validity check is especially important when the item asks for sensitive information.

The SoC developers provide various types of validity and reliability evidence for their measure in the accompanying manual (Hall et al., 1977). For example, they found that teachers' scores on the SoC questionnaire were related to their expressed concerns about an innovation in an interview setting. They also found that, as predicted, teachers' concerns moved along the seven stages of the scale over a two-year period from when an innovation was first introduced to them to its subsequent adoption and implementation in their school.

Results

The procedures used to analyze descriptive research data are fairly simple to understand. The distribution of the sample's scores on each measured variable are analyzed for their central tendency and variability. The **mean** and **standard deviation** are the most commonly used statistics for this purpose. (They were explained in more depth in Chapter 7.)

Figures and graphs can be helpful in presenting statistical results, especially for audiences who are not experienced in reading dense statistical tables. An example of a figure taken from the study by Nippold and her colleagues is shown in Figure 10.2.

The horizontal line (the *x* axis) at the bottom of the figure represents the six age levels that were studied. The vertical line on the left side of the figure (the *y* axis) is the mean number of T-units in each age group's discourse. A T-unit is an occurrence of an independent clause and its accompanying subordinate clauses, if any, while talking (labeled *discourse* in the research report) with another person. A T-unit often consists of one complete sentence.

The frequency of T-units was computed for two types of discourse with each participant for 5 to 8 minutes: (1) conversation about common topics such as school, family, and friends and (2) expository discourse (called *explanation* in the figure), in which the participant explained the rules and strategies of a favorite game or sport.

Figure 10.2 makes it easy to comprehend the results. Individuals' language output during expository discourse (explanation) remains fairly steady until age 13, at which point it steadily increases into adulthood. Language output in conversation is more uneven, with a drop at age 11 and a large spike at age 17. Interestingly, this type of syntactic complexity

FIGURE *10.2* Language Output (Total T-Units Produced) for Conversational and Expository Discourse for Each Age Group

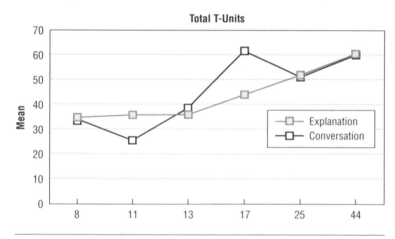

Source: Figure 1 on p. 1054 of Nippold, M. A., Hesketh, L. J., Duthie, J. K., & Mansfield, T. C. (2005). Conversational versus expository discourse: A study of syntactic development in children, adolescents, and adults. *Journal of Speech, Language, and Hearing Research, 48*, 1048–1064. Copyright © 2005 by American Speech-Language-Hearing Association. All rights reserved. Reprinted by permission.

is no greater at age 44 than at age 17. The same results could be shown in statistical tables, but, for most people, these tables are not as easy to comprehend as graphs.

Some descriptive studies involve surveys using questionnaires or brief structured interviews. Because these measures are easy to administer and score, researchers sometimes can form a truly random sample from a defined population. If this is the case, it is appropriate to compute confidence intervals around the sample mean or other descriptive statistic. **Confidence intervals** (also called **margins of error**) provide information about how likely it is that the range of numerical values in the confidence interval contains the actual population parameter. (We explained confidence intervals more fully in Chapter 9.)

Discussion: Implications for Practice

The discussion section of a descriptive research study typically includes a summary of the main findings, an analysis of possible flaws in the design and execution of the study, and implications for further research. The researchers also might discuss implications for professional practice. The following sections discuss some examples.

The 38th PDK/Gallup Poll.   The report of this poll, published in 2006, draws many conclusions about educational practice from the statistical results. The following is one of the main conclusions:

> The public's strong preference is to seek improvement through the existing public schools. Policies shaped with this fact in mind are most likely to gain public approval. (Rose & Gallup, 2006, p. 42)

Those who agree with this finding and implication would be likely to use them to encourage educators, policy makers, and others to focus their energies on the existing public school system rather than creating alternative systems such as charter schools or voucher plans.

Teachers' Beliefs about Inclusive Education.   The journal article at the end of this chapter reports a study of teachers' beliefs and knowledge about inclusion of students with learning disabilities in regular classrooms. The discussion section of the article starts with the following statement:

> The findings from this survey and follow-up telephone interviews revealed three major issues that need to be addressed as school districts attempt to provide inclusive mathematics education to students with LD [learning disabilities], and meet federal and state mandates for inclusion of all students in standardized testing. These issues include (a) the lack of teacher knowledge regarding the mathematical learning needs of included students, (b) the importance of teacher collaboration, and (c) the inadequacy of teacher preparation for inclusion at both the pre-service and in-service levels. (DeSimone & Parmar, 2006, p. 107)

This statement illustrates how descriptive research reveals problems of practice that can prompt improvements in teaching and teacher education.

Status of Equity for Black Undergraduates.   Laura Perna and her colleagues (2006) analyzed data from a large-scale database containing information about the status of equity for black students in enrollment and bachelor's degree attainment at public universities in the southern part of the United States. They found some progress in equity between 1991 and 2001 but concluded that substantial inequities still existed. Perna and colleagues stated several implications for practice based on their findings:

> Blacks will continue to represent about half of all public high school graduates in the South. These projections suggest that higher education institutions must take action now to address inequities for Blacks in undergraduate enrollment and degree completion in the 19 southern and southern-border states. (p. 223)

As a first step toward addressing the persisting inequities for Blacks in enrollment and degree completion, institutional researchers must monitor the status of race equity on their individual campuses. (p. 224)

These statements reveal the power of descriptive research to reveal a widespread problem of practice. Many individuals know only about local problems, because they rely on their own experience for knowledge. Good descriptive research studies can look at conditions on a broader scale by drawing samples from a large defined population. Thus, the researchers can determine how prevalent a problem is, rather than just identifying its presence or absence in a particular community.

Evaluating a Descriptive Research Study

The criteria stated in Appendix 2 are relevant to evaluating a descriptive research study. The following additional criteria, in question-and-answer format, are also useful for judging the soundness of a descriptive research study.

- If the researchers generalize their findings from a sample to a population, have they taken steps to ensure that these generalizations are justified?

  A descriptive research study is done to characterize features of a particular population. If researchers use a sample to represent the population, they need to describe the population in specific detail. If the sample was not randomly drawn from the population, they need to explain how the sample might still be representative of that population.

- If the sample was randomly drawn from a population, did the researchers present a measure of sampling error for their statistical results?

  If the researchers have drawn a random sample from a defined population, they should present a confidence interval for each of their statistical results.

- Did the researchers develop their questionnaire, interview, or observation schedule by doing a pilot study?

  Construction of measures is more difficult than it may seem. Therefore, look for indications that the researchers developed an initial version of their measure, pilot tested it, and then revised it. The mention of pilot testing suggests that a measure is likely to have some level of validity and reliability.

- Are the items in the measure of good quality?

  Writing good items is difficult, whether it be for questionnaires, interviews, or observation schedules. If the research report includes the items, examine them for clarity and relevance. If they are questionnaire items, you can apply the criteria for writing them that we presented earlier in this chapter.

An example of
HOW DESCRIPTIVE RESEARCH CAN HELP IN SOLVING PROBLEMS OF PRACTICE

School curriculum changes in response to larger societal shifts, at least to a certain extent. The following describes one such change happening now.

There's a monumental shift going on in this generation of students. "More and more younger students are fluent . . . in the language of green," said Rachel Gutter, education outreach coordinator for the U.S. Green Building Council in Washington. . . . Students often spearhead green projects because "they don't see the barriers," Gutter said. "An adult may think, 'That's too expensive.' The students are like, 'Let's just raise the money and get it done.'"

> Chandler, M. A. (2008, July 17). Student reaches for the sun and succeeds: Solar panel project at Mason High aims to bring awareness. *The Washington Post*, p. PW08.

The U.S. Green Building Council certifies buildings that meet standards for efficient energy generation and ecofriendly designs. The education outreach coordinator does not specify how large this environmental movement is. Is it something that educators should take notice of? There are many other calls for changes in school curriculum, so educators are faced with the problem of deciding which are a priority. Descriptive research can help educators who face this dilemma.

Quantitative researchers can determine how strong the environmental "green" movement is among students by forming a random sample of students and administering a questionnaire that measures (1) their attitude toward "green" projects, (2) whether they have participated in fund-raising activities for these projects, and (3) how much money they raised. The researchers also can administer attitude scales about the "green" movement to other stakeholders, such as parents, teachers, community members, and policy makers.

The results of this study might determine whether there is sufficient momentum to develop "green" curriculum and fund-raising activities and to determine whether these activities improve students' perceptions of their school and their academic achievement.

Self-Check Test

1. The primary purpose of the National Assessment of Educational Progress is to
   a. collect data about the public's perceptions of the quality of public schools.
   b. collect ideas from educators about how well schools in their district have improved over a five-year period.
   c. determine how well American students are learning selected school subjects.
   d. All of the above.

2. A major feature of descriptive research studies is that
   a. the focus is on discovering cause-and-effect relationships between variables.
   b. the focus is on intensive study of individual cases of a phenomenon.
   c. the variables of interest are identified prior to data collection.
   d. the variables of interest are identified after data collection has been completed.

3. In a cross-sectional longitudinal study, the researchers
   a. select samples that represent different age levels and study all of the samples at the same point in time.
   b. select different samples at different times from a population that does not remain constant.
   c. select a sample and follow it across time.
   d. stratify a population so that the subgroups of interest are well represented across different points in time.

4. The terms *confidence interval* and *margin of error* refer to

   a. a situation in which 10 percent or more of a sample fail to take the research survey.
   b. the likelihood that the confidence interval around a sample statistic fails to include the population parameter.
   c. the likelihood that the distribution of scores in the sample fails to follow a normal curve.
   d. a situation in which the mean, median, and mode for a sample differ significantly from each other.

5. Descriptive research
   a. is limited to the use of survey questionnaires.
   b. is limited to the use of standardized achievement tests.
   c. can make use of any measure that yields quantifiable data.
   d. differs from other types of quantitative research, in that validity and reliability of measurement are not matters of concern.

6. Questionnaires require
   a. validity evidence but not reliability evidence.
   b. reliability evidence but not validity evidence.
   c. both reliability and validity evidence.
   d. the use of demographic items.

7. Questionnaire items
   a. should not be written prior to specification of the constructs that are to be measured.
   b. should be ordered so that difficult items appear last.
   c. can be used to measure the respondents' demographic characteristics.
   d. All of the above.

Chapter References

Hall, G. E., George, A. A., & Rutherford, W. L. (1977). *Measuring stages of concern about the innovation: A manual for the use of the SoC Questionnaire.* Austin: University of Texas Research and Development Center for Teacher Education. (ERIC Document Reproduction Service No. ED147342)

McCaslin, M., Good, T. L., Nichols, S., Zhang, J., Wiley, C. R. H., Bozack, A. R., Burross, H. L., & Cuizon-Garcia, R. (2006). Comprehensive school reform: An observational study of teaching in grades 3 through 5. *Elementary School Journal, 106*(4), 313–331.

Meier, B. (2008, July 29). The evidence gap: A call for a warning system on artificial joints. *New York Times.* Retrieved from www.nytimes.com

National Center for Education Statistics. (n.d.). *National Assessment of Educational Progress. Long-term trend: Reading performance-level descriptions.* Retrieved from http://nces.ed.gov/nationsreportcard/1tt/reading-descriptions.asp

Nippold, M. A., Hesketh, L. J., Duthie, J. K., & Mansfield, T. C. (2005). Conversational versus expository discourse: A study of syntactic development in children, adolescents, and adults. *Journal of Speech, Language, and Hearing Research, 48,* 1048–1064.

Perna, L. W., Milem, J., Gerald, D., Baum, E., Rowan, H., & Hutchens, N. (2006). The status of equity for Black undergraduates in public higher education in the South: Still separate and unequal. *Research in Higher Education, 47*(2), 197–228.

Rose, L. C., & Gallup, A. M. (2006). The 38th annual Phi Delta Kappa/Gallup Poll of the public's attitudes toward the public schools. *Phi Delta Kappan, 88*(1), 41–56.

Schemo, D. J. (2007, March 28). Failing schools see a solution in longer day. *New York Times.* Retrieved from www.nytimes.com

Terman, L. M., & Oden, M. M. (1959). *The gifted group at midlife* (Vol. 5). Stanford, CA: Stanford University Press.

Resources for Further Study

Berends, M. (2006). Survey methods in educational research. In J. L. Green, G. Camilli, & P. B. Elmore (Eds.), *Handbook of complementary methods in education research* (pp. 623–640). Mahwah, NJ: Lawrence Erlbaum.

> The author provides a brief overview of survey methods commonly used in educational research.

Fowler, F. J., Jr. (2008). *Survey research methods* (4th ed.). Thousand Oaks, CA: Sage.

> The author explains various aspects of questionnaires and interviews that you will need to consider if you plan to do survey research.

Rose, L. C., & Gallup, A. M. (2004). Sampling tolerances. *Phi Delta Kappan.* Retrieved from www.pdkintl.org/kappan/kpoll0409sample.htm

> This brief article illustrates sampling errors, using examples from the 36th Annual Phi Delta Kappa/Gallup Poll of the Public's Attitudes toward the Public Schools.

Sue, V. M., & Ritter, L. A. (2007). *Conducting online surveys.* Thousand Oaks, CA: Sage.

> This book provides extensive coverage of the methodology involved in designing and conducting Internet surveys.

Stewart, C. J., & Cash, W. B., Jr. (2008). *Interviewing: Principles and practices* (12th ed.). Boston: McGraw-Hill.

> This book provides extensive coverage of the practical aspects of interviewing and also the theoretical underpinnings of this research methodology.

Sample Descriptive Research Study

Middle School Mathematics Teachers' Beliefs about Inclusion of Students with Learning Disabilities

DeSimone, J. R., & Parmar, R. S. (2006). Middle school mathematics teachers' beliefs about inclusion of students with learning disabilities. *Learning Disabilities Research & Practice, 21*(2), 98–110.

The following journal article deals with an important problem of practice concerning classroom instruction in mathematics. The authors state that only a small percentage of students with disabilities achieve proficiency in mathematics. However, federal legislation has mandated that educators must bring nearly all of these students up to a proficient level.

How can educators achieve this goal? The authors make four recommendations, based on their research findings at the end of the article. After reading the study, you might consider whether you agree with the recommendations or whether you would recommend a different approach.

The authors' research design primarily uses the descriptive methods presented in this chapter. However, they do break the total sample into comparison groups, based on (1) high versus low level of administrator support and (2) more versus fewer years of teaching experience. These analyses involve a group comparison research design and a certain type of statistic (chi-square—χ^2), which are explained in Chapter 11. It is not necessary to read that chapter beforehand in order to understand these analyses at a general level.

You will note, too, that the authors include some qualitative interview data and mention a few research design elements (e.g., constant comparative method; triangulation) that are characteristic of qualitative research. These design elements are explained in Chapter 14.

The authors analyzed the reliability of their primary measure using Cronbach's alpha in the section of their report titled "Survey Instrument." Reliability and Cronbach's alpha were explained in Chapter 6.

The article is reprinted in its entirety, just as it appeared when originally published.

Middle School Mathematics Teachers' Beliefs about Inclusion of Students with Learning Disabilities

Janet R. DeSimone
Lehman College,
City University of New York

Rene S. Parmar
St John's University

ABSTRACT ■ The purpose of this descriptive study was to investigate middle school general education mathematics teachers' beliefs and self-perceived knowledge regarding teaching students with learning disabilities (LD) in inclusive classrooms. Teacher beliefs regarding administrative support and higher education teacher preparation were also examined. The *Survey on Teaching Mathematics to Students With Learning Disabilities in Middle School* was completed by 228 sixth-, seventh-, and eighth-grade general education mathematics inclusion teachers from 19 states. In addition, telephone interviews were conducted with a subset of 26 survey respondents. Frequency analyses were performed on the survey data, with χ^2 tests comparing teachers on demographic variables. Follow-up interview responses were summarized to elaborate on the major research questions. The findings revealed three central issues: (1) teachers had a limited understanding of the mathematics learning needs of students with LD, (2) teacher collaboration was judged to be the most beneficial and available resource by general educators teaching students with LD in inclusive mathematics classrooms, and (3) teachers did not feel that teacher education programs at the preservice level and professional development at the inservice level were adequate in preparing them for teaching students with LD in inclusive mathematics classrooms. Implications and recommendations for teacher preparation and program implementation are provided.

Mathematics has always proved to be a challenging subject, even for general education students, in the United States. When examining the performance of students with disabilities on standardized mathematics assessments, the situation becomes even bleaker. On the National Assessment of Educational Progress (NAEP) only 6 percent of the students with disabilities who participated in the mathematics component of NAEP scored at or above the proficiency level (National Center for Education Statistics, 2004). Considering

that the No Child Left Behind (NCLB) Act of 2001 mandates that all students, with only a few exceptions, master the general education curriculum, participate in standardized assessments, and achieve passing levels of performance, it becomes even more imperative to study the effectiveness of inclusion programs from a variety of perspectives. Furthermore, proportionately, students with learning disabilities (LD) are the largest special education group to be included in general education classes. Forty-nine percent of

DeSimone, J. R., & Parmar, R. S. (2006). Middle school mathematics teachers' beliefs about inclusion of students with learning disabilities. *Learning Disabilities Research & Practice, 21*(2), 98–110.

students classified with specific LD spent 80 percent or more of each school day in a general education classroom. These students are not among the groups exempt from state and national standardized tests (U.S. Department of Education, 2003). Because inclusive practices are rapidly growing, Cochran (1998) is correct in his assessment of the current state of education "all teachers [have] become teachers of special education students" (p. 4). Nowadays, given the expansion of inclusion, general educators, many with little or no special education training, have been assigned the responsibility of teaching students with disabilities.

One of the first steps toward understanding successful instruction in inclusive mathematics classrooms is to understand general educators' beliefs and attitudes regarding inclusion and students with LD. Such insight can help teacher educators and staff development specialists work more effectively with teachers to develop mathematics programming that meets diverse learning needs, to design better-quality teacher preparation, and to establish needed support services at sites where inclusion programs are implemented.

RESEARCH ON TEACHER ATTITUDES TOWARD INCLUSION

There is a body of theoretical literature that posits a relationship between teachers' beliefs and knowledge, and teaching practice (Nespor, 1987). Empirical studies based on this perspective reviewed by Pajares (1992) appear to demonstrate consistently that pedagogy is indeed affected by teacher beliefs, that beliefs are developed early in an individual's teaching career, and are not very easy to change. Some of the research studies that investigate the link between teachers' beliefs and practices regarding inclusion are summarized below.

In their book on successful inclusion programs, Kochhar, West, and Taymans (2000) reported teachers' negative beliefs and feelings as one of the three major barriers to inclusive education. Janney, Snell, Beers, and Raynes (1995) concluded that the more experience general educators had with integrating students with disabilities into the classroom, the more positive were their attitudes. The researchers attributed the general educators' original negative perceptions to the "confusion and uncertainty" (p. 111) that arise when objectives, policies, functions, and responsibilities are altered, sometimes drastically. In their comparison of 78 teachers who worked in inclusion programs and 84 teachers who had not yet started to teach in inclusive settings, McLeskey, Waldron, So, Swanson, and Loveland (2001) found that elementary school teachers with no experience in inclusive settings demonstrated more negative attitudes regarding school readiness, adequacy of resources, academic benefits for students with disabilities, and willingness to collaborate with special education teachers than the group of inclusion teachers. A survey of 127 teachers in grades 1 through 8 by Bender, Vail, and Scott (1995) indicated that teachers who viewed mainstreaming positively were more consistent in employing effective mainstreaming strategies than those teachers with less favorable attitudes.

In their summary of 28 surveys of mainly elementary-level general educators' perceptions of inclusion, Scruggs and Mastropieri (1996) discovered that two-thirds of general educators supported the idea of inclusion, and half of general educators believed that inclusion is indeed beneficial for students with disabilities. However, less than one-third of the general educators thought they had adequate resources, training, and time required to implement inclusive practices successfully. Smith and Smith (2000) interviewed general education elementary school teachers about the factors that contributed to or hindered their success in inclusive classrooms. Data revealed the following four factors as having the greatest effect on general educators' perspectives on teaching students with LD in inclusive classrooms: training (undergraduate and graduate teacher preparation and in-service programs), class load (class size, severity, and range of students' needs), support (administration, special education department, and paraprofessionals), and time (planning lessons and collaborating with special education teachers).

Although the body of research summarized above has provided numerous insights into issues to address when implementing inclusion programs, many aspects remain unexplored. First, the majority of the existing research studies focus on teachers in elementary schools, where included students are placed with a single teacher for most of the school day. In such settings, there is the potential for the general education teacher to develop a strong working relationship with the special education teacher and focus on the learning needs of a few students. In contrast, the present study examines the middle school context, where included students encounter several subject-area teachers within a single day, and mathematics teachers typically do not have long-term contact with any given student or with their special education colleagues. The structure of the elementary school allows for more curriculum flexibility, and included students are frequently reported to be working on materials that are below their grade placement level while placed in inclusive settings. Middle schools have a strong academic focus, teachers feel a great deal of pressure to cover mandated content, and students are expected to be responsible for their own learning to a greater degree than in elementary school. Middle school teachers are more likely to be content-area specialists and to feel responsible for developing student mastery in the area.

A second limitation of existing research on teachers' attitudes toward inclusion is that many of the current studies report attitudes of teachers toward inclusion in general. The present study focuses on the critical subject area of mathematics, where there is an increasing emphasis on student attainment as measured by standardized test scores. Third, many of the existing surveys on teacher attitudes do not specifically focus on students with mild disabilities. However, the research does suggest that teachers have varying attitudes toward inclusion, depending on the nature of the disability of the included student. Finally, the preservice and in-service experiences of elementary and middle school teachers vary greatly. While issues such as literacy development and classroom management dominate the preservice preparation programs for elementary teachers, specific pedagogy in the content area is the focus for middle school teachers. Frequently, the latter group does not feel responsible for differentiating instruction to meet diverse learning needs. The in-service programs and administrative support in middle school tend to be directed toward enhancing specific content area instruction, not providing for diverse programming. To date, no research has specifically considered teachers' beliefs, attitudes, and self-perceived knowledge when actually working with students with LD included in middle school mathematics classes.

PURPOSE OF THE STUDY

This descriptive study attempts to extend the existing research on teachers' beliefs and perceptions, specifically addressing the critical area of mathematics instruction. The purpose of this study was to examine middle school general education mathematics teachers' beliefs and self-perceived knowledge regarding teaching students with LD in inclusive classrooms, and to gain an understanding of teacher perspectives on the application of inclusion in their own schools. The study investigated the following four questions:

1. What are the general beliefs of general education middle school mathematics teachers about inclusion of students with LD?
2. What is the self-perceived knowledge base of general education middle school mathematics teachers regarding the specific learning needs of students with LD who are included in their mathematics classrooms and their ability to adapt instruction for these students?
3. What are the perceptions of middle school general education mathematics teachers regarding administrative support and resources for teaching inclusion?
4. What are the perceptions of middle school general education mathematics teachers regarding the preparation they have received in preservice programs to teach in inclusive classrooms?

The present study reports data from a nationwide survey of middle school mathematics teachers currently teaching in inclusive settings, with follow-up information from telephone interviews conducted with a subgroup of respondents.

METHOD

Survey Component

Surveys were mailed to 361 middle school mathematics inclusion teachers, nationwide, whose names were obtained through contact with professional organizations and school districts. A total of 228 responses were received (63 percent return rate). The demographic characteristics of the respondents are presented in Table 1.

The survey respondents represented 19 different states from all geographic regions of the United States.

TABLE 1   Demographic Variables for Survey Respondents

Variable	Number (%)[a]
Gender	
Female	161 (70.6)
Male	60 (26.3)
Educational level	
Bachelor degree	24 (10.5)
Master's degree (completed or pursuing)	182 (79.8)
Professional diploma (completed or pursuing)	16 (7)
Doctoral degree (completed or pursuing)	6 (2.6)
Years of experience teaching	
1–2	41 (18)
3–8	66 (28.9)
9–14	49 (21.5)
15 or >	72 (31.6)
Years of experience teaching in inclusion settings	
1–2	69 (30.3)
3–5	67 (29.4)
6–10	41 (18)
11 or >	50 (21.9)
No. of math methods courses	
1	51 (22.4)
2	56 (24.6)
3	26 (11.4)
4	19 (8.3)
5	9 (3.9)
6 or >	24 (10.5)
No. of inclusion- or LD-related workshops	
0–2	98 (43)
3–4	62 (27.2)
5–6	22 (9.6)
7–9	10 (4.4)
10 or >	34 (14.9)
Level of support services	
Extremely low	10 (4.4)
Low	39 (17.1)
Average	85 (37.3)
High	64 (28.1)
Extremely high	29 (12.7)
Level of administrative support	
Extremely low	23 (10.1)
Low	47 (20.6)
Average	85 (37.3)
High	49 (21.5)
Extremely high	22 (9.6)

[a]The number of respondents varied because of missing cases.

The regional breakdown was as follows: Mid Atlantic (60.9 percent), New England (19.3 percent), West (7 percent), Southwest (6.6 percent), South (4.4 percent), and Midwest (1.7 percent). Approximately 49 percent of the teachers (n = 110) were from suburban school districts, followed by 25 percent urban (n = 57) and 14.5 percent rural (n = 33). Approximately 11 percent of the respondents (n = 26) did not classify their school district. The majority of teachers taught in schools that had more than 500 students (77.7 percent, n = 177), with the average class size falling between 21 and 30 students. Approximately one-half of the respondents identified themselves as public school teachers (51.4 percent, n = 117); 1 percent (n = 2) indicated they were private school teachers; and the remaining teachers did not describe this aspect of their schools. The sample was a reasonable representation of middle schools across the country in terms of size and community location, as described by the National Center For Educational Statistics (NCES, 2003), in their report on Public Elementary and Secondary Schools. According to the NCES data, the average size for middle schools is 612 students, with 57 percent of schools being located in suburban areas, and 18 percent in major urban areas. However, it is noted that the sample was primarily from the eastern regions in the United States.

Survey Instrument.   The *Survey on Teaching Mathematics to Students with Learning Disabilities in Middle School* (DeSimone & Parmar, 2004) was designed as a three-part questionnaire. Part I (12 items) provided descriptive data regarding the participants and their schools, as well as participants' perceptions of the level of administrative support and available resources for inclusive teaching (*extremely low* to *extremely high*). Part II (14 items) used a 5-point (strongly agree, agree, undecided, disagree, strongly disagree) Likert scale to measure participants' beliefs regarding inclusive mathematics classes, students with LD, and their prior preparation to teach in inclusive classrooms. The items from Parts I and II were adapted from existing research on teachers' beliefs and inclusion (Larrivee & Cook, 1979; Coates, 1989; Chow & Winzer, 1992; McLeskey et al., 2001).

Part III of the questionnaire had two dimensions and used a 4-point (very comfortable, quite comfortable, somewhat comfortable, not comfortable) Likert scale to assess participants' level of comfort in their abilities to both (a) adapt their mathematics instruction for students with various LD learning characteristics (11 items) and (b) adapt their instruction for students with LD in specific topics within the middle school mathematics curriculum (17 items). At the end of the survey, respondents were asked to list their name and telephone number if they were willing to volunteer for a phone interview.

The *Survey* was constructed after an extensive review of literature on teacher beliefs regarding inclusion and mathematics instruction, a compilation of characteristics of students with LD found in major textbooks, and a com-

pilation of mathematics topics from New York State (NYS) curriculum guidelines for grades 7 and 8, which were found to be largely similar across states. The NYS curriculum guidelines are consistent with NCLB goals and also incorporate research from within the United States and abroad on appropriate mathematical content (New York State Education Department, 2005, p. 2). Two procedures were used to establish the validity of the survey instrument. First, a panel of three leading researchers who had experience with teaching mathematics to students with and without LD was asked to review the survey and provide comments, resulting in some changes in wording. Second, a pilot study was conducted by administering the survey to 27 teachers in middle schools in the local area. Separate reliability analyses were conducted for the three parts, and two items were dropped to improve internal consistency, resulting in the following coefficients: *general beliefs* (Cronbach's $\alpha = .75$); the adaptation of instruction to fit the learning *characteristics* of students with LD (Cronbach's $\alpha = .92$); the adaptation of instruction to teach middle school mathematics *topics* effectively to students with LD (Cronbach's $\alpha = .90$); the total instrument (Cronbach's $\alpha = .90$), which were deemed acceptable for the research objectives.

Follow-Up Interview Component

From the 42 survey respondents who had volunteered for follow-up interviews, a purposive sample of 26 was chosen from the nine states with the largest percentage of surveys. The 26 respondents, all public school teachers, were from New York (11), Rhode Island (3), New Hampshire (3), Colorado (3), Texas (2), Massachusetts (1), Pennsylvania (1), West Virginia (1), and Washington (1). The demographic characteristics of the interview participants are presented in Table 2.

For the most part, the interview sample was representative of the original 228 survey respondents, though the former had more years of teaching experience and fewer years of education on average.

Interview Schedule.   The interview schedule (see Appendix) consisted of eight open-ended (semistructured) questions designed to provide further insight into the main constructs found in the survey. The interview schedule was initially piloted with three middle school mathematics teachers to assess the level of clarity of the questions.

Interview data were collected during a span of 6 months. Participants were interviewed for approximately 30 minutes. Telephone interviews were not audiotaped; instead, during the interview, notes were simultaneously entered into a laptop computer. The narrative data were then analyzed using the constant comparative method (as discussed in Bogdan & Biklen, 1998), based on the major areas of the survey. Triangulation of data across sources was achieved, and peer-debriefing methods were used to establish credibility and trustworthiness of the results. The telephone interview responses clarified and elaborated upon the survey responses. Insights into challenges and success factors were obtained that could inform teacher preparation

TABLE 2   Demographic Variables for Interview Participants

Variable	Number (%)
Gender	
Female	21 (80.8)
Male	5 (19.2)
Educational level	
Bachelor degree	8 (30.8)
Master's degree (completed or pursuing)	18 (69.2)
Years of experience teaching	
1–2	2 (7.7)
3–8	11 (42.3)
9–14	7 (26.9)
15 or >	6 (23.1)
Years of experience teaching inclusion	
1–2	6 (23.1)
3–5	6 (23.1)
6–10	9 (34.6)
11 or >	5 (19.2)

programs and classroom practice at sites where inclusive mathematics instruction is being implemented.

FINDINGS

The responses received from the survey and follow-up interviews are summarized below, organized according to major sections of the survey instrument. The responses revealed several issues that would need to be addressed in order to assist middle school mathematics teachers in providing effective instruction in inclusive classrooms.

Research Question 1: Teachers' General Beliefs about Inclusion

Teachers' reported beliefs concerning characteristics of students with LD, inclusion, and teachers' roles and responsibilities in inclusive classrooms are presented in Table 3.

Beliefs about Including Students with LD. Approximately four out of five (80.3 percent) of the survey respondents *agreed* or *strongly agreed* with the statement that students with LD should be afforded every opportunity to learn mathematics with general education students. However, fewer than one-half of the respondents (41.6 percent) believed that students with LD are best taught mathematics in an inclusive classroom, and a large percentage (37.3

percent) of the respondents were still undecided on this issue. The responses indicate a conflict between beliefs regarding equal opportunity for students with LD and reservations about how this equality could be achieved when making instructional or placement decisions. Because the respondents were currently teaching in inclusive classrooms, their responses would indicate that many of them did not personally find the instructional placement to be best for the students with LD in their classrooms. Chi-square tests of significance indicate that teachers in schools with higher levels of administrative support and availability of ancillary support services were significantly more supportive of inclusion ($\chi^2 = 37.72$, $p < .001$).

Beliefs about Implementing Inclusion. Twenty-nine percent of the mathematics teachers *agreed* or *strongly agreed* that middle schools were successfully executing inclusive practices. A fairly large percentage (30.3 percent) of respondents were undecided about the benefits of resource rooms in comparison with inclusive classrooms, and fewer than half (43.9 percent) of the respondents *agreed* or *strongly agreed* with the following statement: "Students with LD who are taught mathematics in inclusive classrooms will have a better chance of succeeding in society than students taught in resource room settings." When asked to rate whether resource rooms were more effective in meeting the mathematics learning needs of students with LD, once again, results were almost evenly split; 31.5 percent *disagreed* or *strongly disagreed*; 36.4 percent *agreed* or *strongly agreed*; and 30.7 percent remained undecided. The varied responses indicated that many middle school mathematics teachers were doubtful that the resource room model effectively ensured learning of mathematics; however, they observed that students were not learning very effectively in inclusive placements either. Chi-square tests of significance once again indicated that teachers in schools with more support felt that inclusion was more effective than those in less supportive schools ($\chi^2 = 85.09$, $p < .001$).

Beliefs about Roles and Responsibilities of the General Educator. Approximately two-thirds of the survey respondents believed that, as general educators teaching students with LD in inclusive mathematics classrooms, they were the ones who were primarily responsible for modifying instruction and ensuring that their students with LD succeeded academically. A large majority (66.7 percent) of respondents *disagreed* or *strongly disagreed* with the statement that students with LD cause the most behavioral problems in inclusive classrooms, though teachers with less experience were more likely to attribute behavioral problems to students with LD.

A sixth-grade teacher from New York, who was interviewed, believed that she was the primary person responsible for her included students, as well as their grades. She stated, "I felt very strongly that these were my kids, and they belonged to my class." Another teacher from New York explained that he planned all of the lessons, which

TABLE 3   General Educators' Beliefs Regarding Inclusion and Students with Learning Disabilities

Beliefs Statement	Number (%)[a]				
	Strongly Agree	Agree	Undecided	Disagree	Strongly Disagree
Beliefs about Including SLD					
SLD should be afforded every opportunity to learn math with general ed students	67 (29.4)	116 (50.9)	25 (11)	17 (7.5)	3 (1.3)
SLD are best taught math in inclusive classrooms	24 (10.5)	71 (31.1)	85 (37.3)	39 (17.1)	9 (3.9)
Beliefs about Implementing Inclusion					
For the most part, middle schools are effectively implementing inclusive programs	12 (5.3)	54 (23.7)	70 (30.7)	62 (27.2)	29 (12.7)
SLD will have a better chance in society learning math in inclusive classrooms than resource rooms	30 (13.2)	70 (30.7)	69 (30.3)	52 (22.8)	6 (2.6)
Resource rooms are effective in meeting the math learning needs of SLD	19 (8.3)	64 (28.1)	70 (30.7)	58 (25.4)	14 (6.1)
Beliefs about Roles and Responsibilities of the General Educator					
General ed teachers are responsible for modifying instruction for SLD	61 (26.8)	89 (39)	26 (11.4)	42 (18.4)	10 (4.4)
General ed teachers are responsible for ensuring that SLD succeed academically	63 (27.6)	94 (41.2)	26 (11.4)	41 (18)	4 (1.8)
SLD cause the most behavioral problems	8 (3.5)	39 (17.1)	29 (12.7)	103 (45.2)	49 (21.5)

Note: SLD = Students with learning disabilities.

[a]The number of respondents varied because of missing cases.

included his modifications, and then the special education teacher would give him some additional ideas on how to modify instruction.

Research Question 2, Part 1: Knowledge of LD

In the second section of the survey, teachers were asked whether or not they felt comfortable adapting instruction to meet specific learning needs. Table 4 presents the percentage of middle school mathematics teachers in each category of response.

Mathematical Learning Needs of Students with LD. More than half of the survey respondents described themselves as either *quite comfortable* or *very comfortable* in their abilities to adapt their instruction to meet the special mathematical needs of students with LD. However, between 5 percent and 13 percent indicated they were *not comfortable* in many areas. The areas of "keeping place," "identifying symbols," and "maintaining attention," had the lowest ratings, followed by "memory of information"

and "written communication." Adapting instruction to help students understand "number line," "follow a sequence of steps," "oral communication," and "using pictures and diagrams" were areas where teachers felt most comfortable. In all areas, responses were generally in the mid-range of *somewhat comfortable* and *quite comfortable.*

Chi-square tests of significance indicated that the teachers with high levels of support in their schools felt most comfortable adapting instruction to meet student needs for all of the specific disability characteristics (χ^2 ranges from 23.97 to 43.05, $p \le .01$). Teachers with more years of experience also felt more comfortable than teachers with fewer years experience. Workshops were found to be beneficial in helping teachers work with students with LD with attention, memory, and communication difficulties. Education level and coursework in mathematics methods had minimal or no effect in this area.

In the interviews, many teachers shared that they struggled with finding ways to increase their included students' levels of motivation and attention, and they named

TABLE 4   Level of Comfort Adapting Instruction to Meet the Needs of Students with Learning Disabilities

Learning Needs	Number (%)[a]			
	Very Comfortable	Quite Comfortable	Somewhat Comfortable	Not Comfortable
Attending to tasks	41 (18)	88 (38.6)	76 (33.3)	16 (7)
Maintaining attention	41 (18)	85 (37.3)	72 (31.6)	25 (11)
Keeping place on pages	43 (18.9)	82 (36)	69 (30.3)	29 (12.7)
Identifying symbols or numerals	36 (15.8)	85 (37.3)	74 (32.5)	29 (12.7)
Using a number line	59 (25.9)	96 (42.1)	59 (25.9)	10 (4.4)
Recalling math facts	46 (20.2)	86 (37.7)	76 (33.3)	16 (7)
Following a sequence of steps to solution	49 (21.5)	94 (41.2)	65 (28.5)	16 (7)
Memory of information in word problems	36 (15.8)	79 (34.6)	89 (39)	20 (8.9)
Oral communication	53 (23.2)	88 (38.6)	74 (32.5)	10 (4.4)
Written communication	43 (18.9)	87 (38.2)	74 (32.5)	20 (8.8)
Interpreting pictures and diagrams	50 (21.9)	96 (42.1)	64 (28.1)	15 (6.6)

[a]The number of respondents varied because of missing cases.

learning characteristics as the characteristics most difficult to address. A seventh-grade teacher from Colorado said, "I guess the lack of motivation for kids [is the hardest to deal with] . . . it's hard to jump start them." Others indicated that "[Getting students with LD interested] takes most of my time and planning" (teacher from New York) and "It takes such an amount of energy not to let [students with LD] be apathetic" (eighth-grade teacher from Colorado).

Research Question 2, Part 2: Teaching Specific Mathematics Topics

Survey respondents were asked to describe their level of comfort in adapting instruction for students with LD in relation to 17 mathematical topics drawn from the NYS Curriculum guidelines (see Table 5).

Specific Mathematics Topics.   According to survey results, the majority of general educators seemed to be most comfortable when teaching students with LD topics where there was extensive use of visual and manipulative materials, such as locating points on a coordinate plane and interpreting line and bar graphs. They seemed to be less comfortable when teaching students with LD to use technology tools such as graphing calculators and computer spreadsheets.

The following topics were rated as *very comfortable* or *quite comfortable*: describing equivalence of fractions, decimals and percents (66.2 percent), performing arithmetic operations on decimals and fractions (68.9 percent), and solving one- and two-step arithmetic word problems (66.3 percent). Yet close to one-half (46.5 percent) of the general education teachers surveyed (*n* = 106) described

themselves as only *somewhat comfortable* (33.33 percent) or *not comfortable* (13.2 percent) in their abilities to modify instruction when describing functional relationships to students with LD. Finally, at least one-fourth of the respondents described themselves as only *somewhat comfortable* in adapting their instruction for students with LD in 12 out of the 17 mathematics topics listed on the survey.

Chi-square tests of significance once again indicated that the most significant factor in teachers' level of comfort is the presence of administrative support and support services (χ^2 ranges from 22.36 to 43.78, $p \leq .01$), followed by years of experience ($\chi^2 = 18.62$ to 27.31, $p \leq .05$). Specific coursework in mathematics methods and workshops did not appear to impact teachers' ratings in this area.

Interview respondents named colored markers, overhead projectors, repetitive practice, reducing the number of examples on tests and homework, small-group work, tiering lessons and spiraling homework, delivering "small pieces [and] chunking material rather than big groups" of information, and teaching "one concept at a time" (teacher from Rhode Island) as different types of instructional modifications. In addition, many teachers emphasized the use of instructional methods based on multiple modalities and being "very structured . . . maintain routine for these kids" (teacher from New Hampshire). Quite a few teachers used the term "differentiated instruction" (e.g., teachers from New York and New Hampshire), yet they could not name specific strategies when asked to elaborate more on this term or provide concrete examples of differentiated instruction. Three teachers said they really did not modify instruction specifically for their students with LD, and more than half of the teachers said they used the same instruc-

TABLE 5 Level of Comfort Adapting Instruction for Specific Mathematics Topics

Topics	Number (%)[a]			
	Very Comfortable	Quite Comfortable	Somewhat Comfortable	Not Comfortable
Reading/writing integers, rational, irrational numbers	63 (27.6)	86 (37.7)	64 (28.1)	12 (5.3)
Equivalence of fractions, decimals, percents	66 (28.9)	85 (37.3)	57 (25)	17 (7.5)
Arithmetic operations—decimals, fractions	70 (30.7)	87 (38.2)	55 (24.1)	12 (5.3)
One- and two-step word problems	64 (28.1)	87 (38.2)	60 (26.3)	14 (6.1)
Inverse relationships between × and /, roots, exponents	44 (19.3)	73 (32)	84 (36.8)	23 (10.1)
Scale drawings	37 (16.2)	90 (39.5)	68 (29.8)	29 (12.7)
Coordinate planes	74 (32.5)	106 (46.5)	36 (15.8)	9 (3.9)
Line and bar graphs	89 (39)	89 (39)	37 (16.2)	8 (3.5)
Compasses, rulers, protractors	65 (28.5)	85 (37.3)	58 (25.4)	16 (7)
Square and cubic units	51 (22.4)	84 (36.8)	71 (31.1)	18 (7.9)
Size, quantity, capacity	56 (24.6)	84 (36.8)	70 (30.7)	14 (6.1)
Graphing calculators	34 (14.9)	49 (21.5)	62 (27.2)	69 (30.3)
Computer spreadsheets	33 (14.5)	57 (25)	69 (30.3)	58 (25.4)
Estimation as problem solving	58 (25.4)	86 (37.7)	62 (27.2)	17 (7.5)
Identifying, describing and creating patterns	70 (30.7)	86 (37.7)	55 (24.1)	11 (4.8)
One- and two-step equations	70 (30.7)	86 (37.7)	51 (22.4)	16 (7)
Describing functional relationships	44 (19.3)	71 (31.1)	76 (33.3)	30 (13.2)

[a]The number of respondents varied because of missing cases.

tional modifications for their lower-end students (teachers from New York and Colorado).

Approximately 18 interview respondents said they had not really altered the curriculum for their included students. A seventh-/eighth-grade teacher from New Hampshire said, "With all the testing we're supposed to teach the same content and try to make the kids learn it. . . . In the middle schools, there's a big push to get kids ready for high school." An eighth-grade teacher from Massachusetts agreed; she stated, "[Teachers] can't change the curriculum. Students have tests to take." A sixth-grade teacher from Texas said, "I do the same curriculum—it just takes longer, and I teach it differently. When I run short on time, I just make the time up in another way." A few of the teachers from Colorado said they "water down the curriculum" and try to emphasize the parts of the curriculum that have "real-world" applications (e.g., time, money). Some teachers from New York said they cover all parts of the curriculum, but do not hold the included students "responsible" or "accountable" for difficult topics such as Pascal's Triangle, graphing calculators, and algebra.

However, a few of the teachers did identify specific curriculum adaptations for their students with LD. A sixth-grade teacher from New Hampshire stated, "For fractions, I only make them do a common denominator . . . and for decimals, I only take my special ed students to the hundredth place. The curriculum requires that they go to the place of one thousand." A seventh-grade teacher from Colorado replied, "I stay away from dividing three-digit numbers into five-digit ones," while an eighth-grade teacher from Rhode Island stated that she "may not cover . . . higher-end word problems" with her inclusion classes. Alternate curricular modifications such as better integration of topics so that all topics could be covered in the allocated time, prioritizing topics to stress important concepts early in the school year, or division of topics between general education teachers and resource room or other teachers, were not mentioned by any of the respondents. Further, 10 teachers named instructional modifications again, when asked to give specific examples of curriculum adaptations.

Participants from New Hampshire, New York, Texas, and Rhode Island all stressed that fractions were very difficult for students with LD to comprehend. A teacher from New Hampshire said, "Cognitively they're [students with LD] not mature enough to understand this." Other topics identified included word problems, decimals, equations with variables and inequalities, geometric formulas where "understanding dimensions [was] tough" (teacher from Pennsylvania), probability, and basic skills such as addition, subtraction, multiplication, and division.

Research Question 3: Support Mechanisms and Resources

Survey respondents and interview participants were asked to comment on the level of administrative support and resources available to aid them in teaching students with LD (see Table 6).

Administrative Support.　Thirty-one percent of survey respondents considered the support level of their school's administration to be *low* or *extremely low* (see Table 1). Almost three-quarters (72.3 percent) of the general educators surveyed believed that students with LD required more time from teachers than general education students. However, more than half (57.5 percent) of the respondents felt that administrators did not give them sufficient time to prepare for their mathematics inclusion classes.

A few of the interview participants believed that their building administration also faced monetary and resource challenges. In some situations, as one New York teacher said, "their [administration] hands are tied," and often administrators have no choice but to implement district-wide policies. However, many participants perceived their administration as being ineffective in offering assistance and solutions. A sixth-grade teacher from New York stated, "Administration doesn't understand the challenges of teaching inclusion." A seventh-grade teacher from New York said, "administration was not very helpful . . . they recognize that inclusion presents problems, but they're not quick to offer advice." In addition, a sixth-grade teacher from New Hampshire replied, "They [administration] don't always focus on making the teacher's job easier. . . . like freeing us up from mundane things . . . free us up for what's important . . . they lose sight of this."

Most teachers were just told that they would be teaching mathematics inclusion and were never asked if they were comfortable with the new assignment. An eighth-grade teacher from New York criticized her administration; she said, "Teachers were not given choices . . . [some] were just assigned inclusion . . . some didn't have any idea what this was . . . they don't want to be teaching inclusion and didn't have a choice." Some of the teachers did not think the administration afforded them adequate and consistent professional development opportunities focused on inclusion. A seventh-grade teacher from Texas commented, "Administration tells you that you need to modify and [they] want to see inclusion work, but they don't help you much. [There is] not much staff development, and it's really sad—especially for the first-year teachers . . . maybe 10 minutes of staff development is on special ed." An eighth-grade teacher from Rhode Island said that her administration was "more supportive the first year [of the inclusion program] . . . no recent workshops [had been planned]" on specific instructional strategies.

Resources.　When asked to rate the level of available support services (e.g., counseling, resource room or teacher, instructional materials, etc.), about one-fifth (21.5 percent) of the survey respondents felt that existing services were below average (see Table 1). Approximately 43 percent of respondents had taken fewer than three workshops related to teaching students with LD. Some of the respondents

TABLE 6　General Educators' Beliefs Regarding Administrative Support and Available Resources

Beliefs Statement	Number (%)[a]				
	Strongly Agree	Agree	Undecided	Disagree	Strongly Disagree
Administrative Support					
In inclusive math classrooms SLD require more time from teachers than general ed students	71 (31.1)	94 (41.2)	24 (10.5)	33 (14.5)	5 (2.2)
General ed teachers are given sufficient time to prepare for teaching math inclusion	9 (3.9)	44 (19.3)	43 (18.9)	83 (36.4)	48 (21.1)
Resources					
Are comfortable team teaching math with special ed teachers	24 (10.5)	82 (36)	76 (33.3)	37 (16.2)	8 (3.5)

[a]The number of respondents varied because of missing cases.

were not required to take any workshops. (See Table 1 for full details on the comprehensive list of categories and percentages.)

Teamwork and collaboration seemed to be an integral resource. According to the survey, approximately 46.5 percent of the general educators *agreed* or *strongly agreed* with the following statement: "General education teachers are comfortable team teaching mathematics with special education teachers." However, more than one fourth (33.3 percent) of the general educators were still undecided concerning their comfort with team teaching.

Although eight of the interview participants did not have a special education teacher or aide in all (or any) of their inclusion classes, most of the interview participants identified other people (e.g., special education teachers, aides, other inclusion teachers, counselors, etc.) as the most significant resource available to them. Much of the interview data supported the theme of teacher collaboration as an important factor in successful inclusive classrooms. A sixth-grade teacher from New York commented, "[We] were given no direction for inclusion . . . I was very lucky to have three other committed educators . . . without them, I wouldn't have gotten half the work done. . . . They were my support . . . the ones I bounced ideas off of . . . [We] shared everything." Another sixth-grade teacher from New Hampshire stated, "It's impossible to do inclusion without collaboration . . . they're [team teachers] my eyes and ears . . . for what I don't always pick up, they catch." A New York eighth-grade teacher explained, "If you don't have a good relationship with your co-teacher, it [inclusion] just doesn't work." An eighth grade teacher from Washington said, "When there's a strong sense of team teaching, everyone enjoys their job more, and the kids are more successful." Other teachers relied on their peers (both special and general education teachers) for "feedback," for the "challenges/benefits . . . of using certain lessons," to "understand [IEP] goals and focus more for the kids," or

just to "hear other perspectives . . . sometimes you get in a fixed pattern on how you teach" (New York teachers). Finally, a sixth-grade teacher from New York summed up teacher collaboration by stating, "Unique ideas are generated through collaboration . . . [You] wouldn't find them in any methods books."

Although some instructional resources were also discussed, such as Web sites, computers and software, overhead projectors, graphing calculators, *Mimeo* technology, manipulatives and other hands-on materials, the interview participants did not seem to rely on these materials as much as assistance from colleagues.

Research Question 4: Strategies from Higher Education Teacher Preparation Programs

Only about one-fourth (27.6 percent) of the respondents agreed that their teacher education programs helped them develop instructional philosophies related to teaching mathematics to students with LD (see Table 7). Half of the respondents thought that their teacher education programs had failed to offer specific information about the characteristics and needs of students with LD in mathematics learning or to offer specific instructional strategies for teaching mathematics to students with LD. Further, as Table 1 shows, more than half (57.1 percent) of the respondents had taken fewer than three mathematics general education methods classes. Ten percent of inclusion mathematics teachers were not exposed to any mathematics methods courses, possibly because this was not a requirement at the time they received certification. Teachers are not provided with opportunities to learn about specific characteristics and needs of students with LD. Further, they have no information on how to tailor instruction to address the specific disabilities demonstrated by students in their classrooms, particularly when covering the curriculum for upper grades. Tests of significance did indicate that teachers in more supportive schools generally rated their level of teacher preparation differently.

TABLE 7   General Educators' Beliefs Regarding Their Teacher Preparation Programs

Beliefs Statement	Number (%)[a]				
	Strongly Agree	Agree	Undecided	Disagree	Strongly Disagree
Teacher ed programs help general ed teachers develop instructional philosophies for teaching math to SLD	5 (2.2)	58 (25.4)	56 (24.6)	77 (33.8)	27 (11.8)
Teacher ed programs offer specific information about characteristics/needs of SLD in math learning	8 (3.5)	52 (22.8)	52 (22.8)	81 (35.5)	33 (14.5)
Teacher ed programs offer specific instructional strategies for teaching math to SLD	5 (2.2)	49 (21.5)	54 (21.9)	84 (35.1)	42 (18.4)

[a]The number of respondents varied because of missing cases.

Twenty of the 26 interviewees believed that their undergraduate and graduate schools did not effectively prepare them to teach mathematics inclusion. Approximately seven of the participants said that they learned "a little" or rated their teacher preparation classes as "fair." One eighth-grade teacher from New York summed up the issue by saying, "My programs prepared me sort of . . . not great but not terrible." Another eighth-grade teacher from New York stated, "[My teacher education program] glossed over special ed and inclusion really quickly." Some of the participants were required to take a special education course in either undergraduate or graduate school, but very few of these courses addressed specific instructional strategies for students with LD. Mainly, the special education courses provided an overview of special education and focused on the various laws associated with special education students. In fact, one participant from New Hampshire recalled learning in her undergraduate and graduate classes that, "When you need to modify lesson plans, you just go to the special ed teacher." Finally, some of the participants commented that anything they learned about inclusive strategies came from "on-the-job training" and the "experience of teaching" (teachers from New York and New Hampshire).

DISCUSSION

The findings from the survey and follow-up telephone interviews revealed three major issues that need to be addressed as school districts attempt to provide inclusive mathematics education to students with LD, and meet federal and state mandates for inclusion of all students in standardized testing. These issues include (a) the lack of teacher knowledge regarding the mathematical learning needs of included students, (b) the importance of teacher collaboration, and (c) the inadequacy of teacher preparation for inclusion at both the preservice and in-service levels.

Issue One: Limited Understanding of Mathematical Learning Needs of Students with LD

Many of the interview participants seemed to lack a strong understanding of specific pedagogical strategies to strengthen the mathematical learning of students with LD. Even though more than one-half of the survey respondents perceived themselves as *quite comfortable* or *very comfortable* in their abilities to adapt instruction for students with LD, a rather alarming percentage (between 5 percent and 13 percent) indicated that they were *not comfortable* meeting the mathematical learning needs of students with LD in many areas. This is problematic considering that two-thirds of the survey respondents, as well as most of the interview participants, believed that they were the primary people responsible for modifying instruction for their students with LD. Also, of great concern was that the majority of participants believed that there was no distinction between a student with LD and a low performing student. Therefore, the participants believed that the modifications

(e.g., slower pace, fewer equations per page, etc.) they used for low-performing students would be sufficient for students with LD. Many of the participants did not seem to understand that students with LD have a whole host of individualized learning challenges that need to be addressed through instructional modifications and individualized lesson plans.

Although some interview participants did name constructive strategies such as chunking material, tiering lessons, and small-group work, there was no mention of other instructional strategies that research has proven effective when teaching mathematics to students with LD. For example, mathematical comprehension of students with LD can be fostered through encouraging these students to "discuss, critique, explain, and when necessary, justify their interpretations and solutions" (Cobb et al., 1991, p. 6). Students with LD can be encouraged to share their mathematical thought processes through journal writing and other forms of written expression (Thornton, Langrall, & Jones, 1998). During the interviews, none of the participants mentioned having students reflect, through words, on the process of solving mathematical equations. In addition, "written communication" was one of the learning needs for which survey respondents felt less comfortable adapting instruction. This indicates a consistency between the survey and interview data and emerges as a key issue in mathematics instruction. In addition, there was no specific mention of using individualized lesson plans, simulations, computer-assisted instruction, self-regulation strategies, or teacher modeling. Such instructional strategies have been found to clarify abstract mathematical concepts and processes by creating concrete illustrations; increase accuracy and understanding of higher-level mathematical concepts; strengthen estimation skills; create kinesthetic awareness; and increase independence, motivation, attention, and coordination for students with LD (Jarrett, 1999; Miller, Butler, & Lee, 1998; Steele, 2002). Although some participants mentioned that instructional resources (e.g., computer software) were available, they said that they did not really rely on such resources. Lastly, the concept of prioritizing lesson objectives for students with LD and focusing on the "big ideas" within the content is critical in mathematics instruction for students with LD, yet none of the participants raised issues related to this. Often, "mathematics programs attempt to cover exhaustive lists of learning objectives, with little or no attempt to prioritize those objectives on the basis of their relative importance later" (Carnine, 1997, p. 135). It is the teacher's responsibility to extract the most significant material and focus on getting students to understand this information.

In addition, participants did not have a sound understanding of the definition of an instructional strategy. For example, none of the participants realized that modifications such as the use of colored markers or overhead projectors are not considered instructional strategies, but are tools to enhance instruction. Many participants mentioned "differentiated instruction," yet they were unable to define this term or give specific examples of what differentiated instruction entails. These results are consistent with the findings of other studies, which have found that general educators did not prepare written, individualized instructional plans for students with LD and did not use many of the instructional methods that researchers have proposed as effective for students with LD (deBettencourt, 1999; Schumm et al., 1995).

Many researchers have argued that curricular modifications and the ways in which the curriculum is delivered are integral to creating effective mathematics programs for students with LD, and instruction should be geared toward the individual needs of students with LD (Carnine, 1998; Jones, Wilson, & Bhojwani, 1998; Montague, 1998; Rivera, 1998). The findings of the present study indicated that the majority of the participants did not modify their mathematics curriculum through prioritizing, better integration of mathematical topics, or dividing difficult topics between general education and special or resource room teachers.

Issue Two: Teacher Collaboration

Results indicated that the most valuable resource for general educators who taught mathematics in inclusion programs was other people—mainly special education teachers, aides, guidance counselors, and/or school psychologists. Teachers in schools with high levels of ancillary support consistently were in favor of inclusion and had higher feelings of efficacy about adapting instruction and curriculum. Many of the interview participants indicated that they met weekly or bi-weekly with the special education experts in their school. Whether it was advice on the ways in which to handle a specific student or simply to gain a deeper understanding of a certain disability, the participants looked to their colleagues who had special education backgrounds to provide them with assistance. Some of the general education participants even sought the counsel of other general educators who taught inclusion. Collaborative strategies and a genuine team mentality were the central reasons the general educators were able to endure the challenges of their mathematics inclusion classes and transform these challenges to some level of success. The results support the findings of Brownell and Pajares (1999), McLeskey and Waldron (2002), and Miller and Savage (1995), who cite collegiality as a key component in the success of inclusion programs.

Issue Three: Inadequacy of Preservice and In-Service Teacher Preparation for Inclusion

Consistent with findings of Smith and Smith (2000) and Rao and Lim (1999), the majority of the respondents in the current study agreed that their preservice teacher preparation programs did not equip them with the necessary skills to face the challenges of teaching students with LD in mathematics inclusive classrooms. Many of the required special education courses were survey type courses that gave an overview of special education, including broad descriptions of disabilities (mainly physical disabilities) and special education laws. The participants had similar reflections on their mathematics methods courses, which neither

addressed inclusion nor discussed specific mathematics instructional strategies for students with LD. Some of the interview participants felt that the most beneficial education came from their actual experience teaching students with LD in inclusive classrooms, their on-the-job-training.

Further, only a small percentage of survey respondents believed that their teacher education programs helped them develop instructional philosophies about teaching mathematics to students with LD. Therefore, teachers felt that they were sent into mathematics inclusive classrooms without being given the opportunity to reflect on their instructional beliefs and create a personalized doctrine to guide them. When teachers are faced with new challenges that they do not feel prepared for, such as teaching students with LD, having a clear set of values and instructional principles to refer to may help alleviate some of the inherent difficulties. Helping teachers develop an innovative and progressive mathematics instructional philosophy is critical, and teacher education faculty must understand that most preservice teachers address mathematics in the way in which they were taught (Parmar & Cawley, 1995). Although perceptions are changing, many preservice teachers still think of mathematics as merely rote memorization and rules. The idea of problem solving and constructivist frameworks is almost unimaginable. As one sixth-grade teacher from New York said, "Strategies are so different than what I remember math being."

As is evident from the survey results, administrative support was a significant factor in how teachers felt about inclusion and about providing effective instruction to address specific learning needs across topics. Training was sporadic or nonexistent in many cases, based on interview responses. Even those who did have some training as first-year inclusion teachers indicated that such training decreased (or was eliminated) after their first year.

Frequently, professional development workshops were seen as ineffective as they did not focus on specific instructional strategies and ways to individualize lesson plans for teaching mathematics to students with LD. Consistent with the findings of Brownell and Pajares (1999), teachers with more intensive and specific professional development felt better prepared to teach in inclusion settings. Administrators must recognize the need for in-service workshops that specifically address mathematical content in areas of identified need such as using technology and teaching with the graphing calculator.

Limitations in Design

The present study extends our understanding of the relationship between teachers' beliefs, their knowledge of disability, and their self-perceived ability to provide mathematics instruction in inclusive settings. However, the current research also had its share of limitations. First, because there was no central mailing list that coincided with the required sample criteria, it was difficult to randomize the sample, as well as obtain an equal representation of respondents from all geographic regions. Second, because classroom observations were not conducted, the data reflect only teachers' perceptions of instruction, which may be quite different from actual practice. These limitations lead to the need for caution when interpreting the study's results.

Implications for Practice

The national data on percentages of students with LD receiving education in general education programs and the findings of the present study lead to some implications for practice.

1. Teachers need to broaden their repertoire of instructional and curricular modifications to better meet the needs of all students. With increasing trends toward inclusion and reductions in support, general education teachers will be taking on more and more responsibilities for included students, and they need to prepare in every way possible. The participants in this study clearly had a limited understanding of effective mathematical instructional methods for students with LD, and even expressed frustration over their perceived inability to motivate their included students. However, the majority of them firmly believed that they were responsible for teaching the students with LD in their inclusive classrooms. Yet, most of the participants never read any research articles or other material that would enhance their understanding of LD and strategies for teaching mathematics to students with LD. It is understandable that with planning, grading, attending meetings, and the everyday routine of actual instruction, a teacher's day is quite hectic, and often there is little time left for additional work. However, general educators must find the time to advance their knowledge regarding mathematics instruction for students with LD.

2. Preservice teacher preparation programs need to be restructured to increase the amount of information provided on the learning needs of included students and pedagogical practices for diverse learners. All mathematics undergraduate teacher education programs should require preservice teachers to spend time observing inclusive classrooms, student teaching in an inclusive classroom, and engaging in discussions of effective strategies for teaching students with LD in inclusive classrooms, particularly for challenging topics such as fractions, decimals, geometric formulas, and computer spreadsheets. It will also prepare them for working with students with attention and motivational difficulties. Using strategies such as class discussions, role playing, and journal writing, teacher education programs could also encourage teachers to reflect on their beliefs, their perceptions, and their knowledge of inclusive practice.

3. In-service teacher training that focuses on particular mathematics topics and strategies for teaching students with LD also appears to be necessary. Workshops need to address more than a few high profile disability categories such as Attention Deficit Hyperactivity Disorder and autism, provide age-appropriate strategies for middle school-age students that are actual instructional modifications rather than just use of tools (highlighter, etc.), and provide information on how to make curricular modifications through prioritization and integration of topics.

4. Teacher collaboration should be fostered through administrative arrangements that allow for joint planning time, conference time, and sustained co-teaching experiences across several years. Teachers also need to work at developing collaborative relationships with professionals outside their immediate subject area or grade level. Colleagues are the most important source of support and information regarding effective inclusive practices.

References

Bender, W. N., Vail, C. O., & Scott, K. (1995). Teachers' attitudes toward increased mainstreaming: Implementing elective instruction for students with learning disabilities. *Journal of Learning Disabilities, 28,* 87–94.

Bogdan, R. C., & Biklay S. (1998). *Qualitative research for education: An introduction to theory and methods* (3rd ed.). Needham Heights, MA: Allyn & Bacon.

Brownell, M. T., & Pajama, F. (1999). Teacher efficacy and perceived success in mainstreaming students with learning and behavior problems. *Teacher Education and Special Education, 22,* 154–164.

Carnine, D. (1997). Instructional design in mathematics for students with learning disabilities. *Journal of Learning Disabilities, 30,* 130–141.

Carnine, D. (1998). Instructional design in mathematics for students with learning disabilities. In D. P. Rivera (Ed.), *Mathematics education for students with learning disabilities* (pp. 119–138). Austin, TX: Pro-Ed.

Chow, P., & Winzer, M. M. (1992). Reliability and validity of a scale measuring attitudes toward mainstreaming. *Educational and Psychological Measurement, 52,* 223–228.

Coates, R. D. (1989). The regular education initiative and opinions of regular classroom teachers. *Journal of Learning Disabilities, 22,* 532–536.

Cobb, P., Wood, T., Yackel, E., Nicholls, J., Wheatley, G., Trigatti, B., & Perlwitz, M. (1991). Assessment of a problem-centered second-grade mathematics project. *Journal for Research in Mathematics Education, 22*(1), 3–29.

Cochran, H. K. (1998). Differences in teachers' attitudes toward inclusive education as measured by the scale of teachers' attitudes toward inclusive classrooms (STATIC). *Proceedings of the Annual Meeting of the Mid-Western Educational Research Association.* Chicago, 3–33.

deBettencourt, L. U. (1999). General educators' attitudes toward students with mild disabilities and their use of instructional strategies: Implications for training. *Remedial and Special Education, 20*(1), 27–35.

DeSimone, J. R., & Parmar, R. S. (2004). *Survey on teaching mathematics to students with learning disabilities in middle school.* Unpublished manuscript, St. John's University, New York.

Janney, R. E., Snell, M. E., Boers, M. K., & Raynea, M. (1995). Integrating students with moderate and severe disabilities: Classroom teachers' beliefs and attitudes about implementing an educational change. *Educational Administration Quarterly, 31,* 86–114.

Jarrett, D. (1999). *The inclusive classroom: Mathematics and science instruction for students with learning disabilities. It's just good teaching.* Portland, OR: Northwest Regional Educational Laboratory.

Jones, E. D., Wilson, R., & Bhojwani, S. (1998). Mathematics instruction for secondary students with learning disabilities. In D. P. Rivera (Ed.), *Mathematics education for students with learning disabilities* (pp. 155–176). Austin, TX: Pro-Ed.

Kochhar, C. A., West, L. L., & Taymans, J. M. (2000). *Successful inclusion: Practical strategies for a shared responsibility.* Upper Saddle River, NJ: Prentice Hall.

Larrivee, B., & Cook, L. (1979). Mainstreaming: A study of the variables affecting teacher attitude. *Journal of Special Education, 13,* 315–324,

McLeskey, J., & Waldron, N. L. (2002). Inclusion and school change: Teacher perceptions regarding curricular and instructional adaptations. *Teacher Education and Special Education, 24,* 41–54.

McLeskey, J., Waldron, N. L., So, T. H., Swanson, K., & Loveland, T. (2001). Perspectives of teachers toward inclusive school programs. *Teacher Education and Special Education, 24,* 108–115.

Miller, K. J., & Savage, L. B. (1995, March). Including general educators in inclusion. In *Reaching to the future: Boldly facing challenges in rural communities. Conference proceedings of the American Council on Rural Special Education.* (ERIC Document Reproduction Service No. ED 381 322)

Miller, S. P., Butler, F. M., & Lee, K. (1998). Validated practices for teaching mathematics to students with learning disabilities: A review of the literature. *Focus on Exceptional Children, 31,* 1–24.

Montague, M. (1998). Cognitive strategy instruction in mathematics for students with learning disabilities. In D. P. Rivera (Ed.), *Mathematics education for students with learning disabilities* (pp. 177–199). Austin, TX: Pro-Ed.

National Center for Education Statistics. (2003). *Overview of public elementary and secondary and districts: School year 2001–02, NCES Report 2003–411.* Washington, DC: Author.

National Center for Education Statistics. (2004). National Assessment of Educational Progress. *The nation's report card: Mathematics highlights 2003, NCES Report 2004–451.* Washington, DC: Author.

Nespor, J. (1987). The role of beliefs in the practice of teaching. *Journal of Curriculum Studies, 19,* 317–328.

New York State Education Department. (2005). *Mathematics core curriculum.* Albany, NY: Author.

Pajam, M. F. (1992). Teachers' beliefs and educational research: Cleaning up a messy construct. *Review of Educational Research, 62,* 307–332.

Parmar, R. S., & Cawley, J. F. (1995). Mathematics curricula frameworks: Goals for general and special education. *Focus on Learning Problems in Mathematics, 17,* 50–66.

Rao, S. M., & Lim, L. (1999, May). *Beliefs and attitudes of preservice teachers towards teaching children with disabilities.* Paper presented at the annual conference of the American Association on Mental Retardation, New Orleans, LA.

Rivera, D. P. (Ed.). (1998), *Mathematics education for students with learning disabilities.* Austin, TX: Pro-Ed.

Schumm, J. S., Vaughn, S., Haager, D., McDowell, J., Rothlein, L., & Saumell, L. (1995). General education teacher planning: What can students with learning disabilities expect? *Exceptional Children, 61,* 335–352.

Scruggs, T. E., & Mastropieri, M. A. (1996). Teacher perceptions of mainstreaming/inclusion, 1958–1995: A research synthesis. *Exceptional Children, 63,* 59–74.

Smith, M. K., & Smith, K. E. (2000). "I believe in inclusion, but. . . ." Regular education early childhood teachers' perceptions of successful inclusion. *Journal of Research in Childhood Education, 14,* 161–180.

Steele, M. M. (2002). Strategies for helping students who have learning disabilities in mathematics. *Mathematics Teaching in the Middle School, 8,* 140–143.

Thornton, C. A., Langrall, C. W., & Jones, G. A. (1998). Mathematics instruction for elementary students with learning disabilities. In D. P. Rivera (Ed.), *Mathematics education for students with learning disabilities* (pp. 139–154). Austin, TX: Pro-Ed.

United States Department of Education. (2003). *Table AB2— Percentage of children ages 6–21 served in different educational environments under IDEA, Part B, by Disability.* Retrieved August 28, 2005, from http://www.ideadata.org/tables27th/ar_ab2.htm.

APPENDIX

NAME:
DATE:
E-MAIL:
STATE:

1. How many years have you been teaching mathematics?
2. How many years have you been teaching mathematics inclusion?
3. How well did your undergraduate or graduate school prepare you for teaching in an inclusive classroom?
4. Please provide some instructional strategies that you utilize for your students with LD.
5. Which specific mathematics topics do you think require instructional adaptations for students with LD?
6. Please provide specific examples of curricular adaptations you have made for your inclusion classes.
7. What resources are currently available to aid you with instructing included students?
8. What has been your greatest challenge in teaching inclusion?

About the Authors

Janet R DeSimone is Assistant Professor of Educational Leadership at Lehman College/CUNY. Her research interests are inclusion, co-teaching, and learning disabilities.

Rene S. Parmar is Professor of Measurement and Evaluation and Special Education at St. John's University. Her research interests are mathematics learning disabilities and educational assessment.

chapter 11

Group Comparison Research

IMPORTANT *Ideas*

1. The improvement of education depends greatly on our ability to discover the causes of problems in educational practice and also the harmful effects that can occur if the problems of practice are not solved.

2. The independent variable is not manipulated in group comparison and correlational research studies.

3. The introductory section of a report of a group comparison study should explain (1) why the study is important, (2) its specific purposes, (3) the variables that were investigated, and (4) the findings from the literature review.

4. A group comparison research design can include multiple independent variables and multiple dependent variables.

5. In an ideal group comparison research design, the sample would be randomly selected from a defined population.

6. A group comparison research design does not impose any restrictions on the instruments that can be used to measure the independent and dependent variables.

7. Commonly used tests of statistical significance in group comparison research include the t test, analysis of variance, and their nonparametric counterparts (the Mann-Whitney U test, the Wilcoxon signed-rank test, the Kruskal-Wallis test, and the chi-square test).

8. The practical significance of statistical results obtained in group comparison research can be determined by computing effect sizes.

9. In the discussion section of a report of a group comparison study, the researchers should (1) summarize the study's findings, (2) consider flaws in the design and execution of the study, and (3) state implications of the study for subsequent research and improvement of professional practice. ■

Key TERMS

analysis of variance	Kruskal-Wallis test of statistical significance	t test
causal relationship		Wilcoxon signed-rank test of statistical significance
construct	Mann-Whitney *U* test of statistical significance	
dependent variable		x variable
effect size	matching procedure	y variable
fixed variable	nonparametric test of statistical significance	
group comparison research	parametric test of statistical significance	
independent variable		
interaction effect	test of statistical significance	

Classification of Quantitative Research Designs

The literature on research methodology does not have consistent terminology for classifying different types of quantitative research designs. This is particularly true of the research designs that we explain in this chapter and the next. Therefore, we start this chapter with a discussion of research designs and our choice of terminology to classify them.

Our starting point is the variables that researchers choose to study. We explained in Chapter 6 that a variable is a quantitative expression of a **construct** that can vary. For example, the construct of self-esteem can be viewed as a variable, because we can imagine variations in this construct: People have different levels of self-esteem, ranging from high to low.

In descriptive research (see Chapter 10), the variables refer to characteristics of the sample—for example, academic achievement, years of education, socioeconomic status, and attitudes. Descriptive research studies do not attempt to determine whether any of these variables has a causal influence on other variables.

All other quantitative research designs, either explicitly or implicitly, conceptualize variables as reflecting a **causal relationship** to each other. If the research study involves two variables, for example, one is usually conceptualized as the cause, and the other is conceptualized as the effect. It is common practice among researchers to label the "cause" variable as the **independent variable** and the "effect" variable as the **dependent variable.** In statistics, the "cause" variable sometimes is labeled the *x* **variable,** and the "effect" variable is labeled the *y* **variable.**

In experimental research designs, the intervention (e.g., an educational program or teaching technique) is the independent variable. The intervention is introduced into an existing situation to determine what effect, or effects, it might have. These effects are the dependent variables.

The labels *descriptive research* and *experimental research* are straightforward and used consistently by researchers. The one exception is that descriptive research sometimes is called *survey research.* However, in some studies, researchers collect data about variables that they have conceptualized to be in a causal relationship to each other, but there is no intervention. Their research designs are neither descriptive nor experimental. They involve two other types of research design, which are the subjects of this chapter and the next.

Nonexperimental Research Involving Causal Relationships

Studies that explore cause-and-effect relationships between variables, but without using the experimental method, have been given various labels in education and other disciplines, including *causal-comparative research, correlational research, ex post facto research, group comparison research,* and *relational research.* Burke Johnson (2001) noted the confusion created by these terms and suggested two new terms—*predictive nonexperimental research* and *explanatory nonexperimental research.* Each of these terms has merit. We mention them here so that you are aware of them should you come across them in reading research reports. Our preference is to distinguish between two types of research designs, both of which are nonexperimental and both of which are used to explore causal relationships between variables.

One type of design involves group comparisons (e.g., comparing the mean scores of two groups on a particular measure), and so we label it *group comparison research.* The other type of design involves the use of correlational statistics, and so we label it *correlational research.*

In previous editions of this book, we used the label *causal-comparative research* instead of *group comparison research,* because the former was commonly used in the research literature. However, Johnson and others criticize the use of this label because it implies that causal-comparative research can be used to explore causal relationships whereas correlational research cannot be similarly used.

As you will see, both of these types of nonexperimental research designs—group comparison research and correlational research—are useful for exploring causal relationships, even though they cannot confirm results to the degree that experimental research can.

The Relevance of Group Comparison Research to Educational Practice

If you reflect on your concerns about educational practice, you are likely to realize that many of them involve cause-and-effect relationships. For example, while we were preparing this edition of the book, the public was deeply troubled when a college student at a state university committed mass murder on campus and then killed himself. The mass media was filled with stories seeking to explain why the student committed these acts. The media response was essentially a concern about cause and effect: What factors (i.e., what causes) led to these violent acts (the effect)?

Consider other phenomena that are raising alarm among educators and other groups— for example, the increasing frequency of obesity among youth, the rising incidence of autism in children, the persistent achievement gap between white students and students of other ethnicities, and the prevalence of bullying behavior on school grounds.

These problems raise a question about cause and effect. Why do these problems occur? Note that this question is based on the premise that the effect (e.g., autism) has already occurred, and now we are looking to the past to determine what caused it. In other words, the focus of the research is on explanation. We observe a certain phenomenon and seek to explain why it has occurred.

Besides explanation, educators are also concerned with prediction. For example, teacher educators and school officials wish to select the best candidates for a teacher education program or teaching position. They ask such questions as "If we select this individual for the program or position, how likely is she to be an effective teacher in the future?"

Elected officials and the general public, too, are concerned about matters involving prediction. If they budget more money for public education, will schools actually improve over time? If they break large schools into smaller schools, will students subsequently feel better about their education and learn more? If charter schools are approved by the government, will public schools suffer adverse consequences?

If we analyze the process of prediction, we realize that it too involves the study of cause and effect, but with a focus on future rather than past occurrences. The cause is a particular action (e.g., selecting particular teacher candidates or increasing a school budget) and the consequence of that action is the effect.

Group comparison research is commonly used to explore possible cause-and-effect relationships such as those just described. We define **group comparison research** as empirical, quantitative studies that either (1) compare groups that differ on the independent variable to determine whether they also differ on the dependent variable or (2) compare groups that differ on the dependent variable to determine whether they also differ on the independent variable.

If the comparison groups differ on the independent variable (e.g., high school graduates vs. dropouts), the purpose of the study will be to predict how they differ on variables that will occur at a later point in time. If the comparison groups differ on the dependent variable (e.g., reading ability), the purpose of the study will be to explain these differences in terms of variables that occurred at an earlier point in time.

Examples of Group Comparison Research

The following are examples of group comparison studies and the problems of practice for which they are relevant. In presenting each example, we label which variables were treated as independent and which were treated as dependent.

New Teachers' Experiences in High-Income and Low-Income Schools

Johnson, S. M., Kardos, S. M., Kauffman, D., Liu, E., & Donaldson, M. L. (2004). The support gap: New teachers' early experiences in high-income and low-income schools. *Education Policy Analysis Archives, 12*(61). Retrieved from http://epaa.asu.edu/epaa/v12n61

Susan Johnson and her colleagues found that new teachers in low-income schools, compared to new teachers in high-income schools, experienced less timely and information-rich hiring, less mentoring from experienced colleagues, and were less likely to be offered a curriculum that was flexible yet aligned with state standards.

In this study, the family income level of the school's students is the independent variable, and new teachers' experience with hiring, mentoring, and curriculum design are the three dependent variables. It is obvious that the family income levels of a school's students occurs earlier in time than the other variables and is hypothesized to affect them. The comparison groups represent differences on the independent variable (family income level).

The researchers recommended that school administrators authorize all schools to hire early so that low-income and high-income schools have equal access to the strongest teaching candidates and that administrators in low-income schools make the effort to place each new teacher with an experienced mentor.

Gender Differences in College Students' Ratings of Professors

Basow, S. A., Phelan, J. E., & Capotosto, L. (2006). Gender patterns in college students' choices of their best and worst professors. *Psychology of Women Quarterly, 30*(1), 25–35.

Few females have had positions as professors in higher education during most of its history. This situation is rapidly changing, as an increasing number of women are hired into faculty positions. It is important to know whether this institutional change has created problems of practice for female faculty and those who interact with them.

The researchers asked college students to describe their best and worst professors. Male students chose a female professor as best less than expected, whereas female students chose a female professor as best as often as expected. Male students generally described their worst female professors as closed-minded and having poor classroom interaction skills.

Both student gender and professor gender are independent variables, and student opinion of a professor's teaching ability is the dependent variable. This classification of the variables reflects the fact that students' gender and professors' gender are established prior in time to college and are thought to affect their views of professors.

The researchers' major recommendation for practice, based on their research findings, is that student evaluations of a professor's excellence should be analyzed carefully for indications of gender bias. They also recommended that if professors wish to receive good student ratings, female professors should try to be accessible to their students, and male professors should try to appear knowledgeable, dynamic, clear, and organized.

Effects of Students' Residential and School Mobility

> Engec, N. (2006). Relationship between mobility and student performance and behavior. *Journal of Educational Research, 99*(3), 167–178.

A substantial percentage of K–12 students change residence and the school they attend each year. There is concern about whether schools adequately meet the academic needs of these mobile students.

The researcher studied several types of student mobility, including moves during a school year. Within this type of mobility, the researcher compared four groups of students: (1) no moves, (2) one move, (3), two moves, and (4) three or more moves. The results indicated that as the number of moves increased, students' academic achievement declined, and they were more likely to experience school suspensions.

Student mobility is the independent variable, and academic achievement and school suspensions are the dependent variables. This is because student moves occurred, and then subsequent academic achievement and suspensions were measured.

The researcher made several recommendations based on these findings, such as the development of student record systems to provide information that helps educators in the new school provide relevant services to mobile students.

Features of a Group Comparison Research Report

Table 11.1 presents typical features of a group comparison study report. In the following sections, we explain each feature and illustrate it with a research study about a type of school scheduling known as block scheduling. At the end of the chapter, you will find another group comparison study investigating whether the academic achievement of children who enter kindergarten at a younger age is better or worse than that of children who enter kindergarten at an older age. The journal report of this study is reprinted in full.

Introduction

The introductory section of a report of a group comparison study should explain (1) why the study is important, (2) its specific purposes, (3) the variables that were investigated, and (4) the findings of the authors' literature review.

Consider the study of block scheduling conducted by Leslie Flynn, Frances Lawrenz, and Matthew Schultz (2005). They started their report by noting that the traditional school schedule in middle schools and high schools includes six or seven time periods. This schedule typically allows only 40 or 50 minutes for each subject. In contrast, block scheduling has a smaller number of time periods, so that each subject can be taught for 85 to 100 minutes. The researchers also noted recent national mandates for standards-based instruction,

TABLE **11.1**   Typical Sections of a Group Comparison Research Report

Section	Content
Introduction	Hypotheses, questions, or objectives are stated. A review of relevant literature is reported. The purpose of the study usually is to explicitly or implicitly study the factors that affect a problem of practice or the consequences resulting from the problem of practice.
Research design	Two or more groups of research participants are specified. If the study examines the factors that caused the groups to be different, the groups will represent the dependent variable, and the factors (i.e., the presumed causes) will be the independent variables. If the study involves prediction, the groups represent variations of the independent variable, and the variables that are measured subsequently are the dependent variables (i.e., the effects).
Sampling procedure	The researchers attempt to select groups of research participants who differ significantly on the independent or dependent variable but are similar in all other respects.
Measures	Virtually any kind of measure can be used to collect data on the independent and dependent variables.
Data analysis	Descriptive statistics for the independent and dependent variables are computed. Commonly used tests of statistical significance for the observed differences between the different groups of research participants are the t test, analysis of variance, analysis of covariance, and the chi-square test.
Discussion	The main findings of the study are summarized. Flaws and limitations of the study are considered. Implications of the findings for further research and professional practice are considered.

which, among other things, require that teachers develop students' problem-solving and higher-order thinking skills.

The researchers hypothesized, "Because many standards-based instructional practices call for in-depth investigations, discussions, and reflections, extended periods associated with block scheduling may act as a catalyst for standards-based teaching techniques that have been neglected in the traditional school schedule" (Flynn et al., 2005, p. 15). Their study was designed to test this hypothesis.

The study also had the intent of helping educators address a problem of practice. The researchers noted that educators currently are being held accountable for student learning and adherence to curriculum standards. The question is whether block scheduling can help educators meet these accountability requirements. As the researchers put it, "The present study provides additional data for school administrators to use in making decisions about school scheduling options" (Flynn et al., 2005, p. 16).

The independent variable in the study (i.e., the presumed cause) was school schedule, which had two values: (1) block scheduling and (2) traditional scheduling. The dependent variable (i.e., the presumed effect) was mathematics teachers' use of 17 standards-based "minds-on" activities reflecting current national standards for mathematics instruction.

Research Design

Researchers typically use a group comparison research design when they are not able to manipulate the independent variable. In the study we are examining, it is difficult to imagine that the researchers could obtain school administrators' permission to select a sample of their traditional schedule schools and randomly assign them to either continue with traditional scheduling or to adopt block scheduling. School systems are not accustomed to this level of experimentation, nor do they have the resources for it.

The alternative is to look for "natural" experiments in which school systems or other agencies, on their own initiative, have instituted the education practices of interest to the researchers. This was the case with the block-scheduling study. The researchers selected schools that had adopted block scheduling and compared them to schools that had retained traditional scheduling.

A group comparison research design is also used when the independent variable involves a personal or group characteristic that cannot be manipulated. Some researchers refer to these variables as **fixed variables,** because they cannot be changed by the researchers or other groups. For example, ethnicity is intrinsic to individuals. Similarly, other characteristics, such as family composition (e.g., two parents, one parent, multigenerational) are determined by factors that are beyond manipulation by an external agency.

The study we are examining here involves one independent variable, school schedule. This basic group comparison research design could be modified to include additional independent variables. For example, all the schools in the sample were middle schools. If the researchers had included high schools with traditional schedules and block schedules, school level would be another independent variable.

The addition of the variable of school level would enable the researchers to determine the effects of time schedule (an independent variable) and school level (another independent variable) on teacher instruction (the dependent variable). Also, the researchers could investigate whether the effects of school schedule varied by school level. For example, they might find that block scheduling affects the instruction of middle school teachers but not the instruction of high school teachers.

A group comparison research design also can include multiple dependent variables. For example, the researchers could examine the effects of block scheduling on these dependent variables—teachers' instruction, teachers' stress level, students' attitude toward school, and students' academic achievement.

Sampling Procedure

As is true of any quantitative research study, researchers who do a group comparison study should select a sample that is representative of the population to which they wish to generalize their results. To achieve this goal, they need to identify the population and randomly select a sample from it.

Typically, researchers lack the resources to define a population and then randomly select participants from it. This is particularly true if the population is distributed across a wide region and if data collection requires direct contact with the sample. Therefore, researchers compromise by selecting an available sample and describing its characteristics in detail. Readers of the report can study these characteristics and make their own determination of the population to which the results might generalize.

In the school schedule study, the researchers' sample included schools from three states. They comment, "Although the sample was not drawn randomly and, therefore, is not necessarily representative of all schools across the three states, it contains a broad range of teachers', principals', and school characteristics" (Flynn et al., 2005, p. 17).

Ideally, the comparison groups should represent different values of the independent variable but be identical in all other respects. Otherwise, we do not know for certain whether observed differences between the comparison groups on the dependent variables are the result of the independent variable or of other variables on which the groups differ.

In the school schedule study, the researchers compared the traditional schedule schools and the block schedule schools on various characteristics. They found that a higher percentage of the traditional schedule schools had small enrollments and more students from poor families. Teachers in both types of schools had a similar amount of teaching experience and professional preparation. However, a significantly greater percentage of teachers in the block schedule schools had earned a degree with a major in mathematics (75 percent vs. 51 percent of the traditional schedule teachers).

One way to make the comparison groups more similar, so as to rule out the possible influence of extraneous independent variables, is to link each research participant in one comparison group with a research participant in the other comparison group who has similar characteristics. This linking procedure, in which one research participant is paired with another because they share a common characteristic, is called a **matching procedure.** It is used occasionally in research, but it has several potential drawbacks. It might result in elimination of some research participants, and it does not ensure that the resulting comparison groups are similar in characteristics that were not matched by the researchers.

Another way to make the comparison groups more similar is to use statistical techniques such as analysis of covariance (see Chapter 9) or multiple regression (see Chapter 12). These techniques are imperfect, but they enable the researchers to estimate whether a specific independent variable has an effect on the dependent variable apart from the effect of other independent variables that were measured.

In the case of the school schedule study, it might have been possible for the researchers to use analysis of covariance to determine the effect of such independent variables as school size and teachers' mathematics training on teachers' instruction (the dependent variable) and also to factor out these effects in determining the effect of school scheduling on teachers' instruction. Stated differently, analysis of covariance provides an estimate of how much school scheduling variations would affect teachers' instruction if the schools and teachers in the two comparison groups were truly similar with respect to school size and teachers' preparation in mathematics.

Measures

The variables studied in a group comparison study can be measured by any of the approaches described in Chapter 6: tests, scales, questionnaires, interviews, and direct observation.

In the block scheduling study, the researchers did not administer their own measures but instead relied on measures and data available from a large multistate study funded by the National Science Foundation. In that study, school principals completed a questionnaire about school characteristics, and teachers completed a questionnaire in which they reported on their classroom activities and use of time during mathematics instruction. The 17 classroom activities are shown in Table 11.2, and the use-of-time variables are shown in Table 11.3.

Results

The usual first step in data analysis for a group comparison study is to compute descriptive statistics, most likely, the mean and standard deviation. These statistics for the block scheduling study are shown in Tables 11.2 and 11.3.

Much can be learned by carefully inspecting the descriptive statistics. Our review of the two tables leads us to conclude that mathematics teachers in block schedule schools provide very similar instruction to that used by mathematics teachers in traditional schedule schools. Differences between means are found for some of the scales, and most indicate that block schedule teachers use standards-based instructional practices slightly more than traditional schedule teachers.

The next step is to determine whether any of the observed differences between means for the two groups are statistically significant. **Tests of statistical significance** were explained in Chapter 9. Commonly used tests of statistical significance in group comparison research are shown in Table 11.4.

The *t* Test in Group Comparison Research.   The researchers in the school schedule study compared two groups, so they used a *t* **test** to determine whether each pair of means differed significantly from each other (see Tables 11.2 and 11.3). We explained the *t* test in Chapter 9. Only two of the comparisons were statistically significant: (1) use of calculators or computers and (2) writing of reflections.

As the number of comparisons increases, so does the likelihood of finding a statistically significant difference by chance. In other words, if this research study were repeated,

TABLE *11.2*   Student Classroom Activities in Traditional and Block Schedule Schools

Student Activity	Schedule	N	Mean	SD	p
Use calculators or computers to solve mathematical problems	Block	69	4.07	0.90	.04*
	Traditional	79	3.70	1.30	
Work on solving real-world problems	Block	70	3.94	1.10	.91
	Traditional	79	3.82	0.97	
Participate in discussions to deepen mathematics understanding	Block	69	3.59	1.02	.07
	Traditional	79	3.24	1.35	
Share ideas or solve problems with each other in small groups	Block	69	3.45	1.08	.49
	Traditional	79	3.32	1.24	
Document and evaluate their own mathematics work	Block	69	3.19	1.36	.34
	Traditional	79	2.96	1.52	
Read from a mathematics textbook in class	Block	70	3.11	1.52	.61
	Traditional	79	3.24	1.48	
Describe what they know about a topic before it is taught	Block	70	2.84	1.19	.32
	Traditional	79	2.65	1.23	
Participate in student-led discussions	Block	69	2.81	1.48	.22
	Traditional	77	2.51	1.48	
Engage in hands-on mathematics activities	Block	70	2.69	0.93	.54
	Traditional	79	2.58	1.12	
Record, represent, and/or analyze data	Block	70	2.64	0.96	.93
	Traditional	79	2.68	1.15	
Complete worksheets that emphasize mastery of essential skills	Block	70	2.50	1.03	.48
	Traditional	79	2.62	0.93	
Write reflections in a notebook or journal	Block	70	2.19	1.38	.00*
	Traditional	79	1.59	1.10	
Model or work on simulations	Block	70	2.07	1.07	.96
	Traditional	79	2.08	1.20	
Read other (nontextbook) mathematics-related materials in class	Block	69	1.91	1.09	.96
	Traditional	79	1.92	1.30	
Make formal presentations in class	Block	69	1.48	0.82	.96
	Traditional	79	1.48	0.89	
Use community resources in the classroom (museums, business people)	Block	69	1.35	0.64	.76
	Traditional	79	1.32	0.63	
Prepare written mathematics reports of at least three pages in length	Block	70	1.07	0.26	.82
	Traditional	79	1.08	0.31	

Note: Means based on 5-point scale: 1 = rarely or never, 2 = once a month, 3 = once a week, 4 = 2–3 times a week, and 5 = daily.

Source: Table 2 on p. 19 of Flynn, L., Lawrenz, F., & Schultz, M. J. (2005). Block scheduling and mathematics: Enhancing standards-based instruction? *NASSP Bulletin, 89*(642), 14–23.

it is possible that a comparison of two means that was statistically significant in the first study might not be statistically significant in the replication study. However, the fact that there is a consistent trend across all comparisons for block schedule teachers to make more use of standards-based instructional practices than the traditional schedule teachers

TABLE **11.3**   Use of Time in Classroom

Activity	Schedule	N	Mean	SD	p
Teacher instructs the class as a whole	Block	70	3.96	0.98	.91
	Traditional	81	3.96	1.02	
Students work individually	Block	68	3.22	0.86	.12
	Traditional	81	3.47	1.05	
Students work in small groups	Block	69	3.14	0.88	.16
	Traditional	78	2.91	1.08	

Note: Means are the percentage of class time based on a 6-point scale: 1 = 0%, 2 = 1–10%, 3 = 11–30%, 4 = 31–50%, 5 = 51–70%, and 6 = 71–100%.

Source: Table 3 on p. 20 of Flynn, L., Lawrenz, F., & Schultz, M. J. (2005). Block scheduling and mathematics: Enhancing standards-based instruction? *NASSP Bulletin, 89*(642), 14–23.

TABLE **11.4**   Statistical Techniques Used to Analyze Group Comparison/Comparative and Experimental Research Data

Test of Statistical Significance	Purpose
Parametric	
t test	Used primarily to determine whether two means differ significantly from each other; also used to determine whether a single mean differs significantly from a specified population value.
Analysis of variance	Used to determine whether mean scores on one or more variables differ significantly from each other and whether the variables interact significantly with each other.
Analysis of covariance	Similar to analysis of variance but permits adjustments to the posttreatment mean scores of different groups on the dependent variable to compensate for initial group differences on variables related to the dependent variable.
Nonparametric	
Mann-Whitney U test	Used to determine whether two uncorrelated means differ significantly from each other.
Wilcoxon signed-rank test	Used to determine whether two correlated means differ significantly from each other.
Kruskal-Wallis test	Used to determine whether the mean scores of three or more groups on a variable differ significantly from one another.
Chi-square test	Used to determine whether two frequency distributions or sets of categorical data differ significantly from each other.

suggests that the populations represented by these two groups actually differ, albeit slightly, in this respect.

The *t* test also can be used to determine whether the variability of scores for two groups is statistically significant. The typical statistic used to describe variability is the standard deviation (SD). If we examine the student activity "Use calculators or computers to solve mathematical problems" in Table 11.2, we see that the SD for the block schedule teachers is 0.90, whereas the SD for the traditional schedule teachers is 1.30.

The SDs are different, but how likely are they to have occurred by chance if, in fact, the block schedule teachers and traditional schedule teachers are two samples drawn from two identical populations? The *t* test for variances can answer this question.

Effect Sizes in Group Comparison Research.   The *t* test is used to determine whether the difference between the means or variances of two groups is statistically significant. However, the *t* test does not provide information relating to two important questions. How large is the difference? Does the difference have practical significance?

Effect sizes were explained in Chapter 8. They were not reported in the school schedule study, but you can calculate them on your own if the research report includes the means and standard deviations of the two groups.

To illustrate, consider the first variable in Table 11.2, "Use calculators or computers to solve mathematical problems." The first step in calculating an effect size is to subtract one group mean from the other. We are interested in knowing how much better block scheduling is than traditional scheduling, so we will subtract the traditional schedule mean (3.70) from the block schedule mean (4.07). The difference is 0.37, which is the numerator in the effect size equation.

The second step is to determine standard deviation, which is the denominator in the effect size equation. The calculation can be done in several different ways. Our choice is to use the standard deviation of the scores of the traditional schedule teachers on this variation (1.30).

Dividing 0.37 by 1.30 yields an effect size of 0.28. This means that the average teacher in the block schedule schools uses calculators or computers during math class at a level that would place him or her at the 61st percentile among teachers in traditional schedule schools. Experts in professional development probably would consider a move from the 50th to the 61st percentile a worthwhile incremental gain in teaching skill.

Analysis of Variance in Group Comparison Research.   **Analysis of variance** is commonly used in group comparison research, so we will explain its features here by using the school schedule study. (Analysis of variance was also discussed in Chapter 9.) Suppose we hypothesize that teachers who have substantial expertise in mathematics will be able to take advantage of block scheduling to use standards-based instructional activities, whereas teachers who lack this expertise will not be able to take advantage of block scheduling in this way. Furthermore, we hypothesize that traditional scheduling hinders both expert and nonexpert teachers, so neither group has the opportunity to make much use of standards-based activities.

Table 11.5 shows hypothetical data for the activity "Writes reflections in a notebook or journal" to illustrate the type of data analyses that would be done to test these hypotheses. Looking at the row means in Table 11.5, we see that expert teachers make greater use of reflection writing (*M* = 2.6) than nonexpert teachers (*M* = 1.8), ignoring the type of school in which they teach. Analysis of variance can determine whether the difference between these means is statistically significant.

Looking at the column means, we see that there is more reflection writing in block schedule schools (*M* = 2.7) than in traditional schedule schools (*M* = 2.0), ignoring variations in teacher expertise. Analysis of variance can determine whether the difference between these means is statistically significant.

Finally, we see an **interaction effect,** meaning that there is a relationship between two variables, but only under a certain condition. In the hypothetical study we are discuss-

TABLE *11.5* Hypothetical Data for the Activity "Writes Reflections in a Notebook or Journal"

Teacher Expertise	Block Schedule School	Traditional Schedule School	Row Means
Expert teachers	3.4	1.8	2.6
Nonexpert teachers	1.8	1.8	1.8
Column means	2.7	2.0	

ing, there is more reflection writing in block schedule schools, but only if the teacher has expertise in mathematics. Furthermore, we do not find that expert teachers assign more reflection writing irrespective of setting; it depends on whether they are teaching in a block or traditional schedule school. Analysis of variance can test whether this interaction effect is statistically significant.

Note that the preceding discussion does not refer to three separate analyses of variance. Rather, one analysis of variance does all three tests of statistical significance and can provide support, or refutation, for the two hypotheses stated above.

The addition of teacher expertise or other factors as an independent variable complicates the school schedule study and requires a more complex test of statistical significance (analysis of variance) than the *t* test. However, it might be a better representation of the complexities of education and yield more insights into the causal relationships that operate within it.

As a research strategy, it is sometimes desirable to study intensively the effects of one independent variable, as was done in the study by Flynn and colleagues. If interesting findings are obtained, subsequent studies can look for more complex causal relationships, as in our hypothetical study involving block scheduling and teacher expertise.

Nonparametric Tests of Statistical Significance.   As we explained in Chapter 9, the *t* test and analysis of variance are parametric tests of statistical significance. A **parametric test of statistical significance** makes several assumptions about the scores of the population represented by the sample used in a research study. One key assumption is that the scores of the population on the measure used in a research study are normally distributed. Another key assumption is that the variances of the scores in the populations being compared are equal.

Researchers typically use a parametric test if these assumptions are not grossly violated. Otherwise, they use a nonparametric counterpart of a parametric test of statistical significance. **Nonparametric tests of statistical significance** do not require satisfaction of the assumptions of a parametric test. The more common nonparametric tests are listed and briefly described in Table 11.4.

Discussion: Implications for Practice

The discussion section of a group comparison research report typically includes a summary of the main findings and analysis of possible flaws in the design and execution of the study. It is particularly important for the researcher or reader to note the inherent limitations of this type of research in demonstrating cause-and-effect relationships. In the school schedule study, for example, the researchers did not manipulate the independent variable by assigning some schools to retain the traditional schedule and others to institute a block schedule. Therefore, we cannot be certain that the finding of a slightly greater use of standards-based class activities was caused by block scheduling or some other factor. We need to be particularly cautious, because the two types of schools differed in other respects besides scheduling. Most notably, the block schedule schools had a higher percentage of teachers who had earned a degree with a major in mathematics.

The discussion section usually contains researcher comments about the implications of the findings for practice. For example, the report of the school-schedule study contains the following statement:

> Simply changing the structure of the school schedule cannot act as the sole catalyst for instructional change. Teachers in block-schedule settings may need to be provided with ongoing professional development to optimize the benefits of the extended period schedule. (Flynn et al., 2005, p. 21)

This recommendation seems reasonable. It also illustrates the point that one research study is rarely definitive. Additional research is needed to ensure that block scheduling, rather than some other factor associated with block scheduling, improves teachers' instruction. Then, a research and development process (see Chapter 20) can be employed to create a professional development program to optimize block scheduling and demonstrate its effectiveness.

Evaluating a Group Comparison Research Study

The criteria stated in Appendix 2 are relevant to evaluating a group comparison research study. The following additional criteria, stated in question-and-answer format, can be used to judge whether a study was weakened by specific problems that can arise in group comparison research.

- Did the researchers specify a cause-and-effect model that links their variables?

  A group comparison design is used to explore possible causal relationships. Therefore, check whether the researchers clearly specified which variables are the presumed causes and which variables are the presumed effects. Also, examine whether the researchers provided a rationale to justify their cause-and-effect model.

- Are the comparison groups similar in all respects except for the variable on which they were selected to differ?

  It is difficult to select two comparison groups that differ only on the variable of interest. Look for evidence of similarity between the two groups on other variables that might have an influence on the cause-and-effect relationship. Also, look for the use of statistical procedures, such as analysis of covariance, to statistically equate the comparison groups on these variables.

- Did the researchers draw tentative, rather than definitive, conclusions about whether observed relationships between independent and dependents are causal in nature?

  Group comparison studies can explore causal relationships, but they cannot demonstrate definitively that variable *A* was influenced by variable *B* or that variable *A* has an effect on variable *B*. Check that the researchers did not use their findings to make a causal claim, for example, a claim that if educators manipulate variable *A* (e.g., implement a procedure such as block scheduling), changes in variable *B* (e.g., improved student learning) will occur.

An example of

HOW GROUP COMPARISON RESEARCH CAN HELP IN SOLVING PROBLEMS OF PRACTICE

Many people believe that physical education is an important part of the school curriculum, because it helps maintain students' fitness. The following news item describes the status of physical fitness in one state.

> In California public schools, kids have been tested for physical fitness for many years. If they could do the push-ups and run a quick mile—great. If not—no big deal.
>
> This spring, that is changing for many of the half-million ninth-graders across the state. For the first time, high school freshmen in many districts must pass five of six fitness exams or face the possibility of extra years in physical education classes.
>
> In [two] districts, about 67 percent of ninth-graders last year met the five-out-of-six passing rate. District representatives expect that number to rise this spring because the tests have been such a big focus this year.
>
> Kollars, D. (2008, April 24). Students' future shapes up: New rules require ninth-graders to pass fitness tests or retake PE. *Sacramento Bee*, p. A1
>
> You might wonder, as we do, why two-thirds of ninth-graders can achieve the passing rate but not the other one-third. If we discover factors that explain the difference between the two groups (those who pass and those who do not pass), this knowledge might pave the way to create programs that help students with low physical fitness well before they are tested in the ninth grade. Group comparison research is well suited for obtaining this type of knowledge, as we explain below.

Researchers can review the research literature and talk to educators to identify possible factors that contribute to good or poor physical fitness. They would define two groups of students: those who meet the five-out-of-six passing standard and those who do not. They could then collect data from the two groups on these factors and then conduct statistical analyses to determine whether the groups differed in these factors and by how much.

A group comparison research design also would be well suited for a prediction study. Researchers would select two groups of ninth-grade students: those who achieve the fitness standard and those who do not. The researchers would make predictions about how these two groups would differ in physical fitness and other outcome variables (e.g., academic achievement) as they matured into adulthood. They could test the predictions by collecting longitudinal data on these outcome variables and analyzing the data to determine whether the two groups differed on them, as predicted.

This example illustrates the versatility of group comparison research for studying causal relationships. In the first study that we described, the purpose is to discover factors (the causes) that influenced students' physical fitness in ninth grade (the effect). In the second study, the purpose is to discover outcomes in later years (the effects) that appear to result from having good or poor physical fitness in ninth grade (the cause).

Both types of research have the potential to contribute to knowledge about students' physical fitness. This knowledge can help educators make a strong case for funding physical fitness programs.

Self-Check Test

1. Prediction research
    a. does not involve the study of causal relationships.
    b. involves the study of causal relationships.
    c. involves the manipulation of independent variables.
    d. involves only the study of dependent variables.
2. A variable is characterized as "independent" if it
    a. is not measured at the time of data collection.
    b. has been measured by individuals not associated with the research study.
    c. is hypothesized to be the effect of particular causes.
    d. is hypothesized to be the cause of particular effects.
3. In a research study that investigates the effects of school budget and instructional use of technology in classrooms,
    a. school budget is the independent variable.
    b. school budget is the dependent variable.
    c. technology use is the independent variable.
    d. it is not possible to identify whether school budget and technology use are independent or dependent variables.
4. In order to infer that two variables are causally related to each other, it is necessary to establish that
    a. both variables represent characteristics of the sample at the same point in time.
    b. the independent variable has an empirical association with more than one dependent variable.
    c. the independent variable occurred prior in time to the dependent variable.
    d. the dependent variable occurred prior in time to the independent variable.
5. A group comparison research design
    a. cannot be used to explore the effects of multiple hypothesized causes.
    b. can be used to explore the effects of multiple hypothesized causes.
    c. assumes that a single cause has a single effect.
    d. assumes that any phenomenon has a single cause.
6. Researchers typically decide to use a group comparison research design when
    a. there are more than three independent variables.
    b. their primary purpose is to describe research participants' scores on variables measured at the same point in time.
    c. their primary purpose is to compare research participants' scores on a measure administered at two different points in time.
    d. they wish to study independent variables that are difficult or impossible to manipulate.

7. The ideal situation in group comparison research is to
    a. select comparison groups that differ on the independent variable but are identical in all other respects.
    b. use a matching procedure to pair each participant in one comparison group with a participant in another comparison group.
    c. use analysis of covariance to equate comparison groups on extraneous variables on which they differ.
    d. select comparison groups that differ on the dependent variable being studied but that are identical on other dependent variables.
8. When used to analyze data in a group comparison study, the *t* test and analysis of variance differ from each other in that only
    a. the *t* test can be used to compare differences between group means.
    b. the *t* test can be used to determine whether the comparison groups differ on more than one dependent variable.
    c. analysis of variance can be used to search for interaction effects.
    d. analysis of variance is considered a parametric test of statistical significance.
9. The practical significance of a statistical result in a group comparison study is best determined by
    a. the effect size statistic.
    b. the *t* test.
    c. analysis of variance.
    d. nonparametric tests of statistical significance.
10. The findings of a group comparison research study
    a. have only theoretical significance.
    b. are of no value unless they are supported by another study that exactly replicates it.
    c. are of tentative value for solving problems of practice.
    d. are educators' best basis for solving problems of practice.

Chapter References

Flynn, L., Lawrenz, F., & Schultz, M. J. (2005). Block scheduling and mathematics: Enhancing standards-based instruction? *NASSP Bulletin, 89*(642), 14–23.

Johnson, B. (2001). Toward a new classification of nonexperimental quantitative research. *Educational Researcher, 30*(2), 3–13.

Resources for Further Study

Gall, M. D., Gall, J. P., & Borg, W. R. (2007). *Educational research: An introduction* (8th ed.). Boston: Allyn & Bacon.

In Chapter 10 of this book, the authors provide an advanced treatment of factors that should be considered in designing a group comparison research study. (In the book the authors describe such research as causal-comparative research.)

Johnson, B. (2001). Toward a new classification of nonexperimental quantitative research. *Educational Researcher, 30*(2), 3–13.

The author explains the essential similarities between group comparison research designs (explained in this chapter), correlational research designs (explained in Chapter 12), and descriptive research designs (explained in Chapter 10). The author also discusses the difficulties that researchers face in demonstrating that two variables are causally related.

Sample Group Comparison Research Study

Academic Performance Gap between Summer-Birthday and Fall-Birthday Children in Grades K–8

Oshima, T. C., & Domaleski, C. S. (2006). Academic performance gap between summer-birthday and fall-birthday children in grades K–8. *Journal of Educational Research, 99*(4), 212–217.

The following journal article addresses a question that faces many parents and kindergarten teachers: Should children who are eligible to enter kindergarten but are substantially younger than the other eligible children be enrolled in kindergarten or should they wait another year? The authors used a group comparison research design to address this question.

The authors designate children who enter kindergarten at a younger age as "summer-birthday children" and children who enter kindergarten at an older age as "fall-birthday children." At the end of the article, the authors clarify the age difference by noting that the summer-birthday children were 7 to 11 months younger than the fall-birthday children.

We recommend that you focus on Table 1 (p. 258) in your initial reading of the article. This table compares the two groups of children by presenting means and standard deviations.

The authors present another statistical analysis, called multiple regression, that we explain in Chapter 12. In simple terms, multiple regression enables researchers to determine how well several factors (factors can be thought of as causes or independent variables) predict a particular outcome, such as reading or math achievement. Table 2 (p. 260) in the article shows that children's ethnicity predicts their academic achievement substantially better than their age or gender. However, age does predict academic achievement to a small degree, at least through the fifth grade.

The article is reprinted in its entirety, just as it appeared when originally published.

Academic Performance Gap between Summer-Birthday and Fall-Birthday Children in Grades K–8

T. C. Oshima
Christopher S. Domaleski
Georgia State University

ABSTRACT ■ Much interest exists among parents and researchers regarding the benefits and drawbacks of delaying kindergarten entrance to acquire academic advantage ("redshirting"). How evident is this assumed advantage at the kindergarten level and beyond? The authors evaluated large-scale test data from Grades K–8 to investigate the difference in performance between younger children (summer birthday) and older children (fall birthday). The performance gap evident in kindergarten decreased rapidly in Grades 1–3 but persisted up to Grade 5, until leveling off at middle school. The performance gap in the early grades that resulted from birth date was much larger than was the gap caused by gender difference.

KEY WORDS ■ academic performance gap, fall- and summer-birthday students, Grades K–8

Headlines in the Atlanta Journal-Constitution ("Kindergarten," 2003) read, "Kindergarten: Is older wiser?" "Some say 'redshirting' improves readiness." The article featured success stories for children with summer birthdays who delayed entrance to kindergarten. Parents of preschoolers, after reading newspaper articles or talking with other parents, or both, are keenly aware that some parents purposefully delay their child's entrance to kindergarten. A number of parents begin the process even earlier by having their child repeat a 3-year-old preschool program. That phenomenon, especially common in affluent communities and among boys, causes parents with a 5-year-old summer-birthday child to wonder whether they should delay enrollment even when their child seems ready for kindergarten.

According to the newspaper article mentioned in the preceding paragraph, "The National Center of Education Statistics repeats that 6% to 9% of kindergarten-aged children in the United States start a year late." However, those figures may be even higher. *Gifted Child Today* ("Delaying Entrance Into Kindergarten," 2004) reported that "According to the Census Bureau, 22% of first graders were 7 or older in Oct. 2002, up from 13% in 1970." "Redshirting" is more common among White parents than it is among parents from other races (Diamond, Reagan, & Bandyk, 2000).

Abundant early childhood research concerns kindergarten readiness (e.g., Andrews & Slate, 2002; Kurdek & Sinclair, 2001), as well as contradicting reports on the benefits of redshirting. Although most researchers seem to agree with the short-term academic and behavioral benefits of redshirting, there is a wide range of conflicting reports on its long-term benefits. Rusch (1998), for example, argued that being an older student in a class can backfire, especially in the upper grades. Conversely, Deutsch (2003) suggested that the youngest children in a classroom suffer more psychiatric disorders than do other students. The benefit (or harm) of redshirting is just a small part of the

problem for an individual. At the classroom level, red shirting widens the age range for students and makes teaching practices more difficult. The presence of substantially older children (i.e., more than a year older) can affect other children academically and socially. Therefore, the increasingly popular trend of delaying kindergarten entry must be evaluated carefully.

To investigate redshirting, researchers should first determine whether there is an academic performance difference between children with summer birthdays and children with fall birthdays. We expected a large difference at the kindergarten level because educators and parents agree that 1 year can make a substantial difference in learning at a young age. Several studies confirm the effect of age on academic achievement at the kindergarten level (e.g., Kurdek & Sinclair, 2001; Meisela, 1992). It is not clear, however, when or if the difference in academic performance diminishes as students grow older. *Gifted Child Today* ("Delaying Entrance Into Kindergarten," 2004) reported that the academic advantages of redshirting diminish by the third grade, whereas Crosser (1991) stated that the difference is still distinct for fifth or sixth graders, especially for boys. Kurdek and Sinclair (2001) found no effects of age for either reading or mathematics achievement at fourth grade.

Our purposes in this study were as follows:

1. To first delineate the difference at the kindergarten level; and
2. To subsequently investigate the difference through the elementary and middle school grades by using a statewide criterion reference test.

METHOD DATA

Data

We used data for kindergarten students from a large dataset, "The Early Childhood Longitudinal Study of the

Journal of Educational Research 99(4), 212–217, 2007. Reprinted with permission of the Helen Dwight Reid Educational Foundation. Published by Heldref Publications, 1319 Eighteenth St., NW, Washington DC 20036-1802. Copyright © 2007.

Kindergarten Class of 1998–1999" (National Center for Education Statistics, 2001). From 21,260 kindergarten students, we identified 3,862 students as "younger children with summer birthdays (June, July, and August)" and 2,693 students as "older children with fall birthdays (September, October, and November)." To qualify for the younger summer-birthday group, the child had to be a first-time kindergarten student who was born in June, July, or August and be less than 67 months of age at the time of fall testing. To be in the older fall-birthday group, the child had to be a first time kindergarten student who was born in September, October, or November and be 67 months of age or older at the time of fall testing. Test data came from two test administration periods (fall and spring). We collected data for elementary and middle grades from a statewide criterion-referenced test administered to approximately 115,000 students per grade in spring 2002. In this southeastern state, children had to have been 5 years old as of September 1 to enter kindergarten. Therefore, children born in the summer were the youngest children in the kindergarten class unless they were held back for a year. For each grade, about 10,000 children qualified as "younger children with summer birthdays"; another 10,000 qualified as "older children with fall birthdays." From each pool of approximately 10,000 students, we randomly selected 3,000 students for the present study. The state reported test scores in Grades 1–8 in scaled scores; a score of 300–349 indicated "meeting expectations," and a score of 350 and over indicated "exceeding expectations."

Analysis

We examined students' reading and mathematics performance in this cross-sectional study. For kindergarten students, we added affective variables (approaches to learning, self-control, and social interaction), as well as physical variables (height and weight). The study also includes demographic variables—race and gender. Race included eight levels for kindergarten students: (a) White, (b) African American, (c) Hispanic—Race Specified, (d) Hispanic—Race Not Specified, (e) Asian, (f) Native Hawaiian, (g) Other—Pacific Islander, (h) American Indian or Alaska Native, and (i) Multiracial, and six levels for Grade 1–8 students: (a) Asian, (b) African American, (c) Hispanic, (d) Native American/Alaskan, (e) White, and (f) Multiracial.

In the first part of the analysis, we investigated the mean difference between the two groups of interest for the age variable (summer- vs. fall-birthday children). To make the comparison meaningful across all kinds of measures and tests, we used effect size *(ES)* as an indicator for the difference throughout this study, as well as the independent *t* test. We calculated *ES* as the mean difference of two groups over pooled standard deviation. We plotted *ES* across grades to observe the general trend over time. We repeated the analysis within each gender group.

In the second part of the analysis, we used multiple regression to compare the relationships between three independent variables (race, gender, and age) and the dependent variables (reading or mathematics) to iden-

tify how age affected the test scores in relation to other demographic variables. Race, gender, and age were categorical variables that we transformed into *k* dummy variables where *k* was the number of categories, minus 1. For race variables for kindergarten students, we created seven dummy variables. For Grades 1–8, we transformed the race variable into five dummy variables (see Pedhazur, 1997 for procedures regarding dummy coding).

RESULTS

Figure 1 shows *ES* for the difference between two groups (older fall-birthday children and younger summer-birthday children) for kindergarten students. Positive *ES* indicates that the mean for the older children was higher than that of the younger children. Stevens (1999) posited that *ES* = .20 is small, *ES* = .50 is medium, and *ES* > .80 is large. Furthermore, Stevens explained that medium *ES* is apparent to a researcher. Stevens provided the IQ difference between semiskilled workers and professionals or managers as an example of medium *ES* (.50). On the basis of Stevens's criteria, the differences of those two groups are considered to be average for academic variables, as well as for physical variables.

Our data show that older kindergarten students are 1.95 in taller than are their younger peers in the fall (*ES* = .50). In other words, older kindergarten students average one half of a standard deviation taller than younger kindergarten students. That physical difference is probably apparent to parents and educators. For academic variables, *ES* also is about .50 (.38 for reading, .55 for mathematics, and .50 for general knowledge). In other words, differences existed between the two groups in academic areas as much as in the physical areas. The differences observed for affective variables (approaches to learning, self-control, and social interaction) were small (see Figure 1). Also shown in Figure 1 is the slight decrease in *ES* from fall to spring, except *ES*

FIGURE 1   Effect Sizes for Younger versus Older Kindergarten Students by Academic, Affective, and Physical Variables

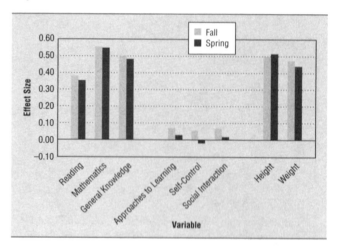

for height, possibly indicating a slight narrowing of the gap during the kindergarten year.

Table 1 reports the means and standard deviations for reading and mathematics scores for the two groups across kindergarten through Grade 8. For kindergarten, the scores are expressed in a T score. The T score is a standardized score with a mean of 50 and a standard deviation of 10. Table 1 also lists p values for the test of equal means

TABLE 1   Means and Standard Deviations for Reading and Mathematics Scores

Grade	Reading			Mathematics		
	Younger	Older	p	Younger	Older	p
Kindergarten[a]						
Fall						
M	44.82	50.75	<.001	47.09	53.48	< .001
SD	16.37	14.61	<.001	11.77	11.52	.901
Spring						
M	46.77	51.62	<.001	48.13	53.85	< .001
SD	14.57	13.05	<.001	10.67	10.32	.430
1[b]						
M	338.31	349.67	<.001	327.85	339.46	< .001
SD	36.30	38.37	.072	29.68	31.98	< .001
2						
M	339.80	348.38	<.001	328.89	335.51	<.001
SD	41.28	43.24	.141	28.87	31.84	< 001
3						
M	338.26	343.61	<.001	328.81	332.47	< 001
SD	34.93	35.75	.293	29.04	29.56	.241
4						
M	343.09	348.37	<.001	317.45	320.64	< .001
SD	43.91	46.84	.002	30.60	31.97	.041
5						
M	334.24	338.06	<.001	324.50	327.94	< .001
SD	33.07	33.62	.239	28.82	29.52	.210
6						
M	343.24	344.68	.205	324.02	324.83	.361
SD	42.78	45.01	.013	33.74	35.01	.018
7						
M	339.96	341.26	.145	321.38	322.61	.072
SD	33.63	35.17	.034	25.73	27.36	.001
8						
M	350.20	351.36	.339	320.49	320.22	.759
SD	46.57	47.51	.402	32.75	33.76	.132

Note. Younger = children with summer (June, July, August) birthdays; Older = children with fall (September, October, November) birthdays.

[a]For kindergarten, n (younger students) = 3,862 and n (older students) = 2,693 in the fall; n (younger students) = 3,718 and n (older students) = 2,586 in the spring. [b]For Grades 1–8, n (younger students) = 3,000 and n (older students) = 3,000.

(independent *t* tests) and equal variances (Levine's test). Because of a large number of significance tests combined with large sample sizes, we used a conservative level of alpha (.001) as an indicator of significance. The differences of means were significant from kindergarten to Grade 5 for reading and mathematics. The differences were not significant for Grades 6–8. Also noteworthy was a consistent trend of standard deviations. For Grades 1–8, although seldom reaching significance, the younger group's variation was less than was that of the older group's variation. That trend reversed for kindergarten students.

To track mean differences over time, we plotted *ES* against Grades 1–8 (see Figure 2; *ES* likely declined rapidly during Grades 1–8). However, a small *ES* (.10) remained during Grades 3–5. *ES* reached near zero for Grades 6–8. Figure 2 also illustrates graphs for girls and boys. For girls, a fairly large *ES* exhibited for mathematics in Grade 1 quickly declined by Grade 2. For boys in Grades 2–8, reading tended to exhibit larger *ES* values than did mathematics, indicating that being a younger aged student may have more effect on reading than on mathematics.

Table 2 shows the results from regression analyses. The R^2 values are reported under race, gender, and age. For example, the R^2 value of .182 under race for kindergarten (fall) for reading indicates that 18.2% of variation in reading can be explained by determining race alone. It is similar that 0.03% and 3.3%, respectively, of variation in reading can be explained by gender and age alone. The R^2_{change} refers to the difference in R^2 between the full model (race, gender, and age as independent variables) and the reduced model (race and gender as independent variables), indicating the unique contribution of age in addition to race and gender. In other words, a significant R^2_{change} indicates that adding age in the model would significantly improve the prediction of the test score when the model already contains race and gender.

One can make several observations from Table 2: First, age (whether a child was younger or older in the class) was a significant predictor for reading and mathematics through Grade 5. Significant R^2_{change} for Grades K–5 also indicated that age improved the prediction after controlling for race and gender. Second, at any given grade, race always had the highest R^2 with the test scores. The effect of race was fairly stable across Grades K–8. Third, gender was a significant predictor for reading but not for mathematics. Fourth, the order of strength for reading in terms of relationship with test scores was race, age, then gender through second grade. For Grades 3–5, the order was race, gender, then age; for Grades 6–8, race then gender. In other words, age was a better predictor of reading than was gender through Grade 2; gender became a better predictor than age for Grades 3–5. Fifth, the order of strength for mathematics was race, then age through Grade 5; race was the only significant predictor for Grades 6–8. For example, at the beginning of the kindergarten year, 10.6% of variation in mathematics scores could be explained by race, and 6.8% could be explained by age. Gender explained little (< 0.1%) variation.

DISCUSSION

For kindergarten students, the difference observed for academic areas (reading, mathematics, and general knowledge) was as large as was the difference for the height of children from the two groups. By spring, the academic difference narrowed somewhat. For elementary school children, *ES* of the difference of the two groups across five grades declined. There was a rapid decrease up to the third grade and a gradual or no decrease between the third and fifth grades; the difference still existed at fifth grade. Conversely, the difference was near zero in the middle school years. Although redshirting is more common for boys (Heart, May, & Kundert, 1996), the gap between the two groups was not always more pronounced for boys.

How large was the impact of age, whether the child was younger or older in the class, on test scores when compared with other demographic variables, such as race and

FIGURE 2 Effect Sizes for Younger versus Older Children over Time (Grades 1–8) for Combined Sample, Female Sample, and Male Sample

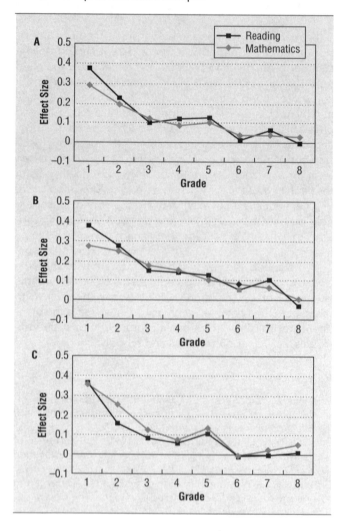

TABLE 2 R^2 Values for Race, Gender, and Age, With Reading or Mathematics as the Dependent Variable

Grade	Reading				Mathematics			
	Race	Gender	Age[a]	R^2	Race	Gender	Age[a]	R^2
Kindergarten								
Fall	.182*	.003*	.033*	.022*	.106*	<.001	.068*	.053*
Spring	.128*	.005*	.028*	.020*	.095*	<.001	.067*	.053*
1	.069*	.016*	.022*	.020*	.084*	<.001	.034*	.031*
2	.084*	.006*	.010*	.011*	.118*	.002	.012*	.011*
3	.104*	.014*	.006*	.006*	.131*	.001	.004*	.004*
4	.120*	.008*	.003*	.003*	.118*	<.001	.003*	.002*
5	.102*	.004*	.003*	.003*	.159*	.001	.003*	.002*
6	.128*	.007*	<.001	<.001	.112*	<.001	<.001	<.001
7	.140*	009*	<.001	<.001	.159*	<.001	<.001	<.001
8	.106*	.007*	<.001	<.001	.128*	<.001	<.001	<.001

[a]Refers to either younger or older students. [b]R^2_{change} refers to the differences in R^2 between the full model (race, gender, and age) and the reduced model (race and gender), indicating the unique contribution of age above and beyond race and gender.

*$p = .001$

gender? Whereas race explained 10–15% of variation in test scores in general, age explained up to about 7% of variation, depending on the grade level. That percentage was much larger than the percentage that we obtained from gender (1% for reading and <.01% for mathematics). In other words, age difference was as important, or more important, than was gender difference in the early grades.

A plethora of research exists on gender differences. For example, many researchers have shown that reading scores for boys are far behind those of girls (e.g., Gambell & Hunter, 1999; Phillips, Norris, Osmond, & Maynard, 2002; Sommers, 2000), a phenomenon that we confirmed. All through Grades K–8, girls outperformed boys. Researchers also suggest that boys outperform girls in mathematics, perhaps more so during adolescence (e.g., Hedges & Newell, 1995; Royer & Wing, 2002). In this study, however, we did not observe gender difference for mathematics. Researchers should acknowledge gender difference in academic performance, as well as identify any difference that may exist by birth date. We showed that differences of birth date can be a much larger factor regarding academic performance than gender differences in the early grades and that the differences continue throughout the elementary school years.

We provide data on the issues related to the controversial practice of academic redshirting. It was not our intention to argue for or against the practice. We did not examine the population that delayed kindergarten entrance. Redshirting is based partly on the assumption that older children have an advantage over younger children in a classroom. We delineated how much difference there actually is in a given grade.

Numerous issues need to be considered before a decision is made regarding whether a parent should hold a summer-birthday child back for a year: (a) Does the child tend to learn better with older peers? (b) Does the child enjoy interacting with older children? (c) Is she or he easily hurt by not being able to perform as well academically (and physically) as her or his peers? and (d) Is the child a boy, and does he have a reading problem? Although any decision concerning academic redshirting at the kindergarten level (or at a younger age) should be individually based, research in these areas (such as type of children who thrive in an environment in which they are the youngest) should help parents make an intelligent decision concerning redshirting, which is a decision that cannot be reversed once it is made.

We showed the magnitude and duration of the academic gap exhibited by age differences of 7 to 11 months (summer-birthday children vs. fall-birthday children). With those objective data, researchers can investigate the practice of redshirting, which has a profound impact on individuals, as well as on teachers and schools.

References

Andrews, S. P., & Slate, J. R. (2007). Public and private prekindergarten programs: A comparison of student readiness. *Educational Research Quarterly, 25,* 59–73.

Bent, D., May, D. C., & Kundert, D. K. (1991). The incidence of delayed school entry: A twelve-year review. *Early Education and Development, 7,* 121–135.

Crosser, S. L. (1991). Summer birth date children: Kindergarten entrance age and academic achievement. The *Journal of Educational Research, 84,* 140–146.

Delaying Entrance into Kindergarten. (2004, Summer). *Gifted Child Today, 27,* 6.

Deutsch, N. (2003). Youngest kids in class suffer more psychiatric disorders. *Medical Post, 39,* 47.

Diamond, K. E., Reagan, A. J., & Bendyk, J. E. (2000). Parents' conception of kindergarten readiness: Relationships with race, ethnicity, and development. *The Journal of Educational Research, 94,* 93–100.

Gambell, T. J., & Hunter, D. M. (1999). Rethinking gender differences in literacy. *Canadian Journal of Education, 24,* 1–16.

Hedges, L., & Nowell, A. (1995). Sex differences in mental test scores, variability and numbers of high-scoring individuals. *Science, 269,* 41–45.

Kindergarten: Is older wiser? (2003, September 20). *The Atlanta Journal-Constitution,* p. G1.

Kurdek, L. A., & Sinclair, R. J. (2001). Predicting reading and mathematics achievement in fourth-grade children from kindergarten readiness scores. *Journal of Educational Psychology, 93,* 451–455.

Meisels, S. (1992). Doing harm by doing good: Iatrogenic effects of early childhood enrollment and promotion policies. *Early Childhood Research Quarterly, 7,* 155–174.

National Center for Education Statistics. (2002). *ECLS-K base year public-use data files and electronic codebook.* Washington, DC: Author.

Pedhazur, E. J. (1997). *Multiple regression in behavioral research: Explanation and prediction* (3rd ed.). New York: Holt, Rinehart and Winston.

Phillips, L. M., Norris, S. P., Osmond, W. C., & Maynard, A. M. (2002). Relative reading achievement: A longitudinal study of 187 children from first through sixth grades. *Journal of Educational Psychology, 94,* 3–13.

Royer, J. M., & Wing, K. E. (2002). Making sense of sex differences in reading and math assessment: The practice and engagement hypothesis. *Issues in Education, 8,* 77–85.

Rusch, L. (1998). Delaying kindergarten. *Parents, 73,* 129.

Sommers, C. H. (2000). *The war against boys: How misguided feminism is hurting our young men.* New York: Simon & Schuster.

Stevens, J. (1999). *Intermediate statistics: A modern approach* (2nd ed.). Hillsdale, NJ: Erlbaum.

chapter 12

Correlational Research

IMPORTANT
Ideas

1. Correlational research designs and group comparison research designs have the same purpose but involve different types of statistical analysis.
2. Correlational research takes into account all the values of at least one of the variables that have been measured in a research study.
3. Correlation coefficients and scattergrams provide information about the direction and degree of relationship between a sample's scores on two or more measures.
4. The relationship between two variables can be positive, negative, nonlinear, or zero.
5. The larger the correlation coefficient, the more accurate researchers can be in using an individual's score on one measured variable to predict his score on another measured variable.
6. In the case of correlation coefficients, researchers typically test the null hypothesis that the correlation coefficient between two variables in the entire population represented by the sample is zero.
7. Multivariate correlational techniques show how three or more variables relate to each other, either for the purpose of explanation or prediction.
8. The introduction of a correlational research report should explain the importance of the study, the research questions to be answered or hypotheses to be tested, the variables of interest, and a review of relevant literature.
9. Correlational research differs from experimental research in that the researchers do not manipulate the independent variable.
10. In correlational research, the researchers should attempt to select a sample that is representative of the population to which they wish to generalize their results.
11. In the discussion section of a report of a correlational study, the researchers should (1) summarize the study's findings, (2) consider flaws in the design and execution of the study, and (3) state implications of the study for subsequent research and improvement of professional practice. ■

Key TERMS

artificial dichotomy	factor analysis	Pearson product-moment
bivariate correlational statistics	hierarchical linear modeling (HLM)	correlation coefficient (*r*)
canonical correlation	independent variable	positive correlation
continuous variable	linear correlation	prediction research
correlational research	line of best fit	predictor variable
correlation coefficient	logistic regression analysis	*r*
criterion variable	moderator variable	scattergram
dependent variable	multiple regression	scatter plot
dichotomous variable	multivariate correlational statistics	statistical significance
differential analysis	negative correlation	structural equation modeling
discriminant analysis	nesting	true dichotomy
effect size	path analysis	

Comparison of Correlational and Group Comparison Research Designs

We recommend that you read Chapter 11, which is about group comparison research designs, before reading this chapter. You will find that group comparison research designs and the research designs presented in this chapter have the same purpose—either to explain why things are a certain way or to predict how things will be in the future.

As in Chapter 11, we will refer here to the presumed cause in a causal relationship as the **independent variable.** We will refer to the presumed effect as the **dependent variable.**

In group comparison studies, groups are formed to represent the independent variable, dependent variable, or both. For example, consider the group comparison studies that we presented in the first part of Chapter 11. The first study investigated the relationship between support for new teachers and school income level. The research design was based on a comparison of two groups of teachers: those who worked in high-income schools and those who worked in low-income schools.

The second study investigated the relationship between students' evaluations of their professors and the effect of student gender and professor gender on those evaluations. The research design was based on a comparison of two groups of professors (male and female) and two groups of students (male and female).

The third study investigated the relationship between student mobility and performance in school. The research design was based on a comparison of four groups: students who made no change in their residence, students who made one move in their residence, students who made two moves, and students who made three or more moves.

If you think about it, you will realize that some of these group comparisons involve only a few of the possible range of values for the variable of interest. For example, consider the first study mentioned, involving a comparison of teachers in high-income schools and low-income schools. The researchers defined a low-income school as one in which more than 50 percent of students qualify for free or reduced-price lunch. They defined a high-income school as one in which less than 15 percent of students qualify for free or reduced-price lunch.

In reality, these two groups represent just two points on a scale that can range from 0 to 100 percent of students qualifying for free or reduced-price lunch. A **correlational research** design would involve forming a sample of schools and using their actual percentages of qualifying students as one of the variables rather than artificially shrinking the percentages into just two categories.

Note, too, that the researchers' definition of high-income and low-income schools eliminates many schools from the sample. Any school having between 15 and 50 percent of qualifying students would not satisfy the criteria, and so we would not learn how the income level of those schools (as measured by free or reduced-price lunch) affects new teachers' experiences in them.

As another example, consider the research study on student mobility. All students with three or more moves are lumped into one category. Thus, we are not able to determine whether students who make four moves have a different level of performance than students who make three moves or whether students who make five moves have a different level of performance than students who make four moves, and so on.

Correlational research would attempt to measure all the values of the variables mentioned and include them in the statistical analysis. In this chapter, we will use the term **continuous variable** to denote a variable all of whose values have been measured by the researchers.

Examples of Correlational Research

The following studies illustrate the relevance of correlational research to problems of practice. In each study, we identify which variables are independent and which are dependent.

Factors Associated with Smoking among Youth

> Chalela, P., Velez, L. F., & Ramirez, A. G. (2007). Social influences, and attitudes and beliefs associated with smoking among border Latino youth. *Journal of School Health, 77*(4), 187–195.

The researchers stated that smoking is a serious problem among adolescents, citing statistics that one-fourth of adolescents are smokers by the time they finish high school. The purpose of this study was to identify social factors (the independent variables) associated with smoking behavior (the dependent variable).

One of the researchers' main findings was that peer influence had the strongest correlation with students' incidence of smoking, which was measured as a continuous variable. Based on this finding, the researchers recommended the development of interventions that help adolescents learn to understand the addictive properties of nicotine and build up skills needed to resist social pressures to smoke.

The Relationship between School Culture and Student Achievement

> Gruenert, S. (2005). Correlations of collaborative school cultures with student achievement. *NASSP Bulletin, 89*(645), 43–55.

The researcher investigated whether a school culture that is collaborative (the independent variable) has an influence on students' academic achievement (the dependent variable). Academic achievement was treated as a continuous variable and measured by standardized tests of reading and language arts. Six aspects of school culture also were measured: (1) school leaders' facilitation of collaboration among the teachers, (2) teacher collaboration, (3) emphasis on teachers' professional development, (4) unity by teachers and the community around the school's mission statement, (5) collegial support among teachers, and (6) partnership among teachers, students, and parents in promoting student performance.

The researcher found that elementary, middle, and secondary schools that had higher levels of each of the six collaborative factors also had higher student scores on the achievement tests. This finding suggests that one key to improving student learning is to promote collaborative efforts among educators and stakeholders that support the school's mission.

Using Infants' Recognition Memory Scores to Predict Adult IQ and Academic Achievement

> Fagan, J. F., Holland, C. R., & Wheeler, K. (2006). The prediction, from infancy, of adult IQ and achievement. *Intelligence, 35,* 225–231.

This study involved basic research (see Chapter 1) on the nature of human intelligence. It tested a theory that conceptualizes intelligence as the ability to process information, investigating whether infants' recognition memory (the independent variable) predicted their IQ and academic achievement in early adulthood (the dependent variables). Scores on each of these measures were treated as continuous variables.

The researchers measured recognition memory by showing each infant a picture for 30 seconds, withdrawing that picture from view, and then showing the same picture now paired with a new picture for several seconds. The amount of time spent looking at the new picture was deemed a measure of recognition memory, based on the assumption that infants will look at the new picture longer if they have already assimilated the information contained in the previously seen picture.

The researchers found that infants' scores on this measure were a good predictor of their IQ scores and academic achievement 21 years later. They concluded, "The present findings support the view that intelligence is continuous over age and that one basis of such continuity lies in the ability to process information" (Fagan et al., 2006, p. 230).

In other professions, it has been found that basic research, in the long term, has the greatest likelihood of improving practice. For example, basic correlational research on intelligence, such as that described above, eventually might identify the fundamental cognitive processes that constitute intelligence. It then might be possible to develop educational programs that enhance these cognitive processes in students (particularly among students with deficits in these processes) and thereby improve their ability to learn.

Correlation between Two Variables

Correlational research is based on a particular type of statistical analysis that yields what are known as correlation coefficients. A **correlation coefficient** is a mathematical expression that provides information about the direction and magnitude of the relationship between a sample's scores on measures of two or more variables. Correlation coefficients can range in value from −1.00 to +1.00.

Statistics courses and textbooks emphasize the mathematic logic, equations, and calculations involved in correlation. Our goal here is different, seeking instead to help you develop an intuitive understanding of correlation by providing simple examples and without presenting formal mathematical equations. This explanation will allow you to understand the features of a correlational research study, a topic that we discuss later in the chapter, while bypassing the technical details.

The Advantages of Continuous Variables

The principal advantage of correlational research is that it provides more information about the sample's scores (or values) on the measured variable than is typically possible with group comparison research. For example, suppose we want to know whether there is a relationship between family poverty and school persistence. Our concern is whether individuals who are living in poverty are more likely to give up on school and remain unemployed or settle into low-wage jobs, thereby perpetuating the poverty cycle.

The National Center for Education Statistics has collected data that allow us to test part of the causal relationship that concerns us, namely the relationship between poverty and school completion. The data are shown in Table 12.1. The first column lists each state; the second column lists the percentage of individuals in each state who are below the

TABLE 12.1   State Comparison of Percentage of Poverty-Level Residents and Percentage of High School Completers

States and District of Columbia	Percentage below Poverty Level	Percentage High School Completion or More	States and District of Columbia	Percentage below Poverty Level	Percentage High School Completion or More
Alabama	16	75	Montana	15	87
Alaska	9	88	Nebraska	10	87
Arizona	14	81	Nevada	11	81
Arkansas	16	75	New Hampshire	7	87
California	14	77	New Jersey	9	82
Colorado	9	87	New Mexico	18	79
Connecticut	8	84	New York	15	79
Delaware	9	83	North Carolina	12	78
District of Columbia	20	78	North Dakota	12	84
Florida	13	80	Ohio	11	83
Georgia	13	79	Oklahoma	15	81
Hawaii	11	85	Oregon	12	85
Idaho	12	85	Pennsylvania	11	82
Illinois	11	81	Rhode Island	12	78
Indiana	10	82	South Carolina	14	76
Iowa	9	86	South Dakota	13	85
Kansas	10	86	Tennessee	14	76
Kentucky	16	74	Texas	15	76
Louisiana	20	75	Utah	9	88
Maine	11	85	Vermont	9	86
Maryland	9	84	Virginia	10	82
Massachusetts	9	85	Washington	11	87
Michigan	11	83	West Virginia	18	75
Minnesota	8	88	Wisconsin	9	85
Mississippi	20	73	Wyoming	11	88
Missouri	12	81	Mean	12.4	80.4

Source: http://nces.ed.gov/programs/digest/d05/tables/dt05_011.asp; http://nces.ed.gov/programs/digest/d06/tables/dt05_020.asp

government's defined poverty level, and the third column lists the percentage of individuals in that state who have completed high school.

The bottom of Table 12.1 shows that the mean poverty percentage for the 50 states plus the District of Columbia is 12.4. We decide to assign the states to two categories: (1) high poverty, if the percentage is 12 or higher, and (2) low poverty, if the percentage is 11 or lower. We find that that the average percentage of individuals who have graduated from high school in low-poverty states is 85 percent. In high-poverty states, the average is 79 percent.

This result supports our theory that poverty affects school persistence. However, it leaves some questions unanswered. For example, we might wonder whether poverty affects school persistence only if it reaches a certain level. Examining Table 12.1, we see that four states (Louisiana, Mississippi, New Mexico, and West Virginia) and the District of Columbia have very high poverty rates (18 percent or more). Perhaps poverty only exerts an influence on school persistence within a state when it is at this high a level. At lower levels, perhaps the effect of poverty is diminished or nonexistent.

Because we only looked at two levels of poverty (low and high) and ignored differences within levels, we cannot test these possibilities. Suppose, however, that we consider poverty as a continuous variable and use statistics that are appropriate for such variables. Then we can examine the effect of poverty on school persistence across all levels of poverty that exist in the 50 states and the District of Columbia. In the following section, you will see how a particular type of visual display, called a scattergram, facilitates this type of examination.

Using Scattergrams to Represent Correlation

A **scattergram** is a graph of the relationship between two variables, such that the scores of individuals on one variable are plotted on the x (horizontal) axis of the graph and the scores of the same individuals on another variable are plotted on the y (vertical) axis. A scattergram is sometimes called a **scatter plot.**

Note that in the previous paragraph we used the term *relationship* in defining a scattergram. Instead, we could substitute the word *co-relationship,* or more simply, *correlation.* Hereafter, we will use the word *correlation,* because that is the term used by statisticians and researchers.

Scattergrams are useful because they provide a simple, clear picture of the correlation between a group's scores on two variables. Figure 12.1 shows a scattergram of the relationship between two variables: (1) the percentage of individuals below the poverty level in each state and (2) the percentage of individuals who earned a high school diploma or higher degree in each state.

You can see that the data in Figure 12.1 for each state and the District of Columbia are represented in the scattergram by a single point. For example, the leftmost point in Figure 12.1 is New Hampshire. This state has the lowest poverty level (7 percent), so its point is at

FIGURE **12.1**   Scattergram of Percentage of Poverty-Level Residents and Percentage of High School Completers

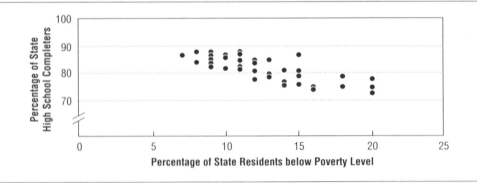

the lowest end of the *x* (horizontal) axis of the scattergram; it has nearly the highest graduation rate (87 percent), so its point is also at the top end of the *y* (vertical) axis.

Negative Correlational Patterns in Scattergrams.

Inspection of the scattergram in Figure 12.1 reveals a *negative* correlation between poverty level and school graduation rate. In other words, as the poverty level increases (going from left to right on the *x* axis), the graduation rate decreases (going from top to bottom on the *y* axis). There is no leveling off of the effect of poverty across the continuum of the 50 states and the District of Columbia. With each increase in the poverty level, there is, with a few exceptions, a decrease in the school graduation rate.

This example illustrates the definition of **negative correlation** as any situation in which higher scores on a measure of one variable are linked to lower scores on a measure of the other variable.

Positive Correlational Patterns in Scattergrams.

As you might imagine, a **positive correlation** occurs when higher scores on a measure of one variable are associated with higher scores on a measure of the other variable. For example, if there had been a positive correlation between poverty level and school graduation rate, higher levels of poverty would be accompanied by higher school graduation rates.

If you examine Figure 12.1, you see that the data points slope down from the left side to the right side of the scattergram. That is the hallmark of a negative correlation. If the data points slope up from the left to the right side of a scattergram, that indicates a positive correlation.

Positive correlations are often found in educational research. For example, in the study of school culture described earlier in the chapter, the researchers found that as the level of collaborative culture in a school increases, the level of student academic achievement tends to increase also. Similarly, in the study of infants' recognition memory, there is a tendency for higher levels of recognition memory to be associated with higher levels of IQ and academic achievement in young adulthood.

Nonlinear Correlational Patterns in Scattergrams.

Most correlational statistics are based on the assumption that if two variables are correlated with each other, the correlation is linear in nature. If a **linear correlation** is perfect in a sample of individuals having scores on two variables, each increase in the score on one variable is accompanied by an increase in the score of the other variable, or conversely each increase in the score on one variable is accompanied by a decrease in the score of the other variable.

For example, consider the scattergram in Figure 12.1. It is easy to visualize a line that runs through all the data points. One end of the line touches the leftmost data point, which represents New Hampshire, the state with the lowest poverty level (7%) and one of the highest school completion rates (87%). The other end of the line touches the average graduation rate (75%) of the District of Columbia, Louisiana, and Mississippi, which also have the three highest poverty levels.

You will see that most of the data points cluster around this straight line. For this reason, we say that the correlation between the two variables is linear. If we used any kind of curve to represent the relationship, it would not show the correlation nearly as well.

In this example, we estimated the line that best represents the data points. Although many of the data points do not fall exactly on the line, they do not deviate much from it. In fact, it is possible to calculate a line that minimizes these deviations to the greatest extent possible. This **line of best fit** can be defined as the line that allows for the best prediction of an individual's score on the *y* axis from knowing her score on the *x* axis. Of course, as in Table 12.1 and Figure 12.1, the scores can represent states rather than individuals (or any other objects of study).

Now we are ready to consider the question of whether all correlations between two variables are best represented by a straight line. In fact, some variables are correlated with each other, but not in a linear manner. For example, consider physical strength and chronological age. As individuals proceed from infancy to adulthood, most will get progressively stronger. As they continue to age, however, their strength will decline. In other words, the correlation between age and strength is positive up to a point, and after that point the correlation is negative.

It may well be that some important relationships between educational variables are nonlinear. For example, Craig Mason and his colleagues (1996) hypothesized a nonlinear relationship between the variables of (1) parental control, (2) problem behavior in adolescents, and (3) problem behavior in the adolescents' peers. Their study focused on the relationship among these variables in African American families.

The researchers presented one of their main findings in the simplified scattergram shown in Figure 12.2. The *x* axis shows different levels of parental behavioral control. This variable was measured by a scale in which the sample of adolescents (ages 12 to 14 at the start of the study) rated their parents' involvement in their day-to-day decision making on such matters as picking out clothes and deciding on a bedtime or curfew. The scale had 28 items, but the researchers decided to simplify the *x* axis of the scattergram by grouping the items into quartiles. For example, the first quartile included the 25 percent of adolescents with the lowest scores on the scale, meaning those who reported that their parents exerted relatively little control over their daily behavior.

The *y* axis represented the change in the adolescents' problem behavior over a one-year period. Problem behavior was measured by asking parents to report how frequently their child engaged in such behavior as gang activity, drug use, stealing, truancy, and fighting. Negative scores on the *y* axis indicated that their child's problem behavior decreased over a period of one year, whereas positive scores indicated an increase in problem behavior.

You will note that Figure 12.2 shows two lines connecting two different sets of data points. This analysis reflects the researchers' interest in peer group influence on adolescents' behavior. The researchers asked each adolescent in the study to rate the extent to which their peers engaged in problem behavior (the same problem behaviors that the parents rated, as

FIGURE *12.2*   Behavioral Control and Peer Problem Behavior Predicting Residualized Change in Parent Reports of Adolescent Problem Behavior

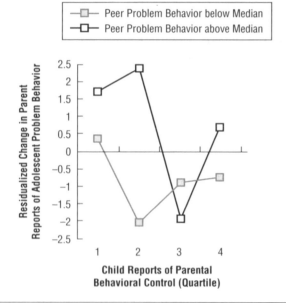

Source: Figure 2 on p. 2123 of Mason, C. A., Cauce, A. M., Gonzales, N., & Hiraga, Y. (1996). Neither too sweet nor too sour: Problem peers, maternal control, and problem behavior in African American adolescents. *Child Development, 67*, 2115–2130.

described in the previous paragraph). The researchers hypothesized that the optimum level of parental control might vary depending on whether a child was associating with friends who were well behaved or who were delinquent.

The scattergram in Figure 12.2 shows that the relationship between parental control and adolescents' problem behavior is nonlinear. If their child associated with well-behaved peers, a modest amount of parental control (level 2 on the *x* axis) was optimal (that is, it was associated with the lowest level of adolescent problem behavior). Exerting more control (levels 3 and 4) or less control (level 1) was not as effective.

A similar pattern was found for children who were associating with peers who exhibited antisocial behavior. A heightened, but not extreme amount of parental control (level 3 on the *x* axis) was optimal (that is, it was associated with the lowest level of adolescent problem behavior). Exerting extreme control (level 4) or less control (levels 1 and 2) was not nearly as effective.

The researchers drew the following conclusions from this and related data analyses in their study:

> In sum, the results generally suggest that when adolescents are part of a more positive peer group, the parenting environment is relatively forgiving. But when their adolescent children are involved with problem peers, the parenting challenge is considerable; underexerting or overexerting control is related to relatively elevated levels of problem behavior in their children. (Mason et al., 1996, p. 2126)

This result illustrates the importance of considering whether the cause-and-effect relationships that are of interest to you in solving problems of practice are linear or nonlinear.

Many of us often assume that more is better or sometimes that less is better. In actuality, there might be an optimal level of an intervention. For example, although we might imagine that more homework is better than less homework, there might instead be an optimal amount. If more homework than the optimum is assigned, students might become discouraged or resentful. If less than the optimum is assigned, students might not get the practice they need to master the curriculum. In other words, the relationship between homework and positive student outcomes might be nonlinear.

Absence of a Correlational Pattern in Scattergrams.   We now have considered correlations between two variables that are positive, negative, or nonlinear. Suppose, though, that the correlation is exactly zero, meaning that scores on one variable are useless in predicting scores on the other variable.

An example of a zero correlation is shown in Figure 12.3. We generated the scattergram by using a set of values between 1 and 9 in a table of random numbers to represent the *x* variable and another set of such values to represent the *y* variable. In effect, we correlated two random sets of numbers with each other. In examining the scattergram, you will observe that the data points do not slope upward or downward or form a nonlinear pattern. If you drew a line representing the midpoint of each set of *y* values for a given *x* value, the line would be horizontal, or nearly so.

The Meaning of Correlation Coefficients for Two Variables

Earlier in the chapter, we provided a definition for the term *correlation coefficient* and indicated that these coefficients can range between +1.00 and −1.00. Now we will examine these ideas more closely by referring to the scattergrams in the previous sections.

In one of our examples, we explored the hypothesis that poverty may correlate with lack of school persistence. The scattergram shown in Figure 12.1 supports the hypothesis, because it shows that higher poverty levels are associated with lower school completion percentages.

Table 12.2 shows the same data as in Table 12.1, but rearranged so that for each poverty level, we see the school completion percentage for all states having that poverty level. Let's examine the range of scores within each state, shown in the third column of Table 12.2. For example, of the six states having a poverty rate of 12 percent, the lowest school

FIGURE *12.3*   Scattergram of Data for Two Variables
Where *r* = .00

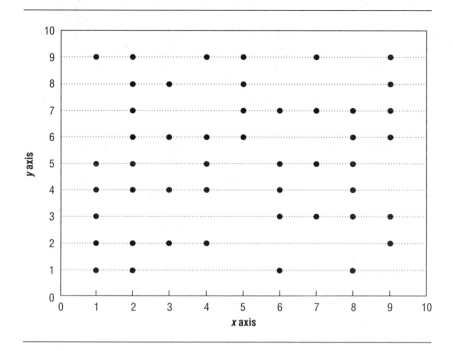

TABLE *12.2*   School Completion Percentages for All States
with Same Poverty Level

State Poverty Levels	Percentage High School Completion or More	Range of School Completion Percentages	Number of Percentage Points in Range
7	87	87–87	0
8	84, 88	84–88	4
9	82, 83, 84, 85, 85, 86, 87, 88, 88	82–88	6
10	82, 82, 86, 87	82–87	5
11	81, 81, 82, 83, 83, 85, 85, 87, 88	81–88	7
12	78, 78, 81, 84, 85, 85	78–85	7
13	79, 80, 85	79–85	6
14	76, 76, 77, 81	76–81	5
15	76, 79, 81, 87	76–87	11
16	74, 75, 75	74–75	1
17			
18	75, 79	75–79	4
19			
20	73, 75, 78	73–78	5
	Total range	74–88	14
	Mean of ranges		4.92

completion rate is 78 percent, and the highest rate is 85 percent. The range of scores then is 7 (85 − 78 = 7). Now let's examine the range of school completion rates for all states, irrespective of poverty level. The total range is 14 and extends from 74 to 88 (see bottom of Table 12.2).

If we did not know a state's poverty level, we could only say that its school completion rate is somewhere between 74 and 88. However, by knowing the state's poverty level, we can predict its school completion rate within a much narrower range. The mean of all the ranges for each poverty level, as shown in Table 12.2, is 5 (the precise mean is 4.92). Thus, for most poverty levels, we can use that information to predict a state's school completion rates typically within 5 percentage points.

The preceding analysis can be used to help us understand what a correlation coefficient means. The question that we wish to answer is, if the total range of school completion rates is 14 and if the range of rates averages 4.92 when we know a state's poverty level, how does 4.92 compare to 14? The answer is that 4.92 is 35 percent of 14 (4.92 ÷ 14 = 0.35).

The final step of the analysis is to consider what 35 percent means. The average range of state school completion rates, when we know a state's poverty level, is 4.92. The total range, when we don't know a state's poverty level, is 14. This means that we have reduced the range by 65 percent (1 − 0.35 = 0.65). This number (.65) is an approximation of the actual correlation coefficient (.77) for the relationship between states' combined poverty level and school completion rate.

The two coefficients (.65 and .77) differ because the computation procedure for a correlation coefficient uses a more mathematically sound indicator of range (the variance, which is described in Chapter 7) and takes into account differences in the score distributions of the two variables. However, the basic meaning of the two coefficients is similar, although a correlation coefficient provides an important bit of information that our use of ranges does not. It specifies whether the relationship between two variables is positive or negative by using plus (+) and minus (−) signs.

In summary, a correlation coefficient tells us how well we can predict the score of an individual (or state, or some other aggregation) on variable y if we know that individual's score on variable x. The higher the value of the correlation coefficient, whether in a positive or a negative direction, the better the prediction.

Keep in mind that prediction is closely related to the idea of causal relationships. If we can predict an individual's score on variable y from her score on variable x, it is likely because the two variables are related to each other in some causal manner. Thus, correlation coefficients serve us well whether we are interested in improving our predictions or in trying to detect possible causal relationships involved in a problem of practice.

Types of Bivariate Correlational Statistics

Table 12.3 lists the most widely used types of **bivariate correlational statistics.** *Bivariate* refers to the fact that the statistic indicates the magnitude of relationship between two, and only two, variables. Probably the best-known of these statistics is *r,* also called the **Pearson product-moment correlation coefficient.** Because r has a small sampling error (see Chapter 6), researchers often compute r for any two sets of scores, even if they are not continuous scores. The other bivariate correlational statistics in Table 12.3 are used less frequently, because they are more appropriate only under the conditions listed in the "Remarks" column.

You will note in Table 12.3 that some of the correlational statistics refer to dichotomous variables. A **dichotomous variable** can only have two values. If the variable expresses a **true dichotomy,** it only has two possible values in reality. For example, high school graduation is a true dichotomy because it only has two values: graduated and not graduated.

In contrast, an **artificial dichotomy** only has two values because they have been created by researchers or others. For example, Table 12.1 shows that the percentage-of-poverty levels across states have many values, ranging from 7 to 20. However, if we wish, we can artificially reduce the range of possibilities to just two values: (1) high-poverty states and (2) low-poverty states.

TABLE *12.3*   Bivariate Correlational Techniques for Different Forms of Variables

Technique	Symbol	Variable 1	Variable 2	Remarks
Product-moment correlation	r	Continuous	Continuous	The most stable technique, i.e., smallest standard error
Rank-difference correlation (*rho*)	ρ	Ranks	Ranks	A special form of product-moment correlation, used when the number of cases is under 30
Kendall's *tau*	τ	Ranks	Ranks	Preferable to *rho* for numbers under 10
Biserial correlation	r_{bis}	Artificial dichotomy	Continuous	Values can exceed 1 and have a larger standard error than r; commonly used in item analysis
Widespread biserial correlation	r_{wbis}	Widespread artificial dichotomy	Continuous	Used when researchers are interested in individuals at the extremes on the dichotomized variable
Point-biserial correlation	r_{pbis}	True dichotomy	Continuous	Yields a lower correlation than r_{bis}
Tetrachoric correlation	r_t	Artificial dichotomy	Artificial dichotomy	Used when both variables can be split at critical points
Phi coefficient	ϕ	True dichotomy	True dichotomy	Used in calculating inter-item correlations
Contingency coefficient	C	Two or more categories	Two or more categories	Comparable to r_t under certain conditions; closely related to chi-square
Correlation ratio, *eta*	η	Continuous	Continuous	Used to detect nonlinear relationships

Source: Adapted from Table 11.5 on p. 348 in Gall, M. D., Gall, J. P., & Borg, W. R. (2007). *Educational research: An introduction* (8th ed.). Boston: Allyn & Bacon. Copyright by Pearson Education. Adapted by permission of the publisher.

Table 12.3 shows that we can calculate a *tetrachoric* correlation coefficient to determine whether the two values of poverty level (high and low) are related to scores on another measured variable. Another option is to think of high-poverty states and low-poverty states as two groups and compare them on another measured variable by doing a *t* test of statistical significance, which we explained in Chapter 11. In doing this, we in fact are using a group comparison research design.

This example illustrates the point that group comparison research designs and correlational research designs generate data that can be analyzed by correlational statistics or group comparison statistics, such as the *t* test and analysis of variance. In fact, researchers increasingly are using correlational statistics to analyze data that involve a group comparison design. This same trend is evident even in experimental research (see Chapter 13), which typically involves comparing two groups (an experimental group and a control group) on one or more outcome variables.

Statistical Significance and Effect Size for Bivariate Correlational Statistics

As we explained in Chapter 9, a test of **statistical significance** indicates the likelihood that the statistical results obtained from the research sample are chance deviations from the statistical results that would have been obtained if the researchers had studied the entire population that the sample represents.

In the case of correlation coefficients, researchers typically test the null hypothesis that the correlation coefficient for the entire population represented by the sample is zero. If the test of statistical significance leads to the rejection of the null hypothesis, researchers conclude, with some level of confidence, that their obtained correlation coefficient reflects a real relationship between the two variables in the population represented by the sample.

In Chapter 8, we explained that **effect sizes** are helpful in determining the practical significance of statistical results. It is possible to convert a correlation coefficient to an effect size. The larger the correlation coefficient, the larger the effect size will be.

Multivariate Correlation

In the preceding sections of this chapter, we focused on the correlation between two variables. We now proceed to consider multiple correlations involving three or more variables.

Research findings for multiple correlations can have significant implications for solving problems of practice. For example, researchers sometimes find that a particular instructional method (variable *A*) improves academic achievement (variable *B*), but not for all students. It might be that it works well for students who have a high level of a certain characteristic (variable *C*), but not students having a low level of the characteristic. Knowledge about the three variables in combination can help educators decide whether to use the new method and for which students.

Various multivariate statistics have been developed for situations such as these. They are called **multivariate correlational statistics,** because they involve the analysis of data for three or more variables in combination with each other. We summarize the more commonly used statistics of this type in Table 12.4 and explain them in the next sections.

TABLE *12.4*   Types of Multivariate Correlational Statistics

Statistic	Purpose
Canonical correlation	To determine the amount of relationship between a set of predictor variables and a set of criterion variables
Differential analysis	To determine whether the amount of relationship between two or more variables is the same for groups having different characteristics
Discriminant analysis	To determine the amount of relationship between a set of predictor variables and a criterion variable whose measurement yields categorical scores
Hierarchical linear regression	To determine whether the amount of relationship between two or more variables is the same at different levels of nesting, for example, individual teachers versus teachers grouped according to the school in which they teach
Logistic regression	To determine the amount of relationship between a set of predictor variables and a criterion variable whose measurement yields dichotomous scores
Multiple linear regression	To determine the amount of relationship between a set of predictor variables and a criterion variable, with the assumption that if there is a relationship, it is linear
Path analysis	To determine whether a set of variables are related to each other in the manner predicted by a theory that hypothesizes causal links between the variables
Structural equation modeling	Has the same purpose as path analysis, but some or all of the variables are measured by two or more tests, scales, or other instruments

Multiple Regression

Earlier in the chapter, we considered the hypothesis that poverty has an influence on school persistence. Using data from the National Center for Education Statistics, we found strong support for the hypothesis. The correlation coefficient between these two variables is .77, but it is not perfect. A perfect correlation coefficient (r) is either +1.00 or –1.00.

The fact that poverty is not a perfect predictor of school persistence is illustrated by the scattergram in Figure 12.1. The points for most values on the x axis are tightly clustered, but they are not identical. Thus, if we know a state's poverty level, we can predict its percentage of high school completers, but not perfectly.

This lack of perfect predictability indicates that other factors besides poverty have an influence on school completion. Therefore, researchers need to consider other factors if they wish to improve their ability to predict an outcome such as completion of high school. As these factors become known, prediction improves and so does our understanding of school completion.

Multiple regression enables researchers to determine (1) how well the scores for each of a set of measured independent variables predict the scores on the measured dependent variable and (2) how well the combination of scores for all the measured independent variables predict the scores on the measured variables. The mathematics used in multiple regression is complex and requires advanced study of statistics. However, we can provide a brief nontechnical explanation here by referring to the data shown in Table 12.2.

Look at the school completion rate for states whose poverty level is 9. There are 10 such states, and their school completion rates vary between 82 and 88. If we used the median rate (85 percent) to predict the rate for a particular state, our prediction would either be correct (the rate for two of the states is 85 percent) or we would be off by just a few points in either direction.

Suppose, though, we found that another factor—for example, state investment in dropout prevention programs—is positively correlated with school completion rates. Also suppose that this investment improves the school completion rate for all states, regardless of poverty level.

In this situation, if we know that the state's poverty level is 9, we can predict that its school completion rate is between 82 and 88 percent, and if we know that the state's investment in dropout prevention programs is high relative to other states, we might be able to make a more precise prediction, for example, that its school completion rate is between 86 and 88 percent. Similarly, if we know that a state's poverty level is 12, we can predict that its school completion rate is between 78 and 85 percent; and if we also know that its investment in dropout prevention programs is low, we might be able to make a more precise prediction, for example, that its completion rate is between 78 and 81 percent.

These examples illustrate the point that multiple independent variables have the potential to improve the precision with which we can predict scores on the dependent variable. Multiple regression is a powerful statistical procedure for determining which combination of independent variables, if any, lead to better predictions than any single independent variable. Also, keep in mind that if an independent variable, or combination of such variables, predicts the dependent variable, a likely reason for this finding is that the independent and dependent variables have a causal relationship with each other.

Discriminant Analysis and Logistic Regression

Multiple regression is used when the scores on the dependent variable are continuous. There are situations, though, when the measure of the dependent variable yields categorical scores. For example, suppose that the scores on the dependent variable consist of three categories indicating whether parents enroll their child in a (1) regular public school, (2) private school, or (3) public charter school.

Now suppose we have identified several independent variables that we think might predict the category in which each child will fall. The appropriate statistical technique for testing these predictions is discriminant analysis. **Discriminant analysis** is a type of multiple regression that enables researchers to determine how well scores on several independent variables predict scores on a dependent variable when those scores are in the form of categories.

Logistic regression analysis also can be used for this purpose, but it is more commonly used when the dependent variable is dichotomous. Examples of dichotomous variables that might be of interest to educators include the following: enrolled in school, not enrolled in school; will be promoted to the next grade, will be held back a grade; has attention deficit disorder, does not have attention deficit disorder.

Canonical Correlation

Canonical correlation is a specialized type of multiple regression used when there are multiple dependent variables that can be viewed as different facets of an underlying factor. For example, suppose that we wish to predict students' attitudes toward school. We might administer separate measures to predict, let's say, their attitude toward their teacher, their program of studies, their homework, and the assessment methods used by the teacher.

One option would be to do separate multiple regression analyses to determine how well the independent variables predict the scores on each attitude measure. However, suppose that bivariate correlational statistics show that scores on each of these attitude measures are correlated with each other. We might conclude, then, that these different attitudes are part of an underlying, generalized positive or negative attitude toward school.

In this case, we can do a single canonical correlation analysis, whose purpose is to determine whether the independent variables predict a composite score that represents the factor underlying the different attitudes. This factor is similar in meaning to the type of factors identified by factor analysis, which we explain in a subsequent section.

Hierarchical Linear Modeling

Suppose we wish to investigate the relationship between the poverty level of students' families and their scores on state-mandated tests of social studies achievement. Further suppose that we have data on these two variables for a random sample of 25 school districts in the state, all 150 high schools within the selected school districts, and all 4,700 ninth-grade students enrolled in the 400 ninth-grade social studies classes in the selected high schools.

Analyzing this situation, we see that (1) each student in this sample has a particular social studies teacher, (2) each social studies teacher works within a particular school, and (3) each school is located in a particular school district. How then should we analyze the relationship between the students' poverty status and their social studies achievement?

We could simply compute a correlation coefficient for the two variables (poverty level and academic achievement) for all 4,700 students in the sample, ignoring the fact that they have different teachers, go to different schools, and reside in different school districts. Or we could compute 400 correlation coefficients (one for the students in each teacher's classroom), ignoring the fact that the classrooms are located in different schools and different school districts. Or we could compute 150 correlation coefficients (one for each of the 150 schools), ignoring the fact that the schools are located in different school districts.

Which data analysis is correct? In fact, all the analyses have merit. We might want to know whether the correlation between students' poverty status and their social studies achievement varies across social studies teachers. If it does, this finding would suggest that some teachers are doing something in their instruction to either mitigate or worsen the effect of students' poverty status on their achievement. Similarly, we might want to know whether the correlation between students' poverty status and social studies achievement varies across schools within a district. If it does, this finding would suggest that certain schools are doing something to either mitigate or worsen the effect of students' poverty status on their achievement.

Researchers conceptualize these complex data sets in terms of **nesting,** which is a situation in which a variable exists at several levels of an organizational structure. They think of students being "nested" in a classroom, meaning that each student is affected by the teacher's behavior and by the other students' behavior. Teachers are "nested" in schools, meaning that they are affected by the behavior of other teachers and staff in the building. Schools are "nested" in districts, meaning that they are affected by the staff of other schools and central offices in the district.

Hierarchical linear modeling (often abbreviated to **HLM**) is a sophisticated statistical technique that enables researchers to determine how the correlation between two variables is affected by different levels of nesting. If no nesting effects are detected, this finding would suggest that the correlation between the variables is robust, in the sense that it is not affected by the organizational structure of the learning environment. If a nesting effect is found, it indicates that the correlation between two variables will be different across different settings.

Larger data sets that include multiple levels of nesting are becoming more common in education. For this reason, there is increasing use of HLM to analyze correlational data.

Path Analysis and Structural Equation Modeling

Path analysis and **structural equation modeling** are sophisticated multivariate techniques for testing causal links among the different variables that have been measured. For example, suppose that researchers hypothesize that, among teachers, (1) childhood travel experiences lead to (2) tolerance for ambiguity and (3) desire for travel as an adult, and that (2) and (3) make it more likely that a teacher will (4) seek an overseas teaching experience and (5) adapt well to the experience.

Path analysis and structural equation modeling are methods for testing the validity of the hypothesized causal links involving these five factors. They differ primarily in that structural equation modeling yields more valid and reliable measures of some or all of the factors. Both approaches are similar, though, in that their goal is to help researchers understand causal relationships rather than to maximize prediction of a criterion variable from some combination of independent variables.

Differential Analysis

Used sometimes in prediction research, **differential analysis** is the technique of using moderator variables to form subgroups when examining the relationship between two other variables. For example, suppose that we have reason to believe that self-esteem has more effect on school performance for students of lower socioeconomic status (SES) than for students of higher SES. Socioeconomic status, then, is a third variable that is thought to mediate the relationship between the first two variables. This third variable is called a **moderator variable** because it affects the strength or direction, or both, of the correlation between the other two variables. It is similar in meaning to the interaction effects sometimes found in analysis of variance (see Chapter 11).

Let's say that the correlation coefficient for the relationship between self-esteem and school performance is .40 for low-SES (socioeconomic status) students and .25 for high-SES students. These results demonstrate that SES moderates the strength of the relationship between self-esteem and school performance.

Factor Analysis

The multivariate correlational techniques that we described in preceding sections have a similar purpose, namely to examine the strength of the relationship between one or more independent variables and one or more dependent variables.

Factor analysis also examines the strength of the relationship between multiple variables, but it does not classify them as independent and dependent. Instead, the purpose of **factor analysis** is to determine whether a set of variables reflects a smaller number of underlying factors.

For example, suppose that researchers have developed measures of eight study skills: (1) organizing one's study materials, (2) time management, (3) classroom listening,

(4) classroom note-taking, (5) planning for assigned papers, (6) writing assigned papers, (7) preparing for tests, and (8) taking tests. The researchers wonder whether these are related skills, meaning that students who are strong in one skill are likely to be strong in all or some subset of the other skills.

Factor analysis examines the sample's scores on all eight variables and determines whether they cluster into a smaller number of factors, based on high correlations among the variables within each cluster. Perhaps the eight study skills reflect three underlying factors: (1) skills that involve writing, (2) skills that involve planning, and (3) skills that involve recall of learned information.

Factor analysis can reveal this underlying structure of factors, if indeed it exists. This is useful research knowledge in its own right. Another benefit is that if a substantial number of measures can be reduced to several factors, subsequent statistical analyses can be simplified.

Features of a Correlational Research Report

Table 12.5 presents typical features of a correlational study report. In the following sections, we discuss each feature and illustrate it with a research study about the validity of an oral reading fluency measure in predicting young children's subsequent reading achievement. At the end of the chapter, you will find an actual correlational study from a journal article that sought to identify factors influencing students' performance in a college course on biopsychology. The article is reprinted in full.

TABLE *12.5*   Typical Sections of a Correlational Research Report

Section	Content
Introduction	Hypotheses, questions, or objectives are stated. A review of relevant literature is reported. The purpose of the study usually is to explicitly or implicitly study the factors that affect a problem of practice or the consequences resulting from a problem of practice.
Research design	If the study is designed to investigate cause-and-effect relationships, at least one variable is designated as the independent variable (i.e., the presumed cause). At least one other variable is designated as the dependent variable (i.e., the presumed effect). If the study focuses on prediction, at least one variable is designated as the predictor variable (also called the independent variable). At least one other variable is designated as the criterion variable (also called the outcome variable or dependent variable). The independent variable must have occurred prior in time to the dependent variable. Typically, at least one of the variables is conceptualized as continuous.
Sampling procedure	The researcher selects a sample of research participants who have the characteristics that are represented by the independent and dependent variables.
Measures	Virtually any kind of measure can be used to collect data on the independent and dependent variables.
Data analysis	Descriptive statistics for the independent and dependent variables are computed. Bivariate correlational statistics are used if the purpose is to determine the relationship between two variables. Multivariate correlational statistics are used if the combined relationship among three or more variables is of interest.
Discussion	The main findings of the study are summarized. Flaws and limitations of the study are considered. Implications of the findings for further research and for professional practice are considered.

Introduction

The introductory section of a correlational research report should explain the importance of the study, the research questions to be answered or hypotheses to be tested, and the variables of interest. It also should include a review of relevant literature so that the reader can understand how the study builds on existing knowledge.

As an example, we consider a prediction research study conducted by Stephen Schilling, Joanne Carlisle, Sarah Scott, and Ji Zeng (2007). **Prediction research** is a type of investigation that involves the use of data collected at one point in time to predict future behavior or events. The researchers started their report by noting that the No Child Left Behind Act makes states, districts, schools, and teachers accountable for students' reading achievement. They then stated a problem of practice, namely that educators need to have valid measures to identify students who are not making adequate progress in reading, so that these students can receive timely instructional support.

Drawing on their review of the literature, the researchers identified a promising measure for this purpose. Called DIBELS (Dynamic Indicators of Basic Early Literacy Skills), this measure assesses oral reading fluency and accuracy. The theory underlying DIBELS is that if students have mastered lower-order reading skills, such as word decoding, they can devote their cognitive resources to mastering higher-order skills involved in reading comprehension.

A major purpose of the study stated by the researchers was "to examine the effectiveness and trustworthiness of DIBELS fluency-based measures as predictors of year-end reading achievement" (Schilling et al., 2007, pp. 430–431). Another purpose was to determine whether certain cut-off scores on DIBELS measures can be used to identify students who will have low scores on a subsequent test of reading achievement if they do not receive any special intervention. Oral reading fluency and accuracy are **predictor variables,** which are variables that are measured at one point in time and then correlated with a criterion variable. Reading achievement is a **criterion variable,** because it is measured at a subsequent point in time and because it is the outcome that researchers are attempting to predict.

Research Design

As with group comparison research, a correlational design usually is chosen because the researchers cannot manipulate the independent variable. In the prediction study we are using as an example, it would not be ethical for the researchers to withhold instruction in oral reading fluency from some children and offer it to others. Therefore, Schilling and his colleagues examined naturally occurring variations among children in their oral reading fluency and accuracy and determined whether these variations predicted their subsequent reading achievement.

As we explained earlier in the chapter, prediction research often is based on hypothesized causal relationships. Predictor variables (also called independent variables) are the presumed causes, and outcome variables (also called dependent variables) are the presumed effects.

In the prediction study we are examining, the predictor variables were measured by a set of DIBELS tests: (1) letter-naming fluency; (2) phoneme-segmentation fluency, which involves asking students to identify separate phonemes in spoken words; (3) nonsense word fluency, which involves asking students to decode three-letter nonsense words; (4) word usage, which involves giving students a word and asking them to use it in a sentence; (5) and oral reading fluency. The researchers studied children in grades 1 to 3, and different groups of these five tests were administered depending on the children's grade level.

The outcome variables were measured by subtests of the Iowa Test of Basic Skills (ITBS): (1) vocabulary, (2) ability to analyze word structure, (3) ability to understand words and phrases presented orally, (4) grammatical knowledge and spelling, (5) reading comprehension, and (6) total reading ability, which is a composite of students' scores on the six subtests.

Sampling Procedure

In doing correlational studies, researchers should select a sample that is representative of the population to which they wish to generalize their results. Ideally, the sample should be randomly drawn from the defined population.

The sample in the reading study consisted of students in districts or local education agencies in the state of Michigan that received Reading First funds during the 2002–2003 school year. Reading First is a program that provides resources to high-poverty, low-achieving schools to help students become successful readers. This sample is appropriate for the purposes of the study, because many students in Reading First schools are particularly at risk for reading failure and therefore it is important to identify these students as soon as possible so they can receive reading interventions that will prevent failure.

A correlational study might include several samples representing different populations. The reading study included samples of children in grade 1, grade 2, and grade 3, which enabled the researchers to determine whether different predictor variables are effective at each grade level. For example, it might be that vocabulary knowledge is a good predictor of reading achievement at the end of grade 1, but not at the end of grade 2.

Measures

As with other quantitative research designs, the independent and dependent variables can be measured by any of the methods described in Chapter 6. These methods include tests, attitude scales, questionnaires, interviews, and direct observation.

The reading study relied on two tests, DIBELS and ITBS, both described above. In addition, Schilling and his colleagues collected demographic data about the students' ethnicity and risk category (economic disadvantage, limited English proficiency, disability status). The methods for collecting these data are not described in the journal article.

Results

Schilling and his colleagues conducted a variety of analyses of their data using correlational statistics. One analysis involved correlating students' scores on the DIBELS measure of oral reading fluency (ORF), administered at the beginning of the school year, with their scores on the ITBS subtests and total test, administered near the end of the school year. The ORF measure involves having each student read aloud three passages. The number of words read correctly in one minute on the middle passage constitutes the student's ORF score.

Table 12.6 shows the result of this correlational analysis. We find that ORF scores correlate fairly highly (usually .50 or above) with all the ITBS subtest scores and total test scores. Correlational statistics on the order of .50 or higher mean that students' ORF scores are good predictors of their ITBS scores. This finding generalizes across grades 2 and 3.

Each correlation coefficient in Table 12.6 involves two variables, making them bivariate coefficients. The specific type of coefficient (see the list in Table 12.3) is not stated in the report. In all likelihood, though, they are product-moment correlation coefficients, because both variables yield continuous scores. Also, product-moment correlation coefficients are so prevalent in research reports that they are rarely identified by name. If researchers use another type of bivariate correlation, they typically label it.

The researchers also used multiple regression to determine whether a combination of DIBELS measures predicts students' scores on the ITBS better than just one of them. One of these analyses is shown in Table 12.7. We see that, for second-graders, ORF scores in the fall are the best predictors of their ITBS reading scores in the winter ($R^2 = .475$). R^2 is simply the square of the correlation coefficient r. It is used to represent the results of a multiple regression analysis because it has desirable mathematical properties.

Looking at Table 12.7, we see that students' word usage scores improve the prediction of their ITBS scores. Combined with the ORF scores, R^2 increases to .488. Adding scores on one more measure (nonsense word fluency) increases the R^2 to .493. Thus, we find that ORF scores are a good predictor of students' ITBS scores, but a combination of scores on

TABLE 12.6   Correlation of DIBELS Oral Reading Fluency and Spring ITBS Subjects for Second and Third Grade

ITBS Subtest	DIBELS Oral Reading Fluency		
	Fall	Winter	Spring
Grade 2:			
Vocabulary	.61	.65	.64
Word analysis	.59	.63	.62
Listening	.29	.33	.33
Language	.59	.65	.64
Reading comprehension	.68	.75	.75
Reading total	.69	.75	.75
Grade 3:			
Vocabulary	.57	.58	.56
Word analysis	.63	.68	.63
Listening	.36	.37	.37
Language	.67	.69	.68
Reading comprehension	.63	.65	.63
Reading total	.65	.67	.65

Note: All $p < .001$.

Source: Table 3 on p. 437 of Schilling, S. G., Carlisle, J. F., Scott, S. E., & Zeng, J. (2007). Are fluency measures accurate predictors of reading achievement? *Elementary School Journal, 107*(5), 429–448.

several DIBELS measures (see the column labeled "Model R^2") improves the prediction, albeit slightly.

Schilling and his colleagues did additional analyses to demonstrate more concretely how the best predictor measure, ORF, can help teachers identify students early in the year who are at risk of reading failure in the spring. One of these analyses, for second-graders, is shown in Table 12.8. ORF scores are divided into three categories. For example, students who accurately read 26 words or less per minute were classified as at risk. Students who read accurately at faster rates were classified as some risk or low risk.

TABLE 12.7   Fall DIBELS Subtests Predicting ITBS Reading Total

Fluency Variable	Partial R^2	Model R^2	F Value*
Oral reading fluency	.475	.475	1,949.64
Word usage	.014	.468	57.76
Nonsense word	.005	.493	19.58

Note: First grade $n = 2,231$ for fall, $n = 2,369$ for winter. Second grade $n = 2,156$ for fall.

*All $p < .001$.

Source: Adapted from Table 4 on p. 438 of Schilling, S. G., Carlisle, J. F., Scott, S. E., & Zeng, J. (2007). Are fluency measures accurate predictors of reading achievement? *Elementary School Journal, 107*(5), 429–448.

TABLE *12.8*   Prediction of ITBS Scores of Second-Graders above and below the 25th Percentile from ORF Fall Status

ITBS Reading Total	Fall DIBELS Oral Reading Fluency			
	At Risk (<26 wpm)	Some Risk (26 wpm–43 wpm)	Low Risk (>43 wpm)	Total ITBS
Below 25th percentile	692	177	37	906
At or above 25th percentile	224	430	599	1,253
Total DIBELS	916	607	636	2,159

Source: Adapted from Table 5 on p. 437 of Schilling, S. G., Carlisle, J. F., Scott, S. E., & Zeng, J. (2007). Are fluency measures accurate predictors of reading achievement? *Elementary School Journal, 107*(5), 429–448.

Now suppose the second-grade data shown in Table 12.8 had been collected in one school year, and we wished to apply it to the following school year. Also, assume that the same instructional conditions and student population remained constant across the two years. What would be our best prediction of whether a particular student would experience reading failure, which we will define as reading below the 25th percentile on the ITBS, or have at least some reading success, which we will define as reading at or above the 25th percentile on the ITBS?

Without any predictive information, our best forecast is that all 2,159 students in the sample will be reading successes. This is because 1,253 students were reading successes. We would be correct for 58 percent of the students (1,253 ÷ 2,159 = 58%). If we predicted instead that all students would be reading failures, we would only be correct for 42 percent of the students (906 ÷ 2,159 = 42%).

Now let's use students' ORF scores in the fall to predict their reading success or failure in the spring. Suppose we know that a student was at risk based on her ORF score. If we predict that the student will be a reading failure, we would be correct for 75 percent of the at risk students (692 ÷ 916 = 75%).

Suppose we know that a student was at some risk based on his ORF score. If we predict that the student will be a reading success, we would be correct for 70 percent of students at some risk (430 ÷ 607 = 70%). Finally, suppose we know that a student was low risk based on the ORF score. If we predict that the student will be a reading success we would be correct for 94 percent of low-risk students (599 ÷ 636 = 94%).

This example illustrates the value of correlational research for the purpose of predicting reading failure. The empirical findings reveal that the use of ORF results in better predictions (75%, 70%, and 94%) than if we had no predictive information at all (42%). If resources for intensive reading instruction are limited, educators might be better advised to focus on students classified by their ORF score as at risk than to distribute the resources equally—and consequently, less intensively—to all students.

Discussion: Implications for Practice

The discussion section of a correlational research report typically includes a summary of the main findings and analysis of limitations and possible flaws in the design and execution of the study. For example, Schilling and his colleagues (2007) made the following observation:

In interpreting these results, the reader should also keep in mind that during the year of this study teachers were encouraged to use DIBELS results to make decisions about reading instruction. (p. 442)

It might be, then, that some students who would have been classified by ORF as at risk or as reading failures at the end of the school year in actuality became reading successes as a result of teachers' interventions. If this were true, it would have the effect of underestimating the predictive validity of ORF. Without teacher intervention, these students would have increased the number of reading failures, thereby increasing the power of low ORF scores to predict low ITBS scores.

The discussion section of a correlational research report sometimes includes comments about implications of the study's findings for practice. For example, in the discussion section of their report, Schilling and his colleagues recommended that teachers use the at risk category of ORF scores to identify students who are likely to be below the 25th percentile on ITBS at the end of the school year. The ORF assessment is relatively simple to administer and score, but it yields valuable information that can help educators pay special attention to students who do not respond to regular classroom instruction and end the year as poor readers.

Evaluating a Correlational Research Study

The criteria stated in Appendix 2 are relevant to evaluating a correlational research study. The following additional criteria, stated in question-and-answer format, are useful for evaluating the quality of correlational research studies. The questions are repeated from Chapter 11 (Group Comparison Research), because they are equally relevant to the evaluation of a correlational research study.

- Did the researchers specify a cause-and-effect model that links their variables?

  A correlational research design is used to determine causal relationships. Therefore, check whether the researchers clearly specified which variables are the presumed causes and which variables are the presumed effects. Also, examine whether the researchers' provided a rationale that explains why one variable is hypothesized to have an effect on another variable.

- Did the researchers express appropriate tentativeness in making causal inferences from their results?

  Correlational research studies can explore causal relationships, but they cannot demonstrate definitively that variable *A* has an effect on variable *B*. Check the report for statements indicating that the researchers avoided drawing strong conclusions of this type or claims that if educators manipulate variable *A* (e.g., implement a new procedure), changes in variable *B* (e.g., improved student learning) will occur.

An *example of*
HOW CORRELATIONAL RESEARCH CAN HELP IN SOLVING PROBLEMS OF PRACTICE

The following is an example of a problem of practice involving advanced placement courses.

A commentary article by Paul Von Blum, a university senior lecturer, titled, "Are Advanced Placement Courses Diminishing Liberal Arts Education?" appeared in the September 3, 2008, issue of *Education Week*. Von Blum states that "my 40 years of undergraduate teaching in the humanities and social sciences, currently at the University of California, Los Angeles, persuade me that Advanced Placement preparation is overrated and may, ironically, diminish rather than advance the deeper objectives of a liberal arts education."

Von Blum claims that high school AP courses are "primarily an exercise in memorization and exam passing." Therefore, in his view, college students with extensive advanced placement (AP) experience in high school can graduate from college with "little feel for authentic learning and few critical-thinking skills."

Von Blum, P. (2008, September 3). Are advanced placement courses diminishing liberal arts education? *Education Week, 28*(2), 26–27.

Many high schools devote a substantial percentage of their budgets to make AP courses available to their students. In addition, students must pay a registration fee for each AP test they take. Von Blum raises the question of whether all this effort and expense results in two desired outcomes: critical-thinking skills and "feel for authentic learning." Is his concern justified? Correlational research studies can help to answer this question.

One of the first steps would be to identify or develop valid measures of critical thinking and "feel for authentic learning," which, in more conventional terms, might be thought of as intrinsic academic motivation. Researchers could select a sample of students who are just about to complete high school. The independent variable would be AP experience, which could be measured by counting the number of AP courses and AP tests taken by these students. Additional measures could be created by weighting each AP course by the student's course grade and by weighting each AP test by the student's test score. The two dependent variables would be students' scores on the measure of critical thinking and on the measure of intrinsic academic motivation. These measures could be administered at the end of the students' high school program and again later to those students in the sample who had graduated from college by a certain date.

If Von Blum's claim is correct, we would expect to find little or no correlation between students' scores on the various AP measures and their scores on the measures of critical thinking and intrinsic academic motivation, either on high school graduation or on college graduation. If the evidence supports Von Blum's claim, it would reveal a significant problem of practice. Educators would need to rethink the value of AP courses in high school and perhaps redesign or eliminate them from the curriculum.

If instead we found a significant positive correlation between students' AP scores and their scores on measures of critical thinking and intrinsic academic motivation, Von Blum's claim would have been refuted. That finding would lead educators, students, and others to have renewed confidence in the effectiveness of AP courses in high school. This confidence might lead educators and policy makers to provide more support for these courses and to encourage more students to take them.

Self-Check Test

1. Correlational research
   a. can be used to explore causal relationships.
   b. can be used to provide conclusive confirmation of causal relationships.
   c. can be used to study causal relationships, whereas group comparison research cannot be used for this purpose.
   d. involves the manipulation of the independent variable, whereas group comparison research does not involve this kind of manipulation.
2. Correlational research is intended primarily for
   a. collapsing a range of observed values of at least one of the measured variables into a single category.

   b. investigating the characteristics of one measured variable in depth.
   c. providing information about all the observed values of at least one of the measured variables.
   d. determining which of the variables being investigated constitutes the independent variable.
3. A correlation coefficient provides information about
   a. the magnitude of the relationship between two variables, but not the direction of the relationship.
   b. the direction of the relationship between two variables, but not its magnitude.
   c. the linearity of the relationship between two variables.

d. the magnitude and direction of the relationship between two variables, but not its linearity.

4. Inspection of a scattergram provides information about whether
   a. data from a sufficient number of research participants are available for exploring a causal relationship.
   b. the correlation between two variables is linear or nonlinear.
   c. the variable on the x axis is the cause or the effect of the variable on the y axis.
   d. All of the above.

5. As a correlation coefficient increases in size, it means that
   a. the direction of the causal relationship between two variables is more uncertain.
   b. the two variables being correlated are more likely to have a nonlinear relationship to each other.
   c. the relationship between the two variables being correlated is more likely to have a negative slope.
   d. scores on one variable are better able to predict scores on the other variable.

6. The null hypothesis in a typical correlational study states that
   a. the true correlation coefficient in the population represented by the research sample has a positive value.
   b. the true correlation coefficient in the population represented by the research sample is zero.
   c. the correlation between the independent variable and the dependent variable is statistically significant.
   d. the effect size for the correlation coefficient is 0.33 or greater.

7. If researchers wish to determine the influence of multiple independent variables on a single dependent variable, the appropriate statistical technique would be
   a. hierarchical linear modeling.
   b. path analysis.
   c. multiple regression.
   d. factor analysis.

8. If researchers wish to determine whether the correlation between two variables is affected by different levels of "nesting," the appropriate statistical technique would be
   a. factor analysis.
   b. hierarchical linear modeling.
   c. discriminant analysis.
   d. canonical correlation.

9. A correlational research design can include
   a. multiple predictor variables.
   b. only one predictor variable.
   c. only predictor and outcome variables that are negatively related to each other.
   d. only predictor and outcome variables that are positively related to each other.

10. In a report of a correlational research study, the researchers should
    a. put greater emphasis on the implications of their findings for theory than for practice.
    b. identify and discuss flaws in the study.
    c. not speculate about whether the observed relationships between variables reflect causality.
    d. not present the corresponding effect sizes for correlation coefficients.

Chapter References

Mason, C. A., Cauce, A. M., Gonzales, N., & Hiraga, Y. (1996). Neither too sweet nor too sour: Problem peers, maternal control, and problem behavior in African American adolescents. *Child Development, 67*, 2115–2130.

Schilling, S. G., Carlisle, J. F., Scott, S. E., & Zeng, J. (2007). Are fluency measures accurate predictors of reading achievement? *Elementary School Journal, 107*(5), 429–448.

Resources for Further Study

Grimm, L. G., & Yarnold, P. R. (Eds.). (2000). *Reading and understanding more multivariate statistics.* Washington, DC: American Psychological Association.

This book and its predecessor, *Reading and Understanding Multivariate Statistics* (1995), provide an overview of multivariate statistical techniques and the types of research questions they can answer. Among the techniques covered are correlation, multiple regression, path analysis, factor analysis, multivariate analysis of variance, and discriminant analysis.

Harrison, D. M., & Raudenbush, S. W. (2006). Linear regression and hierarchical linear models. In J. L. Green, G. Camilli, & P. B. Elmore (Eds.), *Handbook of complementary methods in education research* (pp. 411–426). Mahwah, NJ: Lawrence Erlbaum.

The authors explain two of the multivariate correlational techniques described in this chapter by addressing an illustrative research question. The question concerns whether there is a relationship between the socioeconomic status of students' families and their academic achievement.

Wainer, H., & Velleman, P. F. (2006). Statistical graphics: A guidepost for scientific discovery. In J. L. Green, G. Camilli, & P. B. Elmore (Eds.), *Handbook of complementary methods in education research* (pp. 605–621). Mahwah, NJ: Lawrence Erlbaum.

The authors show how various types of graphs, including scattergrams, help to clarify characteristics of observed relationships between variables.

Sample Correlational Research Study

Correlates of Performance in Biological Psychology: How Can We Help?

Sgoutas-Emch, S. A., Nagel, E., & Flynn, S. (2007). Correlates of performance in biological psychology: How can we help? *Journal of Instructional Psychology, 34*(1), 46–53.

Starting in middle school, most students take subject-matter courses from different teachers. These courses are problematic, because some students learn well in them, but others do not.

In the following study, the researchers attempted to determine factors that cause these differences in academic achievement. A correlational research design was well suited for the study, as the researchers wished to explore the effects of a wide variety of factors. By our count, they investigated 17 different factors (in technical terms, independent variables).

You will find in this journal report that the researchers viewed many of the variables as continuous, and therefore they did correlational statistical analyses. They viewed other variables as categorical and therefore analyzed the data relating to them by a statistical procedure (analysis of variance) appropriate to group comparison designs (see Chapter 11).

The article is reprinted in its entirety, just as it appeared when originally published.

Correlates of Performance in Biological Psychology: How Can We Help?

Sandra A. Sgoutas-Emch,
Erik Nagel, and
Scott Flynn

ABSTRACT ■ Undergraduate students routinely rated science-related courses such as biopsychology as intimidating and very difficult. Identification of factors that may contribute to success in these types of courses is important in order to help increase performance and interest in these topics. To examine what variables are related to performance, we studied undergraduate students enrolled in biopsychology courses. We found grade point average and students' attitudes about science are the best predictors of performance. Level of perceived preparedness, science efficacy, test anxiety, and previous exposure to the course material were also associated. Contrary to previous data, we did not find a significant relationship between gender and race. It appears that to assist students in biopsychology, we need to focus on preparing them better for the course and stimulating a more positive attitude toward the material.

For over 30 years, comparative studies have chronicled the decline of performance in math and science test scores of American children. Internationally, high school seniors in the United States rank among the lowest in both mathematics and science general knowledge (Business Coalition for Education Reform, 2002). For example, an American high school senior's score in the 95th percentile would be equivalent to a score in the 30th percentile in Japan and the 50th percentile in England (Geary, 1996). During the years 1999–2000, of all bachelor's degrees conferred by United States degree-granting institutions, less than 6% were biological and life science degrees (National Center for Education Statistics, 2001a). From 1979 to 1999 the number of people receiving doctoral degrees in the life sciences increased more than 52%; however, the number awarded to American citizens had dropped by over 17% (NCES, 2001b). The proportion of freshmen intending to major in science and engineering fields fell more than 20% over the last 29 years, and the percentage of freshman intending to major in biological sciences has dropped more than 20 points (Higher Education Research Institute, 2002). This performance deficit progressively widens with successive years of schooling, and recent data revealed science majors average a 40% attrition rate, contributing to the United States ranking lower than several other industrialized countries in university degrees in science (Brand, 1995).

Identifying science performance predictors is essential to the exploration of possible reasons and justifications for this issue. Previous research has demonstrated strong correlations between levels of test anxiety and measures of performance (Everson, Tobias, Hartman, & Gourgey, 1993; Paulman & Kennelly, 1984; Tobias, 1979, 1985; Wigfield & Eccles, 1989; Wittmaier, 1972; Wolf & Smith, 1995). Students with higher test anxiety measures were found to be related to lower performance in the course. For instance, one study found relationships between test anxiety in college students, detriments in grade point average, and poor study skills (Culler & Holahan, 1980). This study showed that students with higher grade point averages had better study skills and lower test anxiety scores. Further, research has consistently shown correlations linking achievement to students' self-efficacy and attitude (Germann, 1994). Papanastasiou and Zembylas (2004) reviewed decades of research pertaining to attitudes, finding the attitudes of science students to be positively correlated with academic achievement and participation in advanced science courses. Zohar (1998), for example, found expected success measured with self-efficacy for grade attainment, three days before a test, predicted anxiety levels during an exam.

Quantitative and demographic variables reveal additional correlates of academic performance. Thomas and Schwenz (1998), in an undergraduate biochemistry class, showed that grade point averages and exams revealed the level of understanding of course material. However, in a college biology class, Johnson and Lawson (1998) found prior knowledge of biology had no significant effect on semester scores, quiz scores, or final examination scores.

Demographically, divergence between genders occurs in interest and achievement at the start of high school, growing more prominent as years of education increase (Brownlow, Jacobi, & Rogers, 2000), with United States men having more positive attitudes toward science than women (Czerniak & Chiarelott, 1984; Kahle & Lakes, 1983). However, recent data reveal the total number of women receiving a bachelor's degree in the biological or life sciences has surpassed men. Even more striking was the disparity between races of bachelor's degrees conferred by degree granting institutions. In the 1999–2000 school year, of the 63,532 bachelor's degrees conferred in the United States in the field of biological or life sciences, Black and Hispanic Americans combined received less than 13%, with over 71% issued to White, non-Hispanic Americans (NCES, 2000a). The same racial groups, in the National Center for Education Statistics High School Transcript Study (2000), had mean science and mathematics GPAs lower than all

other subject fields. Showing little change from 1990 to 2000, these data forecast no significant levels of improvement. These trends in mathematics and science scores have added to the growing concern about how Americans will satisfy advancing technological professions, such as neuroscience, in the twenty-first century.

This study examined potential educational and psychological factors that may influence and ultimately predict students' performance in a biological psychology course.

We explore how psychological, social and educational factors may predict performance in biological psychology. In addition, we made comparisons across gender, race, and choice of major.

METHOD

Participants

One hundred and forty-eight undergraduates enrolled in the biopsychology course at the University of San Diego comprised the sample for the current study. The same instructor collected the data over a period of three years. Participation in a research study was a requirement for the course. Alternative choices were given to those students who did not wish to participate in the current study.

Materials

Revised Spielberger State Anxiety questionnaire: (SA; Marteau & Bekker, 1992). This shortened version of the original questionnaire designed by Spielberger (1983) consists of 6 questions from the original scale. The study utilized a 5-point Likert scale with 5 = *the highest level of anxiety* and 1 = *the lowest level of anxiety*. We replaced the phrase used in the questionnaire from how you feel right now to how you feel right now about the course. Scores ranged from 6 to 24. The higher the score, the more anxiety about the course.

Scientific Attitude: (SAT; Moore & Foy, 1997). This is a 40-item test designed to measure the attitude of an individual toward science. A 5-point Likert scale was scored by assigning point values to each of the attitude items (5 = *strongly agree*, 4 = *mildly agree*, 3 = *neutral*, 2 = *mildly disagree*, 1 = *strongly [dis]agree*). The maximum possible score for this section was 140, with the minimum being 28. In addition, six positions are positive and six negative. Positive items: (POSSAT) (5 = *strongly agree* – 1 = *strongly disagree*). Negative items: (NEGSAT) (1 = *strongly agree* – 5 = *strongly disagree*). Scores may range from 12 to 60. The higher the score, the more negative the attitude toward science.

The Test Anxiety Inventory: (TTA; Spielberger, 1980). This is a self-report measure consisting of 20 items, employing a Likert scale from 1–4 (1 = *almost never*, to 4 = *almost always*). Scores may range from a high of 80 to a low of 20. The higher the score, the more test anxiety the person reported.

Science Efficacy: (SCIENCE). This survey was a modification of the math efficacy test designed by Betz and Hackett (1993). Various science courses (16 items) replaced items relating to math courses. The test measured the confidence of the individual in different areas of study, with scores ranging from 0 (*no confidence*), to 9 (*complete confidence*). Scores may range from a high of 135 to a low of 0, with higher scores, indicating greater confidence. The survey included one question (PSYCH) using the same scale to measure confidence in psychology-specific courses.

Biology Knowledge test: This is a 15-question test developed by the instructor to test students' knowledge of biology. Scores were ... the total number correct out of 15. Scores could range from a high of 15 to a low of 0.

Background questionnaire: This questionnaire, developed by the researchers, included questions about year in school, age, sex, ethnic background, current GPA, major, number of science courses taken in college and high school (COLSCI and HSSCI, respectively), level of preparedness for course (1—*not at all* to 10—*very prepared*), as well as whether students had taken biopsychology or cognitive psychology previously.

Procedure

On the first day of class, students enrolled in the course took a biology knowledge test. The instructor explained the study and distributed packets to those who were interested in participating. Other equivalent options to earn their course credit were given to students who did not participate (20%). The analysis did not include the knowledge test scores of non-participating students.

Packets containing the following questionnaires were distributed to students who participated: the shortened version of the Spielberger State Anxiety questionnaire (SA), the Test Anxiety inventory (TTA), the Science Attitude inventory (SAT), a background questionnaire, and the science and psychology efficacy questionnaire. Students completed the packets and returned them to the instructor within two days.

For postcomparisons, another packet of questionnaires was given at the end of the semester. On the last day of class, all members of the course completed the biology knowledge posttest.

Individuals who were not connected with the course scored questionnaires and entered all the data. Student id numbers were coded instead of names in all the questionnaires. Coded under the student identification numbers, average grades and test scores of the course were matched with final grades of the semester.

Statistical Analysis

SPSS completed all the analyses. One-way ANOVA analyzed comparisons between groups. Repeated measures ANOVA compared pre and post data, including the state anxiety measures, knowledge test, and attitude toward science. Spearman correlation coefficients calculated correlations, and simple regression methods provided all the regression analysis. Calculations also yielded means and standard deviations. All missing data were either ignored or if part of a questionnaire, averaged across the other responses in the questionnaire. The analysis did not include

the score, if more than 10% of the data was missing within a questionnaire.

Scores on tests, test average, and overall average grade in the course defined performance. The regression analysis used test average as the dependent variable because overall grade in the course included some variables that were subjective in nature.

RESULTS

Sample Description

The majority of our sample was women (64.2%), senior year (59.5%) and Caucasians (67.6%). The rest of the sample included 14.2% Hispanics, 7.4% Asians, followed by 9.4% who listed themselves as other. Psychology majors were the majority of participants with 89.9%. Only 14.9% of the participants stated they had taken a similar course before. The average age of the sample was 21.25 years of age.

The sample reported an overall GPA of 3.12 ($SD = 0.46$) and an average number of science courses taken during college as 4.59 as compared to 3.97 for high school. On a scale of 1–10 (*most prepared*), the sample reported they felt moderately prepared ($M = 6.21$, $SD = 2.04$) for the course. Of the sample, 14.9% stated that they have taken a similar course before.

Anxiety levels for the course were relatively low ($M = 13.21$, $SD = 4.18$) at the beginning of the course and significantly increased by the end of the course to 15.31 ($SD = 5.48$), [$F(1, 88) = 167.17$, $p < .007$]. Attitude toward science scores started out fairly negative ($M = 132.02$, $SD = 21.99$) and became significantly more positive by the end of the semester ($M = 118.25$, $SD = 19.76$), [$F(1, 76) = 40.07$, $p < .00001$].

Knowledge of the course material significantly improved over time from a pretest score of 8.48 ($SD = 2.12$) to a post-test score of 11.61 ($SD = 1.87$), [$F(1, 88) = 158.04$, $p < .0001$]. Finally, efficacy scores for psychology were fairly high whereas scores for science were relatively low ($M = 7.73$, $SD = 2.10$) and ($M = 42.08$, $SD = 14.49$) respectively.

Correlation

Table 2 shows the correlations between variables. Test average was significantly correlated with all of the variables measured with the exception of number of high school science courses, psychology efficacy, anxiety levels (both pre and post), and negative attitude subscale scores.

Regression Analysis

The dependent variable entered in the analysis was test average. A simple regression analysis was implemented to enter the variables GPA, pretest scores, science efficacy, how prepared for the course, test anxiety, state anxiety, and science attitude scores. The results showed an R square of 0.55; $F(8, 72) = 9.85$, $p < .0001$. GPA (Beta = .66, $p < .0001$) and SAT (Beta = −.16, $p < .06$) were significant predictors of test average. No other significant factors were found.

TABLE 1   Frequency Data of Sample Description Variables

Variable	Percentage
Gender	
Male	34.50
Female	64.20
Race*	
Caucasian	67.60
Hispanic	14.20
Asian	7.40
Other	9.50
Year in School*	
Senior	59.50
Junior	32.40
Sophomore	7.40
Major*	
Psychology	89.90
Biology	2.00
Other	6.20
Taken Course Before	
Yes	14.90
No	84.50

* = Data missing from sample

Sex Differences

Few significant sex differences were reported in the current study, as shown in Table 3. Women reported feeling less prepared for the course, had lower scores on the pretest and more negative attitudes about science both before and after the course. However, although not statistically significant, women did perform better in the course compared to men.

Racial Differences

Because our sample contained such a small percentage of other races with the exception of Caucasian, one group included all individuals who identified themselves as non-Caucasian. ANOVA showed that only efficacy levels for the field of psychology differed between groups with non-Caucasians reporting higher levels of efficacy than Caucasians ($M = 8.31$, $SD = 1.29$) and ($M = 7.54$, $SD = 2.24$) respectively; $F(1, 139) = 4.51$, $p < .03$).

Major vs. Nonmajors

Of the entire sample, only 12 people reported being a major other than psychology. As shown on Table 3, statistically significant differences were found on a number of variables across these groups. Non-majors believed they were more prepared for the course, [$F(1,141) = 6.62$, $p < .01$] reported taking more science courses in college; [$F(1, 143) = 11.28$, $p < .001$] had higher posttest scores, [$F(1,87) = 6.06$, $p < .021$] higher post-anxiety scores, [$F(1,87) = 16.95$, $p < .0001$]. and started with more positive attitudes toward science (NegSAT = $F(1,132) = 24.48$, $p < .0001$; SAT = $F(1,128) = 3.93$, $p < .05$). Non-majors also had significantly different post-positive science attitude scores, [$F(1,85) = 16.35$, $p < .0001$]. Although not significant, the trend of the data was a higher average for the course for non-majors.

In addition, comparisons between those who had previously taken the course with those who had not taken such a course, showed no differences across any of the variables.

DISCUSSION

Data from our study show that GPA and attitude about science were the best predictors of performance. Those students with better GPAs and a more positive attitude about science did better in the course. As seen in previous studies, these variables are related to performance across a variety of courses (Culler & Holahan, 1980; Germann, 1994; Papanastasiou & Zembylas, 2004; Thomas &

TABLE 2   Spearman Correlation Coefficients and N in Parentheses

	GPA	ColSci	Prepared	Pre Test	Post Test	Efficacy	Test Anx	Pre SAT
Test Avg	0.61 (116)**	.18 (120)*	.25 (118)*	.25 (117)*	.48 (109)**	.27 (111)**	−.18 (120)**	−.24 (106)*
Grade	.58 (116)**	.21 (120)*	.21 (118)*	.19 (117)*	.48 (109)**	.30 (111)**	−0.21 (111)**	−.19 (106)

* p < .05

** p < .001

ColSci—number of college science courses

Prepared—how prepared for the course   Test Anx—Test Anxiety Inventory

Efficacy—score on science efficacy scale   PreSat—scores of science attitude before the course

TABLE 3   Means and Standard Deviations across Gender and Choice of Major

	Prepared	Pre-Test	Post-Test	Pre SAT	Post SAT	NEG SAT	POS SAT	Grade
Male	6.67 (1.64)	9.27 (2.13)	11.86 (1.58)	143.90 (19.22)	132.97 (23.14)	21.21 (3.29)	14.00 (3.2)	77.92 (8.28)
Female	5.94 (2.23)*	8.07 (2.03)*	11.57 (1.93)	126.44 (21.14)*	117.15 (18.06)	20.31 (4.36)	13.83 (3.5)	80.54 (7.09)
Major	6.12 (2.03)	8.51 (2.05)	11.45 (1.88)	133.04 (21.96)	119.42 (20.30)	21.13 (3.61)	14.00 (3.4)	78.94 (7.59)
Non Major	7.67 (1.37)*	9.00 (2.59)	13.12 (0.99)*	119.45 (18.90)	108.50 (10.83)	15.27 (5.25)*	12.25 (2.5)	81.27 (10.6)

$p < .05$

SAT = science attitude questionnaire

NEG = negative and POS = Positive

Schwenz, 1998; Wolf & Smith, 1995). Furthermore, course performance in biopsychology was related to several other variables such as level of perceived preparedness, science efficacy, test anxiety, and prior knowledge of material. Therefore, students who came into the course feeling better about their ability to do well in the course, as well as those who had some basic knowledge of the course material, were at an advantage to do better in the class.

Demographically, sex differences in attitudes toward science were consistent with previous research (Czerniak & Chiarelott, 1984; Kahle & Lakes, 1983). Interestingly, although women scored higher on the negative attitudes subscale, they did perform slightly better in the course than men. However, these differences in performance were not statistically significant and may reflect the larger number of female participants in the current study. Moreover, race did not seem to be a factor in performance. Although not reported in this study, performance and grade point average disparities across race have been consistently reaffirmed through a number of research studies (NCES, 2000). One explanation for the discrepancy in our data may be due to the small number of non-Caucasian [participants], prohibiting a meaningful analysis. The combining of groups labeled non-Caucasian was necessary to increase numbers in this group but may have eliminated any existing differences in a specific racial group.

Unlike the demographic variables, choice of major seemed to be important. There were many disparities reported when comparing psychology majors with non-majors. Non-majors reported taking more science courses, feeling more prepared and having a better attitude toward the sciences. In addition, although not statistically significant, they earned higher grades in the course than psychology majors. However, these results should be interpreted carefully, particularly in view of the fact that many psychology majors may have underreported the number of college science courses they had previously taken, neglecting

to consider psychology courses as a science, and very few non-majors participated. Future studies should examine performance and attitude levels in a broader population of students, including more men and individuals of color. Finally, the results may not generalize to other science or psychology courses but may be specific to this area of psychology and this course in particular.

In summary, our results point to the importance of addressing attitudes and knowledge for students to perform better in the biopsychology course. By focusing our efforts early on providing a better background for subjects related to biopsychology and giving extra help for those students with lower GPAs, we may impart an adequate foundation to perform better in science-based coursework. Additionally, by focusing on students' beliefs about their abilities and their preparedness for the course, we may help students to come in with more positive feelings about the course in general. Many unforeseen benefits may follow from addressing these key factors that influence science performance. For example, at the end of the twentieth century, one-third of all science and engineering Ph.D.-holders working in U.S. industry were foreign born (NSF, 2002). Growing political debates about the importing of talent from other countries have raised the issue of the need for more qualified workers within the United States. Future studies need to address possible programs that can increase interest and perceived efficacy for science and math-related careers to help fill the gap in the current employment market.

References

Betz, N. E., & Hackett, G. (1993). *Mathematics Self-Efficacy Scale.* Palo Alto, CA: Mind Garden.

Brand, D. L. (1995). Those students who could have but didn't—Early attrition from college science. *Research & Teaching,* 180–183.

Brownlow, S., Jacobi, T., & Rogers, M. (2000). Science anxiety as a function of gender and experience. *Journal of Science Education and Technology, 42,* 119–131.

Business Coalition for Education Reform. (2002). "What happened to first in the world?" *The Formula for Success.* Retrieved August 9, 2004, from http://www.bcer.org/timss/p5.cfm

Culler, R. E., & Holahan, C. J. (1980). Test anxiety and academic performance: The effects of study-related behaviors. *Journal of Educational Psychology, 72,* 16–20.

Czerniak, C. & Chiarelott, L. (1984*). Science anxiety: An investigation of science achievement, sex and grade level factors.* ERIC: No. ED 243 672.

Everson, H. T., Tobias, S., Hartman, H., & Gourgey, A. (1993). *Test anxiety and the curriculum: The subject matters.* ERIC: No. ED 366 598.

Geary, D. C. (1996). International differences in mathematical achievement: Their nature, causes, and consequences. *Current Directions in Psychological Science, 5,* 133–137.

Germann, P. J. (1994). Testing a model of science process skills acquisition: An interaction with parents' education, preferred language, gender, science attitude, cognitive development, academic ability, and biology knowledge. *Journal of Research in Science Teaching, 31,* 749–783.

Higher Education Research Institute. (2002). Freshman intending to major in selected S&E fields, by race/ethnicity: 1971–2000. *University of California at Los Angeles.* Retrieved July 15, 2004, from http://www.cnc.ac.cn/gb/others/ nsf/200201/pdf/c02.pdf

Johnson, M. A., & Lawson, A. E. (1998). What are the relative effects of reasoning ability and prior knowledge on biology achievement in expository and inquiry classes? *Journal of Research in Science Teaching, 35,* 89–103.

Kahle, J. B. & Lakes, M. K. (1983). The myth of equality in science classrooms. *Journal of Research in Science Teaching, 20,* 131–140.

Marteau, T. M. & Bekker, H. (1992). The development of a six-item short-form of the state scale of the Spielberger State-Trait Anxiety Inventory (STAI). *British Journal of Clinical Psychology, 31,* 301–306.

Moore, R. W. & Foy, R. L. (1997). The Scientific Attitude Inventory: A Revision (SAIII). *Journal of Research in Science Teaching, 34,* 327–336.

National Center for Education Statistics. (2001a). Bachelor's degrees conferred by degree-granting institutions, by racial/ethnic group, major field of study, and sex of student: 1999–2000. *United States Department of Education, National Center System.* Retrieved July 15, 2004, from http://nces.ed.gov/programs/ digest/d01/dt269.asp

National Center for Education Statistics. (2001b). Statistical profile of persons receiving doctor's degrees in the life sciences: 1979–80 to 1998–99. *United States Department of Education, Integrated Postsecondary Education Data System.* Retrieved July 15, 2004, from http://nces.ed.gov/programs/digest/d01/dt306.asp

National Center for Education Statistics. (2002). Comparative indicators of education in the United States and other G-8 countries. *United States Department of Education.* Retrieved July 15, 2004, from http://nces.ed.gov/pubs2003/2003026.pdf

National Center for Education Statistics, High School Transcript Study. (2000). Mean grade point average of high school graduates, by course subject: 1990, 1994, 1998, and 2000. *United States Department of Education, Institution of Education Sciences.* Retrieved October 7, 2004, from http://nces.ed.gov/nationsreportcard/hsts/results/gpa.asp

Papanastasiou, E. C., & Zembylas, M. (2004). Differential effects of science attitudes and science achievement in Australia, Cyprus, and the USA. *International Journal of Science Education, 26,* 259–280.

Paulman, R. G., & Kennelly, K. J. (1984). Test anxiety and ineffective test taking: Different names, same construct? *Journal of Educational Psychology, 76,* 279–288.

Science & Engineering Indicators (2002). Foreign-born scientists and engineers in the U.S. workforce. *National Science Foundation.* Retrieved November 30, 2004, from http://www.nsf.gov/sbe/srs/seind02/pdf/overview.pdf

Spielberger, C. D. (1980). *Test Anxiety Inventory.* Palo Alto, CA: Mind Garden, Inc.

Spielberger, C. D. (1983). *State-Trait Anxiety Inventory.* Palo Alto, CA: Mind Garden, Inc.

Thomas, P. L., & Schwenz, R. W. (1998). College physical chemistry students' conceptions of equilibrium and fundamental thermodynamics. *Journal of Research in Science Teaching, 35,* 1151–1160.

Tobias, S. (1979). Anxiety research in educational psychology. *Journal of Educational Psychology, 71,* 573–582.

Tobias, S. (1985). Test anxiety: Interference, defective skills, and cognitive capacity. *Educational Psychologist, 20,* 135–142.

Wigfield, A., & Eccles, J. S. (1989). Test anxiety in elementary and secondary school students. *Educational Psychologist, 24,* 159–183.

Wittmaier, B. C. (1972). Test anxiety and study habits. *Journal of Educational Research, 65,* 352–354.

Wolf, L. F., & Smith, J. K. (1995). The consequence of consequence: Motivation, anxiety, and test performance. *Applied Measurement in Education, 8,* 227–242.

Zohar, D. (1998). An addictive model of test anxiety: Role of exam-specific expectations. *Journal of Educational Psychology, 90,* 330–340.

chapter 13

Experimental Research

IMPORTANT *Ideas*

1. Educational fads probably would be less prevalent if rigorous experiments testing their effectiveness were required before putting them into practice.

2. The essential feature of an experiment is an intervention by the researchers or collaborators in a particular setting.

3. Experiments typically have four phases: (1) the formation of experimental and control groups, (2) an initial administration of a measure of the outcome variable, (3) the imposition of different conditions on the two groups for a period of time, and (4) a second administration of a measure of the outcome variable.

4. The introduction of a report of an experiment should state its importance, purposes, and variables, as well as including a review of relevant literature.

5. A pretest–posttest control-group experiment with randomization has three features: (1) at least two groups with each one receiving different interventions or one receiving no intervention, (2) random assignment of individuals in the sample to the different intervention or no-intervention conditions, and (3) administration of one or more pretests and posttests.

6. In a pretest–posttest control-group experiment, it is possible for both the experimental intervention and other variables to have a causal influence on the outcome variables.

7. If the experimental data satisfy certain conditions, statistical adjustments (e.g., analysis of covariance) can be made to control for preexisting differences between the experimental and control groups on pretest measures.

8. Of the various quantitative research designs, experiments have the strongest implications for practice, especially if they are conducted in a real-life setting.

9. If random assignment is not possible, a quasi-experiment is a viable option, especially if the experimental and control groups can be matched on critical variables that might affect the posttest variables.

10. Factorial experiments enable researchers to determine whether each of several independent variables has an effect on the dependent variable and also whether a particular independent variable has an effect only under certain conditions.

11. An experiment is internally valid to the extent that extraneous factors can be ruled out as possible causes of observed differences between the experimental and control groups on an outcome variable.

12. The extraneous factors commonly considered to be threats to the internal validity of an experiment in education are history, maturation, testing,

instrumentation, statistical regression, differential selection, selection–maturation interaction, and experimental mortality.

13. The soundness of an experiment is compromised if treatment fidelity departs from the researchers' specifications for each treatment condition or if the treatment lacks sufficient potency.

14. An experiment is externally valid to the extent that the results of an experiment can be generalized to other individuals, settings, and time periods.

15. Single-case experiments involve the application of an intervention to a single individual or a few individuals, whereas group experiments involve the application of an intervention to a substantial sample of individuals or groups.

16. Typical features of a single-case experiment are baseline and treatment conditions, behavior analysis, focus on low-incidence populations, a detailed description of each research participant, repeated administration of one measure, and graphical presentation of data. ■

Key TERMS

A-B-A-B research design	extraneous variable	pretest–posttest control-group experiment with randomization
A-B-A research design	factor	
attrition	factorial experiment	quasi-experiment
baseline condition	group experiment	random assignment
behavior analysis	history effect	reversal phase
behavior modification	independent variable	selection–maturation interaction effect
control condition	instrumentation effect	
dependent variable	interaction effect	single-case experiment
differential-selection effect	internal validity	statistical regression
ecological validity	maturation effect	testing effect
experiment	multiple-baseline research design	treatment condition
experimental condition	population validity	treatment fidelity
experimental mortality	posttest	What Works Clearinghouse
external validity	pretest	

The Relevance of Experimental Research to Educational Practice

Richard Snow, an educational researcher, once described educational innovations as a "garden of panaceas" (Fletcher, Tobias, & Wisher, 2007). Others see educational innovations as fads that come and go. When an innovation is brought into a school district, veteran teachers have been heard to say, "We tried this before and it didn't work. Why are we trying it again?"

Among the innovations currently in vogue are the conversion of a large school into small schools on the same campus, new computer hardware and instructional software, brain-based teaching and learning, teaching to students' different learning styles, charter schools and voucher systems, and summer school and special tutoring for students who are failing to make adequate progress. Each of these innovations has its advocates but also its critics. Even if one takes hold here or there, there is little assurance that it will become institutionalized and improve education over the long term.

What can we do to solve the problem of faddism in educational practice? From a research perspective, two steps are necessary. First, we must support rigorous experiments to determine whether the claims for a particular innovation are valid. Second, we must determine the necessary "buy-ins," pitfalls, and unintended side-effects when moving from experimentation to full-scale implementation and adoption by educators.

In this chapter, we consider what counts as a rigorous experiment. In the chapter on program evaluation (Chapter 20), we consider how researchers go about determining what needs to happen for a particular innovation to become part of the complex world of education practice.

Rigorous experiments in education have now entered the realm of federal policy. In 2005, the U.S. Department of Education issued new regulations that give priority to researchers who propose to conduct rigorous experiments (Glenn, 2005). The **What Works Clearinghouse** was instituted in 2002 by the federal government (see Chapter 5) to highlight innovative programs whose effectiveness has been demonstrated by rigorous experiments.

Of course, experimental evidence alone is not sufficient to improve practice. Educators' advocacy, visionary leadership, clinical skills, and ability to secure financial resources are equally essential. However, in the absence of empirical evidence, these professional skills, even if well-intentioned, can lead down fruitless paths.

Characteristics of Experiments

An **experiment** is an empirical study in which researchers manipulate one variable (e.g., a teaching technique) to determine its effect on another variable (e.g., students' on-task behavior in class). If the experiment is well done, the researchers can conclude that the first variable caused or did not cause a change in the second variable. No other type of quantitative research design (descriptive, correlational, or causal-comparative) is as powerful in demonstrating causal relationships among variables as an experiment.

The essential feature of experiments, as described in the previous paragraph, is manipulation. Experimenters enter a situation and change (i.e., manipulate) some parts of it either themselves or through collaborators. The collaborators might be specially trained research assistants or professional educators.

Another way of describing experimental manipulation is to say that the researcher introduces an intervention into a situation. For example, the researcher might intervene in classroom teachers' regular instruction—with their permission, of course—by having them use an experimental curriculum or teaching method.

Interventions sometimes are called *conditions, experimental conditions, treatment conditions,* or *independent variables* in research reports. For example, the research report might state that the participants were assigned to different experimental conditions. Each **experimental condition** is a situation where a group of research participants receives an intervention to determine its effect on the dependent variable. One of the conditions might be a **control condition,** which is a situation where a group of research participants receives no intervention or an alternative intervention, against whose performance the experimental group's performance is compared.

Group comparison and correlational research do not rely on interventions but rather on naturally occurring variations. For example, some classes have fewer students than others, not because of a researcher's intervention, but because of school policy, scheduling procedures, or other factors. Researchers have discovered that these variations in class size are correlated with student academic achievement; students generally learn more in small classes.

This finding, while intriguing, does not prove that if we reduce class size in a school district, student learning will necessarily improve. Other classroom features might be associated with smaller class size (e.g., more experienced teachers might have priority assignment to smaller classes), and these might be the actual features that cause improvement in student learning.

In an experiment, however, researchers do not rely on naturally occurring variations; instead, they manipulate the situation. In our example, they might make one group of classes smaller while keeping another group of classes at their current size. Moreover, they would try to hold all other factors constant between the two groups of students. Thus, they can attribute any observed differences in student learning to this intervention. Educators then can have confidence that if they manipulate their own situation in the same manner, they will be likely to observe the same effects that the researchers observed.

Phases of an Experiment

After research participants have been selected, an experiment typically involves four phases:

1. A sample of research participants is randomly assigned to either the experimental group or the control group. **Random assignment** means that each participant has an equal chance of being in either group. Thus, previously existing group differences are unlikely to be the cause of observed differences in the outcome variable. For example, if the sample includes a certain percentage of males, random assignment makes it likely that a similar percentage of males will be in the experimental and control groups.

2. Both groups are administered a measure, usually called a **pretest,** which is the same as that administered in phase 4 (the *posttest*). The pretest is a measure that is used to determine whether the experimental and control groups are similar on the variable that the intervention is designed to affect, and it also can be readministered at the conclusion of the intervention to determine the amount of change created by the intervention relative to the control condition.

3. The experimental group is exposed to an intervention, whereas the control group either receives an alternative intervention or no intervention.

4. The experimental and control groups are compared with respect to their scores on the measured variable that the experiment is designed to affect. This variable is called the **dependent variable** (sometimes called the *criterion variable* or *outcome variable*), because participants' scores on a measure of this variable are presumed to be dependent on the intervention introduced by the researchers. The dependent variable is measured by a **posttest,** which is a measure that is administered at the conclusion of the intervention and that is typically the same measure as the pretest.

The majority of this chapter, starting with the next section, is about **group experiments,** that is, experiments that involve samples of research participants, typically 10 or more participants in each experimental condition. In the last part of this chapter, we consider single-case experiments, which involve an intervention with a single research participant or a few participants.

Examples of Experimental Research

The following studies illustrate the relevance of experimental research to problems of practice. In each study, we identify the randomization procedure and the independent and dependent variables.

Effects of Different Class Sizes

Finn, J. D., & Achilles, C. M. (1990). Answers and questions about class size: A statewide experiment. *American Educational Research Journal, 27*(3), 557–577.

One of the most important experiments in education in the past 20 years involved class size (the independent variable). The rigorously designed, large-scale experiment was conducted in actual classrooms. Funded by the Tennessee legislature and commonly known as Project STAR (Student/Teacher Achievement Ratio), this experiment since its publication has served as a model for other experiments funded at the federal and state levels.

Primary school students were randomly assigned to three experimental conditions: (1) one certified teacher and more than 20 students; (2) supplemented classes (one certified teacher, a full-time noncertified teacher's aide, and a class of more than 20 students); and (3) small classes (one certified teacher and approximately 15 students). The students stayed in their assigned condition for up to 4 years—from kindergarten through third grade. Because new students enter a school each year, some students stayed in their experimental condition for 4 years, while students entering later were in their experimental condition for 1, 2, or 3 years.

The dependent variables were achievement in reading, word study, and mathematics, measured at the end of each school year by the Stanford Achievement Test.

Biddle and Berliner (2002) summarized findings for the dependent variable of reading achievement in a graph, shown in Figure 13.1. If you examine the figure, you will see that children in small classes made greater gains in reading achievement than children in the other experimental conditions at each grade level. For example, kindergartners in small classes were half a month ahead of children in large classes by the end of the school year. After 4 years of small classes, the children were 7.1 months ahead of children in large classes.

Another finding shown in Figure 13.1 is that length of time in small classes makes a difference in reading achievement. For example, students who were in small classes for only 2 years (i.e., students who entered the experimental condition in second grade) were 3.3 months ahead in reading achievement, relative to students in large classes, at the end of

FIGURE *13.1*   Average Months of Grade-Equivalent Advantage in Reading Achievement Scores for Students in Small Classes

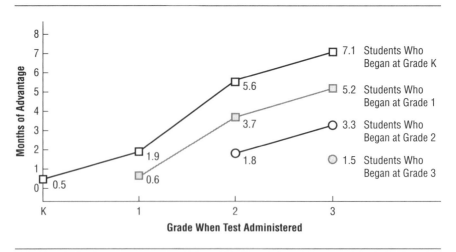

Source: Figure 1 on p. 17 of Biddle, B. J., & Berliner, D. C. (2002). Small class size and its effects. *Educational Leadership, 59*(5), 12–23.

third grade. However, their classmates who had experienced small classes since kindergarten were 7.1 months ahead.

Follow-up research was done to determine the academic achievement of children in the experimental group when they entered standard-sized classes after the end of the third grade, which was the conclusion of the experimental intervention. The follow-up studies indicated that these students had greater academic achievement than other students all the way through high school.

As we stated earlier in the chapter, experimental findings do not necessarily lead directly to improvement in educational practice. Although reduction of class size is demonstrably effective, it is also very expensive. Smaller classes require more teachers and more classrooms, both of which are very costly. It is necessary, then, for policy makers and the general public to weigh costs against benefits and the value they ascribe to those benefits.

Effects of Different Types of History Textbooks

> Harniss, M. K., Caros, J., & Gersten, R. (2007). Impact of the design of U.S. history textbooks on content acquisition and academic engagement of special education students: An experimental investigation. *Journal of Learning Disabilities, 40*(2), 100–110.

The researchers examined U.S. history textbooks and found that they fail to present history as a series of related events and actions and to make these relationships explicit. They identified an experimental textbook that was developed to overcome these failings.

To test the effectiveness of the experimental textbook, they randomly assigned two groups of middle school students (all but one in the eighth grade) who were in special education classrooms or who were identified as low performing to two conditions. The treatment condition consisted of 20 weeks of instruction using the experimental textbook. The control condition consisted of 20 weeks of instruction using a nationally distributed textbook published by Harcourt Brace Jovanovich Holt.

The experiment included administration of measures on a range of student outcome variables: a test that measured mastery of content in both textbooks, a set of items drawn from the National Assessment of Educational Progress, weekly tests of vocabulary terms covered in the textbooks, a test of oral reading fluency, observation of on-task behavior, and ratings of accuracy in answering teachers' questions during instruction. The researchers also measured a set of dependent variables relating to teachers' instructional and classroom-management practices.

The major findings of the experiment were that students who used the experimental textbook earned higher scores on several of the history content tests, demonstrated more on-task behavior, and answered more questions correctly than students who used the conventional history textbook.

This experiment has practical significance, because it demonstrates that the design of textbooks affects student learning. In the case of history textbooks, the findings suggest that explicit statements about the relationships among different historical events and actions facilitates learning for special education students and perhaps for other students as well.

Effects of Different Types of Teacher Education

> Glazerman, S., Mayer, D., & Decker, P. (2006). Alternative routes to teaching: The impacts of Teach for America on student achievement and other outcomes. *Journal of Policy Analysis and Management, 25*(1), 75–96.

Teach for America (TFA) was founded in 1989 to increase the number of teachers available to fill positions in schools that serve predominantly disadvantaged, largely minority populations. TFA recruits receive five weeks of intensive training in education during the summer and then fill regular teaching positions in schools. In contrast, most new teachers receive 1 to 4 years of coursework and field experience before they fill such positions.

Critics of TFA have questioned whether TFA recruits, even though they have strong academic backgrounds, can be as effective as graduates of standard teacher education programs. The researchers conducted an experiment to determine the validity of this criticism.

It was impossible for the researchers to randomly assign individuals to enter the TFA program or a standard teacher education program. Instead, they selected TFA graduates and compared them with non-TFA teachers who taught similar students in similar environments. They were able to ensure similarity by randomly assigning students to classrooms taught by TFA and non-TFA teachers. The students were in grades 1 to 5.

The primary dependent variables were reading and math achievement. Other dependent variables concerned teacher characteristics (e.g., career expectations and professional-development experiences) and student behavior (e.g., disciplinary incidents and retention in grade).

The major findings of the experiment were that students of TFA teachers had higher math achievement than students of non-TFA teachers. Students of TFA and non-TFA teachers had equivalent reading achievement and did not differ in school behavior.

These findings do not support the criticism that TFA teachers are less qualified than graduates of standard teacher education programs. Rather, according to the researchers, the findings support TFA and offer a policy alternative for low-income communities: "From the perspective of a community or a school faced with the opportunity to hire TFA teachers, the findings of this study suggest that TFA offers an appealing pool of candidates" (Glazerman et al., 2006, p. 95).

Features of a Report of a Pretest–Posttest Control-Group Experiment with Randomization

Table 13.1 presents the typical features in a report of an experimental study. In the following sections, we discuss each feature and illustrate it with an experiment involving a program that was designed to teach life skills and drug-avoidance skills to middle school students. The experiment was conducted by Marvin Eisen, Gail Zellman, and David Murray (2003).

Of the various available experimental designs, this study employed the experimental design most respected by researchers. This respect is based on the design's effective controls for threats to the internal validity of an experiment, which are described later in the chapter.

Introduction

The introductory section of a report of an experiment should demonstrate the importance of the experiment, its specific purposes, and the major variables of interest. It also should include a literature review, so that the reader understands how the experiment is likely to make a contribution to research knowledge.

Our example experiment (Eisen et al., 2003) satisfied strong evidence standards, as specified by the What Works Clearinghouse (http://ies.ed.gov/ncee/wwc/references/standards). The researchers started their report by noting the seriousness of substance abuse among teenagers. For example, they cited research findings that 15 percent of eighth-graders had smoked cigarettes and 14 percent had engaged in binge drinking during the month before they were surveyed. They also noted that several substance abuse prevention programs for middle school students have been developed but have not been demonstrated as effective. The purpose of their experiment was to evaluate the effectiveness of another program, Skills

TABLE *13*.1   Typical Features of an Experimental Research Report

Feature	Experimental Research
Introduction	Hypotheses, questions, or objectives are stated. A review of relevant literature is reported. The purpose of the study is to institute an experimental program or other intervention and determine its effects, typically in comparison to one or more control conditions.
Research design	Typically, each research participant is assigned to an experimental condition or a control condition. When possible, the assignment procedure is done randomly so that each participant has an equal chance to be in either condition. Pretests (also called baseline measures or independent variables) typically are administered to determine the participants' status prior to initiation of the experimental and control conditions. Posttests (also called outcome measures, criterion measures, or dependent variables) are administered at the conclusion of the experimental program or other intervention.
Sampling procedure	The researcher selects a sample of research participants who are appropriate candidates to participate in the experimental program or other condition.
Measures	Virtually any kind of measure can be used to collect data on the independent and dependent variables.
Data analysis	Descriptive statistics for the pretest and posttest measures are calculated. The size and statistical significance of the differences between the experimental and control groups on the posttests are determined by analysis of variance or multiple regression. Differences between the groups on the pretest measures are often controlled by analysis of covariance or multiple regression.
Discussion	The main findings of the study are summarized. Flaws and limitations of the study are considered. Implications of the findings for further research and for professional practice are considered.

for Adolescence (SFA), which more than 50,000 trained teachers and other school personnel had used by the end of the 1990s.

Research Design

The key features of a **pretest–posttest control-group experiment with randomization** are contained in its name. You might come across this term in a research report or alternative terms such as *randomized field trial* or *true experiment*.

Inclusion of a Control Group.   The study that we are describing was a control-group experiment because it included at least two groups of research participants, the group receiving the intervention of primary interest and a control group that received another kind of intervention (or none at all). Another possible arrangement might have one group receive the full program while another group receives a scaled-down version of the program and still another group continues with its usual activities.

In the experiment on substance abuse prevention, the experimental group participated in the SFA program. According to the researchers, this program includes processes that "utilize social influence and social cognitive approaches to teach cognitive-behavioral skills for building self-esteem and personal responsibility, communicating effectively, making better decisions, resisting social influences and asserting rights, and increasing drug use knowledge and consequences" (Eisen et al., 2003, p. 887). Students in the control condition received drug education, the elements of which were generally left to the discretion of their teachers and school administrators.

Random Assignment of Research Participants.   The second feature of this experimental design is that the research participants are randomly assigned to the experimental and control conditions. Random assignment should not be confused with random selection, which involves procedures to ensure that all individuals in a defined population have an equal chance of being selected for participation in the research study.

Various procedures can be used to achieve random assignment. For example, we make a list of the names of all the research participants. Then we pick an arbitrary starting point in a table of random numbers. The first listed participant is assigned the starting number, the second participant is assigned the random number just below it, and so on. Then we place the list of names in numerical order using the random numbers assigned to each name. Finally, we assign the first name in the list to, let's say, the experimental condition. We assign the second name to the control condition, the third name to the experimental condition, and so on.

Random assignment does not guarantee that the experimental and control conditions will be equivalent in all possible ways. For example, it is possible, by chance, that a substantially higher percentage of males will wind up in one condition or the other. This is especially possible if the total pool of research participants is small. Randomization only ensures that there is no systematic bias in the assignment of participants to the experimental and control groups. If the randomization procedure results in a substantial disparity between groups on an important variable, the researcher should consider repeating the randomization procedure.

In the case of the SFA experiment, middle schools in 4 of the 10 largest metropolitan areas in the United States were recruited. Those that agreed to the conditions of the experiment were randomly assigned to the experimental and control conditions. Thus, teachers in each school used either the SFA program or their regular substance abuse prevention program.

Administration of Pretests and Posttests.   The third feature of this experimental design is the administration of at least one pretest and one posttest to the participants in the experimental and control conditions. This important feature enables researchers to determine the extent of change or gain created by the experimental condition compared to the control condition.

Scores on the pretest measure also can be used to make a statistical adjustment that equalizes, to a degree, the experimental and control groups on that measure, even though their mean scores are different. If the statistical adjustment works, any observed difference between the two groups on the posttest measure can be attributed to the experimental intervention rather than to preexisting differences on the pretest measure. This statistical adjustment is typically accomplished by analysis of covariance (see Chapter 9) or multiple regression (see Chapter 12).

Variables measured by pretests are considered independent variables because they measure individual characteristics (e.g., academic achievement, attitudes, self-esteem) that exist prior to the beginning of the experimental and control conditions. Variables measured by posttests are considered dependent variables, because they measure individual characteristics following the conclusion of the experimental and control conditions.

In terms of cause and effect, the experimental intervention and control conditions are the causes, and the posttest variables are the effects. Pretest variables also might be causes of these effects. For example, students who score high on a pretest measure of reading are likely to score high on a posttest using the same measure, no matter whether they are in the treatment or control condition.

Sampling Procedure

As with any research design, researchers should select a sample that is representative of the population to which they wish to generalize their results. The researchers who conducted the SFA experiment reported, "Teenage drug usage remains a serious problem in the US, despite efforts by policymakers, health officials, educators, and prevention scientists to reduce it" (p. 884). The prevalence of drug use in this population justifies the researchers' decision to select a sample consisting of teenagers, specifically seventh-graders at the time that they participated in the SFA program or control condition.

The researchers needed to obtain active parental consent for their children to participate in the experiment. Consent was obtained for 71 percent of the students in the participating schools.

The pretests were administered while the sample group was in the sixth grade. The experimental and control conditions occurred during the seventh grade, and a first set of posttests was administered at the end of this grade. Another publication reported the effects of the SFA program on this set of posttests (Eisen, Zellman, Massett, & Murray, 2002). The posttests were readministered at the end of eighth grade to determine the persistence of SFA effects one year later. These are the posttests that we are describing in this section of the chapter.

As one might expect, attrition in the sample occurred from the time of the sixth-grade pretests to the end-of-eighth-grade posttests. The sample that took the eighth-grade posttests included 87 percent of those students who completed the seventh-grade posttests.

Measures

The pretests and posttests used in any experimental design can include any of the measurement methods described in Chapter 6—tests, questionnaires, interviews, and direct observation. In the substance abuse prevention experiment, the pretests and posttests consisted of questionnaires. English and Spanish versions were created, and students could choose the version they preferred to complete. The primary variables measured by the questionnaires were self-reported use of alcohol, cigarettes, marijuana, cocaine/crack, and any other illicit drug during their lifetime and over the 30-day period prior to completing the questionnaire.

In addition, students completed questionnaire items that measured other variables: intent to use drugs in the next three months, beliefs about drug abuse by their friends and peer group, beliefs about whether drug use would make it easier to fit in with others, perceptions concerning harmful effects of drugs, sense of self-efficacy about refusing drugs in various situations, perceived parent monitoring of their whereabouts after school, propensity for sensation seeking, and various demographic characteristics such as gender, family composition, and race/ethnicity.

Results

Analysis of variance (see Chapter 9) can be used to analyze experimental data. In analysis of variance, the two posttest means are compared to determine whether the posttest mean of the experimental condition is significantly greater or less than the posttest mean of the control group.

Analysis of covariance (see Chapter 9) also is used frequently. This statistical technique determines whether the posttest means differ significantly from each other, after adjusting for possible differences in the pretest means of the two groups.

Multiple regression is another method for analyzing experimental data (see Chapter 12). In the substance abuse prevention experiment, the experimental condition (SFA versus the school's regular substance abuse prevention program) constitutes one variable. It is a dichotomous variable because it has only two values: each participating school is coded as SFA or non-SFA. SFA can be given a value of 1, and non-SFA can be given a value of 0, or vice-versa.

Another variable in the correlational analysis is the sample's posttest scores on each posttest measure. If SFA is coded as 1 and non-SFA is coded as 0, a positive correlation coefficient would mean that the students who participated in the SFA program had a higher posttest mean than students who participated in their school's regular substance abuse prevention program. Additional variables (e.g., pretest variables) can be examined to determine whether they predict the sample's posttest scores either independently or in relation to other variables that have been entered into the multiple-regression equation.

Our explanation of analysis of variance, analysis of covariance, and multiple regression simplifies their use in experiments. Understanding how they actually work requires extensive study of statistics. If you have not yet engaged in such studies, you can still learn a lot about the results of an experiment simply by examining the researchers' presentation of descriptive statistics, typically the means and standard deviations.

Eisen and his colleagues (2003) analyzed their data primarily by comparing the percentage of students in the SFA group and control group who engaged in substance use. They adjusted these percentages to account for group differences in substance use prior to the SFA program. The differences were generally small; for example, 22.85 percent of the SFA group drank alcohol over a 30-day period, compared to 23.18 percent of the control group; 11.32 percent of the SFA group smoked marijuana over a 30-day period, compared to 13.79 percent of the control group.

Another finding is that substance use increased significantly from the time the students were in the sixth grade to the time that they were in the eighth grade. For example, the researchers found that 3.5 percent of the combined groups smoked cigarettes over a 30-day period in the sixth grade, but 12.47 percent of the SFA group and 11.48 percent of the control group smoked cigarettes over a 30-day period when they were surveyed in the eighth grade.

One other statistically significant difference was reported by the researchers. They found that, among students who reported being binge drinkers on the pretest questionnaire, a lower percentage (27 percent) of students who had participated in the SFA program reported binge drinking on the posttest questionnaire than students who had participated in their school's regular substance abuse prevention program (37 percent). For students who did not report binge drinking on the pretest, there was no difference in the percentage who reported binge drinking on the posttest (SFA group = 12 percent; control group = 12 percent).

Discussion: Implications for Practice

The discussion section of an experimental research report typically includes a summary of the main findings and an analysis of the study's limitations. Among the limitations described by the researchers who conducted the substance abuse prevention experiment, they noted: "Those students whose parents failed to return the consent form or denied consent cannot be assumed to be the same as those students with more compliant parents" (Eisen et al., 2003, p. 896). This is a legitimate concern because, as we indicated in the section on sampling above, only 71 percent of the parent sample gave consent.

The researchers' report provides various explanations for nonreturn of the parent consent form, such as a student not giving the form to a parent or a parent not being available to read and sign the form. These explanations, among others, suggest that the students who did not return the form have different characteristics than those who did, and these characteristics might have made them more, or less, receptive to the SFA substance abuse prevention program.

Of the various quantitative research designs, experiments typically have the most implications for practice, particularly if they yield positive results for students, educators, or other groups. The reason is that the researchers actually intervened in a situation and improved it. It seems likely then that educators might obtain similar benefits if they replicated the procedures used by the researchers in their own settings. The likelihood of replication of benefits is increased if the experiment was conducted in a real-life setting (e.g., a school) rather than in a laboratory-like situation.

The researchers who conducted the SFA experiment made the following claim based on their findings: "To our knowledge, these results provide the first tangible evidence that elements of a commercially available and widely used prevention program can delay regular marijuana use and reduce binge drinking among early onset drinkers for at least a 1-year post intervention period" (Eisen et al., 2003, p. 896).

Our own speculation is that the SFA program would have been even more beneficial for teenagers if it were extended over several years, rather than being used as a 1-year intervention in the seventh grade. Of course, this remains only a speculation until tested by more experiments.

Other Group Experiment Designs

A pretest–posttest control-group experiment with randomization, as described above, is almost always the preferred experimental design. Other experimental designs are available for special purposes or because of constraints imposed by administrators in the setting where the experiment will be conducted.

Table 13.2 lists experimental designs from which researchers typically choose when planning an experiment. Two of them will be discussed in the following sections. Other designs not listed in the table generally are extensions of them. The most common extension is the incorporation of additional comparison groups into the experimental design. For example, the experimental substance abuse education program was conducted while the students were in seventh grade; the control program was the school's regular substance abuse prevention program. This design could have been extended, let's say, by including an experimental condition in which some of the students participated in the experimental program in the seventh grade and received additional education about substance abuse in the eighth grade. The statistical analysis, then, would have involved comparison of the posttest means for three groups, not two.

Quasi-Experiments

Randomization is fairly easy to achieve under laboratory-like conditions. For example, many experiments about learning processes are conducted with college students, often students enrolled in psychology or education classes. They are asked to come to a special room (a "laboratory" of sorts) and participate in the experimental condition to which they have been randomly assigned. The intervention typically lasts less than an hour. Students might receive grade points or another reward for their participation.

Experiments in real-life school settings (often called *field settings*), especially if they are of extended duration, place many more demands on school personnel. Random assignment of students or classrooms to different experimental conditions can be disruptive to regular school routines. For this reason, school personnel and parents might refuse to consent to this requirement.

The alternatives left to the researchers are either to abandon the experiment or to design it without randomization. If the experimental program or intervention seems promising, it does not make sense to abandon efforts to test its effectiveness. Therefore, researchers choose the other option, a **quasi-experiment,** which is an experiment with experimental and control groups but without random assignment of participants to these groups. This label has negative connotations, but in fact, a quasi-experiment can yield much useful knowledge if steps are taken to make the groups as equivalent as possible when they are selected for participation in the experiment.

The customary procedure is for the researchers to work together with school personnel to select schools and teachers where the experimental program or intervention can be tried. For example, in the substance abuse education experiment, the researchers could search for schools willing to try the SFA program. Once those schools are identified, the researchers and school personnel can form a control group by identifying other schools with characteristics similar to those of the experimental-condition schools. This procedure provides some assurance that any observed differences between the experimental and control group on the posttest are due to the experimental program, not to preexisting differences in the characteristics of concern to the researchers.

Factorial Experimental Designs

In experiments, the term **factor** has the same meaning as the term **independent variable.** Each factor is viewed as an independent variable that exists prior to the dependent variable measured by the posttest and therefore possibly having a causal influence on that variable. The term **factorial experiment** is used to refer to an experiment having more than one factor (i.e., independent variable).

TABLE *13.2*   Types of Experimental Designs

Type of Experimental Design	Comments
Single-Group Designs	
One-shot case study X O	Weakest design. No way to determine amount of change resulting from the intervention.
One-group pretest–posttest design O X O	Weak design. Can be used as an exploratory experiment, particularly if researchers can estimate expected pretest–posttest change in the research participants if they had not received the experimental intervention.
Control-Group Designs	
Pretest–posttest control-group design with randomization R O X O R O Y O	Strong design. The substance abuse education experiment described in this chapter is an example.
Pretest–posttest control-group design without randomization O X O O Y O	Moderately strong design. Sometimes called a quasi-experiment. Because random assignment is lacking, it can be difficult to determine whether differences in pretest–posttest change are due to the experimental condition or to initial differences between the groups.
Posttest-only control-group design with randomization R X O R Y O	Moderately strong design. Its use is recommended when there is reason to believe that administration of a pretest would raise the possibility that posttest differences could be attributed, in whole or in part, to the pretest rather than solely to the experimental intervention.
Posttest-only control-group design without randomization X O Y O	Very weak design. Change from pretest to posttest cannot be determined because no pretest is administered, and it is not possible to determine whether differences on the posttest are due to the experimental intervention or initial differences between the groups.
Factorial Designs	
Two-factor experiments R O X_1 Y_1 O R O X_1 Y_2 O R O X_2 Y_1 O R O X_2 Y_2 O	Strong design. Its purpose is to determine the simultaneous effects of several interventions or participant characteristics on pretest–posttest change. The two-factor design can be extended to include three or more factors.

R = research participants are randomly assigned to the experimental or control condition
O = observation, either a pretest or posttest
X = experimental condition
Y = control or comparison condition

In the substance abuse prevention experiment, teachers, counselors, and other school personnel delivered the SFA program. Suppose we hypothesized that counselors might make the best program instructors because of their specialized training in students' emotional and behavioral problems. To test this hypothesis, we could design an experiment with two factors: type of program and type of instructor, as depicted in the following table:

TYPE OF INSTRUCTOR	TYPE OF PROGRAM	
	SFA Program	School's Regular Program
Teachers	Cell 1	Cell 2
Counselors	Cell 3	Cell 4

You can see that the experimental program has four cells, each of which includes a different program and type of instructor. If we had 40 participating teachers, we could randomly assign them to cells 1 and 2, and if we had 40 participating counselors, we could randomly assign them to cells 3 and 4.

We can use analysis of variance or analysis of covariance to address several questions about the data resulting from this factorial design. First, we can determine whether one type of instructor produces better student outcomes (i.e., less substance abuse at the end of eighth grade) than the other, irrespective of which program they taught. Second, we can determine whether one program produces better student outcomes than the other, irrespective of who taught it.

Third, we can look for program by instructor interactions. An **interaction effect** means that an independent variable has an effect on the dependent variable, but only under certain conditions in the experimental design. For example, it might be that counselors are more effective than teachers for the SFA program, but that counselors and teachers are equally effective when delivering the school's regular program. If we obtained this finding, we would say that an interaction effect occurred.

The factorial design that we are describing has two factors. It also is possible to create experimental designs with three or more factors.

Threats to the Internal Validity of Experiments

Program adoption decisions increasingly are made on the basis of evidence from experiments. Therefore, educators need to understand how to determine whether the evidence is sound. In particular, educators need to be able to judge whether the observed results were caused by the experimental intervention or by one or more extraneous factors.

An **extraneous variable** is a factor other than the treatment variable that might have an effect on the outcome variables. If extraneous variables are present, the researchers will find it difficult to determine the extent to which an observed difference between the experimental and control groups on the dependent variable is caused by the intervention or by one or more extraneous variables.

For example, suppose that, by chance, a higher percentage of male students are in the school's regular program than in the SFA (Skills for Adolescence) program. Suppose, too, that male students have a higher rate of substance abuse than female students.

Now suppose we find that the students in the SFA program have better results on the outcome variables than students in the schools' regular substance abuse prevention program. One explanation for this finding is that the SFA program is more effective. Another explanation, equally plausible, is that the SFA program was not more effective, but it produced better outcomes because it had fewer male participants than the regular substance abuse prevention program. The extraneous variable of gender has made it difficult, if not impossible, to determine the actual impact of the SFA program on the outcome variables.

Ideally, an experiment would have no extraneous factors. Such an experiment would be said to have high **internal validity,** meaning that observed differences between experimental groups on an outcome variable are solely attributable to the treatment variable. If an experiment has low internal validity, it means that observed differences between experimental groups on an outcome variable can be attributed to the treatment variable or to extraneous factors.

Donald Campbell and Julian Stanley (1963) identified eight types of extraneous variables that can affect the internal validity of experiments. Other extraneous variables have been identified, but these eight extraneous variables reflect common challenges to researchers in designing and conducting experiments.

History Effect

If an experimental intervention extends over a substantial period of time, this creates an opportunity for other events to have an effect on the outcome variables. If these other events influence the outcome variables, researchers say that a **history effect** occurred.

In the substance abuse education experiment, the SFA program lasted for a substantial part of sixth grade. During this time and the follow-up period (students were not given the posttest until the end of eighth grade), many other events could have occurred to affect students' substance abuse. However, the experiment included a randomly assigned control group, which presumably would have experienced similar events.

The statistical analysis compared the experimental group relative to the control group, so observed posttest differences would reflect the SFA program's effectiveness over and above the effects of history. Thus, history can be ruled out as an extraneous variable.

Maturation Effect

While an experimental treatment is in progress, certain developmental processes occur in the research participants. For example, participants become older and therefore might experience increased physical fitness, optimism, or some other emotional or physical change, all of which are forms of maturation as defined by Campbell and Stanley. If these developmental changes affect the outcome variables in an experiment, researchers say that a **maturation effect** occurred.

In the experiment we have been analyzing, the SFA program was compared to a randomly formed control group, which had equal time for maturation. Thus, the extraneous variable of maturation was controlled.

Testing Effect

In many educational experiments, a pretest is administered, followed by the treatment and control conditions, concluding with a posttest. If the pretest and posttest are similar or are administered close together in time, research participants might show an improvement on the posttest simply as a result of their experience with the pretest. In other words, they have become test wise.

If repeated administration of a test affects the outcome variable, researchers say that a **testing effect** has occurred. It is unlikely that this extraneous variable was operating in the substance abuse education experiment, because the interval between the pretest and posttest was nearly two years.

Instrumentation Effect

An apparent learning gain from the pretest to the posttest might occur if a different measure was used each time. For example, suppose the pretest in the substance abuse prevention experiment involved interview questions, and the posttest involved the same questions but in a questionnaire format. This procedure would make it nearly impossible to determine whether observed pretest–posttest differences in the experimental group and control group were due to the intervention or to the change in testing procedure. If changes in the measuring instrument affect the results of an experiment, researchers say that an **instrumentation effect** has occurred.

Statistical Regression

Whenever a pretest–posttest procedure is used to assess learning in an experiment, the individuals scoring very high or very low on the pretest will tend to have scores somewhat closer to the mean on the posttest. This phenomenon is known as **statistical regression.**

For example, suppose that the average pretest score of students in the experimental group was at the 15th percentile on national norms for the test. When this group of students take the test again (i.e., the posttest), they are likely to earn a higher mean score, with or without any intervening experimental treatment. The cause of this phenomenon is that the students' low initial score likely results not only from lower ability, but also from chance factors. Perhaps they were feeling ill on the day of the test, or they made unlucky guesses on some test items.

On retesting, these chance factors are unlikely to be present again. Consequently, their test scores will improve independently of the effect of the experimental intervention. Similarly, due to chance factors, when students with very high scores on the pretest are retested, their scores also are likely to regress, that is, move downward towards the mean.

The possibility of statistical regression needs to be considered if all, or most, of the research participants are very high or very low on a key variable in the experiment. For example, an experiment involving highly talented youth might be susceptible to statistical regression on a pretest–posttest measure of achievement. This problem can be avoided if the pretest and posttest are sufficiently difficult that the majority of the research participants do not earn very high scores on them.

Differential Selection

In quasi-experiments, described previously, participants are selected for the experimental and control groups by a procedure other than random assignment. Because the participants in the two groups have been differentially selected, the groups might have different initial characteristics that affect the posttest variable.

If the different initial characteristics of the selected groups affect the outcome variables, researchers say that a **differential-selection effect** has occurred. The presence of this effect makes it difficult to determine the extent to which observed differences between the experimental and control groups on the posttest are caused by the experimental intervention or by differences in the groups' initial characteristics. This problem can be avoided, to a certain extent, by efforts to select control-group participants who are similar to the experimental-group participants on crucial initial characteristics.

Selection–Maturation Interaction

This extraneous variable is similar to differential selection, except that maturation is the specific confounding variable. Suppose that first-grade students from a single school district are selected to receive instruction in a new reading program, whereas the control group is drawn from the population of first-grade students in another school district. Because of different admissions policies in the two school districts, the mean age of students in the control group is 6 months higher than the mean age of students in the experimental group.

Suppose we find that the experimental group made significantly greater achievement gains than the control group. Do these results reflect the greater effectiveness of the experimental treatment or the effects of maturation? Due to differential selection of students into the experimental and control groups, the researchers would not be able to answer this question with any confidence. This situation is called a **selection–maturation interaction effect,** because the experimental and control groups contain participants who are at different developmental levels.

Experimental Mortality

Experimental mortality, more commonly called **attrition,** involves the loss of research participants over the course of the experimental treatment. Attrition can make it difficult to interpret the data if the participants who drop out in the experimental group and control group have different characteristics.

For example, analysis of attrition data in the substance abuse prevention experiment indicated that 37 percent of the students who reported in the pretest questionnaire that they had used marijuana recently failed to complete the eighth-grade posttest questionnaire. In contrast, only 23 percent of the students who did not report using marijuana recently failed to complete this questionnaire. Because of this differential attrition, we cannot be certain of the effectiveness of the SFA program relative to the control condition in helping students avoid marijuana one year after completing the program.

Threats Directly Involving the Experimental Intervention

Educators know that different teachers often implement the same curriculum differently. The essentials of the curriculum might be present in all teachers' classrooms, but some teachers might place more emphasis on certain topics, and other teachers might include topics not in the curriculum. In an experiment, however, all participants need to implement the experimental program as it was designed. Otherwise, the program might be found to be ineffective simply because it was implemented haphazardly. If so, the program might be added to the list of failed innovations, even though it actually might be effective if implemented as intended by its developers. Research reports should include information about this feature of experiments, which is called **treatment fidelity,** defined as the extent to which the experimental intervention is implemented according to the specifications of the researchers or program developers.

In the substance abuse education experiment, the SFA program included 40 sessions, each lasting 35 to 45 minutes. However, the experimenters found variations among teachers in the actual number of sessions that they conducted. The mean number of sessions, based on teacher self-report, was 32.74. Because treatment fidelity relating to this aspect of the experimental program was substantially less than perfect, this departure from the program specifications possibly could have weakened the program's effectiveness.

Another threat relating to experimental programs is the potency of the intervention. A program might be strong or weak in various dimensions, such as duration, intensity, quality of instructional design, and skill of the individuals delivering the program. In medicine, for example, researchers often need to experiment with the proper dosage of a new drug. The drug might be effective, but not if too little or too much is administered or if it is administered for too brief a period of time.

In the substance abuse education experiment, the teachers who delivered the SFA program attended a three-day workshop conducted by certified SFA trainers. Was this a sufficient amount of training? This question was not addressed in the report. However, the fact that program effects on the posttest were found suggests that the amount of training was at least minimally adequate.

Looking at the posttest results from Eisen and his colleagues (2003), we find that the SFA students had better outcomes than the control-group students on several of the variables. However, in our view, the rates of substance abuse in both groups are alarming. It seems that a much stronger program than that tested in the researchers' experiment would be needed to substantially lower the rates of substance use or bring them to a "zero tolerance" level.

Threats to the External Validity of Experiments

Experiments often are expensive to conduct, and therefore the experimental intervention is limited to a relatively small sample in one setting within a limited time frame. If the intervention proves to be effective, though, educators will want to know whether it will work as well in other settings with other individuals. In researchers' terminology, this is a matter of external validity. Experiments have **external validity** to the extent to which their results can be generalized to other individuals, settings, and time periods. Bracht and Glass (1968) ana-lyzed experiments and concluded that they are vulnerable to three external-validity threats: population validity, personological variables, and ecological validity.

Population Validity

In Chapter 6, we defined **population validity** as the degree to which the results of a re-search study can be generalized from the specific sample that was studied to the population from which the sample was drawn. To determine population validity, one must assess the degree of similarity among the research sample that was used in the study, the accessible population from which the research sample was drawn, and the larger target population to which the research results are to be generalized.

The more evidence the researcher provides to establish links between the sample, the accessible population, and the target population, the more confident you can be in gener-alizing the research findings to the target population. The lack of such evidence acts as a threat to the external validity of the experiment.

Educators usually are not as interested in the similarity between the research sample and the target population as in the similarity between the research sample and the indi-viduals in their local setting. To determine this type of similarity, educators should note all relevant information in the research report about the sample, such as age, gender, academic aptitude, ethnicity, socioeconomic status, and the characteristics of the communities in which they live. They can compare the resulting profile with information about the local setting to which they wish to apply the research findings.

Personological Variables

Another factor affecting external validity is the possibility that various personal character-istics of the research sample interact with the experimental intervention. An interaction is present if the experimental results apply to research participants with certain characteristics (e.g., those who have low test anxiety) but not to those with other characteristics (e.g., those who have high test anxiety). If this type of interaction is thought to be likely and important, a factorial experiment (described previously in this chapter) can be conducted to verify its existence and magnitude.

If an experiment has high external validity, the results of the experiment should ap-ply to all kinds of individuals, not just to individuals having a particular characteristic. Of course, if researchers can establish that the results do apply to a population having this characteristic, we can say that the experiment has external validity for that population.

Ecological Validity

Ecological validity is the degree to which an experimental result can be generalized to set-tings other than the one that was studied. It depends on the extent to which the situational conditions that were present during the experiment are similar to the conditions that exist in the setting to which you wish to apply the results. The larger the difference between the experimental setting and the local setting of interest to you, the less confidence you can have that the results of the experiment will apply to it.

Single-Case Experiments

A **single-case experiment** (also called a *single-subject experiment*) is a research study in which the effects of an intervention on a dependent variable are determined by applying that intervention to a single individual. Researchers favor single-case experiments over group experiments when they wish to observe the effects of interventions on specific behaviors and skills of individuals.

Using a single-case experimental design, for example, researchers can diagnose a dyslexic student's reading problem, devise an individualized strategy to solve it, and rigorously test the effectiveness of the strategy through repeated phases of data collection. No matter how uncommon the individual's characteristic, a single-case experiment will permit investigation of the research problem.

Some researchers perceive the single-case experiment as a watered-down version of one of the group-experiment designs presented earlier in this chapter. In fact, single-case experiments are rigorous and time-consuming, and often they involve as much data collection as a design involving experimental and control groups. Furthermore, researchers who conduct single-case experiments are just as concerned about issues of internal and external validity as researchers who conduct group experiments.

The treatment condition in a single-case experiment often involves some form of behavior analysis and behavior modification. **Behavior analysis** involves careful observation of an individual in a setting, determination of dysfunctional behaviors in that setting, and specification of desired behaviors. **Behavior modification** involves techniques such as reinforcement, modeling, and discrimination training to increase or decrease the frequency of specified behaviors.

The purpose of single-case experiments in these situations is to determine whether a particular type of behavior analysis and behavior modification is effective for individuals with a certain type of problem. Therefore, single-case experiments have direct implications for the improvement of professional practice. The titles of the following journal articles illustrate the range of problems that single-case experiments can address:

Didden, R., Korzilius, H., van Oorsouw, W., & Sturmey, P. (2006). Behavioral treatment of challenging behaviors in individuals with mild mental retardation: Meta-analysis of single-subject research. *American Journal on Mental Deficiency, 111*(4), 290–298.

Onslow, M. (2004). Ryan's programmed therapy for stuttering in children and adults. *Journal of Fluency Disorders, 29*(4), 351–360.

Powers, S. W., Piazza-Waggoner, C., Jones, J. S., Ferguson, K. S., Daines, C., & Acton, J. D. (2006). Examining clinical trial results with single-subject analysis: An example involving behavioral and nutrition treatment for young children with cystic fibrosis. *Journal of Pediatric Psychology, 31*(6), 574–581.

Schaefer, J. E. (2002). The effects of peer-buddies on increased initiation of social interaction of a middle school student with Down syndrome and her typical peers. *Down Syndrome Quarterly, 7*(3), 1–8.

In the next sections, we illustrate the features of a single-case experiment by Linda Mechling, David Gast, and Beth Cronin (2006) involving an intervention to improve the task performance of two middle school students with a diagnosis of moderate mental retardation and autism spectrum disorder (ASD).

Although an increasing number of children are being diagnosed as autistic, its incidence in the population is low. Therefore, it would be difficult to form a research sample of sufficient size for one of the group-experiment designs described in the first part of the chapter. A single-case experiment is much more feasible. Moreover, the intervention was designed to change specific behaviors, as determined by a careful behavioral analysis of autistic students' needs. Single-case experiments are particularly appropriate for the study of specific behaviors and their amenability to change.

Features of a Report of a Single-Case Experiment

Table 13.3 presents typical features of a report of a single-case experiment. We describe each of these features in the following sections.

TABLE *13.3* Typical Features of a Research Report for a Single-Case Experiment

Feature	Experimental Research
Introduction	Hypotheses, questions, or objectives are stated. A review of relevant literature is reported. The purpose of the study is to institute an experimental program or other intervention and determine its effects, typically in comparison to one or more control conditions.
Research design	Typically, the research design includes several phases. One or more phases are baseline conditions in which the intervention is absent, and one or more phases are treatment conditions in which the intervention is present.
Sampling procedure	The researchers select one or a few research participants who have a particular problem. The problem typically has behavioral manifestations and a low incidence in the general population.
Measures	The measure typically is an observational scale for counting the frequency of one or more specific behaviors. Trained observers fill out the scale at several fixed intervals during each phase (baseline and treatment) during the course of the experiment.
Data analysis	The usual analysis is to place each bit of observational data on a graph. The y axis of a typical graph represents the frequency of a specific behavior, and the x axis represents the points in time that the behavior was observed.
Discussion	The main findings of the study are summarized. Flaws and limitations of the study are considered. Implications of the findings for further research and for professional practice are considered.

Introduction

The introductory section of the report should demonstrate the significance of the single-case experiment, its specific purposes, and the major variables of interest. It also should include a literature review, so that the reader understands how the present study makes a contribution to research knowledge.

In the autism experiment, the researchers reviewed research findings on the kinds of reinforcers that are effective for autistic children. (*Reinforcer* is a technical term in behavioral theory, similar in meaning to *reward.*) They found that these children like stimuli that are not of interest to nonautistic children and that they like to have choices of rewards. However, their review also discovered that specific reinforcers may lose their effectiveness over time and also that some reinforcers for autistic children are not readily available.

On the basis of this research knowledge, Mechling and her colleagues formulated the purpose for their experiment: "Faced with the need to (a) provide reinforcers to motivate children with ASD and (b) prevent satiation through the use of novel or different stimuli, the current study evaluated the use of video technology as an alternative means for providing choice and access to high-preference items to increase motivation" (p. 8).

Research Design

Single-case experiments can vary in design, but all share two elements: a baseline condition and a treatment condition. A **baseline condition** is the set of typical conditions under which the research participant behaves; it usually is designated as "A." A **treatment condition** is the set of conditions that represent the experimental intervention; it usually is designated as "B." Thus, in an **A-B-A research design,** the experiment includes an initial period of time during which the research participant is observed under typical conditions; next follows the experimental intervention and observation of the research participant under those conditions. Finally, there is a period of time in which the research participant is once again observed under typical conditions.

The autism experiment involved an **A-B-A-B research design.** This design is similar to the A-B-A design just described, except that it involves one more phase, namely reinstatement of the experimental intervention. If the intervention is effective, we would expect to see

- the desired change in the research participant's behavior occur after the intervention (B) is introduced
- a return of the research participant's behavior to its original state (A) after the intervention is stopped
- the desired change in the research participant's behavior recur after the intervention (B) is once again introduced

The A-B-A-B design has strong internal validity, because it includes a **reversal phase,** which involves a second A condition to demonstrate active control of the target behavior by removing the intervention that is hypothesized to have caused the initial change (the initial B condition). Reinstatement of the treatment (the second B condition) provides additional evidence of the intervention effect.

Some behaviors might not reasonably be expected to revert to their original state after the intervention is removed. Also, there might be ethical prohibitions about reinstating the conditions that existed prior to the intervention. For example, suppose a researcher wished to evaluate a counseling intervention designed to reduce a research participant's anxiety level. If the participant's anxiety level lowered during the course of the intervention, the researcher could not ethically withdraw the successful intervention in order to observe whether the client's anxiety level returned to its pretreatment level.

In these situations, researchers would use a **multiple-baseline research design,** which involves using situations other than the naturally occurring condition as a control for determining the presence of intervention effects. For example, the researcher might select three different behaviors that the intervention is hypothesized to improve. If the intervention is applied to the first behavior and it improves while the other two behaviors remain unchanged, this is evidence that the intervention has an effect not attributable to other factors.

The next step is to apply the intervention to the second behavior. If this behavior improves and the third behavior does not, this is more evidence that the intervention is having an effect. Finally, the intervention is applied to the third behavior, and if it too improves, this finding adds to the weight of evidence supporting the effectiveness of the intervention.

In the autism experiment, the two participating students (Donald and Jackson) completed their usual independent work sessions, which were scheduled one or two times per day for 30 minutes each. The work session included three learning tasks, such as reading simple directions, answering "wh-" questions from a story, and using a written menu to order food. Upon completion of their learning tasks, the students had 10 minutes to engage with a preselected reinforcing material or activity.

In the baseline condition (A), the students spent their 10 minutes with one of two reinforcers selected by the teacher. (In the journal article, they are called "tangible reinforcers.") These reinforcers had been previously chosen by the students as their most preferred stimuli. For Donald, the two reinforcers were Dr. Seuss books and sitting inside a tent. For Jackson, they were a pinball game and listening to music.

In the treatment condition (B), the reinforcers were more varied but all involved viewing minute-long computer-based videos. Some of the videos showed the student (Donald or Jackson) interacting with one or the other of his previously chosen preferred stimuli. Others showed the student interacting with a preferred stimulus not available in the classroom setting. For Donald, the preferred stimuli were holiday scenes in the community and expressions of familiar adults. For Jackson, the preferred stimuli were community choirs and his own participation singing in a choir.

During the 10-minute reinforcement period, the student was shown three photos on the computer screen, each representing a preferred stimulus. The student chose one of the photos and then viewed the corresponding 1-minute video. This process was repeated nine more times during the reinforcement period, with an equal number of opportunities to choose each photo.

Sampling Procedure

Single-case experiments typically test the effectiveness of interventions that will be delivered individually to persons with special needs that have a low population incidence (e.g., autism). Therefore, random selection of a sample from a defined population, while a powerful sampling method, is seldom possible.

Instead, the researcher typically prepares a detailed description of each research participant's characteristics, so that educators can decide whether the students whom they are trying to help have similar characteristics. Also, the researcher might replicate the research design with several similar individuals to determine whether the intervention effects recur. If the replication is successful, this finding should increase educators' confidence that the intervention will be effective with students who are similar to those who participated in the experiment.

In the report of the autism experiment, Mechling and her colleagues included two research participants, each of whom completed the experiment independently of the other. Also, they provided a detailed description of each participant. Among other findings, we learn that one of them, Jackson, age 13 years 2 months at the time of the experiment, was diagnosed with autism at age 6 by a professional psychologist and that he was found to have mild mental retardation based on two assessment measures. The other student, Donald, age 14 years 4 months, was diagnosed with autism at age 4 by a licensed psychologist and was found to have moderate mental retardation based on two assessment measures. In addition to providing this information, the researchers described the students' intellectual capabilities and learning needs in some detail.

Measures

Single-case experiments generally do not have pretests and posttests, as is typical of group experiments. Instead, one measure is administered repeatedly to determine whether performance on the measure changes from one condition (baseline or treatment) to another. Most often, the measurement is based on direct observation of the frequency or duration of the behavior that is targeted for change. If the target variable is a learning outcome, a brief test that can be administered repeatedly will be used. If the target variable is an emotional state such as anxiety, a paper-and-pencil scale that measures different levels of the emotional state can be administered.

In the autism experiment, the target behavior was the amount of time that it took Daniel and Jackson to complete the three learning tasks in a work session, which was designed to last approximately 30 minutes. An observer recorded the duration of work sessions in the baseline and treatment conditions.

The observational data would be invalid, of course, if the observer did not record duration times accurately. Therefore, the observer's measurements were checked for reliability by videotaping a third of the work sessions. An independent observer viewed the tapes and recorded work-session durations. This observer's data were found to be highly similar to the data collected by the person who directly observed the two students' behavior.

Results

The results of the autism experiment are shown in Figure 13.2, a form of graphical representation that is standard in reports of single-case experiments. Figure 13.2 contains two graphs, one for each student. The dotted vertical lines in each graph indicate the transition point from one condition (baseline or treatment) to the other. Each data point is the number of minutes that it took for Donald or Jackson to complete all the learning tasks in a work session.

FIGURE *13.2*   Time to Complete Three Tasks across Conditions

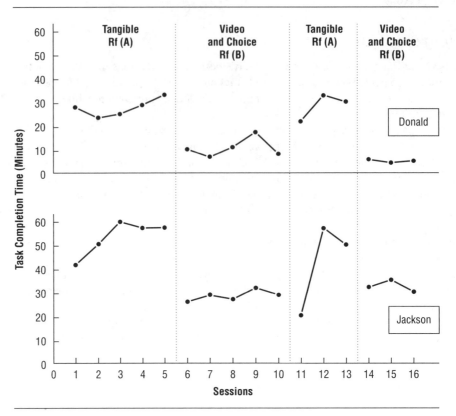

Note: Rf = reinforcement

Source: Figure 1 on p. 11 of Mechling, L. C., Gast, D. L., & Cronin, B. A. (2006). The effects of presenting high-performance items, paired with choice, via computer-based video programming on task completion of students with autism. *Focus on Autism and Other Developmental Disabilities, 21*(1), 7–13. Copyright © 2006 by Sage Publications. Reprinted by permission of Sage Publications.

Inspection of each graph shows clearly that both of them completed their tasks in much less time when their reinforcer consisted of an opportunity to choose a video and then to watch it. The use of a tangible reinforcer was much less effective.

As we explained in our discussion of group experiments, various factors can threaten the validity of causal interpretations made on the basis of experimental results. In the case of the autism experiment, we need to consider the possibility that a factor other than the video-and-choice reinforcer caused Donald and Jackson to complete their learning tasks much more quickly.

The A-B-A-B design used in the experiment and the results shown in Figure 13.2 provide a strong basis for ruling out other factors as possible causal agents. If the availability of a reinforcer, regardless of type, was the causal agent, the duration of the work sessions would be relatively constant across the baseline and treatment conditions. Figure 13.2 rules out this explanation, because the data points vary dramatically across the two conditions.

The timing of the baseline and treatment conditions provides another possible interpretation of cause and effect. The video-and-choice condition came after the tangible reinforcer condition, so one could argue that, by the time it ended, the students had become familiar with the observer and the work session procedures; therefore, they executed the tasks more quickly in the next condition (video and choice).

However, the A-B-A-B design includes two more conditions. When the tangible reinforcer was reintroduced, the students' duration time increased once again. This result rules out familiarity with the observer and procedure as causes of the observed effects.

Descriptive statistics can be computed for data generated in a single-case experiment. For example, the researchers reported that Donald's mean task-completion time across sessions for the first baseline condition (tangible reinforcers) was 27.8 minutes, and the mean task-completion time across sessions for the first video-and-choice condition was 11 minutes. These descriptive statistics are helpful supplements to the information gained from visual inspection of the graphs.

Discussion: Implications for Practice

The discussion section of a report of a single-case experiment typically includes a summary of the main findings, analysis of the study's limitations, and recommendations for further research. For example, in the autism experiment, Mechling and her colleagues noted that the tangible reinforcement condition did not allow the students to choose a reinforcer whereas the video reinforcement condition did. Therefore, we do not know whether it was the (1) opportunity to make choices, (2) viewing of videos, or (3) combination of choice and videos that produced superior results relative to the tangible reinforcement condition. The researchers recommended further research to determine which of these three possibilities made the video reinforcement condition an effective intervention.

Researchers also use the discussion section to consider implications of their findings for professional practice. In the autism experiment, for example, the researchers stated that "results of the current study indicate that providing students the opportunity to view high-preference items and activities via video technology may be a viable means of providing novel, meaningful, and highly preferred stimuli that can function as positive reinforcement" (Mechling et al., 2006, p. 12).

The discovery of this "viable" procedure is likely to be welcomed by parents and teachers of autistic children. It is one more method that they can try out as they strive to promote the learning of this special and increasingly prevalent population. Furthermore, the findings might stimulate the development of new techniques for other groups, including students in the regular school population, so that they, too, learn more effectively.

Evaluating an Experimental Research Study

The criteria stated in Appendix 2 are relevant to evaluating an experimental research study. The following additional criteria, stated in question-and-answer format, can help you judge whether a group experiment was weakened by specific problems that can arise in descriptive research. These criteria are explained in the chapter, so we only mention them briefly here.

- Did the researchers randomly assign the sample to the experimental and control conditions?

  Check the report to determine how the researchers assigned the sample to the different conditions. Randomization procedures do not necessarily result in similar groups, so check whether the researchers compared the randomly assigned groups on demographic variables and other relevant variables. If randomization procedures were not used, it is especially important to check whether the researchers compared the groups to determine how similar they were to each other.

- Did the researchers check for threats to the internal and external validity of the experiment?

  Check the report to determine whether the internal validity of the experiment was subject to any of the eight threats described in the chapter. Similarly, check for any of the three threats to the external validity of an experiment described in the chapter.

- Did the research participants follow the researchers' specifications for the experimental intervention or control conditions?

  Check the report to determine whether the researchers collected data to determine how well the research participants adhered to the intervention or control conditions.

- Was the intervention sufficiently strong?

  Make a judgment about how strong the intervention would need to be in order to have an effect on the dependent variables in the experiment. Then check the report to determine whether the strength of the intervention is consistent with your judgment.

Single-case experiments can also be evaluated by the criteria stated in Appendix 2. In addition, consider the additional criteria stated here.

- Did the experiment contain sufficient data points?

  The dependent variable should have been measured sufficiently often that you can see a clear trend during each of the intervention and control conditions. You can check whether the trends are clear and convincing by examining the graphs that typically are included in reports of this type of research.

- Did the experiment include a control condition?

  Check the report to determine whether the control condition provided an appropriate contrast to the experimental condition. The results for the two conditions should be sufficiently different to convince you that the experimental intervention actually had an effect. If there was an effect, make a judgment about whether it was substantially better than any effect produced by the control condition.

An example of
HOW EXPERIMENTAL RESEARCH CAN HELP IN SOLVING PROBLEMS OF PRACTICE

Educators, publishers, and entrepreneurs are constantly developing new methods to improve student learning. For example, the newspaper *Washington Post* had a news item about an innovative service recently developed by MetaMetrics. The service assigns each student a number, called a Lexile, which corresponds to the student's achievement level on a state's standards-based reading test. Teachers and parents can enter a student's Lexile index into an online database that will list books at the student's reading level.

The *Washington Post* reported that Virginia's Department of Education has adopted MetaMetrics and thinks that it will help students improve their reading skills. The article includes this statement by an individual who works in this department:

"When a child reads on their current reading level, they are more apt to enjoy reading and want to read, instead of being frustrated," said Mark Allan, director of elementary instructional services for the state Department of Education.

Glod, M. (2008, November 13). Tool translates test scores into reading lists. *Washington Post.* Retrieved from www.washingtonpost.com

This educational tool looks like it should be effective, and, in fact, one state department of education has endorsed it. But does it actually work? This question probably is best answered by an experiment such as the one described next.

We first select samples of students at the same grade level who have weak, average, and strong reading skills, as determined by their Lexile score. We then randomly assign students in each of these three groups to an experimental or control group. The experimental group of students will be asked to read the first several pages of a book at their reading level, based on their Lexile score. The control group also will have the same assignment, except that their book will be at a substantially higher reading level than their Lexile score.

Each group will do their reading in a different but equally comfortable setting, with a teacher guiding them through the activity. Following a specified period of time, the students will be asked to complete (1) an attitude scale measuring how well they liked the book and (2) a test measuring their comprehension of the text that they read.

Our hypothesis is that students whose assigned book is at their Lexile score level will have a more favorable attitude toward the book and comprehend it better than students whose assigned book is above their Lexile score level. We also hypothesize that this difference between groups will be found for each of the three subgroups—students with weak, average, and strong reading skills.

If the hypothesis is supported, the experimental results will serve as evidence for use of the Lexile measure in language arts instruction. Of course, the evidence would not be definitive, because the experiment was conducted under laboratory-like conditions. However, the findings could stimulate funding agencies to sponsor larger-scale experiments in natural settings. As evidence grows for or against this educational tool, educators can make informed decisions about whether to adopt it for their school systems.

Self-Check Test

1. Unlike group comparison and correlational research designs, experiments
   a. rely on observations under naturally occurring conditions.
   b. study naturally occurring changes in an experimental group and control group.
   c. introduce an intervention into a laboratory or real-life situation.
   d. have few implications for the improvement of educational practice.

2. The pretest–posttest control-group experiment with randomization
   a. is easy to conduct but has weak internal validity.
   b. is not considered as effective as a quasi-experiment.
   c. is generally regarded as the most powerful of the experimental designs.
   d. uses randomization procedures to select research participants from a defined population.

3. In a pretest–posttest control-group experiment with randomization,
   a. the variable measured by the pretest is the only independent variable.
   b. the variable measured by the pretest is the dependent variable.
   c. the variables measured by the pretest and the experimental intervention are independent variables.
   d. the experimental intervention is the dependent variable.

4. The statistical significance of group differences found in a pretest–posttest control-group experiment with randomization can be determined by
   a. analysis of variance.
   b. analysis of covariance.
   c. multiple regression.
   d. All of the above.

5. A quasi-experimental research design does not include
   a. random assignment of research participants to the experimental and control conditions.
   b. pretests.
   c. posttests.
   d. manipulation of the independent variable.

6. Statistical regression is likely to occur if
   a. the pretest and posttest are administered close together in time.
   b. the research participants score very high or low on the pretest.
   c. the pretest and posttest involve the use of different measuring instruments.
   d. All of the above.

7. An experiment has treatment fidelity if
   a. the experimental treatment is not affected by personal characteristics of the research participants.
   b. the research participants for the experimental and control groups are selected by the same procedure.
   c. the experimental treatment controls for all the extraneous variables to which experiments are susceptible.
   d. the experimental treatment is implemented according to its developers' specifications.

8. All of the following are threats to the external validity of experiments except
   a. lack of population validity.
   b. lack of ecological validity.
   c. selection–maturation interactions.
   d. interactions between personal characteristics of the research sample and the experimental intervention.

9. The baseline condition in a single-case experiment
   a. is the set of typical conditions under which a research participant behaves.
   b. is the set of conditions represented by the experimental intervention.
   c. is not required if an A-B-A-B design is used.
   d. has the same purpose as random assignment of research participants in a group experiment.

10. A typical single-case experiment
   a. has multiple posttests, each measuring a different dependent variable.
   b. has multiple administrations of the same measure, each measuring the same dependent variable.
   c. has two different measures, one measuring the independent variable and the other measuring the dependent variable.
   d. has only one baseline condition.

Chapter References

Biddle, B. J., & Berliner, D. C. (2002). Small class size and its effects. *Educational Leadership, 59*(5), 12–23.

Bracht, G. H., & Glass, G. V (1968). The external validity of experiments. *American Educational Research Journal, 5,* 437–474.

Campbell, D. T., & Stanley, J. C. (1963). Experimental and quasi-experimental designs for research on teaching. In N. L. Gage (Ed.), *Handbook of research on teaching* (pp. 171–246). Chicago: Rand McNally.

Eisen, M., Zellman, G., Massett, H., & Murray, D. (2002). Evaluating the Lions-Quest "Skills for Adolescence" drug education program: First-year behavior outcomes. *Addictive Behaviors, 27*(4), 619–632.

Eisen, M., Zellman, G. L., & Murray, D. M. (2003). Evaluating the Lions-Quest "Skills for Adolescence" drug education program:

Second-year behavior outcomes. *Addictive Behaviors, 28*(5), 883–897.

Fletcher, J. D., Tobias, S., & Wisher, R. A. (2007). Learning anytime, anywhere: Advanced distributed learning and the changing face of education. *Educational Researcher, 36*(2), 96–102.

Glenn, D. (2005, March 11). New federal policy favors randomized trials in education research. *Chronicle of Higher Education,* p. 16.

Mechling, L. C., Gast, D. L., & Cronin, B. A. (2006). The effects of presenting high-preference items, paired with choice, via computer-based video programming on task completion of students with autism. *Focus on Autism and Other Developmental Disabilities, 21*(1), 7–13.

Resources for Further Study

Cook, T., & Sinha, V. (2006). Randomized experiments in educational research. In J. L. Green, G. Camilli, & P. B. Elmore (Eds.), *Handbook of complementary methods in education research* (pp. 551–566). Mahwah, NJ: Lawrence Erlbaum.

   The authors review the fundamentals of experiments and consider the current role of experiments in advancing knowledge about education. They review arguments for and against experiments and make a case for the usefulness of experiments,

especially if complemented by the use of other research methods.

Kennedy, C. H. (2005). *Single-case designs for educational research.* Boston: Pearson.

   The author provides a detailed description of how to do a single-case experiment. The book includes chapters on how to frame research questions, select an appropriate single-case design, measure dependent variables, and analyze data.

Sample Group Experiment

After-School Multifamily Groups: A Randomized Controlled Trial Involving Low-Income, Urban, Latino Children

McDonald, L., Moberg, D. P., Brown, R., Rodriguez-Espiricueta, I., Flores, N. I., Burke, M. P., & Coover, G. (2006). After-school multifamily groups: A randomized controlled trial involving low-income, urban, Latino children. *Children & Schools, 28*(1), 25–34.

The problem of practice addressed in this experiment is the low academic performance and high dropout rate of Latino students. The purpose of the researchers' experiment was to determine whether a specific program to increase Latino parent involvement in their children's education has desirable effects on their academic performance and classroom behavior.

The descriptive statistics in the article are easy to understand. Another set of statistical analyses, reported in Table 3, involves hierarchical regression modeling (see Chapter 12). It provides a more detailed analysis of the effects of the experimental treatment relative to the control condition. The results of the hierarchical regression modeling are fairly consistent with the descriptive statistics in Table 2 and Figure 1 in the article, so an understanding of Table 3, while helpful, is not essential to comprehending the main findings of the experiment.

The article is reprinted in its entirety, just as it appeared when originally published.

After-School Multifamily Groups: A Randomized Controlled Trial Involving Low-Income, Urban, Latino Children

Lynn McDonald, D. Paul Moberg, Roger Brown, Ismael Rodriguez-Espiricueta, Nydia I. Flores, Melissa P. Burke, and Gail Coover

ABSTRACT ■ This randomized controlled trial evaluated a culturally representative parent engagement strategy with Latino parents of elementary school children. Ten urban schools serving low-income children from mixed cultural backgrounds participated in a large study. Classrooms were randomly assigned either to an after-school, multifamily support group (FAST: Families and Schools Together) or to receive eight behavioral parenting pamphlets with active follow-up (FAME: Family Education). Of 180 Latino parents assigned to FAST, 90 percent came once and 85 percent graduated. Two-year follow-up teacher data were collected for 130 Latino children. The teachers, blind to condition, evaluated the children's classroom functioning. Data were analyzed with hierarchical linear modeling, using a conservative, intent-to-treat model. On standardized mental health instruments (Teacher's Report Form of the Child Behavior Checklist; Social Skills Rating System), statistically significant differences favored assignment to FAST rather than to FAME on academic performance and classroom behaviors, including aggression and social skills.

KEY WORDS ■ Hispanics; immigrants; parent involvement; protective factors; social inclusion

A *USA Today* headline reported: "Hispanic population gains fail to translate in classroom . . . Hispanic children face a bleak educational future" (p. A14). Factors cited as relevant to the Latino school dropout rate were poor research, weak accountability, low expectations, and bad communication between Latino parents and schools (Hispanic Population Gains Fail, 2003). The National Center for Education Statistics reported on dropout rates in the United States: "73 percent of all Latino youth graduated from high school compared with 92% [of] white students"

(National Center for Education Statistics, 2003, p. 42). This statistic must be considered in a social context: although 9 percent of white children reside in poverty, 27 percent of Hispanic children reside in poverty in the United States (Suarez-Orosco, Suarez-Orosco, & Doucet, 2003). Almost all growth in the number of U.S. youths over the next 20 years will be among Hispanics (Fry, 2003). Schools need evidence-based approaches to improve communication between Latino parents and schools and address the achievement gap.

The No Child Left Behind Act of 2001 (P.L. 107-110) mandates the achievement of all children and considers parents as critical to achieving successful schools (http://www.ed.gov/print/nclb/overview). Title I specifies that 1 percent of the federal funds going to school districts to serve low-income children must be used for parent involvement. Research linking parent engagement with student outcomes supports these federal policies. Henderson and Mapp's (2002) review shows that parent involvement is positively correlated with school success, but rather than being linear, it is a complex relationship and manifests in various forms. Similarly, Christenson and colleagues' (1992) and Christenson's (2003) research describes the impact of systemic approaches to family, school, and community, which are based on relationships across systems, rather than any one specific form of parent–teacher communication. Epstein's (1991) conceptual framework on parent involvement with schools refers to six forms: parenting, communicating, supporting school, learning at home, decision making, and collaborating with the community (Epstein & Sanders, 2000).

Principals, teachers, and social workers are committed to parent involvement but are frustrated with unsuccessful efforts to achieve this involvement (Allen-Meares, Washington, & Welsh, 1996; Kurtz & Barth, 1989). Parents may be seen as not caring about their child's schooling, rather than as impeded by economic and social policy obstacles (Hewlett & West, 1997; Pena, 2000). Social stressors of poor housing, dangerous neighborhoods, poor transportation, and lack of "living wage" employment, interfere with parental participation in parent–teacher conferences (Garbarino, 1995; Shumow, Vandell, & Posner, 1999). Although parent involvement is supported by federal policies, few strategies have been tested with randomized controlled trials in urban communities.

EVIDENCE-BASED PRACTICES

Educational policy is shifting toward funding evidence-based approaches—that is, tested with randomized controlled trials. The Substance Abuse and Mental Health Services Administration (SAMHSA), U.S. Department of Health and Human Services, funded the National Registry of Prevention Programs and Practices to rigorously assess 1,000 programs with peer reviews, regional technical assistance structures, and state implementation of evidence-based models. Only 54 programs met the criteria for being an evidence-based "model" (Schinke, Brounstein, & Gard-

ner, 2003). Half of the models involved schools; only a few were tested with Latino youths (www.samhsamodels.org). We describe a randomized controlled trial with Latino children of a SAMHSA model, an after-school, multifamily support group model.

FAMILIES AND SCHOOLS TOGETHER (FAST): AN EVIDENCE-BASED SAMHSA MODEL

Families and Schools Together (FAST) is an after-school, multifamily support group to increase parent involvement in schools and improve children's well-being (McDonald, Coe-Braddish, Billingham, Dibble, & Rice, 1991; McDonald, Billingham, Conrad, Morgan, & Payton, 1997). A collaborative, culturally representative, team of parents and professionals facilitates the multifamily group to engage parents into building social networks through the schools. These relationships act as protective factors at several levels of the child's social ecology (Bronfenbrenner, 1979). Teams provide home visits and lead eight weekly multifamily sessions (with five to 15 families); then for two years, parent graduates lead monthly sessions.

There is no formal curriculum or instruction at FAST. Instead, the team leads a structured package of interactive processes at the group sessions to enhance relationships. The activities are based on theory and research: family stress theory (Boyd-Franklin & Bry, 2000; Hill, 1958; McCubbin, Thompson, Thompson, & Fromer, 1998); family systems theory (Alexander & Parsons, 1982; Minuchin, 1974; Rutter, 1999; Satir, 1983); parent-led play therapy (Kogan, 1978; Kumpfer, Molgaard, & Spoth, 1996; Webster-Stratton, 1985); group work (Gitterman & Shulman, 1994); and adult education and community development (Alinsky, 1971; Freire, 1997). Based on experiential learning principles, the repeated encounters build trusting, reciprocal relationships, called "social capital" (Bryk & Schneider, 2002; Putnam, 2000), which are then maintained at monthly groups. McDonald and Sayger (1998) summarize the linkages between these theories and the FAST structured activities.

For the first hour of each FAST session, parents lead communication at their family table, while sharing a meal, singing group songs, and playing family games. The child repeatedly experiences parental hierarchy, embedded compliance requests, and family cohesion, and has fun with his family while at the school. In the second hour, participants separate into peer groups: The children play, and parents meet to talk in small groups, without assigned topics. The groups provide parents with an opportunity to build social connections and a shared identity. The next activity is 15 minutes of cross-generational, dyadic time, when a parent and her child engage in uninterrupted play, in an adaptation of play therapy, with no teaching, bossing, or directing. At the parent-planned graduation, the principal congratulates the parents for their involvement, and the team members present behaviorally specific affirmations to each parent.

These group activities support parents to help their child connect the cultures of home and school (Valenzuela

& Dornbusch, 1994). In the school, with school personnel present, the parents lead the table-based, family activities; without lectures or reading requirements, participants at all levels of English literacy are equally competent. Each FAST team implements the core components (40 percent) while adapting the processes (60 percent) to fit cultural preferences. An example of a core component is "shared governance," whereby the team must represent the social ecology of a child's life, including the culture and language of the neighborhood (Szapocznik & Kurtines, 1993). In addition, a parent with a child at that school partners with professionals from community agencies and the school on the FAST team.

Since its development in 1988, FAST has been implemented, with on-site training and evaluation of child and family outcomes by a national, non-profit organization (www.fastnational.org) at more than 800 schools in 45 states and five countries. Thousands of primarily low-income parents from diverse backgrounds have increased their involvement in schools through FAST: 51 percent white, 23 percent Latino, 20 percent African American, and 1 percent Asian American/Native American. On average, nationally, 80 percent of parents who attend the first session return and graduate from FAST (McDonald & Frey, 1999). In a randomized controlled trial in inner-city New Orleans, parents assigned to FAST compared with parents in the comparison condition were significantly more likely at one-year follow-up to report increased parent involvement in their communities, and to report their children as having decreased aggression and increased social skills (Abt Associates, 2001). Another randomized controlled trial of FAST was conducted in collaboration with three Indian Nations and rural American Indian families; one-year follow-up teacher data showed behavioral outcomes favoring FAST rather than control children (Kratochwill, McDonald, Levin, Young Bear-Tibbetts, & Demaray, 2004).

METHOD

Research Design

Classrooms in 10 urban, elementary schools were randomly assigned to either the treatment (FAST) or the comparison Family Education (FAME) condition. A universal recruitment strategy was used. All families with children in the treatment or comparison condition classrooms were recruited for the study. After exposure to the program, first- and second-year follow-up data were collected for both conditions. This article presents data on the subsample of Latino children. (For complete information about the larger study, see Moberg, McDonald, Brown, & Burke, 2003).

Latino Subsample Characteristics

A total of 473 Milwaukee study children and their families were involved at the baseline data collection of the larger study (FAST = 272 and FAME = 201). Of the original 180 Latino families who participated in this research study, 87 percent of the parents were successfully followed up two years later. Teacher reports could only be collected with specific release forms from the parents interviewed at the two-year point. The Latino subsample with two-year follow-up data by teachers ($n = 130$, with 80 assigned to FAST, 50 assigned to FAME), was similar to the original sample of 180 Latino children at baseline except on gender and grade. More boys were assigned to FAST (54 percent) compared with FAME (28 percent) and more third-graders were in FAST (51 percent) compared with FAME (38 percent) .These group differences were adjusted for in the multivariate analysis described later.

One of the sociodemographic strengths of the subsample of 130 self-identified Latino families was having married parents. More than 70 percent lived in intact family homes (Table 1). The Latino families lived in a relatively stable part of the urban community, and most of their children remained in their original schools over the two years of the study. The Latino families, however, struggled with extremely low incomes: More than 70 percent had annual incomes of less than $20,000, and a third of the families reported incomes less than $10,000. The parents had relatively low educational attainment: Almost half of the parents reported that they had not completed high school, and only 20 percent had more than a high school education. Length of residence in the United States and country of origin were not assessed, although anecdotally most families were of Mexican origin. The average age for the Latino children at baseline was seven years, and slightly more than half were girls.

Procedure

The FAST research project was presented to all elementary school principals in Milwaukee, and they were invited to participate in the study. The 10 schools selected served high rates of Title I-eligible children and served students who were primarily African American (4), Latino (4), and mixed heritage (2). The six schools that served Latino students implemented 12 multifamily group sessions from 1997 to 1999: Four were in Spanish and English, four were in Spanish only, and four were in English (with translators). Program manuals for the team members and all evaluation materials were translated into Spanish; adaptations of activities were planned by each local team.

To recruit families into the study, teachers at each school agreed to offer either program to all children in their classrooms. Classrooms were matched by grade and then randomly assigned to either condition: FAST (intervention) or FAME (comparison). Teachers distributed cards to children to take home to obtain parental consent to being contacted about the study. If parents agreed to participate, there were four in-home interviews: preintervention, postintervention, one year post, and two years post. In addition, parents were paid $25 for each interview. (If not enough parents responded in a school, first- or third-grade classrooms were also recruited). At the two-year postprogram interview, parents were asked to provide releases so that teachers could be contacted for follow-up evaluation. Teachers were generally unaware of the condition of the participating students.

TABLE 1   Baseline Demographics of Children and Families

Demographics	FAST (Treatment) ($n = 80$) (%)	FAME (Comparison) ($n = 50$) (%)
Household Income		
Less than $10,000	37	33
$10,000 or less than $20,000	33	33
$20,000 or less than $30,000	24	22
$30,000 or more	7	13
Parent education		
Less than high school	46	49
High school grad or GED	32	33
Some college or tech school	17	13
College graduate or more	5	4
Marital status		
Married	70	69
Divorced/separated/widowed	14	10
Never married/unmarried couple	16	20
Child's gender*		
Male	54	28
Female	46	72
Child's grade		
First	13	4
Second	27	54
Third	51	38
Fourth	9	4

Notes: FAME = Family Education, FAST = Families and Schools Together.

Percentages may not add to 100 due to rounding.

*Groups differ significantly at $p < .95$. Only self-identified Latino families in the larger study, with two-year follow-up teacher data, are included.

Because randomization was of whole classrooms, parents were assigned to FAST or FAME before the home visits. As discussed in a previous section, families recruited to the FAST condition were offered eight weekly, culturally representative, team led, after-school, multifamily group sessions and parent graduate-led monthly meetings for two years.

The comparison condition families were sent eight weekly mailings of behaviorally oriented parenting skills booklets in English or Spanish (see Channing L. Bete Company, 1997), with follow-up phone calls to see whether they had read the booklets, and an invitation to a formal lecture on "parenting." To engage families in the research study for two years and maintain their addresses over time, both groups of families were mailed regular FAME or FAST newsletters and sent birthday cards from FAME or FAST coordinators.

Measures

Teachers evaluated the children's socioemotional functioning and academic performance by completing two forms that have been used with Latino populations and have been translated into Spanish: (1) the Teacher's Report Form (TRF) of the Child Behavior Checklist (CBCL) (Achenbach, 1991) and (2) the Social Skills Rating System (SSRS) (Gresham & Elliott, 1990). The TRF is a widely used, broad-based, standardized rating scale instrument for socioemotional problems, in the child mental health field, with 120 items that measure problem behaviors on a scale ranging from 1 = never to 3 = often. The TRF, with established validity and reliability, is used to screen children in schools for emotional disturbance. The standardized scores mean that the average level of functioning is 50; at risk is 53 to 56; high risk is 57 to 60; and higher than 60 is clinical. The primary scales are Externalizing (delinquent and aggressive behaviors) and Internalizing (withdrawal, somatic complaints, anxiety, and depression). The TRF Academic Performance scale asks the teacher to assess a child on specific academic skills, including reading, writing, and math, relative to other children at the same grade level.

The SSRS is also a standardized, widely used, multirater instrument, with established validity and reliability. Teachers complete 57 items, including the Academic Competence subscale, which contains nine items that require comparing the child being rated to other students in that specific classroom. The Academic Competence scale includes reading, mathematics, motivation, parental encouragement, and intellectual functioning. The SSRS assesses problem behaviors in the classroom (not used in this study), but its main emphasis is on the child's social skills in the classroom. Questions are about positive behaviors scored with reference to domains of assertiveness, cooperation, and self-control. It has a three-point rating scale (0 = never, 1 = sometimes, 2 = often), indicating the extent to which each item describes a child's behavior.

Data Analysis

An intent-to-treat model was used, which means that families who agreed to be in the study and were assigned to the treatment group condition but did not actually come to any FAST sessions were included in the analysis as part of the treatment group. The classroom teachers of the focal child in either condition completed evaluation forms at pretest, at posttest about three months later, and after two years. Two years later the focal child's current teacher, who was blind to the child's condition, completed the forms. These data are the focus of this article.

Hierarchical repeated measures regression models were used to estimate the net effects of the FAST program after two years, on a range of relevant precursors of substance abuse and on child behavior outcomes based on teacher reports (Moberg et al., 2003). Twelve multifamily group cycles included Latino families, and because the families were assigned to a condition (treatment or comparison), this formed distinctive groupings. A multilevel regression model explicitly models the manner in which families are grouped within cycles and has several advantages. It enables researchers to obtain statistically efficient estimates. By using the clustering information, it provides correct standard errors, confidence intervals, and significance tests, which generally are more conservative than the traditional analyses; and by allowing the use of covariates, it can measure at any level of the hierarchy.

RESULTS

The first key outcome of this study concerns parent engagement. Of the 80 Latino families who agreed to be study participants from classrooms assigned to the FAST condition, 90 percent went once to the after school family support group; of these, 85 percent returned for at least five sessions and graduated. In addition, the FAST families attended an average of 9.9 parent-led family support groups over the next two years. In contrast, of the 50 Latino families who agreed to be study participants from classrooms assigned to FAME, 100 percent were contacted with mailed behavioral parenting booklets, and through mailed newsletters and phone calls; however, only 4 percent attended the FAME formal lecture on parenting.

Did increased parent involvement and participation in FAST affect the Latino children's school performance as assessed by their teacher two years later? To answer this question, we compared results for students in FAST and FAME, using hierarchical linear modeling (HLM) and intent-to-treat analyses. Although the students assigned to FAST had a slightly higher rate of completion of teacher forms than did the control condition (76 percent compared with 67 percent) at two years, this difference was not significant. The teachers were blind to condition—that is, student assignment in the study, and [were] asked to assess the child's academic performance, social skills, and behavior problems. Means and standard deviations for teachers' ratings of students on both the TRF and the SSRS instruments at baseline and at two-year follow-up show that the children assigned to FAST tended to improve their mean scores from pretest to follow-up, whereas FAME students tended to have more negative means from pretest to follow-up (Table 2). Of most note at

TABLE 2   Teacher Evaluations on Classroom Behavior Scales

Teacher's Report Form (TRF)	Baseline		Two-Year Follow-Up	
	M	SD	M	SD
Child Internalizing (anxiety)				
FAME	47.6	8.9	52.0	10.8
FAST	47.5	10.2	51.9	10.5
Child Externalizing (aggression)				
FAME	49.1	8.4	53.5	9.8
FAST	50.1	9.7	51.2	7.9
Academic Performance				
FAME	47.5	9.8	43.6	8.0
FAST	45.8	6.9	46.6	7.8
Social Skills Rating System (SSRS)				
Social Skills				
FAME	104.2	17.4	100.3	16.2
FAST	97.4	17.7	102.4	14.9
Academic Competence				
FAME	95.9	13.8	92.3	13.0
FAST	95.5	11.2	95.0	11.8

FAST (n = 80); FAME (n = 50)

Note: FAME = Family Education; FAST = Families and Schools Together.

two-year follow-up, the means of the students assigned to FAST on the academic performance scale of the TRF were significantly higher (p = .03) than the means for students assigned to the comparison condition.

At the outset, the two groups were similar at baseline on four of the five teacher evaluation measures. One-way ANOVAs comparing the groups found significant baseline differences: FAME students scored higher on the SSRS at baseline than did the FAST students (p = .054). Note that at two-year follow-up, the scores on social skills in the classroom were reversed: FAST students scored significantly higher (meaning that their social skills were better) than those in FAME, who were not exposed to the after-school multifamily groups.

Within[-]group analysis using paired t tests indicated that FAME comparison group students' scores were significantly less favorable than at baseline on each of the five measures analyzed. For those students assigned to FAST, two of the five domain means showed improvement (including the TRF Externalizing scale), two showed no change, and one showed less favorable scores (the TRF Internalizing scale). The ratings were provided independently by different teachers at baseline and at two-year follow-up, but all measures for both groups were significantly correlated over time.

For a more rigorous statistical analysis, these data were analyzed with hierarchical regression models. Table 3 provides the results from the essential data analyses from complex hierarchical regression models. The models take account of the random effect of assignment to FAST or FAME cycle (the grouping variable in the design that con-

FIGURE 1   Teacher Reports of Children's Classroom Aggression (TRF Externalizing)

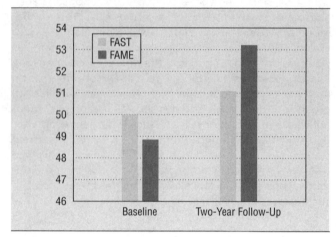

Notes: TRF = Teacher's Report Form of Achenbach's Child Behavior Checklist. FAST = Families and Schools Together. FAME = Family Education. FAST (n = 80), FAME (n = 50)

Only cases with data at both points were included: teachers at two years were not aware of the condition to which the Latino child was assigned. Between group differences were not significant. Baseline to two-year paired t tests were significant at p < .001 for FAME. Hierarchical regression models showed significant effect of FAST condition..

trols for cluster rather than random assignment to condition) as well as a number of other covariates. Coefficients are provided for fixed effects of the FAST condition from hierarchical regression models. Random effects of family/student are nested within [the] cycle of FAST implementation. Models have been adjusted for baseline value of dependent measure, family income, parent education, parent marital status, student sex and grade in school, and student baseline CBCL risk level. The hierarchical regression models indicate a statistically significant program effect of FAST on three of the five teacher variables measured, two years after the intervention (Figure 1). Specifically, on the TRF-CBCL Externalizing Scale (largely due to the aggressive behavior subscale), on the SSRS Total Overall social skills rating, and on the academic performance subscale of the TRF-CBCL. The effect size of these differences is approximately .25 standard deviation units, a moderate effect. Thus, two years after the family support groups, teachers rated Latino students assigned to FAST as having significantly more social skills, less aggressive behavior in the classroom, and better academic skills than those assigned to FAME.

TABLE 3   Fixed Effects of FAST Condition Based on Hierarchical Regression Modeling

Classroom Behavior Scales	Two-Year Follow-Up Teacher Evaluations	
	Coefficient*	SD
TRF Child Internalizing	−0.92	(2.22)
TRF Child Externalizing	−4.68**	(1.57)
TRF Academic Performance	3.06*	(1.50)
SSRS Child Social Skills	4.45*	(2.12)
SSRS Academic Competence	2.48	(1.64)

Note: TRF = Teacher's Report Form of Achenbach's Child Behavior Checklist (CBCL). SSRS = Gresham and Elliot's Social Skills Rating System. FAST = Families and Schools Together. FAME = Family Education. FAST (n = 80), FAME (n = 50).

*Coefficients provided for fixed effects of FAST condition using hierarchical regression models. Random effects of FAST family/student are nested within cycle of FAST implementation. Models have been adjusted for baseline value of dependent measure, for family income, parent education, parent marital status, student sex and grade in school, and student baseline overall CBCL risk level. *p < .05, **p < .001.

DISCUSSION

High engagement and retention rates reflect a possible compatibility of this multifamily group model with the cultural norms of the Latino community. Researchers consistently report on the primacy of the extended family across Latino communities from Latin America, including Mexico,

Cuba, and Puerto Rico (Frauenglass, Routh, Pantin, & Mason, 1997; Perez, Pinzon, & Garza, 1997; Santiago-Rivera, Arredondo, & Gallardo-Cooper, 2002; Zambrana, 1995). The FAST process engages everyone in the family and values their perspective on the primacy of the family, which includes the nuclear and extended family, for example, fathers, mothers, siblings, aunts, uncles, grandparents, and so forth. Personally inviting the whole family to school functions may be particularly effective for Latino families rather than invitations, usually sent home on fliers, issued only to parents. For a school to take the trouble and expend the funds to make a home visit, and host family meals and group activities after school shows the community a respect for the importance of the whole family to be involved for the child's success in school.

Parent participation in after school activities is voluntary, and so attendance alone can be considered to be an objective measure of a program's acceptability in a particular community. Latino parent involvement in these elementary schools increased for parents who participated in FAST. Principals and other school personnel at the six schools serving Latino children reported being pleased with the increased parent involvement and reported increased parent engagement over time at school functions.

The school-based, culturally representative FAST team is trained with role play to show respect both nonverbally and verbally to low-income, ethnic minority parents, and to help children at FAST meetings be respectful to their parents. Respect for the parents as partners in the process of supporting the child to succeed in school is fundamental to FAST. The Latino child observes the school staff being respectful towards his or her parents who might have minimal English language skills or a minimal educational background; this observation supports the child's respect for his or her own parents. This respect for parents is congruent with the reported values of immigrants from Mexico and other Latin American countries (Brown, 1981; Stanton-Salazar, 2001).

FAST offered a structure for meeting other parents and building reciprocal relationships, when other community societal structures are often not available to immigrant parents. FAST team members go to the home and invite families to come to the school for repeated meetings, with time in the evening to network together. Researchers report that the Latino cultures recognize the importance of consistently nourishing support networks by patterns of exchange within one's local community (that is, the social importance of groups) (Gutiérrez & Ortega, 1991; Vega & Kolody, 1985). The mobility of immigration interrupts the familiar extended family and the local networks. Informal, trusted, friendship networks are critical to the survival of ethnic minority families in a majority dominant culture, particularly when struggling with economic hardship.

Chrispeels and Rivero (2000) identified five clarifications that effectively increased Latino parent engagement in schools: (1) actual and perceived school invitations and opportunities to be involved, (2) parents' sense of place in their child's education, (3) parents' knowledge and skills about how to be involved, (4) parents' concept of parenting, (5) parents' aspirations and love for their child. FAST addresses each of these five processes, thereby "helping Latino parents to shift their parenting styles and their engagement with the school, especially with the teacher, when given information and an opportunity to explore how their attitudes and practices affect their children" (Henderson & Mapp, 2002, p. 95).

In addition to effectively engaging Latino parents and increasing their involvement in schools, the teacher evaluations two years later showed that assignment to FAST resulted in significantly better academic performance, decreased problems of aggressive behaviors in the classroom, and increased social skills in the classroom compared with FAME students. The follow-up data showed positive effect[s] in three distinct areas, suggesting that multisystemic, relationship building, multifamily groups are effective with low-income Latino children in school over time.

However, the direction of the change was troubling: By teacher report, the differences between the two conditions were significant because of worsening ratings of the comparison group. This pattern held across all three domains of functioning in the classroom: social skills, classroom aggression, and academic performance. At two years, the FAME students showed decreased academic performance and social skills and increased classroom aggression. Protective factors of multiple relationships across systems of families, schools, and communities may act to shield the FAST Latino child from some of the stresses of racism, poverty, and toxic urban environments.

STUDY LIMITATIONS

The first limitation of this study concerns the comparability of the two study conditions: FAST and FAME. As described earlier, FAME was created as a comparison condition for the FAST intervention. However, a recent study shows that behavioral parenting pamphlets are effective interventions, particularly with active follow-up (Montgomery, Stores, & Wiggs, 2004). The FAME comparison condition of receiving the eight parenting booklets with the active tracking of the families over time may have functioned as an intervention with effects on the children and families. This would suggest that the impact of FAST may actually be considerably stronger than these data show, because the comparison group received a kind of intervention (behavioral parenting pamphlets) rather than treatment as usual or no treatment.

A second limitation of the study was the unknown generalizability of these classroom results to all Latino immigrant populations. A weakness of the study was our lack of specification of the country of origin of the Latino sample and our failure to determine first, second, or third generational status in the United States. In addition, the distribution of the Latino subsample was across six schools serving low-income populations. Of the 12 multifamily group cycles, one-third were in mixed cultural schools, and two-thirds were in monocultural schools. Our sample size and the nonrandom assignment of families to these school settings prevents us from investigating the impact of the language and culture setting on parent involvement rates and classroom impact rates. This should be pursued in future research.

Another limitation was the attrition of the Latino parents over the two-year period, resulting in loss of data on 50 families from the original sample of 180 Latino students at pretest evaluations. This was partly due to family attrition and partly due to failure of some teachers to provide data even when parental release was obtained. Another issue concerns the disproportionate number of boys in the experimental condition compared with the comparison condition. This difference was controlled for in the hierarchical regression.

Although three of the five teacher-reported measures showed significant outcomes, two did not show significant differences: the TRF Internalizing Scale (depression, anxiety) and the SSRS Academic Competence Scale. The implications of the same teachers assessing the same children on two different measures of academic functioning with different results remain unclear.

IMPLICATIONS

The findings from this study suggest that after-school, multifamily groups can increase parent involvement and may help address the achievement gap. However, the lasting effectiveness of the evidence-based intervention is contingent on successful parent engagement and social inclusion. An evidence-based model that builds relationships across systems—the family, the school, and the community—can significantly change outcomes for low-income, culturally marginalized families. This change was achieved in this study through respectful inclusion of the parents in the after-school program, and cultural representation of the child's social ecology in the implementation team. If schools serving Latino students take responsibility for providing evidence-based parent involvement practices, they can support the federal goals of improved academic achievement for all students.

References

Abt Associates. (2001). *National evaluation of family support programs: Volume B. Research studies: Final report.* Cambridge, MA: Author. Retrieved July 10, 2003, from http://www.abtassoc.com/ reports/NEFSP-VolB.pdf

Achenbach, T. M. (1991). *Manual for the Child Behavior Checklist and 1991 Profile.* Burlington: University of Vermont, Department of Psychiatry.

Alexander, J. E., & Parsons, B. V. (1982). *Functional family therapy.* Monterey, CA: Brooks/Cole.

Alinsky, S. D. (1971). *Rules for radicals: A programmatic primer for realistic radicals.* New York: Random House.

Allen-Meares, P., Washington, R. Q., & Welsh, B. L. (1996). *Social work services in schools* (2nd ed.). Boston: Allyn & Bacon.

Boyd-Franklin, N., & Bry, B. H. (2000). *Reaching out in family therapy: Home-based, school, and community interventions.* New York: Guilford Press.

Bronfenbrenner, U. (1979). *The ecology of human development: Experiments by nature and design.* Cambridge, MA: Harvard University Press.

Brown, J. A. (1981). Parent education groups for Mexican-Americans. *Social Work in Education, 3,* 22–31.

Bryk, A. S., & Schneider, B. L. (2002). *Trust in schools: A core resource for improvement.* New York: Russell Sage Foundation.

Channing L. Bete Company. (1997). *Scriptographic parenting booklet series.* South Deerfield, MA: Author.

Chrispeels, J., & Rivero, E. (2000, April). *Engaging Latino families for student success—Understanding the process and impact of providing training to parents.* Presentation at the annual meeting of the American Educational Research Association, New Orleans.

Christenson, S. L. (2003). The family-school partnership: An opportunity to promote the learning competence of all students. *School Psychology Quarterly, 18,* 454–482.

Christenson, S. L., Rounds, T., & Gorney, D. (1992). Family factors and student achievement: An avenue to increase students' success. *School Psychology Quarterly, 7,* 178–206.

Epstein, J. (1991). School and family partnerships. In M. Alkin (Ed.), *Encyclopedia of educational research* (6th ed., pp. 1139–1151). New York: Macmillan.

Epstein, J. L., & Sanders, M. G. (2000). Connecting home, school, and community: New directions for social research. In M. T. Hallinan (Ed.), *Handbook of the sociology of education* (pp. 285–306). New York: Kluwer Academic/Plenum Press.

Frauenglass, S., Routh, D., Pantin, H., & Mason, C. (1997). Family support decreases influence of deviant peers on Hispanic adolescents substance use. *Journal of Clinical Child Psychology, 26*(1), 15–23.

Freire, P. (1997). *Pedagogy of the oppressed.* New York: Continuum.

Fry, R. (2003). *Hispanic youth dropping out of US schools: Measuring the challenge.* Washington, DC: Pew Hispanic Center.

Garbarino, J. (1995). *Raising children in a socially toxic environment.* San Francisco: Jossey-Bass.

Gitterman, A., & Shulman, L. (Eds.). (1994). *Mutual aid groups, vulnerable populations, and the life cycle.* New York: Columbia University Press.

Gresham, F. M., & Elliott, S. N. (1990). *Social Skills Rating System.* Circle Pines, MN: American Guidance Service.

Gutirrez, L. M., & Ortega, R. (1991). Developing methods to empower Latinos: The importance of groups. *Social Work with Groups, 14*(2), 23–42.

Henderson, A. T., & Mapp, K. L. (2002). *A new wave of evidence: The impact of school, family, and community connections on student achievement.* Austin, TX: Southwest Educational Development Lab.

Hewlett, S., & West, C. (1997). *War against parents.* Cambridge, MA: Harvard University Press.

Hill, R. (1958). Social stresses on the family: Generic features of families under stress. *Social Casework, 39,* 139–150.

Hispanic population gains fail to translate in classroom. (2003, January 31). *USA Today,* p. A14.

Kogan, K. L. (1978). Help-seeking mothers and their children. *Child Psychology and Human Development, 8,* 204–218.

Kratochwill, T. R., McDonald, L., Levin, J. R., Young Bear-Tibbetts, H., & Demaray, M. K. (2004). Families and schools together: An experimental analysis of a parent-mediated multi-family group intervention program for American Indian children. *Journal of School Psychology, 42,* 359–383.

Kumpfer, K. L., Molgaard, V., & Spoth, R. (1996). The Strengthening Families Program for the prevention of delinquency and drug use. In R. D. Peters & R. J. McMahon (Eds.), *Preventing childhood disorders, substance abuse, and delinquency* (pp. 241–267). Thousand Oaks, CA: Sage Publications.

Kurtz, D. P., & Earth, R. P. (1989). Parent involvement: Cornerstone of school social work practice. *Social Work, 34,* 407–420.

McCubbin, H. I., Thompson, E. A., Thompson, A. I., & Fromer, J. E. (Eds.). (1998). *Resiliency in Native American and immigrant families.* Thousand Oaks, CA: Sage Publications.

McDonald, L., Billingham, S., Conrad, T., Morgan, A. O. N., & Payton, E. (1997). Families and Schools Together (FAST): Integrating community development with clinical strategy. *Families in Society, 78,* 140–155.

McDonald, L., Coe-Braddish, D., Billingham, S., Dibble, N., & Rice, C. (1991). Families and Schools Together: An innovative substance abuse prevention program. *Social Work in Education, 13,* 118–128.

McDonald, L., & Frey, H. E. (1999). Families and Schools Together: Building relationships [*OJJDP Bulletin*]. Washington, DC: U.S. Department of Justice, Office of Justice Programs, Office of Juvenile Justice and Delinquency Prevention.

McDonald, L., & Sayger, T. V. (1998). Impact of a family and school based prevention program on protective factors for high risk youth: Issues in evaluation. *Drugs and Society, 12,* 61–85.

Minuchin, S. (1974). *Families and family therapy.* Cambridge, MA: Harvard University Press.

Moberg, D. P., McDonald, L. W., Brown, R., & Burke, M. (2003, June). *Randomized trial of Families and Schools Together (FAST).* Paper presented at the Society for Prevention Research 11th Annual Meeting, Washington, DC.

Montgomery, P., Stores, G., & Wiggs, L. (2004). The relative efficacy of two brief treatments for sleep problems in young learning disabled (mentally retarded) children: A randomized controlled trial. *Archives of Diseases of Childhood, 89,* 125–130.

National Center for Education Statistics. (2003). *The condition of education 2003* (NCES 2003–067). Washington, DC: U.S. Government Printing Office.

No Child Left Behind Act of 2001, P.L. 107-110, 115 Stat. 1425 (2002).

Pena, D. C. (2000). Parent involvement: Influencing factors and implications. *Journal of Educational Research, 94*(1), 42–54.

Perez, M. A., Pinzon, H. L., & Garza R. D. (1997). Latino families: Partners for success in school settings. *Journal for School Health, 67,* 182–184.

Putnam, R. (2000). *Bowling alone: The disappearance of civic America.* Cambridge, MA: Harvard University Press.

Rutter, M. (1999). Resilience concepts and findings: Implications for family therapy, *Journal of Family Therapy, 21,* 119–144.

Santiago-Rivera, L., Arredondo, P., & Gallardo-Cooper, M. (2002). *Counseling Latinos and la familia: A practical guide.* Thousand Oaks, CA: Sage Publications.

Satir, V. (1983). *Conjoint family therapy* (3rd ed.). Palo Alto, CA: Science and Behavior Books.

Schinke, S., Brounstein, P., & Gardner, S. (2003). *Science-based prevention programs and principles 2002: Effective substance abuse and mental health programs for every community* (DHHS Publication No. 03–3764). Rockville, MD: U.S. Department of Health and Human Services, Substance Abuse and Mental Health Services Administration, Center for Substance Abuse Prevention.

Shumow, L., Vandell, D. L., & Posner, J. (1999). Risk and resilience in the urban neighborhood: Predictors of academic performance among low-income elementary school children. *Merrill-Palmer Quarterly, 45,* 309–331.

Stanton-Salazar, R. (2001). *Manufacturing hope and despair: The school and kin support networks of U.S.–Mexican youth.* New York: Teachers College Press.

Suarez-Orosco, C., Suarez-Orosco, M., & Doucet, F. (2003). The academic engagement and achievement of Latino youth. In J. Banks & C. McGee-Banks (Eds.), *Handbook of research on multicultural education* (2nd ed., pp. 420–437). San Francisco: Jossey-Bass.

Szapocznik J., & Kurtines, W. M. (1993). Family psychology and cultural diversity: Opportunities for theory, research, and application. *American Psychologist, 48,* 400–407.

Valenzuela, A., & Dornbusch, S. (1994). Familism and social capital in the academic achievement of Mexican origin and Anglo adolescents. *Social Science Quarterly, 75,* 18–36.

Vega, W., & Kolody, B. (1985). The meaning of social support and the mediation of stress across cultures. In W. Vega & M. Mirand (Eds.), *Stress and Hispanic mental health: Relating research to service delivery* (DHHS Publication No. 85–1410, pp. 48–75). Washington, DC: U.S. Government Printing Office.

Webster-Stratton, C. (1985). Predictors of treatment outcome in parent training for conduct disordered children. *Behavior Therapy, 16,* 223–243.

Zambrana, R. E. (Ed.). (1995). *Understanding Latino families: Scholarship, policy, and practice.* Thousand Oaks, CA: Sage Publications.

About the Authors

Lynn McDonald, PhD, MSW, is senior scientist, Wisconsin Center for Education Research, University of Wisconsin-Madison, 1025 West Johnson Street, Madison, WI 53706; e-mail: mrmcdona@wisc.edu. **D. Paul Moberg, PhD,** is deputy director, Population Health Institute, University of Wisconsin-Madison. **Roger Brown, PhD,** is professor of research methodology, School of Nursing and Medicine, University of Wisconsin-Madison, Ismael Rodriguez-Espiricueta, MA, is director, Student Support Services, Central Texas College, Killeen, TX. **Nydia I. Flores, MS,** is bilingual school psychologist, Allen-Field Elementary School, Milwaukee Public Schools. **Melissa P. Burke, BS,** is research specialist, Center for Health Policy and Program Evaluation, University of Wisconsin-Madison. **Gail Coover, PhD,** is research manager, FAST Project, Wisconsin Center for Education Research, University of Wisconsin-Madison. This study was supported by grant DA10067 from the National Institute of Drug Abuse. For more information about FAST, see: www.fastprogram.org.

Sample Single-Case Experiment

Increasing On-Task Behavior in the Classroom: Extension of Self-Monitoring Strategies

Amato-Zech, N. A., Hoff, K. E., & Doepke, K. J. (2006). Increasing on-task behavior in the classroom: Extension of self-monitoring strategies. *Psychology in the Schools, 43*(2), 211–220.

Many students have difficulty staying on-task during classroom instruction. This is a problem because if students are not on-task, their learning suffers.

The following article describes a single-case experiment to test the effectiveness of a new device, called the MotivAider, to solve this problem. The MotivAider is designed to prompt students to self-monitor their on-task behavior, with the ultimate goal of having students internalize self-monitoring without need for the device.

The article is reprinted in its entirety, just as it appeared when originally published.

Increasing On-Task Behavior in the Classroom: Extension of Self-Monitoring Strategies

Natalie A. Amato-Zech
Community Consolidated School District 59

Kathryn E. Hoff and Karla J. Doepke
Illinois State University

ABSTRACT ■ We examined the effectiveness of a tactile self-monitoring prompt to increase on-task behaviors among 3 elementary-aged students in a special education classroom. Students were taught to self-monitor their attention by using the MotivAider (MotivAider, 2000), an electronic beeper that vibrates to provide a tactile cue to self-monitor. An ABAB reversal design was used for each participant. Results indicated that upon implementation of the self-monitoring intervention, students increased on-task behavior from a mean of 55% to more than 90% of the intervals observed. Additionally, teachers and students provided high ratings of treatment acceptability of this self-monitoring intervention. Limitations, implications, and future directions of these findings are discussed.

Self-monitoring among children has been examined extensively as a way to improve attention, academic productivity, and decrease off-task behavior in the classroom (Cole, Marder, & McCann, 2000; Shapiro & Cole, 1994). Self-monitoring involves two processes: self-observation and self-recording. Self-observation requires students to pay attention to a specific aspect of behavior, and discriminate whether the behavior being monitored has occurred. For example, students may be taught to ask themselves "Am I paying attention?" in response to a specific prompt (e.g., when a prerecorded tone sounds). Next, the student records whether the behavior being monitored has occurred (Nelson & Hayes, 1981).

Self-monitoring is an appealing strategy for promoting behavior change. Researchers have demonstrated that students with and without disabilities can learn to use self-monitoring to regulate their own behavior and enhance independent activity (McDougall & Brady, 1998; Shapiro & Cole, 1994). Self-monitoring procedures can decrease reliance on external agents (e.g., teachers, parents, peers) for behavior change, thus facilitating generalization to untrained settings and maintenance of acquired skills (McLaughlin, Krappman, & Welsh, 1985). Further, self-monitoring interventions are easy to use and can be implemented with minimal demands on teacher time or curricular modifications, making them optimal for use in schools (Shimabukuro, Prater, Jenkins, & Edelen-Smith, 1999).

Numerous investigations demonstrate the effectiveness of school-based self-monitoring interventions (Gardner & Cole, 1988; Hughes, Korinek, & Gorman, 1991; McDougall, Farrell, & Hoff, 2004; Shapiro & Cole, 1994). The majority of this research has focused on self-monitoring of attention-to-task, and demonstrates that self-monitoring of attention is effective in decreasing disruptive behavior (e.g., Lam, Cole, Shapiro, & Bambara, 1994) and increasing on-task behavior (e.g., Dalton, Martella, & Marchand-Martella, 1999; Dunlap et. al., 1995; Reid, 1996). Collateral effects of self-monitoring of attention also are apparent, in that self-monitoring of attention is associated with positive changes in academic performance such as academic productivity and academic accuracy (e.g., Harris, Graham, Reid, McElroy, & Hamby, 1994; Maag, Reid, & DiGangi, 1993). Finally, self-monitoring procedures are effective across diverse populations and settings. In particular, research supports the use of self-monitoring for students with emotional and behavioral disorders (Edwards, Salant, Howard, Brougher, & McLaughlin, 1995; McDougall & Brady, 1995; Moore, Cartledge, & Heckaman, 1995; Nelson, Smith, Young, & Dodd, 1991), learning disabilities (Hallahan, Marshall, & Lloyd, 1981; Prater, Hogan, & Miller, 1992; Prater, Joy, Chilman, Temple, & Miller, 1991; Rooney, Hallahan, & Lloyd, 1984), autism (Callahan & Rademacher, 1999; Harrower & Dunlap, 2001; Mancina, Tankersley, Kamps, Kravits, & Parrett, 2004), and mild to severe cognitive impairments (Alberto, Tabs, & Frederick, 1999; Briggs et al., 1990; Gilberts, Agran, Hughes, and Wehmeyer, 2001; Hughes et al., 2002). Further, self-monitoring interventions have proven effective in self-contained resource rooms and general education classroom settings (Dalton et al., 1999; Hughes & Hendrickson, 1987; Moore, Prebble, Robertson, Waetford, & Anderson, 2001; Reid, 1996).

Although research clearly supports the effectiveness of self-monitoring interventions, self-monitoring procedures can be impractical, infeasible, or disruptive in certain classroom settings. To date, the majority of self-monitoring interventions have relied on overt audio cues to prompt students to self-monitor their behavior (McDougall et al., 2004). For example, a tape recorder emits a prerecorded tone and this audible cue prompts a student to record whether they were paying attention (Hallahan et al., 1981). Other audible methods of prompting students in self-monitoring procedures include using a tape recorder with headphones for students to hear the cue, a kitchen timer, or verbal prompts from the teacher (Cole & Bambara, 2000). Although effective, these audible prompts have some potential disadvantages. Noticeable cues (e.g., wearing headphones or audible cues which others can hear) may be perceived as stigmatizing or aversive to the target student participating in the intervention and might be distracting to other students in the classroom who are not directed to self-monitor. Similarly, verbal prompts from a teacher can prove distracting, and requires the teacher to interrupt his or her lesson to provide the prompt. Self-

monitoring methods that are perceived as aversive by students or difficult or distracting for teachers (i.e., low social validity) may reduce the chance that self-monitoring methods will be employed in the classroom (Reid, 1996). Finally, the use of a more stationary self-monitoring prompt may not be portable outside of the classroom (e.g., recess), thus limiting the situations in which the prompt can be used.

Recently, an alternative self-monitoring procedure has emerged that is less intrusive and may prove more practical and feasible for classroom use than traditional aural or verbal prompts. The MotivAider (MotivAider, 2000) is an electronic beeper that vibrates to provide a tactile prompt to self-monitor. The MotivAider attaches to the student's waistband and can be programmed to emit a cue for any desired length of time and on a continuous or intermittent schedule. Although self-monitoring procedures using the MotivAider are promising and have high intuitive appeal, research has not evaluated the efficacy of using the MotivAider for self-monitoring. As such, this is the first known study to analyze the effectiveness of the MotivAider for increasing on-task behavior in the classroom. We sought to extend the self-management literature by examining the use of a tactile self-monitoring cue and contribute to the applied knowledge base by exploring an alternative self-monitoring strategy for the classroom.

METHOD

Participants

Participant selection was based on teacher referral of students with low levels of on-task behavior. Prior to inclusion in the project, these reports were confirmed by the researchers through direct observations in the classroom, with observations indicating that levels of on-task behavior occurred on less than 55% of the intervals observed for all participants.

Three fifth graders participated in this study. Jack and David were both 11-year-old boys who had been given multiple diagnoses of speech and language impairment and specific learning disabilities. Allison was an 11-year-old girl who had been given a diagnosis of emotionally disturbed and speech and language impairment. Each of the students was enrolled in the same self-contained special education classroom.

Setting

The study took place at an elementary school located in the Midwest United States. The classroom was a self-contained, multi-age classroom that included seven students: three third graders and four fifth graders. This self-contained program was a new addition to the continuum of services that existed within the district and was in its first year of implementation. A teacher and a full-time teacher assistant initially staffed the classroom; however, a long-term substitute replaced the teacher midway through the project (i.e., the fifth session of the return to baseline phase for all participants).

Experimental sessions were conducted during a regularly scheduled 45-min period in Reasoning and Writing. Instruction in Reasoning and Writing consisted of direct instruction on language reasoning skills and writing skills and independent seatwork on related materials. The length of time students spent in direct instruction and independent seatwork was consistent throughout the study. During the initial baseline phase and the initial intervention phase, all students received Instruction in Reasoning and Writing at a round table. During the return to baseline phase and throughout the rest of the study, students were sitting at desks during instruction.

Materials

The MotivAider was used for the cue to self-monitor throughout the intervention phase. The MotivAider looks like a pager and attaches to a belt or a waistband. It emits a pulsing vibration, which was used as the cue for participants to self-monitor their behavior. In addition to the MotivAider, all participants used a paper-and-pencil recording system to record whether they were paying attention at the time the MotivAider vibrated.

Measures

On-task behavior.   Direct observation data were collected for on- and off-task behavior using categories from the *Behavioral Observation of the Students in Schools* (BOSS) structured observational code (Shapiro, 1996). On-task behavior was defined as the student actively or passively attending to instruction or assigned work and the absence of off-task behavior during the observed interval. Three possible categories of off-task behavior were recorded: off-task motor, off-task verbal, and off-task passive behaviors. Off-task motor behaviors were defined as any motoric movement that occurred that was not associated with the academic task at hand (e.g., randomly flipping pages in a textbook or out of seat). Off-task verbal behaviors were coded whenever the student made any audible verbalizations that were not relevant to the assigned task or not permitted during the assigned task (e.g., talking to peers, humming, or calling out answers). Off-task passive behaviors occurred whenever there was passive disengagement for a period of at least 3 consecutive seconds (e.g., looking away from assigned material).

Data were collected using a 15-s partial interval recording system. If the student engaged in off-task behavior at any time during the interval, the student's behavior was recorded as off-task rather than on-task for that interval. Direct observations were conducted for 15 min per day, two to three times per week for each student. The first author served as the primary data collector, and the teacher's assistant collected interobserver agreement data.

Interobserver agreement data were collected for 18% of the total sessions observed. Interobserver agreement was calculated by dividing total interval agreements by total intervals observed (Kazdin, 1982). The mean percentage of overall agreement was 96% (range = 92–100%). Additionally, occurrence agreements were calculated on an interval-by-interval basis by dividing the agreements by the total number [of] agreements and disagreements and multiplying by 100. The mean interobserver reliability for the occurrence of off-task behavior was 81% [range = 0 (which occurred when there was only one off-task behavior observed during the session and agreement was not reached)–100%].

Treatment integrity.   Treatment integrity was assessed with a five-item checklist detailing specific steps of the intervention. The primary investigator conducted measures of treatment integrity for 46% of the intervention sessions. Adherence to all steps in the intervention occurred 100% of the time.

Treatment acceptability.   Questionnaires were completed at the end of the study to assess treatment acceptability and feasibility of the self-monitoring intervention using the MotivAider. The classroom teacher, the teacher's assistant, and the long-term substitute completed the later Intervention Rating Profile-20 (IRP-20; Witt & Martens, 1983). This questionnaire consists of 20 items rated on a Likert scale ranging from 0 (*strongly disagree*) to 6 (*strongly agree*). Students were administered a seven-item questionnaire adapted from the Children's Intervention Rating Profile (Turco & Elliot, 1986). This questionnaire consists of seven items rated on a Likert scale of 1 (indicating that the student disagrees with the statement) to 6 (indicating agreement).

Experimental Design and Procedures

An ABAB reversal design was used for each participant in the study, with an extended baseline for the third participant. The specific experimental phases are described next.

Baseline.   Initial baseline observations of student behavior were conducted in Reasoning and Writing as well as Math settings. During baseline, self-monitoring procedures were not in place, and teachers were instructed to use their typical procedures for classroom management (e.g., praising appropriate behavior and redirecting off-task behavior). Additionally, all students in the class participated in a classroom-wide point system, which was in place throughout the study. With this system, each child earned stamps throughout the day for working on his or her personal behavioral goal, and exchanged the stamp sheets at the end of the week for a small incentive. This system was used throughout the course of the study and was not linked to the self-management procedures.

Student training.   Participants were trained to observe and record (i.e., self-monitor) their on-task behavior during two group-training sessions and two practice sessions in the classroom. The training sessions were 30 min in length, and were conducted by the first teacher in her office at the school. During student training, students were taught to identify on- and off-task behaviors using the SLANT strategy (Ellis, 1991). SLANT is an acronym that stands for Sit up, Look at the person talking, Activate thinking, Note key information, and Track the talker. Off-task behavior was defined as the absence of one or more SLANT behaviors. Next, within the training session, students practiced self-monitoring of their on-task behavior, first with an overt audio cue (to ensure they were self-recording accurately and to better provide performance feedback) and then using the MotivAider. Following the two student-training sessions, each student practiced using the MotivAider in the classroom during the 45-min Reasoning and Writing instruction period until they could use the self-monitoring procedures without assistance, as demonstrated by self-recording at the end of each 2-min interval for one entire class session. On the second day of training, all participants were able to self-monitor their on-task behavior and to begin intervention implementation.

Self-monitoring intervention. All participants self-monitored their on- and off-task behavior during Reasoning and Writing instruction. Students wore the MotivAider, which elicited electronic vibrations to cue self-monitoring. When the MotivAider vibrated, students recorded whether they were paying attention at that moment in time by checking "yes, I was paying attention" or "no, I was not paying attention" on a self-monitoring form. After each session, the students returned their completed self-monitoring forms and MotivAider to the classroom teacher. The self-monitoring forms were collected on a weekly basis. After the initial student-training sessions, the classroom teacher was responsible for managing the intervention (i.e., distribution of MotivAiders and self-monitoring forms).

For all participants, the MotivAider was set at 1-min fixed intervals for the first week of the intervention phase; however, at the beginning of the second week of the intervention, the classroom teacher expressed a concern stating that she felt the 1-min cue was too intrusive. After consultation with the teacher about an acceptable cueing interval, the MotivAider was programmed to emit a vibration every 3 min throughout the duration of the study (i.e., the remaining intervention phase and final return to the second intervention phase).

Generalization. Generalization probes were conducted for 10% to 12% of the sessions (i.e., once during each experiment phase). Generalization probes were conducted in a second academic setting (Math) identified by the teacher. The MotivAider was not used in the generalization setting. A direct instruction curriculum (Connecting Math Concepts) was used during this class period.

RESULTS

On-Task Behavior

Figure 1 displays the percentage of intervals of on-task behavior far the three participants. In general, similar results were obtained for each participant in the study. During initial baseline observation, Jack, David, and Allison displayed low levels of on-task behavior (i.e., less than 60% of

intervals observed). During the initial intervention phase, participants' on-task behavior increased and reached above 90% at the end of the phase. When the intervention was discontinued (i.e., return to baseline conditions), there was a steady decrease in on-task behavior. Upon reinstatement of the intervention, on-task behavior immediately improved to more than 90% of the intervals observed and remained stable. Specific results of participants are described next.

Jack. Jack's mean percentage of on-task behavior during baseline occurred for 53% of the intervals (range = 47–61%). His on-task behavior showed a slight increasing trend during baseline; however, the final 3 points in baseline were stable. During the self-monitoring phase, Jack's on-task behavior increased to a mean of 79% of intervals observed (range = 65–95%). When the intervention was discontinued, Jack's on-task behavior displayed a decreasing trend and a mean of 74% of intervals observed (range = 65–81%). When the intervention was reintroduced, Jack's rate of on-task behavior quickly improved to a mean occurrence of 91% intervals observed (range = 85–100%).

The percentage of nonoverlapping data points was calculated to summarize intervention effects. Results indicated that the percentages of nonoverlapping data points between the initial baseline phase and the initial intervention phase, as well as the initial baseline phase and the return to intervention phase, was 100%, suggesting the intervention was consistently associated with behavior change. The percentage of nonoverlapping data points between the initial intervention phase and the return to baseline phase was 54%. The overlapping points between the return to baseline phase and the initial intervention phase consist of the first few data points collected during the intervention, suggesting the intervention did not have an immediate dramatic effect on behavior. Finally, the percentage of nonoverlapping data points between the return to baseline phase and the return to intervention phase was 100%.

Generalization data for Jack indicate his on-task behavior occurred for 55% of the intervals observed during the initial baseline phase. During the self-monitoring phase, Jack's off-task behavior in Math increased to 87% of intervals observed. When the intervention was returned to baseline, Jack's on-task behaviors in Math remained stable, occurring for 85% of the intervals observed. Upon reintroduction of the intervention, Jack's off-task behaviors again remained stable at 85% of the intervals observed.

David. Results indicate that David's on-task behavior during baseline occurred an average of 55% of intervals observed (range = 43–62%). When the self-monitoring intervention was introduced, his on-task behavior showed an increasing trend with a mean of 79% intervals observed (range = 68–93%). When the intervention was discontinued, David's on-task behavior decreased to a mean of 76% intervals observed (range = 70–80%). Upon reinstatement of the intervention, David's on-task behavior increased to an average of 93% of the intervals observed (range = 87–97%).

FIGURE 1   Percentages of Intervals of On-Task Behavior for Jack, David, and Allison

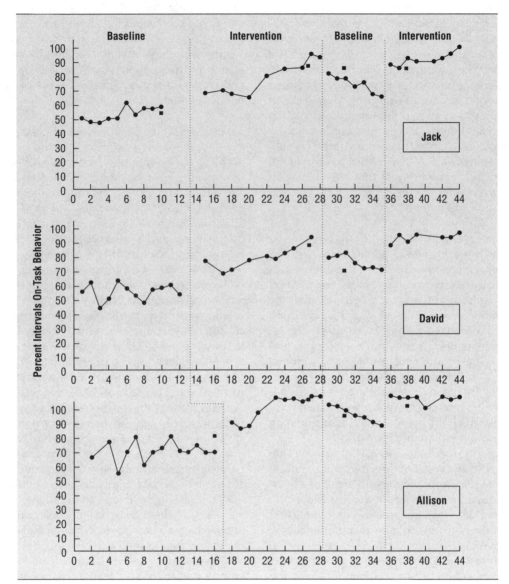

The percentage of nonoverlapping data points between the initial baseline phase and the initial intervention phase was 100% for David, as well as for the initial baseline phase and the return to intervention phase. The percentage of nonoverlapping data points between the initial intervention phase and the return to baseline phase was 22%, suggesting that the intervention did not have an immediate effect on on-task behavior but instead led to a gradual decease in on-task behavior. Finally, the percentage of nonoverlapping data points between the return to baseline phase and the return to intervention phase was 100%.

Generalization data for David indicate that David's on-task behavior in Math during the initial baseline phase, intervention phase, return to baseline phase, and reimplementation of the intervention occurred for 60, 88, 70, and 90% of the intervals, respectively.

Allison.   During the initial baseline phase, Allison's on-task behavior occurred at a mean rate of 56% of the intervals observed (range = 45–67%) and displayed a flat trend. Upon introduction of the self-monitoring intervention, Allison's on-task behavior increased to a mean of 89% of the intervals observed (range = 73–98% of the intervals observed). When the intervention was discontinued, Allison's on-task behavior displayed a steady decreasing trend with a mean of 84% intervals observed (range = 75–91%). When the intervention was reintroduced, Allison's on-task behavior immediately increased to a mean rate of 96% of intervals observed (range = 88–98%).

The percentage of nonoverlapping data points between the initial baseline phase and the initial intervention phase was 100%, as well as for the initial baseline phase and the return to intervention phase. The percentage of nonoverlapping data points between the initial intervention phase and the return to baseline phase was 60%, suggesting that the intervention had a gradual impact on increasing levels of on-task behavior. Finally, the percentage of nonoverlapping data points between the return to baseline phase and the return to intervention phase was 88%. When examining the overlapping data points, there was a single dip in Allison's level of on-task behavior during one intervention session that accounts for the overlap.

Generalization data for Allison indicate that for on-task behavior in Math during the initial baseline phase, intervention phase, return to baseline phase, and reimplementation of the intervention occurred for 67, 95, 83, and 90% of the intervals, respectively.

Treatment Acceptability

Result of the treatment acceptability ratings by classroom personnel were high. The classroom teacher, the teacher's assistant, and the long-term substitute reported total acceptability scores of 115, 102, and 98, respectively, where 120 of 120 indicates the most acceptable score possible. Specifically, results indicated that all teachers strongly agreed on factors such as intervention procedures being beneficial to the student (i.e., two ratings of 5 and one rating of 6), intervention procedures being easy to implement without a lot of training (i.e., two ratings of 6 and one rating of 5), and that overall, the teachers would be willing to use the self-monitoring intervention in the classroom setting (i.e., two ratings of 5 and one rating of 6).

Total acceptability scores on the Children's Intervention Rating Profile for Jack, David, and Allison were 33, 31, and 36 of 42, respectively, where 42 of 42 indicates the most acceptable score possible. All students strongly agreed that they liked the intervention (i.e., three ratings of 6), felt that the intervention would help them in school (i.e., two ratings of 6 and one rating of 5), and did not think there were better ways to help their inattentive behavior (i.e., three ratings of 6).

DISCUSSION

This is the first known investigation of the use of self-monitoring with the MotivAider for increasing the on-task behaviors of elementary-aged students in a special education classroom. Upon implementation of the self-monitoring intervention, students increased levels of on-task behavior from a mean of 55% to more than 90% of the intervals observed. These findings are consistent with prior self-monitoring literature and provide additional empirical support of the effectiveness and acceptability of self-monitoring in the classroom. The data also demonstrate that students with learning and behavioral challenges can effectively use a tactile self-monitoring prompt for behavior change.

The results of this study have several practical implications for use in schools. First, self-monitoring using the MotivAider was easy and relatively time effective. Because the students were responsible for monitoring and recording their own behavior, the intervention was easy to im-

plement and placed few demands on the teachers' time. These are important factors to consider, as interventions requiring low amounts of teacher time are likely to lead to increased follow-through and higher rates of treatment acceptability compared to time-intensive interventions or interventions that take away from classroom instruction (Frith & Armstrong, 1986). Second, students' on-task behaviors increased despite the absence of tangible rewards for doing so (i.e., no complex reinforcement program was required). These results are similar to prior research findings indicating that self-monitoring can produce positive gains without backup consequences (Hallahan & Sapona, 1983; Shimabukuro et al., 1999). These results also are consistent with prior theories indicating that self-monitoring leads to heightened awareness of a target behavior and subsequent behavior change (i.e., reactivity; Kanfer, 1970) and that self-monitoring appropriate behavior can take on motivational properties, providing reinforcement for behavior change (Nelson & Hayes, 1981). The absence of an external reinforcement program can make this intervention more acceptable and less intrusive in the classroom as well as facilitate generalization to untrained settings and skills (McLaughlin et al., 1985). Although these preliminary findings are promising, further research is necessary to explore whether the positive results would maintain over time without additional reinforcement.

Also encouraging were the high intervention acceptability ratings provided by the teachers and the students. Teachers indicated that the intervention was highly acceptable and easy to implement, and responded that they would use the self-monitoring intervention again for a similar problem. Likewise, high ratings of student acceptability revealed that students viewed the MotivAider as a tool to help them stay on task, did not feel the intervention was intrusive in the classroom, and reported that wearing the MotivAider was "cool."

LIMITATIONS

Although we obtained positive results using the MotivAider, there are several limitations to this study worth noting. First, we did not see incomplete return to initial baseline levels when the MotivAider was removed. One possible explanation of this observation is that students were learning to self-manage their behavior; if this were the case, we would not expect a reversal to baseline conditions. Nonetheless, data for all participants clearly demonstrated a decreasing trend of on-task behavior once the MotivAider was removed. Thus, it would appear that students still relied on the MotivAider for behavior change to some extent. It remains to be explored empirically if over time, students can control on-task behavior on their own, without reliance on external prompts, or whether the reactive effects of self-monitoring are more short term and disappear when self-monitoring is discontinued (Nelson, 1977).

Finally, our generalization data must be interpreted with caution, as only one observation per phase was conducted.

When examining these limited data, however, it is surprising to note that for two participants, Allison and David, the generalization probes verbally correspond with the data collected during each phase of the study. For example, during the initial baseline phase, Allison's on-task behaviors in Reasoning and Writing occurred for a mean of 55% of the intervals observed and for 67% of the intervals in the generalization setting (Math). Upon implementation of the intervention, Allison's on-task behaviors increased in the intervention setting and generalization setting where the MotivAider was not being used. It would be interesting to explore whether generalization data collected on a more consistent basis would yield the same results.

FUTURE DIRECTIONS

As this is the first published study that has explored the use of the MotivAider for self-monitoring, future research should include attempts to replicate the results obtained with the use of the MotivAider. Additionally, issues related to long-term use of self-monitoring, such as generalization and maintenance of self-monitoring with the MotivAider across settings and over time, warrant further investigation. Research examining what age ranges and for what behaviors the MotivAider might be most useful would add to the current knowledge base. Finally, future research should explore commensurate changes in academic performance and social acceptance of children using the MotivAider.

In conclusion, self-monitoring using the MotivAider appears to be an effective and practical intervention for increasing on-task behavior for students with learning difficulties and behavioral challenges. Additional research is needed to replicate and extend the findings of this study and to explore ways for students to become an active participant for behavior change.

References

Alberto, P. A., Taber, T. A., & Fredrick, L. D. (1999). Use of self-operated auditory prompts to decrease aberrant behaviors in students with moderate mental retardation. Research in Developmental Disabilities, 20, 429–439.

Briggs, A., Alberto, P., Sharpton, W., Berlin, K., McKinley, C., & Ritts, C. (1990). Generalized use of a self-operated audio prompt system. Education and Training in Mental Retardation, 25, 381–389.

Callahan, K., & Rademacher, J. A. (1999). Using self-management strategies to increase the on-task behavior of a student with autism. Journal of Positive Behavior Interventions, 1, 117–122.

Cole, C. L., & Bambara, L. M. (2000). Self-monitoring: Theory and practice. In E. S. Shapiro & T. R. Kratochwill (Eds.), Behavioral assessment in schools: Theory, research, and clinical foundations (pp. 202–232). New York: Guilford Press.

Cole, C. L., Marder, T., & McCann, L. (2000). Self-monitoring. In E. S. Shapiro & T. R. Kratochwill (Eds.), Conducting school-based assessment of child and adolescent behavior (pp. 121–149). New York: Guilford Press.

Dalton, T., Martella, R. C., & Marchand-Martella, N. E. (1999). The effects of a self-management program in reducing off-task behavior. Journal of Behavioral Education, 9, 157–176.

Dunlap, G., Clarke, S., Jackson, M., Wright, S., Ramos, H., & Brinson, S. (1995). Self-monitoring of classroom behaviors with students exhibiting emotional and behavioral challenges. School Psychology Quarterly, 10, 165–177.

Edwards, L., Salent, V., Howard, V. F., Brougher, J., & McLaughlin, T. F. (1995). Effectiveness of self-management on attentional behavior and reading comprehension for children with attention deficit disorder. Child & Family Behavior Therapy, 17, 1–17.

Ellis, E. S. (1991). SLANT: A starter strategy for class participation. Lawrence, KS: Edge Enterprises, Inc.

Frith, G. H., & Armstrong, S. W. (1986). Self-monitoring for behavioral disordered students. Teaching Exceptional Children, 18(Winter), 144–148.

Gardner, W. I., & Cole, C. L. (1988). Self-monitoring procedures. In E. S. Shapiro & T. R. Kratochwill (Eds.), Behavioral assessment in schools: Conceptual foundations and practical applications (pp. 106–146). New York: Guilford Press.

Gilberts, G. H., Agran, M., Hughes, C., & Wehmeyer, M. (2001). The effects of peer delivered self-monitoring strategies on participation of students with severe disabilities in general education classrooms. Journal of the Association for Persons with Severe Handicaps, 26, 25–36.

Hallahan, D., Marshall, K., & Lloyd, J. (1981). Self-recording during group instruction: Effects on attention to task. Learning Disability Quarterly, 4, 407–413.

Hallahan, D., & Sapora, R. (1983). Self-monitoring of attention with learning-disabled children: Past research and current issues. Journal of Learning Disabilities, 16, 616–621.

Harris, K. R., Graham, S., Reid, R., McElroy, K., & Hamby, R. S. (1994). Self-monitoring of attention versus self-monitoring of performance: Replication and cross-task comparison studies. Learning Disability Quarterly, 17, 121–139.

Harrower, J. K., & Dunlap, G. (2001). Including children with autism in general education classrooms: A review of effective strategies. Behavior Modification, 25, 762–784.

Hughes, C., Copeland, S. R., Agran, M., Wehmeyer, M. L., Rodi, M. S., & Pressley, J. A. (2002). Using self-monitoring to improve performance in general education high school classes. Education and Training in Mental Retardation and Developmental Disabilities, 37, 262–272.

Hughes, C., & Hendrickson, J. (1987). Self-monitoring with at-risk students in the regular class setting. Education and Treatment of Children, 10, 225–236.

Hughes, C. A., Korinek, L., & Gorman, J. (1991). Self-management for students with mental retardation in public school settings: A research review. Education and Training in Mental Retardation, 26, 271–291.

Kanfer, F. H. (1970). Self-monitoring: Methodological limitations and clinical applications. Journal of Consulting and Clinical Psychology, 35, 148–152.

Kazdin, A. E. (1982). Single case research designs: Methods for clinical and applied settings. New York: Oxford University Press.

Lam, A. L., Cole, C. L., Shapiro, E. S., & Bambara, L. M. (1994). Relative effects of self-monitoring on-task behavior, academic accuracy, and disruptive behavior in students with behavior disorders. School Psychology Review, 23, 44–58.

Maag, J. W., Reid, R., & DiGangi, S. A. (1993). Differential effects of self-monitoring attention, accuracy, and productivity. Journal of Applied Behavioral Analysis, 26, 329–344.

Mancina, C., Tankersley, M., Kamps, D., Kravits, T., & Parrett, J. (2000). Reduction of inappropriate vocalizations for a child with autism using a self-management treatment program. Journal of Autism & Developmental Disorders, 30, 599–606.

McDougall, D., & Brady, M. P. (1995). Using audio-cued self-monitoring for students with severe behavior disorders. Journal of Educational Research, 88, 309–318.

McDougall, D., & Brady, M. P. (1998). Initiating and fading self-management interventions to increase math fluency in general education classes. Exceptional Children, 64, 151–166.

McLaughlin, T. F., Krappman, V. F., Welsh, J. M. (1985). The effects of self-recording for on-task behavior of behaviorally disordered special education students. Remedial and Special Education, 6, 42–45.

Moore, D. W., Prebble, S., Robertson, J., Waetford, R., & Anderson, A. (2001). Self-recording with goal setting: A self-management programme for the classroom. Educational Psychology, 21, 255–265.

Moore, R. J., Cartledge, G., & Heckaman, K. (1995). The effects of social skill instruction and self-monitoring on game-related behaviors of adolescents with emotional or behavioral disorders. Behavioral Disorders, 20, 253–266.

MotivAider. (2000). Thief River Falls, MA: Behavioral Dynamics.

Nelson, R. O. (1977). Assessment and therapeutic functions of self-monitoring. In M. Herson, R. M. Eisler, & P. M. Miller (Eds.), Progress in behavior modification (Vol. 5, pp. 263–308). New York: Academic Press.

Nelson, R. O., & Hayes, S. (1981). Theoretical explanations for reactivity in self-monitoring. Behavior Modification, 5, 3–14.

Nelson, J. R., Smith, D. J., Young, R. K., & Dodd, J. M. (1991). A review of self-management outcome research conducted with students who exhibit behavior disorders. Behavioral Disorders, 16, 169–179.

Prater, M. A., Hogan, S., & Miller, S. R. (1992). Using self-monitoring to improve on-task behavior and academic skills of an adolescent with mild handicaps across special and regular education settings. Education and Treatment of Children, 15, 43–55.

Prater, M. A., Joy, R., Chilman, B., Temple, J., & Miller, S. R. (1991). Self-monitoring of on-task behavior by adolescents with learning disabilities. Learning Disabilities Quarterly, 14, 164–177.

Reid, R. (1996). Research in self-monitoring with students with learning disabilities: The present, the prospects, the pitfalls. Journal of Learning Disabilities, 29, 317–331.

Rooney, K. J., Hallahan, D. P., & Lloyd, J. W. (1984). Self-recording of attention by learning disabled students in the regular classroom. Journal of Learning Disabilities, 17, 360–364.

Shapiro, E. S. (1996). Academic skills problems workbook. New York: Guilford Press.

Shapiro, E. S., & Cole, C. (1994). Behavior change in the classroom: Self-management interventions. New York: Guilford Press.

Shimabukuro, S. M., Prater, M. A., Jenkins, A., & Edelen-Smith, P. (1999). The effects of self-monitoring of academic performance on students with learning disabilities and ADD/ADHD. Education and Treatment of Children, 22, 397–414.

Turco, T., & Elliot, S. (1986). Assessment of students' acceptability ratings of teacher initiated interventions for classroom misbehavior. Journal of School Psychology, 24, 277–283.

Witt, J., & Martens, B. (1983). Assessing the acceptability of behavioral interventions used in classrooms. Psychology in the Schools, 20, 510–517.

chapter 14

Case Studies in Qualitative Research

IMPORTANT *Ideas*

1. Unlike case stories in magazines or professional publications for educators, case studies are investigations that attempt to satisfy research standards for validity and reliability.

2. Qualitative research case studies involve intensive inquiry into instances of a phenomenon in its natural context, from both the researchers' (etic) perspective and the research participants' (emic) perspective.

3. Qualitative case studies reflect the interpretivist view, which considers reality as not objective but rather as constructed by each individual.

4. The introductory section of a qualitative case study report typically states questions to be answered, issues to be addressed, or purposes to be achieved.

5. The purpose of most qualitative research case studies is description, evaluation, or explanation of particular phenomena.

6. Selection of qualitative research cases typically is based on purposeful sampling, which involves a search for instances of a phenomenon that are information-rich.

7. Because construction, meaning making, and interpretation are central in qualitative research, the primary instrument of data collection is the researcher.

8. Qualitative researchers often practice reflexivity, engaging in self-reflection to identify, communicate, and attempt to reduce their personal biases with respect to the phenomena being studied.

9. The most common forms of data collection in qualitative research case studies are individual or focus group interviews, participant observation, review of documents and media, and use of paper-and-pencil measures. Interviews are usually open-ended and informal, similar to natural conversation.

10. Interpretational analysis of case study data is based on the principles of grounded theory, which involve coding data segments into categories and grouping them to identify different levels of information that give meaning to the data.

11. Case study researchers typically begin data analysis while still engaged in data collection and continue data collection until additional data contribute nothing new about the phenomenon being studied.

12. Case study researchers sometimes analyze their data through reflective analysis, relying on their own intuition and personal judgment.

13. Case study researchers reflect on the applicability of their findings to other settings and provide thick descriptions of their cases to help readers make their own judgments of applicability.

14. A variety of strategies are available to case study researchers to demonstrate the credibility and trustworthiness of their findings, including usefulness, participant involvement, inclusion of quantitative data, long-term observation, coding checks, member checking, triangulation, and contextual completeness.

15. Qualitative researchers have developed qualitative research traditions over time. These traditions draw on general principles of qualitative research methodology, but they study different types of phenomena and use specialized research techniques to study them. ■

Key TERMS

applicability	fieldwork	positivism
audit trail	focus groups	purposeful sampling
case	grounded theory	qualitative research tradition
case focus	in-depth study	reflective analysis
case story	insider	reflexivity
case study	interpretational analysis	relational pattern
causal pattern	interpretivism	snowball sampling
chain of evidence	key informant	tacit knowledge
coding check	member checking	theme
constant comparison	multivocality	theoretical saturation
constructs	outsider	thick description
critical research	participant observer	triangulation
crystallization	pattern	
emic perspective	performance ethnography	
etic perspective	phenomenon	

How Qualitative Case Study Research Can Help Educators Solve Problems of Practice

In sharing what they know about education, most educators tell stories. They have stories about their own experience as students, often going back to childhood. They have joyful stories about their own successes with particular students and sad stories about others. Many educators can quickly relate insightful, moving descriptions as to why a student like Jimmie or Chaneva or Oliver probably will, or won't, do well in school this year. They often will have ongoing stories about new programs as they proceed to be implemented in their schools.

Many individuals who are preparing to become teachers have told us that they found greater value in their field experience than in their teacher education coursework. Perhaps one reason is that in the field their learning is based more on stories from their fellow student teachers, supervising teachers, and others, as well as from their own and other students' experience. Many of these stories convey to new teachers messages about "the way we do things here" and "what you need to do if you want to get a job in this school district."

Example of a Case Story

Bruce Biddle and Donald S. Anderson (1986) argued that some published qualitative research studies would be better described as case stories than case studies. To illustrate the difference, we present at the end of this chapter an article that appeared in *Teacher Magazine*. (We recommend that you read the article now.)

This article is a case story. A **case story** describes a series of related events in an interesting manner, but it is not intended to provide evidence for judging the validity of the events described or their applicability in other contexts. Nonetheless, this and other case stories are enlightening and interesting, and they give teachers hope that they, too, can improve their classroom instruction.

To what extent are stories like this a sound guide for other educators' practice? This question cannot be answered with any certainty, because the article does not present evidence to validate Ms. Sacks's assertions that her students "worked more productively" and "were surprisingly responsible about their use of time." In the words of Biddle and Anderson, a case story "is designed to illustrate conclusions to which the author is already committed" (p. 239).

In contrast, a **case study** is a systematic qualitative research investigation. It involves in-depth study of instances of a phenomenon in its natural context while conveying both the researchers' and the participants' perspectives and using procedures that test the validity and applicability of its findings. It would be possible for researchers to take Ms. Sacks's insights, based on her own experiences, and test them by a rigorous case study or other research method.

The features of case studies are explained and illustrated in the following sections.

Key Characteristics of Case Studies

Case study research characteristics derive mainly from ethnography, which is one of the earliest forms of qualitative research. Anthropologists typically carry out ethnography by immersing themselves in a different culture and making holistic studies of cultural behavior, beliefs, and artifacts (see Chapter 16).

The next four sections describe key characteristics of a case study, which reflect its foundation in ethnography. We use as an example a case study about bilingual education reported by Ofelia García and Lesley Bartlett (2007).

Study of Particular Instances of a Phenomenon

A case study is conducted to shed light on a particular **phenomenon**—that is, a set of processes, events, individuals, programs, or any other events or circumstances of interest to researchers. Examples of educational phenomena are daily life in a school's computer lab, a particular curriculum, school staff with similar work responsibilities, or school events such as meetings of the district's school board. The researchers must first clarify the phenomenon of interest before they can select for intensive study the **case**, which is the specific instance of the phenomenon, bounded in time and place, that they choose to address in their study.

García and Bartlett's case study involved an analysis of a particular institution providing bilingual education, which is the phenomenon of interest. A phenomenon has many aspects, so researchers must select a focus for their investigation. A **case focus** represents those aspects of the phenomenon on which data collection and analysis will concentrate.

In our example, the researchers wished to study a model of bilingual education different from those found in most bilingual schools. The specific case that they studied as an instance of this phenomenon is Gregorio Luperón High School, a segregated bilingual high school for Latino newcomers in a suburban New York community. Of its 350 students, 85 percent of whom are from the Dominican Republic, 82 percent have been in the United States 3 years or less. The researchers' primary focus for data collection and analysis was the strengths and drawbacks of this type of bilingual high school.

In-Depth Study of the Case

A case study ideally involves **in-depth study** of the phenomenon, meaning that a substantial amount of data are collected about the specific case or cases selected to represent the phenomenon. These data are mainly verbal statements, images, or physical objects, but some quantitative data also might be collected.

The data typically are collected over an extended time period, with several methods of data collection. In our example, the researchers collected data in a variety of ways:

1. Weekly participant observation for a nine-month period in lower-level English as a second language (ESL) and Spanish classes and other content-area classes
2. Seven focus groups conducted in Spanish with newly arrived students enrolled in ESL 1 and 2
3. Interviews with five teachers and two administrators of the school
4. A focus group conducted with some ESL teachers and another with the Spanish teachers
5. Recordings of monthly staff development sessions coordinated by the authors during the first year of the study

The researchers also collected data on their own experience of the school's bilingual program, as well as the research participants' experience. Data collection continued for more than a year.

This extensive data-collection process exemplifies what it means to do an in-depth study of a case. The depth in this case was made possible by the researchers' strategic decision to study a specific instance of the phenomenon of interest rather than a sample of schools, as would be done in a typical quantitative research study.

Study of a Phenomenon in Its Natural Context

Jerome Kirk and Marc Miller (1986) define qualitative research as an approach to social science research that involves "watching people in their own territory and interacting with them in their own language, on their own terms" (p. 9). This approach to research typically involves **fieldwork,** a process in which researchers interact with participants in their natural settings.

In education, fieldwork settings are often schools or other educational institutions, because that is where the research participants of interest to many educational researchers are found. However, we need to remember that students, teachers, and other school participants also have active lives outside these institutional contexts. Thus, you should examine case studies (or any type of research) in education to see whether the researchers conducted fieldwork in other natural sites of teaching and learning, such as the home.

In the bilingual education study, it appears that all data were collected in the school. García and Bartlett state that "most of the teachers are Dominicans, and most of these are immigrants themselves. The principal of the school . . . is also a Dominican" (p. 7). Consistent with its staff and student population and its unique model of bilingual education, "Gregorio Luperón simply teaches most content in Spanish" (p. 17).

Representation of Both the Emic and Etic Perspectives

Case studies seek to develop an understanding of a complex phenomenon as experienced by its participants. In other words, the researchers must come to understand the phenomenon from the research participants' point of view, while maintaining their own point of view. The participants' viewpoint about the phenomenon under study is called the **emic perspective.** Typically, researchers obtain the emic perspective through informal conversations with the case study participants and by observing their natural behavior in the field.

At the same time, the researchers maintain their own perspective as investigators of the phenomenon. Their viewpoint of the phenomenon under study as outsiders, which is called the **etic perspective,** helps them make conceptual and theoretical sense of the case and to report the findings so that their contribution to the literature is clear to other researchers.

In the case study of bilingual education the researchers convey the emic perspective of the participants in varied ways. They include detailed quotations, in both Spanish and English, that reflect students' and teachers' views on various issues, such as the necessity of learning English and the value of students' bilingualism in fostering achievement. In their acknowledgements, the researchers note three research participants who read a first draft of the case study report.

The two researchers, who are employed at the Teachers College of Columbia University, make their etic perspective apparent in several ways. Their study includes a review of bilingual education from the 1960s on, citing political and legislative milestones and describing various models of bilingual education. The researchers enumerate the strengths of Gregorio Luperón's model of bilingual education as perceived by the research participants. They provide a balanced perspective by also discussing the model's limitations, including the social isolation fostered by the school's homogeneous student population. The researchers express their concern that this model for bilingual education might hinder the ability of Dominican students to function effectively beyond their immediate community.

Examples of Case Studies

Case studies, and qualitative research generally, are a rich source of knowledge that educators draw on to identify, explore, and solve their problems of practice. Therefore we want to expand your understanding of the varied kinds of phenomena that case studies address and the approaches used to explore them. To illustrate, consider the following two case studies.

A Case Study of Teacher Development

A researcher (Roza Leikin) and a teacher (Shelly Rota) conducted a collaborative practitioner-oriented study to explore how teachers learn through the process of teaching and reflection (Leikin & Rota, 2006). Rota, an elementary teacher of mathematics, was both the subject and the co-author of the study. The study focused on the teacher's management of whole-class discussion during inquiry-based mathematics instruction in one of her mathematics classrooms.

Rota initiated inquiry-based instruction, which assumes that knowledge is constructed by the learner rather than acquired directly from teachers and other sources, for several reasons. First, she wanted to improve her students' class contributions during instruction and also their learning outcomes. Second, she and Leikin sought to clarify how she, and other teachers, could teach mathematics with less stress and more confidence. Third, they wanted to discover how teachers can encourage students' exploration and understanding of mathematics as opposed to rote learning of mathematical concepts.

Their study analyzed the teacher's change in two aspects of instruction. The first, discussion structure, involves changes in teaching that occur in class discussion as the nature of the mathematical task shifts toward exploration and away from stating facts or seeking to give correct answers. The second, lesson organization, involves changes in how a teacher structures the elements of a lesson.

Leikin and Rota intermittently videotaped 15 months of Rota's lessons and then analyzed the videotaped lessons. The categories for analyzing lesson organization were drawn from previous research. To analyze discussion structure, the researchers developed themes based on grounded theory (Strauss & Corbin, 1990). Three lessons, each representing a different point in Rota's development, were the focus of intensive analysis.

Using timeline diagrams, Leikin and Rota (2006) found that the second and third lessons were better organized than the first lesson "and revealed sharp boundaries between different activities and a clear correspondence between the actual and the intended lesson organization" (p. 51). For example, they found that the teacher needed to reintroduce the task four times during the first lesson because her initial introduction was confusing, whereas "in the second and the third lessons new tasks were presented . . . with a clear connection to relevant learning materials studied earlier" (p. 52).

With respect to classroom discourse, student participation became more active, and the teacher's participation became more responsive as the lessons proceeded. The researchers identified four discussion themes: stimulating initiation, stimulating reply, summary reply, and listening and watching. Within the first three themes, they defined six categories of discussion actions: questioning, translating a representation, exact repetition of students' utterances, constructing a logical chain, stating a fact, and providing feedback.

Leikin and Rota conclude:

> The observed changes in lesson organization, in discussion structure, and in the quality of the discussion actions indicate the development of Shelly's proficiency in managing the inquiry-based lesson. . . . Shelly became more flexible . . . and more able to show trust. (2006, p. 61)

The researchers suggest a model of teacher discussion activity that "is useful for diagnostic purposes" (p. 64) in analyzing teacher proficiency. "For example, the model reveals that the more proficient teacher performs more actions of the stimulated reply type, connected to student conjectures, designing the actual learning trajectory based on student ideas" (p. 64). A similar analysis of student discussion activities also reveals important changes, including taking a more active part in whole-class discussion and becoming more likely to "construct a logical chain" rather than merely "stating a fact" in their statements (p. 62).

Leikin and Rota caution that while teaching actions are teachable, they "are of a heuristic nature, that is, they are not describable by algorithm" (p. 64). In other words, no simplistic formula will help teachers develop proficiency, but rather they must construct their teaching actions flexibly based on a clear conception of their subject, their students, and their own role in the teaching–learning process.

A Case Study of Instructional Technologists' Work

Another case study by Leigh Ausband (2006) examined the involvement of district-level instructional technology (IT) specialists in the curriculum work of one school district. The cases were one former and three current IT specialists in a district in central South Carolina comprising 48 schools. Ausband, previously an IT specialist in this district, was most concerned by the problem of practice of how school districts should define and organize the work of such specialists to increase their impact on curriculum work and thereby on classroom teaching and learning.

The researcher drew on themes and categories generated by previous researchers to describe various aspects of curriculum work on a district level and also various aspects of IT specialists' work. He identified five themes that characterized the district's curriculum work: (1) curriculum and instruction, (2) technical expertise, (3) program management, (4) program coordination, and (5) communication among school staff. He then generated a table comparing the categories of curriculum work and IT work, showing both similarities and differences. He used that table as a framework for analysis of documents, observations of each research participant, and development of questions for individual interviews and a focus group interview. He coded interview transcripts and other data, a methodological procedure discussed in greater depth later in the chapter.

Ausband found that IT specialists' work has evolved to include three new functions: improving and changing curriculum, evaluating instruction, and evaluating programs and research. These new functions reflect the specialists' perceptions that information technology fully corresponds to curriculum work. In the words of one specialist, "I don't think today you can have curriculum without technology. . . . We can't teach today without including technology" (2006, p. 12).

The IT specialists described their actual job responsibilities as including

> working with teachers to help them integrate technology into the curriculum through teaching courses and workshops, helping teachers develop lesson plans that utilized technology, and supporting teachers as they developed their technology portfolios. . . . Through their membership on district-level curriculum committees and the Joint Department Leadership Team, the instructional technology specialists were involved in goal-setting, improving curriculum, planning, evaluating, and updating policies and procedures, dealing with problems, and program management. (Ausband, 2006, p. 13)

Ausband found that IT specialists were concerned about barriers that they felt limited their contributions to curriculum work. These barriers included exclusion from decision making; lack of time to spend working in schools; and communication, relationship, and leadership issues. For example, Ausband states that the IT specialists

> felt the district's curriculum specialists had not changed their focus on curriculum to include technology . . . [and that they] were more curriculum workers than the curriculum specialists themselves because most of the curriculum specialists don't have a clue about technology and don't see it as part of the curriculum. (2006, p. 14)

Drawing on these case study findings, Ausband recommends that IT specialists and curriculum specialists be physically located in the same department within the district organization to facilitate greater cooperation and coordination of their functions. Ausband also suggests the combination of their functions into one IT-curriculum specialist role.

A Case Study of Educational Privatization

Patricia Burch (2006) did a case study to describe the fundamental shifts occurring in K–12 educational privatization in the United States. Educational privatization involves schools contracting with outside firms to carry out essential operations, ranging from specific services to the takeover of entire school systems. Until recently, research on this phenomenon reflected two opposing perspectives: (1) proponent arguments that contracting public education services to nongovernmental parties can improve quality and reduce costs versus (2) opposition arguments that privatization is part of a larger threat to public education, aggravating existing inequities among students differing in ethnicity, social class, and geographic location.

Burch (2006) argues that these perspectives ignore new realities pushing for increased privatization. She draws on organizational field theory, which was developed by sociologists, to understand these new realities. Burch contends that institutions representing three types of organizations (local education agencies, nonprofit and for-profit nongovernmental agencies, and the federal government) all can be considered part of the same organizational field. Interactions across all these organizations was the primary focus of her case study.

Burch used several forms of data collection and analysis in her case study. Examining annual reports and other documents concerning education contracting by government over the past 20 years, she identified four dominant domains of contracting now occurring in the K–12 education sector. She then analyzed policy documents of 10 large school districts, available on the Internet, to examine their contracting activities and also the impact of regulations in the No Child Left Behind Act of 2001.

Her analysis revealed an increase from 40 to 70 percent in companies' annual reported revenues in test development and preparation; from 19 to 46 percent in data management and reporting; from 86 to 300 percent in remedial services; and from 20 to 150 percent in curriculum-specific programming. Burch also found that

> sales of printed materials related to standardized tests nearly tripled between 1992 and 2003, jumping from $211 million to $592 million. . . . One of the four largest companies in the area of test development and preparation generated sales of $4.4 billion and a profit of $560 million in 2003. (2006, p. 2589)

Burch found that, in the past, vendors' primary role was "creating the content of tests and materials designed to increase students' test performance" (2006, p. 2589). The vendors' role now has expanded to include aligning tests with other aspects of district reform agendas. She concludes that vendors "have expanded their role from designers of assessments to designers of systems for monitoring compliance with standards and designers of pre-packaged interventions" (2006, p. 2590).

To situate the new educational privatization in local reform efforts, Burch carried out a three-year qualitative research project in three school districts that reported relying on contracts with vendors in their efforts to implement local reform. She also did an intensive case study of one of the districts.

In her case study, Burch found that reform efforts from 2000 to 2004 continued a prior emphasis on assessment, but "the work moved from a tri-part focus on standardized tests, district-wide performance assessments, and classroom-based assessments to a more exclusive focus on norm-referenced standardized tests" (2006, p. 2598). Burch attributes this shift to "anticipation of the high-stakes accountability reforms legislated under the No Child Left Behind Act" (2006, p. 2598).

The school district that she studied began to spend significantly more money on the purchase of outside products and services. It contracted with a company that initially was local, but was bought by a large national firm. Burch reports that interactions with the national firm were much less personal and less responsive to the school district's needs than they were with the local company.

In the discussion section of her report, Burch speculated that the influence of federal policy contradicts the view of educational privatization as a move away from government regulation and centralized governance. Instead, the expanded federal role in education has shaped the form and level of privatization now occurring.

The Nature of Qualitative Research

We have now explained the basic characteristics of case studies and presented three examples. Later in the chapter, we describe the specific design elements that a report of a case study typically includes. To lay the foundation for our description, we first briefly review the nature of qualitative research.

As we explain in Chapter 1, much of qualitative research is based on a philosophy of epistemology known as interpretivism. According to **interpretivism,** reality is constructed by the individuals who participate in it. Therefore, one can only understand reality and its meaning from the viewpoint of specific individuals, based on their subjective consciousness of experience from moment to moment. Thus, any phenomenon or event—a book, a mountain, or a high school football game—is not seen as having an existence independent of its participants.

A major purpose of qualitative research is to discover the nature of the meanings associated with social phenomena. Case study, the basic method of qualitative research, involves in-depth investigation of the meanings that individuals ascribe to particular instances of a phenomenon, known as cases, in their natural setting.

By contrast, the philosophy of epistemology that characterized most prior investigation in philosophy and science until late in the twentieth century, called **positivism,** assumes that there is a real world "out there," which can be known by using quantitative research strategies similar to those that guide the physical sciences and professions such as medicine and engineering. We suggest that you review Table 1.3 in Chapter 1, which summarizes other ways in which qualitative and quantitative researchers differ in their approach to investigating educational and social phenomena.

Qualitative research sometimes is called case study research because of its focus on cases. However, because some case studies are carried out based on a positivist orientation, we do not refer to qualitative research specifically as case study research. We focus in this chapter on case studies reflecting an interpretivist orientation.

Qualitative Research Traditions

Early in this chapter, we indicated that qualitative research includes a wide variety of research traditions. Each of them involves a community of researchers who have an expressed interest in particular phenomena and agreed methods for studying them. Various researchers (e.g., Gall, Gall, & Borg, 2007; Jacob, 1987; Lancy, 1993; Tesch, 1990) have attempted to identify and classify these **qualitative research traditions.** We present in Table 14.1 the "theoretical traditions" in qualitative research developed by Michael Quinn Patton (2002, p. 132). The table's list of 16 qualitative traditions shows the primary disciplinary roots of each perspective and states central questions that guide qualitative inquiry based on each perspective, providing a good starting point to help you explore particular types of qualitative research that appeal to you.

You should keep in mind that qualitative researchers tend to combine and differentiate these traditions over time. For example, Table 14.1 lists two ethnographic approaches: ethnography (sometimes called *holistic ethnography*) and autoethnography. The *Sage Handbook of Qualitative Research* (Denzin & Lincoln, 2005) includes eight chapters with the word *ethnography* in their titles: (1) critical ethnography, (2) performance ethnography, (3) public ethnography, (4) critical ethnography as street performance, (5) recontextualizing observation: ethnography, (6) autoethnography, (7) online ethnography, and (8) refunctioning ethnography. These chapters reflect the ways in which a qualitative research tradition can morph or expand into various other forms.

While Patton's (2002) list is fairly comprehensive, it does not include some forms of qualitative research that we think also can be considered traditions, namely action research and historical research. Although these forms of qualitative research are among the most general in terms of possible topics, they are very specific in their approach to research.

In the following chapters, we cover five qualitative research traditions that have had a strong influence in education: narrative research in Chapter 15; ethnography and critical research in Chapter 16; historical research in Chapter 17; and action research in Chapter 19. We also include two chapters that involve distinctive uses of qualitative research: mixed-methods research (Chapter 18), which combines quantitative and qualitative research methodologies, and evaluation research (Chapter 20), which draws on qualitative or quantitative methodology, or both.

Features of a Case Study Report

The basic features of a report of a case study are shown in Table 14.2 (on p. 346). In explaining these features in the following sections of the chapter, we will use an illustrative case study

TABLE 14.1   Variety in Qualitative Inquiry: Theoretical Traditions

Perspective	Disciplinary Roots	Central Questions
1. Ethnography	Anthropology	What is the culture of this group of people?
2. Autoethnography	Literary arts	How does my own experience of this culture connect with and offer insights about this culture, situation, event, and/or way of life?
3. Reality testing: Positivist and realist approaches	Philosophy, social sciences, and evaluation	What's really going on in the real world? What can we establish with some degree of certainty? What are plausible explanations for verifiable patterns? What's the truth insofar as we can get at it? How can we study a phenomenon so that our findings correspond, as much as possible, to the real world?
4. Constructionism/ constructivism	Sociology	How have the people in this setting constructed reality? What are their reported perceptions, "truths," explanations, beliefs, and world view? What are the consequences of their constructions for their behaviors and for those with whom they interact?
5. Phenomenology	Philosophy	What is the meaning, structure, and essence of the lived experience of this phenomenon for this person or group of people?
6. Heuristic inquiry	Humanistic psychology	What is my experience of this phenomenon and the essential experience of others who also experience this phenomenon intensely?
7. Ethnomethodology	Sociology	How do people make sense of their everyday activities so as to behave in socially acceptable ways?
8. Symbolic interaction	Social psychology	What common set of symbols and understandings has emerged to give meaning to people's interactions?
9. Semiotics	Linguistics	How do signs (words, symbols) carry and convey meaning in particular contexts?
10. Hermeneutics	Linguistics, philosophy, literary criticism, theology	What are the conditions under which a human act took place or a product was produced that makes it possible to interpret its meanings?
11. Narratology/narrative analysis	Social sciences (interpretive): Literary criticism, literary nonfiction	What does this narrative or story reveal about the person and world from which it came? How can this narrative be interpreted to understand and illuminate the life and culture that created it?
12. Ecological psychology	Ecology, psychology	How do individuals attempt to accomplish their goals through specific behaviors in specific environments?
13. Systems theory	Interdisciplinary	How and why does this system as a whole function as it does?
14. Chaos theory: Nonlinear dynamics	Theoretical physics, natural sciences	What is the underlying order, if any, of disorderly phenomena?
15. Grounded theory	Social sciences, methodology	What theory emerges from systematic comparative analysis and is grounded in fieldwork so as to explain what has been and is observed?
16. Orientational: Feminist inquiry, critical theory, queer theory, among others	Ideologies: Political, cultural, and economic	How is X perspective manifest in this phenomenon?

Source: Exhibit 3.6 on pp. 132–133 of Patton, M. Q. (2003). *Qualitative research & evaluation methods* (3rd ed.). Thousand Oaks, CA: Sage.

TABLE *14.2*   Typical Sections of a Case Study Report

Section	Content
Introduction	Hypotheses, questions, or objectives are stated. Relevant literature is reviewed. The purpose of the study usually is to describe, explain, or evaluate phenomena relating to a problem of practice.
Research design	The researcher describes the specific cases and aspects of the cases that will be studied. The researcher also describes the context surrounding the case and whether the case will be studied from an emic or etic perspective, or both. If the case study is grounded in a particular qualitative research tradition, it, too, is specified.
Sampling procedure	The researcher describes the purposeful sampling strategy that was used in the study and explains why that particular strategy was chosen.
Measures	Case studies typically rely on interviews and observation for data collection. Other measures, including quantitative paper-and-pencil measures, can be used as well.
Data analysis	The researcher describes how interpretational analysis (usually based on grounded theory principles) or reflective analysis was used to make sense of the case study data. The researcher also describes the themes and patterns that were identified as a result of the data analyses.
Discussion	The main findings of the study are summarized. Flaws and limitations of the study are considered. Also, implications of the findings for further research, theory development, and professional practice are considered.

conducted by David Emiliano Zapata Maldonado, Robert Rhoads, and Tracy Lachica Buenavista (2005). The purpose of the case study was to examine an innovative program to improve the retention of ethnic-minority students once they have entered college.

Introduction

In the introductory section of a case study report, researchers usually do not state hypotheses, but they often indicate questions they hope to answer or issues they wish to address. The introduction also describes the general purpose of the case study, which is to describe, explain, or evaluate particular educational phenomena, as explained briefly below.

Description.   The purpose of many case studies is to depict and conceptualize an educational phenomenon clearly. These case studies usually provide a **thick description** of the phenomenon, that is, a set of statements that re-create the situation and its context and give readers a sense of the meanings and intentions that its participants ascribe to it. The term *thick description* originated in anthropology but is now widely used throughout qualitative research.

Evaluation.   Case study researchers have developed several qualitative approaches to evaluation (see Chapter 20). In each approach, researchers conduct a case study about certain phenomena and make judgments about those phenomena. For example, a historical case study carried out by Larry Cuban (1997) bears a title reflecting the case study's evaluative purpose: "Change without Reform: The Case of Stanford University School of Medicine, 1908–1990."

Explanation.   Some case studies seek to explain particular phenomena. The researchers look for relationships among phenomena within a case or across cases. For example, researchers might observe that American teachers in international schools vary (1) in their perceptions of teaching in such schools and (2) in their perceptions of the local culture. Suppose that the researchers find that the teachers' perceptions of teaching are related to their perceptions of the culture. They can therefore say that they have discovered a pattern, that is, a systematic relationship between two or more phenomena within a case or across cases. If a systematic relationship is found but no cause is specified, this is called a **relational pattern.** If one variation appears to have a causal effect on others, it is referred to as a **causal pattern.**

In our judgment, the purpose of the student-initiated retention project (SIRP) case study is primarily explanation, because the researchers state their intention to develop a new theory of the best approach to promote retention of students of color in higher education institutions. Maldonado and his colleagues begin their report by noting that for the past 20 years "few higher education topics have drawn more attention than student retention" (2005, p. 605). The researchers note that colleges and universities are now stressing the need to graduate admitted students within a reasonable time frame, adding that "this is especially true in the case of students of color, who tend to leave colleges and universities at higher-than-average rates" (2005, p. 606). They state that previous retention efforts have met with limited success, so there is a need to look for new approaches.

They then introduce the phenomenon of interest in their research, namely, a student-initiated retention project (SIRP). They explain that "SIRPs represent a unified effort among student organizations to develop programs and support structures that are, in significant ways, *student organized, student run, and student funded* and that primarily serve students of color" (Maldonado et al., 2005, p. 606, italics in original). Such efforts, which have become major programs at many large public universities, aim to increase students' retention and academic success.

Maldonado and colleagues state the following objectives for their research: (1) raising critical questions about dominant retention theories in higher education, (2) developing a new conceptual framework by combining knowledge from a critique of these theories with their own experience working with SIRPs, and (3) applying their conceptual framework to the findings of a case study of the SIRPs at two major universities.

Their conceptual framework involves examining how students' college experience is shaped by, and shapes, the four key concepts of cultural capital, social capital, collectivism, and social praxis. These concepts concern students' individual and organizational power in situating themselves in the college experience and working collectively to transform their higher education experience. A key source in the researchers' literature review for these concepts is Paulo Freire's (1970) critique of the "banking method of education" (p. 613) that views the teacher as the all-knowing keeper of knowledge and students as passively situated, empty receptacles to be filled with facts and information by the teacher.

Research Design

The design of a basic qualitative case study involves the four key characteristics described earlier in the chapter (see pp. 338–340). Our example of case study research involves an examination of SIRPs, considering specific instances at the University of California at Berkeley and another at the University of Wisconsin at Madison. The phenomenon was investigated in its natural context, that is, on the campus of each institution where students of color lived, studied, and participated in their institution's SIRP. An in-depth study was made of these two cases, and the researchers sought to represent both their own (etic) perspective and the student (emic) perspective.

Maldonado and his colleagues (2005) state that their case study of SIRPs builds on the qualitative research tradition of critical theory research. Such research, also known as **critical research,** involves an examination of "the ways that the economy, matters of race, class, and gender, ideologies, discourses, education, religion and other social institutions and cultural dynamics interact to construct a social system" (Kincheloe & McLaren, 2000, p. 281). Critical research is focused on how injustice and subjugation, propagated by members of a society who have power, shape the world view of everyone in the society. Critical researchers strive to engage research participants in efforts to emancipate and empower themselves.

Sampling Procedure

The selection of cases in qualitative research involves **purposeful sampling,** using researcher judgment to select instances that are information-rich with respect to the phenomenon being studied.

Michael Patton (2002) has identified 16 purposeful sampling strategies that case study researchers can use. Many involve selection of cases that represent to different degrees a characteristic of interest to the researchers. For example, a homogeneous sample of students based on math ability would include only students of average math ability, excluding students high or low in math ability. Other strategies reflect a conceptual rationale for selecting cases, such as cases that are well known or politically important.

Maldonado and his colleagues "selected the SIRPs at Berkeley and Madison because of previous knowledge we had about the size and scope of their operations" (2005, p. 616). In our view, this sampling strategy represents what Patton (2002) calls *criterion sampling,* with the criterion being the comprehensiveness of the SIRPs at the two chosen universities.

Maldonado and his colleagues (2005) focused their sampling of research participants on student organizers within each SIRP. These were individuals who were or had been students at the SIRP institution being studied and had actively participated in their SIRP's organization and leadership. Interviews were conducted with 45 student organizers, 34 of whom served SIRP-related functions at the time of the study and 11 of whom had previously worked on SIRP projects. Key informants or other research participants currently at the universities identified these former organizers. A **key informant** is an individual who has special knowledge or status that gives him or her special value in obtaining the emic perspective of the phenomenon being studied.

Selection of student organizers also involved the use of another sampling strategy, **snowball sampling,** in which cases are recommended by individuals who know other individuals likely to yield relevant, information-rich data.

In addition to sampling student organizers, Maldonado and his colleagues (2005) interviewed six full-time professional staff members with knowledge of the SIRPs at their institutions. Including these individuals in the research sample helped ensure that the researchers obtained a thick description of the SIRPs based on the perspectives of different types of individuals involved in the projects.

Data-Collection Procedures

It has been said that the primary instrument of data collection in qualitative research is the researcher himself or herself (Lincoln & Guba, 1985). This view of data collection reflects the centrality of construction, making of meaning, and interpretation in qualitative research.

Case study researchers use any methods of data collection that are appropriate to their purpose. They might begin a case study with one method of data collection and gradually shift to, or add, other methods. The purpose for this data-collection strategy is **triangulation,** also known as **crystallization** (Richardson & St. Pierre, 2005), which involves the use of multiple methods to collect data about the same phenomenon in order to confirm research findings or to resolve discrepant findings. It can also involve the use of different data sources, methods of analysis, or theories to check case study findings. In the next sections, we describe the methods of data collection most often used in case studies.

Interviews.   Researchers often conduct interviews with field participants. They typically use open-ended questions to which the research participants can respond freely in their own terms rather than selecting from a fixed set of responses. The interviews can be informal, occurring in the natural course of conversation. If many respondents are being interviewed, or if more than one interviewer is involved, the researchers might choose to use an interview guide that outlines a set of topics to be explored with each respondent.

Focus groups are a form of group interview in which a number of people participate in a discussion guided by a skilled interviewer. Because the respondents can talk to and hear each other, they are likely to express feelings or opinions that might not emerge if they were interviewed individually.

Observation. Case study researchers often observe individuals in their natural settings over an extensive period of time. Their might videotape their observations and make hand-written or tape-recorded notes. Many researchers strive to become **participant observers,** meaning that they interact personally with participants during activities in the natural setting in order to build empathy and trust and to further their understanding of the phenomenon. These researchers generally take notes on their observations only after they have left the field.

Case study researchers might also make observations of material culture. For example, Peter Manning and Betsy Cullum-Swan (1994) did a case study of McDonald's restaurants using the qualitative research tradition of semiotics, which investigates how both verbal and configural sign systems convey meaning. They studied the meaning of McDonald's sign systems as conveyed by such elements as the design of the menu board, lighting, outdoor playgrounds, food containers and utensils, and the use of the prefix *Mc-* to label food items.

Document and Media Analysis. Case study researchers often study written communications that are found in field settings. In accord with their interpretivist epistemology, these researchers believe that the meaning of a text varies depending on the reader, the time period, the context in which the text appears, and so forth. For example, G. Genevieve Patthey-Chavez (1993) did a document analysis in her case study of the cultural conflict between Latino students and their mainstream teachers in a Los Angeles high school. She interpreted a local newspaper article as revealing the schools' mission to assimilate immigrant students into the mainstream, whether the students wanted to be assimilated or not.

Paper-and-Pencil Measures. In some case studies, research participants are asked to fill out questionnaires, tests, or other self-report measures. Researchers typically use questionnaires when extensive contact with every research participant is not feasible and the desired information is not deeply personal. If well designed, a questionnaire can elicit in-depth information, as illustrated in a study by Ismail Yahya and Gary Moore (1985). These researchers designed a questionnaire that included open-ended questions calling for lengthy replies. They sent the respondents an audiotape with the questionnaire, asking respondents to record their responses on the tape.

Tests are commonly used in quantitative research, but they also can be useful in qualitative case studies. For example, in a case study of the mismatch between a teacher's expectations and the actual reading achievement of two of her first-grade students, Claude Goldenberg (1992) combined qualitative and quantitative methods of data collection. He made qualitative observations of each child's classroom behaviors and administered two standardized tests of reading achievement to each child. Goldenberg found that the child with the lower reading achievement score actually improved in reading, probably due to the teacher's greater involvement, whereas the child with a higher reading achievement score remained in a low reading group.

Data Collection in the Student Retention Study. In the SIRP study, Maldonado and his colleagues (2005) conducted interviews and observations and gathered relevant documents at each site. They made three two-day visits to the Berkeley site and one four-day visit to Madison. Formal structured interviews with each of the 45 research participants, from 1 to 2 hours long, were tape recorded and transcribed verbatim.

At Berkeley, the researchers observed the SIRP organizers while they were in their office, engaging in such activities as planning events and meeting with staff of the recruitment and retention center. At Madison, researchers observed organizers in various informal settings and at their off-campus work site.

Maldonado and his colleagues (2005) mention in their report that two of them were at one time organizers working for SIRPs and that they thus could be viewed as insiders rather than outsiders. In case study research, an **insider** typically is a practitioner who has an internal, or local, perspective on the problems of practice being studied. By contrast, an **outsider** is an individual who has an external perspective on the problems of practice being studied.

Having experience characteristic of insiders undoubtedly gave the researchers credibility and facilitated their entry to the research sites. However, no mention is made in the case study report of any efforts by the researchers to practice **reflexivity,** which is a process of self-reflection that case study researchers use to identify their biases, attempt to take these biases into account in their interpretations, and seek to minimize their effects on data collection and interpretation.

Data Analysis

In case study research, researchers typically begin to analyze data while they are still engaged in data collection. They seek to discover what types of findings are emerging and to add to or modify their data-collection procedures in whatever way they consider best to shed further light on the phenomenon of interest. They continue this process until they have reached **theoretical saturation,** which refers to a point in the process of comparing theoretical constructs and empirical indicators of their meaning when additional data collection and analysis no longer contribute anything new about the phenomenon under investigation. At that point, the researchers conclude their analysis.

Interpretational Analysis.   Case study researchers often use either interpretational analysis (Miles & Huberman, 1984) or reflective analysis (discussed below) to analyze their data. **Interpretational analysis** is the process of closely examining and grouping elements in case study data in order to fully describe, evaluate, or explain the phenomenon being studied. The goal of interpretational analysis is to identify constructs, themes, and patterns that best make meaning of the data from a case study.

Constructs are concepts that are inferred from commonalities among observed phenomena and that are presumed to explain or shed light on the meaning of those phenomena. For example, in Ms. Jones's fifth-grade class, many of the teacher's acts and statements appear to be aimed at keeping order among students. An important construct that might be inferred from observation of Ms. Jones's class is that of classroom management. A **theme** is a salient, recurring feature of a case. Suppose that when Ms. Jones begins presenting on a topic many students begin making jokes, calling out to classmates, or moving around the room. Such behavioral incidents suggest a theme characteristic of the class, namely students actively seeking to interrupt Ms. Jones's teaching activities. **Patterns** represent systematic relationships between two or more phenomena within a case or across cases. If Ms. Jones repeatedly responds to student interruptions by attempting to ignore them and continue her presentation, researchers might presume a causal pattern between her behavior (ignoring interruptions) and students' behavior (continuing interruptions).

A classic model of interpretational analysis is based on grounded theory (Glaser & Strauss, 1967). **Grounded theory** involves the principle that qualitative researchers should *discover* theory that is grounded in the data. They do this by examining data inductively, rather than using the deductive approach of posing a theory or hypotheses in advance to explain what they are studying.

The grounded theory procedure involves (1) recording the data (usually text obtained from interviews or observations), (2) breaking the text into segments (e.g., sentences or lines), (3) defining specific categories to reflect each important conceptual or structural element that appears in the text, and (4) coding each segment for all the categories that apply to that segment. Once all data segments have been coded into categories, the researchers then refine the set of categories through constant comparison, an essential element of grounded theory. **Constant comparison** is a process of comparing instances of each code across segments in order to discover commonalities in the data that reflect the underlying meaning of, and relationships among, the coding categories. It depends not merely on frequency counts, but on the researchers' effort to interpret, that is, give meaning to, the data.

The researchers who studied SIRPs state that they "followed both deductive and inductive strategies" (Maldonado et al., 2005, p. 618) of data analysis. At the beginning of their study they generated hypotheses involving a critique of the traditional views of retention that seek to promote social integration and multiculturalism. Their hypotheses involved efforts to understand the effectiveness of SIRPs from the standpoint of the "conceptual points" of cultural capital, social capital, collectivism, and social praxis (p. 609). As described in the section on findings, the researchers identified three general themes in their data that corresponded closely with these conceptual points from their original research hypotheses. They are thus based on the researchers' deductive approach rather than an inductive approach consistent with grounded theory.

The SIRP researchers indicated, however, that they also used an inductive approach to identify the particular processes associated with successful development and implementation of SIRPs. They generated coding categories by searching through the data for regularities, patterns, and topics that reflected key discoveries about how the student organizers affected, and were affected by, the SIRP at their institution. Through this approach they discovered "unanticipated concerns or areas of understanding in which we had such minimal knowledge that meaningful theories and hypotheses could not be generated a priori" (Maldonado et al., 2005, p. 618). In the findings section we provide examples of the specific patterns that were inductively discovered in the data. The researchers also measured the degree to which two of them agreed in their coding of SIRP data, which, at 85 percent, was considered satisfactory.

Computer Software for Analyzing Qualitative Data.   Like the SIRP study, many published case studies do not mention any use of computer software in their analysis of data. Such case studies involve a manual approach to sorting data segments into categories, for example, with the use of 3×5 cards. However, when case study data involve various forms of media, when the amount of data to be analyzed is very great, or when very complex forms of analysis are desired, a computer software program can speed up the process of data analysis. Consider, for example, three currently available computer software programs for qualitative data analysis.

DataSense markets NVivo, currently in version 8, through the website www.datasense .org/system_requirements.html. The program is described as good for managing complex, unstructured, or multimedia information like field notes, videos, transcripts, and audio recordings. This version supercedes previous versions of QSR International software, including earlier NVivo versions and the NUD*IST (Non-numerical, Unstructured, Data: Indexing, Searching, and Theorising) software program versions 4, 5, and 6.

Qualis Research markets Ethnograph, a software program originally developed for use in ethnographic research, available at www.qualisresearch.com. The website provides a quick tour online showing the basics of creating projects and coding data files.

ResearchWare markets HyperRESEARCH through the website www.researchware .com. This advanced software program allows qualitative researchers to analyze text, graphic, audio, and video data sources. An online tutorial and a free limited edition of HyperRESEARCH are available.

Reflective Analysis.   Interpretational analysis involves an explicit category coding system, as we have described. By contrast, **reflective analysis** requires case study researchers to rely mainly on their own intuition and personal judgment to analyze their data. The resulting findings are thus reflective both in the sense that they mirror the conceptual framework of the particular researcher who did the analysis and in the sense that they result from a deep and deeply personal process of pondering a phenomenon.

Reflective analysis can be compared with artistic endeavors, because visual artists reflect on phenomena that they experience and then portray them to reveal both their surface features and essences. Similarly, expert critics and connoisseurs study a piece of art both to appreciate its esthetic elements and "message" and to make critical judgments about its artistic merit.

Many case study researchers engage in similar reflections and portrayals. For example, some case studies involving evaluation (see Chapter 20) follow a process of reflective analysis known as educational connoisseurship and criticism. Evaluators using this approach both explain the features and purposes of educational programs, products, and methods and help educators to appreciate their strengths and weaknesses. Just as an art or literary critic develops reflective ability with experience, an educational evaluator must build up a store of experience in order to use reflective analysis wisely.

Reflective analysis appears to be the primary way in which findings are generated in highly creative forms of case study research, or qualitative research more generally. Such forms include **performance ethnography,** which involves staged reenactments of the cultural phenomena observed by ethnographers (Alexander, 2005). For example, Joni Jones (2002) staged a production, *Searching for Osun,* that focused on aspects of the deity Osun in Yoruba, a Nigerian culture, "that moved [her] most—dance, music, divination, Osun's relationship to children, 'women's work,' and food preparation" (p. 1). The performers assumed archetypal characters in Yoruba life, and the invited audience entered the performance space as participants, engaging in dance, dining rituals, and other performances characteristic of Yoruba life.

Other forms of reflective analysis result in poetry, oral readings, comedy, satire, and visual social science (Harper, 2005). In qualitative research using these methods, it can be difficult to distinguish between the process of data analysis and the reporting of findings, because the form of reporting itself reflects the manner in which the researchers have analyzed their data.

Laura Richardson (1992) observed that qualitative researchers who use reflective analysis typically have a postmodern sensibility. As we explain in Chapter 1, postmodernism questions all claims to authoritative methods of analysis and reporting, including mainstream scientific reports. A postmodernist would view poetry or street art as just as legitimate a form of case study reporting as more standard forms involving text, quotations, and observation.

Findings

As is typical in case study research, Maldonado and his colleagues (2005) presented their findings as themes derived from verbal data (e.g., field notes, transcripts of interviews, and videotapes). By contrast, quantitative researchers present their findings as statistics derived from numerical data.

The primary findings from the SIRP researchers' deductive approach to data analysis involved identification of three essential concerns or themes focused on making sense of the collective strategies used in student-initiated retention programs. They are described below, along with findings from the researchers' inductive analysis of the data they collected about the SIRPs and from SIRP student organizers.

Theme 1: Developing Necessary Knowledge, Skills, and Social Networks.   Maldonado and his colleagues (2005) tied this theme to the conceptual points of cultural capital and social capital from their original hypotheses. The activities that the SIRPs provided to advance students' academic success, for example, included tutorial programs, study groups, organized study halls, mentoring programs, and direct efforts to assist students of color in interacting with faculty and instructors. As an example, Susan, a Laotian student organizer at Berkeley, learned that questioning her teachers was an acceptable and useful practice, and she credited her involvement in a SIRP with encouragement to "don't just accept knowledge uncritically" (Maldonado et al., 2005, p. 621).

Another inductive finding related to this theme is that SIRPs helped student organizers develop knowledge of both the dominant culture and their own cultural identity, while expanding their capacity to balance participation in each. Additionally, SIRPs developed students' skills in public speaking, leadership, organization, and critical thinking, and also provided a social network that gave ongoing support and resources for dealing with personal issues.

Theme 2: Building a Sense of Students' Commitment to Particular Communities, Including Ethnic/Racial Communities. This theme was tied back to the researchers' conceptual point of collectivism. Based on their inductive analysis, the researchers found that SIRPs "seek to enhance students' commitment to their cultural heritage" (Maldonado et al., 2005, p. 623), which gives students better understanding of the needs of each ethnic community and their role in helping to meet such needs. The SIRPs also built bridges across particular racial/ethnic communities "for the sake of organizing a united community of color" (p. 624).

Theme 3: Challenging Oppressive Social and Institutional Norms. The researchers tied this theme to the conceptual point of social praxis from their deductive analysis. Findings from their inductive analysis showed that the SIRPs engaged students in efforts to promote improved education, protest for change, work institutionally, challenge racism, and serve their racial/ethnic communities. They found that these efforts challenged social and institutional norms that "discourage greater participation by people of color in higher education" (Maldonado et al., 2005, p. 625).

The findings also indicated that SIRP organizers aim to reconstruct the universities "on the basis of cultural norms more consistent with those of their own racial/ethnic communities" (Maldonado et al., 2005, p. 625), and as a result, ultimately improve the retention of students of color. The researchers reported that student organizers and SIRP students engaged in active challenges to racist practices in classrooms and the university as a whole. For example, they worked institutionally to influence university decisions through participation in student government.

The researchers concluded that the vast majority of SIRP programs and activities do resist an assimilationist position, consistent with one of their hypotheses. In other words, the philosophy that guides SIRPs does not emphasize assimilation of students of color to the mainstream culture, but rather it promotes students' intellectual and social development within their own racial/ethnic and collective communities. Because the researchers were committed to a critical research orientation, their report promoted this mission of student-initiated retention projects.

A Hierarchical Approach to Interpretational Analysis. Coding qualitative data is a very common procedure in qualitative data analysis, although the coding process and the resulting levels of coding are not consistently named or carried out among research studies. While not explicitly hierarchical, the process of coding qualitative data into categories typically appears to produce a set of statements that fall into several levels and thus constitute a hierarchy. For example, James McMillan and Sally Schumacher (2006) describe three levels—codes, categories, and patterns—but do not provide data from a single study to illustrate these levels.

To illustrate the levels of a hierarchical coding system, we describe findings from research by Carl Auerbach and Louise Silverstein (2003), based on a theory about the transformation of fathering that is occurring in U.S. culture. In their study of Haitian American fathers Auerbach and Silverstein found data "indicating that these Haitian Christian fathers have constructed a new definition of fatherhood which is more socially progressive and more personally satisfying than the traditional Haitian fathering role" (p. 141).

Auerbach and Silverstein's approach to coding and data analysis involves generating three levels of data, described below and illustrated in Table 14.3.

Level 1: Text-Based Categories. Researchers begin data analysis by selecting segments of text that they see as relevant to the basic concerns of the study. They then develop a set of low-inference text-based categories that paraphrase or generalize those text segments.

An example of a text-based category from Table 14.3 is "1. My dream was to look like my father." The table shows 16 numbered text-based categories.

Level 2: Sensitizing Concepts.   The researchers then organize the text-based categories into clusters of middle-level sensitizing concepts. These concepts reflect tacit or explicit themes that the text categories represent. An example of a sensitizing concept from Table 14.3 is "A. Praising aspects of the traditional Haitian father." The table shows five such concepts, each preceded by a capital letter.

Level 3: Theoretical Constructs.   Finally, the researchers group the sensitizing concepts into high-level theoretical constructs. These theoretical constructs provide the "big picture," or theoretical interpretation, of what the researchers learned from analysis of their data. The following three theoretical constructs are shown in Table 14.3: "I. Bicultural gender role strain," "II. Constructing a more gratifying definition of fatherhood," and "III. A facilitating ideology."

TABLE *14.3*   Example of Theoretical Constructs, Sensitizing Concepts, and Text-Based Categories from Research on Haitian American Fathers

I. Bicultural gender role strain
   A. Praising aspects of the traditional Haitian father — 50%
      1. My dream was to look like my father.
      2. There is no inch of laziness in my father.
      3. I love the way my father treated my mother.
   B. Dissatisfactions with aspects of traditional Haitian fatherhood — 60%
      4. My father never said I love you.
      5. Adults do not play.
      6. When they say your father is coming you run inside.
      7. My father took care of other children and didn't care much for me.

II. Constructing a more gratifying definition of fatherhood
   A. Definition of a "good" father — 100%
      8. My job is to look over the family.
      9. You're not a boss for the children, you're more like a friend.
     10. You have to be there whenever the child needs you.
     11. You call your kid and say I love you.
     12. Jesus was my role model.
   B. An enhanced sense of self — 75%
     13. It has changed you, it has reconstructed you.
     14. You're looking at the children growing it is beautiful

III. A facilitating ideology
   A. God makes all things possible — 75%
     15. We are co-workers in the field of God.
     16. It won't be your doing, it will be God's doing.

Note: $N = 20$. The percentages refer to the percentage of fathers in the sample who used the sensitizing concept.

Source: Taken from Table B-2 on page 146 in Auerbach, C. F., & Silverstein, L. B. (2003), *Qualitative data: An introduction to coding and analysis.* New York: New York University Press.

From the data shown in Table 14.3 we can trace the coding process used by the researchers. For example, the five numbered statements under the Sensitizing Concept "A. Definition of a 'good' father" are all text-based categories that describe specifics of good fathering, from "8. My job is to look over the family" to "12. Jesus was my role model."

In turn the sensitizing concepts "A. Definition of a 'good' father" and "B. An enhanced sense of self" both represent the theoretical construct "II. Constructing a more gratifying definition of fatherhood." At the highest level of analysis we see the three related theoretical constructs noted above.

In summary, Auerbach and Silverstein's research on Haitian American fathers shows how data from a case study can be coded into three hierarchical levels: text-based categories, sensitizing concepts, and theoretical constructs. This approach to interpretational analysis appears easy to learn and promising for studying problems of practice.

Discussion

The discussion section of a case study report typically includes a summary of the research findings, recommendations for practice and future research, and limitations of the study and suggestions for how these could be overcome in future research.

In the discussion section of their report, Maldonado and his colleagues detail some of the proactive efforts made by students involved in the SIRPs to create change. They conclude that these efforts are "consistent with the view of transformative education advanced by Freire (1970)" (2005, p. 633). They also conclude that the SIRP is a better model of student retention than any other described in the literature. Finally, they assert that the student organizers' vision of social change and their contributions to democracy "should extend well beyond simply the scope of their collegiate careers" (2005, p. 634).

These conclusions reflect the researchers' use of critical research as a framework for understanding society and individuals within it. Their endorsement of student-initiated retention projects as essential to the emancipation and empowerment of college students of color is entirely consistent with critical theorists' agenda for research and practice.

Checking the Applicability of Case Study Findings

Quantitative researchers are concerned with whether their findings generalize to samples or populations other than those who participated in a particular research study. Qualitative researchers have a related but different concern: How can educators determine whether the findings of a specific case study are applicable to their own workplace? In general terms, **applicability** refers to an individual's judgment that the findings of a case study can be used to inform a problem of practice in other settings or to serve as evidence for or against a theory of interest.

Case study findings depend on an ongoing interaction between the data and the researchers' creative processes of analysis and interpretation. Therefore, one might argue that the findings are unique to the case that was studied. However, most qualitative researchers believe that case study findings can be applied to other settings.

One approach to determining the applicability of case study findings is to consider the sampling strategy that the researchers used to select the case. If the researchers studied a typical or extreme case, the results should be applicable to other similar cases. Researchers who use a multiple-case design usually conduct a cross-case analysis to help readers determine whether the findings are similar across cases. Demonstration of similarity suggests that the findings will also be applicable to other situations and individuals similar to those studied by the researchers.

Another view about applicability is that the readers of the case study findings are responsible for making this judgment. In this view, readers, not the researchers, need to determine whether the cases that were studied are similar to the situation of interest to the readers. Researchers can help readers make this determination by providing a thick description of the participants and contexts that comprise the case.

Still another view of applicability is that case studies resemble stories in works of literature or "human interest" news accounts. Reading such case studies can deepen your understanding of educational phenomena that interest or concern you. Also, their insights and speculations can help you develop the capacity to explore and refine your educational practice.

Evaluating the Quality and Rigor of a Case Study

The case studies described in this chapter reflect an interpretivist view of reality. This view rejects the notion of an external reality that can be discovered through objective means. Interpretivists instead believe that each researcher, research participant, and reader of a case study report will have his or her own unique interpretation of the meaning and value of the case study.

Researchers who embrace interpretivism use many strategies to demonstrate the credibility and trustworthiness of their findings and methods. In a previous examination of the work of such researchers, we identified 17 such strategies (Gall, Gall, & Borg, 2007). These strategies typically are designed to ensure (1) that the research study has been carefully designed, (2) that sufficient data have been collected to provide rich information about the phenomenon of interest, and (3) that readers will be able to determine whether and how the results can be applied to their own settings.

Below we describe strategies that were used effectively in the case studies discussed in this chapter or in other case studies in the literature. In evaluating case studies that might help solve problems in your own practice, we recommend you examine how well the researchers used strategies such as these to increase the quality and rigor of their research. Table 14.4 lists the strategies and frames them as questions you can ask yourself as you evaluate a case study. We also suggest that you examine Appendix 3, which contains a list of questions to consider when evaluating qualitative research reports.

Usefulness

The most useful case studies focus on topics relevant to readers and provide information that helps them consider approaches to solving specific problems of practice. We selected the case studies described in this chapter with usefulness to educators as a criterion. For example, the case study about teacher learning through teaching inquiry-based math classes (Leikin & Rota, 2006) appears useful to teachers in considering how to assess and improve their skills in guiding student learning. Ausband's (2006) study of instructional technology is useful to educators in considering how to organize and guide the work of instructional specialists in school districts for the greatest impact on teaching and learning.

Participant Involvement

Some case studies involve participants in all phases of the research, from conceptualization of the study to writing the final report. This strategy helps researchers gain understanding of participants' emic perspective and convey it clearly to readers.

Carl Auerbach and Louise Silverstein (2003) note that this strategy improves the opportunity for case study research to contribute to a social-action agenda. Participatory research focuses on participants' voices and acknowledges that individuals' life experience is not standard but varies from one person to the next. It involves designing research in which researchers examine their own biases and address issues that help improve participants' lives.

TABLE *14.4*   Questions to Ask in Evaluating the Quality and Rigor of a Case Study

Evaluative Strategies	Question
Usefulness	Is the study useful in the sense of being relevant to problems of practice?
Participant involvement	Is the emic perspective of the research participants represented in the report?
Inclusion of quantitative data	Are quantitative data used, when relevant, to support qualitative observations?
Long-term observation	Did the researchers observe the case over a sufficiently long period of time?
Coding checks	If data were coded, did the researchers check the reliability of the coding?
Member checks	Did the research participants check the report for accuracy and completeness?
Triangulation	Did the researchers check whether the findings were supported by different data collection methods, data sources, analysts, and theories?
Contextual completeness	Did the researcher provide an in-depth description of the history, setting, participants, and culture within which the case was situated?
Chain of evidence	Are the research questions, data, data analyses, and findings clearly and meaningfully related to each other?
Researcher reflections	Do the researchers state personal assumptions, values, theoretical orientations, and biases that influenced their approach to the case study?

Leikin and Rota's (2006) case study of a teacher learning through teaching reflects this strategy. Rota, the report's coauthor and also the subject of the research, participated fully as a researcher. Chapter 19 on action research further explores research in which practitioners participate as researchers.

Inclusion of Quantitative Data

Case study researchers can supplement important findings by providing results from simple quantitative analyses. Such results enable researchers to show whether specific findings are typical, rare, or extreme.

Burch's case study (2006) about the new trend in educational privatization uses budgetary data to reveal the huge increases in funding to vendors for managing aspects of schools' operations since the passage of the No Child Left Behind Act.

In another case study, Leikin and Rota (2006) provide essential quantitative information about the amount of time a teacher spent on various teaching activities during three lessons at different points in the school year. The observed changes in the teacher's time allocations revealed her growing proficiency in teaching inquiry-based math.

Long-Term Observation

Case study researchers often observe a phenomenon, using various data-collection methods, over a substantial period of time. This data-collection strategy enables them to study a phenomenon in depth and triangulate findings while confirming or disconfirming seeming discrepancies.

In their study of a high school using bilingual education, García and Bartlett (2007) made weekly observations in classes for nine months and participated for a full year in monthly staff development sessions. In their study, Leikin and Rota (2006) intermittently videotaped 15 months of the teacher's math inquiry lessons, from which the three lessons described in the case study were selected. Burch's study of educational privatization (2006) included a 3-year qualitative research project, during which over 250 research participants were interviewed.

Coding Checks

In their case study of student-initiated retention projects (SIRPs), Maldonado and his colleagues (2005) did a coding check of their categories. The purpose of a **coding check** is to determine the reliability with which different researchers classify qualitative data by the same categories. Their check for a sample of data segments revealed an 85-percent level of agreement between two researchers in assigning segments to categories. Then they discussed discrepancies in their coding in order to improve agreement in subsequent coding.

Member Checking

Maldonado and his colleagues (2005) indicate that they employed member checking to increase the authenticity of their findings. **Member checking** is the process of having field participants review research procedures and statements in the research report for accuracy and completeness. They carried out member checking "by sharing interview transcripts with all of the research participants and by sharing early drafts of this article with several volunteer readers from 'bridges' and the MCSC" (p. 619). The researchers also stated that the article was created "in a dialogical manner" (p. 633) with the student activists they studied. These procedures helped to ensure that not only the researchers' etic perspective but also the emic perspective of the research participants were included in the case study.

Triangulation

Case study researchers usually seek to achieve triangulation or crystallization by using different data-collection methods, data sources, analysts, and theories to check their findings. This process might produce convergence, or it might clarify the reasons for apparent contradictions among findings about the same phenomenon. For example, in studies of controversial or stressful phenomena, research participants' self-report data might be inconsistent with data resulting from more direct methods of data collection such as observation or document analysis.

Most of the case studies discussed in this chapter used a range of data-collection methods and strategies to strengthen triangulation. In his study of instructional technology Ausband (2006) analyzed documents, observed three research participants, interviewed each participant individually, and conducted a focus group interview of the three participants.

Maldonado and his colleagues (2005) sought to develop a thick description of each SIRP based on the varied perspectives of those involved in it. Therefore, they conducted in-depth interviews and observations of 45 student organizers and six professional staff members associated with the SIRP at their institution. They also read documents from each site and engaged in various SIRP events.

Contextual Completeness

An important strategy to help readers fully understand a case study involves describing the context in which the case study took place: its history, physical setting, cultural characteristics, social rules, and other features that characterize the setting.

Because participants do not speak with a unified voice in such settings, researchers need to be sensitive to a setting's **multivocality,** that is, a recognition that research participants do not necessarily speak with a unified voice but instead can express diverse interests and viewpoints. They also need to incorporate **tacit knowledge,** the nonverbal cues that convey "the largely unarticulated, contextual understanding that is often manifested in nods, silences, humor, and naughty nuances" (Altheide & Johnson, 1998, p. 492).

García and Bartlett's study (2007) of a segregated bilingual high school in New York included a description of the setting and quotations from students and teachers, reflecting the researchers' attention to the contextual completeness of their report.

Chain of Evidence

To help readers fully understand a case study, the report needs to explain the study design and findings in detail. Perhaps because case studies tend to be long and journals impose length limits, this detail is often lacking. Explanation of a case study's design and findings ideally would provide a **chain of evidence,** which involves making clear, meaningful links between the research questions, raw data, data-analysis procedures, and findings in a case study report.

The chain of evidence often includes an **audit trail,** which is a written record that documents the researchers' procedures for data collection and analysis. An audit trail makes it possible for other researchers to check the soundness of the study's methodology and to use it in subsequent research to replicate or extend the study.

Researcher Reflection

Because the researcher is the primary "measuring instrument" in case studies, researchers can also be a primary source of bias or error that might confound the study's findings. To address this potential problem, researchers sometimes engage in researcher reflection, also known as reflexivity, a process in which researchers ponder their role in the research setting and their assumptions, world view, and personal and theoretical orientation toward the phenomenon being studied. This process helps both to clarify the basis for their etic perspective and, to the extent possible, to remove any unintended bias or error based on such factors.

All the case study researchers whose work we have described in this chapter obviously had personal and professional experience that affected their decision to study the particular phenomena that they studied. However, their case study reports typically give minimal detail about whether researcher reflection occurred. As a result, readers must use their own reflective processes to determine whether bias might have occurred at various points in the research process.

An *example of*
HOW CASE STUDY RESEARCH CAN HELP IN SOLVING PROBLEMS OF PRACTICE

Online courses are proliferating at a rapid rate. Consider what is happening in Florida, according to a newspaper in that state.

> Thousands of Florida students may ditch public elementary and middle schools next year in favor of online classes at home—an option that could change the face of public education.
>
> "I am so excited about this that my goal is to go all the way through 12th grade," said Joni Fussell, whose 8-year-old daughter has been studying at the kitchen computer in their Altamonte Springs home since January.
>
> Florida Virtual School's online courses for high-school students . . . went from students completing 6,765 half-credit courses in 2001 to 137,450 courses last school year.

> Weber, D. (2008, November 10). In Florida, virtual school could make classrooms history. *Orlando Sentinel.* Retrieved from www.orlandosentinel.com

Research sometimes is stimulated by the simple question, "What is going on here?" Undoubtedly, school teachers and administrators are wondering how the on-line learning experience in a different setting than school is affecting students. A case study such as that described below is one option for addressing their curiosity and questions.

Many aspects of online courses are worth investigating, but a case study needs to focus on just a few to allow for thick description. We decided to focus on how parents and students interact with each other and the online course material. Therefore, our case will be a parent and child, similar to the mother and daughter described in the article.

We will limit our sample to just one case, because we will want to make intensive, real-time observations in the family's home while instruction is occurring. If resources are available, we would like to visit the family's home one day per week, randomly selecting the days to visit, over the course of a school term. Our primary instrument for data collection will be note-taking. We will record all salient parent and child comments and their activities as the parent and child engage with online instruction. We also plan to interview the parent and child at planned intervals. In addition, we plan to interview other members of the family and the teacher assigned by the school district to monitor the child's learning.

Our initial research questions are the following: What are the main types of comments that parent and child make to each other as the child interacts with the computer? What are the main activities in which parent and child engage while online instruction is occurring? What do the parent, child, other family members, supervising teachers, and other stakeholders perceive as the main benefits and problems of online instruction? We will consider collecting data relating to other questions that might arise during the course of the study.

Self-Check Test

1. In a qualitative research case study, the researchers strive to do all of the following except
   a. conduct an in-depth study of the phenomenon.
   b. study the phenomenon in its natural context.
   c. maintain an objective perspective on the phenomenon.
   d. reflect the research participants' perspective on the phenomenon being studied.

2. Looking for causal patterns in a case study reflects the goal of _____ a phenomenon.
   a. describing
   b. explaining
   c. evaluating
   d. generalizing

3. Qualitative researchers use purposeful sampling in order to
   a. reduce the chances of selecting atypical cases of the phenomenon to be studied.
   b. eliminate the need to study more than one case.
   c. select cases that are the most convenient for in-depth study.
   d. select cases that are "information-rich" with respect to the purposes of the study.

4. In qualitative research, the primary instrument of data collection typically is
   a. a questionnaire or other self-report measure used to collect data.
   b. audio or video recordings of field events.
   c. the researchers themselves.
   d. researchers' key informants.

5. In interpretational data analysis, researchers consistently
   a. search for patterns inherent in the data.
   b. impose meaning on the data.
   c. search for naturally occurring segments in the data.
   d. use categories developed by other researchers.

6. Researchers who wish to rely on their own intuition and judgment in analyzing case study data will most likely use _____ analysis.
   a. interpretational
   b. structural
   c. reflective
   d. narrative

7. Reflective reporting of a case study tends to involve
   a. an objective writing style.
   b. computer analysis of the data.
   c. a conventional organization of topics.
   d. the strong presence of the researchers' voice.

8. Qualitative researchers believe that the best approach to handling bias in case studies is
   a. honest exploration of the researcher's identity and beliefs as possible biasing factors.
   b. comparison of qualitative data with quantitative data.
   c. having the data collected by individuals who are similar to the field participants.
   d. studying phenomena in which one has a minimal stake.

9. If researchers want to increase the applicability of their case study findings to other settings, it is not advisable to
   a. study an atypical case.
   b. study more than one case.
   c. compare their case to similar cases studied by other researchers.
   d. provide a thick description of their case.

10. Qualitative research traditions typically
    a. do not use methods associated with case study research to investigate phenomena.
    b. are grounded in positivism.
    c. use the research methods of various academic disciplines in the study of phenomena.
    d. are based primarily on models from the physical sciences.

Chapter References

Alexander, B. K. (2005). Performance ethnography: The reenacting and inciting of culture. In N. K. Denzin & Y. S. Lincoln (Eds.), *The Sage handbook of qualitative research* (3rd ed., pp. 411–442). Thousand Oaks, CA: Sage.

Altheide, D. L., & Johnson, J. M. (1998). Criteria for assessing interpretive validity in qualitative research. In N. K. Denzin & Y. S. Lincoln (Eds.), *Handbook of qualitative research* (pp. 485–499). Thousand Oaks, CA: Sage.

Auerbach, C. F., & Silverstein, L. B. (2003). *Qualitative data: An introduction to coding and analysis.* New York: New York University Press.

Ausband, L. T. (2006). Instructional technology specialists and curriculum work. *Journal of Research on Technology in Education, 39*(1), 1–21.

Biddle, B. J., & Anderson, D. S. (1986). Theory, methods, knowledge, and research on teaching. In M. C. Wittrock (Ed.), *Handbook of research on teaching* (3rd ed., pp. 230–252). New York: Macmillan.

Burch, P. E. (2006). The new educational privatization: Educational contracting and high stakes accountability. *Teachers College Record, 108*(12), 2582–2610.

Cuban, L. (1997). Change without reform: The case of Stanford University school of medicine, 1908–1990. *American Educational Research Journal, 34,* 83–122.

Denzin, N. K., & Lincoln, Y. S. (Eds.). (2005). *The Sage handbook of qualitative research* (3rd ed.). Thousand Oaks, CA: Sage.

Freire, P. (1970). *Pedagogy of the oppressed* (M. B. Ramos, Trans.). New York: Grove Press.

Gall, M. D., Gall, J. P., & Borg, W. R. (2007). *Educational research: An introduction* (8th ed.). Boston: Pearson.

García, O., & Bartlett, L. (2007). A speech community model of bilingual education: Educating Latino newcomers in the USA. *The International Journal of Bilingual Education and Bilingualism, 10*(1), 1–25.

Glaser, B., & Strauss, A. (1967). *The discovery of grounded theory.* Chicago: Aldine.

Goldenberg, C. (1992). The limits of expectations: A case for case knowledge about teacher expectancy effects. *American Educational Research Journal, 29,* 517–544.

Harper, D. (2005). What's new visually? In N. K. Denzin & Y. S. Lincoln (Eds.), *The Sage handbook of qualitative research* (3rd ed., pp. 747–762). Thousand Oaks, CA: Sage.

Jacob, E. (1987). Qualitative research traditions: A review. *Review of Educational Research, 57,* 1–50.

Jones, J. (2002). Performance ethnography: The role of embodiment in cultural authenticity. *Theatre Topics, 12*(1), 1–15.

Kincheloe, J. L., & McLaren, P. (2000). Rethinking critical theory and qualitative research. In N. K. Denzin & Y. S. Lincoln (Eds.), *Handbook of qualitative research* (2nd ed., pp. 279–313). Thousand Oaks, CA: Sage.

Kirk, J., & Miller, M. L. (1986). *Reliability and validity in qualitative research.* Beverly Hills, CA: Sage.

Lancy, D. F. (1993). *Qualitative research in education: An introduction to the major traditions.* New York: Longman.

Leikin, R., & Rota, S. (2006). Learning through teaching: A case study on the development of a mathematics teacher's proficiency in managing an inquiry-based classroom. *Mathematics Education Research Journal, 18*(3), 44–68.

Lincoln, Y., & Guba, E. (1985). *Naturalistic inquiry.* Beverly Hills, CA: Sage.

Maldonado, D. E. Z., Rhoads, R., & Buenavista, T. L. (2005). The student-initiated retention project: Theoretical contributions and the role of self-empowerment. *American Educational Research Journal, 42*(4), 605–638.

Manning, P. K., & Cullum-Swan, B. (1994). Narrative, content, and semiotic analysis. In N. K. Denzin & Y. S. Lincoln (Eds.), *Handbook of qualitative research* (pp. 463–477). Thousand Oaks, CA: Sage.

McMillan, J. H., & Schumacher, S. (2006). *Research in education: Evidence-based inquiry* (6th ed.). Boston: Pearson.

Miles, M. B., & Huberman, A. M. (1984). *Qualitative data analysis: A sourcebook of new methods.* Beverly Hills, CA: Sage.

Patthey-Chavez, G. G. (1993). High school as an arena for cultural conflict and acculturation for Latino Angelinos. *Anthropology and Education Quarterly, 24,* 33–60.

Patton, M. Q. (2002). *Qualitative evaluation & research methods* (3rd ed.). Thousand Oaks, CA: Sage.

Richardson, L. (1992). The consequences of poetic representation: Writing the other, rewriting the self. In C. Ellis & M. G. Flaherty (Eds.), *Investigating subjectivity: Research on lived experience* (pp. 125–140). Newbury Park, CA: Sage.

Richardson, L., & St. Pierre, E. A. (2005). Writing: A method of inquiry. In N. K. Denzin & Y. S. Lincoln (Eds.), *The Sage handbook of qualitative research* (3rd ed., pp. 959–978). Thousand Oaks, CA: Sage.

Strauss, A. L., & Corbin, J. (1990). *Basics of qualitative research: Grounded theory procedures and techniques.* Newbury Park, CA: Sage.

Tesch, R. (1990) *Qualitative research: Analysis types & software tools.* Bristol, PA: Falmer.

Yahya, I. B., & Moore, G. E. (1985, March). On research methodology: The cassette tape as a data collection medium. ERIC Document Reference No. ED262098.

Resources for Further Study

Auerbach, C. F., & Silverstein, L. B. (2003). *Qualitative data: An introduction to coding and analysis.* New York: New York University.

> The authors provide an up-to-date, thorough description of the process of coding and analyzing data from qualitative research. They use their own case study of fathers and fathering involving Haitian American, Promise Keeper, and gay fathers to illustrate the process of planning, conducting, and interpreting qualitative research.

Liu, X. (2007). *Great ideas in science education: Case studies of noted living science educators.* Rotterdam, Netherlands: SensePublishers.

> This book is a collection of case studies of eight living educators who have made significant contributions to the field of science education. Using a "history in person" approach, it traces each educator's fruitful research career and shows the potential of his or her work to improve science teaching and learning at all levels. The book illustrates the value of relevant case studies to educators who are concerned with the problem of improving teaching and learning in specific education fields.

Merriam, S. B. (1998). *Qualitative research and case study applications in education.* San Francisco: Jossey-Bass.

> Revised and expanded from Merriam's *Case study research in education* (1988). Provides a detailed description of all phases of qualitative research design in general and in case study research. Includes a detailed description of three actual case studies of adult learners in various contexts.

Sample Case Story

Teaching Secrets: Ask the Kids!

Sacks, A. (2007, September 11). Teaching secrets: Ask the kids! *Teacher Magazine*. Retrieved from www.teachermagazine.org/tm/articles/2007/09/11/03tln_sacks_web.h19.html

Teachers are always looking for new techniques to improve their classroom management. The following article is a case story about one teacher's discovery of a technique that made a difference in her classroom.

After reading this article, we recommend that you read the next article, which reports a case study. By doing so, you can see for yourself the differences between case stories and case studies in purpose and presentation of evidence to support their conclusions.

The article is reprinted in its entirety, just as it appeared when originally published.

Teaching Secrets: Ask the Kids!

Ariel Sacks   It was the middle of my second year of teaching in a high-needs New York City public school. I was finally planning successful lessons and my class of 8th grade transitional English-language learners had become enthusiastic readers of whole novels in English.

So it took me by surprise when, around February, I noticed these same students yawning, poking one another, throwing paper balls, and complaining during class. I bristled at their displays of frustration and heard myself snapping back at them. I was becoming that cranky teacher I vowed never to be.

After weeks of such behavior, I began to get nervous every time this class would enter my room. I tried to make the work more exciting, but nothing seemed to change. Finally, one afternoon, I couldn't take it any longer. My students entered my room and sat down as usual in the

U-shaped configuration of benches called the meeting area. Our agenda was on the board, and I was about to run through it. I had gotten in the habit of doing this as quickly as possible, in my most energetic tone, while I still had the illusion of my students' attention.

But that day I thought to myself, *Why do I keep pretending this is working? Something is wrong.*

"You know what?" I said to the class. "I'm really stressed out. I don't even want to go through the agenda today. Is anyone else feeling stressed?"

My students responded with a resounding, "Yeesssss!" For the first time in weeks, I had everyone's attention.

"Wow," I said. "Let's go around and hear from everyone. Say anything you want. How are you feeling today about school, life—anything?"

I was amazed when one of our school's most academically motivated students, Ana, started us off. "I feel that school is so boring now," she said. "All we want is to talk with our friends."

"Yeah," added Litzabet. "We are so stressed, because of all the tests. One test finishes and you have a test or a project due the next day. We don't get a break! We are, like, oppressed people." ("Oppression" was a literary theme we'd been discussing.)

José said, straight-faced, "Sometimes we just want to have fun."

Suddenly, the whole class was talking at once. I had to remind them to take turns and let everyone be heard. They did, because they really wanted to hear what others thought.

Comments I might have laughed off as adolescent whining on another day, I decided to take seriously. "You never give us popcorn anymore" and "We never watch movies" took on new meaning. The students' pleas for more time to socialize struck me as particularly important in a school that offered no recess, no advisory, and gym and art only once a week. The students' developmental needs were not being met by the school. I would have to do something differently if I expected any real change in my classroom.

We began negotiating. I wrote on the board, "Social time, popcorn, movies, fun." I thanked the students for being honest with me and told them I was willing to make changes to satisfy each one of these requests.

I offered to give them the first five minutes of class for social time. There would be rules, but this would be strictly free time. They could walk around, talk with one another, play cards, etc. But they were not permitted to run, throw, play-fight, use cell phones, or allow the volume in the room to get so loud that they couldn't hear the Tibetan meditation bell that always signals the end of break. They had to come immediately to the meeting area at the sound of the bell. We would then assess how the break went before moving into our agenda for the day.

I never knew so much relief could come from five minutes of freedom! We also decided that if the class worked well Monday through Thursday, we would have popcorn and fun on Friday. We watched movies that related to our literature studies, or we played games. Other times, we needed Fridays to finish work. I found that, when I opened it up for negotiation, the students were surprisingly responsible about that use of time.

Despite some difficult conditions, the rest of the year was a joy. My students and I battled burnout through honest dialogue, and they worked more productively than I had imagined possible. I'll never forget that class for helping me to develop routines I still use—and for showing me what students are capable of when we take time to listen and include them in the decisions of our classrooms.

About the Author

Ariel Sacks is beginning her fourth year of teaching in the New York City schools.

Sample Case Study

General Education Teachers and Students with ADHD: What Modifications Are Made?

Nowacek, E. J., & Mamlin, N. (2007). General education teachers and students with ADHD: What modifications are made? *Preventing School Failure, 51*(3), 28–35.

U.S. schools have several million students with attention deficit hyperactivity disorder (ADHD). Educators are faced with the problem of how to help these students achieve their learning potential.

The following research article presents case studies of four elementary school teachers and four middle school teachers who teach students with ADHD in their classrooms. The researchers studied what teachers knew about this disability and the extent to which they modified their instruction to help their students with ADHD learn effectively.

The article is reprinted in its entirety, just as it appeared when originally published.

General Education Teachers and Students with ADHD: What Modifications Are Made?

E. Jane Nowacek
and Nancy Mamlin

ABSTRACT ■ We investigated 4 elementary school general education teachers' understandings of the characteristics of students with attention deficit hyperactivity disorder (ADHD) and what academic and behavioral modifications they implemented for these learners. Two major findings emerged: (a) teachers provided few modifications for individuals with ADHD and (b) they provided idiosyncratic, nonsystematic modifications. We followed this investigation with a second multiple case study with 2 middle grade teams in which we examined their understanding of the characteristics of students with ADHD and the modifications they made. The two middle grade teams implemented a variety of modifications that they reported were chosen with the developmental level of their students in mind and knowledge of the resources available, rather than the needs of individual students. We found both elementary and middle grades teachers knew key characteristics of students with ADHD. Although they knew the characteristic and needs of these students, there were few modifications that all or a majority of the teachers made at either grade level.

KEYWORDS ■ ADHD, general education, modifications

By 2000, there were four to five million people, mostly school aged, diagnosed with attention deficit hyperactivity disorder (ADHD), twice the estimate given a decade earlier (Mayes, 2002). As described in the *Diagnostic and Statistical Manual of Mental Disorders* fourth edition (DSM-IV, American Psychiatric Association [APA], 1994), this disorder involves inattention, hyperactivity, impulsivity, or a combination of these symptoms. Given that prevalence rates in general education classrooms are estimated to be as high as one to two students per classroom (Barkley, 2000), providing appropriate education poses a challenge.

Although children with ADHD experience significant academic and behavioral difficulties, research suggests that the majority of classroom teachers lack knowledge of what constitutes appropriate interventions and modifications (Parker, 1992). Moreover, a search of the literature revealed few studies that examined teachers' instructional and behavioral modification practices. This is problematic given that many students with ADHD do not qualify for special education programs and, therefore, are the sole responsibility of general education teachers. Furthermore, current laws, such as the Individuals with Disabilities Education Improvement Act (IDEA, 2004), Sec. 504 of the Rehabilitation Act of 1973, and the Americans with Disabilities Act (ADA), support regular class placement for these students (Turnbull, Turnbull, Shank, & Smith, 2004).

Academic Intervention

Although there is little research that specifically addresses interventions for students with ADHD, several academic interventions appear to have promise, including peer tutoring, strategies instruction, and computer-assisted instruction (DuPaul & Eckert, 1998; Spries & Stone, 1989; Pressley & Wolyshyn, 1995). Each of these interventions attempts to address the major symptoms of ADHD: impulsivity, inattention, and hyperactivity.

DuPaul and Eckert (1998) described the use of peer tutoring that may enhance the learning of students with ADHD because it featured one-on-one assistance, individualized pace, continuous prompting, and immediate feedback. In a recent review of research syntheses, Vaughn, Gersten, and Chard (2000) reported that peer tutoring was associated with improved outcomes for all students, including students with ADHD. Another technique, use of a partner board for recognizing good work, led to reliable increases in on-task behavior and reductions in fidgeting (DuPaul & Eckert, 1998; Kemp, Fister, & McLaughlin, 1995).

A second approach, strategy instruction, teaches students to use a set of procedures or strategies that specifically address demands of an academic situation. Although this type of intervention would seem to be an effective way to address needs of students with ADHD, there is scant research in this area. Spries and Stone (1989) investigated directed notetaking [with] students with ADHD. In directed

Reprinted from *Preventing School Failure*, 51(3), 28–35. Reprinted with permission of the Helen Dwight Reid Educational Foundation. Published by Heldref Publications, 1319 Eighteenth St., NW, Washington, D.C. 20036-1801. Copyright © 2007.

notetaking, students are taught a structured split page format for taking notes and a self-questioning strategy for monitoring levels of involvement before, during, and after notetaking and are provided with direct teaching of the notetaking process. This strategy would seem useful for students with ADHD, as taking notes may be more beneficial than is passive listening (DuPaul & Eckert, 1998). There are some benefits to teaching this particular strategy including an increase in the quality of notes, recording of details, on-task behaviors, and improved daily assignment performance. Other interventions that have been suggested in the literature for students with ADHD include providing a listening guide, or partial outline; using framing [cloze procedure]; and allowing tape recording (Chalmers,1991).

In their review, DuPaul and Eckert (1998) reported two empirical studies that addressed computer assisted instruction. To make a difference, software had to offer (a) individual instruction levels, (b) easily readable display formats, (c) self-pacing, (d) motivational features, and (e) game formats with animation. For example, in one study they described, students using computer-assisted instruction completed twice as many problems as a pencil and paper group and spent more time working on problems.

Behavioral Interventions

Self-regulation and self-reinforcement strategies have been effective in addressing behavioral needs, such as impulsivity and poor social skills (Abramowitz & O'Leary, 1991). Self-regulation includes teaching problem-solving techniques, self-evaluation, and self-control (Westby & Cutler, 1994). In one intervention (Shapiro, DePaul, & Bradley-Klug, 1998), two 12-year-old students with ADHD were taught to rate their behaviors by comparing their ratings to those of their teachers. After learning to accurately judge their behavior, comparisons and backup reinforcement in the form of points were gradually reduced and the rating interval was increased until students moved toward complete self-management. In addition, DuPaul and Eckert found that teaching self-regulation strategies was more effective than the use of medication alone, and when combined with medication, had a greater effect. Results of studies have indicated that positive reinforcement is an effective behavioral intervention (DuPaul & Eckert, 1998; Fiore, Becker, & Nero, 1993; Fabiano & Pelham, 2003). For example, Fiore et al. reported positive reinforcement procedures were effective in reducing the activity level and increasing the time on-task of children with ADHD. Fabiano and Pelham similarly found that increasing the opportunities to earn rewards and providing immediate feedback, as well as defining the criteria needed to meet behavioral goals, had "powerful behavioral effects" (p. 127) in an ADHD-diagnosed third grader's behavior in both general and special education classrooms.

In their review of behavioral interventions for students with ADHD, Abramowitz and O'Leary (1991) discussed several studies that used contingency management techniques (e.g., classroom token economies, home-school contingencies) to reduce disruptive behavior. Moreover, teachers can use a combination of functional behavioral assessment and contingency-based techniques to increase appropriate behaviors of their students (Hallahan, Lloyd, Kauffman, Weiss, & Martinez, 2005). Peer-mediated contingency interventions also have had positive results (Northrup, et al., 1995).

Given the limited number of studies in which researchers examined interventions with students with ADHD and the growing number of students identified with ADHD, we wondered what teachers understood about the characteristics associated with ADHD and what modifications and interventions they used with these students. First, we conducted a multiple-case study with elementary school teachers (Study 1). After completing this study we investigated similar issues with middle grade teachers (Study 2), and we considered the relationship between teachers on teams as well as the particular characteristics of young adolescents.

STUDY 1

Method

Participants.   We selected teachers who met three criteria: (a) were identified by their principal as being effective, (b) had at least 5 years teaching experience, and (c) were already teaching students with ADHD. We selected two teachers in primary grades (grades 1–3) and two in upper elementary grades (grades 4–6). During the five-year period preceding our study, all of these educators had participated in staff development that addressed special education, including ADHD.

Ms. Bradley, an educator for over 11 years, taught second grade. With 5 of the 21 students in her class identified as having ADHD and only 1 special education teacher in the school, she reported she experienced little external support. Mr. Campbell was a sixth grade teacher who had been teaching for 28 years. He and one other sixth grade teacher shared responsibility for the 50 sixth-grade students to whom Mr. Campbell taught science, social studies, math, and physical education. At the time of our study, he had 4 students identified with ADHD. Patricia Rossford, a third-grade educator, spent most of her 20 years as a teacher working in an elementary school. During the study, 5 of her 24 students were identified with ADHD. Sandy Wilson, a fourth-grade teacher, had completed 25 years as an elementary school educator. At the time of the study, 1 of her 17 students was classified with ADHD.

Procedure.   After receiving IRB approval, we designed a multiple-case study (Yin, 1994) to investigate four elementary school general education teachers' understanding of the characteristics of students with ADHD and to learn about the academic and behavioral modifications they implemented for these students. Before we began the interviews, the teachers completed a consent form, a demographic information form, and an open-ended question in which they provided their own definition of ADHD. At that time, we described the study and procedures for maintaining their anonymity (e.g., using pseudonyms, destroying tapes). After the interviews, we conducted classroom observations.

Interviews. We asked semistructured questions (Patton, 1990) aligned with the literature in individual interviews. Our questions focused on characteristics of students with ADHD, the academic and behavioral modifications these teachers made, and their methods for promoting acceptance of all students in their classes (see Appendix for questions). After posing each question, we followed up with probes when necessary. These probes covered information such as frequency of modifications, specific types of modifications, and rationale for selecting modifications for certain students. We tape-recorded and transcribed these interviews verbatim. To enhance the rigor of the research, we triangulated the data by conducting classroom observations. To promote reliability (Bogdan & Biklen, 1998), we each took independent field notes during the same observation. In all cases, the data from the field notes converged and were not contradictory. Further, we conducted each interview independently to avoid influence from other participants.

Analysis. We independently coded the data, using the constant comparative method (Bogdan & Biklen, 1998). Several categories emerged from our initial, independent analysis. Next, we compared our codes and negotiated differences, contacting the participants for clarification when necessary. Once we agreed upon the categories, we defined each one to ensure that they were mutually exclusive. Then, we listed all instances of each category by line number and speaker as they appeared in the transcripts. This gave us a visual representation of the frequency of occurrence in each category. In addition, we reviewed the transcripts to discover data that seemed to be particularly salient to the participants. Given the frequency and saliency of categories in the data, two themes emerged: (a) orientation to the class as a whole and (b) idiosyncratic and nonsystematic modifications. First, we discuss the findings from the open-ended question and then discuss these themes.

Results

Although the school context and educational backgrounds differed for each of the teachers, all were familiar with the characteristics of ADHD. Ms. Bradley, for example, described these students as showing "a lot of impulsiveness" and an "inability to stay focused on a task for very long." She further added that they "seem to be loners." When responding to probes about ADHD and its implications for student intelligence and academic ability, Ms. Bradley concluded that "some are bright, some are right-brained and are capable of doing work, if they can stay focused." Ms. Rossford, the other primary grade teacher, agreed that students with ADHD showed an "inability to focus or attend," were "easily distracted," and experienced "difficulty in getting things done." Ms. Wilson summed up the

two upper elementary teachers' understanding of ADHD characteristics as "having difficulty listening, organizing, and following through with work due to (demonstrating) easy distractibility and impulsive behaviors." She further explained that "it [ADHD] covers too much: from the child who never disturbs anybody but never gets anything finished, to those that absolutely take your room apart because they are bouncing off the wall."

Theme 1: Orientation to Class as a Whole. First, the general education teachers in this study were oriented to the class as a whole. They tended to make modifications that maintained the integrity of the academic subject and required little individualization in terms of planning, instruction, and resources. Only one teacher, for example, commented on using school or outside personnel. Ms. Bradley, the second grade teacher, explained that she had "a lot of university volunteers and paid tutors" that enabled her to "break the kids into smaller groups to read." She also commented that in math the "amount (of work) is modified for everybody and it is a reasonable amount." She also reported having "a set schedule (for everyone because) they do much better with structure." The third-grade teacher also commented that the structured setting in her classroom helped these children tremendously, as well as it did all of her students. Mr. Campbell, the sixth-grade teacher, reported helping all his students with time management and by putting notes on the board for his students to copy. All teachers, except Mr. Campbell, shortened some of the assignments they gave to students with ADHD. The few individual academic modifications they made included (a) use of modified spelling lists (second-grade teacher), (b) use of Content Reading in the Secondary Schools (CRISS) strategies (second-grade teacher), (c) permitting dictation to scribe (third-grade teacher), (d) providing copies of book pages so students with ADHD did not have to write down math problems (third-grade teacher), and (e) permitting students with ADHD to choose where they wanted to work (fourth-grade teacher).

Theme 2: Idiosyncratic and Nonsystematic Modifications. The second theme involved the nonsystematic implementation of the few modifications made for students with ADHD. For example, Ms. Bradley reported "some days I let them pick their partners." She also commented that she allowed students with ADHD [to] "have a little more leeway" in discipline situations and gave "them a little bit of flexibility." Mr. Campbell commented similarly that he "made allowances" for their difficulty in focusing on tasks and moved students with ADHD away from others so that they were better able to focus. Our observational data suggested, however, that these modifications were not consistent or predictable. The teachers in our study also reported making other behavioral modifications: (a) attending to grouping arrangements (second- and third-grade teachers), (b) ignoring inappropriate behavior (third-grade teacher), and (c) allowing more frequent movement (fourth-grade teacher). Although we observed instances in which all these modifications were made, we also observed times when they were not.

STUDY 2

Method

Given the paucity of research on interventions or modifications for students with ADHD, it is not surprising that we found little in the literature that specifically addressed modifications made for these students in middle grades. In a 2003 search using the terms "ADHD" and "middle school," we located no research studies and only one study that offered suggestions for middle school teachers (Taylor & Larson, 1998).

Participants. After conducting our initial investigation with elementary school teachers, we wondered if grade level would make a difference in the interventions and modifications teachers make for students with ADHD. We also wondered what the effect of the "team" approach used in middle grades and multiple teachers' rules and requirements would be on students with ADHD.

Therefore, we conducted a second multiple-case study that focused on two small, rural middle grade teams (Grades 6–8) in the South. Although there were no middle schools in the district, the K–8 schools housed middle school students in a separate part of the building and emulated a middle school schedule and philosophy. We interviewed a team of two teachers in each school. The team at Mayfair School included Bob Harrison, who had 8 years of teaching experience, taught social studies to his homeroom and math to sixth-, seventh-, and eighth-grade students and was currently the team leader for the middle grades. The second member of the team, Carol Downing, who had 22 years of teaching experience, taught social studies to her homeroom and language arts to sixth-, seventh-, and eighth-grade students. In a second rural school, Garrison School, Andy Summer and Candace Hoover taught eighth-grade social studies and science, respectively. Mr. Summer had 27 years of experience whereas Ms. Hoover had 21. All of these teachers had at least two students identified as having ADHD in their classes.

Procedure.   In an effort to allow comparisons across Study 1 and Study 2 case studies, we followed the same procedure, interview protocol, and analysis process as we had in Study 1. As in Study 1, each teacher, upon agreeing to participate, completed demographic information and responded to a question regarding their own definition of ADHD. We then asked semi-structured questions (Patton, 1990) and triangulated the data by conducting classroom observations. We initially categorized both the interview and observation data using the main interview questions (see Appendix). From these categories, the final three themes emerged: acceptance, team decisions, and resources. We will first describe the initial categories, then the themes.

Results

As in Study 1, we found that middle grade educators knew key characteristics associated with ADHD as outlined in the DSM-IV (APA, 1994). Specifically, they indicated that students with ADHD experienced difficulty in these areas: (a) attention, (b) hyperactivity, and (c) distractibility. They identified difficulty coming to attention and difficulty sustaining attention as characteristics and commented on the unproductive movement often associated with students with ADHD.

Although all of the teachers in our study knew characteristics associated with ADHD, they used a relatively small number of modifications. Some academic modifications were seen as unnecessary in the middle grades by these teachers. For example, one team of teachers (i.e., Garrison School) pointed out that many interventions had been tried and established in earlier grades. One teacher reported that his team did not do a lot of modifications because of the structure at the middle grades and their teaching styles. He also mentioned that they are trying to get the students ready for high school, where they believed few modifications would be made. These teachers spoke of the academic modifications they made in the classroom for their students with ADHD in three ways: (a) modifications to the assignments themselves, (b) modifications to the environment, and (c) use of another person as an academic support.

These teachers implemented behavioral accommodations that can be grouped into two categories that relate directly to the characteristics the teachers identified: (a) modifications that promoted attention and (b) modifications that allowed movement. For example, teachers attended to grouping arrangements, so that students with ADHD were paired with students without identified disabilities. They reported "giving allowances" for students with ADHD in allowing them to get up and move around the room, or they gave specific tasks to students with ADHD that required their movement in the classroom. For example, the science teacher asked these students to assist with experiments in the classroom, turn on lights, and pass out papers. Finally, teachers commented that the middle-grade setting itself provided some support for students with ADHD because students switched classes and were generally more active in their classes. Candace Hoover at Garrison School reported (in middle grades), "we don't sit at our desks all the time." Her other team member, Andy Sommer, observed that "usually by the time they get to us [in the middle grades], if they're on medication there isn't a need for a lot of physical modification other than the normal things you would do for anybody." From the interviews and observations, three themes emerged: (a) acceptance, (b) team decisions, (c) and resources.

Teacher Acceptance of Students

The participating teachers had several ideas about promoting acceptance among all students. Also, teachers seemed to have their own style of classroom management to enhance acceptance. For example, Bob Harrison said that he "hit problems head-on," whereas his team member, Carol Downing, said that she "tries to be subtle about it." She saw inclusion as promoting acceptance. According to her, students being in the same curriculum and classroom helped them know and accept one another. Downing also focused on self-esteem and read literature in her classes that dealt with differences (e.g., *To Kill a Mockingbird, The Pearl*). All teachers spoke of their actions in the classroom as modeling acceptance. Harrison specifically mentioned modeling respect and patience and Andy Sommer mentioned ignoring inappropriate behaviors. Downing said that she treated all students as capable, focusing on their areas of strength, trying to encourage them. She also mentioned trying to "ward off" situations where things may not turn out as they should. In addition, this teacher used a self-esteem-building curriculum.

Teachers also reported actively involving other students in promoting acceptance. For example, Candace Hoover described the circle discussions she conducted in which students shared good things about another student and then discussed ways in which they could help that student improve. She reported that in her experience, most students were willing to try and work things out and that they were used to adult assistance with this.

Providing structure within the classes also was seen as enhancing acceptance. In a science class, for example, Mrs. Hoover switched groups every 2 weeks, so that eventually each student worked with every other classmate. She also used activities in which she assigned students to groups and did not allow students to choose their own groups to provide control over who worked with whom.

Theme 2: Team Decisions. All the teachers reported working well as members of their middle grades team. As we mentioned earlier, each grade-level team in this study consisted of two teachers. The small size of the team was noted by Mr. Harrison as an advantage. However, he did note that they had no common planning time, and therefore, needed to communicate daily at lunch and in the hallways, a fact mentioned by three of the four teachers in our study. The team at Mayfair had a team meeting once a week, which was described as mostly "taking care of logistics," although these teachers tried to devote at last one meeting a month to curriculum. The teachers described a lot of time on this team as devoted to taking care of discipline issues, not necessarily involving the students with ADHD. At Garrison, Mr. Sommer said that the team made no curriculum decisions because they used the state curriculum. However, that team did decide to have the students move to another teacher or class every 50 minutes, which was seen as a benefit to the students with ADHD. Carol Downing said that they "talked constantly about the kids." Ms. Hoover said that they planned together regarding how to deal with the students with ADHD and that they made a practice of passing along problems and information about students to the next teacher.

Resources

In considering the resources available in the middle grades, all teachers reported using both the professional resources within the school and other people to meet students' needs. Four teachers mentioned using the school-wide assistance team. Mr. Harrison commented

> I think that's been one of the best things that I've had a chance to work on. . . . You're dealing with things that teachers have brought to this committee that there's no simple solution. . . . [On the committee] You've got the guidance counselor, you've got the resource teacher, you've got the speech language (pathologist), you've get the psychologist, you've got the principal, and you have a wide range of classroom teachers. You've got the benefits of all that wisdom around one table, and if there is a solution, it's found out.

Mr. Harrison also identified reviewing student folders as helpful. In addition, three teachers referred to having 504 programs or plans and a professional library in their school as important resources.

Ms. Hoover found peer help—talking with students' previous teachers about "what worked and what didn't" a valuable resource. It is interesting that only one teacher (Mr. Sommer) reported parents as resources. Mr. Harrison remarked: "I should probably tell you that I go look it [information] up, but a lot of times I'll just call the guidance counselor or special education teacher, somebody that deals with it all the time. . . ." The same teacher commented that we "beg for interns, tutors [from the nearby university]. Any help that we can get in our classroom, we want it. Student teachers, we have a high number of student teachers and interns . . . I've got one intern, and I've got two tutors that are [here] during the day, and I have two tutors after school."

His teammate identified the availability of materials such as Franklin spellers and Alpha Smarts as useful. In addition to personnel, records, and materials, two teachers mentioned workshops and inservice programs as being valuable resources. Mr. Harrison commented that school planners given to students by the county provided a vehicle for recording homework and communicating with parents.

Andy Sommer was the only teacher who related resources specifically to the middle grades. He commented that "very few people will volunteer in the upper level. . . . [This year] we've had two [volunteers] so far. This age intimidates the volunteers . . . this age is a real difficult age, because they challenge you at every step of the way."

Limitations.   We conducted one long in-depth interview with each teacher that may limit reliability. However, participants spoke with us on the phone to answer questions and clarify information as required. Furthermore, although this was a multiple-case study, all participants taught in a rural or small university community. Therefore, the findings may not be generalizable to other settings, including larger or more urban communities. Although all of the participants had attended some recent in-service activities regarding students with special needs, only three of the eight teachers had more in-depth instruction in special education (i.e., a university course).

Discussion

After reflecting on the results of these studies, we reached several conclusions. First, both elementary and middle grades teachers knew key characteristics of students with ADHD. They all noted distractibility, impulsiveness, and inability to stay focused on a task. Despite knowing the characteristics and needs of students with ADHD, the majority of teachers made few individual modifications at any grade level. The interview data indicated that teachers had their own idiosyncratic sets of modifications that they used with varying degrees of consistency. Although one explanation for this may be that these were all experienced teachers who, over time, had developed their individual teaching and management approaches, we believe these data have important implications for teacher educators and school districts as they plan professional development programs. First, workshops that focus on characteristics and causes may not provide teachers with sufficient information to modify their practice. Even when given information about modifications for students with special needs, general educators may not have ongoing support to implement changes and refine their practices. For example, Showers, Joyce, and Bennett (1987) estimated that teachers need 25 opportunities to practice a complex strategy to ensure transfer of the strategy to their practice. Given the limited number of specialists in these rural schools, support, too, was limited. Finally, with the increased expectations resulting from high-stakes testing and accountability programs, teachers may feel that individualization is too time consuming, and therefore, implement primarily whole-class strategies (Zigmond & Baker, 1995). Furthermore, Bryant, Dean, Elrod, and Blackbourn (1999) found that rural teachers preferred those modifications that did not change the type or amount of information students had to learn. Moreover, they found that these educators preferred modifications that took the least amount of time to implement and were less likely to separate students with disabilities from those without disabilities.

In general, the middle-grades teachers we observed and interviewed made more academic than behavioral modifications in contrast to the elementary teachers in our study. One middle-grades teacher offered the explanation that these older students regulated their behaviors, either through the use of medication or because they have learned to manage their own behaviors in elementary schools. However, our observational data suggested that students with ADHD in the middle grades we studied continued to be easily distracted and were often inattentive and hyperactive. Although both elementary and middle-grades teachers focused on the whole child, there was an increased emphasis on academics in the middle grades. We conclude that professional development and teacher preparation programs need to help teachers address behaviors that interfere with academics. Our findings support

those of Boyer and Brandy (1997), who found that teachers' most frequently cited concern was the need for training in working with students with disabilities.

The elementary school general educators we interviewed were oriented to the class as a whole and seemed to make limited individual modifications. Two elementary-school teachers discussed the importance of a structured environment for many, if not all, students. The most commonly used modification for students with ADHD was shortening either the work period or assignments. Although three of the four elementary-school teachers modified the length of time or required work, only one reported making other individualized modifications including permitting students with ADHD to dictate their papers and providing copies of math textbook pages so they did not have to copy the problems. However, our observations suggested that these modifications were not consistently implemented.

Similarly, the middle-grades teachers in our study reported making modifications to assignments. As with the elementary teachers, all four middle-grades teachers indicated that they reduced the length of assignments. The team at Mayfair indicated that they also used audiotaped books and read the class materials aloud, provided extended time on tests and written assignments, and gave some differentiated assignments. All the middle-grades teachers also made environmental modifications such as allowing students with ADHD to use the computer for written assignments, checking assignment planners, and reminding students of the materials they would need in the class before class began. Moreover, all four of these teachers indicated that they made use of other people to assist students with ADHD academically. Two teachers reported that they asked the special educator for advice. Other support personnel the teachers mentioned using included the 504 coordinators, volunteers, and peer tutors. In summary, although these middle-grades teachers indicated an awareness of the individual students in their classes and did not discuss students in terms of the whole class, our observational and interview data did not indicate that these general educators made many modifications for individual students. Rather, they knew the resources available to them and used them when they deemed them necessary. This supports Polsgrove and Gable's (2003) observation regarding the inadequate preparation of teachers of students with behavioral problems.

Regarding behavioral modifications, three of the general educators in the four elementary schools we studied discussed providing opportunities for these students to move about the classroom. Two reported applying the rules more flexibly for children with ADHD. Again, our observations suggested that, although these modifications were used, they were not systematically implemented.

The middle-grades general educators in our study discussed behavioral modifications in three categories: enhancing attention, addressing hyperactivity, and promoting acceptance. To increase attention, all four teachers indicated that they paired students with ADHD carefully and monitored group work closely. One teacher reported giving physical and verbal cues whereas his teammate indicated she gave praise for staying on task and completing assignments.

To address hyperactivity, three teachers discussed giving allowances, such as ignoring students with ADHD being out of their seats. We also observed one team member who provided opportunities for students with ADHD to move about the classroom and reported structuring her classroom so that everyone knew where everything was located and could get materials on their own. She further provided opportunities in the lesson for students with ADHD to work with limited distractions.

These four middle-grades teachers were well aware of the implications of working with adolescents. They were concerned about acceptance of all students and students' acceptance of themselves. Although this is a worthy goal, general education preservice training and professional development programs should emphasize that it is not necessarily fair. Rather, as Bryant, et al. (1999) pointed out, "It can mean providing what an individual needs at a given time" (p. 10).

Although the elementary and middle-school teachers we interviewed reported that they attempted to meet the needs of their students with ADHD, they seemed to select modifications that could be performed without advanced planning, that did not require differentiated instruction, or behavioral intervention, or that could be addressed by another professional or support person. Like Lambert, Dodd, Christiansen, and Fishbaugh (1996), we found the implementation of modifications used most often by teachers of students with disabilities: (a) required minimal preparation time, (b) tended to be unresponsive to skill needs of students with disabilities, and (c) were met by adults other than the classroom teacher.

References

Abramowitz, A. J., & O'Leary, S. G. (1991). Behavioral interventions for the classroom: Implications for students with ADHD. *School Psychology Review, 20*(2), 220–234.

American Psychiatric Association. (1994). *Diagnostic and statistical manual of mental disorders* (4th ed.). Washington, DC: Author.

Barkley, R. A. (2000). *Taking charge of ADHD: The complete, authoritative guide for parents* (rev. ed.). New York: Guilford.

Bogdan, R. C., & Biklen, S. K. (1998). *Qualitative research for education: An introduction to theory and methods* (3rd ed.). Needham Heights, MA: Allyn & Bacon.

Boyer, W. A. R., & Brandy, H. (1997). Rural teachers' perceptions of the current state of inclusion: Knowledge, training, teaching practices, and adequacy of support systems. *Exceptionality, 7*, 1–18.

Bryant, R., Dean, M., Elrod, G. F., & Blackbourn, J. M. (1999). Rural general education teachers' opinions of adaptations for inclusive classrooms: A renewed call for dual licensure. *Rural Special Education Quarterly, 18*, 5–12.

Chalmers, L. (1991). Classroom modifications for the mainstreamed student with mild handicaps. *Intervention in School and Clinic, 27*, 40–42, 51.

DuPaul, G. J., & Eckert, T. L. (1998). Academic interventions for students with attention-deficit/hyperactivity disorder: A review of the literature. *Reading & Writing Quarterly: Overcoming Learning Difficulties, 14*, 59–82.

Fabiano, G. A., & Pelham, W. E. (2003). Improving the effectiveness of behavioral classroom interventions for attention-deficit/hyperactivity disorder: A case study. *Journal of Emotional and Behavioral Disorders, 11*, 122–128.

Fiore, T. A., Becker, E. A., & Nero, R. C. (1993). Educational interventions for student's attention deficit disorder. *Exceptional Children, 60*, 163–173.

Hallahan, D. P., Lloyd, J. W., Kauffman, J. M., Weiss, M., & Martinez, E. A. (2005). *Learning disabilities: Foundations, characteristics, and effective teaching* (3rd ed.). Boston: Allyn & Bacon.

Individuals with Disabilities Education Improvement Act (IDEA). S. 1248, 108th Cong. (2003).

Kemp, K., Fister, S., & McLaughlin, P. J. (1995). Academic strategies for children with ADD. *Intervention in School and Clinic, 30*, 203–210.

Lambert, D., Dodd, J. M., Christiansen, L., & Fishbaugh, M. S. E. (1996). Rural secondary teachers' willingness to provide accommodations for students with learning disabilities. *Rural Special Education Quarterly, 15*, 36–42.

Mayes, R. (2002). Rise of ADHD prevalence and psychostimulant use: A historical perspective. Retrieved February 2, 2004, from http://apha.comfex.com/apha/130am/techprogram/paper_46109.htm

Northrup, J., Broussard, C., Jones, K., George, T., Vollmer, T., & Herring, M. (1995). A preliminary comparison of reinforcer assessment methods for children with attention deficit hyperactivity disorder. *Journal of Applied Behavior Analysis, 28*, 235–240.

Parker, H. (1992). *The ADD hyperactivity handbook for schools.* Plantation, FL: Impact Publications.

Patton, M. Q. (1990). *Qualitative evaluation and research methods* (2nd ed.). Newbury Park, CA: Sage.

Polsgrove, L., & Gable, R. A. (2003). Reflections on the past and future (and) like it is: Thoughts on the career of Lewis Polsgrove. *Behavioral Disorders, 28*, 221–228.

Pressley, M., & Wolyshyn, V. (1995). *Cognitive strategy instruction that really improves children's academic performance* (2nd ed.). Boston: Brookline.

Shapiro, E. S., DuPaul, G. J., & Bradley-Klug, K. L. (1998). Self-management as a strategy to improve the classroom behavior of students with ADHD. *Journal of Learning Disabilities, 31*, 545–555.

Showers, B., Joyce, B., & Bennett, B. (1987). Synthesis of research on staff development: A framework for future study and a state-of-the-art analysis. *Educational Leadership, 45*(3), 77–87.

Spries, H. A., & Stone. P. D. (1989). The directed notetaking activity: A self-questioning approach. *Journal of Reading, 33*, 36–39.

Taylor, H. E., & Larson, S. (1998). Teaching children with ADHD—What do elementary and middle grades social studies teachers need to know? *Social Studies 89*, 161–64.

Turnbull, R., Turnbull, A., Shank, M., & Smith, S. (2004). *Exceptional lives: Special education in today's schools* (4th ed.). Upper Saddle River, NJ: Merrill.

Vaughn, S., Gersten, R., & Chard, D. J. (2000). The underlying message in LD intervention research: Findings from research syntheses. *Exceptional Children, 67*, 99–114.

Westby, C. E., & Cutler, S. K. (1994). Language and ADHD: Understanding the bases and treatment of self-regulatory deficits. *Topics in Language Disorders, 14*(4), 58–76.

Yin, R. K. (1994). *Case study research: Design and methods* (2nd ed.). Thousand Oaks, CA: Sage.

Zigmond, N., & Baker, J. M. (1995). Concluding comments: Current and future practices in inclusive schooling. *The Journal of Special Education, 29,* 245–250.

APPENDIX

Interview Questions

Question #1: What does the term *ADHD* mean to you?

Question #2: What characteristics do you associate with students identified as having ADHD?

Question #3: What modifications other than academic modifications do you make in your classroom for students identified as having ADHD?

Question #4: What academic modifications do you make in your classroom for students identified as having ADHD?

Question #5: (asked of middle grades teachers only): What resources are available to you here to work with students with ADHD?

Question #6: (asked of middle grades teachers only): What types of decisions do you make as a team?

Question #7: How do you promote acceptance of all students? Give specific examples.

About the Author

E. Jane Nowacek is a professor of special education at Appalachian State University. *Nancy Mamlin* is an associate professor at Appalachian University.

chapter 15

Narrative Research

IMPORTANT *Ideas*

1. Narrative research involves a systematic study of stories that enables readers to apply the findings to wider issues and solve problems of practice.

2. Narratives are a rich source of data because people have many stories to tell about themselves and their society.

3. Individuals' stories often focus on disruptions, that is, unexpected, difficult, or disturbing occurrences.

4. Narrative research can study all types of narratives, including those of groups, individuals, or researchers; preexisting stories and stories generated during the research process; historical and current stories; and stories that are written, spoken, or performed.

5. Narrative research obtains data from research participants that reflect their natural manner of thinking or speaking, conveying a personal, often emotional flavor.

6. Narratives are a common form of communication among teachers and other educators to learn about their students, practice, and work settings.

7. The primary design of much narrative research involves researchers eliciting individuals' past or unfolding stories and then "retelling" the stories in order to clarify their structure and meaning.

8. Data collection in narrative research relies primarily on interviews, which can be supplemented by other types of data such as memos, photos, and minutes of meetings.

9. Data analysis in narrative research involves identifying key events in an individual's story, organizing those events into a meaningful temporal structure, and then connecting the events and structure to a theoretical framework.

10. Narrative researchers sometimes involve participants collaboratively in analyzing narrative data.

11. Interpretations derived from research participants' stories can help educators make sense of their own stories and the stories of those with whom they work, such as students and colleagues. ∎

Key TERMS

coding frame	narrative	research narrative
commitment script	narrative identity	snowball sampling
dialectic	narrative research	stable story structure
disruption	polarity	story
internal narrative	progressive story structure	
log	regressive story structure	

Narratives as a Focus for Research

In Chapter 14 we introduced you to case study research, which we regard as the most common and basic type of qualitative research. We included a typical case story from *Teacher Magazine* and noted that case stories do not constitute research, because they do not involve the use of accepted research techniques for data collection and analysis or give readers a sound basis for judging their possible theoretical meaning or possible value in addressing problems of practice.

The fact that stories do not constitute research should not be construed to mean that stories are unimportant. Stories are very important in people's lives and are worthy of study in their own right. In fact, the study of people's stories has become increasingly popular among researchers in education and the social sciences. This chapter will help you understand how researchers who study stories go about it. **Narrative research,** which is sometimes called *narrative inquiry,* is the systematic study and interpretation of stories of life experiences and the reporting of such research.

A **story,** according to Livia Polanyi (1985), is the original account of specific events that occurred at specific times in the past. A **narrative,** by contrast, is a later account, in which a precise timeline, made up of discrete moments at which the events took place, is established (Polanyi, 1985).

A **research narrative** can be defined as an organized interpretation of events. Each part of this definition has significance. First, note that a research narrative is organized. Suppose we ask a student teacher to recount her experiences as a student teacher. Her story might jump from event to event, going from an experience at her school to an experience in a university seminar. Some events are simultaneous, some are sequential, and some go back to a previous point in time. The researcher's task is to organize these accounts into a meaningful temporal sequence.

According to the second aspect of our definition, a research narrative not only recounts the events in the research participant's story, but also interprets them. For example, the student teacher might recount experiences of being criticized by the cooperating teacher in whose classroom she is doing her student teaching. Depending on the story of how she reacted to these experiences, the student teacher might be inferred to be demonstrating increasing self-efficacy, and the researcher might then draw on previous research and theory on self-efficacy (Skaalvik & Skaalvik, 2007) for an interpretive framework applicable to student teaching in general.

Perhaps in her story the student teacher blames others for her teaching problems but attributes successes to her own efforts. Such statements might lead the researcher to an interpretation that emphasizes the attributions made by student teachers as they experience problems over the course of their student teaching experience. If so, the researcher might draw on attribution theory (Lam & Law, 2008) for an interpretive framework that might apply to this student teacher's experience or to student teaching in general.

The third part of our definition states that a research narrative is about events. In other words, the narrative states that *A* happened, then *B* happened, and continues until the last event has been recounted. Of course, a story also involves people, settings, emotions, thoughts, and other phenomena. However, these elements of the story are not meaningful in and of themselves. Rather, they acquire meaning as they relate to events in the story. For example, a new teacher might emphasize the emotional highs and lows of her student teaching experience. These emotional fluctuations take on meaning in a research narrative as they become tied to specific events in the teacher's story.

The Difference between Narrative Research and Case Study Research

In narrative research, the story, or set of stories, of one or more research participants could be considered a case. For example, the researcher interviews each participant in-depth, places the participant's story in the context of his life, and encourages the participant to tell the story in a manner that is personally meaningful. As shown in Chapter 14, these research elements are also present in case study research.

The main difference between the two types of research is that case studies seek to investigate a phenomenon in its natural context, whereas narrative research studies seek to make interpretations of a story. To illustrate, suppose a researcher is interested in investigating the student teaching experience. The researcher interviews and observes a student teacher (the research participant) over time and finds that the student teacher makes comments about the cooperating teacher's words or actions, finding some helpful and others irrelevant or even harmful.

The case study researcher might identify this as a theme, namely how a cooperating teacher facilitates or inhibits a student teacher's acquisition of instructional expertise. The researcher then might want to study other cases (i.e., other new teachers who recently completed student teaching) and focus interviews and observations on this theme. He might even interview and observe some cooperating teachers to obtain their perspective on facilitating student teachers' acquisition of expertise.

By contrast, the research participant's story—either in its totality or about certain events within the story—is always the central element in a narrative study. The researcher might make particular note about the cooperating teacher's facilitation or inhibition of the student teacher's expertise, but only in the context of the student teacher's story. Narrative research is thus a specialized type of qualitative research in which the focus of inquiry is the research participants' stories.

Types of Narratives and Narrative Identities

In Western culture, stories constitute much of the natural or enacted dialogue between people: "She said _____ and I said _____ and then she _____ and I _____ . . . ") You likely have heard people telling stories about personal experience that fit this structure and have probably told them yourself, many times. Stories can take varied forms, including orally in conversation or when speaking before a group, and in written form, such as emails, personal journals, and literary compositions.

Internal narratives are probably even more universal. An **internal narrative** is the ongoing stream of thought and self-talk that most individuals engage in during many of their waking moments, whether they are consciously aware of it or not. Researchers have increasingly sought to document the ways in which individuals engage in ongoing internal narrative as they move through their daily experience and how their thoughts about themselves, others, and the broader world affect their lives.

Individuals' ongoing narratives, both shared and internal, bring order and meaning to everyday life. Narrative also provides structure to individuals' very sense of selfhood, or what can be called their **narrative identity.** Because individuals operate in many different social environments and continually experience life changes, it can be argued that they have many narrative identities. Researchers have found that people tend to engage in narrative particularly when they experience a **disruption,** that is, an unexpected, difficult, or disturbing occurrence in life.

In addition to individual narratives, groups, communities, and societies create narratives about their current and past histories. Through narratives, individuals and groups define themselves and clarify the continuity in their life experience. They also create narratives that express their shared aspirations. Narrative research helps to explain how these groups understand themselves through their narratives.

Psychologists have found that individuals' narrative identity relates closely to personal level of well being. In studying young adults' stories about the degree of security they felt in their attachment to their primary caregiver beginning in infancy, Glenn Reisman (2007) found that narratives showing high attachment security during early childhood predicted the observed quality of young adults' romantic relationships and general interpersonal interactions. Reisman concludes that "developing a coherent narrative about early life events serves as a key psychological resource for successfully engaging adult relationships" (p. 4).

Examples of Narrative Research in Education

Much narrative research in education has involved analysis of teachers' stories. This emphasis reflects the central role of storytelling in teachers' work lives. Teachers frequently tell stories to help students learn and also to try to shape students' attitudes and behavior. They share stories with other teachers as part of collegial information sharing and to indoctrinate new teachers into the school culture.

Other narrative studies have focused on the stories of students. Student narratives are often generated from writing assignments like essays or journal entries. Teachers study student narratives both to understand students' life experiences and also to analyze their ability to understand and generate language (Conle, 2003). Beyond such intentional uses, teachers also encounter students' stories in informal conversations before, during, and after class or in chance meetings outside school.

The following are examples of narrative research whose findings are highly relevant to educational problems of practice.

State-Sanctioned Narratives and Student Narratives

Tsafrir Goldberg, Dan Porat, and Baruch Schwarz (2006) analyzed the narrative characteristics of brief student essays generated in response to questions regarding the Melting Pot policy in Israel. This policy concerns Israel's official stance toward the mass immigration of Jews from other nations to Israel in the 1950s. It derives from the Israeli government's intention to create a new nation through the assimilation of Jewish immigrants from other countries with Israel's existing population.

The students, who had not yet formally studied the Melting Pot policy as part of their school's curriculum, were asked to write an essay about (1) what they knew about the policy, (2) whether immigrants were helped or harmed by it, and (3) whether its implementation was essential to the construction of the state of Israel or a destructive political undertaking.

Of the 105 student participants, about half were descendants of Jewish immigrants from Moslem countries (the Mizrahi) and half were descendants of (or were themselves) Jewish immigrants from Christian countries (the Ashkenazi). The researchers analyzed students' narratives individually and then according to their ethnic group (Mizrahi or Ashkenazi) to identify cultural patterns and the level of agreement between the official state narrative of the mass immigration period and student narratives.

The researchers analyzed the student texts both quantitatively and qualitatively. Quantitative analysis was used to determine the percentage of students expressing various viewpoints. Qualitative analysis was used to identify patterns within the students' stories. The researchers drew on sociocultural theory to explain students' use of social representations of the past as a cultural tool for understanding their present life in Israel.

The research report finds that students' stories often diverge from the official Zionist narrative contained in school textbooks, which tend to emphasize the "ordeal of redemption" that portrays the mass immigration policy as necessary and even heroic, and its accompanying difficulties as inevitable. By contrast, students' stories show more differentiated narrative schemes, including "senseless sacrifice" (found in 46 percent of the students' essays), the "tragedy of errors" (in 27 percent of the essays), and the "ordeal of redemption" entwined with suffering and sacrifice (in 25 percent of the essays).

Only the third scheme, with its focus on redemption, resembles the official Zionist narrative. To illustrate the scheme of "senseless sacrifice," the researchers quote Giora, a member of a well-established Ashkenazi family, who summed up the whole immigration-absorption process in six words: "contributed residents, harmed immigrants, a destructive step" (Goldberg et al., 2006, p. 333). The researchers report, "At the other end of the spectrum we find complex accounts such as Alon's, whose father, from a Mizrahi family, immigrated to Israel in a perilous foot trip from Syria" (p. 333):

> The melting pot educational strategy was harmful and discriminated against the immigrants because on the whole it was the long-time residents who set the rules and decided on the education and the immigrants didn't have a say . . . immigrants came with their own knowledge which may have suited the state from which they came but wasn't enough for the state of Israel . . . from that moment the rift began between cultures and classes, that is whoever didn't fit the melting pot belonged "down-there." (p. 333)

Overall, 70 percent of the students expressed critical attitudes toward the Melting Pot policy, and only 18 percent expressed a positive stance. The researchers interpret their findings as reflecting a critical counternarrative of the immigration era, emphasizing Mizrahi immigrants' suppression and "collective amnesia" about the difficulties endured by Ashkenazi immigrants. They attribute students' largely pessimistic view "as an attempt to account for the current social situation as they perceived it, and to establish a horizon of identity and responsibility (or irresponsibility) with respect to it" (Goldberg et al., 2006, p. 344).

This study is useful because it increases educators' understanding of problems of practice that can arise in multicultural education. It helps educators develop sensitivity to the ways in which students make sense of the past and accept or reject the historical narratives conveyed in textbooks. It also can help teachers understand why students from different cultural groups respond differently to historical and current narratives presented in the curriculum. Finally, this narrative research study suggests how essays and other writings of students can be used as a resource for exploring students' attitudes toward individuals from other cultures.

A Teacher's Career Progression

Cheryl Craig (2006) conducted an extended self-narrative inquiry into two career dilemmas she experienced, first when she was a K–12 teacher and second when she was a tenured full professor involved in a local evaluation of a national school reform program. With respect to the reform program, five school principals in a mid-southern state had asked Craig to "join their campuses in this important school reform proposition in the nebulous role as a planning and formative evaluation consultant" (p. 1168). A recent U.S. resident from Canada and relatively new to the nearby university where she was a professor, Craig accepted the offer. With the principals she deliberately negotiated her consulting role to be neither of the schools nor of the school districts, neither of the local reform movement nor of the national reform movement, neither a university employee nor a freelance consultant. In this intermediary zone, I was [to be] positioned "betwixt and between" all of these groups. (p. 1169)

In her research report, Craig focuses on the conflicting stories surrounding the reform effort. For example, she tells of the political shifts surrounding the local reform effort. They included major disagreements about the role of teachers, and changes in leadership when existing leaders became frustrated with the degree to which "highly conservative forces rallied . . . to snuff out the change effort that was challenging, even disturbing, the status quo way of being in the mid-southern state" (2006, p. 1170). She also expresses her concern—her sense of disruption—in seeing how the local reform effort reproduced the standard educational hierarchy in which university academics were treated as higher in status and power than the school teachers with whom they were committed to collaborating.

Craig's own "flesh-and-blood dilemma" (2006, p. 1173) involved her discovery that she alone among the planning and evaluation consultants at the 11 case study sites was evaluated in the publicly distributed school reports, despite prior assurances that "as a matter of professional courtesy" (p. 1171) no one would be individually identified in the reports.

In her efforts to sort out and explain the serious problems that arose in her work on this reform effort, Craig admits that she "did not consciously adjust my way of being to fit the ideologically conservative milieu in which I found my work situated" (2006, p. 1172). She notes that she missed cues about adjustments that might have been appropriate.

Craig concludes her research report by noting the similarity between this dilemma and the earlier one she experienced as a K–12 teacher years before. In the earlier dilemma, she reports finding that

other teachers' and my practical work with K–12 students [were] reduced in importance to test scores from which sweeping generalizations were produced and circulated about all students' performances and all teachers' practices. (2006, p. 1173)

She also notes an important lesson she learned about the phenomenon of educational evaluation:

[I]f the underpinnings of the sacred story of evaluation do not change, it does not matter if the participating evaluators are quantitative researchers or qualitative researchers, or if the evaluated are teachers or planning and evaluation consultants, the hegemonies built into the educational enterprise will continue to play out the same—until the conduct of evaluators and the process of evaluation are themselves reformed alongside the roles and work of those being evaluated. (2006, p. 1174)

The findings of this narrative research study provide a cautionary lesson for school reformers who seek to solve problems of practice. Specifically, we learn that school reform programs, and the program evaluations often tied to them, can themselves become problematic. By reading Craig's narrative, school reform leaders and those involved in program evaluation (see Chapter 20) can glean insights that help them navigate their way among competing stakeholders in the change process.

Stories about What Teaching Is Really Like

Martin Cortazzi (1993) conducted brief individual interviews with 123 British primary teachers from 11 schools. All teachers told at least one story, with most telling between 4 and 10 and one telling 17 narratives, for a total of 856 narratives. In addition, 105 narratives were recorded during teacher meetings or informal conversations. Teachers were informed that "the purpose of the research was to ask about teachers' day-to-day experiences in order to build up a picture of what teaching is really like" (p. 119). The interviews involved questions about six basic teaching-related topics:

1. What happened yesterday/last week? Was it a typical day? Did anything unusual happen?
2. What are the children like in your class this year? Do any children stand out?
3. Have any of the children in your class had a breakthrough recently?
4. Have you ever had any trouble with parents?
5. Have you ever had any disasters in teaching?
6. What is the funniest thing that has ever happened to you in teaching?

When teachers were asked at the end of the interview if they had given a good picture of teaching, most said they had. Cortazzi reports about the interviews:

> Many narratives were performed, especially through quoted dialogue. Teachers animated their stories with gestures and prosody, using great variation in pitch ranges and intonation patterns (noticeably more than in their normal speech) and adopting different tones of voice and accents to imitate children. (1993, p. 119)

The narratives were organized by topic and analyzed to help clarify teachers' thinking and responses in specific teaching situations. To analyze the narratives, Cortazzi used W. Labov and J. Waletsky's (1967) model of language used in social contexts, which identifies six elements in the structure of narratives, as shown in Table 15.1. The optional Coda finishes the narrative by returning listeners to the present moment, similar to "The End" at the conclusion of a movie or novel. An example of narrative analysis using this model is shown in Figure 15.1.

Cortazzi (1993) found that the narrative shown in Figure 15.1 fits well the structure that Labov and Waletsky (1967) posed for narratives. It begins with a brief introduction (Abstract) and then gives listeners information to provide a context for the narrative (Orientation). Next the teacher narrates a longer segment that tells the story (Complication), followed by an explanation of what the story means (Evaluation).

Although the example in Figure 15.1 is shown as having two evaluations, we would classify the second as the Result. Our guess as to why it follows the Coda is that the teacher felt the need to provide a result, which by and large was a repetition of what had already been said in the earlier Evaluation element.

To explain common content found in teacher narratives, Cortazzi identified 10 polarities that he found in many narratives. A **polarity** is a binary opposition that reflects an either–or contrast that is central to the story conveyed in the narrative. The narrative presented in Figure 15.1 reflects several such polarities. For example, the polarity of flexibility versus planning is "about being flexible in order to follow children's interests when

TABLE **15.1**　The Structure of Narratives in the Evaluation Model of Labov and Waletsky

Structure	Question
Abstract	What was this about?
Orientation	Who? When? What? Where?
Complication	Then what happened?
Evaluation	So what?
Result	What finally happened?
Coda	

Source: Table 5 from page 45 of Cortazzi, M. (1993). *Narrative analysis.* London: Falmer.

FIGURE *15.1*   An Example of the Analysis

N13

A   Sometimes I'll just come in and think, 'Oh no, I'm fed up with them, doing maths and English all the time and they are as well' and I just think of something on the spur of the moment.

O   Just before half term, a couple of weeks before half term, they were doing maths, English, maths, English, week in, week out, the same old stuff

C   so I came in after break and I thought, 'This isn't good enough. We'll have to do something different' and I thought, 'Let's try Star Turn.' It just sort of struck me, you know, as I walked through the door. So they got on with their normal work for about ten minutes and all of a sudden I started dragging, getting all these different things together and I dragged that fire extinguisher across the floor and dumped some things, a bowl of wallpaper and a bottle of ink and all this sort of thing, and the kids must have thought I'd gone mad or something. So I put out seven chairs in a circle and they suddenly realized what I was going to do and they were all excited about this and I put one object on each chair and explained what we were going to do, you know. They had thirty seconds each and at the end of thirty seconds I blow the whistle

E   and it was absolutely amazing what I got from them, you know, they were all so eager to try this, even the kind of kids who are normally very quiet. It was absolutely amazing the story lines and the imagination I got from them, you know, and they really enjoyed it

Coda   and we did it a couple of times and we're going to do it this week

E   and I think that must be one of the best lessons that I've ever had, just sort of off the spur of the moment and they really enjoyed it and got some good things out of it. It's the first thing I'd actually done where I could get them to express themselves and talk and explain things, you know, and I was absolutely amazed.

Source: From p. 121 of Cortazzi, M. (1993). *Narrative analysis.* London: Falmer.

something 'cropped up'" (Cortazzi, 1993, p. 125), as opposed to "the need to plan teaching" (Cortazzi, 1993, p. 125). This polarity is illustrated by the teacher's decision to "do something different . . . [and] try Star Turn" (Cortazzi, 1993, p. 121).

Another polarity shown in this narrative involves breakthrough versus incremental learning. Cortazzi describes a breakthrough as "when the actual moments of learning occur" (1993, p. 125) and notes that they are usually described in images. The breakthrough is usually unexplained and remains magical and mysterious. In the teachers' words, it is accidental, unpredictable, or just happens. We see this polarity in the narrative in Figure 15.1 when the teacher states:

it was absolutely amazing what I got from them . . . one of the best lessons that I've ever had, just sort of off the spur of the moment. . . . It's the first thing I'd actually done where I could get them to express themselves and talk and explain things, you know, and I was absolutely amazed.

In teaching, the breakthrough contrasts with and is "balanced by teachers' perceptions of slower continuous incremental learning" (Cortazzi, 1993, p. 128).

Cortazzi's analysis of 96 stories about breakthroughs in children's learning revealed three basic metaphors: learning as a click (e.g., something "clicks"), learning as light (e.g., the light dawns), and learning as movement (e.g., understanding goes up in leaps and bounds). Cortazzi comments, "How teachers think, as they report in stories when they are presumably concentrating on the narrative, can thus be indirectly investigated through narrative analysis" (1993, p. 128).

Two other polarities are reflected in the narrative in Figure 15.1. The enjoyment–grind polarity occurs when teachers are "'amazed', 'thrilled' or 'had great fun'" (p. 131). At the opposite spectrum of this polarity, "teaching was reported as being 'hard work', 'a grind', 'slog' or 'struggle'" (p. 131).

The teacher who related the narrative in Figure 15.1 states not once but three times her amazement at the effects of this lesson on Star Turn: "It was absolutely amazing what I got from them," "It was absolutely amazing," and "I was absolutely amazed." Another polarity that stands out in this narrative is that of social versus cognitive. According to Cortazzi, the social–cognitive polarity

> expresses two key aspects of education which might both be expected to feature in teachers' narratives. In fact, there are few references to the cognitive pole. Even in narratives specifically about children's learning few details are given about exactly what was learnt, or how. In contrast, the social pole is continually mentioned: Teachers repeatedly stress children's "interest", "involvement", "enjoyment", "excitement." (1993, pp. 131–132)

The narrative shown in Figure 15.1 refers to the children being "all excited about this" and repeats twice that "they really enjoyed it" (1993, p. 121).

Cortazzi continues his analysis by comparing teachers' perceptions of planning and learning and how they relate to teacher flexibility and student breakthrough. The analysis reveals that, while teachers affirm that they plan classroom work, many narratives address their flexibility in responding to children's interest and enjoyment, which creates the opportunity for breakthroughs in students' learning. Overall, focus on cognitive aspects of learning, and on teacher planning, was covered minimally in these primary teachers' narratives.

Cortazzi's (1993) analysis of teacher narratives reveals much about how teachers think "in the moment" when interacting with students during lessons. Such research can help teachers, and other educators who supervise, train, or collaborate with them, address many problems of practice. Narrative research findings might help teachers rethink ways to teach that are fun and motivating but also promote desired student learning on a consistent basis. For example, a teacher educator could help teachers generate narratives to gain insights into how they can plan lessons that encourage students' creativity and enjoyment, instead of waiting for accidental breakthroughs. The case study of teacher development in Chapter 14 illustrates such teacher planning.

Features of a Narrative Research Report

Narrative research about education has become increasingly varied in design, focus, and application. It has no standard methodology. We describe features mentioned in some narrative research literature, but the possibilities extend beyond our description. Common features of a narrative research report are summarized in Table 15.2.

Introduction

The introductory section of a narrative research report includes a statement of its purpose, questions, or hypotheses, and a review of relevant literature. For example, Dan McAdams and Regina Logan (2006) authored a chapter in a book about research on the creation of self in narrative. They describe their report as an exploratory study of the life stories of individual university professors. In an exploration of the development of narrative identity, they wanted to find patterns that link the creative work and personal lives of such individuals. The researchers sought to articulate a model of creative work among professors, looking for "parallels between work and love" in their careers (p. 106).

TABLE *15.*2   Typical Sections of a Narrative Research Report

Section	Content
Introduction	Questions or objectives are stated. A review of relevant literature is reviewed. The purpose of the study usually is to describe, explain, or evaluate phenomena relating to a problem of practice.
Research design	The typical narrative research study has two main phases: (1) eliciting stories from the research participants that are relevant to the study's purposes and (2) retelling the story as an organized interpretation of the story's events.
Sampling procedure	The researcher describes the purposeful sampling strategy that was used in the study and explains why that particular strategy was chosen.
Measures	Narrative research studies typically rely on the use of interviews to solicit the participants' stories. Other measures, including quantitative measures, can be used as well.
Data analysis	The data analysis will vary, depending on whether the purpose of the study is description, explanation, or evaluation. The analysis results in an organized retelling of the story that includes relevant events and the context surrounding each event. Story structures that are in the existing literature on narrative research methodology, or a structure created by the researcher, can be used to interpret the research participants' stories.
Discussion	The main findings of the study are summarized. Flaws and limitations of the study are considered. Also, implications of the findings for further research, theory development, and professional practice are explored.

A major purpose of any narrative research study is description, and the researchers' report describes what happened in each professor's story. However, the report is not exactly the word-for-word story as recounted by the research participant. As we stated earlier in the chapter, the participants' stories need to be "retold," so that each relates an organized series of events, settings, characters, thoughts, and emotions.

Another purpose of many narrative research studies is explanation, in which the researcher seeks to find causal patterns within the story. For example, if the story contains a disruption the researcher might inquire about factors that caused the disruption to occur and also about its consequences. Researchers can look for explanations within the story itself or draw on theories that appear relevant to the story.

Narrative research studies generally do not seek to predict future outcomes beyond the end of a study. However, it is appropriate for researchers to ask participants what they think is likely to happen beyond the story's ending. Indeed, it might be of research value to do a subsequent narrative research study to see how a story continued to unfold beyond the time period of the initial study.

A narrative research study might also have an evaluative purpose, with participants making their own evaluations or the researcher making evaluative comments, both of which characterize Cortazzi's (1993) study of teacher narratives.

Research Design

The design of a narrative research study includes two phases. In the first phase, the researcher elicits a story from the participant that includes phenomena of interest to the researcher. In the second phase, the researcher "retells" the story by systematically interpreting and organizing the events recounted by the participant.

In their narrative study of university professors, McAdams and Logan (2006) started by eliciting stories that would clarify their focus of inquiry, namely the interplay between educators' creative work and their personal lives. They collected a sample of stories and then, in the second phase, analyzed them for insights into the interplay between these two arenas of lived experience.

Sampling Procedure

Any of the types of purposeful sampling used in case study research (see Chapter 14) can be used in a narrative research study. For their narrative research study, McAdams and Logan (2006) interviewed 15 professors, sampling individuals in the sciences, engineering, and the humanities. They selected professors whom their colleagues regarded as unusually creative and productive in scholarly endeavors. This sampling approach represents what Patton (2002) calls **snowball sampling,** in which cases are recommended by individuals who know other individuals likely to yield relevant, information-rich data. McAdams and Logan (2006) then focused their narrative analysis on two men and two women: a professor of computer science at a major research university, a professor of literature at a small liberal arts college, a professor of romance languages at a large public university, and a history professor who returned to the university after a successful business career.

Data-Collection Procedures

One approach to narrative research is to generate a self-narrative, as in Craig's (2006) research report, described in a previous section, about her dilemmas in crossing the boundaries between K–12 and higher education. However, interviewing is the primary data-collection procedure in narrative research. Researchers have found that most participants will spend ample time and provide personal details about their lives when invited to tell their stories to a respectful listener. Participants appreciate the opportunity to have researchers help them understand significant life events, although researchers sometimes need to meet with some participants several times to win their confidence and help them adopt a reflective frame of mind about their life experiences. Researchers should also collect background information and personal information from each participant, which often proves to be useful during the data-analysis phase. Other kinds of data are often collected in narrative research to enrich and supplement interview data. For example, researchers can encourage participants to keep a personal journal, provide photographs depicting significant life experiences, or make video recordings in which they, and possibly others, recount their stories.

McAdams and Logan (2006) conducted individual interviews with each creative academic in their sample. They asked participants to describe the overall trajectory of their scholarly lives and then to focus on four particular scenes that stand out in their story: (1) an opening scene that reveals how the individual's interest in that specific area of scholarship originated, (2) a professional high point, (3) a low point, and (4) a turning point. The focus of the interviews was on individuals' scholarly lives, and the extent to which they dovetail with or conflict with their personal lives.

In conducting interviews, researchers need to consider their position with respect to controlling the narrative. They might choose to remain neutral and minimize their own talk during the interview in order to foster free-flowing communication from the research participants. On the other hand, they might wish to structure their own language so as to shape the participants' responses in particular ways. They also need to consider what types of probes to use in following up on ambiguous or interesting points.

Instead of interviewing individuals, researchers can conduct focus groups with groups of research participants (see Chapter 14). Focus groups are particularly useful for developing a collective or group narrative.

Whether the interviews are conducted with individuals or groups, researchers typically record them and later have them transcribed into written form. Verbatim transcripts are valuable because they accurately capture what participants say, and a researcher or team of researchers can review them repeatedly. Also, the transcripts facilitate data analysis.

Some researchers use existing narratives, as in the study described previously involving student essays about the great immigration to Israel in the 1950s. Memoirs, films, and other media also provide existing narratives for analysis. For example, Jennifer Terry (2007) did a narrative analysis in which she traced how the author Toni Morrison shaped "her own potent narrative act" (p. 93) in her fourth novel *Song of Solomon* in order to give voice to African American experience and cultural identity and to craft a counternarrative to traditional descriptions of historical structures of power in the United States.

Data Analysis

Data analysis begins at the point when the researcher becomes familiar with the narratives that she has generated or selected for study. For example, if narratives are obtained from interviews, researchers often prepare a log of each interview shortly after concluding it. A **log** is a record of the topics covered in a specific interview, along with notations of any interesting occurrences (especially disruptions) and how they were handled. The log helps researchers highlight important aspects of the narrative—for example, nonverbal features such as facial expressions or laughter that might give keys to the meaning of particular comments. Also, the interviewer might note her own thoughts and emotional reactions during the interview. The researcher's thoughts and reactions are important data, because the narrative that is reported is a joint production of the research participant and the researcher.

The interpretive phase of data analysis can take various forms, depending on whether the researcher's purpose is description, explanation, or evaluation. If the purpose is description, the researcher will need to organize the data into a coherent story. This task requires interpretive skill, as the data might include one or more interviews and the researcher's later reactions to the participant's responses, as well as supplementary information from memos, documents, and other artifacts related to the story. Also, the researcher will need to depict the context for each event, which might include its setting, the individuals who played a role in the event, and their behavior, thoughts, and emotions.

In reading across their summaries of each narrative, researchers begin to get an idea of the main issues that have been raised. They can then develop a coding frame that can be applied to the various narratives. A **coding frame** is an analytic framework designed to capture the overall meaning of the narratives and the particular issues raised in them. The story structure in Table 15.1 is an example of a coding frame.

If the interpretive phase of data analysis focuses on explanation, the researcher will need to weave the events of the story into a structure that reveals causal relationships. All stories have a structure, the simplest being beginning, middle, and end. The narrative structure developed by Labov and Waletsky (1967), shown in Table 15.1, is an elaboration of this basic structure. Both these structures organize the story events, but not in a manner that has explanatory value.

Ken Gergen and Mary Gergen (1984) identified three structures that are particularly useful for finding meaning in people's life stories. The first, a **progressive story structure,** conveys events to demonstrate progress toward a goal. The second, a **regressive story structure,** presents events as obstacles to achieving a goal or as a defeat leading to abandonment of the goal. The third is a **stable story structure,** in which events lead to little or no change in the individual's circumstances.

These three structures each organize the events of a story, and each can be elaborated on to explain how one event led to another. For example, the researcher might view the participants as active agents who try to control their own destiny, which would include self-determined goals. If the story has regressive elements, the researcher can analyze the obstacles that the participant encounters, the strategies used to overcome them, and any further reaction depending on whether the strategy is successful or not.

If the interpretive phase of data analysis focuses on evaluation, the researcher will want to analyze the data for the participants' evaluation of programs, individuals, and other phenomena that form the content of the story. The researcher will seek to interpret why the individual made these determinations and their consequences.

The purpose of McAdams and Logan's (2006) data analysis was explanatory. They wanted to understand how professors' creative work and personal lives mutually affected each other. Their analysis of the stories they elicited from the professors, supplemented by their previous study of highly creative individuals such as Darwin, led them to generate the following theoretical analysis:

> In sum, the narratives illustrate how the protagonist (a) encounters an early question or problem in childhood or adolescence that drives intellectual work thereafter; how the question (b) suggests an idealized image of something or someone in the world that (c) illuminates or embodies a personal aesthetic; how the question/image/aesthetic (d) sets up a corresponding dialectic, pitting contrasting proclivities or trends in life sharply against each other; and how this dialectic, which operates to organize one's story of creative work, may (e) play itself out in the personal realm as well, sometimes organizing certain aspects of one's story of love, family, and personal relationships. (p. 93)

The key construct in this theoretical model is the concept of the dialectic. A **dialectic** is an oppositional relationship between an important value or perspective in an individual's life story and a countervailing, equally powerful value or perspective.

For example, the life narrative of the professor of literature is strongly centered on her religious conversion to Christianity and her study of medieval religion. McAdams and Logan (2006) found the central dialectic in the life of Professor Rubin (a pseudonym) to be the choice "between unity and disintegration" (p. 100). Her conversion and decision to focus her academic career on a specific period of religion represent the perspective of unity in the central dialectic in Rubin's story. It is opposed by the perspective of "disintegration," a term she uses to characterize her previous life during which she had felt "in exile" (p. 96) from the "inner spiritual, intellectual, emotional sense" (p. 96) of grounding that she was led to following her conversion.

The use of the concept of dialectic to explain a life story is further illustrated in McAdams and Logan's analysis of their data involving Jerry Dennett (a pseudonym), a professor of computer science at a major U.S. research university. He teaches courses on robotics, computer programming, and artificial intelligence (AI). Since the sixth grade, Dennett has wanted to build the perfect robot, and he still does. He is interested in how the mind works and aims to build systems that can interact with an unpredictable environment and respond appropriately. Robots are systems that must "see" the physical environment, perform tasks, and move in an efficient, goal-directed manner, avoiding any and all collisions. In short, they need to be self-regulating, just like the people they are meant to imitate—or replace.

McAdams and Logan found that "problems involving collisions and self-regulation are front and center in Dennett's life story" (2006, p. 91). Since graduate school he has had five serious romantic relationships with women, including one whom he married and then divorced. In the narrative interview he described each as having characteristics he longed to have but, like his father, being out of his control. The narrative describes him as still trying to "design" the perfect self-regulated companion.

The dialectic in this professor's life, then, is described thus: "Dennett's image of the perfect robot and the aesthetic it illustrates set up a powerful dialectic in his narrative identity . . . a signal opposition is that between the self-regulated and graceful movements of the perfect robot . . . and the chaotic, clumsy, and unpredictable actions" (McAdams & Logan, 2006, p. 95) that he has observed not only in some robots but also in the closest relationships of his life.

McAdams and Logan interpret Dennett's life story as a commitment script, which they explain as follows:

> The gifted protagonist enjoys a special advantage early in life, commits the self to realizing the potentials that come from that advantage, and continues to persevere through difficult times, believing that suffering will ultimately be redeemed. (2006, p. 94)

A **commitment script** can be defined then as an early decision to focus one's life in a particular direction that appears to offer a unique advantage for the individual, the pursuit of which the individual regards as worth the experience of whatever obstacles might arise along the way. In our view, a commitment script is similar to Gergen and Gergen's (1984) concept of a progressive story structure, which we explained earlier in this chapter.

In Dennett's case, the commitment script began when Dennett showed precocious skills in his sixth-grade class on computer programming. Prior to that, he had been an underperforming student, but his grades soon improved, and he started researching computers and robots at the local Radio Shack. From that point on, the robot became "the idealized image of Dennett's professional life story. It is a picture of what he wants to make or achieve" (McAdams & Logan, 2006, pp. 93–94). This goal has enabled him "to persevere through difficult times, believing that suffering will ultimately be redeemed" (p. 94).

Discussion

The discussion section of a narrative research report is similar to that of a case study report (see Chapter 14). The main findings of the study are summarized, flaws and limitations of the study are considered, and implications of the findings for practice and further research are explored. The criteria for determining the applicability and quality of a case study are equally appropriate for narrative studies.

Narrative accounts, such as those presented in the study by McAdams and Logan (2006), contain truths that may apply to individuals in your own life. For example, they can help you understand how particular students or colleagues develop unique interests and how those interests affect, or are affected by, their personal lives. In particular, the study can develop your sensitivity to conflicts (or dialectics) that students and colleagues must strive to resolve in order to achieve a sense of identity and self-fulfillment.

Evaluating a Narrative Research Study

Narrative research is grounded in qualitative methods of inquiry. Therefore, you can evaluate these research studies using Appendix 3. The following are two additional questions that will help you evaluate the quality of a narrative research study.

- Did the researcher elicit sufficient detail about the participants' stories?

   Participants might recount their stories in a superficial way, focusing primarily on the who, what, and where of events. In a good narrative study, the researcher will probe the participants' statements to determine how they felt about these events, their inner motivations, and their explanations about why events unfolded as they did.

- Does the researcher provide a credible interpretation of the story?

   A report of a narrative research study must include an interpretation of the participants' stories. You will need to judge whether the interpretation is justified by the empirical data, namely the story details that are included in the report.

An *example of*
HOW NARRATIVE RESEARCH CAN HELP IN SOLVING PROBLEMS OF PRACTICE

The current composition of America's teacher workforce is problematic for many people. Their concern is whether the workforce sufficiently represents this country's diverse population. One of their concerns is reflected in the following news item.

If it didn't run afoul of employment laws, principal Thomas DeVito would consider taking out the following newspaper advertisement: "Wanted: Male teachers."

At his Ferryway School, where boys slightly outnumber girls, male teachers are a rare species, presiding over only four of the 35 classrooms. . . .

The same scenario is playing out across the state and the nation, where the number of male teachers is dwindling despite a recent focus on drawing more men into classrooms. In Massachusetts, only 24 percent of teachers last year were men compared with 32 percent 15 years ago, according to the most recent state data. Nationally, a quarter of teachers are men, a 40-year low.

Vaznis, J. (2008, November 16). Hunt is on for more men to lead classrooms. *Boston Globe*. Retrieved from www.boston.com

How can schools attract more men into teaching if, as principal DeVito stated, they can't advertise for them? We need research to answer this question. A narrative research study might be one possibility.

Although male teachers are a minority in the workforce, they do exist. Researchers might identify a small sample of males—perhaps a few just beginning their teaching careers, a few who are midcareer, and a few who have been teaching a long time. They also might consider including male teachers at different levels of schooling—elementary, middle, and high school.

The researchers can use individual interviews to solicit the male teachers' stories, asking a variety of questions. How did you get into teaching? What other careers did you pursue? Can you think of incidents while being a teacher that were particularly rewarding? Frustrating? What would you say to men who might be thinking about teaching as a career?

The resulting stories might yield insights into factors that draw men into teaching and that keep them there or drive them out. These insights can suggest strategies that administrators and teacher educators can use to increase the percentage of male teachers in schools. In addition, the researchers could write up the stories in such a way that they can be used by career counselors to help men form a picture about the kind of lives they might lead if they chose teaching as a career.

Self-Check Test

1. Narrative researchers study narratives because
   a. storytelling is central to how human beings make meaning of their lives.
   b. narrative is a common form of communication in most cultures.
   c. narratives provide great insights into people's life challenges.
   d. All of the above.
2. Researchers have found that individuals' narratives about their earliest life experiences with caregivers tend to
   a. have little relevance to their current relationships.
   b. accurately predict the quality of their current relationships.
   c. reveal few detailed memories of negative early life experiences.
   d. reveal few detailed memories of positive early life experiences.
3. Compared to the data collected by quantitative researchers, narrative research data are more likely to

   a. be highly personal, emotional, and focused on significant events.
   b. not require systematic analysis in order to convey their meaning.
   c. reveal discrepancies between participants' actual and reported experiences.
   d. allow comparisons between different cultural groups.
4. The primary design of much narrative research involves researchers _____ as the main data-collection technique.
   a. analyzing existing narratives using a new theory
   b. conducting interviews of research participants
   c. reflecting on their own life experiences
   d. All of the above.
5. Focus groups are primarily used in narrative research to
   a. obtain self-narratives from individual research participants.
   b. determine whether individuals' narrative accounts are accurate.

c. develop a collective or group narrative.

d. compare narratives obtained from different cultural groups.

6. Making a log of a narrative interview helps researchers
   a. highlight important aspects of the narrative.
   b. note nonverbal features that seem significant.
   c. become familiar with the narratives selected for study.
   d. All of the above.

7. Researchers develop a coding frame of a narrative primarily to
   a. break the narrative into themes.
   b. specify the issues raised in the narrative.

c. put the events covered by the narrative into temporal order.

d. interpret the narrative in relation to a theoretical framework.

8. In narrative research a commitment script involves
   a. a narrative reflecting an individual's perseverance in pursuing an early life goal.
   b. a verbal protocol researchers use to ensure that all interview topics are covered.
   c. a conflict between an individual research participant's personal and professional goals.
   d. a theory that helps researchers interpret the meaning of individual narratives.

Chapter References

Conle, C. (2003). An anatomy of narrative curricula. *Educational Researcher, 32*(3), 3–15.

Cortazzi, M. (1993). *Narrative analysis.* Washington, DC: Falmer.

Craig, C. J. (2006). Dilemmas in crossing the boundaries: From K–12 to higher education and back again. *Teaching and Teacher Education, 23*(7), 1165–1176.

Gergen, K. J., & Gergen, M. M. (1984). The social construction of narrative accounts. In K. J. Gergen & M. M. Gergen (Eds.), *Historical social psychology* (pp. 173–190). Hillsdale, NJ: Lawrence Erlbaum.

Goldberg, T., Porat, D., & Schwarz, B. B. (2006). "Here started the rift we see today": Student and textbook narratives between official and counter memory. *Narrative Inquiry, 16*(2), 319–347.

Labov, W., & Waletsky, J. (1967). Narrative analysis: Oral versions of personal experience. In J. Helm (Ed.), *Essays on the verbal and visual arts* (pp. 12–44). Seattle, WA: American Ethnological Society.

Lam, S., & Law, Y. (2008). Open attitudes, attribution beliefs, and knowledge of Hong Kong teacher interns in an era of education reform. *Asia Pacific Journal of Education, 28*(2), 177–187.

McAdams, D. P., & Logan, R. L. (2006). Creative work, love, and the dialectic in selected life stories of academics. In D. P. McAdams, R. Josselson, & A. Lieblich (Eds.), *Identity and story: Creating self in narrative* (pp. 89–108). Washington, DC: American Psychological Association.

Patton, M. Q. (2002). *Qualitative research and evaluation methods* (3rd ed.). Thousand Oaks, CA: Sage.

Polanyi, L. (1985). *Telling the American story: A structural and cultural analysis of conversational storytelling.* Norwood, NJ: Ablex.

Reisman, G. I. (2007, Fall). The legacy of early experience: Prospective and retrospective evidence for enduring effects. *Psychology Times, 1,* 4.

Skaalvik, E. M., & Skaalvik, S. (2007). Dimensions of teacher self-efficacy and relations with strain factors, perceived collective teacher efficacy, and teacher burnout. *Journal of Educational Psychology, 99*(3), 611–625.

Terry, J. (2007). Buried perspectives: Narratives of landscape in Toni Morrison's *Song of Solomon. Narrative Inquiry, 17*(1), 93–118.

Resources for Further Study

Chase, S. E. (2005). Narrative inquiry: Multiple lenses, approaches, voices. In N. K. Denzin & Y. S. Lincoln (Eds.), *Sage handbook of qualitative research* (3rd ed., pp. 651–679). Thousand Oaks, CA: Sage.

A sociology and women's studies professor, Chase analyzes the forms of narrative research and issues facing narrative researchers and refers to her own research on the narratives of women school superintendents. Gives a good picture of the complexities and varieties of narrative inquiry and its value in shedding light on the lives of those involved in educational endeavors.

Connelly, F. M., & Clandinin, D. J. (2006). Narrative inquiry. In J. L. Green, G. Camilli, & P. B. Elmore (Eds.), *Handbook of complementary methods in education research* (pp. 477–487). Mahwah, NJ: Lawrence Erlbaum.

Lays out starting points for narrative inquiry; explains three commonplaces of this approach, namely temporality, sociality, and place; describes considerations in designing a narrative inquiry; and provides guidelines on moving from the original field text to a research text.

Freidus, H. (2002). Narrative research in teacher education: New questions, new practices. In N. Lyons & V. K. LaBoskey (Eds.), *Narrative inquiry in practice: Advancing the knowledge of teaching* (pp. 160–172). New York: Teachers College Press.

Summarizes a 3-year study in which researchers sought to provide professional development to experienced teachers implementing an instructional program involving promotion of student literacy. Through focus groups and interviews as exemplars of narrative research practice, teachers' perceptions of validation, community, and professional growth emerged as themes.

Sample Narrative Research Study

"How Will I Get Them to Behave?": Pre Service Teachers Reflect on Classroom Management

Stoughton, E. H. (2007). "How will I get them to behave?": Pre service teachers reflect on classroom management. *Teaching and Teacher Education, 23*(7), 1024–1037.

Preservice teachers often struggle to make sense of discrepancies between their own views about teaching, their university professors' views of teaching, and what they learn from observing and working with experienced teachers in actual classrooms.

The author of this article did a narrative research study to examine these discrepancies with respect to one critical aspect of teaching—classroom management. Her narrative analyses provide a basis for educators to consider how best to help preservice teachers develop a sound, ethical professional identity from their diverse, and often disparate, learning experiences at the university and in the schools.

The article is reprinted in its entirety, just as it appeared when originally published.

"How Will I Get Them to Behave?": Pre Service Teachers Reflect on Classroom Management

Edy Hammond Stoughton
*Department of Teacher Education,
School of Education,
Indiana University,
11470 Valley Meadow Drive,
Zionsville, IN 46077, USA*

ABSTRACT ■ This study examines how pre-service teachers think about disconnections between what they believe about teaching, what they learn in their university coursework, and what they observe of behaviour management practices in public school classrooms. Based on the reflective writings of teacher education students at an urban Midwestern university in the United States, this narrative research leads to a deeper understanding of how teacher educators can support and challenge future teachers in their ability to think critically and thoughtfully in developing their identities as future educators.

KEYWORDS ■ Teacher education; Critical inquiry; Behaviour management; Teacher socialization; Pre service teachers; Narrative research; Teacher reflection

1. INTRODUCTION

> If we are going to prepare teachers to work intelligently and responsibly in a society that is increasingly diverse in race, language, and culture, then we need more teachers who are actively willing to challenge the taken-for-granted texts, practices, and arrangements of schooling through participation in systematic and critical inquiry. (Cochran-Smith, 2004, p. 62)

What is the impact on the developing teaching identities of novice teachers when what they have learned about critical awareness and issues of social justice in progressive teacher education programmes come up against traditional structures in American public school settings? How do they negotiate meaning between what they have come to understand about teaching and what they see in practice?

These questions are important for the growing number of teacher educators in the United States, and elsewhere, who believe that preparing teachers who are sensitive and reflective decision makers able to work against the technicalization and reductionism of the current educational climate depends to a great extent on teacher education that develops a stance of thoughtful inquiry concerning dominant practices. University programs based on this foundation emphasize a critical inquiry stance in which there is in-depth consideration of the sociocultural and sociopolitical implications of schooling as well as one's own cultural embededness and preconceptions. In this process novices and experienced educators come together to examine multiple perspectives on complex questions and to interrogate and critique existing frameworks and taken-for-granted practices aligned with Friere's (1971) idea of transformational dialogue. A space is also opened up where important questions can be asked about "what should be in relation to moral and ethical issues in education" (Kincheloe, 2004, p. 103).

However, the intersection between social justice teachings, the individual and cultural backgrounds that preservice teachers bring with them, and the context of public schools can frequently result in disarticulations and contradictions as these novice teachers struggle to make sense of who they want to be professionally. They frequently conceptualize their own schooling experiences as "prototypical and generalizable toward the teaching profession" (Fajet, Bello, Leftwich, Mesler, & Shaver, 2005, p. 718). This leads to the question of how they negotiate interactions between the very different understandings represented in these disparate contexts. Do they find themselves straddling two worlds (Smagorinsky, Cook, Moore, Jackson, & Fry, 2004) "caught in the middle between what the university is encouraging them to think and do and what the school-based teachers they work with advocate?" Is there, as Brouwer and Korthagen (2005) suggest, a tendency for a rift to develop between the teachings of their teacher education programs and the teachers in their classroom assignments whom they come to view as the "realistic role models, as the people who 'know' how one should go about teaching" (p. 155)? Or does the process of negotiating and problematizing these conflicting frameworks challenge future educators to construct a more thoughtful and nuanced teaching identity?

One area of classroom practice that leads to particularly intense questioning among novice educators is the issue of student behaviour. Typically this is a crucial subject that lies at the forefront of concern for future teachers (McNally, I'anson, Whewell, & Wilson, 2005). There are several reasons for this. The control of behaviour of the children in one's classroom is an area into which socialization of beginning teachers in school norms is emphasized. There is widespread agreement among school personnel that classroom management is an essential part of their work particularly in light of the frequently expressed perception that children are becoming increasingly unruly and difficult to teach, especially in inner city schools. As a school administrator in a large urban school corporation recently stated, *"Discipline is the biggest problem we face"* (pers. commun., April 2005). Discipline issues are rated consistently as a leading cause of teacher stress and burnout (Lewis, Romi, Qui, & Katz, 2005). According to Ayers (2004) effective behaviour management "is one of the most persistent perceived needs of preservice teachers; for many it is practically the sina qua non of teaching itself, (p. 89). A substantial body of research points to the importance

school administrators place on a teacher's ability to control disruptive students (Brophy & McCaslin, 1992). As Brophy and McCaslin (1992) found, principals tend to rate highly teachers who they perceive as skilled classroom managers on the basis of their ability to "control" disruptive students. Therefore, to a great extent, beginning teachers understand that a large part of the evaluation of their effectiveness will depend on how well they are perceived to be able to control behaviour in their classes and yet there is a deep apprehension about their ability as inexperienced educators to perform successfully in this complex area. This leads to concerns about how these future teachers make sense of what they experience in their public school assignments in terns of the management of children's behaviour and the part those experiences play in their developing teaching identities. In addition, there is a recognition among both experienced and novice educators that the way schools deal with the behaviour—and misbehaviour—of students has important implications in terms of the educational establishment's assumptions, expectations, and attitudes toward children and learning (Ayers, 2003; Caine & Caine, 1997; Raider-Roth, 2005; Watts & Ereveles, 2005).

Questions about matters of discipline are certainly not limited to American teachers, but are of concern for the international teaching community as well. Student behaviour management was rated as the second most significant factor causing stress among 400 teachers in Hong Kong studied by Chan (1998). In a survey of teachers in Australia, Israel, and China, a substantial percentage of those questioned considered discipline to be either of moderate or major concern (Lewi[s] et al., 2005). In addition, McNally, I'anson, Whewell, and Wilson (2005) report that in Scotland "the management of pupil behaviour is considered a major policy priority" (p. 169) according to the *Times Educational Supplement* in January 2004 that decried the poor behaviour of students in the United Kingdom and the inability of teachers to exert authority in their classrooms. Therefore, although this study centers on how teacher preparation students think about classroom behaviour practices in the context of American public schools, the findings can be widely applicable. Issues of discipline and classroom climate (Lewis et al., 2005; McNally et al., 2005); exclusion (Warren, 2005); and the ways novice teachers think about possible disconnections between university teaching and "practical" considerations in the formation of a teaching identity (Brouwer & Korthagen, 2005; Shkedi & Laron, 2004) are of international concern.

The large, urban Midwestern university where I instruct pre-service teachers brings teachers-in-training together into cohorts of approximately 25 students which are based in public schools both for classroom experience and for their university seminars. The rationale for this arrangement stems from a belief that conversations are enriched and extended when practical experiences in schools are closely linked with theoretical input (Brouwer & Korthagen, 2005). The university instructors seek to develop a dialogic pedagogy which begins with the experiences of students and their responses to themes and problems they identify and which engages them in a critical discourse about those issues (Kincheloe, 2004). A number of the seminar discussions are grounded in an examination of the "critical dissonance between what students learn about teaching and learning at the university and what they already know and continue to learn about them in the schools" (Cochran-Smith, 2004, p. 25). The seminar in this initial semester developed to enlarge student thinking about issues of diversity, difference, and culture is grounded in readings and discussions of the critical pedagogy of Friere and Nieto; the importance of meaningful curriculum and the construction of knowledge based on the works of Dewey, Piaget and Vygotsky; and an understanding of the social construction of disability.

One of the topics covered is classroom management. Individual interviews and class discussions indicated that students identified this as a subject about which there is a fairly wide disparity between what is taught in university classes and seminars and the theoretical construct upon which many behavioural plans are based. As one student related, *"The teacher gives away tickets for certain things such as turning in homework and passing certain tests. Once children have collected so many tickets they can go to the candy jar. This goes totally against what we have been discussing in class about intrinsic motivation and best practices."*

2. THE STUDY

This study developed from discussions and student writings in two cohorts of elementary pre-service teachers for which I was the instructor during the 2004–2005 academic year. It asks questions about how those pre-service teachers constructed their understanding of behaviour management in their first sustained experience in public school classrooms, and how they incorporated what they learned from their education courses, their cooperating teachers, and their own initial teaching experiences and how they framed and evaluated these practices. It is based on the understanding that "one cannot help teachers develop their classroom management skills without addressing their emotional responses to the events around them and the attitudes, values, and beliefs that underlie these responses" ([V]an den Berg, 2002, p. 586). The study also examines if, and in what ways, these novice teachers are able to go beyond questions of simply "what works" to reflect more deeply on behaviour practices and to decide how they fit with their beliefs about justice and equity. As McNally et al. (2005) note, although most beginners are looking for "practical things that will work in the short term as one of their main objectives is, understandably, to get order in order to teach" (p. 180), an overemphasis on "tips" risks the absence of central principles to guide their practice. Therefore, an objective of this research is to discover how teacher education students can be supported in an "ongoing process of self-examination and reframing" (Greenman & Dieckman, 2004, p. 241) in which they find possibilities for deepened understanding and a heightened critical awareness that will enable them to question established practices including underlying assumptions and beliefs in this important area.

Written reflections were used as the basic analytical tool in this study. The students were asked to respond in reflective journal entries to the question. *"Discuss the philosophy and tone of the behavioural expectations and practices in your assigned classroom and talk about how well you think these might work for you in your own classroom and what, if anything, do you think you would do differently."* Journal entries were analyzed on the basis of what these future teachers understand about classroom management practices they observed in public schools and how they incorporated those ideas into their understanding of teaching and learning.

3. REFLECTIVE WRITING AS A VEHICLE FOR EXAMINING POSSIBILITIES

> Reflection is a disciplined way of assessing situations, imagining a future different from today, and preparing to act. (Ayers, 2004, p. 110).

Reflection can be significant in promoting self-awareness with the benefit of coming to a sense of understanding of oneself and one's reactions and perceptions. Reflective journals can also be important in providing protected spaces for developing, critiquing, and sharing reactions to experiences and perceptions. Through reflection, pre-service teachers are encouraged to revisit an event and see it through multiple perspectives making connections between experiences and values and beliefs. Oliver and Lalik (2000) discovered in their research among girls that the privacy of journal writing provides a feeling of safety that allowed the girls to feel freer to express opinions that might seem risky in group conversations. They speak of journals as a way for students to "facilitate finding a voice, a voice needed before any kind of dialogue can ever take place between them and their culture" (p. 114). Reflective journal writing, in providing a forum for students to express their questions and concerns and receive feedback from others in the learning community, is an important part of building knowledge about teaching and learning. As Lowenstein points out, "Journals enable students to raise awareness of their ways of making sense of the world, but also to assess these ways and make choices about what counts as sensible or legitimate" (p. 54). Therefore, a careful study of the reflective journal writings completed as a course requirement can provide insight into the conceptual models that are being constructed. Providing an opportunity to write about their perplexities and concerns not only allows students to step back from situations and consider them from a different perspective, but it also helps their instructors gain insight into what students are thinking and how they might be helped to reframe and rethink troubling issues. These written reflections and the ways in which university instructors respond to them, have the potential to open up conversations that can help novice teachers make sense of what they are seeing and experiencing and the meaning those experiences have for them.

4. NARRATIVES AS A WAY OF CONSTRUCTING IDENTITY

> Narrative is a fundamental human way of giving meaning to experience. In both telling and interpreting experiences, narrative mediates between an inner world of thought-feeling and an outer world of observable actions and states of affairs. (Garro & Mattingly, 2000, p. 1).

In studying the way that the two cohorts of pre-service teachers responded to the situated cognitions they acquired through being in schools I analyzed their journal writings through the lens of narrative analysis. My choice of method derives from a belief that narratives express a worldview, and that we come to terms with our experiences and develop and negotiate our identities largely through the stories we construct and the discourse we use in telling those stories (Fairclough, 1995; Polkinghorne, 1988; Titscher et al., 2000). The ways in which stories about teaching are constructed, retold, and interpreted help to define how we structure reality. There are major ideological effects in the ways discursive practices represent and position situations and people as well as relationships between people (Titscher et al., 2000).

Studying narratives in an effort to understand the "main story line" can provide important insight into how meaning is constructed. Therefore, I considered it to be important in analyzing these student writings to look closely at how they chose to represent what they saw and how they expressed their expectations and understandings of the classroom culture in which they participated. I studied the selected set of journal entries and surrounding conversations to examine the different voices this group of students was internalizing and in what ways. A central question was how their narratives fit in the multiple discourses of social justice, student behaviour, school practices, and the university voice as they constructed images of teacher identities.

One's personal experiences and conflicting beliefs and values are not the only forces that are significant in developing one's identity. Other people's storied constructions of reality also play a part, particularly others who, in our estimation, have compelling claims to speak with authority (Sfard & Prusak, 2005). Sfard and Prusak contend that "significant narrators, the owners of the most influential voices, are carriers of those cultural messages that will have the greatest impact on one's actions" (p. 18). Therefore, in my analysis I looked for instances in which students either challenged or acquiesced to the authoritative voices of classroom teachers as they defined appropriate practices including how to think about children and their behaviour. How did these teachers-in-training attempt to mediate between conflicting versions of reality in constructing their own central narratives as future teachers? If, as Brouwer & Korthagen (2005) contend, novice teachers often come to regard classroom teachers as the most knowledgeable

authorities concerning educational practices, was this apparent in these particular journal entries?

In analyzing the reflective writings I considered both the overall meaning that individual students gave to their experiences and emergent themes that the narratives had in common (Garro & Mattingly, 2000; Polkinghorne, 1988; Strauss, 1987; Titscher, Meyer, Wodak, & Vetter, 2000). I also looked for the dynamic tensions within themes and ways in which "prevailing themes in the text both resonate and clash with one another" (Raider-Roth, 2005, p. 187). I examined how the discourses used in the reflections tended to either naturalize or problematize social practices (Fairclough, 1995). Finally, I studied the pieces of writing recursively comparing the discourse of teacher education as evidenced in classroom discussions and the way experiences were narrated.

The thinking behind these student writings was further explored and extended in several subsequent class discussions centering around the journal entries which provided a means of member checking. Triangulation was provided through a comparison of the reflections across participants, through my regular observations in the classrooms described in the journal entries, and by sharing the completed study with the students. Student responses to their reading of the study largely centered around their positive reactions to the validation of their voices and their questions including Kaitlin's response that, *This makes me feel that I'm on the right track to becoming a teacher."*

5. CONTEXTUALIZING THE STUDY

5.1. Participants

The participants in this study were pre-service teachers attending a large university of approximately 30,000 students located in a major metropolitan area in the Midwest. At the time of the study they were enrolled in two separate sections of Block I, the initial teacher preparation semester. Each group spent two full days each week on-site at public elementary schools. One afternoon a week they met with a team of two instructors for coursework in Math and English. In the afternoon of the alternate day they met with a team of two other instructors to learn about teaching diverse learners. I was the special education professor for the team.

Discussion in the section of the course that featured diversity issues was complicated and made especially significant by the fact that there was very little diversity in these two groups of students. The overwhelming number of the cohort members were middle class White females in their 20s and early 30s who had attended secondary school in small towns or suburbs where there were few persons whose race and ethnicity were not like their own. One cohort of 22 students was composed of 20 European American females, one African American female, and a European American male. All 26 students in the other class were European American with 24 females and 2 males. To complicate this demographic, the university has a strong and long-standing commitment to the highly diverse urban schools in the city and, therefore, field placements are typically located in inner city schools. This created a certain amount of initial uncertainty and apprehension among a number of students as they indicated that they felt rather fearful and unsure about what to expect in their placements in city schools that were quite different from their familiar school contexts.

5.2. Schools

The two cohorts of students were placed for their field experience in three elementary schools (Grades K–5) all serving low-income populations. Although the schools had highly diverse student populations, the faculties of the schools, following the wide-spread pattern of teachers in today's urban schools in the United States, were overwhelmingly European American females (Cochran-Smith, 200[4]; Goodwin, 2004; Lowenstein, 2005).

Brookview [pseudonym] is located in an area of the city characterized by a growing population of Hispanic families. At the time of this study, 80% of the students were Hispanic, 15% were African American, and 5% were European American. All but five of the teaching staff—two African American females, two African American males and a Hispanic male—were European American females. A number of classroom assistants were Hispanic. These employees served as a bridge to the significant number of students who spoke little, or no, English.

The demographic of Heritage [pseudonym] was 70% European American, 20% African American, and 10% Hispanic. During the 2004–2005 school year, the teaching staff at Heritage was totally comprised of European American females. The only male presence was the European American male principal. The majority of the European American students live in the immediate neighborhood whereas most of the African American students ride a bus to school. The principal reported in an interview that the African American children represent the poorest students and that all of them participate in the Free and Reduced lunch program. In the same interview the principal referred to the Hispanic students as the lowest performing group in the school.

Woodridge [pseudonym] is located on the edge of a traditionally rural area that is rapidly becoming urbanized as the city encroaches on surrounding farmland. The demographic composition of the school is 44% African American, 54% European American, and 2% Hispanic. Again, the teaching staff was overwhelmingly White and female. The Principal at Woodridge was an African American male and, in addition, there was an African American male physical education teacher. There were no Hispanic teachers at Woodridge.

6. CLASSROOM MANAGEMENT AT BROOKVIEW, HERITAGE, AND WOODRIDGE

The three elementary schools in this study all followed a philosophy about behaviour control in their classrooms that was quite similar. Their procedures were equally uniform. This conformity to a common philosophy was characterized by an emphasis on order, obedience to authority,

and externally enforced control over problem behaviour (Brophy & McCaslin, 1992). Standard practices were confirmed both by student descriptions and by classroom observations. The accepted format for classroom management in all of the schools consisted of three essential parts: clearly defined rules that students must follow at all times, positive recognition for following the rules, and consequences that are applied when students do not follow the rules. Consequences were given to children in public ways largely with the expressed purpose of serving the function of deterrence. They were arranged in an escalating hierarchy and were expected to be carried out with unvarying consistency.

Journal excerpts from teacher education students in each of the three schools provide a general overview of the behavioural philosophies at use in the classrooms they observed. Although I have chosen three entries as representative, all of the journal entries described basically the same model.

Bethany reports from her second grade classroom at Brookview:

> My teacher, Mrs. D___, has a "bad" behaviour system and a "good" behaviour system. If the students do something that she doesn't like, they have to move their "pin" from one big colored circle to another. As they move to a different color they have time taken off their recess. If they move to the red circle, they lose all of their recess and have to call home. If the students do something that the teacher likes, they earn a Mega smile. This is a piece of yellow paper that they keep together with their group's Mega Smiles. The group that has the most at the end of the week gets rewarded with Snickers bars.

Stacey writes about her first grade class at Heritage:

> The discipline system in place in my mentor teacher's classroom is a pull-card system. The system has 5 colors—green, blue, yellow, brown, and red. The first time students are told to pull a card, they get up and go to the board and place the first color in the back of the stack. Green is the color which the students start out with in the beginning of the week. Blue is their first warning. Yellow is the next color in the lineup and means that the student misses 5 minutes of recess. Brown means the student misses the whole recess. The final color is red and that color means they need to call a parent.

Diane describes her assigned kindergarten classroom at Woodridge:

> Each student has a card that starts on green for good behaviour. If they disrupt class they have to switch the card to yellow and sit in time-out for five minutes. Time-out is a chair that is placed near the cards and away from the rest of the students. The card has to be automatically changed to yellow if the student did not do homework the previous night and it is also moved for disruptive behaviour. If the student is still disruptive, then the card has to be switched to red and their guardian is called.

Sometimes the procedures are quite a bit more elaborate as in the case of the "star stick" used by a 2nd grade class at Brookview described by Mary Ann. It seems that the "star stick" is a dowel rod containing four painted sections—red, yellow, orange, and green. There is a clothespin for each child with his or her number on it. At the start of each day all clothespins are on green. After one infraction the clothespin is moved to the yellow section. The penalty for that movement is that the child must spend 10 minutes of recess walking around the perimeter of the playground. If the clothespin must be moved to orange, the child spends the entire recess marching around the playground perimeter. A move to red means that the child spends recess walking and a call is placed to his or her parents. Mary Ann was quite taken with this plan as she demonstrated by going on to say enthusiastically:

> The best thing about the "star stick" is that it moves! It is light and moves with the students when they go to "specials." So any person in the school can move the pin on the "star stick!"

Most of the classrooms had an additional isolation policy that was ostensibly used for infractions that were too egregious or disruptive to be dealt with through normal channels. However, in certain contexts and with certain children, these arrangements seemingly became normalized with some children permanently separated from their classmates. Typical journal entries noted practices that were similar to those Mindy wrote about when she noted that, *"I know a few of the 'hard-to-control' children have their desks set off from the rest of the class."*

7. A RANGE OF OPINIONS AMONG NOVICE TEACHERS ABOUT CLASSROOM MANAGEMENT PLANS

On one level this seemed to be an easy topic for these pre-service teachers to write about. Behaviour management plans were an important and pervasive element in each of their classrooms and were frequently referenced throughout the school day. The aspect of the assignment that proved to be more difficult for Block I students was trying to sort through their feelings about how disciplinary concerns were addressed in their particular classrooms. Only 3 of the 48 students who completed the assignment were quite sure that they would structure their own classrooms in a similar way. On the other end of the spectrum, 8 of the 48 students were extremely uncomfortable with the behavioural procedures in use in the classroom to which they had been assigned. The majority of the students were either somewhat or decidedly ambivalent about the practices they observed.

In looking at the three groups in terms of possible factors that might account for their divergent reactions, there were two rather interesting differences. The group of students who disagreed with classroom behavioural practices tended to include more non-traditional students in that several were older and had children of their own. Whereas the ambivalent group also contained a number of non-traditional students, the group that was unreservedly in agreement was made up wholly of younger, unmarried students. Another distinctive commonality shared by the students who were adverse to practices in effect in their schools was that all of them indicated that they remembered very vividly quite negative school experiences. There seemed to be a sensitivity to teaching practices perceived as repressive or unjust and a desire to do things differently. This sentiment was expressed by Megan who said that, *"I lived through miserable times at school, but there was one teacher who made a difference in my life and I want to be like her."* In addition, students who were planning on becoming special education teachers were all in the groups that either were ambivalent or who disagreed with behavioural practices. Further examining these patterns would be an interesting topic for further research with future cohorts of pre-service teachers.

The differences in how these three groups of students deconstructed what they observed concerning the management of student behaviour can be seen in the following comments selected from each of three positions.

7.1. Those who approved: "I believe that rules dictate behaviour"

The three teacher education students who wrote in very positive terms about behaviour management in their public school classrooms stressed that what they most appreciated about their particular setting was that order was efficiently maintained. They evidenced a strongly utilitarian orientation: a system of classroom control is good if it works smoothly. A fairly consistent theme among this group of novice teachers was a belief in the positive outcome of having predictable expectations and established procedures. Amy expressed the belief that in her third grade classroom at Brookview:

> The teacher's good technique for handling behaviour issues is because the students know what the expectations are. They know what is expected and what is inappropriate and they obey that.

In a similar vein, Lisa, who was assigned to a fourth grade class at Woodridge stated that:

> I would set up my classroom in exactly the same way. Behaviour expectations need to be put out there early on. If children know what is expected and what the consequences are, then they are likely to think twice before acting a certain way.

Brooke, although somewhat uncertain at first, came to accept the classroom teacher's expert knowledge as the best way to deal with behaviour:

> At first I thought the teacher was being hard on the students. It seemed as though the entire day was centered on disciplining children. However, now that I have seen more and become better acquainted with the students, I think the teacher has to have this sort of discipline policy in place to keep the attention of the children and to keep some order in the classroom. The children do respond, and it does get their attention when their sticks are taken away. I think I would tweak things a little to show more understanding of their emotional needs, but overall I think it is a very effective approach to discipline.

Overall, these students agreed with the necessity of establishing a smooth-running classroom and, in accordance with Amy's observation that, *"Procedures are the most important thing in having a smooth running classroom,"* they believed the best way to achieve that goal was to set clear expectations right from the beginning and to hold firm to them.

7.2. Those who disagreed with procedures: "I have concerns about how behaviour is addressed"

The objections of the 8 pre-service teacher[s] who were not in agreement with the procedures for behaviour control in their public school classrooms fell into several general areas. Both intuitively and through class readings and discussions in their university seminars, these future teachers had come to believe that lasting and positive change in the way a child acts in school requires more than paper "Mega Smiles," Snickers bars, or changing colored tags. They questioned the implicit as well as the explicit purposes behind decisions made about how to shape student behaviour. They further wondered if classroom procedures supported children in finding better ways of acting as well as a reason for changing their behaviour, or if they were simply *"a means to keep social control through training"* as Chris contends in his journal entry. The following reflections speak to worries about the lack of efficacy, and in some cases futility, of existing behaviour procedures—at least for certain students:

> It seems to always be the same few students and they do not appear surprised that they have had to move their pins.

> I have not noticed a significant decrease in behaviour problems from those students who have been asked to pull cards.

> The fact that the same names are usually on the board to miss recess just goes to show that this is not effective for them.

Katherine had a more global objection to the classroom management practices in her assigned classroom:

> I feel that Mrs. R's. class is out of her control a lot of the time and that she spends most of her day trying to get them to be quiet and do their work. I have never seen a class that is so focused on behaviour, but their behaviour is generally out of the teacher's control. I have used this experience as a looking glass into a class environment I do not want to have as a teacher. I will have a classroom where the children want to learn and where motivation is intrinsic.

As Caroline writes, it is the students who *"Never have the opportunity to experience the rewards"* that this group of student teachers in Block I found to be a troubling indictment of the system's lack of effectiveness. In addition, contradictions between practices that appeared demeaning and ostracizing and "expert" practitioner knowledge claiming that these practices were the best way to deal with difficult students confused and puzzled them and provided hopeful openings for further questioning and critical conversation.

7.3. Those who were unsure: "I have to keep sifting through my brain and critically thinking about why I would or would not want to use these practices in my classroom someday"

The large group of students who wavered between acceptance and rejection of current practices was not so certain as the first group about either the efficacy or the desirability of the ways of controlling behaviour that they saw in their classrooms. These future teachers were much more ambiguous about the success of the interventions. One of the most frequently expressed sources of this ambivalence was the tension some students felt between an orderly classroom atmosphere and one that was over-controlling, inflexible, and focused too heavily on obedience. What was the line, they wondered, between enforcing of necessary classroom rules and a structure in which compliance is enforced in authoritarian or punitive ways? This inner conflict was expressed by Jennifer who wrote:

> In my classroom I definitely see that the teacher is in charge of the entire classroom. I think that some of her ways of managing a classroom are great and others I want to steer clear of. I like that she always sticks to the rules and the students know what their punishment will be if they don't. I like that everything she does is very orderly. But she has little tolerance for students who don't follow the rules. Her teaching style is very rigid—don't talk unless talked to, stay in your seat etc.

In a recent article Lisa Delpit (2003) deplores the vast amounts of energy and time that teachers are expected to spend on "keeping track of points related to non-instructional tasks and preventing any kind of deep instruction" (p. 17). Likewise, Katy, as well as a number of other students, expressed a concern about an overemphasis on obedience to the possible detriment of other, more important, concerns in her journal entry:

> I'm torn between liking the cards and not liking the cards. I don't mind the "pulling the card idea" but I don't agree with having to spend all day long trying to make sure the books are flat, pencils down, eyes on me, ears open, bottoms on the seat, etc. I believe that most of Mrs. T's time is spent 'managing' her class instead of teaching.

8. CONFLICTING NEEDS

For this study I focus on the journal entries of a group of students who were opposed to behaviour practices and the group of students who were ambivalent about them. I chose those two groups of reflective writings to analyze because of the important role they could potentially play in discussions of dominant practices.

The 8 students who did not agree with the existing programmes for behaviour control are significant in that they are the people who can provide leadership in making a shift in thinking among cohort members as they push their fellow pre-service teachers to go beyond "the ways things are" to consider "the way they should be."

A number of these students went beyond voicing their concerns about specific procedures to reflect on what they would do in terms of the climate they wanted their classrooms to have. They saw building relationships as a key component in encouraging positive behaviour. Elements of a developing teaching philosophy are apparent in the following journal excerpt:

> I would not set up a behaviour system in my classroom that only supports students who are already disciplined and are high achievers. I would want to gain the attention and respect of all students by including all children. If you can give a child even a pinch of confidence and encouragement, they are more likely to respect you and themselves and, in the end, achieve goals higher than they could ever imagine.

The 37 students who expressed uncertainty about behavioural practices are also important because they are at the point where they are questioning and yet are unsure of where they stand or how they can resolve their questions. Ambivalence can be a failure to deal with conflict pointing to the need to provide critical lenses that encourage these novice teachers to consider unexamined issues and unexplored possibilities. As Madeline Grummet (conference presentation, Purdue University, February, 2006) pointed out, pre-service teachers are often convinced of ethical orientations, but it is too frequently a "polemic of complaint and not questioning." Smagorinsky et al. (2004) spoke to the importance of stretching these students to think more deeply about what puzzles them when they wrote that, "Student teachers who never face philosophical contrast or conflict may well face an ideological meltdown when moving to settings that invalidate their ideals" (p. 22). Therefore, it is important to use the disjunctures they experience to lead to reflective questioning (Fecho, Graham, & Hudson-Ross, 2005). Their perplexities and concerns can serve as a catalyst for deepened inquiry and thoughtful dialogue. During a class discussion following the journaling exercise, Matt expressed his concern about the exclusion of certain students. As the discussion, continued Matt was able to make the connection that all of the excluded students were African American boys. His new awareness led to a deeper and more critical exploration of sociocultural issues. In deconstructing their reflections we must dig deeply into their questions and uncertainties supporting these novice teachers in developing a thoughtful, ethical framework upon which to base their identities as future teachers. They need help in dealing critically and thoughtfully with what they are seeing and in deepening their inquiry, making more explicit their values and beliefs through thoughtful dialogue that can lead to "existential struggle and transformation" (Jupp, 2005, p. 22). They are in the process of developing their own personal interpretive frameworks through which they can perceive and give meaning to teaching. The challenge in working with this group is to open up conversations that not only question practices but begin thinking in an intentional way about how to do things differently.

The most common concern running through the reflections of those 45 students was the dichotomy many students felt between the need to maintain order and other values that figured prominently in their developing teaching philosophies such as the importance of building community and meeting individual student needs. The two groups came together over this issue that was very much a point of struggle within and among these novice teachers over such social justice issues as inclusiveness, equal access, and providing opportunities for all students to achieve their potential. Although they did not consistently cite seminar literature or philosophical orientations they did employ a rhetoric of ethical orientation positioning. Several of the students expressed some concern over how their ideas would work "in practical terms," yet they all indicated a commitment to a supportive, prosocial community as a crucial foundation for learning, and they showed a recognition that learning and teaching are inherently relational activities (Raider-Roth, 2005).

Two common themes emerged from the narratives of the two groups of students: those undecided and those opposed. There was a feeling among a number of these future teachers that the philosophy and practice of how teachers reacted to student behaviour was expedient rather than educational and that responses were frequently concerned with "putting out fires" rather than helping children learn how to be more successful classroom participants. The second common theme that appeared in many of the papers was a concern about the exclusion and ostracism of students who were considered discipline problems.

8.1. "This form of punishment has no lasting effects on the kids"

In several of the journal entries a concern was expressed about the ultimate purposes of behaviour management programmes. It appeared to the journal writers that the object of many interventions was to stop misbehaviour as quickly and efficiently as possible without considering how to help children learn more effective ways to handle similar situations in the future (Brophy & McCaslin, 1992). They expressed discomfort about the fact that it appeared that teacher needs for order, obedience, and compliance were served rather than student needs for understanding and growth. There was generalized agreement in classroom discussions that behaviour plans must be about more than maintaining order, they must also deal with inculcating an understanding of the reasons behind the rules. As Ellen wrote, *"I don't think her behaviour management does much to the extent of teaching the students about appropriate behaviours and decision-making. Instead it is just a means of stopping the behaviour as soon as possible."* This parallels Covaleskie's (2005) assertion that, "Children must develop a framework within which they can make good choices about how to act, and we must help them do so" (p. 50). The following two excerpts, both from cohort members in the ambivalent group also speak to this point:

> I believe that students need reason and purpose in order to intrinsically motivate them to develop their own plan for

success. Students of this age should be learning the real reasons they need to make good decisions. If we instill in them why we want them to behave instead of just saying "go, pull your card," it may affect their decision making. The problem with this form of punishment is that it does nothing to correct the behaviour, just the symptoms. It focuses on what I believe to be not as important as other things.

8.2. "For a student to feel unwelcome into the classroom community is simply unacceptable"

The clearest disjunction between disciplinary practices and ideas of social justice was in what these two groups of future teachers considered to be the injustice and ostracism inherent in exclusionary forms of punishment. Separating out students due to their poor behaviour had the effective of marginalizing them from social and academic participation and was seen as problematic not only because of the effect on the student who was marginalized, but also because of the negative effect such actions had on the climate of the classroom and particularly on the creation of a safe and inclusive classroom community. Seven of the eight students who expressed disagreement with dominant practices and 12 of the students who were ambivalent expressed concern about students who were separated from their classmates frequently for extended periods of time. These prospective teachers were troubled by practices that polarized students and labeled some students as "less than". There was also an understanding of the pervasive influence teacher attitudes and actions have on children. The importance of teacher modeling including public criticism and ridicule was noted by Megan, who stated poignantly that *"The teacher has targeted one child in her room to feel her wrath which has a much longer arm than just her own. Her wrath extends through the arms of Kevin's peers also."* Paul writes about his perceptions of the negative consequences of isolation both on the student and his classmates in a fifth grade classroom:

> There is one student whose desk is located in the left rear of the classroom, nowhere near any of his classmates. I was shocked and dismayed, especially when everything I was learning in Block 1 discusses inclusion and classroom community. I do not believe isolating students with behavioural problems will do anything to improve a student's behaviour. First, the isolated student is not learning how to get along with his fellow classmates. It is impossible for him to discuss class work with other students if he is not allowed to sit near anyone else. Therefore, he is behind in classroom assignments and has no chance at all for success. All I can see is a student who is set up to fail. Second, his isolation cannot help in building a classroom community. From my observations, the rest of the class, including the teacher has total disdain for the student. If anything goes wrong in the classroom, he is usually blamed for it. I may not have all the answers of how to deal with students with behaviour problems, but I do know that isolating a student is not how the problem is solved.

Anne also wrote of the negative effects of exclusionary practices:

> Students with behavioural problems sat alone at different corners. There was a student whose desk was in the corner of the room facing the window. She seemed like an outcast who did not belong. It was difficult for her to participate in class discussions because she was not facing the classroom like other students. She had to turn her head to see the board and look at the teacher, which seemed very uncomfortable. She seemed as if she was not part of the class.

The nature of negative self-fulfilling prophecies inherent in differential treatment was noted by Beth:

> Some students are set aside in the room and treated as outcasts because of their behaviour. It appears to me that these students act the way they do because of the way they are treated. Two students especially are set off to the side in the back and are surrounded by empty boxes and desks so as not to be able to draw attention to themselves and disrupt the classroom. However, these same students are the ones who are always interrupting and acting out.

Because of the prominence of exclusionary practices in their reflections, and also because of the clear disconnection such practices presented with university teachings, this issue opened up important possibilities for critical conversations that could help students make connections between their beliefs about teaching and learning and classroom practice. The significance of this topic also lies in the near universality of the removal of certain children. In a subsequent discussion every Block I student in both cohorts indicated that the practice of isolating students because of their behaviour was standard practice in their classrooms.

The ambivalence and wavering between ethical values and efficacy expressed in the following journal entry points up the need for conversations to explore issues more deeply:

> In Mrs. F's. classroom when I first attended, there were two desks that were away from the rest of the class. I had asked her "why" on the second visit, and she responded by saying they have talking issues. The two girls were separated from each other and from the rest of the class. The one girl has made her way back into the group setting, while the other girl is still sitting away from the class. I do know that this type of technique for talking seems to be working for the girls. *What else could you do if they just don't stop talking?*

Thoughtful analysis and authentic dialogue based on these reflective writings have great potential for growth and transformation. The questions these students ask are the kinds of questions that are important to foreground in our work with future teachers as we support them in becoming the thoughtful and caring educators that are needed in our schools.

9. DISCUSSION

> The challenge of teaching is to decide who you want to be as a teacher, what you care about and what you value, and

how you will conduct yourself in classrooms with students. (Ayers, 2001, p. 23).

What do we hope students in our teacher education programs understand as they prepare to enter the teaching profession, and how will we assess what they are actually understanding? Teacher educators concerned about the complex challenges and ethical choices facing young teachers, must find ways to help novice teachers not only teach successfully in the complex contexts of public schools in the 21st Century, but also find ways to transform those contexts. How can teacher education programs support future educators in developing thoughtful frameworks that will equip them to meet the needs of a widely diverse population of children and be able to "reinvent classroom knowledge and discourse so that it builds on, and is attentive to, the resources of all children" (Cochran-Smith, 2004, p. 62)? We, as teacher educators, are challenged to consider carefully the perplexities our students express and find ways to move them from where they are to where they need to be as ethically aware teachers.

This study is based on narrative analysis of journal writings as a reflective tool in teacher education. A careful and thoughtful analysis of such writings can provide teacher educators with a clearer understanding of their students' thinking and thus can become a powerful tool in providing a context for important discussions paving the way for authentic transformation in the way future teachers look at how to work with children in their classrooms. Studying student voices through these writings can also help us examine our own practices and reflect on what we are teaching and how it is being received.

In looking at implications for my work, I found both the language of critique and the language of possibility in these journal entries. Particularly for those students who were having trouble deciding what they believed, this exercise in reflective writing played an important role in creating protected spaces where they could interrogate and deepen their thinking (Oliver & Lalik, 2000).

In their writing about behaviour practices, the two cohorts of future teachers struggled with competing discourses concerning institutional needs for order and the individual needs of children. They struggled with tough questions related to the validity of "expert knowledge" and "the unitary visions of teachers' roles and behaviours that they believed were valued in their schools" (Vinz, 1996, p. 55). I found in a number of these student writings a willingness to think analytically about taken-for-granted practices. I was encouraged to find that there appeared to be a wrestling with the complexity of behaviour interventions leading some students to reject simplistic, one-dimensional solutions. A number of students showed in their writings an intuitive knowledge backed up by seminar discussions that behaviour management is integrally linked with the culture of the classroom and is, further, ultimately related to the ethical values and commitments that teachers bring to their work with children.

A significant number of the prospective teachers who participated in this study seemed be internalizing and in-

corporating into their developing teaching philosophies ideas about social justice and fair and equitable treatment of all students in inclusive learning communities that were fostered in the university teacher education program. Ideas that were featured prominently in seminar conversations were frequently referenced in comments such as, *"I want my classroom to be a place where students want to attend everyday and I want to have a positive learning environment like the ones we learned about in class discussions."* That many of these teachers-in-training took a critical look at classroom management practices led me to be optimistic about the possibility for them to continue to be open to discovering more nuanced ways of establishing classrooms where fewer children are written off as incorrigible or "hopeless" and where all children are able to contribute their unique promise and potential. Yet, at the same time I was concerned about how to most effectively respond to the ambivalence and conflicting values that remained with a number of the cohort members. This points up the clear need to continue to explore ways to connect school practices with university teachings and existing predispositions.

10. IMPLICATIONS AND DIRECTIONS FOR RESEARCH

The findings of this study of how two groups of pre-service teachers were beginning to construct their teaching identities in the face of conflicting knowledge claims raise further questions and point out directions for future work. Making personal decisions about the values one holds as a teacher is a developmental process. As Ayers (2004) contends, "Our stories are dynamic and in-motion, always changing with new conditions, and always suggesting alternative outcomes" (p. viii). This leads to concerns about the ways in which the understandings and knowledge structures of these novice teachers will change and evolve in their future classroom experiences. There is a need to continue to confront their unanswered questions and issues of ambivalence as well as support and further develop the beliefs that they hold firmly. Without this continued critical pressure there may well be a tendency to see behavioural methodologies with which they initially disagreed as "the way things are" as they become inculcated into dominant practices. A significant question raised by this research study involves whether the attitudes of these students will change when, as they proceed in their teacher preparation program, the balance shifts to spending more extended time in schools and less time in university seminars. This connects to the concern expressed by Fajet et al. (2005) that becoming overwhelmed with the challenges of learning to teach, they may "revert to teaching how they were taught which sometimes means that they teach in ways quite different from what they learn in their teacher preparation programs" (p. 725).

A further area of these research findings points to the need for further work and study. The students showed a lack of connection between their developing beliefs and the larger cultural context including little problematizing of how the classroom culture intersects with the culture of the school and of the larger society. This finding is in agreement with Shkedi and Laron's (2004) contention that:

> Beginning student teachers typically have given little thought to the contexts of teaching—not to the larger societal context, nor to the features of communities, schools, and classrooms that influence teaching and learning. (p. 696).

Although in seminar discussions several of the students were troubled by the fact that most of the children who were marginalized were African American, there was a hesitancy on the part of a large number of students to go further in analyzing the "othering" of certain students and the connection of that positioning with issues of cultural difference and power. They stopped short of looking at possible connections between "common sense" professional practices and embedded cultural assumptions. They did not seem to be at the point where they could consider the "normal practices of schooling as processes of instituting a particular social imaginary" (Warren, 2005, p. 244), uncovered in a study of similar processes of exclusion among African-Caribbean young men in schools in the United Kingdom. Their critique, which was centered around the humanistic position of a sense of unfairness, needs to be extended to questioning the wider practices of schooling. This kind of critical analysis is particularly important in light of the cultural encapsulation of these preservice teachers and the differences between the social, racial, and ethnic makeup of public school faculties and that of the children.

Teacher education programs need to continue to explore difficult questions with students if we are to counteract both the unquestioned acceptance of "common sense" wisdom and the pull of familiar ways of doing things. It is crucial to continue to provide spaces where future teachers can do the important work of examining what is, what can be, and the implications of their choices for themselves as teachers, for the children they teach, and for the schools and communities we hope to build.

References

Ayers, W. (2001). *To teach: The journey of a teacher.* New York: Teachers College Press.

Ayers, W. (2003). *On the side of the child: Summerhill revisited.* New York: Teachers College Press.

Ayers, W. (2004). *Teaching the personal and the political: Essays on hope and justice.* New York: Teachers College Press.

Brophy, J., & McCaslin, M. (1992). Teachers' reports of how they perceive and cope with problem students. *The Elementary School Journal, 93*(1), 3–66.

Brouwer, N., & Korthagen, F. (2005). Can teacher education make a difference? *American Educational Research Journal, 42*(1), 153–223.

Caine, N., & Caine, G. (1997). *Education of the edge of possibility.* Alexandria, VA: Association for Supervision and Curriculum Development.

Chan, D. W. (1998). Stress, coping strategies, and psychological distress among secondary teachers in Hong Kong. *American Educational Research Journal, 35*(1), 145–163.

Cochran-Smith, M. (1995). Color blindness and basket making are not the answers: Confronting the dilemmas of race, culture, and language diversity in teacher education. *American Educational Research Journal, 32*(3), 493–522.

Cochran-Smith, M. (2004). *Walking the road: Race, diversity, and social justice in teacher education.* New York: Teachers College Press.

Covaleskie, J. F. (2005). Discipline and morality: Beyond rules and consequences. In D. Evans (Ed.), *Taking sides: Clashing views on controversial issues in teaching and practice* (pp. 49–57). Dubuque, IA: McGraw Hill/Dushkin.

Delpit, L. (2003). Educators as "seed people" growing a new future. *Educational Researcher, 32*(7), 14–21.

Fajet, W., Bello, M., Leftwich, S. A., Mesler, J. L., & Shaver, A. N. (2005). Pre-service teachers' perceptions in beginning education classes. *Teaching and Teacher Education, 21,* 717–727.

Fairclough, N. (1995). *Critical discourse analysis: The critical study of language.* London: Longman Group, Inc.

Fecho, B., Graham, P., & Hudson-Ross, S. (2005). Appreciating the wobble: Teacher research, professional development, and figured worlds. *English Education, 37*(3), 174–190.

Friere, P. (1971). *Pedagogy of the oppressed.* New York: Seabury.

Garro, L. C., & Mattingly, C. (2000). Narrative as construct and construction. In C. Mattingly, & L. C. Garro (Eds.), *Narrative and the cultural construction of illness and healing* (pp. 1–49). Berkeley: University of California Press.

Goodwin, A. L. (2004). Exploring the perspectives of teacher educators of color: What do they bring to teacher education? *Issues in Teacher Education, 13*(2), 7–24.

Greenman, N. P., & Dieckmann, J. A. (2004). Considering criticality and culture as pivotal in transformative teacher education. *Journal of Teacher Education, 55*(3), 240–245.

Kincheloe, J. L. (2004). *Critical Pedagogy.* New York: Peter Lang.

Lewis, R., Romi, S., Qui, X., & Katz, Y. J. (2005). Teachers' classroom discipline and student misbehaviour in Australia, China, and Israel. *Teaching and Teacher Education, 21,* 729–741.

Lowenstein, K. (2005). Readings of diversity from an undergraduate foundations course. *Multicultural Education,* Winter, 15–22.

McNally, J., I'anson, J., Whewell, C., & Wilson, G. (2005). "They think that swearing is okay": First lessons in behaviour management. *Journal of Education for Teaching, 31*(3), 169–185.

Oliver, K. L., & Lalik, R. (2000). *Bodily knowledge: Learning about equity & justice with adolescent girls.* New York: Peter Lang.

Polkinghorne, D. E. (1988). *Narrative knowing and the human sciences.* Albany: State University of New York Press.

Raider-Roth, M. B. (2005). *Trusting what you know: The high stakes of classroom relationships.* San Francisco: Jossey-Bass.

Shkedi, A., & Laron, D. (2004). Between idealism and pragmatism: a case study of student teachers' pedagogical development. *Teaching and Teacher Education, 20,* 693–711.

Smagorinsky, P., Cook, L. S., Moore, C., Jackson, A. Y., & Fry, P. G. (2004). Tensions in learning to teach: Accommodation and the development of a teaching identity. *Journal of Teacher Education, 55*(1), 8–23.

Sfard, A., & Prusak, A. (2005). Telling identities: In search of an analytic tool for investigating learning as a culturally shaped activity. *Educational Researcher, 34*(4), 14–22.

Strauss, A. L. (1987). *Qualitative analysis for social scientists.* Cambridge: Cambridge University Press.

Titscher, S., Meyer, M., Wodak, R., & Vetter, E. (2000). *Methods of text and discourse analysis.* London: Sage Publications.

Van den Berg, R. (2002). Teachers' meanings regarding educational practice. *Review of Educational Research, 72*(4), 577–625.

Vinz, R. (1996). *Composing a teaching life.* Portsmouth, NH: Boynton/Cook.

Warren, S. (2005). Resilience and refusal: African-Caribbean young men's agency, school exclusions, and school-based mentoring programmes. *Race, Ethnicity, and Education, 8*(3), 243–259.

Watts, I. E., & Etevelles, N. (2004). These deadly times: Reconceptualizing school violence by using critical race theory and disability *studies. American Educational Research Journal, 41*(2), 271–299.

chapter 16

Ethnography and Critical Research

IMPORTANT *Ideas*

1. Critical ethnography is a qualitative research tradition that combines ethnography, which is the earliest qualitative research tradition, and critical research, a more recent tradition.

2. Ethnography involves in-depth study of a cultural entity in its natural context, from both the researchers' (etic) and research participants' (emic) perspective.

3. Culture, the central focus of ethnography, is what makes human beings unique as a species.

4. Culture is the pattern of traditions, symbols, rituals, and artifacts that characterize a particular society or group of individuals.

5. Ethnographers explain cultural phenomena by revealing aspects of the culture that are so central that most culture members appear to be almost unaware of them.

6. Educational ethnographers study the process of both cultural acquisition (how individuals learn to function in the culture) and cultural transmission (how a culture passes on its characteristics to new members).

7. Technology has created new opportunities for participant observation and thick description, two of the main characteristics of ethnographic research.

8. Critical research focuses on the negative effects of unequal power relationships found in most cultures and on the reasons for and means to reverse them.

9. Critical researchers have a value orientation aimed at highlighting and reversing oppressive cultural practices that are taken for granted by most mainstream researchers.

10. Critical research in education draws on several research and theoretical traditions, particularly cultural studies and critical pedagogy.

11. Critical ethnography uses various ethnographic methods to explore unequal power relationships in educational settings and their meaning to research participants and to researchers themselves.

12. Compared to other qualitative research approaches, critical ethnography puts particular emphasis on research strategies designed to validate various types of truth claims of researchers and research participants.

13. Critical ethnographers seek to shed light on the culture of the specific sites that they study, to clarify system relationships common to those and similar sites studied by other researchers, and to pose theoretical explanations of such relationships. ■

Key TERMS

agency	emic perspective	normative–evaluative truth claims
anti-oppressive education	epistemology	norms
border pedagogy	ethnography	objective truth claims
conscientization	ethnology	participant observation
critical ethnography	etic perspective	postmodernism
criticalists	feminisms	praxis
critical pedagogy	hegemony	privilege
critical research	hermeneutic circle	reconstructive analysis
cultural acquisition	holistic description	reproduction
cultural studies	holistic ethnography	subjective truth claims
cultural transmission	instrumental rationality	text
culture	internalized oppression	thick description
deconstruction	meaning fields	troubling
dialogical data generation	microethnography	voice
emancipation	monological data collection	

The Use of Critical Ethnography to Study Problems of Practice in Education

This chapter describes a relatively new qualitative research tradition, critical ethnography. We show how it builds on two other qualitative research traditions, ethnography and critical research.

We begin the chapter with a brief introduction to ethnography, followed by a description of the impact of critical research on this tradition. The rest of the chapter focuses on the goals and methods of critical ethnography as applied to education.

The Characteristics of Ethnographic Research

Ethnography is the firsthand, intensive study of the features of a specific culture and the patterns in those features. Reports of ethnographic research help readers develop understanding of their own culture and of cultures much different from their own. Ethnography began in the field of anthropology. Many of its design features resemble those of qualitative case studies, which are described in Chapter 14. In fact, David Lancy (1993) claims that ethnography is "the prototype for the qualitative method" (p. 66).

The case or cases studied in ethnography can range from a single individual to an entire community, society, or institution. In ethnographic research, as in qualitative case study research, the researcher

- studies particular instances of a phenomenon (in ethnographic research, the case is a culture or some aspect of culture).

- makes an in-depth study of the phenomenon of interest.
- studies the phenomenon in its natural context.
- represents both the field participants' (emic) and researchers' (etic) perspectives.

Focus on Culture or Aspects of Culture

Culture is the central concept in ethnographic research. **Culture** can be defined as the pattern of traditions, symbols, rituals, and artifacts that characterize a particular society or group of individuals. Many early ethnographers lived in non-Western societies for an extended time period. They often examined specific phenomena, such as religious ceremonies, marriage, and kinship, that appeared to be ritualized in such societies. They believed that study of those phenomena in so-called "primitive" cultures might reveal universal patterns in the development of such phenomena.

Early ethnographers sought to provide a **holistic description,** which is a comprehensive analysis and description of the unique cultural patterns of a group of people who live close together in a specific geographical region. Their work represents the research tradition called **holistic ethnography.** The studies of Margaret Mead (1930) and Bronislaw Malinowski (1922) are widely known examples of such research.

Ethnographers believe that the influence of culture in human beings' lives is what makes us unique as a species. Culture allows a particular group of people to live together and thrive through a system of shared meanings and values. On the other hand, that same system also involves opposition to or oppression of groups whose cultures represent different shared meanings and values. Investigating this process of cultural oppression is central to critical ethnography, which we discuss later in the chapter.

Individuals display beliefs and behaviors that reflect the various cultures of which they are members, for example, their racial group, age group, religious affiliation, and occupation. Researchers have found that certain aspects of culture have a particularly strong influence on individual and group life, including family structure, socialization processes, religious affiliations, leisure activities, and ceremonial behavior. For example, ethnographers investigating education might focus on rituals marking transitional events in the lives of students in school, such as entry into kindergarten, receipt of report cards, summer vacation, and school graduation.

Closer examination of actual ethnographies reveals that the culture of a given society or social group is not a consistent whole but more closely resembles what Murray Wax (1993) called "a thing of shreds and patches" (p. 101). Each ethnographic study contributes fragments of information to a broad description of the culture. The patchwork development pattern means that certain aspects of the culture are better defined than others. For example, in U.S. schools more research exists about teacher culture than about the culture of school leaders, partly because groups in power are less inclined to reveal characteristics of their culture to outsiders.

Lancy (1993) notes that today's world is becoming increasingly homogeneous with respect to culture. He argues that wealth, rather than influences unique to geographic location, is now the principal factor that differentiates the lifestyles of specific cultural groups.

Instead of making a comprehensive study of a culture as a whole, most current ethnographers focus their research studies on a particular aspect of culture within a specific cultural group or society, which is sometimes referred to as **microethnography.**

An ethnography by Kathleen Hogan and Catherine Corey (2001) exemplifies this more focused approach. The researchers became guest science teacher–researchers in one fifth-grade classroom to observe "what happens as teachers work to create a scientific culture in their classrooms" (p. 215). The class was instructed to follow the norms of experimental science (such as rigor, control, and collaboration) in testing plant growth in the classroom. Students were guided to plan an experiment to compare different compost mixtures in stimulating plant growth and also reviewed other students' plans for conducting the experiment.

The researchers found that in designing their experiments and in giving peer feedback, students expressed the individualistic goals typical in most classrooms, not those consistent with scientific norms about how best to support knowledge claims. For example, most students wanted to have their own plants to control, and they expressed criticism rather than supportive comments of others' plans. Hogan and Corey's (2001) ethnography suggests that teachers can improve the way they guide students' learning of science by considering not only students' knowledge about scientific concepts, but also the cultural norms and values that students bring to such learning endeavors.

Naturalistic Study of Individuals in the Field

Many ethnographers today study subcultures in their own geographic vicinity, carrying out data collection in the natural setting of the members of the culture. They rely on unobtrusive data-collection methods like informal observations and conversations, with which field participants will be comfortable. Also, they usually seek to immerse themselves in the setting, both to increase participants' trust of them and to deepen their own understanding of cultural phenomena.

Making the Familiar Strange

Traditionally, ethnographers have sought to "make the familiar strange" (Spindler & Spindler, 1992). This goal involves analyzing a cultural phenomenon from the researcher's **etic perspective,** which is the perspective of an outsider, to whom the phenomenon is strange, while also seeking to understand it from the participants' **emic perspective,** which is the perspective of an insider, to whom it is familiar.

Ethnographers can make the familiar strange in at least three ways. First, they can immerse themselves in a culture far different from their own. Second, they can study a subculture within their own community with which they are unfamiliar. Third, they can investigate a subculture with which they are familiar but look at it from the perspective of another subculture rather than from their own subculture's perspective.

Exemplifying this third approach, African American professor D. Soyini Madison (2005) describes her participation in street performance ethnography in Ghana to protest the killing of a young African American man, Amadou Diallo, by four New York police officers. Reflecting that racism "is alive and still hurting people" (p. 539) both in "the home of my heart, Africa" (p. 539) and in the "the home of my birth, the United States" (p. 539), she cites three verbatim exchanges from a website nearly three years later celebrating Diallo's shooting and exulting over White Power, Hitler, and white people.

Another way an ethnographer can make the familiar strange is to reflect light on the particular phenomena of which members of a culture are seemingly unaware because they appear to take them for granted. For example, an ethnographer studying the culture of college sports teams might notice patterns of acceptable and unacceptable behavior beyond those contained in the game rules, such as differences in how starters and bench players cluster around the coach during time-outs.

Thick Description

In writing their research report, ethnographers typically generate a thick description of the cultural phenomenon they are studying. A **thick description** describes the field setting in great detail and uses extensive quotations from field participants. It is intended to bring the culture alive for the reader. Ethnographers sometimes write their descriptions in the present tense, which enhances the impression of the permanence, or even universality, of what is being described. Such ethnographic reports tend to promote the sense that the description applies not just to the specific cases that were studied, but also to similar cases that might have been studied.

Differences between Ethnographies and Basic Case Studies

Ethnographies have special characteristics beyond those of basic qualitative research case studies (see Chapter 14). They usually involve a longer, more in-depth period of data collection than a typical case study. Also, ethnographers often make a comparative study of a particular phenomenon as it manifests itself in different cultures, which is called **ethnology.** By contrast, case study researchers usually limit themselves to a single cultural context. Most important, while educational case studies can focus on any aspect of education, educational ethnographies focus specifically on aspects of culture that influence schooling or the teaching–learning process.

Educational ethnographers have done considerable research on learning as a cultural process. They have addressed the issue of whether learning is primarily a process of cultural acquisition or of cultural transmission. **Cultural acquisition** refers to the process by which individuals seek to acquire, or in some cases avoid acquiring, the concepts, values, skills, and behaviors that are reflected in the common culture. By contrast, **cultural transmission** is the process by which the larger social structure intentionally intervenes in the lives of new members of the culture in order to promote or, sometimes discourage, the learning of particular concepts, values, skills, or behaviors that are reflected in the common culture.

The relative importance of cultural acquisition and cultural transmission plays a central role in ethnographers' efforts to understand the achievement gap among students. The achievement gap refers to persistent differences in the level of educational achievement and retention that have been documented for members of various cultural (that is, racial and ethnic) groups attending schools in the United States and other Western cultures.

David Lancy (1993) cites a number of ethnographic research studies, conducted primarily between 1960 and 1980, exploring adaptation to public schooling by young people whose cultures were in transition. The cultures that were studied included villages in Africa and Papua New Guinea as well as Native American and Black communities in the United States. Lancy states:

> All document persistent "failure" in the sense that one sees little pleasure in either the teaching staff or the children. There is no evidence that students are making satisfactory academic progress, enabling them to "climb out of the ghetto," "leave the reservation," or "become self-sufficient." Increasingly, anthropologists who study minority education now take student failure as their point of departure. (p. 41)

Lancy's review leads him to question a frequent assumption of critical researchers that "minority student failure can inevitably be traced to the fact that children who are poor, don't speak English, or are culturally different are inevitably given prejudicial treatment by public schools" (p. 50). He cites his own study of the U.S. Agency for International Development's effort to build rural schools in Liberia in the 1960s:

> The informal, casual nature of instruction, characteristic of the village, no longer applies in school. Now, in a relatively short period of time . . . students must master whole volumes of new information in a foreign language. The result . . . was "indoctrination without education." Students become indoctrinated with Western values and aspirations, reject the traditional values of the village, but the quality of instruction is so poor, they don't learn enough to succeed at increasingly higher levels in the education system. (1993, pp. 39–40)

In seeking the cause of many U.S. minority students' lower level of academic success compared to that of students in the mainstream culture, the African American scholar John Ogbu (1978) carried out research based on a theoretical model of education and caste focused on learning as cultural acquisition. Ogbu claims that native-born members of minority groups who have suffered a long history of economic discrimination withhold their investment in education because they do not perceive it as having any economic payoff.

Other qualitative researchers interested in cultural acquisition have studied how individuals' sense of agency is formed. **Agency** refers to individuals' assumed ability to shape the conditions of their lives, whatever their cultural situation.

Ethnographers George Spindler and Louise Spindler (1992) observe that focus on cultural acquisition as the primary explanation of the achievement gap makes it easy to slip into a "blame-the-victim" interpretation of individuals' learning problems. They argue that ethnography can best contribute to the understanding of learning by showing how societies use their cultural resources to organize the conditions and purposes of learning. Their research thus focuses on cultural transmission, that is, how schools and other agents facilitate or hinder specific types of learning by individuals from various cultures. We will return to the topic of the achievement gap in our discussion of critical ethnography.

Examples of Ethnographic Research

The following two examples of research represent contemporary uses of ethnography to understand problems of practice in education.

An Ethnography of Video Blogging

> Young, J. R. (2007, May). An anthropologist explores the culture of video blogging. *Chronicle of Higher Education, 53*(36), p. A42.

Modern technology, particularly the Internet, has greatly affected the design and findings of ethnographic research. Young describes the work of Michael Wesch, an assistant professor of cultural anthropology at Kansas State University, who began a collaborative ethnography of the online community with nine of his undergraduate students.

Calling themselves the Digital Ethnography Working Group, Wesch and his students undertook a study of the culture of YouTube, a website to which thousands of people have posted videos that they recorded themselves. The working group uploaded a video about social networking and other interactive tools known as Web 2.0 to YouTube. Their online reports, available on the group's website (http://mediatedcultures.net) focus on video bloggers, including both Wesch's students and other people who responded with their own videos.

One group video of the Digital Ethnography Working Group, titled "A Vision of Students Today," shows a large university lecture hall, at first empty and then filled with hundreds of students. One at a time students hold up diary-like signs describing the disconnects in their experience of learning in the university context versus in the world as a whole, as in the following examples:

- 18% of my teachers know my name.
- I will be $20,000 in *debt* after graduation!
- Over 1 billion people make less than $1 a day.
- I did not create the problems
- But they are *my* problems.

Since its posting hundreds of people have responded to that video with their own video blogs, or *vlogs*, as they have become known.

Because ethnography involves participant observation (defined below), the making and sharing of videos online is a perfect medium for carrying out this form of research and learning worldwide. Videos like this might encourage teachers and students to use YouTube or other online sites to investigate their own and other students' perspectives about social issues. They could also examine how the learning process is affected by students having access to video blogs as opposed to only lectures or written material.

An Ethnography of Studying

Anderson, K. T., & McClard, A. P. (1993). Study time: Temporal orientations of freshmen students and computing. *Anthropology and Education Quarterly, 24,* 159–177.

Anderson and McClard, with two other research team members, explored the meanings that university students attribute to the construct of study, their perceived and actual use of time, and the effects of computers on these aspects of student culture.

The research team spent an entire academic year in the field, investigating most of the residents of a freshman residence hall at a university recently outfitted with computers. Participant observation was their chief method of data collection. **Participant observation** is a process in which researchers assume a meaningful identity within the group while maintaining their role as researchers. One of the researchers actually lived in the residence hall for the entire study year, thus serving as an almost constant participant observer.

Data were also collected through formal and informal interviews and from written questionnaires. The questionnaire data included quantitative measures of students' self-reported use of computers and their time allocations to study and other activities. Another form of quantitative data was collected directly by a computer program that tracked the amount of each student's use of computers in the residence hall network. These examples illustrate how quantitative measures can contribute to the qualitative study of a culture.

In their research report Anderson and McClard use several long quotes from individual students to explain the meaning of the constructs of *study* and *time* from the students' emic perspective. Study breaks were found to be an integral part of what students describe as study time. Indeed, students often spent more time on study breaks than in what the researchers considered to be actual study.

Because study breaks were a social activity, the researchers originally had the perspective that most students goofed off a lot. However, from the students' perspective study breaks were an essential part of their study time. From the students' standpoint, many academic problems that they worked out during a break with other students could not have been worked out as effectively in more formal settings or on their own. They viewed study breaks as a secure environment for testing ideas. The researchers likened college students' use of time as more similar to the time orientation of farmers than of 9-to-5 workers.

This study has implications for teachers of students of all ages. It suggests that teachers who want to help students learn to the best of their ability need to understand study from the students' perspective. They might want to address uses of study time and help students develop study skills. They could also encourage, and provide a setting for, students to work together in study groups.

Critical Research as a Field of Inquiry and Practice

We turn now to an examination of critical research and its contributions to the study of education. **Critical research** (sometimes called *critical theory,* based on its strong theoretical orientation) involves a broad range of methods designed to uncover and help remedy the negative effects of unequal power relationships that prevail in the global community and in most cultures within it.

Researchers who carry out critical research are sometimes called **criticalists** because they specialize in critical inquiry and praxis. In qualitative research, **praxis** is a form of practical activity aimed at "doing the right thing and doing it well in interactions with fellow humans" (Schwandt, 2001, p. 207).

The concern for improving education through research is not unique to critical researchers, of course. Much existing educational research, whether qualitative or quantitative, also aims to improve the learning and opportunities of nonprivileged groups. However, critical research differs from other forms of research because of its specific focus on social justice and its efforts to highlight (through research and theory) and to reverse (through praxis) causes of cultural inequities. Because of their profound impact on almost every individual in society, schools and other educational systems deserve the particular attention of critical researchers.

Examples of Issues Studied by Criticalists

Hardly a day goes by without television news, magazines, and online news sources reporting on ways in which political interests have dominated, distorted, or fabricated the information people receive about issues central to their own and others' social well-being. For example, the Associated Press featured a story about a report released in June 2008 by the office of the inspector general of the National Aeronautics and Space Administration (NASA). The report stated that NASA had "marginalized or mischaracterized" studies on global warming between 2004 and 2006 and had canceled a press conference on ozone pollution because it was too close to the 2004 presidential election ("Watchdog," 2008).

Today's news media increasingly include stories about personal economic and health disasters that individuals are experiencing. For example, the Associated Press reported that throughout the United States food banks today are finding more clients but receiving fewer donations to meet their needs (Nieves, 2008). The article adds:

> April saw the biggest jump in food prices in 18 years, according to the Labor Department. At the same time, workers' average weekly earnings, adjusted for inflation, dropped for the seventh straight month . . . In Baton Rouge, La., the public school system has found students hoarding their free and reduced-price lunches so they can bring them home to eat at night. (Nieves, 2008, p. A-5)

Critical research goes beyond standard reports of such events in an effort to understand and challenge the underlying political and economic forces that lead to and maintain problems such as these.

Critical research in education can be regarded as one form of anti-oppressive education. According to Kevin Kumashiro (2002), **anti-oppressive education** "involves constantly *looking beyond* what we teach and learn" (p. 6), for the critical purpose of troubling education and educational research. **Troubling** means exposing the assumptions underlying widely accepted but oppressive cultural practices that traditional educational practices help maintain.

Challenging the claims of quantitative research to being more rigorous, objective, or valid than qualitative research, Carspecken has developed a methodological theory for conducting critical social research using methods of research design and interpretation that can withstand rigorous tests of validation. His research shares the value orientation of critical research, seeking to address what is hidden or concealed by the dominant, or mainstream, powers operating in education (Carspecken, 1996). Carspecken's model of critical ethnography (to be discussed later in the chapter) is critical both in value orientation and in its methodological objectivity.

Two criticalists described the main assumptions held by such researchers (Kincheloe & McLaren, 1994). As in Carspecken's summary of their assumptions, we group them into two categories—those reflecting criticalists' value orientation and those related to their epistemological orientation. We describe the assumptions in the next sections.

The Value Orientation of Critical Research

Critical researchers make four assumptions about society. These assumptions, described next, reflect the high value they place on social justice.

The Tendency to Privilege and Oppress.   Criticalists argue that every society systematically privileges certain cultural groups and oppresses other cultural groups. **Privilege** is the disproportionate power, resources, and life opportunities held by members of culturally dominant groups in society. It is reinforced by the wider society through **hegemony,** which refers to the ways in which privileged cultural groups maintain domination over other groups through various cultural agencies that exert power.

According to Peter McLaren (2003), the political, criminal justice, and educational systems are the three cultural agencies that most clearly reflect and promote hegemonic interests. The privileged always have an interest in preserving the status quo in order to protect their advantages. Critical research seeks to disclose the true interests (i.e., the needs, concerns, and advantages) of different groups and individuals, including both those who are privileged and those who are oppressed.

The Maintenance of Low Privilege.   Criticalists believe that privilege is maintained in part through **internalized oppression,** which is the process by which individuals unwittingly help maintain their own lack of privilege through thoughts and actions consistent with a lesser social status. Through this process, **reproduction** of their oppression occurs, meaning that new members who are born to or join the culture accept, and behave consistently with, hegemony. In McLaren's terms, hegemony involves "a struggle in which the powerful win the consent of those who are oppressed, with the oppressed unknowingly participating in their own oppression" (1998, p. 182).

Critical research strives to highlight the factors that lead nonprivileged individuals to behave consistently with their lesser social status. Through the use of interviews and examination of narratives, it seeks to convey the sense of frustration and powerlessness that accompanies many individuals' awareness of the entrenched limits on their opportunities to realize their potential. Perhaps most important, such research directly seeks to provide insights to guide oppressed groups toward greater autonomy and, ultimately, **emancipation,** the actions and changes in consciousness of and toward the members of oppressed cultural groups that help free them from oppression.

The Multifaceted Nature of Oppression.   Criticalists argue that the tendency to focus on one type of oppression (for example, racism) obscures the connections among forms of oppression and the weight of their joint operation in a given individual's life. To understand and combat oppression, they believe it is necessary to identify all the cultural categories that operate to separate and oppress people and to examine their joint effects.

In *Troubling Education,* Kumashiro (2002) uses the stories of queer activists whom he interviewed to illustrate this phenomenon by "reading" their multiple identities, cultures, and experiences of oppression. Kumashiro includes a poem about Pab, a teenage activist born in Nepal now living in the United States who identifies as a lesbian. Through the poem Kumashiro demonstrates the "impossibility of identity" experienced by queer Asian American women, caught up in the conflicting cultural expectations involving Asian, Asian American, female, and heterosexual identities. Pab, like other Asian American women who are queer, is "often invisible both in Asian American communities and mainstream society" (p. 95).

The Role of Mainstream Research in Maintaining Oppression.   Critical researchers believe that mainstream research practices help reproduce systems of oppression that are based on class, race, gender, and other cultural categories. They observe that, despite a gradual increase in academic diversity, the majority of educational research is still based on positivist epistemology (see Chapter 1) and carried out by middle- or upper-class white males. This research rests on assumptions about science, truth, and good that such researchers tend to accept as universal.

According to critical researchers, mainstream research has actually served to maintain the oppression of groups who represent other cultural categories. Critical researchers particularly oppose educational research that focuses on prediction and control for the purpose of maximizing educational productivity. In their view, such research reflects the operation of **instrumental rationality,** which is a cultural preoccupation with means over ends or purposes. Rex Gibson (1986) views the IQ testing movement as a key example of the short-comings and injustices resulting from this preoccupation:

> Instrumental rationality is the cast of thought which seeks to dominate others, which assumes its own rightness to do so, and which exercises its power to serve its own interests. Coldly fol-lowing its narrow principle of efficiency and applying a crude economic yardstick, its results are all too obvious . . . the interests least served are those of comprehensive schools and pupils from working class homes. (pp. 8–9)

Critical theorists would likely view the current reliance on standardized testing to evaluate and enforce standards of student achievement as a manifestation of educational systems' preoccupation with instrumental rationality.

The Epistemological Orientation of Critical Research

Epistemology is a branch of philosophy devoted to the study of the nature of knowledge and the process by which knowledge is acquired and validated. Critical researchers make epistemological assumptions in their methods of acquiring knowledge, as we describe below.

Power Relationships That Underlie Knowledge.

Criticalists assume that all thought is mediated by socially and historically constructed power relations. This assumption im-plies that the beliefs and knowledge of students, teachers, and other groups involved in education are inevitably affected by their experiences with power and dominance, both within and outside the educational system. As a result, their beliefs and knowledge can only be understood in reference to the unique context in which they are expressed.

For example, say that a student ignores a teacher's command to stop talking. Depend-ing on students' views of the teacher, their history of experience with that classmate, and what else is occurring in the classroom when the teacher utters his command, some students might regard the talking student as a troublemaker, while others might see him as a buddy or hero.

Acccording to criticalists, any educational phenomenon can be subjected to contextual analysis to determine how it reflects power relations. For example, McLaren (2003) argues that multiculturalism—a movement aimed at improving relationships among students of different cultures and increasing their conformance to society's educational expectations—is still largely a mainstream, progressive agenda, exceedingly important but conceptually and politically compromised from the start.

A critical ethnography by Joan Parker-Webster (2001) illustrates the problems that educators can encounter in their attempts to implement multicultural themes in reading and language arts curricula. Parker-Webster found vastly different understandings of what themes should be incorporated in the curricula between white and African American teach-ers in training. For example, she quotes a white teacher, Sandra: "So, anything that's differ-ent than what you live normally would mean multicultural. You know, just like, you know, the um, homosexual thing" (p. 44). Parker-Webster comments: "This response reflects the tension between Sandra's outwardly liberal stance that embraces differences, and her deep-seated belief that emphasizes sameness" (p. 44) as the core of what multiculturalism should be about.

The Value-Laden Nature of Knowledge.

Criticalists believe that facts can never be isolated from the domain of values and prevailing assumptions about what is valued. Thus, they reject the notion that research about teaching and learning can ever be a neutral or value-free process. Indeed, critical researchers question the notion of objective reality itself. Like other qualitative researchers, critical researchers believe that all so-called facts about human nature and behavior are socially constructed, thus open to many interpretations and modifiable through human action.

Critical research is sometimes associated with postmodernism. In Chapter 1 we explain that **postmodernism** is a philosophy based on the assertion that no one approach to developing knowledge about the human world is privileged over (that is, better than) any other. Critical researchers are skeptical of any theory or method that claims to have timeless or universal application to understanding or improving the human condition. However, they remain committed to forms of social inquiry and action that promote the emancipation of nonprivileged individuals and groups, thereby affirming what Kincheloe and McLaren (1994) call "resistance postmodernism" (p. 144).

Critical researchers also argue that ideas about how teaching and learning operate always involve preformed systems of values and beliefs, which usually reinforce the power of dominant groups in society. Some critical researchers (Apple, 2003) claim that even the most seemingly "common-sense" educational concepts, such as achievement, reform, innovation, and standards, are categories constructed by, and serving the interests of, privileged groups in the educational hierarchy.

The Role of Capitalist Culture in Framing Knowledge.

Criticalists believe that every human "text" can be interpreted in relation to the cultural context of capitalist production and consumption. In critical research, the term **text** refers to any object, event, or instance of discourse that possesses communicative value. For a criticalist, the form and content of most texts reflect the values of the dominant culture and therefore are consistent with standards derived from a capitalist value framework.

Viewing most texts in education and research as problematic (that is, tending to misrepresent an individual's lived experience), criticalists subject such texts to deconstruction. **Deconstruction** is the critical analysis of texts based on the assumption that a text has no fixed meaning and that unrestricted efforts to interpret a text can yield multiple, often contradictory meanings. In deconstructing a teacher's letter to her students' parents, for example, a critical researcher would examine possible connotations of each term, opening the text to multiple interpretations, with none privileged over any other.

Take professional sports as another example of a cultural text to be deconstructed. Most people regard football games and golf tournaments on television as a form of entertainment and a road to riches for a few outstanding athletes. Now consider the following deconstruction (Bourdieu, 1991):

> More than by the encouragement it gives to chauvinism and sexism, it is undoubtedly through the division it makes between professionals, the virtuosi of an esoteric technique, and laymen, reduced to the role of mere consumers, a division that tends to become a deep structure of the collective consciousness, that sport produces its most decisive political effects. (p. 364)

For criticalists, professional sports also highlight numerous issues of oppression that need much further examination—such as the extent of violence both during games and in the personal lives of some athletes, physical ailments that may arise for athletes in later life, and the difficulty for the average fan in affording a ticket to a professional sporting event.

Critical researchers are at the forefront in investigating educational influences in society beyond those of schools, particularly the products of popular corporate culture. Increasingly, the common discourse and interests of young people (and perhaps most people) lie in what is loosely called the "entertainment media," including movies, songs, and even advertising. In *Kinderculture: The Corporate Construction of Childhood,* Shirley Steinberg and Joe Kincheloe (1997) argue that the prevailing economic and technological climate in the United States has created a crisis of childhood through the increasing role of corporations as educators of young people and the growing presence of corporate products, images, and messages within as well as outside the schools.

Steinberg and Kincheloe make a strong case that the impact of corporate culture on education requires a new response from educators who have embraced traditional forms of cultural transmission. Paolo Freire (1974) refers to these traditional forms as the banking model of learning, in which knowledge is "deposited" into passive students' minds and then is expected to be displayed, or "withdrawn," at the teacher's request. Freire, who educated and encouraged the activism of laborers in his native Brazil, "created a notion of teaching as mining where first and foremost the teachers [sic] responsibility is to pull knowledge out—to build upon the knowledge students bring to the pedagogical situation" (Hughes, 2008, p. 249).

As indicated in the signs described earlier from Michael Wesch's video "A Vision of Students Today," criticalists have found that factors like debt, poverty, and huge impersonal lecture classes are central to the educational experience of many students in today's institutions of higher learning (Young, 2007). They believe that educators at every level need to examine and address how these factors might hamper students' motivation and learning.

The Role of Cultural Texts in Maintaining Privilege.   Cultural texts (including but not limited to language) are probably the most powerful means of expressing and maintaining differences in privilege. Criticalists view any discourse, object, or event as having communicative value and thus able to be analyzed as a text.

Criticalists claim that individuals' awareness can be expanded or constrained by the texts they experience and use to encode their experience. The formal and informal language in classrooms (including body language, gestures, or the absence of response), and instructional programs involving different forms of discourse (such as bilingual education or whole-language instruction) are examples of how educators use language to maintain or contest hegemony.

Critical researchers use the concept of *voice* to study texts that express domination or oppression in the educational system (Giroux, 1992). **Voice** refers to the degree to which the communications of individuals occupying particular social identities are privileged, silenced, muted, or empowered through discourses that maintain or contest dominant and subordinate cultures in a society.

In her book on critical pedagogy, Joan Wink (1997) uses the concept of conscientization to suggest how marginalized voices can be brought to the forefront of public discourse. **Conscientization,** a term coined by Friere (1974) in *Pedagogy of the Oppressed,* is a process by which individuals come to understand their role in maintaining cultural processes that are not consistent with their basic values and subsequently to find voice to question and change their role.

Wink uses an example of conscientization about family involvement to illustrate teachers' need to have "the voice and the courage to question ourselves and the role we are playing in maintaining educational processes that we do not value" (1997, p. 26). Rainey and Carmen, two teachers in a school with a high proportion of Latino students, were discussing what their students' families needed. Rainey was a new teacher who had never been around Mexican kids before but really wanted to help her kids learn. Carmen taught in Spanish and had been around Mexican kids all her life. During their talk, Rainey said she could do a computer search of the university library holdings to identify what Latino families need. Carmen nodded, then added, "Or, we could ask the families" (1997, p. 31). At the next family meeting, the teachers asked, and the families told them their needs.

To us this example of exploring family needs does not discount research. Rather it expresses the importance of teachers doing research directly with the parents and students who are their clients instead of relying solely on knowledge available in mainstream research literature. Wink's book gives numerous examples of how teachers' actions, particularly their use of language in interactions with students, can empower or disempower specific individuals every day.

The Contribution of Criticalist Thinking to Research

The eight assumptions presented above reveal how criticalists think about the purpose of research. On the one hand, they assume that cultural oppression has widespread effects and is largely taken for granted in the broader research community. On the other hand, they seek to balance their criticism with hope and a deep belief that the emancipation of nonprivileged groups will improve the lives of all groups and individuals. Critical researchers also question the authority of their own emancipatory agenda, by deconstructing their statements expressing that agenda. They emphasize that any issue never has one essential, universal answer, but that a key role of education is to encourage continual questioning and discussion of the meaning and impact of each issue.

Some individuals denounce critical research as promoting a negative view of capitalism, of the worldwide spread of the market culture, and of the politics of the United States and other Western societies. While it shares with Marxism a critique of the inequities of the capitalist system, critical research promotes democratic principles as the best way to discover and correct these inequities, standing "in opposition to crude material or economic determinism" (Seymour-Smith, 1986, p. 59). The scholarship on which critical research is based can stimulate much critical reflection about dominant forms of educational practice and research.

Foundations of Critical Research in Education

We now move to a discussion of the major foundations, theoretical orientations, and design characteristics of critical research in education. We start by describing two bodies of inquiry within the critical research tradition that have had a significant impact on education—cultural studies and critical pedagogy. Then we briefly consider the central role of theory in critical research. The rest of the chapter presents the qualitative research tradition of critical ethnography, which represents a blending of the traditions of ethnography and critical research.

Cultural Studies

Cultural studies, an early qualitative research tradition found in some traditional academic disciplines, has inspired some new ones. Cultural studies researchers explore the economic, legal, political, and other socially constructed underpinnings of cultural phenomena (Nelson, Treichler, & Grossberg, 1992) while deconstructing many aspects of capitalist culture, giving particular attention to works in literature, art, and history as sources to be examined.

Many of the writings of cultural studies researchers are quite abstract and do not appear to involve fieldwork. However, cultural studies has direct relevance to educational practice. Their descriptive analyses often include critiques of the settings (e.g., schools, universities) and genres (e.g., conferences, journals) in which educators carry out their work.

The cultural categories of gender and race are specialized fields of study within cultural studies. Feminist research, sometimes called **feminisms** to reflect its diverse foci and methods, has paid particular attention to studying how the cultural meanings that circulate through females' everyday lives shape their lived cultures and experiences (Olesen, 1994). Critical feminists have also done much work to identify and deconstruct cultural texts, such as those in film and popular literature, that depict women mainly as (1) sexual objects for men but also (2) responsible for domesticity, housework, child rearing, and caregiving while still considered (3) the weaker or secondary sex and (4) normally as well as normatively heterosexual (Agger, 1992). Later in the chapter we discuss an example of critical feminist research concerning the depiction of young women's sexuality in an educational context.

With respect to race, cultural studies researchers have carried out research on each of the commonly identified racial or ethnic groups. While members of the cultural groups being studied have conducted some of this research, white researchers have conducted the majority. According to African American scholar John Stanfield II (1994), the dominance of what he calls mainstream researchers in this body of work has distorted the findings and tended to conceal, rather than highlight, the contributions of nonwhite racial and ethnic groups to society. Stanfield argues that mainstream researchers have sought to fit their analyses of African American culture into "the more orthodox norms of social scientific communities" (p. 177) and thus have "ignored, marginalized, or reinterpreted" (p. 177) the very aspects of African American intellectuals' lives that are the most empowering and normality-revealing.

The **norms** to which Stanfield refers can be defined as unstated sets of rules and assumptions that guide individuals' beliefs and social acts, in this case, those of mainstream (that is, white) intellectuals. Stanfield urges divergence away from those norms, including previous mainstream forms of investigation, and toward the use of indigenous qualitative methods that draw from the cosmos of people of color. For example, he recommends "the collection of oral histories that allow the examined people of color to articulate holistic explanations about how they construct their realities" (1994, p. 185). He also urges researchers engaged in such research to discard their own notions of time, space, and spirituality in order to grasp the meaning of indigenous people's stories.

A new thread of cultural studies recently initiated by the U.S. Army (Mulrine, 2008) also has educational implications. This work aims to improve U.S. military personnel's understanding of, and hence their effectiveness in working with, individuals and cultural groups in other countries where U.S. troops are deployed. According to Anna Mulrine's news article, the University of Foreign Military and Cultural Studies at Fort Leavenworth recently installed its first team of graduates (nicknamed the Red Team) in Baghdad. Mulrine reports:

> The Red Teamers' job . . . involves questioning prevailing assumptions to avoid "getting sucked into that groupthink" . . . having someone inside that says, "Wait a minute, not so fast." (2008, p. 30)

Red Teamers investigated the impact of using dogs in U.S. military operations in Iraq, a culture in which citizens generally regard dogs as unclean and, occasionally, evil. Another task involved pinpointing what Iraqis considered to be their own "greatest generation," similar to how people in the U.S. tend to regard its World War II vets.

Lt. Col. Ragland, the Red Team commander, reported that he got little support when he proposed employing 12-year-old Iraqis to do odd jobs, "a practice contrary to U.S. child labor laws" (Mulrine, 2008, p. 32). He continues:

> We have a preconceived image of an American 12-year-old. But in Iraq, they may be, in everything but age, the head of the household—engrossed in the economy, governance, day-to-day life. . . . We've mirror-imaged it. (2008, p. 32)

According to Mulrine, the policy of not hiring 12-year-olds "perhaps ceded some chance to help and influence everyday Iraqis" (2008, p. 32).

This example illustrates some of the issues that cultural studies workers face, and how their learning helps them confront and attempt to resolve different values and biases within their own culture and other cultures.

Critical Pedagogy

Because of its commitment to foster emancipation from oppression, critical research in education is closely connected to educational practice. Here we define **critical pedagogy** as teaching practices that are based on the goals and values of critical research.

One example of critical pedagogy is the work of the James and Grace Lee Boggs Center in Detroit. This form of critical pedagogy operates independently of, or across, most types of educational institutions. Described on its website (www.boggscenter.org), the center's work involves sponsorship of community-building activities designed to motivate all the community's children to learn and at the same time reverse the physical deterioration of its neighborhoods. These efforts include community gardening, mural painting programs, and other ways to build a foundation for systems change.

An activist for over 60 years, Boggs finds hope in her observation that "the new generation, which is beginning to discover its mission, is more open than the generation that led the movement in the 1960s" (1998, p. 272). In another publication Boggs (2003a) argues that we must be the change that we want to see in the world:

> Children need to be given a sense of the unique capacity of human beings to shape and create reality in accordance with conscious purposes and plans. Learning . . . is not something you can make people do in their heads with the perspective that years from now they will be able to get a good job and make a lot of money. (p. 5)

Boggs continues to promote critical pedagogy through the center and her worldwide networking efforts. A recent article in the *Christian Science Monitor* about the numerous community programs building gardens in Detroit's vacant land parcels gives the center credit for beginning the urban garden movement (Bonfiglio, 2008).

The Role of Theory in Critical Research

Critical research emphasizes theory to explain society and explore approaches to foster the emancipation of oppressed groups. For example, Henry Giroux (1988) developed a body of critical theory that can be applied to education in the United States and other Western cultures. Giroux's theory begins with the assumption that U.S. public education is in crisis. He sees this condition reflected most clearly in the contrast between hegemonic rhetoric that equates U.S. culture with democracy in its ultimate form and increasing indicators of the falsity of this rhetoric. As examples, he cites decreasing voter participation (though this trend was reversed in the 2008 presidential election), rising illiteracy rates among the general population, and a growing opinion among U.S. citizens that social criticism and social change are irrelevant to the maintenance of U.S. democracy.

Giroux seeks to replace the "politics of difference" that he views as characteristic of most standard dialogue about educational problems and solutions. In his view, standard educational dialogue favors a focus on the "democratic" treatment of difference. As a result, it can exhibit one of two oppressive tendencies. The first tendency involves the implication that individuals in certain cultural categories are superior to others—for example, old to young, heterosexual to homosexual, or able to disabled—because of inherent cultural or individual factors that presumably demonstrate and justify their supposed superiority.

The second tendency encourages students to buy into the notion of sameness—that cultural differences are irrelevant and thus should be ignored (as in the old notion of "color blindness") or actively eliminated. This second tendency promotes the view that school, and American society overall, is basically a "melting pot," in which cultural differences should be erased over time in the interests of promoting social harmony.

By contrast, Giroux (1988) proposes a postmodern (see Chapter 1), liberatory theory of critical pedagogy termed **border pedagogy.** *Border* reflects the view that cultural differences between individuals and groups are permeable and changing, not captured in the rigid either–or nature of conventional social categories. Thus in exploring cultural phenomena, this theory rejects both the concepts of better–worse and of sameness as the basis for describing or valuing the cultural characteristics of different individuals or cultural groups.

Giroux contends that "the struggle over public schools cannot be separated from the social problems currently facing this society. These problems are not only political in nature but are pedagogical as well" (1992, p. 199). If based on Giroux's theory, schools and pedagogy would be organized around a sense of purpose that makes the centrality of difference a critical notion of citizenship and democratic public life. In the pedagogy envisioned by this theory, educators at all levels of schooling would engage in redefining the nature of intellectual work and inquiry itself. The goal would be for educators and their students to "become knowledgeable and committed actors in the world" (1988, p. 208).

Giroux argues that if his theory were seriously applied in schools students would no longer study unified subjects like reading, language arts, or science. Instead, they would explore the "borderlands" between diverse cultural histories as sites for critical analysis and a potential source of experimentation, creativity, and possibility. Students would also explicitly study the sources and effects of power in their own experience, seeking to understand how forms of domination are historically and socially constructed. Teachers would explore the ways in which they can use their authority to aid students' emancipation from internalized oppression and external sources of domination. Finally, students would be educated to read critically the ways in which various forms of discourse regulate the cultural texts that they encounter as learners and to see the different ideological interests that such texts express.

The work of Stanfield, Mulrine, Boggs, and Giroux can all be considered as contributions to the field of critical pedagogy. "Critical Pedagogy: Where in the World Did It Come From?" is a chapter in the third edition of Wink's book on critical pedagogy (2004) that provides brief summaries of the work of many other theorists in the critical theory tradition.

Features of a Critical Ethnographic Research Report

Critical ethnography is a structured approach to critical research in which the research methods of ethnography are used to study power relationships and forms of oppression within particular cultures. To illustrate the design elements of critical ethnography we describe a research study conducted by Carspecken (1996) evaluating Project TRUST, a school extraction (also known as pullout) program for low-achieving students exhibiting a high level of school mobility. Project TRUST was established by one of Carspecken's former students in the school where he served as vice principal.

Carspecken's description of Project TRUST includes all the stages that his model of critical ethnography includes, and it describes problems that are still characteristic of many schools today. More recent critical ethnographies have been carried out by Carspecken's students (Carspecken & Walford, 2001), but they are less comprehensive in their design.

Introduction

Carspecken's (1996) report begins with a description of West Forest School (a pseudonym), an elementary school serving a low-income neighborhood in Houston that had previously served white middle-class families. After a severe downturn in the local economy, this school absorbed a large number of impoverished minority students who showed a high mobility rate from one school to another.

Robert, the school's vice principal, set up an extraction program that pulled the low-income students out of class to reduce "frequent classroom disruptions" (p. 32). Carspecken commented:

> Robert was well aware of the fact that extraction policies often damage students through stigmatization, but he thought this risk could be ameliorated by keeping the TRUST students up-to-date on their academic programs and returning them to the normal classrooms as soon as possible. (1996, p. 32)

Robert also wanted to raise the students' self-awareness and self-esteem and improve their conflict resolution skills while they were in the extraction program.

Carspecken claims that such programs usually seek to *control* disruptive students more than they actually *help* them. He wanted to see if that generalization applied to Project TRUST, but also "to understand more about the effects of extraction as well as refine our present understanding of power, culture, identity, and social reproduction" (1996, p. 28). The school administration saw Carspecken's role as simple—"to find out whether or not TRUST worked" (1996, p. 33). Carspecken viewed his role as more complex: to determine if disruption rates were in fact curbed by TRUST and if conflict resolution skills and self-esteem were higher after students' participation in TRUST.

Before entering the field, critical ethnographers specify their research questions. They also explore their value orientations, so that they can raise awareness of their biases and consider how to counter them. Carspecken (1996) sought to formulate general, flexible questions, while being fairly comprehensive. He listed the general topics in which he was interested, including the procedure for assigning students to Project TRUST; what was taught and learned in the TRUST classroom; and the project's relationship to the school, the neighborhood, and broader socioeconomic forces. His report focuses on using the Project TRUST research findings to explain recommendations for carrying out the various design elements of critical ethnography.

Research Design, Sampling, Measures, and Results

Carspecken's (1996) methodology for a critical ethnography involves five stages.

Stage One: Monological Data Collection.   **Monological data collection** means that only the researcher "speaks" at this stage, writing the primary record from the perspective of a relatively uninvolved observer. This perspective corresponds to the etic perspective that researchers convey in qualitative case study research. The researcher seeks to be unobtrusive, a passive observer recording a thick description of field participants' verbal and nonverbal behavior from the researcher's perspective.

The researcher thereby seeks to produce objective data that are similar to what other observers would likely obtain if they carried out the same study. Such data are intended to support **objective truth claims,** which are claims open to multiple access, that is, accessible to, generally agreed on by, and thus able to be directly validated by, various observers.

To produce such data during Stage One, the researcher uses low-inference vocabulary, frequent time notations, occasional bracketed observer comments, context information, and italics for verbatim speech acts. Such data enable the researcher to compare information obtained from the researcher's (etic) perspective during Stage One with data obtained during Stage Three, which seeks the participants' (emic) perspective and places the researcher in the role of "a facilitator of talk and discussion" (p. 52).

Carspecken provides a rich introduction to Project TRUST, describing the crumbling neighborhood surrounding the school and the idealism and commitment he observed in a white teacher named Alfred. Carspecken's thick description of the Project TRUST classroom includes a diagram of the room's arrangement and detailed notes on student interactions he observed.

Carspecken (1996) also provides monological data based on a detailed account of the interaction between Samuel, a student of mixed African American and white ethnicity, and the teacher, Alfred, at a point when the class was supposed to begin taking a test. The following description lists several highlights from the account:

- descriptions of participants' actions (e.g., "Samuel throws test on the floor. Hums a cheerful song," p. 53)
- student and teacher comments in italics (e.g., from Alfred, *"We're at a critical point,"* p. 54) and the researcher's low-inference descriptions (e.g., for Alfred, "Tone still calm," p. 54).
- two observer comments noting the researcher's interpretations of specific statements from participants (e.g., for Alfred, "As if, 'You know what is going on as well as I do, you are just refusing to talk about it. But I am patient,'" p. 54).

These excerpts represent the researcher's efforts to describe expressions of power as the teacher and student argue about taking the test.

Stage Two: Preliminary Reconstructive Analysis.   Critical ethnographers next analyze the primary record to determine interaction patterns and their apparent meanings. **Reconstructive analysis** is the process of researchers' *reconstruction* of the data obtained during previous stages, explicitly stating possible meanings of specific statements and actions and beginning the process of coding the data.

Reconstructive analysis involves coding **meaning fields,** which are the possible intended meanings of participants' statements or nonverbal behavior that others in the setting might themselves infer. Coding begins at a low level of inference, as in the following example of low-level code: "Reasons for not doing classwork: (a) Sick, (b) 'Having a bad day,' (c) 'It's too hard'" (Carspecken, 1996, p. 148). Coding then moves to higher levels of inference, "Student conflicts: (a) Student reprimanding other student, (b) 'Your mama'" (p. 148). Such codes clarify cultural themes and system factors that are derived from the primary record but that research participants rarely mention directly. Carspecken explains that the researcher "must become a 'virtual participant' in order to articulate the meaning fields" (p. 98).

Below is a segment of the researcher's initial meaning reconstructions for the interaction between Samuel and Alfred referred to previously. The notation *A* designates the teacher Alfred, who is the subject of the entry; *OC* designates an observer's comment by the researcher; *MF* conveys the meaning field laying out the researcher's interpretation of possible meanings of the previous statement with (*OR*) used to indicate an alternate possible meaning.

> A: Alfred looks up in Samuel's direction with placid, smooth facial features [OC: as if bland, nonchalant, "no big deal"].
> A: *Samuel let's go now and take that test.* Addresses Samuel in matter-of-fact way, as if "no big deal, time to take the test, as we both know."
> [MF: *Alfred conveys social distance in his behavior; no greeting, no smile. He looks at papers first, then mentions the test implying that the test and his relationship with Samuel are just one of many things now on his mind. (OR) Alfred's actions indicate controlled nervousness. He is leery of beginning a conflict with Samuel and delays by looking at the papers*] (Carspecken, 1996, p. 97)

During Stage Two researchers also speculate about participants' **subjective truth claims.** These are the researcher's inferences of what an individual research participant would claim based on the participant's specific thoughts and feelings that can only be accessed indirectly.

During this stage researchers also ask participants to generate positions which allow the researchers to infer participants' **normative–evaluative truth claims,** which are claims that reflect social agreements on the rightness, goodness, and appropriateness of various types of activities. During this stage participants often express new or unanticipated comments compared to their comments during Stage One.

To illustrate Stage Two data, Carspecken presents a conversation between Alfred and Samuel about Samuel's home and family situation, involving questions about whether his mother was at home the previous night, where she went, and Samuel's beliefs and feelings about her possible actions while she was out. Examples of the truth claims that the researcher inferred from Alfred's comments in talking with Samuel are shown, in the format that the researcher depicted them.

Possible subjective claims

Foregrounded, Immediate

"I care about you," "I want to understand you," "I want to help you cope with your problems"

Less Foregrounded, Less Immediate

"I am a kind and caring teacher" (identity claim), "I am sincere"

Possible objective claims

Quite Foregrounded, Quite Immediate

"Events are occurring in your home that many children would report as upsetting"

Highly Backgrounded, Remote, Taken-for-Granted

"You live in a home," "You live with other people—mother and grandmother" (OR—just possible) "Black families have many domestic problems"

Possible normative–evaluative claims

Quite Foregrounded, Quite Immediate

"It is good to talk about feelings"

Less Foregrounded, Less Immediate

(OR) "Your mother's behavior is bad" (Carspecken, 1996, p. 112).

Inferring meaning involves hermeneutics, a process through which researchers seek to understand human phenomena by analyzing how each part of a text relates to the whole. Given the above interaction as an illustration, each specific comment by Alfred represents a part, and all of Alfred's comments and nonverbal behavior during the recorded episode represent the whole.

Carspecken describes the entire process of interpretation of the meaning of a text as the **hermeneutic circle.** This process includes five features that "raise awareness of an inference process we all employ tacitly in everyday life" (p. 102). These features are explained in the following list from the researcher's perspective:

1. Taking the position of the participant, by imagining oneself in the participant's situation and "occupying virtually the positions of the others in the setting" (p. 99) in order to interpret the meaning of the situation.

2. Becoming culturally familiar with different research participants so as to be able to recognize specific statements as culturally typical or "uniquely constructed from culturally typical interactions" (p. 99).

3. Reflecting on the cultural norms the researcher employs in efforts to define the typical cultural representations of research participants. As an example, Alfred remains silent when Samuel does not begin taking the test after Alfred's second comment. Carspecken (1996) speculates that Alfred's silence means he is uncertain what to do next or wants Samuel to sense that he needs to respond or wants Samuel to understand that a sanction will occur unless he responds. Then the researcher tests these possible cultural norms by examining previous data involving the same research participants or collecting additional data on them.

4. Making tacit comparisons between the norms that the researcher claims as valid and those that individual research participants seem to claim as valid. As an example, Alfred tends to wait longer to respond than Carspecken takes to be the norm. The researcher would need to make repeated observations of Alfred to confirm or disconfirm this inference.

5. Distinguishing between the effects of individual personality patterns (e.g., vocal tones and facial expressions) and culturally determined patterns in the observed behaviors of specific research participants.

Stage Three: Dialogical Data Generation.   At Stage Three, researchers begin **dialogical data generation,** which is the process of creating a dialogue in which researchers help participants explore issues with their own vocabulary, metaphors, and ideas. They use such dialogical data to test the validity of the subjective and normative–evaluative truth claims that they have posed as being characteristic of particular research participants.

Researchers need to specify interview questions for each topic area of interest, including (1) very concrete "lead-off questions, each designed to open up a topic domain" (Carspecken, 1996, p. 157), (2) "covert" questions that researchers do not want to ask explicitly because they could lead the interview too much but that they want the interviewee to address, and (3) possible follow-up questions, to ensure that the research participant has said enough about each topic area.

Researchers' responses to participants' statements can range on a 6-point scale from "1. bland encouragement" to "6. high-inference paraphrasing." The higher the number, the less often the researcher should use that response. The resulting data often challenge information from previous stages and give the participants more control over the research process, as Carspecken emphasizes:

> Interviews and group discussions produce many subjective truth claims: claims that people believe, feel, intend, value, and experience various things within a realm closed off to others . . . the realm of privileged access. We depend on honest and accurate self-reports to learn about the subjective states of others. (1996, p. 165)

Carspecken lists procedures that help strengthen Stage Three claims, including (1) checking whether the individual was consistent in comments made during recorded interviews, (2) interviewing the same individuals repeatedly, (3) engaging in member checks (see Chapter 14), and (4) using nonleading interview techniques. Carspecken believes that researchers must be open to being "wounded" through fieldwork, because what one learns "is going to effect [sic] you existentially" (p. 169). He adds:

> The more we reduce those modes of power that prevent all people from having an equal voice, the more open we must be to existential threats. But being "wounded" through conducting research with integrity is ultimately going to be more empowering for us because it will change us, broaden our horizons, help us grow as human beings. (1996, p. 170)

Carspecken notes that this process resembles cathartic validity (Lather, 1986), whereby "the researcher allows herself to change and grow through field work . . . in ways that often challenge oppressive cultural forms" (p. 170).

Stage Four: Discovering System Relationships. Carspecken's discussion of the Project TRUST research findings is not confined to a particular stage of his model but can be briefly summarized.

With respect to reducing classroom disruptions, Project TRUST appears to have had some success. Two field journal entries from Carspecken's primary record during Stage One state: "Last year at this same date Robert had 600 referrals, this year he has had only half that number" (1996, p. 51). "Those present commented that disruption referrals have gone down since TRUST began because it is viewed as a stigma to go there" (p. 51).

With respect to Project TRUST students' learning conflict resolution skills (one of the goals the school administration had for the project), Carspecken provides some affirmative evidence. Specifically, he observed some teacher–student interactions in which "conflicts were resolved noncoercively" (p. 152). He also found evidence that students "had actually internalized covert messages about self and choice" (p. 152), based on observations of student–student interactions "when students used expressions in nonclassroom contexts that I had seen Alfred teach them" (p. 152).

We found no specific discussion of whether changes occurred in students' self-esteem based on their participation in Project TRUST.

During Stage Four researchers compare the findings from the specific site being investigated with findings from other sites involving a similar research focus. In this manner, they discover system relationships, that is, broad similarities that reveal common cultural features in the behavior of participants across different sites. Such system relationships appear similar to cross-case generalizability (see Chapter 14), because they allow readers to determine the extent to which the findings from one site are applicable to other sites.

In Project TRUST, one system relationship is how individual students sought to "renegotiate" stressful classroom settings by their expressed dominance of, or subordination to, other students. For example, the behavior in school of Samuel, a mixed-race student living with a white mother and white grandmother, was characterized by a system relationship that Carspecken called *cultural isomorphisms*. As reflected in Project TRUST, cultural isomorphisms involved research participants' efforts to change the interactive pattern of the school setting to more closely resemble the outside culture in which they felt more comfortable.

According to Carspecken (1996), Samuel "frequently employed themes learned from home to defend himself from feelings of low self-respect in school" (p. 198). When attempting to renegotiate stressful classroom settings, such as teacher efforts to explain academic concepts, "Samuel would often bid for a session of chit-chat on themes that were rewarding for him at home . . . where the rules for a positive identity were under his control" (p. 198).

The type of system relationships found in Carspecken's research is also prevalent in Paul Willis's classic study (1977) of working-class "lads," identified by Carspecken as one of the first critical ethnographies ever conducted. Willis discovered correspondences, which he termed *reproductive loops,* between the lads' behavior in three different social sites—school, home, and job setting. He found that the lads sought to avoid activities in school (e.g., doing the assigned work) that could conceivably help them move out of the working class into the middle class but which the lads viewed as a rejection of their home-based culture. In Willis's discussion of the lads' home site, he observes that all the lads' fathers had stayed within the working class in seeking work. Then the lads, in turn, moved into jobs involving physical labor when they left school.

Stage Five: Seeking Explanations of the Findings through Social-Theoretical Models.   At Stage Five the level of inference rises, as the researcher explores how the interests and power relations discovered at Stage Four can serve as explanatory factors. In the Project TRUST research, Carspecken (1996) shows parallels between the classic research of Willis and the efforts of TRUST participants to negotiate their cultural heritage in a way that provided some opportunity to maintain dignity and self-respect. For example, Carspecken reports that Project TRUST students favored video games, TV shows, and types of popular music depicting violence, race relations, and traditional gender stereotypes. Carspecken interprets the themes of these media elements as reflecting the harsh living conditions of most families in Park Forest and the surrounding community. He also notes the efforts of the TRUST students to challenge those conditions, for example, by talking tough and tending to glamorize violence.

These themes and insights can be interrelated and tied together by a theoretical construct—*reproduction*—posed by Willis (1997) and mentioned by Carspecken (1996) that clarifies similarities between Willis's research findings and those of the Project TRUST study. In this context reproduction means that individuals act in a manner consistent with broadly distributed conditions, particularly the existing long-term social systems of which they are a part. It corresponds to our earlier definition of *reproduction,* because it shows how the Project TRUST students accept, and behave consistently with, the oppressive cultural patterns of their society.

In Willis's (1977) research, the history of family employment experienced by the parents of the lads was a social system that the lads reproduced through their behavior during and after their schooling. Social systems are thus human activities, like work, that have become patterned and continue to exist because they are continuously reproduced. Despite some positive results of Project TRUST, Carspecken's discussion of "Stage Five and the TRUST Study" (1996, p. 205) makes it clear that the Project TRUST students, like Willis's working class "lads," largely reproduced the social conditions that surrounded them.

Conclusion

Carspecken (1996) summarizes the cultural conditions characteristic of children from Project TRUST as follows:

- having to grow up fast and to continually defend themselves physically
- school as a place they had to go to but not a place around which their plans could revolve
- school as a place dominated by others of different racial and class categories who sought to impose authority on students

• home as a source of harsh discipline, accompanied by parents' resistance to any efforts of others to dominate them

Carspecken also describes the effects of these conditions:

Thus these children negotiated for harsh authority relations at school (the only form of authority they respected) while simultaneously resisting vigorously any form of authority. The culture of the neighborhood was not conducive to success at school. School work was rarely supported in the home, and few adults known by these children owed anything to past schooling for whatever life successes they displayed. In the school, teachers like Alfred strived hard to help these children but found their hands tied in many ways. (1996, p. 206)

Carspecken then depicts the circumstances of West Forest even more broadly as tied to "the economic system of the United States, the economic circumstances of Houston, the conjuncture of race and class categories within our society, and the political power of the middle and upper-middle classes to establish educational policies in their interests" (1996, p. 206).

Carspecken notes that during periods of economic decline, typically lower-class people lose jobs in large numbers and then are reabsorbed into menial positions when the economy picks up. He notes that state laws controlling curriculum and pedagogy limit the school system's efforts to prepare all students for well-paying jobs. He concludes: "Schools end up keeping children like those in the TRUST study off the streets, but the students [are] ill prepared to do anything but unskilled labor" (1996, p. 206).

Evaluating Ethnographies and Critical Ethnographies

Research conducted by ethnographers and criticalists is grounded in qualitative methods of inquiry. Therefore, you can evaluate these research studies using Appendix 3, on the questions to ask yourself when evaluating qualitative research reports.

Ethnographers and criticalists typically focus on selected cases as they seek to understand a culture or the power relationships within a society. You can evaluate their case research by using strategies to evaluate the quality and rigor of a case study described in Chapter 14.

The distinction between emic and etic perspectives is particularly important in ethnographies and critical ethnographies. Therefore, you should evaluate how well these perspectives were represented during data collection and analysis. The following are several questions for you to consider as you read research reports of this type.

• Does the report include an emic perspective?

Examine the report for evidence that researchers took care to collect data about the participants' view of their own culture and their role in it. Examples of such evidence are quoted statements from participants, their writings and other forms of communication, and logs of their activities.

• Does the report include an etic perspective?

Examine the report for evidence that the researchers engaged in self-reflection about their personal values and beliefs concerning the phenomena being studied. The researchers also should try to identify personal biases that might distort their data collection and analysis. These reflections should occur during all phases of the study and especially when the phenomena are controversial or markedly different from the researchers' own background and experiences.

An example of

HOW ETHNOGRAPHY AND CRITICAL RESEARCH CAN HELP IN SOLVING PROBLEMS OF PRACTICE

In 2006 the U.S. Department of Education relaxed restrictions on single-sex education in public schools. Currently at least 442 U.S. schools offer single-sex classes, according to the National Association for Single Sex Public Education.

The Mobile, Alabama, *Press-Register* reported on a local middle school that recently started offering single-sex classes for all academic subjects. Educators at this school claimed that this arrangement helps all students learn more, because teachers can shape instruction to the different needs of male and female learners. Reported benefits include being able to give boys a "brain break" once or twice during a class session so they can move around, and freeing girls to speak up more during lessons. The school's principal was quoted on the increase of average daily attendance by 2 percent and the decreased number of students being sent to the office. Not everyone was completely pleased with single-sex classes, though.

> Emily Martin, deputy director of the ACLU's Women's Rights Project, said the rationale that boys and girls learn differently is troubling if it leads to different teaching programs that could lead to unequal education.
>
> Leonard Sax with the National Association for Single Sex Public Education said some children benefit from it while others do not. Sax recommends public schools let parents choose.
>
> Havner, R. (2008, November 24). Single-sex classes attracting both praise and concern. *Press-Register*, Mobile, Alabama. Retrieved from www.al.com/news/press-register

These concerns about single-sex education raise questions about power relationships and oppression, for example: Are schools reproducing patterns of gender discrimination and inequity that might negatively affect all students? Do single-sex classes oppress specific types of students by offering inferior instruction? What makes it appropriate to separate students by gender in school when, in the larger society, people generally are not separated in that way? How do same-sex classes address the needs of students who identify as gay, lesbian, bisexual, intersex, or transgendered, in terms of both class placement and their treatment by other students?

We can describe a critical ethnography that would be helpful for answering questions such as these.

The researchers can decide to study one all-male class and one all-female class in the same academic subject in a school that has instituted same-sex education. The sample is limited, but it enables them to collect intensive ethnographic data over an extensive time period, perhaps as much as a school year.

To maintain the culture of the classroom, a male researcher is assigned to the all-boy class and a female researcher to the all-girl class. They might choose to embed themselves in the classroom culture as participant observers by engaging in the same learning activities as the students.

The researchers take extensive notes on class activities, both formal (e.g., a teacher lecture) and informal (e.g., student-to-student chats or student use of cell phones or iPods). They note any remarks or actions that reflect stereotyping based on gender or sexual orientation, either by students or the teacher. They also examine homework assignments and quizzes and observe students outside the classroom while on school grounds. If they can observe parent interactions with their children or the school staff without being obtrusive, they do so. The researchers analyze their classroom and outside the classroom data to determine whether the information reflects gender stereotypes or oppressive power relationships such as bullying. The two ethnographers initially analyze their data separately. Then they compare their observations and interpretations as a check on the trustworthiness of their findings.

Self-Check Test

1. When researchers study a subculture in their own vicinity about which they know little beforehand, they are primarily fulfilling the intent of ethnographic research to
   a. carry out naturalistic observations of participants in the field.
   b. make the familiar strange.
   c. provide a thick description of a cultural phenomenon.
   d. do a cross-cultural comparison.

2. Ethnographers focus on the study of culture because they believe that
   a. the influence of culture on human beings is what makes them unique as a species.
   b. the study of primitive cultures can show how Western cultures evolved.
   c. an increasing number of distinct cultures are emerging in the world.
   d. the similarities observed between people from different parts of the world are best explained in terms of cultural factors.

3. In providing a description of a cultural phenomenon, ethnographers generally seek to
   a. examine the phenomenon in more than one culture.
   b. emphasize the perspective of high-status members of the culture.
   c. use their own perspective to reconcile conflicting views of the phenomenon.
   d. balance the emic and etic perspectives.

4. Some educational ethnographers view the typically lower academic performance of students from certain ethnic groups as due to their tendency to withhold investment in education because they do not perceive it as having any economic payoff, an explanation that views student performance as being affected by
   a. cultural acquisition.
   b. cultural assimilation.
   c. school organization.
   d. teacher bias.

5. In today's world the primary characteristic that differentiates the lifestyles of different cultural groups is typically
   a. educational level.
   b. wealth.
   c. nationality.
   d. religion.

6. In the view of critical researchers, mainstream research practices have maintained cultural oppression primarily by

a. neglecting the study of racial and ethnic minorities.
b. upholding hegemonic assumptions about truth, science, and good.
c. questioning the meaning of all texts.
d. not distinguishing between the effects of class, race, and gender on individuals' cultural attainments.

7. Criticalists refer to the tendency of certain researchers to become preoccupied with means over ends or purposes as
   a. instrumental rationality.
   b. voice.
   c. cultural assimilation.
   d. deconstruction.

8. Hegemony refers to
   a. emancipatory methods as conceptualized by criticalists.
   b. a conception of social justice advocated by criticalists.
   c. differences among the emic perspectives of the members of a nonprivileged cultural group.
   d. the domination of nonprivileged cultural groups by privileged cultural groups.

9. Deconstruction of a text involves
   a. rephrasing it in language that culturally oppressed groups can understand.
   b. specifying the cultural themes and system factors reflected in it.
   c. asking the members of the culturally dominant group to clarify its meaning.
   d. examining its connotations and various possible meanings.

10. In critical ethnography, it is desirable to
    a. involve field participants in all phases of data collection.
    b. demonstrate consistency between the data collected through passive observation and the data collected through dialogue with field participants.
    c. analyze the findings from the specific research site in terms of existing or emergent theory about system relationships.
    d. primarily collect data that meet objective truth claims.

11. An example of schools' reproduction of cultural oppression is
    a. teaching students from poor backgrounds skills associated with obedience and students from affluent backgrounds skills associated with achievement.
    b. designing sexuality education programs focused on premarital abstinence.
    c. teaching history in a way that characterizes the portrayals in textbooks as factual.
    d. All of the above.

12. A criticalist's deconstruction of a chapter of a high school textbook on U.S. history would most likely result in
   a. identification of the actual meaning of the text.
   b. identification of multiple, often contradictory meanings of the text.
   c. an interpretation consistent with mainstream views of U.S. history
   d. All of the above.

13. Conscientization is a process designed to
   a. improve students' classroom behavior.
   b. encourage individuals to question and change oppressive cultural practices.
   c. promote more classroom activities involving multicultural themes
   d. All of the above.

Chapter References

Agger, B. (1992). *Cultural studies as critical theory*. Washington, DC: Falmer.

Anderson, K. T., & McClard, A. P. (1993). Study time: Temporal orientations of freshmen students and computing. *Anthropology and Education Quarterly, 24,* 159–177.

Apple, M. W. (2003). *The state and the politics of knowledge*. New York: Routledge Falmer.

Boggs, G. L. (1998). *Living for change: An autobiography*. Minneapolis: University of Minnesota Press.

Boggs, G. L. (2003a, January). *We must be the change*. Paper based on a presentation at the University of Michigan, 2003 Martin Luther King Symposium, Ann Arbor, MI. Retrieved from www3.boggscenter.org

Boggs, G. L. (2003b, February). A paradigm shift in our concept of education. Paper presented at the workshop *Transnationalism, ethnicity, and the public sphere* at the Center for Critical Theory and Transnational Studies, University of Oregon, Eugene, OR.

Bonfiglio, O. (2008, August 21). Detroit grows green. *Christian Science Monitor,* p. 17.

Bourdieu, P. (1991). Sport and social class. In C. Mukerji & M. Schudson (Eds.), *Rethinking popular culture: Contemporary perspectives in cultural studies* (pp. 357–373). Berkeley: University of California Press.

Carspecken, P. F. (1996). *Critical ethnography in educational research: A theoretical and practical guide*. New York: Routledge.

Carspecken, P. F., & Walford, G. (Eds.). (2001). *Critical ethnography and education*. Oxford, UK: Elsevier Science.

Freire, P. (1974). *Pedagogy of the oppressed*. New York: Seabury.

Freire, P. (1994). *Pedagogy of hope: Reliving pedagogy of the oppressed*. New York: Continuum.

Gibson, R. (1986). *Critical theory and education*. London: Hodder & Stoughton.

Giroux, H. A. (1988). Critical theory and the politics of culture and voice: Rethinking the discourse of educational research. In R. R. Sherman & R. B. Webb (Eds.), *Qualitative research in education: Focus and methods* (pp. 190–210). New York: Falmer.

Giroux, H. A. (1992). Resisting difference: Cultural studies and the discourse of critical pedagogy. In L. Grossberg, C. Nelson, & P. A. Treichler (Eds.), *Cultural studies* (pp. 199–212). New York: Routledge.

Hogan, K., & Corey, C. (2001). Viewing classrooms as cultural contexts for fostering scientific literacy. *Anthropology and Education Quarterly, 32,* 214–243.

Hughes, S. A. (2008). Teaching theory as "other" to white urban practitioners: Mining and priming Freirean critical pedagogy in resistant bodies. In J. Diem & R. J. Helfenbein (Eds.), *Unsettling beliefs: Teaching theory to teachers* (pp. 245–271). Charlotte, NC: Information Age.

Kincheloe, J., & McLaren, P. (1994). Rethinking critical theory and qualitative research. In N. K. Denzin & Y. S. Lincoln (Eds.), *Handbook of qualitative research* (pp. 138–157). Thousand Oaks, CA: Sage.

Kumashiro, K. (2002). *Troubling education: Queer activism and anti-oppressive pedagogy*. New York: Routledge Falmer.

Lancy, D. F. (1993). *Qualitative research in education: An introduction to the major traditions*. White Plains, NY: Longman.

Madison, D. S. (2005). Critical ethnography as street performance: Reflections of home, race, murder, and justice. In N. K. Denzin & Y. S. Lincoln (Eds.), *The Sage handbook of qualitative research* (3rd ed., pp. 537–546). Thousand Oaks, CA: Sage.

Malinowski, B. (1922). *Argonauts of the Western Pacific*. New York: Dutton.

McLaren, P. (1998). *Life in schools: An introduction to critical pedagogy in the foundations of education* (3rd ed.). New York: Longman.

McLaren, P. (2003, February). Critical pedagogy in the age of neoliberal globalization: The domestication of political agency and the struggle for socialist futures. Paper presented at the workshop *Transnationalism, ethnicity, and the public sphere* at the Center for Critical Theory and Transnational Studies, University of Oregon, Eugene, OR.

Mead, M. (1930). *Growing up in New Guinea: A comparative study of primitive education*. New York: William Morrow.

Mulrine, A. (2008, May 26). To battle groupthink, the army trains a skeptics corps. *U.S. News & World Report,* pp. 30, 32.

Nieves, E. (2008, May 27). Food banks finding more clients, fewer donations. Mobile, AL: *Register-Guard,* pp. A-1, A-5.

Nelson, C., Treichler, P. A., & Grossberg, L. (1992). Cultural studies: An introduction. In L. Grossberg, C. Nelson, & P. A. Treichler (Eds.), *Cultural studies* (pp. 1–22). New York: Routledge.

Ogbu, J. U. (1978). *Minority education and caste: The American system in cross-cultural perspective*. New York: Academic Press.

Olesen, V. (1994). Feminisms and models of qualitative research. In N. K. Denzin & Y. S. Lincoln (Eds.), *Handbook of qualitative research* (pp. 158–174). Thousand Oaks, CA: Sage.

Parker-Webster, J. (2001). In P. F. Carspecken & G. Walford (Eds.), *Critical ethnography and education* (pp. 27–60). Oxford, UK: Elsevier Science.

Schwandt, T. A. (2001). *Dictionary of qualitative inquiry* (2nd ed.). Thousand Oaks, CA: Sage.

Seymour-Smith, C. (Ed.). (1986). *Dictionary of anthropology*. Boston: G. K. Hall.

Spindler, G., & Spindler, L. (1992). Cultural process and ethnography: An anthropological perspective. In M. D. LeCompte, W. L. Millroy, & J. Preissle (Eds.), *Handbook of qualitative research in education* (pp. 53–92). San Diego, CA: Academic Press.

Stanfield, J. H. II (1994). Ethnic modeling in qualitative research. In N. K. Denzin & Y. S. Lincoln (Eds.), *Handbook of qualitative research* (pp. 175–188). Thousand Oaks, CA: Sage.

Steinberg, S., & Kincheloe, J. (1997). *Kinderculture: The corporate construction of childhood.* Boulder, CO: Westview.

Watchdog says NASA censored studies. (2008, June 3). Mobile, AL: *Register-Guard,* p. A9.

Wax, M. (1993). How culture misdirects multiculturalism. *Anthropology and Education Quarterly, 24,* 99–115.

Willis, P. (1977). *Learning to labour: How working class kids get working class jobs.* London: Gower.

Wink, J. (1997). *Critical pedagogy: Notes from the real world.* White Plains, NY: Longman.

Wink, J. (2004). *Critical pedagogy: Notes from the real world* (3rd ed.) Boston: Addison-Wesley Longman.

Young, J. R. (2007). An anthropologist explores the culture of video blogging. *Chronicle of Higher Education, 53*(36).

Resources for Further Study

Anderson-Levitt, K. M. (2006). Ethnography. In J. L. Green, G. Camilli, & P. B. Elmore (Eds.), *Handbook of complementary methods in education research* (pp. 279–295). Mahwah, NJ: Lawrence Erlbaum.

A clear summary of the purpose and methods of ethnography and its history in education. The author discusses the ethnographer's responsibility to research participants and gives a brief overview of research design and analysis in ethnography.

Angrosino, M. V. (2005). Recontextualizing observation: Ethnography, pedagogy, and the prospects for a progressive political agenda. In N. K. Denzin & Y. S. Lincoln (Eds.), *The Sage handbook of qualitative research* (3rd ed., pp. 729–745). Thousand Oaks, CA: Sage.

Analyzes the central and evolving role of observation in ethnographic research, its relevance to service learning as a pedagogy for social justice, and current postmodernist, ethical, and epistemological issues related to observational research.

Carspecken, P. F., and Walford, G. (Eds.). (2001). *Critical ethnography and education.* Kidlington, UK: Elsevier Science Ltd.

Describes the University of Houston approach to critical ethnography formulated by Phil Carspecken. Following a summary of Carspecken's distinctive theory that guided their work, seven chapters describe specific research studies carried out by his graduate students. Research topics include preservice teachers' views of multicultural literature; students' and teachers' negotiations of meaning concerning norms in teaching about violence and oppression; how African American students react to standardized testing; and the power relations observed in instructional supervision, in a constructivist charter school, and in a restructured school.

Wink, J. (2004). *Critical pedagogy: Notes from the real world* (3rd ed.). Boston: Addison-Wesley Longman.

Authored by an academic who draws heavily on her own and other teachers' K–12 teaching experiences, the book provides a clear analysis of critical research applied to teaching and other aspects of educational practice. The book explains the language of critical pedagogy and discusses the work of various scholars in the critical theory tradition. It encourages teachers to constantly rethink their assumptions and suggests many classroom activities to foster teachers' and students' empowerment. The third edition includes new chapters on learning models and parental involvement.

Sample Critical Ethnography

From Gangs to the Academy: Scholars Emerge by Reaching Back through Critical Ethnography

Gordon, J. A. (2002). From gangs to the academy: Scholars emerge by reaching back through critical ethnography. *Social Justice, 29*(4), 71–81.

How do college students whose background includes gang affiliation differ from traditional college students? The following article addresses this question.

Seven self-identified gang members were enrolled in the author's undergraduate education course on "Race, Culture, and Class." With her support and guidance, each described their gang experience in a course "fishbowl," a process of critical pedagogy from which they and other students learned a great deal. Then each gang-affiliated student carried out critical ethnographic research with other gang members they knew.

The study focuses on the problems and opportunities that the student researchers experienced from conducting their own critical ethnographic research. It offers a very different view of the research process than any other reprinted article in this book.

The article is reprinted in its entirety, just as it appeared when originally published.

From Gangs to the Academy: Scholars Emerge by Reaching Back through Critical Ethnography

June A. Gordon | Four foot eight, flashing eyes, red nails, and skimpy clothes with a cocky air, *she* exuded defiance and demanded space. She hung with the Latinos in the class, but loosely so. Primed for a fight, her curiosity got the better of her as she ventured into my office after class one day at the University of California, Santa Cruz. She wanted to know how I knew what I did about the issues being discussed in class, issues she had never heard discussed in an Education course before. She wanted to share, as I had done, something about her life. Arriving in this country at age 12 after five of her brothers had died in an apartment fire back in Mexico, she struggled to gain some respect. They had called her "killer" as she set about to prove to her peers within Los Angeles gang culture that despite, or perhaps because of, her mixed heritage (African and Mexican), she should be accepted. School had been a battlefield. She was now at university, in my class.

He was declared illiterate at age 14. Leaving home half way through middle school to save himself from his alcoholic, drug-addicted parents, he hooked up with an older cousin, living tenaciously on the edges of urban culture while working full time and trying to stay in school. According to him, "gangs were just a part of the scenery." His family belonged to gangs; he was born into it. *La familia* crossed international borders, making the profit margin a temptation even to someone who was trying to stay out of the flow. He ended up in prison, where he learned to read for the first time and received his GED. Five years later, he is at university, in my class. These are only two stories; there are many, many more.

Urban youth gang involvement as a factor in college achievement is a neglected area of educational research. Gang culture is no longer something that is left in the streets. It has permeated life in California to such a degree that a large proportion of urban youth are affected, whether by choice or by circumstances. Given the prevalence of gang affiliation among our youth, it should come as no surprise that some of these young people are not only successful high school students, but are also moving into prestigious universities and colleges.

The work reported here documents the process of students self-identifying as gang members, the author's interviews with them, and their induction into an ethnographic research project whereby they interviewed other gang members and people who had been affected by, or associated with, gangs. The purposes of the work were threefold: (1) to enable college students, who perceived themselves as marginalized due to their gang affiliation, to make the linkage between their past and present; (2) to deconstruct the assumptions around gang affiliation and the reasons for gang membership; and (3) to explore the role and image of academics in gang life. This article is *not* about the research findings based on the interviews conducted by the students, but rather about the use of ethnographic research as pedagogy for engagement and retention. In the following pages, I will explain how the project was formed, how the research was conducted, and describe the nature of the transformative process for both informants and students.

CONTEXT

While teaching an undergraduate education course, "Race, Culture, and Class," I realized that I had at least seven gang members in the class. These were the ones who owned up to it; as we came to find out, there were more who had been radically affected by gangs: losing a brother, a father, a friend, a lover. The disclosures originally came through early class writing assignments and private conversations with me. Later, more open discussions evolved in response to class readings and lectures on the larger context of urban education. Around the second week of the quarter, students had to select a research topic that interested them from a range of current issues that were found to be most pressing in urban schools. Several students, including many middle-class, non-urban educated students, chose "violence and gangs" as their topic. I found this to be an interesting comment on *perceptions* of urban schools. As the rough drafts for the paper began to come in around week five of the quarter, I realized that although middle-class white students carefully cited research, their assumptions about the causes of violence and gangs did not fit

Source: Reprinted from Gordon, J. A. (2002). From gangs to the academy: Scholars emerge by reaching back through critical ethnography. *Social Justice, 29*(4), 71–81. www.socialjusticejournal.org

with my own knowledge of gangs. More important, they did not fit with some of the stories their fellow students had written to me or spoken privately with me about their gang affiliation.

To many of the middle-class students, a gang member was someone from a low-income, "broken" home who had no supervision and a family that could care less about her or his education or future. This was not the case for at least half the students with whom I had spoken concerning their own gang experience. I felt that the best education I could provide for the class would be if the students who had spoken to me about gang affiliation could share some of their experience with their peers. Five of them agreed, and we discussed the format and possible scenarios that might evolve. On an appointed day, I announced that we would hold a "fishbowl," with five student volunteers discussing among themselves their experiences and perspectives on violence and gangs in urban schools. These students sat in the center of a very large classroom while the rest of the class (about 75 students) circled around, sitting or standing to hear. The testimonies and revelations were powerful and painful. The class response ranged from shock to disbelief. Most had never imagined the lives some of these students had lived, and, I assure you, they did not disclose the half of it.

Because of this forum, many of the observing students questioned the assumptions that most of the media and the academic literature professed. A few of those who had researched violence and gangs for their final paper wanted to start over, beginning with in-depth interviews with their peers who had just spoken. Although they did not get anywhere with this idea, I acknowledged the validity of their reasoning and decided to pursue it on a different level. For the gang-involved students, the disclosure showed them even more vividly the naiveté on the part of their peers, most of whom wanted to become urban teachers. Given the fishbowl experience, as well as the misrepresentation of gang culture in the academic literature, the gang-involved students confided privately that they felt more clearly than ever the discrepancy between their lives "back home" and their college existence. Hearing this, I invited the students who had participated in the fishbowl, or had had their lives touched by gangs, to begin the process of bridging these two worlds through research and critical dialogues in their communities.

STUDENT RESEARCHER PERSONAL ESSAYS

Before commencing the interviews with their friends, family, and associates, I asked the student researchers to write about their life experiences and what affected their decision to move toward academic success and, hence, their arrival at a major research university. Here are some examples:

Example #1:

Throughout my life, certain aspects have remained constant, such as family, school, friends, and gang-related issues.

I don't know whether to say that I've been unfortunate to have experienced the environment that fosters gang-related activity, or to see it as an enriching experience that no one will ever take away from me (I choose the later). It is fair to say that it has been very difficult to get to the university and sometimes even harder to be retained here. I'll proceed to write a little on how gangs have touched this scholar boy.

As I was growing up in the San Joaquin Valley, I can remember seeing and being around people that chose to claim a niche in society. This niche to them (as well as for myself for a portion of my life) is their *barrio*. As a kid, I was influenced by the gang bangers that live around me. Then, at about the age of 13, I chose to give in. I was an active member of the . . . , a gang in the outer limits of the city of X. At this time of my life, I was pretty heavy into the gang scene. My parents not being too aware of what I was involved in, moved further into the city of X. They now live in the north side of the city, which is the nice part of the city.

The weird thing about my experiences is that throughout the 11 months I was heavy into gangs, I still took care of business in the classroom. I didn't let my grades suffer because of my second life outside of school. Moving out of my old neighborhood was the biggest factor that helped me to see what was going on in my life. Gang activity has been the cause of many fatalities of close friends and major crossroads in my life. At this time, I choose not to talk a lot about these experiences in detail. I see it as being my past. Sometimes it is good to leave the past where it belongs, in the past. But at the same time, you should never forget who you are as a person and where you come from. I use the things that have happened to me as motivation to become a better person and to succeed in life.

Example #2:

My only exit from my world is by writing poetry. I am not going to say that gangs messed up my life because they didn't; they help me. Of course, there are things which are not right, but, hey, who is out there to help youth and guiding them the right way? Nobody. Each day the world is becoming more and more fucked up.

I hope that with this confession you don't judge me or misunderstand my point. This is the first time I write something like this so, if at any time it seems that I was trying to make it short, it was because the issues are very strong. Or, if I made it too long, it was because I'm OK talking about certain things. I'll leave you with a note: This is nothing compared to all the shit that is constantly eating my insides; one thing I have learned from all this is that I have learned to move on.

Example #3:

I want to return to something that I feel is important to share with you. What specific thing happened to me in jail that changed my life? The thing that fully kicked me in the ass was that I, for the first time, realized that I was functionally illiterate. I couldn't even read and understand a newspaper article without someone else's help. I can still remember lying in that jail cell and silently crying because I had realized for the first time in my life what I was a piece of shit, illiterate, Mexican drug dealer, convicted felon, and in jail. If I didn't do something about it soon, I would probably spend the better portion of my life there.

I don't know if I've even come close to describing how powerful of an event that was in my life, but I have done my best. My life since then has been a continual struggle to continue to move forward. Trying all the while as much as possible not to look back at where I came from, focusing more on where I am and where I'm going. I don't feel as though I relate to anyone here because of what I've lived through, let alone feeling that I belong here at U.C. But, it scares me to even think about where my life would be if I were not.

RESEARCH GROUP FORMATION AND DATA ANALYSIS

Seven students (three males and four females) agreed to the group independent research project that lasted for about one year. The average age was 21, as some had spent three to four years at community college before arriving at university. For the first two to three weeks of the project I worked intensely with the student researchers to provide them with training in basic qualitative research methods: how to identify respondents, opening up dialogue around difficult issues, confidentiality, probes, and general ethnographic protocol. At the beginning, we met every week in my office at night for two to three hours to deal with the difficulties of acquiring interviews and fostering a dialog among the student researchers themselves. It must be remembered that these students came to me as individuals, not as a group. To a large extent, they were in hiding about their past, not only due to the stereotypes that other college students might lay upon them, but also due to issues of privacy. Most were still very well connected to their communities and retained alliances, not to mention different identities, "back home." Although these students may have suspected each other's potential association with gangs before coming together as a research group, there was no verification of this or a desire for confirmation. In some cases, it was a matter of safety, in others, life and death.

Part of moving through the layers of distrust entailed negotiating a set of interview questions acceptable to all concerned. Significant time was spent discussing what was appropriate and how the questions should be, and could be, varied depending on the context, the person. After some powerful testimony that defended what would work when, they reached consensus on the following questions:

Name, age, status, occupation, city, ethnicity? Age joined? For how long? Composition: ethnicities involved? Why join? Friends: pressure/felt left out? Born into/parents gang members? Poverty/quick money? Isolation/perceived that family didn't love/support them? School: Attitude towards, drop out, views on education? Jumped in? Related activities: Steal, drugs, sex, violence? Family affected? Parents, siblings? When/why leave gang? Friend killed? How out? Jumped, walked, left city? Regrets? After gang, what?

Though they acknowledged that some of these questions were loaded and not all would be asked if the situation proved too hot or unsafe, they felt that all of the questions were important and useful in understanding the complexity of what was going on. Once the interviewing began, we met every two weeks to give them more time to conduct the interviews and to write up their impressions of what they were finding and experiencing. On each occasion, the group reviewed the content and process of the data collection, discussing the following issues:

What is emerging, new, constant? Do we need to reevaluate the probes used to access information? Should the interview questions be expanded and/or tightened up? Who else needs to be included and why?

In some cases, student researchers coded their own data; in most cases, they transcribed and translated their own tapes or field notes. The student researchers and I analyzed each interview, and we identified recurring themes. At the beginning of the transcript, the student researchers provided a brief sketch of the informant and the context of the interview. At the end of the transcribed interview, they wrote a reflection on how the experiences of the informant related to themselves and their community. Further writing reflected their responses to the process of revisiting the topic of gang affiliation, as well as doing so in an academic context. Similarly, part of their write-up for each interview related their own views on how authentic the recounting was, how they were perceived by their respondent, and how the conversation affected their own understanding of their past, present, and future.

INTERVIEWS AND STUDENT RESEARCHER REFLECTION

Example #1 (from an interview with a 19-year-old gang member):

What do you think is important or a good strategy to help the gang community?

Like the parents are just [he hesitates and needs more clarity on the educational aspect] . . . I think, um, like student-teacher relationships really work a lot; like, to me, my counselor, she was a really helpful lady. She used to check on me regularly and stuff, and make sure I was doing the things that I was doing. I have my mom and she also showed interest in what I was doing 'cause she wanted me to do something else with my life. Well, basically, the change has to with yourself; you have to have your mindset, but with the help of somebody else, with some type of family support is the best. At school, too, you know, you just got to believe in yourself and think that you are capable of doing something else besides what you are doing. And when you become educated, like I don't know, you begin to think in a different way and question a lot of things that you used to do in the past; and that is pretty helpful in a way you define your future.

Reflection of the interviewer:

This interview was interesting. I can connect to some things, but I also don't connect with others. I think it's all where you're coming from and the experiences that you carry with you. It was difficult trying to get him to talk, but it was an experience trying to explain to someone that comes from the same place that you're coming from. Here is my personal stereotype: we are all not the same and obviously, we don't think the same. We all have our different ideas because of our different experiences, but in the long run, they all connect.

Interview example #2 (begins with commentary by student researcher):

At the age of 17, little is feared. The stage of invincibility makes him feel even stronger. XX gets up every morning to iron his pants for school. Thin, fine lines make his size 46 Frisco Ben pants look sharp. The following interview was made possible through my cousin. The thing that is so unusual about him is that he manages to maintain a B average at school while living *la vida loca* (crazy life). How can this possibly be true? How does he do it and why?

What do you seek in a gang?

Power, protection, fun, excitement, partying, and meeting girls.

How do you manage to maintain a B average at school?

I balance my time between schoolwork and my homeys. I know that school is also important to me because I don't want to be in this type of shit forever.

Is this a stage that you are going through in your life?

I guess so, I mean, I can see myself down the road with some type of future besides gangs. Also, almost everyone that lives here in East L.A. is involved in a gang sometime in their life.

Are you afraid of dying?

Maybe at the moment I am not, but when it comes down to the 187, I might not be that hard.

What is of greater importance, your education or your barrio?

At the moment, both are equal priorities to me: keeping my grades up and showing love for the hood, that's what it's all about. With time, I know that I have to value my education more than anything, or else I won't get any place in life.

Do your parents care that you are involved?

They have talked to me about it in the past, but what can they do? The way I see things is if I keep up my grades, my parents won't give me any trouble with my social life.

Reflection on the interview:

My cousin is now in his last semester of school. He has high aspirations of going to college after he graduates. XX is a very smart and capable student that chose to follow a gang during this stage in his life. Both school and his barrio play an important part in his life; it was very interesting to me to see this unusual case. I can relate to my cousin in many ways. I have been there and done that. Making time for both school and your barrio is not an easy thing to maintain. You have to watch your grades, but most important of all, your back. I believe that my cousin will get ahead in life as he becomes educated further. Knowledge will open his eyes to the reality of the world. At the moment, he is considering U.C. Irvine, Santa Cruz, Riverside; he hopes to be an anthropologist one day.

Example #3 (reflection by a student researcher on an interview):

These were the questions I asked my brother. I quickly learned things about him that I never before knew. Being part of his family, I knew for a fact that he received all the attention and love from my parents. So why did he decide to join a gang? I agree that in most cases joining a gang is just a fact of life. On the other hand, my brother led me to believe that even though one has the love and support of family members, this did not affect his decision about joining. This interview goes to show how gang activity is purely based on the drug trade market. I believe that it is not about defending one's communities from outsiders, but rather gangs are seen as an opportunity to attain identity, respect, money, girls, and most important of all, power.

Over the course of almost a year, the seven student researchers conducted 57 interviews with individuals on how gang involvement interacts with academic achievement before and during college. Much of the work was translated from Spanish, and some of it remains in Spanglish. Research sites included Los Angeles, Sacramento, Salinas, Watsonsville, San Jose, and Santa Cruz.

DISCUSSION

One of the most salient forces undermining higher education is disengagement (Astin, 1993). Students leave college for a variety of reasons, but often due to an inability to find a connection between their personal lives before college and the work that is required for success in higher education. This is particularly true for students of color and working-class students who do not see the relevance of a detached liberal arts education to the demands of their lives "back home" (Duster, 1991; Gordon, 1997). For many of these students, their past life was just that—passed, hidden, and disconnected from their current pursuits. This disjunction can cause resentment, friction, and distancing from the very environment they need to engage to succeed. For first-generation college students, the situation is compounded in a variety of ways.

Separation from family: First, there is the separation of self from family. Although part of growing up involves creating a unique identity, when that development takes place in isolation from the family context, the new identity can be perceived as determined by outside influences. The inability and the inappropriateness of sharing the realities of college life with one's family and friends often inhibit fluid communication and create distance. Intellectual growth at school can create emotional tension at home. For working-class kids, one might even ask if it is possible to really "go home" once you have gone away to university.

Separation from other students: Second, first-generation students experience separation of self from other students. Isolation kicks in when working-class students on prestigious university campuses believe that they are alone in dealing with this schizophrenic existence. As a result, they resist sharing with peers, faculty, or staff members what is happening to them. They hesitate to talk about their past, their family, their trials, or their lives "back home."

Masking of self: Third, masking of self becomes a necessary survival skill. Political rhetoric and bravado at times are used to mask the confusion, loneliness, and academic gaps of many working-class students who lack the social or academic preparation to enable them to move securely in this new environment. Maintaining a facade and performing acceptably for peers and family at home and at school drains energy that could be used for academic achievement.

Hesitancy to ask for assistance: Fourth, because of separation, isolation, and masking, first-generation students do not ask for assistance (Fullilove and Treisman, 1990). Working-class kids are taught self-reliance and they fear exposure of weaknesses, particularly if accepted to an elite university and/or are the first to leave their community. Unaware of differences in cultural capital and the ways in which educational background privileges some students over others, they would rather "go it alone" than collaborate with those they assume to be different from them. They carry the burden of family pride mixed with fear of failure. In reality, they know that their success in the context of their community is dubious in comparison to their middle- and upper-middle-class college peers. Revealing inadequacies would jeopardize their status. They cannot go back, but experience a paralysis that prevents them from moving forward as they search for the skills and knowledge to negotiate the system.

School knowledge can be empowering for subordinate groups, as long as it respects, and even draws upon, the cultural resources of those groups. Similarly, retention data on first-generation college students, particularly if they are students of color, demonstrate that students who connect with a faculty member through research that is perceived to be beneficial to both sides tend to achieve academically and graduate at a higher rate (Astin, 1993). Following the insights of Claude Steele (Hummel and Steele, 1996), I have found that engaging students in authentic research and inquiry brings about their own best efforts and eventual success.

The integration of research, teaching, and service, as well as bringing research to bear on the needs of the community, especially the need to understand, is not new. The sources for this approach include the many strands of critical pedagogy that seek to involve the student as an active participant in the learning process through cultural awareness and community service, as developed by Freire (1970), Horton and Freire (1990), and Shor (1980). Learning that provides opportunities for active involvement in research in schools and communities to enhance the professional development of educators has been a part of Becker's (1998) work over the years. This is clearly articulated in articles on critical ethnography (Carspecken, 1996), an approach that combines attention to the demands of social justice within the study of marginalized communities.

CONCLUSION

The integration of research and pedagogy was designed to reconnect marginalized youth who had been unable to link their past affiliation with gang culture to their current collegial life; it also gives them an opportunity to see themselves as experts in a contentious area of study. The collaborative project connected students who were struggling with similar issues in isolation with an instructor specializing in comparative urban education, as well as with individuals in urban communities who were aware of the choices these students had made.

Because of the work, these students were able to integrate the many phases of their lives and come out of "hiding." They realized that their expertise and knowledge are important and valued, especially as they inform educators working with youth and add to a greater understanding of culture. The training in ethnographic research enabled them to perceive themselves for the first time as potential scholars, rather than as marginalized college students, thereby increasing their retention and providing them with direction and confidence toward careers in public school teaching, counseling, and related professions. All seven student researchers have gone on to graduate school. In short, I found that returning students to their communities as researchers provided a form of critical engagement that reached multiple goals.

The results from the research process provide a basis for interpretations both of college experience for former youth gang members and of educational perceptions and aspirations among a sample of college-age participants in urban gangs. This form of research offers one example of how critical ethnography can add significantly to teacher preparation in a diverse undergraduate cohort. The process illustrates how ethnographic research pedagogy creates opportunities for increased awareness of students' multiple identities as we teach them to simultaneously interrogate privileged assumptions of the Other. Clearly, without an understanding of the complexity of the lives of youth, educators blindly create ineffective programs or place students in categories labeled "at-risk." A shift in the political landscape of higher education is essential as educators ask about and listen to the experience of those they serve.

References

Astin, Alexander W. 1993 *What Matters in College: Four Critical Years Revisited.* San Francisco: Jossey-Bass.

Becker, Howard S. 1998 *Tricks of the Trade: How to Think about Your Research While You're Doing It.* Chicago: University of Chicago Press.

Carspecken, Phil F. 1996 *Critical Ethnography in Educational Research.* New York and London: Routledge.

Duster, Troy 1991 *The Diversity Project: Final Report.* Berkeley, CA: University of California.

Freire, Paulo 1970 *Pedagogy of the Oppressed.* New York: Continuum.

Freire, Paulo and Donaldo P. Macedo 1995 "A Dialogue: Culture, Language, and Race." *Harvard Educational Review 65,* 3: 377–402.

Fullilove, Robert E. and Phillip Uri Treisman 1990 "Mathematics Achievement Among African American Undergraduates at the University of California, Berkeley: An Evaluation of the Mathematics Workshop Program." *Journal of Negro Education 59,3:* 463–478.

Gordon, June A. 1997 "A Critical Interpretation of Policies for Minority Culture College Students." *NA CA DA Journal 17,1:* 15–21.

Horton, Myles and Paolo Freire 1990 *We Make the Road by Walking: Conversations on Education and Social Change.* Philadelphia: Temple University Press.

Hummel, M. and Claude Steele 1996 "The Learning Community: A Program to Address Issues of Academic Achievement and Retention." *Journal of Intergroup Relations 23,2:* 28–32.

Shor, Ira 1980 "The Working Class Goes to College." Ira Shor (ed.), *Critical Teaching in Everyday Life.* Boston: South End Press: 1–44.

About the Author

June A. Gordon, Ph.D., is Assistant Professor of Education at Crown College, University of California, Santa Cruz, CA 95064 (e-mail: jagordon@cats.ucsc.edu). Her teaching includes courses in the sociology of education, with an emphasis on international and comparative urban education. Her research focuses on the attitudes of teachers from different cultures toward their profession and how this affects the access and success of marginalized youth in England, Japan, and the U.S. Her publications include The Color of Teaching *(RoutledgeFalmer, 2000)* and Beyond the Classroom Walls: Ethnographic Inquiry as Pedagogy *(Routledge Falmer, 2002).*

chapter 17

Historical Research

IMPORTANT *Ideas*

1. Historical research relies primarily on qualitative approaches to data collection and analysis.

2. Historical research is relevant to educators in several ways: as content for school curriculum, as a basis for understanding current practices and policies, and as a resource for planning the improvement of education.

3. Historians find data about the past by consulting search engines and bibliographic indexes to find secondary and primary sources and by collecting oral histories.

4. The past is preserved in the form of documents, records, photos and other visual media, stories that are continually retold within a society's oral traditions, relics, and other quantitative materials such as census data and statistical summaries.

5. The validity of historical data is established through a process of external criticism as well as internal criticism.

6. Historians continually reconstruct the past as their interests and questions change.

7. Historians use key concepts and causal inference to interpret their data about the past.

8. As in other forms of research, historians need to take care in generalizing their findings beyond the persons and settings that they have directly studied.

9. The study of quantitative data can strengthen the generalizability of historical interpretations and provide a common-man perspective on the time period being studied.

10. Unlike other types of research reports, historical reports usually present findings in the form of a story, organized around key time periods that have thematic significance for the historian.

11. Reports of historical studies generally have many notes, with each note referring to a primary or secondary source that supports a particular finding or claim. ■

Key TERMS

archive	historical research	reconstructionist
bias	internal criticism	record
concept	oral history	relic
document	presentism	repository
external criticism	primary source	revisionist historian
forgery	quantitative historical materials	search engine
futurology	quantitative history	secondary source

The Nature of Historical Research

Nearly everyone reads histories—histories of countries, of wars, of organizations, or of people in biographies and autobiographies. They watch histories on TV such as the Civil War series by Ken Burns. Many movies also base their drama on events of historical significance—*Titanic, The Queen,* and *United 93* come to mind.

In this chapter, we examine the research process used to produce a history. **Historical research** is the process of systematically searching for and organizing data to better understand past phenomena and their likely causes and consequences.

Contemporary historians tend to dismiss most historical literature of bygone eras as mere chronicles of events and lives. Their own writings generally are shorter, subordinating historical facts to an interpretive framework within which those facts are given meaning and significance. In this chapter we treat historical research as a qualitative research tradition because of its reliance on, although not exclusive use of, qualitative approaches to data collection and analysis.

The types of research that we describe in other chapters of this book involve the creation of data. For example, researchers create data when they make observations or administer tests to determine the effectiveness of an instructional program. In contrast, historical researchers primarily discover data that already exist in such sources as diaries, official documents, and relics. On occasion, though, historical researchers interview individuals to obtain their recollections of past events. This form of historical research, called *oral history,* does involve data creation.

The Role of Historical Research in Education

Many journal articles and books about the history of education are published each year. The following list illustrates the range of possible topics.

Berube, M. R. (2004). *Radical reformers: The influence of the left in American education.* Greenwich, CT: Information Age Publishing.

Campbell, C., & Sherrington, G. (2006). *The comprehensive public high school: Historical perspectives.* New York: Palgrave Macmillan.

Erickson, C. K. (2006). "We want no teachers who say there are two sides to every question": Conservative women and education in the 1930s. *History of Education Quarterly, 46*(4), 487–502.

Johnson, W. G. (2008). "Making learning easy and enjoyable": Anna Verona Dorris and the visual instruction movement, 1918–1928. *Linking Research and Practice to Improve Learning, 52*(4), 51–58.

Kohlstedt, S. G. (2008). "A better crop of boys and girls": The school gardening movement, 1890–1920. *History of Education Quarterly, 48*(1), 58–93.

Why would anyone wish to study these past events when there are so many current problems in education to be solved? One answer to this question is the truism, "Those who ignore the lessons of the past are doomed to repeat them."

Another answer is that studying the past helps us understand why things are the way they are today. Powerful forces have shaped our current education system, and they continue to keep it in place. For example, two of the historical studies cited above concern the influence of conservative groups and radical reformers on educational practice. An understanding of those forces might help us to understand, for example, whether current educational reforms will take hold, be modified, or disappear.

Some historical studies trace the growth of an educational practice and identify key figures in that growth. The study of Anna Verona Dorris cited above serves that purpose. The researcher identifies her seminal contribution to what we now know as instructional technology. As professionals, we need real-life heroes to inspire us and demonstrate that improvement of educational practice actually can happen.

Before reading the history of the school gardening movement cited above, we did not realize that there once was such a movement. This historical study is interesting in its own right, but it also serves another purpose. It provokes educators to think about the implications of the school gardening movement for present-day schooling, nearly a century after it came and went. For example, the study suggests how the school curriculum might play a role in addressing current concerns about the health of the natural environment.

In short, historical research gives us a way to engage in a continuing dialogue with the past. What we know about past events changes as we ask new questions. What we learn about the past gives us new ways of thinking about the present and stimulates our thinking on improving the practice of education.

Revisionist History

Some historical researchers, generally called **revisionist historians** or **reconstructionists,** carry out research to point out aspects of a phenomenon that they believe were missed or distorted in previous historical accounts. Their larger goal is to sensitize educators to past practices that appear to have had unjust aims and effects but have continued into the present and thus require reform. For example, a study of educational innovation in mid-nineteenth-century Massachusetts demonstrated how it functioned to serve dominant economic interests and thwart many people's democratic aspirations (Katz, 1968).

As another example, a study of schooling in the Southwest in the first half of the twentieth century found a widespread practice of separate schooling for Mexican American children (Gonzalez, 1990). Gonzalez concluded that this practice was encouraged by the economic interests of white communities in this part of the United States. These studies alert educators to the possibility of similar problems with current educational practices and innovations so that they can be avoided or corrected.

There is debate about whether and how educational historians should raise findings such as these in the arena of educational policy making. Some historians believe that they should influence policy making directly, whereas others believe that historians might corrupt the integrity of their discipline by becoming too closely involved with the policy-making process. Donato and Lazerson (2000) reviewed these differing views and made their own recommendation:

[E]ducational policies are proposed and implemented in the context of historical moments. Invariably, the policies rest on assumptions about the past; they rest on the stories people believe about the past. Educational historians have an obligation to thrust their stories into the policy arena for if they do not, the stories that become the common view will be told by others who often have little stake in the integrity of historical scholarship. Or, even worse, their stories will go unnoticed altogether. (p. 10)

Another viewpoint, which we espouse, is that educators and policy makers should search for all relevant evidence, including revisionist histories, when thinking about how to best solve a problem of practice.

Futurology

A type of research called **futurology** specifically examines what the future is likely to be. Some futurology studies are based on surveys of current trends, while others use simulation and gaming involving various imagined future scenarios. The predictions are based largely on statistical logic or rational reasoning derived from the study of past events.

Another purpose of historical research, then, is to assist educators in defining and evaluating alternative future scenarios involving a particular educational phenomenon. If we know how certain individuals or groups have acted in the past, we can predict with a certain degree of confidence how they will act in the future. For example, we can make a good prediction of how specific legislators will vote on an upcoming education bill by doing research on their past voting records.

Methods of Historical Research

In the next sections of this chapter, we describe the process of historical research as a series of steps: (1) identifying historical sources, (2) validating historical evidence, and (3) interpreting historical data. Keep in mind, though, that many researchers skip back and forth among these steps. For example, consider the research process used by one historian (Carr, 1967):

> For myself, as soon as I have got going on a few of what I take to be the capital sources, the itch becomes too strong and I begin to write—not necessarily at the beginning, but somewhere, anywhere. Thereafter, reading and writing go on simultaneously. The writing is added to, subtracted from, re-shaped, cancelled, as I go on reading. The reading is guided and directed and made fruitful by the writing: the more I write, the more I know what I am looking for, the better I understand the significance and relevance of what I find. (pp. 32–33)

Carr's process might remind you of processes found in case study research (see Chapter 14). There is an initial research plan, but as data are collected and analyzed, new research questions can be framed, new research participants can be added, and new sources of data can be identified.

Identifying Historical Sources

As we have explained, historians primarily seek to discover rather than create data that are relevant to their research problem. Those data are available in various sources, which historians identify by reflecting on the types of sources likely to exist, which individuals or institutions are likely to have produced them, and where they are likely to be stored. These reflections are the basis for an initial search plan. As their interpretive framework develops, or as their sources point them toward new sources, historians can revise their tentative search plan.

Historians generally use the types of sources that we describe in Chapter 3—search engines and bibliographic indexes to find secondary and primary sources.

Search Engines and Bibliographic Indexes

A literature search for historical research studies usually begins with the use of a search engine. You will recall from Chapter 4 that a **search engine** is software that enables you to search through a database of publications to identify those relevant to your research topic. Hard-copy bibliographic indexes also are preliminary sources that can be used for this purpose.

Many of the general search engines and bibliographic indexes that we describe in Chapter 4 are useful for doing a search of historical literature. In addition, you might want to make use of search engines and bibliographic indexes to identify researchers who have conducted historical studies in your area of interest. Figure 17.1 lists search engines and bibliographic indexes that you might find particularly useful.

FIGURE *17.1*   Search Engines and Hard-Copy Indexes for Historical Research

---

America: History and Life
   A search engine for identifying journal articles about U.S. and Canadian history from prehistory to the present. Santa Barbara: ABC-CLIO.

Biography and genealogy master index www.gale.com
   A hard-copy index to biographical sketches of several million contemporary and historical figures from around the world. Updated annually.

Biography Reference Bank www.hwwilson.com/Databases/biobank.htm
   A search engine for identifying biographical information, photos, and articles about more than 550,000 individuals.

Directory of genealogical and historical libraries, archives and collections in the US and Canada. (2002). Boulder, CO: Iron Gate.
   A hard-copy index of over 14,000 collections of genealogical and historical materials located in libraries, genealogical societies, and museums.

Fritze, R. H., Coutts, B. E., & Vyhnanek, L. A. (2003). *Reference sources in history: An introductory guide* (2nd ed.). Santa Barbara, CA: ABC-CLIO.
   A comprehensive guide to reference books in the field of history.

Historical Statistics of the United States hsus@cambridge.org
   A source of quantitative data relating to American history. The data are organized into five categories: population, work and welfare, economic structure and performance, economic sectors, and governance and international relations. Available in electronic and hard-copy formats.

National Union Catalog of Manuscript Collections www.loc.gov/coll/nucmc/nucmc .html
   A search engine for identifying historical documents and archives of national interest.

United States Newspaper Program www.neh.gov/projects/usnp.html
   A microfilm collection of newspapers published in the United States from the eighteenth century to the present. The program also maintains an electronic database of newspapers.

Secondary Sources

A **secondary source** in historical research is a document or other record, such as a video file, in which the author describes events not from direct witness but instead from descriptions of events generated by other individuals who witnessed or participated in them. Many newspaper articles and TV news broadcasts are secondary sources, because the reporters relied on interviews with eyewitnesses to obtain the information. Annual reports of educational programs and school operations also are secondary sources if they are prepared by individuals who relied on data collected from other individuals, such as school administrators and teachers.

Most historians read a substantial number of secondary sources early in the research process in order to clarify their research problem and determine the types of primary sources that are relevant. Sometimes they decide to just accept the information given in a secondary source about a relevant primary source rather than tracking down the primary source itself. In other cases, historians might decide they need to examine the primary source directly. In making this decision, they consider the reputation of the author of the secondary source, the degree of compatibility between that author's interpretive framework and their own, and the feasibility of gaining access to the primary source.

Primary Sources

A **primary source** in historical research is any source of information (e.g., a diary, a song, a map, a set of test scores, or objects) preserved from the past or created to document a past phenomenon by someone who witnessed or participated in it. Historians rely on four main types of primary sources: (1) text and other media, (2) oral history, (3) relics, and (4) quantitative materials. We describe each of these types of primary sources in the following sections.

Text and Other Media.   Text materials, whether written or printed, are the most common primary source for historical research. Lincoln and Guba (1985) classify such materials as either a **document,** which is prepared for personal use only (e.g., a letter to a friend or a private diary), or a **record,** which has an official purpose (e.g., a legal contract, a will, or a newspaper article). Documents and records might contain handwritten, typed, or computer-generated text. They might be published or unpublished, representing various genres (e.g., newspaper articles, poetry, or novels).

The text materials examined by historians might include materials intentionally written to serve as a record of the past, such as a memoir or a school yearbook. Other text materials might be prepared only to serve an immediate purpose (e.g., school memos or teacher-prepared tests), with no expectation of any later use as a historical source.

Increasingly, visual media are used to store and communicate information—for example, TV, film, CDs, DVDs, digital photos, and Web-based streaming videos. Grosvenor and Lawn (2001) claim that these media can yield important evidence about historical events and practices in education.

Oral History.   Many cultures use ballads, tales, and other forms of spoken language to preserve a record of past events for posterity. Historical researchers can make recordings of these oral accounts and use them as primary sources. Another possibility is to conduct interviews of individuals who witnessed or participated in events of potential historical significance, recording and transcribing the interviews to produce a written record. The use of existing oral accounts of the past, or the collection of these oral accounts, constitutes what is commonly called **oral history.**

An example of oral history is *Missing Stories,* a book by Kelen and Stone (1996). These researchers studied eight cultural communities in the state of Utah. They conducted lengthy interviews with 352 individuals, taped the interviews, and transcribed them. The book presents the stories of 88 of the individuals, who share recollections of their past as it relates to the community that each represents.

For example, the epilogue to the chapter on the Chicano-Hispano community is the story of a Chicano woman who is an assistant principal of an intermediate school. She describes her father's struggle to obtain an education and become a teacher and how she as an educator continues his commitment to "reject rejection," despite living in an environment still tempered with racial stereotypes.

Relics.   A **relic** is any object that provides information about the past. School supplies, computers, a blueprint of a school building, textbooks, worksheets, and instructional games are examples of relics that researchers could examine for information about past educational practices. Sheumaker and Wajda (2007) have compiled an encyclopedia of such objects, as well as other aspects of material culture, that reveal glimpses of past periods in the United States.

Quantitative Historical Materials.   **Quantitative historical materials,** which provide numerical information about educational phenomena, are another important primary source. Like documents and records, they are recorded and preserved in some print form or as computer files. Census records, school budgets, school attendance records, teachers' grade sheets, test scores, and other compilations of numerical data can provide useful data for historians. Later in the chapter, we discuss the interpretive uses of quantitative materials in historical research.

Archives.   Primary sources such as diaries, manuscripts, or school records, and relics such as old photographs or classroom paraphernalia might be found in regional museums or archives. **Archives,** also known as **repositories,** are special locations for storing primary sources, particularly very old or rare primary sources, in order to preserve them in good condition and control access to them.

Historians often must follow particular procedures to gain access to a primary source, such as making a written request to an archive for permission to study the records. They might be asked to indicate the length of time they will need the records, how they will record information, and perhaps even the use to which they plan to put the information.

Validating Historical Evidence

Educators who wish to apply the findings of historical research need assurance that the historical sources on which historians have based their interpretations are valid. Otherwise, their views of present practices will be distorted by incorrect accounts of past events. The disturbances in contemporary society created by Holocaust denial stories, presumably based on "sound" historical evidence, provide a cautionary tale about the need for strong validation procedures in historical research. Historical sources are valid to the extent that they are authentic and contain accurate information. In the following sections, we describe procedures for validating historical sources against these criteria.

Procedures for Determining the Authenticity of Historical Sources

Determining the authenticity of primary sources in historical research is called **external criticism.** The process of external criticism is concerned not with the content of the primary source but with whether the apparent or claimed origin of the source corresponds to its actual origin. The term *origin* refers to such matters as author, place of origin, date of publication, and publisher or sponsoring institution, all of which are usually found in the citation for a primary source.

Citation data may seem clear and concrete, but there may be further problems with it. While the author of a primary source usually is listed in the source itself, this indicator may not be reliable. Some primary sources, such as recorded speeches, are ghostwritten by someone other than the individual identified as the author. In other cases, authors use pseudonyms to conceal identity. If a primary source lists multiple authors, it might be impossible to determine who wrote the parts relevant to a historical research problem. Still another issue relating to authorship is the possibility of **forgery,** a fabrication claiming to be genuine—for example, a diary written by someone other than the person listed as the author whose experiences are described.

The place of origin of a primary source often is apparent from where it is stored, or from indications in the source itself. The date of origin might be more difficult to ascertain. If no date is given, it might be possible to infer the date from references in the primary source or from its sequential location in a file cabinet. Dates on primary sources should be viewed critically, because people sometimes make errors. For example, at the start of a new year it is not uncommon for someone to make the mistake of recording the previous year.

To determine the authenticity of a primary source, historians generate and test alternative hypotheses about each aspect of its reputed origin. For example, they might hypothesize that a subordinate in an organization wrote a particular primary source rather than the person designated as the author. If they collect information showing that this and other alternative hypotheses are untenable, they increase the probability, although never to the point of absolute certainty, that the source is genuine. Any doubts that a historian has about the authenticity of a source should be noted in the research report.

Procedures for Determining the Accuracy of Historical Sources

The process of determining the accuracy of information in a primary historical source is called **internal criticism.** In doing internal criticism, researchers ask questions about the material. Is it likely that people would act in the way that the writer described? Is it physically possible for the events described to have occurred this close together in time? Do the budget figures mentioned by the author seem reasonable?

A researcher's sense that an event or situation described in a historical source is improbable might not be a sufficient basis for discounting the source. Most people can recall highly improbable events that have actually occurred during their lifetime.

Internal criticism requires researchers to judge both the reasonableness of the statements in a historical source and the trustworthiness of the person who made the statements. Criteria used to judge the trustworthiness of a source's author include (1) the author's presence or absence during the events being described, (2) whether she was a participant in or an observer of the events, (3) her qualifications to describe such events accurately, (4) her level of emotional involvement in the situation, and (5) whether she might have a vested interest in the outcomes of the event.

Even competent and truthful witnesses often give different versions of events. When researchers discover widely differing accounts of an event, they need not conclude that all are equally true or false. As Carr (1967) notes, "It does not follow that, because a mountain appears to take on different shapes from different angles of vision, it has objectively either no shape at all or an infinity of shapes" (pp. 30–31). Carr argues that the historian's task is to combine one or more witnesses' accounts, admittedly subjective, and to interpret them (also a subjective process) in an attempt to discover what actually happened.

Accounts of historical events need to be checked carefully for **bias,** a set way to perceive events such that certain types of facts are habitually overlooked, distorted, or falsified. Individuals with strong motives for wanting a particular version of a described event to be regarded as "the truth" are likely to produce biased information. Historians examine such factors as ethnic background, political party, religious affiliation, and social status of those whose views are conveyed in a historical source, in an effort to appraise the likelihood of bias. They also examine use of emotionally charged or intemperate language, which can reflect commitment to a particular position on an issue.

If researchers discover a difference between someone's public and private statements, the discrepancy does not necessarily mean that the public statements have no value as historical evidence. Rather, the discrepancy itself is evidence about the person making the statement and about the social environment in which the person functioned.

Interpreting Historical Data

In explaining internal criticism, we noted that witnesses to an event report different impressions based on their competence, personal position, and relationship to the event. Historical researchers are in a similar position. Historians will write different histories about the past depending on the evidence that they have chosen to collect and how they have interpreted it.

Because history inevitably involves interpretation, historical researchers continually reconstruct the past as their interests and questions change. For example, revisionist historians have become prominent voices in education in recent decades. As we explained earlier in the chapter, these researchers take a different view of educational history than the conventional or popular view.

Historical researchers need to be especially careful to avoid a type of interpretive bias. **Presentism** is the interpretation of past events based on concepts and perspectives from more recent times. Historical researchers need to discover how various concepts were used in the time period and setting that they are investigating, rather than attach present meanings to them. For example, the concept of *school principal* has changed over time, as you will find in the journal article reprinted at the end of this chapter.

Causal Inference in Historical Research

An essential task of historical research consists of investigating the causes of past events, as in the following examples of causal questions. What events gave rise to the intelligence testing movement? Why did U.S. educators so readily adopt the British open-classroom approach several decades ago? How did the role of school principals originate in this country?

Causal inference in historical research is an interpretive process that results in a conclusion that one set of events brought about, directly or indirectly, a subsequent set of events. Historians cannot demonstrate through direct observation that one past event caused another, but they can make explicit the assumptions that underlie their causal inferences.

Some historians make the assumption that humans act similarly across cultures and time. Thus, they might use a currently accepted causal pattern to explain an apparently similar pattern in the past. For example, a researcher might find an instance in nineteenth-century U.S. education when students at a particular college stopped attending classes and began making public protests against college administrators. Suppose that the researcher also discovered that this event was preceded by administrative rulings at the college that diminished students' rights and privileges. He might infer that these rulings led to the student revolt, using as his rationale that a similar chain of events precipitated student protests in many U.S. colleges during the 1960s.

Other historians generally believe, however, that historical events are unique, and therefore history does not repeat itself. In this view, occurrences at one point in time can illuminate, but do not explain, occurrences at another point in time. Also, historians who see past occurrences as harbingers of later events must be wary of presentism, which we described above as the use of concepts that now have different meanings to interpret events from an earlier time period.

Historians invoke various types of causes in their attempts to explain past events. They might attribute past educational occurrences to the actions of certain key persons, to the operation of powerful ideologies, to advances in science and technology, or to economic, geographical, sociological, or psychological factors.

Some historians take an eclectic view and explain past events in terms of a combination of factors. For example, Tyack (1976) studied the rise of compulsory education in the United States. He explained that until about 1890, Americans built a broad base of elementary schooling that attracted ever-growing numbers of children. During that period most states passed compulsory attendance legislation but did little to enforce those laws. Tyack calls this phase the *symbolic* stage of compulsory schooling.

Tyack concluded that a second stage, which he calls the *bureaucratic* stage, began in the United States shortly before the turn of the twentieth century. He notes that during this era

> school systems grew in size and complexity, new techniques of bureaucratic control emerged, ideological conflict over compulsion diminished, strong laws were passed, and school offi-cials developed sophisticated techniques to bring truants into schools. By the 1920s and 1930s increasing numbers of states were requiring youth to attend high school, and by the 1950s secondary school attendance had become so customary that school-leavers were routinely seen as dropouts. (1976, p. 60)

The question arises—why did schooling in the United States gradually become com-pulsory under force of law? Tyack examined five causal interpretations to see how well each answered this question. For example, the ethnocultural interpretation argues that compul-sory education came about because of the belief that it would inculcate a single "correct" standard of behavior. This interpretation is based in part on a recognition of efforts then be-ing made to address challenges to the U.S. economy and culture resulting from the influx of immigrants from southern and eastern Europe. This influx provoked considerable concern among some of the religious and ethnic groups already established in this country.

Another interpretation, drawn from the economic theory of human capital, states that compulsory schooling grew out of a belief that education would improve the productivity and manageability of the workforce.

Each of Tyack's interpretations of the main reason for the growing strength of compul-sory schooling in the United States explains some historical evidence, leaves other evidence unexplained, and suggests new lines of research. Tyack notes that such alternative interpre-tations help historians "to gain a more complex and accurate perception of the past and a greater awareness of the ambiguous relationship between outcome and intent—both of the actors in history and of the historians who attempt to recreate their lives" (1976, p. 89).

The more historians learn about the antecedents of a historical event, the more likely they are to discover possible alternative causes of the event. Therefore, it probably is more defensible to identify an earlier event as *a* cause, rather than *the* cause, of a later event. Moreover, by their choice of language in the research report, historians can convey their interpretation of the strength of the causal link (e.g., "It was a major influence . . ." or "It was one of many events that influenced . . .") and of its certainty (e.g., "It is highly likely that . . ." or "It is possible that . . .").

Generalizing from Historical Evidence

Like other qualitative researchers, historical researchers do not seek to study all the indi-viduals, settings, events, or objects that interest them. Instead, they usually study only one or several cases. The case that is chosen is determined partly by the availability of sources. For example, suppose that a historian wished to examine the diaries, correspondence, and other written records of elementary school teachers in the 1800s in order to understand teaching conditions during that time. The study necessarily would be limited to teachers whose writings had been preserved and to which the researcher could gain access.

Before generalizing the study's findings to other teachers of the period, the researcher should consider whether other teachers would have provided similar data. One way to determine whether similar results would be found for other types of teachers would be to examine how teachers in different circumstances viewed their teaching experience. For example, the researcher might ask whether teachers who wrote about their work for pub-lication described similar conditions as did teachers who wrote about their work in private diaries and correspondence.

Another potential problem in historical interpretation involves the generalizability of historical data relating to a single individual. For example, a historian might discover a primary source in which an educator stated an opinion about a particular educational issue. The statement does not prove that this educator held the same opinion at a later or earlier time. The researcher must look for more data that will help establish whether the expressed opinion was characteristic of this educator.

Using Quantitative Materials in Historical Research

One reason for the growing use of quantitative materials in historical research is that conclusions based on large amounts of carefully selected quantitative data probably are more generalizable than conclusions based on case studies. Another benefit of quantitative materials is that they allow researchers to characterize the historical views and experiences of many people, which sometimes is referred to as the "common-man approach" to historical research. In contrast, older historical studies tend to focus on a few prominent individuals.

Button (1979) referred to the common-man approach as "history from the bottom up—grassroots history" (p. 4). Because historical records typically give minimal attention to grassroots perspectives, Button argues that historians must mine every source to reflect those perspectives:

> For instance, for a quantitative study of Buxton, a black antebellum haven in Ontario, it is necessary to assemble data from perhaps fifteen thousand entries in the census manuscripts of 1861, 1871, and 1881; from town auditors' accounts, and church records. . . . The research necessity for compilation and statistical treatment, by unfortunate paradox, produces history almost without personalities, even without names. Still, this new history has and will produce new understandings and will counterweight our long-standing concern for "the better sort." (p. 4)

Studies of this type are called **quantitative histories,** because they make use of an electronic database containing numerical data that typically are analyzed using a computer and statistical techniques.

Features of a Historical Research Report

Reports of historical research differ from other research reports. One of the main differences is that many of them are published as books rather than as journal articles. The reason for book publication is that historians often tell stories that have a broad sweep.

For example, biographies of educators might encompass their entire lives. Certain phases of an educator's life, especially during the professional career, might require separate chapters. In describing critical life phases, the historian needs to make sense of the educator's actions and contributions by setting them in relevant contexts—political, economic, cultural, among others—both at the local and broader levels.

Historical research studies that are published in journals do not follow the same format as quantitative studies and most qualitative studies. Instead, most of the article is a story: a chronology of events, the characters involved in them, the settings, and the larger forces in society that influenced the actions and thoughts of the characters. The researcher's interpretations are interwoven throughout the story.

The reprinted article at the end of this chapter, which concerns the history of the school principalship in the United States, illustrates this form of reporting. First we will analyze another historical account. Our purpose is to note certain features that you are likely to find in educational histories.

Statement of Purpose

Tracy Steffes (2008) conducted a historical study of rural schools from 1900 to 1933. Although more than a century has passed since the start of that period, her study of rural schools' problems and the solutions tried is quite relevant to current educational problems. The main problem of rural schools then was that they had vastly fewer resources compared to urban schools, an inequality still experienced in today's poor school districts.

As in some other historical reports, Steffes stated her purpose as a thesis, that is, as a proposition that she set forth and supported through evidence and argument:

> The Rural School Problem, this article argues, helped to stimulate and legitimate significant new interventions into local schools and define the forms of state aid, regulation, and bureaucracy in a formative period of state development. (p. 181)

In other words, Steffes proposed to demonstrate that a particular problem of practice led to the development of state departments of education and their particular ways of relating to local school systems. Most of the article provides historical evidence and interpretations to support this thesis.

Historical Chronology

Many reports of historical studies are organized chronologically. This is true of the rural school study, which covers 1900 to 1933. Steffes (2008) organized her report into four main sections, each having its own thematic label, as shown in the following list, with a summary of the significant events that each thematic label encompasses:

- *Definition of the Rural School Problem.* A rural school system at the turn of the twentieth century usually consisted of a single one-room school. Gradually, people realized that these schools were lagging behind the sophisticated urban schools that were expanding as a result of industrialization. Educators and public leaders perceived that the gap between rural and urban schools might threaten the nation's economy and social fabric.

- *The Failure of Local School Reform to Solve the Rural School Problem.* Reform efforts to improve local rural schools met with limited success. These efforts, occurring in the 1910s and 1920s, included raising local taxes to increase support and consolidating schools by closing down several small sites and building a larger, modern facility. Another effort involved replacing local school district control with county-level governance, which included a county board of education, a county superintendent and staff, and county taxation to fund schools. It became apparent that county governance worked to an extent but that the rural populace wanted to retain as much local control as possible.

- *Equalizing Opportunity in the Countryside: State Aid and Standards.* World War I revealed that draftees had high rates of illiteracy and physical unfitness. Public concern about this problem put pressure on states to take action. They needed to find a way to ensure that all schools, including rural schools, provided sound education. One of the main solutions was for states to provide financial aid to local school systems to support such reforms as consolidation of schools. In the 1910s and 1920s, states increasingly had tied financial aid to required adherence to state-defined standards. This solution had the effect of leaving behind low-performing school districts that could not raise matching funds for state aid or that made the investment to receive state aid, but only met minimal state standards in return.

- *Leadership and Supervision: State Departments of Education.* As state governments took increasing responsibility for helping rural and other schools needing resources beyond local government's ability to provide, many states began developing state departments of education. The average number of persons working in such departments grew from less than 3 in 1890 to almost 54 in 1930. These state departments increasingly took on the role of supervising local school districts. Supervisory personnel could not coerce conformity to state standards, but they found various ways to encourage and persuade local schools to meet state standards and implement "best practices."

This thematic chronology helps us see a pattern in various events involving local school districts, county districts, and state departments of education. The desire for local control meant that school communities were more likely to commit financial and emotional support to their schools, but it also resulted in some communities having low-performing schools.

State departments of education faced the difficult task of helping these low-performing schools improve without resorting to coercive measures that would be seen as a violation of the near-sacred principle of local control.

Lessons to Be Learned from a Historical Study

Some historians interpret their findings, but leave it to readers to draw their own implications for problems of practice. Others suggest lessons that can be learned from the findings, as does Steffes in her study of rural schools. She offers several lessons, but with the qualification that "the lessons to be learned from the relationship between local control and growing state centralization are neither simple nor straightforward" (2008, p. 219).

Steffes observes that today the interrelationships of local, state, and federal control over education is problematic. Researchers have found that educators are resistant to the requirements of the federal No Child Left Behind (NCLB) Act and state-mandated testing of students. Educators do not want federal and state governments overriding the local decision making of those closest to the students, namely their parents and educators.

One of the main lessons that Steffes learned from her study of rural schools from 1900 to 1933 is that local control of schools, with the support of county and state initiatives, can act as a positive force for educational improvement but also as a negative force. Here is what she states about local control as a positive force:

> Local control harnessed local pride and boosterism in support of schooling which helped to encourage emulation of best practices as well as experimentation and innovation. . . . Perhaps most importantly, the close identification of a community with "its" local school helped to encourage higher levels of school spending and investment, even in the face of generalized anti-tax sentiment. (2008, p. 217)

There also were negative consequences.

> The system that emerged in this period did help to ease some rural and urban disparities and establish an absolute bottom limit, but it also accepted and further entrenched racial and economic inequality. Leaving enforcement to localities meant allowing them to ignore minority populations and tying finance to local property tax in districts of unequal wealth meant that economic disparities would be a permanent and acceptable fixture of school governance. (2008, p. 218)

On the matter of minority populations, Steffes provides evidence that some rural school districts did not enforce school attendance for Mexican and African American students or provide them transportation to consolidated schools.

Steffes' history of rural schools from 1900 to 1933 does not tell us the best role for federal, state, and local governments in improving schools. What it does tell us is that some intergovernmental arrangements have had positive outcomes but also negative side effects. This knowledge can help us think more deeply about how to improve schools in the future. For example, we might conclude that no one level of control—local, state, or federal—is sufficient to improve education. Also, no one level of control can be dismissed as irrelevant. Educators and policy makers at all levels need to come together and figure out how to coordinate efforts to maximize positive outcomes and close loopholes that adversely affect some students or communities.

Historical Concepts

Earlier in the chapter, we noted that a historian might refer to concepts that originated in a particular time period. The researcher needs to avoid presentism by defining the concept as it was used in that time period, not today. Supervision is a key concept in the rural school research report. In describing the rise of state departments of education, Steffes claims that supervision was one of the "major projects of emerging state bureaucracies and they defined their roles in terms of it" (2008, p. 208).

Supervision in education can have various meanings in today's world. Supervision might mean observing teachers or schools to assess whether they are meeting certain standards, or more simply, to check that they are not engaged in inappropriate actions. Supervision might also mean observing teachers or schools for the purpose of helping them improve. To avoid the error of presentism, we need to check which of these meanings, or other meanings, were intended by use of the term in the past.

Because supervision was a central concept in the study, Steffes took care to explain its meaning in historical context.

> "Supervision" entailed both inspection and guidance and was designed to bring professional leadership to local school workers. Supervision required sending state officers into the field to observe teachers and local administrators at work, offer suggestions for improvement, diffuse new practices and ideas, and coordinate local efforts. . . . While couched as a program of improvement, supervision also carried a significant quest for greater uniformity of "best practices" as defined by the profession. (2008, p. 208)

This nuanced description of supervision as practiced in the early 1900s helps us understand it, not as seen in our own experience but rather as it existed in that particular time period.

Evaluating Historical Research

Historical research studies in education tend to be more difficult to evaluate than other kinds of research. The reason is that reports of historical research generally do not include a discussion of the methodology used to collect evidence and interpret it. Nonetheless, it is important to read the reports with a critical perspective.

The following questions can help you maintain a critical perspective as you read historical research reports.

- Does the report refer to primary sources?

  Interpretations of past events are likely to be more credible if they are based on the historian's examination of documents written by individuals who participated in or witnessed those events.

- Does the report refer to the use of external criticism of primary sources?

  It seems unlikely that documents of interest to educational historians are forgeries or of uncertain origin. However, if a document referring to a past event is essential to the study, it is worth asking whether there is any possibility that it is a forgery or written by someone other than the listed author.

- Does the report refer to the use of internal criticism to check the accuracy of statements made in historical sources?

  Earlier in the chapter, we stated five criteria for judging the trustworthiness of a source's author: (1) the author's presence or absence during the events being described; (2) whether she was a participant in or an observer of the events; (3) her qualifications to describe such events accurately; (4) her level of emotional involvement in the situation; and (5) whether she might have a vested interest in the outcomes of the event.

- Do the historian's interpretations reflect bias?

  Bias is certainly possible in historical research. Revisionist historians have identified evidence about past events that were overlooked or ignored by other historians. Check for indications, usually subtle, that the historian has a vested interest in portraying a particular view about an educational event.

- Does the report include credible causal inferences?

  Societal events and individual actions often are influenced by multiple factors. Check the historical report for interpretations that examine only one factor, to the possible exclusion of other important factors. Also, consider whether the causal inferences are supported by the evidence presented in the report.

- Does the historian overgeneralize from the evidence presented in the report?

  Historians generally focus on the study of particular individuals or events, but use them to make generalizations about larger trends in education. Examine whether these generalizations are justified by the evidence presented in the report.

- Does the historian use educational concepts in an appropriate manner?

  As we explain earlier in the chapter, educational concepts in use today might have had a different meaning in the past. Therefore, check whether the historian determined how these concepts were defined and used during the time encompassed by the study.

An example of
HOW HISTORICAL RESEARCH CAN HELP IN SOLVING PROBLEMS OF PRACTICE

Recent decades have seen the emergence of charter schools as an alternative to traditional public schools, with advocates claiming they are more innovative and effective than traditional public schools. A recent radio broadcast provided an interesting perspective on the charter school movement, as indicated by its opening statements.

> Nearly 20 years after Minnesota passed the nation's first charter school law, charters in the Twin Cities continue to perform worse, are more segregated than traditional public schools and are forcing those traditional public schools to become more segregated.
>
> These are the findings of a new report called "Failed Promises"—from the Institute on Race and Poverty at the University of Minnesota.
>
> Weber, T. (2008, November 26). Study: Charter schools promote segregation, perform worse than traditional schools. Retrieved from http: //minnesota.publicradio.org

The legislators who passed the charter school law undoubtedly did not think these schools would prove so controversial. The report cited in the broadcast calls them "failed promises." However, the broadcast also referred to several charter schools where administrators and parents are happy. One such charter school has a high percentage of Hmong students who are recent arrivals to the United States. The school's principal states, "With the number of parents I talk to, they put the issues of 'welcoming' and 'comfort' ahead of education. . . . I can understand because if your kids don't feel comfortable in a setting, how do you expect them to learn?"

Does the current situation reflect the intents and hopes of those who advocated for and passed the charter school law? This is a question that calls for a historical research study, such as the one we describe below. The question is particularly interesting, because Minnesota was the first state to pass this type of law and therefore has a longer historical record to examine.

Historical research has no prescribed methodology, so our study can go in various directions. We might start with a careful review of the text of the law, focusing on its intents, hoped-for outcomes, and rationale. From there, we can search for documents such as memos written by the legislators, budgetary analyses, letters and papers submitted by advocacy groups, and legal opinions, supplemented by collecting oral histories from legislators and stakeholders who were involved in various activities leading up to enactment of the law.

The research analysis might focus on a comparison of that time period with the present situation, as represented by the "Failed Promises" report and other relevant documents pertaining to charter schools in Minnesota. If time and resources are available, it would be worthwhile to study other critical periods in Minnesota's charter school movement between its inception and now.

This historical study would provide an important perspective for helping educators and other stakeholders to decide next steps. For example, a historical perspective might show stakeholders that today's charter schools are operating in a manner that appears consistent with the mission laid out for them in the original law, but that they need more resources and some modifications. Or the study might find that charter schools have strayed far from the law's original intent and need to be reconceptualized.

Without the perspective provided by historical research, educators could be caught up in a continuing state of confusion, not knowing where they have been and where they are likely to be heading, in relation to charter schools or other educational movements.

Self-Check Test

1. All educational researchers can be regarded as historians, primarily because they
   a. review past research as a basis for designing their own research studies.
   b. study causal relationships among observed phenomena.
   c. interpret the practical significance of their research findings.
   d. suggest desirable directions for future research on the topics they have studied.

2. In historical research, the literature review typically
   a. is a relatively minor part of the research process.
   b. provides the research data.
   c. is conducted after the data have been analyzed.
   d. focuses on secondary sources.

3. In historical research, a private journal written by a nineteenth-century school principal most likely would be classified as a
   a. secondary source.   c. relic.
   b. document.   d. record.

4. In historical research, physical objects preserved from the period being studied are called
   a. records.   c. repositories.
   b. secondary sources.   d. relics.

5. The procedure for determining whether a source of historical data is authentic sometimes is called
   a. internal criticism.   c. external criticism.
   b. historiographical validation. d. revisionism.

6. Internal criticism of documents is used to
   a. detect forgeries.
   b. determine whether the author and date of publication are valid.
   c. determine the extent of a document's dissemination.
   d. determine the accuracy of the information in the text of documents.

7. In historical research, presentism refers to the
   a. belief that the present is more important than the historical past.
   b. use of contemporary concepts to interpret past events.
   c. belief that the future cannot be predicted based on study of past events.
   d. set of assumptions underlying revisionist history.

8. Historical researchers generally consider quantitative materials superior to other types of primary sources for examining
   a. the unique aspects of a historical event.
   b. the history of nonliterate cultures.
   c. population characteristics and trends during a historical period.
   d. accounts of prominent individuals of past periods.

9. Causal inference in historical research is a process by which researchers
   a. use interpretation to ascribe causality to a sequence of historical events.
   b. narrow the cause of a historical phenomenon to one set of factors.
   c. explain past events in terms of contemporary concepts.
   d. take a critical view of past practices that previously were viewed positively.

Chapter References

Button, H. W. (1979). Creating more usable pasts: History in the study of education. *Educational Researcher, 8*(5), 3–9.

Carr, E. H. (1967). *What is history?* New York: Random House.

Donato, R., & Lazerson, M. (2000). New directions in American educational history: Problems and prospects. *Educational Researcher, 29*(8), 4–15.

Gonzalez, G. (1990). *Chicano education in the era of segregation.* Philadelphia: Balch Institute Press.

Grosvenor, I., & Lawn, M. (2001). Ways of seeing in education and schooling: Emerging historiographies. *History of Education, 30,* 105–108.

Katz, M. B. (1968). *The irony of early school reform: Educational innovation in mid-nineteenth century Massachusetts.* Cambridge, MA: Harvard University Press.

Kelen, L. G., & Stone, E. H. (1996). *Missing stories.* Salt Lake City: University of Utah Press.

Lincoln, Y. S., & Guba, E. G. (1985). *Naturalistic inquiry.* Beverly Hills, CA: Sage.

Sheumaker, H., & Wajda, S. T. (Eds.). (2007). *Material culture in America.* Santa Barbara, CA: ABC-CLIO.

Steffes, T. L. (2008). Solving the "Rural School Problem": New state aid, standards, and supervision of local schools, 1900–1933. *History of Education Quarterly, 48*(2), 181–220.

Tyack, D. B. (1976). Ways of seeing: An essay on the history of compulsory schooling. *Harvard Educational Review, 46,* 55–89.

Resources for Further Study

Barzun, J., & Graff, H. F. (2004). *The modern researcher* (6th ed.). Belmont, CA: Wadsworth.

> This is one of the classic books about historical research methodology. The authors provide a comprehensive description of historical researchers' work, including strategies for fact finding, criticism, interpretation, and reporting.

Henry, A. (2006). Historical studies: Groups/institutions. In J. L. Green, G. Camilli, & P. B. Elmore (Eds.), *Handbook of complementary methods in education research* (pp. 333–355). Mahwah, NJ: Lawrence Erlbaum.

> The author describes a revisionist approach to conducting historical research. She advocates for historians who are "on the margins" and marginalized groups who have been underrepresented or misrepresented in mainstream historical research.

Rury, J. L. (2006). Historical research in education. In J. L. Green, G. Camilli, & P. B. Elmore (Eds.), *Handbook of complementary methods in education research* (pp. 323–332). Mahwah, NJ: Lawrence Erlbaum.

> The author provides an overview of current approaches to historical research and a good reference list for further study of particular topics.

Yow, V. R. (2005). *Recording oral history: A guide for the humanities and social sciences* (2nd ed.). Walnut Creek, CA: AltaMira.

> The author explains interviewing strategies and the ethical issues involved in oral history. The book includes an in-depth description of three types of oral history projects: community studies, biographies, and family histories.

Sample Historical Research Study

Go to the Principal's Office: Toward a Social History of the School Principal in North America

Rousmaniere, K. (2007). Go to the principal's office: Toward a social history of the school principal in North America. *History of Education Quarterly, 47*(1), 1–22.

What *is* the role of the school principal? What *should* the role of the school principal be? Educators and others have struggled with these questions for decades.

The following article does not answer these questions directly but does put them into historical perspective. As we see how the role of school principal has evolved, we develop an understanding of the complex, conflicting demands that are placed on today's principals. With this understanding, we perhaps are in a better position to define the role so that principals can be more effective.

Go to the Principal's Office: Toward a Social History of the School Principal in North America

Kate Rousmaniere | Of the many organizational changes that took place in public education in North America at the turn of the last century, few had greater impact on the school than the development of the principal. The creation of the principal's office revolutionized the internal organization of the school from a group of students supervised by one teacher to a collection of teachers managed by one administrator. In its very conception, the appointment of a school-based administrator who was authorized to supervise other teachers significantly restructured power relations in schools, realigning the source of authority from the classroom to the principal's office. Just as significant was the role that the principal played as a school based representative of the central educational office. Created as a conduit between the district and the classroom, the principal became an educational middle manager in an increasingly complex school bureaucracy.

The introduction of the principal's office radically changed the overall machinery of how public education was delivered from central authorities to the classroom. Located as the connecting hinge between the school and the district, the principal was critical to the success of newly designed school systems in the early twentieth century, in much the same way that the middle manager in business reinforced the development of corporate enterprise. Business historian Alfred Chandler describes how the creation of middle managerial structures helped to consolidate the control of independent businesses under a corporate umbrella. Modern administrative practices, including scientific management, greased the wheels of this development, providing managerial techniques, a hierarchical decision-making structure, and an occupational culture of rationality. Middle managers were the engine behind bureaucracy, providing the smooth transition of responsibilities—what Chandler described as "vertical integration"—from the central office to the shop floor.[1]

Like the foreman in the factory and the mid-level executive in the office building, the school principal was an administrator who was responsible for day-to-day building operations rather than strategic policy decisions. Standing between the district and the classroom, principals were, as C. Wright Mills described such white-collar positions, "the assistants of authority" whose power was derived from others, and who were responsible for implementing managerial decisions but had limited opportunities for influencing those decisions.[2] Like other middle managers, the principal had a "dual personality," standing "on the middle ground between management and employee," as both a loyal sergeant to a distant supervisor and a local administrator who had to negotiate with workers in order to get the job done properly.[3] Larry Cuban aptly describes principals' historic and contemporary role as "positioned between their superiors who want orders followed and the teachers who do the actual work in the classrooms, . . . [principals'] loyalties are dual: to their school, and to headquarters."[4]

In this essay, I offer a framework for understanding the overall development of the principal's office in the United States and Canada from the late nineteenth century to the present. I argue that the school principal replaced the nineteenth century head teacher, exchanging an informal position of a teacher who took on administrative tasks with an administrator who supervised teachers. This is what I refer to as the development of the "principal's office:" the creation of both the administrative position of the principal *and* the physical office in the school building.

---

[1]Alfred Chandler, *The Visible Hand: The Managerial Revolution in American Business* (Cambridge, MA: Belknap Press, 1977).

[2]C. Wright Mills, *White Collar: The American Middle Classes* (New York: Oxford University Press, 1951), 74.

[3]Nelson Lichtenstein, "'The Man in the Middle': A Social History of Automobile Industry Foreman," in *On the Line: Essays in the History of Auto Work*, ed. Nelson Lichtenstein and Stephen Meyer (Urbana: University of Illinois Press, 1989), 161–62; Geoff Mason, "Production Supervisors in Britain, Germany, and the United States: Back from the Dead Again?" *Work, Employment, and Society* 14, (2000): 626–27.

[4]Larry Cuban, *The Managerial Imperative and the Practice of Leadership in Schools* (Albany: SUNY Press, 1988), 61.

From Rousmaniere, K. (2007) Go to the principal's office: Toward a social history of the school principal in North America. *History of Education Quarterly, 47*(1), 1–22.

The essay is organized in the following way. First, I comment briefly on the historiography of the principal. Next, I introduce the nineteenth century predecessor to the principal—the head teacher, or principal teacher. I then describe how certain professionalization strategies led to the identification of the principal as the iconographic white man in the principal's office. I argue that the creation of the principal's office as the figurehead of North American schools involved the cementing of institutional and personal definitions of gender and race in school leadership. But ultimately, the middle manager location of the principal undermined its professional status. For all the efforts to lift the principal above the classroom teacher, the principal's office remained stubbornly embedded *in* the school, a middle manager position wedged between the classroom and the district.

WHERE IS THE PRINCIPAL'S OFFICE?

Given the significance of the principal's office in the development of modern schooling, it is surprising how little we know about it. There are no articles on the history of the public school principal in the *History of Education Quarterly*, the leading American journal in the field for the past forty-five years. In the *Historical Studies in Education* bibliography of over 850 references on the history of Canadian education published since 1980, there are only two essays specifically on the principal. A May 2006 survey of a leading history of education bibliographic listserve found no references to the principal out of 1,400 scholarly articles published since 1997.[5]

Whole volumes on the history of education refer to the historical development of school finance, curriculum, district policies, architecture, and student life; analyze the impact of desegregation, feminization, consolidation, and centralization; and describe the roles of teachers, superintendents, parent and community leaders, and government officials, with virtually no mention of the school building principal. The principal is missing from both the political history of school administration and the social history of schools. It's as if the principal did not exist at all, except to appear occasionally, without elaboration or explanation, as a spontaneous actor in the experience of a teacher or the development of a school.

The sole exception to this historiographical pattern is a pocket of studies on African American principals. Through the late twentieth century, black principals were completely excluded from predominantly white public schools in both the legally segregated southern United States and in the north where virtually no African American held a principalship in any school with even a minority white population until the 1960s. In their racially segregated school systems, black principals played a critical role, serving as important role models and respected servant leaders in their communities. Historians have examined black school leaders in racially segregated schools with significantly more interest than any historians have expressed about white majority principals, and this research provides a unique model of scholarship on the historical significance of school leaders.[6]

Why has it been so easy for historians to side step the school principal? I suggest three reasons.

The first reason is that histories of educational administration are written primarily by scholars with limited historical training in order to frame prescriptive guidance for contemporary school leaders. The focus has been on categorizing occupational themes for contemporary reflection rather than the analysis and interpretation of historical evidence.[7] A second reason that the principal has been bypassed is that historians of education have tended to encapsulate the entire field of school administration in

[5]h-education@h-net.msu.edu. This is not to say that the topic has been completely ignored. Recent scholarship on the history of the principalship in North America includes in addition to Larry Cuban's volume, Kathleen Brown, "Pivotal Points: History, Development, and Promise of the Principalship," in *Sage Handbook of Educational Leadership,* ed. Fenwick W. English (University of North Carolina: Sage Publications 2005), 109–141; Rebecca H. Goodwin, Michael L. Cunningham and Teresa Eager, "The Changes Role of the Secondary Principal in the United States: An Historical Perspective," *Journal of Administration and History* 37, (April 2005): 1–17; Thomas Fleming, "British Columbia Principals: Scholar-Teachers and Administrative Amateurs in Victorian and Edwardian Eras, 1872–1918," in *School Leadership: Essays on the British Columbia Experience, 1872–1995,* ed. Thomas Fleming (Bendall Books, 2001), 249–85; Thomas Fleming, "Our Boys in the Field: School Inspectors, Superintendents, and the Changing Character of School Leadership in British Columbia," in *Schools in the West: Essays in Canadian Educational History,* ed. Nancy M. Sheehan, J. Donald Wilson, and David C. James (Calgary: Detselig Enterprises, 1986), 285–303. Oral histories and biographical studies comprise a bulk of new scholarship on the history of the principal: Cecelia Reynolds, "Changing Gender Scripts and Moral Dilemmas for Women and Men in Education, 1940–1970," in *Women and School Leadership: International Perspectives,* ed. Cecilia Reynolds (Albany: SUNY, 2002), 29–48; James M. Wallace, *The Promise of Progressivism: Angelo Patri and Urban Education* (New York: Peter Lang, 2006).

[6]Carol F. Karpinski, "Bearing the Burden of Desegregation: Black Principals and *Brown,*" *Urban Education* 41, (May 2006): 237–276; Linda C. Tillman, "African American Principals and the Legacy of *Brown,*" *Review of Research in Education,* (2005): 101–146; Adah Ward Randolph, "The Memories of an All-Black Northern Urban School: Good Memories of Leadership, Teachers, and the Curriculum," *Urban Education* 39, (November, 2004): 596–620 and "Resisting Oppression through Education: Ethel Thompson Overby, 1912–1958," *Journal of Black Studies* (forthcoming); Vanessa Siddle Walker, "Organized Resistance and Black Educators' Quest for School Equality," *Teachers College Record* 107, (March 2005): 355–388.

[7]H. Warren Button, "Doctrines of Administration: A Brief History," *Educational Administration Quarterly* 2, (Autumn 1966): 216–224; Phillip Hallinger, "The Evolving Role of American Principals: From Managerial to Instructional to Transformational Leaders," *Journal of Educational Administration* 30, (1992): 35–48; Lynn G. Beck and Joseph Murphy, *Understanding the Principalship: Metaphorical Themes, 1920s–1990s* (New York: Teachers College Press, 1993); Thomas E. Glass, et al., *The History of Educational Administration Viewed Through its Textbooks,* (Lanham, MD: Scarecrow, 2004).

the popular historical trope of the "administrative progressive." This is the familiar argument that educational reformers in the late nineteenth century divided into two groups: pedagogical progressives who promoted a child centered, humanistic approach to education, and administrative progressives who advocated for the development of school systems driven by values of fiscal economy and organizational accountability. This division of educational history into administrative and pedagogical progressive camps was proposed by David Tyack over thirty years ago and has never been seriously revisited. We universally characterize the entirety of school leadership history by single phrases or metaphors such as "the cult of efficiency," "scientific management," and Tyack's own term "administrative progressives."[8]

Two points about the administrative progressive model are worth expanding here. First, in these histories, the occupational roles of principal and superintendent are often lumped uncritically together and seen as a one-dimensional cabal of administrative power.[9] Largely ignored are distinctions between building, local and central administrators. There are few fine-grained analyses of how administrative roles emerged and developed at all levels of the educational structure.[10] Secondly, these studies tend to focus on policy development and the institutionalization of bureaucratic authority through scientific management. The collapsing of all administrators into a pot of scientific management has colored our understanding of school organization so that we see the work of teachers and administrators as separate and antagonistic, driven by different values, ideologies, and purposes. In these studies of "system builders," we forget that local school administrators often had tenuous connections to central office power.

A final, impressionistic observation about why historians of education have ignored principals is simply a personal predilection against them. In our own life history, many of us remember an inspiring teacher, but we may remember the principal only for an unfortunate, and assuredly unfair, disciplinary encounter. For women and people of color the principal was often a position not of us, and not attainable.[11] Personal experience is reinforced by a long cultural history of alienation between school administration and classroom teaching: teachers who become administrators are often seen as crossing a boundary much like the River Styx—a one-way passage to a place not all that pleasant. The principal's office holds an unsavory tinge, and the people who sit in that office are viewed with some misgivings. Memory and methodology reinforce each other: when historians write about the introduction of scientific management and the consolidation of authority in early twentieth century schools, the principal becomes folded into a battalion of upper level administrators who inflicted orders from distant offices.

Historians have largely side stepped the school principal as a central figure in the history of school life, as well as the history of school system development. A cursory overview of that history suggests that we cannot understand the development of early schools and early school systems without understanding the changing role of the principal.

THE MAKING OF THE PRINCIPAL TEACHER

Before there was a principal's office, the school was essentially the teacher, and that teacher worked as instructor and building manager. The administrative structure of the school was simple: in the United States, a superintendent, and in Canada, an inspector, oversaw district operations from afar; local school boards exerted more immediate authority from the community. The teacher managed the school and taught students in a building consisting solely of classroom space. For the most part, the teacher worked alone, under broad administrative directives.

The first principals' positions were created in mid-nineteenth century urban districts to address the organizational demands of the new graded school where students were classified by age and achievement and placed in separate classrooms under a single teacher. With teachers and students divided into different graded compartments, a head teacher, or teaching principal, was assigned to act as an overarching authority to the whole, organizing the separate courses of study, administering discipline, and supervising the operation of all the classes in order to, as the American school reformer Henry Barnard wrote, "secure the harmonious action and progress of each department."[12] By the late nineteenth century in both America and Canada, most urban school systems

[8]Ira E. Bogotch, "A History of Public School Leadership: The First Century, 1537–1942," in *Sage Handbook of Educational Leadership* ed. Fenwick W. English (Chapel Hill: University of North Carolina, Sage Publications), 7–33.

[9]The bulk of historical studies of educational administration are on district leadership: David Tyack and Elisabeth Hansot, *Managers of Virtue: Public School Leadership in America, 1820–1980*, (Boston: Basic Books 1982); Jackie Blount, *Destined to Rule the Schools: Women and the Superintendency, 1873–1995* (Albany: SUNY Press, 1998); Bruce Curtis, *True Government by Choise Men? Inspection, Education, and State Formation in Canada West* (Toronto: University of Toronto Press, 1992); Raymond E. Callahan, *Education and the Cult of Efficiency* (Chicago: University of Chicago Press, 1962).

[10]Kathleen Murphey's fine study of the late nineteenth century institutional development of Fort Wayne Indiana's school system is one of the few exceptions. Kathleen A. Murphey, "Common School or 'Our Best System'? Tracking School Reform in Fort Wayne, Indiana, 1853–75," *Historical Studies in Education* 11, (Fall 1999): 188–211. See also Michael F. Murphy, "Unmaking and Remaking the 'One Best System': London, Ontario, 1852–1860," *History of Education Quarterly* 37, (Fall 1997): 291–310.

[11]Blount, *Destined to Rule the Schools*, 153–56.

[12]"Henry Barnard on the significance of school grading," in *Education in the United States: A Documentary History*, Vol. 3, ed. Sol Cohen (New York: Random House, 1974), 1322; Frederick Dean McCluskey, "Introduction of Grading into the Public Schools of New England," *The Elementary School Journal* 21 (October 1920).

had graded elementary and secondary schools with some form of a building administrator who reported to a district officer.[13]

The work of nineteenth century principals was based mostly on expediency, and not on the improvement of either learning or school operations. The principal's job was little more than a routine administrator: according to one historian, merely "a mechanic who was serving an unsophisticated machine."[14] Distinguishing leadership opportunities were few and far between. For example, in 1841, school trustees in Cincinnati, Ohio (one of the first cities that authorized the position) gave the principal the responsibility of monitoring examinations and seeing that the bell was rung for each class to come in; in 1847 the duty of ringing the bell for recess was added; the following year the principal was authorized to suspend pupils for profane language and to prevent pupils from leaving school without permission.[15]

There was no systematic process to the authorization of these first school principals. In his history of school administration in British Columbia, Thomas Fleming describes the "organizational incrementalism" whereby "one-room elementary schools grew room-by-room until they became institutions large enough to require supervision by a head teacher or principal." The process occurred over a century in North America "without any preconceived design for the shape of the institutions to come, without any overarching view of the structures required to manage such schools, and without much thought about who should manage them." Growing schools might be governed by the longest serving teacher, or the teacher most liked by the school board, or by the only teacher willing to do the work. Experience as a teacher was the sole prerequisite for the position. Fleming observes that "circumstance, rather than ambition, preparation, or talent" led to the identification of head teachers so that "supervisory and organizational chores were undertaken for decades by untrained individuals on a piecemeal basis, as something to be done before or after instruction."[16]

These early administrators worked in a world almost entirely free of job descriptions, legal guidelines, or professional support, and their relationship with both their superiors and their staff were unregulated, often lead-

ing to conflict. As the administrative framework of school districts developed, principals and district officers jostled for authority over their different pieces of the emerging educational enterprise. Local and district administrators argued over which office had the right to promote, assign, and examine pupils, hire and fire teachers, purchase books, and control building maintenance.[17] School board minutes reveal squabbles at the most intricate levels of the work day. Ontario principals in 1909, for example, collectively objected to the Ministry of Education for requiring a specific method of examination of teachers' notebooks. Such "matters of detail," the principals argued, were local "questions of judgment."[18]

While battling intrusions from above, principals also defended their authority from those below. Relieved from the head teachers' menial duties of building maintenance, the principal now had to direct others to do that work, a managerial task that often caused discord within the building. Ontario principals in the 1890s believed that although some of their authority had increased, in other areas, including the heating and ventilation of the classroom, they were "powerless" and as a result, the occupants of schools were "being slowly poisoned" by negligent caretakers.[19] In some cities, regulations outlined the responsibilities of principal and engineer, such as in Chicago in 1905 where the Board wrote in excruciating detail about whose responsibility it was to open the school, keep the keys, sweep the halls, and monitor the furnace.[20] In relations with the local community, too, the principal's authority was not absolute: parents and teachers could, and did, appeal to district officials for review of a principal's decision on discipline or managerial practice.[21]

By the end of the nineteenth century, then, the principal teacher or head teacher, was a shadowy figure on the educational landscape. In one and two room schools in rural communities across North America, the principal simply did not exist, since staffing in local schools depended upon the fiscal resources and generosity of local school boards.[22] But urban schools were only marginally more systemic in their appointment of school leaders. In his

---

[13]David Tyack and Elisabeth Hansot, *Learning Together: A History of Coeducation in American Schools* (New Haven: Yale University Press, 1990), 82–83; Alison Prentice, *The School Promoters: Education and Social Class in Mid-Nineteenth Century Upper Canada*, (Toronto: McClelland and Stewart), 17; Charles E. Phillips, *The Development of Education in Canada* (Toronto: W. J. Gage and Co., 1957), 8.

[14]Rafael Alexander Lewy, "The Secondary School Principal in Theory: An Examination of Major Theoretical Trends of the Principalship in the United States Between 1917 and the Early Thirties," (Ph.D. diss., University of Illinois, 1965), 18.

[15]Paul Revere Pierce, *The Origin and Development of the Public School Principalship*, (Chicago: University of Chicago, 1935), 11–12, 26–27.

[16]Fleming, "British Columbia Principals," 251–52.

[17]Pierce, *Origin and Development of the Public School Principalship*, 40–46, 50–51, 89–99; Lewy, "The Secondary School Principal," 23.

[18]Edwin C. Guillet, *In the Cause of Education: Centennial History of the Ontario Educational Association, 1861–1960* (Toronto: University of Toronto Press, 1960), 237.

[19]Guillet, *In the Cause of Education*, 135.

[20]Pierce, *Origin and Development of the Public School Principalship*, 52–53.

[21]See for example, "The Brantford 'School Difficulty'" and "An Inspector Investigates a Local Conflict," in Alison L. Prentice and Susan E. Houston, *Community School and Society in Nineteenth Century Canada*, 107–115, 122–27 (Toronto: Oxford University Press, 1975).

[22]D. A. Lawr and R. D. Gidney, "Who Ran the Schools? Local Influence on Education Policy in Nineteenth Century Ontario," *Ontario History 72*, (September 1980): 131–143.

1892 expose of American urban schools, Joseph Rice described a variety of different responsibilities for principals, from Philadelphia where they were "lords and masters of their own schools" to Indianapolis where each school had a principal, but their duties barely extended beyond teaching and general supervision over the building. In some cities, one principal was in charge of a number of schools; in others, the principal was little more than a clerk whose main job was to keep attendance.[23]

THE MAKING OF THE PRINCIPAL'S OFFICE

Pivotal to the reshaping of the irregular head teacher into a professional office in the early twentieth century was the realignment of the principal's affinity away from the classroom teacher and towards the district officer. In 1923, Ellwood P. Cubberley described the significance of the principal's relationship with the district office as

> analogous in the business world to that of the manager of a town branch of a public utility to the general superintendent of the business; to that of the manager of a single department to the general manager of a department store; to that of the superintendent of a division of a railroad to the president of the company; or that of the colonel of a regiment to the commanding general of an army.[24]

The first step toward professionalizing the principal was to distinguish between mundane administrative tasks and supervisory responsibilities. The first, observed one reformer, "is mere shop keeping; the second is educational statesmanship."[25] Supervision enhanced [the] principal's cultural authority over the school: as Charles H. Judd saw it, only the principal's "true scientific supervision" would "convert the school into a laboratory of human engineering."[26] As Seattle's superintendent promised in 1933, all education would be improved by the principal's "well lubricated, frictionless operation of the machinery."[27] Supervision also increased [the] principal's actual authority to hire and fire, assign extra duties, and recommend teachers and staff for promotion. Later in the century, Willard Elsbree and Edmund Reutter specifically referred to these attributes when they described the principal as "a kind of foreman who through close supervision

helped to compensate for ignorance and lack of skill of his subordinates."[28]

And principals had an increasing number of subordinates in the expanding bureaucratic system. In their famous community study of Middletown, Robert and Helen Lynd pointed out that in 1890, the superintendent was the only person in the school system who did not teach; but by the 1920s there was "a whole galaxy of principals, assistant principals, supervisors of special subjects, directors of vocational education and home economics, deans, attendance officers, and clerks who do no teaching but are concerned in one way or another with keeping the system going."[29] The growing demands on principals to manage this staff led to their removal from the classroom: teaching principals remained prominent in smaller and rural schools, but by the mid-1930s, 70% of American urban principals in elementary schools had no teaching responsibilities.[30] Recognition of the new authority of the principal led to the construction of a separate principal's office that often included special accommodations for a secretary, filing clerks, and a waiting room.[31] By the 1920s, public address systems linked the principal's office with classrooms, emphasizing how the principal was both apart from, and constantly overseeing, teachers.[32]

The second step in the professionalization of the principal was the tightening of academic qualifications for the position, and specifically increasing the distinctions between administrator and teacher preparation. In 1906, Ellwood P. Cubberely, a newly minted graduate from one of the first doctoral programs in educational administration, proposed that each state offer an administrative certificate for educators seeking appointment to leadership positions, arguing that specified coursework in administration was an avenue toward "professionalizing educational leadership."[33] Between 1923 and 1934, the number of American states that distinguished teacher from administrator certificates more than tripled from 7 to 27. By the 1950s one-third of all states and half of all Canadian

[23]Joseph Mayer Rice, *The Public-School System of the United States* (New York: Arno Press, 1969), 113, 149.

[24]Ellwood P. Cubberley, "The Principal and the Principalship," *The Elementary School Journal* 23, (January, 1923): 342.

[25]Quoted in Leonard V. Koos, James M. Hughes, and Percival W. Huston, *Administering the Secondary School* (New York: American Book Company, 1940), 455.

[26]Quoted in Edward A. Krug, *The Shaping of the American High School, 1920–1941* (Madison: University of Wisconsin Press, 1972), 160.

[27]Worth McClure, "The Organizing Administrative Work of the School Principal," in *Modern School Administration: Problems and Progress*, ed. John C. Almack (Boston: Houghton Mifflin, 1933), 119.

[28]Willard S. Elsbree and E. Edmund Reutter, Jr., *Principles of Staff Personnel Administration in Public Schools* (New York: Teachers College, 1954), 231.

[29]Quoted in David Tyack, *The One Best System: A History of American Urban Education* (Cambridge: Harvard University Press, 1974), 185.

[30]Bess Goodykoontz and Jessie A. Lane, *The Elementary School Principalship* (U.S. Department of the Interior Bulletin, 1938, no. 8), 9.

[31]Pierce, *Origin and Development of the Public School Principalship*, 47–48. See also Antonio Vinao, "The School Head's Office as Territory and Place: Location and Physical Layout in the First Spanish Graded School," in *Materialities of Schooling: Design, Technology, Objects, Routines*, ed. Martin Lawn and Ian Grosvenor (Oxford: Symposium Books, 2005), 56.

[32]Krug, *The Shaping of the American High School*, 162.

[33]As cited in Roal F. Campbell, Thomas Fleming, L. Jackson Newell, and John W. Bennion, *A History of Thought and Practice in Educational Administration* (New York: Teachers College Press, 1987), 75.

provinces stipulated specific academic requirements for the principalship.[34] In the years after the Second World War, the new academic field of educational administration developed a knowledge base that increasingly distinguished administrative and pedagogical areas of research and that fragmented educational administrators into specialty groups—principals separated from superintendents and assistant superintendents, and from the panoply of other administrative experts in school finance, law, building management, and curriculum.[35] Such specialization solidified the identity of school administrators as uniquely prepared professionals with distinct skills. In 1962, an educator at the University of Calgary could conclude that "No longer is the administrator simply a teacher with intuitive understanding of some problems of school-community relationships."[36]

But these efforts to distinguish the principal from the teacher were compromised by the unavoidable fact that the principal remained in the school with teachers. Educational administrators struggled with this tension, constructing tortured arguments about how the principal both was and was not a teacher. For example, in 1910 Frank McMurry described principals as "professional leaders" whose primary affinity still should be to teachers, while at the same time they should also be "teachers of teachers."[37] The tangled irony of the principal's role was often symbolized by their physical office. Having left the classroom to address new administrative responsibilities, principals were then criticized for not paying enough attention to classroom matters. Such comments often referred specifically to the principal's office which, now that it was created to house the new building authority, was seen as the last place that the truly inspired principal should be. In 1924, Chicago's superintendent urged principals to get "out of the office chairs and into the work area."[38] Cubberley applauded the work of an elementary principal in Salt Lake City who was always "somewhere in the rooms busy with his work, instead, of sitting on his chair in his office."[39] Administrative reformers who assigned principals mountains of paper work now criticized principals for being a "Director of Routine" rather than leading "educational engineering and

generalship."[40] Yet routine efficiency was also valued by district officials who were more likely to assess a principal on specific clerical matters than on instructional supervision or leadership style.[41]

Teachers' attitudes about the newly empowered school head also reflected the ambiguity of the principal's office. The increasing prestige of the principal concerned many teachers who reported abuses by their local administrator, what one teachers' council in Chicago in 1921 called the assumption on the part of some principals that their office carried with it "the right to be an autocrat, a boss, or a czar, instead of a leader in educational ideals."[42] When teachers began to form protective organizations in the early twentieth century, some excluded principals, seeing them as part of an encroaching administrative force that restricted the independence of the classroom teacher.

But teachers' antipathy to building principals was not universal. Teachers often expressed loyalty to their school head, appreciating the discipline and order provided by a principal who might act, as one Toronto teacher approvingly described it, as a "benevolent dictator."[43] Rural teachers in newly consolidated schools balanced their loss of autonomy in the one-room school with the relief from administrative and disciplinary responsibilities that their new principal assumed.[44] As Richard Quantz argued, some women teachers held complex attitudes about working relationships in their school house, leading many to accept their principal's authority.[45] Furthermore, the demands of teachers' organizations were primarily directed not at building principals but at district policies over salaries, pensions, tenure, and working conditions, and principals were largely powerless in determining these matters. Some teachers' associations did allow principals into their ranks, electing them as leaders in the organization, and filing grievances on their behalf.[46]

Nor were principals themselves easily seduced into the administrative hemisphere. Principals shared with teachers a common boss who was not always attuned to local contexts. Failure on the part of a principal to abide by a

---

[34]Glass, *The History of Educational Administration Viewed through its Textbooks*, 62; W. N. Toombs, "Administrative Requirements of Principals and Superintendents," *Canadian Education and Research Digest*, 2 (March 1962): 64.

[35]Keith Goldhammer, "Evolution in the Profession," *Educational Administration Quarterly* 19, (Summer 1983): 249–272; Frank W. Hart, "Special Certification as a Means of Professionalizing Educational Leadership," *Teachers' College Research* 27, (1925): 121; B. H. Peterson, "Certification of School Administrators in the United States," *School and Society* 45, (1937): 784–86.

[36]Toombs, "Administrative Requirements of Principals and Superintendents," 64.

[37]As quoted in Cuban, *The Managerial Imperative*, 6.

[38]As quoted in Pierce, *Origin and Development of the Public School Principalship*, 82.

[39]As quoted in Cuban, *The Managerial Imperative*, 58–59.

[40]As quoted in Krug, *Shaping of the American High School*, 33.

[41]Cuban, *The Managerial Imperative*, 56.

[42]Group Council 29, Bryn Mawr School, Chicago, October 21, 1921, Box 48, Folder August-October 1921, Chicago Teachers' Federation General Files, Chicago Historical Society.

[43]Kristin R. Llewellyn, "Gendered Democracy Women Teachers in Post-War Toronto," *Historical Studies in Education* 18, (Spring 2006): 21.

[44]Margaret K. Nelson, "From the One-Room School House to the Graded School: Teaching in Vermont, 1910–1950," *Frontiers: A Journal of Women's Studies* 7, (1983): 14–20.

[45]Richard Quantz, "The Complex Visions of Female Teachers and the Failure of Unionization in the 1930s: an Oral History," *History of Education Quarterly* 25, (Winter, 1985): 439–458.

[46]John E. Lyons, "Ten Forgotten Years: The Saskatchewan Teachers' Federation and the Legacy of the Depression" in *Schools in the West*, ed. Sheehan et al., 113–129.

district officer's expectations might end a career: As one British Columbia principal was warned by a district official, "There are a lot of Siberia's out there" where a disobedient principal could be exiled.[47] Some principals shared teachers' concerns over district intrusions and were themselves committed activists for improving school funding, class size, and local autonomy, working with teachers to undermine the impact of district regulations.

The process of professionally distinguishing between principals and teachers was also complicated by the fact that principals were always required to have experience as teachers. Teachers' continued loyalty to principals was often rooted on their common experience in the classroom. In 1895, women teachers in a primary school in New York City objected to the appointment as principal of their school of a male grammar school teacher who had less experience than their own head teacher. The teachers argued that because their own Miss Eghert had been in their school for many years, she was "imbued with the atmosphere of the school," and best knew its needs and interests.[48] This experience qualified her for the position more than any outsider. Margaret Haley made a similar argument thirty years later in Chicago, when she criticized principals whose "sole claim to fitness for the position is that of having written an examination on academic subjects with particular emphasis on theory and method of teaching."[49]

Leading figures in new educational administration graduate programs disagreed, arguing that school administrators' work required "the endorsement of educational experts."[50] But even as academic qualifications for the principalship increased, experience in the classroom remained a requirement. For example, in the checklist of qualifications for the principalship that was devised by the Chicago Board of Examiners in 1930, an applicant's experience as a teacher was weighed as twice as important as a bachelors and masters degree.[51] Even as aspiring principals were increasingly required to take written tests and submit academic credentials, their experience as teachers remained the prominent qualification.

By the mid twentieth century, the principal's office existed, but its professional status was uncertain. It was not always clear if the principal was a teacher or an administrator, or where the loyalties and professional attributes of the principalship lay. Standing on the middle ground between the district and the classroom, the principal was both and neither administrator and teacher.

THE MAKING OF THE MAN IN THE PRINCIPAL'S OFFICE

Reformers' ambivalence about the professional status of the principal's office was accompanied by concerns about who sat in that office. The elementary principalship presented a special professional problem because, well into the twentieth century, it retained many of the characteristics of the old head teacher with its expansive job description, teaching responsibilities, and low status.[52] Most troubling was that the bulk of elementary principals were women. The elementary school had long been considered both the domain of women and an institution that resisted formal bureaucratic order. Compared with the secondary school with its subject areas, curriculum aligned toward vocational or collegiate preparation, and college educated teachers, the elementary school was a disordered mass of small children, integrated curriculum, and women teachers with insignificant certificates and Normal School degrees. As Marta Danylewycz and Alison Prentice argued in their study of women teachers in nineteenth century schools in Montreal and Toronto, bureaucratizing school systems institutionalized gender inequality, offering "radically different opportunities to the men and women who staffed the schools."[53] Because elementary schools were bureaucratized later than secondary schools, particularly in rural areas, women remained in those leadership positions for significantly longer. The result, as David Tyack and Elisabeth Hansot note, was that through much of the twentieth century, the elementary principalship offered women perhaps "the greatest opportunity for autonomy and educational leadership."[54]

In the United States between 1900 and the 1950s, over two-thirds of American elementary schools had women principals. Most of these positions were in rural schools, but women were also prominent in city schools, holding over three-fourths of elementary principalships in cities under 30,000, and well over half in many of the largest American cities.[55] In Canada, women elementary principals were particularly prominent in the west. Through the First World War, at least one half of all elementary principals in the city of Victoria were women, and through the 1940s almost 80% of elementary principals in Winnipeg were women.[56]

---

[47]Fleming, "Our Boys in the Field," 290.

[48]Wayne Urban, *Why Teachers Organized* (Detroit: Wayne University Press, 1982), 30.

[49]*Margaret Haley's Bulletin*, 31 January 1928, 107.

[50]As quoted in Callahan, *Education and the Cult of Efficiency*, 250–51.

[51]Pierce, *Origin and Development of the Public Principalship*, 175–76.

[52]Goodykoontz and Lane, *The Elementary School Principalship* 4, 7; James F. Hosic, "College Course for Elementary School Principals," *Teachers College Record* 27, (1926): 792.

[53]Marta Danylewycz and Alison Prentice, "Teachers, Gender, and Bureaucratizing School Systems in Nineteenth Century Montreal and Toronto," *History of Education Researcher* 24, (Spring 1984): 75–100.

[54]As quoted in Kathleen Weiler, *Country Schoolwomen: Teaching in Rural California, 1850–1950* (Stanford: Stanford University Press, 1998), 21.

[55]Tyack and Hansot, *Managers of Virtue*, 183; Goodykoontz and Lane, *The Elementary School Principalship*, 12; Pierce, *Origin and Development of the Public School Principalship*, 172.

[56]Fleming, "British Columbia Principals," 258–59; Mary Kinnear, " 'Mostly for the Male Members': Teaching in Winnepeg 1933–1966," *Historical Studies in Education* 6, (Spring 1994): 5, 13.

In comparison, women were virtually excluded from the more prestigious and higher paying secondary school principal's office. In both Canadian and American cities, women secondary school principals could be counted on one hand, and were usually employed in all-girls' schools, small schools or vocational schools.[57]

Gendered differences in elementary and secondary school principalships were embedded in the structure of the two positions. High school principals were more likely than their peers in the elementary schools to have clerical help, separate conference rooms, and assistant principals; one 1929 study reported the suggestive finding that high school principals were three times more likely to dictate letters than were elementary principals, indicating that secondary principals were three times more likely to have a secretary to whom to dictate.[58] Even the earliest secondary schools required their principals hold an advanced degree, thereby excluding women who had limited access to universities, while elementary principals required only minimal qualifications through much of the twentieth century.[59] Elementary principals were more likely than secondary principals to teach classes, be involved in direct interaction with children on the playground and lunch room, and in community and welfare organizations.[60] Early twentieth century architectural plans represented the occupational difference in material terms: the high school principal's office was positioned on the first floor, at the entrance to the school building to symbolize the principal as the public face of the school. In the elementary school, the principal's office was often on the second floor, embedded in the core of the school. Differential salaries reflected differential status: across Canada and the United States, elementary principals earned between two-thirds and three-fourths of secondary principals.[61] For those educators seeking promotion, experience as an elementary principal was considered less valuable than experience as a secondary principal. In turn of the century New York City, elementary principals were denied the opportunity even to apply for secondary principalship positions because, according to the school superintendent, the experience of managing an elementary school was simply not enough of a qualification for leading "a great city high school."[62]

To early twentieth century school reformers, the low status, expansive job description and continued feminization of the elementary principalship gave the position a decidedly unprofessional character. According to one observer in 1926, the elementary principalship, was not a professional position but merely "a function" that varied "with varying situations."[63] Reformers initiated a variety of strategies to redesign the elementary principalship, clarifying its job description, qualifications and credentialing processes, and replacing women principals with men.

In the 1920s, university programs in educational administration began to shape and categorize the work of the elementary school principal by offering specific courses on child study and elementary level administration.[64] Access to these programs was explicitly limited to men through recruitment practices and gender quotas in graduate programs. In both Canada and the United States, male veterans returning from the First and Second World Wars received tuition waivers for graduate courses.[65] Married men were particularly targeted to resolve a perceived masculinity crisis caused by too many women in elementary schools. The athletic, married male principal offered school districts a vision of stability, heteronormativity, and professionalism.[66] Further excluding women from administration was that, although teaching experience remained a requirement for the principalship, experience in the elementary school was considered less favorably than in secondary schools, as seen in the New York City case noted earlier. And in the Chicago certification checklist of 1930 cited above, elementary teachers required two years more of teaching experience than secondary teachers to qualify for the principalship.[67]

[57]Kinnear, "Mostly for the Male Members," 5; Susan Gelman, "Women Secondary School Teachers: Ontario, 1871–1930," (Ph.D. diss., University of Toronto 1994), 88–91; Dan Harrison Eikenberry, "Status of the High School Principal" (Department of the Interior, Bureau of Education. Bulletin 1925, no. 24), 43; Frank Kale Foster, "Status of the Junior High School Principal," (Department of the Interior, Bureau of Education. Bulletin 1930, no. 18), 15, 46; Andrew Fishel and Janice Pottker, "Women in Educational Governance: A Statistical Portrait," *Educational Researcher* 3, (July-August 1974): 4–7; Cecelia Reynolds, "Naming the Experience: Women, Men and Their Changing Work Lives as Teachers and Principals," (Ph.D. diss., University of Toronto, 1987), 98–99.

[58]Goodykoontz and Lane, *The Momentary School Principalship*, 12; Fred C. Ayer, "The Duties of the Public School Administrator, III," *American School Board Journal* 78, (April 1929): 40.

[59]Peterson, "Certification of School Administrators," 785; Ontario Department of Education, A *History of Professional Certificates* (Ontario Department of Education Toronto, 1935), 68.

[60]Ayer, "The Duties of the Public School Administrator," 40.

[61]Pierce, *Origin and Development of the Public School Principalship*, 188; salary estimates from the annual "Blue Books:" *Schools and Teachers of the Province of Ontario* (Toronto: Legislative Assembly of Ontario).

[62]Pierce, *Origin and Development of the Public School Principalship*, 163.

[63]Hosic, "College Courses for the Elementary Principal," 792; Goodykoontz and Lane, *The Elementary School Principalship*, 6.

[64]Hart, "Special Certification as a Means of Professionalizing Educational Leadership," 121; Goodykoontz and Lane, *The Elementary School Principalship*, 17–30.

[65]Ontario Department of Education, *History of Professional Certificates*, 50; Blount, "Manliness and the Gendered Construction of School Administration," 64.

[66]Jackie M. Blount, *Fit to Teach: Same-Sex Desire, Gender, and School Work in the Twentieth Century* (Albany: SUNY, 2005), 84. See also Catherine A. Lugg, "Sissies, Faggots, Lezzies, and Dykes: Gender, Sexual Orientation, and the New Politics of Education?" *Educational Administration Quarterly* 39, (February 2003): 95–134.

[67]Pierce, *Origin and Development of the Public School Principalship*, 175–76. There was also an "age penalty" that subtracted points for any principal applicant over the age of 54, thereby flatly denying experienced teachers credit for their years of work.

The work of elementary teaching, done primarily by women, was flatly counted as less significant for school leadership than similar work in the secondary school.[68]

Another strategy that effectively re-organized women out of the elementary principalship was school amalgamation and consolidation that systematically dismantled small elementary schools where women had been principals, and replaced them with large schools that were, in the words of one school reformer "large enough to be of interest to a man."[69] Kathleen Weiler describes how school consolidation excluded women principals in two rural counties in California between 1930 and 1950, when the number of women principals declined from almost twice the number of men principals, to one quarter.[70] A similar pattern occurred in Ontario where province-wide school consolidation in 1967 decreased the number of one-room schools from 1,400 to 500 in a two-year period.[71] Before the consolidation law was enacted, women held 26% of all principalships; three years later, they had dropped to 8%.[72]

In cities, the amalgamation of schools led to similar results. In 1917 the Hamilton, Ontario school district had 20 elementary schools, four of which had women principals. Eleven years later, the total number of schools in the city had increased to 26, in spite of the fact that four schools had closed, and those were the very schools that had women principals in 1917. Of the original women principals, only one retained an administrative position at another, smaller school. (Notably, in 1965, Hamilton still had only four women principals, even though there were now 75 schools.[73])

By the 1960s, the principalship in both Canada and the United States had been culturally reconstructed to align with gendered norms. Institutional and personal definitions of manhood and womanhood played out in school staffs with the woman in the classroom and the man in the principal's office.[74] The impact of these processes on women principals was devastating. Across the United States, the number of women school principals plummeted from well over a half before World War II to less than a quarter in the 1970s. The percentage of women principals in Winnipeg declined between 1943 and 1956 from 46% to 33%. In 1967, in the urban area of Lower Mainland of British Columbia, 5 out of 250 principals were women; although 99 women continued to lead small rural schools in the region.[75] A 1968 survey of the elementary principalship in the United States reflected the legacy of this gendered professionalization process. Compared to their male peers in the principal's office, women principals had more experience as elementary teachers and longer tenure in the school system. But women principals were less likely to hold the formal professional credentials for the position, including a masters degree, a professional license, and membership in a professional association.[76]

THE MAKING OF THE WHITE MAN IN THE PRINCIPAL'S OFFICE

Until the late 1950s, American educational administrators worried less about black principals than they did about women because black principals were essentially invisible to the public school system. Employed only in racially segregated schools, black educators worked in almost complete isolation from whites, whether in legally segregated schools in the South, or in de facto segregated schools in the North. A number of scholars have argued that black schools in the South before the school desegregation mandates of the 1950s were fiscally impoverished but rich in community support. The unintended consequences of white neglect, argues Vanessa Siddle Walker and others, was that black schools built their own communities of academic excellence, commitment to students, and neighborhood support that were a beacon of achievement for African Americans.[77] Chief among the assets of the black school was the principal.

From the mid-nineteenth through the mid-twentieth century, black principals in racially segregated schools of the South were important role models and respected leaders in their communities, often comprising the bulk of the black middle class, and serving as central liaisons between the school and the family. The black principal was regarded as a professional, responsible for

[68]For one unique exception to the exclusion of women through certification, see Anne Drummond, "Gender, Profession, and Principals: The Teachers of Quebec Protestant Academies, 1875–1900," *Historical Studies in Education* 2, (Spring 1990): 59–71.

[69]Cited in Blount, *Destined to Rule the Schools*, 123.

[70]Weiler, *Country Schoolwomen*, 240.

[71]Robert M. Stamp, *The Schools of Ontario 1876–1976* (Toronto: University of Toronto Press, 1982), 208.

[72]Shirley Stokes, "The Career Patterns of Women Elementary School Principals in Ontario," (master's thesis, University of Toronto, 1974), 1.

[73]*Schools and Teachers of the Province of Ontario.*

[74]Rosabeth Moss Kanter, *Men and Women of the Corporation* (New York: Basic Books, 1977); Angel Kwolek-Folland, *Engendering Business: Men and Women in the Corporate Office, 1870–1930* (Baltimore: Johns Hopkins University Press, 1994).

[75]Charol Shakeshaft, *Women in Educational Administration* (Newbury Park, CA: Sage, 1989), 20; Karin L. Porat, "The Woman in the Principal's Chair in Canada," *Phi Delta Kappan 67*, (December 1985): 297–98; Bernice McDonough, "Women Haven't a Chance in Our School System," *The B.C. Teacher 46*, (May-June 1967): 354–56; Kinnear, "Mostly for the Male Members," 3–5.

[76]Department of Elementary School Principals, National Education Association, *The Elementary School Principalship in 1968* (Washington, DC: Department of Elementary School Principals, 1968).

[77]Vanessa Siddle Walker, *Their Highest Potential: An African American School Community in the Segregated South* (Chapel Hill: University of North Carolina Press, 1996); Frederick A. Rodgers, *The Black High School and its Community*, (Lexington, MA: Lexington Books, 1975); Vivian Gunn Morris, *The Price They Paid: Desegregation in an African American Community* (New York Teachers College Press, 2002).

upholding the black school as the cultural symbol of the community's aspirations for its youth.[78] Ironically, black principals often had more authority than many of their white counterparts, due to the neglect of white school boards and superintendents. Ignored by district [offices], black principals could hire and fire teachers, design programs and command respect from parents, students, and staff.[79]

Black principals held local authority, but they had no independent financial power or access to resources outside the black community beyond what they could negotiate out of white administrators.[80] Furthermore, unlike many white principals, black principals at all levels were more likely to teach and be engaged in a wide variety of activities from teaching to community work to political advocacy. In this way, all black principals shared the same broad and diverse occupational responsibilities as white women elementary school principals. Similar too, was that black principals received only a fraction of the salary of any white male principal.[81]

The maintenance of a segregated system of schooling ensured black principals a culturally significant role, and the dismantling of this system destroyed that. When Southern school districts were forced to desegregate after the Supreme Court's 1954 *Brown v. Board of Education* decision, white leaders complied by closing segregated black schools. The result all across the South was the destruction of thousands of community based black schools and staff. While black teachers became scarce under this process, black principals faced literal extinction. In the decade after *Brown,* the number of black principals in the South was reduced by 90%.[82] In the late 1960s, when the enforcement of desegregation was at its peak in the American South, black principals were eliminated with what one investigating body called "avalanche-like force and tempo."[83] Numbers show the stark reality that faced black principals: Between 1964 and 1971 in Alabama, the number of black secondary school principals fell from 134 to 14; in Virginia, from 107 to 16; in each Texas and North Carolina, 600 black principals lost their jobs. In Maryland, the number of black principals decreased by 27%, while the number of white principals increased 167%. Most of these former principals were reassigned to minor administrative jobs working under white principals, or returned to the classroom, or left education altogether.[84]

The ejection of the black principal from schools left the black community without one of its most professional icons. It interrupted the recruitment and promotion paths for young black teachers and excluded a voice advocating for black children at the administrative level. It meant not only the loss of one of the few professional positions reserved for highly educated African Americans, but also "a loss of tradition of excellence, a loss of black leadership as a cultural symbol in the black community, and a loss of expertise of educators who were committed to the education of black children."[85] The loss continues: in 2002, less than 10% of all American principals were African American, and only 4% were Hispanic, at a time when students of color constitute a majority of enrollment in urban public school systems.[86] Even in urban schools with predominantly minority student populations, only one-third of all principals are African American.[87]

CONCLUSION: GO TO THE PRINCIPAL'S OFFICE

The loss of the black principal mirrors the story of the removal of white women principals from elementary schools, and both cases speak to the impact of organizational change on school culture. The occupation of the principal in elementary schools and in black schools continued the tradition of the head teacher: the *educator* who took on administrative tasks, versus the *administrator* who supervised teachers. As the principalship became a more formalized position, it was designed to be more closely aligned to and responsive to district offices than to teachers' classrooms. The new configuration of the principal's office conformed with traditional social expectations for men, and its recruitment and hiring practices explicitly excluded women and people of color. But ironically, even as the principals' office marginalized others, the principal remained in a subsidiary position: marginalized in the middle of a vast bureaucracy.

As educational historians have long argued, the development of a bureaucratic school system in the late 19th and early 20th centuries created a seismic shift in the organizational character of North American schools. In

---

[78]Tillman, "African American Principals and the Legacy of *Brown*," 102; Jacqueline Jordan Irvine, "An Analysis of the Problem of Disappearing Black Educators," *The Elementary School Journal* 88, (May 1988): 509.

[79]Tillman, "African American Principals," 109.

[80]J. Irving and E. Scott, "The Professional Functions of Negro Principals in the Public Schools of Florida in Relation to Status," *The Journal of Negro Education* 13, (Spring 1944): 171, 73.

[81]Ibid.

[82]Johnny S. Butler, "Black Educators in Louisiana: A Question of Survival," *The Journal Negro Education* 43, (Winter 1974): 22.

[83]Cited in *Tillman,* "African American Principals," 112.

[84]Karpinksi, "Bearing the Burden of Desegregation," 251; Robert Hooker, "Displacement of Black Teachers in the Eleven Southern States," *Afro-American Studies* 2, (December 1971): 165–180; Simon O. Johnson, "A Study of the Perceptions of Black Administrators Concerning the Roles of the Black Principal in Florida During the Period 1973–78," *The Journal of Negro Education* 46, (Winter 1997): 53; Everett E. Abney, "The Status of Florida's Black School Principals," *The Journal of Negro Education* 43, (Winter 1974): 3–8.

[85]Tillman, "African American Principals," 112–13.

[86]Education Writers Association, "Searching for a Superhero: Can Principals Do it All?" Washington, DC: Educational Writers Association, 2002.

[87]Tillman, "African American Principals," 112–13.

this essay, I have traced the role of the principal in those massive organizational changes. I suggest that the peculiar position of the principal as a middle manager with a "dual personality," standing between the classroom and the district, provides a fresh insight into how school systems slowly lumbered into their contemporary model. The school principal continues to represents the on-going tension between central and local management, between policy development and policy implementation, and between the formal bureaucratic aspects of school administrative work and the informal, relational and immediate demands of daily school life. However much effort has been made to separate the principal from the teacher and to design it as an authoritative and professional profession, the principalship has remained tethered to the classroom and the teacher. That legacy continues in the workload of contemporary principals who juggle a diverse array of responsibilities from supervision of staff to instructional design to disciplining of students to community relations to crisis management. Not surprisingly, there is a shortage of school principals, and, also not surprisingly, a shortage of women and people of color expressing interest in the principalship. More historical studies of the school principal may provide further insight into the curious combination of marginality and centrality of the principal in school organization and culture.

About the Author

Kate Rousmaniere is Professor of Educational Leadership at Miami University, Ohio. This essay was the History of Education Society Presidential Address delivered at the joint annual meeting of the History of Education Society and the Canadian History of Education Association, Ottawa, October 2006.

The author thanks the following for their help with the essay's conception and construction: Catherine Lugg, Jim Burchyett, Bob Hampel, Wayne Urban, Richard Quantz, Harry Smaller, Kim Underwood, Kathleen Knight Abowitz, Adah Ward Randolph, and Cecelia Reynolds.

chapter 18

Mixed-Methods Research

IMPORTANT *Ideas*

1. Researchers need multiple research methods, because a method that is well suited for one purpose, such as the study of individuals' overt behavior, might be poorly suited for another purpose, such as the study of individuals' inner lives.

2. Mixed-methods research uses both quantitative and qualitative techniques, either concurrently or sequentially, to address the same or related research questions.

3. Mixed-methods research designs differ from each other in (1) whether the quantitative and qualitative methods are used concurrently or sequentially, and if sequentially, which method is used first, (2) whether more emphasis is placed on qualitative methods or quantitative methods, and (3) whether an explicit theoretical perspective is used to guide the entire study.

4. Mixed-methods research designs vary depending on whether their purpose is to (1) use qualitative methods to explain quantitative findings, (2) use a theoretical perspective to guide the design of the study and interpretation of its findings, or (3) use qualitative and quantitative methods to triangulate findings.

5. The introductory section of a mixed-methods research report should explain the importance of the study, state the research questions or hypotheses that guided the study, and present a review of relevant literature.

6. In a mixed-methods study, the sampling procedures for the quantitative and qualitative components will vary; however, it is generally desirable to select a sample that is representative of a defined population.

7. Mixed-methods research imposes no restrictions on the types of measures that can be used.

8. Mixed-methods research reports include both quantitative results (typically based on statistical analyses) and qualitative results (typically based on the search for themes in observational or verbal data).

9. The discussion section of a mixed-methods research report should include a summary of the findings, reflections on the implications of the findings for research and practice, and a consideration of the study's limitations. ■

Key TERMS

concurrent-triangulation research design	sequential-explanatory research design	sequential-transformative research design
mixed-methods research		

The Need for Multiple Research Methods

No single research methodology, even experimentation, is sufficient for examining all facets of education from all perspectives. For this reason, different communities of researchers have formed over time in order to study particular educational problems using their own special methods. We have described the primary research methods in Parts III and IV of this book.

In the past 30 years or so, individual research methods have typically been grouped into two categories: quantitative and qualitative. Research methodologists have debated about how these two types of research differ and whether one is superior to the other. To a certain extent, qualitative research expanded in the 1970s and 1980s as a reaction to perceived inadequacies of quantitative research methods (Teddlie & Tashakkori, 2003).

Research in education and the social sciences has now reached the point where quantitative and qualitative research methodologies coexist in a state of mutual respect. Indeed, there is increasing awareness that both methodologies can be used in a single study to address the same research question. This type of inquiry typically is called mixed-methods research.

We define **mixed-methods research** as a type of study that uses both quantitative and qualitative techniques for data collection and analysis, either concurrently or sequentially, to address the same or related research questions. Given this definition, it is easy to see that you will need expertise in both quantitative and qualitative research methodology in order to design a mixed-methods study.

As a starting point for explaining mixed-methods research, we will describe a problem of educational practice and show how it can be illuminated by using quantitative or qualitative methods, or both. To help us, we repeat here a table that first appeared in Chapter 1, here labeled Table 18.1, listing the key differences between quantitative and qualitative research methods. It lists key features of each approach and sets them in contrast to each other.

Our example problem of educational practice comes from a recent report, *Diploma to Nowhere*, published by Strong American Schools (2008), a major advocacy organization for educational reform. The report was summarized in many newspapers in September 2008, including *USA Today:*

> It's a tough lesson for millions of students just now arriving on campus: Even if you have a high school diploma, you may not be ready for college.
>
> In fact, a new study calculates, one-third of American college students have to enroll in remedial classes. The bill to colleges and taxpayers for trying to bring them up to speed on material they were supposed to learn in high school comes to between $2.3 billion and $2.9 billion annually. ("Colleges," 2008)

The report documents a serious problem of practice. In the next sections, we explain how this problem can be addressed by posing different research questions, each requiring a different methodology—quantitative, qualitative, and mixed methods.

TABLE 18.1   Differences between Quantitative and Qualitative Research

Quantitative Researchers	Qualitative Researchers
Assume an objective social reality.	Assume that social reality is constructed by the participants in it.
Assume that social reality is relatively consistent across time and settings.	Assume that social reality is continuously constructed in local situations.
View causal relationships among social phenomena from a mechanistic perspective.	Assign human intentions a major role in explaining causal relationships among social phenomena.
Take an objective, detached stance toward research participants and their setting.	Become personally involved with research participants, to the point of the sharing perspectives and assuming a caring attitude.
Study populations or samples that represent populations.	Study cases.
Study behavior and other observable phenomena.	Study the meanings that individuals create and other internal phenomena.
Study human behavior in natural or contrived settings.	Study human actions in natural settings.
Analyze social reality into variables.	Make holistic observations of the total context within which social action occurs.
Use preconceived concepts and theories to determine what data will be collected.	Discover concepts and theories after data have been collected.
Generate numerical data to represent the social environment.	Generate verbal and pictorial data to represent the social environment.
Use statistical methods to analyze data.	Use analytic induction to analyze data.
Use statistical inference procedures to generalize findings from a sample to a defined population.	Generalize case findings by determining their applicability to other situations.
Prepare impersonal, objective reports of research findings.	Prepare interpretive reports that reflect researchers' constructions of the data and an awareness that readers will form their own constructions from what is reported.

Source: Table 1.2 on p. 32 in Gall, M. D., Gall, J. P., & Borg, W. R. (2007). *Educational research: An introduction* (8th ed.). Boston: Allyn & Bacon. Copyright by Pearson Education. Reprinted by permission of the publisher.

A Research Question That Requires a Quantitative Research Method

One research question raised by *Diploma to Nowhere* is whether the percentage of college students who need remedial instruction varies by the high school they attended. We raise this question because we wonder whether some high schools do a better job of preparing their students for college than others.

Answering this question clearly requires a quantitative study using descriptive research methodology (see Chapter 10). We might form a random sample of high schools from the population of all U.S. high schools, identify the students who graduated from each of the sampled high schools in a given year and completed at least one year of college, and determine the percentage of students from each high school who required remedial instruction at their college.

A Research Question That Requires
a Qualitative Research Method

The newspaper article that we mentioned includes a brief vignette about a particular student, Christina, who was an "A" student when she took high school English, but found herself placed in a remedial course when she entered Long Beach Community College in California.

The article includes a few statements by Christina about her frustration with needing remedial instruction and her perception that her high school teachers did not demand enough of her. These comments raise several research questions for us. How demanding did Christina find her teachers to be during the time that was going through high school? Did she have control over what those academic demands were? And what kind of high school experience would she like if she could repeat those years?

Answering these research questions clearly calls for a qualitative study using case study methodology. We are interested in one particular student, and we are interested in her perceived reality. Moreover, our implied perspective is not neutral, because we are wondering about the power relationships involved in high school and college instruction. Did this student have any power to control the academic demands of her curriculum, and was she given information (e.g., the intellectual demands of college and careers) that would have helped her make informed decisions about which courses to take?

A Research Question Answerable by Either Quantitative
or Qualitative Research Methods

Now we will consider a different question raised by *Diploma to Nowhere:* Why do some high school graduates need to take remedial courses in college? It is not immediately clear whether this research question requires the use of a quantitative or qualitative research method. In fact, both types of methodologies can be used to address the question. Using Table 18.1, we outline two studies, one quantitative and the other qualitative, that could shed light on why some high school graduates need to take remedial courses in college.

Study of Cases versus Study of Populations or Samples.   Our qualitative study will rely on the study of a single case. We will identify a high school that has an above-average percentage of graduates who require remedial instruction when they reach college. By intensive study of this school, we hope to discover factors that account for their graduates' need for remedial instruction.

Our quantitative study will rely on the study of two samples of college students. One sample will comprise college freshmen who do not need remedial instruction. The other sample will comprise college freshmen who are enrolled in remedial courses. Both samples will be drawn from the same university. By studying these samples, we hope to identify factors that are associated with the need for remedial instruction.

Causality as Intentional versus Mechanistic.   Qualitative researchers generally assume that people can form intentions to achieve certain goals. In other words, they can shape their own cause-and-effect relationships. In our qualitative study, then, we will interview selected high school students to determine what they are doing to prepare themselves for college. We also will interview some of their teachers about what they are doing to prepare students for college. We will synthesize what we learn from these interviews and then interview several university professors to determine their views of students' and teachers' preparation efforts.

Our quantitative study will involve a nonexperimental group comparison design (see Chapter 11), which makes no assumption about intentionality. We will compare our sample remedial and nonremedial college freshmen on quantitative measures of personality characteristics, academic achievement, and study skills. Variables on which these two groups differ will be considered as possible causes of students' placement into remedial courses.

In this research design, the factors are viewed as characteristics of students rather than as dynamic intentions that students continually form as active agents controlling their own destiny.

Discovery of Concepts or Theories versus Use of Known Concepts or Theories. In our qualitative study, we will make audio recordings of our student and teacher interviews. We might conduct additional interviews with school administrators and counselors, parents, classmates, and others depending on what we learn from the initial interviews. Using the procedures of grounded theory (see Chapter 14), researchers will analyze the interview data by coding segments into categories and grouping them to identify constructs, themes, and patterns that should help reveal which factors possibly predispose students to need remedial instruction in college.

In our quantitative study, we will start by reviewing the research literature to determine what is already known about the factors causing students to need remedial college instruction. We also will learn how these factors have been measured quantitatively. In addition, we might identify other factors by examining relevant existing theories (e.g., theories of student motivation and self-concept). We will select the most promising causative factors and compare the two groups (remedial and nonremedial college freshmen) on them. Factors on which the two groups differ will be viewed as possible causes of students' remediation status when they enter college.

In the qualitative study, then, the purpose is to discover concepts and theories. In the quantitative study, the purpose is to use known concepts and theories to create new research knowledge.

Analysis of the Illustrative Quantitative and Qualitative Studies.   The preceding sections demonstrate how a quantitative study and a qualitative study might have contrasting features, yet address the same research question. We could elaborate on this analysis by using other features listed in Table 18.1, but they are sufficiently clear to enable you to do this analysis on your own.

Note that our analysis does not privilege either the quantitative or the qualitative research approach. Both of the outlined research studies have value and can contribute important knowledge that addresses our research question: Why do some high school graduates need to take remedial courses in college?

Note, too, that we have described each study as separate from the other. In fact, we could have designed this investigation as a single study, not two. It would simply be a larger study, requiring a "mix" of two methodologies—one quantitative, the other qualitative. Each methodology would complement the other, in that each might identify different factors that result in college-level remedial instruction.

In the next sections, we analyze in more detail how quantitative and qualitative methods can be "mixed" in a single study, so that they complement each other rather than constituting stand-alone studies.

Types of Mixed-Methods Research

As the mixed-methods approach to research has evolved in recent decades, researchers have created design variations that suit their particular purposes. Some researchers (e.g., Creswell, Plano Clark, Gutmann, & Hanson, 2003) have developed typologies to classify these design variations and help researchers realize their options when designing a mixed-methods study.

No one of these typologies has become the accepted standard for mixed-methods researchers. However, there is one point of consensus: The term *mixed methods* applies only to studies that employ both quantitative and qualitative methods. Thus, a study that employed two quantitative research methods (e.g., descriptive research and an experiment) or two qualitative research methods (e.g., narrative study and critical ethnography) would not constitute a mixed-methods study. To be classified as mixed-methods research, the study must have design elements that genuinely reflect some or all of the features of both qualitative and quantitative research, as listed in Table 18.1.

Typologies of mixed-methods research designs have separate classifications for designs in which quantitative and qualitative methods are used concurrently and those in which they are used sequentially. Some typologies also distinguish between a sequential design in which quantitative methods are used first and a sequential design in which qualitative methods are used first. Several of the typologies differentiate whether quantitative methods or qualitative methods were given more emphasis in the study. Finally, a typology might discriminate between mixed-methods studies that are guided by a theoretical perspective and mixed-methods studies that are not.

In the following sections, we present several types of mixed-methods designs that appear particularly useful for developing knowledge to help educators solve problems of practice. We classify each example using typologies developed by John Creswell, Vicki Plano Clark, Michelle Gutmann, and William Hanson (2003). The examples illustrate three of the major mixed-method designs that they present.

Using Qualitative Methods to Explain Quantitative Findings

Researchers can design a quantitative research study in two phases. The first phase is a standard quantitative study using one of the designs described in Part III of this book. The second phase is a qualitative study to help them understand the research findings of the first phase. The inclusion of this second phase can help the researchers understand their quantitative findings, especially if they are exploring educational phenomena about which little is known. Because this type of study includes both quantitative and qualitative methods, it qualifies as a mixed-methods design.

L. Brent Igo, Kenneth Kiewra, and Roger Bruning (2008) used this type of mixed-methods design in a study of students' note-taking behavior. The first phase of the study was an experiment involving students' note-taking behavior while studying text-based sources on the Web. Previous research had found that the majority of students prefer to copy and paste selected sections of the text onto a computer file (perhaps using software such as Microsoft Word) rather than typing their own notes.

However, at least one previous study cited by Igo and his colleagues found that most high school students in advanced placement courses preferred typing their own notes. Another study found that limiting the amount of Web-based text that students could copy and paste was beneficial to learning. Students were required to paste their notes into an electronic chart that only allowed seven words per cell. An explanation for the positive effect of this restriction is that limiting the amount of text that can be pasted requires students to engage in deep processing of the text in order to decide which words to copy and paste.

Igo and his colleagues (2008) designed an experiment in which college students were randomly assigned to four different treatment conditions. In each condition, students studied a 1,796-word Web document about three learning theories. They copied and pasted their notes into an electronic chart containing 3 columns (one for each learning theory) and 11 rows (each row involving a different topic, such as definition, assumptions, and impact on instruction). Depending on the experimental condition to which they had been assigned, students could copy and paste (1) 7 words, (2) 14 words, (3) 21 words, or (4) an unlimited number of words into each cell.

After studying the text and copying and pasting (7, 14, 21, or an unrestricted number of words) on Day 1, students took three tests assessing recall of facts, concept recognition, and relational inferences on Day 2. The researchers' hypothesis predicted that

> students assigned to the 7-word, 14-word, and 21-word copy-and-paste conditions will
> perform better on tests assessing (a) cued recall of facts, (b) recognition of concepts, and

(c) inferences regarding relationships among text ideas than students in the unrestricted copy-and-paste condition. (Igo et al., 2008, p. 153)

Their rationale for the hypothesis was that restrictions on note-taking compel students to engage in deeper cognitive processing of the text.

The test results are shown in Table 18.2. To the researchers' surprise, their hypothesis was not supported by the empirical results. Students in the unrestricted copy-and-paste condition demonstrated superior learning to students in two of the restricted conditions (14 words and 21 words), and they learned as well as students in the 7-word condition.

This unexpected finding led the researchers to pose the question, "Why did students in the unrestricted pasting group perform as well as those in the 7-word restricted pasting group?" (Igo et al., 2008, p. 157). They answered this question by using qualitative methods in the second phase of their study. They analyzed the students' note-taking charts and also interviewed 12 of the research participants—several from each of the four experimental conditions.

The researchers learned from their analysis of students' note-taking charts that students in the unrestricted condition copied and pasted many fewer words per cell ($M = 24$) than was found in a previous research study ($M = 42$). Also, in the previous study, students who pasted the most words performed poorer on the posttests than students who posted the fewest words.

Thus, it appears that students in the unrestricted group in the present study were relatively selective in what they copied and pasted, even though they were free to paste as many notes as they wished. Their self-imposed selectivity means that they probably engaged in more cognitive processing of the text than the researchers expected.

Igo and his colleagues (2008) also interviewed students about their cognitive processes while copying and pasting and whether they modified their notes after copying them into the chart cells and, if so, why. The researchers made verbatim transcripts of the interviews and then analyzed them.

The analysis revealed that three different processes can occur in the copy-and-paste method when studying Web-based text. The student can read the text and copy a section (7, 14, 21, or unlimited words) into the chart cell; they can completely replace what they copied by copying another section of the text; or they can modify the copied section.

TABLE 18.2   Means and   Standard Deviations for Experimental Groups

	Unrestricted	21-Word Restricted	14-Word Restricted	7-Word Restricted
Fact test				
M	4.77	2.63	2.00	4.87
SD	3.79	2.44	1.84	3.84
Relational test				
M	2.73	1.00	0.54	2.39
SD	2.41	1.45	0.88	2.21
Concepts test				
M	8.05	6.96	6.67	7.87
SD	2.88	2.42	2.44	2.32

Source: Table on p. 156 of Igo, L. B., Kiewra, K. A., & Bruning, R. (2008). Individual differences and intervention flaws: A sequential explanatory study of college students' copy-and-paste note taking. Journal of Mixed Methods Research, 2(2), 149–168. Copyright © 2008 by Sage Publications. Reprinted by permission of Sage Publications.

The researchers identified five themes in the transcripts, which, in brief, revealed that students in the unrestricted group focused almost entirely on the text, whereas students in the other three groups found themselves focusing both on the text and on the copy-and-paste restrictions, which sometimes proved distracting. For example, here is what one student in the unrestricted group stated: "I just put in the [sentence] that I thought fit the category best. . . . I didn't want to change what I had. . . . I just went with my instinct about it" (Igo et al., 2008, p. 161). In contrast, a student in the 21-word group stated: "In some cells, I had things that didn't need to be there. . . . I took them out," and "I usually took a couple of sentences that sounded good and then put them in [the cell] and trimmed them down to 14 words" (Igo et al., 2008, pp. 163–164).

The 7-word group expressed fewer copy-and-paste distractions than the 14-word and 21-word groups. This qualitative finding led the researchers to conclude that the lower frequency of distractions led them to perform more like the unrestricted group. It also led them to conclude that the greater frequency of distractions encountered by the 14-word and 21-word groups caused them to have the lowest learning levels of the four experimental groups.

Igo and his colleagues (2008) distilled their conclusions to make several practical recommendations to teachers whose students use the copy-and-paste method while reading Web-based text. Primarily, they recommend that teachers prompt the students to be selective in how much of the text they copy and paste. They suggest that teachers might encourage students just to copy and paste key sentences or the main idea stated in a paragraph. The goal, in other words, is not note-taking for its own sake, but rather note-taking that facilitates deep processing of the information contained in the text.

According to the mixed-methods typology of Creswell and his colleagues (2003), the design of this study is sequential explanatory. According to them, a **sequential-explanatory research design** involves the collection and analysis of quantitative data followed by the collection and analysis of qualitative data, which are then used to explain the quantitative findings.

Using a Theoretical Perspective to Guide a Mixed-Methods Study

John Parmelee, Stephynie Perkins, and Judith Sayre (2007) conducted a mixed-methods study to explore how political ads affect college students. They used framing theory to guide their research design and interpretations. According to this theory, mass media and other social entities focus individuals' attention on certain events and not others in order to shape their perceptions of social reality.

R. M. Entman (1993) explained the framing process: "To frame is to select some aspects of a perceived reality and make them more salient in a communicating text, in such a way as to promote a particular problem definition, causal interpretation, moral evaluation, and/or treatment recommendation for the item described" (p. 52).

Parmelee and his colleagues drew on framing theory to help them understand why young people generally have a relatively low voter turnout in elections. The specific election of interest was the 2004 presidential election in which George W. Bush and John Kerry were the Republican and Democratic candidates, respectively.

Qualitative data collection and analysis constituted the first phase of the mixed-methods study. The researchers selected a sample of 32 college students, ages 18 to 28, which included registered Democrats, Republicans, and independents, as well as nonregistered voters. The students were organized into four focus groups and shown eight political ads sponsored by Kerry's and Bush's campaigns. Each focus group was asked to discuss three main topics:

- In what ways have political ads successfully or unsuccessfully spoken to you in the past?
- How did the ads shown in the study speak to you?
- What would you do to make political ads better engage college students? (Parmelee et al., 2007, p. 188)

The researchers made an audiotape recording of each focus group discussion, created a verbatim transcript of each recording, and then analyzed the transcripts for themes using the method of constant comparison (see Chapter 14). The themes resulting from this qualitative analysis are shown in Figure 18.1.

Parmelee and his colleagues interpreted the themes to mean that the ads created frames of little relevance to college students. Also, negative ads confirmed their preexisting cynicism toward adult authority figures.

The quantitative phase of the study involved a content analysis of the eight Bush and Kerry TV ads for issues that they mentioned. The content analysis revealed 13 issues: abortion, education, environment, health care, jobs, Medicare/Social Security, outsourcing, prescription drugs, stem cells, taxes, tuition assistance, terrorism, and the war in Iraq. The researchers also coded whether the ads were framed by visually showing 18- to 24-year-olds or by including statements that mentioned young adults.

The content analysis revealed that only one of the eight ads was framed to address college students. Furthermore, this ad only covered one of the 13 issues mentioned above. The researchers quoted one of the research participants, a 22-year-old college student, to convey the impact of this framing of the presidential campaign by TV:

> I just feel like all these ads are addressing the same thing, and they're kind of disregarding our age group. And it's kind of like a put-down, like we're not going to vote, you know? So maybe if they'd address it more towards our age group, we'd be more involved. (Parmelee et al., 2007, p. 191)

Parmelee and his colleagues explained these findings in terms of framing theory. They concluded that the framing of the political issues in the TV ads had the effect of limiting

FIGURE *18.1*   Emergent Focus Group Themes

1. Political advertising fails to engage participants because their issues are not addressed or are not addressed from their perspective:
   a. health insurance (they cannot afford health plans or had other concerns)
   b. educational issues (ads fail to include discussion of issues important to higher education, such as tuition assistance)
   c. the war in Iraq
   d. the war on terror
   e. jobs
   f. taxes

2. Ads ignore college student demographic in visual inclusion of actors from this demographic

3. Students cynical about negative nature of many ads

4. Students attracted to humor in some ads

5. Participants prefer to use Internet sites or other sources for political information

6. Suggested that political ads would be more relevant for this demographic if they discussed issues important to age group

7. Ads would gain legitimacy if they emphasized the importance of voting in general

Source: Table 1 on p. 190 of Parmelee, J. H., Perkins, S. C., & Sayre, J. J. (2007). "What about people our age?" Appling qualitative and quantitative methods to uncover how political ads alienate college students. *Journal of Mixed Methods Research, 1*(2), 183–199. Copyright © 2008 by Sage Publications. Reprinted by permission of Sage Publications.

their meaning and importance to college students, characterizing this effect as "the frame of omission" (2007, p. 192). The researchers mention several recommendations for changing this frame, such as having ads mention the relevance of the issues to young people and drawing on students' sensibilities and mannerisms.

Educators might draw other lessons from the study's findings for improving schooling. For example, they might review the social studies curriculum to determine whether issues of historical importance are framed in a manner that includes individuals of the same age group as the students and that motivates students by making reference to their particular way of seeing the world.

The researchers stated that their mixed-methods study was based on a sequential-transformative research design. According to Creswell and his colleagues (2003), a **sequential-transformative research design** involves the use of a theoretical perspective to guide both the qualitative and quantitative phases of data collection, analysis, and interpretation; either the qualitative or the quantitative phase can occur first. In the case of this study, framing theory was the theoretical perspective that guided the study's methodology and interpretation of the findings.

Using Qualitative and Quantitative Methods to Triangulate Findings

Lynn Hoffman and Katharyn Nottis (2008) conducted a mixed-methods study to learn how eighth-grade students become motivated to do their best on a state-mandated high-stakes test. The journal article that reports their study is reprinted at the end of this chapter. We briefly describe it here, because it illustrates a particular mixed-methods research design.

Among the research questions guiding the study were the following two: "What strategies do students perceive as influential in motivating them during a high-stakes testing situation?" and "How do students articulate elements of effective test preparation?" (p. 212).

Hoffman and Nottis collected two types of data to answer these questions. One was a quantitative measure consisting of a 20-item questionnaire, illustrated by the following two items from the questionnaire:

- I appreciated the morning announcements and posters from the Student Government Association wishing us good luck on the test.
- I wanted to help prove that our eighth grade class is the best. (2008, p. 221)

Students responded to each item on a 5-point scale, with 1 indicating no influence on performance and 5 indicating a great deal of influence on performance.

Qualitative data also were collected immediately after students completed the questionnaire. Students were asked to write a letter to their school principal in which they offered ideas about how to help students work hard so they would do well on the high-stakes test. Hoffman and Nottis analyzed the letters qualitatively to identify common themes in their content.

The next step was to jointly interpret the quantitative and qualitative results: "Themes developed from the analysis of qualitative data were compared again with findings from the quantitative data to determine points of convergence or divergence" (2008, p. 214). Findings from analysis of the questionnaire data generally were supported by the qualitative data. For example, the two questionnaire items with the highest scores were: "Wanted to attend the picnic after testing" and "Appreciated edible treats provided by the teacher during the test." This finding was corroborated by comments in the students' letters to the principal, for example: "Knowing that we had a great picnic to look forward to made me want to do my best. It provided something special for our hard work and I knew that if I did not work hard, I did not deserve the picnic" (p. 215). This convergence from two different data sources—one qualitative and the other quantitative—serves to strengthen the validity of the findings.

In the typology of Creswell and his colleagues (2003), Hoffman and Nottis's (2008) mixed-methods study followed a concurrent-triangulation design. A **concurrent-triangulation research design** involves collecting qualitative and quantitative data at approximately the same time and then determining whether the findings generated by analysis of each type of data corroborate the other.

Note that, in this definition, we use the term *corroborate* to indicate that two sets of data analyses yield similar results. Researchers also use other terms that have the same meaning. Hoffman and Nottis use *convergence*. Creswell and his colleagues (2003) use the terms *confirm, cross-validate,* and *corroborate* (p. 229) interchangeably to refer to the interpretation of quantitative and qualitative findings as similar or different. They use still another term, *triangulation,* in their label for this research design. We present all these terms here, because you might come across any or all of them in reading reports of mixed-methods research.

Reading a Mixed-Methods Research Report

Reports of mixed-methods studies vary in how they are organized. Quantitative and qualitative methods and results can be presented in various sequences, depending on the study's purpose. Nonetheless, there are commonalities across reports of mixed-methods research. To illustrate these commonalities, we use as our example a mixed-methods study by Meg Schleppenbach, Lucia Flevares, Linda Sims, and Michelle Perry (2007). The study examined a common problem of practice in mathematics instruction, namely how teachers should respond to student errors during mathematics instruction.

Introduction

In the introductory section of a mixed-methods research report, the researchers should explain the importance of the study and the research questions to be answered or hypotheses to be tested. They should provide a justification for the use of mixed methods to study these questions or hypotheses. They also should provide a review of relevant literature.

In the introduction to their research report, Schleppenbach and her colleagues noted that the *Professional Standards for Teaching Mathematics,* published by the National Council of Teachers of Mathematics (1991), emphasizes the importance of student discourse as a way to promote students' learning of mathematics. Discourse does not primarily help students get more "right" answers but rather helps students think about and understand mathematics.

The researchers' primary purpose in conducting the study was to explore how students' errors in mathematics, and teachers' responses to them, can promote mathematical discourse and understanding. They focused on students' errors because their review of the literature suggested that this classroom phenomenon might have particular value for promoting these goals. For example, they cited an experiment (Borasi, 1994) that found students' errors, if used properly by teachers, could be "springboards for inquiry" into mathematical concepts and reasoning.

The researchers chose to examine students' errors from multiple perspectives. This goal was accomplished by observing how teachers in two different cultures, Chinese and American, respond to student errors. To keep the study focused, Schleppenbach and her colleagues framed three questions:

> Do the instructional practices of Chinese teachers look different from those of U.S. teachers in terms of responses to errors? If so, how are they different? And finally, what can we learn from these differences? (2007, p. 134)

The researchers expanded on the third question by saying that they particularly wanted to learn from their data analyses whether some teacher practices are more effective than others in encouraging mathematical discourse, inquiry, and understanding. This statement demonstrates the researchers' interest in applying their research findings to educational practice.

Research Design

Schleppenbach and her colleagues (2007) did not explicitly label their research as a mixed-methods design. However, it is clear that the design involved the use of both quantitative and qualitative research methodology. They used quantitative research methods to collect observational data about teacher and student behavior in actual classroom settings. They also interviewed the teachers about the observed lesson and their philosophy of teaching and used qualitative methods to analyze interview responses.

Most important, the researchers integrated the two data sources to pursue a larger goal: "These [interview] statements and [classroom] practices were integrated into a presentation of four themes regarding beliefs and practices surrounding errors, with the goal being to examine how teachers' beliefs about the use of errors translated into inquiry-based practice regarding errors" (2007, p. 137). This statement indicates that the researchers did not subordinate quantitative data to qualitative data, or the reverse. Instead, they respected both types of data as sources for speculating about what teachers can do to promote student inquiry, discourse, and understanding during mathematics instruction.

Sampling Procedure

Mixed-methods research can accommodate various sampling procedures. The researchers' selection among these procedures will depend on the quantitative and qualitative methodologies that they plan to use to address their research questions or hypotheses.

Whatever the sampling procedures, it is desirable to select a sample, at least for the quantitative phase of the study, that is representative of a defined population. By doing so, readers of the research report will be able to determine whether the findings are likely to generalize to the population of interest to them. Purposeful sampling strategies (see Chapter 14) generally are used for the qualitative phase of the study.

Schleppenbach and her colleagues (2007) selected their sample to represent various populations: 10 first-grade teachers and 14 fifth-grade teachers from China and 5 first-grade teachers and 12 fourth- and fifth-grade teachers from the United States. This sampling procedure enabled them to study student errors during instruction on two mathematical topics: place value in first grade and manipulation of fractions at the fourth- or fifth-grade level. Manipulation of fractions is taught at the fifth grade in China and at either the fourth or fifth grade in the United States.

The researchers acknowledged that the participating teachers constituted a convenience sample (see Chapter 6) rather than a randomly drawn sample from a defined population. For this reason they state, "Because we did not randomly select the teachers, we naturally exercise caution in drawing inferences" (2007, p. 135).

The schools in which the teachers in the two countries worked were not matched. Therefore, we cannot be certain whether variations in student and teacher behavior reflect cultural or other factors. However, the researchers note that cross-cultural comparisons were not the key interest of their study. Rather, their interest was in observing a wide range of teacher behavior and beliefs in order to generate good ideas about how teachers might use student errors to promote mathematical inquiry, discourse, and understanding.

Measures

Mixed-methods research imposes no restrictions on the types of measures that are permissible. Any of the measures described in Chapter 6 or the chapters in Part IV can be used to collect data.

Schleppenbach and her colleagues (2007) used videotape to record 46 mathematics lessons taught by their sample of 24 Chinese teachers and 17 U.S. teachers. They analyzed only the parts of each lesson that involved whole-class instruction. Their two-fold rationale for this decision was based on the difficulty of hearing verbal interaction during small-group work and seatwork and their belief that norms for discourse and inquiry are established most strongly for students during whole-class instruction.

The researchers' report does not include the questions they asked in the teacher interviews. Also, they do not indicate whether all teachers were asked the same questions and whether follow-up questions were asked following particular teacher statements. The researchers do state that the interview was designed to elicit teacher comments about how they prepared the lesson that was videotaped, the major points of the lesson, incidents during the lesson that surprised them, their methods for addressing student differences in mathematical ability, and their philosophy of mathematics instruction.

Results

Descriptive and inferential statistics generally are used to analyze the quantitative data in a mixed-methods study. Analytic techniques used in case study research (see Chapter 14) generally are applied to the qualitative data. The quantitative and qualitative analyses are often presented separately and then integrated in a subsequent section. This was the case in the study of mathematics instruction that we are using as an example.

Quantitative Results.   Schleppenbach and her colleagues (2007) counted the number of student errors that occurred during whole-class instruction in each videotaped lesson. They also computed the amount of time that whole-class instruction occurred during the lesson. Dividing error frequency by the time measure yielded the variable, number of errors per minute.

The researchers found that the mean number of errors per minute varied little across lesson types (place value and fractions) and the teachers' country (China and the United States). The lowest mean number of errors per minute was 0.40 for U.S. place-value lessons (compared to 0.50 for the Chinese lessons), and the highest mean number of errors per minute was 0.55 for U.S. fraction lessons (compared to 0.44 for the Chinese lessons). We find, then, that students make errors while learning mathematics fairly frequently—approximately one every two minutes during whole-class instruction.

The researchers developed a coding scheme to categorize the types of responses that teachers made in response to student errors. Some of the response types are teacher statements, and others are teacher questions. These two categories and the subcategories under each of them are listed in the first column of Table 18.3. The statistics shown in Table 18.3 are student errors in lessons about place value. Results for the lessons about fractions were similar.

Schleppenbach and her colleagues (2007) found that teachers in both countries were more likely to respond to a student error with a question than a statement. Most commonly, they asked the same question to the same student who made the error or redirected the same question to another student.

The primary cultural difference revealed by the statistics in Table 18.4 is the relative emphasis on statements and questions after a student made a mathematical error. Although both Chinese and American teachers were more likely to respond to a student error with a question than a statement, Chinese teachers did so more often.

These quantitative results tell us something about the prevalence of student errors during mathematics instruction and how teachers respond to them. They provide a window into teachers' classrooms, but they do not tell us why teachers respond the way they do to student errors and whether one type of response is better than another. For answers, we need to look at the results of the researchers' qualitative analyses.

Qualitative Results.   The researchers derived four themes from the interview data and from an analysis of the videotaped lessons.

1. *Creating a classroom environment that supports errors.* The teachers expressed the belief that student errors are a good way for helping them discover the students' learning needs. Therefore, they try to convey to students that they should feel free to make errors, as one Chinese teacher stated:

I won't discourage [the children who make mistakes] and will let them speak out their ideas confidently. It doesn't matter if you say it wrong. If only you dare say it, you're so great. In this way all the students can fully express themselves, and their problems can be exposed and resolved in a timely manner. (Schleppenbach et al., 2007, p. 140)

This belief in the value of student errors is supported by the researchers' quantitative finding that errors are, in fact, prevalent—approximately one every two minutes.

2. *Creating "good mistakes."* Some teachers in the sample deliberately asked questions that some students would answer incorrectly. For example, in a fractions lesson, a teacher asked students how they would write "one whole." Evidently, students had just been taught that a fraction with the same numerator and same denominator equals 1. Therefore, some students stated that sixteen-sixteenths is "one whole." The teacher used this error as an opportunity to note that sixteen-sixteenths has 16 parts, and therefore is not a single whole thing.

The researchers commented that the elicitation of "good mistakes" might be a productive way for teachers to encourage mathematical inquiry and discourse among students.

3. *Review, review, and review again.* Some of the teachers commented that review is a powerful technique for helping students learn from their errors. For example, they refer to

TABLE *18.3*   Mean Proportion of Each Type of Teacher Response to Student Errors in Chinese and U.S. Lessons about Place Value

Type of Teacher Response	Mean Proportion for Chinese Teachers	Mean Proportion for U.S. Teachers	t value
Teacher Statement	.16	.34	2.65*
Tells the student the answer is wrong	.03	.10	0.92
Gives the correct answer	.08	.05	0.89
Ignores the error	.02	.05	0.77
Provides explanation or direction	.04	.14	2.32*
Students spontaneously correct themselves	.003	0	0.69
Teacher Question	.84	.66	2.65*
Re-asks the question	.28	.15	1.76
Clarifies the question	.11	.03	2.76*
Asks for an addition to the answer	.09	0	5.57**
Asks for certainty about the answer or agreement with it	.11	.25	3.33*
Redirects the question	.22	.24	0.28
Asks for student explanation of the answer	.03	0	1.61

*p < .05

**p < .001

Source: Adapted from Table 1 on p. 139 of Schleppenbach, M., Flevares, L. M., Sims, L. M., & Perry, M. (2007). Teachers' responses to student mistakes in Chinese and U.S. mathematics classrooms. *Elementary School Journal, 108*(2), 131–147.

Chinese teachers' practice of having a student remain standing after they made an error. The teachers asked other students to provide the correct answer. Then the teachers asked the student who made the error to repeat the correct answer aloud.

This is a form of review, in that the student who made the error had the opportunity to review it and replace it with the correct answer. Another type of review used by Chinese teachers is a remedial class where students who make repeated errors can receive instruction that addresses the learning problems that result in these errors.

4. *Students working through errors.* The researchers found in their quantitative results that Chinese teachers more often asked questions after a student error than did American teachers. They analyzed their qualitative data in search of an explanation of this cultural difference.

Their analysis led the researchers to explain: "We concluded that the emphasis on questions by the Chinese teachers was a matter of encouraging students to work through their errors rather than correcting their errors immediately" (Schleppenbach et al., 2007, p. 143). The Chinese and American teachers who engaged in this practice did so in various ways, such as having students work more problems to see if they could discover the errors in their thinking or by asking other students to help them.

Discussion

As is typical in reports of other kinds of research, reports of mixed-methods research often include a summary of their findings and extend them by exploring their implications for practice and further research. For example, Schleppenbach and her colleagues repeat their finding that errors in mathematics instruction are common and then speculate that "students' self-esteem does not suffer and they are better able to correct mistakes and learn more mathematics than when errors are discouraged" (2007, p. 145).

This speculation, which derives from the researchers' analysis of teacher interviews and videotaped lessons, can be tested by further research. Researchers can use qualitative or quantitative methods, or a combination of both, to determine whether student outcomes (self-esteem and mathematics learning) are different in classrooms where errors are encouraged and respected than in classrooms where they are not.

The researchers also reflect on their findings about how teachers correct students' errors—whether to correct the error immediately or to ask questions that encourage students to work their way through the error to a correct answer. They state, "Obviously there is a fine line between giving students time to correct their errors and letting the discussion about an error go on too long" (Schleppenbach et al., 2007, p. 145). Researchers can speculate about what this "fine line" is and design a study to explore, quantitatively, qualitatively, or both, decision rules about when, and for how long, it is best to let students' discover for themselves the source of their mathematical errors.

Educators, too, can reflect on the researchers' findings and consider experimenting with the way they handle students' errors in mathematics and other curriculum subjects. They can do this informally and collegially or more formally through action research (see Chapter 19).

Limitations of the research study are also considered in the discussion section of a report of a mixed-methods study. For example, Schleppenbach and her colleagues obtained richer quantitative and qualitative data by studying both Chinese and U.S. classrooms. However, their sampling approach still leaves room for further exploration using other cultures.

The researchers commented that "we did not see such high-level discourse practices surrounding errors as students debating each other about the plausibility of an error" (2007, p. 146). They noted that this type of practice is recommended by the National Council of Teachers of Mathematics and by experts on mathematics instruction. This limitation can be addressed by additional studies in which researchers identify classrooms where this practice occurs and study its possible strengths and weaknesses.

Evaluating Reports of Mixed-Methods Studies

The most essential feature of mixed-methods research studies is that they employ both quantitative and qualitative methodologies. Therefore, in evaluating them, you can employ both Appendix 2 on evaluating a quantitative research report and Appendix 3 on evaluating a qualitative research report. In addition, you can pose the following questions specific to evaluating reports of mixed-methods studies.

• Did the researchers use both quantitative and qualitative methods in their study?

   If the answer to this question is no, it is not a mixed-methods study. Rather, it should be analyzed to identify which of the other research designs covered in this book was actually used.

• Did the researchers combine quantitative and qualitative methods so that they shed more light on the research problem than either method would have alone?

   In this chapter, we described three productive uses of a mixed-methods design: (1) using qualitative methods to explain quantitative findings; (2) testing the validity and utility of a theory to explain both quantitative and qualitative data; and (3) using qualitative and quantitative methods to triangulate research findings.

An example of
HOW MIXED-METHODS RESEARCH CAN HELP IN SOLVING PROBLEMS OF PRACTICE

Many of us grew up at a time when our parents—and we—did not know how we were doing in school until the teacher gave us a report card once or twice a term. Online grading systems are changing all that, as you can see in the following newspaper article, which we have excerpted.

> Parents and students in a growing number of Washington area schools can track fluctuations in a grade-point average from the nearest computer in real time. . . .
>
> A student can log on at school, or a parent at work, to see the immediate impact of a missed assignment on the cumulative grade. . . .
>
> Children harbor mixed feelings about the march of educational technology. Honor-roll students tend to appreciate 24/7 access to grades more than those with checkered academic records.
>
> De Vise, D. (2008, November 3). Online grading systems mean no more changing D's to B's. Retrieved from www.washingtonpost.com

Online grading appears to be a step forward in the use of technology to improve learning. But is it in fact a step forward? Research is needed to determine how well online grading works, both on its own and in comparison with traditional grading. Mixed-methods research can provide answers, as we demonstrate.

We suggest a mixed-methods study in which the first phase is an experiment using quantitative methodology. Schools in which teachers use traditional grading methods will constitute the sample. The schools will be randomly assigned to two conditions. Schools in the experimental condition will move to an online grading system. Schools in the control condition will retain their usual grading system.

   Once the online grading system has been well established, we will compare the grades of students in the experimental and control conditions. We also might administer standardized achievement tests and a rating scale measuring attitudes toward school to determine whether the two groups differ on these measures.

The newspaper article cited above suggests that high-achieving students might benefit from online grading more than low-achieving students. We can test this possibility by forming students in the experimental condition into two groups (high-achieving and low-achieving) based on their scores on standardized achievement tests. We will follow the same procedure for students in the control condition. Our data analysis will determine whether the online grading system has differential effects on high-achieving and low-achieving students.

The second phase of the study will involve case studies, using qualitative methodology. Our cases will be a small number of randomly selected students in the experimental and control conditions. We will interview control group students to learn their reactions to their customary grading system, and we will interview experimental group students to learn their reactions to online grading.

We expect that our qualitative data will help us interpret the findings from the experiment. For example, suppose we find that students earn higher grades if they have access to online grading. This finding in itself does not tell us why this effect occurred. Case study data might provide an explanation.

A mixed-methods study of this type is likely to be more useful to educators who are considering an online grading system than either a stand-alone quantitative study or a stand-alone qualitative study.

Self-Check Test

1. Well-designed experiments that yield statistically significant findings about a problem of practice
   a. are sufficiently conclusive that mixed-methods research is not necessary.
   b. still will leave important unanswered questions that can be addressed by multiple-methods research.
   c. can best be replicated through qualitative research studies.
   d. constitute a type of mixed-methods research if observational data are collected and quantified.

2. One of the main rationales for mixed-methods research is that
   a. qualitative measurements are imprecise, and therefore they need to be checked by quantitative measurements.
   b. some readers of a research report will find more meaning in statistical results, and other readers will find more meaning in case stories and themes.
   c. the value of qualitative research is heavily disputed, and therefore a qualitative study gains in legitimacy if supplemented by a quantitative component.
   d. research participants are more likely to take tests if they know that they also will be interviewed.

3. A mixed-methods study in which qualitative methods are used to explain quantitative findings can be classified as a
   a. sequential-explanatory design.
   b. sequential-exploratory design.
   c. sequential-transformative design.
   d. sequential-triangulation design.

4. A mixed-methods study that is guided by an explicit theoretical perspective can be classified as a
   a. sequential-explanatory design.
   b. sequential-exploratory design.
   c. sequential-transformative design.
   d. sequential-triangulation design.

5. The purpose of triangulation in a mixed-methods study is to determine whether
   a. the researchers have coded verbal transcripts similarly.
   b. the quantitative and qualitative findings support previous research on the same topic.
   c. there are points of convergence between the quantitative and qualitative results.
   d. the research participants agree with the researchers' depiction of themes in the qualitative data.

6. In a mixed-methods study,
   a. the same sampling procedure must be used to select a sample for both the quantitative and qualitative phases.
   b. it is inappropriate to use random sampling procedures.
   c. the cases to be studied in the qualitative phase should determine the sample that is selected for the quantitative phase.
   d. it is desirable to select a sample for the quantitative phase that is representative of a defined population.

7. In a mixed-methods study, it is common to see
   a. a presentation of the quantitative results and discussion of their significance, followed by a presentation of the qualitative results and discussion of their significance.
   b. the presentation of quantitative and qualitative results in separate sections.
   c. a sequence in which each qualitative result is followed by the presentation of a corresponding quantitative result.
   d. separate presentations of the quantitative and qualitative results, but without an integrated interpretation of both sets of results.

Chapter References

Borasi, R. (1994). Capitalizing on errors as "springboards for inquiry": A teaching experiment. *Journal for Research in Mathematics Education, 25,* 166–208.

Colleges spend billions on remedial classes to prep freshman. (2008, September 19). *USA Today.* Retrieved from www.usatoday.com/neus/education/2008-09-15-colleges-remedialclasses_N.htm

Creswell, J. W., Plano Clark, V. L., Gutmann, M. L., & Hanson, W. E. (2003). Advanced mixed methods research designs. In A. Tashakkori & C. Teddlie (Eds.), *Handbook of mixed methods in social and behavioral research* (pp. 209–240). Thousand Oaks, CA: Sage.

Entman, R. M. (1993). Framing: Toward clarification of a fractured paradigm. *Journal of Communication, 43,* 51–58.

Hoffman, L. M., & Nottis, K. E. K. (2008). Middle school students' perceptions of effective motivation and preparation factors for high-stakes tests. *NASSP Bulletin, 92*(3), 209–223.

Igo, L. B., Kiewra, K. A., & Bruning, R. (2008). Individual differences and intervention flaws: A sequential explanatory study of college students' copy-and-paste note taking. *Journal of Mixed Methods Research, 2*(2), 149–168.

National Council of Teachers of Mathematics (NCTM). (1991). *Professional standards for teaching mathematics.* Reston, VA: Author.

Parmelee, J. H., Perkins, S. C., & Sayre, J. J. (2007). "What about people our age?" Applying qualitative and quantitative methods to uncover how political ads alienate college students. *Journal of Mixed Methods Research, 1*(2), 183–199.

Schleppenbach, M., Flevares, L. M., Sims, L. M., & Perry, M. (2007). Teachers' responses to student mistakes in Chinese and U.S. mathematics classrooms. *The Elementary School Journal, 108*(2), 131–147.

Strong American Schools. (2008). *Diploma to nowhere.* Retrieved from www.strongamericanschools.org/diploma-nowhere

Teddlie, C., & Tashakkori, A. (2003). Major issues and controversies in the use of mixed methods in the social and behavioral sciences. In A. Tashakkori & C. Teddlie (Eds.), *Handbook of mixed methods in social and behavioral research* (pp. 3–50). Thousand Oaks, CA: Sage.

Resources for Further Study

Hanson, W. E., Creswell, J. W., Plano Clark, V. L., Petska, K. S., & David, J. (2005). Mixed methods research designs in counseling psychology. *Journal of Counseling Psychology, 52*(2), 224–235.

> Various typologies have been developed to classify the designs used in mixed-methods research. This article provides a brief introduction to the typologies and describes two of them in detail.

Smith, M. L. (2006). Multiple methodology in education research. In J. L. Green, G. Camilli, & P. B. Elmore (Eds.), *Handbook of complementary methods in education research* (pp. 457–475). Mahwah, NJ: Lawrence Erlbaum.

> The author provides a brief overview of multiple-methods research and describes examples of its use in her studies of state-mandated assessment and assessment of Outward Bound.

Tashakkori, A., & Teddlie, C. (Eds). (2003). *Handbook of mixed methods in social and behavioral research.* Thousand Oaks, CA: Sage.

> This book contains 26 chapters written by experts in mixed-methods research. If you are planning a mixed-methods study, the chapters on research designs, sampling strategies, data-collection strategies, methods of data analysis, and integrating mixed-methods results will be particularly useful.

Sample Mixed-Methods Research Study

Middle School Students' Perceptions of Effective Motivation and Preparation Factors for High-Stakes Tests

Hoffman, L. M., & Nottis, K. E. K. (2008). Middle school students' perceptions of effective motivation and preparation factors for high-stakes tests. *NASSP Bulletin, 92(3),* 209–223.

Student performance on high-stakes tests, such as those mandated by state departments of education, is of great importance to educators. The results of these tests usually are a matter of public record and therefore a visible reflection of educators' effectiveness.

Students might not share these concerns, either not realizing or caring about the test results. The problem, then, is how to motivate students to do their best on these tests. Should educators appeal to extrinsic or intrinsic sources of motivation, and which ones? These are among the questions that the authors of the following journal article sought to answer by doing a mixed-methods study.

Middle School Students' Perceptions of Effective Motivation and Preparation Factors for High-Stakes Tests

Lynn M. Hoffman
Katharyn E. K. Nottis

ABSTRACT ■ This mixed-methods study examines young adolescents' perceptions of strategies implemented before a state-mandated "high-stakes" test. Survey results for Grade 8 students (N = 215) are analyzed by sex, academic group, and preparation team. Letters to the principal are reviewed for convergence and additional themes. Although students were most motivated by extrinsic rewards, those whose teachers developed students' self-efficacy and positively used attribution theory were less influenced. Letters revealed parental impact on students' attitudes and performance. Implications are addressed.

KEYWORDS ■ high-stakes tests; student motivation; test preparation; teacher role in test preparation and administration

The passage of the No Child Left Behind Act (2002) has ushered in an era of increased accountability for students' academic performance that has resulted in a proliferation of assessment programs, including mandated testing implemented by the states. This legislation, and the provisions developed from it, are designed to identify and reward school programs where students meet proficiency standards and to provide evidence needed to alter or eliminate programs where such progress is not seen (Popham, 2004; Thomas, 2005). Maintaining student motivation during "high-stakes" testing can be especially challenging for school personnel, as students' motivation and performance are often dependent on their learning environment (Anderson & Midgley, 1997; Brophy, 1998). In an effort to prepare and motivate students to perform successfully on an impending high-stakes state assessment, school administrators and teachers inevitably initiate an array of strategies to prepare and motivate students to perform successfully. Fedore (2006) listed a number of test preparation strategies that school personnel typically employ, including posters, "practice packets," entertainment on test days, and breakfast.

Review of Related Literature

The value of the preparation and implementation strategies associated with high-stakes testing can be examined from a variety of theoretical perspectives. Self-efficacy or the belief in one's possession of and ability to access and use skills needed to accomplish a task is based on feedback that is received from significant others (Bandura, 1997). Individuals obtain their most powerful feedback through enactive mastery, or their ability to perform a task successfully (Bandura, 1986). Students may enhance their enactive mastery by performing well on tasks similar to the test embedded within regular instruction or on prior simulations of the high-stakes test. In addition, self-efficacy is developed through vicarious experiences and verbal feedback from valued models. Students are more likely to imitate these models if they feel they have a greater chance of being reinforced (Slavin, 2003). Finally, individuals' ability to achieve self-efficacy is enhanced when learning occurs in a low-stress, positive environment (Bandura, 1986, p. 79).

Weiner (1986) has suggested that students' perceptions of their academic ability influence their performance. Attribution theory postulates that students develop perceptions of their ability as either modifiable or fixed. When students believe that their poor performance is caused by external factors beyond their control, they tend to give up easily (Weiner, 1986). On the other hand, students who attribute their lack of success to underdeveloped skills, poor habits, or lack of personal effort will persist until a task is mastered (Weiner, 1986). These theories serve to focus on the importance of meeting the needs of the individual or adjusting and modifying students' learning environments to ensure their optimal performance. How do teachers communicate to students whether their ability is fixed or modifiable, along with their expectations for students' success?

Previous research has found that students' perceptions of high-stakes tests and their performance can vary by grade level and school location (Wheelock, Bebell, & Haney, 2000a, 2000b). Wheelock et al. (2000a, 2000b)

Hoffman, L. M., & Nottis, K. E. K. Middle school students' perceptions of effective motivation and preparation factors for high-stakes tests. *NASSP Bulletin, 92*(3), 209–223. Copyright © 2008 by Sage Publications. Reprinted by permission of Sage Publications.

analyzed elementary and secondary students' drawings created shortly after their high-stakes testing in Massachusetts. Unlike Triplett and Barksdale's (2005) analysis of elementary students' drawings and their written descriptions of them that found nervousness and anger to be prominent themes, Wheelock et al. (2000a) found that approximately 40% of the 411 student self-portraits reflected either students' willingness to comply with test demands without comment or their positive perceptions of the test and their confidence in their ability to perform successfully. However, the other 60% produced pictures that reflected anxiety, anger, pessimism, boredom, or loss of motivation as a result of their participation in the high-stakes testing. Wheelock et al. (2000a) determined that these negative emotions were confined primarily to secondary students in the sample, or those in Grades 8 and 10. Fourth graders tended to portray themselves as self-assured test takers, attending to the test, whereas 8th and 10th graders more frequently showed themselves as alienated from the testing process. Later, Triplett, Barksdale, and Leftwich (2003) reported that eighth grade students in a new sample expressed no concern about testing; instead, their concerns focused on peer relationships.

Differences in students' perceptions of the high-stakes testing have also been found depending on school location. Wheelock et al. (2000a) found that overall, suburban students were less likely to describe the test in negative terms than students in urban schools and were less apt to categorize themselves as angry, bored, or uninvested in the testing process. In addition to location differences, research has also suggested that teachers hold different roles in the testing process that can be either helpful or detrimental to students. Triplett and Barksdale (2005) found four roles illustrated in 19 of the 225 drawings they collected from children in Grades 3 through 6: "monitor, coach, comforter, and uninterested observer" (p. 248). The researchers concluded that "having a comforter close by may ameliorate children's feelings of isolation and alienation. Having a coach close by may decrease children's feelings of powerlessness and increase their self-confidence" (Triplett & Barksdale, 2005, p. 257). These research reports suggest that suburban middle school students' perceptions of a high-stakes testing situation and its effect on them are affected not only by their location and grade level but also by students' perceptions of their teachers' behavior during the testing process as well.

Administrators and teachers faced with the responsibility of preparing students for high-stakes tests routinely attempt to positively affect students' engagement, effort, and performance. Strategies are often selected and implemented based on adults' intuitive sense of what might be effective with their student population or on the perceived success of certain activities implemented in other schools (Fedore, 2006). However, adolescents themselves can talk about their own school culture and their feelings surrounding it. Chang (1992) noted that "the reality they present in their own voices is more valuable than the reality constructed solely by researchers" (p. 4) or that created by school administrators and teachers who make decisions based on their own perceptions of what is meaningful to students (Bernhardt, 2004). Students' voices, rather than adults' intuitive sense alone, should guide the use of strategies used during high-stakes testing to enhance students' performance.

THE CURRENT STUDY

It can be a challenge to motivate students to perform to their ability in high-stakes testing situations (Anderson & Midgley, 1997; Brophy, 1998; Covington, 1992). Students' levels of self-efficacy and attributions for success or failure can affect their performance. Additionally, there is some research to support developmental and school location differences in performance on and perceptions of these tests (Wheelock et al, 2000a, 2000b). Students in elementary school appear to respond differently from those in secondary school, as do those' in urban versus nonurban schools (Triplett et al., 2003). In addition, students' drawings have indicated that teachers play different roles in the high-stakes testing process (Triplett & Barksdale, 2005).

Previous research has grouped the responses of 8th and 10th grade students together as "secondary" (Wheelock et al., 2000a, 2000b), which may not adequately capture the more nuanced perceptions of either middle or high school students. There is a need to examine the responses of each group more closely. In addition, the roles of teachers found in students' drawings indicate that teacher attitude and comments may affect the success of any motivational strategies incorporated. There continues to be a need to examine the effect of teachers on motivational strategies selected for high-stakes test preparation.

This pilot study was designed to obtain a more detailed view of suburban, middle school students' perceptions of strategies that were effective in obtaining their best efforts when taking a high-stakes test. The researchers also examined how those perceptions varied by different subgroups. Questions that guided the study were as follows:

1. What strategies do students perceive as influential in motivating them during a high-stakes testing situation?
2. Do students' perceptions of influential strategies and initiatives vary based on their sex, academic program, or teaching team?
3. How do students articulate elements of effective test preparation?

METHOD

Design

A mixed-methods approach with both quantitative and qualitative methodologies was conceptualized using a triangulation design (Fraenkel & Wallen, 2009); both quantitative and qualitative data were collected at the same time and given equal priority. Data were analyzed separately and then examined together to see whether there was a convergence on a particular interpretation of the effectiveness of strategies used to motivate students. Quantitative methods were used to address the first two research questions, and qualitative methods were used to address the third.

A within-subjects posttest design with no control groups was used for the quantitative phase of the study. Responses to individual survey questions were examined using descriptive statistics. The Mann-Whitney U test was used to compare the preference of different student groups (male versus female, gifted and talented [GT] versus academic program, and Preparation and Teaching Team L versus Preparation and Teaching Team R) for individual test strategies. Students' letters to the principal were also reviewed and analyzed to determine points of collaboration or disagreement with quantitative survey results.

Content analysis of student letters was done for the qualitative portion of the study. Analytic induction was used. This method of qualitative analysis allows the researcher to start with a proposition or theory-driven hypotheses and then to use the qualitative data obtained to verify them (Patton, 2002). Students' letters to their principal were analyzed to determine their vision of optimal testing practices that positively influenced their motivation and to identify how their perceptions about successful motivational strategies might differ based on their sex, academic level, or teaching team. In the process of analyzing students' responses, the researchers were able to determine how students' ideas fit with the list of strategies implemented prior to the testing session. In addition, students' responses allowed identification and development of new patterns, contrary examples, and a deeper understanding of both the quantitative data and the original framework of adult generated strategies and interventions.

Participants

Grade 8 students (N = 215) in a suburban 6–8 middle school in a mid-Atlantic state participated in this pilot study. School wide, according to district reports, students were 80.9% White, 9.1% Asian, 7.6% African American, and 2.9% Hispanic. Of the total population, 11.2% were classified as English for Speakers of Other Languages (ESOL), 10.5% eligible for free and reduced lunch, and 10.2% receiving special education services. This middle school reported an 11.3% mobility rate. There were 109 males and 106 females in the sample studied. ESOL students with minimal proficiency and severely learning-disabled students who were taught in a self-contained setting were excluded from the study, as they were not required to take the state-mandated test and followed an adjusted curriculum. Mainstreamed ESOL and special needs students were included in this sample.

There were two academic groupings of students: GT (n = 104) and academic (n = 111). Students in the GT group were enrolled in one or more academic classes designated as GT. These students had been identified prior to middle school, and some as early as Grade 3, through a combination of review of School Ability Index (SAI) scores culled from the Otis Lennon School Ability Test (Otis & Lennon, 1996), performance on the California Test of Basic Skills (McGraw Hill, 1989), classroom performance, and teacher, parent, and self-evaluations and recommendations. In addition, students were divided into two preparation teams, R (n = 110) and L (n = 105), which also served as their teaching teams during the school year. These teams comprised teachers of English, math, social studies, and science. Each teaching and test preparation team taught five sections of students designated as GT or academic. The R team contained 57 GT and 53 academic students, and the L team comprised 47 GT and 58 academic students. There were 58 males and 52 females in the R team and 51 males and 54 females on the L team.

Instrument

A researcher-developed, 20-item questionnaire was used. Participants were given a five-choice Likert-type scale format ranging from 1 = *not at all* to 5 = *a great deal* in response to the stem "influenced my performance." Items used in the questionnaire corresponded to the known initiatives and strategies that the administrative team had put into place prior to the testing (see the appendix for a copy of the instrument). The assessment was determined to have face validity (Krathwohl, 1998); it appeared valid to test takers. No reliability testing was done. In addition to completing the questionnaire, students wrote letters to the school principal describing which factors were most influential in gaining their best efforts.

Procedure

Participants completed the questionnaire 2 weeks after taking a high-stakes, statewide test. Students were also asked to write a letter to their principal describing why they believed students were so successful with the test. At their teachers' discretion, some sections of students completed the letters as an in-class assignment; other students completed the letters for homework and returned their letters separately from the questionnaires to their English teachers.

In this mixed-methods study, the quantitative and qualitative data were analyzed separately. Researchers first reviewed the quantitative results to determine the relative value of elements in the testing and preparation process from students' perspectives. Evidence of differences in response patterns based on students' sex, academic program, and teaching team were noted and helped to inform the qualitative analysis that followed. Triplicate copies of all letters were made, coded by students' sex, academic program, and teaching team. Analysis of qualitative data involved multiple readings of the students' letters to their principal by both researchers, with an initial process of "sorting and sifting" through the material, looking for common themes, similar phrases, and patterns (Miles & Huberman, 1994). Themes and commonalities aligned with the implemented strategies were named, recorded, and coded wherever they appeared. When the coding of students' comments was complete, comments were grouped by theme according to their category of team, academic program, and sex, and response patterns based on students' teaching team, academic program, and sex were noted. Themes developed from the analysis of qualitative data were compared again with findings from the quantitative data to determine points of convergence or divergence (Fraenkel & Wallen, 2009). Additional themes not suggested by the survey were also identified.

RESULTS

External Rewards Were Motivational

Students indicated that they were most motivated to perform during the high-stakes test by extrinsic rewards, expectations they would be successful, familiarity with the test format, and knowing the Grade 8 assistant principal might review their responses in the future. Table I shows the mean, median, and mode scores for each questionnaire response. The three measures of central tendency are provided as an indicator of whether the data are skewed, although the median was considered the primary measure of central tendency because of the ranked data (Hopkins, Hopkins, & Glass, 1996). Wanting to attend the grade-level picnic after the testing period and the dispersal of edible treats by teachers during the lengthy testing sessions had the highest median scores.

Qualitative data from the student letters supported these findings. A female GT student on the R team echoed the sentiment expressed repeatedly by her classmates when she wrote:

> Knowing that we had a great picnic to look forward to made me want to do my best. It provided something special for our hard work and I knew that if I did not work hard, I did not deserve the picnic.

A male GT student on the same team commented, "I always work harder with a short, sweet incentive [sic] such as snacks." Students repeatedly mentioned their appreciation of the candy treats provided by their teachers during testing. Another student on the same team noted, "I think that giving students candy during the testing was positive because the sugar gave us more energy to do the tasks each day."

Students were least motivated by announcements and posters presented by student government members or seeing their classmates in a commercial about the testing on the local education channel. In addition, students reported that they did not find the test items intrinsically interesting. In their letters to the principal, students described the test

TABLE 1   Influence of Factors in Descending Order

Factor	M	SD	Median	Mode
Wanted to attend the picnic after testing	4.12	1.27	5.0	5.0
Appreciated edible treats provided by teacher during the test	3.98	1.29	5.0	5.0
Felt confident about completing assigned tasks	3.99	1.02	4.0	5.0
Were familiar with test terminology and format	3.87	1.19	4.0	5.0
Desired to maintain school's reputation as high-achieving school	3.65	1.36	4.0	5.0
Desired to prove that their eighth grade class was the best	3.60	1.45	4.0	5.0
Knew parents expected them to do their best	3.51	1.39	4.0	5.0
Remembered teachers' comments about the importance of the test	3.46	1.29	4.0	4.0
Knew the test was important because of special meetings with the principal and assistant principal	3.38	1.28	3.0	3.0
Did well on the prior practice test	3.27	1.29	3.0	3.0
Knew the assistant principal might read their responses	3.11	1.53	3.0	5.0
Know their individual scores would be available if requested in the fall	3.03	1.48	3.0	5.0
Responded to encouraging comments by teachers during the test	2.96	1.28	3.0	3.0
Tasks were similar to ones done regularly in class	2.92	1.31	3.0	4.0
Appreciated the morning announcements and encouraging posters created by the Student Government Association	2.56	1.45	2.0	1.0
Found the testing tasks interesting	2.34	1.07	2.0	3.0
Saw the Cable TV spot with classmates discussing the test	1.46	1.13	1.0	1.0

as easier than prior practice tests and classroom exercises and the tasks as uninteresting. A male GT student in the R team noted, as a suggestion for future tests that "tasks that are more interesting will help, too. The Archimedes tasks that I had were extremely boring."

Girls Valued Practice More Than Boys

There was one significant difference found in students' perceptions of the effectiveness of the strategies based on sex. Girls were significantly more influenced by the similarity between tasks done in class throughout the year and tasks on the test ($Z = -1.959$, $p = .05$). A female student in an academic section of the L team noted, "All the reviewing we did on circle graphs, reading for information, and writing prompts all got me well prepared." Another wrote, "The practice test was very helpful . . . because it showed us what to expect when we started the actual testing. The practice problems we had in class were helpful, too."

Students' Academic Level Dictated Their Strategy Preferences

There were three significant differences found in students' perceptions of the effectiveness of the strategies based on class type (GT versus academic). Academic students found the testing tasks to be significantly more interesting than GT students ($Z = -2.230$, $p < .05$). In addition, academic students were significantly more positively affected by seeing classmates on TV ($Z = -2.010$, $p < .05$). By contrast, the GT students were significantly more affected by their success on a prior practice test than the academic students ($Z = -3.014$, $p < .01$). A female GT student wrote:

> During classes this year, the teachers would include a drill or an activity for class that that would be in a typical format of a test question. This helped us a lot because we were able to see what a real test question may be like and we would be able to see how the format was. This also helped because we were more able to become more comfortable with these questions so that at the time of the test, we would be used to seeing questions like that.

Preparation Teams Made a Difference

Students in the R preparation team reported that they were significantly more positively affected by the following strategies than their peers on the L team: finding the tasks interesting ($Z = -2.933$, $p < .01$), knowing parents would expect good scores ($Z = -2.021$, $p < .05$), desiring to attend the picnic ($Z = -2.051$, $p < .05$), knowing scores would be available in the fall ($Z = -2.136$, $p < .05$), meeting with the principal prior to testing ($Z = -2.610$, $p < .01$), responding to morning announcements and posters ($Z = -4.758$, $p < .01$), hearing encouraging teacher comments during testing ($Z = -2.856$, $p < .01$), and doing well on the practice test ($Z = -2.549$, $p < .05$).

Students in the L team appeared to be less affected than R team members by many of the external strategies employed by teachers and administrators to enhance their test performance. However, L team students' written comments may provide some of the reasons for the differences between the teams' reactions. L team students repeatedly referred to the "self-pride" that propelled them to be successful with the test. A GT male student explained:

> You need self pride to do well on the test. You have to be proud that you're taking a test which the score counts as part of all the other students [sic] test scores combined. . . . Self pride is having self-confidence in doing the test.

Other students used the term *legacy* to describe their desire to maintain their school's excellent reputation. A female GT student wrote, "The students want to keep up the legacy. For several years now, (the school) had the highest test scores in _____ and the surrounding counties. The students feel a little pressure to 'keep the streak going.'"

In addition, letters to the principal revealed that L team teachers had eliminated homework across the board for the duration of the testing period and had adjusted the workload in classes held after each day's testing to reduce students' fatigue. This female academic student's comments were representative of several from all student groups in the L team:

> Another thing that motivated me was that I didn't have the stress of classwork and homework. I'm very glad I didn't because I could focus in the test, not the homework and classwork I had to do.

Another student, in commenting on the value of the reduced class work and homework expectations the L team teachers provided, described how her life changed for the better during the testing period, at least:

> Not having homework was a big help. When I would come home from testing, I would have no homework. Since this occurred, I got more sleep and I ate better. Some mornings when I wake I am very tired. During the week of testing, I was not because I had a chance to go to sleep earlier and eat a good breakfast and dinner.

Parents Influenced Students' Test Performance

Although parental influence was not included as an element in the survey instrument, its importance to students surfaced in their letters. Repeatedly, students in each team and academic group noted that their parents' behavior influenced their test performance. An R team academic male appreciated his parents' "support and encouraging words" on testing days. A GT female on the L team commented that "the _____ School parents made sure their children had a full night's rest. They made sure we ate proper breakfasts. Our parents taught us to strive for our best and not settle for less." Finally, a female academic student on the R team noted that the support of the parent who sent her off to school each day of the testing saying "good luck, or do a good job on the test was very good for me."

Resistance Was Evident, Especially among GT Boys

For the most part, students' comments reflected their co-operation with teachers and the principal in their preparation for the high-stakes tests and in their execution of them. However, a small number of boys used their letters to the principal to express either their resentment of the test itself or their disagreement with the methods of preparation and practice that other students described as valuable. An academic male from the L team noted that he performed his best on the test, even though "we, the students, are forced to take this test against our will." A male GT student on the R team explained that he was immune to any strategies that the principal might put into place. He wrote, "If you think it helps, then you can do whatever you want. You're the principal. No one can stop you from making a decision. Everyone has to follow what you say."

Another GT male suggested that the school "forsakes any real teaching in favor of phony practices and pep talks to motivate the students." He described the test preparation and strategies as attempts to "boost the school's inflated ego." He suggested a different approach: "Tell us that you would like us to do our best as a favor to you. Then quit the pointless drilling, have us taught the real stuff so the test will be honest." He continued to explain that his approach would work "because they [the students] are nice people." Finally, another GT male student from the R team offered a colorful suggestion for the test itself, which he perceived as something mandated by the principal in conjunction with state politicians:

> It's a useless and worthless test and the only good purpose, I think, it should be used for would be to start a fire, to light up other tests, in order to incinerate them and lift them from the face of the Earth in a gigantic bonfire.

DISCUSSION AND EDUCATIONAL IMPLICATIONS

This group's performance, as published on their state's Department of Education Web site, placed them among the highest scoring Grade 8 students in their county and state for that year's test administration. Practice tests and regular course content presented and assessed in the upcoming testing format provided ample opportunities for students to develop the enactive mastery that Bandura (1997) considers critical for effective mastery. GT students, in particular, indicated that taking the simulated test in April was instrumental to their success with the state assessment. Weiner's (1986) attribution theory would suggest that either the GT students performed well on the practice test, thereby increasing their confidence that they would be successful when the real test was administered, or they would perceive a lack of success on the practice test as modifiable in time for the May administration through extra effort, more practice, or increased attention. On the other hand, academic students may have experienced less success with the practice test and believed that their lower performance was fixed, thus interpreting poor performance on the practice test as a precursor of poor performance on the end-of-year state assessment. Overall, however, knowing that Grade 8 students from their school had been highly successful in past years with this assessment may have served to reinforce the belief that they too would be successful, regardless of students' individual performance on the practice test.

Students' comments to their principal reflected the importance of establishing an optimal balance between encouragement and support and overkill. Students on the R team, more significantly affected by a variety of external actions by teachers and administrators than their L team counterparts, were also more apt to comment on the pressure and stress they felt while preparing for and taking the test. A female student advised the principal not to "put so much pressure on us. I know it is a big deal and you want us to do well, but we could do better if we were more relaxed." Another student who missed a portion of the week-long testing because of illness wrote, "I could not help being sick with such a high fever, but after all of the pressure (to attend and do well) I felt so guilty."

Based on the frequency of references to "self-pride" as a motivator among L team members, it appears that teachers made ample use of attribution theory (Weiner, 1985) to motivate their students, demonstrating their confidence in students' ability to perform well, and appealing to students' ability to build a positive legacy for their grade and school. Another difference that became apparent through students' letters was that L team teachers eliminated homework across the board for the duration of the testing period. In addition, they adjusted the workload in classes held after each day's testing to reduce students' fatigue. Students repeatedly expressed their gratitude for teachers' consideration. A female academic student wrote, "Another thing that motivated me was that I didn't have the stress of classwork and homework. I'm very glad I didn't because I could focus on the test, not the homework and classwork I had to do." Another student on the L team noted, "I think our having no homework made us think and believe we had to put all of our effort into the _____ testing." A male GT student referred to the homework reprieve when he stated, "This kindness was one of the reasons we tried hard on our testing." L team students described their teachers' enthusiasm about the test and their desire not to let their teachers down by performing poorly. A male GT L team member reflected the reciprocal nature of his performance when he stated, "The teachers depend on us to do well. Kids don't usually like to let people down."

Feedback from four major sources of self-efficacy knowledge (enactive mastery, vicarious experiences, verbal persuasion, and attention to the affective state) may have been embedded inadvertently in the strategies and initiatives selected by teachers and school administrators to enhance students' performance (McCabe, 2003). Kagan (1992) has suggested that teachers develop their beliefs about students and their learning based primarily on their own experiences or on the shared experiences of colleagues. This practical knowledge that teachers develop over time informs their practice (Fenstermacher, 1994). Although the actions of teachers and administrators in this case may have been aligned with the theoretical base described here, it is probable that they did not act based on their propositional knowledge or as a direct result of research findings or understanding of educational theory (Smith, 1989).

Based on the information in students' letters, it appears that R team teachers relied most heavily on the development of enactive mastery and verbal persuasion to prepare their students for the upcoming high-stakes test, whereas teachers on the L team also emphasized an attention to students' affective state before and during the testing period. Triplett and Barksdale (2005) previously described these teaching roles as "coach" and "comforter" respectively, (p. 248). Perhaps L team students, confident in their ability to handle the test successfully because their teachers knew they would, needed less external reinforcement than R team students to do their best. Also, the decisions that L team teachers made to offer extra encouragement and support before and during the test sessions and their efforts to minimize students' workload and stress also appear to be more clearly aligned with Triplett and Barksdale's recommendation that teachers reconceptualize their role in test preparation as "comforters and coaches"(p. 257). Given the significant differences in the perceptions of the effectiveness of several strategies among students taught by one teaching team rather than the other, we are reminded once again of the power teachers possess to influence and reinforce, or not, their students' perceptions of school events and initiatives.

Limitations to the Study

There are a number of limitations in this pilot study that should be recognized and addressed in future studies. First, there was no reliability testing of the current instrument. Second, the current questionnaire asked students about school-initiated strategies. The qualitative data revealed that beyond school strategies, students were also influenced by their parents and had feelings about the testing process in general. Insights from the qualitative data should be used to design a more comprehensive questionnaire for future studies, and reliability testing should be done on that instrument. Finally, the sample for this study was from a high-performing, suburban district with a predominantly White student population. Future studies should examine whether similar pretest strategies are equally motivating to students in urban and rural schools and schools with other racial compositions. Schools with larger subgroups of students of color would allow for the additional disaggregation of responses by race and perhaps yield additional, alternative student suggestions about effective test preparation (Bernhardt, 2004).

Despite these limitations, insights from this study can guide school administrators as they craft their own successful preparation plans for students taking high-stakes tests. These findings suggest that there are multiple ways for administrators to encourage optimal test performance results. As Foster (2004) suggests, "conducting internal and external scans of school environments lays the groundwork for creating welcoming and effective schools where students feel that their concerns and interests play an important role" (p. 46). Soliciting information directly from students is an important element of such an "internal scan." Communication with parents about their important role in supporting students throughout the testing process, including making them aware of test dates and the rigors of testing, and offering concrete suggestions about steps they can take to help their children prepare for it may enhance students' attitude and performance. Helping teachers recognize and develop their roles as "coaches" and "comforters" may be a caring, low-cost, and effective way to support students before and during high-stakes testing while ensuring their best efforts, as suggested by Triplett and Barksdale (2005). Encouraging teachers to focus on the development of students' self-confidence, "self-pride," and community spirit that leads to an interest in school legacy building through high performance, instead of an exclusive reliance on external rewards for test effort, would strengthen students' personal sense of efficacy and motivation to learn, which would benefit them long after the testing was completed.

References

Anderson, L. H., & Midgley, C. (1997). Motivation and middle school students. In J. L. Irvin (Ed.), *What current research says to the middle level practitioner* (pp. 41–48). Columbus, OH: National Middle School Association.

Bandura, A. (1986). *Social foundations of thought and action: A social cognitive theory.* Englewood Cliffs, NJ: Prentice Hall.

Bandura, A. (1997). *Self-efficacy: The exercise of control.* New York: Longman.

Bernhardt, V. (2004). *Data analysis for continuous school improvement.* Larchmont, NY: Eye on Education.

Brophy, J. (1998). *Motivating students to learn.* Boston: McGraw-Hill.

Chang, H. (1992). *Adolescent life and ethos: Ethnography of a US high school.* Washington, DC: The Falmer Press.

Covington, M. V. (1992). *Making the grade: A self-worth perspective on motivation and school reform.* New York: Cambridge University Press.

Fedore, H. (2006). De-stressing high stakes testing for NCLB. *Education Digest, 71*(6), 23–28.

Fenstermacher, G. D. (1994). The knower and the known: The nature of knowledge in research on teaching. In L. Darling-Hammond (Ed.), *Review of research in education: Vol 20* (pp. 3–56). Washington, DC: American Educational Research Association.

Foster, L. (2004). Great expectations: Reflections on the 50th anniversary of Brown v. Board of Education. *Principal Leadership (Middle School Edition), 4*(9), 41–48.

Fraenkel, J. R., & Wallen, N. E. (2009). *How to design and evaluate research in education* (7th ed.). New York: McGraw-Hill.

Hopkins, K. D., Hopkins, B. R., & Glass, G. V. (1996). *Basic statistics for the behavioral sciences* (3rd ed.). Boston: Allyn and Bacon.

Kagan, D. M. (1992). Implications of research on teacher beliefs. *Educational Psychologist, 27*, 65–90.

Krathwohl, D. R. (1998). *Methods of educational and social science research: An integrated approach* (2nd ed.). Long Grove, IL: Waveland.

McCabe, P. (2003). Enhancing self-efficacy for high stakes reading tests. *The Reading Teacher, 57*(1), 12–20.

McGraw Hill. (1989). California test of basic skills Level 4, survey battery (4th ed.). Monterey, CA: CTB/McGraw Hill.

Miles, M., & Huberman, A. M. (1994). *Qualitative data analysis.* Thousand Oaks, CA: Sage.

No Child Left Behind Act of 2002. Pub. L. No. 107-110, 115 Stat. 1425 (2002). Retrieved October 6, 2006, from http://www.ed.gov/legislation/ESEA02/

Otis, A., & Lennon, R. (1996). *The Otis-Lennon School Ability Test Seventh Edition.* Retrieved October 6, 2006, from http://harcourtassessment.com/haiweb/cultures/en-us/product detail.htm?pid=OLSAT

Patton, M. Q. (2002). *Qualitative evaluation and research methods* (3rd ed.). Thousand Oaks, CA: Sage.

Popham, W. J. (2004). *America's "failing" schools: How parents and teachers can cope with No Child Left Behind.* New York: Routledge Falmer.

Slavin, R. B. (2003). *Educational psychology: Theory and practice* (7th ed.). Boston: Allyn & Bacon.

Smith, M. L. (1989). Teachers' beliefs about retention. In L. A. Shepard & M. L. Smith (Eds.), *Flunking grades: Research and policies on retention* (pp. 132–150). Philadelphia: Falmer.

Thomas, R. M. (2005). *High stakes testing: Coping with collateral damage.* Mahwah, NJ: Lawrence Erlbaum.

Triplett, C. F., & Barksdale, M. A. (2005). Third through sixth graders' perceptions of high-stakes testing. *Journal of Literacy Research, 32*(2), 237–260.

Triplett, C. F., Barksdale, M. A., & Leftwich, P. (2003). Children's perceptions of high stakes testing. *Journal of Research in Education, 13*(1), 15–21.

Weiner, B. (1986). *An attributional theory of motivation and emotion* (Springer series in social psychology). New York: Springer-Verlag.

Wheelock, A., Bebell, D., & Haney, W. (2000a, November 2). Student self-portraits as test-takers: Variations, contextual differences, and assumptions by motivation. *Teachers College Record* (ID Number: 10635). Retrieved January 11, 2007, from http://www.tcrecord.org

Wheelock, A., Bebell, D., & Haney, W. (2000b, November 2). What can student drawings tell us about high stakes testing in Massachusetts? *Teachers College Record* (ID Number: 10634). Retrieved January 11, 2007, from http://www.tcrecord.org

About the Authors

Lynn M. Hoffman, an associate professor of education at Bucknell University in Lewisburg, PA, is a former middle and high school principal. Her teaching is devoted to the preparation of outstanding future teachers and principals, while she researches issues relating to school culture.

Katharyn E. K. Nottis is an associate professor of education at Bucknell University in Lewisburg, PA. An educational psychologist, she is primarily interested in conceptual learning in science and gender issues. Her teaching interests are in educational psychology and in the preparation of novice teachers.

APPENDIX
Grade 8 Student Survey

NAME: _____   DATE: _____

(School) students worked very hard on their (state) tests. Please indicate whether the following factors impacted on your efforts to work as hard as you did.

Please circle the number for each response that best expresses your feelings.	Influenced my performance				
	Not at all			A great deal	
1. I found the tasks interesting.	1	2	3	4	5
2. I felt confident that I could do the assigned tasks.	1	2	3	4	5
3. I knew that (Assistant Principal) might read my responses.	1	2	3	4	5
4. I wanted to help maintain [School's] reputation as the best middle school in (Name) County.	1	2	3	4	5
5. I knew my parents expected me to do well.	1	2	3	4	5
6. I wanted to attend the (Name) picnic.	1	2	3	4	5
7. I knew my individual scores would be available from (Assistant Principal) in the fall.	1			4	5
8. I appreciated the treats that teachers gave us during testing.	1	2	3	4	5
9. I remembered teachers' comments about the importance of the test.	1	2	3	4	5
10. I knew the tasks were important because we met with the principal and assistant principals before the test.	1	2	3	4	5
11. I appreciated the morning announcements and posters from the Student Government Association wishing us good luck on the test.	1	2	3	4	5
12. I responded to encouraging comments that teachers made while we were taking the test.	1	2	3	4	5
13. I found the tasks similar to the ones I did all year.	1	2	3	4	5
14. I wanted to help prove that our eighth grade class is the best.	1	2	3	4	5
15. I knew the terminology and the requirements of the test, like labeling all of my answers.	1	2	3	4	5
16. I did well on the practice test we took in April.	1	2	3	4	5
17. I saw the cable TV spot featuring Grade 8 students about the tests.	1	2	3	4	5

The (School) staff will be working on strategies to get next year's eighth graders ready to be successful on their (State) tests. Think about all of the things that parents, teachers, and administrators said or did this year that encouraged you to do your best. Now, write (the Principal) a letter offering your ideas or strategies that work to help students work hard and do well on their (State) tests.

_____

_____

_____

_____

_____

_____

_____

chapter 19

Action Research

1. Action research is more closely tied to educators' practice than other types of research, so it possesses great potential to solve problems of practice.
2. Educators carry out action research projects for various purposes—personal, professional, and political.
3. After carrying out an action research project, educators report their findings to colleagues in some form and often decide on a new course of action for continuing their research.
4. Systematic data collection, analysis, and reflection are what distinguish action research from educators' other approaches to problem solving.
5. A good action research project provides educators an understanding of new practices and empirical data that show the results of those practices on teaching and learning in a real-life setting.
6. Action research benefits educators by improving their theories of education, their work with students, and their interactions with colleagues.
7. By following the principles of action science, educators can identify and address discrepancies between their espoused beliefs and their actual behavior.
8. Action research is carried out primarily by insiders with an internal perspective on the problems of practice being studied, but outsiders can help in research design, interpretation of findings, helping insiders address strong feelings about the topics being studied, and contributing support for personal and social change.
9. Action researchers can use a number of validity criteria to help them design their research to achieve maximum credibility and trustworthiness. ■

Key TERMS

action research	insider	process validity
action science	insider research	reflection
catalytic validity	intentionality	self-study research
collaborative action research	outcome validity	systematicity
democratic validity	outsider	teacher research
dialogic validity	participatory action research	theory-in-action
espoused theory	practitioner research	

The History of Action Research

Action research is a form of research carried out by educators in their everyday work settings for the purpose of improving their professional practice. This form of research corresponds to what some researchers call **practitioner research** (Zeichner & Noffke, 2001), **teacher research** (Cochran-Smith & Lytle, 1999), **insider research** (Kemmis & McTaggart, 2000), and **self-study research** (Zeichner & Noffke, 2001). When researchers and participants collaborate in solving a problem of practice, it is sometimes called **participatory action research** (Reason & Bradbury, 2001).

Social psychologist Kurt Lewin (1946) helped popularize action research during World War II. He observed that much research resulted in scholarly publications that had little effect on professionals' work or on the broader society. Lewin developed action research as a form of investigation that community members and working professionals could do together to promote positive social change.

In one study, Lewin assembled small groups of housewives to consider the use of organ meats in family meals. At the time, the U.S. government was seeking to promote these cheaper cuts of meat because of a wartime shortage in meat supplies. Lewin's action research project showed the value of group discussion in changing people's attitudes and behavior about a significant social problem.

Action research was popular in the social sciences during the 1940s and 1950s in the United States. Its use declined subsequently, because most academic researchers, and the public as well, considered *research* to mean primarily experimentation carried out in laboratory settings. Australian and British educators brought action research back to the forefront in the 1960s, and they continue to use this approach extensively. Action research has also again become popular in the United States, especially among teachers who carry out studies as part of their teacher education preparation program.

Using Action Research to Address Problems of Practice

Action research has more practical purposes than formal research. The quality of an action research project depends on how well it serves educators' immediate, local needs. As a result, action research is easier to design and carry out as part of an educator's everyday practice than a formal research study.

Table 19.1 summarizes the characteristics of action research compared to those of formal research. These characteristics highlight its relevance as a tool for educators seeking to

TABLE *19.1*   Characteristics of Action Research Compared to Formal Research

Research Overview	Action Research	Formal Research
Purpose	Solve a local problem of practice	Produce generalizable knowledge
Focus of study	A problem or goal related to one's own practice	A problem or question of concern to educational researchers
Topic selection	Limited review of research literature, emphasizing secondary sources	Extensive review of research literature, emphasizing primary sources
Researcher Characteristics		
Researcher affiliation	One or more school-based educators, perhaps in collaboration with university faculty	University researchers
Researcher qualifications	Practical experience with the problem; basic knowledge/experience in research	Substantial knowledge of the research literature and training in research methods
Research Characteristics		
Sample selection	Convenience sample of one's own clients/students	Random or representative sample from a defined population
Research method	Easily implementable procedures, emergent design, short time frame	Rigorous research design and controls, long time frame
Measures	Simple or available	Selection based on evidence of validity and reliability
Data collection and analysis	Emphasis on descriptive statistics and practical significance of the results	Emphasis on in-depth qualitative coding and interpretation or on tests of statistical significance
Research report	Informal sharing with colleagues or publication through an online network	Published report or formal presentation at a conference
Application of results	Make changes to one's practice if the findings justify them	Add to the knowledge base of education

improve some aspect of their practice. As the table shows, action research has a different orientation, and is typically simpler, than formal research in every respect.

Examples of Action Research Studies

Action research studies are done by practitioners in various professional disciplines, including education. Educators might conduct studies for personal reasons or to fulfill degree and licensure requirements. They might test a theory of their own or draw on other theoretical perspectives. Critical research, which advocates democratic changes in education (see Chapter 16), is one such theoretical perspective (Carr & Kemmis, 1988). The following sections present several examples of action research studies done by teachers.

Bullying in Middle School

Drosopoulos, J. D., Heald, A. Z., & McCue, M. J. (2008). *Minimizing bullying behavior of middle school students through behavioral intervention and instruction.* Chicago: St. Xavier University. ERIC Document Reproduction Service No. ED500895.

Three teachers conducted this study as a master's degree requirement. They initiated the study by administering questionnaires to students and parents about the incidence of bullying. Among other findings, they learned that half of the students had been bullied at least once.

The teachers experimented with various interventions to reduce the incidence of bullying, including some that directly involved students as research participants. For example, the students created and posted antibullying posters in bullying hot spots in school, and they wrote and performed an antibullying rap song in class.

The teachers made direct observations of students at various sites in the school to determine the incidence of bullying before and after these interventions. They found that various types of bullying decreased by 31 percent overall, and name-calling decreased the most.

Teachers presented their own perceptions of the change. For example, one teacher stated,

> Once they were taught the definition of bullying, the many different kinds of bullying, and how it can cause life long mental scars, most [students] were ashamed of the actions they had taken against other people at some point in the past. . . . [N]ow that I know the impact this intervention program has had on students, I will implement it every semester for the rest of my teaching career. (Drosopoulos et al., 2008, p. 70)

The teacher researchers submitted their paper to ERIC, and the full text is available on its website (www.eric.gov).

The Needs of College Students in China

Schippers, M. (2008). *Student support in China: Addressing the perceived needs of undergraduate English department students.* ERIC Document Reproduction Service No. ED499780.

This action research study was conducted by Margriet Schippers, a Western-culture instructor who had been teaching at a Chinese university for 10 years. To learn more about her students' needs she initiated her own study by taking the role of a teacher–researcher. Combining both quantitative and qualitative methods, she interviewed a sample of students and administered a questionnaire to another sample.

Schippers found that the students expressed needs for study skills, including time management, and guidance on how to adapt to college life, develop confidence, and plan for a career. The students expressed dissatisfaction with current university efforts to foster their emotional and social development and with the university's use of monitors (teacher aides).

These findings provided the basis for Schippers to propose action in the form of offering a new student support course that would teach "teamwork (students learn about role differentiation and find out their preferred . . . team role, Gardner's Multiple Intelligences (students learn more about their strong and weaker points), basic counseling skills, study skills such as time management skills and note taking, presentation skills, job interview techniques, Maslow's hierarchy of needs, the reflective diary tool, and goal setting" (p. 48). Schippers also noted a personal benefit—"professional development for me as a teacher in that I have become more aware of students' wishes and weaknesses that need addressing in class" (p. 19).

This study illustrates the fact that action research need not involve an immediate change in professional practice. An action research study can involve careful analysis of an existing situation to discover needs and opportunities that set the stage for subsequent design of an intervention and application in the context of professional practice.

The Effectiveness of Reciprocal Teaching

Holt, C. (2008). *Does reciprocal teaching increase student achievement in 5th grade social studies?* Retrieved December 18, 2000, from http://actionresearch .altec.org

The teacher–researcher, Crystal Holt, conducted an action research study in her classroom of students who were struggling with social studies because of poor reading skills. She decided to try a teaching technique called *reciprocal teaching,* which had been found to be effective in formal research studies. In this technique, the teacher and students take turns in leading conversations about the meaning of text passages. The leader makes efforts to summarize the text, ask questions about it, clarify its statements, and predict what will come next.

Holt conducted an experiment with her 22 students in which half the students read textbook material, listened to the teacher talk about it, and took whole-group notes. The other half read the same textbook material but engaged in reciprocal teaching. She consulted with three other teachers in designing the reciprocal teaching intervention.

Holt found that the reciprocal teaching group made much greater gains from a pretest to a posttest on social studies than did the conventional instruction group. Moreover, she achieved an insight into her professional practice:

> Before doing this research, I had a lot of problems with students talking out and making inappropriate comments during instructional time. Now that I have implemented the reciprocal teaching technique into my daily routine I have noticed that the inappropriate talking has ceased while higher-order thinking and comments are coming more and more into play. I truly believe that the students behave better when given an outlet to talk.

These comments illustrate an important feature of action research. Although one can read about the benefits of a technique like reciprocal teaching in professional publications, action research makes these benefits tangible by allowing researchers to see them occurring in their own work site.

Design Features of Action Research

Our explanation of how to design an action research project draws on the model of action research developed by Jeffrey Glanz (1998). To his six steps we have added a final step, namely, reporting the findings of action research. Action researchers do not always perform the steps in the order presented here. Sometimes action researchers begin by taking a new action before collecting any data (Schmuck, 1997). Similarly, while in Glanz's model reflection follows action taking, reflection is appropriate at various points during a project.

Some models of action research describe a definite beginning and end. This description is generally accurate when action research is carried out as part of a degree or course requirement. However, when educators incorporate action research into their everyday work, it is more likely to become an ongoing cycle of activity.

We describe the typical steps in an action research project by referring to a study conducted by Wallace Shilkus (2001).

Step One: Selection of a Focus for the Study

Shilkus (2001), an industrial arts middle school teacher, had recently returned to graduate education as a student after 17 years of teaching. Shilkus was "curious about the ways in which the industrial arts were relevant to middle school students" (p. 143). He had several goals for his action research project, which he undertook as part of coursework toward a master's degree. Specifically, he wanted to explore teaching methods to activate students' multiple intelligences and explore different ways to reach all students, including hard-to-motivate students.

Undertaking his research at a time when industrial arts was being cut from many schools' curriculum offerings, Shilkus also wanted to demonstrate the contribution of industrial arts to students' intellectual development, especially in middle school. He wanted to help others become aware of the importance of the "endangered subject" (p. 144) of industrial arts.

In his action research study, Shilkus used both cross-tutoring and peer-tutoring approaches in guiding students' design and construction of CO_2-powered race cars. He arranged to have his seventh- and eighth-grade industrial arts "veteran" students first tutor fourth-grade "rookies" at his school and then the adults in his own graduate education class.

Step Two: Data Collection

Shilkus's middle school students, their fourth-grade "rookie" partners, and his graduate school classmates all engaged in providing data for the action research project and in sharing their discoveries to learn and help others learn.

In his transportation technology classes Shilkus had observed that a wide range of student abilities was needed to produce a successful CO_2-powered race car. He found Howard Gardner's theory of multiple intelligences (Gardner, 1983) helpful in defining the types of skills students would need to learn to experience success in the class. Shilkus reports, "Student journal keeping assisted me . . . in identifying students' strengths and weaknesses" (2001, p. 145). This process was important, because he wished to ensure pairings of students who would be compatible with each other. Also, Shilkus continually observed the classroom activities and administered pre- and postsurveys to all three groups of research participants.

After analyzing each set of data, Shilkus added other data-collection strategies. He asked his adult classmates to make journal entries describing the classroom atmosphere. Also, he made a videotape of a two-hour lab in which the middle school students tutored the adults in design and construction of their race cars, as well as a subsequent videotape of an elimination car race for all participants.

Step Three: Analysis and Interpretation of the Data

Shilkus wrote descriptions of students' design, construction, and tutoring activities in class, with specific examples:

> In many cases, I saw a marked improvement in class participation and behavior. Students were forming a tutoring system in the classroom too, not just with their tutees. I observed many students who asked for additional work; they wanted and enjoyed helping someone else. I was witnessing a form of community being born. (2001, p. 146)

At the elimination car race, "some members of my middle school class commented that the fourth-grade sketches were better than the adult sketches" (p. 148). A postactivity questionnaire revealed that participants liked making the cars more than designing them.

Adults reported insights that they gained from being in the role of student in an unfamiliar context. For example, the comment of a home economics teacher in Shilkus's graduate education class confirmed for him the importance of teachers being able to put themselves in their students' shoes when they design instruction: "I know now some of the frustrations my kids must feel in my sewing class. . . . As much as I like to think I can see things through a student's eyes, it's refreshing to be proved wrong on this point!" (2001, pp. 148–149).

Shilkus concluded from his research project that basing his class teaching activities on the multiple intelligences framework helped him reach more of the hard-to-motivate students, promoted students' socialization skills, and appealed to their varied learning styles.

Step Four: Taking Action

Action research typically involves making changes in one's behavior and observing the consequences. As described, Shilkus engaged in a variety of actions: using both cross tutoring and peer tutoring, having veteran students tutor a fourth-grade class of "rookies," and having the veterans tutor the adults in his own graduate education class. Shilkus coached his veteran students in their role as tutors, and helped the "rookies" and the adults take the role of industrial arts students, a role with which most of them were unfamiliar.

Step Five: Reflection

Reflection is a process in which educators step back from the fast-paced and problem-filled world of practice in order to ponder, and possibly share with others, ideas about the meaning, value, and impact of their practice. This type of reflection can lead educators to make new commitments, discover new topics to explore through action research, and achieve new insights into the strengths and weaknesses of their current practice.

Shilkus does not specifically mention his use of reflection in his report, but he gives many examples of how his thought processes changed during, and after, the action research project. For example:

> I've noticed changes in myself and my students as a result of this project. Presenting information in different manners has made it possible to reach more students, not just the students who excel in traditional classes. . . . I can only hope my students learn as much as I did during this project. (2001, p. 149)

David Hobson (2001) views journaling as a critical tool for generating a "written record of practice" (p. 19). Figure 19.1 provides our summary of his suggestions for keeping an action research journal as a basis for reflection.

FIGURE 19.1 Suggestions for Keeping an Action Research Journal

1. Use 8 ½" × 11" pages and put them in a 3-ring binder so that pages can be removed, added, or rearranged. For ease of carrying, you might prefer a 6" × 9" binder, blank lesson plan book, Post-It note pad, or spiral-bound notebook.
2. Date and time each entry to facilitate viewing developments processes over time. Start each entry on a new page, so that the pages can be grouped to reflect recurring patterns or reconstruct sequences.
3. Make time for journaling by picking a regular time free of interruption or writing in class while your students are writing.
4. Use descriptive writing to record directly observed/experienced details for later review.
5. Use reflective writing to comment, associate, and make meaning.
6. Use double-entry journal writing with a description in one column and reflection in the other column.
7. Keep a daily log to help reveal priorities and to note what absorbs your attention and what continuing issues predominate.
8. Name each important teacher you have known, and describe each one. Look for commonalities; describe the stepping-stones in your experience of teaching and reflect on your development over time.
9. Examine the materials you have been reading and bring the results of your investigations into your journal.
10. Develop a "journal of the journals," going back through your entire journal to seek themes and highlight passages, and have a friend read aloud the lines you have highlighted.
11. Ask your students to turn in "exit slips" at the end of each class reflecting on their learning, questions, and expectations.

Source: Adapted from Hobson, D. (2001). Action and reflection: Narrative and journaling in teacher research. In G. Burnaford, J. Fischer, & D. Hobson (Eds.), *Teachers doing research* (2nd ed., pp. 7–27). Mahwah, NJ: Lawrence Erlbaum.

Step Six: Continuation or Modification of Practices

The postactivity survey showed that Shilkus's research participants preferred making the race car to designing it. Therefore, he decided that he needed to make the design of the race car "even more interesting for my students" (2001, p. 148). His observations of the quality of his students' suggestions for the race car design and competition led Shilkus to add a critique unit to all his car-racing classes. From the students' critiques he learned that they appreciated seeing a finished product before they began their own car design and construction. Therefore, he changed his teaching unit to allow students to examine the cars being designed by others as they progress. This activity provides feedback and motivation to all the students, both those designing the cars and those observing the design process.

Step Seven: Preparing a Report of the Findings

Shilkus's action research report is one of a number of detailed examples in *Teachers Doing Research* (Burnaford, Fischer, & Hobson, 2001). It is thus a polished, published example of action research and illustrates the value of an action researcher being part of a professional development program. Through his program Shilkus was able to interact with, learn from, and include as research participants his graduate student colleagues. He also received guidance from the course instructors, who edited the book in which Shilkus's research report is published.

Reports of action research projects can be disseminated in other media besides journals and books. Cochran-Smith and Donnell (2006) observe that action research has led to "new ways to store, retrieve, code, and disseminate practitioners' inquiries in the form of CD-ROMs, Web sites, and other electronic innovations as well as new modes of public presentation and publication, such as multivoiced conversations, readers theater, poetry, and so on" (p. 512).

How Action Research Differs from Educators' Other Approaches to Problem Solving

Table 19.1 describes how action research differs from formal research. Here we consider briefly how action research differs from educators' typical approaches to solving problems of practice. Typically teachers talk to colleagues, attend workshops, pick up ideas from professional magazines, or rely on their own hunches as a guide to trying something new in their practice.

The question must be asked: Do the ideas derived from these approaches actually affect student learning? Mixed evidence from the National Assessment of Educational Progress and the No Child Left Behind Act as to the overall quality of student learning in the United States suggests that such approaches, despite their popularity, are not highly effective. Action research possesses two important features beyond those of most other approaches to solving problems of practice—systematicity and intentionality.

Cochran-Smith and Donnel (2006) have used these concepts to clarify the unique characteristics of practitioner research, including action research. They describe **systematicity** as involving "ordered ways of gathering and recording information, documenting experiences inside and outside of the contexts of practice, and making some kind of written record . . . [and] ordered ways of recollecting, rethinking, and analyzing events for which there are only partially written records" (p. 510).

Intentionality, in turn, "refers to the planned and deliberate rather than spontaneous nature of practitioner inquiry" (Cochran-Smith & Donnel, 2006, p. 510). Many teachers frequently examine assignments, test results, and the other forms of student documents routinely generated in schools. Action research encourages teachers to generate additional data to look specifically at what they do and what results they observe in students from what they do. They thus can gather new data on student learning and highlight the specific relationships between their varied teaching choices and student learning.

In some reports of action research, the authors limit their description of findings to statements that students "responded positively" or "did better" after a new action was undertaken. To have the greatest impact on their own and others' practice, we recommend that in reports of action research authors explain specifically the actions they took, as well as the procedures of data collection, analysis, and interpretation that provided the basis of the results they obtained.

Purposes and Benefits of Action Research

Action research is sometimes regarded as having three main purposes—personal, professional, and political (Zeichner & Noffke, 2001). In practice, as reflected in the set of actual research studies cited in this chapter, most educators carry out action research for reasons that appear to blend these purposes. Below we briefly summarize some of the benefits of action research, referring back to Shilkus's (2001) study to illustrate each one.

1. *Contribution to the theory and knowledge base that educators need to enhance their practice.* Educators who carry out action research learn to reconstruct educational theory and findings in terms that are understandable to them. Based on this understanding, they can develop more effective practices in their work settings. Shilkus's use of cross tutoring and peer tutoring illustrates his application of new concepts to his teaching repertoire.

Educators who have the opportunity to try out new teaching strategies can in turn contribute to the teaching profession and to the education research literature. For example, Madeline Hunter (1994) was the director of the laboratory school at the University of California, Los Angeles, when she began informally experimenting with ways to improve teachers' classroom instruction. Her individual creativity resulted in the development of a method of instruction called ITIP (Instructional Theory into Practice), which has had a major impact on teaching practice and stimulated many formal research studies of its effectiveness.

2. *Support of the professional development of educators.* Shilkus's report shows how his action research increased his competence in applying research findings, carrying out research himself, and reporting the research. He not only developed needed skills in doing research, but he also improved his ability to read, interpret, and apply the research of others. Furthermore, the education course that he completed while doing his research contributed to his completion of a master's degree.

3. *Build a collegial networking system.* **Collaborative action research** is carried out by two or more educators involved in the same type of practice (e.g., K–12 teaching) or from more than one type of practice (e.g., K–12 teachers and university teacher educators). The collaboration might also extend to the clients for whom the research activities are intended.

For example, Shilkus's research collaborators included his own middle school students, the fourth-grade student "rookies" and their teacher, and his graduate education classmates. They were involved not only as research participants but also in the design and conduct of the research itself. Shilkus thus built a rich communication network, reducing the isolation often experienced by individual teachers and providing opportunities for future collaborative work.

4. *Help identify problems and seek solutions in a systematic fashion.* Shilkus's action research required that he and his students and teaching colleagues define problems of practice clearly, identify and try out possible solutions systematically, and reflect on and share the

results of their efforts. Thus, systematic action research enables educators to break out of the rut of institutionalized, taken-for-granted routines. It generates hope and motivation to solve seemingly intractable problems in the workplace.

5. *Can be used at all levels and in all areas of education practice.* Shilkus's study not only cut across two levels of schooling (fourth-graders and his middle school students), but also included both his school and the university where he and his classmates were studying. Action research can be carried out in specific classrooms or departments, throughout an educational institution, or at the regional, national, or international level.

Applying Action Science to Action Research

Action science, a theory developed by Chris Argyris and Donald Schön (1974), can help action researchers design their action research to produce effective change in their practice. **Action science** is an approach to help educators discover and reconcile differences between their **espoused theory,** that is, their *beliefs* about how they deal with specific problems of practice, and their **theory-in-action,** that is, their actual *behavior* as they engage in their work.

For example, suppose that Sophie, a ninth-grade history teacher, believes that she fosters higher-order thinking when questioning her students. If in fact she actually asks mostly knowledge and comprehension questions, she is not tapping the higher cognitive levels that are specified in models of thinking (e.g., Bloom, 1956; Wiggins & McTighe, 1998).

Action research could help demonstrate this discrepancy and the problems it causes. Suppose that Sophie undertook action research to improve her questioning strategies. She could collect data on both her specific actions and students' responses to them. For example, she could videotape herself as she carries out a lesson for subsequent self-analysis—a method known as *microteaching* that was once widely used in teacher education (MacLeod, 1995). She could fill out an observation scale to assess the extent to which she carried out the actions that she intended to carry out. She could also ask colleagues or teacher educators from a university to observe and give her feedback.

Sophie could look specifically for instances that reveal differences between her espoused theory and her theory-in-action. Then she could take new actions to bring her behavior closer to her beliefs about what she wants to accomplish.

A study by Thomas Hatch (1998) illustrates the value of action science in identifying problems of practice. In 1991 the New American Schools Development Corporation issued a request for proposals. In response, four large-scale school-improvement organizations formed a collaborative effort called the Authentic Teaching Learning and Assessment for All Students (ATLAS) Communities Project. Their stated goal was to effect change in schools nationwide. Hatch outlines major differences in the espoused theories of the leaders of these organizations, which contributed to very different approaches to basic schooling dilemmas. Hatch concludes that these differences "made it extremely difficult to make decisions and to carry out the collaborative work that school improvement required" (p. 24).

The Insider–Outsider Issue in Collaborative Action Research

Whether the promise of action research is realized depends to a great extent on the participants in action research projects. Some educators who engage in action research (typically, K–12 teachers) view themselves as **insiders,** that is, individuals with an internal perspective on the problems of practice being studied. They might argue against collaborating with **outsiders,** such as university professors or researchers from a research organization, who are viewed as having an external perspective on those problems. Stephen Kemmis and Robin McTaggart (2000) argue that reliance on the interpretations of outsiders might disempower teachers and might imply that "outsider" research is more valid than teacher research.

In a subsequent publication, McTaggart (2003) addresses the insider–outsider issue from a different perspective. He argues that scholars such as university professors can best add value to K–12 educators' practice through participatory action research endeavors. McTaggart asserts that educational practice involves not only K–12 teaching, but all the major functions of various educational systems or institutions. He explains that all educators engage in some aspect of practice and can affect other aspects of practice through collaborative efforts. Therefore, he argues that to be effective, the action undertaken through action research must affect all the critical aspects of educational practice: curriculum, administrative practice, teacher education, and the conduct and publication of educational research.

McTaggart (2003) identifies three ways in which scholars such as university professors, who would be considered outsiders in relation to K–12 teaching, can contribute through action research to solving K–12 teachers' problems of practice. First, he sees such scholars as able to help ensure that action research insiders adequately test the credibility of evidence in support of particular research findings and interpretations. This involves "an ongoing sociopolitical process. . . . in situ with participants" (p. 9) that depends on systematic data collection and analysis.

Second, McTaggart urges scholars to support insiders and research participants in expressing their feelings about what is being studied, which are often strong and can help or hinder subsequent action. McTaggart argues that outsiders can also help insiders determine which of those feelings are justified and which are better to reframe or set aside in the interests of social change.

Third, McTaggart sees scholars as able to contribute critical support for the development of personal political agency among research participants and provide critical mass for a commitment to change. He admits, though, that outsiders' typical privileged institutional settings may have deskilled them for such collaborative roles. He nonetheless asserts that if they will "insinuate themselves into political life" (p. 14), they will gradually be able to become equal players with insiders in a truly participatory action research process.

Evaluating the Credibility and Trustworthiness of Action Research Projects

Action researchers need to consider ways to design and carry out their research so that the resulting actions, and the reports on them, are credible and trustworthy both to the researchers and to others. Some action research projects rely primarily on quantitative research designs. You can evaluate these projects using the criteria shown in Appendix 1 and the design-specific criteria for descriptive research (see Chapter 10), group comparison research (see Chapter 11), correlational research (see Chapter 12), and experimental research (see Chapter 13).

Other action research projects reply primarily on qualitative research designs. You can evaluate these projects using the criteria shown in Appendix 3. The suggested strategies for evaluating case studies (see Chapter 14) are also relevant. In addition, you can apply five validity criteria developed by Gary Anderson and Kathryn Herr (1999) specifically for evaluating action research studies: (1) outcome validity, (2) process validity, (3) democratic validity, (4) catalytic validity, and (5) dialogic validity. We describe each validity criterion next. We also cite actual research studies and refer to specific strategies used in each study to increase that type of validity.

As you read about these criteria, keep in mind that you may encounter action research projects that are not presented in a complete, formal report. You can overcome this limitation by interviewing the action researcher—and perhaps colleagues and clients, too—in order to learn more about the project. That process should give you the necessary information to evaluate a specific action research study using these or other validity criteria.

Outcome Validity

Outcome validity concerns the extent to which actions occur that lead to a resolution of the problem that prompted the action research study. Rigorous action research, of course, seeks not only to solve a specific problem. It also aims to help researchers reframe the problem in a more complex way, which often leads to a new set of questions or problems to be addressed. Thus, this criterion also stresses the importance of reflection and the continuing introduction of new actions to address ongoing or emerging problems.

Barbara Levin and Tracy Rock (2003) studied five pairs of preservice and experienced teachers who engaged in collaborative action research projects during the preservice teachers' professional development internship in the experienced (mentor) teachers' classrooms. Levin and Rock analyze interviews with, and written and audiotaped reports from, the participants. They present findings about the costs of collaboration (for example, time pressures, dependence on someone else to fulfill one's responsibilities, or limited access to one's mentor). As important, they demonstrate that the project had beneficial outcomes for the preservice teachers (for example, generating their mentors' perspective, support, and feedback).

Process Validity

Process validity concerns the adequacy of the processes used in different phases of an action research project. Framing and solving problems in a way that promotes the researchers' ongoing learning is one aspect of process validity. Triangulation (the inclusion of multiple perspectives or data sources) also contributes to process validity. If the action research project is reported through narratives such as poems, folktales, or anecdotes, readers need to know whether they depict accurately what occurred, rather than being purely subjective accounts or interesting exaggerations.

Martha Stevens (2001) carried out action research while teaching mainstreamed sixth-graders with learning disabilities. She used a continual process of exploration of students' learning, and corresponding change of her actions, to improve the learning environment. For example, she modified the curriculum to encourage greater use of self-management by students. Based on her review of research on teaching reading to students with learning disabilities, she also scaffolded information in the regular education texts for her students by recording it on audiotape and rewriting the assignments at a simpler reading level. The adequacy of these processes is shown in six years of data reflecting good student progress in both reading and writing skills, including improvements in test scores and grades both in her classes and in mainstreamed settings.

Democratic Validity

Democratic validity refers to the extent to which an action research project is done in collaboration with all the parties who have a stake in the problem being investigated. It also involves determination of whether the multiple perspectives and material interests of all stakeholder groups have been taken into account. Here multiple perspectives are viewed not as a basis for triangulation of data sources but as an issue of ethics and social justice.

Shilkus's action research (2001) provides an outstanding example of including multiple perspectives in the problem of making industrial arts instruction an active learning process for all participants. He included as data sources, and actually as coresearchers, not just his middle school students, but also fourth-grade "rookie" students and his graduate education classmates.

Catalytic Validity

Catalytic validity involves the extent to which an action research project reorients, focuses, and energizes participants so that they become open to a transformed view of reality in relation to their practice. Action researchers strengthen this aspect of validity by keeping a research journal to record their reflections and changing perceptions.

This criterion also addresses the extent to which practitioner research realizes an emancipatory potential. In other words, catalytic validity addresses an action research project's success in fostering the widespread engagement of educators and education stakeholders in an active quest for ending oppression and promoting social justice.

For example, Anchalee Chayanuvat and Duangta Lukkunaprasit (1997), two English-language instructors at a university in Thailand, conducted action research to help enhance the English-language skills of gifted students entering their university. Their findings included recommendations for a special English class for gifted students, with:

> more emphasis on speaking and writing, inclusion of external reading materials which are more difficult and challenging, and exploitation of students' learning activities outside class in our English program, e.g., an oral discussion following the watching of an assigned film. (p. 164)

Chayanuvat and Lukkunaprasit provide evidence that the provision of this type of class helped emancipate their students by giving them increased opportunities to express their giftedness and make learning gains not otherwise possible.

Dialogic Validity

Dialogic validity refers to the use of extensive dialogue with peers in the formation and review of the action researcher's findings and interpretations. It can be met by doing action research collaboratively. It is also enhanced by the researcher engaging in critical and reflective dialogue with other researchers or with a "critical friend" who serves as a devil's advocate for alternative explanations of research data. Efforts to ensure the "goodness-of-fit" of the action research problem and findings with the intuitions of the practitioner community also improves dialogic validity.

Stevens's (2001) action research projects with her mainstreamed sixth-graders involved an impressive amount of dialogue between her and her students, the students' other teachers, and the students' parents. The other teachers' positive responses to her program outcomes and materials also reflect "goodness-of-fit" with the teaching community in her middle school.

An *example of*
HOW ACTION RESEARCH CAN HELP IN SOLVING PROBLEMS OF PRACTICE

Students and others often question the value of homework, as illustrated in these excerpts from a recent newspaper article:

> For years, students, parents, teachers and Ph.D.s have debated the value of homework in general, yielding mixed but impassioned opinions. When it comes to giving homework over Thanksgiving and other school breaks, opinions are equally mixed—and passionate.
>
> Some teachers, such as English teacher [BN], don't give anything beyond extra credit or makeup work.
>
> Others, such as [SC], a second-grade teacher . . . , say they assign homework over breaks for students' own good.
>
> Schencker, L. (2008, November 26). School's out, but homework's not. *Salt Lake Tribune*. Retrieved from www.sltrib.com

The article also mentions parents, students, and professors who are either for or against assigning homework to be completed during holiday breaks from school. They express a surprising range of opinions about this issue. This controversy can stimulate an action research project, as we illustrate.

Suppose you are a teacher with the choice to assign homework over a holiday break. You know that students are expected to be prepared for school tests and for state competency examinations. On the pro side, you believe that homework helps them review and extend their learning beyond what you and your students cover in class. On the con side, you feel that you and your students need a true break during holiday periods.

To help you decide on a strategy you could first review some research on homework as to the pros and cons of assigning homework at all, and specifically during school breaks. You could also talk to other teachers in your school and get their opinions. In the process, suppose that you discover another teacher at your grade level (Joan) who also wonders about the value of homework. You could do collaborative action research with Joan, in one of her classes and one of your classes. Your goal could be to determine whether assigning homework over school breaks is a good idea and if so, what type of homework is most appropriate.

You and Joan could design a questionnaire asking students to rate their attitudes about homework in general and over holiday breaks. It could also ask students to rate different types of homework as to how positively or negatively they would feel about having each type during a holiday break.

To help you find out more about individual students' attitudes, you could also include room for student comments on the questionnaire. If you ask students to sign their questionnaires, you could look for differences between the responses of higher-achieving and lower-achieving students.

When the next holiday break comes, you could give no homework while Joan tries out an approach to homework that students rated. You could then have students in your class rate how positively they felt about getting no homework while the other class rates the approach Joan used. You could also give an examination on the material covered before the holiday break and compare the performance of the students who got homework during the break with the performance of students who had no homework.

The findings from this action research might help you and Joan develop a homework policy that fosters student learning. You and Joan could also share the results with your students, which might reduce their resistance to homework you assign in the future.

Self-Check Test

1. Action research has all the following purposes except
   a. supporting the professional development of practitioners.
   b. building theory and generalizable knowledge.
   c. building a collegial networking system among educators.
   d. helping practitioners identify problems and seek solutions systematically.

2. The quality of an action research project is *least* dependent on its
   a. use of well-designed methods of data collection and analysis.
   b. promotion of collaboration between the researcher and his or her colleagues.
   c. contribution to the knowledge base for education.
   d. impact on the researcher's practice.

3. Reflection by action researchers
   a. is particularly important at the start of an action research project.
   b. occurs primarily during data analysis and interpretation.
   c. involves pondering the meaning, value, and impact of one's actions.
   d. requires dialogue with the research participants.

4. The problem to be addressed by an action research project typically is identified by
   a. educators' consideration of obstacles to achieving their work goals.
   b. reviews of the education literature.
   c. a systematic needs assessment.
   d. consultation with outsiders.

5. Action researchers who publish their studies in the research literature are primarily motivated by the desire to
   a. present generalizable findings to the widest possible audience.
   b. encourage other educators to undertake action research on problems of practice.
   c. demonstrate the rigor that action research can involve.
   d. enhance their status in their local educational context.
6. For an action research project to be considered a success, it is important that the researchers
   a. receive extensive preparation to develop their research knowledge and skills.
   b. review the education literature before designing the action to be taken.
   c. discuss the theoretical implications of their results.
   d. apply the findings to their own practice.
7. According to Robin McTaggart, scholars can best contribute to collaborative action research with K–12 educators by
   a. promoting adherence to positivist principles of objectivity.
   b. providing structure for the research design.
   c. providing critical mass for a commitment to change.
   d. All of the above.

8. Considering the multiple perspectives and interests of all stakeholders in an action research project is a strategy that directly increases its _____ validity.
   a. democratic
   b. catalytic
   c. dialogic
   d. process
9. Educational action research differs most from formal research in
   a. its focus on improving teaching and learning.
   b. its use of deliberate inquiry and ordered ways of gathering and recording information.
   c. its conduct of research on aspects of the researchers' own practice.
   d. its applicability to all levels and types of education practice.
10. Action science can best inform action research with respect to
    a. identifying and resolving discrepancies between participants' espoused theories and theories-in-action.
    b. determining the appropriate participants for collaborative action research.
    c. enabling insiders to free themselves from the disempowerment of working with outsiders.
    d. increasing the political impact of research findings.

Chapter References

Anderson, G. L., & Herr, K. (1999). The new paradigm wars: Is there room for rigorous practitioner knowledge in schools and universities? *Educational Researcher, 28*(5), 12–21, 40.

Argyris, C., & Schön, D. A. (1974). *Theory in practice: Increasing professional effectiveness.* San Francisco: Jossey-Bass.

Bloom, B. S. (Ed.). (1956). *Taxonomy of educational objectives: Classification of educational goals. Handbook 1: Cognitive domain.* New York: Longman.

Burnaford, G., Fischer, J., & Hobson, D. (Eds.) (2001). *Teachers doing research* (2nd ed.). Mahwah, NJ: Lawrence Erlbaum.

Carr, W., & Kemmis, S. (1988). *Becoming critical: Educational knowledge and action research.* London: Falmer.

Chayanuvat, A., & Lukkunaprasit, D. (1997). Classroom-centered research at Chulalongkorn University Language Institute. In S. Hollingsworth (Ed.), *International action research: A casebook for educational reform* (pp. 157–167). London: Falmer.

Cochran-Smith, M., & Donnell, K. (2006). Practitioner inquiry: Blurring the boundaries of research and practice. In J. L. Green, G. Camilli, & P. B. Elmore (Eds.), *Handbook of complementary methods in education research.* Washington, DC: American Educational Research Association.

Cochran-Smith, M., & Lytle, S. L. (1999). The teacher research movement: A decade later. *Educational Researcher, 28*(7), 15–25.

Drosopoulos, J. D., Heald, A. Z., & McCue, M. J. (2008). *Minimizing bullying behavior of middle school students through behavioral intervention and instruction.* Chicago: St. Xavier University. ERIC Document Reproduction Service No. ED500895.

Glanz, J. (1998). *Action research: An educational leader's guide to school improvement.* Norwood, MA: Christopher-Gordon.

Hatch, T. (1998). The differences in theory that matter in the practice of school improvement. *American Educational Research Journal, 35,* 3–31.

Hobson, D. (2001). Action and reflection: Narrative and journaling in teacher research. In G. Burnaford, J. Fischer, & D. Hobson (Eds.), *Teachers doing research* (2nd ed., pp. 7–27). Mahwah, NJ: Lawrence Erlbaum.

Holt, C. (2008). *Does reciprocal teaching increase student achievement in 5th grade social studies?* Retrieved from http://actionresearch.altec.org

Hunter, M. (1994). *Enhancing teaching.* New York: Macmillan.

Kemmis, S., & McTaggart, R. (2000). Participatory action research. In N. K. Denzin & Y. S. Lincoln (Eds.), *Handbook of qualitative research* (2nd ed., pp. 567–605). Thousand Oaks, CA: Sage.

Levin, B. B., & Rock, T. C. (2003). The effects of collaborative action research on preservice and experienced teacher partners in professional development schools. *Journal of Teacher Education, 54,* 135–149.

Lewin, K. (1946). Action research and minority problems. *Journal of Social Issues, 2*(4), 34–46.

MacLeod, G. (1995). Microteaching in teacher education. In L. W. Anderson (Ed.), *International encyclopedia of teaching and teacher education* (2nd ed., pp. 573–577). Tarrytown, NY: Elsevier Science.

McTaggart, R. (2002). Action research scholar: The role of the scholar in action research. In M. P. Wolfe & C. R. Pryor (Eds.), *The mission of the scholar: Research and practice* (pp. 1–16). New York: Peter Lang.

Reason, P., & Bradbury, H. (Eds.). (2001). *Handbook of action research: Participative inquiry and practice.* Thousand Oaks, CA: Sage.

Schippers, M. (2008). *Student support in China: Addressing the perceived needs of undergraduate English department students.* ERIC Document Reproduction Service No. ED499780.

Schmuck, R. A. (1997). *Practical action research for change.* Arlington Heights, IL: IRI/Skylight.

Shilkus, W. (2001). Racing to research: Inquiry in middle school industrial arts. In G. Burnaford, J. Fischer, & D. Hobson (Eds.), *Teachers doing research* (2nd ed., pp. 143–149). Mahwah, NJ: Lawrence Erlbaum.

Stevens, M. C. (2001). Laptops: Language arts for students with learning disabilities: An action research curriculum development project. In G. Burnaford, J. Fischer, & D. Hobson (Eds.), *Teachers doing research* (2nd ed., pp. 157–170). Mahwah, NJ: Lawrence Erlbaum.

Wiggins, G., & McTighe, J. (1998). *Understanding by design.* Alexandria, VA: Association for Supervision and Curriculum Development.

Zeichner, K. M., & Noffke, S. E. (2001). Practitioner research. In V. Richardson (Ed.), *Handbook of research on teaching* (4th ed., pp. 298–330). Washington, DC: American Educational Research Association.

Resources for Further Study

Burnaford, G., Fischer, J., & Hobson, D. (Eds.). (2001). *Teachers doing research* (2nd ed.). Mahwah, NJ: Lawrence Erlbaum.

> Presents guidelines for the conduct of teacher research in local, university, and national or international settings. The many detailed examples of teachers doing research are well designed, clearly written, and inspiring.

Fishman, S. M., & McCarthy, L. (2000). *Unplayed tapes: A personal history of collaborative teacher research.* Urbana, IL: National Council of Teachers of English.

> Summarizes the authors' experiences in conducting and guiding others in the conduct of "insider–outsider" collaborative teacher research.

Marion, R., & Zeichner, K. (2001). *Practitioner resource guide for action research.* Oxford, OH: National Staff Development Council. ERIC Document Reproduction Service No. ED472207.

> A compilation of resources for practitioner research, including information about practitioner research networks, journals, and online sites presenting action research studies, funding sources, and a bibliography on sources for designing action research.

Sample Action Research Study

Student-Generated Discussion in the Senior Secondary English Classroom

Lehmann, A. W. (2000). Student-generated discussion in the senior secondary English classroom. *Networks: An On-line Journal for Teacher Research, 3*(2). Available at http://journals .library.wisc.edu/index.php/networks/article/view/142/141

The following journal article reports a qualitative action research study that was published online. The article is reprinted in its entirety, just as it appeared when originally published. It is preceded by comments specially prepared by the article's author for this book.

Many teachers would like students to become active learners in class by speaking to each other and the teacher about ideas expressed in their curriculum materials. Also, they would like students to initiate more questions. In this article, we learn how a teacher–researcher conducted an experiment in her classroom to achieve these goals.

RESEARCHER'S
Comments

Prepared by
A. W. Lehmann

It was my good fortune a few years ago to pursue a master's degree from the University of Northern British Columbia. Of the courses in the stream through which I personally navigated, several focused on the pragmatics of speech in the classroom. Some investigations were devoted to habits of instruction that can so easily become paradigms of classroom management. Others explored the differences between didactic instruction and narrative. Constructivist literature emphasized the significance of student engagement and participation in classroom activity, and so on.

Overall, these courses' most lasting impression on me was the conviction that the common discourse of classrooms, including both the oral interchanges between instructors and students and conversations among students themselves, is of exceptional importance to learning that lasts. In constructing my own learning about this issue, I wished to explore further, by examining my own teaching, the kinds of departures from habitual practices that might more effectively generate student engagement. I wanted to see the effects of meaningful oral activities that were both student-driven *and* productive toward curricular goals, a combination that can prove elusive. Teachers love to promote curricular aims, but often students' interests lie elsewhere. Students love to talk, but frequently not as enthusiastically about classwork as about their personal lives and social priorities.

Discourse dynamics are extremely complicated, despite their surface simplicity. Before one even begins to assess or interpret the denotations of the messages being exchanged, there are numerous elements to consider. The nature of the venue, the participants' ages and genders, the relative social power of the speakers and listeners, and all the tacit understandings implicit in culture, tradition, and social expectation combine to provide the framework in which messages are exchanged.

Then, once such verbal exchange is under way, other considerations arise. For example, whose agenda is being served (is the conversation aimless or directed, and if the latter, by whom)? Is there an understood common purpose to the interchange? Is there mutual understanding of vocabulary and idiom? Of course, if each time we teachers began a lesson in a classroom situation we tried to attend to all these concerns, we would probably stop up our mouths and ears and cower in despair. The priorities of getting on with the job prevent most such analysis.

Despite such a daunting truth, the challenge of improving student speaking and listening in class and developing student participation in discourse while increasing its utility in positive directions is one that doesn't go away. For teachers to rely on the occasional "teachable moment" to generate student involvement in curricular goals through class discussion has always seemed too haphazard and too inadequate for professional practice. However, if and when such moments occur, we naturally embrace them strongly. Can we, though, devise useful strategies that are more consistently successful? This is a useful question, and perhaps it is natural that we recognize that questioning itself is key.

Although we all use questions quite naturally in our daily lives—asking directions, trying to locate products, investigating details in personal relationships, and so on—in education questions often have a kind of delayed utility. For example, if one asks a store clerk in which aisle one can find the canned tuna and the clerk responds "Aisle 4," the answer fulfills the question's purpose, and the episode is finished. Some questions in the language arts classroom are of just that sort, pragmatic tools for helping youngsters learn to use both the jargon and the concepts of grammar, syntax, composition, analysis, and criticism. However, in the open-ended universe of literary study, it often seems as if our queries never cease, with one question leading to the next in a continual chain toward an elusive goal of more comprehensive understanding—of what? Of ourselves? Of society? Of the world?

Such open-ended questions, the ones with no easy answers, are often, paradoxically, both the most frustrating and the most satisfying. As Leonard Cohen once sang, "I never had a secret chart/to get you to the heart/of this or any other matter." The world of literature is mysterious not only because it reflects a mysterious world, but also because our continual wrestling match with language often leaves us unsatisfied as to the delivery of completely definitive meanings. It is our questions, though, that create the boundaries and forms of our exploration.

Teachers, naturally, direct a great deal of the questioning in classrooms, sometimes to wonderfully beneficial effect. It is to be expected, though, that although curricular purposes will shape much of the direction and form of their questions, teachers' personal biases, judgments, and values will also mold them. By contrast, students may have questions whose boundaries are not necessarily congruent with those of the instructor or of their peers.

Adventures in English Literature is one of the common texts used in British Columbia to teach a historical overview of English literature. Surely if teachers expect students to participate in this adventure in a whole-hearted way, we must encourage the exploration of literature *as an adventure,* and encourage, embrace, and address genuine student questions about it. I use the adjective *genuine* in contrast to the "red herring" questions youngsters sometimes ask in the hope of drawing the class away from its intended purposes.

In addressing the puzzle of the role of questions amid the greater discourse in senior secondary language arts, I decided to pursue the theory that perhaps student questions have been insufficiently appreciated and underutilized. Teachers have always valued genuine questions from their students. Our difficulty has been, however, to design into our classroom planning successful, systematic, and reliable methods of encouraging such questions, of allowing them a respected place on the floor of discussion, and of using them to enhance overall learning.

To that end I devised the strategy outlined in the paper that follows. It is to be hoped that the methods outlined may prove useful as guides toward more successful approaches, to the ultimate benefit of the whole learning community.

Student-Generated Discussion in the Senior Secondary English Classroom

A. W. Lehmann

ABSTRACT ■ The purpose of this research study was to devise and test a method of encouraging, and subsequently managing, student-generated discussion of English literature within a senior secondary classroom. The students would provide not only the discussion itself, but also a "client's-eye" evaluation of the process. Accordingly, students were engaged in part of the initial clarification of the study's purposes and procedures, produced the bulk of the discussion which constituted the content for the method being examined, and provided a post-discussion evaluation which could be compared to earlier comments. A simple qualitative analysis of written comments provided by the students and of my own notes and reactions to the discussion allowed me to define more clearly some observations about the dynamics of discussion and to select some directions for further investigation. It would be premature to draw any definitive conclusions based on this study alone, but some of the observations are constructively suggestive.

PRELIMINARY CONSIDERATIONS

Classroom discussions can be wonderfully valuable for constructing and sharing knowledge. Often, however, the origin of these discussions and their movement toward the success described above is haphazard and fortuitous. I hoped to be able to prompt students to generate discussion that accomplished the valuable goals mentioned, in addition to ameliorating two main problems that are common in classroom activity. The first is that in many classroom discussions three or four voices dominate the interchange of ideas, and at least as many students never participate at all. The second is that many discussions are focused upon issues or ideas that the instructor has defined rather than upon considerations and questions which the students might find more significant or personally meaningful. Thus, the method that I adopted was meant to obviate these problems by requiring at least the limited

Source: Lehmann, A. W. (2000). Student-generated discussion in the senior secondary English classroom. *Networks: An On-line Journal of Teacher Research* 3(2). Retrieved October 31, 2008, from http://journals.library.wisc.edu/index.php/networks/index

participation of each student at one or more levels of the discussion and by having the students set the questions for the discussion's foci.

There were several questions that I hoped the project would illuminate. First, I desired a clearer profile of student attitudes to discussion in an average class. Second, I wished to discover students' feelings about teacher evaluation of their discussions; that is, should student discussions be graded and if so, how? Third, I wished to supplement my observations of the success or failure of the method of discussion with those of the students. Do they like the method, and do they find it educationally productive? Do their comments as participants describe much the same features that a teacher might observe?

A limiting factor was the brevity of the actual research period. The learning that needs to be negotiated by any class trying a new procedure is one that cannot be mastered immediately. Consequently, the limited success of the method we tried is probably not clearly indicative of the successes or failures that use of such a method might obtain over a longer period. Nonetheless, some constructive information was obtained.

Several authors and researchers provided useful ideas for the direction of the project. Sara Allen's (1992) paper on student-sustained discussion explored the limits to allowing students to manage a discussion without teacher interference. Her method of non-evaluative analysis of her classroom discussions influenced some of my questions.

Douglas Barnes (1991) provided some interesting observations on the methods of and reasons for using small group discussions. Particularly useful were the chapters on learning in small groups (pp. 34–70) and the teacher's control of knowledge (pp. 108–134).

Neil Mercer (1995) makes extensive reference to Barnes. In some ways he recapitulates Barnes' observations, particularly in his support of Barnes' argument that there is a difference between discussion in a classroom and educationally appropriate discussion, the latter being characterized by "learners (a) sharing the same ideas about what is relevant to the discussion; and (b) having a joint conception of what is trying to be achieved by it" (p. 96).

Borich's (1992) comprehensive text includes a chapter on cooperative learning and the collaborative process. It examines in detail the rationale for cooperative learning strategies; discusses the roles of both student and teacher; and outlines methods for specifying the goal of such activities, structuring the student task, teaching and evaluating the process itself, monitoring group performance, and subsequent debriefing (pp. 320–333). These ideas were particularly useful in designing my project. As well, Borich's explanations about the appropriate times for direct instruction supported my own decision about using direct instruction in part of the project's method (p. 187).

Two other texts, Richmond and McCroskey's (1992) *Power in the Classroom*, and Stewart's (1985) *How to Involve the Student in Classroom Decision Making* provided insights into problems that might accrue due to disciplinary anomalies. Morgan and Saxton (1994) provided valuable comments on the nature of questioning, whether by instructor or by student. Although I didn't use their specific categories, their text was helpful in clarifying my own approach, which follows.

METHOD

Before beginning this project, I followed the consent/assent procedures that are standard protocol within the school district (School District #82 has in policy a comprehensive procedure to deal with any research efforts in the district that involve children in any way, to ensure their privacy and safety). University ethics approval procedures were followed, as well. These completed, I turned to the project itself.

I first "floated" the idea of doing research in the classroom with my twelfth grade English class to see how they would feel about having their work made the subject of research. They were a normally inquisitive group of youngsters with a fairly equal spread of ability, ambition, gender, and so forth. They seemed interested in the idea, and when I submitted the information letter and the consent/assent forms for them to examine and sign or have signed, nearly every one of them immediately signed and returned the assent forms. Within about a week and a half we were prepared to proceed. Those students who failed to obtain permission to participate went to the library to finish reading the novel which was subject of the discussion, *A Prayer for Owen Meany* by John Irving, under the supervision of the librarian.

My first step was to try to obtain an informal overview of student attitudes toward classroom discussion in general, based on their previous experience. I asked them to compose brief responses, three or four sentences long, to the following clusters of questions. (a) How would you characterize yourself as a participant in classroom discussions: As an eager participant; as an occasional participant; as one who prefers to listen and observe; or as one who commonly "tunes out," for whatever reason? (b) Is classroom discussion, in your experience, a good place to develop skills in listening and speaking, and to develop critical tolerance toward others' points of view? Why or why not? (c) If these learning outcomes are important, as the Ministry of Education believes, should student participation in discussions be graded, and if so, how? (d) Is classroom discussion an effective means for taking responsibility for your own learning, that is, for generating questions and seeking out their answers? Why or why not? Students were asked to identify themselves with pseudonyms or to leave the papers unsigned altogether, in the expectation that anonymity would encourage honesty in their responses.

I was moderately surprised at the energy with which the students tackled these questions. Time that I had scheduled for this phase of the project had to be extended so that students could get down all their ideas, and I suspect some of them had more to say but were directed forward onto the next question before they could completely explore their own thinking. Nonetheless, their responses presented an interesting spectrum of student experience, including personal descriptions, confessions and opinions.

I created a summary form loosely based on ideas presented by Miles and Huberman (1994) for compiling the student responses to these questions along with some of their more germane quotes. I read all of the student submissions and transferred, usually by quotation but occasionally by paraphrase, their attitudes and ideas to the summary form. One weakness of this method is that I served as editor of their thoughts, only pulling out their more insightful or well-stated contributions to be included. It may be that something important was omitted, although I went through their responses more than once in order to be reasonably rigorous. As well, had I had the time to interview each of the students orally, I could have asked for clarification of some of the ideas they presented. Some statements were either contradictory or so poorly stated grammatically that they were unusable. I didn't like leaving too much out, but some of the data either repeated things that had previously been said or were so general or clichéd as to be relatively valueless for the purposes of the summary.

I randomly assigned students to numbered small groups. The groups were numbered one through six to match the chapter numbers of our novel with which I wanted each group to deal. Thus group one would work on the first chapter, group two on the second chapter, and so on.

As part of preparation for their discussions, I provided the class with some brief direct instruction on the nature of questions and questioning. I explained to them three categories of questions: literal questions, inferential questions, and elaborative questions. Literal questions are those that can be answered by simple reference to the text. For example, how did Johnny Wheelwright's mother die? An inferential question requires both information from the text and knowledge or speculation on the part of the person seeking an answer in order to deal with it satisfactorily. An example, based on clues from the story, is what might some reasons be for Owen's attitudes toward his parents? Here students might provide ideas from their own family relationships and relate them to evidence available in the text. An elaborative question is one that requires synthesis or evaluation to address it fully. It, too, should have some referents in the text to tie it to the rest of the discussion. A suitable example is, did Dan exhibit the characteristics of a good father? Why or why not? (The three samples above are based upon *A Prayer for Owen Meany*.) I provided them with examples of those distinctions so that, within the context of the exercise, they could explore several dimensions of questioning, and also so that they could be directed toward creating more complex questions for discussion purposes. I wanted to avoid a discussion based solely or even primarily on literal level, search-type questions, which tend to simplify and deaden discussion rather than to encourage it.

Each student was given the same assignment, which was to compose a question from each level of complexity,

based on the chapter his or her group had been assigned. A few students asked brief questions of clarification regarding the levels of question described above, but within a few minutes all seemed to understand. I allowed them a full weekend to read any necessary material (some students were still behind in the reading) and to compose their questions.

On the following Monday, we divided into our groups by chapter. Each small group (the largest had four students, the smallest two) was instructed to select a spokesperson by consensus. Then the groups were to share their questions, one level at a time (literal level first, then inferential, then elaborative). At this stage we ran into a small but annoying difficulty. Only about half the class had actually prepared their questions. Thus, those reliable students who were prepared had to wait patiently while their less reliable group partners hastily cobbled together something to contribute to the day's activity. (This particular hazard of group work, the differential reliability of students, is a common detraction from the success of group activities at the secondary level.) After fifteen minutes or so we were once again under way. Students shared and discussed their questions well, appearing to be on topic and on task, and requiring little in the way of instructor intervention to get the job done. I circulated among the groups, noting the progress of their discussion, which lasted twenty to thirty minutes. At the end of their discussions each group was instructed to select, by consensus, one question from either the inferential or elaborative level to present to the full class group discussion to come. They spent ten minutes or so debating the relative merits of the questions they had discussed and selected their questions for the full class discussion by the end of the period.

The following day we gathered as a large group and began sharing the questions. The discussion went well, with rarely a lapse of energy. Some of the questions were more challenging or appealing to the group than others, and the time devoted to them reflected this. Others were a little obscure and "fizzled out" in the large-group discussion.

During the last twenty minutes of the class we did a post-discussion evaluation, or debriefing, as Borich (1992) would have termed it (p. 331). Once again, this was done through soliciting written answers from the students to specific questions about the discussion as well as the process we used to approach it and carry it out. They were as follows: (a) Do you think a two-level discussion (first small group, then larger group) encourages broader participation by students in the discussion? (b) Are student-generated questions superior or inferior to questions generated by your instructor or that emerge by chance? Explain. (c) Was it useful to you to have a knowledge of various levels of questioning? (d) How would you evaluate the successes or failures of the discussion method we used? (e) If we could eliminate the bureaucratic impedimenta (permission slips, etc.) would you like to use this method again? Why or why not?

The participating students readily addressed these questions, providing on average a page to a page and a half of commentary in response. I analyzed their responses in much the same way as I did the pre-discussion responses. I devised a summary form onto which I mapped student responses into categories. Again, I included quotations or paraphrases which seemed most to characterize or explain the reasons behind their attitudes.

RESULTS

Pre-Discussion Attitudes

The pre-discussion background research led to some useful anecdotal information. The class divided itself almost evenly among three categories of participation in discussion: eager participants, occasional participants and listener/observers. Only one student admitted to habitually tuning out, stating that "wonderland is a good place to be if the topic's boring." Eager participants made such statements as, "I love to argue." "I actively participate and then sit back . . . to get a feel of how people react to my opinions." "It's exciting." Even one student who was a self-described avid participant admitted, "I try to zone out . . . it never lasts very long." Apparently the lure of discussion was far stronger to this student than the appeal of daydreaming.

Others who described themselves as occasional participants seemed, in some ways, more thoughtful. One stated, "I like to feel I have something really relevant to say before I say anything." Another commented, "I prefer to think out my arguments [so as not] to look stupid." Several would speak based on the immediacy and power of their emotions. "If [my] opinion is challenged I will speak up and defend it." "[I participate] when I have something really important to share." Two students wanted to defend personal identity and beliefs: "I try to be my own voice [rather than] go with what the majority thinks." "I'll speak out quite loudly . . . when it has something to do with my faith."

Listener/observers had a third cluster of perspectives. Some were simply shy. "I don't like the attention I bring myself." "I don't want people to judge me for something I said in class." Others claimed uncertainty or lack of knowledge. "Usually I am quite unsure of myself." "[Sometimes] I don't fully understand what is being discussed." Another group remained quiet because they felt other, more aggressive, students would have covered the topic adequately by the time they felt like contributing. "The issue is usually burnt out before I voice my opinion."

A sizable majority of students, whatever their own proclivities toward contributing to a discussion, felt that the classroom is a good place to learn listening and speaking skills, and critical tolerance toward others' ideas. There were many caveats, though. One observed that classroom discussion works because it is "mostly controlled." Another felt that discussions are excellent, but only useful if the class is "mature enough and tolerant enough to allow this to happen." Discussions could, in this student's view, be quite destructive when they became personal, "cruel," with "insults." A student who professed to love discussion also confessed that "after a discussion I'm often mad, un-

able to listen, and during and after the discussion I can be quite mean," which rather reinforces the previous student's comments. Some students complained about others' lack of attention. One stated, "I don't think teachers push hard enough to get those few involved and they fall behind." And one blunt student averred that "some people just don't have the know-how to say what they think." Many students, though, recognized that discussions are an excellent forum in which to "widen your understanding of [a] topic" or to be "exposed to many ideas," to get "less nervous," to "develop confidence in speaking and get better at taking 'mental notes.' " One claimed, "That is the way I learn things best" (giving support to theories about preferential learning styles), and another went so far as to make the claim that "in a Utopian classroom all class would be is discussions."

The question about grading discussions generated many interesting and somewhat contradictory ideas. Those in favour of grading them outnumbered those opposed by about three to two, but there were very few constructive ideas about how their contributions to discussion should be graded. There were some astute comments on the problem. As one person put it, "Some [students] are active, some are not; some make themselves heard a lot when they don't have much to say," an observation that shows an awareness not only of the quantity of someone's participation, but also of the quality. Another very clearly pointed out that inopportune timing "makes late speakers' contributions less 'valuable,' thus penalizing shy students," who presumably might speak up later when they got their courage up. One student noted that students are more likely to "speak their minds when they're not worried about a grade," suggesting that some students feel that their opinions might be vulnerable to a low grade due to a teacher who holds a counter-opinion, or that the process of public evaluation inhibits their expressive ability due to a kind of performance anxiety.

Many other unanswered questions about grading discussion activity were raised, either as direct questions or as pithy observations. "How can you put weight on a particular aspect of a discussion [as opposed to another aspect]?" "People [who are] above . . . the activity . . . should be penalized for it." Presumably losing the grade would be the penalty for not participating. "Teacher input would be much more useful [than a number]." Apparently this student would prefer verbal feedback. "It's hard to put a mark on a statement." "A mouthy person should not be marked on the same level as a quiet person." One student made a useful connection between discussion and written activities, suggesting that we "grade essays on the same topic after discussion, or look at notes taken during the discussion," which is quite insightful and pragmatic.

Addressing the problem of personal responsibility for learning and its relation to discussions is a considerably more difficult question. One student expressed the idea that in discussion "your mind doesn't have a chance to wonder [wander?]. This almost forces you to have self-responsibility of your own learning." Another felt it is "good for finding personal answers." A third made the connection that shy students fail to participate, which in turn leads them to devalue the activity because the greatest benefits accrue to those who do participate. "We can ask questions about what we don't understand," said one, indicating a willingness for self-direction. Another acerbically remarked, "The best way to gain knowledge is to shut your mouth and listen, [and] ask questions when you don't understand."

These students showed an alert sensitivity to the problems inherent in classroom discussion. They were able to describe vividly their own strengths and weaknesses as well as to put themselves imaginatively into others' positions, for example, that of another student who might be shy or aggressive, or that of the instructor trying to evaluate the whole process. They also demonstrated strong approval of discussions as learning tools, even if not all students wanted to be actively involved.

Post-Discussion Research

One aim of this research was to evaluate the method we used in our discussion of a novel. Was the division of the discussion into two levels helpful? Was the instruction on levels of questioning useful? How effective was the student-generation of questions? These considerations were to lead to decisions whether or not to try this method again, or to modify it in some ways and then try again.

In answer to the first question regarding whether or not the two-tier discussion process was effective in broadening the discussion, the students were generally of agreement that it was, though three respondents disagreed. One felt that the small groups "pressured [shy students] into stating an opinion; later in the big group their opinion was more likely to come up [than if they had remained silent]." Students felt that in the small group they did not "have to worry about being judged," because "in the small group you formed similar ideas . . . in the large group . . . you felt . . . the small group supported your ideas. It was not like you were alone." Group solidarity can lend confidence. "It gives a chance to organize thoughts," "you can compare and contrast more easily with [the] smaller group before taking the idea to the larger group," and it probably allows "for more involvement." A more avid participant observed that "a couple of shy people in my small group were actively participating." Nonetheless, of the three who felt there was not any real difference between this method and other discussions, one felt that only "the group that made up the question" really benefited, and another felt that often the student "didn't really have [his] own voice."

On the value of student-generated questions, students were fairly evenly divided. Many felt such an approach clearly superior. Students could "focus on the things that interest us" and could "ask about things we did not understand." "Student questioning gives the students a feeling of importance and acknowledgment." However, a considerable number felt student questions were worse, especially if "major points are missed." "Usually the instructor

has a firmer grasp on the material in discussion and can therefore focus the questions on the more important aspects." "Sometimes the teacher seems to ask a question on the more difficult concept which most people need to discuss to understand it better." A few felt there was little difference between student-generated and teacher-generated questions, and questions that emerge organically or by hazard from the story were admired by a few. "Chance allows a discussion to flow. If students are thorough, [missing important points] shouldn't be a problem." "Questions due to chance are probably the best. Some teachers feel that they [must] have specific answers and some students cannot make up good questions." The final word by one was, "A question is a question." Does it matter whose question it is if it is a good one, one that generates reflective discussion?

There was a mixed evaluation of the direct instruction on questioning strategies (the division of questions into literal, inferential, and elaborative levels). Several suggested that it was not important. "I don't think it made much of a difference." "My life hasn't been changed too much by the new knowledge." "I don't think you need to have a knowledge of questions." One held the middle ground. "It is useful . . . in a limited way . . . [it] allows one to organize thoughts and questions for writing in a more orderly fashion . . . beyond this [it is] little more than trivia." Positive responses included, "I learned something new." "The knowledge of these levels will affect the end result in the long run." "It expands your knowledge . . . forcing you to really think about the chapter and its connections to the rest of the world."

There was little consensus as to the success of the exercise. Some felt it was very useful; others had serious reservations. On the positive side, students had a chance "to see what things interest others . . . and maybe have things pointed out to us that we might otherwise have missed." It was "an excellent example of two heads being better than one." "Getting in groups was good." In a more ambiguous response, one student rated the process "a 6 out of 10." "Some people weren't done the book," which limited the participation. "It could have been better. Many people . . . weren't really interested in the questions being discussed." "It took two classes and we were still rushing to get through it all, so the efficiency can be questioned. The student questions were not very effective." And as usual, there were complaints about those few "who don't know when to stop or be quiet," or who "ramble incoherently."

Most students wanted to try again, and they provided some interesting suggestions. One was "to post the questions a day or two before the discussion." Another, from a student who likes discussions to be "fast and fight-like," was a request for a little more freedom. "Do the questions have to be about the novel?" asked one. Several pointed out that the bureaucratic problems to do with consent shrank our class, and recommended trying again with "more people." Only one student said, "No. This method just won't work for me, anyway."

DISCUSSION

It must be noted that a few students chose not to provide assent or neglected to get parental consent for this project; this factor probably skewed my classroom sample to include a greater proportion of students who are actually interested in English discussion or in academic pursuits in general. Nonetheless, for the majority who were involved, the following findings are suggestive.

The purpose of this project was to get a clear profile of student attitudes to discussion in a twelfth grade English class. This was accomplished. Its results were heartening, although they may have been somewhat sanitized by student efforts to please their teacher or to prevent getting a low reputation that might eventually affect their marks. (I made it clear that this project would have nothing to do with the calculation of their English 12 grade, but students are occasionally somewhat skeptical of authority and some may have decided to "play it safe.") I consider the results heartening because of the relatively high level of attention to discussion that was reported by students. There was only one student who confessed to enjoying "tuning out," and even that was in response to topics that are "boring." There may have been a few more such students, but they were not evident in the responses submitted, for whatever reasons.

The second consideration of importance was whether and how to evaluate this activity. The dominant ethos in senior secondary tends toward the evaluation of everything. Anything done for its own sake is usually extra-curricular. It is very common for students to ask, "Do we get marks for this?" in a tone of voice as if to suggest, "If we don't, why should we bother?" And indeed, unless the fear of poor marks threatens, a significant number of students will not participate. Further, as we well know, even this does not motivate a considerable minority of students. As a teacher somewhat habituated to this state of affairs, I would likely try to connect this activity in future to some form of evaluation, and some of the student suggestions mentioned above are good ideas. The students raised some good objections to grading, though, and evaluation of this kind of activity often seems either "fuzzily" inexact or somewhat pointless. It is difficult enough to distinguish reliably between A and B, let alone between 73% and 74%. If the instructor spends all his/her time filling out some kind of checklist monitoring who was talking, how many times, how forcefully, how many comments were questions, how many were answers, and so on, what kind of contribution is he/she likely to make to actually encouraging the discussion through immediately constructive feedback? Perhaps one student comment is most pragmatic. He claimed that we should not mark discussion directly because participation, whether as a speaker or a listener, would lead to better grades anyway, indirectly. Students who "tuned out" would not learn, and their work that was graded (essays and so on) would suffer accordingly. Those who participated would improve their thinking and, by extension, the content and style of their written work.

Finally, did the students find the exercise a successful one, that they would readily repeat? Many students, especially shy ones, found the two-level discussion liberating, and that it enhanced their participation. Less important to them was the theoretical nature of questioning. Rather they preferred to attend to questions that grew organically from their discussions, to focus on their content and meaning as opposed to their level of abstraction. As for the source of the questions, it appears that students were engaged by the process of questioning, but that they also were attuned to the importance of instructor expertise.

Did student perceptions mirror my own? I, like several of my student critics, found some of the questioning to be weak. I, too, was irked by one or two students who had little of significance to say but who "rambled incoherently" before I could tactfully grant someone else the floor. I agree with the youngster who felt that classroom discussion works best when it is controlled to prevent cruelty and insults, and although some increased freedoms from one-speaker-at-a-time decorum might result in greater entertainment value, I think that we should not aspire to model the classroom on Jerry Springer. I do not think that "fast" discussions characterized by "fights" are educationally defensible.

FURTHER RESEARCH

Like most of the student respondents, I would like to try this method again. Further useful observations could be made toward refinements that would improve discussion considerably and make it a more predictable process than simply capitalizing on what used to be labeled "the teachable moment."

The comparatively high level of student attention drawn to discussion, as shown by the student responses in this project, is fascinating in that it is almost surely higher than that given to lecture-style presentations by the instructor or to most presentations by their fellow students. There is something in the spontaneous give-and-take of discussion, an element of unpredictability and challenge, that is absent in the other forms of discourse cited above, and this feature might account for the higher attention. If this is true, then any methods that we can utilize to energize and foster productive discussion in our classrooms should be pursued.

I was particularly struck by the following final message by one of the students.

> I really liked this experiment, not quite chemistry, but very fun. I really like the fact that here we get to have a say in the way that we are learning, we get more emotionally involved and therefore we can take it more seriously. It's not just a marks thing, it's us getting to be us and learning through the best way we see fit.

With such a positive endorsement, it would be difficult not to pursue this method further.

References

1. Allen, S. (1992). Student-sustained discussion: When students talk and the teacher listens. In N. A. Branscombe, D. Goswami, & J. Schwartz (Eds.), *Students teaching: Teachers learning* (pp. 81–95). Portsmouth, NH: Boynton/Cook.
2. Barnes, D. (1991). *From communication to curriculum* (2nd ed.). Portsmouth, NH: Boynton/Cook.
3. Borich, G. (1992). *Effective teaching methods* (2nd ed.). Toronto: Maxwell MacMillan Canada.
4. Irving, J. (1989). *A Prayer for Owen Meany.* New York: Random House.
5. Mercer, N. (1995). *The guided construction of knowledge: Talk amongst teachers and learners.* Philadelphia, PA: Multilingual Matters.
6. Miles, M. B., & Huberman, A. M. (1994). *Qualitative data analysis: An expanded sourcebook* (2nd ed.). Thousand Oaks, CA: Sage.
7. Morgan, N., & Saxton, J. (1994). *Asking better questions: Models, techniques and classroom activities for engaging students in learning.* Markham, ON: Pembroke.
8. Richmond, V. P., & McCroskey, J. C. (1992). *Power in the classroom: Communication, control and concern.* Hillsdale, NJ: Lawrence Erlbaum.
9. Stewart, W. J. (Ed.) (1985). *How to involve the student in classroom decision making.* Saratoga, CA: R & E Publishers.

About the Author

A. W. Lehmann is a teacher in School District No. 82, Terrace, BC, Canada. Correspondence concerning this article should be addressed to A. W. Lehmann, English Department, Caledonia Senior Secondary School, 3605 Munroe Street, Terrace, British Columbia, Canada, V8G 3C4.

chapter *20*

Evaluation Research

IMPORTANT *Ideas*

1. Evaluations of programs are difficult, because programs seldom are uniformly effective, and different stakeholders define effectiveness differently.
2. Programs typically include curriculum materials, instructional methods, assessment procedures, and perhaps a professional development component. In addition, each program functions within a distinct culture.
3. Evaluation research is value-laden and political at every stage of the process.
4. The identification of a program's stakeholders and their concerns is important in most evaluation studies.
5. The model of objectives-based evaluation focuses on how well a program helps students achieve specified learning objectives.
6. The model of needs assessment is designed to identify discrepancies between an existing condition and a desired condition, so that educators can decide whether to improve a current program or develop a new one.
7. The CIPP model of program evaluation is comprehensive, because it is designed to assess all aspects of a program: stakeholders' needs and problems, competing alternatives, work plans and budgets, program activities, and program effectiveness.
8. The model of responsive evaluation involves the use of qualitative methods to identify and describe the issues and concerns of a program's stakeholders. Open, safe dialogue among stakeholders is critical to this evaluation model.
9. Research and development (R & D) is a systematic model for developing programs and products that are evidence-based. Formative and summative evaluation are integral components of this model.
10. Reports of evaluation studies generally are organized in the format of quantitative research reports, qualitative research reports, or mixed-methods reports.
11. The Joint Committee on Standards for Educational Evaluation, which includes representatives from 12 major educational organizations, has created a set of criteria for judging the quality of educational programs and products. ■

Key TERMS

CIPP model	National Assessment of Educational Progress	responsive evaluation
context evaluation		stakeholder
effectiveness evaluation	needs assessment	summative evaluation
emergent design	objectives-based evaluation	sustainability evaluation
evaluation research	performance objective	transportability evaluation
formative evaluation	process evaluation	
impact evaluation	product evaluation	
input evaluation	program	
Joint Committee on Standards for Educational Evaluation	program culture	
	research and development (R & D)	

The Use of Evaluation Research in Educational Decision Making

Evaluation research in education is the process of using quantitative or qualitative methods, or both, to arrive at judgments about the effectiveness of particular aspects of education. The process of arriving at these judgments is complicated, because "effectiveness" is a multifaceted concept, meaning different things to different stakeholders. Also, educational programs and processes seldom are uniformly effective. Typically, they are found to have benefits and drawbacks, and they might be effective only under certain conditions.

Despite its complexity, evaluation research has become increasingly important in education. Public schooling is essential in a democratic society, but it is also expensive. For this reason, the general public and policy makers want to know whether their money is well spent. In practice, this means that they want to fund programs that work and eliminate programs that do not work.

The prominence of evaluation's role in governmental funding and decision making is illustrated by a recent evaluation conducted by the Academic Competitiveness Council, which was commissioned by the U.S. Congress. The following is an excerpt from an ERIC abstract (Document Reference No. ED496649) of the Council's report on its evaluation findings:

> The Academic Competitiveness Council (ACC) is responsible for reviewing the effectiveness of existing federally funded Science, Technology, Engineering, and Math (STEM) programs, and for improving the state of STEM education in the United States. To this end, it has conducted a review of program evaluations submitted by 115 STEM programs. The ACC's review revealed that, despite decades of significant federal investment in science and math education, there is a general dearth of evidence of effective practices and activities in STEM education, and there is evidence of ineffective duplication of efforts.

If educators take no action in response to this kind of evaluation, there is a risk that funding for science education and other educational programs gradually will diminish. This scenario could unfold if policy makers and other groups came to believe that educational programs in general, not just the ones evaluated by the Academic Competitiveness Council, are ineffective and not capable of improvement by education professionals.

Our illustration involves evaluation at a macro level. Closer to home, consider how evaluation research might affect you as an educator. During your career, you might be asked to learn about a new program and teach in it or administer it. For example, suppose you are teaching in a regular school and are asked to teach in a new charter school instead. Undoubtedly, you will be interested in what is known about the effectiveness of this new school. Who is it intended for? Is there evidence that it produces better outcomes than traditional schools? What are the risks and drawbacks of this type of school? Would you be comfortable teaching in it?

Evaluation studies in the literature might help you answer these important questions. If none are available, you and your colleagues will need to learn about the program as you implement it. If the program is effective, all is well. If not, you might find yourself asking why the program was not researched beforehand to discover its pitfalls.

The purpose of this chapter is to help you learn about the effectiveness of programs not only from your personal experience with them but also from the findings of evaluation research.

Examples of Evaluation Research

Researchers do evaluation studies on many aspects of the education enterprise. The titles of the following journal articles suggest how wide the range is.

> Arancibia, V., Lissi, M. R., & Narea, M. (2008). Impact in the school system of a strategy for identifying and selecting academically talented students: The experience of Program PENTA-UC. *High Ability Studies, 19*(1), 53–65.
>
> Black, E. W., Fertig, R. E., & DiPietro, M. (2008). An overview of evaluative instrumentation for virtual high schools. *American Journal of Distance Education, 22*(1), 24–45.
>
> Eteokleous, N. (2008). Evaluating computer technology integration in a centralized school system. *Computers & Education, 51*(2), 669–686.
>
> Gaudet, C. H., Annulis, H. M., & Kmiec, J. J. Jr. (2008). Building an evaluation framework for a competency-based graduate program at the University of Southern Mississippi. *Performance Improvement, 47*(1), 26–36.
>
> Pence, H. M., & Macgillivray, I. K. (2008). The impact of an international field experience on preservice teachers. *Teaching and Teacher Education, 24*(1), 14–25.
>
> Schull, C. P., & Anderson, E. A. (2008). The effect of home visiting and home safety on children's school readiness. *European Early Childhood Education Research Journal, 16*(3), 313–324.

You can find many more examples of evaluation research at the website for the What Works Clearinghouse (http://ies.ed.gov/ncee/wcw), described in Chapter 5. The U.S. Department of Education sponsors and funds this agency, reflecting its increasing emphasis on evaluation research to guide policy making and influence the direction of school reform initiatives.

Programs as a Focus of Evaluation Research

A moment's reflection will help you realize that evaluation permeates the entire education enterprise. Teachers evaluate students' academic achievement and behavior. Administrators evaluate teachers. School boards evaluate school districts. School districts evaluate individual schools. Textbook adoption committees evaluate new textbooks.

Our focus in this chapter, though, is on methods for evaluating programs. We define a **program** as a systematic sequence of materials and activities designed to achieve explicitly stated goals and be used in many different settings. In education, a program typically includes curriculum expressed in text materials and other media, instructional methods, assessment procedures, and perhaps a staff development component to help educators implement it properly. All of these components are packaged so that they can be implemented in many different school sites. For example, elementary textbook series in reading produced by major publishers qualify as programs by this definition.

Saville Kushner and Clem Adelman (2006) claim that programs include more than these components:

> [P]rograms typically exhibit a "program culture." This is to say that they have rules, rituals, roles, a tension between the individual and the collective, a recognizable texture to their social processes, and a broadly agreed boundary that demarcates thoughts and actions that are or are not of this program. . . . People fit into programs, but programs also fit into people's lives. (p. 712)

Based on this statement, we define **program culture** as the rules, rituals, and roles that accompany the technical specifications of a program and also the tensions that come into play when the needs and desires of individuals in the program conflict with these specifications.

Program culture becomes an important consideration when educators are asked to adopt a new program that will replace the one they are already using. They are likely to wonder how much work the adoption of the new program will add to their already busy schedules. They might wonder, too, about the motivations of those promoting the new program, especially if they like the existing program. These concerns can be mitigated to an extent if evaluation evidence attesting to the program's effectiveness is available.

Evaluation Research as a Political Activity

All research involves values. For example, the fact that researchers choose to study one educational problem rather than another reflects a value judgment that it is more important, worthwhile, or interesting, or that it is more likely to attract funding and advance the researchers' careers.

Evaluation research is even more value-laden, because the researchers' explicit goal is to make value judgments about a program based on their empirical findings. Furthermore, individuals who are affected by the program will make value judgments about whether evaluations of it were fair and relevant.

If everyone affected by a program shares the same values, an evaluation study can probably proceed smoothly. However, this is seldom the case when educational programs are involved. An educational program has many features, and some might appeal to certain individuals and repel others. Therefore, individuals and organized groups are likely to compete with each other for power to make decisions about the program, such as whether to adopt or reject it, or how to evaluate it to highlight its strengths, or perhaps how to evaluate it in order to minimize or conceal its weaknesses.

This competition for power and influence in evaluating programs, especially when the stakes are high, makes evaluation research an inherently political activity. The intensity of the politics can increase if the program has prominent cultural features—for example, a program for ethnic-minority groups designed and evaluated by ethnic-majority educators and researchers.

Because program evaluation is inherently political, researchers have found it helpful to identify all relevant stakeholders at the outset of an evaluation study. A **stakeholder** is an individual who is involved in the phenomenon that is being evaluated or who may be affected by the findings of an evaluation. Identifying all the stakeholders affected by an educational program is not always easy. However, it is essential to be as inclusive as possible. Otherwise, some stakeholders' voices might be left unheard, thereby compromising the integrity of the evaluation study.

Models of Evaluation Research

In the course of doing evaluation studies over a period of decades, researchers have reflected on their work and created formal models of how evaluations should be done. Daniel Stufflebeam and Anthony Shinkfield (2007) identified and compared 26 of these evaluation models.

In the following sections, we describe five of these models, because they have achieved some prominence in the literature and because they illustrate the range of variation among models. They vary primarily in whether they focus on stakeholder perspectives and program culture or on the program's effectiveness in achieving measurable objectives.

If you plan to do a program evaluation, knowing about these models can help you in deciding which one best suits your purpose. If you are a stakeholder in an evaluation study, knowing about these models will give you a better sense of the study's goals and procedures.

Objectives-Based Evaluation

Objectives-based evaluation focuses on the extent to which an educational program helps students achieve the intended learning objectives associated with it. The **National Assessment of Educational Progress** (NAEP), which we describe in Chapter 10, is an example of this evaluation model. NAEP is a federally funded project that annually determines how well students are performing on measures of learning objectives in reading, mathematics, science, writing, history, geography, and other school subjects.

NAEP is based on the model of curriculum, instruction, and evaluation developed by Ralph Tyler (1949), who claimed that school instruction should be organized around specific curriculum objectives and that the success of such instruction should be judged on the basis of how well students reach those objectives.

The U.S. school system largely follows the principles of Tyler's model to this day. Classroom, district, state, and federal assessments are, for the most part, evaluations of how well students perform on measures of curriculum objectives. Programs designed to tie teachers' incentive pay to student learning outcomes and programs to identify and remediate "failing" schools also exemplify the Tyler model.

Educational experiments reflect objectives-based evaluation if they compare the learning gains of students in an innovative program with those of students receiving a traditional program or no program. Some of these studies are collected and reviewed by the What Works Clearinghouse in an effort to provide educators with evaluation evidence about particular educational programs.

Needs Assessment

Needs assessment is a set of procedures for identifying and prioritizing needs related to societal, organizational, and human performance (McKillip, 1987). A *need* usually is defined as a discrepancy between a desired and an existing state or condition.

For example, Richard Mihans (2008) analyzed a previously published survey of school staffing (National Center for Education Statistics, 2006). He found that 64,954 elementary and secondary public schools had teaching vacancies in the 2003–2004 school year. Teaching vacancies are projected to soar, even while student enrollments are also projected to increase for decades to come. Thus, there is a discrepancy between the existing number of teachers and the desired number of teachers.

This discrepancy constitutes a need, or in other words, a problem of practice. Mihans suggests that a key approach to solving it is to retain the teachers who are already in the profession. He identifies five conditions that are likely to accomplish this goal: (1) higher salaries, (2) more support from administrators, (3) more opportunities to be mentored, (4) better working conditions, and (5) more professional autonomy.

Mihans's analysis of a particular need in the education system and proposal for solutions can be used as a basis for developing programs to improve teacher retention. These programs, of course, should be evaluated to determine their effectiveness.

Needs assessment can be thought of as the first stage in program development. By evaluating existing conditions, researchers can determine whether they are satisfactory or in need of improvement. The availability of research data to establish a need should make it easier to argue for resources to improve existing programs or develop new ones.

The Context-Input-Process-Product (CIPP) Model

Stufflebeam (2003) developed the **CIPP model** to help educators evaluate programs, although the model also can be used to evaluate projects, personnel, institutions, and other entities. The acronym CIPP refers to four types of evaluation (context, input, process, product) that should be performed if one wishes to conduct a truly comprehensive assessment of a program as it unfolds over time.

- **Context evaluation** assesses needs, assets, and problems of the stakeholders, staff, and beneficiaries of the program.
- **Input evaluation** assesses competing alternatives, work plans, and budgets for the program under consideration.
- **Process evaluation** documents and assesses program activities.
- **Product evaluation** assesses whether the program succeeded.

Product evaluation has four subparts:

- **Impact evaluation** assesses whether the program reached the right target audience.
- **Effectiveness evaluation** assesses the quality and significance of the program's outcomes.
- **Sustainability evaluation** assesses whether the program is institutionalized successfully in the short term and long term.
- **Transportability evaluation** assesses whether the program can be adapted and institutionalized in other settings.

Stufflebeam (2007) developed sets of checklist items to guide evaluators and stakeholders through each of these types of evaluation as well as other aspects of evaluation, such as making contractual agreements for the evaluation and writing a final report. To illustrate, we show the checklist items for effectiveness evaluation in Table 20.1.

Most program developers and administrators probably do not have the resources to perform a program evaluation that encompasses the entire CIPP model. However, they can review all the items and select those that are most important and feasible for their particular situation.

Responsive Evaluation

Stake (2004) developed one of the first qualitative approaches to evaluation. **Responsive evaluation** focuses on identifying and describing stakeholders' issues (i.e., points of contention among different stakeholders) and concerns (i.e., matters about which stakeholders feel threatened or that they want to substantiate). Concerns and issues tend to provide a wider and different focus for an evaluation study than the program objectives that are central to objectives-based evaluation.

The four phases of responsive evaluation are (1) initiating and organizing the evaluation, (2) identifying key issues and concerns, (3) gathering useful information, and (4) reporting results and making recommendations. During the first phase, stakeholders are identified; also, the evaluator and client negotiate a contract to specify such matters as the phenomena to be evaluated, the purpose of the evaluation, rights of access to records, and guarantees of confidentiality and anonymity.

TABLE *20.1*   Effectiveness Evaluation

Effectiveness evaluation documents and assesses the quality and significance of outcomes.

Evaluator Activities	Client/Stakeholder Activities—Assessment/Reporting Outcomes
☐ Interview key stakeholders, such as community leaders, beneficiaries, program leaders and staff, and other interested parties, to determine their assessments of the program's positive and negative outcomes.	☐ Use effectiveness evaluation findings to gauge the program's positive and negative effects on beneficiaries.
	☐ As relevant, use the effectiveness evaluation findings to gauge the program's positive and negative effects on the community/pertinent environment.
☐ As feasible and appropriate, conduct in-depth case studies of selected beneficiaries.	☐ Use the effectiveness evaluation findings to sort out and judge important side effects.
☐ Engage an evaluation team member and program staff to supply documentation needed to identity and confirm the range, depth, quality, and significance of the program's effects on beneficiaries.	☐ Use the effectiveness evaluation findings to examine whether program plans and activities need to be changed.
☐ As appropriate, engage an evaluation team member to compile and assess information on the program's effects on the community.	☐ Use the effectiveness evaluation findings to prepare and issue program accountability reports.
☐ Engage a goal-free evaluator* to ascertain what the program actually did and to identify its full range of effects—positive and negative, intended and unintended.	☐ Use the effectiveness evaluation findings to make a bottom-line assessment of the program's success.
☐ Obtain information on the nature, cost, and success of similar programs conducted elsewhere and judge the subject program's effectiveness in contrast to the identified "critical competitors."	☐ Use needs assessment data (from the context evaluation findings), effectiveness evaluation findings, and contrasts with similar programs elsewhere to make a bottom-line assessment of the program's significance.
☐ Compile effectiveness evaluation findings in a draft report (that may be incorporated in a larger report) and present it to the client and agreed-on stakeholders.	
☐ Discuss effectiveness evaluation findings in a feedback session.	
☐ Finalize the effectiveness evaluation report and present it to the client and agreed-on stakeholders.	
☐ Incorporate the effectiveness evaluation findings in an updated program profile and ultimately in the final evaluation report.	

*A goal-free evaluator is a contracted evaluator who, by agreement, is prevented from learning a program's goals and is charged to assess what the program is actually doing and achieving, irrespective of its aims. This technique is powerful for identifying side effects or unintended outcomes, both positive and negative, and for describing what the program is actually doing, irrespective of its stated procedures.

Source: Adapted from The Evaluation Center, Evaluation Checklists Website: www.wmich.edu/evalctr/checklists/cippchecklist_mar07 .pdf. Retrieved November 7, 2008.

In the second phase, key issues and concerns are identified through direct involvement with a variety of stakeholders. The evaluators seek to clarify the values of different stakeholders that underlie the issues and concerns expressed. For example, in examining a particular school system's governance structure, the evaluators might discover that some stakeholders value a high-quality curriculum and accountability, whereas others place greater value on equality of representation in decision making and a rational decision-making process.

In the third phase of the evaluation, the evaluators collect more information about the concerns, issues, and values identified by the stakeholders, descriptive information about the phenomena being evaluated, and standards to be used in making judgments about it.

The final phase of a responsive evaluation involves preparing reports of results and recommendations. Frequently a case study reporting format (see Chapter 14) is used to describe the concerns and issues identified by stakeholders. The evaluators, in negotiation with stakeholders, then make judgments and recommendations based on the information that has been collected.

In doing a responsive evaluation, evaluators do not specify a research design at the outset of their work. Instead, they use an **emergent design,** meaning that the design of the evaluation changes as evaluators gain insights into stakeholders' primary issues and concerns. Consistent with the analytic methods associated with grounded theory (see Chapter 14), responsive evaluators continue obtaining information from stakeholders until the information they are receiving becomes redundant with information already collected.

Dialogue among stakeholders is central to responsive evaluation. However, dialogue might or might not resolve issues and concerns about the program being evaluated. Tineke Abma (2006) claims that the actual goal of dialogue is not necessarily agreement. "Dialogue may lead to consensus, but it is also considered successful if personal and mutual understanding has increased or if the understanding of differences is enhanced" (p. 31). Abma's eight guidelines for responsive evaluators to follow in order to facilitate open dialogue among diverse stakeholders are listed in Figure 20.1.

All types of research methodology require researchers to be sensitive to the needs of their participants. The participants in program evaluation are stakeholders who are embedded in a political process, and therefore, evaluators need to use guidelines, such as those presented in Figure 20.1, to ensure that the stakeholders feel safe in providing evaluative data. They are more likely to feel safe if they see that the evaluator respects them and if they know that there will be no political reprisals for anything they say.

Responsive evaluation is grounded in qualitative methodology, but it is not alone in this respect. Stufflebeam and Shinkfield (2007) describe other evaluation models that use qualitative methodology.

Educational Research and Development

Evaluation plays a key role in educational **research and development (R & D).** R & D is a systematic process for developing, improving, and assessing educational programs and materials (referred to hereafter as *products*). A term sometimes used to describe R & D, *research-based product development,* conveys the fact that (1) the goal is to develop a product based as much as possible on research findings and that (2) the development process will be research-based. If you want to develop your own product (e.g., software or a set of curriculum guides), you might be able to accomplish this goal as a thesis or dissertation by developing the product while also doing research on it.

Dick, Carey, and Carey (2005) advocate the systems approach model of educational R & D. The 10 steps of this model are shown in Figure 20.2. Step 1 involves needs assessment, which we have described in a previous section. In this model, a needs assessment is carried out in order to identify the goals of the product to be developed.

Step 2, instructional analysis, involves identification of the specific skills, procedures, and learning tasks that are seen as desirable or necessary to reach the instructional goals.

FIGURE *20.1*   Eight Guidelines for Creating Effective Dialogues among Stakeholders in a Responsive Evaluation Study

1. *Identify and include everyone who is a stakeholder in the program being evaluated.*   Treat stakeholders as partners and collaborators in the evaluation. Pay particular attention to individuals who might feel silenced by other stakeholders.

2. *Show respect to all stakeholders.*   Show respect to stakeholders, especially those who feel silenced or without power, by conducting in-depth, informal interviews with them on a one-to-one basis.

3. *Build trust.*   Build trust by interviewing stakeholders and by participating, as equals, with them in activities on the stakeholders' own "turf."

4. *Examine the stakeholders' environment to determine their need for privacy.*   Find out whether stakeholders have concerns that their comments about the program might put them in jeopardy. Respect their rights to privacy and anonymity.

5. *Form homogeneous discussion groups.*   If certain stakeholders feel vulnerable, put them in their own discussion group. Seeing others who are like themselves might help stakeholders feel comfortable about expressing their concerns about the program.

6. *Use stories to create an open dialogue.*   Ask stakeholders to share stories about experiences that convey their concerns about the program. Individuals often become more comfortable in a group if they share stories with each other.

7. *Avoid subtle mechanisms of exclusion.*   Look for signs that certain stakeholders, especially those who have a lower status, are being excluded from participating in a group dialogue. Some members of a group might try to silence other members by nonverbal expressions or critical remarks; be sure to foster expression by everyone.

8. *Interact with all stakeholder groups.*   If stakeholders form groups that have different status with respect to the program (e.g., administrators, staff, clients, community members), be impartial. A responsive evaluator should be a spokesperson for all the groups and convey each group's distinctive perspective to the other groups.

Source: Adapted from Abma, T. A. (2006). The practice and politics of responsive evaluation. *American Journal of Evaluation, 27*(1) 31–43.

Step 3 is designed to identify the level of entry behaviors (sometimes called enabling objectives) that learners bring to the learning task. It also involves identification of other characteristics of the learners that might affect learning (e.g., specific personality traits such as test anxiety) and the settings in which the instruction will occur and in which the learned skills will ultimately be used.

During Step 4, the developers write **performance objectives,** which are descriptions of the behaviors that the learners will be able to demonstrate after instruction. Then assessment instruments to test achievement of the objectives are developed (Step 5); the appropriate instructional strategy is formulated (Step 6); and instructional materials are developed or possibly selected from available materials (Step 7).

Steps 8, 9, and 10 of the R & D systems model involve the distinction between formative and summative evaluation, which was formulated by Scriven (1967). Scriven found

FIGURE *20.2*   Steps of Systems Approach Model of Educational Research and Development

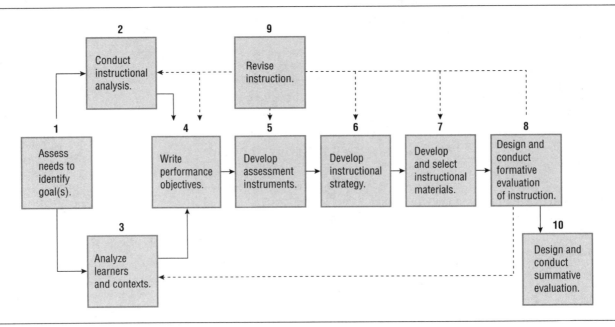

Source: Adapted from figure on pp. xxii–1 in Dick, W., Carey, L., & Carey, J. O. (2005). *The systematic design of instruction* (6th ed.). Boston: Allyn & Bacon. Published by Allyn and Bacon, Boston, MA. Copyright © 2005 by Pearson Education. Adapted with permission from the publisher.

that, in practice, evaluation serves two different functions, which he called *formative evaluation* and *summative evaluation.*

Step 8, **formative evaluation,** involves collecting data about an educational product while it is under development. This is done to help the developers and evaluators decide whether the product needs revision before release and, if so, what revisions are necessary. Formative evaluation is also used to determine whether the prospects for an eventually effective product are low, and if so, to reach a decision that further product development should be terminated and the product should not be released.

As shown in Figure 20.2, formative evaluation can occur at all the earlier stages of the development process. For example, the developers might carry out a formative evaluation of the product's objectives during Step 4, examining such issues as the clarity and comprehensiveness of the objectives. Based on the results, they might eliminate some objectives, rewrite others, or add new objectives. Once they have developed instructional materials (Step 7), they might do more formative evaluation and further revise the performance objectives, perhaps so that the objectives better match the content of the instructional materials.

A more thorough formative evaluation is also conducted when a prototype of the product (that is, a relatively complete set of the necessary elements) is available. This formative evaluation involves a field test of the product. Compared to implementation of the completed product, a field test is a trial of the product (1) with a smaller number of research participants, (2) more hands-on involvement of the developers, and (3) a more controlled environment than the real-life conditions in which the final product is meant to be used.

At some point in your career, you might find yourself involved in a formative evaluation of a program or product. Your knowledge about evaluation research will help you to be a good participant in the formative evaluation process. Your expert feedback can serve as one basis for improving the program or product, so that it is effective for many other educators later on.

Step 10, summative evaluation, is conducted once the development process (i.e., Steps 1 through 9) has been completed. The purpose of **summative evaluation** is to determine whether the completed product achieves its objectives under real-life conditions. Summative evaluation also might involve comparing the effectiveness of the completed product with that of competing products.

Summative evaluation usually is carried out by someone other than the developers, but it also can be done by members of the development team if appropriate controls are used to minimize researcher bias. If a summative evaluation demonstrates that the product is effective, we can characterize it as being evidence-based. In Chapter 1, we explained that evidence-based practice is becoming increasingly important in education and other professional fields.

Most evaluation studies of programs that appear in the education literature are summative evaluations. As an educator examining the evaluation research literature, you probably will be most interested in summative evaluations of instructional programs, methods, and materials that have been tested under conditions similar to your work environment. These evaluations will help you determine whether these products will be effective under conditions similar to your own situation.

How to Read an Evaluation Research Report

Many evaluation studies are done under contract for a school system, governmental agency, or other organization. These reports serve local purposes and might contain sensitive information. Therefore, they are rarely available in the published literature.

Some of the intended readers of these reports might have little knowledge of research methods and terms. Therefore, the evaluation reports are likely to be nontechnical. The emphasis is on the implications of the findings rather than on the methods used to generate them.

Other evaluation studies are conducted to assess programs that are widely used or that show promise of solving an important problem of practice. These studies generally are conducted with the intent that they will eventually be reported in wide-circulation educational journals. These are the kinds of reports that we consider here.

We start by noting that most evaluation studies use quantitative, qualitative, or mixed methods. If an evaluation study uses quantitative methods, the report will be organized like the reports of quantitative methods described in Part III. Many of these reports are experiments that are designed to test the effectiveness of a program. An example is the experiment by Gerald Knezek and Rhonda Christensen (2008) whose purpose was to evaluate technology-intensive programs at the primary grade level. The abstract for the article, downloaded from ERIC, is shown in Figure 20.3. As you read the abstract, you will see that the study uses quantitative methodology. Specifically, it is an experiment (see Chapter 13).

If a program evaluation uses qualitative methods, on the other hand, it most likely will be a case study. Therefore, the report probably will be organized like the reports

FIGURE 20.3   Abstract of Evaluation Study Using Quantitative Methods

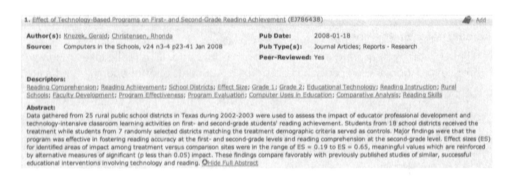

1. Effect of Technology-Based Programs on First- and Second-Grade Reading Achievement (EJ786438)   Add

Author(s): Knezek, Gerald; Christensen, Rhonda   Pub Date: 2008-01-18
Source: Computers in the Schools, v24 n3-4 p23-41 Jan 2008   Pub Type(s):   Journal Articles; Reports - Research
                                                                  Peer-Reviewed: Yes

Descriptors:
Reading Comprehension; Reading Achievement; School Districts; Effect Size; Grade 1; Grade 2; Educational Technology; Reading Instruction; Rural Schools; Faculty Development; Program Effectiveness; Program Evaluation; Computer Uses in Education; Comparative Analysis; Reading Skills

Abstract:
Data gathered from 25 rural public school districts in Texas during 2002-2003 were used to assess the impact of educator professional development and technology-intensive classroom learning activities on first- and second-grade students' reading achievement. Students from 18 school districts received the treatment while students from 7 randomly selected districts matching the treatment demographic criteria served as controls. Major findings were that the program was effective in fostering reading accuracy at the first- and second-grade levels and reading comprehension at the second-grade level. Effect sizes (ES) for identified areas of impact among treatment versus comparison sites were in the range of ES = 0.19 to ES = 0.65, meaningful values which are reinforced by alternative measures of significant (p less than 0.05) impact. These findings compare favorably with previously published studies of similar, successful educational interventions involving technology and reading. ○Hide Full Abstract

described in Chapter 14. An example is an evaluation study by Patrick McQuillan and Yves Salomon-Fernandez (2008) whose purpose was to determine how the staff of underperforming schools responded to state-led interventions to improve the students' academic achievement. The schools were underperforming as defined by the No Child Left Behind Act (NCLB), which mandates that schools make adequate yearly progress toward proficiency for all students in English/language arts and mathematics by 2014.

The researchers collected qualitative data from staff at two underperforming middle schools and one underperforming high school. They interviewed 16 teachers and administrators at these schools, made observations at each school on two occasions, and analyzed various documents. The teachers and administrators constituted the stakeholders for this study

McQuillan and Salomon-Fernandez (2008) used the method of constant comparison based on grounded theory (see Chapter 14) to identify themes and patterns in the data. Their report lists 11 themes, each of which reflects the stakeholders' perspective on state-level interventions. Each theme is illustrated by interview comments made by the teachers and administrators. Figure 20.4 presents two of the themes, one positive and one negative, to illustrate the results of this evaluation study.

FIGURE **20.4**   Themes and Quotes from a Report of a Qualitative Evaluation of a State-Level Intervention on Underperforming Schools

---

Theme 1: Benefits of State Intervention

Administrator Statement

"I can't tell you how much support, cooperation I've gotten from teachers. . . . Most people here spend a great deal of time after school, they go the extra mile. . . . This has forced [teachers] to examine what they do. . . . I thank [Massachusetts Comprehensive System] for bringing my staff together and making them even more unified. . . . This has been my most rewarding experience in education." (p. 17)

Teacher Statement

"It has had a positive impact in terms of the lower end of the teaching staff who didn't necessarily give a lot of thought and consideration to what they were doing. They've had to raise the bar. [In fact,] we've all stepped up to the [challenge]. . . . [W]e've been forced to look at ourselves and reflect more. And that's been the positive part." (p. 18)

Theme 2: Negative Impacts of Interventions on Schools

Teacher Statement

"We have not been able to operate as a real school because all our attention has been focused on doing what the DOE [Department of Education] wants. . . . It's not like we're doing things because it's best for our kids. . . . [I]t's always around the parameters set by the DOE. You do something and you have to think, 'Is this going to fit within the guidelines of DOE? Will it meet DOE expectations?' " (pp. 20–21)

Administrator Statement

"I'm constantly preparing information for the state and . . . it really takes me away from instruction and working in classrooms. . . . It takes a lot of energy. . . . It's a good thing to have oversight, but there are limits. . . . It's the most frustrating part of my job." (p. 21)

Source: McQuillan, P. J., & Salomon-Fernandez, Y. (2008). The impact of state intervention on "underperforming" schools in Massachusetts: Implications for policy and practice. *Education Policy Analysis Archives, 16*(18), 1–40.

These findings can help other stakeholders (e.g., federal and state officials, educators' professional organizations) understand the impact of external mandates on those who must implement them. Better solutions to problems of educational practice are more likely if all stakeholders can have their concerns and aspirations heard and respected.

Evaluating an Evaluation Research Study

You can judge the quality of most evaluation research reports by answering the questions listed in Appendix 2 (for a quantitative study), Appendix 3 (for a qualitative study), and Appendix 4 (for specific research designs).

In addition, you can refer to the authoritative standards for program evaluation developed by the **Joint Committee on Standards for Educational Evaluation** (1994). The committee consisted of representatives from 12 major educational organizations, including the American Association of School Administrators, the American Federation of Teachers, and the American Educational Research Association.

The standards are shown in Figure 20.5. You will see that there are 30 standards, which are grouped under four criteria: utility, feasibility, propriety, and accuracy. You can use these standards to judge the adequacy of evaluation research studies that you read or to design your own evaluation research.

The Joint Committee excluded the evaluation of educators from their consideration of program evaluation, because they previously had developed a separate set of personnel evaluation standards (Joint Committee, 1988). They also developed a separate set of standards for assessing evaluation practices in elementary and secondary classrooms (Joint Committee, 2002).

An *example of*
HOW PROGRAM EVALUATIONS CAN HELP IN SOLVING PROBLEMS OF PRACTICE

A major problem in education is that some students do not adjust well to the curriculum and regulations of mainstream schools. For this reason, educators have developed alternative models of schooling, such as described in the following brief news item.

> Four L.A. teens say they were on the verge of becoming dropouts, but the individualized attention they got from the staff at Hollywood's Alternative Education and Work Center helped them set a new direction, and now all four plan to attend college.
>
> *ASCD SmartBrief*, July 18, 2008, summarizing an article in the *Los Angeles Times*, July 17, 2008.

School and government officials might wonder whether this alternative model is worth expanding regionally or perhaps nationally, so that other potential dropouts might benefit. However, the second-hand testimonials in the news item are slim evidence of the program's effectiveness. Evaluation research can provide better evidence, as we explain below.

Experts in program evaluation can present various evaluation models to educators, administrators, and other stakeholders. Objectives-based evaluation, needs assessment, CIPP, and responsive evaluation are some of the available options.

FIGURE 20.5   Criteria and Related Standards for Effective Evaluation

Utility: The extent to which the evaluation is informative, timely, and useful to the affected persons.

1. *Stakeholder identification.* All the groups affected by the evaluation should be identified.
2. *Evaluator credibility.* The evaluator should be competent and trustworthy.
3. *Information scope and selection.* The information to be collected should pertain directly to the evaluation questions and stakeholder concerns.
4. *Values identification.* The evaluators' basis for making value judgments from the obtained results should be made clear.
5. *Report clarity.* The evaluators' report should be comprehensive and easily understood.
6. *Report timelines and dissemination.* Evaluation reports, including interim reports, should be disseminated to users in a timely manner.
7. *Evaluation impact.* The evaluation should be conducted so as to encourage appropriate action by the stakeholders.

Feasibility: The extent to which the evaluation design is (1) appropriate to the setting in which the study is to be conducted and (2) cost-effective.

1. *Practical procedures.* The evaluation procedures should be practical and minimally disruptive to participants.
2. *Political viability.* The evaluators should obtain the cooperation of affected interest groups and keep any of them from subverting the evaluation process.
3. *Cost effectiveness.* The benefits produced by the evaluation should justify the resources expended on it.

Propriety: The extent to which the evaluation is conducted legally and ethically.

1. *Service orientation.* The evaluation should help stakeholders meet the needs of all their clients and the larger society as well.
2. *Formal agreements.* The formal parties to the evaluation should state their obligations and agreements in a written contract.
3. *Rights of human subjects.* The rights and welfare of persons involved in the evaluation should be protected.
4. *Human interactions.* Evaluators should show respect in their interactions with persons involved in the study.

5. *Complete and fair assessment.* The strengths and weaknesses of the entity being evaluated should be explored completely and fairly.
6. *Disclosure of findings.* Individuals with a legal right to know and those affected by the results should be informed about the evaluation results.
7. *Conflict of interest.* If a conflict of interest should arise, it should be treated openly and honestly.
8. *Fiscal responsibility.* Expenditure of resources for the evaluation should be prudent and ethically responsible.

Accuracy: The extent to which the evaluation produces valid, reliable, and comprehensive information for making judgments of the evaluated program's worth.

1. *Program documentation.* All pertinent aspects of the program being evaluated should be described in detail.
2. *Context analysis.* Aspects of the program's context that affect the evaluation should be described in detail.
3. *Described purposes and procedures.* The evaluation's purposes and procedures should be described in detail.
4. *Defensible information sources.* Sources of data should be described in sufficient detail that their adequacy can be judged.
5. *Valid information.* The data-collection procedures should yield valid interpretations.
6. *Reliable information.* The data-collection procedures should yield reliable findings.
7. *Systematic information.* The evaluation data should be reviewed and corrected, if necessary.
8. *Analysis of quantitative information.* Analysis of quantitative data in an evaluation study should be thorough and should yield clear interpretations.
9. *Analysis of qualitative information.* Analysis of qualitative data in an evaluation study should be thorough and should yield clear interpretations.
10. *Justified conclusions.* Evaluators should provide an explicit justification for their conclusions.
11. *Impartial reporting.* Evaluation reports should be free of bias and of the personal feelings of any of those connected to the evaluation.
12. *Meta-evaluation.* The evaluation should be subjected to formative and summative evaluation using this list of standards.

Source: Adapted from Joint Committee on Standards for Educational Evaluation (J. R. Sanders, Chair). (1994). *The program evaluation standards* (2nd ed.). Thousand Oaks, CA: Sage.

It is likely that these stakeholders have a variety of questions, all driven in part by concerns about the costs and benefits of funding this particular model of schooling for potential drop-outs. Is the Alternative Education and Work Center a good environment for these students? Are students acquiring worthwhile knowledge, skills, and values? Is the school being managed effectively? Are the school's curriculum, schedules, and other organizational features sufficiently documented that they can be incorporated into other new or existing schools?

If the stakeholders want all these questions answered, the CIPP model of program evaluation might be a good option. The stakeholders can go to the CIPP website and review the checklist items listed there. They can choose those parts of the model (impact, effectiveness, sustainability, transportability) that are most appropriate to their concerns.

The evidence provided by this type of program evaluation can be helpful to the stakeholders in deciding what to do next. For example, they might find that the Alternative Education and Work Center is helping some potential dropouts, but not others. This finding possibly could lead them to provide funding for the school's administrators to expand curriculum and resources to reach students whose needs are not currently being met.

Self-Check Test

1. Program culture refers to the
   a. explicit and tacit views of those involved in a program evaluation study.
   b. the roles and relations between program developers and educators.
   c. the rituals, rules, and roles that come into play as individuals become involved with a program.
   d. a model of evaluation research that focuses on the study of the culture into which a program needs to fit.

2. A stakeholder is
   a. the individual who initiates the request for an evaluation.
   b. anyone who will be affected by the evaluation findings.
   c. an evaluator who assesses a program by analyzing costs relative to benefits.
   d. an evaluator who uses personal interpretation to evaluate a phenomenon.

3. The work of the National Assessment of Educational Progress and the What Works Clearinghouse is based primarily on
   a. needs assessment.
   b. the CIPP model.
   c. objectives-based evaluation.
   d. All of the above.

4. Needs assessment typically involves
   a. measurement of the discrepancy between an existing condition and a desired condition.
   b. interviews of stakeholders to identify what they require for a program to function efficiently.
   c. estimation of the costs and benefits of a proposed intervention.
   d. the determination of which program, in a set of possible programs, should have priority for funding.

5. The CIPP model of evaluation focuses on
   a. stakeholder needs and problems.
   b. a program's work plans and budgets.
   c. a program's impact and transportability.
   d. All of the above.

6. A central feature of responsive evaluation is its
   a. focus on identifying the issues and concerns of stakeholders.
   b. specification of the evaluation design prior to data collection.
   c. concern with the goals and objectives of the program being evaluated.
   d. specification of procedures for reconciling the different perspectives of various stakeholders.

7. The primary purpose of formative evaluation in educational R & D is to
   a. demonstrate the effectiveness of a program under operational conditions.
   b. evaluate the program once the development process has been completed.
   c. obtain information to guide revision and further development of the program.
   d. satisfy the oversight mandates of the agency funding the program's development.

8. Unlike formative evaluation, summative evaluation of a program generally
   a. occurs throughout the R & D process.
   b. is conducted to determine whether development of the product should be discontinued.
   c. is conducted to determine why stakeholder groups have different views of the program's effectiveness.
   d. is conducted to determine the effectiveness of the completed program.

9. Reports of program evaluation studies
   a. are rarely published, because the evaluation process reveals sensitive political matters that stakeholders wish to keep private.
   b. are only published in professional journals if the study involves the objectives-based model of evaluation.
   c. generally are organized more like reports of historical studies than like reports of case studies.
   d. generally are organized like reports of quantitative research studies and case studies.

10. The program evaluation standards of the Joint Committee on Standards for Educational Evaluation
    a. are suitable for the evaluation of teachers and school administrators.
    b. are suitable for use by teachers in constructing their own tests.
    c. were developed by a committee representing major educational organizations in the United States.
    d. does not specify ethical standards for conducting program evaluation, because standards of this type differ greatly across school districts and other agencies.

Chapter References

Abma, T. (2006). The practice and politics of responsive evaluation. *American Journal of Evaluation, 27*(1), 31–43.

Bollag, B. (2007). Federal programs to improve science education are not well reviewed, panel finds. *Chronicle of Higher Education, 53*(37), A19.

Dick, W., Carey, L., & Carey, J. O. (2005). *The systematic design of instruction* (6th ed.). Boston: Allyn & Bacon.

Joint Committee on Standards for Educational Evaluation. (1988). *The personnel evaluation standards: How to assess systems for evaluating educators.* Thousand Oaks, CA: Corwin.

Joint Committee on Standards for Educational Evaluation. (1994). *The program evaluation standards: How to assess evaluations of educational programs* (2nd ed.). Thousand Oaks, CA: Sage.

Joint Committee on Standards for Educational Evaluation. (2002). *The student evaluation standards: How to improve evaluations of students.* Thousand Oaks, CA: Corwin.

Knezek, G., & Christensen, R. (2008). Effect of technology-based programs on first- and second-grade reading achievement. *Computers in the Schools, 24*(3–4), 23–41.

Kushner, S., & Adelman, C. (2006). Program evaluation: A democratic process. In J. L. Green, G. Camilli, & P. B. Elmore (Eds.), *Handbook of complementary methods in education research* (pp. 711–726). Mahwah, NJ: Lawrence Erlbaum.

McKillip, J. (1987). *Need analysis: Tools for the human services and education.* Thousand Oaks, CA: Sage.

McQuillan, P. J., & Salomon-Fernandez, Y. (2008). The impact of state intervention on "underperforming" schools in Massachusetts: Implications for policy and practice. *Education Policy Analysis Archives, 16*(18), 1–40.

Mihans, R. (2008). Can teachers lead teachers? *Phi Delta Kappan, 89*(10), 762–765.

National Center for Education Statistics. (2006). *2003–04 Schools and staffing survey.* Retrieved from http://nces.ed.gov/pubsearch/pubsinfo.asp?pubid=2006313

Scriven, M. (1967). The methodology of evaluation. In R. E. Stake (Ed.), *Curriculum evaluation: American Educational Research Association Series on Evaluation, No. 1* (pp. 39–83). Chicago: Rand McNally.

Stake, R. E. (2004). *Standards-based and responsive evaluation.* Thousand Oaks, CA: Sage.

Stufflebeam, D. L. (2003). *The CIPP model for evaluation.* In T. Kellaghan and D. L. Stufflebeam (Eds.), *The international handbook of educational evaluation* (Chapter 3). Boston: Kluwer Academic Publishers.

Stufflebeam, D. L. (2007). *CIPP evaluation model checklist* (2nd ed.). Retrieved from www.wmich.edu/evalctr/checklists/cippchecklist_mar07.pdf

Stufflebeam, D. L., & Shinkfield, A. J. (2007). *Evaluation theory, models, and applications.* San Francisco: Jossey-Bass.

Tyler, R. W. (1949). *Basic principles of curriculum and instruction: Syllabus for Education 360.* Chicago: University of Chicago Press.

Resources for Further Study

Altschuld, J. W., & Witkin, B. R. (1999). *From needs assessment to action: Transforming needs into solution strategies.* Thousand Oaks, CA: Sage.

> The authors explain how to conduct a needs assessment and use the results to create an action plan for organizational change.

Evaluation Center at Western Michigan University. (n.d.). Evaluation checklists. Retrieved from www.wmich.edu/evalctr/checklists

> This website provides checklists that evaluators can use to design and conduct evaluation projects of various sorts. Each checklist is accompanied by a supporting rationale grounded in the evaluation literature and lessons learned from practice.

Patton, M. Q. (2002). *Qualitative research and evaluation methods* (3rd ed.). Thousand Oaks, CA: Sage.

> The author explains how to conduct an evaluation study using qualitative research methods. Among the topics covered are ethical issues in evaluation, focus groups, computer-assisted analysis of data, and criteria for judging the quality of qualitative evaluation studies.

Sanders, J. R., & Sullins, C. D. (2006). *Evaluating school programs: An educator's guide* (3rd ed.). Thousand Oaks, CA: Corwin.

> This book is for educators who need to conduct mandated evaluations of school programs. The authors present a five-step model for evaluation that is efficient, responsive to No Child Left Behind guidelines, and oriented to school improvement.

Worthen, B. R., Sanders, J. R., & Fitzpatrick, J. L. (2004). *Program evaluation: Alternative approaches and practical guidelines* (3rd ed.). Boston: Allyn & Bacon.

> The authors explain the purposes of program evaluation and provide detailed treatment of seven different approaches to program evaluation. The book gives practical guidelines for planning, conducting, and using evaluations.

Sample Evaluation Research Study

Divergence in Learning Goal Priorities between College Students and Their Faculty: Implications for Teaching and Learning

Myers, C. B. (2008). Divergence in learning goal priorities between college students and their faculty: Implications for teaching and learning. *College Teaching, 56*(1), 53–58.

The following article reports an evaluation study to assess the priorities that college faculty and students place on eight learning goals. The study also examines whether faculty and students have different priorities. In this respect, the study can be viewed as a needs assessment. If faculty priorities are considered the desired condition, we can examine the student priorities to determine whether they are aligned with the faculty priorities. If discrepancies are found, stakeholders can consider how students might develop in the direction of the faculty's priorities or whether faculty and students jointly need to reconsider their priorities.

The researchers' data analysis involved the use of simple descriptive statistics and a measure of effect size. The effect size statistic is explained in Chapter 8.

Divergence in Learning Goal Priorities between College Students and Their Faculty: Implications for Teaching and Learning

Carrie B. Myers

ABSTRACT ■ Using a sample of 751 undergraduate students and 85 of their faculty, the author examined the extent of faculty-student differences in their priorities placed on eight learning goals. The findings show that students placed significantly more importance on career preparation, scientific reasoning, personal development, and art and cultural appreciation and that faculty placed significantly more importance on critical thinking and mastery of discipline content. Students and their faculty did not differ significantly on the priorities they placed on basic academic skills, citizenship, and values. The implications of these findings are discussed in terms of curriculum development and an increasing belief that student development and learning are improved when curricula assess and incorporate students' goals and priorities.

KEYWORDS ■ faculty, goals, learning, students, teaching

There is an interesting paradox in higher education: curriculum reform and design are supposed to be in the best interest of student development and learning, but these students have little input into curriculum and teaching decisions. Although many educators advocate a student-centered environment (Barr and Tagg 1995; Stiggins 2001), the extent to which this occurs in the college classroom is limited. Three learning and educational theories—metacognition (personal), cognition, and multicultural (social)—contend that student development and learning are improved when curricula assess and incorporate students' goals and priorities (Baxter Magolda 1992; Dillard and Blue 2000). Perhaps curriculum design is devoid of student input because research on college students' values concerning education and learning priorities in their courses is limited. In this article, I (1) present theory and research that support the need to incorporate students and their values into curriculum reform and (2) use assessment data to measure student and faculty priorities across eight learning goals and test the extent to which students and faculty prioritize similar goals.

RATIONALE

Three educational theories strongly suggest that curriculum reform should incorporate student perceptions, goals, and expectations to facilitate student development and, therefore, learning. First, metacognitive theory emphasizes that both student and faculty should be aware of the student's self-perception of his of her learning to best assist the student in that learning (Butler and Winne 1995). Education is a combination of the needs and processes of individual students and the faculty's ability to understand these processes. By assessing student perceptions, faculty provide feedback to students to help them create their own understanding and meaning of course content. Two studies support the metacognitive model. King and Baxter Magolda (1999; Baxter Magolda 1999) followed about eighty students through college and into young adulthood. In qualitative interviews, these students reported that their development of self—goals, values, convictions, and construction of knowledge—occurred in courses where they were empowered and given a voice. Further, the students reported that most faculty were too rigid, did not promote the development of individual belief systems and goals, and were entirely responsible for course content and structure without asking for the input of students.

Second, the cognitive model posits that the assessment of students' prior knowledge and experiences is important to their development because faculty can link the presentation of new information and knowledge in class to the students' existing knowledge. Filip, Moerkerke, and Martens (1996) conducted a metaanalysis of 129 studies on the effect of poor knowledge on achievement. They found 118 studies that reported significant effects of prior knowledge on achievement where prior knowledge predicted about 50 percent of the variance in achievement. Prior knowledge includes all subjective information and experiences that each student takes with him or her into each course. As an extension, curriculum that is informed by and linked to the students' prior goals and perceptions may enhance the development and learning processes of each student.

Third, multicultural theory promotes the move to a student-centered curriculum and an emphasis on student development by incorporating the students' cultural diversity. Each student hails from a diverse cultural, social, and ideological background, and the design and content of curriculum should be a reflection of these diverse backgrounds. Dillard and Blue argue, "We must acknowledge that in our classrooms there will be a myriad of perspectives held by our students, some of which may be contradictory to the ones we hold. Our task is one of structuring the curriculum to help our students and ourselves 'center' our personal histories and experiences" (2000, 197). Further, Inglebret and Pavel (2000) contend that culturally diverse students have unique learning styles. To connect with students, a teacher must acknowledge the unique perspectives and values they bring to the classroom.

These three theories on development and learning do not discount the importance of faculty input in curriculum decisions. The theories emphasize, however, that teaching and learning should be more symmetrical and iterative by assessing and then incorporating students' experiences, goals, and values. Current research, however, finds that the shaping of curriculum is mostly by the personal experiences and goals of individual faculty and is devoid of students' input or research on students (Kennedy 1994). Data from six surveys (between 1968 and 1992) of more than 50,000 college faculty showed little change in faculty goals over the twenty-four-year period (Tice and Dey 1997). The need to understand the students' goals has hastened when one considers the significant changes in the demographic profiles of college students between 1968 and 1992 (e.g., increases in the number of women, racial minorities and immigrants, nontraditional students, return students, and part-time students [Keller 2001]).

PRIOR RESEARCH

A successful student-centered curriculum requires a basic understanding of student values and the extent to which faculty and students share similar goals and perceptions. A limited line of research finds that significant disparities exist between college students and faculty. Peterson and Chinen (2000) studied 378 graduate students in business school and 321 business school professors and found that the professors' perceptions of the rank-ordered goals of students were significantly dissimilar to the students' own rankings in eleven of eighteen categories. Almost all of the professors, however, reported that knowing their students' goals is important to their approach to teaching, but few used explicit means to uncover their students' goals. In a study of 224 faculty and undergraduate students, MacLellan (2001) found wide disparities between students and faculty regarding perceptions about the purpose and procedures of assessment. For example, 69 percent of faculty but only 5 percent of students reported that assessment was frequently used to motivate learning. The biggest disparity between faculty and students occurred in perceptions about what classroom activities composed the bulk of assessment. Of the nine modes (e.g., multiple choice, participation in labs), student and faculty perceptions were similar only on one. This last finding is important as it relates to the concept of met expectations in college classrooms. *Met expectations* refers to the degree to which students' expectations of pedagogy and assessment align with the behaviors and practices of faculty (Kolb, Osland, and Rubin 1995). Research finds that student attrition is associated with unmet expectations (Darkenwald and Gavin 1987).

Given this limited line of research, it is not clear what factors contribute to disparities in learning goals between faculty and students. Research on the general goal orientations of college students, however, may shed light on some important factors. Research finds that learning values differ by a student's sex, major, and class standing (Colbeck, Cabrera, and Terenzini 2001; Paulsen and Wells 1998). For faculty-student similarity in goals, major field and class standing may be very important because faculty-student contact is greater for juniors and seniors and for students majoring in the social sciences and humanities (Kuh and Hu 2001). Research also shows that student perceptions are different in lower- and upper-level courses (Colbeck et al. 2001), perhaps a reflection of the value difference by class standing. Finally, there is some evidence that faculty-student disparities may be greater for nonmajors than majors, partly because of discipline-specific knowledge and norms (Wilson 2001).

METHOD

Sample

The data for this analysis come from a teaching, learning, and technology center at a large northwestern public university. The center functions mainly as a support system for faculty who wish to incorporate technology into their classroom. The center also assists faculty with more general pedagogy issues and operates an assessment division that evaluates the impact, satisfaction, and effectiveness of technology that is incorporated into classrooms. The center creates and supports various educational tools that are located online and allow students to interact asynchronously with the faculty and each other. Faculty generally use the educational tools to complement their face-to-face lectures.

Faculty who use the educational tools were asked to participate in the formative assessment process. The formative assessment process involved three surveys—two geared toward students and one aimed at faculty. Generally, the content of the questions was identical for students and faculty. A Web site address of the faculty survey was sent to all faculty using the technologies. Once the instructor completed and submitted the survey, a link for the student surveys was attached to their online space.

This article uses data from 751 undergraduate students and 85 of their faculty who completed these formative survey questionnaires in either the fall of 2000 or the spring 2001. The response rate for faculty was nearly ninety percent, but only forty percent for the students. Ancillary analyses show (results available on request) that there are no consistent patterns of nonresponse among the students. Students who responded are not from selective colleges, disciplines, or departments or differentially linked to faculty respondents. A random sample was not feasible because of the nature of the investigation. The data are from a convenience sample. Admittedly, the nonrandom sample limits the ability to generalize to the larger population of college students. Therefore, the results presented here will be most useful when compared in context to other existing studies.

Learning Goals

Data from a parallel question on the faculty and student surveys were used to assess the similarity in general edu-

cational and learning goals between students and their faculty. The specific wording of the question in the student survey was "How important is it to you to achieve the following from this course?"; the faculty survey said "Indicate the priority you place on each of the following learning outcomes in this course." Faculty and students could respond with 4 = very important, 3 = somewhat important, 2 = not very important, or 1 = not important at all. The eight learning outcomes listed in both surveys were (1) critical thinking skills, (2) basic academic skills, (3) career preparation, (4) scientific reasoning, (5) personal development, (6) mastery of discipline content, (7) citizenship and values, and (8) art and cultural appreciation. These goals are a slight modification of the Teaching Goal Inventory developed by Angelo and Cross (1993). The survey's purpose was not to address discipline- or course-specific topics but rather to assess general educational and learning goals and priorities.

Additional Variables

The surveys also contain data on the general characteristics of the students and on a limited number of characteristics of their instructor and the course in which the students were enrolled. Most of these variables receive empirical support that show they affect the educational and learning goals of students and faculty. Student characteristics include their sex and age, whether they took the course as an elective, requirement, or other (e.g., personal or professional enrichment), and their major. The only faculty characteristic is their sex. Course characteristics include whether the course comprised predominately majors, nonmajors, or both, and the level of the course (i.e., lower undergraduate, upper undergraduate). These variables are used to adjust the student and faculty learning goal means that are analyzed below.

RESULTS

Table 1 presents the means and standard deviations and the results from the weighted paired t-tests of differences in means between faculty and student on the value they place on each learning goal. Briefly, by estimating a paired t-test (versus a standard t-test) each of the faculty's scores was matched (i.e., paired) with the scores from the specific students in his or her course. Then, a weight adjusts for the different number of students in each class that contributes to the overall statistics. Finally, all means are controlled for the aforementioned student, faculty, and course characteristics.

Looking at the mean scores for faculty and students shows that each group places high priorities on a slightly different set of learning goals. For faculty, the highest priorities are placed on critical thinking, basic academic skills, and mastery of discipline content. Students also value basic academic skills, but similarly value personal development and career preparation. These last two goals prioritized by students reveal a substantive divergence between faculty and students. Specifically, the goals prioritized by faculty

TABLE 1   Learning Outcome Priorities of Students and Their Faculty: Means, Standard Deviations, and Statistical Tests of Differences

Learning Outcome	Faculty		Students		Difference in Priorities	Cohen's | d |
	Mean	Standard Deviation	Mean	Standard Deviation		
Priority placed on:						
Critical thinking	3.87	0.49	3.12	0.66	0.75***	1.29
Basic academic skills	3.51	0.78	3.42	0.66	0.09	0.12
Career preparation	2.75	0.89	3.33	0.94	−0.58***	0.63
Scientific reasoning	2.43	1.00	2.97	0.84	−0.54***	0.5
Personal development	3.19	0.86	3.55	0.75	−0.36**	0.45
Mastery of discipline content	3.50	0.81	3.18	0.74	0.32**	0.41
Citizenship and values	3.02	0.81	2.88	0.84	0.14	0.17
Art and cultural appreciation	2.67	0.91	3.04	0.88	−0.37**	0.41

Note: The means and standard deviations presented in the table are unweighted and adjusted for student, faculty, and course characteristics. Statistical tests for the differences in priorities were estimated by a weighted paired *t*-test.

*$p < .05$ **$p < .01$ ***$p < .001$ (two-tailed)

pertain directly to learning and thinking progress, whereas two of the three goals prioritized by students pertain more to individual and affective progress. Surprisingly, both faculty and students placed a relatively low priority on scientific reasoning.

This theme of divergence continues when looking at the statistical differences in means. On the one hand, students and their faculty place statistically similar priorities on basic academic skills, citizenship, and values. On the other hand, faculty and students have statistically different priorities across six of the eight learning goals. Faculty place significantly more importance on critical thinking (mean = 3.87) than do students (mean = 3.12), and more importance on mastery of discipline content (mean = 3.50) than do students (mean = 3.18). Students, however, place significantly more importance on four learning goals than do faculty: career preparation (mean = 3.33 versus 2.75), scientific reasoning (mean = 2.97 versus 2.43), personal development (mean = 3.55 versus 3.19), and art and cultural appreciation (mean = 3.04 versus 2.67). All of these differences are significant at $p < .01$. Again, these differences have been adjusted for several relevant student, faculty, and course characteristics.

How large are these differences substantively? To determine the practical size of these differences, I calculated a Cohen's *d* for each of the significant differences. Cohen (1988) defined effect sizes as "small" for a *d* about 0.20, "medium" for a *d* about 0.50, and "large" for a *d* 0.80 or larger. Among the learning goals valued higher by faculty, the size of the difference in means between faculty and students on critical thinking is quite large (*d* = 1.29), whereas the difference in means on mastery of discipline content is close to a medium effect size (*d* = .41). Among the learn-

ing goals valued higher by students—career preparation, scientific reasoning, personal development, and art and cultural appreciation—the effect sizes of the differences in means on all are of a medium effect size. These results suggest that faculty and students differ both statistically and practically on the values they place on six of the eight learning goals under study.

DISCUSSION AND IMPLICATIONS

The findings indicate faculty and students not only have a different set of learning goals that each prioritizes but that they also disagree more than they agree on the value of eight common learning goals. The results for the effect sizes of these differences indicate that most were medium in size. Further, it is possible that the cumulative effect of these medium differences is certainly greater than any single effect, given that most or all of these learning goals are simultaneously present in any one course. For example, imagine a course where the relative goals of the instructor and students followed the patterns in this study—the instructor prioritizes critical thinking and mastery of discipline content and the students prioritize career preparation, scientific reasoning, personal development, and art and cultural appreciation. Although the effect of the different relative priorities for any one goal may be medium, the cumulative effect of instructor-student differences across all the learning goals may be quite large.

The patterns found in this research suggest that teaching and learning and, ultimately, student development may be affected by the different learning goals held by students and their faculty. Indeed, Dillard and Blue (2000) argue that curriculum development is a collaborative effort between teachers and students, and teachers' interpretation of what is important to teach can be informed by understanding and knowing their students' goals and values. According to Parkay and Hass (2000), teachers should seek the input of students about clarifying and modifying classroom learning objectives. Hass compares curriculum planning to a democratic society where students are "the major untapped resource. . . . Students are in the best position to explain many of the advantages and deficiencies of the present curriculum" (2000, 303). Although the goals of students and faculty do not have to be identical, they should overlap in a significant way such that faculty and students learn together (Barr and Tagg 1995; Parkay and Hass). So, how do faculty and students become aware of each other's goals? There are many possibilities, but three strategies are most probable: formative assessment, research on teaching and learning, and faculty-student communication.

Formative assessment is a learner-centered movement that encourages faculty to focus on the student-learning component of teaching (Angelo and Cross 1993; Huba and Freed 2000). Faculty use student feedback to understand what students do and do not understand, identify barriers to learning, and clear up any misconceptions and miscommunication. Angelo and Cross argue that faculty and students need better ways to monitor learning throughout the semester, and formative assessment is one method to encourage a continuous flow of accurate information on student learning.

With educational research the focus is on faculty development—the improvement of teaching and education through the systematic study of research on teaching and learning (Cross and Steadman 1996). According to Boyer (1990), using research to inform teaching is the scholarship of application, where faculty apply what is known about teaching and learning—including learning goals—to the teaching process. Furthermore, this process is recursive: as faculty learn more about teaching, they become better teachers, which inspires them to learn more about teaching. This feedback process has tangible benefits for students as it positively affects the development of achievement, motivation, and the self (Anderson, Green, and Loewen 1988; Ross 1992).

The third method is faculty-student communication, which is one of the seven principles of good practice in undergraduate education (Chickering and Gamson 1987). Research has shown conclusively that faculty-student communication increases faculty and student awareness of each other's goals and, in turn, enhances student development (Astin 1993). Cabrera et al. (2002) found that student-faculty collaboration is positively associated with the development of cognitive and affective outcomes (personal development, understanding science and technology, appreciation for art, and analytical skills) and openness to diversity. Faculty-student contact can take place both in and out of the classroom and such contact increases the extent to which faculty can influence student development

and increases the intrinsic value students place on learning (Terenzini et al. 1995).

Interpretation of the results and the direction of future research are guided by both the findings and limitations of this study. First, it is unclear the extent to which the low student response rate (40 percent) tempers the ability to fully generalize the findings, although this response rate is similar to or better than many large web-based surveys of college students. For example, the National Survey of Student Engagement (NSSE) is an annual survey of about 60,000 first-year and senior-year college students, where data are collected about sixty-seven college experiences (e.g., courses taken, perceptions of campus environment). The response rate for the Web-based-only mode of the 2000 NSSE was 40 percent. The 2001 Your First College Year (YFCY) survey—designed in part as a follow-up survey to the 2000 Cooperative Institutional Research Program Freshman Survey—contained an experimental survey administration to assess the effectiveness of traditional versus Web-based survey methods (Sax, Gilmartin, and Bryant 2003). The response rates for the Web-only survey were between 17.1 percent and 19.8 percent, whereas the response rate for the paper-only survey was 22 percent. What are the general biases because of low response rates? Krosnick (1999) argues that low response rates do not necessarily allow bias to contaminate the findings, especially when there are no real differences between the characteristics of respondents and nonrespondents. As reported above in the Methods section, ancillary analyses found no discernible patterns of nonresponse for this current study, thus reducing the likelihood of bias. This finding is similar to that of Sax, Gilmartin, and Bryant, where gender was the only consistent predictor of nonresponse to the Web-based YFCY survey (i.e., female students were more likely to participate than male students). Further, with respect to biases because of mode of survey, Carini et al. (2003) found that after controlling for student and institutional characteristics, there are only small distinctions in patterns of responses between students who completed the NSSE in Web-based versus paper mode. Although the low response rate of this current research should not be dismissed, most evidence suggests that the response rate did not significantly bias the findings overall. Further research, however, with a higher response rate, is certainly needed.

Second, this study was conducted at a single public research university in the northwest. Although there is not an a priori reason to suggest this university is unique, future research should be conducted at private, liberal arts, historically black, and community universities and colleges to form a critical mass of findings. Third, the faculty involved in this study voluntarily used the university's teaching and learning center's resources. This suggests that the convenience sample of faculty may have self-selected characteristics that affected the results. Results from a university-wide random sample of faculty could be compared with the findings in this study to detect any self-selection biases. Fourth, the sample of students and faculty was predominately white. It is possible that the results would be different or shed more light on faculty-student goals if the sample were more racially, demographically, and socially diversified, similar to the diversification of universities and colleges nationwide. Fifth, this study focuses on eight specific learning goals; other patterns may be found with a different set of learning goals.

Further research should replicate and expand this study with these limitations in mind. However, the current results also point to other types of future research. Most notably, research should examine what faculty, students, and administration can do to increase the awareness and similarity of faculty-student goals and priorities, how to instruct faculty to understand their students' goals, and the benefits that confer when the goals of faculty and students overlap. The focus of this research must be directed toward the behaviors of academic and student affairs, higher administration, individual departments and academic units, student and faculty groups, and lines of communication between faculty. One possibility is the creation of a community of inquiry, which comprises faculty, staff, students, and administrators that come together for the common purpose of discussing, assessing, and supporting techniques and outcomes of teaching and learning (Thomas 1997). Palincsar, Magnusson, and Marano (1998) describe a teaching community as that which relies on diverse expertise to contribute to the intellectual resources of the community. The benefits of creating a genuine academic community of interest ultimately extend to student development.

References

Anderson, R., M. Greene, and P. Loewen. 1988. Relationships among teachers' and students' thinking skills, sense of efficacy, and student achievement. *Alberta Journal of Educational Research* 34:148–65.

Angelo, T. A., and K. P. Cross. 1993. *Classroom assessment techniques: A handbook for college teachers.* San Francisco: Jossey-Bass.

Astin, A. W. 1993. *What matters in college: Four critical years revisited.* San Francisco: Jossey-Bass.

Barr, R. B., and J. Tagg. 1995. From teaching to learning: A new paradigm for undergraduate education. *Change* 27:12–25.

Baxter Magolda, M. B. 1992. Students' epistemologies and academic experiences: Implications for pedagogy. *Review of Higher Education* 153:265–87.

———. 1999. The evolution of epistemology: Refining contextual knowing at twentysomething. *Journal of College Student Development* 40:333–44.

Boyer, E. L. 1990. *Scholarship reconsidered: Priorities of the professoriate.* San Francisco: Jossey-Bass.

Butler, D. L., and P. H. Winne. 1995. Feedback and self-regulated learning: A theoretical synthesis. *Review of Educational Research* 65:245–82.

Cabrera, A. F., J. L. Crissman, E. M. Bernal, A. Nora, P. T. Terenzini, and E. T. Pascerella. 2002. Collaborative learning: Its impact on college students' development and diversity. *Journal of College Student Development* 43:20–34.

Carini, R. M., J. C. Hayek, G. D. Kuh, J. M. Kennedy, and J. A. Ouimet. 2003. College student responses to web and paper surveys: Does mode matter? *Research in Higher Education* 44:1–19.

Chickering, A. W., and Z. F. Gamson. 1987. Seven principles for good practice in undergraduate education. *American Association of Higher Education Bulletin* 40:3–7.

Cohen, J. 1988. *Statistical power analysis for the behavioral sciences.* 2nd ed. Hillsdale, NJ: Lawrence Erlbaum.

Colbeck, C. L., A. F. Cabrera, and P. T. Terenzini. 2001. Learning professional confidence: Linking teaching practices, students' self perceptions, and gender. *Review of Higher Education* 24:173–91.

Cross, K. P., and M. H. Steadman. 1996. *Classroom research: Implementing the scholarship of teaching.* San Francisco: Jossey-Bass.

Darkenwald, G. G., and W. J. Gavin. 1987. Dropout as a function of discrepancies between expectations and actual experiences of the classroom social environment. *Adult Education Quarterly* 37:152–63.

Dillard, C. B., and D. A. Blue. 2000. Learning styles from a multicultural perspective: The case for culturally engaged education. In *Curriculum planning: A contemporary approach,* ed. F. W. Parkay and G. Hass, 196–201. Boston: Allyn and Bacon.

Filip, J., G. Moerkecke, and R. Martens. 1996. Integrating assessment, learning and instruction: Assessment of domain-specific and domain-transcending prior knowledge and progress. *Studies in Educational Evaluation* 224:309–39.

Hass, G. 2000. Who should plan the curriculum? In *Curriculum planning: A contemporary approach,* ed. F. W. Parkay and G. Hass, 301–4. Boston: Allyn and Bacon.

Huba, M. E., and J. E. Freed. 2000. *Learner-centered assessment on college campuses: Shifting the focus from teaching to learning.* Boston: Allyn and Bacon.

Inglebret, E., and D. M. Pavel, 2000. Curriculum planning and development for Native Americans and Alaska natives in higher education. In *Curriculum planning: A contemporary approach,* ed. F. W. Parkay and G. Haas, 493–502. Boston: Allyn and Bacon.

Keller, G. 2001. The new demographics of higher education. *Review of Higher Education* 243:219–35.

Kennedy, M. F. 1994. Instructional design or personal heuristics in classroom instructional planning. *Educational Technology* 34:17–25.

King, P. M., and M. B. Baxter Magolda. 1999. *A developmental perspective on learning: Journal of College Student Development* 40:599–609.

Kolb, D. A., J. S. Osland, and L. M. Rubin. 1995. *Organizational behavior: An experiential approach.* Englewood Cliffs, NJ: Prentice-Hall.

Krosnick, J. A. 1999. Survey research. *Annual Review of Psychology* 50:537–67.

Kuh, G. D., and S. Hu. 2001. The effects of student-faculty interaction in the 1990s. *Review of Higher Education* 24:309–32.

MacLellan, E. 2001. Assessment for learning: The differing perceptions of tutors and students. *Assessment and Evaluation in Higher Education* 26:307–18.

Palincsar, A. S., S. J. Magnusson, and N. L. Marano. 1998. Designing a community of practice: Principles and practices of GisML community. *Teaching and Teacher Education* 141:5–19.

Parkay, F. W., and G. Hass, ed. 2000. *Curriculum planning: A contemporary approach.* Boston: Allyn and Bacon.

Paulsen, M. B., and C. T. Wells. 1998. Domain differences in the epistemological beliefs of college students. *Research in Higher Education* 39:365–54.

Peterson, R. T., and K. Chinen. 2000. Student objectives for gateway jobs: The keys to effective teaching. *Business Education Forum* 551:36–38.

Ross, J. A. 1992. Teacher efficacy and the effect of coaching on student achievement. *Canadian Journal of Education* 17:51–65.

Sax, L. J., S. K. Gilmartin, and A. N. Bryant. 2003. Assessing response rates and non-response bias in Web and paper surveys. *Research in Higher Education* 44:409–32.

Stiggins. R. J. 2001. *Student-involved classroom assessment.* Upper Saddle River, NJ: Prentice-Hall.

Terenzini, P. T., L. Springer, E. T. Pascarella, and A. Nora. 1995. Academic and out-of-class influences on students' intellectual orientations. *Review of Higher Education* 19:23–44.

Thomas, J. C. 1997. Community of inquiry and differences of the heart. *Thinking* 13:42–48.

Tice, A. G., and E. L. Dey. 1997. Trends in faculty teaching goals: A longitudinal study of change. *Journal of College Student Development* 38:527–34.

Wilson, J. A. 2001. Pseudoscientific beliefs among college students. *Reports of the National Center for Science Education* 21:9–13.

About the Author

Carrie B. Myers is an assistant professor in the department of education at Montana State University. Her research mainly focuses on institutional and instructional determinants of faculty roles and activities.

Self-Check Test Answers

Chapter 1: Using Research Evidence to Improve Educational Practice
1. b   2. d   3. a   4. d   5. c   6. b   7. b   8. a   9. d   10. c

Chapter 2: Doing Your Own Research: From Proposal to Final Report
1. b   2. d   3. a   4. c   5. a   6. b   7. d   8. c   9. a   10. b

Chapter 3: Conducting and Writing Your Own Literature Review
1. b   2. b   3. c   4. a   5. c   6. d   7. b   8. a   9. c   10. d

Chapter 4: Using Search Engines in a Literature Review
1. b   2. c   3. d   4. a   5. a   6. b   7. d   8. c   9. d   10. b

Chapter 5: Making Use of Available Literature Reviews
1. d   2. a   3. c   4. c   5. a   6. b   7. d   8. c   9. b   10. a

Chapter 6: Analyzing and Evaluating Reports of Quantitative Research Studies
1. b   2. c   3. c   4. a   5. d   6. b   7. b   8. a   9. a

Chapter 7: Using Descriptive Statistics to Study Problems of Practice
1. b   2. d   3. b   4. c   5. a   6. b   7. d   8. a   9. c   10. d

Chapter 8: The Practical Significance of Statistical Results
1. c   2. d   3. a   4. a   5. b   6. c   7. b   8. d   9. d   10. b

Chapter 9: Tests of Statistical Significance
1. c   2. b   3. c   4. a   5. b   6. d   7. a   8. b   9. b   10. d

Chapter 10: Descriptive Research
1. c   2. d   3. a   4. b   5. c   6. c   7. d

Chapter 11: Group Comparison Research
1. b   2. d   3. a   4. c   5. b   6. d   7. a   8. c   9. a   10. c

Chapter 12: Correlational Research
1. a   2. c   3. d   4. a   5. d   6. b   7. c   8. b   9. a   10. b

Chapter 13: Experimental Research
1. c   2. c   3. c   4. d   5. a   6. b   7. d   8. c   9. a   10. b

Chapter 14: Case Studies in Qualitative Research
1. c   2. b   3. d   4. c   5. b   6. c   7. d   8. a   9. a   10. c

Chapter 15: Narrative Research
1. d   2. b   3. a   4. b   5. c   6. d   7. b   8. a

Chapter 16: Ethnography and Critical Research
1. b   2. a   3. d   4. a   5. b   6. b   7. a   8. d   9. d   10. c   11. d   12. b   13. b

Chapter 17: Historical Research
1. a   2. b   3. b   4. d   5. c   6. d   7. b   8. c   9. a

Chapter 18: Mixed-Methods Research
1. b   2. d   3. a   4. c   5. c   6. d   7. b

Chapter 19: Action Research
1. b   2. c   3. c   4. a   5. b   6. d   7. c   8. a   9. c   10. a

Chapter 20: Evaluation Research
1. c   2. b   3. c   4. a   5. d   6. a   7. c   8. d   9. d   10. c

Guide for Outlining a Quantitative or Qualitative Research Proposal

This form consists of a list of items in the form of questions and directions. By completing each item, you can create an outline of a research proposal. The outline then can be elaborated into a formal research proposal. To learn more about each part of the outline, review Chapter 2.

1. Purpose of Study

    A. The purpose of this study is to _____. (State the purpose succinctly in one or two sentences)
    B. What previous research is your study most directly based on? (Select three to five publications that are absolutely central)
    C. How does your study build on previous research?
    D. How will your study contribute to educational research and practice?

2. Research Questions, Hypotheses, Variables, and Case Delineation

    A. List your research questions or hypotheses.
    B. If you propose to test hypotheses, describe briefly the theory from which the hypotheses were derived.
    C. If your study is quantitative in nature, list the variables that you will study. For each variable, indicate whether it is an independent variable, a dependent variable, or neither.
    D. If the study is qualitative in nature, describe the case features on which data collection and analysis will focus.

3. Literature Search

    A. List the search engines and indexes that you will use to identify relevant publications.
    B. List the keywords and descriptors that you will use with search engines and indexes.
    C. Identify published literature reviews (if available) relating to your study.

4. Research Design

    A. Describe the research design that you selected for your study: descriptive, causal-comparative, correlational, experimental, case study, specific qualitative research tradition, evaluative research, or action research.
    B. If your study is quantitative in nature, what are the threats to the internal validity of your research design? (Internal validity means the extent to which extraneous variables are controlled, so that observed effects can be attributed solely to the independent variable.) What will you do to minimize or avoid these threats?
    C. If your study is quantitative in nature, what are the limitations to the generalizability (i.e., external validity) of the findings that will result from your research design? What will you do to maximize the generalizability of your findings?
    D. If your study is qualitative in nature, what criteria do you consider to be relevant to judging the credibility and trustworthiness of the results that will be yielded by your research design?

5. Sampling

A. If your study is quantitative in nature, describe the characteristics of the population that you will study.

B. If your study is qualitative in nature, describe the phenomenon you wish to study and the cases that comprise instances of the phenomenon.

C. Identify your sampling procedure and sampling unit.

D. Indicate the size of your sample, and explain why that sample size is sufficient.

E. Indicate whether the sample will be formed into subgroups, and if so, describe the characteristics of the subgroups.

F. If your study will involve the use of volunteers, explain whether their characteristics will affect the generalizability of the research findings.

6. Methods of Data Collection

A. For each of the variables that you plan to study (see 2.C), indicate whether you will measure it by a test, questionnaire, interview, observational procedure, or content analysis. Indicate whether the measure is already available or whether you will need to develop it.

B. For each measure stated above, indicate which types of validity and reliability are relevant and how you will check them.

C. If your study is qualitative in nature, indicate whether your data collection will focus on etic or emic perspectives or both, how you will collect data on each case feature that you have chosen for study (see 2.D), and the nature of your involvement in the data-collection process.

7. Data-Analysis Procedures

A. What descriptive statistics and what inferential statistics, if any, will you use to analyze each of your research questions or hypotheses?

B. If your study is qualitative in nature, indicate whether you will use an interpretational, structural, or reflective method of analysis.

8. Ethics and Human Relations

A. What risks, if any, does your study pose for your research participants? What steps will you take to minimize these threats?

B. Will the study need to be approved by an institutional review board? If yes, describe the approval process.

C. How will you gain entry into your proposed research setting, and how will you gain the cooperation of your research participants?

9. Timeline

A. Create a timeline listing in order all the major steps of your study. Also indicate the approximate amount of time that each step will take.

Questions to Ask Yourself When Evaluating a Report of a Quantitative Study

The following questions can be used to help you evaluate each section of a quantitative research report. For each question we indicate the type of information that you will need to identify in the report to answer the question, and we provide a sample answer. The examples are drawn from our experience in evaluating quantitative research studies.

Quantitative studies encompass various research designs. For design-specific questions to use in evaluating quantitative studies, see Appendix 4.

Introductory Section

1. Are the research problems, methods, and findings appropriate given the researchers' institutional affiliations, beliefs, values, or theoretical orientation?

   Information needed. The researchers' institutional affiliation often is given beneath the title of a published research report, or it might be at the end of the report or at the end of the journal in which the report appears. Also look for any information in the report that indicates the researchers' beliefs, values, or theoretical orientation with respect to education and how that affected their research.

   Example. Most of the researchers' prior work has focused on cognitive models of learning. Therefore, they designed their research to show the advantages of cognitively oriented teaching methods compared to behaviorally oriented teaching methods.

2. Do the researchers demonstrate any favorable or unfavorable bias in describing the subject of the study (e.g., the instructional method, program, curriculum, etc., that was investigated)?

   Information needed. Identify any adjectives or other words that describe an instructional method, program, curriculum, and so forth, in clearly positive or negative terms.

   Example. The researchers described the group of students who served as research participants as difficult to handle, unmotivated, and disorganized. No evidence was presented to support this characterization. In the absence of evidence, this description might indicate a negative attitude toward the children who were studied.

3. Is the literature review section of the report sufficiently comprehensive, and does it include studies that you know to be relevant to the problem?

   Information needed. Examine the studies mentioned in the report. Note particularly if a recent review of the literature relevant to the research problem was cited, or if the researchers mentioned an effort to make their own review comprehensive.

   Example. The researchers stated the main conclusions of a previously published comprehensive literature review on the instructional program that they intended to study. They demonstrated clearly how their study built on the findings and recommendations of this review.

4. Is each variable in the study clearly defined?

   Information needed. Identify all the variables (also called *constructs*) that were studied. For each variable, determine if and how it is defined in the report.

   Example. One of the variables studied is intrinsic motivation, which is defined in the report as the desire to learn because it increases self-esteem. This definition is not consistent with other definitions in the research literature, which state that intrinsic motivation is the desire to learn because of the satisfaction that comes from the act of learning and from the content being learned.

5. Is the measure of each variable consistent with how the variable was defined?

   Information needed. Identify how each variable in the study was measured.

   Example. The researchers studied self-esteem but did not define it. Therefore, it was not possible to determine whether their measure of self-esteem was consistent with their definition.

6. Are the research hypotheses, questions, or objectives explicitly stated, and if so, are they clear?

   Information needed. Examine each research hypothesis, question, or objective stated in the report.

   Example. The researcher stated one general objective for the study. It was clearly stated, but it did not provide sufficient information concerning the specific variables that were to be studied.

7. Do the researchers make a convincing case that a research hypothesis, question, or objective was important to study?

   Information needed. Examine the researchers' rationale for each hypothesis, question, or objective.

   Example. The researchers showed how the hypothesis to be tested was derived from a specific theory. They also showed that if the hypothesis was confirmed by the study, it would add support to the validity of the theory, which is currently being used in the design of new reading curricula.

Method Section

8. Did the sampling procedures produce a sample that is representative of an identifiable population, or generalizable to your local population?

   Information needed. Identify the procedures that the researchers used to select their sample.

   Example. The researchers selected several classes (not randomly) from one school. The only information given about the students was their average ability and gender distribution. I cannot tell from this description whether the sample is similar to students in our schools.

9. Did the researchers form subgroups to increase understanding of the phenomena being studied?

   Information needed. Determine whether the sample was divided into subgroups, and if so, why.

   Example. The researchers showed the effects of the instructional program for both boys and girls; this information was helpful. However, they did not show the effects for different ethnic subgroups. This is an oversight, because the program might have a cultural bias that could have an adverse effect on some ethnic subgroups.

10. Is each measure appropriate for the sample?

    Information needed. Determine whether the researchers reported the population for whom the measure was developed.

Example. The ABC Reading Test was developed 20 years ago for primary grade students. The current study also involves primary grade students, but the test may no longer be valid, because students and the reading curriculum have changed considerably over the past 20 years.

11. Is each measure in the study sufficiently valid for its intended purpose?

    Information needed. Examine any evidence that the researchers presented to demonstrate the validity of each measure in the study.

    Example. The XYZ Test was used because it purportedly predicts success in vocational education programs. However, the researchers presented evidence from only one study to support this claim, involving a vocational education program that was quite different from the one they investigated.

12. Is each measure in the study sufficiently reliable for its intended purpose?

    Information needed. Examine any evidence that the researchers presented to demonstrate the reliability of each measure in the study.

    Example. The researchers had observers rate each student's on-task behavior during Spanish instruction in a sample of 30 classrooms. Inter-rater reliability was checked by having pairs of observers use the rating system in the same five classrooms. The pairs typically agreed on 90 percent of their ratings, which indicates good reliability.

13. If any qualitative data were collected, were they analyzed in a manner that contributed to the soundness of the overall research design?

    Information needed. Determine whether the researchers report qualitative information about the research participants, procedures, or findings.

    Example. In seeking to explain the absence of differences between the experimental and control groups' classroom behavior, the researcher mentioned information shared by the students' teacher that students in the control group classroom had reacted positively to the observer's presence.

14. Were the research procedures appropriate and clearly stated so that others could replicate them if they wished?

    Information needed. Identify the various research procedures that were used in the study and the order in which they occurred.

    Example. The researchers administered three types of pretests during one class period the day before the experimental curriculum was introduced. The pretests, though brief, might have overwhelmed the students, so that they could not do their best work. Also, some aspects of the experimental curriculum (e.g., the types of seatwork activities) were not clearly described in the research report, and the researchers did not indicate how soon the posttests were administered after the curriculum was completed.

Results Section

15. Were appropriate statistical techniques used, and were they used correctly?

    Information needed. Identify the statistical techniques described in the report.

    Example. The researchers calculated the mean score for students' performance on the five tests that were administered. However, they did not give the range of scores (i.e., lowest score and highest score). This would be helpful information, because they studied a highly heterogeneous group of students.

16. Was the practical significance of statistical results considered?

    Information needed. Look for the presence of effect-size statistics or interpretation of descriptive statistics in terms of normative standards.

Example. The researchers found a difference between the mean scores of the experimental and control groups on a measure of science achievement. They computed an effect-size statistic to determine the percentile of the average student in the experimental group relative to the score distribution of students in the control group.

Discussion Section

17. Do the results of the data analyses support what the researchers conclude are the findings of the study?

    Information needed. Identify what the researchers considered to be the major findings of the study.

    Example. The researchers concluded that the experimental treatment led to superior learning compared to the control treatment, but this claim was true for only two of the four criterion measures used to measure the effects of the treatments.

18. Did the researchers provide reasonable explanations of the findings?

    Information needed. Identify how the researchers explained the findings of the study and whether alternative explanations were considered.

    Example. The researchers concluded that the narrative version of the textbook was less effective than the traditional expository version. Their explanation was that the story in the narrative version motivated students to keep reading, but that it also distracted them from focusing on the factual information that was included in the test. They presented no evidence to support this explanation, although it seems plausible.

19. Did the researchers relate the findings to a particular theory or body of related research?

    Information needed. Identify any theory or body of related research to which the researchers refer in discussing their findings.

    Example. The researchers discussed the conceptual implications of their findings in relation to theories of reinforcement on learning and task performance.

20. Did the researchers draw sound implications for practice from their findings?

    Information needed. Identify any implications for practice that the researchers drew from their findings.

    Example. The researchers claimed that teachers' morale would be higher if administrators would provide more self-directed staff development. However, this recommendation is based only on their questionnaire finding that teachers expressed a desire for more self-directed staff development. The researchers are not justified in using just this bit of data to claim that teachers' morale will improve if they get the kind of staff development that they prefer. This type of claim requires evidence from experiments.

21. Did the researchers suggest further research to build on their results, or to answer questions that were raised by their findings?

    Information needed. Identify any suggestions that the researchers make for further study of the topic, and the questions that such study might answer.

    Example. The researchers noted that students showed greater levels of problem behavior during the reversal phase of the experiment than during the baseline phase. They recommended further research to explore the conditions under which such "post-reversal intensification" tends to occur.

Questions to Ask Yourself When Evaluating a Report of a Qualitative Study

The following questions can be used to help you evaluate each section of a qualitative research report. For each question we indicate the type of information that you will need to identify in the report to answer the question, and we provide a sample answer. The examples are drawn from our experience in evaluating qualitative research studies.

Qualitative studies encompass various research designs. For design-specific questions to use in evaluating qualitative studies, see Appendix 4.

Introductory Section

1. Are the research problems and methods appropriate given the researchers' institutional affiliations, beliefs, values, or theoretical orientation?

   Information needed. The researchers' institutional affiliation often is given beneath the title of a published research report, or it might be at the end of the report or at the end of the journal in which the report appears. Also look for any information in the report that indicates the researchers' beliefs, values, or theoretical orientation with respect to education and how that affected their research.

   Example. The researchers taught in inner-city schools for many years before doing this study. This experience would give them knowledge of the issues facing inner-city students and teachers.

2. Do the researchers demonstrate any favorable or unfavorable bias in describing the subject of the study (e.g., the instructional method, program, curriculum, etc., that was investigated)?

   Information needed. Identify any adjectives or other words that describe an instructional method, program, curriculum, and so forth, in clearly positive or negative terms.

   Example. The researchers used a qualitative research method known as *educational connoisseurship and criticism* to study a high school football team. This method is inherently evaluative, so it is no surprise that the researchers made many judgments—both positive and negative—about the impact of the team on individual players.

3. Is the literature review section of the report sufficiently comprehensive? Does it include studies that you know to be relevant to the problem?

   Information needed. Examine the studies mentioned in the report. Note particularly if a recent review of the literature relevant to the research problem was cited or if the researchers described their efforts to make their own review comprehensive.

   Example. The researchers completed their literature search prior to beginning data collection. This procedure is not desirable in qualitative research, because questions and hypotheses are bound to arise as the data are collected. They should have done an ongoing literature search to discover what other researchers have found concerning the emerging questions and hypotheses.

Research Procedures

4. Did the sampling procedure result in a case or cases that were particularly interesting and from which much could be learned about the phenomena of interest?

    Information needed. Identify the type of purposeful sampling that the researchers used to select their sample.

    Example. The researchers used intensity sampling to select a high school principal who had received several awards and widespread recognition for "turning her school around." She was a good case to study, given the researchers' interest in administrators' instructional leadership.

5. Were the data-collection methods used in the research appropriate for the phenomena that the researchers wanted to explore?

    Information needed. Examine any evidence that the researchers presented to demonstrate the soundness of their data-collection methods.

    Example. The researchers' primary data-collection method was participant observation. Several quotations suggest that they were accepted as honorary members of the groups they observed. Thus, it appears that they had good access to the kinds of events and behavior about which they wished to collect data.

6. Was there sufficient intensity of data collection?

    Information needed. Identify the time period over which an individual, setting, or event was observed, and whether the observation was continuous or fragmented. If documents were analyzed, identify how extensive the search for documents was and how closely the documents were analyzed. If interviews were conducted, did the researchers build sufficient rapport with field participants before asking in-depth questions, and did they reexplore sensitive topics in subsequent interviews in order to check their data?

    Example. The researchers' goal was to learn how elementary school teachers established classroom routines and discipline procedures at the beginning of the school year. They observed each teacher every day for the first three weeks; this is a good procedure. They assumed, however, that routines and discipline procedures would be explained at the start of the school day, and so they observed only the first hour of class time. The validity of this assumption is questionable.

7. Were the data collected in such a way as to ensure a reflection of the field participants' emic perspective?

    Information needed. Examine any information that the researchers present to demonstrate that they sought to reflect the emic perspective of field participants.

    Example. The researchers wished to learn about children's views of preschool, but noted that children in the culture they studied often become uncomfortable when adults ask them questions in a formal setting. The researchers made the children more comfortable by setting up a playlike environment and asking questions unobtrusively as the interviewer and children played.

8. Did the researchers triangulate their data sources and data-collection methods to test the soundness of the findings?

    Information needed. Examine such information as whether the data obtained from two or more data-collection methods were compared for evidence of confirmation or of meaningful discrepancies.

    Example. The researcher obtained both observational data on students' self-references when with their peers and interview data about students' self-perceptions from one-on-one conversations with the researcher.

9. Were the research procedures appropriate and clearly stated so that others could replicate them if they wished?

    Information needed. Identify the various research procedures that were used in the study and the order in which they occurred.

Example. The researchers' main data-collection procedure was to ask students questions as they attempted to solve mathematics problems. The problems and questions are available upon request, so it seems that the study could be replicated.

Research Findings

10. Did the report include a thick description that gives a thorough sense of how various individuals responded to the interview questions and how they behaved?

    Information needed. Identify the amount of vivid detail that is included about what the individuals being studied actually did or said.

    Example. The researchers identified 10 issues that mentor teachers faced in working with beginning teachers. Unfortunately the issues were described in rather meager detail, with no examples of what they looked like in practice.

11. Was the research report written in a style that brings to life the phenomenon being studied?

    Information needed. Identify any use of visual or literary structures (e.g., drawings, use of similes or metaphors) or unusual genres (e.g., poetry, songs, storytelling) that are meant to convey the unique perspective of individuals in the field.

    Example. The historical research report included photographs to convey what one-room schools and their teacher and students looked like at the turn of the century. A typical school song of the period was included, as well as a harrowing newspaper account of a boy who became lost in the woods while on his way to school during the winter.

12. In summarizing the findings, did the report present any specific questions or hypotheses that emerged from the data that were collected?

    Information needed. Identify each research hypothesis or question that is stated in the report and how they are based on the study data.

    Example. The researchers focused almost entirely on writing a narrative account of the events leading up to the teachers' strike. There was no attempt to develop hypotheses about why these events happened, which could be tested in subsequent research.

13. If any quantitative data were collected, were they described and analyzed appropriately?

    Information needed. Identify any quantitative data in the report.

    Example. The researchers studied three teachers' aides and made such comments as "They spent most of their time helping individual children and passing out or collecting papers." Time is easily quantified, so the researchers could have collected some time data and reported means and standard deviations.

14. Did the researchers establish a strong chain of evidence?

    Information needed. Identify information in the report that explains the researchers' reasoning with respect to their decisions from the beginning to the end of the study.

    Example. The researchers wanted to study how recent immigrants adapted to the manner in which students interact with each other in inner-city high schools. They trained high school students from each immigrant culture to collect observational and interview data. They explained that they chose this method of data collection because they assumed that the students would be able to obtain more valid data than adult researchers could obtain. This explanation appears reasonable, and therefore it contributes to the chain of evidence supporting the soundness of the study's findings.

15. Did the researchers use member checking to ensure that the information they presented about field participants was accurate and reflected field participants' perceptions?

    Information needed. Identify information indicating that the researchers asked individuals to review statements in drafts of the researchers' report for accuracy and completeness.

Example. The researchers asked several members of each of the groups they studied—students, teachers, and parents—to review drafts of the report. An individual who spent considerable time on that task and provided helpful feedback was listed as one of the report authors.

Discussion

16. Did the researchers reflect on their own values and perspectives and how these might have influenced the study outcomes and describe steps that were taken to minimize their effect?

    Information needed. Look for information in which the researchers describe their own thoughts or feelings about the phenomenon being investigated, and how they took their personal reactions into account in collecting and analyzing the data.

    Example. The report referred to a discussion among the researchers about their personal disappointment at the ways some students treated other students during the research observations. It noted the researchers' agreement to behave in a respectful and friendly manner toward every individual in the field and then to journal about their personal feelings after each field session.

17. Were multiple sources of evidence used to support the researchers' conclusions?

    Information needed. Identify the researchers' conclusions and how each of them was supported by the data analyses.

    Example. The researchers concluded that textbook adoption committees were frustrated by the paucity of written information provided by publishers and their inability to question publishers' representatives in person. This frustration was documented by analysis of interviews with selected members of the textbook adoption committees, field notes made by the researchers during committee meetings, and letters written by the chair of the committee to the director of textbook adoption in the state department of education.

18. Did the researchers provide reasonable explanations of the findings?

    Information needed. Identify how the researchers explained the findings of the study and whether alternative explanations were considered.

    Example. The researchers found that peer coaching did not work at the school they studied, and they attributed its failure to the lack of a supportive context, especially the lack of a history of collegiality among the teaching staff. Another plausible explanation, which they did not consider, is that the teachers received inadequate preparation in peer coaching.

19. Was the generalizability of the findings appropriately qualified?

    Information needed. Identify whether the researchers made any statements about the generalizability of their findings. If claims of generalizability were made, were they appropriate?

    Example. The researchers made no claims that the results of their case study could be generalized to anyone other than the teacher who was studied. It is unfortunate that they did not discuss generalizability, because the findings have significant implications for practice, if in fact they apply to other teachers. There are not enough data about the teacher's professional education for readers to generalize on their own.

20. Did the researchers draw reasonable implications for practice from their findings?

    Information needed. Identify any implications for practice that the researchers drew from their findings.

    Example. The researchers found that students who volunteer for community service derive many benefits from the experience. Therefore, they encourage educators to support community service programs for their students. This recommendation seems well grounded in their findings about the benefits of community service that students in their study received.

Design-Specific Questions to Ask Yourself When Evaluating a Research Report

Appendix 2 lists questions that will help you evaluate any report of a quantitative study. Appendix 3 is similar, except that it applies to reports of qualitative studies. In this appendix, we list additional questions that apply to evaluating the specific research design used in a study. We elaborate on these questions in the chapters from which they are drawn. You can find these elaborations simply by turning to the last section of the chapter pertaining to the research design. Alternatively, you can turn to the book's table of contents to find them.

Descriptive Research Studies (Chapter 10)

- If the researchers generalize their findings from a sample to a population, have they taken steps to ensure that these generalizations are justified?
- If the sample was randomly drawn from a population, did the researchers present a measure of sampling error for their statistical results?
- Did the researchers develop their questionnaire, interview, or observation schedule by doing a pilot study?
- Are the items in the measure of good quality?

Group Comparison Research (Chapter 11)

- Did the researchers specify a cause-and-effect model that links their variables?
- Are the comparison groups similar in all respects except for the variable on which they were selected to differ?
- Were the researchers' conclusions about possible causal relationships expressed in tentative, exploratory language rather than as definite claims?

Correlational Research (Chapter 12)

- Did the researchers specify a cause-and-effect model that links their variables?
- Were the researchers' conclusions about possible causal relationships expressed in tentative, exploratory language rather than as definite claims?

Group Experiments (Chapter 13)

- Did the researchers randomly assign the sample to the experimental and control conditions?
- Did the researchers check for attrition of research participants over the course of the experiment?
- Did the researchers check for threats to the internal and external validity of the experiment?
- Did the research participants follow the researchers' specifications for the experimental intervention or control conditions?
- Was the intervention sufficiently strong?

Single-Case Experiments (Chapter 13)
- Did the experiment contain sufficient data points?
- Did the experiment include a control condition?

Case Studies (Chapter 14)
- Is the study useful in the sense of being relevant to problems of practice?
- Is the emic perspective of the research participants represented in the report?
- Are quantitative data used, when relevant, to support qualitative observations?
- Did the researchers observe the case over a sufficiently long period of time?
- If data were coded, did the researchers check the reliability of the coding?
- Did the research participants check the report for accuracy and completeness?
- Did the researchers check whether the findings were supported by different data collection methods, data sources, analysts, and theories?
- Did the researcher provide an in-depth description of the history, setting, participants, and culture within which the case was situated?
- Are the research questions, data, data analyses, and findings clearly and meaningfully related to each other?
- Do the researchers state personal assumptions, values, theoretical orientations, and biases that influenced their approach to the case study?

Narrative Research (Chapter 15)
- Did the researcher elicit sufficient detail about the participant's stories?
- Does the researcher provide a credible interpretation of the story?

Ethnography and Critical Research (Chapter 16)
- Does the report include an emic perspective?
- Does the report include an etic perspective?

Historical Research (Chapter 17)
- Does the report refer to primary sources?
- Does the report refer to the use of external criticism of primary sources?
- Does the report refer to the use of internal criticism to check the accuracy of statements made in historical sources?
- Do the historian's interpretations reflect bias?
- Does the report include credible causal inferences?
- Does the historian overgeneralize from the evidence presented in the report?
- Does the historian use educational concepts in an appropriate manner?

Mixed-Methods Research (Chapter 18)
- Did the researchers use both quantitative and qualitative methods in their study?
- Did the researchers combine quantitative and qualitative methods so that they shed more light on the research problem than either method would have alone?

Action Research (Chapter 19)
- Do the researchers state actions that occurred to solve the problem that prompted the study?
- Do the researchers validate their findings by triangulating them using multiple perspectives or data sources?
- Do the researchers explain how the study contributed to their professional development?
- Did the researchers collaborate with all the individuals who have a stake in the problem being investigated?

- Do the researchers state how the project energized the participants so they became open to new viewpoints about their work?
- Did the researchers engage in a dialogue with their peers in framing their findings and interpretations?

Evaluation Research (Chapter 20)

- Was the study informative, timely, and useful for the stakeholders?
- Was the evaluation design appropriate to the setting in which the study was conducted?
- Was the evaluation design cost-effective?
- Was the evaluation study conducted legally and ethically?
- Did the evaluation study produce valid, reliable, and comprehensive information for making judgments about the evaluated program's worth?

Glossary

A-B-A-B research design   a type of single-case experiment in which the researchers institute a baseline condition (*A*), administer the treatment (condition *B*), institute a second baseline condition (the second *A*), and readminister the treatment (the second *B*), while measuring the target behavior repeatedly during all conditions.

A-B-A research design   a type of single-case experiment in which the researchers institute a baseline condition (*A*), administer the treatment (condition *B*), and institute a second baseline condition (the second *A*), while measuring the target behavior repeatedly during all conditions.

abstract   a brief summary of the information contained in a publication, usually written either by the author or an indexer who works for the publisher of a search engine.

accessible population   a feasible population from which a sample can be drawn for a research study.

action research (also called *insider research, participatory action research, practitioner research, self-study research, teacher research*)   research that is carried out by practitioners, usually in their own workplace, to improve their professional practice.

action science   in action research, the use of the theory of action to help professionals discover and address discrepancies between their espoused theories about how they work and their theories-in-action, which is their actual work behavior.

age equivalent   a derived score that represents a given raw score on a measure as the average age of the individuals in the norming group who earned that score.

ageism   in critical theory, the devaluation and exploitation of individuals within a certain age range.

agency   in qualitative research, individuals' assumed ability to shape the conditions of their lives.

analysis of covariance   a statistical procedure for determining whether the difference between the mean scores of two or more groups on a measure is statistically significant, after adjusting for initial differences between the groups on a pretest.

analysis of variance   a statistical procedure for determining whether the difference between the mean scores of two or more groups on a measure is statistically significant.

AND connector   a search engine feature that enables the user to identify only those bibliographic citations in a database that include both of two keywords.

anti-oppressive education   an approach to educational inquiry and practice that involves questioning traditional educational practices in order to expose and correct underlying forms of cultural oppression maintained by such practices.

APA Presidential Task Force on Evidence-Based Practice   a commission established by the American Psychological Association to determine research-based and expertise-based standards for psychologists to use in their professional practice.

applicability   in case study research, an individual's judgment that a study's findings can be used to inform a problem of practice in other settings or to test a theory.

applied research   research that is designed to yield findings that can be used directly to improve practice.

archive (also called *repository*)   a facility for storing documents to preserve them in good condition and control access to them.

artificial dichotomy   a variable that has only two values, both of them created by researchers or others.

attrition (also called *experimental mortality*)   in experiments, the loss of research participants over the course of the experimental treatment.

audit trail   in a research study, a detailed record of the researcher's procedures so that other researchers can check the soundness of the study's methodology or use it to replicate the study.

baseline condition   in single-case experiments, the *A* condition or conditions, during which the individual's behavior is observed under natural conditions.

basic research   research that is designed to understand processes and structures that underlie observed behavior.

behavior analysis   in single-case experiments, a procedure for careful observation of an individual in a setting, typically for the purpose of determining dysfunctional behaviors and specifying desired behaviors.

behavior modification   in single-case experiments, the use of techniques such as reinforcement, modeling, and discrimination training to increase or decrease the frequency of specified behaviors.

bell-shaped curve   see *normal probability distribution.*

bias   a mental set to perceive events in such a way that certain types of facts are habitually overlooked, distorted, or falsified.

bibliographic citation   a statement that describes a publication—typically its author, title, publisher, publication date, page numbers if an article or book chapter, and a brief abstract.

bivariate correlational statistic   a statistic that describe the magnitude of the relationship between a sample's scores on two measures.

border pedagogy   in critical theory, an approach to educational practice that conceives the differences between individuals and ethnic groups as permeable and changing, as opposed to the more rigid, either–or nature of conventional social categories.

canonical correlation   a type of multiple regression analysis that involves use of a sample's scores on two or more measures to predict their score on an index that is a composite of their scores on two or more criterion measures.

case   in qualitative research, a particular instance of a phenomenon, bounded in time and place, that is selected for study.

case delineation   in case study research, the process of focusing the investigation on a limited number of features of the phenomenon.

case focus   those aspects of the phenomenon on which data collection and analysis will concentrate.

case story   a description of a series of events that usually is meant to be informative and entertaining, but without evidence for judging the validity of the description or its applicability to other settings.

case study   a type of qualitative investigation that usually involves the in-depth study of instances of a phenomenon in its natural context, both from the participants' and researchers' perspective, and with concern for the validity and applicability of the findings.

catalytic validity   in action research, a judgment about the extent to which an action research project reorients, focuses, and energizes participants so that they become open to a transformed view of reality in relation to their practice.

categorical scale (also called *nominal scale*)   a measure whose values are categories that have the properties of being mutually exclusive and not orderable.

causal-comparative research   see *group comparison research.*

causal pattern   in case study research, a systematic relationship that is observed between particular phenomena within a case or across cases and that is presumed to be causal.

causal relationship (also called *cause-and-effect relationship*)   in quantitative research, a hypothesis or empirical demonstration that one variable, which is the assumed cause and is measured at a certain point in time, has an influence on another variable, which is the assumed effect and is measured at a later point in time.

ceiling effect   a situation in which some research participants earn the maximum score on a test or a score close to it, because their achievement level exceeds the highest achievement level measured by the test.

central tendency   a point in a distribution of scores, such as the mean or median, that is representative of the scores in the distribution.

chain of evidence   a judgment of the soundness of a study's findings based on clear, meaningful links among the study's research questions, the raw data, the data-analysis procedures, and the findings.

chart essay   a visual presentation that focuses the audience's attention on particular findings from a research study or research review.

chi-square (χ^2) test   a nonparametric test of statistical significance that is used to accept or reject the null hypothesis when the data are frequency counts on two or more categorical scales.

CIPP model   see *Context-Input-Process-Product (CIPP) model*.

citation   see *bibliographic citation*.

citation manager   software that enables the user to record bibliographic citations so they can be stored and retrieved easily and systematically.

citation pearl growing   the use of a relevant publication (the "pearl") to search for other relevant publications.

clinical expertise   the ability to make informed, ethical judgments about whether a particular professional practice is both evidence-based and appropriate for the needs of an individual student or other client.

closed-ended item   in an attitude scale or other measure, an item that requires an individual to make a forced choice between the options that it lists.

Cochrane Collaboration   an organization that synthesizes research findings on medical interventions in order to promote the practice of evidence-based medicine.

coding check   the determination of the reliability of data by calculating the level of agreement between different researchers who coded it into categories.

coding frame   in narrative research, an analytic framework for capturing the overall meaning of stories and the issues they raise.

cohort study   research in which a group of individuals is surveyed at multiple data-collection points, with the provision that a different sample from the group will be included at each of the data-collection points, for the purpose of studying how the group changes over time and possible reasons for the changes.

collaborative action research   a type of investigation in which different professionals, sometimes from different organizations or disciplines, work together to collect data about a problem of practice, analyze the data, report the results to stakeholders, and implement a plan of action to solve the problem.

commitment script   in narrative research, story elements that indicate an early decision to focus one's life in a particular direction that appears to offer a unique advantage for the individual, sufficiently so that the individual is willing to confront obstacles that might arise along the way.

comparison groups   in group comparison research, two or more samples that are selected because they naturally possess different levels of a variable; in experiments, two or more samples that are formed in order to test different interventions or control conditions.

concept   a construct that is used to group individuals, events, or objects that share one or more attributes.

concurrent evidence of test validity (also called *concurrent validity*)   the extent to which individuals' scores on a new test correspond to their scores on a more established test of the same construct, which is administered shortly before or after the new test.

concurrent-triangulation research design   in mixed-methods research, the collection of qualitative and quantitative data at approximately the same time, followed by analysis of findings from both types of data to determine whether they corroborate each other.

concurrent validity   see *concurrent evidence of test validity*.

confidence interval   a range of values of a sample statistic that is likely to include its population parameter.

confidence limit   the upper or lower value of a confidence interval.

conscientization   in critical theory, a process in which individuals come to find their voice and courage to question and change their role in maintaining cultural processes that are not consistent with their basic values.

consequential evidence of test validity   the extent to which the values implicit in the constructs measured by a test and its intended uses are consistent with the values of test takers, those who will use the test results to make decisions, and other stakeholders.

consequential validity   see *consequential evidence of test validity*.

constant   a construct that is part of the design of a research study but is not allowed to vary among the research participants.

constant comparison   in qualitative research, the process of comparing instances of data that have been classified by a particular code, in order to discover commonalities in these data that reflect the meaning of the code and that differentiate it from other codes.

constructs   concepts that are inferred from commonalities among observed phenomena.

construct validity   see *validity*.

content analysis   the study of the information contained in a document or other form of communication by developing categories to code the information and analyzing the frequency of each category.

content-related evidence of test validity (also called *content validity*)   the extent to which the items in a test represent the domain of content that the test is designed to measure.

content validity   see *content-related evidence of test validity*.

context evaluation   in the CIPP model, assessment of the needs, assets, and problems of the stakeholders, staff, and beneficiaries of the program.

Context-Input-Process-Product (CIPP) model   a type of evaluation research that is used to assess various aspects of a program—needs, problems, budgets, competing alternatives, functions, effectiveness—as it unfolds over time.

continuous variable   a variable all of whose values have been measured, typically by an interval or ratio scale with an indefinite number of points along its continuum.

control condition   in an experiment, a situation in which a group of research participants receive no intervention or an alternative intervention, against whose performance the experimental group's performance is compared.

convergent evidence of test validity   the extent to which individuals' scores on a test correlate positively with their scores on other tests that are hypothesized to measure the same construct.

correlational research   a type of quantitative investigation that seeks to discover the direction and degree of the relationship among variables through the use of correlational statistics.

correlation coefficient   a mathematical expression of the extent to which a sample's distribution of scores on two or more measures are related to each other.

criterion variable   in experimental research, a variable that is measured after the intervention and that the intervention is intended to affect; in correlational research, a variable for which there is a measure that is administered to a sample to determine whether their scores on it can be predicted by their scores on other measures.

critical ethnography   a qualitative research tradition that combines critical theory and ethnographic methods to study power relationships and forms of oppression in a culture.

criticalists   researchers or theorists who attempt to use their investigations as a form of social or cultural criticism.

critical pedagogy   any applied system of teaching and learning that is based on the goals and values of critical research.

critical research (also called *critical theory*)   a qualitative research tradition that seeks to uncover the nature of power relationships in a culture and help to emancipate members of the culture from the forms of oppression that operate within it.

Cronbach's alpha   a reliability coefficient used to quantify the extent to which an individual's scores across different items on a test are consistent with each another.

cross-sectional study   a type of research in which changes in a population over time are studied by collecting data at one point in time from samples that vary in age or developmental stage.

crystallization   see *triangulation*.

cultural acquisition   the process by which individuals seek to acquire, or to avoid acquiring, the concepts, values, skills, and behaviors that are reflected in the common culture.

cultural studies   a qualitative research tradition that investigates the economic, legal, political, and other underpinnings of cultural phenomena as expressed in literature, art, history, and other disciplines.

cultural transmission   the process by which the larger social structure intentionally intervenes in individuals' lives in order to promote, or sometimes to discourage, the learning of particular concepts, values, skills, or behaviors.

culture   the pattern of traditions, symbols, rituals, and artifacts that characterize a particular group of individuals and that they transmit from one generation to the next or from current members to newly admitted members.

database   in a search engine, the citations for all the publications that it indexes.

deconstruction   the critical analysis of texts, based on the assumptions that a text has no definite meaning, that words can refer only to other words, and that "playing" with a text can yield multiple, often contradictory interpretations.

democratic validity   a judgment about the credibility of an action research project based on the extent to which the perspectives and interests of all stakeholders were taken into account.

dependent variable   a variable that researchers hypothesize occurs after, and as an effect of, another variable (called the *independent variable*) that occurs naturally or as the result of an intervention.

descriptive research   a type of quantitative investigation that seeks to portray characteristics of a sample or population by measuring prespecified variables.

descriptive statistics   mathematical techniques for organizing, summarizing, and displaying a set of numerical data.

descriptor   in a literature search, a term that an individual uses to locate publications that have been classified by it.

dialectic   in narrative research, an oppositional relationship between an important value or perspective in an individual's life story and a countervailing, equally powerful value or perspective.

dialogical data generation   a stage of a critical ethnography project in which researchers collect data by having the research participants explore issues with their own vocabulary, metaphors, and ideas.

dialogic validity   a judgment about the credibility of an action research project based on the extent to which colleagues shared in the development of the practitioner/researcher's findings and interpretations.

dichotomous variable   a variable that has only two values.

differential analysis   a method for determining whether an observed relationship between two variables for the entire research sample is the same for subgroups that have been formed by using a moderator variable.

differential-selection effect   in quasi-experiments, the selection of participants for the experimental and control groups by a procedure other than random selection.

directional hypothesis   a prediction that one group of research participants will have a higher average score on a measure than another group.

direct observation   the collection of data while the research participants are engaged in some form of behavior or while an event is occurring.

discriminant analysis   a type of multiple regression that enables researchers to determine how well a sample's scores on measures of several independent variables predict their scores on a measure of a dependent variable whose scores are in the form of categories.

disruption   in narrative research, an unexpected, difficult, or disturbing occurrence in one's life that is given meaning by an interpretive process.

document   in historical research, a type of text material that is prepared for personal use rather than for an official purpose.

ecological validity   in experiments, an estimate of the extent to which the findings can be generalized to the naturally occurring conditions of a local setting.

educational research   the systematic collection and analysis of empirical data in order to develop various kinds of valid, generalizable knowledge—descriptions of educational phenomena; predictions about future events or performance; evidence about the effects of experimental interventions; or explanations of observed phenomena in terms of basic processes that underlie them.

Educational Resources Information Center (ERIC)   a federally funded agency that maintains a search engine and database of bibliographic citations for education-related documents.

effect size   a statistic that represents the magnitude of the difference between the average scores of two groups on a measure or the magnitude of the relationship between the distribution of scores on two measures for a sample.

effectiveness evaluation   in the CIPP model, a process for assessing the quality and significance of a program's outcomes for the individuals who participate in it.

emancipation   in critical theory, a process of generating action and consciousness raising in and toward oppressed cultural groups in order to free them from their oppression.

emergent design   a form of evaluation in which the focus of evaluation changes as evaluators gain insights into stakeholders' primary issues and concerns.

emic perspective   in qualitative research, the research participants' perceptions and understanding of their social reality.

enculturation   the process by which cultural practices and beliefs are transferred to the youth or other new members of a culture.

epistemology   the branch of philosophy that studies the nature of knowledge and the process by which knowledge is acquired and validated.

ERIC   see *Educational Resources Information Center (ERIC).*

espoused theory   in action science, professionals' beliefs about how they deal with problems of practice.

ethnography   the first-hand, intensive study of the features of a specific culture.

ethnology   the comparative study of a particular phenomenon as it manifests itself in different cultures.

ethnoscience   the study of a culture's semantic systems for the purpose of revealing the cognitive structure of the culture.

etic perspective   in qualitative research, the researchers' conceptual and theoretical understanding of the research participants' social reality.

evaluation research   a systematic process of making judgments about the merit, value, or worth of programs, organizations, and other phenomena.

evidence-based practice   the art of solving problems of practice through the integration of the best available research combined with the practitioner's clinical expertise and values.

Excel   a software program, available in Office for Windows or Mac, for computing statistics commonly used by in educational research.

experiment   a type of quantitative investigation that involves the manipulation of a treatment variable to determine its effect on one or more dependent variables.

experimental condition   in an experiment, a situation in which a group of research participants receive an intervention to determine its effect on the dependent variable.

experimental mortality   see *attrition.*

exploratory case study method   a method for synthesizing the findings of case studies, in addition to relevant quantitative studies and nonresearch accounts, so as to identify both the unique characteristics of each case and their commonalities.

external criticism   in historical research, the process of determining the authenticity of a historical source, that is, whether the apparent or claimed origin of the source corresponds to its actual origin.

external validity   in quantitative research, the extent to which the results of a study can be generalized to individuals and situations beyond those involved in the study.

extraneous variable   a factor, other than the treatment variable, on which the experimental groups vary and which possibly affects the dependent variable.

face validity   the extent to which an informal inspection of a test's items indicates that they cover the content that the test is claimed to measure.

factor (also called *latent variable*)   in factor analysis, a mathematical expression of a feature shared by a particular subset of quantitative variables that have been found to be intercorrelated; in experimental design, a term synonymous with *independent variable.*

factor analysis   a correlational procedure for reducing a set of measured variables to a smaller number of factors.

factorial experiment   an experiment having more than one factor, or in other words, more than one independent variable.

feminisms   various forms of study of females' lived experiences and the manner in which those experiences are shaped by cultural phenomena; also known as *feminist research.*

fidelity of implementation   the extent to which individuals who carry out a program or procedure conform to the specifications established by its developers or other individuals.

fieldwork   in qualitative research, the researchers' collection of data while interacting with research participants in their natural settings.

fixed variables   in a group comparison research design, a characteristic of individuals or groups that cannot be manipulated.

focus groups   a type of group interview in which individuals, led by a skilled interviewer, can talk to each other, perhaps expressing feelings and opinions that might not emerge if they were interviewed individually.

forgery   in historical research, a document or relic that is claimed to be the work of a particular individual, but that was actually fabricated by someone else.

formative evaluation   a type of evaluation that is carried out while a program or product is under development, in order to decide whether and how it should be improved, or whether it should be abandoned.

fugitive literature   publications that are not widely disseminated or easy to obtain.

futurology   in historical research, a type of investigation that uses such methods as analysis of past events and simulations in order to predict possible futures.

F **value**   a statistic that is computed in an analysis of variance and used to decide whether to accept or reject a null hypothesis.

gain score   a measure of an individual's score on a posttest minus that individual's score on a pretest.

grade equivalent   a derived score that represents a student's raw score on a test as the grade level of students in the norming group who, on average, earned that score.

grounded theory   in qualitative research, the principle that researchers should develop theory inductively by examining their data directly and without external influence, rather than by creating a theory in advance of what they are studying.

group comparison research (also called *causal-comparative research*)   a type of quantitative investigation in which groups that differ on the independent variable are compared to determine whether they also differ on the dependent variable or in which groups that differ on the dependent variable are compared to determine whether they also differ on the independent variable.

group experiment   in experimental research, a design in which each treatment and control condition includes a sample of research participants, rather than a single case.

growth model   an approach to measurement and statistical analysis of students' learning over time in order to assess their learning gain.

hegemony   the maintenance of privileged groups' dominance over subordinate groups through the cultural agencies they control.

hermeneutic circle   the process of understanding any text or other form of communication by interpreting it as a whole in terms of one's understanding of its various parts.

hierarchical linear modeling (HLM)   a statistical technique for determining whether the correlation between two variables is affected by different levels of nesting.

high-inference variable   a variable that requires the researcher to make an inference from observed behavior to underlying factors, such as cognitive and emotional processes, that it expresses.

historical research   a type of investigation that involves a systematic search for data to answer questions about a past phenomenon, in order to better understand the phenomenon and its likely causes and consequences.

history effect   in experiments, the effect on the dependent variable of events that occur while the experimental intervention is in progress, but that are not part of the intervention.

holistic description   a comprehensive description and analysis of the unique cultural patterns of a group of people who live close together in a specific geographical region.

holistic ethnography   a qualitative research tradition that involves efforts to provide a comprehensive description and analysis of the entire culture of a group of people who live close together in a specified geographical region.

hypothesis   a prediction, derived from a theory or speculation, about how two or more variables will be related to each other.

impact evaluation   in the CIPP model, an assessment of whether a program reached the appropriate target audience.

independent variable   a variable that researchers hypothesize occurred before, and had an influence on, another variable (the *dependent variable*).

in-depth study   in qualitative research, the collection of a substantial amount of data, typically using different methods and extending over a long period of time, in order to develop a deep understanding of a case.

inferential statistics   mathematical procedures that enable researchers to make inferences about a population's characteristics based on the descriptive statistics that are calculated from data for a sample that was selected to represent the population.

input evaluation   in the CIPP model, the assessment of competing alternatives, work plans, and budgets for a particular program.

insider   in action research and qualitative research, a practitioner or other individual in the setting being studied who is viewed as having direct knowledge of the problem that is being investigated.

insider research   see *action research.*

Institute of Education Sciences   an agency of the U.S. Department of Education that has the mission of supporting scientifically based research to improve student learning outcomes.

institutional review board   a committee within a recognized institution that follows a protocol to ensure that research participants are protected from harm and risk of harm.

instrumental rationality   a preoccupation with means over ends; in critical theory, a term used to characterize research and theory that emphasizes prediction, control, and the maximization of productivity rather than emphasizing deliberation about which ends have the most value.

instrumentation effect   in experiments, a change from the pretest to the posttest that is due to changes in the nature of the measuring instrument rather than to the experimental treatment.

intentionality   in action research, practitioner inquiry that is planned and deliberate rather than spontaneous.

interaction effect   in experiments, a situation in which an independent variable has an effect on the dependent variable, but only under certain conditions in the experimental design.

internal criticism   in historical research, the process of determining the accuracy and worth of the information contained in a historical source.

internal narrative   in narrative research, the ongoing stream of thought and self-talk that most individuals engage in during many of their waking moments, whether they are conscious of it or not.

internalized oppression   in critical theory, the process by which individuals unwittingly maintain their own lack of privilege through thoughts and actions consistent with a lesser social status.

internal validity   in experiments, the extent to which extraneous variables have been controlled by the researchers such that any observed effects can be attributed solely to the treatment.

interpretational analysis   the process of examining qualitative data to identify constructs, themes, and patterns that can be used to describe and explain the phenomenon being studied.

interpretivism   an epistemological position that social reality has no existence apart from the meanings that individuals construct for them in a continuous process as they participate in social reality.

inter-rater reliability   the extent to which the scores assigned by one rater agree with the scores assigned by other raters who have observed the same events or analyzed the same tests or other materials.

interval scale   a measure that lacks a true zero point and for which the distance between any two adjacent points is the same.

interview   the collection of data through direct interaction between the researcher and the individuals being studied.

item consistency   the extent to which all the items on a test measure the same construct, as determined by one of several correlational methods.

item response theory   a theory of psychological measurement which assumes that individuals with different amounts of an ability will perform differently on an item measuring that ability; also, an approach to test construction in which the difficulty level of the items presented to each individual are matched with his or her ability level as determined by performance on earlier test items.

Joint Committee on Standards for Educational Evaluation   a committee with representatives from 12 major educational organizations whose mission it is to create standards for evaluating the quality of educational programs.

key informant   in qualitative research, any individual who has special knowledge or status that make him especially important in obtaining an emic perspective of the social reality being studied.

keyword   a word or phrase that a search engine will use to identify all entries in its database, such as bibliographic citations and website addresses, containing that word or phrase.

Kruskal-Wallis test of statistical significance   a nonparametric test of statistical significance that is used to determine whether the observed difference between the distribution of scores for more than two groups on a measured variable is statistically significant.

latent variable   see *factor.*

latent variable causal modeling   see *structural equation modeling.*

linear correlation   a statistical approach for analyzing the distribution of a sample's scores on two measures, based on the assumption that as scores in one distribution increase, scores in the other distribution will also increase.

line of best fit   in correlational research, the line on a scattergram that allows for the best prediction of an individual's score on the y axis from knowing the score on the x axis.

Listserv   a software program for managing Internet bulletin boards and discussion forums, so that their subscribers can interact with each other.

literature review   in research, a synthesis of what is known about a particular topic or problem, based on a systematic search for relevant publications, using standard search procedures and criteria for judging the soundness of research evidence.

log   in interviews, a record of the topics covered in a specific interview, accompanied by notations of any interesting occurrences (especially disruptions) and how they were handled.

logistic regression analysis   a type of multiple regression in which a sample's scores on two or more measures is used to predict their scores on a categorical measure.

longitudinal research   a type of quantitative investigation that involves describing changes in a sample's characteristics or behavior patterns over a period of time.

low-inference variable   a variable that only requires the observer to examine a behavior and then decide whether it is an instance of a particular behavioral construct.

Mann-Whitney U test of statistical significance   a nonparametric test of statistical significance that is used to determine whether the observed difference between the distribution of scores for each of two groups on a measured variable is statistically significant.

margin of error   a range of values derived from known statistics for a random sample that is likely to include a population parameter of interest.

matching procedure   in experimental or group comparison research, a technique used to equate groups on extraneous independent variables so that if group differences are observed on a dependent variable, this effect cannot be attributed to the extraneous variables, but instead to the independent variable of interest to the researchers.

maturation effect   in experiments, a change from the pretest to the posttest that is due to developmental changes in the research participants during the course of an experiment rather than to the intervention.

mean   a measure of central tendency that is calculated by summing the individual scores of the sample and then dividing the total sum by the number of individuals in the sample.

mean absolute deviation   in a score distribution, the mean of all the amounts by which each score deviates from the actual mean of the scores, ignoring whether the deviation from the mean is positive or negative.

meaning fields   in critical theory, the possible intended meanings of a participant's statements or nonverbal behavior that others in the setting themselves might infer.

measurement error   the difference between the scores that individuals actually obtain on a test and their true scores if it were possible to obtain a perfect measure of their performance.

median   a measure of central tendency corresponding to the middle point in a distribution of scores.

member checking   a procedure used by qualitative researchers to check their reconstruction of the field participants' emic perspective by having them review statements in the research report for accuracy and completeness.

meta-analysis   a method for combining the statistical results from different quantitative research studies on the same phenomenon into a single statistic called an *effect size*.

microethnography   the study of specific aspects of the culture of a specific subgroup of members of the culture, instead of making a comprehensive study of a culture as a whole.

mixed-methods research   a type of study that uses both quantitative and qualitative techniques for data collection and analysis, either concurrently or sequentially, to address the same or related research questions.

mode   a measure of central tendency that identifies the most frequently occurring score in a distribution of scores.

moderator variable   in correlational research, a variable, *Z,* that affects the extent to which variable *X* predicts variable *Y,* such that the correlation between *X* and *Y* for some values of *Z* is different from the correlation between *X* and *Y* for other values of *Z.*

monological data collection   in critical ethnography, a stage of a research project in which only the researchers "speak," compiling a thick description of field participants' activities that is written from the perspective of an uninvolved observer.

multiple-baseline research design   in single-case experiments, using situations other than the naturally occurring condition as a baseline control for determining the presence of intervention effects.

multiple regression   a statistical procedure for determining the magnitude of the relationship between a criterion variable and a combination of two or more predictor variables.

multivariate correlational statistics   a set of statistics that describe the magnitude of the relationship between three or more variables.

multivariate descriptive statistics   a type of statistic that is used to describe the relationship between the distributions of scores on two or more measures.

multivocality   a situation in which the participants in a culture or societal group do not speak with a unified voice but instead express diverse interests and viewpoints.

narrative   in narrative research, a story in which a precise time line, made up of discrete moments at which events took place, is established.

narrative identity   a sense of self that develops from the stories that an individual constructs from his or her experiences.

narrative research   the systematic study and interpretation of stories of life experiences.

narrative summary   a method for synthesizing qualitative research findings that involves using a consistent writing style to create a brief description of each study.

National Assessment of Educational Progress (NAEP)   a congressionally mandated, large-scale, continuing assessment of what a representative sample of students in the United States know and can do in various subject areas.

needs assessment   a set of procedures for identifying and prioritizing needs, which consist of discrepancies between desired and existing conditions.

negative correlation   a correlation between two score distributions, *X* and *Y,* such that the higher the score for variable *X,* the lower the corresponding score for variable *Y.*

nesting   a situation in which a variable exists at several levels of organizational structure, such as students being "nested" in a classroom, classrooms being "nested" in a school, and schools being "nested" within a school district.

No Child Left Behind Act   a set of regulations approved by the U.S. Congress that impose various educational requirements on all states, including the requirement to specify standards of achievement in basic skills that all students in certain grades are expected to meet.

nominal scale (also called *categorical scale*)   a measure whose values are categories that have the properties of being mutually exclusive and not orderable.

nonparametric test of statistical significance   a type of test of statistical significance that does not depend on assumptions about the distribution or form of scores on the measured variables.

normal curve   see *normal probability distribution.*

normal curve area   the amount of area in the normal curve between the mean, which has a *z* score of 0, and another *z* score.

normal probability distribution   (also called *normal curve* and *bell-shaped curve*) a distribution of scores that are clustered around each side of the mean in a symmetrical bell-shaped curve when plotted on a graph.

normative–evaluative truth claims   in critical ethnography, assumptions about the world as it is or should be that reflect existing social agreements on the rightness, goodness, and appropriateness of various types of activities.

norming group   a large sample that represents a defined population and whose scores on a test provide a set of standards to which the scores of individuals who subsequently take the test can be referenced.

norm-referenced test   a test that is intended for wide use and that is accompanied by tables of norms, so that local users can compare their students' scores with those of students in the general population who are at the same age or grade level.

norms   unstated background sets of rules and assumptions that influence individuals' social acts.

NOT connector   a search engine feature that enables the user to exclude bibliographic citations in a database that have a particular keyword.

null hypothesis   a prediction that the researcher hopes to reject by using a test of statistical significance.

objectives-based evaluation   the use of quantitative or qualitative methods to determine how well a program or curriculum materials help students achieve specified learning outcomes.

objective truth claims   in critical ethnography, assertions that are open to multiple access, meaning that they are accessible to examination and generally agreed on and therefore can be directly validated by various observers.

observer bias   an observer's mental set to perceive events in such a way that certain events or behaviors are overlooked, distorted, or falsified.

one-tailed test of statistical significance   a test that evaluates the null hypothesis in one direction, for example, a test that considers the possibility that the mean score for population *A* is greater than the mean score for population *B*, but not that the mean score for population *B* is greater than the mean score for population *A*.

open-ended item   in an attitude scale or other measure, an item that allows any response an individual wishes to make.

oral history   a type of historical research in which individuals who witnessed or participated in past events are asked to recount their recollections of those events.

OR connector   a search engine feature that enables the user to identify bibliographic citations in a database that include one or the other of two keywords.

ordinal scale   a measure whose different values can be placed in order of magnitude, but the difference between any two sets of adjacent values might differ.

outcome validity   a judgment about the credibility of an action research project based on the extent to which new actions lead to a resolution of the problem that prompted the project.

outlier   an individual or situation that differs greatly in some manner, such as having an extreme score on a measure, from other cases that are studied.

outsider   in action research, an individual who works outside the setting being studied and who is viewed as having an external perspective on the problem of practice being investigated.

p   see *probability (p) value.*

panel study   research in which the same sample is surveyed at more than one data-collection point in order to explore changes in specific individuals and possible reasons for those changes.

parameter   a statistic that applies to the entire population rather than just to a sample.

parametric test of statistical significance   a type of test of statistical significance that depends on certain assumptions about the distribution and form of scores on the measured variables.

participant observer   in qualitative research, researchers' assumption of a meaningful identity within the group being studied while maintaining their role as observers collecting research data.

participatory action research   see *action research.*

path analysis   a statistical multivariate method for testing the validity of a theory about causal links between three or more measured variables.

pattern   in case study research, a systematic relationship between two or more types of phenomena within a case.

pdf file   an electronic copy of a document created by the software program Adobe Acrobat.

Pearson product-moment correlation coefficient (r value)   a widely used statistic that indicates the degree of relationship between the distributions of scores on two measures for a sample.

peer-reviewed journal   in research, a periodical in which the articles have been evaluated by authorities for the quality and relevance of the research that they report.

percentile rank   a type of rank score that represents a given raw score on a measure as the percentage of individuals in the sample or norming group whose score falls at or below that score.

performance ethnography   staged reenactments of cultural phenomena observed by ethnographers.

performance measure   a test that evaluates individuals' skill by having them complete a complex task, sometimes involving a real-life situation.

performance objective   in research and development, a specific statement of what learners will be able to do after receiving instruction provided by a program or curriculum materials.

phenomenon   in qualitative research, any process, event, or characteristic that will be the subject of inquiry.

Phi Delta Kappa/Gallup Polls   an annual national poll, jointly sponsored by the Gallup organization and the educational organization Phi Delta Kappa, to determine the public's attitude about various aspects of U. S. schools.

polarity   in narrative research, a binary opposition that reflects an either–or contrast that is central to the story conveyed in the narrative.

population   the complete set of individuals, groups, events, or other entity that is the subject of inquiry.

population validity   the degree to which the results of a research study can be generalized from the specific sample that was studied to the population from which the sample was drawn.

positive correlation   a correlation between two score distributions, X and Y, such that the higher the score for variable X, the higher the corresponding score for variable Y.

positivism   an epistemological position that asserts that there is a reality "out there" that is available for objective study through scientific means similar to those that were developed in the physical sciences.

postmodernism   a broad social and philosophical movement that questions assumptions about the rationality of human action, the use of positivist epistemology, and any human endeavor (e.g., science) that claims a privileged position with respect to the search for truth.

posttest   in experiments, a measure that is administered following the intervention in order to determine the effects of the treatment.

practical significance   in statistics, a statistical result that has meaningful consequences for individuals to whom the result applies.

practitioner research   see *action research.*

praxis   in critical theory, the process of transforming theory into practice so as to do the right thing and do it well in interacting with one's fellow human beings.

prediction research   an investigation that involves the use of data collected at one point in time to predict future behavior or events.

predictive evidence of test validity (also called *predictive validity*)   the extent to which the scores of individuals on a measure administered at one point in time predict their scores on a measure administered at a subsequent point in time.

predictive validity   see *predictive evidence of test validity.*

predictor variable   a variable that researchers measure at one point in time and then correlate with a criterion variable that is measured at a later point in time.

presentism   a type of bias in historical research that involves interpreting past events by using concepts and perspectives that originated in more recent times.

pretest   in experiments, a measure that is administered prior to a treatment in order to provide a basis for comparison with the posttest.

pretest–posttest control-group experiment with randomization   an investigation that includes an intervention, a pretest and posttest, a group that receives the intervention, and one or more groups that do not receive the intervention or that receive another intervention, with random assignment of the sample to the groups.

primary source   in general research, a publication written by the individuals who actually conducted the investigation presented in the publication; in historical research, any source of information from witnesses or participants that has been preserved from the past.

privilege   in critical theory research, the disproportionate power, resources, and life opportunities that are granted to members of culturally dominant groups in a society; also, to grant such power to a specific group or individual.

probability (*p*) value   a mathematical expression of the likelihood that a statistical result for a sample randomly drawn from a defined population was obtained by chance.

process evaluation   in the CIPP model, an assessment of program activities.

process validity   the adequacy of the processes used in different phases of an action research project.

product evaluation   in the CIPP model, an assessment about the success of a program.

product-moment correlation coefficient (*r*)   a mathematical expression of the direction and magnitude of the relationship between two measures that yield continuous scores.

program   a systematic, transportable sequences of materials and activities that are designed to achieve explicitly stated goals.

program culture   the rules, rituals, and roles that are involved in implementing a program; also, the tension between an individual's needs and preferences and the demands of the program.

progressive discourse   the prevailing scientific view that anyone at any time can offer a criticism about a particular research study or research methodology and that if it proves to have merit, it will be listened to and accommodated.

progressive story structure   in narrative research, a story in which the events demonstrate progress toward a goal.

proportional random sampling   a variation of stratified random sampling that is designed to ensure that the proportion of individuals in each subgroup in the sample is the same as their proportion in the population.

Publication Manual of the American Psychological Association   a book containing style specifications that are widely used in preparing dissertations, journal articles, and other reports in education.

purposeful sampling   in qualitative research, the process of selecting cases that are likely to be "information-rich" with respect to the purposes of a particular study.

***p* value**   see *probability value.*

qualitative research   generally, a type of inquiry grounded in the assumption that individuals construct social reality in the form of meanings and interpretations and that these constructions are transitory and situational; the dominant methodology is to discover these meanings and interpretations by studying cases intensively in natural settings.

qualitative research tradition   an approach to inquiry involving a group of qualitative researchers and scholars who hold a similar view of the nature of social reality, the research questions that are important to ask, and the techniques needed to answer them; also, the work of such individuals.

quantitative historical materials   materials containing numerical information that are preserved and can be used as a primary source in historical research.

quantitative history   an approach to historical research that involves the use of an electronic database containing numerical data that typically are analyzed by computer-based statistical techniques.

quantitative research   inquiry that is grounded in the assumption that features of the social environment constitute an objective reality that is relatively constant across time and settings; the dominant methodology for inquiry involves collecting numerical data on the observable behavior of samples and subjecting these data to statistical analysis.

quasi-experiment   an experimental study in which research participants for the experimental and control groups are selected by a procedure other than random selection.

questionnaire   a set of questions in paper-and-pencil or computer format that typically measure many variables.

r   see *Pearson product-moment correlation coefficient.*

R & D   see *research and development.*

random assignment   in experiments, the process of assigning individuals or groups to the experimental and control treatments such that each individual or group has an equal chance of being in either treatment condition.

random sample   a group in which each member of the group was chosen entirely by chance from the population.

range   a statistic that measures the amount of dispersion in a score distribution; it is equal to the difference between the highest and the lowest score plus 1.

rank (also called *ranking*)   a number that expresses the position of an individual's score on a measure relative to the positions of other individuals' scores.

ratio scale   a type of measurement in which the values of the variable can be ordered, the interval between any two adjacent values is equal, and there is a true zero point.

raw score   the numerical value that the individual obtains on the scale that the measure employs, without any further statistical manipulation.

reconstructionist (also called *revisionist historian*)   a historian who in researching a phenomenon believes that some aspects of the situation were missed or distorted in previous historical accounts.

reconstructive analysis   the process by which critical ethnographers analyze the data collected during monological data generation in order to describe interaction patterns among field participants and the apparent meaning of those patterns.

record   a type of document that is prepared with an official purpose, as contrasted with material prepared for personal use only.

reflection   in action research, the process by which practitioners step back from the world of practice and ponder and share ideas about the meaning, value, and impact of their work.

reflective analysis   in qualitative research, a type of data analysis in which researchers rely on their own intuition and personal judgment to analyze the data that have been collected.

reflexivity   in qualitative research, the researchers' act of inquiring about themselves as constructors and interpreters of the social reality that they study.

refutation   the process of submitting the knowledge claims of science to empirical tests that allow them to be challenged and disproved.

regressive story structure   in narrative research, a story in which the events present either obstacles to achieving a goal or possibly a defeat leading to abandonment of the goal.

relational pattern   in case study research, a systematic relationship that is observed between particular phenomena within a case or across cases that is not presumed to be causal.

reliability   the extent to which a test or other measure is free of measurement error.

reliability coefficient   a type of correlation coefficient that quantifies the extent to which a test or other measure is free of measurement error.

relic   in historical research, any object whose physical properties provide information about the past.

replication   the process of repeating a research study with different research participants under similar conditions in order to increase confidence in, or extend, the original study's findings.

repository (also called *archive*)   a facility for storing documents to preserve them in good condition and control access to them.

representativeness check   in qualitative research, a procedure used to determine whether a finding is typical of the field site from which it was obtained.

reproduction   in critical theory, the view that many of the learning problems experienced by members of low-income and ethnic-minority groups result from educational practices that maintain and reinforce the cultural oppression of such groups.

research and development   a systematic process involving the development and refinement of educational programs and materials through formative and summative evaluation.

research narrative   in narrative research, an organized interpretation of events.

response-process evidence of test validity   the extent to which the process used by an individual in taking a test are consistent with the particular construct or constructs that the test presumably measures.

responsive evaluation   a type of evaluation research that focuses on stakeholders' issues and concerns.

reversal phase   in single-case experiments, the process of withdrawing the treatment (condition *B*) so as to reinstitute the baseline condition (*A*).

revisionist historian   see *reconstructionist*.

***r* value**   see *product-moment correlation coefficient*.

sample of convenience   see *volunteer sample*.

sampling error   the difference between a statistic for a sample and the same statistic for the population from which the sample was randomly drawn.

scale   a set of numbers that represent the range of values of a variable.

scattergram (also called *scatter plot*)   a graph depicting the correlation between two variables, with the scores on one variable plotted on the *x* axis and the scores on the other variable plotted on the *y* axis of the graph.

scatter plot   see *scattergram*.

Scheffé's test   a type of *t* test that is used to compare pairs of means for three or more groups.

search engine   computer software that helps users sort through a database to identify documents or other items that satisfy user-specified criteria.

secondary source   in literature reviews, a publication in which the author reviews research or other work that was carried out by someone other than an author; in historical research, a document or other communication in which an author who was not a direct witness describes an event.

selection–maturation interaction effect   in experiments, a change from the pretest to the post-test that is due to developmental differences between the experimental and control groups during the course of the experiment rather than to the intervention.

self-study research   see *action research*.

sequential-explanatory research design   in multiple-methods research, the collection and analysis of quantitative data followed by the collection and analysis of qualitative data, which are then used to explain the quantitative findings.

sequential-transformative research design   in multiple-methods research, the use of a theoretical perspective to guide both the qualitative and quantitative phases of data collection, analysis, and interpretation; either the qualitative or the quantitative phase can occur first.

simple random sampling   a procedure in which all the individuals in the defined population have an equal and independent chance of being selected as a member of the sample.

single-case experiment   a type of experiment in which an intervention is applied to one or a few individuals in order to determine its effect on one or more dependent variables.

skewness   a nonsymmetrical distribution of scores in which the majority of scores are clustered on one side of the mean and the other scores trail off on the other side of the mean.

snowball sampling   in qualitative research, a type of sampling in which information provided by one or more initially selected cases leads to other individuals who are likely to yield relevant, information-rich data.

stable story structure   in narrative research, a story in which the events lead to little or no change in the individual's circumstances.

stakeholder   an individual who is involved in a phenomenon that is being evaluated or who may be affected by or interested in the findings of the evaluation.

standard deviation   a statistic that indicates how much a set of scores deviates from the mean score.

standard error of measurement   a statistic that is used to estimate the probable range within which an individual's true score on a test falls.

standard score   an expression of an individual's raw score on a test or other measure in another form, namely, a score based on the standard deviation of the score distribution.

Standards for Educational and Psychological Testing   a definitive guide, published by several professional organizations, for determining the quality of tests and other measures.

statistic   any number that describes a characteristic of a sample's scores on a measure.

statistical regression   the tendency for individuals who score either very high or very low on a measure to score nearer to the mean when the measure is readministered.

statistical significance   an inference, based on a statistical test, that the results obtained for a research sample are of a sufficient magnitude to reject the null hypothesis.

status model   a method of evaluating schools' ability to promote students' academic achievement in which students at a particular grade level are tested each year, and the achievement test scores of students at that grade level in year X are compared with the scores of students at the same grade level in year Y.

story   in narrative research, an individual's account of events that occurred at specific times in the past.

stratified random sampling   a procedure involving the identification of subgroups with certain characteristics in the population and drawing a random sample of individuals from each subgroup.

structural equation modeling (also called *latent variable causal modeling*)   a statistical procedure for testing the validity of a theory about the causal links among variables, each of which has been measured by one or more different measures.

subjective truth claims   in critical ethnography, assertions by field participants about their state of being to which there is privileged access, meaning that only the individual has access to the experience on which the claim is based.

sum of squares   the total amount of variability in a set of scores, determined by computing the sum of all the squared deviations (each raw score minus the mean) for the scores.

summative evaluation   a type of evaluation that is conducted to determine the worth of a fully developed program in operation, especially in comparison with competing programs.

survey research   a form of descriptive investigation that involves collecting information about research participants' beliefs, attitudes, interests, or behavior using standard questionnaires, interviews, or paper-and-pencil tests.

sustainability evaluation   in the CIPP model, an assessment of whether a program is institutionalized successfully in a particular setting in the short term and long term.

systematicity   in action research, an ordered way of recording and analyzing experiences inside and outside the contexts of practice.

table of norms   a presentation of possible raw scores for a test or other measure and, for each score, its age equivalent, grade equivalent, or other numerical value based on a large norming group.

tacit knowledge   implicit meanings that the individuals being studied either cannot find words to express or that they take so much for granted that they do not refer to them.

target population   the entire group of individuals or other entities that have the characteristics that interest researchers and to which they wish to generalize the findings of their study.

teacher research   see *action research*.

test   a measure of an individual's knowledge, depth of understanding, or skill within a curriculum domain, which typically yields a total score for the number of items answered correctly.

testing effect   in experiments, the effect of repeated administrations of a test or other measure on the posttest.

test of statistical significance   a mathematical procedure for determining whether the researchers' null hypothesis can be rejected at a given probability level.

test–retest reliability (also called *test stability*)   the extent to which individuals' scores on one administration of a test are consistent with their scores on another administration of the test after a delay.

test stability   see *test–retest reliability*.

test validity   see *validity*.

text   in critical theory, any cultural discourse, object, or event that possesses communicative value; in particular, communications that express and maintain differences in privilege among cultural groups in society.

theme   in qualitative research, a salient, recurrent feature of the case being studied.

theoretical saturation   the outcome of the process of comparing theoretical constructs and empirical indicators of their meaning until additional data collection and analysis no longer contribute anything new about the phenomenon under investigation.

theory   an explanation of observed phenomena in terms of a set of underlying constructs and a set of principles that relate the constructs to each other.

theory-in-action   in the theory of action, the actual behavior of professionals as they engage in their work.

thick description   in qualitative research, a richly detailed report that re-creates a situation and as much of its context as possible, including the meanings and intentions inherent in the situation.

transportability evaluation   In the CIPP model, an assessment of whether a program can be adapted and institutionalized in other settings.

treatment condition   in experiments, the intervention that is administered to the experimental group to determine its effect on the dependent variable.

treatment fidelity   the extent to which the experimental intervention is implemented according to the specifications of the researchers or program developers.

trend study   a research study that describes change by selecting a different sample at each data-collection point from a population that does not remain constant.

triangulation (also called *crystallization*)   in qualitative research, the use of multiple data-collection methods, data sources, analysts, or theories to increase the soundness of research findings.

troubling   in anti-oppressive education, the process of questioning widely accepted but oppressive cultural practices.

true dichotomy   a variable that has only two values in reality.

true score   the score that an individual would receive if it were possible to obtain a perfect measure of performance.

truncation   a procedure for searching an electronic database for any words that contain the same stem, such as the stem *sign* retrieving *signature, signing,* and *signs.*

t **test**   a test of statistical significance that is used to determine whether the null hypothesis that two sample means come from identical populations can be rejected.

t **test for independent means**   a *t* test in which it is assumed that the two populations from which the two samples were drawn are not related to each other.

t **test for related means**   a *t* test in which it is assumed that the two populations from which the two samples were drawn are related to each other.

Tukey's test   a type of *t* test for comparing pairs of means for three or more groups.

two-tailed test of statistical significance   a test that evaluates the null hypothesis in both directions, for example, a test that considers the possibility that the mean score for population *A* is greater than the mean score for population *B* and also the possibility that the mean score for population *B* is greater than the mean score for population *A*.

Type I error   the rejection of the null hypothesis when it is actually true.

Type II error   the acceptance of the null hypothesis when it is actually false.

validity   in research generally, the soundness of research findings based on the satisfaction of specific criteria for the research design that generated the findings; in testing, the degree to which evidence and theory support the interpretation of test scores in the context that they will be used.

value   a discernible point in a variable.

variable   a quantitative expression of a construct, indicating the possible number of ways that individuals or other entities can vary with respect to the construct.

variance   a statistical measure of the extent to which scores in a distribution deviate from the mean, computed for a sample by dividing the sum of squares by the sample size minus one ($n - 1$).

voice   in critical theory, the extent to which individuals occupying particular social categories or identities are privileged, silenced, muted, or empowered through the operation of discourses that maintain or contest dominant and subordinate cultures in a society.

volunteer sample (also called *sample of convenience*)   a sample based on individuals' expression of willingness to participate in a research study rather than on a systematic sampling strategy.

What Works Clearinghouse   an agency within the U.S. Department of Education that creates databases and user-friendly reports about research evidence relating to interventions that claim to improve student learning and other outcomes.

Wilcoxon signed-rank test   a nonparametric counterpart of the *t* test of statistical significance.

wildcard   a part of the truncation feature of search engines that involves the use of a symbol, typically an asterisk (*), to find all words in an electronic database that have the same stem.

x **variable**   an independent variable that researchers assume has a causal influence on another variable, called the dependent variable or *y* variable.

y **variable**   a dependent variable that researchers assume was caused by another variable, called the independent variable or *x* variable.

z-**score**   an expression of a raw score as a standard score that indicates the raw score's distance from the score distribution's mean in standard deviation units.

Name Index

Subject Index